COMPLETE GUIDE TO
American
Bed and Breakfast

COMPLETE GUIDE TO

American Bed and Breakfast

FOURTH EDITION

By RIK BARNES

PELICAN PUBLISHING COMPANY
GRETNA 1996

First printing, January 1986
Second printing, May 1986
Second edition, October 1987
Third edition, May 1991
Fourth edition, January 1996

*The word "Pelican" and the depiction of a pelican are trademarks
of Pelican Publishing Company, Inc., and are registered
in the U.S.Patent and Trademark Office.*

ISBN 1-56554-036-0
ISSN 1059-6917

Maps by Michael Forsythe

*Information in this guidebook is based on authoritative data available at the time of
printing. Prices and other information concerning the businesses listed are subject to
change without notice. Readers are asked to take this into account when consulting
this guide.*

Manufactured in the United States of America
Published by Pelican Publishing Company, Inc.
1101 Monroe Street, Gretna, Louisiana 70053

Contents

Introduction

Compiling this guidebook has afforded me an interesting perspective on the lodging industry in general and, of course, the Bed and Breakfast segment in particular. One obvious trend is that Bed and Breakfast Inns (country inns, homestays, urban inns, etc.) continue to grow in popularity by leaps and bounds.

Clearly the popular perception of the Bed and Breakfast life-style attracts many people. Continued corporate downsizing all across the country has resulted in many middle-upper managers with entrepreneurial aspirations searching for a fulfilling business of their own. "We had such a good time at that inn on our last vacation, who wouldn't want to own and operate a nice, little inn in the wine country, or a B and B in the historical district of a cute little town?" However, the turnover rate (between my third and fourth editions there were more than 500 inns that had gone out of business) indicates that many entrepreneurs discover, after investing their time, energy, and money in their dream business, that operating a good inn requires more dedication and attention than they are willing to spend. It takes hard work to present a "comfortable and relaxed" atmosphere.

The number of "Bed and Breakfasts" is swelled also by lodging establishments eager to cash in on the "trend" by marketing themselves as Bed and Breakfast Inns when their only connection is that they offer travelers a bed and, yes, they do serve breakfast. Having thrown out these words of caution to the discerning traveler, defining "Bed and Breakfast Inns" remains a difficult task, and therein lies part of their charm. Municipalities all across America are struggling with legal definitions that will allow each inn's personality to shine through the requisite zoning laws, standardization of quality control, and insurance regulations while they redefine their tax base. There is such a wide variety of architectures and locations, so many varied sizes and shapes, so many different price ranges that to severely and artificially legislate the category may unfairly exclude some wonderful inns—such is the price of success!

Realizing that the lines between, and even within, the various categories often blur from one B and B to the next, following is an attempt to help describe the different types of B and B establishments:

B and B Homestay. Most are hosted by the homeowner who shares his or her private home with paying guests. The "innkeeper" generally makes available one to four bedrooms and common rooms to occasional guests. Breakfast is, typically, the only meal served (although other meals may be available by negotiation) and is included in the charge for the room. Homestays are usually unregulated under various zoning provisions, but the majority of this country's homestays are affiliated with one or more reservation services/agencies, most of whom regularly inspect the properties for which they make reservations.

Guesthouse. Guesthouses welcome B and B guests on a regular basis and longer, even indefinite stays are welcome. Some guesthouses are in unhosted houses; that is, the owners turn over the entire house, apartment, loft, boat, etc. to the paying guest. Breakfast is included in the charge for the room (often it is "self-served" from a kitchen to which the guest has access). Other meals may also be made available.

B and B Inn. This is a professional business property with usually more than eight rooms, primarily used for lodging. The owners may or may not live on the premises. This business is subject to all local, state, and federal regulations. There is a wide variety of inns available, each with its own particular individuality. Breakfast is the only meal served and is included in the charge for the room.

Country Inn. This is a professional business property that offers accommodations and dining. Usually a restaurant on the premises serves all meals to guests (although it is not unusual for breakfast to be the only meal included in the charge for the room) and the general public. This business is subject to all local, state, and federal regulations. Country inns usually offer more than eight guest rooms.

B and B Reservation Service/Agency. This is a business that helps travelers arrange all of the details of B and B stays—primarily in homestays and guesthouses rather than inns—offering the convenience of a variety of lodgings with just one phone call. The agency or service also may develop and train B and B hosts, usually personally inspects all accommodations, screens and matches guests to appropriate B and Bs, and generally handles all of the administrative details of arranging the reservation. Many agencies and services make available directories with descriptions of affiliated B and Bs, and some provide the full range of services one would expect from a travel agency. Remuneration for services rendered is typically in the form of a commission paid by the innkeeper, although some services charge "membership" fees.

I continue to stay at inns, guesthouses, and homestays when I travel and also depend on many traveling friends, agents, readers, and even innkeepers to keep me up-to-date on various lodgings. The goal of this edition, however, is not to simply list every inn in the country, but to allow the innkeepers, for a nominal fee, to describe their own accommodations. Most innkeepers will be happy to respond to your request for their brochures and rate cards.

I have assumed, for the sake of each inn's description, that the reader knows something about the geographical area; for example, the description of an inn in Denver won't include the fact that the guest has "access to the Rocky Mountains," and the description of a homestay in Key West won't include the fact that "deep sea fishing is available."

Once again, the listings are organized alphabetically by state, city, and inn. Each city has a numeric code that relates to its location within a quadrant on the map at the beginning of each chapter. The reader should realize that the very nature of a guidebook such as this is that it is out of date, particularly as it relates to room charges, even before it is released, and use this information as a guideline. The reader should always call the innkeeper or service/agency and not be shy about discussing any appropriate details prior to making reservations. A courteous traveler will always make reservations and cancellations as far in advance as possible.

As always, I look forward to hearing about your traveling experiences. If you know of an inn, guesthouse, or homestay that should be included in the next edition—or if you think I have included one that, in your opinion, should not be included—please let me know by writing to me (Rik Barnes, Complete Guide to American Bed and Breakfast, c/o Pelican Publishing Company, P.O. Box 3110, Gretna, LA 70054).

Thank you for your interest in America's Bed and Breakfasts, and happy trails to you!

LIST OF ABBREVIATIONS

AE	American Express
apts.	apartments
avail.	available
bldgs.	buildings
brk.	breakfast
cont. brk.	continental breakfast
dbl.	double room
DC	Diners Card
DS	Discover Card
hr.	hour
incl.	included
MC	Master Card
min.	minimum
pkgs.	packages
pvt. bath	private bath
req.	required
sgl.	single room
V	Visa
wknds.	weekends
*	inn will pay commission to travel agency

EXPLANATIONS

Afternoon refreshment	generally indicates that, in addition to breakfast, nonalcoholic refreshments, i.e., tea, cookies, hot chocolate, etc., are available to guests during the day.
Evening refreshment	generally indicates that, in addition to breakfast, alcoholic beverages, i.e., wine, port, etc., are available—oftentimes in conjunction with nonalcoholic refreshments—to guests during the day.
Handicapped access	indicates an inn that, for common rooms and at least one guest room, has the facilities for wheelchair access

Most Major Cards	indicates that inn will accept at least three major credit cards
Seasonal variations	indicates that room charges vary throughout the year, i.e., some inns have higher rates during fall foliage season, some inns have lower rates in the winter, etc.
Small private parties accommodated	generally indicates an inn that has the facilities for and/or special interest in hosting weddings, business conferences, family reunions, etc.

Note: In entries with more than one phone number listed, the last number is the fax number. (Unless the last number is an 800-number, in which case there is no fax number.)

Alabama

Alabama

ANNISTON (1)

THE VICTORIA

The Victoria
1604 Quintard Ave., Box 2213, Anniston, AL 36201
(205) 236-0503, (205) 236-1138
Innkeeper: Jean Ann Oglesby
Rooms: 44 rooms plus 4 suites, all w/pvt. bath, phone, TV. Located in 3 bldgs.
Rates: $69/room, $80-$145/suite, all incl. cont. brk., evening refreshment
Credit cards: Most major cards
Restrictions: No pets. Smoking restricted. Deposit req. 72-hour cancellation notice
   req. during special events.
Notes: Three-story Victorian Inn with parquet floors, carved mantels, 3-story turret
built in 1888. Restored and expanded in 1985. Four dining rooms, piano lounge,
glass-enclosed veranda, covered walkways, verandas, gazebos, outdoor atrium, swimming pool. Furnished with antiques. Restaurant on premises. Listed on the National Register of Historic Places. Small private parties accommodated.

BIRMINGHAM (1)

The Pickwick Hotel
1023 20th St. S., Birmingham, AL 35205
(205) 933-9555, (800) 255-7304, (205) 933-6918
Innkeeper: Manager
Rooms: 35, plus 28/suites, all w/pvt. bath, phone, TV
Rates: $69-$99/room, $82-$129/suite, all incl. cont. brk., evening refreshment. Dis-
   count avail. for extended stay.
Credit cards: Most major cards
Restrictions: Deposit req. for pets. Smoking restricted.
Notes: Parlor. Handicapped access.*

RIVER VIEW B & B

FLORENCE (1)

River View B & B
Rte. 7, Box 123G, Florence, AL 35630
(205) 757-8667
Innkeeper: Buddy and Edith Meeks
Rooms: 1, plus 1 suite w/TV, all w/pvt bath
Rates: $75/room, $85/suite, all incl. full brk., afternoon refreshment
Credit cards: MC, V
Restrictions: No children, pets, smoking. Deposit req. 24-hour cancellation notice req.
Notes: Architecturally designed, contemporary home located on Tennessee River bank in wooded area. Patio. Decks. Sailboats.*

LIVE OAKS BED & BREAKFAST

GENEVA (3)

Live Oaks Bed & Breakfast
307 S. Academy St., Geneva, AL 36340
(205) 684-2489
Innkeeper: Horace and Pamela Newman

Rooms: 3 w/pvt. bath, phone, TV
Rates: $40, incl. full brk.
Credit cards: DC
Restrictions: No pets, smoking.
Notes: Built in 1918. Fully restored. Porch, gazebo, sun room, living room. Private entrance.

JEMISON (2)

Horse Shoe Bunk House
356 County Road 164, Jemison, AL 35085
(205) 646-4109

Innkeeper: Kay RedHorse
Rooms: 2 w/pvt. bath
Rates: $45, incl. full brk.
Credit cards: None
Restrictions: No children under 15, pets, smoking.
Notes: Decorated in cowboy & indian style.

The Jemison Inn
212 Hwy. 191, Jemison, AL 35085
(205) 688-2055, (800) 438-3042

Innkeeper: Nancy and Joe Ruzicka
Rooms: 3, incl. 1 w/pvt. bath
Rates: $55-$60, incl. full brk., afternoon refreshment
Credit cards: Most major cards
Restrictions: No children under 12, pets, smoking. Deposit req. 7-day cancellation notice req.
Notes: Two-story inn furnished with antiques. Swimming pool. Small private parties accommodated. Handicapped access.*

RED BLUFF COTTAGE

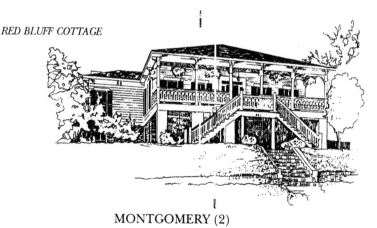

MONTGOMERY (2)

Red Bluff Cottage
551 Clay St., Box 1026, Montgomery, AL 36101
(205) 264-0056, (205) 262-1872

Innkeeper: Mark and Anne Waldo
Rooms: 3 plus 1 suite, all w/pvt bath, phone

Rates: $65/room $65-$75/suite, all incl full brk.
Credit cards: Most major cards
Restrictions: No pets. Smoking restricted. $20.00 deposit req. 7-day cancellation notice req.
Notes: Raised cottage built in 1987 as Inn. Dining room, living room. Sitting room with TV. Music room with piano and harpsichord on second floor. Guests have access to kitchen. Decorated with family antiques. Crib available. Upstairs porch with view of river and State capitol. Lower porch with mattress swing. Gazebo. Fenced play yard. Off-street parking available.*

TALLADEGA (2)

The Governor's House
Rte. 6, Box 392, Talladega, AL 35160
(205) 763-2186
Innkeeper: Mary Sue and Ralph Gaines
Rooms: 3, incl. 1 w/pvt. bath
Rates: $60-$70, incl. full brk., afternoon refreshment. Discount avail. for rental of entire house.
Credit cards: None
Restrictions: No children under 12, pets. Smoking restricted. One night's deposit req.
Notes: Two-story house on working farm overlooking Logan Martin Lake. Built in 1850 for Governor Lewis Parsons. Moved to 139-acre Meadowlake Farm in, and has operated as Inn since May 1990. Living room with TV and books. Furnished with antiques and handmade quilts. Watch hay being harvested in season. Horses in pastures. Front porch with wicker swing and rockers. Lighted tennis courts. Fishing in stocked bass pond. Boat rides on pond, with wine and cheese available. Lunch and picnic baskets available.

Historic Oakwood B & B
715 E. North St., Talladega, AL 35160
(205) 362-0662
Innkeeper: Al and Naomi Kline
Rooms: 4
Rates: $55, incl. full brk.
Credit cards: None
Restrictions: No children under 10, pets, smoking. $25.00 deposit req.
Notes: Two-story antebellum Federal-style house built in 1847. Furnished with heirloom antiques.

Alaska

ANCHORAGE (3)

Arctic Loon Bed and Breakfast
P.O. Box 110333, Anchorage, AK 99511
(907) 345-4935, (907) 345-4936
Innkeeper: Janie and Lee Johnson
Rooms: 2 plus 1 suite, all w/phone, TV, incl. 2 w/pvt. bath
Rates: $60-$75/room, $75-$90/suite, all incl. full brk. Seasonal variations.
Credit cards: AE, MC
Restrictions: No pets, smoking. Two night's deposit req. 7-day cancellation notice
 req. 2-night min. stay.
Notes: 6,500-square-foot Scandinavian house with views of the Anchorage Bowl,
Alaska Range across Cook Inlet, and Mt. McKinley. Furnished with European and
Alaskan artwork, antiques. Rosewood grand piano and pool table. 8-person Jacuzzi
hot tub, sauna. Exercise room available. Some Norwegian spoken.*

Bed and Breakfast on the Park
602 West 10th Ave., Anchorage, AK 99501
(907) 277-0878
Innkeeper: Helen Tucker and Stella Hughton
Rooms: 3 w/pvt. bath, phone, TV
Rates: $65-$75, incl. full brk. Seasonal variations.
Credit cards: Most major cards
Restrictions: No children under 10, pets, smoking. Deposit req. 7-day cancellation
 notice req.
Notes: Log cabin built in 1946 as a church. Renovated in and has operated as Inn
since 1991. Gardens.*

Burns' B & B
4169 Westwood Dr., Anchorage, AK 99517
(907) 248-1530, (800) 999-9551 voice mail # 982, (907) 277-5024
Innkeeper: Mary Jo and Mike Burns
Rooms: 2 w/pvt. bath, incl. 1 w/phone, plus 1 suite w/pvt. bath, phone, fireplace,
 TV
Rates: $70-$80/room, $140/suite, all incl. cont. brk. Seasonal variations. Discount
 avail. for extended stay.
Credit cards: None
Restrictions: No pets, smoking. One night's deposit req. 3-day cancellation notice
 req., less $10.00 fee.
Notes: Spanish-style house built in 1980. Family room with TV, board games, and
wood stove. Laundry facilities, freezer space available. Special dietary arrangements
possible. Gardens, lawn, flowering trees. Bicycles and guided hiking trips by
innkeeper avail.*

EAGLE RIVER (3)

The Log House B & B
10925 Corrie Way, Eagle River, AK 99577
(907) 694-9231

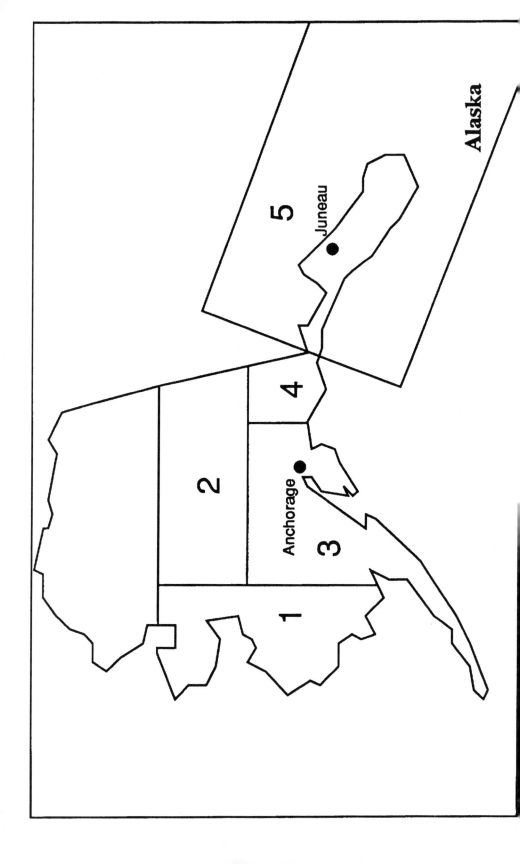

Innkeeper: Joyce Simmons
Rooms: 2, incl. 1 w/pvt bath, all w/TV
Rates: $60-$100, incl. full brk.
Credit cards: MC, V
Restrictions: Smoking restricted. Min. one night's deposit req. 14-day cancellation notice req.
Notes: Log house located on 1.5 wooded acres overlooking Anchorage and Eagle River Valley. Living room with native stone fireplace. Landscaped yard. Picnic table. Barbeque. Flower gardens. Special dietary needs considered. Giftshop with Alaskan-made gifts on premises. Limited freezer and storage space available.

FAIRBANKS (2)

A Pioneer Bed & Breakfast
1119 Second Ave., Fairbanks, AK 99701
(907) 452-5393, (907) 452-4628

Innkeeper: Jack and Nancy Williams
Rooms: 3 w/pvt. bath, phone, TV
Rates: $65, incl. full brk.
Credit cards: Most major cards
Restrictions: Pets restricted. Deposit req.
Notes: One-story authentic Pioneer log cabin built in 1906. Outdoor barbecue. Handicapped access.*

ALASKA'S 7 GABLES

Alaska's 7 Gables
P.O. Box 80488, Fairbanks, AK 99708
(907) 479-0751, (907) 479-2229

Innkeeper: Paul and Leicha Welton
Rooms: 9, w/phone, TV, incl. 8 w/pvt. bath, plus 3 suites w/pvt. bath, phone, TV. Located in 2 bldgs.
Rates: $70-$95/room, $75-$150/suite, all incl. full brk. Seasonal variations. Discount avail. for extended stay.
Credit cards: Most major cards
Restrictions: One night's deposit req. 2-day cancellation notice req.
Notes: Tudor-style passive solar house with natural wood paneling, cathedral ceilings, wine cellar, and wedding chapel built near river in 1982. Floral solarium with antiqued stained-glass and indoor waterfall. Conference room, library collection. Luggage, game and ski storage available. Jacuzzis, laundry, bicycles, canoes available. Spanish, some German spoken. Handicapped access.*

BELL HOUSE BED & BREAKFAST

Bell House Bed & Breakfast
909 Sixth Ave., Fairbanks, AK 99701
(907) 452-3278
Innkeeper: Kathryn LaSalle
Rooms: 3
Rates: $55-$65/incl. full brk. Seasonal variations.
Credit cards: Most major cards
Restrictions: No children, pets, smoking. One night's deposit req. 10-day cancellation notice req. during peak season.
Notes: Two-story Old Cape Cod-style house built in 1937. Named for owner's collection of bells. Library/sitting room with antique pump organ, piano, fireplace. Dining room, sun deck. Lawn swing and bench on grounds. Board games, jigsaw puzzles, books available. Resident cats.*

BIRCH GROVE INN B & B

Birch Grove Inn B & B
691 DePauw Dr., Box 81387, Fairbanks, AK 99708-1387
(907) 479-5781, (907) 479-5781
Innkeeper: Greg and Theresa Ely
Rooms: 3
Rates: $45-$80, incl. full brk., evening refreshment. Seasonal variations. Discount avail. for extended and senior citizen stays.
Credit cards: Most major cards

Restrictions: No pets. Smoking restricted. One night's deposit req. 72-hr. cancellation notice req., less $10.00 fee. Closed Oct.–Jan.
Notes: Three-story chalet-style house surrounded by birch trees. Living room with fireplace, Alaskan videos, board games. Reading room. Furnished with antiques and Alaskan art. Children's playhouse. Fishing and gold panning equipment available. Tours and excursions can be arranged. Airport and train depot pickup. Some German spoken.*

The Blue Goose Bed & Breakfast
4466 Dartmouth, Fairbanks, AK 99709
(907) 479-6973, (800) 478-6973, (907) 457-6973
Innkeeper: Susan and Ken Risse
Rooms: 3 w/TV, incl. 1 w/pvt. bath
Rates: $55-75, incl. full brk., afternoon refreshment. Discount avail. for extended stay. Seasonal variations.
Credit cards: Most major cards
Restrictions: No pets. Smoking restricted. 50% deposit req. 2-day cancellation notice req.
Notes: Tri-level frame house. Living room, kitchen/dining area. Mini-library with VCR, board games, piano, toys. Furnished with antiques. Telephone available. Two resident children and one resident dog.*

MARILYN'S BED & BREAKFAST

Marilyn's Bed & Breakfast
651 Ninth Ave., Fairbanks, AK 99701-4506
(907) 456-1959
Innkeeper: Marilyn Nigro
Rooms: 3 w/TV
Rates: $55-$70, incl. cont. brk.
Credit cards: Most major cards
Restrictions: No children under 12, pets, smoking. One night's deposit req. 2-day cancellation notice req.
Notes: Two-story house. Easy walk to town. Resident dog.*

Stone Frost Downtown Inn
851 Sixth Ave., Fairbanks, AK 99701
(907) 457-5337, (907) 474-0532

Innkeeper: Randi Reed-Helton
Rooms: 5, no pvt. bath, plus 1 suite w/pvt bath, all w/phone, TV
Rates: $45-$65/room, $75-$85/suite, all incl. full brk., afternoon refreshment. Seasonal variations.
Credit cards: MC, V
Restrictions: Smoking restricted. 20% deposit req. 3-day cancellation notice req.
Notes: Built in 1928 as two-story rooming house. Located in residential area. Decorated with antiques. Yard with gazebo.*

GUSTAVUS (5)

A Puffin's Bed & Breakfast
P.O. Box 3, Gustavus, AK 99826
(907) 697-2260 (summer), 789-9787 (winter), (907) 697-2258

Innkeeper: Chuck and Sandy Schroth
Rooms: 5 cabins w/pvt. bath, incl. 3 w/fireplace. Located in 5 bldgs.
Rates: $70-$75, incl. full brk. Discount avail. for senior citizens. Special pkgs. avail.
Credit cards: Most major cards
Restrictions: No smoking. 50% deposit req. 14-day cancellation notice req., less
    10% fee. Closed Oct.–April.
Notes: Modern cabins with wood heat and electricity located on five wooded acres.
Separate lodge for reading, socializing, and relaxing. Furnished with Alaskan arts
and crafts. Gustavus dock and airport pick-up, bicycles available. Handicapped access.*

Glacier Bay Country Inn
P.O. Box 5, Gustavus, AK 99826-0005
(907) 697-2288, (907) 697-2289

Innkeeper: Al and Annie Unrein
Rooms: 9, incl. 8 w/pvt. bath
Rates: $238, incl. all meals. Special pkgs. avail.
Credit cards: Most major cards
Restrictions: No pets. Smoking restricted. 50% deposit req. 45-day cancellation
    notice req., less $25.00 fee. Closed Oct. 1–April 30. Due to small size and short
    season, singles may be asked to share. Access only by plane or boat.
Notes: Hand-built in 1979 by the innkeepers with multi-angled roofs, dormer windows, log beamed ceilings from trees cleared from their property. Has operated as
inn since 1986. Dining room, garden kitchen. Lounge with board games, books.
Furnished with Alaskan art and artifacts. Wide porch with rockers. Fishing, whale-watching tours, *flight-seeing*, National Park walk and Glacier Bay tours organized.
Transfers to and from airport, bicycles available. Winter address, Oct. through
April: P.O. Box 2557, St. George, UT, 84771, (801) 673-8480, FAX (801) 673-8481.

Good Riverbed and Breakfast
P.O. Box 37, Gustavus, AK 99826
(907) 697-2241, (916) 697-2241

Innkeeper: S. Burd
Rooms: 5, no pvt. bath. Located in 2 bldgs.
Rates: $50-$70, incl. cont. brk. Discount avail. for extended stay.
Credit cards: None
Restrictions: No infants, pets. $20.00 deposit req. 14-day cancellation notice req.
    Closed Labor Day–Memorial Day.

GOOD RIVERBED AND BREAKFAST

Notes: Three-story log house with dovetail corners, maple hardwood floor, wooden beams and handmade tiles. Common room with harpsichord overlooking garden. Library with board games. Root cellar. Decorated with original painting by Alaskan artists. Log cabin with no running water available. Bicycles available.

Gustavus Inn at Glacier Bay
P.O. Box 60, Gustavus, AK 99826
(907) 697-2254

Innkeeper: David and JoAnn Lesh
Rooms: 13, incl. 7 w/pvt. bath
Rates: $130/adult, $65/child aged 4-12, all incl. 3 meals. Special pkgs. avail.
Credit cards: Most major cards
Restrictions: Pets welcome with prior approval only. Smoking discouraged. Min. one night's deposit req. 60-day cancellation notice req., less $25.00 fee.
Notes: Two-story inn built in 1928 in the Salmon River meadow. Has operated as inn since 1965. Dining room, library, hearth room, garden, wine and root cellar, bar, country kitchen. Bicycles, fishing poles, kayaks, airport pickup, picnics, seafood dinner available. Special diets accommodated. Thunder Bay and Glacier Bay boat tours and charter fishing available. Winter address: 7920 Outlook, Prairie Village, KS, 66208, (913) 649-5220.*

HOMER (3)

Kachemak Bay Wilderness Lodge
P.O. Box 956, Homer, AK 99603
(907) 235-8910, (907) 235-8911

Innkeeper: Mike and Diane McBride
Rooms: 1 w/pvt. bath, plus 4 cabins w/pvt. bath, incl. 3 w/fireplace. Located in 5 bldgs.
Rates: $3900 for 5-day/4-night pkg., incl. all meals, transportation, full guide service. Seasonal variations.
Credit cards: None
Restrictions: No pets. 50% deposit req. 60-day cancellation notice req. 4-night min. stay. Closed mid-Dec.–May.
Notes: Main lodge with large stone fireplace located on banks of untouched peninsula. Has operated as an Inn since 1972. Community bath and shower. Dining room with picture window, outdoor pavilion. Separate Finnish Sauna with sod roof. Four

log cabins with woodburning heaters, homemade quilts, sitting porch, private outside privy. Vegetable and herb garden. Canoes, kayaks available. Salmon and trout fishing. Hiking. Dig for clams and mussels. Boat and floatplace access only.*

JUNEAU (5)

Alaska Wolf House
P.O. Box 21321, Juneau, AK 99802
(907) 586-2422, (907) 586-2422

Innkeeper: Philip and Cloris Dennis
Rooms: 3, plus 2 suites, incl. 2 w/pvt. bath, kitchen, all w/phone, TV
Rates: $55-$75/room, $95/suite, all incl. full brk.
Credit cards: None
Restrictions: Well-behaved children welcome. No pets, smoking. Min. 2-night nonrefundable deposit req.
Notes: Western red cedar log house. Located on side of Mt. Juneau. Off-season address: P.O. Box 743, Wimberly, TX 78676.

PEARSON'S POND LUXURY INN

Pearson's Pond Luxury Inn
4541 Sawa Circle, Juneau, AK 30324-8723
(907) 789-3772, (907) 789-6722

Innkeeper: Steve and Diane Pearson
Rooms: 1 w/pvt. bath, phone, TV, plus 2 suites w/phone, TV, incl. 1 w/pvt. bath. Kitchens available.
Rates: $69-$139/room, $79-$149/suite, all incl. full brk., evening refreshment. Seasonal variations. Discount avail. for extended stay. Special pkgs. avail.
Credit cards: Most major cards
Restrictions: No children under 3, pets, smoking. Min. one night's deposit req. Min. 3-day cancellation notice req. 3-night min. stay from June–August.
Notes: Two-story modern cedar house surrounded by rain forest, overlooking Mendenhall Glacier. Pond. Private decks, sitting and dining areas. Bicycles, row boats, fishing poles, laundry facilities, freezer, health club privileges available. Starlit spa, fireplace. Handicapped access.*

KETCHIKAN (5)

Ketchikan B & B
1508 Water St., Box 5015, Ketchikan, AK 99901
(907) 225-8550, (907) 247-0200

Innkeeper: Bente Andersen
Rooms: 2, incl. 1 w/pvt. bath, TV, phone, refrigerator, coffee nook plus 1 suite w/pvt. bath, TV, phone, refrigerator, coffee nook. Located in 2 bldgs.
Rates: $65-$75/room, $150/suite, all incl. full brk. Seasonal variations.
Credit cards: Most major cards
Restrictions: Pets, smoking restricted. One night's deposit req. 2-day cancellation notice req., less fee.
Notes: Located on historical street. Common area, laundry facilities. Special dietary needs considered. Taxi and airport shuttle service available. Danish spoken.

KODIAK (3)

Kodiak Bed and Breakfast
308 Cope St., Kodiak, AK 99615
(907) 486-5367, (907) 486-6567

Innkeeper: Mary Monroe
Rooms: 2, no pvt. bath
Rates: $80, incl. full brk. Discount avail. for extended stay.
Credit cards: Most major cards
Restrictions: No smoking. One night's deposit req. 2-day cancellation notice req.
Notes: Two-story private contemporary house built in and has operated as inn since 1985. Sitting room with TV overlooking boat harbor. Breakfast area, outside deck. Summer ferry available from Homer or Seward. Air access all year 'round.

NENANA (2)

Finnish Alaskan Bed & Breakfast
Mi. 302.1 Parks Hwy., Box 274, Nenana, AK 99760
(907) 832-5628, (907) 832-5656

Innkeeper: Carl and Gerrie Jauhola
Rooms: 1 w/pvt. half bath, phone, TV, plus 1 suite w/pvt. bath, fireplace, TV, plus 1 apt. w/pvt. bath, kitchen, TV, fireplace. Located in 2 bldgs.
Rates: $50/room, $65/suite, $75/apt., all incl. full brk. Discount avail. for extended stay. Seasonal variations.
Credit cards: AE, MC
Restrictions: No children under 6 months. Smoking restricted. One night's deposit req. 2-day cancellation notice req., less $15.00 fee.
Notes: Two-story log cabin. Dining room, library. Patio. Finnish sauna.*

PALMER (3)

Hatcher Pass Bed and Breakfast
HC 01, Box 6797-D, Palmer, AK 99645
(907) 745-4210, (907) 745-4210

Innkeeper: Dick and Roxie Anderson
Rooms: 3, no pvt. bath, incl. 1 w/TV. Located in 3 bldgs.
Rates: $65, incl. full brk. Seasonal variations. Discount avail. for extended stay.
Credit cards: Most major cards

Restrictions: Smoking restricted. One night's deposit req. 7-day cancellation notice req.

Notes: Log cabins decorated with artifacts of yesteryear. Breakfast served in main house.*

STERLING (3)

Angler's Lodge
P.O. Box 508, Sterling, AK 99672
(907) 262-1747, (907) 262-6747
Innkeeper: Roger Byerly
Rooms: 7, incl. 4 w/pvt. bath. Located in 2 bldgs.
Rates: $100, incl. cont. brk. Seasonal variations. Special pkgs. avail.
Credit cards: MC, V
Restrictions: Smoking restricted. 50% deposit req.
Notes: Located on the banks of the Kenai River. Guided fishing trips organized.*

TOK (4)

Cleft of the Rock B & B
Sundog Trail, Box 122, Tok, AK 99780
(907) 883-4219, (800) 478-5646 in AK, (907) 883-4219
Innkeeper: John and Jill Rusyniak
Rooms: 3 w/pvt. bath, plus 2 suites w/TV, no pvt. bath. Located in 3 bldgs.
Rates: $60-$80/room, $75-$85/suite, all incl. full brk., afternoon refreshment. Seasonal variations.
Credit cards: MC, V
Restrictions: No smoking. $25.00 deposit req. 3-day cancellation notice req.
Notes: Offering Christian hospitality. Fax, modem, and computer services available.*

TRAPPER CREEK (3)

North Country B & B
P.O. Box 13377, Trapper Creek, AK 99683
(907) 733-3981
Innkeeper: Mike and Sheryl Uher
Rooms: 5, incl. 4 w/pvt. bath plus 1 suite w/pvt. bath, TV, plus 1 cabin. Located in two bldgs.
Rates: $85/room, $120/suite, $65/cabin, all incl. cont. brk.
Credit cards: Most major cards
Restrictions: Deposit req. 3-day cancellation notice for full refund. No smoking.
Notes: Built in 1993. All rooms have private outside entrance. The cabin on the lake sleeps 2 adults in the loft. Recreation room below guest rooms is furnished with a pool table, TV, breakfast bar, and laundry facilities.

YUKON DON'S

WASILLA (3)

Yukon Don's
2221 Yukon Cir., 1830 E Parks Hwy. 386, Wasilla, AK 99654
(907) 376-7472, (907) 376-6515

Innkeeper: Don and Kristan Tanner

Rooms: 3 w/pvt. bath, phone, incl. 1 w/TV, plus 2 suites w/pvt. bath, phone, incl. 1 w/TV

Rates: $55-65/room, $85-$105/suite, all incl. cont. brk. Discount avail. for extended stay.

Credit cards: None

Restrictions: No smoking. Deposit req. 3-day cancellation notice req. 2-night min. stay in suite.

Notes: One-story, colony-era barn converted to home and Inn. Lounge overlooking Chugach Mountains. Furnished with Alaska decor, log partitions, log bar. Sauna, exercise room, hot tub. Provisions for tours, fishing, hiking, canoeing trips available.*

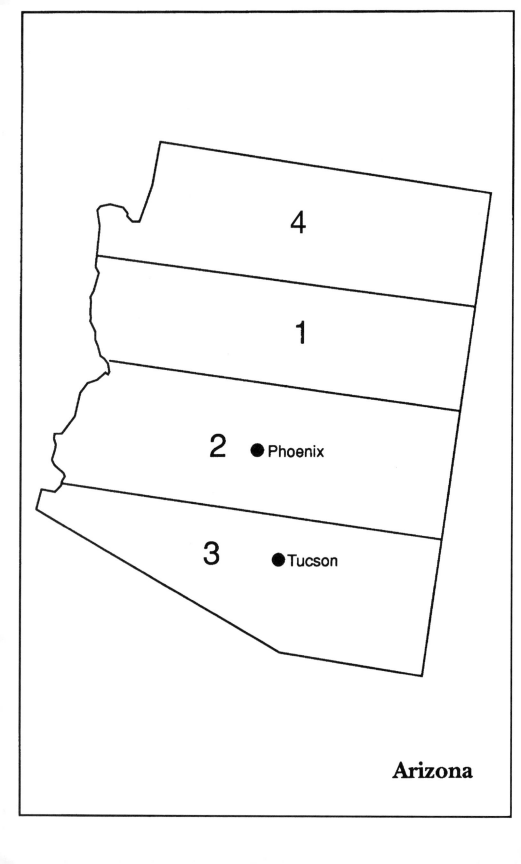

Arizona

The Greenway House
401 Cole Ave., Bisbee, AZ 85603
(602) 432-7170, (800) 253-3325
Innkeeper: Joy O'Clock, Dr. George Knox
Rooms: 8 suites w/pvt. bath, kitchenette, incl. 3 w/phone and 3 w/TV. Located in
   2 bldgs.
Rates: $75-$125, incl. cont. brk. Discount avail. for extended stay.
Credit cards: Most major cards
Restrictions: No children under 12, pets, smoking. Deposit req. 72-hour cancellation notice req. 2-night min. stay req.
Notes: Craftsman-style mansion and Carriage House built in 1906. Fully restored
with air conditioning. Furnished with antiques. Billiard room with pool table, shuf-
fleboard, jukebox, slot machine, TV, bar. Spanish spoken. Handicapped access.

Main Street Inn
26 Main St., Bisbee, AZ 85603
(602) 432-5237
Innkeeper: Walter Kuehl and Jim Grosskopf
Rooms: 8, plus 1 suite
Rates: $45-$75/room, $95-$110/suite, all incl. full brk.
Credit cards: Most major cards
Restrictions: No pets. Smoking restricted. Deposit preferred. 24-hour cancellation
   notice req.
Notes: Built in 1888 with bay windows. Furnished in Southwestern style. Quiet room
and separate TV lounge. Small private parties accommodated.*

School House Inn
818 Tombstone Canyon, Box 32, Bisbee, AZ 85603
(602) 432-2996, (800) 537-4333
Innkeeper: Marc and Shirl Negus
Rooms: 6 w/pvt. bath, plus 3 suites w/pvt. bath
Rates: $45-$55/room, $65-$85/suite, all incl. full brk. Discount avail. for mid-week
   stay.
Credit cards: Most major cards
Restrictions: No children under 13, pets. Smoking restricted. Deposit req. 2-day
   cancellation notice req.
Notes: Two-story historic brick school built in 1918. Has operated as an Inn since
1989. Copies of original school blueprints in main stairway. Family room with TV,
board games. Furnished with antiques. Balcony, shaded patio with brick barbecue
fireplace, swing, fountain.

Kelly's Whistlestop B & B
107 Perry Rd., Box 236, Dragoon, AZ 85609
(602) 586-7515
Innkeeper: Jim and Katy Kelly

Rooms: 2, no pvt. bath. Located in 2 bldgs.

Rates: $50-$55, incl. full brk. Discount avail. for extended stay.

Credit cards: None

Restrictions: No children under 12. Smoking restricted. One-night's deposit req. 3-day cancellation notice req.

Notes: Rammed earth passive solar buildings located in a high desert range on the Southern Pacific rail line. Dining room with 12-foot windows in main house. Guest house has common sitting room with kitchenette. Deck overlooking mountain.

FLAGSTAFF (1)

Arizona Mountain Inn
685 Lake Mary Rd., Flagstaff, AZ 86001
(602) 774-8959

Innkeeper: The Wanek family

Rooms: 3 suites w/pvt. bath, TV, incl. 2 w/fireplace

Rates: $60-$90, incl. cont. brk., evening refreshment

Credit cards: Most major cards

Restrictions: No pets, smoking. Full prepayment req. 2-night min. stay on wknds.

Birch Tree Inn
824 W. Birch Ave., Flagstaff, AZ 86001-4420
(602) 774-1042, (602) 774-8462

Innkeeper: Sandy and Ed Znetko, Donna and Rodger Pettinger

Rooms: 5, incl. 3 w/pvt. bath, phone

Rates: $60-$85, incl. full brk., afternoon refreshment. Seasonal variations. Discount avail. for extended stay.

Credit cards: Most major cards

Restrictions: No children under 5, pets, smoking. Full prepayment req. 72-hour cancellation notice req., less $10.00 fee per day. 2-night min. stay on holiday wknds.

Notes: Two-story house with Greek columns built in 1917. Parlor with fireplace. Game room with billiard table, piano, board games. Dining room, patio, wraparound porch. Furnished in country style with antiques, heirlooms. Off-street parking available.*

INN AT FOUR TEN

Inn at Four Ten
410 N. Leroux St., Flagstaff, AZ 86001
(602) 774-0088

Innkeeper: Howard and Sally Krueger

Rooms: 3, incl. 1 w/pvt. bath, plus 6 suites w/pvt. bath, incl. 1 w/fireplace. Located in 2 bldgs.
Rates: $55-$85/room, $70-$85/suite, $80-$85/fireplace suite, all incl. full brk., afternoon refreshment. Seasonal variations.
Credit cards: Most major cards
Restrictions: No pets, smoking. Min. 50% deposit req. 7-day cancellation notice req. 2-night min. stay for holidays, wknds. from May 1–October 31
Notes: Built in 1907 as a family residence. Fully renovated and decorated with antiques, stained-glass, lace. Living room with books, music, board games. Patio, gazebo, porch swing. Handicapped access.

FREDONIA (4)

Jackson House B & B
90 N. Main St., Fredonia, AZ 86022
(602) 643-7702, 643-7204

Innkeeper: Darol and Georgia Heaton
Rooms: 6, incl. 2 w/TV. No pvt. bath.
Rates: $38-$50, incl. expanded cont. brk.
Credit cards: Most major cards
Restrictions: No smoking. Deposit req. 5-day cancellation notice req. Closed Nov. 1–April 30.
Notes: Two-story house built in early 1900s.

GLOBE (2)

Noftsger Hill Inn
425 North St., Globe, AZ 85501
(602) 425-2260

Innkeeper: Frank and Pamela Hulme
Rooms: 2 plus 2 suites all w/pvt. bath, incl. 2 w/fireplace, 1 w/TV
Rates: $45-$65, incl. full brk. Discount avail. for extended stay.
Credit cards: Most major cards
Restrictions: No children under 4, pets, smoking. Deposit req. 10-day cancellation notice req.
Notes: Two-story building originally built as a school house in 1907. Renovated in 1991. Decorated in mining era antiques and art. Limited handicapped access.*

Pinal Mountain B & B
360 Jess Hayes Rd., Box 1593, Globe, AZ 85502
(602) 425-2563, (502) 425-0113

Innkeeper: Peter and Carol DeNinno
Rooms: 2 w/pvt. bath, phone, cable TV/VCR
Rates: $60-$75, incl. cont. brk. Discount avail. for extended stay.
Credit cards: None
Restrictions: No pets, smoking. One night's deposit req.
Notes: Working horse farm located at the foot of Pinal Mountains next to the Besh-Ba Gowah Salado Indian Ruins. Full kitchen facilities. Living room. Sitting porch. Guest may bring own horses. Stabling facilities available. Rose garden. Resident animals.

HEREFORD (3)

Ramsey Canyon Inn
31 Ramsey Canyon Rd., Hereford, AZ 85615
(602) 378-3010
Innkeeper: Ronald and Shirlene De Santis
Rooms: 6 plus 2 cottages w/kitchen, all w/pvt. bath. Located in 2 bldgs.
Rates: $90-$95/room, incl full brk. $95-$115/cottage
Credit cards: Most major cards
Restrictions: No children under 13, pets. Smoking restricted. Full prepayment req.
  2-week cancellation notice req., less $15.00 fee. 2-night min. stay during holidays
  and for cottages.
Notes: Located at 5,400-ft. elevation with stream. Furnished with antiques. Limited
handicapped access.

PATAGONIA (3)

The Patio B & B
277 McKeown Ave., Box 271, Patagonia, AZ 85624
(602) 394-2671
Innkeeper: Kathy Lundy
Rooms: 2 plus 1 cottage, all w/pvt. bath, TV, incl. 1 w/fireplace. Located in 2 bldgs.
Rates: $60/room, $75/cottage, all incl. full brk. Discount avail. for extended stay.
Credit cards: Most major cards
Restrictions: No smoking.
Notes: Cottage built as miner's home. Cottage guests have access to full kitchen.
Handicapped access.

PHOENIX (2)

Maricopa Manor
15 W. Pasadena Ave., Phoenix, AZ 85013
(602) 274-6302, (602) 766-3904
Innkeeper: Mary Ellen and Paul Kelley
Rooms: 5 suites w/pvt. bath, phone, TV. Located in 3 bldgs.
Rates: $79-$159, incl. cont. brk. Discount avail. for extended stay. Seasonal varia-
  tions.
Credit cards: Most major cards
Restrictions: No pets, smoking. Deposit req. 7-day cancellation notice req., less
  $15.00 fee.
Notes: Spanish styled manor house built in 1928. Gathering room with outside
deck. Formal living, dining, music rooms. Patio, gazebo spa. Furnished with an-
tiques, art. Small private parties accommodated.

PRESCOTT (1)

Mt. Vernon Inn
204 N. Mt. Vernon Ave., Prescott, AZ 86301
(602) 778-0886
Innkeeper: Sybil and John Nelson
Rooms: 4 w/pvt. bath, phone, plus 3 guesthouses w/pvt. bath, phone, TV, kitchen.
  Located in 4 bldgs.

Rates: $70-$80/room, $90-$110/guesthouse, all incl. full brk., afternoon refreshment. Discount avail. for extended, mid-week stay. Seasonal variations.
Credit cards: Most major cards
Restrictions: Pets, smoking restricted. One night's deposit req. Min. 3-day cancellation notice req. Children welcome in cottages. 2-night min. stay on holiday wknds.
Notes: Two-story Victorian house built in 1900. Two parlors. Dining room with fireplace. Sitting room with TV, VCR. Greek Revival side porch. Furnished with antiques. Board games available. Handicap access.*

The Prescott Country Inn
503 S. Montezuma St., Prescott, AZ 86303
(602) 445-7991
Innkeeper: Morris and Sue Faulkner
Rooms: 15 cottages w/pvt. bath, phone, TV, incl. 4 w/fireplace. Located in 6 bldgs.
Rates: $89-$149, incl. cont. brk. Discount avail. for mid-week and senior citizen stays. Seasonal variations.
Credit cards: MC, V
Restrictions: No pets. Smoking restricted. Deposit req. 2-day cancellation notice req., less $15.00 fee. 2-night min. stay on wknds. and holidays.
Notes: American, French, and English-style country cottages established in 1940. Individual and private decks, porches, patios. Parking at front door. Decorated with quilts, live plants, collectibles, art.*

SCOTTSDALE (2)

Inn at the Citadel
8700 E. Pinnacle Peak Rd., Scottsdale, AZ 85255
(602) 585-6133, (800) 927-8367, (602) 585-3255
Innkeeper: Manager
Rooms: 11 suites w/pvt. bath, phone, TV, incl. 6 w/fireplace
Rates: $265, incl. cont. brk. Seasonal variations.
Credit cards: Most major cards
Restrictions: No smoking. Pets restricted. One-night's deposit req. 7-day cancellation notice req. 2-night min. stay.
Notes: Excercise equipment, computer, and fax facilities available. Small private parties accommodated. Handicapped access. Spanish spoken.*

Valley O'the Sun B & B
P.O. Box 2214, Scottsdale, AZ 85252
(602) 941-1281, (800) 689-1281
Innkeeper: Kathleen Curtis
Rooms: 3 w/TV, phone, incl. 1 w/pvt. bath
Rates: $35, incl. cont. brk.
Credit cards: None
Restrictions: No children under 10, pets. Smoking restricted. Min. one night's deposit req. 7-day cancellation notice req., less $15.00 fee.
Notes: Private home located in college area of Tempe. Has operated as inn since 1983. Airport pick-up available.

SEDONA (1)

B & B at Saddle Rock Ranch
P.O. Box 10095, Sedona, AZ 86336
(602) 282-7640

Innkeeper: Fran and Dan Bruno
Rooms: 2 plus 1 suite, all w/pvt. bath, fireplace, TV. Located in 2 bldgs.
Rates: $110-$120/room, $130/suite, all incl. full brk., afternoon refreshment. Seasonal variations. Dicount avail. for extended stay.
Credit cards: None
Restrictions: No children under 14, pets, smoking. Deposit req. 10-day cancellation notice req., less $15.00 fee. 2-night min. stay. 3-night min. stay on some holdays.
Notes: One- and two-story ranch houses built with timber beams, rustic adobe and red rock walls, wood and flagstone floors in the 1920s. Fully renovated. Located on 3 hillside acres, adjoining National Forest. Has been in Old West motion pictures. Rock-walled breakfast room. Parlor. Library with fireplaces, books, games, antique pump organ. Decorated with art by local artists. Furnished in antiques. Decks, gardens. Pool and whirlpool spa open in season. Discounted off-road tours available. French, German, Spanish, Italian spoken.

Briar Patch Inn
HC 30, Box 1002, Sedona, AZ 86336
(602) 282-2342, (602) 282-2342

Innkeeper: Edward and Jo Ann Olson
Rooms: 16, incl. 9 suites, all w/pvt. bath, incl. 12 w/fireplace. Located in 14 bldgs.
Rates: $135-$195, all incl. full brk. and afternoon refreshment.
Credit cards: MC, V
Restrictions: No pets. Smoking restricted. One night's deposit req. 10-day cancellation notice req., less $10.00 fee. 2-day min. stay in peak season. 3-day min. stay on holidays.
Notes: Cabins, some w/decks and creek view, located on 9 acres. Furnished in Southwestern style. Live classical music. German and Spanish spoken.*

Canyon Villa B & B Inn
125 Canyon Circle Dr., Box 204, Sedona, AZ 86336
(602) 284-1226, (800) 453-1166, (602) 284-2114

Innkeeper: Chuck and Marion Yadon
Rooms: 11 w/pvt. bath, phone, TV, incl. 4 w/fireplace
Rates: $95-$155, all include full brk., afternoon refreshment
Credit cards: Most major cards
Restrictions: No children under 10, pets, smoking. Deposit req. 7-day cancellation notice req. 2-night min. stay on wknds.
Notes: Two-story Inn fully insulated for weather. Living and dining rooms overlook red rocks and canyons. Private patios or balconies in guest rooms. Pool, fireplace. Received AAA Four Diamond and Mobil Guide's Four Star awards. Handicapped access.*

Casa Sedona
55 Hozoni Dr., Sedona, AZ 86336
(602) 282-2938, (800) 525-3756, (602) 282-2259

Innkeeper: Misty and Lori Zitko, Dick Curtis
Rooms: 11 w/pvt. bath, phone, fireplace, terrace, spa tub. Located in 2 bldgs.

Rates: $95-$150, incl. full brk. Special pkgs. avail.

Credit cards: Most major cards

Restrictions: No children under 10, pets, smoking. One-night's deposit req. 72-hour cancellation notice req. 2-night min. stay on wknds. and holidays.

Notes: Two-story inn. Sierra room with TV, music center. Library with fireplace. Sunrise alcove, dining room, kitchen. Two patios. Handicapped access.*

COUNTRY ELEGANCE B & B

Country Elegance B & B
P.O. Box 1257, Sedona, AZ 86339
(602) 634-4470

Innkeeper: Rita Sydelle

Rooms: 3 w/TV, incl. 2 w/pvt. bath, 1 w/kitchen

Rates: $70-$95, incl. full brk.

Credit cards: None

Restrictions: No children under 10, pets, smoking. Deposit req. 7-day cancellation notice req., less $15.00 fee. 2-night min. stay.

Notes: Located in pastoral setting on a mini-farm. Arizona room with views. Library. Living room with fireplace. Furnished by Interior Designer/Innkeeper. Egg-laying chickens, organic vegetable gardens, fruit trees. Fishing in fish pond.

Country Gardens B & B
P.O. Box 2603, Sedona, AZ 86339
(602) 282-1343

Innkeeper: Rod and Judy Snapp

Rooms: 3 suites w/phone, TV, pvt. bath; 2 w/fireplaces, 1w/Jacuzzi

Rates: $115-$165, incl. 3-course gourmet brk. by chef/owner. Discount avail. for extended stay.

Credit cards: None

Restrictions: No pets, smoking. 50% deposit req. 7-day cancellation notice req., less $15.00 fee. 2-night min. stay on wknds.

Notes: Southwest Country estate nestled in the pinon forest of Sedona. Antiques throughout inn.

Cozy Cactus Bed & Breakfast
80 Canyon Circle Dr., Sedona, AZ 86351-8678
(602) 284-0082, (800) 788-2082

Innkeeper: Bob and Lynne Gillman
Rooms: 5 w/pvt. bath
Rates: $75-$90, incl. full brk. Discount avail. for extended and senior citizen stays.
Credit cards: Most major cards
Restrictions: No pets. Smoking restricted. Deposit req. 7-day cancellation notice
   req., less $15.00 fee. 2-night min. stay on wknds.
Notes: Ranch-style house located at the foot of Castle Rock. Great room. Unique
furnishings include family heirlooms and theatrical memorabilia. Each pair of bed-
rooms shares a sitting room featuring a fireplace and small kitchen. Patio. Tour
arrangements available. Italian spoken.*

Graham's Bed & Breakfast Inn
150 Canyon Circle, Sedona, AZ 86351
(602) 284-1425, (800) 228-1425, (602) 284-0767
Innkeeper: Roger and Carol Redenbaugh
Rooms: 5 w/pvt. bath, phone, TV, pvt. balcony, incl. 3 w/fireplace, plus 1 suite
   w/pvt. bath, TV, laser disc player, Jacuzzi, fireplace, pvt. patio.
Rates: $95-$155/room, $195/suite, all incl. full brk., afternoon refreshment. Dis-
count avail. for extended stay.
Credit cards: Most major cards
Restrictions: No pets. Smoking restricted. Deposit req. 7-day cancellation notice
   req., less $15.00 fee. 2-night min. stay on wknds. 3-night min. stay on some holi-
   days.
Notes: Modified two-story Southwestern-style house with lawn and fountain around
entryway. Has operated as Inn since 1985. Living room with fireplace, TV, stereo,
board games. Dining room with fireplace. Decorated in Southwestern style with art-
deco and Early American antiques, wicker. Some rooms w/VCR, Jacuzzi. Swimming
pool, spa, covered patio/porch. Giftshop on premises. Bicycles, gift certificates
available. Handicapped access.

Lodge at Sedona
125 Kallof Pl., Sedona, AZ 86336
(602) 204-1942, (800) 619-4467, (602) 204-2128
Innkeeper: Barb and Mark Dinunzio
Rooms: 11 w/pvt. bath, phone, incl. 2 w/fireplace, plus 2 suites w/pvt. bath, phone,
   fireplace, TV
Rates: $85-$125/room, $165-$195/suite, all incl. full brk., afternoon refreshment
Credit cards: Most major cards
Restrictions: No pets. Smoking restricted. Deposit req. 7-day cancellation notice
   req. 2-night min. stay on wknds. and holidays.
Notes: Two-story rustic house built in 1959 as a doctor's home. Recently restored.
Operated as an inn since 1991. Surrounded with pine trees. Five common rooms
including a boardroom for meetings, fireside parlor, library, morning porch, all ac-
cented with rough-hewn timbers and native red sandstone. Furnished with antiques. Handicapped access. Small private parties accommodated.*

Rose Tree Inn
376 Cedar St., Sedona, AZ 86336
(602) 282-2065
Innkeeper: Rachel M. Gillespie
Rooms: 1 w/TV, plus 3/suites w/kitchen. Located in 2 bldgs.

Rates: $82/room, $89-$116/suite. Seasonal variations. Discount avail. for extended stay.
Credit cards: MC, V
Restrictions: No children under 12, pets. Smoking restricted. 50% deposit req. Min. 2-day cancellation notice req. 2-night min. stay on wknds.
Notes: Country style inn. Kitchen, library, Jacuzzi, gas grill. Lawn games. Small private parties accommodated.*

Territorial House An Old West B & B
65 Piki Dr., Sedona, AZ 86336
(602) 204-2737, (800) 801-2737, (602) 204-2230
Innkeeper: John and Linda Steele
Rooms: 3 w/pvt. bath, TV, incl. 2 w/phone, plus 1 suite w/pvt. bath, phone, fireplace, TV
Rates: $90-$130/room, $120/suite, all incl. full brk., evening refreshment. Seasonal variations. Discount avail. for extended stay.
Credit cards: Most major cards
Restrictions: No pets. Smoking restricted. Deposit req. 7-day cancellation notice req., less $15.00 fee. 2-night min. stay on wknds. and holidays.
Notes: Territorial-style native stone and cedar house built in 1974. Has operated as inn since 1993. Saltillo-tiled kitchen. Stone fireplace, three redwood decks. Some rooms incl. whirlpool tubs, private stairways, private balconies, telescopes, VCR, hardwood floors, marble Jacuzzi, gas fireplace.*

SIERRA VISTA (3)

San Pedro B & B
P.O. Box 885, Sierra Vista, AZ 85636-0885
(602) 458-7626
Innkeeper: Sue and Bob Walker
Rooms: 1 plus 1 suite, all w/pvt. bath. Located in 2 bldgs.
Rates: $50/room, $65/suite, all incl. full brk.
Credit cards: None
Restrictions: No children under 12, pets. Smoking restricted. One night's deposit req. 7-day cancellation notice req., less $10.00 fee. 2-night min. stay.
Notes: Two-story hacienda. Located on 5 acres. Decorated with Southwestern furnishings and collectibles. Game room with TV, pool table. Swimming pool. Spa. Garden courtyard with Mexican fountain.*

TOMBSTONE (3)

Priscilla's B & B
101 N. 3rd St., Tombstone, AZ 85638
(602) 457-3844
Innkeeper: Barbara and Larry Gray
Rooms: 3 w/sink, no pvt. bath
Rates: $39-$55, incl. full brk. Discount avail. for extended stay.
Credit cards: Most major cards
Restrictions: Smoking restricted. Deposit req. 24-hour cancellation notice.
Notes: Two-story Victorian, country house built in 1904. Furnished with antiques. Dining room, garden, paths. Spanish spoken.

TUCSON (3)

Casa Alegre Bed and Breakfast
316 E. Speedway, Tucson, AZ 85705
(602) 628-1800, (602) 792-1880

Innkeeper: Phyllis Florek
Rooms: 4 w/pvt. bath, incl. 1 w/fireplace
Rates: $70-$85, incl. full brk. Seasonal variations. Discount avail. for extended and
senior citizen stays.
Credit cards: Most major cards
Restrictions: No children, pets. Smoking restricted. Min. 50% deposit req. 7-day
cancellation notice req., less one-night's fee.
Notes: Craftsman-style bungalow built in 1915. Located in central Tucson. Formal
living room with rock fireplace. Mahogany and leaded-glass cabinetry and hard-
wood floors. Furnished with antiques that reflect Tucson's history. Patio, pool, and
Jacuzzi. Spanish spoken.*

Casa Tierra
11155 W. Calle Pima, Tucson, AZ 85743
(602) 578-3058

Innkeeper: Karen and Lyle Hymer-Thompson
Rooms: 3 w/pvt. bath, refrigerator, microwave oven
Rates: $70-$85, incl. full vegetarian brk. Discount avail. for extended stay.
Credit cards: None
Restrictions: No children under 3, pets, smoking. 50% deposit req. 7-day cancella-
tion notice req. 2-night min. stay.
Notes: Rustic adobe house built in 1989 on five acres of secluded desert. Entryways
with vaulted brick ceilings, interior arched courtyard. Family dining room. Fur-
nished in Mexican decor. Rooms have private patios. Hot tub outdoors. Spanish
spoken.

Catalina Park Inn
309 E. 1st St., Tucson, AZ 85705
(602) 792-4541, (602) 792-4541

Innkeeper: Mark Hall, Paul Richard
Rooms: 2 plus 1 suite, all w/pvt. bath, phone, TV. Located in 2 bldgs.
Rates: $90-$115/room, $130/suite, all incl. cont. brk.
Credit cards: MC, V
Restrictions: No children under 10, pets. Smoking restricted. One-night's deposit
req. 7-day cancellation notice req.
Notes: Two-story Italianate house built in 1927. Living room with fireplace,
study/gameroom, 2 verandas.*

Copper Bell B & B
25 N Westmoreland Ave., Tucson, AZ 85745
(602) 629-9229

Innkeeper: Hans H. Kraus, Gertrude M. Eich
Rooms: 8, plus 1 suite, all w/pvt. bath. Located in 2 bldgs.
Rates: $55-$65/room, $85/suite, all incl. lunch and dinner. Discount avail. for ex-
tended stay.
Credit cards: None

Restrictions: No children under 12, pets. Smoking restricted. 10% deposit req., 7-day cancellation notice req., less 10% fee. 2-night min. stay.

Notes: Lava stone house built with German doors and windows from 1907 to 1920. German copper bell located in arched porch. Living room with fireplace. Heirloom furnishings. French, German spoken.

EL PRESIDIO BED & BREAKFAST INN

El Presidio Bed & Breakfast Inn
297 N. Main Ave., Tucson, AZ 85701
(602) 623-6151

Innkeeper: Patti Toci

Rooms: 1 plus 1 suite w/fireplace, plus 2 guesthouses, all w/pvt. bath, phone, TV. Located in 2 bldgs.

Rates: $75/room, $85-$110/suite, all incl. full brk., afternoon refreshment. Discount avail. for extended stay. Seasonal variations.

Credit cards: None

Restrictions: No children under 12, pets. Smoking restricted. 50% deposit req. 14-day cancellation notice req. Closed July.

Notes: Victorian adobe house built in 1879 as American Territorial blend of Mexican and American building traditions. Located in El Presidio Historic District. Courtyards with fountains, gardens. Furnished in Old Mexican style with antiques. Listed on the National Register of Historic Places. Small private parties accommodated.*

Hideaway B & B
4344 E. Poe St., Tucson, AZ 85711
(602) 323-8067

Innkeeper: Dwight and Ola Parker

Rooms: 1 suite w/pvt. bath, TV, VCR, phone

Rates: $55, incl. full brk.

Credit cards: None

Restrictions: No pets, smoking. Deposit req. 7-day cancellation notice req. 3-night min. stay.

Notes: Private bungalow for two. Spacious yard w/patio. Guests have access to refrigerator.

La Posada del Valle
1640 N. Campbell Ave., Tucson, AZ 85719
(602) 795-3840

Innkeeper: Tom and Karin Dennen
Rooms: 5 w/pvt. bath, incl. 2/w phone. Located in 2 bldgs.
Rates: $90-$115, incl. brk., lunch, afternoon refreshment. Seasonal variations. Discount avail. for extended, mid-week, or senior citizen stays.
Credit cards: Most major cards
Restrictions: No children under 12, pets, smoking. Deposit req. 14-day cancellation notice req.
Notes: Southwest adobe inn built in 1929. Sun porch overlooking landscaped yard. Private entrances. Living room, dining room. Furnished with period antiques, art-deco pieces. Courtyard with fountain, gardens. Spanish spoken.*

Natural B & B
3150 E. Presidio Rd., Tucson, AZ 85716
(602) 881-4582, (602) 326-1385

L. Marc Haberman
Rooms: 3 w/phone, TV, incl. 2 w/pvt bath
Rates: $55-$65, incl. full brk. Discount avail. for extended and senior citizen stays.
Credit cards: Most major cards
Restrictions: No pets. Smoking restricted. No street shoes inside. Deposit req. 2-day cancellation notice req., less $5.00 fee.
Notes: Located in quiet neighborhood. Living room with fireplace. Patio, private sun decks. Vegetarian food. Special diets accommodated. Massage, holistic health counseling, secretarial services available. Lunch available. Laundry service, airport transportation available. German and Spanish spoken. Limited handicapped access.

The Peppertrees Bed & Breakfast
724 E. University Blvd., Tucson, AZ 85719
(602) 622-7167, (800) 438-5763, (602) 622-5959

Innkeeper: Marjorie Martin
Rooms: 3 w/pvt. bath, plus 2 guesthouses w/pvt. bath, phone, TV, living room, dining area, kitchen, laundry, pvt. patio. Located in 3 bldgs.
Rates: $68-$88/room, $140/suite, all incl. full brk. Seasonal variations. Discount avail. for extended stay.
Credit cards: Most major cards
Restrictions: No pets. Children, smoking restricted. One night's deposit req. 7-day cancellation notice req. 2-night min. stay on major holiday wknds.
Notes: Territorial house built in 1905. Fully restored in 1981. Has operated as inn since 1988. Sitting room, library. Dining room with French doors leading to garden. Furnished with period antiques. Patio with fountain. Innkeeper is author of cookbook. Special diets, small private parties accommodated. Airport pick-up available. Some French, Spanish spoken.*

Quail's Vista
826 E. Palisades Dr., Tucson, AZ 85737
(602) 297-5980

Innkeeper: Barbara Jones
Rooms: 2 w/pvt. hall bath, plus 1 suite w/phone, fireplace, TV
Rates: $65/room, $85/suite, all incl. cont. brk. Discount avail. for extended stay.
Credit cards: None
Restrictions: No pets. Smoking restricted. Min. one-night's deposit req. 14-day cancellation notice req., less $10.00 fee.

QUAIL'S VISTA

Notes: Earth and adobe "Santa Fe" house with 27' walls. Great room with TV Satellite, VCR/CD. Furnished with Native American artifacts and Mexican tile decor. Redwood deck with view of mountains. Swim/steam hot tub. Innkeeper is professional tour guide, will help with planning as time permits.*

YUMA (3)

Casa de Osgood
11620 Ironwood Dr., Yuma, AZ 85367
(602) 342-0471
Innkeeper: Chris and Vickie Osgood
Rooms: 1 suite w/pvt. bath, phone, fireplace, TV
Rates: $65, incl. full brk.
Credit cards: None
Restrictions: No pets, smoking, alcohol. Min. one-night's deposit req. 7-day cancellation notice req., less $5.00 fee.
Notes: Private home with view of Gila Mountains. Veranda. Sundeck. Airport pickup available.

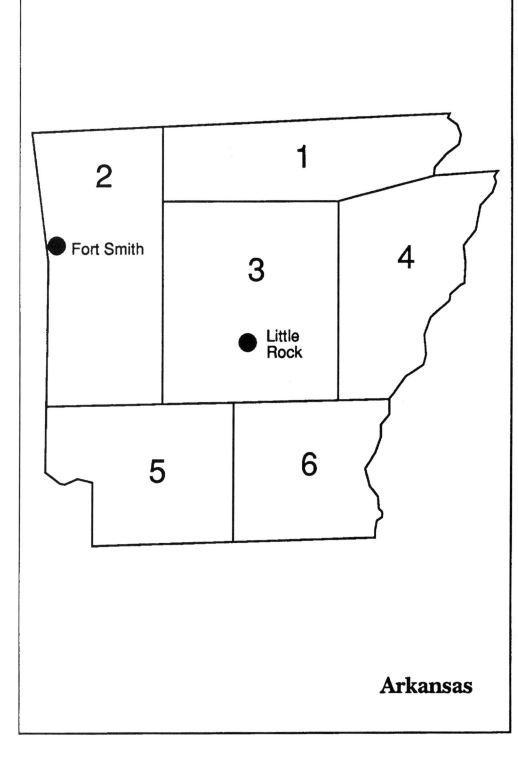

Arkansas

Arkansas

CROSSETT (6)

THE TRIESCHMANN HOUSE BED & BREAKFAST

The Trieschmann House Bed & Breakfast
707 Cedar, Crossett, AR 71635
(501) 364-7592
Innkeeper: Pat and Herman Owens
Rooms: 3, incl. 1 w/pvt. bath, phone, electric fireplace
Rates: $50-$60, incl. full brk.
Credit cards: Most major cards
Restrictions: No pets, smoking. 2-day cancellation notice req.
Notes: One-story house built in 1903. Located in a forested area. Furnished with period furniture. Grounds include pecan trees, wicker swing. Front porch with wicker swing and furniture.

EUREKA SPRINGS (2)

Arbour Glen B & B
7 Lema St., Eureka Springs, AR 72632
(501) 253-9010, (800) 515-GLEN
Innkeeper: Jeff
Rooms: 1 plus 2 suites, all w/pvt. bath, TV
Rates: $65-$75/room, $75-$95/suite, all incl. full brk., afternoon refreshment. Discount avail. for extended and mid-week stays. Seasonal variations.
Credit cards: Most major cards
Restrictions: No pets, smoking. One night's deposit req. 10-day cancellation notice req., less $15.00 fee. Min. 2-night stay on wknds. and holidays.
Notes: Built in 1896 overlooking Eureka Springs historic district. Veranda with swing overlooking garden with fish pond, fountain. Decorated with antiques, handmade quilts, Victorian touches.*

Arsenic & Old Lace
60 Hillside Ave., Eureka Springs, AR 72632
(501) 253-5454, (800) 243-5223

Innkeeper: Gary and Phyllis Jones
Rooms: 5 w/pvt. bath, incl. 1 w/fireplace, 2 w/TV
Rates: $90-$150, incl. full brk., afternoon refreshment. Seasonal variations. Discount avail. for extended stay.
Credit cards: MC, V
Restrictions: No children under 14, pets, smoking. Deposit req. 7-day cancellation notice req. 2-night min. stay in season.
Notes: Three-story Queen Ann Victorian inn built in 1992. Located on one acre of landscaped English perennial gardens adjacent to trolley line and train terminal in historic district. Library with TV, VCR, selection of old movies. Jacuzzis in some baths. Parlor with piano. Guest sing-alongs. Morning room. Furnished with lace curtains and ceiling fans, stained glass, original art. Wrap-around verandas with wicker furniture, rocking chairs, porch swings.*

Bridgeford House
263 Spring St., Eureka Springs, AR 72632
(501) 253-7853

Innkeeper: Denise and Michael McDonald
Rooms: 3, plus 1 suite, all w/pvt. bath, TV
Rates: $85/room, $95/suite, all incl. full brk., afternoon refreshment. Seasonal variations. Discount avail. for extended stay.
Credit cards: Most major cards
Restrictions: 7-day cancellation notice req. 2-night min. stay on wknds. 3-night min. stay on holidays.
Notes: Gingerbread house built in 1884. Parlor. Furnished with period antiques. Air-conditioned. Porches with wicker furniture.*

Carriage House
75 Lookout Lane, Eureka Springs, AR 72632
(501) 253-5259, (501) 253-5259

Innkeeper: Pamela Doyle
Rooms: 2 suites w/pvt. bath, phone, cable TV, incl. 1 w/Jacuzzi. Located in 2 bldgs.
Rates: $105-$115, incl. afternoon refreshment. Seasonal variations.
Credit cards: Most major cards
Restrictions: No children under 5, smoking.
Notes: Carriage House built approx. 1895. Garden with brick patio, hot tub. Hayloft bedroom with skylight. Fireplace stove. Pool table and pinball machine. Living room w/fireplace. Furnished in country decor.

CLIFF COTTAGE B & B

Cliff Cottage B & B
42 Armstrong St., Eureka Springs, AR 72632
(501) 253-7409, (800) 799-7409
Innkeeper: Sandra Smith
Rooms: 2 plus 2 suites, all w/pvt. bath, TV, inc. 2 w/Jacuzzi. Located in 2 bldgs.
Rates: $85-$100/room, $110-$125/suite, all incl. cont. brk., evening refreshment.
Seasonal variations. Discount avail. for extended and mid-week stays.
Credit cards: Most major cards
Restrictions: No children, pets. Smoking restricted. One night's deposit req. 14-day
cancellation notice req., less $20.00 fee. 2-night min. stay req. on wknds.
Notes: Built in 1892 on a bluff. Fully restored in 1992. Located in Historic Downtown. Dining room. Great room with fireplace, petite swuare grand piano forte,
vaulted ceiling. Victorian furnishings. Decks, Victorian gardens. Listed in the National Register of Historic Places. Small private parties accommodated. Wedding
consultant avail. French, Spanish, German spoken.*

Crescent Cottage Inn
211 Spring St., Eureka Springs, AR 72632
(501) 253-6022, (501) 253-6234
Innkeeper: Ralph and Phyllis Becker
Rooms: 3 plus 1 suite, all w/pvt. bath, phone, TV
Rates: $75-$115/room, $90/suite, all incl. full brk., afternoon refreshment. Sea-
sonal variations. Discount avail. for extended stay.
Credit cards: Most major cards
Restrictions: No children, pets, smoking. 50% deposit req. 10-day cancellation
notice req. Closed Jan.–Feb. 2-night min. stay on wknds.
Notes: 2-story Victorian structure built in 1881 by first governor of Arkansas. Fully re-
stored. Furnished with antiques. Two double Jacuzzi whirlpool spas. Back porch overlooks the hills. Listed on the National Register of Historic Places. Spanish spoken.*

DAIRY HOLLOW HOUSE

Dairy Hollow House
515 Spring St., Eureka Springs, AR 72632
(501) 253-7444, (800) 562-8650
Innkeeper: Crescent Dragonwagon, Ned Shank
Rooms: 3 plus 3 suites, all w/pvt. bath, fireplace. Located in 2 bldgs.
Rates: $125-$145/room, $145-$155/suite, all incl. full brk. Seasonal variations.
Credit cards: Most major cards

Restrictions: Children restricted. No pets, smoking. One night's deposit req. 10-day cancellation notice req. 2-night min. stay on wknds. 3-night min. stay on holidays and Oct. craft wknd.

Notes: Two-story Ozark farmhouse built in 1888. Restored and operated as Inn since 1981. Also late '40s "bungalow" style house with tile work throughout. Both decorated with regional antiques, handmade quilts. Each with own living/sitting room. One with private balcony. Parlor with board games. Hot tub. Porch with swing and rockers overlooks flower garden. Herb garden. Restaurant on premises. Three-time winner of "Best Country Inn of the Year." Innkeeper has written the *Dairy Hollow House Cookbook*. Murder-mystery weekends. Limited French spoken.

Dr. R. G. Floyd House
246 Spring St., Eureka Springs, AR 72632
(501) 253-7525

Innkeeper: Georgia and Bill Rubley

Rooms: 4 incl. 1 suite, all w/pvt. bath, phone, TV, 2 w/fireplace. Located in 2 bldgs.

Rates: $80/room, $150/suite, all incl. full brk., afternoon refreshment. Discount avail. for extended stay.

Credit cards: Most major cards

Restrictions: No children under 14. Pets, smoking restricted. 50% deposit req. 10-day cancellation notice req. less $15.00 fee. 2-night min. stay req.

Notes: Queen Anne Victorian house with covered porches built in 1893 by doctor specializing in spring water healing. Victorian-style carpeting wall and ceiling papers. Furnished with antiques. Limestone terrace garden. Board games available. Limited handicapped access.*

HARVEST HOUSE

Harvest House
104 Wall St., Eureka Springs, AR 72632
(501) 253-9360

Innkeeper: Bill and Patt Carmichael

Rooms: 5, incl. 4 w/pvt. bath, 1 w/Jacuzzi

Rates: $60-$90, incl. full brk. Seasonal variations. Discount avail. for extended stay.

Credit cards: Most major cards

Restrictions: No children under 12. Smoking restricted. One-night's deposit req. 7-day cancellation notice req.

Notes: Victorian house built in 1910. Located in the Historic District. Decorated with antiques and collectibles. Common area with TV. Screened gazebo. Off-street parking available. Handicapped access. Resident dog and cat.*

The Heartstone Inn and Cottages
35 Kings Hwy., Eureka Springs, AR 72632
(501) 253-8916

Innkeeper: Bill and Iris Simantel

Rooms: 7 plus 3 suites, all w/pvt. bath, cable TV, incl. 1 w/fireplace, plus 2 cottages

Rates: $67-$80/room, $85-$118/suite, $95-$115/cottages, all incl. full brk. Seasonal variations. Discount avail. for extended stay.

Credit cards: Most major cards

Restrictions: No children, pets. Smoking restricted. 50% deposit req. 7-day cancellation notice req., less $10.00 fee. 2-night min. stay on wknds. 3-night min. stay for some holidays.

Notes: Two-story Victorian house, surrounded by picket fence, with 10-foot ceilings, oak and pine floors. Located in historic district. Furnished with antiques, quilts. Front porch with rockers. Kitchen. Gardens, gazebo. Deck with umbrella tables overlooks wooded ravines. Old fashioned trolley stops at front door. Off-street parking, golf privileges available. Small private parties accommodated. Limited handicapped access.*

Pond Mountain Lodge and Resort
RR 1, Box 50, Eureka Springs, AR 72632
(501) 253-5877

Innkeeper: Judy Jones

Rooms: 2, plus 4 suites, all w/pvt. bath, TV, VCR, microwave, coffe maker, incl. 1 w/fireplace, 2 w/kitchenette, 2 w/Jacuzzi. Located in 2 bldgs.

Rates: $62-$80/room, $88-$125/suite, all incl. full brk., evening refreshment. Seasonal variations. Discount avail. for extended and mid-week stays.

Credit cards: Most major cards

Restrictions: No pets, smoking. Min. one night's deposit req. 3-day cancellation notice req., less $20.00 fee.

Notes: Large rambling ranch house built in 1955 as a summer vaction home of Carl Koch, inventor of the Toni home permanent. Renovated in and has operated as inn since 1992. Located on 209 acres. Vaulted ceiling living room with fireplace. Front veranda. Video and reading library. Game room with billiards. Swimming pool. Picnic area. Two spring-fed ponds stocked for fishing. Horseback riding. Hiking trails. Small private parties accommodated. Limited handicapped access.*

RED BUD MANOR

Red Bud Manor
7 Kings Highway, Eureka Springs, AR 72632
(501) 253-9649

Innkeeper: Tandy and Shari Bozeman

Rooms: 3 w/pvt. bath, cable TV, refrigerator
Rates: $65-$109, incl. full brk. Seasonal variations.
Credit cards: MC, V
Restrictions: Smoking restricted. One night's deposit req. 10-day cancellation notice req., less $15.00 fee. 2-night min. stay on some wknds.
Notes: Victorian house. Fully restored. Dining room, screened porch, Jacuzzis. Furnished with family heirlooms, Victorian antiques.*

Rock Cottage Gardens
10 Eugenia St., Eureka Springs, AR 72632
(501) 253-8659, (800) 624-6646
Innkeeper: Steve Roberson
Rooms: 5 cottages w/pvt. bath, Jacuzzi, cable TV, refrigerator w/beverages
Rates: $95, incl. full brk. Seasonal variations.
Credit cards: Most major cards
Restrictions: No children under 16, pets. Smoking restricted. Min. 50% deposit req. 14-day cancellation notice req., less $20.00 fee. 2-night min. stay on wknds. 3-night min. stay for special events.
Notes: Five rock cabins with vaulted ceilings built in 1930. Renovated in 1992. Decorated with antiques. Flower and herb gardens. Off-street parking available. Located on trolley route.*

SINGLETON HOUSE

Singleton House
11 Singleton, Eureka Springs, AR 72632
(501) 253-9111, (800) 833-3394
Innkeeper: Barbara Gavron
Rooms: 3 plus 2 suites, all w/pvt. bath, incl. 3 w/TV. Cottage w/Jacuzzi. Located in 2 bldgs.
Rates: $65-$69/room, $75-$95/suite, $95/cottage, all incl. full brk. Discount avail. for extended stay.
Credit cards: Most major cards
Restrictions: No pets. Smoking, children restricted. One night's deposit req. 14-day cancellation notice req., less $10.00 fee. Cottage closed Nov.–May.
Notes: Queen Anne Victorian Inn built in the 1890s. Located on hillside overlooking garden with covered arches, arbors, and lily-filled goldfish pond, nature library.

Balcony. Decorated in eclectic style with antiques, folk art, curiosities. Small private parties accommodated.*

HILL AVENUE BED AND BREAKFAST

FAYETTEVILLE (2)

Hill Avenue Bed and Breakfast
131 South Hill Ave., Fayetteville, AR 72701
(501) 444-0865
Innkeeper: Cecelia and Dale Thompson
Rooms: 1, plus 1 suite w/TV
Rates: $40/room, $50/suite, incl. full brk.
Credit cards: None
Restrictions: No children, pets, smoking
Notes: Two-story house located in residential neighborhood. Dining room. Porch with chairs.

HARDY (1)

The Olde Stonehouse Inn
511 Main St., Hardy, AR 72542
(501) 856-2983
Innkeeper: David and Peggy Johnson
Rooms: 6, incl. 5 w/portable phone, plus 2 suites w/fireplace, TV, all w/pvt. bath. Located in 2 bldgs.
Rates: $55-$65/room, $85/suite, all incl. full brk., afternoon refreshment. Special pkgs. avail.
Credit cards: None
Restrictions: No children under 13, pets. Smoking restricted. Deposit req. 7-day cancellation notice req. 2-night min. stay on wknds.
Notes: Two-story native-stone house built in early 1930s. Living room with stone fireplace, antiques, and reproductions. Dining room with oak claw-footed dining table. Sitting area with board games, CDs and tapes. Furnished in 1930s decor.

Front porch with rocking chairs. Side porch with white wicker furniture. Gift certificates available.*

HEBER SPRINGS (3)

Oak Tree Inn
Hwy. 110 West, Heber Springs, AR 72543
(501) 362-7731

Innkeeper: Freddie Lou Lodge
Rooms: 6 w/pvt. whirlpool bath, incl. 5 w/fireplace, plus 4 cabins w/kitchen, laundry, fireplace. Cottage avail.
Rates: $75-$85/room, $110-$140/cottage, all incl. full brk., evening dessert. Discount avail. for mid-week stay.
Credit cards: Most major cards
Restrictions: No pets. Children, smoking restricted. One night's deposit req. 7-day cancellation notice req. 2-night min. stay in cottage.
Notes: Two-story inn located on the Little Red River. Decorated with antiques, contemporary pieces. Swimming pool, tennis court. Limited handicapped access.*

EDWARDIAN INN

HELENA (4)

Edwardian Inn
317 Biscoe, Helena, AR 72342
(501) 338-9155

Innkeeper: Jerri Steed
Rooms: 9 w/pvt. bath, phone, TV, plus 8 suites w/pvt. bath, phone, TV, incl. 2 suites w/fireplace. Located in 2 bldgs.
Rates: $50-$70/room, $56-$89/suite, all incl. cont. brk. Special pkgs. avail.
Credit cards: Most major cards
Restrictions: No smoking. Pets restricted. Deposit req. for large groups. 24-hour cancellation notice req.
Notes: Three-story brownstone and brick mansion with quarter-sawn oak woodwork —floors, ceilings, staircases, paneling, and columns—built in 1904. Fully restored in 1982. Has operated as inn since 1984. Second floor sitting room. Wrap-around porches, sun porch, conference room. Furnished in Edwardian style with antiques.

Newly restored addition, the 1858 Allin House has suites for long-term travelers. Handicapped access. Small private parties accommodated.

HOT SPRINGS NATIONAL PARK (3)

WILLIAMS HOUSE B & B INN

Williams House B & B Inn
420 Quapaw Ave., Hot Springs Ntl. Pk., AR 71901-5201
(501) 624-4275
Innkeeper: Mary and Gary Riley
Rooms: 3 plus 2 suites, all w/pvt. bath. Located in 2 bldgs.
Rates: $65-$80/room, $75-$90/suite, all incl. full brk., evening refreshment
Credit cards: Most major cards
Restrictions: No children under 12, pets. Smoking restricted. One night's deposit req. 7-day cancellation notice req., less one night's fee. 2-night min. stay on wknds. and holidays from March 1–April 30 and Oct.
Notes: Two-story Victorian brownstone and brick Carriage House built in 1890. Reception hall with baby grand piano, fireplace. Game room with cable TV, board games. Furnished with antiques and primitives. 2-story wrap-around porches overlooking gardens. Hammock, picnic tables. Listed on the National Register of Historic Places.*

MOUNTAIN VIEW (1)

Wildflower B & B
On the Square, Box 72, Mountain View, AR 72560-0072
(501) 269-4383, (800) 591-4879
Innkeeper: Todd and Andrea Budy
Rooms: 8, incl. 6 w/pvt. bath, some w/kitchenette
Rates: $41-$85, incl. cont. brk.
Credit cards: Most major cards
Restrictions: No pets, smoking. One night's deposit req. 7-day cancellation notice req. Bakery closed Jan.
Notes: Two-story Craftsman-style building built in 1918. Fully restored in 1985. Located on the historic courthouse square. Decorated in European style. Wraparound

WILDFLOWER B & B

porch. Bakery and bookshop on premises. Listed on the National Register of Historic Places. Some French spoken.

SPRINGDALE (2)

Faubus House on Governor's Hill
P.O. Box 142, Springdale, AR 72765-0142
(501) 738-1114, (800) 737-2005
Innkeeper: Melba English
Rooms: 6 w/pvt. bath, phone, TV, fireplace, plus suite w/pvt. bath, phone, TV, fireplace
Rates: $175/room, $325/suite, all incl. full brk. Seasonal variations. Discount avail. for extended stay.
Credit cards: MC, V
Restrictions: No children, pets. Smoking restricted. One night's deposit req. 7-day cancellation notice req.
Notes: Wood and glass house with flagstone floors, built from 1964 to 1967 overlooking the Ozark Mountains. Former residence of Governor Orval Faubus. Located on twenty-two acres. Natural stone pillars. Redwood and mahogany trim. Club Room, living area with 4 native stone fireplaces. Governor's study. Dining room furniture handmade by local craftsmen. Expanses of bevelled glass. Each guest room with private entrance. Olympic-sized swimming pool. Walkway on grounds is natural trail through rock formation. Courtesy lunch available. Small private parties accommodated. Handicapped access.*

California

Forest Manor
415 Cold Springs Rd., Angwin/Napa Valley, CA 94508
(707) 965-3538, (800) 788-0364, (707) 965-3303
Innkeeper: Harold and Corlene Lambeth
Rooms: 3 suites w/pvt. bath, refrigerator, incl. 2 w/fireplace, 1 w/spa
Rates: $90-$239, incl. full brk., afternoon refreshment. Seasonal variations.
Credit cards: MC, V
Restrictions: No children under 16, pets, smoking. One night's deposit req. 7-day
    cancellation notice req., less $10.00 per-night fee.
Notes: Three-story English Tudor manor with vaulted ceilings and hand-hewn
beams built in 1981. Located on twenty wooded hillside acres adjoining 100-acre
vineyard. Breakfast room with fireplace. Game rooms with pool table, ping-pong
table, board games, TV with VCR. Furnished with English antiques, Persian carpets,
Oriental art. Deck overlooking swimming pool, Jacuzzi. Forest trail, spring, waterfall, deer. Phones and TV available. Spanish and Thai spoken.*

APTOS (9)

MANGELS HOUSE

Mangels House
570 Aptos Creek Rd., Box 302, Aptos, CA 95003
(408) 688-7982
Innkeeper: Jacqueline and Ron Fisher
Rooms: 6 w/pvt. bath, incl. 1 w/fireplace
Rates: $105-$135, incl. full brk. Discount avail. for extended stay.
Credit cards: Most major cards
Restrictions: No children under 8. Pets, smoking restricted. Full prepayment req. 7-
    day cancellation notice req., less $10.00 fee. 2-night min. stay on wknds. Closed
    Dec. 24–26.
Notes: Italianate Victorian mansion built in 1886 as country home for sugar baron.
Located on four acres with garden, orchard next to 10,000-acre Nisene Marks For-
est. Fully restored in and has operated as inn since 1979. Wrap-around verandas
with swings. Sitting room with fireplace, concert grand piano. Library, dining room,

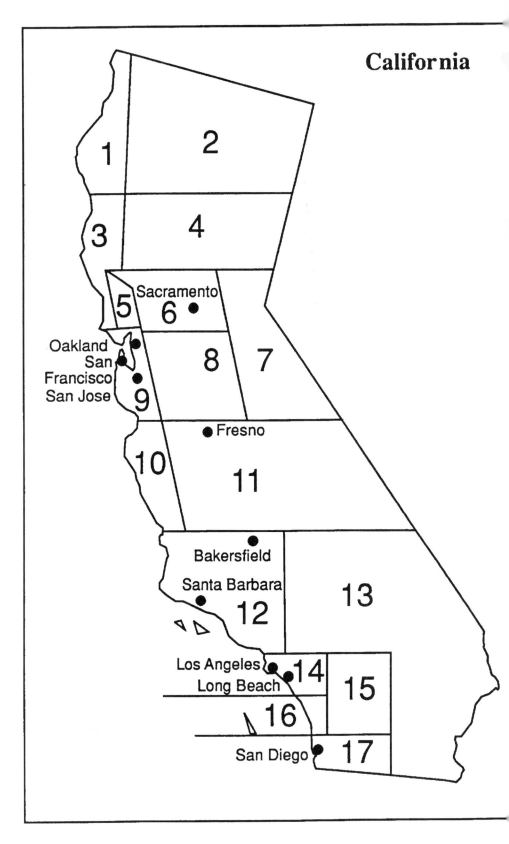

tape library. Decorated in eclectic style. Furnished with antiques. French, Spanish spoken.*

ARNOLD (7)

Lodge at Manuel Mill
P.O. Box 998, Arnold, CA 95223
(209) 795-2622

Innkeeper: Ann Saunders
Rooms: 5 w/pvt. bath, working stove
Rates: $90-$120, incl. full brk. Discount avail. for extended, mid-week, and senior citizen stays.
Credit cards: MC, V
Restrictions: No children under 10, pets, smoking. 50% deposit req. 3-day cancellation notice req., less 10% fee. 2-night min. stay on wknds. and holidays.
Notes: 1800s lumber mill on the banks of old Mill Pond. Located on 43 acres. Common room with fireplace. Decorated with antiques. Gazebo. Outdoor activities available. Small private parties accommodated.*

AVALON (16)

Gull House
344 Whittley Ave., Box 1381, Avalon, CA 90704-1381
(310) 510-2547, (310) 510-7606

Innkeeper: Bob and Hattie Michalis
Rooms: 3 w/TV, incl. 2 w/pvt. bath, plus 2 suites w/pvt. bath, TV, fireplace, refrigerator
Rates: $95-$110/room, $125-$135/suite, all incl. cont. brk. Discount avail. for senior citizens. Seasonal variations.
Credit cards: None
Restrictions: No pets, smoking. Full prepayment req. 10-day cancellation notice req., less min. $25.00 fee. 2-night min. stay. Closed Nov. 1–April 1.
Notes: Each suite includes living room, morning room, separate entrance. Patio, swimming pool, spa, gas BBQ. Taxi passes from and to Avalon ferry terminal available.*

BENICIA (9)

Captain Walsh House Inn
235 E. L St., Benicia, CA 94510
(707) 747-5653

Innkeeper: Reed and Steve Robbins
Rooms: 4 w/pvt. bath, incl. 3 w/fireplace, 2 w/phone, 1 w/TV
Rates: $110-$125 incl. full brk., evening refreshment. Discount avail. for extended stay.
Credit cards: Most major cards
Restrictions: No pets, smoking. Credit card deposit req. 7-day cancellation notice req.
Notes: Gothic Revival building built in Boston in 1849. Later shipped to Cape Horn. Restored and opened as an inn in 1991. Selected by *Better Homes & Gardens* as one of the three best decorated inns in the U.S. Handicapped access.

BERKELEY (9)

Hillegass House
2834 Hillegass Ave., Berkeley, CA 94705
(510) 548-5517, (800) 400-5517, (510) 548-5517
Innkeeper: Richard Warren
Rooms: 4 w/pvt. bath, phone
Rates: $80-$90, incl. full brk. Discount avail. for extended, mid-week, and senior citizen stays.
Credit cards: None
Restrictions: No pets, smoking. Deposit req. 7-day cancellation notice req., less $10.00 fee. 2-night min. stay on wknds.
Notes: Two-story house built in 1904. Dining room, parlor, sun room, multilevel deck. Furnished in eclectic style with antiques. Garden. Sauna. French and Spanish spoken.*

BERRY CREEK (4)

Lake Oroville B & B
240 Sunday Dr., Berry Creek, CA 95916
(916) 589-0700
Innkeeper: Cheryl and Ron Dambereger
Rooms: 6 w/pvt. bath, incl. 5 w/whirlpool tub
Rates: $65-$110, incl. brk.
Credit cards: Most major cards
Restrictions: No pets. Smoking restricted. Deposit req. 5-day cancellation notice req., less 10% per night fee.
Notes: Built in 1992 as an inn. Located on 40 acres. Parlor with bay windows, fireplace, TV, VCR, library of cassettes and books. Billiard room, sun room. Covered wraparound porches, brick patio. R.V. and boat parking available. Guided fishing and lake tours organized. Small private parties accommodated.

BIG BEAR CITY (15)

Gold Mountain Manor
1117 Anita, Box 2027, Big Bear City, CA 92314
(909) 585-6997
Innkeeper: John and Conny Ridgway
Rooms: 5 plus 2 suites, all w/pvt. bath incl. 6 w/fireplace
Rates: $75-$180, incl. full brk., afternoon refreshment. Seasonal variations. Discount avail. for mid-week stay.
Credit cards: MC, V
Restrictions: No smoking. Credit card deposit req. 7-day cancellation notice req. 2-night min. stay on wknds.
Notes: Three-story log and stone mansion built in 1931. Fully restored. Located on one wooded acre at 7,000 ft. elevation. Veranda. Bird's eye maple floors, beamed ceilings. Parlor with rock fireplace. Game room with TV/VCR, pool table, phone. Furnished with antiques. Massage available. French, Dutch, German spoken. Small private parties accommodated. *

BIG BEAR LAKE (15)

Knickerbocker Mansion
869 S. Knickerbocker, Box 3661, Big Bear Lake, CA 92315
(909) 866-8221, (909) 866-6942

Innkeeper: Clee Langley and Karen Bowers
Rooms: 9, incl. 4 w/pvt. bath, 9 w/TV, plus 2 suites w/pvt. bath, fireplace, TV. Located in 2 bldgs.
Rates: $110-$140/room, $195-$225/suite, incl. full. brk., afternoon refreshment. Seasonal variations. Discount avail. for mid-week stay.
Credit cards: Most major cards
Restrictions: No pets, smoking. One-night's deposit req. 10-day cancellation notice req. 2-night min. stay on July–April wknds. 3–4-night min. stay on holidays.
Notes: 3-story house built of vertical logs in the 1920s and carriage house. Has operated as inn since 1985. Located on 2.5 acres. 2nd-floor porch with hammock, rockers overlooking Lake Arrowhead. Sun deck with Jacuzzi. Living room with musical instruments, Victrola, board games Lawn games available. Limited handicapped access. Small private parties accommodated. Picnic lunches and Saturday dinners available.*

BIG SUR (10)

Ventana Inn
Highway 1, Big Sur, CA 93920
(408) 667-2331, (408) 667-2419
Innkeeper: Robert Bussinger
Rooms: 55 w/pvt. bath, phone, TV, incl. 46 w/fireplace, plus 4 suites w/pvt. bath, phone, fireplace, TV. Located in 14 bldgs.
Rates: $195-$485/room, $350-$890/suite, all incl. cont. brk., evening refreshment. Seasonal variations.
Credit cards: Most major cards
Restrictions: No children, pets. Smoking restricted. Deposit req. 72-hour cancellation notice req. 2-night min. stay on wknds. 3-night min. stay on holiday wknds.
Notes: Weathered cedar buildings located on 243 acres overlooking Big Sur coast. Operated as an inn since 1975. Private balconies and patios. Dining terrace. Paneled cedar and glass dining room with ocean and mountain views. Two swimming pools, hot tub, sauna. Restaurant and giftshop on premises. Massage, facials and manicures available. Hiking. Handicapped access. French and Spanish spoken.*

BISHOP (11)

The Matlick House
1313 Rowan Lane, Bishop, CA 93514
(619) 873-3133
Innkeeper: Ray and Barbara Showalter
Rooms: 5 suites w/phone, no pvt. bath
Rates: $79-$89, incl. full brk., evening refreshment
Credit cards: Most major cards
Restrictions: No children under 14, pets, smoking. Deposit req. 7-day cancellation notice req., less $15.00 fee.
Notes: Ranch house built in 1906. Fully renovated. Parlor. 2-story wrap-around screened verandas overlooking Sierra Nevada and White Mountains.

BRIDGEPORT (7)

The Cain House
340 Main St., Box 454, Bridgeport, CA 93517
(619) 932-7040, (619) 932-7419

Innkeeper: Chris and Marachal Gohlich
Rooms: 7 w/pvt. bath, phone, fireplace, TV
Rates: $80-$135, incl. full brk., evening refreshment
Credit cards: Most major cards
Restrictions: No pets, smoking. Credit card deposit req. 48-hour cancellation notice req. Closed Nov.–Apr.
Notes: Two-story inn built in 1930. Fully renovated. Located on .5 acre in the Eastern Sierra Mountains.*

CALISTOGA (5)

Calistoga Country Lodge
2883 Foothill, Calistoga, CA 94515
(707) 942-5555
Innkeeper: Rae Ellen
Rooms: 5 w/pvt. bath, incl. 4 w/phone, 2 w/TV, plus 1 suite w/pvt. bath
Rates: $95-$125/room, $205/suite, all incl. full brk., evening refreshment. Seasonal variations. Discount avail. for extended stay.
Credit cards: Most major cards
Restrictions: No children under 12, pets, smoking. One-night's deposit req. 72-hour cancellation notice req. 2-night min. stay on wknds. and holidays.
Notes: California ranch house built in 1917. Fully restored. Located in the foothills of the Mayacamas Mountains. Decorated in Southwest style.

Christopher's Inn
1010 Foothill Blvd., Calistoga, CA 94515
(707) 942-5755
Innkeeper: Christopher Layton
Rooms: 9 w/pvt. bath, incl. 5 w/TV, plus 1 suite w/pvt. bath, fireplace, TV
Rates: $120/room, $135/suite, all incl. cont. brk.
Credit cards: Most major cards
Restrictions: No pets, smoking. Children restricted. One night's deposit req. 7-day cancellation notice req., less $10.00 fee. 2-night min. stay on wknds. Mar 1–Nov 30, excluding major holidays and Napa Valley events.
Notes: Two-story Georgian style house. Once 3 separate buildings, built in 1940s, surrounded by extensively landscaped grounds. Furnished with antiques and Laura Ashley decor. Some guest rooms offer private patios, gardens. Lawn games. Flowering trees, rose gardens. Small private parties accommodated. Innkeeper is architect and landscape designer.*

Culvers, A Country Inn
1805 Foothill Blvd., Calistoga, CA 94515
(707) 942-4535
Innkeeper: Meg and Tony Wheatley
Rooms: 6, no pvt. bath
Rates: $105-$115, incl. full brk., afternoon refreshment
Credit cards: None
Restrictions: No children under 16, pets, smoking. One night's deposit req. 7-day cancellation notice req., less $20.00 fee. 2-night min. stay on holiday and summer wknds.
Notes: 3-story house built in 1875 in country Victorian style. Fully restored, decorated with period antiques. Has operated as inn since 1983. Breakfast room, formal

dining room, living room with fireplace, player piano. Wrap-around porch, swimming pool, Jacuzzi, sauna.*

Foothill House
3037 Foothill Blvd., Calistoga, CA 94515
(707) 942-6933, (707) 942-5692
Innkeeper: Doris and Gus Beckert
Rooms: 3 suites w/pvt. bath, fireplace, refrigerator, some w/Jacuzzi, plus 1 cottage.
  Located in 2 bldgs.
Rates: $$130-$170/suite, $220/cottage, all incl. full brk., evening refreshment
Credit cards: Most major cards
Restrictions: No children under 12, pets, smoking. One night's deposit req. 7-day
  cancellation notice req., less $10.00. 2-night min stay on wknds.
Notes: Farmhouse built in 1897 overlooking Mount St. Helena. Has operated as inn
since 1982. Sun room, terrace. Furnished with country antiques.*

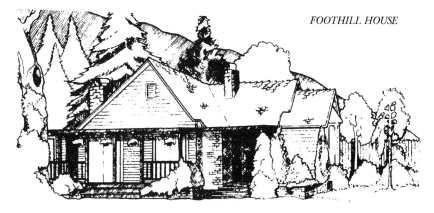

FOOTHILL HOUSE

Hillcrest Bed and Breakfast
3225 Lake County Hwy., Calistoga, CA 94515
(707) 942-6334
Innkeeper: Debbie O'Gorman
Rooms: 6 w/pvt. bath, incl. 4 w/phone, plus 1 cottage w/pvt. bath. Located in 2
  bldgs.
Rates: $70-$90/room, $100/cottage, all incl. cont. brk. on wknds. Seasonal varia-
  tions. Discount avail. for mid-week stay.
Credit cards: None
Restrictions: One night's deposit req. 72-hour cancellation notice req. 2-night min.
  stay on holidays and wknds.
Notes: Modern, rambling country hilltop house located on 40 acres. Family owned
since 1870. Parlor with Steinway piano, fireplace. Balconies and dining room over-
looking Napa Valley. Decorated with antiques, family heirlooms, Oriental rugs.
Swimming pool, spa, gardens, hiking trails. Fishing pond on property. Trampoline,
BBQ available. Small private parties accommodated.*

The Pink Mansion
1415 Foothill Blvd., Calistoga, CA 94515
(707) 942-0558, (800) 238-7465

Innkeeper: Jeff Seyfried, Toppa Epps
Rooms: 3 plus 2 suites, all w/pvt. bath, phone, incl. 1 w/fireplace, 2 w/TV
Rates: $105/room, $165/suite, all incl. full brk. Discount avail. for senior citizens. Seasonal variations.
Credit cards: Most major cards
Restrictions: No children under 12, smoking. One night's deposit req. 7-day cancellation notice req., less $10.00 fee. 2-night min. stay on wknds.
Notes: Two-story Victorian house with turret built in 1875. Fully restored. Living room with fireplace. Dining room, sitting room, library, parlor. Furnished with antiques. Garden. Bicycles available. Handicapped access. Spanish spoken.*

Quail Mountain B & B Inn
4455 N. St. Helena Hwy., Calistoga, CA 94515
(707) 942-0316

Innkeeper: Don and Alma Swiers
Rooms: 2 plus 1 suite, all w/pvt. bath, phone, deck
Rates: $100-$110/room, $125/suite, all incl. full brk., evening refreshment
Credit cards: MC, V
Restrictions: No children, pets, smoking. One night's deposit req. 5-day cancellation notice req., less 10% fee. 2-night min. stay on wknds. and holidays.
Notes: Contemporary-style inn built in 1984. Located on twenty-six forested acres with two streams. Furnished with antiques and art. Solarium with fireplace. Sitting room. Deck overlooking Napa Valley. Swimming pool, whirlpool. Garden, orchard, vineyard on premises.*

Trailside Inn
4201 Silverado Trail, Calistoga, CA 94515
(707) 942-4106, (707) 942-4702

Innkeeper: Randy & Lani Gray
Rooms: 3 suites w/pvt. bath, fireplace, kitchen, porch. Located in 2 bldgs.
Rates: $120, incl. cont. brk., evening refreshment. Discount avail. for mid-week stay.
Credit cards: Most major cards
Restrictions: No pets, smoking. Deposit req. 48-hour cancellation notice req. 2-night min. stay on wknds.
Notes: Farmhouse built in the 1930s overlooking Three Palms Vineyard. Furnished with antiques. Bar-b-que available.*

CALOMA-LOTUS (7)

Golden Lotus
1006 Lotus Rd., Box 830, Caloma-Lotus, CA 95651
(916) 621-4562

Innkeeper: Bruce and Jill Smith
Rooms: 6, no pvt. bath
Rates: $85-$95, incl. full brk. Discount avail. for mid-week and extended stays, newlyweds, 6-room bookings.
Credit cards: Most major cards
Restrictions: No smoking. One-night's deposit req. 7-day cancellation notice req., less $10.00 fee.
Notes: Two-story pre-Victorian brick and frame house built in 1857. Operated as an inn since 1990. Located on the American River. Covered wrap-around veranda. Library with board games. Common room with player piano. Restaurant, antique

store, tea room on premises. Herb and flower gardens. Fishing, gold panning. El Dorado County Historical Site. Small private parties accommodated.*

CAMBRIA (10)

Pickford House
2555 Macleod Way, Cambria, CA 93428
(805) 927-8619
Innkeeper: Anna Larsen
Rooms: 8 w/pvt. bath, incl. 3 w/fireplace
Rates: $85-$125, incl. full brk., evening refreshment
Credit cards: MC, V
Restrictions: No pets, smoking. Full prepayment req. 7-day cancellation notice req.
  2-day min. stay on holiday wknds.
Notes: Country inn within view of Hearst Castle overlooking Rancho Santa Rosa and Santa Lucia Mountains. Parlor with backbar, antiques, fireplace.

The Squibb House
4063 Burton Dr., Cambria, CA 93428
(805) 927-9600, (805) 927-9606
Innkeeper: Bruce Black, Martha Gibson, Linda Finley
Rooms: 5 w/pvt. bath, fireplace
Rates: $95-$125, incl. cont. brk., evening refreshment. Seasonal variations.
Credit cards: MC, V
Restrictions: No children, pets, smoking. Deposit req. 7-day cancellation notice req.
  2-night min. stay on busy wknds.
Notes: Two-story Victorian house built in 1877. Has operated as school. Fully restored in and has operated as inn since 1994. Main parlor, porch. Garden with gazebo. Innkeepers collect Squibb photos, paintings and mementos. Small private parties accommodated.*

CARLSBAD (17)

Pelican Cove Inn
320 Walnut Ave., Carlsbad, CA 92008
(619) 434-5995
Innkeeper: Kris and Nancy Nayudu
Rooms: 6 plus 2 suites, all w/pvt. bath, fireplace, TV
Rates: $85-$175, incl. full brk.
Credit cards: Most major cards
Restrictions: No children under 9, pets, smoking. Deposit req. 7-day cancellation notice req. 2-night min. stay on wknds.
Notes: Cape Cod-style inn built in 1987. Located 200 yards from beach. Parlor, breakfast nook. Sundeck, roof veranda, gardens, gazebo. Handicapped access. Phones available.*

CARMEL (10)

Happy Landing Inn
Monte Verde at 6th, Box 2619, Carmel, CA 93921
(408) 624-7917
Innkeeper: Robert Ballard and Dick Stewart

Rooms: 5 w/pvt. bath, TV, incl. 1 w/fireplace, plus 2 suites w/pvt. bath, fireplace, TV. Located in 3 bldgs.
Rates: $90-$120/room, $155/suite, all incl. cont. brk. Seasonal variations.
Credit cards: MC, V
Restrictions: No children under 12, pets, smoking. One night's deposit req. 72-hr. cancellation notice req. 2-night min. stay on wknds.
Notes: Built in 1925 as family retreat. Living room with fireplace. Lobby. Furnished with antiques. Cathedral ceilings, stained-glass windows. Award-winning central garden with flagstone paths, gazebo, fish pond. Private parties accommodated. Japanese spoken.

Sea View Inn
Camino Real, Box 4138, Carmel, CA 93921
(408) 624-8778
Innkeeper: Marshall and Diane Hydorn
Rooms: 8, incl. 6 w/pvt. bath
Rates: $80-$115, incl. expanded cont. brk., afternoon and evening refreshment
Credit cards: MC, V
Restrictions: No children under 12, pets, smoking. First and last night's deposit req. 7-day cancellation notice req., less $5.00 fee. 2-night min. stay on wknds. 3-night min. stay on holidays.
Notes: Three-story Victorian wood-shingled house built in 1906. Living room, dining room, each with fireplace. Decorated with antiques and paintings done by the innkeeper. Secluded garden.*

CHICO (4)

The Esplanade B & B
620 The Esplanade, Chico, CA 95926
(916) 345-8084
Innkeeper: Lois Kloss
Rooms: 6 w/TV, incl. 5 w/pvt. bath, 1 w/phone
Rates: $45-$65, incl. full brk., evening refreshment
Credit cards: MC, V
Restrictions: Smoking restricted. Deposit req.
Notes: Two-story house built in 1904. Parlor, garden patio, dining room.*

CLOVERDALE (3)

Ye Olde Shelford House
29955 River Rd., Cloverdale, CA 95425
(707) 894-5956
Innkeeper: Ina and Al Sauder and Perry and Denise DuBois
Rooms: 6 w/pvt. bath. Located in 2 bldgs.
Rates: $85-$110, incl. full brk., afternoon refreshment
Credit cards: Most major cards
Restrictions: No smoking. Credit card deposit req. 7-day cancellation notice req. 2-night min. stay on wknds. and holidays.
Notes: Two-story Victorian house built about 1885. Carriage house with sun deck, parlor overlooking valley. Fully restored. Game room, formal dining room. Wraparound porch with swing overlooking vineyards. Furnished with antiques, homemade quilts. Hot tub, swimming pool, gazebo. Bicycles, surry rides, antique auto tours and tubes for Russian River tubing available. Handicapped access.*

COLOMA (6)

Coloma Country Inn
345 High St., Box 502, Coloma, CA 95613
(916) 622-6919

Innkeeper: Alan and Cindi Ehrgott

Rooms: 5, incl. 3 w/pvt. bath, plus 2 suites, incl. 1 w/pvt. bath. Located in 2 bldgs.

Rates: $89-$99/room, $120-$155/suite, all incl. full brk., afternoon refreshment. Special pkgs. avail.

Credit cards: None

Restrictions: No pets, smoking. 50% deposit req. 10-day cancellation notice req., less $25.00 fee

Notes: Victorian farmhouse and carriage housebuilt in 1852. Situated on 5 acres. Located in the 300-acre Gold Discovery State Park in the Sierra Nevada foothills. Furnished with antiques, quilts. Garden gazebo. Bicycles, balloon rides available. Spanish and French spoken.*

DAVENPORT (9)

New Davenport Bed & Breakfast Inn
31 Davenport Ave., Davenport, CA 95017
(408) 425-1818, (408) 423-1160

Innkeeper: Bruce and Marcia McDougal

Rooms: 11 plus 1 suite, all w/pvt. bath, phone, fireplace. Located in 2 bldgs.

Rates: $70/room, $115/suite, all incl. cont. brk. on wknds., restaurant discount, evening refreshment. Seasonal variations.

Credit cards: Most major cards

Restrictions: No children under 2, pets, smoking. Deposit req. 4-day cancellation notice req. 2-night min. stay on holiday wknds.

Notes: Built in 1900 and 1977 across from beach. Sitting room, patio, restaurant, pottery, import gallery. Furnished with antiques, local art and crafts. Restaurant on premises. Spanish spoken.*

DULZURA (17)

Brookside Farm
1373 Marron Valley Rd., Dulzura, CA 92017
(619) 468-3043

Innkeeper: Edd and Sally Guishard

Rooms: 8 w/pvt. bath, incl. 5 w/fireplace, plus 2 suites. Located in 4 bldgs.

Rates: $755-$95/room, $115/suite, incl. cont. brk. Discount avail. for mid-week stay. Special pkgs. available.

Credit cards: Most major cards

Restrictions: No children under 12, pets, smoking. Deposit req. 7-day cancellation notice req. 2-night min. stay for some rooms.

Notes: Three-story main farmhouse, restored wellhouse and restored chicken house built about 1928. Fully renovated in 1983. Located on four acres with stone barn, stream. Sitting room with wood stove. Dining room with stone fireplace, Victrola, piano. Furnished with vintage pieces. Spa, sauna, vegetable garden, berry patch, grape arbor. Terrace. Lawn games. Dinners available on weekends. Handicapped access. Small private parties accommodated. Resident farm animals. Spanish spoken. Handicapped access.*

ELK (3)

Elk Cove Inn
6300 S. Hwy. 1, Box 367, Elk, CA 95432
(707) 877-3321, (800) 275-2967, (707) 877-1808
Innkeeper: Elaine Bryant
Rooms: 10 w/pvt. bath, incl. 6 w/fireplace. Located in 3 bldgs.
Rates: $108-$198, incl. full brk., afternoon and evening refreshment. Seasonal variations. Discount avail. for mid-week stay.
Credit cards: MC, V
Restrictions: No children, pets, smoking. Full prepayment req. Min. 7-day cancellation notice req., less $10.00 per night fee. 2-night min. stay on wknds. and holidays.
Notes: Two-story Victorian house with mansard roof built in 1883. Located on bluff overlooking the ocean. Has operated as inn since 1968. Front porch. Dining room, common rooms with TV, books, board games. Furnished with antiques. Gazebo, gardens, private steps to beach. Cabins available. French and German dinner available. Spanish spoken.*

EUREKA (1)

Carter House Victorians
301 "L" St., Eureka, CA 95501
(707) 444-8062, (707) 444-8062
Innkeeper: Mark and Christi Carter
Rooms: 26, incl. 3 w/fireplace, plus 6 suites w/fireplace incl. 1 w/two fireplaces, all w/pvt. bath, phone, TV. Located in 3 bldgs.
Rates: $95-$185/room, $155-$225/suite, all incl. full brk., afternoon and evening refreshment. Discount avail. for mid-week stays.
Credit cards: Most major cards
Restrictions: No pets, smoking. One-night's deposit req. 3-day cancellation notice req.
Notes: Four-story Victorian mansion recreated in 1981 from original 1884 building plans. Exterior built of clear heart redwood, interior of polished redwood and oak floors. Bay window in entryway. Furnished with Victorian antiques, Oriental rugs, contemporary paintings, ceramics by local artists. Three parlors with two marble fireplaces and fifty-foot chimneys. Organic gardens. Four-star dining room. Wine shop, restaurant on premises. 1958 Bentley available for limousine service. Handicapped access. French, German, Italian spoken.*

Daly Inn
1125 H St., Eureka, CA 95501
(707) 445-3638, (800) 321-9656, (707) 444-3636
Innkeeper: Sue and Gene Clinesmith
Rooms: 3, incl. 1 w/pvt. bath, 1 w/fireplace, plus 2 suites w/pvt. bath
Rates: $65-$100/room, $120/suite, all incl. full brk., evening refreshment. Seasonal variations. Discount avail. for mid-week stay.
Credit cards: Most major cards
Restrictions: No children under 12, pets. Smoking restricted. Credit card deposit req. 7-day cancellation notice req., less $15.00 fee.
Notes: Three-story Colonial Revival style house built in 1905. Fully restored. Christmas ballroom with dumb waiter. Four fireplaces. Dining room. Furnished with turn-of-the-century antiques. Victorian gardens.*

DALY INN

An Elegant Victorian Mansion
1406 C St., Eureka, CA 95501
(707) 444-3144, (800) 386-1888
Innkeeper: Doug and Lily Vierra
Rooms: 3 incl. 1 w/pvt. bath, 1 w/phone, plus 1 suite w/pvt. bath, phone
Rates: $85-$110/room, $135/suite, incl. full brk. Seasonal variations. Special pkgs. avail.
Credit cards: MC, V
Restrictions: No children under 15, pets, smoking. Full prepayment req. 7-day cancellation notice req., less $10.00 fee.
Notes: Two-story Queen Anne Victorian mansion with gingerbread porches, gables built in 1888. Fully restored. Two parlors, library, sitting room, dining room. Furnished with period antiques. Hot tub, Finnish sauna, gazebo. Flower gardens. Tennis court. Lawn games, bicycles available. Laundry service. Listed on the National Register of Historic Places. French, Dutch, German spoken.

AN ELEGANT VICTORIAN MANSION

Old Town Bed and Breakfast Inn
1521 Third St., Eureka, CA 95501-0710
(707) 445-3951, (800) 331-5098, (707) 445-8346
Innkeeper: Leigh and Diane Benson
Rooms: 6, incl. 4 w/pvt. bath, 1 w/wood stove, 1 w/TV

Rates: $75-$150, incl. full brk., evening refreshment. Seasonal variations. Discount avail. for extended and military stays.
Credit cards: Most major cards
Restrictions: No children under 10, pets, smoking. Deposit req. 3-day cancellation notice req.
Notes: Two-story Greek Revival Italianate house built from solid virgin redwood in 1871 as home for lumber baron. Exterior walls are four inches of solid wood. Located on wooded grounds with flower gardens. Dining room, living room with fireplace, kitchen with woodburning stove. Furnished with period pieces. Teak hot tub. Phones available. Italian and Spanish spoken. Resident cats.*

A Weaver's Inn
1440 B St., Eureka, CA 95501
(707) 443-8119
Innkeeper: Bob and Dorothy Swendeman
Rooms: 3 incl. 1 w/pvt. bath, 1 w/fireplace, plus 1 suite w/pvt. bath, fireplace
Rates: $60-$70/room, $85/suite, all incl. full brk.
Credit cards: Most major cards
Restrictions: No smoking. One-night's deposit req. 3-day cancellation notice req.
Notes: Two-story Queen Anne/Colonial Revival house built in 1883. Remodeled in 1907. Porch. Fiber artist studio with spinning wheel, antique loom, fireplace. Victorian parlor with piano. Dining room. Fenced flower and Japanese garden. Croquet. Dinner available some evenings.

FERNDALE (1)

THE GINGERBREAD MANSION INN

The Gingerbread Mansion Inn
400 Berding St., Box 40, Ferndale, CA 95536
(800) 952-4136, (707) 786-4000, (707) 786-4381
Innkeeper: Ken Torbert
Rooms: 5 w/pvt. bath, incl. 2 w/fireplace, 2 w/TV, plus 4 suites w/pvt. bath, incl. 2 w/fireplace
Rates: $115-$155/room, $145-$185/suite, all incl. full brk., afternoon refreshment. Seasonal variations. Discount avail. for extended stay.

Credit cards: Most major cards

Restrictions: No children under 10, pets, smoking. Full prepayment req. Min. 7-day cancellation notice req., less $10.00/night fee. 2-night min. stay on wknds., holidays, and special events.

Notes: Queen Anne Victorian/Eastlake-style inn trimmed with gingerbread built in 1899 as doctor's residence. Expanded into hospital in 1920. Renovated in 1981. Operated as an inn since 1983. Located in State Historical Landmark village. Turreted, carved and gabled. Veranda. Four parlors, with books, board games, incl. two with fireplace. Formal dining room. Furnished with Victorian antiques. Formal English gardens. Bicycles available.*

SHAW HOUSE INN

Shaw House Inn
703 Main St., Box 1125, Ferndale, CA 95536-1125
(707) 786-9958, (707) 786-9958

Innkeeper: Ken and Norma Bessingpas

Rooms: 6, w/pvt. bath

Rates: $75-$135, incl. full brk.

Credit cards: Most major cards

Restrictions: No children under 4, pets, smoking. Full prepayment req. 7-day cancellation notice req., less $10.00 fee. 2-night min. stay during Fair and Feb. 13.

Notes: Gabled Gothic carpenter house built in 1854 with 1-acre garden along Francis Creek. Parlor, library with fireplace, kitchen with woodburning stove, formal dining room, 2 porches, balconies, deck overlooking creek. Furnished with antiques, art collections, memorabilia. Listed on the National Register of Historic Places.*

FISH CAMP (7)

Karen's B & B Yosemite Inn
1144 Railroad Ave., Box 8, Fish Camp, CA 93623
(209) 683-4550, (800) 346-1443, (209) 683-4550

Innkeeper: Karen Bergh and Lee Morse

Rooms: 3 w/pvt. bath

Rates: $85, incl. full brk., afternoon refreshment

Credit cards: None

KAREN'S B & B YOSEMITE INN

Restrictions: No pets, smoking. Min. one night's deposit req. Min. 7-day cancellation notice req., less $10.00 fee. 2-night min. stay on major holidays. No radio, TV, music, or sound equipment in upstairs guest areas.
Notes: Two-story contemporary country house built in 1989. Located at 5,000-ft. elevation amid pine and cedar trees. Wrap-around covered porches. Sitting room with gas fireplace. Living room with wood stove, piano, TV, VCR. Library, dining room. Deck.*

FORESTHILL (7)

Tin Roof B & B
24741 Foresthill Rd., Box 671, Foresthill, CA 95631
(916) 367-4466
Innkeeper: Clyde and Judith Larrew
Rooms: 3 w/pvt. bath
Rates: $85, incl. full brk. Seasonal variations. Discount avail. for extended stay.
Credit cards: Most major cards
Restrictions: No pets, smoking. Deposit req. 48-hour cancellation notice req.
Notes: Two-story house built in 1875. Wrap-around porch. Knotty pine walls, antiques. Barn. Orchard. Art studio and shop. Small private parties accommodated. Gold panning tours. Resident cat.*

FORT BRAGG (3)

The Grey Whale Inn
615 N. Main St., Fort Bragg, CA 95437
(707) 964-0640, (707) 964-4408
Innkeeper: John and Colette Bailey
Rooms: 8 w/pvt. bath, phone, incl. 1 w/fireplace, 1 w/TV, plus 6 suites w/pvt. bath, phone, incl. 2 w/fireplace, 5 w/TV
Rates: $75-$100/room, $120-$140/suite, all incl. full brk. Seasonal variations. Discount avail. for corporate stays.
Credit cards: Most major cards
Restrictions: Children restricted. No pets, smoking. One night's deposit req. 7-day cancellation notice req. 2-night min. stay on wknds. 3-night min. stay on holidays.

Notes: Four-story redwood Classic Revival structure built in 1915 as a hospital. Fully restored. Renovated in 1971. Has operated as family-run inn since 1978. Extra wide hallways and doorways. High ceilings. Parlor. Recreation room with TV, VCR, library, fireplace. Porch, deck, patios. Ocean views. Grounds received the 1989 Mayor's Well Done Award for outstanding landscape care. Spanish, German spoken. Handicapped access.*

GEYSERVILLE (5)

Campbell Ranch Inn
1475 Canyon Rd., Geyserville, CA 95441
(707) 857-3476, (800) 857-3476
Innkeeper: Mary Jane and Jerry Campbell
Rooms: 4 w/pvt. bath, plus 1 cottage w/pvt. bath, fireplace, TV. Located in 2 bldgs.
Rates: $100-$165, incl. full brk., evening dessert
Credit cards: MC, V
Restrictions: No children under 10, pets, smoking. Credit card deposit req. 3-day cancellation notice req. 2-night min. stay on wknds. 3-night min. stay on major holidays wknds.
Notes: Private ranch. Located on thirty five-acre hilltop. Living room, family room, each with fireplace. Tennis court, swimming pool, hot tub spa, ping-pong, croquet. Terrace overlooking Sonoma wineries, vineyards, flower gardens. Daily excursions arranged. Bicycles available. Masseuse available.*

CAMPBELL RANCH INN

GRASS VALLEY (7)

Murphy's Inn
318 Neal St., Grass Valley, CA 95945
(916) 273-6873, (916) 273-6873
Innkeeper: Tom and Susan Myers and Linda Jones
Rooms: 4 w/pvt. bath, phone, TV, incl. 1 w/fireplace, plus 4 suites w/pvt. bath TV, incl. 3 w/fireplace, 2 w/phone. Located in 2 bldgs.
Rates: $75-$100/room, $115-$135/suite, all incl. full brk., afternoon refreshment.
Credit cards: Most major cards
Restrictions: No pets, smoking. Deposit req. 7-day cancellation notice req., less $10.00 fee. 2-night min. stay on June–Dec. wknds.

Notes: Two-story Colonial Victorian-style inn built in 1866. Surrounded by ivy topiary. Two sitting rooms with fireplaces. Dining room, parlor with fireplace. Decorated with some antiques. Sundeck with swimming pool/spa.*

GROVELAND (8)

Evergreen Lodge
33160 Evergreen Rd., Groveland, CA 95321
(209) 379-2606
Innkeeper: John and Kay Bargmann
Rooms: 16, plus 2 suites, all w/pvt. bath, TV. Located in 10 bldgs.
Rates: $70-$90/room, $80-$100/suite, all incl. full brk. Discount avail. for extended stay. Special pkgs. avail.
Credit cards: Most major cards
Restrictions: No pets, smoking. One night's deposit req. 48-hr. cancellation notice req. 2-night min stay on wknds. Closed Nov.–March.
Notes: One-story lodge and cabins. Has operated as an Inn since 1924. Surrounded by forest. General store and restaurant. Handicapped access.*

EVERGREEN LODGE

The Groveland Hotel
18767 Main St., Box 289, Groveland, CA 95321
(209) 962-4000, (800) 273-3314, (209) 962-6674
Innkeeper: Peggy A. Mosley
Rooms: 14 w/pvt. bath, phone, TV, plus 3 suites w/pvt. bath, phone, fireplace, TV. Located in 2 bldgs.
Rates: $85-$105/room, $165/suite, all incl. cont. brk., evening refreshment. Seasonal variations. Discount avail. for mid-week stay, Oct. 15–April 15. Special pkgs. avail.
Credit cards: Most major cards
Restrictions: No smoking. Pets restricted. 24-hour cancellation notice req., less $10.00 fee.
Notes: Two-story Monterey Colonial adobe building built in 1849 and two-story Queen Anne building built in 1914. Both recently restored. Balconies. Parlor with

books, games, fireplace and TV. Restaurant on premises. Small private parties accommodated. Handicapped access.*

GUALALA (3)

NORTH COAST COUNTRY INN

North Coast Country Inn
34591 S. Hwy. 1, Gualala, CA 95445
(707) 884-4537, (800) 884-4537

Innkeeper: Loren and Nancy Flanagan
Rooms: 4 suites w/pvt. bath, fireplace, deck. Located in 4 bldgs.
Rates: $135, incl. full brk.
Credit cards: Most major cards
Restrictions: No children under 12, pets, smoking. One night's deposit req. 5-day cancellation notice req. 2-night min. stay on wknds. 3-night min. stay on holidays.
Notes: Cluster of redwood buildings nestled in a redwood and pine forest. Located on a hilltop overlooking Mendocino Coast. Open beam ceilings. Furnished with American country pine antiques, art treasures, collectibles, memorabilia. Gardens with lawn, brick pathways and fruit trees. Gazebo, hot tub, spa, wrap-around sun deck with ocean view. Antique shop on premises.*

GUERNEVILLE (3)

Ridenhour Ranch House Inn
12850 River Rd., Guerneville, CA 95446
(707) 887-1033, (707) 869-2967

Innkeeper: Diane and Fritz Rechberger
Rooms: 7 w/pvt. bath, incl. 1 w/fireplace, 3 w/TV, plus 1 suite w/pvt. bath, TV. Located in 2 bldgs.
Rates: $95-$130/room, $120/suite, all incl. full brk., evening refreshment
Credit cards: Most major cards
Restrictions: No pets, smoking. One night's deposit req. 7-day cancellation notice req., less $10 fee. 2-night min. stay on wknds.
Notes: Ranch house built in 1906 of heart redwood. Located on 2.5 wooded acres. Has operated as inn since 1980. Decorated with American and English antiques. Living room with fireplace. Parlor with board games. Formal dining room, country kitchen. Garden terrace, hot tub. Lawn games. Orchards. Dinners available. Small private parties accommodated. Handicapped access. German spoken.*

Santa Nella House
12130 Hwy. 116, Guerneville, CA 95446
(707) 869-9488

Innkeeper: Ed and Joyce Ferrington
Rooms: 4 w/pvt. bath, fireplace
Rates: $75-$95/room incl. full brk., afternoon refreshment. Discount avail. for midweek stay.
Credit cards: Most major cards
Restrictions: No pets, smoking. Children restricted. Deposit req. 7-day cancellation notice req. 2-night min. stay on wknds.
Notes: Two-story bucolic country Victorian-style farmhouse with high ceilings, built in 1870. Located in Redwood Forest. Wrap-around veranda. Living room with wood stove. Parlor/music room, library. Country kitchen with wood stove, bay window. Furnished in period antiques. Gazebo, hot tub.*

SANTA NELLA HOUSE

HALF MOON BAY (9)

Old Thyme Inn
779 Main St., Half Moon Bay, CA 94019
(415) 726-1616

Innkeeper: George and Marcia Dembsey
Rooms: 6 plus 1 suite, all w/pvt. bath, phone, fireplace, TV, incl. 3 w/whirlpool tub.
Rates: $75-$150/room, $165-$220/suite, all incl. full brk., evening refreshment. Discount avail. for senior citizens.
Credit cards: MC, V
Restrictions: No children under 6, pets, smoking. One-night's deposit req. 7-day cancellation notice req., less $10.00 fee. 2-night min. stay on summer wknds.
Notes: Two-story Queen Anne Victorian redwood inn built in 1899. Fully restored. Parlor with wood stove, books, games. Furnished with antiques and period art. Herb/flower garden with over fifty varieties. Small private parties accommodated. Spanish spoken.*

Zaballa House
324 Main St., Half Moon Bay, CA 94019
(415) 726-9123

Innkeeper: Kerry Pendergast
Rooms: 9 w/pvt. bath, incl. 4 w/fireplace, 2 w/TV
Rates: $90-$135, incl. full brk., evening refreshment. Discount avail. for mid-week stay.
Credit cards: Most major cards
Restrictions: No children under 6, smoking. Credit card deposit req. 48-hour cancellation notice req.
Notes: Blue clapboard house built in 1859, the oldest house in Half Moon Bay. Fully remodeled. Has operated as inn since 1988. Parlor with fireplace. Furnished with antiques, grandfather clocks, oil paintings. Some rooms with whirlpool tubs. Flower gardens.*

HEALDSBURG (5)

Frampton House
489 Powell Ave., Healdsburg, CA 95448
(707) 433-5084
Innkeeper: Paula Bogle
Rooms: 3 w/pvt. bath
Rates: $70-$90, incl. full brk., evening refreshment. Discount avail. for extended and senior citizen stays.
Credit cards: MC, V
Restrictions: No children under 12, pets, smoking. Credit card deposit req. 5-day cancellation notice req., less $10.00 fee.
Notes: Queen Anne Victorian redwood house built in 1908. Solarium. Sitting room with wine bar, fireplace, library, board games. Furnished with oak antiques in Victorian style. Garden, swimming pool, spa, sauna, ping-pong.*

The George Alexander House
423 Matheson St., Healdsburg, CA 95448
(707) 433-1358, (800) 310-1358, (707) 433-1367
Innkeeper: Christian and Phyllis Baldenhofer
Rooms: 4 w/pvt. bath, incl. 2 w/fireplace
Rates: $80-$130, incl. full brk.
Credit cards: Most major cards
Restrictions: No pets, smoking. One-night's deposit req. 7-day cancellation notice req. 2-night min. stay during holiday wknds.
Notes: Queen Anne Victorian house built in 1905. Furnished with antiques, art and oriental rugs. Two large parlors, one with fireplace. Board games avail. Resident cats.*

Grape Leaf Inn
539 Johnson St., Healdsburg, CA 95448
(707) 433-8140
Innkeeper: Karen and Terry Sweet
Rooms: 6, plus 1 suite, all w/pvt. bath, incl. 5 w/whirlpool tub
Rates: $95-$140/room, $150/suite, all incl. full brk., evening refreshment. Seasonal variations. Discount avail. for mid-week stay.
Credit cards: Most major cards
Restrictions: No children under 12, pets, smoking. One night's deposit req. 48-hr. cancellation notice req. 2-night min. stay on wknds.

Notes: Queen Anne Victorian inn built in 1900. Veranda. Parlor with fireplace, board games. Living/dining room with fireplace. Flower garden. Furnished with antiques. Wine tasting from local winery.*

Haydon Street Inn
321 Haydon St., Healdsburg, CA 95448
(707) 433-5228

Innkeeper: Joanne Claus and Sophia
Rooms: 8 plus 1 suite, incl. 4 w/pvt. bath. Located in 2 bldgs.
Rates: $75-$150/room, $105/suite, all incl. full brk., afternoon refreshment. Discount avail. for mid-week stay.
Credit cards: MC, V
Restrictions: No children under 10, pets. One night's deposit req. 7-day cancellation notice req., less $10.00 fee. 2-night min. stay on wknds.
Notes: Queen Anne house with hardwood floors built in 1912. Gothic-style cottage built in 1987. Located on wooded grounds with country flower gardens. Dining room, double parlor, wrap-around veranda. Furnished with French and American antiques, custom down comforters, Dhurrie rugs. Decorated with designer wallcoverings.*

Healdsburg Inn on the Plaza
110 Mattheson, Box 1196, Healdsburg, CA 95448
(707) 433-6991

Innkeeper: Genny Jenkins and LeRoy Steck
Rooms: 10 w/pvt. bath, phone, TV, incl. 3 w/fireplace
Rates: $135-$175, incl. full brk., evening refreshment. Seasonal variations. Discount avail. for mid-week and extended stays.
Credit cards: MC, V
Restrictions: No pets. Smoking and children restricted. Credit card deposit req. 3-day cancellation notice req., less $15.00 fee.
Notes: Two-story brick Victorian iron-front building built in 1900. Fully restored. Overlooks historic town square. Covered porch extends along entire rear of the building. Bay windows, vaulted glass skylights, roof garden/solarium. Lounge with board games, TV, books. Furnished with American antiques. Two giftshops, bakery, art gallery with grand staircase on premises. Limited handicapped access.*

Madrona Manor, A Country Inn
1001 Westside Rd., Healdsburg, CA 95448
(707) 433-4231, (707) 433-0703

Innkeeper: John and Carol Muir
Rooms: 18 w/pvt. bath, phone, incl. 15 w/fireplace, plus 3 suites w/pvt. bath, phone, fireplace. Located in 4 bldgs.
Rates: $135-$185/room, $185-$225/suite, all incl. full brk.
Credit cards: Most major cards
Restrictions: Children, pets, smoking restricted. One-night's deposit req. 5-day cancellation notice req., less $10.00 fee. 2-night min. on wknds. in mansion.
Notes: Three-story Victorian mansion built in 1881. Located on eight wooded acres with citrus grove, swimming pool. Has operated as inn since 1981. Music room with original rosewood piano, fireplace. Lounge area with billiards. Furnished with antiques, Persian carpets. Gourmet restaurant on premises. All meals available. Spanish spoken. Handicapped access.*

Raford House
10630 Wohler Rd., Healdsburg, CA 95448
(707) 887-9573, (707) 887-9597
Innkeeper: Carole and Jack Vore
Rooms: 7, incl. 5 w/pvt. bath, 2 w/fireplace
Rates: $85-$135/room, $150/suite, all incl. full brk., evening refreshment
Credit cards: Most major cards
Restrictions: No children, pets, smoking. One-night's deposit req. 7-day cancellation notice req., less $20.00 fee. 2-night min. stay on wknds.
Notes: Three-story Queen Anne Victorian house built in 1880s. Remodeled in and has operated as inn since 1981. Located on 4 acres of lawns and gardens with picnic tables. Front porch overlooking vineyards. Patios overlooking flower gardens. Sun room, dining room with fireplace. Furnished with period pieces. Sonoma County Historical Landmark. Suites available.*

HOPLAND (3)

Thatcher Inn
13401 S. Highway 101, Hopland, CA 95449
(707) 744-1890, (800) 266-1891, (704) 744-1219
Innkeeper: Carmen Gleason
Rooms: 18 plus 2 suites, all w/pvt. bath, phone
Rates: $90-$105/room, $120-$150/suite, all incl. full brk. Special pkgs. avail.
Credit cards: Most major cards
Restrictions: No pets, smoking. Deposit req. 5-day cancellation notice req.
Notes: Three-story Victorian-style structure. Recently underwent $800,000 restoration. Dining room. Library with fireplace. Lobby bar, patio. Swimming pool.*

IDYLLWILD (15)

The Inn at Pine Cove
P.O. Box 2181, Idyllwild, CA 92549-2181
(909) 659-5033
Innkeeper: Lisa Gabriel and Patick Black
Rooms: 6 w/pvt. bath, incl. 3 w/fireplace, plus 3 suites w/pvt. bath. Located in 3 bldgs.
Rates: $80-$100, incl. full brk., afternoon refreshment. Discount avail. for mid-week stay.
Credit cards: MC, V
Restrictions: No pets, smoking. One-night's deposit req. 5-day cancellation notice req. 2-night min. stay on wknds. 3-night min. stay on holidays.
Notes: A-frame chalets. Located at 6,500 ft. elevation on 3 wooded acres. Common room with fireplace. Decks, porches. Small private parties accommodated. Limited handicapped access.*

Wilkum Inn B & B
P.O. Box 1115, Idyllwild, CA 92549-1115
(909) 659-4087
Innkeeper: Barbara Jones and Annamae Chambers
Rooms: 5, incl. 2 w/pvt. bath, plus 1 apt. w/pvt. bath, fireplace
Rates: $65-$95/room, $85-$95/apt., all incl. expanded cont. brk., afternoon and evening refreshment. Discount avail. for extended stay.

WILKUM INN B & B

Credit cards: None
Restrictions: No pets, smoking. Deposit req. 7-day cancellation notice req., less
    $5.00 per-night fee. 2-night min. stay on wknds. 3-night min. stay on holidays. 2-
    night min. stay in apt.
Notes: Two-story shingle house built in 1938. Located in the San Jacinto Mountains.
Common room with rock fireplace. Furnished with family antiques, collectibles. Re-
frigerators and microwaves available. Limited handicapped access. Some Spanish,
sign language spoken.*

INDEPENDENCE (11)

Winnedumah Hotel
211 N. Edwards, Box 147, Independence, CA 93526
(619) 878-2040

Innkeeper: Marvey Chapman and Alan Bergman
Rooms: 20, incl. 5 w/pvt. bath
Rates: $40-$51, incl. cont. brk.
Credit cards: Most major cards
Restrictions: Deposit req. 24-hr. cancellation notice req. 2-night min. stay on holi-
    day wknds.
Notes: 2-story inn built in 1927 on landscaped yard. Has operated as hotel since
1927. Located at the foot of the Eastern Sierras. Lobby with fireplace. Furnished in
period style. Dining room. Restaurant. Box lunches avail. Small private parties ac-
commodated. Handicapped access.*

INVERNESS (3)

Fairwinds Farm B & B Cottage
P.O. Box 581, Inverness, CA 94937
(415) 663-9454

Innkeeper: Joyce Godfield
Rooms: 1 cottage w/fireplace, TV, VCR
Rates: $125, incl. full brk., afternoon refreshment. Discount avail. for extended stay.
Credit cards: None

Restrictions: No pets, smoking. Deposit req. 14-day cancellation notice req. 2-night min. stay on wknds.
Notes: Cottage located atop Inverness Ridge in 75,000 acres of wilderness. Play-house with toys, instruments for children. Barnyard animals. Deck top hot tub, garden with ponds, waterfall, swing. Sign language spoken.

Patterson House
12847 Sir Fr. Drake Blvd., Box 13, Inverness, CA 94937
(415) 669-1383
Innkeeper: Rosalie H. (Missy) Patterson
Rooms: 5 w/pvt. bath
Rates: $125-$145, incl. cont. brk. (Tues.–Fri.), full brk. (Sat.–Mon.). Discount avail. for mid-week stay.
Credit cards: MC, V
Restrictions: No children under 9 on wknds., pets, smoking. Full prepayment req. 7 day cancellation notice req. 2-night min. stay on holiday wknds.
Notes: Three-story Craftsman style brown-shingled house built in 1916. Wrap-around deck with view of Tomales Bay. Living room with fireplace, piano. Dining room.*

Sandy Cove Inn
P.O. Box 869, Inverness, CA 94937
(415) 669-2683, (800) 759-2683, (415) 669-7511
Innkeeper: Kathy and Gerry Coles
Rooms: 3 suites w/pvt. bath, phone, fireplace, refrigerator. Located in 2 bldgs.
Rates: $115-$175, incl. full brk., afternoon refreshment. Seasonal variations. Discount avail. for senior citizen, AAA, and extended stays.
Credit cards: Most major cards
Restrictions: No pets, smoking. Full prepayment req. 14-day cancellation notice req., less $10.00 per night fee.
Notes: Cape Code-style inn. Located on four acres. Solarium. Furnished with antique-finished pine furniture. Decorated with original artwork, Turkish kilim rugs. Swimming pool. Certified massage therapy, picnic lunches available. Small boat storage and launching, kayak and bicycle rental arranged.

IONE (6)

The Heirloom
214 Shakeley Ln., Box 322, Ione, CA 95640
(209) 274-4468
Innkeeper: Patricia Cross and Melisande Hubbs
Rooms: 6, incl. 4 w/pvt. bath, 3 w/balcony, 3 w/fireplace. Located in 2 bldgs.
Rates: $60-$92, incl. full brk., afternoon refreshment. Discount avail. for extended stay.
Credit cards: Most major cards
Restrictions: No children under 8, pets. Smoking restricted. One night's deposit req. 72-hour cancellation req. 2-night min. stay on wknds. from April–Dec.
Notes: Two-story Colonial-style antebellum mansion built in 1863. Located on 1.5 acres. Living room with fireplace, game table, 120-year-old square grand piano. Balcony overlooking private garden, veranda. Furnished with period pieces, family antiques. Hammocks, swings, croquet, bicycles, glider. Limited handicapped access.*

JACKSON (6)

GATE HOUSE INN

Gate House Inn
1330 Jackson Gate Rd., Jackson, CA 95642
(209) 223-3500, (800) 841-1072, (209) 223-3500
Innkeeper: Keith and Gail Sweet
Rooms: 4 plus 1 suite, all w/pvt. bath, incl. 2 w/fireplace. Located in 2 bldgs.
Rates: $85-$95/room, $120/suite, all incl. full brk. Discount avail. for mid-week stay.
Credit cards: Most major cards
Restrictions: No children under 12, pets. Smoking restricted. One night's deposit
   req. 7-day cancellation notice req., less $10.00 fee. 2-night min. stay on wknds.
   March 15–Dec. 15.
Notes: Two-story Victorian style inn built in 1902. Located on 1 acre. Has operated
as inn since 1981. Dining room. Screened room with BBQ, table tennis, exercise
machines. Porches with wicker furnishings. Decorated with Victorian period fur-
nishings. Swimming pool, patio. Summer House cottage includes double Jacuzzi.
Angel gift house on premises. Spanish spoken. Handicapped access. Listed on the
National Register of Historic Places.*

JAMESTOWN (8)

Historic National Hotel
77 Main St., Box 502, Jamestown, CA 95327
(209) 984-3446
Innkeeper: Stephen Willey
Rooms: 11, incl. 5 w/pvt. bath
Rates: $65-$80, incl. expanded cont. brk. Discount avail. for mid-week stay. Special
   pkgs. avail.
Credit cards: Most major cards
Restrictions: No children under 8. Pets restricted. Deposit req. 72-hour cancellation
   notice req.
Notes: Built as hotel in 1859. Fully restored in turn of the century style. Dining
room. Garden courtyard with grape arbor. Furnished in gold rush theme with antiques. Restaurant, saloon with original redwood bar on premises. TVs, picnic baskets available. Small private parties accommodated. Spanish and German spoken.*

The Palm Hotel
10382 Willow St., Box 677, Jamestown, CA 95327
(209) 984-3429
Innkeeper: Richard and Sandra Allen
Rooms: 7 w/TV, incl. 3 w/pvt. bath, plus 2 suites w/pvt. bath, TV.
Rates: $60-$80/room, $90-$120/suite, incl. full brk. Seasonal variations. Discount
   avail. for mid-week stay. Special pkgs. avail.
Credit cards: Most major cards

Restrictions: No pets, smoking. Deposit req. 5-day cancellation notice req. 2-night min. stay for mid-week discount.
Notes: 3-story Victorian house built about 1890, remodeled and furnished with antiques. Lobby with marble-topped bar. Upstairs and downstairs porches. Phones available. Handicapped access.

JULIAN (17)

Julian Gold Rush Hotel
2032 Main St., Box 1856, Julian, CA 92036
(619) 765-0201
Innkeeper: Gig and Steve Ballinger
Rooms: 17, incl. 4 w/pvt. bath, plus 1 suite, w/pvt. bath, fireplace. Located in 3 bldgs.
Rates: $64-94/room, $110-$145/suite, all incl. full brk., afternoon refreshement. Discount avail. for senior citizens.
Credit cards: Most major cards
Restrictions: No pets. Min. one night's deposit req. 2-day cancellation notice req.
Notes: Victorian hotel built of redwood, cedar, oak and pine in 1897. Lobby with woodburning stove. Parlor with games. Two backyard native stone patios. Decorated in turn of the century style with American antiques. Listed on the National Register of Historic Places. German spoken.*

KERNVILLE (11)

Kern River Inn
119 Kern River Dr., P.O. Box 1725, Kernville, CA 93238-1725
(619) 376-6750
Innkeeper: Mike and Marti Meehan
Rooms: 6 w/pvt. bath, incl. 3 w/fireplace
Rates: $89, incl. full brk., afternoon refreshment. Seasonal variations.
Credit cards: Most major cards
Restrictions: No children under 12, pets, smoking. One night's deposit req. 7-day cancellation notice req. 2-night min. stay on wknds. from April–October.
Notes: 2 story Victorian Inn with wrap-around front porch overlooking Kern River. Built in 1991. Located in the Sequoia National Forest in the Southern Sierra Nevada Mountains. Whirlpool tubs available.

KINGS CANYON NATIONAL PARK (11)

Montecito-Sequoia Lodge
Gens. Hwy 1, Sequoia Nat'l Forest, Kings Canyon Nat'l Pk., CA 93633
(800) 227-9900
Innkeeper: Virginia C. Barnes
Rooms: 32 plus 4 suites, all w/pvt. bath, plus 8 cabins w/fireplace. Located in 4 bldgs.
Rates: $138/room, suite, $98/cabin, all incl. full brk., dinner. Seasonal variations. Discount avail. for senior citizen and mid-week stays.
Credit cards: Most major cards
Restrictions: No pets. Full pre-payment req. $25.00 cancellation fee req. 2-night min. winter stay.
Notes: Rustic mountain inn. Heated pool and spa. Horseshoes, tennis available.*

KLAMATH (1)

Requa Inn
451 Requa Rd., Klamath, CA 95548
(707) 482-8205, (707) 482-0844
Innkeeper: Sue Reese, Leo and Melissa Chavez
Rooms: 9 plus 1 suite, all w/pvt. bath
Rates: $70-$80/room, $85/suite, all incl. full brk. Discount avail. for extended stay.
  Seasonal variations.
Credit cards: Most major cards
Restrictions: No pets, smoking. 24-hour cancellation notice req.
Notes: Two-story in built in the 1880s. Dining room. Parlor with fireplace over-looking Klamath River. Spanish spoken.

LA JOLLA (17)

Bed & Breakfast Inn at La Jolla
7753 Draper Ave., La Jolla, CA 92037
(619) 456-2066, (619) 454-9055
Innkeeper: Pierrette Timmerman
Rooms: 16, incl. 15 w/pvt. bath, 13 w/phone, 3 w/fireplace
Rates: $85-$225, incl. full brk., evening refreshment. Discount avail. for senior citi-zen stays.
Credit cards: Most major cards
Restrictions: No pets. Smoking restricted. One night's deposit req. 7-day cancella-tion notice req. 2-night min. stay on wknds.
Notes: Cubist-style house and annex built in 1913. Library/sitting room, dining room, patio, sun deck. Original gardens planted by Kate Sessions. Furnished in cot-tage style. Picnic lunch available. Once the home of John Philip Sousa. Listed as San Diego Historical Site. Handicapped access. Spanish and French spoken.*

Prospect Park Inn
1110 Prospect St., La Jolla, CA 92037
(619) 454-0133, (800) 433-1609 (US), (800) 345-8577(C), (619) 454-2056
Innkeeper: Brigitte Schmidt, Jean Beazley, Manager
Rooms: 16 plus 3 suites, 4 studios, all w/pvt. bath, phone, TV, incl. 3 w/full kitchen.
  Some w/balconies.
Rates: $90-$120/room, $200-$260/suite, $95-$115/studio, all incl. cont. brk., after-noon refreshment. Seasonal variations. Discount avail. for mid-week stay.
Credit cards: Most major cards
Restrictions: No pets, smoking. Deposit req. 2-day cancellation notice req.
Notes: Fully remodeled in 1987. Library, reception area, conference room. Sun deck overlooking Cove. Furnished in contemporary style. German, French, and Spanish spoken. Small private parties accommodated. Free parking available.*

LAGUNA BEACH (16)

The Carriage House
1322 Catalina St., Laguna Beach, CA 92651
(714) 494-8945
Innkeeper: Dee and Tom Taylor
Rooms: 6 suites w/pvt. bath, TV, several w/kitchen

THE CARRIAGE HOUSE

Rates: $95-$150, incl. expanded cont. brk., bottle of wine, afternoon refreshment. Seasonal variations. Special pkgs. avail.

Credit cards: Most major cards

Restrictions: Pets restricted. One night's deposit req. 7-day cancellation notice req., less $10.00 fee. 2-night min. stay on wknds. 3-night min. stay on holidays.

Notes: Colonial New Orleans-style carriage house built in 1920. Dining room, sitting room. Furnished with antiques. Double-bricked courtyard with moss hanging from Carrotwood tree, fountain, flowers. Small private parties accommodated.*

Casa Laguna Inn
2510 S. Coast Hwy., Laguna Beach, CA 92651
(800) 233-0449, (714) 494-5009

Innkeeper: Louise Gould and Joan Kerr

Rooms: 21 w/pvt. bath, cable TV, incl. 2 w/fireplace. Cottage avail. Located in 5 bldgs.

Rates: $69-$120/room, $99-$150/suite, $139-$205/cottage, all incl. cont. brk., evening refreshment. Seasonal variations.

Credit cards: Most major cards

Restrictions: Deposit req. 72-hour cancellation notice req. 2-night min. stay on holidays.

Notes: Spanish Revival-style mission house and cottage built in the early 1930s. Built as guest facilities for the historic Villa Rockledge overlooking ocean. Library. Furnished with antiques and contemporary pieces. Gardens, bell tower, Bird aviary, patios, deck, heated swimming pool. Spanish spoken.*

Eiler's Inn
741 S. Coast Hwy., Laguna Beach, CA 92651
(714) 494-3004

Innkeeper: Henk and Annette Wirtz

Rooms: 11 w/pvt. bath, plus 1 suite w/pvt. bath, fireplace

Rates: $100-$130/room, $175/suite, all incl. full brk., evening refreshment. Seasonal variations.

Credit cards: Most major cards

Restrictions: No pets. Full deposit req. 5-day cancellation notice req., less $10.00 fee.

Notes: Inn named for Eiler Larsen, official greeter of Laguna Beach. Common room with fireplace. Furnished with antiques, special linens. Brick courtyard with fountain. Sun deck with ocean view. Classical guitarist on Saturdays and special occasions. German, French, Danish, spoken.*

LAKE ARROWHEAD (15)

Bluebelle House B&B
263 S. Hwy. 173, Box 2177, Lake Arrowhead, CA 92352
(909) 336-3292, 1-800-429-BLUE
Innkeeper: Rick and Lila Peiffer
Rooms: 5, incl. 3 w/pvt. bath
Rates: $85-$120, incl. full brk., evening refreshment. Discount avail. for senior citizen and mid-week stays.
Credit cards: MC, V
Restrictions: No children under 10, pets, smoking. One night's deposit req. 7-day cancellation notice req., less $15.00 fee. 2-night min. stay on wknds, 3-night min. stay on holiday wknds.
Notes: Two-story house built in the 1950s. Fully redecorated in 1983. Parlor with rock fireplace, library, board games, TV. Dining room. Deck with hammock. Furnished in country English decor with collectibles, mementoes, fine art. Lawn games available. Innkeepers are interior designer, wood craftsman.

Bracken Fern Manor
815 Arrowhead Villas Rd., Box 1006, Lake Arrowhead, CA 92352
(909) 337-8557, (909) 337-3323
Innkeeper: Cheryl Weaver
Rooms: 7 w/pvt. bath, plus 3 suites w/pvt. bath, incl. 1 w/Jacuzzi
Rates: $80-$100/room, $130-$175/suite, all incl. full brk. Seasonal variations. Discount avail. for senior citizen, group, extended and mid-week stays.
Credit cards: Most major cards
Restrictions: No children under 5, pets, smoking. Deposit req. 3-day cancellation notice req., less 15% fee. 2-night min. stay on holidays.
Notes: Three-story building built in 1929 as a resort. Fully restored. Art gallery/library, parlor with fireplace, game room. Furnished with antiques. Sauna, wine tasting cellar, garden spa. Spanish spoken.*

Prophets' Paradise B & B
26845 Modoc Lane, Box 2116, Lake Arrowhead, CA 92352
(909) 336-1969
Innkeeper: Laverne and Tom Prophet, Jr.
Rooms: 1 w/pvt. bath, plus 2 suites w/pvt. bath, incl. 1 w/fireplace, 2 w/TV, 1 w/Jacuzzi
Rates: $90/room, $110-$160/suite, all incl. full brk., hors d'oeuvres
Credit cards: MC, V
Restrictions: No children under 2, smoking. Deposit req. 72-hour cancellation notice req., less $15.00 fee. 2-night min. stay on wknds.
Notes: Five-story mountain tudor style inn built in 1984. Located on an alpine hillside. Leaded and stained-glass windows, open beam ceilings. Common room with brick fireplace. Full gym with weights, exercise equipment. Billard room. Furnished with antiques, angel collection. Bicycles, horseshoes, hiking available. Private tennis court and beach in summer.*

LITTLE RIVER (3)

The Inn at Schoolhouse Creek
7051 N. Highway One, Little River, CA 95456
(707) 937-5525
Innkeeper: Linda Wilson and Peter Fearey
Rooms: 5 w/pvt. bath, incl. 3 w/fireplace, plus 2 suites w/pvt. bath, fireplace, plus 4 cottages w/pvt. bath, fireplace, kitchen, incl. 1 w/refrigerator. Located in 8 bldgs.
Rates: $60-$85/room, $85-95/suite, $85-120/cottage. Discount avail. for mid-week stays from Oct. 15–May 15.
Credit cards: MC, V
Restrictions: Small children welcome in cottages only. Smoking restricted. Deposit req. 3-day cancellation notice req., less $10.00 fee. 2-night min. stay on wknds.
Notes: Located on 10 acres once part of a large coastal ranch built in 1862. All rooms/cottages have ocean views. Ledford home serves as lounge w/fireplace. Breakfast available on an optional plan. Limited handicapped access.*

LODI (6)

Wine & Roses Country Inn
2505 W. Turner Rd., Lodi, CA 95242
(209) 334-6988, (209) 334-6570
Innkeeper: Kris Cromwell, Del and Sherri Smith
Rooms: 7 plus 3 suites, all w/pvt. bath, phone, TV
Rates: $99-$110/room, $145/suite, all incl. full brk., evening refreshment. Discount avail. for mid-week stay.
Credit cards: Most major cards
Restrictions: No pets. Smoking restricted. Deposit req. 14-day cancellation notice req., less $10.00 fee.
Notes: Two-story Victorian farmhouse. Located on five wooded acres with flower gardens. Sitting room with fireplace. Dining room, library, meeting room, terrace. Furnished with antiques, handmade comforters, artwork, collectibles. Lawn games available. Restaurant on premises. All meals available. Small private parties accommodated. Spanish spoken. Handicapped access.

LONG BEACH (14)

Lord Mayor's Inn
435 Cedar Ave., Long Beach, CA 90802
(310) 436-0324, (310) 436-0324
Innkeeper: Laura and Reuben Brasser
Rooms: 5 w/pvt. bath, phone, sundeck access
Rates: $85-$105, incl. full brk., afternoon refreshment
Credit cards: Most major cards
Restrictions: No pets, smoking. Deposit req. 7-day cancellation notice req.
Notes: Two-story Edwardian house built in 1904. Veranda with granite pillars. Dining room, library, living room. Furnished with antiques. Recipient of Great American Home Award from the National Trust for Historic Preservation. Danish, Dutch spoken.*

LOS ANGELES (14)

Norja Bed & Breakfast Inn
1139 S. Tremaine Ave., Los Angeles, CA 90019
(213) 933-3652, (310) 285-9440
Innkeeper: Norja Bercy
Rooms: 4, incl. 1 w/pvt. bath, plus 1 suite w/pvt. bath, phone
Rates: $65-$85/room, $110-$125/suite, all incl. full brk., afternoon refreshment. Seasonal variations. Special pkgs. avail.
Credit cards: MC
Restrictions: No pets, smoking. One-night's deposit req. 7-day cancellation notice req., less 20% fee.
Notes: Spanish mansion built in 1929. Surrounded by flower gardens and lawns. Features antiques, collectables, fresh flowers, feather pillows, down comforters on full or king canopy beds, lace on windows and linens. Small private parties accommodated. TV, all meals available. Spanish spoken.*

SALISBURY HOUSE BED & BREAKFAST

Salisbury House Bed & Breakfast
2273 W. 20th St., Los Angeles, CA 90018
(213) 737-7817, (800) 373-1778
Innkeeper: Sue and Jay German
Rooms: 3 w/phone, refrigerator, incl. 1 w/pvt. bath, plus 2 suites w/pvt. bath, phone, refregerator, incl. 1 w/TV
Rates: $75-90/room, $90-$100/suite, all incl. full brk., afternoon refreshment. Discount avail. for group and extended stays.
Credit cards: Most major cards
Restrictions: No children under 10, pets, smoking. Min. one night's deposit req. 72-hr. cancellation notice req.
Notes: Three-story Craftsman-style house built in 1909. Located in West Adams district. Restored with original stained and leaded-glass, wood-beamed ceilings. Formal dining room. Living room with fireplace, TV. Board games, grand piano, CD player. Furnished with antiques. Porch and garden. Small private parties accommodated. French and Spanish spoken.*

LOS OSOS (10)

Gerarda's B & B
1056 Bay Oaks Dr., Los Osos, CA 93402
(805) 534-0834

Innkeeper: Gerarda Ondang
Rooms: 2 w/cable TV, w/pvt. bath
Rates: $35-$45, incl. full brk.
Credit cards: Most major cards
Restrictions: No children, pets, smoking. Deposit req. 5-day cancellation notice req.
Notes: Dutch kitchen. Flower gardens. Handicapped access. Dutch, Indonesian spoken.

LOTUS (7)

Golden Lotus
1006 Lotus Rd., Box 830, Lotus, CA 95651-0830
(916) 621-4562
Innkeeper: Bruce and Jill Smith
Rooms: 6 w/pvt. bath
Rates: $85-$95, incl. full brk. Discount avail. for mid-week, group and extended stays.
Credit cards: Most major cards
Restrictions: Well-behaved pets welcome. No smoking. Full pre-payment req. 7-day
    cancellation notice req., less $10.00 fee.
Notes: Two-story red brick and frame house built in 1857. Located on the south
fork of the American River. Has operated as inn since 1990. Each guest room dec-
orated in different theme. Library. Herb and flower gardens. Board games avail-
able. Restaurant, antique store, tea room on premises. Whitewater rafting available.
El Dorado County Historical Site # 37.*

KRISTALBERG B & B

LUCERNE (5)

Kristalberg B & B
P.O. Box 1629, Lucerne, CA 95458
(707) 274-8009
Innkeeper: Merv Myers
Rooms: 2, incl. 1 w/pvt. bath, fireplace, TV, plus 1 suite w/pvt. bath, TV
Rates: $55-$90/room, $125-$150/suite, all incl. expanded cont. brk., evening re-
    freshment. Seasonal variations. Discount avail. for mid-week and off-season stays.
Credit cards: Most major cards

Restrictions: No children under 12. Smoking restricted. Deposit req. 7-day cancellation notice req.

Notes: Two-story house located on mountain overlooking Mount Konocti and Ckear Lake. Has operated as inn since 1988. Parlor, formal dining room. Furnished with 18th-century Italian and 20th-century American decor. German, Spanish, French spoken.*

MALIBU (14)

Casa Larronde
P.O. Box 86, Malibu, CA 90265
(310) 456-9333

Innkeeper: Charlou Larronde

Rooms: 2 w/pvt bath, incl. 1 suite w/phone, fireplace, TV

Rates: $110/room, $125/suite, all incl. full brk., evening refreshment

Credit cards: Most major cards

Restrictions: No pets. Smoking restricted. Deposit req. 7-day cancellation notice req., less $20.00 fee. Closed July 1–Oct. 10.

Notes: Located on a private beach. Suite has floor to ceiling glass bordering private deck. Handicapped access.

MAMMOTH LAKES (7)

TAMARACK LODGE

Tamarack Lodge
Twin Lakes Rd., Box 69, Mammoth Lakes, CA 93546-0069
(619) 934-2442, (619) 934-2281

Innkeeper: David and Carol Watson

Rooms: 10 w/phone, incl. 5 w/pvt. bath, plus 1 suite w/pvt. bath, phone, plus 25 cabins w/phone, incl. 8 w/fireplace.

Rates: $45-$150/room, $100-$180/suite, $75-$390/cabin. Seasonal variations. Discount avail. for winter mid-week stays.

Credit cards: Most major cards

Restrictions: No pets. Smoking restricted. 50% deposit req. 21-day cancellation notice req., less $20.00 fee.

Notes: Lodge built in 1924. Located on 20 acres on Twin Lakes. Sitting room with piano, lobby with fireplace, deck with swing. Furnished with knotty pine furniture.

Restaurant and cross-country ski rental shop on premises. Boats and canoes available. Limited handicapped access. Spanish spoken.*

MARINA DEL REY (14)

Mansion Inn
327 Washington Blvd., Marina Del Rey, CA 90291
(310) 821-2557, (800) 828-0688, (310) 827-0289
Innkeeper: Richard Hunnicutt
Rooms: 38 w/pvt. bath, phone, plus 5 suites w/pvt. bath, phone, TV
Rates: $69-$89/room, $95-$125/suite, all incl. cont. brk. Seasonal variations. Discount avail. for extended and senior citizen stays.
Credit cards: Most major cards
Restrictions: No pets. Credit card deposit req. 48-hour cancellation notice req.
Notes: French, Spanish, Norwegian, Swedish spoken. Handicapped access.*

Marina B & B
P.O. Box 11828, Marina Del Rey, CA 90295
(310) 821-9862
Innkeeper: Peter and Carolyn Griswold
Rooms: 1 suite w/pvt. bath, and TV
Rates: $50-$80, incl. cont. brk. Discount avail. for extended stay.
Credit cards: Most major cards
Restrictions: No pets. Smoking restricted. Deposit req.
Notes: Two-story house built in 1990. Suite located on second floor with private entrance, bath, kitchen, dining and sleeping areas. Access to deck.*

MARIPOSA (8)

Dubord's Restful Nest
4274 Buckeye Creek Rd., Mariposa, CA 95338
(209) 742-7127, (209) 742-6888
Innkeeper: Huguette Dubord
Rooms: 3 w/pvt. bath, TV
Rates: $75-$85, incl. full brk. Seasonal variations.
Credit cards: Most major cards
Restrictions: No pets. Smoking restricted. One night's deposit req. 2-day cancellation notice req., less $10.00 fee. 2-night min. stay.
Notes: Located on eleven wooded acres with fishing pond, swimming pool. Common room, dining room, kitchen. Wrap-around deck. BBQ, lawn games, archery practice range (bring your own arrows) available. French spoken.

Finch Haven Bed & Breakfast
4605 Triangle Rd., Mariposa, CA 95338
(209) 966-4738, (209) 966-7615, (209) 966-4738
Innkeeper: Bruce and Carol Fincham
Rooms: 2 w/pvt. bath
Rates: $65, incl. expanded cont. brk.
Credit cards: Most major cards
Restrictions: No pets. Smoking restricted.

Notes: Wildlife setting. Built in 1990. Furnished in country style. Spanish spoken. Bruce was a ranger in Yosemite National Park. Carol is a teacher. Limited handicapped access.*

Oak Meadows, Too B & B
5263 Hwy. 140 N., Box 619, Mariposa, CA 95338
(209) 742-6161, (209) 966-2320
Innkeeper: Frank Ross and Kaaaren Black
Rooms: 5 w/pvt. bath, plus 1 suite w/pvt. bath. Located in 2 bldgs.
Rates: $59-89/room, $79/suite, incl. expanded cont. brk.
Credit cards: Most major cards
Restrictions: No children under 12, pets, smoking. One night's deposit req. 3-day cancellation notice req. Closed Dec. 24, 25.
Notes: New England-style inn built in 1985. Living room with stone fireplace, board games. Breakfast room, porches. Decorated with handmade quilts. Air-conditioned. French and some German spoken.*

OAK MEADOWS, TOO B & B

The Pelennor Bed & Breakfast
3871 Hwy. 49 S., Mariposa, CA 95338
(209) 966-2832
Innkeeper: Dick and Gwen Foster
Rooms: 4, no pvt. bath
Rates: $45, incl. full brk. Discount avail. for group and extended stays.
Credit cards: Most major cards
Restrictions: Smoking restricted. One night's deposit req. 24-hour cancellation notice req.
Notes: Two-story house. Located on fifteen acres in the Sierra foothills. Common room with wood stove, kitchenette. Sun deck, sauna, lap pool, spa. Decorated with tartans from Scottish clans. Innkeepers play bagpipes.

McCLOUD (2)

McCloud Guest House
606 W. Colombero Dr., McCloud, CA 96057
(916) 964-3160

Innkeeper: Dennis and Pat Abreu, Bill and Patti Leigh
Rooms: 5 w/pvt. bath, incl. 1 w/fireplace
Rates: $75-$90, incl. cont. brk.
Credit cards: Most major cards
Restrictions: No children, pets. Smoking restricted. One night's deposit req. 7-day cancellation notice req., less $10.00 fee. 2-night min. on some holiday wknds. Sweater or jacket req. for dinner.
Notes: Two-story house built in 1907 as residence of president of McCloud River Lumber Company. Renovated in and has operated as inn since 1984. Foyer with fireplace. Game room with hand-carved pool table, library, sun room. Wrap-around veranda with wicker furniture. Restaurant on premises. Herbert Hoover, Jean Harlowe slept here.

McCLOUD HOTEL

McCloud Hotel
408 Main St., McCloud, CA 96057
(916) 964-2822, (800) 964-2823, (916) 964-2844
Innkeeper: Lee and Marilyn Ogden
Rooms: 14 plus 4 suites, all w/pvt. bath, phone
Rates: $68-$88/room, $120-$130/suite, all incl. expanded cont. brk., afternoon refreshment. Discount avail. for senior citizens and AAA stays and through 1996.
Credit cards: MC, V
Restrictions: No children, pets, smoking. One night's deposit req. 10-day cancellation notice req., less $10.00 fee.
Notes: Three-story hotel built in 1916. Fully restored in 1995. Registered as a national landmark. Lobby with fireplace. Library with board games. Handicapped accessable.

MENDOCINO (3)

Agate Cove Inn
11201 N. Lansing, Box 1150, Mendocino, CA 95460
(707) 937-0551
Innkeeper: Sallie McConnell, Jake Zahavi
Rooms: 10 cottages, w/pvt. bath, phone, incl. 9 w/cable TV. Located in 10 bldgs.
Rates: $79-$189, incl. full brk., evening refreshment. Seasonal variations. Discount avail. for winter mid-week stay.
Credit cards: Most major cards

Restrictions: No pets, smoking. Deposit req. 7-day cancellation notice req., less
$15.00 fee. 2-night min. stay on wknds. 3-night min. stay on holidays.
Notes: Farmhouse built in the 1860s. Cottages built about 1980. Located on bluff
overlooking ocean. Furnished in country style. Breakfast room with ocean view.
Kitchen with antique woodstove. Living room. Landscaped gardens. Spanish, Hebrew, French spoken.

Brewery Gulch Inn
9350 Coast Hwy. 1, Mendocino, CA 95460
(707) 937-4752
Innkeeper: Linda and Bill Howarth
Rooms: 5, incl. 3 w/pvt. bath, 2 w/fireplace, 3 w/phone, 2 w/phone
Rates: 85-$130, incl. full brk. Seasonal variations.
Credit cards: Most major cards
Restrictions: No children, pets, smoking. One night's deposit req. 5-day cancella-
tion notice req. 2-night min. stay on wknds. 3-night min. stay on holidays.
Notes: Victorian farmhouse built in the 1860s. Fully restored. Common room. Fur-
nished with antiques. Limited handicapped access.*

HEADLANDS INN

Headlands Inn
Howard at Albion, Box 132, Mendocino, CA 95460
(707) 937-4431
Innkeeper: David and Sharon Hyman
Rooms: 5 w/pvt. bath, fireplace. Located in 2 bldgs.
Rates: $110-$180, incl. full brk., afternoon refreshment
Credit cards: Most major cards
Restrictions: No children under 16, pets, smoking. Min. one night's deposit req. 7-
day cancellation notice req. 2-night min. stay on wknds. 3-night min. stay on hol-
idays.
Notes: Victorian house built in 1868 as a barber shop. Expanded in 1873. Restored
in 1979. Parlor with fireplace. Sitting room with games, books, magazines, fruit,
candy. Front deck overlooking English garden and ocean. Furnished with period
antiques, local artwork. Guest rooms with antique armoires, featherbeds, down
comforters, european reading pillows, handmade quilts. English-style garden.
Handicapped access.

John Dougherty House
571 Ukiah St., Box 817, Mendocino, CA 95460
(707) 937-5266

Innkeeper: David and Marion Wells

Rooms: 3 w/pvt. bath, incl. 2 w/woodburning stove, plus 3 suites w/pvt. bath, incl. 2 w/woodburning stove, 1 w/fireplace. Located in 2 bldgs.

Rates: $95-$115/room, $115-$175/suite, all incl. full brk., evening refreshment. Seasonal variations.

Credit cards: Most major cards

Restrictions: No children under 12, pets, smoking. One-night's deposit req., 7-day cancellation notice req., less $15.00 fee. 2-night min. stay on wknds. 3-night min. stay on holiday wknds.

Notes: Built in 1867, one of oldest houses in Mendocino. Main house furnished with period country antiques. New England style keeping room with fireplace. Limited handicapped access.*

JOSHUA GRINDLE INN

Joshua Grindle Inn
44800 Little Lake, Box 647, Mendocino, CA 95460
(707) 937-4143, (800) GRI-NOLE

Innkeeper: Jim and Arlene Moorehead

Rooms: 10 w/pvt. bath, incl. 6 w/fireplace. Located in 3 bldgs.

Rates: $95-$155, incl. full brk., afternoon refreshment. Discount avail. for mid-week stay. Seasonal variations.

Credit cards: Most major cards

Restrictions: No pets, smoking. Deposit req. 7-day cancellation notice req., less $10.00 fee. 2-night min. stay on wknds. 3-night min. stay on holiday wknds.

Notes: Main house, cottage, water tower built in 1879 by town banker, Joshua Grindle. Located on two acres. Parlor with fireplace, antique pump organ, board games. Furnished with early-American antiques. Each guest room has sitting room and two have ocean view. Partial handicapped access available.

MacCallum House Inn
45020 Albion St., Box 206, Mendocino, CA 95460
(707) 937-0289

Innkeeper: Melanie and Joe Reding

Rooms: 19, incl. 7 w/pvt. bath, 2 w/fireplace, plus 1 suite w/pvt. bath, fireplace. Located in 8 bldgs.

Rates: $75-$140/room, $180-$240/suite, all incl. cont. brk. Discount avail. for senior citizen and mid-week, winter stays.
Credit cards: MC, V
Restrictions: No pets, smoking. First and last nights deposit req. 7-day cancellation notice req., less $10.00 fee.
Notes: Gingerbread Victorian mansion built in 1882. Operated as an inn since 1974. New England style porch. Multi-paned sun parlor. Furnished with antiques, original Tiffany lamps, Persian rugs. Barn, carriage house, garden gazebo, water tower. Restaurant on premises.*

Mendocino Farmhouse
P.O. Box 247, Mendocino, CA 95460
(707) 937-0241, (707) 937-1086

Innkeeper: Marjorie and Bud Kamb
Rooms: 3 w/pvt. bath, fireplace, plus 1 cottage w/pvt. bath, fireplace. Located in 2 bldgs.
Rates: $85-$95/room, $105-$110/suite, all incl. full brk. Seasonal variations. Discount avail. for mid-week stay.
Credit cards: Most major cards
Restrictions: No children under 8, pets, smoking. One night's deposit req. 7-day cancellation notice req., less $15.00 fee. 2-night min. stay on wknds. 3-night min. stay on holidays.
Notes: Victorian farmhouse surrounded by redwood forest. Eclectic collection of books, music. Furnished with country antiques. Gardens, pond, meadow. Limited handicapped access.

Mendocino Village Inn
44860 Main St., Box 626, Mendocino, CA 95460
(707) 937-0246, (800) 882-7029

Innkeeper: Bill and Kathleen Erwin
Rooms: 12, incl. 10 w/pvt. bath, 7 w/fireplace, plus 1 suite w/pvt. bath, fireplace.
Rates: $65-$145/room, $175/suite, all incl. full brk., afternoon refreshment. Discount avail. for extended stay.
Credit cards: Most major cards
Restrictions: No children under 10, pets, smoking. Full prepayment req. 72-hr. cancellation notice req., less $10.00 fee. 2-night min. stay on wknds. 3-night min. stay on some holidays.
Notes: Queen Anne Victorian house built in 1882. Guest rooms individually decorated with a different theme. Furnished with Navajo rugs, Indian art. Some rooms with ocean view and private entrance. Frog pond. Handicapped access. French and Spanish spoken.

Whitegate Inn
499 Howard St., Box 150, Mendocino, CA 95460
(707) 937-4892, (707) 937-1131

Innkeeper: George and Carol Bechtloff
Rooms: 5 w/pvt. bath, incl. 4 w/fireplace, 3 w/TV, plus cottage w/pvt. bath, fireplace, TV, deck, refrigerator. Located in 2 bldgs.
Rates: $99-$175/room, $165/cottage, all incl. full brk., evening refreshment. Seasonal variations. Discount avail. for mid-week stay.
Credit cards: Most major cards

Restrictions: No pets. Children, smoking restricted. Full prepayment req. 7-day cancellation notice req., less $15.00 fee. 2-night min. stay on wknds. and in August. 3-night min. stay on holiday wknds.

Notes: Built as a private 2-story residence in 1880. Fully refurbished and redecorated. Furnished with antiques, down comforters, lace-edged sheets, individual sitting room. Parlor with fireplace. Hamilton pump organ, original light fixtures throughout, chandeliers of crystal and handpainted porcelain, Oriental rugs. Surrounded by picket fence. English garden. Some guests have access to refrigerator. Resident cat.

MILL VALLEY (9)

Mountain Home Inn
810 Panoramic Hwy., Mill Valley, CA 94941
(415) 381-9000

Innkeeper: Lynn M. Saggese
Rooms: 10 w/pvt. bath, phone, incl. 3 w/fireplace
Rates: $131-$215, incl. full brk.
Credit cards: Most major cards
Restrictions: No pets. Smoking restricted. Deposit req. 5-day cancellation notice req.
Notes: Located on Mount Tamalpais. Terrace overlooking San Francisco Bay. Lounge, bar, dining room with fireplace. Restaurant on premises. Decks. Herb, vegetable, and flower gardens. Handicapped access.*

MONTARA (9)

Goose and Turrets B & B
835 George St., Box 937, Montara, CA 94037-0937
(415) 728-5451

Innkeeper: Raymond and Emily Hoche-Mong
Rooms: 5 w/pvt. bath, incl. 2 w/fireplace
Rates: $85-$110, incl. full brk., afternoon refreshment. Discount avail. for extended, mid-week and senior citizen stays.
Credit cards: Most major cards
Restrictions: No pets, smoking. Credit card deposit req. 3-day cancellation notice req., less $10.00 fee.
Notes: Northern Italian villa-type inn built 1908 as a country club. Operated as an inn since 1986. Sitting room with wood stove, games table, piano, tape deck, library. Dining room. Furnished in eclectic style with family antiques, collectibles, original art. Yard with swing, pond, fountain. Pick-up at Half Moon Bay airport and Pillar Point harbor available. Bocce ball court. French spoken. Resident geese.*

MONTEREY (10)

The Jabberwock
598 Laine St., Monterey, CA 93940
(408) 372-4777

Innkeeper: Jim and Barbara Allen
Rooms: 7, incl. 3 w/pvt. bath, 1 w/fireplace
Rates: $100-$180, incl. full brk., evening refreshment
Credit cards: MC, V

Restrictions: No pets. Smoking restricted. Full prepayment req. 7-day cancellation notice req. 2-night min. stay on wknds. 3-night min. stay on holidays.

Notes: Three-story post-Victorian house built in 1911 located on ½ acre. Dining room with fireplace. Living room with board games. Furnished with antiques, period furniture. Veranda overlooking Monterey Bay. Special Aquarium tickets available.

MORAGA (9)

HALLMAN B & B

Hallman B & B
309 Constance Pl., Moraga, CA 94556
(510) 376-4318

Innkeeper: Frank and Virginia Hallman

Rooms: 2 w/phone, TV

Rates: $60, incl. full brk. Discount avail. for extended stay.

Credit cards: Most major cards

Restrictions: No pets, smoking. One night's deposit req. 3-day cancellation notice req. Closed various times for vacation.

Notes: Private home built about 1970. Living room with fireplace, dining room. Furnished with antiques, contemporary pieces. Terrace, solar-heated swimming pool, spa.

MOUNT SHASTA (2)

Mt. Shasta Ranch Bed & Breakfast
1008 W. A. Barr Rd., Mount Shasta, CA 96067
(916) 926-3870, (916) 926-6882

Innkeeper: Bill and Mary Larsen

Rooms: 5, no pvt. bath, plus 4 suites w/pvt. bath, plus cottage w/pvt. bath, all w/TV. Located in 2 bldgs.

Rates: $45-$60/room, $80/suite, $95-$110/cottage, all incl. full brk. Discount avail. for extended stay.

Credit cards: Most major cards

Restrictions: Children welcome in cottage and main house. No pets. Smoking restricted. 3-day cancellation notice req. Min. 2-and 3-night stay summer wknds and all holidays.

Notes: House has rock fireplace. Cottage w/handicapped access. *

MUIR BEACH (9)

The Butterfly Tree
20 Sunset Way, Muir Beach, CA 94966
(415) 383-8447, (415) 383-8447
Innkeeper: Karla Andersdatter
Rooms: 2 w/pvt. bath, phone,
Rates: $105-$130, incl. cont. brk. Discount avail. for extended stay.
Credit cards: None
Restrictions: No pets, smoking. One night's deposit req. 7-day cancellation notice req., less $35.00 fee. Closed for Christmas holidays.
Notes: Located in the Golden Gate National Recreation Area. Common room with fireplace. Front veranda, porch. Monarch butterflies arrive from Nov.–March. Spanish spoken. Innkeeper is poet, author, artist. Mailing address: P.O. Box 790, Sausalito, CA 94966.

Pelican Inn
10 Pacific Hwy., Muir Beach, CA 94965-9729
(415) 383-6000
Innkeeper: R. Barry Stock
Rooms: 7 w/pvt. bath
Rates: $140-$155, incl. full brk.
Credit cards: Most major cards
Restrictions: No pets. One night's deposit req. 72-hr. cancellation notice req., less $10.00 fee. Closed Christmas Day.
Notes: Two-story inn. Tudor architecture with antiques. Dining room with fireplace, lounge with fireplace and 16th-century Tudor bar. Terrace. Indoor games, reading room, hiking, biking, fishing, surfing. Restaurant serving English cuisine.

1880 DUNBAR HOUSE

MURPHYS (8)

1880 Dunbar House
271 Jones St., Box 1375, Murphys, CA 95247
(209) 728-2897, (209) 728-1451
Innkeeper: Bob and Barbara Costa

Rooms: 3 plus 1 suite, all w/pvt. bath, wood stove, refrigerator, TV/VCR, classic-video collection. Suite w/Jacuzzi.

Rates: $105/room, $145/suite, all incl. full brk., afternoon and evening refreshment.

Credit cards: Most major cards

Restrictions: No children under 10, pets. Smoking restricted. One-night's deposit req. 5-day cancellation notice req., less $10.00 fee. 2-night min. stay on wknds.

Notes: Two-story Italianate-style house built in 1880. Parlor with fireplace. Dining room. Porches with wicker rockers. Decorated in country style with antiques. Century-old gardens.*

NAPA (5)

Arbor Guest House
1436 G St., Napa, CA 94559
(707) 252-8144

Innkeeper: Bruce and Rosemary Logan

Rooms: 3 plus 2 suites, all w/pvt. bath, incl. 2 w/wood burning fireplace, 1 w/gas fireplace. Located in 2 bldgs.

Rates: $85-$115/room, $135-$165/suite, all incl. full brk. Seasonal variations.

Credit cards: MC, V

Restrictions: No children under 10, pets, smoking. One night's deposit req. 3-day cancellation notice req. 2-night min. stay on wknds. and holidays.

Notes: Colonial Revival-style Main House and Carriage House built in 1906. Surrounded by a vine-covered arbor. Garden patio. Dining room. Furnished with antiques. Handicapped access.*

Blue Violet Mansion
443 Brown St., Napa, CA 94559-3349
(707) 253-2583, (707) 257-8205

Innkeeper: Bob and Kathy Morris

Rooms: 6 w/pvt. bath, incl. 4 w/fireplace, plus 1 suite w/pvt. bath, fireplace

Rates: $115-$195/room, $165-$240/suite, all incl. full brk., evening refreshment. Seasonal variations. Discount avail. for mid-week stay. Special pkgs. avail.

Credit cards: Most major cards

Restrictions: Deposit req. 10-day cancellation notice req., less 10% fee. 2-night min. stay on wknds.

Notes: Queen Anne Victorian mansion located on one acre of gardens, built in 1886. 2 parlors, sun room, gazebo with swings, rose garden, grape-arbored deck, hammock area. Picnic lunch and dinner available by request. Bicycles, massages available.*

Cedar Gables Inn
486 Coombs St., Napa, CA 94559
(707) 224-7969, (707) 224-4838

Innkeeper: Margaret and Craig Snasdell

Rooms: 5 w/pvt. bath, incl. 2 w/fireplace, plus 1 suite w/pvt. bath. Some rooms w/whirlpool tubs.

Rates: $79-$149, incl. full brk., evening refreshment. Seasonal variations.

Credit cards: Most major cards

Restrictions: No pets, smoking. Deposit req. 7-day cancellation notice req. 2-night min. stay on wknds. from April–October.

Notes: Two-story Old England-style Inn with winding staircases built in 1892 as a wedding gift. Furnished with antiques. Family room with fireplace. Dining room, sun room.*

Churchill Manor
485 Brown St., Napa, CA 94559
(707) 253-7733, (707) 253-8836
Innkeeper: Joanna Guidotti, Brian Jensen
Rooms: 10 w/pvt. bath, phone, incl. 3 w/fireplace
Rates: $75-$145, incl. full brk., afternoon and evening refreshment
Credit cards: Most major cards
Restrictions: No children under 12, pets. Smoking restricted. Deposit req. Min. 7-day cancellation notice req. 2-night min. stay on wknds.
Notes: Three-story mansion. Located on one acre. Wrap-around veranda with white columns. Sun room with marble floor. Parlor with fireplace, grand piano, TV/VCR. Furnished with antiques, Oriental rugs. Lawn games, board games, bicycles available. Spanish spoken. Listed on the National Register of Historic Places.*

Country Garden Inn
1815 Silverado Trail, Napa, CA 94558
(707) 255-1197, (707) 255-3112
Innkeeper: Lisa and George Smith
Rooms: 6 w/pvt. bath, incl. 1 w/fireplace, 2 w/Jacuzzi, plus 4 suites w/pvt. bath, Jacuzzi, fireplace. Located in 3 bldgs.
Rates: $115-$165/room, $175-$195/suite, all incl. full brk., afternoon and evening refreshment. Seasonal variations. Discount avail. for extended, mid-week stays.
Credit cards: MC, V
Restrictions: No children under 16, pets, smoking. One night's deposit req. 3-day cancellation notice req., less 10% fee. 2-night min. stay on wknds.
Notes: Two-story Coach house built in the 1850s. Located on 1.5 wooded acres. Living room with fireplace. Furnished with English pine antiques. Brick and stone pathways, garden terrace, circular rose garden with lily pond, fountain. Decks. Handicapped access.*

Cross Roads Inn
6380 Silverado Trail, Napa, CA 94558
(707) 944-0646, (800) 822-5151
Innkeeper: Sam and Nancy Scott
Rooms: 4 suites w/pvt. bath, phone, TV
Rates: $175-$200, incl. full brk., afternoon and evening refreshment
Credit cards: MC, V
Restrictions: No children under 16, pets, smoking. Deposit req., 7-day cancellation notice, 2-night min. stay on wknds.
Notes: Three-story retreat situated on 23 acres of wine country. Suites are all individually decorated, Jacuzzi spas. View of vineyards and mountains. Hiking trails. Assistance for winery, hot-air balloon tours, and more.

Hennessey House
1727 Main St., Napa, CA 94558
(707) 226-3774, (707) 226-2975
Innkeeper: Lauriann Delay, Andrea Weinstein
Rooms: 10 w/pvt. bath, incl. 4 w/fireplace, 1 w/TV. Located in 2 bldgs.

Rates: $70-$155, incl. full brk., evening refreshment. Seasonal variations.
Credit cards: Most major cards
Restrictions: No pets, smoking. Deposit req. 72-hour cancellation notice req., less
$15.00 fee. 2-night min. stay on wknds.
Notes: Two-story Eastlake Queen Anne Victorian house with Georgian-style panelling and Carriage House built in 1889. Fully refurbished in 1986. Formal dining
room with handpainted pressed-tin ceiling. Parlor with board games. Enclosed
porch with wicker furniture. Furnished with English and Belgian antiques. Garden
with fountain, sauna. Bicycle rental available. Part of the Joseph Mathews Winery
enclave. Listed on the National Register of Historic Places. Guests have access to
nearby health club.*

HENNESSEY HOUSE

Inn on Randolph
411 Randolph St., Napa, CA 94559
(707) 257-2886, (707) 257-8756
Innkeeper: Deborah Coffee
Rooms: 4 w/pvt. bath, incl. 2 w/fireplace, plus 1 suite w/pvt. bath
Rates: $109-$164/room, $159/suite, all incl. full brk., afternoon refreshment. Sea-
sonal variations. Discount avail. for mid-week, extended, senior citizen and group
stays.
Credit cards: MC, V
Restrictions: No pets. Smoking restricted. One-night's deposit req. 72-hour cancellation notice req., less $10.00 fee. 2-night min. stay on wknds. & holidays.
Notes: Two-story Gothic Rivival multi-gabled farmhouse with bay window, beveled
porch posts, hardwood floors, built in 1860. Fully restored. Decorated in Victorian
style with antiques. Parlor with gas fireplace, original built-in desk. Dining room
with gas fireplace and baby grand piano. Sunroom with french doors leading to garden deck. Board games, books available. Lawns and gardens. Gazebo. Croquet.
Phone available upon request.*

La Belle Epoque
1386 Calistoga Ave., Napa, CA 94559
(707) 257-2161, (707) 226-6314
Innkeeper: Merlin and Claudia Wedepohl
Rooms: 6 w/pvt. bath, incl. 2 w/fireplace, 1 w/TV, plus 1 suite w/pvt. bath, fireplace, TV
Rates: $110-$160 incl. full brk., evening refreshment. Seasonal variations.

LA BELLE EPOQUE

Credit cards: Most major cards
Restrictions: No children under 10, pets, smoking. Credit card deposit req. 5-day cancellation notice req. 2-night min. stay on wknds. 3-night min. stay on major holidays.
Notes: Three-story, multi-gabled Queen Anne house built in 1893 with carved dormers, original stained-glass windows in transoms and semi-circular windows and high-hipped roof. Located in Napa's Calistoga Historic District. "Painted lady" style color scheme. Furnished with Victorian antiques. Dining room w/fireplace, 2 parlors, 1 with TV, wine tasting room, wine cellar. Massages available.*

La Residence Country Inn
4066 St. Helena Hwy. N., Napa, CA 94558
(707) 253-0337, (707) 253-0382

Innkeeper: David R. Jackson and Craig E. Claussen
Rooms: 17 plus 3 suites, all w/pvt. bath, phone, TV. Located in 2 bldgs.
Rates: $115-$185/room, $185-$235/suite, all incl. full brk., evening refreshment. Special pkgs. avail.
Credit cards: Most major cards
Restrictions: No pets, smoking. Deposit req. 7-day cancel notice req. 2-night min. stay on holiday wknds.
Notes: Gothic Revival house built in 1870 and French-style barn. Located on 2 wooded acres. Dining room, sitting room. Guests have access to kitchen. Furnished with French, English, American antiques. Spa, hot tub. Handicapped access.*

The Napa Inn
1137 Warren St., Napa, CA 94559
(707) 257-1444

Innkeeper: Doug and Carol Morales
Rooms: 4 plus 2 suites, all w/pvt. bath, incl. 2 w/fireplace
Rates: $120-$135/room, $160-$170/suite, all incl. full brk., afternoon refreshment. Discount avail. for mid-week stay.
Credit cards: Most major cards
Restrictions: No children under 12, pets, smoking. One night's deposit req. 7-day cancellation notice req. 2-night min. stay on March–November wknds.

Notes: Three-story Queen Anne Victorian house built at the turn of the century. Parlor, formal dining room. Furnished with Victorian antiques. Country garden with picnic/sitting area.*

Old World Inn
1301 Jefferson St., Napa, CA 94559
(707) 257-0112
Innkeeper: Diane Dumaine
Rooms: 8 w/pvt. bath
Rates: $105-$140, incl. full brk., afternoon refreshment
Credit cards: Most major cards
Restrictions: No pets, smoking. One night's deposit req. 7-day cancellation notice req. 2-night min. stay on Apr. 1–Nov. 30 wknds.
Notes: Victorian house with wood shingles, clinker brick, leaded and beveled glass built in 1900. Parlor, morning room, each with fireplace. Porches, Jacuzzi. Decorated in continental style with Scandinavian flavor. Furnished with painted Victorian and antique furniture.*

OLD WORLD INN

Stahlecker House Bed & Breakfast Country Inn & Gardens
1042 Easum Dr., Napa, CA 94558
(707) 257-1588, (707) 224-7429
Innkeeper: Ron and Ethel Stahlecker
Rooms: 2, incl. 1 w/fireplace, plus 1 suite w/fireplace, all w/pvt. bath, TV
Rates: $108-$145/room, $185/suite, all incl. full brk., afternoon refreshment. Discount avail. for military.
Credit cards: Most major cards
Restrictions: No children, pets, smoking. 7-day cancellation notice, less $10.00 per night fee. 2-night min. stay on wknds. & holidays.
Notes: Sitting with fireplace, TV. Reading rooms. Gardens, sun deck.

NEEDLES (13)

Old Trails Inn
304 Broadway, Needles, CA 92363
(619) 326-3523, (619) 326-1254
Innkeeper: Hank and Edna Wilde

OLD TRAILS INN

Rooms: 4 cabins w/kitchenette. Located in 4 bldgs.
Rates: $50, incl. cont. brk.
Credit cards: MC, V
Restrictions: No children under 8. Pets, smoking restricted. One night's deposit req. 14-day cancellation notice req., less $10.00 fee.
Notes: One-story tourist cabins built in 1930. Restored in 1992. Breakfast room, greeting room, sitting room with cards, board games. turn-of-the-century photographs, camera collection, and memorabilia on walls. Furnished with antique and classic 1930s furniture. Park-like court with patio, tile walkway.

NEVADA CITY (7)

Downey House
517 West Broad St., Nevada City, CA 95959
(916) 265-2815, (800) 258- 2815
Innkeeper: Miriam Wright
Rooms: 6 w/pvt bath
Rates: $75-$100, incl. full brk. Discount avail. for extended and mid-week stays. Seasonal variations.
Credit cards: MC, V
Restrictions: No pets. Smoking restricted. One night's deposit req. 7-day cancellation notice req.
Notes: Eastlake Victorian house built in 1870. Located on 1/4 acre. Parlor. Sunroom with cable TV. Garden room with phone. Furnished with antiques. Veranda, terrace.*

The Emma Nevada House
528 E. Broad St., Nevada City, CA 95959
(916) 265-4415, (800) 916-3662
Innkeeper: Ruth Ann Riese
Rooms: 6 w/pvt. bath, incl. 1 w/fireplace
Rates: $100-$150, incl. full brk., afternoon refreshment. Discount avail. for senior citizen and mid-week stays.
Credit cards: Most major cards
Restrictions: No children under 12, pets, smoking. One night's deposit req. 7-day cancellation notice req. 2-night min. stay on wknds. from May–Dec.
Notes: Victorian house built in 1856. Fully restored in 1993. Has operated as an inn since 1994. Livingroom with fireplace. Game room with antique slot machine, TV,

THE EMMA NEVADA HOUSE

VCR, books, board games. Sun room with five walls of floor-to-ceiling windows, deck. Wrap-around front and back porches overlooking garden. Emma Nevada, a 19th-century opera star, lived here as a child. Small private parties accommodated.

The Parsonage
427 Broad St., Nevada City, CA 95959
(916) 265-9478, (916) 265-8147
Innkeeper: Deborah Dane
Rooms: 6 w/pvt. bath, incl. 1 w/fireplace, 2 w/TV
Rates: $65-$125, incl. expanded cont. brk., afternoon refreshment. Discount avail. for extended and mid-week stays.
Credit cards: MC, V
Restrictions: Children restricted. No pets, smoking. 7-day cancellation notice req. 2-night min. stay on wknds. & holidays.
Notes: Two-story house built in 1885. Has operated as inn since 1986. Parlor, formal dining room, family room. Furnished with family antiques. Veranda.*

NEWPORT BEACH (16)

Doryman's Inn
2102 West Ocean Front, Newport Beach, CA 92663
(714) 675-7300, (714) 675-7300
Innkeeper: Jeannie and Richard Lawrence
Rooms: 8 plus 2 suites, all w/pvt. bath, phone, cable TV, fireplace, sunken tub
Rates: $135-$225/room, $230-$275/suite, all incl. cont. brk. Discount avail. for mid-week stay.
Credit cards: Most major cards
Restrictions: No children, pets, smoking. One-night's deposit req. 72-hour cancellation notice req., less $25.00 fee.
Notes: Located on the Pacific Ocean. Guest rooms reflect influence of classic Victorian designs. Furnished with French and American antiques. Fern-filled skylights over Italian marble sunken tubs. Floral draperies and bedspreads, gilt-edged beveled mirrors, etched French glass fixtures. Parlor, patio. Rooftop sunbathing deck.*

Little Inn on the Bay
617 Lido Park Dr., Newport Beach, CA 92663
(800) 438-4466, (714) 673-8800

Innkeeper: Michael and Fi Palitz
Rooms: 17 plus 13 suites, all w/pvt. bath, phone, TV. Located in 2 bldgs.
Rates: $100/room, $125/suite, all incl. expanded cont. brk., evening refreshment.
    Discount avail. for mid-week stay.
Credit cards: Most major cards
Restrictions: Deposit req. 7-day cancellation notice req.
Notes: All guests receive a complimentary bay cruise. Bicycles available. Handi-
capped access. Many languages spoken.*

NIPTON (13)

HOTEL NIPTON

Hotel Nipton
72 Nipton Rd., HCI Box 357, Nipton, CA 92364
(619) 856-2335, (702) 896-6846
Innkeeper: Roxanne and Gerald Freeman
Rooms: 4, no pvt. bath
Rates: $49.05, incl. cont. brk.
Credit cards: Most major cards
Restrictions: No pets. Credit card deposit req. 48-hour cancellation notice req.
Notes: Built in 1910. Fully restored. Central parlor with historical photographs. Fur-
nished in southwestern style with antiques. Outdoor Jacuzzi. Cactus garden.

OAKHURST (7)

Chateau du Sureau
48688 Victoria Lane, Box 577, Oakhurst, CA 93644
(209) 683-6860
Innkeeper: Ema Kubin-Clanin
Rooms: 9 w/pvt. bath, phone, fireplace. Located in 2 bldgs.
Rates: $260-$360, incl. full brk.
Credit cards: Most major cards
Restrictions: 50% deposit req. 7-day cancellation notice req., less 10% fee. 2-night
    min. stay on holiday wknds.
Notes: Two-story 19th-century French Chateau. Located on hilltop on seven acres.
Dining room. Red clay floor tiles, wrought iron balconies. Common room with fire-
place, piano. Garden with fountain. Restaurant on premises. Handicapped access.
German and Spanish spoken.*

CHATEAU DU SUREAU

OAKLAND (9)

Dockside Boat & Breakfast
77 Jack London Sq., Oakland, CA 94607
(510) 444-5858, (510) 444-0420
Innkeeper: Rob Harris
Rooms: 15 yachts, all w/TV, stereo, bath, coffee maker, flowers, incl. 5 suites
Rates: $95-$150/room, $175-$325/suite, all incl. cont. brk. Seasonal variations. Discount avail. for mid-week, extended stay. Special pkgs. avail.
Credit cards: Most major cards
Restrictions: No children under 8, pets, high-heel shoes. Smoking restricted. 50% deposit req. 30-day cancellation notice req., less 25% fee. 2-night min. stay on holiday wknds.
Notes: Sailing and motor yachts available for dockside lodging at Jack London Square in Oakland, Pier 39 in San Francisco, and San Diego. Private charters, catered dinner, limosine service, floral arrangements, concierge service available. Spanish spoken.*

DOCKSIDE BOAT & BREAKFAST

OCCIDENTAL (3)

The Inn at Occidental
3657 Church St., Box 857, Occidental, CA 95465
(707) 874-1047, (707) 874-1078

Innkeeper: Jack Bullard
Rooms: 6 plus 2 suites, incl. 1 w/fireplace, all w/pvt. bath, phone, TV
Rates: $95-$145/room, $140-$195/suite, all incl. full brk., afternoon refreshment. Discounts avail.
Credit cards: Most major cards
Restrictions: No children under 10, pets, smoking. One night's deposit req. 10-day cancellation notice req., less $10.00 fee. 2-night min. stay on wknds. from April–Oct.
Notes: Three-story Victorian house built in 1887. Restored in 1988 with fir floors, wainscotted hallways. Parlor with library, fireplace. Dining room. Decorated with antiques and original art from innkeeper's collection. Covered porches with wicker furniture, balustered railings overlooking courtyard garden. Handicapped access. Small private parties accommodated.*

OLEMA (9)

Roundstone Farm
P.O. Box 217, Olema, CA 94950
(415) 663-1020
Innkeeper: Inger Fisher and Barbara Hand
Rooms: 5 w/pvt. bath, fireplace
Rates: $115-$135, incl. full brk. Seasonal variations. Discount avail. for extended stay.
Credit cards: Most major cards
Restrictions: No children under 6, pets, smoking. 5-day cancellation notice req. 2-night min. stay on wknds.
Notes: Board and batten cedar farmhouse designed by a solar architect. Located on ten-acre horse ranch in the Golden Gate National Recreation area. Living room with 16-ft. ceiling, skylight, board games, library. Decorated with contemporary artwork. Deck overlooking valley, pond. Patio garden. Bicycles available.*

THE INN AT SHALLOW CREEK FARM

ORLAND (4)

The Inn at Shallow Creek Farm
4712 Road DD, Route 3, Box 3176, Orland, CA 95963
(916) 865-4093

Innkeeper: Kurt and Mary Glaeseman
Rooms: 2 w/phone, plus 1 suite w/pvt. bath, phone, plus cottage w/wood-burning stove, sunporch, kitchen. Located in 2 bldgs.
Rates: $55/room, $65/suite, $75/cottage, all incl. full brk.
Credit cards: Most major cards
Restrictions: No pets, smoking. One-night's deposit req. 6-day cancellation notice.
Notes: Two-story turn-of-the-century farmhouse. Located on working farm with orange orchard. Furnished with antiques. Country dining room, sunporch. French, German and Spanish spoken.*

JEAN'S RIVERSIDE B & B

OROVILLE (4)

Jean's Riverside B & B
45 Cabana Dr., Oroville, CA 95965
(916) 533-1413

Innkeeper: Jean Pratt
Rooms: 7 plus 2 suites, all w/pvt. bath, TV, phone, incl. 4 w/fireplace
Rates: $55-$85/room, $95-$105/suite, all incl. full brk., evening refreshment. Discount avail. for extended stay.
Credit cards: Most major cards
Restrictions: No children, pets. Smoking restricted. Deposit req. 7-day cancellation notice req., less cancellation fee.
Notes: Private home on 5 wooded acres alongside Feather River. Private Jacuzzis and old-fashioned wood-burning stoves. Deck. Small private parties accommodated. Lawn games, canoes, gold panning, fishing, musical instruments available. Handicapped access.*

PACIFIC GROVE (10)

Centrella Bed & Breakfast Inn
612 Central Ave., Pacific Grove, CA 93950
(408) 372-3372, (800) 233-3372 (US), (408) 372-2036

Innkeeper: Joe Megna
Rooms: 18 w/phone incl. 16 w/pvt bath, 5 w/TV, plus 3 suites w/pvt bath, phone, TV, plus 5 cottages w/pvt. bath, phone, fireplace, TV. Located in 5 bldgs.

Rates: $90-$125/room, $150/suite, $175-$185/cottage, all incl. expanded cont. brk., evening refreshment. Special pkgs. avail. Seasonal variations.
Credit cards: Most major cards
Restrictions: No pets, smoking. One night's deposit req. 72-hr. cancellation notice req., less $10.00 fee. 2-night min. stay on wknds.
Notes: Three-story Victorian-style inn with turrets, bay windows built in 1889. Fully restored in 1982. Parlor with fireplace. Dining room. Sun porch overlooking gardens. Furnished in Laura Ashley decor with antiques. Small private parties accommodated. Handicapped access. Listed on the National Register of Historic Places. Spanish, Italian, Portugese spoken.*

Gosby House Inn
643 Lighthouse Ave., Pacific Grove, CA 93950
(408) 375-1287, (408) 655-9621
Innkeeper: Shirley Butts
Rooms: 22, incl. 20 w/pvt. bath, phone, incl. 12 w/fireplace. Located in 2 bldgs.
Rates: $85-$150, incl. full brk., afternoon and evening refreshment
Credit cards: Most major cards
Restrictions: No pets, smoking. One night's deposit req. 48-hour cancellation notice req.
Notes: Two-story Queen Anne-style mansion with rounded corner tower built in 1887. Has operated as inn since 1887. Front parlor with fireplace. Side parlor with antique doll collection. Decorated with polished natural woods, floral-print wall papers. Furnished with period antiques. Garden with winding brick path, tables, chairs. Small private parties accommodated. Newspapers provided. Listed on the National Register of Historic Places. Handicapped access.*

Martine Inn
255 Ocean View Blvd., Pacific Grove, CA 93950
(408) 373-3388, (408) 373-3896
Innkeeper: Don and Marion Martine
Rooms: 17 w/pvt. bath, phone, incl. 10 w/fireplace, plus 2 suites w/pvt. bath, phone, incl. 1 w/fireplace. Located in 2 bldgs.
Rates: $125-$230/room, $280/suite, all incl. full brk., afternoon refreshment
Credit cards: Most major cards
Restrictions: No pets. Smoking restricted. Full prepayment req. 72-hour cancellation notice req., less $10.00 fee. 2-night min. stay on wknds. 3-night min. stay on holiday wknds.
Notes: Mediterranean-style house built in 1899, overlooking coast. Remodeled in 1908, 1925, 1972. Game room, library, parlor, dining room, sitting rooms, solarium, Jacuzzi, sauna, enclosed courtyard with Oriental fountain and pond. Conference rooms. Furnished with Victorian antiques. Small private parties accommodated. Picnic lunches available. Handicapped access. French, Italian, Spanish, Portugese spoken.

PALM SPRINGS (15)

Casa Cody B & B Country Inn
175 S. Cahuilla St., Palm Springs, CA 92262
(619) 320-9346, (619) 325-8610
Innkeeper: Frank Tysen and Therese Hayes

CASA CODY B & B COUNTRY INN

Rooms: 10 w/pvt. bath, phone, TV, incl. 4 w/fireplace, plus 6 suites w/pvt. bath, phone, TV, incl. 2 w/fireplace, plus 1 cottage w/pvt. bath, phone, TV. Located in 3 bldgs.

Rates: $65-$105/room, $125-$175/suite, $125/cottage, all incl. cont. brk. Seasonal variations. Discount avail. for mid-week and extended stays.

Credit cards: Most major cards

Restrictions: Credit card deposit req. 72-hour cancellation notice req. 2-night min. stay on wknds. 3-night min. stay on holidays.

Notes: Single story early California Hacienda style buildings built as a lodge in the 1920s, restored in 1987. Sante Fe decor. Located near San Jacinto Mountain. Landscaped grounds include two swimming pools, whirlpool spa. Handicapped access. French and Dutch spoken.*

Orchid Tree Inn
261 S. Belardo Rd., Palm Springs, CA 92262
(619) 325-2791, (800) 733-3435, (619) 325-3855

Innkeeper: Bob and Karen Weitham

Rooms: 26 w/pvt. bath, phone, TV, plus 15 suites, w/pvt. bath, phone, TV, incl. 5 w/fireplace. Located in 19 bldgs.

Rates: $50-$105/room, $70-$270/suite, incl. cont. brk. Nov.–May. Seasonal variation. Discount avail. for seniors, extended stay.

Credit cards: Most major cards

Restrictions: No pets. Smoking restricted. Min. one night's deposit req. 7 day cancellation notice req. 2-night min. stay on wknds. from Jan.–May & most holidays.

Notes: Two swimming pools, spa, gardens. Guests have access to 30 full kitchens. Some Spanish spoken.*

Villa Royale Inn
1620 S. Indian Trail, Palm Springs, CA 92264
(619) 327-2314, (800) 245-2314, (619) 322-3794

Innkeeper: Bob Lee

Rooms: 23 plus 10 suites, all w/pvt. bath, phone, TV, incl. 16 w/fireplace. Located in 7 bldgs.

Rates: $75-$165/room, $150-$270/suite, all incl. cont. brk. Discount avail. for extended stay. Seasonal variations in Summer.

Credit cards: Most major cards

Restrictions: No children under 16, pets. Smoking restricted. One night's deposit req. 10-day cancellation notice req. 2-night min. stay on wknds. 3-night min. stay on holidays.

Notes: European style country inn located on 3.5 landscaped acres. Multiple interior courtyards. Dining room. Each room decorated in decor of different European country. Outdoor living room with fireplace, Italian wicker chairs. Private patios, spa, two swimming pools, Jacuzzi, tennis courts. Bicycles available. European country-style restaurant on premises. Limited handicapped access. Spanish spoken.*

PALO ALTO (9)

Adella Villa
P.O. Box 4528, Palo Alto, CA 94027-4021
(415) 321-5195, (415) 325-5121

Innkeeper: Tricia Young
Rooms: 4, plus 1 suite, all w/pvt. bath, phone, TV, some w/Jacuzzi
Rates: $105, incl. full brk., evening refreshment. Rates higher during Stanford graduation period. Discount avail. for senior citizens.
Credit cards: Most major cards
Restrictions: No children under 10, pets. Smoking restricted. 3-day cancellation notice req. 2-night min. stay.
Notes: Two-story Italian Renaissance villa built in the 1920s. Located on one wooded acre. Sitting room with fireplace, projection TV, VCR, and video library. Shiatsu massage lounge chair. Dining room, music room, laundry room. Swimming pool, BBQ. Manicured gardens with Japanese koi pond. Bicycles provided. Airport pickup available. Fax and copy machine available. On site parking. German, Spanish spoken. *

Hotel California
2431 Ash St., Palo Alto, CA 94306
(415) 322-7666, (415) 321-7538

Innkeeper: Andy and Michelle Hite
Rooms: 20 w/pvt. bath, phone, TV
Rates: $48-$60, incl. cont. brk.
Credit cards: Most major cards
Restrictions: No children under 10, pets, smoking. Deposit req. 24-hour cancellation notice req.
Notes: Two-story hotel with courtyard. Furnished with turn-of-the-century pieces. Guests have access to kitchen and laundry facilities. Bakery on premises.

The Victorian on Lytton
555 Lytton Ave., Palo Alto, CA 94301
(415) 322-8555, (415) 322-7141

Innkeeper: Susan Hall
Rooms: 10 w/pvt. bath, phone, incl. 1 w/fireplace, 8 w/TV. Located in 2 bldgs.
Rates: $98-$185, incl. cont. brk., evening refreshment
Credit cards: Most major cards
Restrictions: No pets, smoking. Deposit req. 10-day cancellation notice req., less 10% fee.
Notes: Victorian house built in 1895. Fully restored in 1986. Living room. Furnished with period antiques. Breakfast served in room. English garden. Handicapped access.*

PARKFIELD (11)

Parkfield Inn
Parkfield Rte., Box 3560, Parkfield, CA 93451
(805) 463-2421, (805) 463-2323
Innkeeper: John and Barbara Varian
Rooms: 6 w/pvt. bath
Rates: $45-$65, incl. cont. brk. Seasonal variations. Discount avail. for mid-week stay.
Credit cards: MC, V
Restrictions: No pets, smoking. Deposit req. 7-day cancellation notice req.
Notes: Ranch-style log house built in 1991 adjoining 20,000 acre ranch in "Old West" setting. Gathering room with TV, fireplace, full library. Hardwood floors. Furniture made from logs and other antique materials. Furnished in southwest, rustic decor. Porch made of railroad ties. Fireplace built of river rock found on property. Lawns. Fishing, swimming, biking, hiking on ranch. Antique farm equipment abound. Cafe with full menu on premises. Small private parties accommodated. Handicapped access.*

PLACERVILLE (6)

The Chichester-McKee House
800 Spring St., Placerville, CA 95667-4424
(916) 626-1882, (800) 831-4008
Innkeeper: Doreen and Bill Thornhill
Rooms: 3 w/pvt. half-bath
Rates: $75-$85, incl. full brk.
Credit cards: Most major cards
Restrictions: No pets. Smoking restricted. Credit card deposit req. 5-day cancellation notice req., less $8.00 fee.
Notes: Two-story Victorian mansion built in 1892 on 1 acre with gardens. Fully restored in 1978. Has operated as inn since 1984. Dining rooms, parlor with pump organ, fireplace, board games. Stained glass. Solarium. Library with fireplace. Furnished with antiques. Flower garden. Phones available. Resident dog.*

River Rock Inn
1756 Georgetown, Placerville, CA 95667
(916) 622-7640
Innkeeper: Dorothy Irvin
Rooms: 3 w/pvt. bath, TV, incl. 2 w/phone, plus 1 suite w/pvt. bath, TV
Rates: $75/room, $90/suite, all incl. full brk. Discount avail. for extended stay.
Credit cards: D
Restrictions: No pets, smoking
Notes: Built in1960. Living room with fireplace, TV. Dining room. Kitchen with wood stove. Deck with hot tub overlooking American River. Furnished in country style with some antiques. Fishing, panning for gold. Limited handicapped access.*

PLYMOUTH (6)

Amador Harvest Inn
12455 Steiner Rd., Plymouth, CA 95669
(209) 245-5512
Innkeeper: Bobbie Deaver
Rooms: 3 plus 1 suite, all w/pvt. bath

Rates: $85-$95/room, $110/suite, all incl. full brk., afternoon refreshment
Credit cards: Most major cards
Restrictions: No children under 12, pets, smoking. Credit card deposit req. 7-day cancellation notice req.
Notes: Two-story house on working farm. Living room with fireplace, reading room. Croquet, wine tasting.

POINT REYES STATION (3)

Carriage House
325 Mesa Rd., Box 1239, Point Reyes Station, CA 94956
(415) 663-8627, (415) 663-8431

Innkeeper: Felicity Kirsch
Rooms: 2 suites w/pvt. bath, fireplace, TV, kitchen
Rates: $120, incl. full brk., afteroon refreshment. Discount avail. for extended and mid-week stays. Seasonal variations.
Credit cards: None.
Restrictions: No pets. Smoking restricted. 50% deposit req. 7-day cancellation fee, less $10.00 fee. 2-night min. stay on wknds.
Notes: Two-story Inn built in 1920s, remodelled in 1990. Furnished with antiques and folk art. Giftshop. Small private parties accommodated. Garden with BBQ overlooking the Inverness Ridge. Giftshop and gallery on premises.*

Cricket Cottage
P.O. Box 627, Point Reyes Station, CA 94956
(415) 663-9139

Innkeeper: Penelope Livingston, James Stark
Rooms: 1 cottage w/pvt. bath, hot tub, fireplace
Rates: $125, incl. full brk.
Credit cards: Most major cards
Restrictions: No pets. Smoking restricted. One night's deposit req. 7-day cancellation notice req., less $10.00 fee. 2-night min. stay on wknds. and holidays.
Notes: A cottage in a garden setting with Franklin fireplace, private hot tub. Spanish spoken.

Ferrando's Hideaway
12010 Highway 1, Box 688, Point Reyes Station, CA 94956
(415) 663-1966, (415) 663-1825

Innkeeper: Greg and Doris Ferrando
Rooms: 2 w/pvt. bath, phone, pvt. entrance, patio, plus 1 cottage w/pvt. bath, TV, VCR, stereo, deck, kitchen, phone. Located in 2 bldgs.
Rates: $95-$110/room, $110-$120/cottage, all incl. full brk.
Credit cards: None
Restrictions: No pets, smoking. Deposit req. 7-day cancellation notice req., less $15.00 fee per night. 2-night min. stay on wknds.
Notes: Main house built in 1972. Sitting room with wood stove. Breakfast room, patios. Vegetable garden. Outdoor hot tub. Massage therapist, TV and VCR avail. German spoken.

Marsh Cottage
P.O. Box 1121, Point Reyes Station, CA 94956
(415) 699-7168

MARSH COTTAGE

Innkeeper: Wendy Schwartz
Rooms: 1 cottage w/pvt. bath, fireplace, kitchen
Rates: $95-$110, incl. full brk. Discount avail. for extended stay.
Credit cards: Most major cards
Restrictions: No pets, smoking. Deposit req. 7-day cancellation notice req., less
$10.00 fee. 2-night min. stay on wknds. 3-night min. stay on holiday wknds.
Notes: Built in the style of a Cape Cod country cottage in the 1930s. Located on a
salt/freshwater marsh along Tomales Bay. Antiques. Covered front porch and sun
deck with furnishings. Board games, guidebooks, binoculars.

Thirty-Nine Cypress
39 Cypress Rd., Box 176, Point Reyes Station, CA 94956
(415) 663-1709
Innkeeper: Julia and Barbara
Rooms: 3 w/pvt. bath
Rates: $100-$125, incl. cont. brk. Discount avail. for extended stay.
Credit cards: Most major cards
Restrictions: No children under 6, smoking. Pets restricted. One-night's deposit
req. 7-day cancellation notice req., less $20.00 fee. 2-night min. stay on wknds.
Notes: Passive solar-heated redwood house. Located in 3½-acre meadow overlook-
ing 200 acres of pastureland, a stream and the Inverness Ridge. Living room with
fireplace, dining room. Furnished with antiques, original artwork, Oriental rugs.
Garden. French spoken.*

The Tree House
P.O. Box 1075, Point Reyes Station, CA 94956
(415) 663-8720
Innkeeper: Lisa Patsei
Rooms: 3 incl. 1 suite, all w/phone, TV, incl. 1 w/fireplace. Located in 2 bldgs.
Rates: $80/room, $95/suite, all incl. full brk. Discount avail. for extended stay.
Credit cards: Most major cards
Restrictions: No smoking. Deposit req. 3-day cancellation notice req., less $10.00
fee.
Notes: Studio with fireplace. Furnished with antiques. Wet bar. Large deck. Board
games. Italian spoken.*

QUINCY (4)

THE FEATHER BED

The Feather Bed
542 Jackson St., Box 3200, Quincy, CA 95971
(916) 283-0102
Innkeeper: Bob and Jan Janowski
Rooms: 5 w/pvt. bath, phone, incl. 2 w/fireplace, 1 w/TV, plus 1 cottage and 1
guesthouse w/pvt. bath, fireplace. Located in 3 bldgs.
Rates: $70-$85/room, $85-$100/other, all incl. full brk., afternoon refreshment.
Discount avail. for single business guests.
Credit cards: Most major cards
Restrictions: No pets, smoking. One night's deposit req. 6-day cancellation notice
req. 2-night min. stay on major holidays.
Notes: Queen Anne-style house with Greco-Roman facade built in 1893. Renovated
at the turn of the century. Restored in 1979. Brick patio with flower gardens. Parlor. Phones available. Front porch with swing. Furnished with antiques. Bicycles, off-
street parking, airport pickup available. Limited handicapped access.*

REDDING (2)

Cabral House on Chestnut
1752 Chestnut St., Redding, CA 96001
(916) 244-3766
Innkeeper: Ann and Louie Cabral Jr.
Rooms: 3 w/pvt. bath.
Rates: $75-$125/room, incl. full brk., evening refreshment. Discount avail. for mid-
week stay.
Credit cards: Most major cards
Restrictions: No children under 12, pets. Smoking restricted. Deposit req. 7-day
cancellation notice req., less fee.
Notes: Private home decorated from "Golden Era" of the 1920s to 1940s. Gardens,
porch, and patio. Resident pets.*

Palisades Paradise B & B
1200 Palisades Ave., Redding, CA 96003
(916) 223-5305
Innkeeper: Gail Goetz
Rooms: 2 suites w/TV

PALISADES PARADISE B & B

Rates: $55-$80, incl. full brk., afternoon refreshment. Discount avail. for extended stay.

Credit cards: Most major cards

Restrictions: No children under 8. Smoking restricted. Pets welcome with prior arrangement. Deposit req. 5-day cancellation notice req., less $10.00 fee.

Notes: Two-story house overlooking the Sacramento River and city. Living room with fireplace, wide-screen TV/VCR. Old-fashioned porch swing under the oak tree. Garden spa.*

Tiffany House Bed & Breakfast Inn
1510 Barbara Rd., Redding, CA 96003
(916) 244-3225

Innkeeper: Roberta and Arthur Dube

Rooms: 3 w/pvt. bath, plus 1 cottage w/pvt. bath, fireplace, spa. Located in 2 bldgs.

Rates: $75-$95/room, $125/cottage., all incl. full brk., evening refreshment. Discount avail. for extended and mid-week stays.

Credit cards: Most major cards

Restrictions: No children under 5, pets. Smoking restricted. Deposit req. 7-day cancellation notice req., less $10.00 fee.

Notes: Two-story Victorian house on hilltop with view of Mt. Lassen range. Parlor, drawing room, dining room. Organ with sheet music, board games, books, TV/VCR, movies. Two fireplaces. Furnished in antiques. Shaded deck with porch swing, chairs. Lawn games. Swimming pool and gazebo. Special arrangements available. Airport transportation available. Limited handicapped access.*

REDLANDS (15)

Morey Mansion
190 Terracina Blvd., Redlands, CA 92373
(909) 793-7970, (909) 793-7870

Innkeeper: Dolly Tavares Wimer

Rooms: 4 w/pvt. bath, phone, fireplace, TV, plus 1 suite w/phone, fireplace, TV

Rates: $109-$145/room, $145-$185/suite, all incl. cont. brk. Discount avail. for extended stay.

Credit cards: Most major cards

Restrictions: No smoking. 7-day cancellation notice req., less $15.00 fee.

Notes: Victorian house with French Mansard roof, onion dome, beveled windows, French stained-glass and wrap-around veranda built in 1889. Operated as Inn since 1991. Staircase railing with carved serpentine dragon tails. Hand-carved oak woodwork throughout house. Reception Hall built to resemble captain's quarters of a ship. Historical Landmark. Small private parties accommodated. Spanish and Portuguese spoken.*

REDONDO BEACH (14)

Ocean Breeze B & B
122 S. Juanita Ave., Redondo Beach, CA 90277-3435
(310) 316-5123
Innkeeper: Norris and Betty Binding
Rooms: plus 1 suite, all w/pvt. bath, TV
Rates: $30-$40/room, $45-$50/suite, all incl. cont. brk. Discount avail. for extended
  stay.
Credit cards: None
Restrictions: No children under 5, pets, smoking. Deposit req. 14-day cancellation
  notice req., less deposit. 2-night min. stay on wknds.
Notes: Private house built in 1940. Has operated as inn since 1987. Furnished with
Oriental rugs. Guests have access to kitchen. Bicycles, beach towels available.

SACRAMENTO (6)

Abigail's
2120 G St., Sacramento, CA 95816
(916) 441-5007, (800) 858-1568, (916) 441-0621
Innkeeper: Susanne and Ken Ventura
Rooms: 5 w/pvt. bath, phone, incl. 2 w/TV
Rates: $95-$135, incl. full brk., evening refreshment. Discount avail. for mid-week
  stay.
Credit cards: Most major cards
Restrictions: No pets. Smoking restricted. One night's deposit req. 7-day cancellation notice req., less 10% fee. 2-night min. stay on holidays. 3-night min. stay on
  Memorial Day wknd.
Notes: Two-story Colonial Revival mansion built in 1912. Living room with fireplace, sitting room with piano, board games, dining room. Furnished with antiques, family memorabilia. Garden, patio, hot tub in secluded garden. Vegetarian dietary needs met. Refrigerator available. Resident cats.*

Amber House
1315 22nd St., Sacramento, CA 95816
(916) 444-8085, (800) 755-6526, (916) 447-1547
Innkeeper: Michael and Jane Richardson
Rooms: 9 w/pvt. bath, phone, TV, radio-cassette, incl. 5 w/Jacuzzi. Located in 2
  bldgs.
Rates: $85-$195, incl. full brk., afternoon refreshment. Discount avail. for mid-week
  stay.
Credit cards: Most major cards
Restrictions: No pets. Children and smoking restricted. One night's deposit req.
  Min. 2-day cancellation notice req.
Notes: California Craftsman house built in 1905. Dining room, library. Living room with antique pocket doors, boxed beam ceiling, clinker brick fireplace, hardwood

AMBER HOUSE

floors. Veranda. Furnished with English period antiques, beveled- and stained-glass windows, original oil paintings, Oriental rugs. Airport pickup, bicycles. Small private parties accommodated. Spanish and French spoken.*

SAINT HELENA (5)

Ambrose Bierce House
1515 Main St., Saint Helena, CA 94574
(707) 963-3003
Innkeeper: Jane Hutchings Gibson
Rooms: 2 plus 1 suite, all w/pvt. bath
Rates: $99-$109/room, $139/suite, all incl. cont. brk.
Credit cards: Most major cards
Restrictions: No children under 12, pets, smoking. One night's deposit req. 7-day cancellation notice req., less $10.00 fee. 2-night min. stay on wknds.
Notes: Two-story Victorian house with exterior staircase built in 1872. Sitting room, dining room, upstairs porch. Furnished with period antiques. Decorated with Laura Ashley wallpapers. Air-conditioned. Flower gardens. Former home of author Ambrose Bierce. Off-street parking, bicycles available.*

Asplund Conn Valley Inn
726 Rossi Rd., Saint Helena, CA 94574
(707) 963-4614
Innkeeper: Elsie Asplund Hudak
Rooms: 3 w/refrigerator, incl. 1 w/pvt. bath
Rates: $95-$115, incl. full brk., bottle of Napa Valley wine, afternoon refreshment. Seasonal variations. Discount avail. for extended and mid-week stays.
Credit cards: Most major cards
Restrictions: No pets, smoking. Deposit req. 72-hour cancellation notice req. 2-night min. stay on wknds. from April 1–October 31.
Notes: 36-year old ranch style house. Common room with fireplace, library, TV. Furnished with antiques. Terraces overlooking vineyard, gardens. Volleyball, lawn games. Finnish spoken. Handicapped access.*

Bartels Ranch & Country Inn
1200 Conn Valley Rd., Saint Helena, CA 94574
(707) 963-4001, (707) 963-5100

BARTELS RANCH & COUNTRY INN

Innkeeper: Jamie Bartels
Rooms: 3 w/pvt. bath, phone, TV, incl. 1 w/fireplace, plus 1 suite w/pvt. bath, phone, fireplace, TV
Rates: $135-$225/room, $225-$275/suite, all incl. cont. brk., evening refreshment. Seasonal variations. Discount avail. for senior citizen, mid-week and extended stays.
Credit cards: Most major cards
Restrictions: Children welcome with prior notification only. No pets. Smoking restricted. Full prepayment req. 14-day cancellation notice req., less $15.00 fee. 2-night min. stay on wknds. 3-night min. stay on holidays.
Notes: Ranch-style house built in 1979. Located on 60 acres in Napa Valley wine country. Library. Recreation room with fireplace, pool table, ping-pong table, TV. Swimming pool with Jacuzzi, sauna. Redwood decks. Furnished in eclectic style with some antiques. Handicapped access. Bicycles available. Lunch, dinner available. Masseuse. Wine country tours. Small private parties accommodated. Spanish spoken.*

Cinnamon Bear Bed & Breakfast
1407 Kearney St., Saint Helena, CA 94574
(707) 963-4653
Innkeeper: Genny Jenkins and LeRoy Steck
Rooms: 3 w/pvt. bath
Rates: $135-$155, incl. full brk., afternoon refreshment, evening cookies. Seasonal variations. Discount avail. for mid-week stay.
Credit cards: MC, V
Restrictions: No pets. Children, smoking restricted. Credit card deposit req. 3-day cancellation notice req., less $15 fee.
Notes: Arts and Crafts house built in 1904. Living room with fireplace. Parlor with board games. Dining room. Front porch with chairs. Furnished with period antiques, Oriental rugs, teddy bears.*

Hilltop House B & B
9550 St. Helena Rd., Box 726, Saint Helena, CA 74574
(707) 944-0880
Innkeeper: Annette Gevarter
Rooms: 2 w/pvt. bath, TV, plus 1 suite w/pvt. bath, phone, TV

Rates: $115-135/room, $155-$175/suite, incl. full brk., refreshment. Discount avail. for mid-week and extended stays.
Credit cards: Most major cards
Restrictions: No children under 6, pets, smoking. 5-day cancellation notice req. 2-night min. stay in season.
Notes: Hot tub, hiking trails. Handicapped access.*

Villa St. Helena
2727 Sulphur Springs, Saint Helena, CA 94574
(707) 963-2514
Innkeeper: Ralph and Carolyn Cotton
Rooms: 3 suites w/pvt. bath, phone, incl. 2 w/fireplace
Rates: $155-$245, incl. cont. brk., evening refreshment
Credit cards: Most major cards
Restrictions: Children over 14 welcome with prior approval. No pets. Smoking restricted. Deposit req. 7-day cancellation notice req., less $10.00 fee. 2-night min. stay on wknds.
Notes: Three-story Mediterranean-style villa. Located on twenty-acre estate overlooking Napa Valley. One of only two California homes designed by Robert M. Carrere. Used in the 1940s and 1950s as hideaway for Hollywood celebrities. Wood-paneled library. Living room with beamed ceiling, stone fireplace. Solarium, verandas. Furnished in eclectic style with period antiques. Courtyard with swimming pool. *Falcon Crest* used this inn as set.*

Wine Country Inn
1152 Lodi Ln., Saint Helena, CA 94574
(707) 963-7077, (707) 963-9018
Innkeeper: Jim Smith
Rooms: 20 w/pvt. bath, phone, incl. 13 w/fireplace, plus 4 suites w/pvt. bath, phone, incl. 2 w/fireplace. Located in 3 bldgs.
Rates: $126-$144/room, $193/suite, all incl. cont. brk. Discount avail. for mid-week stay, January–mid-April. Seasonal variations.
Credit cards: MC, V
Restrictions: No pets. One night's deposit req. 72-hr. cancellation notice req., less $10.00 fee. Fireplaces inoperable mid-April–mid-October.
Notes: Two-story inn with turret built in 1975. Located on knoll overlooking vineyards. Common room with fireplace. Furnished with country antiques. Swimming pool, whirlpool. Some Spanish spoken.*

SAN CLEMENTE (16)

Casa De Flores
184 Avenue La Cuesta, San Clemente, CA 92672
(714) 498-1344
Innkeeper: Marilee Arsenault
Rooms: 2 suites w/pvt. bath, TV/VCR, incl. 1 w/fireplace
Rates: $75-$100, incl. full brk., afternoon refreshment. Discount avail. for mid-week stay.
Credit cards: Most major cards
Restrictions: No children, pets. Smoking restricted. One night's deposit req. 14-day cancellation notice req. 2-night min. stay on wknds. & holidays

Notes: Two-story Spanish style house built in 1974 with ocean view. Has operated as an inn since 1988. Over 400 video movies. Nintendo and Super NES. Full-size pool table. Garden with over 1,000 orchids. Sand chairs and beach towels. Guests have access to washer/dryer, refrigerator. Can accommodate special diets.*

SAN DIEGO (17)

The Elsbree House
5058 Naragansett Ave., San Diego, CA 92107
(619) 226-4133, (619) 223-4133
Innkeeper: Katie and Phil Elsbree
Rooms: 7 w/pvt. bath, phone, pvt. entrance
Rates: $75-$85, incl. cont. brk. Discount avail. for extended stay.
Credit cards: None
Restrictions: No pets, smoking. One night's deposit req. 10-day cancellation notice req., less $25.00 fee.
Notes: Cape Cod-style house. Living room with fireplace, game table. Patio, balcony. Winner of the Ocean Beach Planning Board Enhancement Award.

Harbor Hill Guest House
2330 Albatross St., San Diego, CA 92101
(619) 233-0638
Innkeeper: Dorothy A. Milbourn
Rooms: 4 suites plus Carriage House, all w/pvt. bath, phone, refrigerator, cable TV. Located in 2 bldgs.
Rates: $65-$90, incl. cont. brk., afternoon refreshment
Credit cards: Most major cards
Restrictions: No pets. Smoking restricted. One-night's deposit req. 72-hour cancellation notice req.
Notes: Three-level house built in 1920. Located on Bankers Hill overlooking the harbor. Upper level with outside entry, lobby, kitchenette. Redwood sun deck with patio tables and chairs, BBQ grill, access to gazebo in garden. Sundeck level with private entry, lobby, kitchen. Carriage House with private balcony. Entire house may be rented.*

Keating House
2331 2nd Ave., San Diego, CA 92101
(619) 239-8585
Innkeeper: Larry Vlassoff
Rooms: 8, incl. 2 w/pvt. bath, 1 w/fireplace. Located in 2 bldgs.
Rates: $50-$85, incl. full brk., afternoon refreshment. Discount avail. for extended stay.
Credit cards: Most major cards
Restrictions: No pets. Smoking restricted. One night's deposit req. 72-hour cancellation notice req. 2-night min. stay on holiday wknds.
Notes: Two-story Victorian house with gabled roofs, octagonal windowed turret and Guest Cottage built in 1888. Foyer, parlor, veranda, music room with stenciled frieze. Gardens. Located on Bankers Hill. Limited handicapped access. French spoken.*

Vera's Cozy Corner
2810 Albatross St., San Diego, CA 92103
(619) 296-1938

Innkeeper: Vera V. Warden
Rooms: 1 cottage w/pvt. bath, TV. Located in 2 bldgs.
Rates: $40-$50, incl. cont. brk. Discount avail. for senior citizens.
Credit cards: Most major cards
Restrictions: No children, pets, smoking. One night's deposit req. 2-night min. stay.
Notes: Colonial style house with black shutters. View of San Diego Bay. Dining room. Juice from trees on property. Flower-filled patio. French and German spoken.

SAN FRANCISCO (9)

A Room at the Inn
1458 Kansas St., San Francisco, CA 94107
(415) 821-4454

Innkeeper: Salvatore Verruggio
Rooms: 2 w/pvt. bath, fireplace, incl. 1 w/phone, plus 1 suite w/pvt. bath, fireplace, phone
Rates: $95/room-suite, incl. cont. brk., evening refreshment. Discount avail. for extended stay.
Credit cards: Most major cards
Restrictions: No pets, smoking
Notes: Queen Anne Victorian house built in 1898. Fully restored. Common rooms with 2 pianos, including 1 player piano. Furnished with antiques, collectibles. French and American Sign Language spoken.*

ALAMO SQUARE INN

Alamo Square Inn
719 Scott St., San Francisco, CA 94117
(415) 922-2055, (800) 345-9888, (415) 931-1304

Innkeeper: Wayne Corn, Klaus May
Rooms: 10 w/pvt. bath, phone, 3 w/fireplace, plus 3 suites w/pvt. bath, phone, 2 w/fireplace, 3 w/TV. Located in 2 bldgs.
Rates: $85-$135/room, $125-$275/suite, all incl. full brk. Seasonal variations. Discount avail. for extended stay.
Credit cards: Most major cards

Restrictions: No pets. Smoking restricted. Two night's deposit req. 7-day cancellation notice req., less $10.00 fee. 2-night min. stay on wknds. & holidays.
Notes: Complex of two Victorian mansions. Queen Anne and Neo-Classical Revival styles, built in 1895 and 1896. Fully restored since 1977. Parlor, large Norman hall, sitting room with fireplaces. Formal dining room, morning room. Oak floors, wood paneling, stained-glass skylight. Decorated in Victorian style with Oriental rugs, European pieces. Large garden complex with decks. Off-street parking available. French and German spoken.*

Amsterdam Hotel
749 Taylor St., San Francisco, CA 94108
(415) 673-3277, (415) 673-0453
Innkeeper: Kanti Gopal
Rooms: 34 w/TV, incl. 30 w/phone, 1 w/Jacuzzi and wet bar
Rates: $79-$129, incl. cont. brk. Seasonal variations.
Credit cards: Most major cards
Restrictions: No pets. Deposit req. 48-hour cancellation notice req.
Notes: Three-story European-style hotel built in 1909. Located on Nob Hill. Spanish spoken.*

Casa Arguello
225 Arguello Blvd., San Francisco, CA 94118
(415) 752-9482
Innkeeper: Emma Baires and Marina McKenzie
Rooms: 5 w/TV, incl. 2 w/pvt. bath.
Rates: $42-$72, incl. cont. brk.
Credit cards: Most major cards
Restrictions: No pets, smoking. Deposit req. 7-day cancellation notice req. 2-night min. stay.
Notes: Private town house between the Richmond district and Pacific Heights near Golden Gate Park. Foyer, living room. Dining room with chandelier. Furnished with antiques. Spanish spoken.

Chez Duchene
1075 Broadway, San Francisco, CA 94133
(415) 441-3160
Innkeeper: Jay Duchene
Rooms: 1 w/pvt. bath
Rates: $90, incl. cont. brk.
Credit cards: None
Restrictions: No pets, smoking. One-night's deposit req. 2-night min. stay.
Notes: Three-story Victorian row house. Bay view.

Edward II Bed and Breakfast Inn
3155 Scott St., San Francisco, CA 94123
(415) 922-3000, (415) 931-5784
Innkeeper: Robert and Denise Holland
Rooms: 25 w/phone, TV, incl. 20 w/pvt. bath, plus 6 suites w/pvt. bath, phone, kitchen, TV. Located in 4 bldgs.
Rates: $67-$89/room, $135-$200/suite, all incl. cont. brk., evening refreshment
Credit cards: Most major cards

Restrictions: No pets. Smoking restricted. Deposit req. 3-day cancellation notice req. 2-night min. stay on wknds.
Notes: Three-story redwood European-style inn built in 1915 for the Panama-Pacific International Exposition. Located in the Marina District. Furnished in English country decor. Carriage house apartment suites. Whirlpool baths available. English pub, old-world bakery, restaurant on premises. Limited handicapped access.*

Golden Gate Hotel
775 Bush St., San Francisco, CA 94108
(415) 392-3702, (415) 392-6202
Innkeeper: John and Renate Kenaston
Rooms: 23 w/TV, incl. 14 w/pvt. bath, 11 w/phone
Rates: $55-$99, incl. cont. brk., afternoon refreshment
Credit cards: Most major cards
Restrictions: Pets, smoking restricted. One night's deposit req. 48-hour cancellation notice req.
Notes: Edwardian hotel built in 1913. Located on Nob Hill. Parlor with fireplace. Front and back bay windows. Birdcage elevator. Wicker and antique furnishings. Original art. Antique claw foot tubs. German, French, Spanish spoken.*

Grove Inn
890 Grove St., San Francisco, CA 94117
(415) 929-0780, (800) 829-0780, (415) 929-1037
Innkeeper: Klaus & Roselta Zimmerman
Rooms: 19 plus 1 suite, all w/phone, TV, incl. 13 w/pvt. bath
Rates: $50-$85/room, $115/suite, incl. cont. brk.
Credit cards: Most major cards
Restrictions: No pets, smoking. Deposit req. 10-day cancellation notice req., less $10.00 fee.
Notes: 1885 Italianate Victorian located in Alamo Square Historic District. Restored in 1983. Italian, German, Spanish spoken.*

The Inn San Francisco
943 S. Van Ness Ave., San Francisco, CA 94110
(415) 641-0188, (800) 359-0913, (415) 641-1701
Innkeeper: Marty Neeley
Rooms: 11 w/pvt. bath incl. 5 w/phone, TV plus 6 suites w/pvt. bath, phone, TV. Located in 2 bldgs.
Rates: $75-$145/room, $165-$195/suite, all incl. full brk. Special pkgs. avail.
Credit cards: Most major cards
Restrictions: Call in advance for pets. Smoking restricted. One-night's deposit req. 7-day cancellation notice req. 2-night min. stay on wknds.
Notes: Two-story Italianate Victorian mansion with marble fireplaces built in 1872 as horse breeding and training estate. Fully restored. Double parlors. Lounge with cable TV. Library, rooftop deck. Furnished in Victorian style with period antiques, Oriental carpets. English garden, gazebo, Jacuzzi, redwood hot tub. Total solar energy system. Limited reserved parking available. Chinese, Spanish, some French spoken.*

The Monte Cristo
600 Presidio Ave., San Francisco, CA 94115
(415) 931-1875, (415) 931-6005

Innkeeper: George Yuan
Rooms: 14, incl. 11 w/pvt. bath, phone, cable TV, plus 1 suite w/pvt. bath
Rates: $63-$98/room, $108/suite, all incl. expanded cont. brk., evening refreshment. Discount avail. for extended stay.
Credit cards: Most major cards
Restrictions: No pets. Smoking restricted. Deposit req. 7-day cancellation notice req. 2-night min. stay on wknds.
Notes: Built in 1875 as saloon and hotel. Has served as bordello, refuge after the 1906 earthquake, and speakeasy. Fully restored, furnished with authentic period pieces. Spanish spoken.*

Subtleties: Carol's Cow Hollow Inn
2821 Steiner St., San Francisco, CA 94123
(415) 775-8295, (415) 775-8296
Innkeeper: Carol Blumenfeld, Alex Sachal
Rooms: 3 w/pvt. bath, phone, TV
Rates: $95-$125, incl. full brk. Discount avail. for senior citizens.
Credit cards: MC, V
Restrictions: No pets. Smoking restricted. One night's deposit req. 7-day cancellation notice.
Notes: Three-story Pacific Heights English beach house-style inn built in 1908. Foyer with Steinway piano. Living room with fireplace. Dining room, kitchen, breakfast room overlooking terace and garden. Third-story balcony overlooking Golden Gate Bridge. Decorated with innkeeper's original oil paintings. Innkeeper's family has lived in San Francisco for 7 generations. French, Spanish, German, Russian spoken. *

Union Street Inn
2229 Union St., San Francisco, CA 94123
(415) 346-0424
Innkeeper: Helen Stewart, Jamie Bailey
Rooms: 6 w/pvt. bath, phone, incl. 3 w/TV. Located in 2 bldgs.
Rates: $135/inn, $225/Carriage House, all incl. cont. brk., afternoon refreshment
Credit cards: Most major cards
Restrictions: No pets, smoking. Min. one night's deposit req. 7-day cancellation notice req. 2-night min. stay on wknds.
Notes: Two-story Edwardian house built in 1901. Carriage House with Jacuzzi overlooks garden. Has operated as inn since 1980. Parlor with fireplace, bay windows. Garden patio, sun deck. Furnished in period style with antiques. Spanish spoken.*

Victorian Inn on the Park
301 Lyon St., San Francisco, CA 94117
(415) 931-1830, (800) 435-1967, (415) 931-1830
Innkeeper: William and Lisa Benau
Rooms: 10 plus 2 suites, all w/pvt. bath, phone, TV, incl. 4 w/fireplace
Rates: $99-$159/room, $159-$315/suite, all incl. cont. brk., evening refreshment. Special pkgs. avail. November–April. Discount avail. for seniors, mid-week, corporate and extended stays.
Credit cards: Most major cards
Restrictions: No pets. Smoking restricted. First and last nights' deposit req. 7-day cancellation notice req. 2-night min. stay on wknds. 3-night min. stay on holiday wknds.

VICTORIAN INN ON THE PARK

Notes: Three-story Queen Anne Victorian inn built in 1897. Fully restored. Library with TV. Parlor with fireplace. Dining room with oak paneling. Sitting room. Furnished with Victorian antiques. Small private parties accommodated. Listed on City and State Registers of Historic Places. Portugese, French, Spanish spoken.*

Washington Square Inn
1660 Stockton St., San Francisco, CA 94133
(415) 981-4220, (800) 388-0220, (415) 397-7242
Innkeeper: Brooks Bayly
Rooms: 15 w/phone, incl. 10 w/pvt. bath
Rates: $85-$180, incl. cont. brk., afternoon refreshment
Credit cards: Most major cards
Restrictions: No pets, smoking. One night's deposit req. 24-hour cancellation notice req.
Notes: Two-story inn located in the North Beach. Lounge with fireplace. Decorated with English and French antiques. Concierge service available.*

SAN GREGORIO (9)

Rancho San Gregorio
Rt. 1, Box 54, San Gregorio, CA 94074
(415) 747-0810, (415) 747-0184
Innkeeper: Bud and Lee Raynor
Rooms: 3 w/pvt. bath, incl. 2 w/fireplace, plus 1 suite w/pvt. bath, fireplace
Rates: $80-$95/room, $145/suite, all incl. full brk., afternoon refreshment. Discount avail. for mid-week stay.
Credit cards: Most major cards
Restrictions: No pets. Smoking restricted. Deposit req. 7-day cancellation notice req.
Notes: Two-story mission-style country retreat with redwood beams, terra cotta tile floors built in 1971. Located on fifteen wooded acres with a creek. Library of books, games and VCR films. Dining room. Furnished with carved-oak antiques. Rooms are decorated with American antiques and family pieces. Some rooms feature hide-abeds, wood-burning stove, VCR, refrigerator, private deck, soaking tub, claw-foot

RANCHO SAN GREGORIO

tub, stained-glass window. Courtyard with cactus, decks, patio, gazebo. Lawn games available. Small private parties accommodated.*

SAN LUIS OBISPO (10)

Arroyo Village Inn
407 El Camino Real, Arroyo Grande, San Luis Obispo, CA 93420
(805) 489-5926

Innkeeper: Gina
Rooms: 2 plus 5 suites, all w/pvt. bath, phone
Rates: $95-$125/room, $125-250/suite, all incl. full brk. Seasonal variations. Discount avail. for mid-week, extended stay.
Credit cards: Most major cards
Restrictions: No pets, smoking. 14-day cancellation notice req., less $25.00 fee.
Notes: Victorian-style inn built in 1984. Decorated with Laura Ashley prints and antiques. Window seats, skylights, balconies. Dining room, parlor with fireplace. Italian and Spanish spoken. TVs available.*

SANTA BARBARA (12)

Bath Street Inn
1720 Bath St., Santa Barbara, CA 93101
(805) 682-9680, (800) 788-2284

Innkeeper: Susan Brown, Lynn Kirby
Rooms: 10 w/pvt. bath, incl. 2 w/phone, fireplace, TV. Located in 2 bldgs.
Rates: $95-$150, incl. full brk., afternoon and evening refreshment. Discount avail. for mid-week stay.
Credit cards: Most major cards
Restrictions: No pets. Smoking restricted. Min. one night's deposit req. Min. 3-day cancellation notice req. 2-night min. stay on wknds.
Notes: Three-story Queen Anne Victorian inn. Garden. Living room. Dining room. Furnished with period antiques. Small private parties accommodated. Bicycles available.*

Casa Del Mar
18 Bath St., Santa Barbara, CA 93101
(805) 963-4418, (800) 433-3097, (805) 966-4240

Innkeeper: Mike and Becky Montgomery
Rooms: 14 w/pvt. bath, phone, TV, incl. 1 w/fireplace, plus 6 suites w/pvt. bath, phone, TV, kitchen, incl. 5 w/fireplace. Located in 4 bldgs.
Rates: $59-$159/room, $89-$179/suite, all incl. cont. brk., evening refreshment. Seasonal variations. Discount avail. for extended winter, commercial & mid-week stays.
Credit cards: Most major cards
Restrictions: No children under 1. Smoking restricted. Deposit req. 48-hour cancellation notice req.
Notes: Two-story Mediterranean-style villa with white stucco walls and red tiled roofs. Sun-deck surrounded by gardens and flowers. Paths. Located 50 meters from the beach. Courtyard whirlpool spa. Fax machine, 24-hour telephone services, modem hookups. Handicapped access. German spoken. Resident cat.*

Glenborough Inn
1327 Bath St., Santa Barbara, CA 93101
(805) 966-0589, (805) 564-2369
Innkeeper: Michael, Steve, Ken
Rooms: 8 w/phone, incl. 2 w/pvt. bath, plus 3 suites w/pvt. bath, fireplace, phone. Located in 3 bldgs.
Rates: $70-$125/room, $145-$165/suite, all incl. full brk., evening refreshment. Discount avail. for mid-week stay.
Credit cards: Most major cards
Restrictions: No children under 12, pets. Smoking restricted. Full prepayment req. Min. 3-day cancellation notice req., less $15.00 fee. 2-night min. stay on wknds. 3 night min. stay on holidays.
Notes: Two-story Craftman's style Main House built in 1906. One-story Victorian Cottage built in early 1880s. White House is a California Classic. Parlor, patio, deck, hot tub. Furnished with antiques. New Orleans-style garden. Spanish and sign language spoken.*

Long's Seaview B & B
317 Piedmont Rd., Santa Barbara, CA 93105
(805) 687-2947
Innkeeper: LaVerne Long
Rooms: 1 w/pvt. bath, cable TV
Rates: $79, incl. full brk. Discount avail. for extended stay.
Credit cards: None
Restrictions: No children under 12, pets, smoking. Deposit req. 7-day cancellaiton notice req. 2-night min. stay preferred.
Notes: Ranch-style house. Patio overlooking private orchard, garden, ocean. Furnished with family antiques.

The Old Yacht Club Inn
431 Corona Del Mar Dr., Santa Barbara, CA 93103
(805) 962-1277, (805) 962-3989
Innkeeper: Nancy Donaldson and Sandy Hunt
Rooms: 9 w/pvt. bath, phone. Located in 2 bldgs.
Rates: $90-$150, incl. full brk., evening refreshment. Seasonal variations. Discount avail. for mid-week & senior citizen stays.
Credit cards: Most major cards

Restrictions: No pets, smoking. Deposit req. 3-day cancellation notice req. 2-night min. stay on wknds.

Notes: Built in 1912 as a private home. Renovated in and has operated as inn since 1980. Common room with brick fireplace and grand piano. Covered porch, back yard deck. Furnished with period pieces, European and early American antiques, Oriental rugs. Hitchcock House with front room, fireplace, front porch, back deck. Gourmet dinners served on Saturdays. Guests have golf privileges at private country club. Cable TV avail. upon request. Spanish spoken.*

Olive House
1604 Olive St., Santa Barbara, CA 93101
(805) 962-4902, (800) 786-6422, (805) 899-2754

Innkeeper: Lois Gregg

Rooms: 6 w/pvt. bath, phone, incl. 1 w/fireplace, 2 w/hot tubs, 3 w/TV

Rates: $105-$175, incl. full brk., afternoon and evening refreshment. Discount avail. for mid-week stay. Seasonal variations.

Credit cards: Most major cards

Restrictions: No pets, smoking. One night's deposit req. 7-day cancellation notice req., less $10.00 fee. 2-night min. stay on wknds. 3-night min. stay on major holidays.

Notes: California craftsman-style house built in 1904. Moved to present site and fully restored in 1980 with bay windows, window seats, stained and leaded-glass, coffered ceilings. Completely refurbished in 1990. Redwood-paneled living room with fireplace, stone hearth, studio grand piano, library, board games. Dining room, sun deck. Furnished eclectically with antiques. Garden. Off-street parking available. Resident dog.*

The Parsonage
1600 Olive St., Santa Barbara, CA 93101
(805) 962-9336

Innkeeper: Hilde Michelmore and Jane Fair

Rooms: 5 plus 1 suite, all w/pvt. bath, phone, incl. 1 w/solarium porch

Rates: $95-$140/room, $185/suite, incl. full brk. Discount avail. for extended and off-season, mid-week stays.

Credit cards: Most major cards

Restrictions: No children under 12, pets, smoking. Deposit req. 7-day cancellation notice req. 2-night min. stay on wknds. 3-night min. stay on holidays.

Notes: Queen Anne Victorian house built in 1892 as a parsonage for the Trinity Episcopal Church. Operated as an inn since 1980. Fully restored. Grand lobby, redwood staircase. Living room with fireplace. Dining room, sun deck. Furnished with antiques, Oriental rugs. German spoken. Handicapped access.*

Simpson House Inn
121 E. Arrellaga, Santa Barbara, CA 93101
(805) 963-7067, (800) 676-1280, (805) 564-4811

Innkeeper: Gillean Wilson, Glyn and Linda Davies

Rooms: 6 w/pvt. bath, phone, incl. 1 w/fireplace, plus 7 suites w/pvt. bath, phone, fireplace, TV. Located in 5 bldgs.

Rates: $105-$165/room, $205-$245/suite, incl. full brk., evening refreshment. Seasonal variations. Special pkgs. avail.

Credit cards: Most major cards

SIMPSON HOUSE INN

Restrictions: No pets. Smoking restricted. Min. one night's deposit req. 7-day cancellation notice req. 2-night min. stay on wknds. 3-night min. stay on holidays.

Notes: Eastlake-style Victorian house built in 1874 on an acre of English gardens. Fully restored in 1976. Has operated as inn since 1985. Formal dining room. Sitting room with fireplace, library. Furnished with antiques, fine art, English lace, Oriental rugs. Some guest rooms have deck and Jacuzzi tub. Garden verandas with teak floors, white wicker furniture. Lawn games, bicycles. Beach and picnic equipment avail. Small private parties accommodated. Spanish spoken. Handicapped access.*

The Upham Hotel
1404 De La Vina St., Santa Barbara, CA 93101
(805) 962-0058, (805) 963-2825

Innkeeper: Jan Martin Winn

Rooms: 46 w/pvt. bath, phone, TV, incl. 7 w/fireplace, plus 3 suites w/pvt. bath, phone, TV, incl. 1 w/fireplace, plus 8 cottage rooms. Located in 8 bldgs.

Rates: $110-$160/room, $175-$325/suite, $175/cottage, all incl. cont. brk., evening refreshment. Seasonal variations. Discount avail. for corporate, senior citizen, AAA stays.

Credit cards: Most major cards

Restrictions: No pets. Smoking restricted. One night's deposit req. 3-day cancellation notice req. 2-night min. stay on wknds.

Notes: Two-story Victorian-style hotel with cupola and cottages built with redwood timbers and square-head nails in 1871. Located on one acre with flower gardens, hammock, spa. Lobby, meeting rooms, garden veranda. Living room with fireplace. Restaurant on premises.*

SANTA CRUZ (9)

Chateau Victorian
118 First St., Santa Cruz, CA 95060
(408) 458-9458

Innkeeper: Alice June

Rooms: 7 w/pvt. bath, fireplace. Located in 2 bldgs.

Rates: $110-$140, incl. expanded cont. brk., evening refreshment. Discount avail. for extended stay.

Credit cards: Most major cards

Restrictions: No children, pets, smoking. One night's deposit req. 2-day cancellation notice req.
Notes: Victorian house built about 1885, converted to apartments in the 1950s. Fully renovated in and has operated as Inn since 1983. Lounge, dining area. Furnished with individual color schemes, carpeted. Garden, brick patio. Front terrace, secluded deck.

CHATEAU VICTORIAN

Inn Laguna Creek
2727 Smith Grade, Santa Cruz, CA 95060
(408) 425-0692

Innkeeper: Gay Carlson and Jim Holley
Rooms: 2, no pvt. bath, plus 1 suite w/pvt. bath, TV
Rates: $95/room, $125-$180/suite, incl. full brk., afternoon refreshment. Seasonal variations. Discount avail. for extended stay.
Credit cards: Most major cards
Restrictions: No pets, smoking. One night's deposit req. 4-day cancellation notice req. 2-night min. stay on holiday wknds.
Notes: Modern design structure built in 1975. Sitting room with wet bar, refrigerator, microwave oven, VCR, games. Book and video library. Furnished with antiques and contemporary furniture. One suite has a private solarium. Picnic area and natural gardens. Sun deck, hot tub. Handicapped access.

Pleasure Point Inn B & B
2-3665 E. Cliff Dr., Santa Cruz, CA 95062
(408) 475-4657

Innkeeper: Barbara and Gary Pasquini
Rooms: 2 w/pvt. bath, phone, plus 1 suite w/pvt. bath, phone, TV
Rates: $115-$125/room, $135/suite, incl. cont. brk., evening refreshment. Discount avail. for extended stay.
Credit cards: MC, V
Restrictions: No pets. Smoking restricted. Deposit req. 2-day cancellation notice req., less $10.00 fee. 2-night min. stay.
Notes: Restored beach-front house built in the 1940s. Fully remodeled in 1982. Common room with fireplace overlooking Monterey Bay. Furnished in beach decor. Handicapped access.

SANTA MONICA (14)

The Channel Road Inn
219 W. Channel Rd., Santa Monica, CA 90402
(310) 459-1920, (310) 454-9920

Innkeeper: Kathy Jensen
Rooms: 12 plus 2 suites, all w/pvt. bath, phone, TV
Rates: $95-$180/room, $175-$200/suite, all incl. full brk., afternoon and evening
refreshment. Discount avail. for mid-week stay.
Credit cards: Most major cards
Restrictions: No pets. Smoking restricted. One night's deposit req. 3-day cancella-
tion notice req.
Notes: Three-story shingle-clad Colonial Revival house built in 1910 with hardwood
floors, overlooking the ocean. Renovated in and has operated as inn since 1988.
Living room, library, each with fireplace. Breakfast room. Furnished with antiques,
white wicker, Oriental rugs, Amish quilts. Hillside spa. Bicycles available. Spanish
spoken. Handicapped access.*

THE WHITE GABLES INN

SANTA PAULA (12)

The White Gables Inn
715 E. Santa Paula St., Santa Paula, CA 93060
(805) 933-3041

Innkeeper: Bob and Ellen Smith
Rooms: 2 plus 1 suite, all w/pvt. bath
Rates: $85-$95/room, $115/suite, all incl. full brk. Seasonal variations. Discount
avail. for mid-week stay.
Credit cards: MC, V
Restrictions: No children, pets, smoking. One-night's deposit req. 72-hour cancel-
lation notice req., less $15.00 fee.
Notes: Three-story Queen Anne Victorian house built in 1894. Fully restored. Lo-
cated in the historical district of Santa Paula. Wrap-around porch. Dining room.
Parlor with fireplace, piano and TV. Furnished with antiques. Phone available. A
Heritage Landmark.

SANTA ROSA (5)

THE GABLES

The Gables
4257 Petaluma Hill Rd., Santa Rosa, CA 95404
(707) 585-7777, (707) 584-5634
Innkeeper: Michael and Judy Ogne
Rooms: 5 plus 2 suites, all w/pvt. bath, incl. 3 rooms and 1 suite w/fireplace. Located in 2 bldgs.
Rates: $95/room, $135-$175/suite, all incl. full brk., afternoon refreshment. Discount avail. for extended stay.
Credit cards: Most major cards
Restrictions: No pets, smoking. Deposit req. 7-day cancellation notice req., less $10.00 fee. 2-night min. stay on wknds. 3-night min. stay on some holiday wknds.
Notes: Two-story Victorian house built in 1877 located on 3½ acres. Handicapped access.*

Melitta Station Inn
5850 Melita Rd., Santa Rosa, CA 95409
(707) 538-7712
Innkeeper: Diane Crandon, Vic Amstadter
Rooms: 6, incl. 4 w/pvt. bath
Rates: $70-$90, incl. full brk., evening refreshment. Seasonal variations.
Credit cards: Most major cards
Restrictions: No children under 8, pets, smoking. One night's deposit req. 7-day cancellation notice req., less $10.00 fee. 2-night min. stay on wknds.
Notes: Turn-of-the-century redwood railroad station converted to inn. Sitting room with wood stove. Balcony. Furnished with antiques, country collectibles. Herb garden. Meeting room available.

Vintners Inn
4350 Barnes Rd., Santa Rosa, CA 95403
(707) 575-7350, (800) 421-2584, (707) 575-1426
Innkeeper: Cindy Young and John Duffy
Rooms: 44 w/pvt. bath, phone, cable TV, incl. 23 w/fireplace. Suites avail. Located in 3 bldgs.
Rates: $118-$168/room, $155-$195/suite, all incl. cont. brk. Discount avail. for midweek and group stays.
Credit cards: Most major cards

Restrictions: No pets. One night's deposit req. 72-hr. cancellation notice req. 2-night min. stay on wknds. Apr.–Oct.

Notes: European-style hotel with beamed ceilings, balconies. Located within 50-acre Le Carrefour Vineyards. Library, breakfast room, each with fireplace. Furnished in Country French style with pine furniture, brass and porcelain fixtures. Central landscaped plaza with fountains, flower-bordered tile walkways. Spa and sundeck. Small private parties accommodated. Spanish spoken. Handicapped access. *

SARATOGA (9)

The Inn at Saratoga
20645 4th St., Saratoga, CA 95070
(408) 867-5020, (408) 741-0981

Innkeeper: Jack Hickling

Rooms: 41 plus 4 suites, all w/pvt. bath, phone, TV

Rates: $145-$245/room, $390-$440/suite, all incl. cont. brk., afternoon refreshment. Discount avail. for AAA and senior citizens.

Credit cards: Most major cards

Restrictions: No pets. Deposit req. 48-hour cancellation notice req.

Notes: 5-story modern replacement for the original 1912 Saratoga Inn. Located on Saratoga Creek near Wildwood Park. Lobby patterned after an English country inn, terrace above the brook. Towel-warmers in bathrooms. Whirlpool baths. Computer capabilities. Spanish spoken. Handicapped access.*

SEAL BEACH (16)

Seal Beach Inn & Gardens
212 Fifth St., Seal Beach, CA 90740
(310) 493-2416, (310) 799-0483

Innkeeper: Marjorie Bettenhausen Sschmaehl

Rooms: 11 plus 12 suites, all w/pvt. bath, phone, TV, incl. 2 suites w/fireplace. Penthouse avail. Located in 3 bldgs.

Rates: $118/room, $155-$185/suite, $255/penthouse, all incl. full brk., evening refreshment. Discount avail. for senior citizen, AAA, corporate and extended stays.

Credit cards: Most major cards

Restrictions: No pets, smoking. One night's deposit req. 72-hour cancellation notice req.

Notes: French Mediterranean-style inn with 300-year old French iron work built in 1923. Completely restored. Victorian library with fireplace. Tea Room. Old Mediterranean tile murals. Furnished with antiques. Brick courtyard overlooking gardens with fountains. Antique fences and streetlights. Swimming pool. Small private parties accommodated. Handicapped access.*

SEQUOIA NATIONAL PARK/LEMON (11)

Lemon Cove B & B Inn
33038 Sierra Hwy., Sequoia National Park/Lemon, CA 93244
(209) 597-2555, (800) 240-1466

Innkeeper: Patrick and Kay Bonette

Rooms: 9, incl. 7 w/pvt. bath, 2 w/fireplace, 3 w/TV. Located in 2 bldgs.

Rates: $55-$89 incl. full brk., evening refreshment

Credit cards: Most major cards

Restrictions: No pets, smoking. One night's deposit req. 48-hour cancellation notice req. 2-night min. stay on holidays.
Notes: Two-story building. Located in the Sierra Foothills. Balconies with mountain view. Furnished with antiques. Parlor with piano. Orange groves.

SHINGLETOWN (4)

WESTON HOUSE

Weston House
Red Rock Rd., Box 276, Shingletown, CA 96088
(916) 474-3738

Innkeeper: Angela and Ivor Weston
Rooms: 3, incl. 2 w/pvt. bath, 1 w/woodstove, plus 1 suite w/pvt. bath, kitchenette, woodstove. Located in 2 bldgs.
Rates: $75-95/room, $105/suite, all incl. full brk., afternoon refreshment
Credit cards: Most major cards
Restrictions: No pets. Smoking restricted. One night's deposit req. 7-day cancellation notice req., less $10.00 fee.
Notes: Multi-level shingled house overlooking dormant volcanos and mountains. Large common room with VCR, stereo, books, games. Furnished in antique and eclectic decor. Lap pool, sun deck, hot tub, massage available. Flower and vegetable gardens. Private balconies and decks. Can accommodate special diets. Handicapped access.

SONOMA (5)

Sparrow's Nest Inn
424 Denmark St., Sonoma, CA 95476
(707) 996-3750

Innkeeper: Thomas and Kathleen Anderson
Rooms: 1 cottage w/pvt. bath, phone, TV/VCR
Rates: $85-$105, incl. full brk.
Credit cards: Most major cards
Restrictions: Pets, smoking restricted. Deposit req. 2-day cancellation notice req., less $15.00 fee.
Notes: Private cottage located in countryside. Living room, full kitchenette. Furnished with Laura Ashley bedding. Covered porch. English flower gardens, courtyard.

Victorian Garden Inn
316 E. Napa St., Sonoma, CA 95476
(707) 996-5339, (707) 996-2446
Innkeeper: Donna Lewis
Rooms: 3, incl. 2 w/pvt. bath, plus 1 suite w/pvt. bath, fireplace. Located in 2 bldgs.
Rates: $79-$119/room, $139/suite, all incl. full brk, afternoon refreshment
Credit cards: Most major cards
Restrictions: No pets. Children and smoking restricted. Min. one night's deposit
   req. Min. 7-day cancellation notice req., less $10.00 fee. 2-night min. stay on
   wknds. 3-night min. stay on holiday wknds.
Notes: Greek Revival farmhouse built in 1870. Located on one wooded acre. Rooms
also available in renovated water tower. Parlor with fireplace, board games. Dining
room. Furnished with antiques, pump organ. Patios, veranda, swimming pool.
Innkeeper is interior designer. Small private parties accommodated. Spanish spoken.*

SOQUEL (9)

BLUE SPRUCE INN

Blue Spruce Inn
2815 Main St., Soquel, CA 95073-2412
(408) 464-1137, (800) 559-1137, (408) 475-3976
Innkeeper: Pat and Tom O'Brien
Rooms: 5 w/pvt. bath, incl. 4 w/phone, fireplace, 2 w/pvt. spa, 1 w/TV, VCR, pvt.
   phone. Located in 3 bldgs.
Rates: $80-$125, incl. full brk., evening refreshment. Seasonal variations. Special
   pkgs. avail.
Credit cards: Most major cards
Restrictions: No pets. Smoking restricted. One night's deposit req. 3-day cancellation notice req., less $10.00 fee. 2-night min. stay on wknds.
Notes: Original two-story farm house built in 1875, along with the barn and carriage house make up this inn. Fully renovated. Opened in 1990. Parlor. Two sitting
rooms with bay window seat, wood-burning fireplace. Decorated with original local
art. Garden in back with arbor and deck. Hot tub. Spanish spoken.*

SUMMERLAND (12)

INN ON SUMMER HILL

Inn on Summer Hill
2520 Lillie Ave., Summerland, CA 93067
(805) 969-9998, (800) 845-5566, (805) 969-9998

Innkeeper: Verlinda Richardson

Rooms: 15, plus 1 suite, all w/pvt. bath, phone, Jacuzzi, fireplace, TV/VCR. Located in 2 bldgs.

Rates: $160-$195/room, $225-$275/suite, all incl. full brk., evening refreshment. Discount avail. mid-week, for senior citizen, auto club. Special pkgs. avail.

Credit cards: Most major cards

Restrictions: No children under 10, pets. Smoking restricted. Full pre-payment req. 5-day cancellation notice req. less $10.00 fee. 2-night min. stay on wknds. and holidays.

Notes: California Craftsman style inn built in 1989 with oceanview. Dining room features teapot collection. Great room. Furnished in English country-style with pine furniture and paneling, original art, embroidered fabric from Austria. Belgium carpets on pine floors. Concierge service, gift and picnic baskets, gift certificates, fax machine avail. Resident cat. Handicapped access.*

Summerland Inn
2161 Ortega Hill Rd., Summerland, CA 93067-1209
(805) 969-5225

Innkeeper: James R. Farned and Farah Unwalla

Rooms: 11 w/pvt. bath, phone, cable TV, incl. 2 w/fireplace. Located in 2 bldgs.

Rates: $90-$140, incl. expanded cont. brk. Discount avail. for mid-week stay.

Credit cards: Most major cards

Restrictions: No pets, smoking. Deposit req. 3-day cancellation notice req., less fee. 2-night min. stay on wknds.

Notes: New England Colonial style house. Living room with fireplace, conference room, dining room, foyer. Decorated with folk art, antiques. Small private parties accommodated. Handicapped access.*

SUSANVILLE (4)

The Roseberry House
609 North St., Susanville, CA 96130
(916) 257-5675

Innkeeper: Bill and Maxine Ashmore
Rooms: 3 plus 1 suite, all w/pvt. bath
Rates: $55-$65/room, $80/suite, all incl. full brk.
Credit cards: Most major cards
Restrictions: No children under 10, pets, smoking.
Notes: Two-story country Victorian house built in 1902. Porch, balcony. Library
with TV. Dining room. Furnished with antiques. Bicycles available.

SUTTER CREEK (6)

Grey Gables Inn
161 Hanford St., Box 1687, Sutter Creek, CA 95685
(800) 473-9422

Innkeeper: Roger and Sue Garlick
Rooms: 8 w/pvt. bath, fireplace
Rates: $85-$125, incl. full brk., afternoon and evening refreshment
Credit cards: Most major cards
Restrictions: No children, pets, smoking. One-night's deposit req. 7-day cancella-
tion notice req., less $10.00 fee. 2-night min. stay on wknds. and holidays.
Notes: Two-story English country manor house. Decorated with antiques. Formal
dining room. Parlor with double alcove. Terraced garden. Fountains. Handicapped
access.*

Sutter Creek Inn
75 Main St., Box 385, Sutter Creek, CA 95685
(209) 267-5606

Innkeeper: Jane Way
Rooms: 17 plus 1 suite, all w/fireplace. Located in 5 bldgs.
Rates: $88-$95, incl. full brk., afternoon refreshment. Discount avail. for mid-week
and senior citizen stays.
Credit cards: None
Restrictions: No children under 12, pets. Smoking restricted. Deposit req. 2-night
min. stay on wknds.
Notes: Greek Revival redwood house built in 1859. Located on one acre. Parlor with
board games, piano, library. Dining room/kitchen w/fireplace. Furnished in modern eclectic style with some antiques. Lawns with hammocks, chaise lounges, tables
with umbrellas. Massages and handwriting analysis available.*

TAHOE CITY (7)

Chaney Guest House
4725 W. Lake Blvd., Box 7852, Tahoe City, CA 96145
(916) 525-7333, (916) 525-4413

Innkeeper: Gary and Lori Chaney
Rooms: 1 plus 2 suites, 1 apt., all w/pvt. bath, phone, incl. 1 w/cable TV. Located
in 2 bldgs.
Rates: $100-$115/room, $100-$110/suite, $115/apt., all incl. full brk., evening re-
freshment.

Credit cards: None

Restrictions: No children under 12, pets, smoking. 50% deposit req. Min. 2-week cancellation notice req. 2-night min. stay on wknds.

Notes: Two-story house with eighteen-inch-thick stone walls built in 1928. Has operated as Inn since 1989. Living room with cathedral ceiling, fireplace, chandelier. Dining room with carved wooden staircase. Three patios with stone arches and walls overlooking the lake. Private beach with pier on Lake Tahoe. Bicycles and paddle boats available for rent. Resident dog.*

MAYFIELD HOUSE

Mayfield House
236 Grove St., Box 5999, Tahoe City, CA 96145
(916) 583-1001

Innkeeper: Cynthia and Bruce Knauss

Rooms: 4, no pvt. bath, plus 1 suite w/TV, no pvt. bath

Rates: $85-$95/room, $115/suite, all incl. full brk., evening refreshment. Seasonal variations. Discount avail. for extended stay.

Credit cards: Most major cards

Restrictions: No children under 15, pets, smoking. 50% deposit req. 2-week cancellation notice req., less $10.00 fee. 2-night min. stay during high season.

Notes: Built in 1932. Fully refurbished in 1979. Living room with fireplace. Dining room, breakfast room, patio. Furnished with down comforters and pillows, fresh flowers. Small private parties accommodated.*

River Ranch
P.O. Box 197, Tahoe City, CA 96145
(916) 583-4264, (916) 583-7237

Innkeeper: Pete Friedrichsen

Rooms: 19 w/pvt. bath, phone, TV. Located in 2 bldgs.

Rates: $90-$110, incl. cont. brk. Seasonal variations. Discount avail. for mid-week stay. Special pkgs. avail.

Credit cards: Most major cards

Restrictions: No pets, smoking. One night's deposit req. 3-day cancellation notice req. 2-night min. stay on wknds.

Notes: Two-story shingle lodge originally built in 1890s. New structure built in 1950, renovated in 1960. Furnished in Early American antiques. Restaurant on premises, with lunch and dinner available. Patio overlooking river and pond, which is termination point of 4-mile raft trip down Truckee River. Small private parties accommodated. Free shuttle bus service. Swimming, horseback riding, hiking and fishing. Bicycles. Limited handicapped access.*

TEMECULA (15)

Loma Vista B & B
33350 La Serena Way, Temecula, CA 92390
(909) 676-7047
Innkeeper: Betty and Dick Ryan
Rooms: 6 w/pvt. bath, incl. 3 w/pvt. balcony
Rates: $95-125, incl. brk., evening refreshment. Discount avail. for mid-week stay.
Credit cards: Most major cards
Restrictions: No pets, smoking. 7-day cancellation notice req. 2-night min. stay in balcony rooms on wknds.
Notes: Two-story California mission-style house built in 1987. Located on hilltop. Patio overlooking vineyards, citrus groves. Spanish spoken.*

TEMPLETON (10)

Templeton Manor
1442 Ridge Rd., Templeton, CA 93465
(805) 434-1529, (805) 434-3540
Innkeeper: Billie and Tony Castiglia
Rooms: 1 w/pvt. bath, plus 1 cottage w/pvt. bath, fireplace. Located in 2 bldgs.
Rates: $105-$125/room, $125-$150/cottage, incl. full brk. Seasonal variations. Discount avail. for extended stay.
Credit cards: Most major cards
Restrictions: No children, pets. Smoking restricted. One night's deposit req. 7-day cancellation notice req.
Notes: Single-story white brick rancho house built in 1920 on 20 acres. Living room with TV, collection of old movies. Patio. Pond, 3-hole golf course, gazebo, lawn games. Swimming pool available in season. Multiple gardens. Massage therapy and yoga classes available. Italian, German and French spoken.*

TRUCKEE (7)

Truckee Hotel
10007 Bridge St., Truckee, CA 96161
(916) 587-4444, (800) 659-6921, (916) 587-1599
Innkeeper: Rachelle L. Pellisier
Rooms: 29 plus 8 suite, incl. 8 w/pvt. bath, 3 w/TV
Rates: $60-$125/room, $80-$115/suite, all incl. cont. brk. Seasonal variations.
Credit cards: Most major cards
Restrictions: No pets, smoking. 3-day cancellation notice req., less one night's fee.
Notes: 3-story Victorian hotel built about 1863. Parlor with fireplace. Furnished with period antiques. Restaurant on premises.

UKIAH (3)

Vichy Springs
2605 Vichy Springs Rd., Ukiah, CA 95482
(707) 462-9515, (707) 462-9516

Innkeeper: Gilbert and Majorie Ashoff
Rooms: 12 plus 2 suites, all w/pvt. bath, phone, incl. 2 w/fireplace. Located in 3 bldgs.
Rates: $125/room, $150-$160/suite, all incl. full brk. Discount avail. for extended stay.
Credit cards: Most major cards
Restrictions: No pets. Smoking restricted. Deposit req. 4-day cancellation notice req.
Notes: Hot tub, Olympic-size pool. Spanish spoken.*

VALLEY CENTER (17)

LAKE WOHLFORD B & B

Lake Wohlford B & B
27911 N. Lake Wohlford Rd., Valley Center, CA 92082
(619) 749-1911, (800) 831-8231
Innkeeper: Tatiana Ovanessoff
Rooms: 5, incl. 3 w/pvt. bath
Rates: $88-$128, incl. full brk., afternoon refreshment. Discount avail. for extended stay.
Credit cards: MC, V
Restrictions: Children welcome during "Children's Week." No pets, smoking. Full pre-payment req. 7-day cancellation req., less $10.00 per night fee. 2-night min. stay on wknds.
Notes: Two-story mountain lodge style house. Located on 48 acres with jogger's path. Common room with fireplace. Decorated with twig furniture, wildlife art, and sculptures. Veranda. Hammock by creek. Guided nature walks, picnic baskets and bicycles, catering available. Resident ducks, roosters and peacocks. French, Spanish spoken. Limited handicapped access.*

VALLEY FORD (3)

Valley Ford Hotel
14415 Hwy. One, Valley Ford, CA 94972
(707) 876-3600, (800) 696-6679, (707) 876-3603
Innkeeper: Ed and Peg Duffy
Rooms: 7 w/pvt. bath, phone, fireplace

Rates: $80, incl. full brk. Seasonal variations. Discount avail. for senior citizens, mid-week stays.

Credit cards: Most major cards

Restrictions: Children discouraged. No pets, smoking. $80 deposit req. 3-day cancellation notice req. 2-night min. stay on holidays.

Notes: Two-story house built in 1864, renovated in 1990. Antique pine furnishings. Meeting rooms, library, full bar and Basque restaurant on premises. Garden courtyard. Small private parties accommodated. Handicapped access. *

VENTURA (12)

Bella Maggiore Inn
67 S. California St., Ventura, CA 93001
(805) 652-0277, (800) 523-8479 (in California only)

Innkeeper: Thomas Wood

Rooms: 21 w/pvt. bath, phone, TV, incl. 4 w/fireplace, plus 3 suites w/pvt. bath, phone, TV, incl. 2 w/fireplace

Rates: $75-$150/room, $135/suite, all incl. full brk., afternoon refreshment. Discount avail. for AAA, senior citizen, mid-week stays.

Credit cards: Most major cards

Restrictions: No children under 13, pets. One night's deposit req. 48-hour cancellation notice req., less $15.00 fee.

Notes: Spanish Colonial Revival-style house built in the 1920s. Fully renovated in 1984. Lobby with fireplace, grand piano, antiques, original artwork, Italian chandeliers. Courtyard with fountain. Sun deck roof garden and sitting area. Some rooms have spas or bathtubs, semi-private balconies, bay window seats, hideaways, wet bar, microwave and refrigerator. Handicapped access. Small private parties accommodated.*

La Mer Bed & Breakfast
411 Poli St., Ventura, CA 93001
(805) 643-3600, (805) 485-5430

Innkeeper: Gisela and Michael Baida

Rooms: 5 w/pvt. bath, incl. 1 w/fireplace

Rates: $100-$155, incl. full brk., bottle of wine or champagne. Discount avail. for mid-week stay. Special pkgs. avail.

Credit cards: MC, V

Restrictions: No children. Smoking restricted. One night's deposit req. 7-day cancellation notice req., less $15.00 fee. 2-night min. stay on wknds. Closed Dec. 25.

Notes: Cape Cod Victorian house overlooking ocean built in 1890. Bavarian breakfast room, dining room, living room. Decorated to capture the feeling of specific European countries–France, Germany, Austria, Norway, England. Furnished with antiques. Certified massage therapist, picnic baskets available for small fee. On-site parking. German, Spanish spoken.*

WESTPORT (3)

Howard Creek Ranch
40501 N. Hwy 1, Box 121, Westport, CA 95488
(707) 964-6725

Innkeeper: Charles and Sally Lasselle Grigg

Rooms: 7, incl. 4 w/pvt. bath, 1 w/fireplace plus 3 cabins, all w/pvt. bath, fireplace. Located in 5 bldgs.

HOWARD CREEK RANCH

Rates: $55-$125, incl. full brk.
Credit cards: Most major cards
Restrictions: Children, pets welcome with prior notification only. Smoking restricted. Deposit req. 7-day cancellation notice req.
Notes: Redwood farmhouse built in 1871. Located on 2,000-acre sheep and cattle ranch with freshwater stream, three miles of sandy beach frontage. Parlor with fireplace. Furnished with antiques, collectibles. Sauna, hot tub. Massage available. German, Italian, Dutch spoken.*

WHITTIER (14)

Coleen's California Casa
P.O. Box 9302, Whittier, CA 90608
(310) 699-8427

Innkeeper: Coleen Davis
Rooms: 3 plus 2 suites, all w/pvt. bath, phone, TV. Located in 2 bldgs.
Rates: $75/room, $95/suite, all incl. full brk., evening refreshment. Discount avail. for extended stay.
Credit cards: None.
Restrictions: No pets, smoking. Full prepayment req. 2-week cancellation notice req. 2-night min. stay.
Notes: Ranch-style house built in 1960. Patio, deck overlooking Catalina Island. Dinner available. Handicapped access. Spanish spoken.*

YOUNTVILLE (5)

Maison Fleurie
6529 Yount St., Yountville, CA 94599
(707) 944-2056

Innkeeper: Roger Asbill
Rooms: 13 w/pvt. bath, phone, incl. 6 w/fireplace. Located in 3 bldgs.
Rates: $110-$190, incl. full brk., evening refreshment
Credit cards: Most major cards

Restrictions: No pets, smoking. One night's deposit req. 48-hr. cancellation notice req.

Notes: Built about 1873 of brick and native fieldstone as Victorian hotel. Dining room with wine cellar. Lobby with fireplace. Furnished with antiques. Decorated in French country style. Swimming pool, Jacuzzi, enclosed spa, gardens. Bicycles available. Some rooms w/patios. Handicapped access.*

Colorado

ALAMOSA (7)

Cottonwood Inn
123 San Juan Ave., Alamosa, CO 81101
(719) 589-3882

Innkeeper: Julie and George Mordecai-Sellman
Rooms: 4, incl. 2 w/pvt. bath, 1 w/phone, plus 3 suites w/pvt. bath, phone. Located in 2 bldgs.
Rates: $58-$79/room, $79/suite, all incl. full brk., afternoon refreshment. Special pkgs. avail. Discount avail. for mid-week stay.
Credit cards: Most major cards
Restrictions: No pets, smoking. One night's deposit req. 7-day cancellation notice req., less $15.00 fee. 2-night min. stay on wknds. during special events.
Notes: Two-story craftsman-style house built at the turn of the century. Has operated as inn since 1987. Living room, dining room. Parlor with fireplace, TV, VCR, library. Veranda with swings. Furnished with antiques, artwork. Winter weekend retreats/workshops organized. Small private parties accommodated. Spanish spoken.*

ALLENSPARK (2)

Allenspark Lodge
184 Main, Box 247, Allenspark, CO 80510
(303) 747-2552

Innkeeper: Mike and Becky Osmun
Rooms: 14, incl. 8 w/pvt. bath, plus 1 suite w/pvt. bath, fireplace
Rates: $45-$75/room, $80/suite, incl. cont. brk. Discount avail. for extended stay. Seasonal variations.
Credit cards: Most major cards
Restrictions: No children under 14, pets, smoking. 50% deposit req. 15-day cancellation notice req.
Notes: An authentic hand hewn lodge built in the 1930s. Great room with native stone fireplace. Game/reception room. Hot tub.*

ASPEN (5)

Boomerang Lodge
500 W. Hopkins, Aspen, CO 81611
(303) 925-3416, (800) 992-8852, (303) 925-3314

Innkeeper: Charles Paterson
Rooms: 26 plus 8 suites all w/pvt. bath, phone, TV, incl. 10 rooms & 7 suites w/fireplace. Located in 3 bldgs.
Rates: $106-$219/room, $170-$219/suite, $213-$469/apt., all incl. cont. brk., winter afternoon refreshment. Seasonal variations. Discount avail. for senior citizens.
Credit cards: Most major cards
Restrictions: No pets, smoking. Deposit req. Min. 30-day cancellation notice req. during winter. 15-day cancellation notice during summer, less $10.00 per person fee.

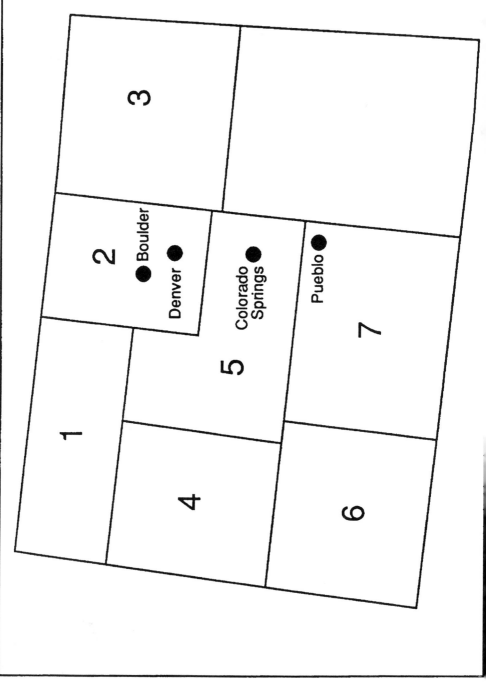

Colorado

Notes: Three-story ski lodge design by owner-architect and influenced by his teacher, Frank Lloyd Wright. Opened in 1956. Located in Aspen's West End and within walking distance to downtown. Rooms and fireplace apartments have a sunny patio or balcony. Upper lounge, copper hooded fireplace, pool, whirlpool and sauna. Handicapped access, in town shuttle van available.*

Christmas Inn
232 W. Main St., Aspen, CO 81611
(303) 925-3822
Innkeeper: Lynn Durfee
Rooms: 24 rooms w/pvt. bath, phone, cable TV
Rates: $40-$138, incl. full brk., afternoon refreshment in winter. Seasonal variations.
Credit cards: Most major cards
Restrictions: No pets. Smoking restricted. 50% deposit req. 30-day cancellation notice req., less $25.00 fee. Closed April 15–June 9, except Memorial Day wknd. 2-night min. stay on winter wknds.
Notes: English Tudor-style inn. Fully renovated in 1985. Lobby. California sun deck with glass walls on three sides overlooking Aspen Mountain. Jacuzzi, sauna, porch, courtyard. Off-street parking available. Handicapped access.*

Crestahaus Lodge
1301 E. Cooper Ave., Aspen, CO 81611
(303) 925-7081, (800) 344-3853, (303) 925-1610
Innkeeper: Melinda Goldrich
Rooms: 30 w/pvt. bath, phone, TV, incl. 1 suite w/pvt. bath, phone, TV. Located in 3 bldgs.
Rates: $115-$185/room, $155-$235/suite, all incl. expanded cont. brk., evening refreshment. Seasonal variations. Discount avail. for extended and group stays.
Credit cards: Most major cards
Restrictions: Pets, smoking restricted. Full prepayment req. 30-day cancellation notice req., less 10% fee.
Notes: Two-story lodge with two guest lounges with fireplaces. Volleyball and outdoor pool open in summer and fall. Hot tub, sauna. BBQ. Garden area. Bicycles available for rent. Ski lockers, airport transportation, laundry facilities. Small private parties accommodated. Spanish spoken. Handicapped access.*

Snow Queen Victorian Lodge
124 E. Cooper St., Aspen, CO 81611
(303) 925-8455, (303) 925-6971, (303) 925-8455
Innkeeper: Norma Dolle and Larry Ledingham
Rooms: 4 w/pvt. bath, phone, TV, plus 2 suites w/phone, incl. 1 w/kitchen
Rates: $108-$138, incl. cont. brk. Seasonal variations. Discount avail. for extended stay.
Credit cards: Most major cards
Restrictions: No pets. 50% deposit req. Min. 30-day cancellation notice req., less $20.00 per person fee. 3-night min. stay req. Closed April 15–May 15.
Notes: Two-story Victorian house built in 1886. Parlor with fireplace, TV. Outdoor hot tub. Some German and Spanish spoken.

BASALT (4)

Shenandoah Inn
0600 Frying Pan Rd., Box 578, Basalt, CO 81621
(303) 927-4991

Innkeeper: Bob and Terri Ziets
Rooms: 2 w/pvt. bath, phone, plus 2 suites
Rates: $75-$85/room, $65-$75/suite, all incl. full brk., afternoon refreshment. Seasonal variations. Discount avail. for extended stay.
Credit cards: Most major cards
Restrictions: No children under 12, pets. Smoking restricted. 50% deposit req. 14-day cancellation notice req. 2-night min. stay on wknds.
Notes: Contemporary western Colorado Bed and Breakfast, situated on 2 riverfront acres on the Frying Pan. Dining room, living room share a 16-foot high rock fireplace. Library with cable TV, VCR, books, magazines, games. Decks, hot tub. Small private parties accommodated. French, Spanish spoken.*

BOULDER (2)

Magpie Inn on Mapleton Hill
1001 Spruce St., Boulder, CO 80302
(303) 449-6528

Innkeeper: Nancy Raddatz and Teresa Koby
Rooms: 7, incl. 5 w/pvt. bath, 2 w/fireplace. Suite avail.
Rates: $72-$118, incl. cont. brk.
Credit cards: Most major cards
Restrictions: No pets, smoking. 2-day cancellation notice req.
Notes: Three-story Victorian mansion. Marble fireplaces, fine paintings, old local photographs. Furnished in antiques.

BRECKENRIDGE (5)

Allaire Timbers Inn
9511 Hwy #9, Box 4653, Breckenridge, CO 80424
(303) 453-7530, (800) 624-4904

Innkeeper: Kathy and Jack Gumph
Rooms: 8 w/pvt. bath, phone plus 2 suites all w/pvt. bath, phone, fireplace
Rates: $115-$175/room, $150-$250/suite, incl. full brk., afternoon refreshment. Seasonal variations.
Credit cards: Most major cards
Restrictions: No children under 13, pets, smoking. 50% deposit req. Min. 13-day cancellation notice req., less full fee unless room rebooked.
Notes: New two-story log B&B. Great room with fireplace, Sunroom, and loft. Outdoor spa with view of the Ten Mile range. Inn furnished with combined contemporary southwest and rustic log pieces. Guest rooms are all individually decorated and all have decks with mountain views. Suites offer a private hot tub and fireplace. Member of Distinctive Inns of Colorado and Special Places for the Discerning Traveler. "Top 10 Outstanding New Inns in America–1993" by Inn Marketing Review. Handicapped access available. *

The Cotten House Bed & Breakfast
102 S. French St., Box 387, Breckenridge, CO 80424
(303) 453-5509

Innkeeper: Pete and Georgette Contos
Rooms: 3, incl. 1 w/pvt. bath, 1 w/TV
Rates: $50-$90, incl. full brk., afternoon refreshment. Seasonal variations. Special pkgs. avail.

Credit cards: Most major cards
Restrictions: No pets, smoking. One night's deposit req. Cancellation notice req.,
  less 15% fee.
Notes: Two-story Victorian built in 1886. Common room with TV, VCR, stereo
books, games. Ski storage and telephone available. Listed in the National Historic
Register. Greek and French spoken.

Hunt Placer Inn
275 Ski Hill Rd., Box 4898, Breckenridge, CO 80424
(970) 453-7573, (800) 472-1430, (970) 453-2335
Innkeeper: Gwen and Carl Ray
Rooms: 8 w/pvt. bath, deck, incl. 3 w/fireplace
Rates: $115-$175, incl. full brk., afternoon refreshment. Seasonal variations.
Credit cards: Most major cards
Restrictions: No children under 12, pets, smoking. Min. one night's deposit req.
  Full deposit refunded, less $20.00 fee, upon min. 14-day cancellation only if room
  re-rented. 2-night min. stay on wknds. 7-night min. stay from Christmas–New
  Years.
Notes: European chalet-style inn built in 1994. Decorated in style ranging from
Gold Rush to Britannia. Small private parties accommodated. Handicapped access.
German spoken.*

Little Mountain Lodge
98 Sunbeam Dr., Box 2479, Breckenridge, CO 80424-2479
(303) 453-1969, (303) 454-1919
Innkeeper: Lynn and Truman Esmond
Rooms: 8 w/pvt. bath, phone, TV, plus 2 suites w/pvt. bath, phone, fireplace, TV
  All rooms have pvt. decks or patios.
Rates: $110-$175/room, $140-$210/suite, all incl. full brk., afternoon refreshment.
  Seasonal variations.
Credit cards: Most major cards
Restrictions: No children under 12, pets, smoking. 50% deposit req. 3-night min.
  stay.
Notes: New custom log lodge. Wood gurning fireplace in main room. Lower level
has large screen TV, pool table, outdoor hot tub. Business center with copier and
fax. French, German spoken. Handicapped access.*

The Ridge Street Inn
212 N. Ridge St., Box 2854, Breckenridge, CO 80424
(303) 453-4680
Innkeeper: Carol Brownson
Rooms: 5 w/TV, 3/pvt. bath, plus 1 suite w/pvt. bath, TV
Rates: $55-$90/room, $80-$100/suite, all incl. full brk., afternoon refreshment. Seasonal variations.
Credit cards: Most major cards
Restrictions: No children under 6, pets, smoking. 2 night's deposit req. 30-day cancellation notice req., less $10.00 fee. 5-night min. stay in winter. 2-night min. stay
  in summer.
Notes: Two-story Victorian style inn built in 1890. Parlor with bay windows, fire-
place. Furnished with antiques. Kitchen available to guests in the evening.*

Williams House - 1885 B & B
303 N. Main St., Box 2454, Breckenridge, CO 80424
(303) 453-2975, (800) 795-2975
Innkeeper: Diane Jaynes, Fred Kinat
Rooms: 4 rooms, plus 1 suite, all w/pvt. bath, incl. 1 suite w/fireplace, TV. Located
  in 2 bldgs.
Rates: $89-$135/room, $150-$200/suite, all incl. full brk., afternoon refreshment.
  Seasonal variations.
Credit cards: Most major cards
Restrictions: No children, pets, smoking. Deposit req. 30-day cancellation notice
  req., less $20.00 fee.
Notes: Originally built in 1885, this house features 2 parlors with Victorian fire-
places, a TV in the rear parlor. Outdoor hot tub. Suite located in Victorian Cottage,
which features a Jacuzzi for two, mantled fireplace, sitting area with TV and refrig-
erator. Handicapped access. Resident beagle.*

BUENA VISTA (5)

Cottonwood Hot Springs Inn
18999 County Rd. 306, Buena Vista, CO 81211
(719) 395-6434, 395-2102
Innkeeper: Cathy Manning and Jim Gerhordt
Rooms: 12 plus 4 cabins w/kitchenette, all w/pvt. bath. Located in 5 bldgs.
Rates: $42-$52/room, $55-135/cabin, all incl. cont. brk. Seasonal variations. Dis-
  count avail. for extended and mid-week stays.
Credit cards: Most major cards
Restrictions: 25% deposit req. 72-hour cancellation notice req. 3-night min. stay in
  cabins from July 1–Aug. 31.
Notes: Dining room with fireplace. Decorated in rustic style. Exercise and weight
room. Hot mineral spa and sauna. Teepee, dormitory and camping also avail. Small
private parties accommodated. Limited handicapped access.

CARBONDALE (4)

Ambiance Inn
66 N. 2nd St., Carbondale, CO 81623
(303) 963-3597, (800) 350-1515
Innkeeper: Norma and Robert Morris
Rooms: 3 w/pvt. bath, plus 1 suite w/pvt. bath, refrigerator, sunroom, TV
Rates: $60-$80/room, $80-$120/suite, all incl. full brk. Discount avail. for extended
  stay
Credit cards: MC, V
Restrictions: No children under 7, pets, smoking. Deposit req. 25-day cancellation
  notice req., less $25.00 fee.
Notes: Contemporary chalet-style house built in 1975. Dining room. Sitting room,
library. Furnished in ski lodge decor, Victorian, southwest and island furnishings.
Patio. Dinner available. Dietary restrictions accommodated. Picnic basket avail-
able.*

Mt. Sopris Inn
0165 Mt. Sopris Ranch Rd., Box 126, Carbondale, CO 81623
(303) 963-2209, (800) 437-8675

Innkeeper: Marion and Les Perkins
Rooms: 5 w/pvt. bath, TV, phone, incl., 4/suites, w/pvt. bath, fireplace, TV, phone. Located in 3 bldgs.
Rates: $85-$125/room, $125-$250/suite, incl. full brk.
Credit cards: MC, V
Restrictions: No children under 10, pets, smoking. Deposit req. 7-day cancellation notice req. less $25.00 fee.
Notes: Two-story building sits on 14 acres of land, 775 feet crystal river flows at the base of forty-foot-high bluff. Terrace, pool, Jacuzzi. llamas in the pastures. The great room features a 15' wide floor to ceiling river rock fireplace. 7' grand piano. Lawn games. Small private parties accommodated. Handicapped access.*

CIMARRON (7)

The Inn at Arrowhead
21401 Alpine Plateau Rd., Cimarron, CO 81220
(303) 249-5634, (303) 249-2802
Innkeeper: Mg. Anjani Ammen
Rooms: 12 incl. 1 suite, all w/pvt. bath and fireplace
Rates: $69-$79/room, $99/suite, all incl. full brk.
Credit cards: Most major cards
Restrictions: No pets. Smoking restricted. 50% deposit req. 7-day cancellation notice req. 30-day Holiday cancellation notice req.
Notes: 2-story house. Located at 9,300 ft. elevation. Lounge with pool table. Lobby with fireplace, satellite TV, VCR, board games. Hot tub on second-floor deck. Restaurant on premises. Rooms include carpet, fireplaces, lights around vanities, chests, closets, paperback books, writing desks, rocking chairs, and radios. Small private parties accommodated. Handicapped access.*

SHAMROCK RANCH

COALMONT (1)

Shamrock Ranch
4363 JCR 11, Coalmont, CO 80430
(303) 723-8413
Innkeeper: Cindy and Bruce Wilson
Rooms: 2, plus 4 cabins. Located in 2 bldgs.
Rates: $70-$80/room, $255/cabin, all incl. full brk., dinner, afternoon refreshment.

Credit cards: Most major cards
Restrictions: No pets. Smoking restricted. 50% deposit req. 60-day cancellation notice req., less 10% fee.
Notes: Spruce log lodge, built in the 1930s. Furnished with antiques. Inside or outdoor dining. Hot tub. Organized fishing trips available. Sacked lunch available.*

COLORADO SPRINGS (5)

Cheyenne Canon Inn
2030 W. Cheyenne Blvd., Colorado Springs, CO 80906
(719) 633-0625, (719) 633-8826
Innkeeper: John and Barbara Starr
Rooms: 5 plus 2 suites, all w/pvt. bath, phone, TV
Rates: $75-$110/room, $110-$115/suite, all incl. full brk., afternoon refreshment.
Seasonal variations. Discount avail. for senior citizens and extended stays.
Credit cards: Most major cards
Restrictions: No pets, smoking. 50% deposit req. 72-hour cancellation notice req.
Notes: Mission-style mansion built in 1921. Terraced rock gardens. Great room with mission antiques, library with rock fireplace, dining room with built-in sideboard and original stained-glass, front porch with a view of Cheyenne Mountain. Two creeks join in front of house. Private hot tub room. French spoken.

Holden House 1902 B & B Inn
1102 W. Pikes Peak Ave., Colorado Springs, CO 80904
(719) 471-3980
Innkeeper: Sallie and Welling Clark
Rooms: 2 plus 4 suites, all w/pvt. bath., incl. 4 suites w/fireplace. Located in 3 bldgs.
Rates: $70-$75/room, $90-$105/suite, all incl. full brk., afternoon refreshment.
Credit cards: Most major cards
Restrictions: No children, pets, smoking. Min. one night's deposit req. Min. 30-day cancellation notice req., less $15.00 fee. 2-night min. stay on wknds. 3-night min. stay on holidays or special events.
Notes: Two-story Colonial Revival Victorian house built in 1902. Rooms filled with period furnishings, tubs, fireplace. Furnished with antiques, period wallpaper. Resident cats.*

HOLDEN HOUSE 1902 B & B INN

The Painted Lady B & B
1318 W. Colorado Ave., Colorado Springs, CO 80904-4023
(719) 473-3165
Innkeeper: Valerie and Zan Maslowski
Rooms: 4, incl. 2 w/pvt. bath
Rates: $55-$75/room, incl. full brk., afternnon refreshment. Discount avail. for extended stay.
Credit cards: Most major cards
Restrictions: No children under 10, pets, smoking. Min. one night's deposit req. 8-day cancellation notice req., 30-day cancellation notice req. for holidays and special events, less $10.00 per night fee. 2-night min. stay during holidays and special events.
Notes: Restored 1894 Victorian house with gingerbread trim, wraparound porches, coach lights. Parlor. Guest rooms feature lace curtains and period furnishings. Claw foot "tub for two." Off-street parking. Resident cat.*

ROOM AT THE INN

Room at the Inn
618 N. Nevada Ave., Colorado Springs, CO 80903
(719) 442-1896
Innkeeper: Chick, Jan and Kelly McCormick
Rooms: 3 w/pvt. bath, incl. 1 w/fireplace, plus 4 suites w/pvt. bath, incl. 2 w/fireplace. Located in 2 bldgs.
Rates: $80-$105/room, $95-$115/suite, all incl. full brk., afternoon refreshment. Discount avail. for extended and charitable organization stays.
Credit cards: Most major cards
Restrictions: No children under 12, pets, smoking. Min. 50% deposit req. 14-day cancellation notice req., less $15.00 fee.
Notes: Three-story Queen Anne-style house with three-story turret, seven kinds of fish scale siding, multiple gables and oak staircase, built in 1896. Cottage. Formal parlor with library, board games. Wrap-around porch. Sun deck with hot tub. Furnished with Oriental rugs and antiques from the Rennaissance, Revival, Eastlake and Empire periods. Bicycles available.*

CREEDE (7)

Creede Hotel
P.O. Box 284, Creede, CO 81130
(719) 658-2608

Innkeeper: Kathy and Rich Ormsby
Rooms: 6, all w/pvt. bath. Located in 2 bldgs.
Rates: $49-$79, incl. full brk. Seasonal variations. Discount avail. for extended stay.
Credit cards: Most major cards
Restrictions: No pets. Smoking restricted. Deposit req. 7-day cancellation notice
    req.
Notes: Two-story building built in 1892. Balcony and picnic areas. Limited handi-
capped access.*

CRESTED BUTTE (5)

Purple Mountain Lodge
714 Gothic Ave., Box 897, Crested Butte, CO 81224
(303) 349-5888

Innkeeper: Walter and Sherron Green
Rooms: 5 incl. 3 w/pvt. bath
Rates: $70-$85, incl. full brk. Seasonal variations. Discount avail. for extended stay
Credit cards: Most major cards
Restrictions: Smoking restricted. 50% deposit req. 14-day cancellation notice req.
    2-night min. stay req.
Notes: Lodge, originally built above town in 1927, was moved, refurbished and has
operated as an inn since 1979. Surrounded by mountains, meadows. Living room
with massive stone fireplace, cable TV. Sun room with spa. Dining room. Innkeep-
ers lived in Switzerland and Argentina.*

DENVER (2)

Capitol Hill Mansion
1207 Pennsylvania, Denver, CO 80203
(303) 839-5221, (303) 839-9046

Innkeeper: Kathy Robbins and Chuck Hillestad
Rooms: 5 w/pvt. bath, phone, TV, plus 3 suites w/pvt. bath, phone, TV, incl. 2
    w/fireplace, 1 w/kitchen. All w/refrigerator.
Rates: $79-$139/room, $99-$139/suite, all incl. cont. brk., afternoon refreshment
Credit cards: Most major cards
Restrictions: No pets, smoking. Min. one night's deposit req. 5-day cancellation no-
    tice req.
Notes: Three-story, Richardsonian Romanesque style house with patterned plaster
and golden oak paneling, built in 1891. Exterior of ruby sandstone, high turrets,
soaring chimneys, balconies. Sweeping staircase, stained and beveled glass window.
Public parlors with board games, puzzles, books. Alarm system. Furnished in designer decor and original art. Coffee makers, hair dryers in all rooms. Fax and
copier machine available. Listed on National Register of Historic Places. Free parking. Handicapped access.*

Castle Marne
1572 Race St., Denver, CO 80206
(303) 331-0621, (800) 926-2763, (303) 331-0623

Innkeeper: The Peiker Family
Rooms: 7 plus 2 suites, all w/pvt. bath, phone
Rates: $70-$150/room, $150-$180/suite, all incl. full brk., afternoon refreshment.
Credit cards: Most major cards

Restrictions: No children under 10, pets, smoking. Deposit req. 30-day cancellation notice req.

Notes: Three-story Victorian mansion built in 1889. Fully restored with hand-rubbed woods, circular stained-glass window, peacock windows, ornate fireplaces. Formal dining room, parlor. Veranda with swing overlooking Victorian garden. Furnished with period antiques, family heirlooms. Board games available. Small private parties accommodated. Hungarian, Spanish, Russian spoken. Listed on the National Register of Historic Places.*

CASTLE MARNE

Haus Berlin Bed and Breakfast
1651 Emerson St., Denver, CO 80218
(303) 837-9527, (303) 837-9527

Innkeeper: Christina and Dennis Brown

Rooms: 3 w/pvt. bath, phone, incl. 2 w/TV, plus 1 suite w/pt. bath, phone, TV

Rates: $85-$100/room, $120/suite, all incl. expanded cont. brk., afternoon refreshment. Discount avail. for extended stay and return guests.

Credit cards: Most major cards

Restrictions: No children, pets, smoking. One night's deposit req. 7-day cancellation notice req.

Notes: Three-story Victorian townhouse built in 1892. Listed on the National Register of Historic Places. Fresco morning parlor with leaded and bottle glass window. Comtemporary sitting room. French breakfast area. Furnished in eclectic and antiques with down comforters and ironed European and American linen. Courtyard with flower garden, tables and chairs in backyard. German spoken.*

Holiday Chalet
1820 E. Colfax Ave., Denver, CO 80218
(303) 321-9975, (800) 626-4497, (303) 377-6556

Innkeeper: Bob and Margo Hartmann

Rooms: 10 suites w/pvt. bath, phone, TV, kitchen

Rates: $54-$68, incl. cont. brk. Discount avail. for extended stay and senior citizens.

Credit cards: Most major cards

Restrictions: No smoking. Pets restricted. One night's deposit req. 2-day cancellation notice req.

Notes: Three-story Victorian chalet built in 1896. Converted to a AAA hotel in 1952. Public rooms with Victorian family heirlooms, period wallpapers, stained-glass. Many pieces throughout were found during an archaeological dig in the basement. Third floor gathering place/library with games, reading, piano. Some guest rooms with sunrooms, eating areas, fireplaces. Gardens. Guest passes to Denver Athletic Club available. Some Spanish and some German spoken.*

Queen Anne Inn
2147 Tremont Place, Denver, CO 80205
(303) 296-6666, (800) 432-4667, (303) 296-2151

Innkeeper: Tom King
Rooms: 10 w/pvt. bath, phone, incl. 2 w/TV, plus 4 suites w/pvt. bath, phone, TV, incl. 1 w/fireplace. Located in 2 bldgs.
Rates: $75-$125/room, $135-$155/suite, all incl. full brk., afternoon refreshment. Special pkgs. avail. Discount avail. for mid-week stay. Seasonal variations.
Credit cards: Most major cards
Restrictions: No children under 12, pets, smoking. One night's deposit req. 3-day cancellation notice req. 2-night min. stay for 3-day holiday wknds.
Notes: Two side-by-side three-story Queen Ann Victorian houses built in 1879 and 1886. by Frank Edbrooke of Brown Palace fame. Located in Clements Historic District. Foyer with grand oak staircase. Living room, dining room, private garden. Furnished with heirloom antiques, reproductions and original works by regional artists. Mountain, city skyline, park or garden view from each room. Off-street parking, bicycles, horse-drawn carriage rides, all meals available. Small private parties accommodated. Spanish, some French spoken. Limited handicapped access.*

SWAN MOUNTAIN INN

DILLON (5)

Swan Mountain Inn
P.O. Box 2900, Dillon, CO 80435
(303) 453-7903, (800) 578-3687

Innkeeper: Steve Gessner
Rooms: 4, incl. 3 w/pvt. bath and TV
Rates: $50-$100, incl. full brk. Seasonal variations. Discount avail. for extended stay. Special pkgs. avail.

Credit cards: Most major cards

Restrictions: No pets. Smoking restricted. 2-night min. stay on wknds. in high and regular season.

Notes: Two-story wood house with two fireplaces located on Summit County bike path in Breckenridge. Furnished with antiques and down comforters. Two decks and large front porch. Robes provided for outdoor hot tub. Restaurant and full service bar on premises. Guests have access to laundry facilities. Small private parties accommodated. Limited handicapped access.

DOLORES (6)

Historic Rio Grande Southern Hotel
101 S. 5th., Box 516, Dolores, CO 81323
(303) 862-7527

Innkeeper: Cathy and Fred Green

Rooms: 7 plus 1 suite, incl. 3 w/pvt. bath

Rates: $35-$60/room, $120/suite, all incl. full brk.

Credit cards: MC, V

Restrictions: No pets. 2-day cancellation notice req., less one night's fee.

Notes: Restaurant on premises.*

DURANGO (6)

The Leland House B & B
721 E. Second Ave., Durango, CO 81301
(303) 385-1920, (303) 385-1967

Innkeeper: Kirk Komick and Diane McConn

Rooms: 10 incl. 6 suites, all w/pvt. bath, phone, TV, incl. 4 w/kitchenette, 6 w/full kitchen

Rates: $85-$95/room, $125-135/suite, all incl. full brk., afternoon refreshment. Seasonal variations. Special pkgs. avail.

Credit cards: Most major cards

Restrictions: No children under 2, pets, smoking. One night's deposit req. 7-day cancellation notice req.

Notes: Two-story brick building built in 1927 as an apartment house. Restored and began operation in 1993. Located in Historic downtown Durango. Decorated with rustic antiques and photos, memorabilia, and biographies of historic figures associated with the property.*

Lightner Creek Inn
999 CR 207, Durango, CO 81301
(303) 259-1226, (303) 259-0732

Innkeeper: Julie and Richard Houston

Rooms: 7 incl. 5 w/pvt.bath, 6 w/phone, 2 w/TV

Rates: $55-95, incl. full brk., afternoon refreshment. Special pkgs. avail. Seasonal variations.

Credit cards: Most major cards

Restrictions: No children under 10, pets, smoking. 50% deposit req. 14-day cancellation notice req., less $20.00 fee. 2-night min. stay on holidays.

Notes: Built in 1903 on 20 acres with mountain and creek views, surrounded by Wildlife Reguge. Sun room, library, fireplaces. Furnished with Victorian antiques. Hot tub and gazebo. Small private parties accommodated. Handicapped access.*

LIGHTNER CREEK INN

Logwood Bed and Breakfast
35060 U.S. Hwy. 550 N., Durango, CO 81301
(303) 259-4396, (800) 369-4082
Innkeeper: Greg and Debby Verheyden
Rooms: 6 w/pvt. bath, phone
Rates: $65-$90, incl. full brk., afternoon refreshment, evening dessert. Seasonal
variations. Discount avail. for extended winter stay.
Credit cards: Most major cards
Restrictions: No children under 8, pets, smoking. Deposit req. 2-week cancellation
notice req., less $15.00 fee. Closed April 15–May 15, Oct. 15–Thanksgiving.
Notes: Three-story western red cedar log inn built in 1988. Located on the Animas
River. Common room with fireplace, library. Wrap-around deck with hammock.
Covered porch. Resident cats.*

River House B & B Inn
495 Animas View Dr., Durango, CO 81301
(303) 247-4775, (303) 259-1465
Innkeeper: Crystal Carroll, Kate and Lars Enggren
Rooms: 5 w/pvt. bath, plus 2 suites w/pvt. bath, TV
Rates: $60-$85, incl. full brk.
Credit cards: Most major cards
Restrictions: No pets, smoking. Min. one night's deposit req. 14-day cancellation
notice req., less $15.00 fee. 2 night min. stay on wknds.
Notes: One level southwestern house overlooking the Animas River. Living room
with fireplace and wet bar. Common room with large screen TV, VCR, piano, antique snooker table. Atrium with fountain. Decorated with original local art. Ski
shuttle buss service at front door. Flagstone patio. Theraputic spa. Massage or hyp-
nosis session available. Special diets accommodated. Small privage parties accommodated. Handicapped access. Innkeeper is massage therapist and clinical
hypnotherapist. Some Spanish spoken.*

Scrubby Oaks B & B
1901 Florida Rd., Box 1047, Durango, CO 81302
(970) 247-2176

RIVER HOUSE B & B INN

Innkeeper: Mary Ann Craig
Rooms: 7, incl 3 w/pvt. bath
Rates: $65-$75, incl. full brk., afternoon refreshment
Credit cards: None
Restrictions: No pets, smoking. 50% deposit req. 14-day cancellation notice req., less $10.00 fee. Closed Oct. 25–Thanksgiving and March 31–last wknd. in April.
Notes: Private home located on ten acres overlooking Animas Valley. Country kitchen with fireplace, brick walls, quarry tile floors. Patios with tables and chairs. Living room with fireplace. Recreation room with pool table, dart board, TV, weights. Family room with fireplace, TV, VCR. Furnished with family antiques, art works, books. Sauna, gardens. Board games available. Resident dog.*

Strater Hotel
699 Main Ave., Durango, CO 81301
(303) 247-4431, (800) 247-4431, (303) 259-2208
Innkeeper: Rod Barker
Rooms: 92 plus 1 suite, all w/pvt. bath, phone, TV
Rates: $78-$105. Seasonal variations. Special pkgs. avail. Discount avail. for senior citizen stay.
Credit cards: Most major cards
Restrictions: No pets. Smoking restricted. One night's deposit req. 24-hour cancellation notice req.
Notes: Four-story rede brick and chiseled stone Victorian Hotel built in 1887. Fully renovated. Lobby. Furnished in Victorian style with antiques. World's largest collection of Victorian walnut furniture. Restaurant, saloon with live ragtime piano on premises. Small private parties accommodated.*

ESTES PARK (2)

Black Dog Inn
650 S. St. Vrain Ave., Box 4659, Estes Park, CO 80517
(303) 586-0374
Innkeeper: Pete and Jane Princehorn

Rooms: 4, incl 2 w/pvt bath, plus 1 suite w/pvt. bath, fireplace, whirlpool, library, refrigerator. Located in 2 bldgs.

Rates: $65-$75/room, $120/suite, all incl. full brk. Special winter pkgs. avail.

Credit cards: MC, V

Restrictions: No children under 15, pets, smoking. Min. one night's deposit req. 15-day cancellation notice req., less $15.00 fee. 2-night min. stay for suite and on wknds. in pvt. bath rooms.

Notes: Built in 1910. Located on one wooded acre. Living room with fireplace, TV, VCR with over 120 movies. Family room with piano, library. Dining room. Guests have access to kitchen. Furnished with antiques. Resident dog.*

ROMANTIC RIVERSONG

Romantic Riversong
1765 L. Broadview, Box 1910, Estes Park, CO 80517
(303) 586-4666

Innkeeper: Gary and Sue Mansfield

Rooms: 4 plus 5 suites, all w/pvt. bath, incl. 8 w/fireplace. Located in 4 bldgs.

Rates: $145-$165/room, $145-$195/suite, all incl. full brk. Special pkgs. avail.

Credit cards: MC, V

Restrictions: No children under 12, pets, smoking. Two night's deposit req. Min. 30-day cancellation notice req., less $15.00 fee. 2-night min. stay. 3-night min. stay on holidays.

Notes: Two-story main house, carriage house. Located along stream on thirty wooded acres at foot of Giant Track Mountain. Has operated as inn since 1986. Breakfast room. Main room with library, fireplace. Furnished with locally hand-crafted log and birch furniture and antiques. Gazebo by pond. Dinner available. Handicapped access.*

FRISCO (5)

Mar Dei's Mountain Retreat
221 S. 4th Ave., Box 1767, Frisco, CO 80443
(303) 668-5337

Innkeeper: Jack and Carmen Galbraith

Rooms: 5 incl 2 w/pvt bath, phone, 1 w/TV plus 1 suite w/TV

Rates: $15-$100 incl. cont. brk. Discount avail. for extended and senior citizen stays.

Credit cards: Most major cards
Restrictions: No pets. Deposit req. Cancellation notice req., less $10.00 fee.
Notes: Two-story mountain retreat with fireplaces. Outdoor hot tub. Free shuttle service in Summit County during ski season.

FRUITA (4)

Stonehaven B & B
798 N. Mesa, Fruita, CO 81521
(303) 858-0898
Innkeeper: Amy Kadmas and Vance I. Norris
Rooms: 4, incl. 1 suite, 2 w/pvt. bath, 1 w/phone
Rates: $34-$45/room, $85/suite, incl. full brk.
Credit cards: Most major cards
Restrictions: Pets and smoking restricted. Deposit preferred. 7-day cancellation notice req.
Notes: Victorian house with hardwood floors, wrap-around veranda built in 1906. Furnished with antiques. Children's playground, steam room. Guests have access to cable TV. Small private parties accommodated.

GEORGETOWN (2)

Hardy House B & B Inn
605 Brownell, Box 156, Georgetown, CO 80444
(303) 569-3388
Innkeeper: Carla and Mike Wagner
Rooms: 3, plus 1 suite, all w/pvt. bath, TV/VCR
Rates: $73-$77/room, $87-$102/suite, all incl. full brk., afternoon refreshment. Special pkgs. avail.
Credit cards: MC, V for deposit only
Restrictions: No children under 12, pets, smoking. 7-day cancellation notice req., less $15.00 fee. 30-day cancellation notice req. for special events, ski groups, holidays.
Notes: Cape Cod Victorian house built in 1880. Parlor with potbellied stove. Rooms furnished with feather comforters. Hot tub. Special-occasion dinners available.

GLENWOOD SPRINGS (4)

The Kaiser House
P.O. Box 1952, Glenwood Springs, CO 81602
(303) 945-8827, (303) 945-8826
Innkeeper: Ingrid Eash
Rooms: 8 w/pvt. bath, incl. 3/TV
Rates: $60-$120, incl. full brk., afternoon refreshment. Seasonal variations. Discount avail. for extended stay.
Credit cards: Most major cards
Restrictions: No children under 8, pets, smoking. 7-night cancellation notice req. 2-night min. stay on wknds. 3-night min. stay on holidays.
Notes: Three-story Queen Anne Victorian house built in 1902. Renovated in 1988. Located at 932 Cooper Ave. Dining room, breakfast area. Decorated in Victorian style. Private patio. Hot tub.*

GOLDEN (2)

Antique Rose B & B
1422 Washington Ave., Golden, CO 80401
(303) 277-1893, (303) 278-9747
Innkeeper: Sharon Bennetts
Rooms: 3 plus 1 suite, all w/pvt. bath, phone, TV, incl. 2 w/whirlpool
Rates: $75-$90/room, $115/suite, all incl. full brk. Discount avail for mid-week and
    senior citizen stays.
Credit cards: MC, V
Restrictions: No pets, smoking. Deposit req. $15.00 cancellation fee.
Notes: Two-story Queen Anne Victorian house with gables and dormers built in
1880s. Recently renovated. Dining room. Furnished in Victorian style. Guests have
access to FAX, copy machine and IBM-compatible computer. Small private parties
accommodated.*

GREELEY (2)

Sterling House B & B
818 12th St., Greeley, CO 80631
(303) 351-8805
Innkeeper: Lillian Peeples
Rooms: 1 w/pvt. bath, phone, TV, plus 1 suite w/pvt. bath, TV, phone
Rates: $49, incl. full brk. Discount avail. for extended stay.
Credit cards: MC, V
Restrictions: No children under 10, pets. Smoking restricted. One night's deposit
    req.
Notes: Built in 1886. Was home to a cattle baron. Furnished with period furnishings
of the 1880s. German spoken.*

GREEN MOUNTAIN FALLS (5)

Outlook Lodge B & B
6975 Howard St., Box 5, Green Mountain Falls, CO 80819-0005
(719) 684-2303
Innkeeper: Hayley and Pat Moran
Rooms: 6 plus 2 suites, incl. 4 rooms w/pvt. bath. Located in 2 bldgs.
Rates: $45-$55/room, $70/suite, all incl. full brk. Discount avail. for extended stay.
Credit cards: MC, V
Restrictions: No pets, smoking. One night's deposit req. 7-day cancellation notice
    req., less one night's fee. 2-night min. stay for holidays.
Notes: Built in1889 on Pikes Peak as parsonage for historic Little Brown Church in
the Wildwood. the lodge has hosted many of guests since 1950s. Small parlor used
as reading room. Large parlor with TV, fireplace. Dining/game room, veranda.
Decorated in German/American atmosphere. Furnished with Victorian antiques.
Patio, BBQ. Guests have access to kitchen. Small private parties accommodated.*

GUNNISON (5)

Mary Lawrence Inn
601 N. Taylor St., Gunnison, CO 81230
(303) 641-3343
Innkeeper: Jan Goin

MARY LAWRENCE INN

Rooms: 3 w/pvt. bath, plus 2 suites w/pvt. bath, phone
Rates: $69/room, $85-$135/suite, all incl. full brk., afternoon refreshment. Special
  pkgs. avail.
Credit cards: Most major cards
Restrictions: No pets, smoking. 50% deposit req. 14-day cancellation notice req.,
  less $15.00 fee.
Notes: Two-story Italianate Victorian house built in 1885. Restored in 1988. Sitting
room with books, board games. Dining room. Furnished with antiques, collectibles.
Enclosed porch. Fenced yard with deck, play house and picnic area. Resident dog.
Limited handicapped access.*

HESPERUS (6)

Blue Lake Ranch
16919 State Hwy. 140, Hesperus, CO 81326
(303) 385-4537, (303) 385-4088
Innkeeper: David and Shirley Alford
Rooms: 8 incl. 4 suites, all w/pvt. bath, phone, TV, incl. 1 room & 3 suites w/fire-
  place. Located in 5 bldgs.
Rates: $85-$150/room, $132-$225/suite, all incl. full brk., afternoon refreshment.
  Discount avail. for extended stay.
Credit cards: Most major cards
Restrictions: No pets, smoking. 50% deposit req. 2-week cancellation notice req.,
  less $30.00 fee. 2-night min. stay.
Notes: European style country estate located on 100 acres with lake, flower gardens.
Furnished in southwestern style. Hot tub overlooking La Plata Mountains. Handi-
capped access. German spoken.*

IDAHO SPRINGS (2)

St. Mary's Glacier B & B
336 Crest Dr., Idaho Springs, CO 80452
(303) 567-4084, (303) 567-4084
Innkeeper: Jackie and Steve Jacquin
Rooms: 4 plus 1/suite, all w/pvt. bath. Located in 1 bldg.
Rates: $75-$125/room, $125-$150/suite, all incl. full brk.

ST. MARY'S GLACIER B & B

Credit cards: MC, V
Restrictions: No children, pets, smoking. Deposit req. 14-day cancellation notice req.
Notes: Two story country house. Located at 10,500-foot elevation. Fireplace in the parlor, library, hot tub, a hammock for two. Decorated with exquisite paintings.*

LEADVILLE (5)

Apple Blossom Inn
120 W. 4th St., Leadville, CO 80461
(719) 486-2141, (800) 982-9279
Innkeeper: Maggie Senn
Rooms: 8, incl. 3 w/pvt. bath, 1 w/fireplace
Rates: $59-$79, incl. full brk., afternoon refreshment. Discount avail. for senior citizens. Special pkgs. avail.
Credit cards: Most major cards
Restrictions: No pets, smoking. One night's deposit req. 14-day cancellation notice req.

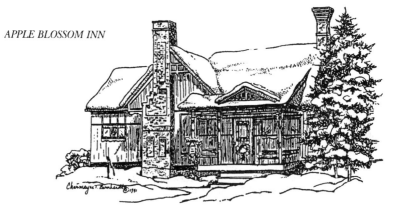

APPLE BLOSSOM INN

Notes: Two-story Victorian-style inn with stained-glass windows, fireplaces, built in 1879. Furnished in antiques. Guests have access to recreation center. Limited handicapped access.*

Delaware Hotel
700 Harrison Ave., Leadville, CO 80461
(719) 486-1418, (800) 748-2004, (719) 486-2214
Innkeeper: Susan and Scott Brackett
Rooms: 32 w/pvt. bath, TV, plus 4 suites w/pvt. bath, TV
Rates: $60-90/room, $90-$100/suite, all incl. full brk. Special pkgs. avail.
Credit cards: Most major cards
Restrictions: No pets. Deposit req. 3-day cancellation notice req.
Notes: Three-story Victorian hotel with oak paneling, crystal chandeliers, built in 1886. Fully renovated in 1992. Lobby with grand piano. Furnished with antiques, lace curtains. Jacuzzi. Special Theme Weekends offered. Small private parties accommodated. Restaurant on premises. Handicapped access.*

DELAWARE HOTEL

The Ice Palace Inn
813 Spruce St., Leadville, CO 80461
(719) 486-8272
Innkeeper: Giles and Kami Kolakowski
Rooms: 2, plus 1 suite, all w/pvt. bath
Rates: $79-$99/room, $109/suite, incl. full brk. Seasonal variations.
Credit cards: None
Restrictions: No pets, smoking. One night's deposit req. 10-day cancellation notice req.
Notes: Three-story Victorian Inn built in 1903 using the lumber from the original Ice Palace, built in 1896, which burned down. Formal dining room. Parlor with gas fireplace. Game room. Furnished with antiques. Antique shop on premises.*

LOVELAND (2)

Lovelander B & B Inn
217 W. 4th St., Loveland, CO 80537
(303) 669-0798, (303) 669-0797

LOVELANDER B & B INN

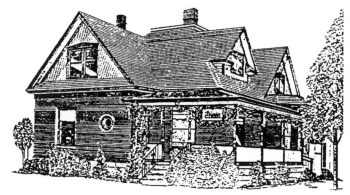

Innkeeper: Marilyn and Bob Wiltgen
Rooms: 11, all w/pvt. bath, phone, incl. 1 w/fireplace
Rates: $74-$125, incl. full brk., afternoon refreshment. Discount avail. for mid-week, extended and senior citizen stays.
Credit cards: Most major cards
Restrictions: No children under 10, pets, smoking. One night's deposit req. 7-day cancellation notice req., less $15.00 fee.
Notes: Two-story Victorian house with stained-glass built in 1902. Parlor with fireplace. Library with TV. Dining room. Furnished with antiques. Wrap-around front porch, flagstone terrage with flowers and herbs, decks. Summer picnic baskets available. Small private parties accommodated. Limited handicapped access.*

MANCOS (6)

Lost Canyon Lake Lodge
15472 County Rd., 35-3, Mancos, CO 81328
(800) 992-1098
Innkeeper: Beth Newman and Ken Nickson
Rooms: 5 w/pvt. bath.
Rates: $70-$90, incl. full brk., evening refreshment. Seasonal variations. Discount avail. for extended stay.
Credit cards: Most major cards
Restrictions: No pets, smoking. One night's deposit req. 7-day cancellation notice req., less $15.00 fee.
Notes: Two-story contemporary log house built in 1983. Located on 20 forested acres, overlooking Canyon Lake Reservoir. Common room with 18' moss rock fireplace. Games, reading material, TV/VCR, movies and tapes. Country kitchen. Hot tub. Wrap-around decks. Guests have access to laundry facilities, phone, refrigerator/freezer. Picnic lunch available. Two resident dogs.*

MANITOU SPRINGS (5)

Gray's Avenue Hotel
711 Manitou Ave., Manitou Springs, CO 80829
(719) 685-1277
Innkeeper: Dona Lee Gray

Rooms: 8 plus 1 suite, incl. 3 w/pvt. bath
Rates: $45-$65/room, $55-$65/suite, all incl. full brk. Discount avail. for extended
  stay.
Credit cards: Most major cards
Restrictions: No children under 10, pets, smoking. Deposit req. 3-day cancellation
  notice req.
Notes: Three-story Queen Anne Victorian shingle inn built in 1886 as one of the
town's original hotels. Formal living room. Library/family room with TV, VCR. Din-
ing room. Furnished with antiques. Listed on the National Register of Historic
Places.

Victoria's Keep
202 Ruxton Ave., Manitou Springs, CO 80829
(719) 685-5354, (800) 905-5337
Innkeeper: Marvin and Vicki Keith
Rooms: 3 plus 2 suites, all w/pvt. bath, fireplace, incl. 1 w/Jacuzzi, 1 w/phone
Rates: $65-$120, incl. full brk., evening refreshment. Discounts avail.
Credit cards: Most major cards
Restrictions: No smoking. Credit card deposit req. 7-day cancellation notice req.
Notes: Two-story Queen Anne Victorian house with wraparound porch and turret,
built in 1892. Living room, front parlor. Dining room with fireplace. Decorated with
stained-glass windows, period wall coverings and wainscotting. Spa. Bicycles avail-
able.*

MINTURN (5)

Eagle River Inn
145 N. Main St., Box 100, Minturn, CO 81845
(303) 827-5761, (800) 344-1750, (303) 827-4020
Innkeeper: Jane Leavitt
Rooms: 12 w/pvt. bath, cable TV
Rates: $89-$190, incl. full brk., evening refreshment
Credit cards: Most major cards
Restrictions: No children under 12, pets, smoking. Deposit req. 14-day cancellation
  notice req., less min. $10.00 fee.
Notes: Adobe inn built in 1894. Renovated in 1986. Sitting room. Lobby with bee-
hive fireplace. Deck overlooking the Eagle River. Furnished in rustic southwestern
style with Indian pottery, rugs. Hot tub.*

MONTROSE (6)

The Uncompahgre Lodge
21049 Uncompahgre Rd., Montrose, CO 81401
(303) 240-4000, (800) 820-1713-4819
Innkeeper: Richard and Barbara Helm
Rooms: 8 w/pvt. bath, TV
Rates: $45-$65, incl. full brk. Seasonal variations. Discount avail. for Senior citizens
  & Govt. employees.
Credit cards: Most major cards
Restrictions: No smoking. $30.00 deposit req. 7-day cancellation notice req.
Notes: Converted school building built in 1914, once used for social functions.
Completely restored with 12 and 14 foot ceilings and remodeled. Decorated in

Early American, and safari decor. Dining room, gathering room with TV/VCR. FAX available. Handicapped access. French, Spanish spoken.*

OURAY (6)

The Damn Yankee
100 6th Ave., Box 709, Ouray, CO 81427
(303) 325-4291, (800) 845-7512, (303) 325-0502
Innkeeper: Mike Manley
Rooms: 8 plus 2 suites, all w/pvt. bath, phone, cable TV
Rates: $58-$115/room, $125-$145/suite, all incl. full brk., afternoon refreshment. Seasonal variations. Discount avail. for extended winter stay.
Credit cards: Most major cards
Restrictions: No children under 12, pets, smoking. 50% deposit req. 7-day cancellation notice req.
Notes: Three-story house built in 1981. Fully rebuilt and remodeled in 1990. Parlor with baby grand piano, wood-burning stove. Third-story enclosed viewing tower. Gazebo with hot tub overlooking stream. All guest rooms have private exterior entrances and share a common interior foyer.*

Historic Western Hotel B & B
210 7th Ave., Box 25, Ouray, CO 81427
(303) 325-4645
Innkeeper: Tom and Tammy Kenning
Rooms: 12, incl. 2/suites w/pvt. bath
Rates: $48/room, $78/suite, all incl. full brk.
Credit cards: Most major cards
Restrictions: No pets, smoking. One night's deposit req. One day cancellation notice req., less $10.00 fee.
Notes: All wood building built in 1894. Located on the western slopes. Furnished w/antiques. Restored to the turn-of-the-century charm with full bar and restaurant on premises. Jewelery store, hot springs pool. Listed in the National Historic Register. Limited handicapped access.

The Manor Bed & Breakfast
317 Second St., Box 745, Ouray, CO 81427
(303) 325-4574
Innkeeper: Joel and Diane Kramer
Rooms: 7 w/pvt. bath
Rates: $65-$80, incl. full brk., afternoon refreshment. Seasonal variations. Discount avail. for extended stay.
Credit cards: MC, V
Restrictions: No children under 12, pets, smoking. Min. one night's deposit req. 10-day cancellation notice req., less $20.00 fee.
Notes: Three-story Georgian-Victorian hybrid manor house built in 1890. Parlor with TV, fireplace. Furnished with period pieces. Common area with phone. Patio, porch, second-floor balcony overlooking grounds, terraced gardens. Lawn games available. Massages available. Listed on the National Register of Historic Places. Recipient of The Historical Society's Preservation Award.*

St. Elmo Hotel
426 Main St., Box 667, Ouray, CO 81427
(303) 325-4951, (303) 325-0348

ELMO HOTEL

Innkeeper: Dan and Sandy Lingenfelter
Rooms: 7 plus 2 suites, all w/pvt. bath
Rates: $58-$84/room, $65-$94/suite, incl. full brk. Seasonal variations. Special
pkgs. avail.
Credit cards: Most major cards
Restrictions: No pets, smoking. Min. one-night's deposit req. 7-day cancellation
notice req. 2-night min. stay on holidays.
Notes: Built in 1898. Fully restored with leaded-glass, brass, polished wood and wallpapers of the Victorian era. Lobby. Parlor with TV, library. Breakfast room. Furnished with antiques. Hot tub, indoor sauna. Restaurant on premises. Guests have
access to ½ price lift tickets.*

PAGOSA SPRINGS (6)

Echo Manor Inn
3366 Hwy. 84, Pagosa Springs, CO 81147
(303) 264-5646, (303) 264-4617

Innkeeper: Sandy and Ginny Northcutt
Rooms: 9, incl. 5 w/pvt. bath, incl. 2/suites w/pvt. bath, 1 w/fireplace
Rates: $75-$125, incl. full brk. Discount avail. for extended stay.
Credit cards: Most major cards
Restrictions: No children under 10, pets, smoking. One night deposit req. 14-days
min. cancellation notice req., less $10.00 fee. 2-night min stay. 3-night min. stay
during Christmas.
Notes: The four-story Dutch Tudor tower sits on 10,000 sg. ft. over looking San Juan
Mountains. Complete w/turrets, tower, and gables. French country breakfast room,
porch with hot tub in the middle. Game room, deck. Small private parties accommodated.*

PUEBLO (7)

Abriendo Inn
300 W. Abriendo Ave., Pueblo, CO 81004
(719) 544-2703, (719) 544-1806

Innkeeper: Kerrelyn M.Trent
Rooms: 7, incl. 1 suite, all w/pvt. bath, phone, TV

ABRIENDO INN

Rates: $49-$85/room, $78-$83/suite, all incl. full brk.

Credit cards: Most major cards

Restrictions: No children under 7, pets. Smoking restricted. Deposit req. 7-day cancellation notice req.

Notes: Three-story four-square mansion built in 1906 for brewing magnate Martin Walter. Renovated in 1989. Dining room with oak wainscoting. Grand foyer with spiral staircase, stained-glass windows, fireplace. Living room, porches. Furnished with antiques, quilts, crocheted bedspreads, armoires and brass and fourposter beds. Listed on the National Register of Historic Places. Small private parties accommodated. Resident cats.*

REDSTONE (5)

Cleveholm Manor/Redstone Castle
0058 Redstone Blvd., Redstone, CO 81623
(303) 963-3463, (303) 963-1751

Innkeeper: Rose Marie Johnson and Cyd Lange

Rooms: 13, incl. 5 w/pvt. bath, plus 3 suites w/pvt. bath, incl. 1 w/fireplace

Rates: $95-$125/room, $180/suite, all incl. expanded cont. brk. Discount avail. for mid-week stay. Special pkgs. avail.

Credit cards: Most major cards

Restrictions: No smoking. 50% deposit req. 2-day cancellation notice req.

Notes: Stone manor house built in 1898. Located in Rocky Mountain setting. Fully restored with inlaid floors, gold leaf ceilings, marble fireplaces. Library, music room, game room, armory, board room, sun parlor, grand room with huge fireplace, dining room. Full bar. Decorated with tiffany chandeliers, Persian rugs, silk damask, leather and velvet wall coverings. Guests have access to kitchen. Lawn games. 200 acres of private trails. Small private parties accommodated. Spanish, French, German spoken. Handicapped access.*

SALIDA (5)

The Tudor Rose
6720 Paradise Rd., Box 89, Salida, CO 81201
(719) 539-2002, (800) 379-0889

Innkeeper: Jon and Terre Terrell

Rooms: 4 w/phone, TV, no pvt. bath, plus 2 suites, w/phone, TV, incl. 1 w/pvt. bath

Rates: $50-$65/room, $80-$105/suite, all incl. full brk. Discount avail. for extended stay. $7/horse, $4/dog.

Credit cards: Most major cards

Restrictions: No children under 1, smoking. Full pre-payment req. 72-hour cancellation notice req.

Notes: Two-story country tudor manor house built in 1979. Located on 37 wooded acres on Pinon Hill. Has operated as inn since 1995. Queen Anne-style living room. Den with TV, VCR, board games. Wine cellar. Deck with hot tub overlooking mountains. Horse stalls and paddocks, pet pens available.

SNOWMASS (5)

Starry Pines
2262 Snowmass Creek Rd., Snowmass, CO 81654
(303) 927-4202

Innkeeper: Shelley Burke

Rooms: 3 w/pvt. bath, incl. 1 apt. w/phone

Rates: $80/room, $100/apt., all incl. cont. brk., afternoon refreshment. Seasonal variations. Discount avail. for mid-week and extended stays.

Credit cards: Most major cards

Restrictions: No children under 7, pets, smoking. One night's deposit req. 30-day cancellation notice req., less $20.00 fee.

Notes: Contempory mountain house built in 1984. Balcony overlooking trout stream. Common room with vaulted ceiling, fireplace and TV. Hot tub. Picnic area. Horseshoes. Horses boarded.*

STEAMBOAT SPRINGS (1)

Oak Street B & B
P.O. Box 772434, Steamboat Springs, CO 80477
(303) 870-0484, (303) 870-0484

Innkeeper: Gary and Marianne Osteen

Rooms: 6 plus 6 suites, all w/pvt. bath, TV. Located in 2 bldgs.

Rates: $45-$95/room, $55-$110/suite, all incl. full brk. Seasonal variations.

Credit cards: MC, V

Restrictions: No pets, smoking. Deposit req. Cancellation notice req. 2-night min. stay.

Notes: Victorian house with private cottages built in 1930. Decorated with antiques. Meeting rooms available. Small private parties accommodated.*

Vista Verde Ranch, Inc.
P.O. Box 465, Steamboat Springs, CO 80477
(303) 879-1413, (800) 526-7433

Innkeeper: John and Suzanne Munn

Rooms: 3 plus 8 cabins w/fireplace, all w/pvt. bath. Located in 9 bldgs.

Rates: $300-$400, incl. full brk., lunch, dinner

Credit cards: None

Restrictions: No children under 5, pets, smoking. 25% deposit req. 60-day cancellation notice req.

Notes: Working cattle ranch. Hot tub. Sauna. Transportation to ski area. Ranch rodeo, mountain biking, fishing, barn dancing, supervised children's activities, cattle drives in June and September, rock climbing, river rafting, hot-air ballooning,

VISTA VERDE RANCH, INC.

hiking, cross country skiing, sleigh rides, dog sledding all organized. Spanish, French spoken. *

TELLURIDE (6)

Alpine Inn B & B
440 W. Colorado Ave., Box 2398, Telluride, CO 81435-2398
(303) 728-6282, (303)728-3424
Innkeeper: Denise and John Weaver
Rooms: 8, incl. 5 w/pvt. bath, TV, plus 1 suite w/pvt. bath, TV
Rates: $50-$180/room, $95-$200/suite, all incl. full brk., afternoon refreshment, apres ski in winter. Seasonal variations.
Credit cards: Most major cards
Restrictions: No children under 10, pets, smoking. Deposit req. Cancellation notice req., less fee. 3-night min. stay in winter. 7-night min. stay during summer festivals.
Notes: Two-story Victorian inn built in 1903 with a view of Imogene Falls. Parlor with fireplace. Sunroom. Furnished with handmade quilts and antiques. Front porch with wicker furniture. Hot tub.*

Bear Creek Bed and Breakfast
221 E. Colorado Ave., Box 2369, Telluride, CO 81435
(303) 728-6681, (800) 338-7064
Innkeeper: Colleen and Tom Whiteman
Rooms: 7 plus 3 suites, all w/pvt. bath, cable TV, phone. Located in 2 bldgs.
Rates: $55-$160/room, $80-$190/suite, all incl. full brk., afternoon and evening refreshment, discount lift tickets. Seasonal variations. Discount avail. for senior citizen, world ski association & extended stays.
Credit cards: Most major cards
Restrictions: No children under 10, pets, smoking. 50% deposit req. Min. 20-day cancellation notice req., less min. $25.00 fee. Min. stay req. on holidays, major festivals, regular ski season.
Notes: European style inn with sauna, steam room, central fireplace, roof-top deck.*

Johnstone Inn
403 W. Colorado, Box 546, Telluride, CO 81435
(303) 728-3316, (800) 752-1901, (303) 728-6395
Innkeeper: Bill Schiffbauer
Rooms: 8 w/pvt. bath, phone
Rates: $70-$140, incl. full brk. Seasonal variations.
Credit cards: Most major cards
Restrictions: No children under 10, pets, smoking. 50% deposit req. Min. 21-day
cancellation notice req., less $20.00 fee.
Notes: Restored Victorian inn built in 1894. Sitting room with fireplace. Victorian
marble and brass baths. Outdoor hot tub.*

The San Sophia
330 Pacific Ave., Box 1825, Telluride, CO 81435
(303) 728-3001, (800) 537-4781
Innkeeper: Gary and Dianne Eschman
Rooms: 16 w/pvt. bath, phone, cable TV
Rates: $70-$210, incl. full brk., afternoon refreshment. Seasonal variations. Special
pkgs. avail.
Credit cards: Most major cards
Restrictions: No children under 10, pets, smoking. $50.00 deposit req. Min. 30-day
cancellation notice req., less $20.00 fee. Closed April 8–May 4, Oct. 24–Nov. 24.
Min. stay req. during holidays and festivals.
Notes: New England/Victorian inn built in 1988. Bay windows overlooking water-
falls, 13,000 foot peaks, Coronet Creek. Observatory with telescope, maps. Li-
brary/lounge with collection of local and historical references. Dining area, decks.
Furnished in period country style with brass beds, handmade quilts. English garden, gazebo with sunken Jacuzzi. Concierge service, ski locker area, covered parking available.*

THE SAN SOPHIA

WINTER PARK (2)

Alpen Rose
244 Forest Tr., Box 769, Winter Park, CO 80482
(303) 726-5039

Innkeeper: Rupert and Robin Sommeraver
Rooms: 5 w/pvt. bath, phone, incl. 2 w/TV
Rates: $65-$95, incl. full brk., afternoon refreshment. Seasonal variations. Discount avail. for extended stay, directly-booked return visits.
Credit cards: Most major cards
Restrictions: No children under 12, pets, smoking. Min. one-night's deposit req. 7-day cancellation notice req. less $20.00 fee. 3-night min. stay in winter.
Notes: Two-story private home operated as inn since 1989. Decorated with Austrian furnishings. Located on wooded area. Queen-sized feather beds. Outdoor hot tub. Ice skating. Snow tubing. Sleigh rides. Common room with view of mountains. Deck. Handicapped access. German spoken.

WOODLAND PARK (5)

Woodland Inn Bed & Breakfast
159 Trull Rd., Woodland Park, CO 80863-9027
(719) 687-8209, (800) 226-9565, (719) 687-3112

Innkeeper: Nancy and Frank O'Neil
Rooms: 4, incl. 1 w/pvt. bath
Rates: $45-$65, incl. full brk. Seasonal variations. Discount avail. for extended and mid-week stays.
Credit cards: MC, V
Restrictions: Smoking restricted. One night's deposit req. 7-day cancellation notice req.
Notes: Two-story country inn built in 1955. Located on twelve wooded acres with vegetable, flower and herb gardens. Has operated as inn since 1995. Dining room with fireplace. Parlor, recreation room. Guest rooms decorated in country style with each room having a theme designed around woodland flowers and vines. Covered patio with BBQ grill. Lawn and board games available. Small private parties accommodated. Innkeeper is a licensed hot air balloon pilot. Resident dog and cat.*

YELLOW JACKET (6)

Wilson's Pinto Bean Farm
P.O. Box 252, Yellow Jacket, CO 81335
(303) 562-4476

Innkeeper: Arthur and Esther M. Wilson
Rooms: 2, no pvt. bath
Rates: $40-$50, incl. full brk. Seasonal variations.
Credit cards: None
Restrictions: No smoking.
Notes: Two-story farmhouse. Homecooked meals made from vegetables and fruit from owner's garden and meat grown on the farm.

Connecticut

CHESTER (5)

Inn at Chester
318 W. Main St., Chester, CT 06412
(203) 526-9541, (203) 526-4387
Innkeeper: Deborah Moore
Rooms: 42 w/pvt. bath, phone, TV, incl. 1 w/fireplace, plus 1 suite w/pvt. bath, phone, fireplace, TV
Rates: $85-$175/room, $195-$205/suite, all incl. cont. brk.
Credit cards: Most major cards
Restrictions: Deposit req. 24-hour cancellation notice req. 2 night min. stay on holiday wknds.
Notes: Two-story farmhouse, parts of which were built in the 1700s, located on 12 acres. Gameroom, with pool table, board games. Exercise room with sauna and massages available. Furnished with antiques and reproductions, oriental rugs and art work. Air-conditioned. Tennis and lawn games available. Restaurant and Tavern on premises. All meals available. Resident cat. Limited handicapped access.*

INN AT CHESTER

CLINTON (5)

Captain Dibbell House
21 Commerce St., Clinton, CT 06413
(203) 669-1646
Innkeeper: Helen and Ellis Adams
Rooms: 4 w/pvt. bath
Rates: $65-$85, incl. full brk., afternoon refreshment. Discount avail. for extended & senior citizen stays. Seasonal variations.
Credit cards: Most major cards
Restrictions: No children under 14, pets, smoking. Min. one night's deposit req. 7-day cancellation notice req. 2-night min. stay during holidays.

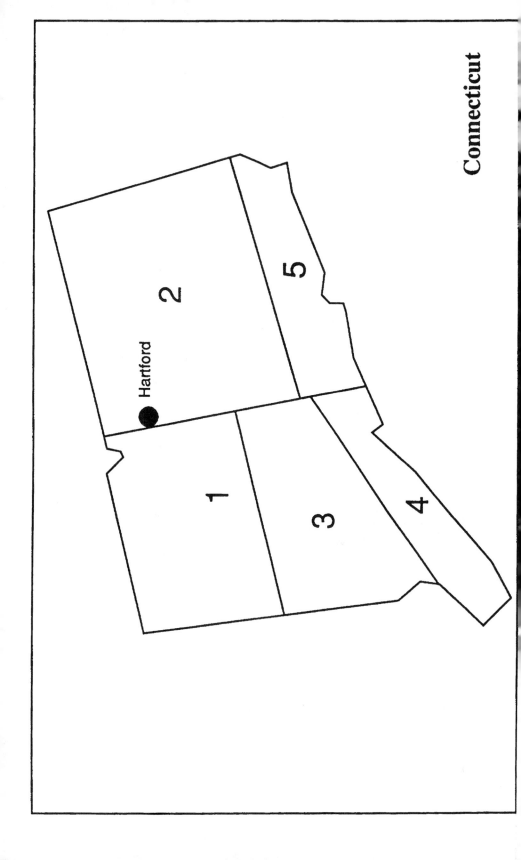

Connecticut

Notes: Three-story Victorian house built in 1866. Located on .75 acre with gazebo overlooking flower gardens, wisteria-covered footbridge. Living room with fireplace, player piano, TV, library. Dining room. Furnished with antiques, family heirlooms, auction finds. Special diets accommodated. Bicycles, beach chairs and towels, board games available. Complimentary bottle of champagne for guests celebrating a special occasion. Innkeepers collect original art by New England artists.*

COLCHESTER (2)

Hayward House Inn
35 Hayward Ave., Colchester, CT 06415
(860) 537-5772
Innkeeper: Bettyann and Stephen J. Possidento
Rooms: 2 w/pvt. bath, fireplace, plus 5 suites w/pvt. bath, incl. 3 w/TV, 1 w/fireplace. Located in 3 bldgs.
Rates: $65-$125/room, $65-$125/suite. Discount avail. for mid-week and extended stays.
Credit cards: Most major cards
Restrictions: No smoking. Prior approval req. for pets. Deposit req. 7-day cancellation notice req. 2-night min. stay on holiday wknds.
Notes: Restored Georgian Colonial from 1767, located on the Town Green in Colchester. Some guests have access to fully equipped kitchens.*

CORNWALL BRIDGE (1)

Cornwall Inn
Route 7, Cornwall Bridge, CT 06754
(800) 786-6884
Innkeeper: Emily and Lois, Robyn and Ron
Rooms: 11 plus 1 suite, incl. 11 w/pvt. bath. Located in 2 bldgs.
Rates: $50-$120/room, $85-$150/suite, all incl. full brk. Discount avail. for mid-week stay.
Credit cards: Most major cards
Restrictions: One night's deposit req. 7-day cancellation notice req., less $25.00 fee.
Notes: Two-story country inn built in 1871. Sitting room. Outdoor pool. Lounge and restaurant on premises. Handicapped access.*

COVENTRY (2)

Maple Hill Farm
365 Goose Lane, Coventry, CT 06238-1215
(800) 742-0635
Innkeeper: Tony Felice and Marybeth Gorke-Felice
Rooms: 4, incl. 1 w/pvt. bath
Rates: $65-$75, incl. full brk. Discount avail. for extended stay.
Credit cards: MC, V
Restrictions: No children under 3, pets. Smoking restricted. One night's deposit req. 2-week cancellation notice req., less $5.00 fee. Min. stay on Univ. of Conn. graduation, and parents' wknd.
Notes: Farmhouse built in 1731. Parlor with fireplace, videos and board games. Keeping room with fireplace, originally the kitchen. Breakfast room. Solarium with hot tub. Screened porch. Picnic areas, swimming pool. Spanish spoken.*

DURHAM (5)

The Durham B & B
36 Carriage Dr., Durham, CT 06422
(203) 349-3513

Innkeeper: Jack and Marge Stahl
Rooms: 3, no pvt. bath
Rates: $45-$60, incl. cont. brk.
Credit cards: None
Restrictions: Well-behaved pets welcome. No smoking. One night's deposit req. 24-hour cancellation notice req. Periodically closed.
Notes: Two-story Colonial house built in 1967. Sunroom, porch. Family room with TV. Upstairs sitting room with phone. Furnished in traditional style. Swimming pool. Children's crib, board and lawn games available. Flower and vegetable gardens. Russian spoken.

ESSEX (5)

The Griswold Inn
36 Main St., Essex, CT 06426
(203) 767-1776, (203) 767-0481

Innkeeper: William and Victoria Winterer
Rooms: 25 incl. 11 suites, all w/pvt. bath, phone, incl. 6 w/fireplace. Located in 4 bldgs.
Rates: $90/room, $95-$175/suite, all incl. cont. brk.
Credit cards: Most major cards
Restrictions: One night's deposit req. 48-hr. cancellation notice req.
Notes: Has operated as inn since 1776. Bar with potbellied stove, 4 dining rooms with fireplace, library of firearms dating from 15th century.

GLASTONBURY (2)

Butternut Farm
1654 Main St., Glastonbury, CT 06033
(203) 633-7197, (203) 633-7197

Innkeeper: Don Reid
Rooms: 2 w/pvt. bath, phone plus 2 suites w/pvt. bath, phone, TV, and 1 apt. Located in 2 bldgs.
Rates: $68/room, $73-$78/suite, $88/apt., all incl. full brk.
Credit cards: AE
Restrictions: Well-behaved children welcome. No pets, smoking. Deposit req., 10-day cancellation notice req., less $5.00 fee.
Notes: Colonial house with pumpkin-pine floors built in 1720. Fully restored. Furnished with 18th-century Connecticut antiques. Located on working farm. Wide brick fireplaces. Breakfast room. Herb gardens. Resident dairy goats, chickens, pigeons, pheasants, ducks, and a goose. German and French spoken.

Udderly Wooly Acres
581 Thompson St., Glastonbury, CT 06033-4030
(203) 633-4503

Innkeeper: Joan and Tom Kemble
Rooms: 1 w/pvt. bath, plus 1 suite w/pvt. bath
Rates: $40/room, $75/suite, all incl. full brk.

Credit cards: Most major cards
Restrictions: No smoking, pets. Deposit req. 15-day cancellation notice req.
Notes: Farmhouse built in 1820. Located on twenty acres. Guests have access to fresh vegetables, fruit, milk, eggs, and cheese in season.

HARTFORD (2)

THE 1895 HOUSE B & B

The 1895 House B & B
97 Girard Ave., Hartford, CT 06105
(203) 232-0014
Innkeeper: Connie and Bob Davis
Rooms: 2, no pvt. bath, w/phone, TV, plus 1 suite w/pvt. bath, TV, phone, seating area, sleep sofa, refrigerator
Rates: $60/room, $75/suite, all incl. full brk., afternoon refreshment. Seasonal variations. Discount avail. for senior citizens.
Credit cards: Most major cards
Restrictions: Children, pets, smoking restricted. Deposit req. Min. 24-hour cancellation notice req. Min. stay req., May–October.
Notes: Colonial Revival was built in 1895, and designed by a woman. Under present management since 1989. Fireplace, leaded windows. Dining room with a crystal chandelier and bay window. French, Italian.*

IVORYTON (5)

Copper Beech Inn
46 Main St., Ivoryton, CT 06442
(203) 767-0330
Innkeeper: Eldon and Sally Senner
Rooms: 13 w/pvt. bath, incl. 9 w/cable TV. Located in 2 bldgs.
Rates: $100-$160, incl. cont. brk. Seasonal mid-week variations.
Credit cards: Most major cards
Restrictions: No children under 8, pets. Smoking restricted. One night's deposit req. 5-day cancellation notice req. 2-night min. stay on wknds.
Notes: Victorian mansion with hardwood floors and Carriage House built in 1886. Refurbished in and has operated as inn since the early 1970s. Located on seven wooded acres with turn of the century gardens near Connecticut River. Three dining

rooms, foyer, porch. Furnished in country style with antiques, period furniture, Oriental rugs. Seasonal Award-winning country French restaurant, antique oriental porcelain gallery on premises. Limited handicapped access.

COUNTRY GOOSE B & B INN

KENT (1)

Country Goose B & B Inn
211 Kent Cornwall Rd., Kent, CT 06757-1203
(203) 927-4746
Innkeeper: Phyllis Dietrich
Rooms: 3, incl. 2 w/pvt. bath
Rates: $80, incl. cont. brk. Seasonal variations.
Credit cards: Most major cards
Restrictions: No children, pets, smoking. One night's deposit req. 7-day cancellation notice req., less $10.00 fee. 2-night min. stay on wknds. Closed March 1–April 10.
Notes: 18th-century Colonial house. Under present ownership for 7 years. Library with vintage magazines, formal parlor. Antique furnishings, watercolors by local artists. Original country kitchen with a working beehive oven. Gazebo in back meadow.

LEDYARD (5)

Applewood Farms Inn
528 Colonel Ledyard Hwy., Ledyard, CT 06339
(203) 536-2022, (203) 536-4019
Innkeeper: Tom and Frankie Betz
Rooms: 4 plus 2 suites, incl. 5 w/pvt. bath, 4 w/fireplace
Rates: $115-$125/room, $150/suite, all incl. full brk.
Credit cards: MC, V
Restrictions: No children under 10. Smoking restricted. Deposit req. 2-night min. stay on wknds. 3-night min. stay on holiday wknds.
Notes: Farmhouse built in 1826.*

MADISON (5)

Tidewater Inn B & B
949 Boston Post Rd., Madison, CT 06443-1190
(203) 245-8457, (800) 693-6198, (203) 245-8058
Innkeeper: Damon and Maryann Lizzi
Rooms: 10 incl. 2 suites, all w/pvt. bath, TV, incl. 2 w/fireplace
Rates: $100-$110/room, $150-$175/suite, all incl. full brk. Seasonal variations. Discount avail. for Corporate travelers.
Credit cards: Most major cards
Restrictions: No children under 13, pets, smoking. Full prepayment req. 2-night min. stay on July and Aug. wknds.
Notes: Built in late 1800s. Furnished with antiques and oriental carpets. Common room with baby grand piano and fireplace.

MYSTIC (5)

Harbour Inne & Cottage
15 Edgemont St., RFD 1 Box 398, Mystic, CT 06355
(860) 572-9253
Innkeeper: Charley Lecouras, Jr.
Rooms: 7 incl. 1 cottage, all w/pvt. bath, cable TV, incl. 2 w/fireplace. Located in 2 bldgs.
Rates: $35-$95/room, $125-250/cottage. Seasonal variations.
Credit cards: Most major cards
Restrictions: Deposit req. 2-week cancellation notice req. less 20% fee.
Notes: Picnic tables overlooking Mystic River. Guests have access to kitchen. Canoes, rowing boats available. Greek spoken. Handicapped access.*

PEQUOT HOTEL B & B

Pequot Hotel B & B
711 Cow Hill Rd., Mystic, CT 06355
(860) 572-0390, (203) 536-3380
Innkeeper: Nancy Mitchell
Rooms: 2 plus 1 suite, incl. 2 w/fireplace, all w/pvt. bath

Rates: $110-$115/room, $85/suite, all incl. full brk., evening refreshment. Seasonal variations.
Credit cards: Most major cards
Restrictions: No pets, smoking, 14-day cancellation notice req.
Notes: Greek Revival-style inn built in 1840 as stagecoach stop. Authentically restored. Located on 23 wooded acres with ponds and gardens. Two parlours with fireplaces, library, screened porch. Lawn games available.

NOANK (5)

PALMER INN

Palmer Inn
25 Church St., Noank, CT 06340
(203) 572-9000

Innkeeper: Patricia Ann White
Rooms: 6 w/pvt. bath, phone, incl. 1 w/fireplace
Rates: $125-$195, incl. cont. brk., afternoon refreshment
Credit cards: Most major cards
Restrictions: No children under 16, pets, smoking. 50% deposit req. 14-day cancellation notice req., less $20.00 fee. 2-night min. stay on wknds. from June–October.
Notes: Mansion built at turn of the century. Features antique furnishings, working fireplace in parlor, mahogany staircase, original wall-coverings, stained-glass windows. Sailing and Art classes offered. Victorian Christmas weekends offered.

NEW LONDON (5)

Queen Anne Inn
265 Williams St., New London, CT 06320
(860) 447-2600, (800) 347-8818

Innkeeper: Tracey and Jim Cook
Rooms: 10 plus 1 suite, incl. 8 w/pvt. bath, incl. 2 w/fireplace, 3 w/cable TV, 3 w/phone
Rates: $78-$145/room, $155/suite, all incl. full brk., afternoon refreshment. Discount avail. for mid-week, extended and off-season stays. Special pkgs. avail.
Credit cards: Most major cards

Restrictions: No children under 12, pets. Smoking restricted. One night's deposit req. 7-day cancellation notice req. 2-night min. stay on New Year's Eve and Valentine's Day.

Notes: Three-story Queen Anne Victorian mansion with tower built in 1880. Fully restored in 1989. Parlor, foyer, dining room, each with fireplace. Library, wraparound porch, Jacuzzi. Furnished with period antiques, artwork. Decorated in nautical theme. Antiques gallery on premises. Small private parties accommodated.*

NEW MILFORD (3)

The Homestead Inn
5 Elm St., New Milford, CT 06776
(203) 354-4080, (203) 354-7046

Innkeeper: Rolf and Peggy Hammer
Rooms: 14 w/pvt. bath, phone, cable TV. Located in 2 bldgs.
Rates: $72-$95, incl. cont. brk.
Credit cards: Most major cards
Restrictions: No pets. Smoking restricted. Deposit req. 2-day cancellation notice req. 2-night min. stay from May 1–Oct. 1, holidays and special wknds.
Notes: Two-story Victorian inn built in 1853. Has operated as inn since 1928. Lobby, living room. Front porch with rocking chairs. Rear patio. 6-room motel also on premises. Off-street parking available. Limited handicapped access.*

NORFOLK (1)

Manor House
69 Maple Ave., Box 447, Norfolk, CT 06058
(203) 542-5690, (203) 542-5690

Innkeeper: Hank and Diane Tremblay
Rooms: 7 w/pvt. bath, incl. 2 w/fireplace, plus 1 suite w/pvt. bath. Some rooms w/pvt. balconies, soaking tub, Jacuzzi.
Rates: $95-$160/room, $110-$160/suite, all incl. full brk., evening refreshment
Credit cards: Most major cards
Restrictions: No children under 8, pets, smoking. Deposit req. 10-day cancellation notice req., less $15.00 fee. 2-night min. stay on wknds. 3-night min. stay for holidays.
Notes: Two-story Victorian Tudor manor house built in 1898. Located on five acres with beehives, raspberry patch. Cherry-panelled foyer with Tiffany windows. Living room with fireplace, compact disc collection, piano. Sun porch, library, dining room. Furnished with antiques. Carriage, sleigh, hay rides available. Small private parties accommodated. French spoken.*

Mountain View Inn
69 Litchfield Rd., Rt. 272, Box 467, Norfolk, CT 06058
(203) 542-5595, (203) 542-6895

Innkeeper: Michele Sloane
Rooms: 7 w/pvt. bath, incl. 6 w/phone
Rates: $70-$125, incl. full brk. Seasonal variations. Discount avail. for mid-week stay.
Credit cards: Most major cards
Restrictions: No children under 12, pets. 50% deposit req. 14-day cancellation notice req. 2-night min. stay on holidays and during fall foliage.

MOUNTAIN VIEW INN

Notes: 2-story Victorian house built in 1875. Dining room, foyer, living room, bar, each with fireplace. Garden porch. Decorated with period furnishings. Restaurant on premises. All meals available. Small private parties accommodated.*

OLD GREENWICH (4)

Harbor House Inn
165 Shore Rd., Old Greenwich, CT 06870
(203) 637-0145, (203) 637-0145
Innkeeper: Dolly Stutting and Dawn Browne
Rooms: 23 w/TV, incl. 17 w/pvt. bath
Rates: $85-95, incl. cont. brk. Seasonal variations.
Credit cards: Most major cards
Restrictions: No pets, smoking. Deposit req. 2-day cancellation notice req.
Notes: Located near the ocean. Guests have access to kitchen, laundry facilities.

OLD LYME (5)

Old Lyme Inn
85 Lyme St., Box 787, Old Lyme, CT 06371
(860) 434-2600, (800) 434-5352, (860) 434-5352
Innkeeper: Diana Field Atwood
Rooms: 13 w/pvt. bath, phone, TV
Rates: $98-$144, incl. cont brk. Discount avail. for seasonal mid-week stay.
Credit cards: Most major cards
Restrictions: Min. $60.00 deposit req. 48-hour cancellation notice req. Closed Jan. 1–14.
Notes: Farmhouse with curly maple staircase, ornate iron fence built in the 1850s. Fully restored in 1976. Banistered front porch. Meeting room. Library with fireplace, TV. Four dining rooms, one with 19th-century chestnut paneling. Cocktail lounge with Victorian bar, fireplace. Furnished with handpainted murals, Empire and Victorian antiques. Gourmet restaurant on premises. Small private parties accommodated. Handicapped access.*

POMFRET CENTER (2)

Karinn B & B
330 Pomfret St., Pomfret Center, CT 06259
(203) 928-5492

Innkeeper: Karen Schirack, Ed Wurzel
Rooms: 6 w/pvt. bath, incl. 3 w/fireplace. Suites avail.
Rates: $70-$80/room, $90/suite, all incl. full brk., afternoon refreshment.
Credit cards: None
Restrictions: Well-mannered pets welcome. Smoking restricted. Min. 50% deposit req. 14-day cancellation notice req.
Notes: Three-story house built in the early 1900s as school for girls. Operated as inn from 1930-1960. Fully renovated in, and has operated as B & B since 1991. Grand foyer, library, TV room, music/bar room, game room. Porch, deck overlooking landscaped gardens. Furnished with leather, antiques, Oriental rugs.

RIDGEFIELD (3)

West Lane Inn
22 West Ln., Ridgefield, CT 06877
(203) 438-7323, (203) 438-7325

Innkeeper: Maureen Mayer
Rooms: 18 plus 2 suites, all w/pvt. bath, phone, cable TV, incl. 2 w/fireplace. Located in 2 bldgs.
Rates: $100-$165, all incl. cont. brk. Seasonal variations.
Credit cards: Most major cards
Restrictions: No pets. Credit card deposit req. 7-day cancellation notice req.
Notes: Victorian building built in 1847. Fully renovated in 1978. Breakfast room overlooking gardens. Pantry for light dining. Lobby with oak paneling, fireplace. Wrap-around front porch. Tennis court.

SIMSBURY (1)

Simsbury 1820 House
731 Hopmeadow St., Simsbury, CT 06070
(203) 658-7658, (203) 651-0724

Innkeeper: Wayne Bursay
Rooms: 30, plus 4 suites, all w/pvt. bath, phone, cable TV. Located in 2 bldgs.
Rates: $85-$125/room, $115-135/suite, all incl. cont. brk. Special pkgs. avail. Seasonal variations.
Credit cards: Most major cards
Restrictions: Deposit req. 2-day cancellation notice req. Min. stay on wknds., some holidays in spring and fall,
Notes: Handicapped access.*

TOLLAND (2)

Tolland Inn
63 Tolland Green, Tolland, CT 06084-0717
(203) 872-0800

Innkeeper: Susan Geddes Beeching and Stephen Beeching
Rooms: 7, incl. 5 w/pvt. bath, 1 w/fireplace, hot tub, 2 w/TV, plus 1 suite w/pvt. bath, TV, kitchen
Rates: $40-$120/room, $70-$90/suite, all incl. full brk., afternoon refreshment. Seasonal variations.
Credit cards: Most major cards
Restrictions: No children under 10, pets, smoking. One night's deposit req. 14-day cancellation notice req. 2-night min. stay on May–Oct. wknds.

Notes: Three-story colonial house built in 1800. Restored in and has operated as an inn since 1985. Three common rooms with hand-built furniture, fireplace, sunporch. Furnished with antiques.*

WESTBROOK (5)

Talcott House Bed & Breakfast
161 Seaside Ave., Box 1016, Westbrook, CT 06498
(203) 399-5020, (800) 972-6094
Innkeeper: Jim Fitzpatrick
Rooms: 4 w/pvt bath, phone, incl. 1/pvt. veranda
Rates: $125-$135, incl. full brk. Discount avail. for extended stay.
Credit cards: MC, V
Restrictions: No children under 11, pets, smoking. 50% deposit req. 2-night min. stay on wknds.
Notes: Two-story restored New England house. Located on oceanfront. Living room with fireplace. Lawn with view of water. Small private parties accommodated. *

WETHERSFIELD (3)

Chester Bulkley House B & B
184 Main St., Wethersfield, CT 06109
(203) 563-4236
Innkeeper: Frank and Sophie Bottaro
Rooms: 4, incl. 3 w/pvt. bath, 3 w/phone, plus 1 suite w/pvt. bath, phone.
Rates: $65-$85/room, $130/suite, all incl. full brk., afternoon refreshment. Discount avail. for mid-week stay.
Credit cards: Most major cards
Restrictions: No pets, smoking. Min. one night's deposit req. 7-day cancellation notice req.
Notes: Two-story Greek Revival structure with wide pine floors, hand carved woodworkbuilt in 1830. Fully renovated. Decorated with period pieces. Fresh cut flowers. Cot available. Parlor with working fireplace. Formal dining room with working fireplace. Television in common sitting room. Catering services available. Italian spoken.*

Delaware

CLAYMONT (1)

Darley Manor Inn
3701 Philadelphia Pike, Claymont, DE 19703-3413
(302) 792-2127, (800) 824-4703
Innkeeper: Ray and Judith Hester
Rooms: 2 w/pvt. bath, phone, TV, plus 3 suites w/pvt. bath, phone, TV, incl. 1 w/fireplace.
Rates: $59/room, $69-79/suite, all incl. full brk., afternoon refreshment. Discount avail. for extended stay.
Credit cards: Most major cards
Restrictions: No children under 12, pets. Smoking restricted. One night's deposit req. 72-hour cancellation notice req. 2-night min. stay at Thanksgiving and Christmas.
Notes: 2-story Manor house built in the late 1700s, expanded in 1840 and 1850. Fully renovated in 1991. Has operated as inn since 1993. Living room. Parlor with player piano. Library, meeting room, reading room. Wrap-around enclosed porch with wicker furniture, rocking chairs. Azalea garden with benches and 2-seat lawn swing, fountains, gazebo. All rooms include queen-sized beds, private baths, air conditioning, TV/VCR, and phones. Suites have refrigerators, coffee pots, and "warming" ovens. Listed on the National Historic Register. Small private parties accommodated.*

DEWEY BEACH (4)

Barry's Gull Cottage
116 Chesapeake St., Box 843, Dewey Beach, DE 19971
(302) 227-7000 in season, (703) 560-8127, (302) 227-7000
Innkeeper: Bob and Vivian Barry
Rooms: 3, incl. 1 w/pvt. bath, 1 w/phone, 1 w/fireplace, 1 w/TV
Rates: $85-$100, incl. full brk., afternoon and evening refreshment
Credit cards: Most major cards
Restrictions: No children under 13, pets, smoking. 50% deposit req. 14-day cancellation notice req., less $10.00 fee. 2-night min. stay on wknds. 3-night min. stay on holiday wknds.
Notes: Beach House Cottage built in 1962. Gull Cottage is a contemporary Nantucket-style Summer House one block from the ocean. The cottage received a First Honor Award from the American Institute of Architects, House and Home and Life Magazines in the Homes for Better Living Program. It is filled with antique wicker, quilts, and stained-glass. The B & B was opened in 1985, and was completely renovated in 1989. The renovation included adding a galley, lovers' suite and private bath, enlarging the porch, installing an enclosed hot tub, two decks, and twelve sky lights. There is a common TV, VCR, player piano, and fireplace. German spoken.

LEWES (4)

New Devon Inn
142 2nd St., Box 516, Lewes, DE 19958
(302) 645-6466, (800) 824-8754

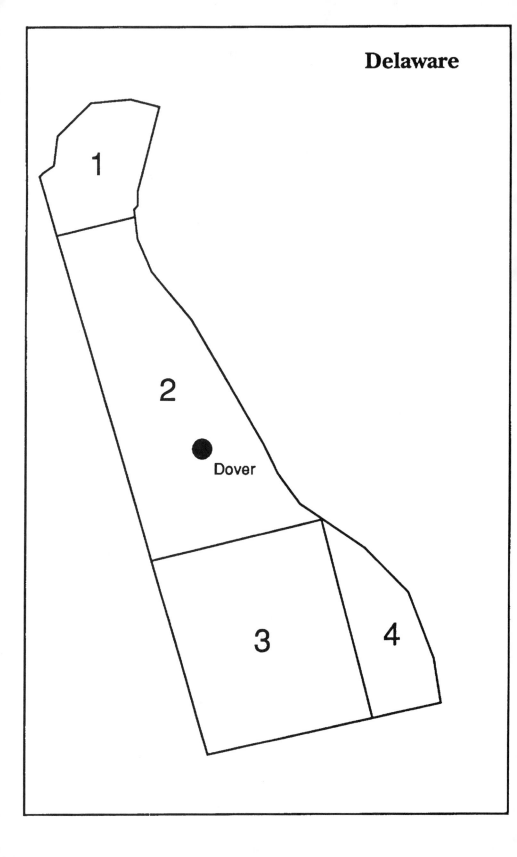

Innkeeper: Dale Jenkins, Bernie Nash
Rooms: 24 plus 2 suites, all w/pvt. bath, phone
Rates: $60-$105/room, $105-$145/suite, all incl. cont. brk. Seasonal variations. Discount avail. for mid-week stay. Special pkgs. avail.
Credit cards: Most major cards
Restrictions: No children under 16, pets. One night's deposit req. 3-day cancellation notice req. 2-night min. stay for in-season wknds. 3-night min. stay for some special events.
Notes: Three-story inn. Located in historic district. Furnished with antiques. Small private parties accommodated. Listed on the National Register of Historic Places.*

NEW CASTLE (1)

Jefferson House B & B
The Strand at the Wharf, New Castle, DE 19720
(302) 322-8944, (302) 325-1025
Innkeeper: Martha Rispoli
Rooms: 1 w/pvt. bath, phone, screened porch, plus 3 suites w/pvt. bath, TV, kitchen, incl. 2 w/fireplace, phone. Located in 2 bldgs.
Rates: $54-$85, incl. cont. brk. Discount avail. for extended stay.
Credit cards: Most major cards
Restrictions: No pets. Deposit req. 10-day cancellation notice.
Notes: 200-year old river front hotel. Jacuzzi.*

William Penn Guest House
206 Delaware St., New Castle, DE 19720
(302) 328-7736
Innkeeper: Richard and Irma Burwell
Rooms: 4, no pvt. bath
Rates: $45-$70, incl. cont. brk.
Credit cards: None
Restrictions: No children under 12, pets, smoking. Deposit req. 3-day cancellation notice req.
Notes: Brick house built in 1692. Located across from village green. Living room, patio. Furnished in 18th-century style. Italian spoken.

REHOBOTH BEACH (4)

Royal Rose Inn
41 Baltimore Ave., Rehoboth Beach, DE 19971
(302) 226-2535
Innkeeper: Kenny and Cindy Vincent
Rooms: 7, incl. 3 w/pvt. bath
Rates: $35-$115, incl. cont. brk. Seasonal variations. Discount avail. for mid-week stays. Special pkgs. avail.
Credit cards: None
Restrictions: No children under 6, pets, smoking. Deposit req. 72-hour cancellation notice req., less $15.00 fee. 2-night min. stay on wknds.
Notes: Beach cottage with screened porch. built in the 1920s. Furnished with antiques, period funiture.

Tembo Bed & Breakfast
100 Laurel St., Rehoboth Beach, DE 19971
(302) 227-3360

Innkeeper: Gerry and Don Cooper
Rooms: 6, incl. 1 w/pvt. bath
Rates: $60-$95/shared bath, $80-$95/pvt. bath, all incl. cont. brk.
Credit cards: None
Restrictions: No children under 12, smoking. Pets restricted. 50% deposit req. 14-day cancellation notice req. 2-night min. stay on wknds. from May 15–Sept. 30. 4-night min. stay on some holidays.
Notes: Two-story frame cottage built in 1935. Living room with fireplace. Furnished in early American style with antiques, fine art by Delaware artists, hand-braided rugs, elephant collection. Lawn and gardens with picnic table, brick walkways. Enclosed front porch with rockers, swing. Beach chairs, off-street parking available. Guests have access to kitchen. French spoken in summer.

SMYRNA (2)

The Main Stay
41 S. Main St., Smyrna, DE 19977
(302) 653-4293
Innkeeper: Phyllis E. Howarth
Rooms: 1 plus 1 suite
Rates: $45, incl. full brk.
Credit cards: Most major cards
Restrictions: No children under 8. Pets, smoking restricted.

District of Columbia

Capitol Hill Guest House
101 Fifth St. N.E., Washington, DC 20002
(202) 547-1050
Innkeeper: Mark
Rooms: 10
Rates: $45-$85, incl. cont. brk. Seasonal variations. Discount avail. for senior citizens.
Credit cards: Most major cards
Restrictions: No children under 8, pets, smoking. Deposit req. 7-day cancellation notice req.
Notes: Three-story Victorian rowhouse built in early 1900s. Located in historic district. Formerly home to U.S. Congressional Pages. Original woodwork and appointments. Small private parties accommodated. American sign language spoken.*

Kalorama Guest Houses
1854 Mintwood Pl. N.W., Washington, DC 20009
(202) 667-6369, (202) 319-1262
Innkeeper: Tami, John, Carlotta
Rooms: 28, incl. 12 w/pvt. bath, plus 2 suites. Located in 3 bldgs.
Rates: $45-$95/room, $85-$110/suite, all incl. cont. brk., evening aperitif. Discount avail. for extended and group stays.
Credit cards: Most major cards
Restrictions: Deposit req. 7-day cancellation notice req.
Notes: Victorian town houses built at the turn of the century. Located in the Embassy District. Parlor with fireplace. Breakfast room, garden courtyard. Furnished with Victorian antiques, artwork, Oriental carpets. Small private parties accommodated.*

The Reeds
P.O. Box 12011, Washington, DC 20005
(202) 328-3510, (202) 332-3885
Innkeeper: Janet Armbruster
Rooms: 7, incl. 1 apt., all w/TV, phone, incl. 1 w/pvt. bath
Rates: $50-$80/room, $65-$85/apartment, all incl. cont. brk. Seasonal variations. Discount avail. for extended stay.
Credit cards: Most major cards
Restrictions: No pets, smoking. $50.00 deposit req. Min. 48-hour cancellation notice req., less $15.00 fee. 2-night min. stay.
Notes: Three-story Victorian house with stained-glass, lattice porch built in 1890s. Has operated as Inn since 1984. Furnished with Victorian antiques. Player piano. Garden, terrace, fountains. Central air conditioning. Spanish, French spoken.

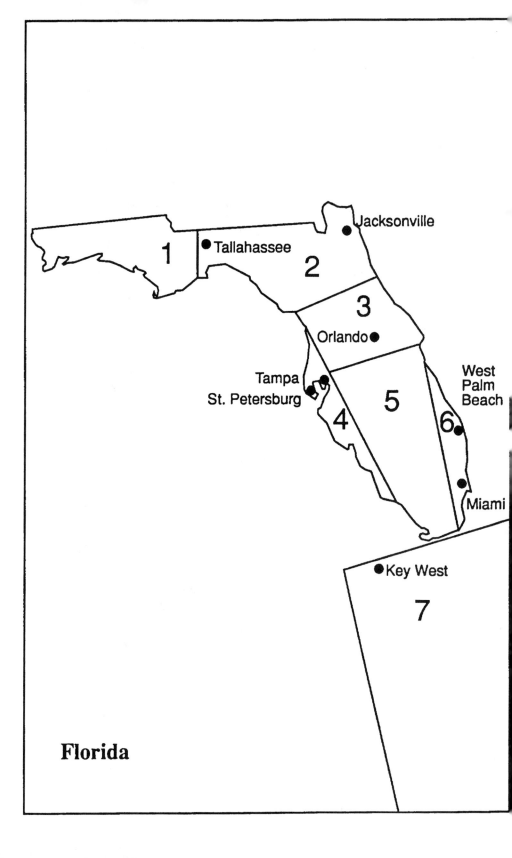

Florida

AMELIA ISLAND (2)

The 1735 House
584 S. Fletcher Ave., Amelia Island, FL 32034
(800) 872-8531, (904) 261-9200
Innkeeper: Gary and Emily Grable
Rooms: 6 suites w/pvt. bath, phone, TV. Located in 2 bldgs.
Rates: $85-95, incl. cont. brk. Special pkgs. avail.
Credit cards: Most major cards
Restrictions: No children under 12, pets. Smoking restricted. Min. one night's deposit req. Cancellation notice req. 2-night min. stay on wknds.
Notes: Two-story New England style beach house built in the 1920s. Living room. Furnished in nautical style with antiques. Lighthouse accomodations also available.*

Elizabeth Point Lodge
98 S. Fletcher, Amelia Island, FL 32034
(904) 277-4851, (904) 2776500
Innkeeper: David and Susan Caples
Rooms: 25 plus 3 suites, all w/pvt. bath, phone, cable TV. Located in 3 bldgs.
Rates: $95-$150, incl. full brk., evening refreshment. Discount avail. for AAA, and senior citizen stays.
Credit cards: Most major cards
Restrictions: No pets. Smoking restricted. Min. 50% deposit req.
Notes: Three-story 1890s "Nantucket shingle" style ocean front house. Has operated as inn since 1991. Furnished with fresh flowers and maritime photos. Sun room. Wrap-around porch with rockers. Fitness programs, daily special events for children and adults, bicycles, beach equipment, airport pick-up available. Handicapped access.*

The Fairbanks House
227 S. Seventh St., Amelia Island, FL 32034
(904) 277-0500, (800) 261-4838, (904) 277-3103
Innkeeper: Nelson and Mary Smelker
Rooms: 6 plus 4 suites, all w/pvt. bath, phone, TV. Located in 3 bldgs.
Rates: $85-$130/room, $125-$150/suite, all incl. cont. brk., afternoon refreshment. Discount avail. for extended and mid-week stays.
Credit cards: Most major cards
Restrictions: No pets. Smoking restricted. Deposit req. 7-day cancellation notice req.
Notes: Two-story Italianate villa with tower built in 1885. Fully restored. Located on one acre. Foyer with polished hardwood floors. Living room and formal dining room, each with fireplace. Furnished with antiques, period pieces and Oriental rugs. Four piazzas, courtyard, swimming pool, gardens. Small private parties accommodated. Listed on the National Register of Historic Places.*

BIG PINE KEY (7)

BARNACLE B & B

Barnacle B & B
Rte. 1, Box 780A, Big Pine Key, FL 33043
(305) 872-3298

Innkeeper: Wood and Joan Cornell
Rooms: 4 w/pvt. bath, phone, TV. Located in 2 bldgs.
Rates: $75-$100, incl. full brk.
Credit cards: Most major cards
Restrictions: No children. Deposit req. 10-day cancellation notice req. 2-night min. stay.
Notes: Two-story star-shaped villa with atrium built in 1980, hot tub. Cottage with patio overlooking pond. Private ocean beach with boat ramp, dock. BBQ, rafts, rubber boat, kayak, bicycles available. French spoken.*

Deer Run
Long Beach Dr., Box 431, Big Pine Key, FL 33043
(305) 872-2015

Innkeeper: Sue Abbott
Rooms: 2 w/pvt. bath, TV, plus 1 suite w/pvt. bath, TV
Rates: $75/room, $85/suite, incl. full brk. Seasonal variations.
Credit cards: Most major cards
Restrictions: No children, pets, smoking. 50% deposit req. 14-day cancellation notice req. 2 night min. stay.
Notes: Cracker-style, air-conditioned house located on oceanfront. Furnished with antiques, wicker, rattan. Bahama Fans. Veranda and spa. Handicapped access.*

CORAL GABLES (6)

Hotel Place St. Michel
162 Alcazar Ave., Coral Gables, FL 33134
(305) 444-1666, (305) 529-0074

Innkeeper: Stuart Bornstein
Rooms: 27 plus 3 suites, all w/pvt. bath, phone, TV.

Rates: $125/room, $165/suite, all incl. cont. brk., fruit basket. Discount avail. for seniors citizens.
Credit cards: Most major cards
Restrictions: No pets. Credit card deposit req. 48-hour cancellation notice req.
Notes: 3-story Spanish-style stone, stucco, and tile hotel built in 1926. Fully restored to original character with hand-tiled floors, vaulted ceilings, brass elevator. Furnished with antiques. Air conditioning. Lobby, piano bar, rooftop garden. French restaurant on premises. Spanish, French spoken. Handicapped access.*

DAYTONA BEACH (3)

Captain's Quarters All Suite Inn
3711 S. Atlantic Ave., Daytona Beach, FL 32127
(800) 332-3119
Innkeeper: Todd Morgan
Rooms: 25 suites w/pvt. bath, kitchen, phone, TV, incl. 2 w/VCR, 1 w/fireplace.
Rates: $65-$165, incl. full brk.
Credit cards: Most major cards
Restrictions: No pets. Deposit req. 48-hour cancellation notice req. Min. stay req. for special events.
Notes: Ocean front inn with private balconies. Handicapped access.

Coquina Inn
544 S. Palmetto Ave., Daytona Beach, FL 32114
(904) 254-4969, (800) 727-0678
Innkeeper: Jerry and Susan Jerzykowski
Rooms: incl. 1 w/TV, plus 1 suite, all w/phone
Rates: $75-$105/room, $195/suite, all incl. brk. Seasonal variations.
Credit cards: Most major cards
Restrictions: No children under 12, pets, smoking. 72-hour cancellation notice req. 14-day notice req. during holidays and peak season.
Notes: Three-story Coquina rock English house, polished wood floors, red tile roof built in 1912. Drawing room with fireplace and grand piano. Sunroom, dining room, second-floor terrace. Furnished with antiques. Garden patio. Bicycles, picnic lunches, shuttle service from Halifax Harbor Marina available.

DESTIN (1)

Henderson Park Inn Beachside B & B
2700 Hwy. 93 E., Destin, FL 32541
(904) 837-3700, (800) 336-4853, (904) 837-5390
Innkeeper: Susie Nunnelley
Rooms: 37 suites w/pvt. bath, phone, TV, incl. 2 w/firplace. Located in 2 bldgs.
Rates: $75-$260, incl. full brk. Seasonal variations.
Credit cards: Most major cards
Restrictions: No pets. $50.00 deposit req. 14-day cancellation notice req., less $50.00 fee. 3-night min. stay.
Notes: Queen Anne style house w/green mansard roof built in 1992. Not one room resembles the other. Decorated with portraits from the Impressionist period, Handcrafted Queen Anee antique reproductions. Pool, beachside sundeck. Barbecue, picnic area, beach chairs, umbrellas. Restraunt, Common area w/woodburning fireplace on premises. Guests have access to tennis, deep sea fishing, diving. Small private parties accommodated. Handicapped access.*

EAST LAKE WEIR (3)

Lakeside "Country" B & B
P.O. Box 71, East Lake Weir, FL 32133-0071
(904) 288-1396, (904) 237-0258
Innkeeper: Sandy and Bill Bodner
Rooms: 6 plus 1 suite, incl. 6 w/pvt. bath, 2 w/fireplace, TV
Rates: $45-$65/room, $75-$90/suite, all incl. full brk. Discount avail. for extended
stay. Seasonal variations.
Credit cards: None
Restrictions: No children under 4. Smoking restricted. One night's deposit req. 5-
day cancellation notice req. 2-night min. stay on holiday wknds.
Notes: Two-story lakeside inn built in 1882. Living room. Parlor with TV. Victorian
furnishings. Off-street parking available. Canoes available. *

LAKESIDE "COUNTRY" B & B

EDGEWATER (3)

Colonial House
110 E. Yelkca Terrace, Edgewater, FL 32132
(904) 427-4570
Innkeeper: Eva Brandner
Rooms: 3, w/pvt. bath, phone, TV
Rates: $52-$69, incl. full brk. Seasonal variations.
Credit cards: None
Restrictions: No children under 8, pets. Smoking restricted. Min. 20% deposit req.
2-night min. stay.
Notes: Two-story Colonial house built in 1928. Furnished in contemporary style.
Heated pool and Jacuzzi. German and French spoken.*

FERNANDINA BEACH (2)

The Bailey House
28 S. 7th St., Box 805, Fernandina Beach, FL 32034
(904) 261-5390
Innkeeper: Tom and Jenny Bishop

THE BAILEY HOUSE

Rooms: 5 w/pvt. bath, TV, incl. 2 w/fireplace
Rates: $75-$105, incl. expanded cont. brk. Seasonal variations.
Credit cards: Most major cards
Restrictions: No children under 10, pets, smoking. One night's deposit req. 2-day cancellation notice req. 2-night min. stay on holidays and special wknds. Closed on the Wednesday prior to Thanksgiving.
Notes: Queen Anne Victorian house with turrets, gables, bay windows built in 1895. Reception hall with wide stairway, fireplace, stained-glass windows. Parlor with pump organ, Victrola. Dining room. Veranda with swing, wicker rocking chairs. Furnished with period antiques. Pickup at City Marina and Amelia Island airport available by arrangement. Bicycles, including bicycle-built-for-two, available. Listed on the National Register of Historic Places. Handicapped access.*

Hoyte House
804 Atlantic Ave., Fernandina Beach, FL 32034
(904) 277-4300, (904) 277-9626
Innkeeper: Riat and John Kovacevich
Rooms: 8 plus 1 suite, all w/pvt. bath, phone, TV, incl. 4 w/fireplace
Rates: $75-$110/room, $120/suite, all incl. full brk. Discount avail. for extended and mid-week stays, and for senior citizens.
Credit cards: Most major cards
Restrictions: No children under 12, pets. Smoking restricted. Min. one night's deposit req. Min. 14-day cancellation notice req.
Notes: Queen-Anne style house built in 1905. Parlor with fireplace. Living room with fireplace. Furnished with antiques, reproductions. Board games and piano available. Off-street parking available. Handicapped access.*

The Phoenix's Nest
619 S. Fletcher Ave., Fernandina Beach, FL 32304
(904) 277-2129, (904) 261-2661
Innkeeper: Harriett Johnston Fortenberry
Rooms: 5 suites w/pvt. bath, TV
Rates: $65-$85, incl. cont. brk.
Credit cards: Most major cards
Restrictions: One night's deposit req. 72-hour cancellation notice req.

Notes: Two story house built in 1938. Each suite has own entrance and an ocean view. Guests have access to tennis and pool priviledges offered at nearby club. Bikes, boogie boards, VCRs, a video library, and 250-year-old magazine collection, fishing gear available.*

GAINESVILLE (2)

Magnolia Plantation
309 S.E. 7th St., Gainesville, FL 32601
(904) 375-6653
Innkeeper: Cindy and Joe Montalto
Rooms: 6, incl. 4 w/pvt bath, 2 w/fireplace
Rates: $60-$90, incl. full brk, refreshment. Discount avail. for extended and mid-week stays.
Credit cards: Most major cards
Restrictions: No children under 6, pets. Smoking restricted. One night's deposit req. 7-day cancellation notice req. 2-night min. stay for special events.
Notes: Two-story French Second Empire Victorian Mansion built in 1885. Fully restored. Veranda, gazebo. Garden with waterfalls and reflecting pond.*

HOLMES BEACH (4)

Harrington House B & B
5626 Gulf Dr., Holmes Beach, FL 34217
(813) 778-5444, (813) 778-0527
Innkeeper: Frank and Jo Davis
Rooms: 13 w/pvt. bath, fireplace, cable TV
Rates: $79-$169, incl. full brk. Discount avail. for extended and mid-week stays, May–Dec.
Credit cards: Most major cards
Restrictions: No children under 12, pets, smoking. One night's deposit req. 14-day cancellation notice req. Min. 2-night stay on wknds. and holidays.
Notes: Three-story beach house built in 1925. Remodeled in and has operated as inn since 1989. Living room with eighteen-ft. ceiling, fireplace. Breakfast room. Decks on three levels, walled courtyard. Furnished in eclectic style. Most guest rooms have balconies overlooking swimming pool, Gulf of Mexico. Handicapped access.*

JACKSONVILLE (2)

House on Cherry Street
1844 Cherry St., Jacksonville, FL 32205
(904) 384-1999, (904) 981-2998
Innkeeper: Carol Anderson
Rooms: 4 suites w/pvt. bath, TV, portable phone
Rates: $70-$85, incl. full brk., evening refreshment
Credit cards: MC, V
Restrictions: No children under 10, pets, smoking. One night's deposit req. 3-day cancellation notice req. 2-night min. stay during special events.
Notes: Colonial house built in 1912. Moved to its present location in 1919. Screened porch overlooking the St. John's River. Decorated with period antiques, Oriental rugs, tall case clocks, pewter, and collectibles. Recipient of 1989 Preserva-

tion Award from Jacksonville Historic Landmarks Commission. Innkeeper collects decoys. Air-conditioned.*

KEY WEST (7)

Andrew's Inn
Zero Whalton Ln., Key West, FL 33040
(305) 294-7730, (305) 294-0021
Innkeeper: Tim Gatewood
Rooms: 9, incl. 2-br. house, all w/pvt. bath, phone, TV. Located in 2 bldgs.
Rates: $98-$158, $178-278/house, all incl. full brk., open bar. Seasonal variations.
Credit cards: Most major cards
Restrictions: No children under 12, pets. 2-night deposit req. 7-day cancellation notice req.
Notes: Private entrances. Deck. French and Spanish spoken.*

The Banyan Resort
323 Whitehead St., Key West, FL 33040
(305) 296-7786, (800) 225-0639, (305) 294-1107
Innkeeper: Gilbert Russell and Martin J. Bettercourt
Rooms: 38 suites w/pvt. bath, phone, TV, kitchen, pvt. patio or balcony, fans. Located in 8 bldgs.
Rates: $115-$245. Seasonal variations. Discount avail. for extended stay.
Credit cards: Most major cards
Restrictions: No pets. Children restricted. Deposit req. 2-week cancellation notice req. 2-night min. stay on wknds. 3-night min. stay on holidays.
Notes: Six historic homes on the National Register of Historic Places. Tiki bar. 2 pools, outdoor Jacuzzi.*

DUVAL HOUSE

Duval House
815 Duval St., Key West, FL 33040
(305) 294-1666, (305)292-1701
Innkeeper: Richard Kamradt
Rooms: 29, incl. 4 suites, incl. 28 w/pvt. bath, 8 w/TV. Located in 7 bldgs.
Rates: $85-175/room, $120-200/suite, all incl. cont. brk. Seasonal variations. Discount avail. for mid-week stay.

Credit cards: Most major cards
Restrictions: No children under 10, pets. One night's deposit req. 7-day cancellation notice req.
Notes: Victorian buildings built in 1880s as a cigar factory. Breakfast room, TV room. Furnished with wicker, antiques, ceiling fans. Swimming pool, sun deck, tropical gardens.*

Heron House
512 Simonton St., Key West, FL 33040
(305) 294-9227, (305) 294-5692
Innkeeper: Fred Geibelt, Robti Framarin
Rooms: 20 w/pvt. bath, incl. 12 w/TV. Located in 4 bldgs.
Rates: $75-$195, incl. full brk. Seasonal variations.
Credit cards: Most major cards
Restrictions: No children under 16, pets. 2-night's deposit req. 14-day cancellation notice req., less 2-night's fee. Min. stay for special events.

Island City House Hotel
411 William St., Key West, FL 33040
(305) 294-5702, (800) 634-8230, (305) 294-1289
Innkeeper: Stan and Janet Carneal
Rooms: 24 suites w/pvt. bath, phone, TV. Located in 3 bldgs.
Rates: $95-$210, incl. cont. brk. Seasonal variations. Discount avail. for extended stay.
Credit cards: Most major cards
Restrictions: No pets. Deposit req. 7-day cancellation notice req.
Notes: Two-story Victorian mansion built in the 1880s. Converted into hotel in 1889. Fully restored with third floor added in 1912. Furnished in the turn of the century decor with antiques. Guests have access to kitchens, laundry facilities. Spacious private porches, ceiling fans. Swimming pool, deck, patio, Jacuzzi set in floral garden. French and German spoken. Will arrange snorkeling, fishing charter, diving, sailing adventures.*

THE POPULAR HOUSE

The Popular House
415 William St., Key West, FL 33040
(800) 438-6155

Innkeeper: Jody Carlson
Rooms: 6 plus 2 suites, incl. 4 w/pvt. bath. Located in 2 bldgs.
Rates: $69-$99/room, $79-$200/suite, all incl. cont. brk. Seasonal variations.
Credit cards: Most major cards
Restrictions: Children, smoking restricted. No pets. Deposit req. 14-day cancella-
tion notice req., less $10.00 fee. May req. min. stay.
Notes: Three-story Victorian house built about 1898. Decorated in Carribean style.
Jacuzzi and sauna. Listed on the National Register of Historic Places.*

SEASCAPE

Seascape
420 Olivia St., Key West, FL 32040-7441
(305) 296-7776, (305) 296-7776
Innkeeper: Alan Melnick
Rooms: 5 w/TV
Rates: $69-$109, incl. cont. brk., evening refreshment in winter. Seasonal variations.
Credit cards: Most major cards
Restrictions: No children under 15, pets. Smoking restricted. Two night's deposit
req. 14-day cancellation notice req., less $10.00 fee.
Notes: Built circa 1889. Recently restored. Features a tropical garden, heated
pool/spa, and sundecks. Listed on the National Register of Historic Places.

Tropical Inn
812 Duval, Key West, FL 33040
(305) 294-9977
Innkeeper: Dennis Beaver, Amanda Kesar
Rooms: 4, plus 3 suites, all w/pvt. bath, TV. Located in 2 bldgs.
Rates: $72-$98/room, $108-$139/suite. Seasonal variations.
Credit cards: Most major cards
Restrictions: One night's deposit req. 10-day cancellation notice req., less $5.00 fee.
2-night min. stay on wknds.
Notes: Two-story conch house. Fully restored. Listed on the National Register of
Historic Places.

Whispers B & B
409 William St., Key West, FL 33040
(305) 294-5969, (800) 856-7477
Innkeeper: John Marburg
Rooms: 7 w/TV, incl. 5 w/pvt. bath
Rates: $69-$150/room, incl. full brk. Seasonal variations.
Credit cards: Most major cards

WHISPERS B & B

Restrictions: No children under 8, smoking. Call about pets. Min one night's deposit req. 14-day cancellation notice req. 2-night min. stay on wknds. 3-night min. stay on holidays.

Notes: Older part of house built circa 1845. Newer part of house, built circa 1866, reflects a typical Greek Revival floor plan, but with Victorian embelleshments. The scuttles, porches, shuttered windows, and numerous doors show the Bahamian influence. Guests have access to private beach, workout room, and swimming pool. Listed on the National Register of Historic Places.*

MICANOPY (2)

Herlong Mansion
P.O. Box 667, Micanopy, FL 32667
(904) 466-3322

Innkeeper: H.C. (Sonny) Howard, Jr.
Rooms: 7 w/pvt. bath, plus 3 suites w/pvt. bath
Rates: $50-$105/room, $105-$135/suite, incl. full brk. Discount avail. for mid-week stay.
Credit cards: Most major cards
Restrictions: No pets, smoking. Deposit req. 7-day cancellation notice req. 2-night min. stay on football wknds.
Notes: Two-story Mid-Victorian house with leaded-glass windows, mahogany inlaid oak floors, Tiger oak and walnut paneling. Built in 1845. Encased within brick Classic Revival Southern Colonial design in 1910. Parlor. Furnished with period antiques. Front veranda with swings, rocking chairs. Garden with oak and pecan trees.*

Shady Oak B & B
P.O. Box 327, Micanopy, FL 32667
(904) 466-3476

Innkeeper: Frank James
Rooms: 4 plus 1 suite, all w/pvt. bath, TV
Rates: $75-$125, incl. full brk.
Credit cards: Most major cards
Restrictions: Smoking restricted. Deposit req. 7-day cancellation notice req., less $10.00 fee. 2-night min. stay on Gator home football wknds.

Notes: 19th-century mansion furnished with crafts, collectibles, and antiques. Screened porch. Located near University of Florida, theatres, gardens, and art centers.

MOUNT DORA (3)

The Emerald Hill Inn
27751 Lake Jem Rd., Mount Dora, FL 32757
(904) 383-2777, (904) 383-6701
Innkeeper: Diane Deckinger, Michael Wiseman
Rooms: 3 plus 1 suite, incl. 3 w/pvt. bath
Rates: $75-$115/room, $150/suite, all incl. expanded cont. brk. Discount avail. for extended stay.
Credit cards: MC, V
Restrictions: No children under 10, pets. Smoking restricted. 50% deposit req. 7-day cancellation notice req. 2-night min. stay on wknds, holidays, special events.
Notes: Ranch-style house built in 1941. Living room with cathedral ceiling, fireplace. Dining room with fireplace. Common room with phone, TV. Patio. Board games available. Dock on the lake. Handicapped access.*

Farnsworth House
1029 E. 5th Ave., Mount Dora, FL 32757
(904) 735-1894
Innkeeper: Dick and Sandra Shelton
Rooms: 5, incl. 3 suites, all w/pvt. bath, TV, kitchen w/microwave. Located in 2 bldgs.
Rates: $75-$95, incl. cont. brk. Discount avail. for senior citizen, off-season and extended stays.
Credit cards: Most major cards
Restrictions: No children under 12, pets, smoking. Min. one night's deposit req. 3-day cancellation notice req., less $15.00 fee.
Notes: Two story house built in late 1800s by Leander Farnsworth. Renovated in 1944 into apartment and carriage houses. Screened porch.*

Raintree House
1123 Dora Way, Mount Dora, FL 32757
(904) 383-5065, (904) 383-1920
Innkeeper: Dottie Smith
Rooms: 3 w/pvt. bath
Rates: $75-$100, incl. cont. brk., evening refreshment. Discount avail. for mid-week stay.
Credit cards: Most major cards
Restrictions: No children under 12, pets. Smoking restricted. Deposit req. 7-day cancellation notice req. Min. 2-night stay on festival wknds.
Notes: 1940s-era Raintree house. Large shade trees. Common room with TV, fireplace. Dining room. Decorated with Oriental, English, and American antiques, paintings, and prints. Porch.*

OCALA (3)

Seven Sisters Inn
820 S. E. Fort King St., Ocala, FL 34471
(904) 867-1170, (904) 732-7764

SEVEN SISTERS INN

Innkeeper: Bonnie Morehardt and Ken Oden
Rooms: 3 w/pvt. bath, phone, incl. 2 w/TV, plus 4 suites w/pvt. bath, incl. 2 w/phone
Rates: $105/room, $135/suite, incl. full brk., afternoon refreshment. Discount avail. for mid-week, senior citizen, and AAA stays. Special pkgs. avail.
Credit cards: Most major cards
Restrictions: No children under 12. Pets, smoking, restricted. One night's deposit req. 7-day cancellation notice req., less $10.00 fee.
Notes: Three-story Queen Anne-style Victorian mansion with gables, bays, red brick chimneys built in 1888. Fully restored in 1985. Club room with library, TV, board games. French Monet breakfast room. Furnished with antiques. Balustered porch. Flowering walkways, lawn games. Murder Mystery weekends. Small private parties accommodated. Spanish spoken. Limited handicapped access.*

ORANGE PARK (2)

The River Suites at the Club Continental
2143 Astor St., Box 7059, Orange Park, FL 32073
(904) 264-6070, (904) 264-4044

Innkeeper: Karrie Massee and Caleb Massee
Rooms: 16 w/pvt. bath, phone, TV, plus 6 suites w/pvt. bath, phone, TV, incl. 2 w/fireplace. Located in 2 bldgs.
Rates: $55-$130/room, $75-$115/suite, all incl. cont. brk. Discount avail. for extended stay.
Credit cards: Most major cards
Restrictions: Deposit req. 72 hour cancellation notice.
Notes: Mediterranean architecture mansion built in 1923. Pool, tennis, live entertainment, Jacuzzi, courtyards, gardens, private balconies, refrigerators, cable TV, microwaves available. Handicapped access.*

ORLANDO (3)

Court-Yard at Lake Lucerne
211 N. Lucern Circle E., Orlando, FL 32801
(800) 444-5289, (407) 246-1368

Innkeeper: Charles Meiner, Paula Bowers

Rooms: 6 plus 16 suites, all w/pvt. bath, phone, TV. Located in 3 bldgs.
Rates: $65-$85/room, $85-$125/suite, all incl. cont. brk., bottle of wine. Discount avail. for extended stay.
Credit cards: Most major cards
Restrictions: No pets. Smoking restricted. One night's deposit req. 2-day cancellation notice req.
Notes: Victorian style house built in 1883. Tropical gardens. Parlor with fireplace. Furnished with antiques.*

Perri House
10417 S. R. 535, Orlando, FL 32836
(407) 876-4830, (407) 876-0241
Innkeeper: Nick and Angi Perretti
Rooms: 6 w/pvt. bath, phone, TV
Rates: $69-$89, incl. cont. brk. Discount avail. for extended stay and senior citizens. Seasonal variations.
Credit cards: Most major cards
Restrictions: No pets, smoking. Deposit req. 3-day cancellation notice req. Min. stay req. on holiday wknds. and special events.
Notes: Country estate located on 20 acres. Screened gazebo. Sundeck. Pool and spa. Bird watchers paradise.*

RUSKIN (4)

RUSKIN HOUSE B & B

Ruskin House B & B
120 Dickman Dr. S.W., Ruskin, FL 33570-4649
(813) 645-3842
Innkeeper: Dr. A. M. Miller
Rooms: 2 plus 1 suite, all w/pvt. bath, phone, TV.
Rates: $45-55/room, $65/suite, all incl. cont. brk. Discount avail. for extended stay.
Credit cards: None
Restrictions: No children under school age, pets. Smoking restricted. Deposit req. 2-week cancellation notice req.
Notes: Two-story water-front house with high ceilings and hardwood floors, built in 1910. Located on three acres. Furnished in period antiques. Verandas on both stories.

Guests have access to laundry facilities and refrigerator. French spoken. Limited handicapped access.*

SAINT AUGUSTINE (2)

Carriage Way Bed and Breakfast
70 Cuna St., Saint Augustine, FL 32084
(904) 829-2467
Innkeeper: Bill and Diane Johnson
Rooms: 9 w/pvt. bath, phone, incl. 1 w/fireplace
Rates: $69-$105, incl. full brk., afternoon refreshment. Discount avail. for mid-week and senior citizen stays.
Credit cards: Most major cards
Restrictions: No children under 8, pets. Smoking restricted. Deposit req. 7-day cancellation notice req. 2-night min. stay on wknds.
Notes: Victorian house built in 1883. Located in historic district. Furnished with antiques and reproductions. Breakfast in bed, picnics, carriage tours, bicycles available.*

CASA DE LA PAZ B & B

Casa De La Paz
22 Avenida Menendez, Saint Augustine, FL 32084
(904) 829-2915
Innkeeper: Jan Maki
Rooms: 6 incl. 2 suites, all w/pvt. bath, TV, incl. 1 w/fireplace
Rates: $70-$110, incl. full brk., afternoon refreshment. Discount avail. for senior citizen, AAA, and extended stays.
Credit cards: Most major cards
Restrictions: No children, pets, smoking. Deposit req. 24-hour cancellation notice req. 2-night min. stay on wknds.
Notes: Two-story Mediterranean style building overlooking Mantanzas Bay. Porch with white wicker furnishings. Living room with fireplace. Walled garden.*

Castle Garden
15 Shenandoah St., Saint Augustine, FL 32084
(904) 829-3839

Innkeeper: Bruce Kloeckner
Rooms: 4 w/pvt. bath, incl. 1 w/phone, plus 2 suites w/pvt. bath—Jacuzzi, TV, incl. 1 w/phone
Rates: $55-$79/room, $100-$150/suite, all incl. full brk., evening refreshment. Discount avail. for extended, mid-week and senior citizen stays.
Credit cards: Most major cards
Restrictions: No children on wknds, pets. Smoking restricted. Min. one night's deposit req. 7-day cancellation notice req., less $10.00 fee. 2-night min. stay on wknds.
Notes: Castle of Moorish Revival design built in 1894. Coquina stone exterior. Solid wood floors. Furnished with antiques. Sun porch. Outdoor flower gardens. Bicycles available. Small private parties accommodated.*

The Kenwood Inn
38 Marine St., Saint Augustine, FL 32084
(904) 824-2116, (904) 824-1689
Innkeeper: Mark, Kerrianne, and Caitlin Constant
Rooms: 10 w/pvt. bath, phone, including 6 w/TV, plus 4 suites w/pvt. bath
Rates: $65-$95/room, $95/suite, all incl. full brk. Discount avail. for senior citizens.
Credit cards: Most major cards
Restrictions: No children under 8, pets, smoking. One night's deposit req. 7-day cancellation notice req. 2-night min. stay on wknds. 3-night min. stay on holiday wknds.
Notes: Three-story Victorian house with high ceilings built approx. 1865 as private residence. Fully renovated in 1984. Has operated as inn since 1886. Redecorated in 1989. Living room, dining room. Sun room with TV. Porches, walled courtyard with wrought-iron furniture and fish pond. Furnished with antiques, family pieces. Swimming pool, sunning area. Pecan, grapefruit, plum trees on grounds.*

OLD CITY HOUSE INN

Old City House Inn
115 Cordova St., Saint Augustine, FL 32084
(904) 826-0113, (904) 829-3798
Innkeeper: Robert and Alice Compton
Rooms: 5 w/pvt. bath, TV

Rates: $60-$105, incl. full brk., evening refreshment. Discount avail. for extended and mid-week stays.
Credit cards: Most major cards
Restrictions: Smoking restricted. Deposit req. 7-day cancellation notice req. 2-night min. stay on wknds. 3-night min. stay on some holidays.
Notes: Two-story Colonial Revival inn built in 1873. Fully restored in 1990. Located in historic district. Veranda, courtyard. Bicycles available. Award-winning restaurant/bar on premises.*

Old Powder House Inn
38 Cordova St., Saint Augustine, FL 32084
(904) 824-4149, (800) 447-4149
Innkeeper: Al and Eunice Howes
Rooms: 8 w/pvt. bath, plus 1 suite w/pvt. bath, TV
Rooms: $59-$95/room. $109/suite, all incl. full brk., afternoon and evening refreshment. Seasonal variations. Special pkgs. avail.
Credit cards: Most major cards
Restrictions: No children under 8, pets. Smoking restricted. Min. 7-day cancellation notice req. 2-night min. stay on wknds.
Notes: Two-story Victorian house built in 1899. Originally housed gun powder for nearby fort. Elaborate woodwork, high ceilings. Dining room. TV available. Furnished with antiques. Wrap-around verandas. Bicycles, including bicycle-built-for-two. 10-person Jacuzzi.*

St. Francis Inn
279 St. George St., Saint Augustine, FL 32084
(904) 824-6068, (800) 824-6062
Innkeeper: Stan and Regina Reynolds
Rooms: 14 w/pvt. bath, cable TV, incl. some w/fireplace. Located in 3 bldgs.
Rates: $49-$115, incl. cont. brk., admission to oldest house. Discount avail. for extended stay.
Credit cards: MC, V
Restrictions: Children restricted. No pets, smoking. One night's deposit req. 7-day cancellation notice req.
Notes: Three-story Spanish Colonial coquina house built in 1791. Expanded in 1888. Remodeled in 1925. Living room with TV. Balcony and patio overlooking garden courtyard. Swimming pool. Bicycles available.*

ST. FRANCIS INN

St. Francis Inn

The Secret Garden Inn
56½ Charlotte St., Saint Augustine, FL 32084
(904) 829-3678

Innkeeper: Nancy Noloboff
Rooms: 3 suites w/pvt. bath, phone, TV, kitchen, deck or patio
Rates: $79-$99, incl. cont. brk. Discount avail. for mid-week stay.
Credit cards: MC, V
Restrictions: No pets, smoking. One night's deposit req. 7-day cancellation notice
  req. 2-night min. on wknds. 3-night min. stay on some holidays.
Notes: Two-story house built in 1920s, named for Frances Hodgson Burnett's clas-
sic children's book. Has operated as an inn since 1991. All meals brought to suites.
Furnished with antiques and modern amenities. Garden, courtyard.

Southern Wind B & B
18 Cordova St., Saint Augustine, FL 32084
(904) 825-3623

Innkeeper: Dennis and Jeannette Dean
Rooms: 9 w/pvt. bath, TV, plus 5 suites w/pvt. bath, TV, incl. 1 w/fireplace. Cottage
  available. Located in 2 bldgs.
Rates: $60-$129/room, $75-$105/suite, all incl. full brk., evening refreshment. Sea-
  sonal variations. Discounts avail.
Credit cards: Most major cards
Restrictions: No children, pets. Smoking restricted. One night's deposit req. Min.
  7-day cancellation notice req. 2-night min. stay on wknds.
Notes: Two-story house, built of coquina masonry with columns. Formal dining
room. Furnished with antiques. Verandas. Nearby cottage suitable for families.*

Wescott House
146 Avenida Menendez, Saint Augustine, FL 32084
(904) 824-4301

Innkeeper: David and Sharon Dennison
Rooms: 8 w/pvt. bath, phone, cable TV, incl. 3 w/fireplace
Rates: $95-$150, incl. full brk. Seasonal variations.
Credit cards: MC, V
Restrictions: Children restricted. Deposit req. 7-day cancellation notice req. 2-night
  min. stay on wknds.
Notes: Built circa 1880s. Restored in 1983. Located on the Intracoastal Waterway. Fur-
nished with antigues, oriental rugs, brass, china, and crystal. Bicycles available for rent.*

WESCOTT HOUSE

SAINT PETERSBURG (4)

Bayboro House B & B on Old Tampa Bay
1719 Beach Dr. S.E., Saint Petersburg, FL 33701
(813) 823-4955, (813) 823-4955

BAYBORO HOUSE B & B ON OLD TAMPA BAY

Innkeeper: Gordon and Antonia Powers
Rooms: 4, incl. 1 suite, all w/pvt. bath, TV. Apartment avail.
Rates: $75-$85/room, $110/suite, $550 per week/apt., all incl. cont. brk., evening
    refreshment. Discount avail. for extended stay.
Credit cards: MC, V
Restrictions: No children, pets. Smoking restricted. Deposit req. 14-day cancellation
    notice req.
Notes: Two-story Queen Ann Victorian house built in 1905 on waterfront. Has op-
erated as an inn since 1982. Formal dining room. Parlor. Furnished with antiques.
Verandah with rockers, swing, chaise and wicker chairs. Beach towels, chairs avail-
able. Air-conditioned. Phone, fax, answering machine available.*

SAINT PETERSBURG BEACH (4)

Island's End Resort
1 Pass-A-Grille Way, Saint Petersburg Beach, FL 33706
(813) 360-5023, (813) 367-7890
Innkeeper: Millard and Jone Gamble
Rooms: 6 cottages, incl. 1 w/atrium and pvt. swimming pool, all w/pvt. bath, phone,
    cable TV/VCR/HBO. Located in 4 bldgs.
Rates: $68-$160, incl. cont. brk. 3 days per week. Seasonal variations.
Credit cards: MC, V
Restrictions: No pets. Min. $250 deposit req. 14-day cancellation notice req. 4-night
    min. stay on holidays.
Notes: Located directly on waterfront, bordered by Gulf of Mexico. Guests have ac-
cess to fully equipped kitchen, laundry facilities, babysitting. Gazebo. Dock avail-
able for fishing, shelling. Snorkeling, deep-sea fishing trips organized.
Handicapped access possible. Lithuanian, Latvian, Russian spoken.

SEASIDE (1)

The Dolphin Inn at Seaside
107 Savannah St., Box 4732, Seaside, FL 32459
(904) 231-5477, (800) 443-3146, (904) 231-1973,

Innkeeper: Mac McCullen, Nancy Judkins
Rooms: 2 w/pvt. bath, TV, VCR, refrigerator, incl. 1 w/phone
Rates: $95, incl. cont. brk.
Credit cards: Most major cards
Restrictions: No pets. Smoking restricted.
Notes: 3-story Victorian cottage with stained-glass windows and dolphin-shaped gingerbread trim. Guest rooms open onto veranda with view of the Gulf of Mexico. Shell collection. Common kitchen, living room, dining room. Spanish spoken.

THE BANYAN HOUSE

VENICE (4)

The Banyan House
519 S. Harbor Dr., Venice, FL 34285
(813) 484-1385, (813) 484-8032

Innkeeper: Chuck and Susan McCormick
Rooms: 1 plus 8 suites, all w/pvt. bath, cable TV, incl. 5 w/phone. Located in 3 bldgs.
Rates: $59/room, $79/suite, all incl. cont. brk. Discount avail. for extended stay. Seasonal variations.
Credit cards: None
Restrictions: No children under 12, pets. Smoking restricted. Min. $25.00 deposit req. 21-day cancellation notice req. 2-night min. stay.
Notes: Two-story Mediterranean-style house built in 1926. Living room with high beamed ceilings, Italian tile floors, sculptured fireplace. Garden courtyard, swimming pool, Jacuzzi, solarium. Bicycles, laundry services available.

WEST PALM BEACH (6)

West Palm Beach B & B
419 32nd St. Old Northwood, West Palm Beach, FL 33407-4809
(407) 848-4064, (407) 842-1688
Innkeeper: Dennis Keimel
Rooms: 2 w/pvt. bath, TV, plus Carriage House w/pvt. bath, TV, kitchennette. Located in 2 bldgs.
Rates: $75-$85/room, $95/Carriage House, all incl. cont. brk. Seasonal variations. Discount avail. for extended stay.
Credit cards: Most major cards
Restrictions: No children, pets, smoking. Deposit req. 2-week cancellation notice req. 2-night min. stay/room, 3-night min. stay/Carriage House during high season.
Notes: Cottage-style house with hardwood floors, carved fireplace built in 1937 as a private residence. Renovated and restored. Garden room, living room. Decorated in style influenced by tropical Florida and the Islands with art work by Eileen Seitz. White picket fence. Pool and sundeck. Bicycles available. Located in the Old Northwood Historic District.

Georgia

AMERICUS (4)

The Pathway Inn
501 S. Lee St., Americus, GA 31709
(912) 928-2078, (800) 889-1466, (912) 928-2078

Innkeeper: David and Sheila Judah
Rooms: 5 w/pvt. bath, phone, TV
Rates: $70-$110, incl. full brk., evening refreshment. Discount avail. for mid-week stay.
Credit cards: Most major cards
Restrictions: Small pets welcome. Smoking restricted. One night's deposit req. 72-hour cancellation notice req.
Notes: Two-story Greek Revival inn built in 1906. Has operated as inn since 1994. Parlor with grand piano. Library. Veranda with rocking chairs. Furnished with antiques.*

ATLANTA (2)

Ansley Inn
253 15th Street N.E., Atlanta, GA 30309
(404) 872-9000, (800) 446-5416, (404) 892-2318

Innkeeper: Tim Thomas
Rooms: 29, incl. 3 w/fireplace, plus 4 suites, all w/pvt. bath and Jacuzzi, wet bar, phone, cable TV.
Rates: $115-$157/room, $210-$500/suite, all incl. cont. brk., afternoon refreshment. Discount avail. for mid-week, extended stay.
Credit cards: Most major cards
Restrictions: Deposit req. 3-day cancellation notice req.
Notes: Two-story English Tudor mansion with Italian marble floors built in 1907. Has operated as boarding house for young, single women. Refurbished in 1987. Dining room, living room, parlor. Furnished with Chippendale, Queen Anne and Empire antiques, Oriental carpets. Concierge service, conference facilities, health club privileges, all meals available. Audio-visual equipment, fax and copy service available. Small private parties accommodated. Handicapped access.*

Beverly Hills Inn
65 Sheridan Dr. N.E., Atlanta, GA 30305-3121
(404) 233-8520, (800) 331-8520, (404) 233-8520

Innkeeper: Mit Amin
Rooms: 18 suites w/pvt. bath, phone, TV, kitchen
Rates: $74-$160, incl. cont. brk.
Credit cards: Most major cards
Restrictions: One night's deposit req. 72-hour cancellation req.
Notes: Three-story symmetrical inn built in 1929 with natural wood floors. Has operated as inn since 1982. Located in Buckhead area. Decorated with period furniture. Garden room, patio, library, Civil War room. Parlor with baby grand piano. TV lounge, laundry, game area, private balconies. Guests have access to Buckhead Towne Club. Handicapped access.*

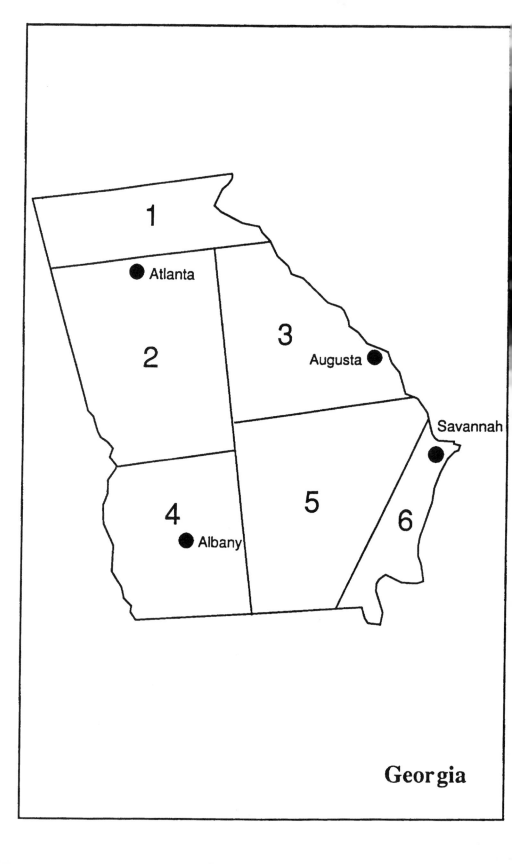

Georgia

BEVERLY HILLS INN

Little Five Points B & B
466 Seminole Ave., Atlanta, GA 30307
(404) 524-7660, (404) 524-7660

Innkeeper: Jane and Andy Fillo
Rooms: 1 plus 1 suite, all w/pvt. bath, phone, TV
Rates: $50-$80, incl. cont. brk. Discount avail. for extended stay.
Credit cards: Most major cards
Restrictions: No children, pets, smoking. 72-hour cancellation notice req.
Notes: Craftsman cottage with 11-ft. ceilings built in 1905. Fully restored. Private media room, living room. Swimming pool, Jacuzzi.*

Oakwood House
951 Edgewood Ave. N.E., Atlanta, GA 30307
(404) 521-9320

Innkeeper: Judy and Robert Hotchkiss
Rooms: 4 w/pvt. bath, phone
Rates: $60-$90, incl. cont. brk. Seasonal variations. Discount avail. for extended stay.
 Special pkgs. avail.
Credit cards: Most major cards

OAKWOOD HOUSE

Restrictions: No pets. Smoking restricted. Credit card number will hold room. Min. 72-hour cancellation notice req., less one night's fee. 2-night min. stay for special event periods.

Notes: Two-story frame house original woodwork, shutters and lace curtains built in 1911. Furnished in eclectic style. Two rooms have exposed brick hearths. Common areas have books, dark wicker and outdoor decks overlooking the oak tree. FAX, copier, word processor for guest use.*

The Woodruff Bed & Breakfast
223 Ponce de Leon Ave., Atlanta, GA 30308
(404) 875-9449, (404) 875-2882

Innkeeper: Joan and Douglas Jones

Rooms: 11 plus 2 suites, all w/phone, incl. 10 w/pvt. bath, 2 w/fireplace, 3 w/TV

Rates: $69-$250/room, $99-$295/suite, all incl. full brk. Discount avail. for extended stay.

Credit cards: Most major cards

Restrictions: No pets. Smoking restricted. 2-day cancellation notice req.

Notes: Three-story Victorian house with heart-carved stairways built in 1906. Fully restored. Living room, dining room, foyer, porches. Furnished with antiques. Spanish/French spoken.*

AUGUSTA (3)

The Oglethorpe Inn
836 Greene St., Augusta, GA 30901
(404) 724-9774, (706) 823-6623

Innkeeper: Fran Upton

Rooms: 16 plus 3 suites, all w/pvt. bath, phone, TV, incl. 10 w/fireplace. Located in 3 bldgs.

Rates: $85/room, $85-$150/suite, all incl. full brk. Discount avail. for senior citizens. Seasonal variations.

Credit cards: Most major cards

Restrictions: Smoking restricted. Deposit req. 2-day cancellation notice req.

Notes: 2 Victorian houses and carriage house. Built in late 1800s. Furnished with antiques. Outdoor hot tub. Private dinners available. Small private parties accommodated. *

BLAIRSVILLE (3)

Souther Country Inn
2592 Collins Lane, Blairsville, GA 30512
(706) 379-1603, (706) 379-3095

Innkeeper: Linda Sudnik

Rooms: 8, incl. 1 suite w/pvt. bath

Rates: $75-$85/room, $125/suite, all incl. full brk. Seasonal variations.

Credit cards: Most major cards

Restrictions: No children under 10, pets, smoking. 50% deposit req. One night's cancellation fee. 2-night min. stay on wknds.

Notes: Handicapped access.*

CLARKESVILLE (1)

Glen-Ella Springs
Bear Gap, Rte.3, Box 3304, Clarkesville, GA 30523
(706) 754-7295, (706) 754-1560

Innkeeper: Barrie and Bobby Aycock
Rooms: 14 w/pvt. bath, phone plus 2 suites w/pvt. bath, phone, fireplace
Rates: $100/room, $150/suite, all incl. full brk.
Credit cards: Most major cards
Restrictions: No pets. Smoking restricted. Deposit req. 72-hour cancellation notice req. 2-night min. stay on wknds, June–Nov.
Notes: Built about 1890. Fully restored in 1986. Located on seventeen acres with herb and perennial gardens surrounded by the Chattahoochee National Forest. Lobby, dining room, conference room. Sun deck overlooking swimming pool. Furnished with antiques, reproductions. Handicapped access. All meals available. Listed on the National Register of Historic Places.*

DARIEN (6)

Open Gates
Vernon Square, Box 1526, Darien, GA 31305
(912) 437-6985

Innkeeper: Carolyn Hodges
Rooms: 4, incl. 2 w/pvt. bath
Rates: $48-$53, incl. full brk., evening refreshment. Discount avail. for extended stay.
Credit cards: None
Restrictions: Children, pets, smoking restricted. 2-night min. stay on most wknds.
Notes: Built in 1876 as home for timber baron. Common room with Steinway piano, library. Furnished with antiques, family collections. Bicycling, canoeing. Private garden entrance to guest rooms.*

FLOWERY BRANCH (2)

WHITWORTH INN

Whitworth Inn
6593 McEver Rd., Flowery Branch, GA 30542
(404) 967-2386

Innkeeper: Kenneth and Christine Jonick
Rooms: 10 w/pvt. bath, incl. 3 w/TV
Rates: $55-$65, incl. full brk.
Credit cards: MC, V
Restrictions: No pets, smoking. Deposit req. 24-hour cancellation notice req.

Notes: Country inn located on five wooded acres. Two living rooms, dining room. Small private parties accommodated. Spanish spoken. Handicapped access.*

HAMILTON (2)

Wedgwood Bed and Breakfast
123 Old College St., Box 115, Hamilton, GA 31811
(404) 628-5659
Innkeeper: Hanice Neuffer
Rooms: 3 w/pvt. bath
Rates: $65-$75, incl. full brk. Seasonal variations.
Credit cards: Most major cards
Restrictions: No pets, smoking. Deposit req. 48-hour cancellation notice, less $5.00 fee. 2-night min. stay on some holidays and wknds.
Notes: Greek Revival house built in 1850. Library, living room with piano, den with VCR, screened porch with swing, patio. Furnished with period antiques. Decorated in Wedgewood blue with white stenciling.

HELEN (1)

Habersham Hollow Country Inn and Cab
Route 6, Box 6208, Helen, GA 30523
(706) 754-5147
Innkeeper: C. J. and Maryann Gibbons
Rooms: 3 w/pvt. bath, TV, plus 1 suite w/pvt. bath, TV, fireplace, pvt. porch. Located in 2 Cabins.
Rates: $95 and up/room, $125 and up/suite, $85 and up/cabin, all incl. cont. brk.
Credit cards: Most major cards
Restrictions: No children, smoking. 50% deposit req. 14-day canellation notice req.
Notes: Located on seven wooded acres. Cabins include fireplaces, wood, A/C, heat, color TV, deck with picnic table and grill, well-mannered pets welcome. Rooms open on to covered porch with rocking chairs.

MACON (2)

1842 Inn
353 College St., Macon, GA 31201
(912) 741-1842
Innkeeper: Phillip Jenkins
Rooms: 21 w/pvt. bath, cable TV, incl. some w/fireplace and whirlpool bath. Suite avail. Located in 2 bldgs.
Rates: $95-$125/room, $190-$250/suite. all incl. cont. brk, afternoon refreshment. Discount avail. for mid-week stay.
Credit cards: Most major cards
Restrictions: No Children under 12, pets. Credit card deposit req.
Notes: Greek Revival antebellum inn and adjoining Victorian house. Parlors. Library. Decorated with English antiques, Oriental carpets, tapestries and paintings. Courtyard and garden. Overnight shoe shines available. Listed on the National Register of Historic Places. Four Diamond Award winner. Small private parties accommodated. Handicapped access.*

MOUNTAIN CITY (1)

THE YORK HOUSE

The York House
York House Rd., Box 126, Mountain City, GA 30562
(800) 231-9675

Innkeeper: Jimmy and Phyllis Smith

Rooms: 12 plus 1 suite, all w/pvt. bath, cable TV, incl. 1 w/fireplace

Rates: $64-$69/room, $74-$79/suite, all incl. cont. brk. Special pkgs. avail.

Credit cards: Most major cards

Restrictions: No pets. Smoking restricted. Min. one night's deposit req. 10-day cancellation notice req.

Notes: Two-story Victorian house built as an Inn in 1896. Located on four wooded acres with two acres of lawns, spring house, picnic table. Parlor with fireplace, piano, TV. Game room with fireplace, community kitchen. Porch with rocking chairs. Second-story veranda. Decorated with period antiques. Featured in the movie *Deliverance*. Listed on the National Register of Historic Places. German and French spoken.*

NEWNAN (2)

Parrott-Camp-Soucy House
155 Greenville St., Newnan, GA 30263
(404) 253-4846

Innkeeper: Rick and Helen Cousins

Rooms: 4 w/pvt. bath, phone, fireplace

Rates: $95-$125, incl. full brk., afternoon and evening refreshment. Discount avail. for extended stay.

Credit cards: MC, V

Restrictions: No children under 15, pets. Smoking restricted.

Notes: Two-story Second Empire Victorian house built in 1842, redesigned in 1886 from Greek Revival house with oak, mahogany, cherry and maple wood throughout. Renovated in 1986 with thirteen foot ceilings, carved mantles, staircase and alcoves, original stained-glass windows and reproduction Victorian wallpapers. Located on four acres of formal gardens. Ladies parlor. formal dining room, library with columned fireplace, books, cassettes, and classic movie videos. Upstairs living hall with board games. Verandahs with cut-outs on railings. Heated swimming pool. Spa with gazebo. French and Spanish spoken. *

PARROTT-CAMP-SOUCY HOUSE

ST. MARY'S (6)

The Goodbread House
209 Osborne St., St. Mary's, GA 31558
(912) 882-7490

Innkeeper: Betty and Beorge Krauss
Rooms: 4 rooms w/pvt. bath, fireplace
Rates: $50-$60, incl. full brk., evening refreshment
Credit cards: Most major cards
Restrictions: None
Notes: Victorian house built circa 1870. Fully restored. Located in the heart of the National Register Historic District of St. Mary's, Georgia. Features high ceilings, seven fireplaces, upstairs and downstairs verandas, pine floors, original wood trim, and antiques.

The Historic Spencer House Inn
101 E. Bryant St., St. Mary's, GA 31558
(912) 882-1872

Innkeeper: Tom and Janet Murray
Rooms: 13 plus 1 suite, all w/pvt. bath, phone, TV
Rates: $65-$85/room, $100/suite, all incl. cont. brk.
Credit cards: Most major cards
Restrictions: No pets. Smoking restricted. Deposit req. 48-hour cancellation notice
    req. 2-night min. stay on holiday wknds.
Notes: Two-story Victorian inn with elevator, built as a hotel in 1872. Three verandas, dining room, parlor, meeting room, lobby. Furnished with antiques. Giftshop on premises. Bicycles available. Handicapped access.*

SAINT SIMONS ISLAND (6)

Little St. Simons Island
P.O. Box 21078, Saint Simons Island, GA 31522
(912) 638-7472, (912) 634-1811

Innkeeper: Debbie McIntyre
Rooms: 10 plus 1 suite, all w/pvt. bath, fireplace. Located in 4 bldgs.
Rates: $175-390/room, $300-$440/suite, incl. 3 meals daily. Seasonal variations.

Credit cards: Most major cards
Restrictions: No children under 6, pets. Smoking restricted. Deposit req. 45-days cancellation notice req. 2-night min. stay.
Notes: Island located on 10,000 acres, privately owned since 1908. Decks with rocking chairs to view river and marshes. Horseback riding, canoeing, fishing equipment, boats available.*

SAUTEE (1)

The Stovall House
Rte. 1, Box 1476, Sautee, GA 30571
(404) 878-3355
Innkeeper: Ham Schwartz
Rooms: 5 w/pvt. bath, incl. 1 w/fireplace
Rates: $70, incl. cont. brk. 10% discount for 3 or more nights stay. $63 Dec.-March
Credit cards: MC, V
Restrictions: No pets. Smoking restricted. Deposit req. 72-hour cancellation notice req.
Notes: Victorian farmhouse built in 1837. Located on twenty-eight acres. Restored in and has operated as inn since 1983. Parlor with fireplace, library, board games. Dining room. Wrap-around porch with rockers, mountain views. Furnished with antiques. Restaurant on premises. Small private parties accommodated. Listed on the National Register of Historic Places. Limited handicapped access.

SAVANNAH (6)

17 Hundred 90 Inn and Restaurant
307 E. President St., Savannah, GA 31401
(912) 236-7122, (800) 487-1790, (912) 236-7123
Innkeeper: Manager
Rooms: 13 plus 1 suite, all w/pvt. bath, phone, TV, incl. 12 w/fireplace
Rates: $89-$129, incl. cont. brk., evening refreshment. Discout avail. for mid-week and senior citizen stays. Seasonal variations.
Credit cards: Most major cards
Restrictions: Pets restricted. One night's deposit req. 2-day cancellation notice req.
Notes: Garden room. Dining room with fireplace. Furnished with Scalamandre Fabric and original antiques. Restaurant on premises.*

Ballastone Inn and Townhouse
14 E. Oglethorpe Ave., Savannah, GA 31401
(912) 236-1484, (800) 822-4553 in GA, (912) 236-4626
Innkeeper: Richard Carlson, Tim Hargus
Rooms: 15 w/pvt. bath, phone, TV, incl. 7 w/fireplace, plus 8 suites w/pvt. bath, phone, TV, incl. 6 w/fireplace. Located in 2 bldgs.
Rates: $95-$155/room, $175-$200/suite, all incl. cont. brk. Discount avail. for mid-week stay.
Credit cards: Most major cards
Restrictions: No children under 12. Pets restricted. Credit card number or full deposit req. 96-hour cancellation notice req.
Notes: Four-story Victorian-style antebellum mansion built in 1838. Townhouse was built in 1930s. Inn was fully restored in 1980 with Queen Anne staircase, elevator, ceiling fans. Parlor, library, full service bar, landscaped courtyard, garden. Furnished

BALLASTONE INN AND TOWNHOUSE

with 18th- and 19th-century furniture, art. Concierge service, off-street parking available. Handicapped access.*

Eliza Thompson House
5 W. Jones St., Savannah, GA 31401
(912) 236-3620, (800) 348-9378, (912) 238-1920
Innkeeper: Arthur Smith
Rooms: 25, w/pvt. bath, phone, cable TV. Located in 2 bldgs.
Rates: $88-$108, incl. full brk., evening refreshment. Seasonal variations.
Credit cards: Most major cards
Restrictions: Pets and smoking restricted. Deposit req. 2-day cancellation notice req.
Notes: Three-story Victorian town house with heart pine floors, built in 1847. Located in historic district. Parlor with "honor bar." Landscaped courtyard with 3 fountains. Furnished with antiques. Secretarial, concierge services available. Small private parties accommodated. Catering available. Spanish spoken.*

FOLEY HOUSE INN

Foley House Inn
14 W. Hull St., Savannah, GA 31401
(912) 232-6622, (800) 647-3708, (912) 231-1218

Innkeeper: Susan Steinhauser
Rooms: 20 w/pvt. bath, phone, cable TV, fireplace. Located in 2 bldgs.
Rates: $85-$195, incl. full brk., evening refreshment. Seasonal variations. Special
pkgs. avail.
Credit cards: Most major cards
Restrictions: No children under 6 months, pets. Smoking restricted. Deposit req.
72-hour cancellation notice req.
Notes: Three-story Victorian townhouses built in 1896. Fully restored in 1982. Parlor with hand-carved fireplace. Patio with hot tub. Two courtyards with fountains.
Furnished with antiques, reproductions, Oriental rugs. Concierge services available. Rated in Vacation magazine as one of the ten most romantic inns.*

The Forsyth Park Inn
102 W. Hall St., Savannah, GA 31401
(912) 233-6800
Innkeeper: Virginia and Hal Sullivan
Rooms: 8 w/pvt. bath, TV, incl. 3 w/fireplace, plus 2 suites w/pvt. bath, TV. Located
in 2 bldgs.
Rates: $85-$165/room, $115-$165/suite, all incl. cont. brk., evening refreshment.
Discount avail. for mid-week stay. Seasonal variations.
Credit cards: Most major cards
Restrictions: No pets. Deposit req. Min. 3-day cancellation notice req.
Notes: Two-story Queen Anne Victorian mansion with sixteen-foot ceilings, parquet
floors built in 1893. Parlor. Furnished with Queen Anne English antiques, reproductions, Oriental rugs. Veranda overlooking 75-acre Forsyth Park. Walled garden.
Some French spoken.*

THE FORSYTH PARK INN

Joan's on Jones
17 W. Jones St., Savannah, GA 31401
(912) 234-3863, (912) 234-1455
Innkeeper: Joan and Gary Levy
Rooms: 2 suites w/pvt. bath, phone, TV, kitchen
Rates: $85-$95, incl. cont. brk., evening refreshment
Credit cards: Most major cards

Restrictions: No smoking. Pets restricted. One night's deposit req. 14-day cancellation notice req. 2 night min. stay on wknds.

Notes: Three-story Victorian house in National Historic Landmark District. Original heart-pine floors, Savannah grey brick walls. Suites have their own sitting rooms, one with patio on garden, and antique furnishings. Air-conditioned. Some French spoken. Handicapped access.

LION'S HEAD INN

Lion's Head Inn
120 E. Gaston St., Savannah, GA 31401
(912) 232-4580, (912) 232-7422

Innkeeper: Christy Dell'Orco

Rooms: 4 w/pvt. bath, phone, TV, fireplace, plus 2 suites w/pvt. bath, phone, TV, incl. 1 w/fireplace

Rates: $85-$110/room, $110/suite, incl. expanded cont. brk., evening refreshment. Seasonal variations. Discount avail. for mid-week and senior citizen stays.

Credit cards: Most major cards

Restrictions: No pets. Smoking restricted. One night's deposit req. 7-day cancellation notice req. 2-night min. stay on wknds. and holidays.

Notes: Three-story Federal-style townhouse built in 1883. Located in historic district. Oak wood floors. Detailed wood and plaster molding, Savannah gray bricks, jib windows. Formal dining room with Waterford crystal chandelier. Double parlor, library. Furnished with Federal antiques. Veranda, marble courtyard with flowers. Handicapped access.*

Pulaski Square Inn
203 W. Charlton St., Savannah, GA 31401
(912) 232-8050, (800) 227-0650

Innkeeper: J. B. and Hilda Smith

Rooms: 8 plus 6 suites, incl. 6 w/cable TV, fireplace, pvt. bath, kitchen. Located in 2 bldgs.

Rates: $48-$88/room, $125/suite, all incl. full brk. Seasonal variations.

Credit cards: MC, V

Restrictions: No pets. Deposit req. 7-day cancellation notice req.

Notes: 4-story masonry townhouse built in 1853. Carriage House. Located in historic area. Restored with original random-width heart pine flooring, marble mantels, chandeliers. Furnished with antiques, traditional pieces, Oriental carpets. Garden courtyard.*

Remshart-Brooks House
106 W. Jones St., Savannah, GA 31401
(912) 234-6928

Innkeeper: Anne E. Barnett
Rooms: 1 suite w/pvt. bath, phone, TV
Rates: $75-$115, incl. cont. brk.
Credit cards: None
Restrictions: No children under 12, pets. One night's deposit required. 7-day cancellation notice req., less $5.00 fee. 2-night min. stay on wknds.
Notes: Four-story rowhouse built in 1853. Completely restored. Living room with antique game table. Kitchen. Furnished with country antiques. Terrace garden. Private front and rear entrances. Off-street parking available.*

REMSHART-BROOKS HOUSE

THOMSON (3)

1810 West Inn
254 N. Seymour Dr. NW, Thomson, GA 30824
(706) 595-3156, (800) 515-1810

Innkeeper: Virginia White
Rooms: 10 w/pvt. bath, phone, incl. 4 w/fireplace, plus 2 suites w/pvt. bath, phone, incl. 1 w/TV. Located in 3 bldgs.
Rates: $45-$64/room $65-$75/suite, all incl. cont. brk., evening refreshment. Discount avail. for group and mid-week stays.
Credit cards: Most major cards
Restrictions: No children under 12, pets. Smoking restricted. 2-day cancellation notice req.
Notes: Farmhouse and two country houses built in 1810. Located on 12 acres. Kitchen, screened veranda. Decorated with family memorabilia and antiques. Small private parties accommodated. Resident peacocks.*

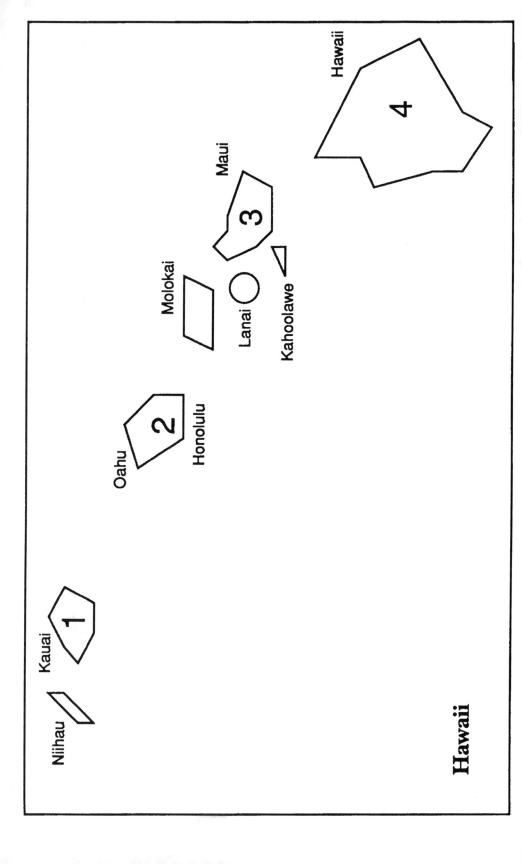

Niihau

Kauai

1

Oahu

2

Honolulu

Molokai

Lanai

Kahoolawe

Maui

3

Hawaii

4

Hawaii

Hawaii

HAIKU, MAUI (3)

Pilialoha B & B Cottage
255 Kaupakalua Rd., Haiku, Maui, HI 96708
(808) 572-1440, (808) 572-4612
Innkeeper: Bill and Machiko Heyde
Rooms: 1 cottage w/pvt. bath, kitchen, phone, TV, VCR, laundry facilities
Rates: $85, incl. cont. brk., afternoon refreshment. Dicount avail. for extended stay.
Credit cards: Most major cards
Restrictions: No pets. Smoking restricted. 50% deposit req. 14-day cancellation notice req.
Notes: Cottage fully furnished with vacation items such as picnic coolers, beach chairs/mats/towels, snorkel gear, informative books and videos. Breakfast brought to the cottage daily. Rose and flower garden. Japanese spoken.

HANA, MAUI (3)

Hana Plantation House
P.O. Box 489, Hana, Maui, HI 96713
(800) 228-4262, (808) 248-7867
Innkeeper: Blair Shurtleff
Rooms: 9 suites plus 1 studio, all w/pvt. bath, incl. 8 suites w/phone, TV. Located in 10 bldgs.
Rates: $70-$195, Discount avail. for extended stay.
Credit cards: Most major cards
Restrictions: No pets. Smoking restricted. 50% deposit req. 10-day cancellation notice req., less 10% fee. Min. 2-night stay.
Notes: 10 houses with living and dining areas, covered lanai's, outdoor decks with Jacuzzi tub/shower, tropical gardens. Small private parties accommodated.*

WAIPIO WAYSIDE B & B INN

HONOKAA, HAWAII (4)

Waipio Wayside B & B Inn
P.O. Box 840, Honokaa, Hawaii, HI 96727
(808) 775-0275, (800) 833-8849

Innkeeper: Jacqueline Horne
Rooms: 4, incl. 1 w/pvt. bath, plus 1 suite w/pvt. bath
Rates: $60-$90/room, $90-$100/suite, all incl. full brk. Dicount avail. for extended
    stay.
Credit cards: MC, V
Restrictions: No pets. Smoking restricted. One night's deposit req. 14-day cancella-
tion notice req., less $15.00 fee.
Notes: Sugar plantation manager's house built in 1938. Fully renovated. Deck with
2 double hammocks, gazebo. Living room with TV, VCR, video movies, handmade
Koa backgammon board, assortment of books on Hawaii from birding to history to
language. Furnished with family antiques, Chinese rugs.*

KAILUA, OAHU (2)

Akamai B & B
172 Kuumele Place, Kailua, Oahu, HI 96734
(808) 261-2227, (800) 642-5366
Innkeeper: Diane and Joe Van Ryzin
Rooms: 2 studios w/pvt. bath, phone, TV, kitchenette
Rates: $65, incl. full brk.
Credit cards: Most major cards
Restrictions: No children, pets, smoking. $14.00 per night deposit req. 3-night min.
    stay.
Notes: Library. Laundry facilities. Lanai, swimming pool, barbecue. Handicapped
access. French spoken.

Arnold & Leona's Vacation Rental
1191 Kupau St., Kailua, Oahu, HI 96734
(808) 261-2285
Innkeeper: Arnold and Leona Pereza
Rooms: 2 bdrm. apt w/pvt. bath, entrance, kitchen, balcony.
Rates: $95, incl. cont brk. first day
Credit cards: None
Restrictions: No pets. Smoking restricted. 2-night's deposit req. 2-day cancellation
    notice req. 3-night min. stay.
Notes: Dining room. Guests have access to washer, dryer and gas grill. Off-street
parking, evening airline service available.*

KAILUA-KONA, HAWAII, (4)

Hale' Maluhia B & B
76-770 Hualalai Rd., Kailua-Kona, Hawaii, HI 96740
(808) 329-5773, 329-1123, (800) 559-6627, (808) 326-5487
Innkeeper: Ken and Ann Smith
Rooms: 5 w/pvt. bath, TV, plus 2 cotages. Located in 3 bldgs.
Rates: $55-$110/room, $125-$210/suite, all incl. expanded cont. brk., evening re-
freshment. Discount avail. for extended stay. Special pkgs. avail.
Credit cards: Most major cards
Restrictions: Pets, smoking restricted. 50% deposit req. 30-day cancellation notice
    req.

Notes: Built in the 1970s. Has operated as Inn since 1991. Located on one-acre Hawaiian/Japanese garden setting at 900-ft. elevation. Library/game room with TV, VCR, video library, pool table, piano. Furnished with Victorian and Hawaiian antiques, wicker. Guests have access to lanais, kitchen facilites, stone spa, hot tub. Beach equipment, snorkle gear available. German, Japanese spoken. Handicapped access.*

KAMUELA, HAWAII (4)

Mountain Meadow Ranch
P.O. Box 1361, Kamuela, Hawaii, HI 96743
(808) 775-9376, (800) 535-9376
Innkeeper: Michael Cowan
Rooms: 4, no pvt. bath. Located in 2 bldgs.
Rates: $55, incl. cont. brk.
Credit cards: Most major cards
Restrictions: No pets, smoking. 72-hour cancellation notice req.
Notes: Located half-way between Kona and Hilo, 11 miles from Waipio Valley. Sauna available.

KAPAA, KAUAI (1)

Alohilani Bed & Breakfast
1470 Wanaao Rd., Kapaa, Kauai, HI 96746
(808) 823-0128, (800) 533-9316, (808) 823-1028
Innkeeper: Sharon C. Mitchell
Rooms: 1 cottage w/kitchen, pvt. bath, TV, plus 2 suites w/pvt. bath, microwave oven, refrigerator, TV. Located in 2 bldgs.
Rates: $95/cottage, $85/suite, all incl. cont. brk. Discount avail. for extended stay.
Credit cards: None
Restrictions: No pets, smoking. 50% deposit req. 3-night min. stay.
Notes: Tropical garden setting. Furnished with some antiques. Private sitting area in each guest room, plus sofa bed, ceiling fans, deck or lanai. Reservations for island activities can be arranged.*

House of Aleva
5509 Kuamo'o Rd., Kapaa, Kauai, HI 96746
(808) 822-4606
Innkeeper: Ernest and Anita Perry
Rooms: 3 w/phone, TV, incl. 1 w/pvt. bath
Rates: $40-$55, incl. cont. brk. Seasonal variations.
Credit cards: None
Restrictions: No children, pets. Smoking restricted. Deposit req.
Notes: Two-story house. Guests have access to beach towels/mats, snorkel gear, laundry facilities.*

Kealia Ridge Guest House
5366 Kumole St., Kapaa, Kauai, HI 96746
(808) 822-2886, (800) 316-8849, (808) 246-2618
Innkeeper: John and Paula Reardon
Rooms: 3 suites w/pvt. bath, incl. 2 w/TV
Rates: $600/week, incl. cont. brk. Seasonal variations. Discount avail. for group stay.

Credit cards: None
Restrictions: No pets, smoking. 50% deposit req. 48-hour cancellation notice req., less $85.00 fee. 3-night min. stay.
Notes: Guests have access to kitchen. Wrap-around deck.*

KEAAU, HAWAII (4)

Rainforest Retreat Guest Ranch
HCR 1 Box 5655, Aulii & 36th, Keaau, Hawaii, HI 96749
(808) 982-9601, (808) 966-6898
Innkeeper: Lori Cambell, Mark Wilmm, Lynn Bob
Rooms: 1 room, plus 1 suite, all w/pvt. bath, phone
Rates: $59/room, $69/suite, all incl. full brk.
Credit cards: MC, V
Restrictions: No pets. Smoking restricted. One night's deposit req. 24-hour cancellation notice req.
Notes: Two story house offers views of Mauna Kea and a hot tub. Located near Hawaii Volcanoes National Park, tide pools, snorkeling bays, and tropical flower gardens.*

KEALAKEKUA, HAWAII (4)

Merryman's
P.O. Box 474, Kealakekua, Hawaii, HI 96750
(808) 323-2276
Innkeeper: Don and Penny Merryman
Rooms: 3 plus 1 suite, all w/pvt. bath, TV
Rates: $75-$95/room, $95/suite, all incl. full brk.
Credit cards: Most major cards
Restrictions: No pets. Smoking restricted. Deposit req. Cancellation notice req.
Notes: Beach supplies available.*

KIHEI, MAUI (3)

Jasmine House
883 Kupulau Dr., Kihei, Maui, HI 96753
(808) 875-0400, (800) 604-4233, (808) 875-7324
Innkeeper: Art and Pat Pryor
Rooms: 4, plus 1 suite, plus cottage, all w/pvt. bath. Located in 2 bldgs.
Rates: $110-$125/room, $225/suite, $150/cottage, all incl. cont. brk., evening refreshment.
Credit cards: Most major cards
Restrictions: No children under 16, pets. Smoking restricted. 50% deposit req. 14-day cancellation notice req., less 50% fee.
Notes: Two-story, colonnaded buildings. Located at 800-ft. elevation. Breakfast porch overlooking Pacific Ocean. Furnished with touches of Europe and the South Sea islands. Fruit trees, rose and spice gardens. Stress-reduction program available. Innkeeper Pat is a gourmet cook. Innkeeper Art is an enthusiast of early American history and the Oriental martial arts.*

Whale Watch House
726 Kumulani Dr., Kihei, Maui, HI 96753
(808) 879-0570, (808) 874-8102

Innkeeper: Patricia and Patrick Lowry
Rooms: 4 incl. 2 w/refrigerator, plus 2 suites w/kitchen, all w/pvt. bath, phone, TV. Located in 2 bldgs.
Rates: $65/room, $85/suite, all incl. cont. brk. Discount avail. for senior citizen and extended stays.
Credit cards: Most major cards
Restrictions: No children under 12, pets. Min. one night's deposit req. 60-day cancellation req. 3-night min. stay.
Notes: Cedar pole house, bordering dormant volcano. Tropical garden with swimming pool and waterfall. Private entrances and decks. Two-story cottage w/thatched roof and handicapped access. Furnished with Oriental, English, and tropical American antiques.*

KILAUEA, KAUAI (1)

Hale' Ho'o Maha
P.O. Box 422, Kilauea, Kauai, HI 96754
(808) 828-1341, (808) 851-0291
Innkeeper: Kirby Guyer-Searles, Toby Searles
Rooms: 3 w/cable TV, phone, incl. 1 w/pvt. bath, 1 w/fireplace
Rates: $55-$70, incl. cont. brk., evening refreshment. Discount avail. for extended stay.
Credit cards: Most major cards
Restrictions: No children under 12, pets. 50% deposit req. 30-day cancellation notice req. 2-night min. stay.
Notes: Located on cliffs overlooking Hanalei Valley, Princeville. Has operated as inn since 1983. Living room, dining room, kitchen, lanai. Tropical garden. Common rooms with complete entertainment center, color cable TV, fireplace, salt water aquarium and bar area. Boogie boards, beach mats, towels, BBQ, laundry facilities available. Inn's name is Hawaiian for House of Rest. Spanish spoken.*

KOLOA, KAUAI (1)

Gloria's Spouting Horn B & B
4464 Lawai Beach Rd., Koloa, Kauai, HI 96756
(808) 742-6995
Innkeeper: Gloria and Bob Merkle
Rooms: 3 w/cable TV, refrigerator, ceiling fan, incl. 3 w/pvt. bath
Rates: $125-$150, incl. expanded cont. brk., evening refreshment. Discount avail. for extended stay.
Credit cards: Most major cards
Restrictions: No children under 14 pets. Smoking restricted. 3-night's deposit req. Min. 30-day cancellation notice req., less $25.00 fee. 3-night min. stay. Guests must remove shoes prior to entering.
Notes: Tropical beach house 40-ft. from beach. Located within walking distance of the Spouting Horn. Dining room. Living room with piano, cable TV, VCR, board games, library. Furnished with English walnut and American oak antiques. Coconut palm hammock and lanai overlooking surf.

Victoria Place
3459 Lawai Loa Lane, Koloa, Kauai, HI 96756
(808) 332-9300
Innkeeper: Edee Seymour

Rooms: 3 plus studio apt., all w/pvt. bath, incl. 1 w/kitchen and laundry
Rates: $55-75/room, $95/studio, all incl. cont. brk., popcorn. Seasonal variations.
Credit cards: None
Restrictions: No children under 15, pets. Smoking restricted. 2-night deposit req.
    30-day cancellation notice req.
Notes: Two-story house. Has operated as inn since 1987. Lanai overlooking jungle,
cane fields, Pacific Ocean. Parlor with library, board games. Swimming pool, tropi-
cal flower gardens. Snorkels, fins available. Handicapped access.*

KULA, MAUI (3)

Kula View B & B
140 Holopuni Rd., Box 322, Kula, Maui, HI 96790
(808) 878-6736
Innkeeper: Susan Kauai
Rooms: 1 suite w/pvt. bath
Rates: $85, incl. cont. brk. Discount avail. for extended stay.
Credit cards: None
Restrictions: No children under 12, pets, smoking. 2-night min. stay.
Notes: Located at 2,000 ft. above sea level in rural area on slopes of dormant vol-
cano Haleakala. Private upper level suite surrounded by herb and flower garden.
Reading area, wicker breakfast nook with mini-fridge. Private entrance and deck.*

LAHAINA, MAUI (3)

Garden Gate Bed & Breakfast
P.O. Box 12321, Lahaina, Maui, HI 96761
(808) 661-8800, (808) 667-7999
Innkeeper: Ron and Welmoet Glover
Rooms: 1 w/pvt. bath, plus 1 suite w/pvt. bath, phone, TV. Located in 2 bldgs.
Rates: $50/room, $95/suite, all incl. full brk. Seasonal variations.
Credit cards: Most major cards
Restrictions: No pets. Smoking restricted. One night's deposit req. 14-day cancella-
    tion notice req., less $25.00 fee. Min 3-night stay.
Notes: Common room with phone, TV, books. Decorated with tropical garden-like
decor. Stream and fountain located in the garden. Some Spanish spoken.*

Old Lahaina House
P.O. Box 10355, Lahaina, Maui, HI 96761
(800) 847-0761, (808) 667-5615
Innkeeper: John and Sherry Barbier
Rooms: 3 plus 2 suites, all w/phone, TV, incl. 2 w/pvt. bath
Rates: $45-$60/room, $79-$95/suite, all incl. cont. brk.
Credit cards: Most major cards
Restrictions: No pets. Smoking restricted. 50% deposit req. 14-day cancellation no-
    tice req. 3-night min. stay.
Notes: Decorated in Hawaiian Isles. Tropical courtyard. Chemical-free swimming
pool.*

Tony's Place
13 Kauaula Rd., Lahaina, Maui, HI 96761
(808) 661-8040

Innkeeper: Tony Mamo
Rooms: 3, no pvt. bath
Rates: $55, incl. morning coffee or tea
Credit cards: Most major cards
Restrictions: No children under 7, pets. Smoking restricted. $100 deposit req. 30-day cancellation notice req. 2-night min. stay.
Notes: Bungalow built in 1990. Living and dining areas. Desk with phone and phone books. Porch area for guest use and smoking. Library. Guests have access to kitchen and laundry rooms. Coolers, beach mats available.

LANAI CITY, LANAI (3)

Hotel Lanai
P.O. Box A-119, Lanai City, Lanai, HI 96763
(808) 565-4700, (808) 321-4666, (808) 565-4713
Innkeeper: Richard Wood and Stacy Pierce
Rooms: 11 incl. 1 cottage, all w/phone, fireplace. Located in 2 bldgs.
Rates: $95/room, $135/cottage
Credit cards: Most major cards
Restrictions: No pets. One night's deposit req. 48-hour cancellation notice req.
Notes: Built in 1823. Retains original structure, but has recently undergone a complete renovation of guest rooms, kitchen, bar, dining, and public areas. Guest rooms feature country pine furnishings, patchwork quilts, hardwood floors. Enclosed veranda. Lawn games, horseback riding, swimming, snorkeling, sailing, and hiking activities available. Handicapped access.*

OCEAN VIEW, HAWAII (4)

South Point Bed & Breakfast
P.O. Box 6589, Ocean View, Hawaii, HI 96704
(808) 929-7466
Innkeeper: Cid and Randy Newberg
Rooms: 3 w/pvt. bath, incl. 1 w/pvt. deck
Rates: $55-$65, incl. full brk. Discount avail. for extended stay.
Credit cards: Most major cards
Restrictions: No pets. Smoking restricted. 2-day cancellation notice req.
Notes: Contemporary house built in 1982. Located at 2,000 ft. elevation in Ocean View Estates, thirty miles south of Capt. Cook. Wrap-around lanai overlooking gardens, ocean.*

PA'AUILO, HAWAII (4)

Sud's Acres B & B
43-1973 Paauilo Mauka Rd., Box 277, Pa'auilo, Hawaii, HI 96776-0277
(808) 776-1611, (808) 776-1592, (800) 735-3262
Innkeeper: Anita and Suds Suderman
Rooms: 2 w/pvt. bath, TV, incl. 1 w/pvt. entrance, plus 1 cottage w/microwave, TV. Located in 2 bldgs.
Rates: $65, incl. cont. brk. Discount avail. for extended stay.
Credit cards: Most major cards
Restrictions: No pets. $10.00 deposit req.
Notes: Phone in main house. Handicapped access.*

PUNALUU, OAHU (2)

Kahana Kai Estate
53-103 Kamehameha Hwy., Punaluu, Oahu, HI 96717
(808) 237-8431, (800) 462-4805, (808) 237-7343
Innkeeper: Larry and Sandra Thomas
Rooms: 3, no pvt. bath, plus 2 suites w/pvt. bath, phone, TV. Located in 2 bldgs.
Rates: $75/room, $150-$300/suite, all incl. cont. brk. Discount avail. for extended stay.
Credit cards: MC, V
Restrictions: No children under 1, pets. One night's deposit req. 3-week cancellation notice req.
Notes: Private estate with private gardens, Jacuzzi, and spas. Furnished in European and Asian styles. Grounds include croquet and practice putting green. Video available. 40' Catamaran available for charter. Private dock. Snorkle gear provided. Small private parties accommodated.

VOLCANO, HAWAII (4)

Chalet Kilauea at Volcano
P.O. Box 998, Volcano, Hawaii, HI 96785
(808) 967-7786, (800) 937-7786, (808) 967-8660
Innkeeper: Brian and Lisha Crawford
Rooms: 3 plus 1 suite w/pvt. entrance, pvt. bath, TV, radio, mini-kitchen, plus 5 vacation homes w/kitchen, wood-burning stove, fireplace
Rates: $75-$225, incl. full brk., afternoon refreshment
Credit cards: Most major cards
Restrictions: Deposit req. 72-hour cancellation notice req.
Notes: Jacuzzi, fireplace, library, garden. Gathering place with art, books, music, fireplace. Dining room. Rental cars available.

Hale' Ohia Cottages
P.O. Box 758, Volcano, Hawaii, HI 96785
(808) 967-7986, (800) 455-3803, (808) 967-8610
Innkeeper: Michael Tuttle
Rooms: 3 w/pvt. bath, plus 3 suites w/pvt. bath, incl. 2 w/fireplace. Located in 4 bldgs.
Rates: $60-$95, incl. cont. brk. Discount avail. for extended stay.
Credit cards: Most major cards
Restrictions: No pets. Smoking restricted. One night's deposit req. 14-day cancellation notice req., less 10% fee.
Notes: Located in botanical garden developed over a period of 60 years. Wisteria-covered gazebo. Breakfast is brought to your room. Handicapped access.*

Kilauea Lodge
P.O. Box 116, Volcano, Hawaii, HI 96785
(808) 967-7366
Innkeeper: Albert and Lorna Jeyte
Rooms: 11 w/pvt. bath, incl. 5 w/fireplace, plus 1 suite w/pvt. bath, fireplace. Located in 3 bldgs.
Rates: $90-$115/room, $115-$125/suite, all incl. full brk.
Credit cards: Most major cards

Restrictions: No pets. Smoking restricted. Deposit req. 72-hour cancellation notice
    req. less $10.00 fee.
Notes: Built in 1938 as a YMCA. Dining room with fireplace. Common room with
fireplace and library. Hardwood floors, koa tables. Gourmet restaurant on
premises. Handicapped access. German spoken.

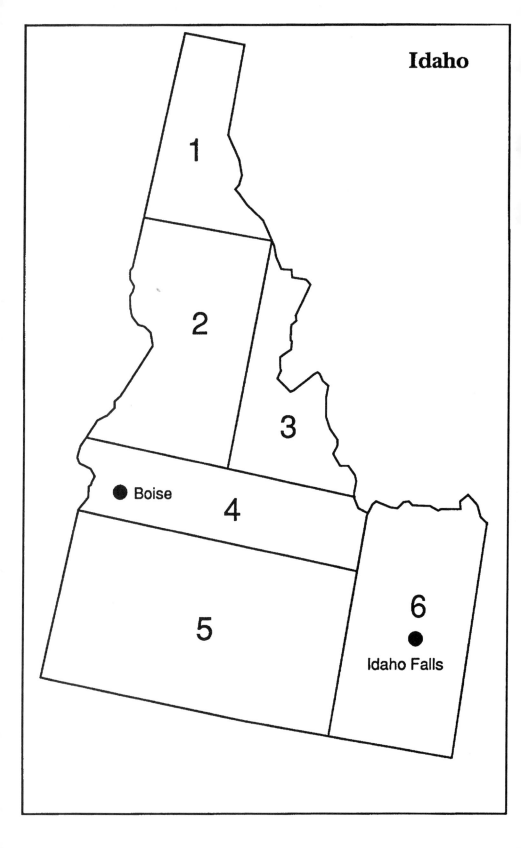

Idaho

1

2

3

● Boise

4

5

6

● Idaho Falls

Idaho

COEUR D'ALENE (1)

Greenbriar Inn
315 Wallace, Coeur d'Alene, ID 83814
(208) 667-9660, (800) 369-0026
Innkeeper: Kris McIlvenna
Rooms: 6 w/pvt. bath, incl. 4 w/phone, plus 2 suites w/pvt. bath, phone
Rates: $45-$80/room, $70-$125/suite, all incl. full brk., evening refreshment. Discount avail. for extended, govt., and sr. citizen stays. Seasonal variations. Special pkgs. avail.
Credit cards: Most major cards
Restrictions: No children under 3, pets, smoking. Deposit req. for 3-night stay. 7-day cancellation notice req.
Notes: Three-story red brick house built in 1908, with mahogany woodwork, winding staircases, hand-stenciled walls, gabled ceilings. Once operated as a boarding house. Parlor with fireplace. Library, TV room, front porch, hot tub. Furnished in French country decor with period antiques including down comforters from Ireland. Special workshops organized. Canoe and bicycle rental, all meals and gourmet catering available. Listed on the National Register of Historic Places. Small private parties accommodated. French spoken.*

GREENBRIAR INN

Gregory's McFarland House
601 Foster Ave., Coeur d'Alene, ID 83814
(208) 667-1232
Innkeeper: Winifred, Stephen, and Carol Gregory
Rooms: 5 w/pvt. bath
Rates: $90-$120, incl. full brk. Seasonal variations.
Credit cards: MC, V
Restrictions: No children under 14, pets, smoking. Deposit req. 14-day cancellation notice req. 2-night min. stay during high season and on holidays.
Notes: Three-story historical house built in 1905. Dining room. Living room. Family entertainment room with TV/VCR, phone, pool table. Decorated with lace, English

chintz, family heirlooms. Deck and summer house. Resident minister and professional photographer available for weddings.*

Warwick Inn
303 Military Dr., Coeur d'Alene, ID 83814
(208) 765-6565
Innkeeper: Jim and Bonnie Warwick
Rooms: 2 incl. 1 w/pvt. bath, plus 1 suite w/pvt. bath
Rates: $75/room, $105/suite, all incl. full brk., evening refreshement
Credit cards: Most major cards
Restrictions: No children under 12, pets. Smoking restricted. Deposit req. 7-day
  cancellation notice req., less 15% fee. 2-night min. stay on holidays. Reservations
  req.
Notes: Restored two-story house built in the early 1900s. Located in wooded area.
Fully renovated. Library, front porch, rear deck, patio. Furnished in Victorian and
Country French decor. Winner of Excellence in Lodging, and Preferred Establishment awards. Special dietary needs accommodated. Picnic baskets available with 2
day notice. Resident dogs.*

FISH HAVEN (6)

Bear Lake B & B
500 Loveland Lane, Fish Haven, ID 83287
(208) 945-2688
Innkeeper: Esther Harrison
Rooms: 4 incl. 1 w/pvt. bath, phone, TV
Rates: $65-$75, incl. full brk.
Credit cards: Most major cards
Restrictions: No children under 12, pets, smoking. Credit card deposit req.
Notes: Log home with deck, giftshop. Recreation room with TV, VCR. Outdoor
Jacuzzi. Cross-country skiing. German spoken.

IDAHO CITY (4)

Idaho City Hotel
215 Montgomery St., Idaho City, ID 83631
(208) 392-4290, (208) 392-4505
Innkeeper: Don and Pat Campbell
Rooms: 5 w/pvt. bath, TV, plus 1/suite w/pvt. bath, phone, TV. Located in 2 bldgs.
Rates: $31-$37/rooms, $43-$47/suites
Credit cards: Most major cards
Restrictions: Deposit req. 12-hour cancellation notice req.
Notes: Restored Old West inn furnished with antiques. Natural hot water swimming
pool. Lounge. Guests have access to kitchen. Ice-cream shop on premises.

IRWIN (6)

Swan Valley B & B
535 Swan Ln., Box 115, Irwin, ID 83428
(208) 483-4663, (800) 241-7926
Innkeeper: Jack and Kathy Lee
Rooms: 4, w/pvt. bath
Rates: $85 incl. full brk. Seasonal variations.

Credit cards: Most major cards
Restrictions: No pets. Smoking restricted. 25% deposit req. Reservations req.
Notes: Two-story log-cabin lodge. Located in wooded area on Snake River. Spa. Fireplace. Big screen TV. Cooking area. Barbeque area. Lounging deck. Guided fishing and scenic float trips available. Transportation to airport available. Handicapped access by June 1995.*

KOOSKIA (2)

Three Rivers Bed & Breakfast
HC75, Box 61, Lowell Hwy. 12, Kooskia, ID 83539
(208) 926-4430
Innkeeper: Mike and Marie Smith
Rooms: 15 w/pvt. bath, TV, incl. 2 w/fireplace, plus 15 suites w/pvt. bath, TV incl. 2 w/fireplace, plus motel. Located in 15 bldgs.
Rates: $50-$95/room, $50-$95/suite, $39/motel, all incl. full brk., evening refreshment. Seasonal variations.
Credit cards: Most major cards
Restrictions: Closed Nov.–Mar.
Notes: Main house built in 1924. Cabins, campsites built in early 1960s. Located on eighteen acres hill where the Lochsa and Selway Rivers combine to form the Clearwater River. Grocery store, giftshop, restaurant with antique pool table on premises. Front deck with Jacuzzi hot tub. Picnic table, swimming pool, lawn games available. Handicapped access. Small private parties accommodated. Raft trips offered. Bicycle for rent. Chinese spoken.*

LACLEDE (1)

River Birch Farm
P.O. Box 280, Laclede, ID 83841
(208) 263-3705
Innkeeper: Charles and Barbra Johnson
Rooms: 5, no pvt. bath
Rates: $65-$130, incl. full brk.
Credit cards: MC, V
Restrictions: No children under 12. Pets, smoking restricted. Deposit req. Min. 7-day cancellation notice req. 2-night stay during high season.
Notes: Two-story farmhouse built in 1903. Living room with fireplace. Den with TV/VCR. Dining room overlooking rvier. Wrap-around front deck overlooking scenic river. Hot tub house. Outside patio tables and chairs. Barbeque available. Outdoor activities available. Swedish spoken.*

LAVA HOT SPRINGS (6)

Riverside Inn
255 Portneuf, Box 127, Lava Hot Springs, ID 83246-0127
(203) 776-5504, (800) 733-5504, (208) 776-5504
Innkeeper: Duke and Joan Walden
Rooms: 16, incl. 12 w/pvt. bath
Rates: $45-$75, incl. cont. brk. Discount avail. for mid-week stay. Seasonal variations.
Credit cards: Most major cards
Restrictions: No smoking. Deposit req. 7-day cancellation notice req. 2-night min. stay on holidays.

Notes: Built in 1914 as hotel. Decorated with quilts, and antique dressers. Indoor swimming pools. Outdoor hot tub. Mineral hot springs. Small private parties accommodated.

LEWISTON (2)

Shiloh Rose B & B
3414 Selway Dr., Lewiston, ID 83501
(208) 743-2482
Innkeeper: Dorthy Mader
Rooms: 1 suite w/pvt. bath, phone, wood stove, TV, VCR
Rates: $65, incl. full brk. Discount avail. for extended stay.
Credit cards: MC, V
Restrictions: No children under 11, pets. Smoking restricted. One night's deposit req. 7-day cancellation notice req.
Notes: Common room with upright grand piano. Decorated in Country-Victorian style. Backyard garden.*

McCALL (2)

Northwest Passage B & B Lodge
201 Rio Vista, Box 4208, McCall, ID 83638
(208) 634-5349, (800) 597-6658, (208) 634-4977
Innkeeper: Steve and Barbara Schott
Rooms: 5/rooms, incl. 1 w/fireplace and TV, plus 2 suites, incl. 1 w/TV, and 1 apt., all w/pvt. bath
Rates: $60/room, $70-$80/suite, $150/apt, all incl. full brk., afternoon and evening refreshment. Discount avail. for extended stay.
Credit cards: Most major cards
Restrictions: Children, pets restricted. Deposit req. 14-day cancellation notice req. less $20.00 fee. 2-night min. stay on holiday wknds., winter carnival.
Notes: Two-story pine inn used in filming 1938 movie Northwest Passage. Located in wooded area. Two stone fireplaces. Pool table. Family room. Corrals provided. Snow trails.

SMITH HOUSE

SHOUP (3)

Smith House
49 Salmon River Rd., Shoup, ID 83469
(208) 394-2121, (800) 926-5915
Innkeeper: Aubrey & Marsha Smith
Rooms: 4, 1 w/pvt. bath, plus 1 suite. Located in 2 bldgs.
Rates: $35-$42/room, $54/suite, all incl. cont brk., evening refreshment. Discount
avail. for group, extended stays. Closed Nov.16–Mar.14.
Credit cards: Most major cards
Restrictions: Smoking restricted. One night's deposit req. 7-day cancellation notice
req.
Notes: Split-level log house. Has operated as inn since 1987. Located by Salmon
River on over 3 wilderness acres. Old fashioned gas lamps in rooms. Living/dining
room with stone fireplace. Library/game room. Deck overlooking river. Hot tub.
Vineyard. Orchard. Vegetable gardens. Fruit trees. Fishing, hunting, float trips, hiking. Giftshop on premises.

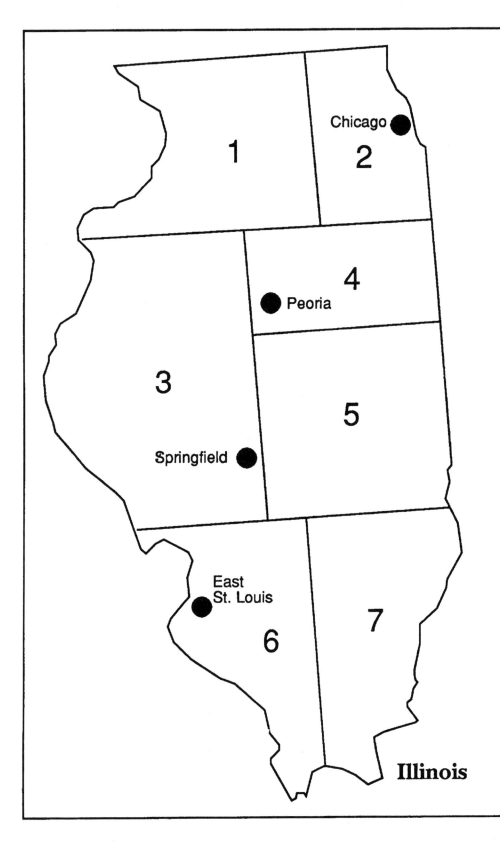

Illinois

Illinois

CARLYLE (6)

Country Haus
1191 Franklin St., Carlyle, IL 62231
(618) 594-8313
Innkeeper: Ron and Vicki Cook
Rooms: 5 w/pvt. bath, phone
Rates: $45-$55, incl full brk., afternoon refreshment. Discount avail. for mid-week
stay.
Credit cards: Most major cards
Restrictions: No pets, smoking. Deposit req. Cancellation notice req., less $10.00
fee.
Notes: Built between 1898 and 1904 in Eastlake style. Library with TV, stereo.
Pantry with board games and snacks. Dining room. Country decor includes a few
antiques and reproduction pieces.*

The Victorian B & B
1111 Franklin St., Carlyle, IL 62231
(618) 594-8506, (800) 594-8505
Innkeeper: Mary and Dennis Mincks
Rooms: 3 w/phone, incl. 2 w/TV
Rates: $55, incl. full brk., afternoon refreshment. Discount avail. for government
employees.
Credit cards: Most major cards
Restrictions: No children under 5, pets, smoking. One night's deposit req. 7-day
cancellation notice req., less $15.00 fee.
Notes: 3-story Victorian house with hardwood floors built approx. 1890. Foyer with
fireplaces, curving staircase, original stained-glass windows. Designated a Clinton
County Historical Landmark. Handicapped access. French spoken.

CHAMPAIGN (5)

The Golds B & B
2065 County Rd. E., Champaign, IL 61821
(217) 586-4345
Innkeeper: Bob and Rita Gold
Rooms: 3 No pvt. bath.
Rates: $40-$45, incl. cont. brk. Discount for extended stay.
Credit cards: None
Restrictions: No children under 5. No pet, smoking. One night's deposit req.
Notes: Two-story farmhouse built in 1874 with walnut stairway, early American sten-
ciling on the walls. Fully restored. Located on six acres. Parlor with Edison victrola.
Living room with fireplace, satellite TV, wide range of CDs. Dining room, kitchen,
parlor, side porch, deck. Furnished in country style with antiques. Resident cats.*

Norma's Hideaway
1714 Scottsdale Dr., Champaign, IL 61821
(217) 359-5876
Innkeeper: Norma R. Kite

Rooms: 3
Rates: $60, incl. full brk.
Credit cards: Most major cards
Restrictions: Smoking restricted. Deposit req. 14-day cancellation notice.
Notes: 2-story house built approx. 1964. Front room, family room, dining room, and kitchen. Furnished in a blend of country and traditional styles. Guests have access to TV, VCR, board games. Resident dogs.

CHICAGO (2)

Lakeshore Drive B & B
Lincoln Park, Chicago, IL 60614
(312) 404-5500

Innkeeper: Barbara Marquard
Rooms: 1 w/pvt. bath, phone, cable TV
Rates: $75, incl. cont. brk. Discount avail. for extended stay.
Credit cards: None
Restrictions: No children, pets, smoking. Deposit req. 2-night min. stay.
Notes: Wrap-around views of Lake Michigan, Lincoln Park, and Chicago skyline. Rooftop garden.*

COLLINSVILLE (6)

Maggie's Bed & Breakfast
2102 N. Keebler Rd., Collinsville, IL 62234
(618) 344-8283

Innkeeper: Maggie Leyda
Rooms: 3, w/pvt. bath, cable TV, incl. 2 w/fireplace, plus 1/suite, w/pvt. bath, TV, fireplace.
Rates: $35-$70/room, $55-$70/suite incl. full brk. Discount avail. for extended stay.
Credit cards: MC, V
Restrictions: Pets allowed w/arrangments. No smoking. Deposit req. 2-day cancellation notice req.
Notes: Two-story cottage built in 1900. Has operated as Inn since 1984. Gazebo, hot tub, garden, foyer. Furnished with family antiques. Innkeeper has quilt collection. Handicapped access.

DU QUOIN (6)

Francie's Bed & Breakfast Inn
104 S. Line St., Du Quoin, IL 62832
(618) 542-6686

Innkeeper: Tom and Francie Morgan
Rooms: 2 plus 2 suites, all w/pvt. bath, TV, radio, phone
Rates: $60/room, $75-$80/suite, all incl. full brk., evening refreshment. Discount avail. for extended stay. Special pkgs. avail.
Credit cards: MC, V
Restrictions: Children restricted. No smoking. Deposit req. Cancellation notice req.
Notes: Restored turn-of-the-century orphanage. Bikes, lawn games available. Small private parties accommodated.*

ELDRED (3)

Bluffdale Vacation Farm
R # 1, Eldred, IL 62027
(217) 983-2854
Innkeeper: Bill and Lindy Hobson
Rooms: 5 plus 4 suites, all w/pvt. bath, incl. 2 w/fireplace. Located in 3 bldgs.
Rates: $62-$80, incl. full brk.
Credit cards: Most major cards
Restrictions: No pets. Smoking restricted. Deposit req.
Notes: Farmhouse built in 1828. Located on 320-acre working grain and hog farm next to Illinois River. In the same family for eight generations. Has operated as inn since 1962. Swimming pool, hot tub, fishing pond, recreation house with square dances. Furnished with antiques. Hay rides, bonfires with sing-alongs, boats, horse riding available. Limited handicapped access.*

EVANSTON (2)

The Margarita European Inn
1566 Oak Ave., Evanston, IL 60201
(708) 869-2273, (708) 869-2353
Innkeeper: Judith Baker
Rooms: 46, incl. 9 w/pvt. bath, 20 w/phone, 3 w/TV, plus 4 suites w/pvt. bath, phone, incl. 3 w/TV.
Rates: $45-$90/room, $90-$140/suite, all incl. cont. brk.
Credit cards: Most major cards
Restrictions: No pets.
Notes: Five-story Georgian mansion, originally a woman's private club. Parlor with molded fireplace and floor-to-ceiling arched windows. Rooftop garden, paneled library, conference room with large screen TV. Restaurant on premises. Small private parties accommodated. Handicapped access.*

GALENA (1)

Belle Aire Mansion
11410 Rte. 20 West, Galena, IL 61036
(815) 777-0893
Innkeeper: Jan and Lorraine Svec
Rooms: 5 incl. 2 suites, all w/pvt. bath, incl. 3 w/fireplace, 1 w/TV
Rates: $65-$80/room, $90-$135/suite, all incl. full brk. Discount avail. for senior citizens.
Credit cards: Most major cards
Restrictions: No pets, smoking. Deposit req. 3-day cancellation notice req. 2-night min. stay on wknds.
Notes: Antebellum Federal-style house built in 1836. Located on eleven manicured acres with barn, windmill. Living room with TV, VCR, piano. Upper and lower verandas. Furnished in Victorian style with antiques, reproductions.

Brierwreath Manor B & B
216 N. Bench St., Galena, IL 61036
(815) 777-0608
Innkeeper: Mike and Lyn Cook
Rooms: 1 plus 2 suites, all w/pvt. bath, incl. 1 w/fireplace

BREIRWREATH MANOR B & B

Rates: $75-$85, incl. full brk. Seasonal variations.
Credit cards: Most major cards
Restrictions: No children, pets, smoking. One night's deposit req. 3-day cancellation notice req. 2-night min. stay on wknds.
Notes: Two-storyhouse built in 1884. Wrap-around porch with antique rockers and swing. Parlor with cable TV. Dining room. Furnished antiques and period pieces.

The Goldmoor
9001 Sand Hill Rd., Galena, IL 61036-9341
(815) 777-3921, (800) 255-3925, (815) 777-3993
Innkeeper: James C. Goldthorpe
Rooms: 4 plus 2 suites, all w/pvt. bath, phone, TV, incl. 2 w/fireplace
Rates: $75-$95/room, $135-$225/suite, all incl. full brk. Discount avail. for midweek stay. Special pkgs. avail.
Credit cards: Most major cards
Restrictions: Dogs welcome. Smoking restricted. Full prepayment req. 7-day cancellation notice req. 2-night min. stay on wknds.
Notes: Two-story country estate overlooking the Mississippi River Valley. Bicycles available. Sauna and spa. Handicapped access available.*

Park Avenue Guest House
208 Park Ave., Galena, IL 61036
(815) 777-1075, (800) 359-0743
Innkeeper: Sharon and John Fallbacher
Rooms: 3 w/pvt. bath, incl. 2 w/fireplace, 1 w/TV, plus 1 suite w/pvt. bath, fireplace
Rates: $65-$85/room, $100-$110/suite, all incl. expanded cont. brk. Discount avail. for mid-week, extended, and senior citizen stays.
Credit cards: Most major cards
Restrictions: No children under 12, pets. Smoking restricted. Full deposit req. 5-day cancellation notice req. 2-night min. stay on wknds.
Notes: Two-story Queen Anne house with tower built in 1893. Original ornate woodwork. Two parlors, one with fireplace, TV, VCR. Formal dining room. Furnished with antiques. Wrap-around screened porch overlooking gazebo, Victorian gardens. Special Christmas decorations. Air-conditioned.

Stillwaters Country Inn
7213 W. Buckhill Rd., Galena, IL 61036
(800) 767-0223, (312) 528-6313

Innkeeper: George and Leann

Rooms: 3 suites w/pvt. bath, phone, fireplace, kitchen, deck, TV, VCR, CD player and pvt. entrance

Rates: $80-$120, incl. cont. brk. Discount avail. for mid-week and extended stays. Seasonal variations. Children under 12: half price, under 6: free.

Credit cards: MC, V

Restrictions: No pets. Full prepayment req. $75.00 security deposit req. 2-night min. for most stays.

Notes: Furnished with antiques. Located on 17 wooded acres. Vegetable, herb, rock gardens, grape arbors, patio, deck, sauna, steam, sunken tub. BBQ available. Camping and other programs available. Innkeeper is holistic psychologist offering workshops.*

GALESBURG (3)

Seacord House B & B
624 N. Cherry St., Galesburg, IL 61401-2731
(309) 342-4107

Innkeeper: Gwen and Lyle Johnson

Rooms: 3

Rates: $35-40, incl. full brk.

Credit cards: MC, V

Restrictions: No children under 12, pets, smoking. Deposit req. 2-day cancellation notice req.

Notes: Victorian house built in the 1890s. Parlor with fireplace, library. Furnished with family antiques. Patio, front porch with swing. Lawn games available.

SEACORD HOUSE B & B

GENEVA (2)

Oscar Swan Country Inn
1800 W. State St., Rte. 38, Geneva, IL 60134
(708) 232-0173

Innkeeper: Hans and Nina Heymann

Rooms: 8 w/phone, TV, incl. 6 w/pvt. bath, 1 w/fireplace

Rates: $75-$150, incl. full brk. Seasonal variations. Discount avail. for senior, extended and mid-week stays.
Credit cards: Most major cards
Restrictions: Deposit req. 2-day cancellation notice req.
Notes: Two-story Colonial Revival Williamsburg-style inn built in 1902. Remodeled in 1950s. Has operated as inn since 1983. Located on seven acres with gardens. Furnished with antiques. Living room, breakfast conservatory with fifteen-ft. ceiling. Italian marble floors. Swimming pool. Guests have access to local health club. Small private parties accommodated. German spoken.*

GOLCONDA (7)

Marilee's Guesthouse
Washington & Monroe, Box 8627, Golconda, IL 62938
(618) 683-2751, (800) 582-2563
Innkeeper: Marilee Joiner
Rooms: 3 w/phone
Rates: $45.00, incl. full brk.
Credit cards: Most major cards
Restrictions: No pets. Deposit req.
Notes: Bungalow-style house with beamed ceilings. Located near the Ohio River. Living room. Boat hookup available.

GURNEE (2)

Sweet Basil Hill Farm
15937 W. Washington St., Gurnee, IL 60031
(708) 244-3333, (800) 225-4372, (708) 263-6693
Innkeeper: Teri and Bob Jones
Rooms: 1, plus 2 suites, all incl. pvt. bath, phone, TV. Guesthouse avail.
Rates: $85/room, $85-$130/suite, $100-$160/guesthouse, all incl. full brk., afternoon refreshment. Discount avail. for mid-week stay. Seasonal variations.
Credit cards: Most major cards
Restrictions: No pets, smoking. One night's deposit req. 21-day cancellation notice req.
Notes: Cape Cod-style house built in 1950. Located on seven wooded acres. Has operated as inn since 1990. Common room with fireplace, chess board, spinning wheel. Breakfast room. Furnished in Victorian style with English pine antiques. Herb, flower gardens. Grounds include hammock and swing. VCR and tape collection available. Innkeepers are actor, photographer and jazz musician. French spoken. Resident sheep, llamas.*

HARRISBURG (7)

House of Nahum
90 Sally Holler Lane, Harrisburg, IL 62946
(618) 252-1414
Innkeeper: Sona Thomas
Rooms: 4 w/pvt. bath
Rates: $65.00, incl. full brk., afternoon refreshment, evening dessert
Credit cards: Most major cards
Restrictions: No children, pets. Smoking restricted. 50% deposit req. 7-day cancellation notice req.

Notes: Built in 1993. Located on 5 acres. Common room with piano and antique games. Old-fashioned veranda with swing and wicker furniture. Hammock, flower garden and deck.*

HIGHLAND (6)

Phyllis's B & B
801 9th St., Highland, IL 62249
(618) 654-4619
Innkeeper: Bob and Phyllis Bible
Rooms: 5, incl. 3 w/pvt. bath
Rates: $55.00, incl. full brk. Discount avail. for mid-week and extended stays.
Credit cards: MC, V
Restrictions: No children under 12, pets, alcohol. Smoking restricted. One night's
    deposit req. 7-day cancellation notice req., less $15.00 fee.
Notes: Built circa 1900. Sitting room with fireplace, TV, reading and board games.
Decorated in antiques and reproductions. Giftshop on premises.

MOSSVILLE (4)

Old Church House Inn
1416 E. Mossville Rd., Box 295, Mossville, IL 61552
(309) 579-2300
Innkeeper: Dean and Holly Ramseyer
Rooms: 2, incl. 1 w/pvt. bath
Rates: $55-$99, incl. expanded cont. brk., afternoon refreshment
Credit cards: MC, V
Restrictions: No children under 10, pets, smoking. Min. one night's deposit req.
    14-day cancellation notice req., less $15.00 fee.
Notes: Two-story, Colonial-style Presbyterian church built in 1869. Located along
the Illinois River. 18' ceilings, tall, arched windows. Living room with fireplace,
board games, ladder up to library. Dining room, balcony. Furnished with Victorian
antiques. Rose and vegetable gardens. Fruit trees. Picnic lunch available. Listed on
the National Historic American Building Survey.

MOUNT CARMEL (7)

Living Legacy Homestead
RR 2, Box 146A, Mount Carmel, IL 62863
(618) 298-2476
Innkeeper: Edna Schmidt Anderson
Rooms: 3, incl. 1 w/pvt. bath, 2 w/phone and TV, plus 1 cottage. Located in 2 bldgs.
Rates: $40-$70, incl. full brk., afternoon refreshment. Discount avail. for extended
    and senior citizen stays.
Credit cards: None
Restrictions: No pets, smoking. Deposit req. Cottage avail. in season.
Notes: Two-story log house built in the 1870s. Farmhouse built in 1902. Located on
10 acres. Barnsiding, log walls. Loft houses giftshop. Gathering room with parlor
games, player piano, historical memorabilia. Dining room. Wood-burning cook-
stove in kitchen. Furnished with antique and period furniture. Flower, vegetable,
herb gardens. Orchard, meadow, farm buildings. All meals available.

The Poor Farm B & B
Poor Farm Rd., Mount Carmel, IL 62863
(618) 262-4663, (800) 646-3276
Innkeeper: Liz and John Stelzer
Rooms: 2 plus 2 suites, all w/pvt. bath, phone, TV
Rates: $45/room, $85/suite, all incl. full brk. Discount avail. for extended stay.
Credit cards: Most major cards
Restrictions: No pets. Smoking restricted. One night's deposit req. 7-day cancellation notice req.
Notes: Two-story brick building built in 1915 for the homeless. Common room with antique player piano, Victrola and board games. Furnished with antiques. Private luncheons or dinner parties avail. Handicapped access.*

THE POOR FARM B & B

MUNDELEIN (2)

Round Robin Guesthouse
231 E. Maple Ave., Mundelein, IL 60060
(708) 566-7664, (708)566-1895
Innkeeper: George and Laura Loffredo
Rooms: 6, incl. 2 w/pvt. bath, phone, plus 1 suite, w/pvt. bath, phone
Rates: $40-$65/room, $85-$110/suite, all incl. full brk. Discount avail. for mid-week stay.
Credit cards: MC, V
Restrictions: No pets, smoking. Deposit req. 2-day cancellation notice req.
Notes: Victorian house built in 1909. One suite offers a fireplace and all rooms have central air and ceiling fans. Front porch with swing. Hostess plays piano during breakfast.*

NAUVOO (3)

Ancient Pines B & B
2015 E. Parley St., Nauvoo, IL 62354
(217) 453-2767
Innkeeper: Genevieve Simmems
Rooms: 3
Rates: $39, incl. full brk. Seasonal variations.
Credit cards: Most major cards

Restrictions: No pets, smoking. Deposit req. 3-day cancellation notice req.
Notes: Two story brick Victorian built in 1900. Parlor, dining room, library. Board games, music, books. Furnished with antiques. Front verandah, side porch. Herb and rose gardens.

Mississippi Memories
Riverview Heights, Box 291, RR1, Nauvoo, IL 62354
(217) 453-2771
Innkeeper: Marge and Dean Starr
Rooms: 3 w/pvt. bath, phone, plus 1 suite w/pvt. bath, phone, TV, fireplace
Rates: $58/room, $75/suite, all incl. full brk.
Credit cards: Most major cards
Restrictions: Children restricted. No smoking, pets, alcohol. Deposit req. 3-day cancellation notice req.
Notes: Five-level brick house. Located on wooded setting. Common room with fireplace, piano. Dining room with fireplace. Kitchen. Furnished with antiques. Two decks overlooking Mississippi River. Handicapped access.*

MISSISSIPPI MEMORIES

ROCK ISLAND (1)

The Potter House
1906 7th Ave., Rock Island, IL 61201
(309) 788-1906, (800) 747-0339
Innkeeper: Gary and Nancy Pheiffer
Rooms: 4 w/pvt. bath, phone, TV, incl. 1 w/fireplace, plus 2 suites w/pvt. bath, phone, TV. Located in 2 bldgs.
Rates: $60-$85/room, $70-$100/suite, all incl. full brk. Discount avail. for extended and mid-week stays.
Credit cards: Most major cards
Restrictions: No pets, smoking. Deposit req. 7-day cancellation notice req., less fee. 2-night min. stay on holidays, special event wknds and peak season wknds.
Notes: Three-story Colonial Revival mansion built in 1907. Living room with fireplace. Dining room, solarium, parlor with player piano, central hall with open staircase. Embossed leather wallcoverings. Board games, puzzles, books. VCR available. Stained-glass windows. Furnished with antiques. Lawn games. Listed on the National Register of Historic Places. Bicycles available. Tours can be arranged.*

Top O'The Morning
1505 19th Ave., Rock Island, IL 61201
(309) 786-3513
Innkeeper: Sam and Peggy Doak
Rooms: 2 plus 1 suite, all w/pvt. bath
Rates: $40-$80, incl. full brk.
Credit cards: None
Restrictions: No pets, smoking. Deposit req. 7-day cancellation notice req., less $10.00 fee.
Notes: Brick prairie-style mansion with slate roof and copper guttering built by president of Rock Island Railroad in 1912. Located on 3.5 wooded acres with gardens on bluff overlooking the Mississippi River. Living room, dining room, each with natural fireplace. Redwood deck, screened porch.

Victorian Inn B & B
702 20th St., Rock Island, IL 61201
(309) 788-7068
Innkeeper: David and Barbara Parker
Rooms: 5 w/fireplace, plus 1/suite w/phone
Rates: $55-75/room, $125/suite all incl. full brk.
Credit cards: MC, V
Restrictions: No pets. Smoking restricted. Deposit req. 2-day cancellation notice req.
Notes: Two-story Victorian hosue built in 1888. Located on 2/3 acre on the Eaton Gardens. Illuminated glass tower windows, french doors, spacious living room, dining room with oak ceiling beams and paneling crowned by turn of the century tapestries. Porch, fireplace, giftshop. Listed in the National Register of Historic Places.*

SPARLAND (4)

Hillside
304 North St., Sparland, IL 61565
(309) 246-4650, (309) 246-2455

Innkeeper: Louis and Marjorie Lenz
Rooms: 3 w/phone. 2 w/TV. 1w/pvt. bath.
Rates: $50/room, incl. cont. brk.
Credit cards: Most major cards
Restrictions: No children, pets. one night's deposit req. 14-day cancellation notice
 req. 2-night min. stay on wknds.
Notes: Victorian structure built approx. 1870. Located on a bluff overlooking the
Illinois Valley and River. Two bedrooms open onto a 1,500-sq.-ft. deck overlooking
valley. Furnished with antiques. *

SPRINGFIELD (3)

Flagg Stopp Inn
RR 16 Box 175, Springfield, IL 62707
(217) 527-1599
Innkeeper: Alan and Josephine Lichtenberger
Rooms: 5 w/pvt. bath
Rates: $50-$75, incl. cont. brk.
Credit cards: Most major cards
Restrictions: No children under 16, pets, smoking. One night's deposit req. 24-hour
 cancellation notice req.
Notes: Two-story Greek Italianate mansion built in 1871 on 300 acres. Locate in
Sherman. Restored in 1989. Furnished in Victorian style. Marble and cast-iron fire-
places. Wrap-around porch. Original light fixtures. Listed in the U.S. Historical
Records.

STOCKTON (1)

Hammond House
323 N. Main St., Stockton, IL 61085
(815) 947-2032
Innkeeper: LaVonneda and Spencer Haas
Rooms: 5 rooms, plus 3 suites, all w/pvt. bath, TV
Rates: $55-$150/room, $85-$150/suite, all incl. full brk.
Credit cards: Most major cards
Restrictions: No children under 13, pets, smoking. 72-hour cancellation notice.
Notes: Greek revival was built in 1900. Color cable TV, central air, double deck and
flower garden. Guest suites have double whirlpools.

URBANA (5)

Shurts House B & B
710 W. Oregon St., Urbana, IL 61801
(217) 367-8793, (217) 344-1615
Innkeeper: Bruce and Denni Shurts
Rooms: 3, no pvt. bath, plus 3 suites w/pvt. bath, phone, TV, incl. 1 w/Jacuzzi, VCR,
 kitchen. Located in 2 bldgs.
Rates: $75-$100/room, $100-$200/suite, all incl. full brk., afternoon refreshment.
 Discount avail. for extended stay.
Credit cards: Most major cards
Restrictions: No pets, smoking. Deposit req.
Notes: Three-story red brick English Tudor style building built in 1909. Walnut
wood trimmed interior furnished with antiques. Livingroom with fireplace, board

games. Sun deck, swimming pool. Guests have access to bicycles. Handicapped access.*

WATERLOO (6)

Senator Rickert Residence B & B
216 E. Third St., Waterloo, IL 62298-1609
(618) 939-8242
Innkeeper: Ed and Kathi Weilbacher
Rooms: 1 w/pvt. bath, phone, TV
Rates: $75.00, incl. full brk. Discount avail. for mid-week stay.
Credit cards: Most major cards
Restrictions: No pets, smoking. One night's deposit req. 7-day cancellation notice
   req.
Notes: One-story, brick, French country villa built in 1866. Some restoration is ongoing. Dining room. Furnished with antiques.

WILLIAMSVILLE (3)

BED & BREAKFAST AT EDIE'S

Bed & Breakfast at Edie's
233 E. Harpole, Williamsville, IL 62693
(217) 566-2538
Innkeeper: Edie Senalik
Rooms: 4, no pvt. bath
Rates: $45-$85, incl. cont. brk.
Credit cards: None
Restrictions: No pets, smoking. $25.00 deposit req. 3-day cancellation notice req.
Notes: Two-story mission-style house built in 1915. Dining room. Furnished in the period of the home. Wrap-around veranda, patio. Small private parties accommodated.

WINNETKA (2)

Chateau des Fleurs
552 Ridge Rd., Winnetka, IL 60093
(312) 256-7272

Innkeeper: Sally Ward
Rooms: 3 w/pvt. bath, phone, TV, incl 1 w/Jacuzzi
Rates: $95, incl. full brk., afternoon refreshment
Credit cards: None
Restrictions: No children under 11, pets, smoking. One night's deposit req. 21-day cancellation notice req. 2-night min. stay on wknds.
Notes: Authentic French Country house built in 1936. Located on .75 acre of expansive lawns and English gardens. Formal dining room, living room with Baby Grand piano, library and game room each with fireplace. 55-inch TV with a taped-movie library. Breakfast room. Furnished with antiques. Sun porch, swimming pool.*

YORKVILLE (2)

Silver Key B & B
507 W. Ridge St., Yorkville, IL 60560
(708) 553-5612
Innkeeper: Jerry Lunch
Rooms: 2 w/TV, VCR, no pvt. bath, plus 1 suite w/pvt. bath, TV, VCR
Rates: $50-$75/room, $99/suite, all incl. cont. brk., evening refreshment. Discount avail. for mid-week and extended stays.
Credit cards: None
Restrictions: No pets. Smoking restricted. One night's deposit req. 24-hour cancellation notice req., less $5.00 fee. 2-night min. stay on holiday wknds.
Notes: Two-story house built in 1901. Owner forged a key of silver for main entrance, which has been handed down to each owner. Located in historic district. Living room with fireplace. Dining room. Library with wide selection of movies. Some German spoken.*

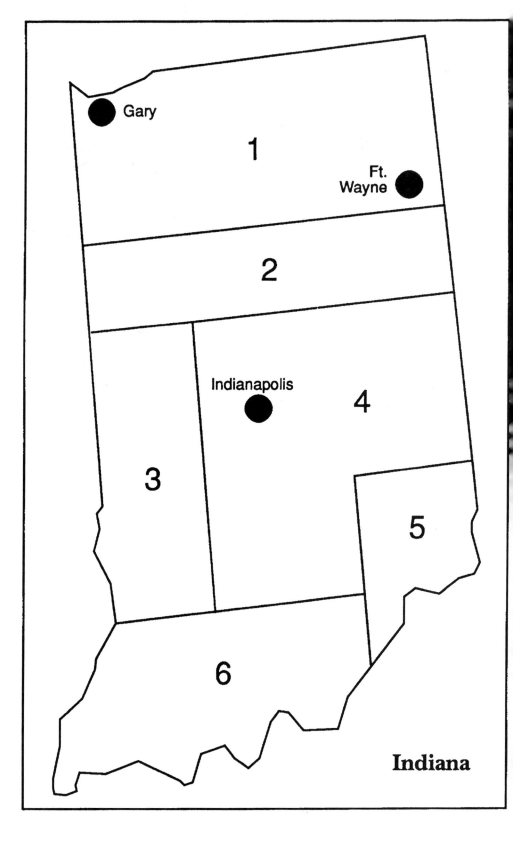

Indiana

Indiana

BLOOMINGTON (4)

The Grant Street Inn
310 N. Grant St., Bloomington, IN 47408
(812) 334-2353, (812) 331-8673
Innkeeper: Kelly Staggs
Rooms: 12 w/pvt. bath, phone, TV, incl. 2 w/fireplace, plus 2 suites w/pvt. bath, phone, TV, incl. 2 w/fireplace
Rates: $75-$95/room, $100-$150/suite, all incl. full brk., afternoon refreshment. Discount avail. for extended, corporate, and senior stays.
Credit cards: Most major cards
Restrictions: No children. 24-hour cancellation notice req.
Notes: Main section of inn built in 1883, originally the Ziegler House. Parlor and rooms decorated with antique style furniture. Handicapped access.*

Scholars Inn
801 N. College Ave., Bloomington, IN 47404
(812) 332-1892, (800) 765-3466, (812) 335-1490
Innkeeper: Nickky Jackson
Rooms: 5 w/pvt. bath, phone, TV, incl. 1 w/fireplace
Rates: $69-$135, incl. cont. brk. Discount avail. for mid-week stay. Seasonal variations.
Credit cards: Most major cards
Restrictions: No children under 15, pets, smoking. 50% deposit req. 72-hour cancellation notice req.
Notes: Two-story brick mansion built in 1894. Gathering room. Garden room with fountain wall. Common room with fireplace. Furnished with antiques, Oriental rugs.

BUFFALO (2)

Sluyter Haus
P.O. Box 238 Hwy. 119, Buffalo, IN 47925
(219) 278-6308, (219) 627-3293
Innkeeper: Clara Sluyter
Rooms: 2 plus 1 suite, no pvt. bath
Rates: $45, incl. full brk.
Credit cards: None
Restrictions: No children under 12, pets. Smoking restricted. $10.00 deposit req.
Notes: Porch with swing. Parlor. Access to kitchen. Furnished with antiques. Hot tub. Outdoor barbeque available. Small private parties accommodated.

CHESTERTON (1)

Gray Goose Inn
350 Indian Boundry, Chesterton, IN 46304
(800) 521-5127
Innkeeper: Tim Wilk
Rooms: 5 plus 3 suites, all w/pvt. bath, phone, fireplace, TV

Rates: $80-$95/room, $110-$135/suite, all incl. full brk. Discount avail. for midweek stay.

Credit cards: Most major cards

Restrictions: No children under 12, pets. Smoking restricted. One night's deposit req. 10-day cancellation notice req. 2-night min. stay on holiday wknds.

Notes: Two-story English Country House built in 1939. Located on 100 acres. Overlooking private lake. Dining room. Common room. Some rooms with Jacuzzi. Decorated with 18th-century English antiques. Sun porch. Small private parties accommodated. Resident dogs.*

CLINTON (3)

Pentreath House
424 Blackman St., Clinton, IN 47842-2007
(317) 832-2762

Innkeeper: Lou and Laura Savage

Rooms: 3, incl. 2 w/pvt. bath, TV. Suite avail.

Rates: From $45, incl. cont. brk. Discount avail. for extended stay except during festivals.

Credit cards: None

Restrictions: No children under 6, pets. Deposit req. during festivals. 7-day cancellation notice req. 2-night min. stay during Covered Bridge Festival wknds.

Notes: Two-story Edwardian style house built in 1926. Located in heart of covered bridge country. Has operated as an inn since 1990. Living room with TV, music. Brousing library, extensive video collection, games. Furnished with antiques. Front porch. Resident cat.*

PENTREATH HOUSE

CRAWFORDSVILLE (3)

Sugar Creek Queen Anne
901 W. Marhet, Box 726, Crawfordsville, IN 47933
(317) 362-4095

Innkeeper: Hal and Maryalice Barbee

Rooms: 3 plus 1/suite, all w/pvt. bath, phone. Located in 2 bldgs.

Rates: $60, incl. full brk.

Credit cards: None
Restrictions: No pets, smoking. Deposit req. 7-day cancellation notice req., less $25.00 fee.
Notes: 2-story Victorian house built in 1900. Rose garden, Jacuzzi. Guests have access to limo ride.

GOSHEN (1)

Waterford Bed and Breakfast
3004 S. Main St., Goshen, IN 46526
(219) 533-6044
Innkeeper: Judith Forbes
Rooms: 4, incl. 2 w/pvt. bath
Rates: $55, incl. full brk. Discount avail. for extended stay.
Credit cards: None
Restrictions: No children under 8, pets, smoking. $20.00 deposit req. 7-day cancellation notice req., less $5.00 fee.
Notes: Brick Italianate house built in 1854. Located on two landscaped acres .5 block from Elkhart River. Common room with fireplace, cable TV, library, phone, board games. Large grounds with lawn games available. Furnished with local antiques. Listed on the National Historic Register.

HUNTINGTON (2)

Purviance House B & B
326 S. Jefferson, Huntington, IN 46750
(219) 356-4218, 356-9215
Innkeeper: Bob and Jean Gernand
Rooms: 5, incl. 4 w/TV
Rates: $45-$55, incl. full brk., afternoon refreshment. Discount avail. for extended stay.
Credit cards: Most major cards
Restrictions: No pets, smoking. $25.00 deposit req. 3-day cancellation req.
Notes: An 1859 Italianate/Greek Revival mansion listed in National Register of Historic Places. Decorated with period furnishings. Features include solid cherry winding staircase, parlors with 4 fireplaces, library, and original interior shutters.

INDIANAPOLIS (4)

Le Chateau Delaware Inn
1456 N. Delaware St., Indianapolis, IN 46202
(317) 636-9156
Innkeeper: Mignon Wyatt
Rooms: 5, w/pvt. bath, incl. 1 w/fireplace
Rates: $75-$175/room, $150/suite, all incl. full brk. Seasonal variations. Discount avail. for extended stay.
Credit cards: None
Restrictions: No children under 10, pets, smoking. Deposit req. 2-day cancellation notice req., less $15.00 fee.
Notes: Two-story manor built in 1906. Living room. Dining room. Furnished with antiques and other period accessories. Off-street parking available. Small private parties accommodated.*

LE CHATEAU DELAWARE INN

Tranquil Cherub
2164 N. Capitol Ave., Indianapolis, IN 46202
(317) 923-9036

Innkeeper: Thom and Barb Feit
Rooms: 3, incl 1 w/pvt. bath, plus 1 suite w/pvt. bath, phone, fireplace, TV
Rates: $55-$65/room, $85/suite, all incl. full brk. Discount avail. for extended and
mid-week stays. Seasonal variations.
Credit cards: MC, V
Restrictions: No children under 6, pets. Smoking restricted. Min. one night's de-
posit req. 5-day cancellation notice req., less $10.00 fee.
Notes: Greek Revival house with oak staircase, pier mirror, built in eary 1900s.
Room decor range from Victorian to Art Deco. Formal dining room. Furnished
with antiques. Suite decorated with old steamer trunk, period dresses and children's toys. Back deck overlooking lily ponds. Airport pickup available. Resident
dog and cat.*

TRANQUIL CHERUB

LaGRANGE (1)

The 1886 Inn
212 W. Factory St., Box 5, LaGrange, IN 46761
(219) 463-4227, (219) 463-7489

Innkeeper: Duane and Gloria Billman, Kelly Shank
Rooms: 1 plus 3 suites, all w/pvt. bath, phone
Rates: $79, incl. expanded cont. brk.
Credit cards: Most major cards
Restrictions: No children, pets, smoking. Deposit req. Cancellation notice req., less
  fee.
Notes: Two-story red brick mansion with arched doorways, ash woodwork, stairway
with ornate newel post built in 1886. Furnished with antiques.

MADISON (5)

Autumnwood B & B
165 Autumnwood Lane, Madison, IN 47250
(812) 265-5262
Innkeeper: Lynda Jae Breitweiser
Rooms: 9 w/pvt. bath
Rates: $85, incl. cont. brk., afternoon refreshment
Credit cards: MC, V
Restrictions: No pets. Smoking restricted. $25.00 deposit req. 14-day cancellation
  notice req.
Notes: Two-story inn built about 1840. Located on hill overlooking city and Ohio
River. Furnished with Victorian antiques. Parlor. Patio with fountain. Limited hand-
icapped access.*

Schussler House B & B
514 Jefferson St., Madison, IN 47250
(812) 273-2068
Innkeeper: Bill and Judy Gilbert
Rooms: 3 w/pvt. bath
Rates: $85, incl. full brk., afternoon refreshment
Credit cards: Most major cards
Restrictions: No children under 12, pets, smoking. One night's deposit req. Min.
  24-hour cancellation notice req.
Notes: Federal/Classic Revival house built in 1849. Recently renovated. Located in
historic district. Front parlor, dining room.*

METAMORA (5)

The Thorpe House
Clayborne St., Box 36, Metamora, IN 47030-0036
(317) 647-5425, (317) 932-2365
Innkeeper: Jean and Mike Owens
Rooms: 4 w/pvt. bath, plus 1 suite w/pvt. bath
Rates: $70/room, $125/suite, all incl. full brk., evening refreshment
Credit cards: Most major cards
Restrictions: $20.00 deposit req. 3-day cancellation notice req., less $10.00 fee. 2-
  night min. stay on holiday and special event wknds.
Notes: Two-story house with gingerbread adornment built in 1840. Restored in
1985 by the current innkeepers. Furnished with antiques, many of which are for
sale. Restaurant and shops on premises. Small private parties accommodated.
Guests arriving by train can be met by horsedrawn carriage. Limited handicapped
access.*

MICHIGAN CITY (1)

Creekwood Inn
Rte. 20-35 at I-94, Michigan City, IN 46360
(219) 872-8357

Innkeeper: Mary Lou Linnen, Mary Ellen Hatton, Peggie Wall
Rooms: 12, plus 1 suite, all w/pvt. bath, phone, TV, incl. 3 w/fireplace
Rates: $95-$125/room, $102-$150/suite, all incl. cont. brk. Discount avail. for extended, mid-week, senior citizen stays.
Credit cards: Most major cards
Restrictions: Deposit req. 14-day cancellation notice req. 2-night min. stay on wknds. Closed for 10 days in March.
Notes: Two-story English Cotswold-style house with wood plank-covered floors, handhewn ceiling beams, built in the 1930s. Renovated as an inn in 1984. Located on 30 acres. Some rooms have private deck. Parlor with fireplace, bay window. Suite includes meeting room, wet bar. Screened porch. Small private parties accommodated. Handicapped access.*

Hutchinson Mansion Inn
220 W. 10th St., Michigan City, IN 46360
(219) 879-1700

Innkeeper: Ben and Mary Duval
Rooms: 5 plus 5 suites, all w/pvt. bath, phone. Located in 2 bldgs.
Rates: $70-$102/room, $92-$133/suite, all incl. full brk. Discount avail. for mid-week, extended stay. Seasonal variations.
Credit cards: Most major cards
Restrictions: No pets. Children, smoking restricted. One night's deposit req. 7-day cancellation notice req. 2-night min. stay on holiday wknds. and special events.
Notes: Three-story house built in 1876. Stained glass windows, high-beamed and decorated ceilings. Furnished with antiques. Parlor, library, gardens, lawn games. Handicapped access.*

HUTCHINSON MANSION INN

MIDDLEBURY (1)

Bee Hive B & B
P.O. Box 1191, Middlebury, IN 46540
(219) 825-5023

Innkeeper: Herb and Treva Swarm
Rooms: 3, no pvt. bath, plus 1 cottage w/pvt. bath. Located in 2 bldgs.
Rates: $52-$70, incl. full brk., afternoon refreshment
Credit cards: MC, V
Restrictions: No pets, smoking, alcohol. Deposit req. 10-day cancellation notice
    req., less $10.00 fee.
Notes: Two-story country inn. Decorated with handmade quilts, collectibles, origi-
nal paintings. Amish tours available.

Varns Guest House
205 S. Main St., Box 125, Middlebury, IN 46540
(219) 825-9666
Innkeeper: Carl and Diane Eash
Rooms: 5 w/pvt. bath, phone, fireplace
Rates: $69, incl. cont. brk.
Credit cards: MC, V
Restrictions: No pets, smoking. 50% deposit req. 7-day cancellation notice req., less
    $10.00 fee.
Notes: Built in 1898, totally remodeled and redecorated in 1988 by original owner's
great-granddaughter. Living room with brick fireplace. Wrap-around front porch
with swing, wicker furniture. Furnished with solid cherry pieces.*

MONTICELLO (2)

1887 Black Dog Inn
2830 Untalulti, Monticello, IN 47960
(219) 583-8297
Innkeeper: Tom and Joyce Condo and Bo
Rooms: 6 w/pvt. bath, phone, TV
Rates: $69, incl. full brk. Discount avail. for extended stay.
Credit cards: Most major cards
Restrictions: No children under 8. Smoking restricted. Deposit req. 14-day cancel-
    lation notice req.
Notes: Two-story farm style house. Located on 3 acres on Lake Shafer. Has operated
as an inn since 1991. Furnished with New England antiques. Boating, fishing. Pool
and lawn games. Garden with benches, summer porch with wicker furniture. Small
private parties accommodated. Guests have access to refrigerator. Handicapped access.

NAPPANEE (1)

Olde Buffalo Inn
1061 Parkwood Dr., Nappanee, IN 46550
(219) 773-2223
Innkeeper: Ann and Larry Lakins
Rooms: 5 w/phone, TV, incl. 2 w/pvt. bath
Rates: $65, incl. full brk.
Credit cards: Most major cards
Restrictions: No children under 15, pets, smoking. Deposit req. 7-day cancellation
    notice req., less $10.00 fee.
Notes: Originally a farm house, built in 1840s on 2.5 acres. Completely restored,
and added onto in 1970s. Original basement transformed into a reproduction of a
tavern found in Williamsburg, Virginia. Common area with a baby grand piano and

chess. Air conditioned. Red barn, red brick sidewalks, traditional windmill, enclosed by a white picket fence. Basketball court in barn. Nature walks. Resident pets.

NASHVILLE (4)

STORY INN

Story Inn
6404 S. State Rd. 135, Box 64, Nashville, IN 47448
(812) 988-2273, (812) 988-6516
Innkeeper: Bob and Gretchen Haddix
Rooms: 2 rooms plus 2 suites plus 9 cottages, all w/pvt. bath, phone, fireplace. Located in 6 bldgs.
Rates: $65/room, $75/suite, $85-$95/cottage, all incl. full brk.
Credit cards: Most major cards
Restrictions: No pets, smoking. Deposit req. 7-day cancellation notice req., less $5.00 fee. 2-night min. stay, Sept.–Nov.
Notes: Two-story general store and buggy factory rebuilt after fire 1916. Fully restored. Upstairs living room. Furnished with period antiques. Landscaped gardens. Gourmet restaurant on premises. Small private parties accommodated. Handicapped access available in cottage.

NEW ALBANY (6)

Honeymoon Mansion B & B
1014 E. Main St., New Albany, IN 47150
(800) 759-7270
Innkeeper: Franklin and Beverly Dennis
Rooms: 6 suites w/pvt. bath, TV, VCR, incl. 5 w/marble Jacuzzi, 1 w/fireplace
Rates: $68-$135, incl. full brk. Discount avail. for mid-week, extended, and senior citizen stays. Special pkgs. avail.
Credit cards: None
Restrictions: No children under 12, pets. Smoking restricted. $50.00 deposit req. 96-hour cancellation notice req., less 15% fee.
Notes: Victorian mansion built around 1850. National Historic Landmark. Wedding chapel.*

PAOLI (6)

BRAXTAN HOUSE INN

Braxtan House Inn
210 N. Gospel St., Paoli, IN 47454
(812) 723-4677
Innkeeper: Duane and Kate Wilhelmi
Rooms: 6 w/pvt. bath
Rates: $55-$75, incl. full brk., afternoon refreshment. Discount avail. for senior citizen and extended stays.
Credit cards: Most major cards
Restrictions: No pets. Smoking restricted. One night's deposit req. 72-hour cancellation notice req., less $10.00 fee. 2-night min. stay during ski season and Kentucky Derby wknd.
Notes: Three-story Queen Anne Victorian house built in 1893. Fully restored. Original oak, cherry and maple woodwork. Stained glass windows. Parlor with books, puzzles, games, TV. Second floor sitting room with library. Children's toys, games, videos. Furnished with antiques. Listed on the National Register of Historic Places. Child care available.

ROCKVILLE (3)

Suit's Us
514 N. College St., Rockville, IN 47872
(317) 569-5660
Innkeeper: Bob and Ann McCullough
Rooms: 3 plus 1 suite, all w/pvt. bath, TV
Rates: $50-$65/room, $100-$125/suite, all incl. mid-week cont. brk., wknd. full brk.
Credit cards: Most major cards
Restrictions: No pets. Smoking restricted. Min. $20.00 deposit req. 3-day cancellation notice req.
Notes: Two story Victorian inn with spiral hanging staircase built in 1883. Front porch. Formal living room. Library. Guests have access to exercise equipment.

SOUTH BEND (1)

Queen Anne Inn
420 W. Washington, South Bend, IN 46601
(219) 234-5959, (219) 234-4324

Innkeeper: Pauline and Bob Medhurst
Rooms: 5 w/pvt. bath, phone, TV, plus 1 suite w/pvt. bath, phone, TV, fireplace
Rates: $65-$85/room, $95/suite, all incl. full brk. Discount avail. for mid-week and extended stays.
Credit cards: Most major cards
Restrictions: No pets, smoking. One night's deposit req. 7-day cancellation notice req.
Notes: Two-story Queen Anne neoclassical house with tiger oak staircase, hand-painted silk wallpaper, built in 1893 as a wedding gift to owner's daughter. Library, music room. Front porch with swing. Second-floor landing. Features Frank Lloyd Wright bookcases. Board games, dinner available. Small private parties accommodated.*

SYRACUSE (1)

ANCHOR INN B & B

Anchor Inn B & B
11007 N. State Rd. 13, Syracuse, IN 46567
(219) 457-4714
Innkeeper: Robert and Jean Kennedy
Rooms: 8, incl. 5 w/pvt. bath
Rates: $40-$65 incl. full brk. Discount avail. for extended stay. Seasonal variations.
Credit cards: MC, V
Restrictions: No children under 12, pets, smoking. Deposit req. Min. 7-day cancellation notice req.
Notes: Three-story American four-square house built in 1905. Front porch overlooking golf course. Cottage graden. Furnished in country style with antiques.

WARSAW (1)

The Candlelight Inn
503 E. Ft. Wayne St., Warsaw, IN 46580
(219) 267-2906, (800) 352-0640, (219) 269-4646
Innkeeper: Ron and Lori McSorley
Rooms: 10 plus 2 suites, all w/pvt. bath, phone, AC, fireplace, cable TV. Located in 2 bldgs.

Rates: $59-$125/room, $110-$135/suite, all incl. full brk., cookies on nightstand. Discount avail for mid-week stay.

Credit cards: Most major cards

Restrictions: No children under 16, pets. Smoking restricted. 7-day cancellation notice req.

Notes: Two-story Victorian house with porch built in 1860s. Restored in 1985 with rich wood, historic wallpapers, and antiques.

WEST LAFAYETTE (2)

Kent House Inn
223 S. Chauncey, West Lafayette, IN 47906
(317) 743-3731

Innkeeper: Sally McKinney

Rooms: 3, incl. 2 w/pvt. bath, 1 w/fireplace, 1 w/TV

Rates: $60-$80, incl. expanded cont. brk., evening refreshment. Seasonal variations.

Credit cards: Most major cards

Restrictions: No children under 14, pets, smoking. One night's deposit req. 7-day cancellation notice req., less $15.00 fee.

Notes: Two-story Victorian house with multiple gables built in the late 1800s. Carved oak woodwork and hardwood floors. Parlor with stained, leaded-glass, pump organ. Dining room, morning room. Furnished with antiques, lace curtains.

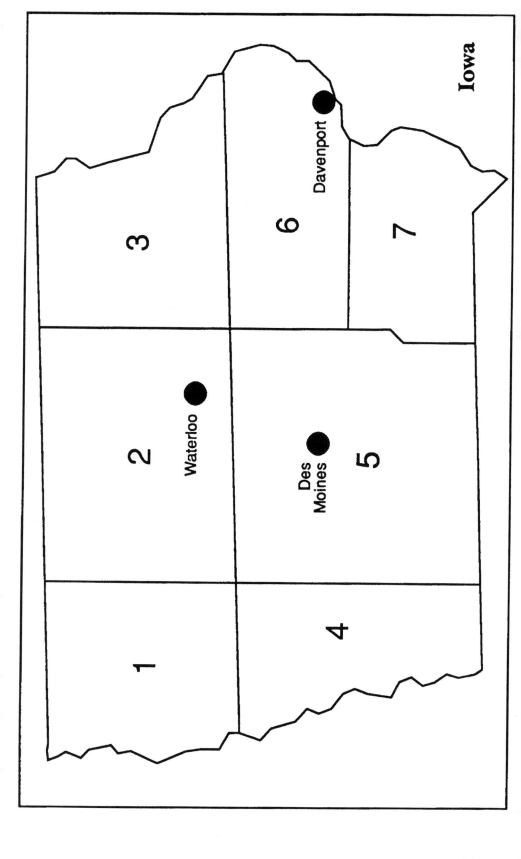

Iowa

Iowa

ADAIR (4)

Lalley House
701 5th St., Adair, IA 50002
(515) 742-5541
Innkeeper: Kay & Danny Faga
Rooms: 5 w/pvt. bath, phone, TV. Located in 2 bldgs.
Rates: $65-$95/room, $125/cabin, all incl. full brk., afternoon refreshment, evening dessert. Discount avail. for mid-week stay.
Credit cards: Most major cards
Restrictions: No children under 12, pets, smoking.
Notes: Built in the early 1900s. Porches, whirlpools, breakfast. Log cabin built in 1850 offers privacy. Decorated with hearts by its Irish builder. Biking, golf, tennis, fishing available. Handicapped access.

ATLANTIC (4)

Chestnut Charm Bed & Breakfast
1409 Chestnut, Atlantic, IA 50022
(712) 243-5652
Innkeeper: Barbara Stensvad
Rooms: 4 w/pvt. bath, incl. 2 w/phone, plus 1 suite w/pvt. bath, phone
Rates: $55-$75/room, $85/suite, all incl. full brk.
Credit cards: Most major cards
Restrictions: No young children, pets, smoking. 50% deposit req. 5-day cancellation notice req. less $10.00 fee.
Notes: Two-story Victorian carriage house with hardwood floors built in 1898. Parlor with piano. Sunroom. Patio with fountain. Air-conditioned. Special diets accommodated with advance notice. Small private parties accommodated.*

BATTLE CREEK (1)

Inn at Battle Creek
201 Maple St., Battle Creek, IA 51006
(712) 365-4949, (712) 365-4949
Innkeeper: Rod and Nancy Pearson
Rooms: 4 w/pvt. bath, TV
Rates: $65., incl. full brk.
Credit cards: Most major cards
Restrictions: No pets, smoking. One night's deposit req. 14-day cancellation notice req. Closed Jan.
Notes: Queen Anne Victorian house built in 1897. Fully restored. VCR and movies. Furnished with antiques. Restaurant on premises with seasonal hours. Air-conditioned. Listed on the National Register of Historic Places.*

CALMAR (3)

Calmar Guesthouse
103 N. St., Calmar, IA 52132
(319) 562-3851

CALMAR GUESTHOUSE

Innkeeper: Lucille B. Kruse
Rooms: 5
Rates: $45, incl. full brk.
Credit cards: Most major cards
Restrictions: No pets, smoking. Deposit req. 4-day cancellation notice req.
Notes: Two-story Victorian mansion built in 1890. Recently restored. Office with ceiling, walls, floor made of wood. Living room with stained-glass window. Stained-glass window in entry hallway. Sitting room with cable TV. Dining room. Air conditioned.

CEDAR FALLS (3)

Carriage House Inn B & B
3030 Grand Blvd., Cedar Falls, IA 50613
(319) 277-6724

Innkeeper: Mel & Sandy McCleary
Rooms: 1 w/pvt. bath, plus 2 suites w/pvt. bath, phone, TV, fireplace, all w/whirlpool. Located in 2 bldgs.
Rates: $85/room, $120/suite, all incl. full brk., afternoon refreshment. Discount avail. for corporate stay.
Credit cards: Most major cards
Restrictions: No children, pets, smoking. One night's deposit req. 7-day cancellation notice req., less $10.00 fee.
Notes: Two-story Victorian house with Cameo windows, golden oak staircase and bannister, fireplace built in the early 1800s. Furnished with antiques and period lighting. Gazebo. Spanish spoken.

COUNCIL BLUFFS (4)

Lion's Den
136 S. 7th St., Council Bluffs, IA 51501
(712) 322-7162

Innkeeper: Jerry and Kathy Gilmore
Rooms: 1 5-room suite w/pvt. bath, phone, fireplace, TV
Rates: $100, incl. full brk., evening refreshment.
Credit cards: MC, V

Restrictions: No children under 5. 50% deposit req. 7-day cancellation notice req., less 25% fee.
Notes: Two-story Gothic house built in 1900. Lounge, book and video library, Jacuzzi, sauna. Furnished with antiques and collectables. Victorian porch with swing. Guests have access to exercise equipment.

DES MOINES (5)

Carter House Inn
640 20th St., Sherman Hill, Des Moines, IA 50314-1001
(515) 288-7850
Innkeeper: Penny Schiltz
Rooms: 4, incl. 2 w/pvt. bath
Rates: $50-$60, incl. full brk.
Credit cards: MC, V
Restrictions: No children, smoking. Deposit req. 7-day cancellation notice req.
Notes: Victorian house built in 1870s. Renovated in 1988. 2 parlors. Library. Dining room. Decorated in period furnishings. Small private parties accommodated.*

DUBUQUE (3)

Juniper Hill Farm
15325 Budd Rd., Dubuque, IA 52001
(319) 582-4405, (800) 572-1449, (319) 583-6607
Innkeeper: Ruth and Bill McEllhiney
Rooms: 1 w/pvt. bath, plus 2 suites w/pvt.bath, incl. 1 w/phone, 1 w/TV
Rates: $70/room, $90-$130/suite, all incl. full brk., afternoon refreshment. Discount avail. for mid-week stay.
Credit cards: Most major cards
Restrictions: No children under 4, pets. Smoking restricted. One night's deposit req. 3-day cancellation notice req. 2-night min. stay on wknds.
Notes: Built in 1940. Fully renovated. Located on 40 wooded acres with stocked fishing pond, including 6 acres of manicured lawns and flower beds. Gathering room with 1900 wood burning stove. Atrium with TV. Furnished in modified country decor. Year-round outdoor hot tub.

THE RICHARDS HOUSE

The Richards House
1492 Locust St., Dubuque, IA 52001-4714
(319) 557-1492

Innkeeper: Michelle Delaney
Rooms: 5, incl. 3 w/pvt. bath, phone, 2 w/fireplace, plus 1 suite w/pvt. bath, fireplace, all w/cable TV
Rates: $40-$75/room, $50-$85/suite, all incl. full brk., afternoon refreshment. Seasonal variations. Discount avail. for group, extended and mid-week stays. Special pkgs. avail.
Credit cards: Most major cards
Restrictions: Pets restricted. Smoking restricted. One night's deposit req. 3-day cancellation notice req.
Notes: Four-story stick-style Victorian mansion built in 1883 with seven varieties of woodwork and nine patterns of Lincrusta-Walton wall coverings. Located in Jackson Park National Register District. Furnished with period pieces. Over eighty stained-glass windows. Music room with grand piano. Dining room with fireplace. Special diet needs accommodated with advance notice.*

FOREST CITY (2)

1897 Victorian House B & B
306 S. Clark, Forest City, IA 50436
(515) 582-3613
Innkeeper: Richard and Doris Johnson
Rooms: 3 plus 2 suites all w/pvt. bath, 3 w/phone, 1 w/TV
Rates: $69/room, $79-$89/suite, all incl. full brk.
Credit cards: MC V
Restrictions: No children, pets, smoking, alcohol. $20.00 deposit req.
Notes: Three-story Victorian House built in 1897. Dining room, porch. Decorated with quilts, lace curtains, hooked rugs and antiques. Antique shop on premises. Small private parties accommodated.

FORT MADISON (7)

KINGSLEY INN

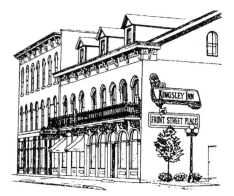

Kingsley Inn
707 Ave. H, Fort Madison, IA 52627
(319) 372-7074
Innkeeper: Myrna Reinhard
Rooms: 14 w/pvt. bath, phone, TV
Rates: $55-$105, incl. cont. brk. Seasonal variations. Seasonal variations.
Credit cards: Most major cards

Restrictions: No children under 12, pets. Smoking restricted. Deposit req. 24-hour cancellation notice req.

Notes: Victorian inn with three-story glass atrium building built in 1808 on the banks of the Missipppi. Winding walnut staicase, glass-front elevator, pool. Courtyard, restaurant, lounge on premises. Furnished with period antiques. Small private parties accommodated.*

GREENFIELD (5)

The Wilson Home B & B
RR 2, Box 132-1, Greenfield, IA 50849
(515) 743-2031
Innkeeper: Wendy and Henry Wilson
Rooms: 2 w/pvt. bath, phone, TV
Rates: $75, incl. full brk.
Credit cards: Most major cards
Restrictions: Pets, smoking restricted. $25.00 deposit req. 48-hour cancellation notice req.
Notes: Two-story farmhouse with cherry woodwork, fireplace, built in 1918. Expanded in 1961. Dining room, library. Furnished with antiques. Lower deck, upper deck, indoor swimming pool. Guests have access to kitchen. Hunting packages avail. Handicapped access.*

HOMESTEAD (6)

Die Heimat Country Inn
Amana Colonies, Main St., Homestead, IA 52236
(319) 622-3937
Innkeeper: Warren and Jacki Lock
Rooms: 19 w/pvt. bath, TV
Rates: $41-$63, incl. full brk. Discount avail. for winter and group stays.
Credit cards: Most major cards
Restrictions: No pets. Smoking restricted. Deposit req. 24-hour cancellation notice req.
Notes: Built as stagecoach stop in 1854 of native stone, timbers. Fully restored, redecorated in 1963. Lounge. Guest rooms individually furnished with walnut and cherry furniture from the historic Amana Colonies. Decorated with paintings, keepsakes, heirlooms. Shaded lawn with wooden glider. Hay rides and sleigh rides arranged. Small private parties accommodated. Die Heimat is German for *The Home Place.*

IOWA CITY (6)

Haverkamps' Linn Street Homestay
619 N. Linn St., Iowa City, IA 52245
(319) 337-4363
Innkeeper: Clarence and Dorothy Haverkamp
Rooms: 3, no pvt. bath
Rates: $30-$45, incl. full brk.
Credit cards: None
Restrictions: No pets, smoking. $10.00 deposit req. 5-day cancellation notice req., less $10.00 fee.

Notes: Two-story Edwardian-style house built in 1908. Reception room with hat collection, 1934 Mills slot machine. Living room. Library with TV. Front porch with swing. Furnished with antiques.*

MAQUOKETA (6)

Squiers Manor
418 W. Pleasant St., Maquoketa, IA 52060
(319) 652-6961
Innkeeper: Virl and Kathy Banowetz
Rooms: 5 w/pvt. bath, phone, TV, plus 1 suite w/pvt. bath, phone, TV, fireplace.
Rates: $65-$95/room, $125/suite, all incl. full brk., evening dessert
Credit cards: Most major cards
Restrictions: No pets. Smoking restricted. Deposit req. 7-day cancellation notice req.
Notes: Queen Anne brick mansion built in 1882. Restored in 1990. Original features include walnut, cherry and butternut woodwork, brass hardware, stained and frosted glass, brass gas and electric chandeliers. Decorated with period antiques.

MARENGO (6)

Loy's Farm Bed & Breakfast
2077 KK Ave., RR #1, Marengo, IA 52301
(319) 642-7787
Innkeeper: Loy and Robert Walker
Rooms: 3, incl. 1 w/pvt. bath, fireplace, TV
Rates: $50-$60, incl. full brk.
Credit cards: None
Restrictions: Pets, smoking restricted. Deposit req. 7-day cancellation notice req.
Notes: Two-story farm house built in 1976. Has operated as Inn since 1985. Located on 2500 acre working corn and hog farm. Spacious lawn with swing set, sandbox, flower gardens. Living room with fireplace, TV. Recreation room with pool table, table tennis, shuffleboard, board games. Country kitchen, screened porch overlooking countryside. Manufacturing and farm tours available. Resident farm animals.

MITCHELLVILLE (5)

Whitaker Farms
11045 NE 82nd Ave., Mitchellville, IA 50169
(515) 967-3184
Innkeeper: Virginia & John Whitaker
Rooms: 1 suite w/phone
Rates: $65, incl. full brk.
Credit cards: Most major cards
Restrictions: Smoking restricted. 50% deposit req.
Notes: Farmhouse surrounded by trees. Decorated with farmhouse antiques. Pick-your-own strawberries in summer and pumpkins in fall.

MONTPELIER (6)

Varners' Caboose B & B
204 E. 2nd St., Box 10, Montpelier, IA 52759
(319) 381-3652
Innkeeper: Bob and Nancy Varner

Rooms: 1 suite w/pvt. bath, kitchen, TV
Rates: $55, incl. full brk. Discount avail. for extended stay.
Credit cards: Most major cards
Restrictions: Pets restricted. No smoking. $20.00 deposit req. 7-day cancellation notice req.
Notes: Rock Island Line caboose set on its own track behind innkeeper's house, which was the original Montpelier Depot. Common room with TV.*

PELLA (5)

AvondGloren (Sunset View) B & B
984 198th Pl., Box 65, Pella, IA 50219
(515) 628-1578, (515) 628-2401
Innkeeper: Henry and Luella Bandstra
Rooms: 3, no pvt. bath
Rates: $40-$50, incl. cont. brk., afternoon refreshment. Discount avail. for extended and senior citizen stays.
Credit cards: Most major cards
Restrictions: No pets, smoking. One night's deposit req. 7-day cancellation notice req. Closed Jan.–March.
Notes: One-story brick house. Family room with TV and fireplace. Flower gardens and deck. Handicapped access.

ROCKWELL CITY (2)

Pine Grove B & B
2361 270th St., Rockwell City, IA 50579
(712) 297-7494
Innkeeper: David & Marcia Ahlrichs
Rooms: 2 rooms w/phone, TV
Rates: $55, incl. full brk., evening dessert
Credit cards: Most major cards
Restrictions: No pets, smoking.
Notes: Farmhouse built in the early 1900s. Sun porch, dining room. Furnished with antiques and quilts.

ST. ANSGAR (2)

Blue Bell Inn
513 W. 4th St., St. Ansgar, IA 50472
(515) 736-2225
Innkeeper: Sherrie Hansen
Rooms: 4, incl. 3 w/pvt. bath, TV, plus 2 suites w/pvt. bath, fireplace, TV
Rates: $50-$80/room, $110-$120/suite, all incl. full brk. Discount avail. for midweek and extended stays.
Credit cards: MC, V
Restrictions: Children welcome at owner's discretion. No pets, smoking. 50% deposit req. Min. 7-day cancellation notice req., less $10.00 fee applied to gift certificate.
Notes: Three-story Victorian house with fireplaces, wood floors, tin ceilings with ornate moldings, leaded-glass, stained-glass and crystal chandeliers in bay and curved window pockets, and eight foot maple pocket doors, built in 1896. Maple bannister winds to second floor balcony overlooking maples trees, flowers and fish pond.

Third-floor Jacuzzi. Decorated in Queen Anne Victorian style. Guests have access to kitchenette. Videos, board games available. Small private parties accommodated. Limited German spoken. *

SPENCER (1)

Hannah Marie Country Inn
4070, Hwy. 71, Spencer, IA 51301
(712) 262-1286, 332-7719
Innkeeper: Mary Nichols
Rooms: 4 w/pvt. bath. Located in 2 bldgs.
Rates: $50-$90, incl. full brk., afternoon refreshment
Credit cards: Most major cards
Restrictions: Pets restricted. No smoking. 50% deposit req. Cancellation notice req., less fee on holidays. Closed Dec. 19–April 1.
Notes: Country Victorian house built in 1910. Restored in 1985. Has operated as inn since 1987. Located on 200-acre corn and soybean farm. One house is country-gentleman's home, decorated with items from travels to Spain, Italy and Provence. One guest room decorated with 'Sherlock Holmes' items, another with 'Teddy' Roosevelt touches. Dining room. Veranda with rockers. Gardens. Special children's lunches with Queen of Hearts organized. Lawn games, rope swing available. Sign language.*

WALNUT (4)

Antique City Inn B & B
400 Antique City Dr., Walnut, IA 51577
(712) 784-3722
Innkeeper: Sylvia Reddie
Rooms: 5, incl. 1 w/pvt. bath
Rates: $40, incl. full brk.
Credit cards: Most major cards
Restrictions: No children under 12, pets, smoking. One night's deposit req. 24-hour cancellation notice req.
Notes: Two-story Victorian house built in 1911. Restored to its original state. Furnished with Victorian period pieces. Wrap-around porch. Surrounded by a town full of antiques shops and malls. All meals available. Small priviate parties accommodated.

WATERLOO (2)

Wellington B & B
800 W. Fourth St., Waterloo, IA 50702
(319) 234-2993
Innkeeper: Jim and Reatha Aronson
Rooms: 1 plus 2 suites, all w/pvt. bath, phone, TV
Rates: $75-$85, all incl. full brk.
Credit cards: Most major cards
Restrictions: No pets, smoking. One night's deposit req. 14-day cancellation notice req.
Notes: Colonial revival-style house built in 1900. Parlor, library, oak staircase and piazza. Turn-of-the-century furnishings incl. crystal chandelier and pump-organ.

Wood-carved moldings and parquet flooring. Perennial gardens. Listed on the National Register of Historic Places. *

WAVERLY (2)

Villa Fairfield B & B
401 Second Ave. SW., Waverly, IA 50677
(319) 352-0739
Innkeeper: Inez Boevers-Christensen
Rooms: 2, plus 2/suites
Rates: $55/room, $75/suite, incl. full brk. Seasonal variations
Credit cards: MC, V
Restrictions: Smoking restricted. Deposit req. 24-hour cancellation notice req.
Notes: Two-story, soft red brick, Italianate Victorian house with maple and oak flooring, marble fireplace, built in 1876. Furnished w/family antiques. General store on premises. Spanish, Portuguese spoken.*

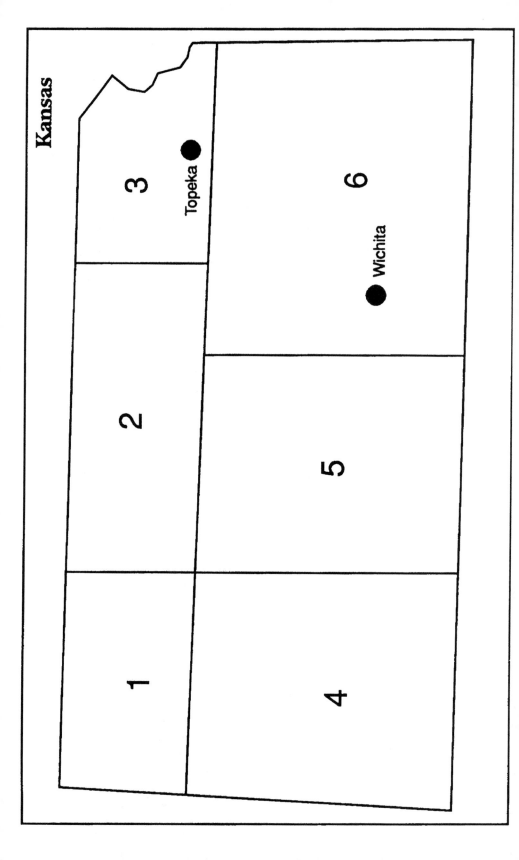

Kansas

ABILENE (6)

Victorian Reflections
820 N.W. Third St., Abilene, KS 67410
(913) 263-7701, (913) 263-7701
Innkeeper: Don and Diane McBride
Rooms: 3 w/pvt. bath, plus 1 suite w/pvt. bath, TV
Rates: $45-$55/room, $65-$75/suite, all incl. full brk. Discount avail. for extended stay. Special pkgs. avail.
Credit cards: Most major cards
Restrictions: No children under 10, pets, smoking. 50% deposit req. 2-day cancellation notice req.
Notes: Three-story Victorian inn built about 1890. Parlor with library, board games, TV, phone. Dining room. Furnished with antiques. Curved stairway. Tennis, swimming pool. Small private parties accommodated. Antique and giftshop on premises.*

ATWOOD (1)

Country Corner
South Hwy. 25, Atwood, KS 67730-88
(913) 626-9516
Innkeeper: Charles and Connie Peckham
Rooms: 2, no pvt. bath, incl. 1 w/phone.
Rates: $30-$40, incl. expanded cont. brk. Discount avail. for children.
Credit cards: Most major cards
Restrictions: No pets. Smoking restricted.
Notes: Two-story country house with fireplace. Furnished with antiques, family heirlooms, and hand-crafted items. Handicapped access.

BASEHOR (3)

Bedknobs & Biscuits
15202 Parallel, Basehor, KS 66007
(913) 724-1540
Innkeeper: Soni Mance
Rooms: 3 w/pvt. sitting room, ceiling fans, skylights, incl. 1 w/pvt. bath
Rates: $55, incl. full brk., evening refreshment. Discount avail. for extended stay.
Credit cards: Most major cards
Restrictions: No children under 8, pets. Smoking restricted. 50% deposit req. 7-day cancellation notice req. 7-night min. stay.
Notes: Beamed gathering room, walls covered in hand-painted vines. Quilts, lace curtains, stained-glass windows. Books, TV. Flower, herb garden overlooking cornfield.

EMPORIA (6)

Plumb House B & B
628 Exchange, Emporia, KS 66801
(316) 342-6881

Innkeeper: Barbara Stoecklein
Rooms: 5, incl. 2 w/pvt. bath, 1 w/phone, TV, plus 2 suites incl. 1 w/pvt. bath, phone, TV
Rates: $45-$55/room, $65-$75/suite, incl. full brk., afternoon refreshment. Discount avail. for extended, senior citizen and mid-week stays.
Credit cards: MC, V
Restrictions: No pets. Smoking restricted. Min. $25.00 deposit req. 7-day cancellation notice req., less $10.00 fee.
Notes: Three-story Victorian house built in 1910. Located downtown. Decorated with beveled glass windows, pocket doors, fainting couches and antique furnishings. Large front porch with stone arch leads to flower garden area and lily pond. Small private parties available. Guided tours, kennel arrangements available.

FORT SCOTT (6)

THE CHENAULT MANSION

The Chenault Mansion
820 S. National Ave., Fort Scott, KS 66701
(316) 223-6800
Innkeeper: Bob and Elizabeth Schafer
Rooms: 5 w/pvt. bath, incl. 2 suites w/pvt. bath, phone, TV
Rates: $64-$70/room, $75/suite, all incl. full brk.
Credit cards: Most major cards
Restrictions: No pets. Smoking restricted. One night's deposit req. 5-day cancellation notice req., less $10.00 fee.
Notes: Built in 1887 with curved glass windows, stained and leaded-glass, ornate cherry, gun, ash and oak woodwork, pocket doors, and fireplaces. Victorian parlor. Furnished with antiques and china, glass collection. Open for tours daily.*

The Courtland B & B Inn
121 E. First St., Fort Scott, KS 66701
(316) 223-0098, (316) 223-4666
Innkeeper: Barbara Kelly and Darcy Heiser-Beck
Rooms: 15 w/pvt. bath

Rates: $55-$85, incl. full brk. Discount avail. for extended, senior citizen, and group stays.

Credit cards: Most major cards

Restrictions: No children under 10, pets. Smoking restricted. 7-day cancellation notice req.

Notes: Two-story building built in 1906 as the Railroad Hotel. Furnished with Victorian antiques. Gathering room with large lace curtained windows and tin ceiling. Giftshop, cafe, and art gallery on premises.

GIRARD (6)

LaForges Bed & Breakfast Inn
505 N. Summit, Girard, KS 66743
(316) 724-4767

Innkeeper: Janice LaForge

Rooms: 4, no pvt. bath, incl. 1 w/phone

Rates: $45, incl. full brk., afternoon refreshment. Discount avail. for extended stay.

Credit cards: None

Restrictions: Pets welcome with advance notice. Smoking restricted. One night's deposit req. 5-day cancellation notice req., less $10.00 fee.

Notes: The two-sory brick house built in 1907. Dining area. Small private parties accommodated. Resident dog.

MELVERN (6)

SCHOOLHOUSE INN

Schoolhouse Inn
106 East Beck, Melvern, KS 66510
(913) 549-3473

Innkeeper: Rudy and Alice White

Rooms: 4, incl. 2 w/pvt. bath. Seasonal variations.

Rates: $45-$55, incl. full brk.

Credit cards: MC, V

Restrictions: No pets, smoking. Deposit req. 2-day cancellation notice req.

Notes: Two-story house built as schoolhouse in 1870. Converted into residence in 1890s. Located on ½ acre of heavy timbers and stone from nearby quarries. Furnished with antiques and contemprary furniture. Entered on the Kansas Historical Register in 1986.

MORAN (6)

Hedge Apple Acres B & B, Inc.
Rte. 2, Box 27, Moran, KS 66755
(316) 237-4646
Innkeeper: Jack and Ann Donaldson
Rooms: 6, no pvt. bath, incl. 1 w/fireplace
Rates: $65, incl. full brk. Discount avail. for extended and mid-week stays, except on holidays.
Credit cards: Most major cards
Restrictions: No pets. Smoking restricted. $20.00 deposit req. 14-day cancellation notice req.
Notes: Brick ranch bldg. located on 80 acres of lake and timber. 65-sq.-ft. family room with TV, fireplace. Porch, deck. Lawn games available. Small private parties accommodated.*

NICKERSON (5)

Hedrick B&B Inn
7910 N. Roy L Smith Rd., Nickerson, KS 67561
(316) 422-3245,
Innkeeper: Betty Van Osdol
Rooms: 6 plus 1 suite, all w/pvt. bath, phone, TV
Rates: $75/room, $100/suite, all incl. full brk.
Credit cards: Most major cards
Restrictions: No pets. Smoking restricted. Deposit req. 10-day cancellation notice req.
Notes: Two-story Western town-front with swinging doors. Located on Exotic Animal Farm. Balcony completely surrounds Inn and overlooks exotic animals. Decorated with murals of animals on farm, mosquito netting, zebra sheets, and Peruvian rugs. Giftshop, snack bar on premises. Children must be supervised at all times. Guests invited to help with chores. Farm tours, camel rides, pony rides, hayrack rides and campfire weiner roasts available. Small private parties accommodated. Handicapped access.

SYRACUSE (4)

Braddock Ames Bed and Breakfast
201 N. Ave. B & Main, Syracuse, KS 67878
(316) 384-5218
Innkeeper: Dorothy Braddock Fouts and Lois Jacobs
Rooms: 3 w/TV, no pvt. bath
Rates: $45-$65, incl. brk.
Credit cards: None
Restrictions: No children under 12, pets, smoking.
Notes: Built in 1930 as senior-citizen residential hotel. Two renovated and fully restored lobbies. Health food breakfast, 'Tanking' rides available. Handicapped access.

WICHITA (6)

Inn at the Park
3751 E. Douglas, Wichita, KS 67218
(316) 652-0500

Innkeeper: Michelle Hickman

Rooms: 7 w/pvt. bath, phone, TV, incl. 2 w/fireplace, plus 4 suites w/pvt. bath, phone, TV, fireplace. Located in 2 bldgs.

Rates: $75-$105/room, $110-$135/suite, all incl. cont. brk. Discount avail. for extended stay.

Credit cards: Most major cards

Restrictions: No children under 10, pets. Smoking restricted. Deposit req. 24-hour cancellation notice req.

Notes: Three-story brick mansion built in 1909. Completely renovated and redecorated. Carriage house offers two private suites. Handicapped access.*

Max Paul, an Inn
3910 E. Kellogg, Wichita, KS 67218
(316) 689-8101, (316) 687-1159

Innkeeper: Roberta Eaton

Rooms: 6 w/pvt. bath, phone, cable TV, plus 8 suites w/pvt. bath, phone, TV, incl. 4 w/fireplace. Located in 3 bldgs.

Rates: $59-79/room, $84-$149/suite, all incl. cont. brk.

Credit cards: Most major cards

Restrictions: No pets. Children restricted. 24-hour cancellation notice req. Closed Dec. 24, 25.

Notes: Three Tudor cottages built in the 1930s. Fully restored. Living room with fireplace, bay window. Breakfast room, conference room. Exercise room with Jacuzzi. Furnished with European antiques, Persian rugs. Private decks overlooking garden with arbor, pond. Small private parties accommodated. French spoken.

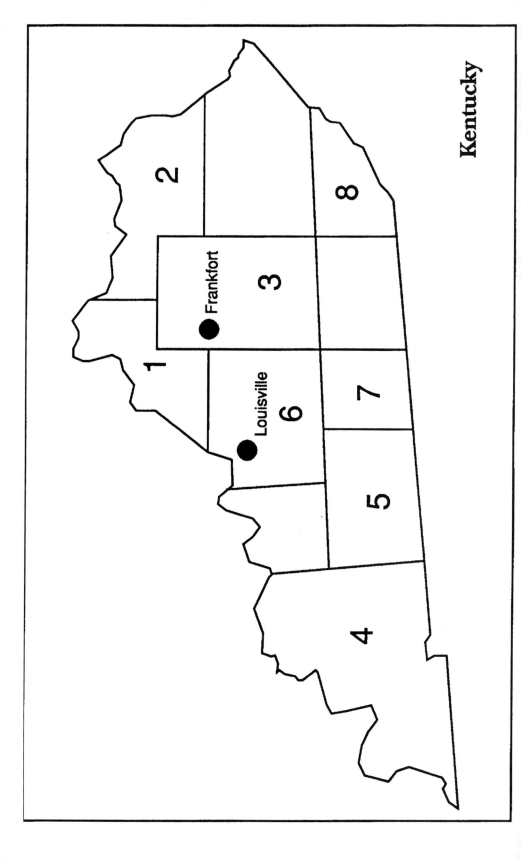

Kentucky

Kentucky

AUBURN (5)

Auburn Guesthouse
421 W. Main, Auburn, KY 42206
(502) 542-6019
Innkeeper: David and Joy Williams
Rooms: 5, incl. 2 w/pvt. bath
Rates: $35-$55, incl. full brk. Discount avail. for extended and senior citizen stays.
Credit cards: None
Restrictions: No children under 5, pets. Smoking restricted. $10.00 deposit req. 10-day cancellation notice req.
Notes: Two-story Southern Colonial mansion. Located at Shakertown and South Union Hwy. Living room. Lounge. Cable TV. *

BARDSTOWN (6)

Bruntwood Inn
714 N. Third St., Bardstown, KY 40004
(502) 348-8218
Innkeeper: Susan Danielak
Rooms: 5, incl. 4 w/pvt. bath, plus 4 suites w/pvt. bath
Rates: $75-$85/room, $140/suite, all incl. full brk.
Credit cards: Most major cards
Restrictions: No pets, smoking. $50.00 deposit req. 7-day cancellation notice req.
Notes: Two-story Southern house. Dining room, grand entrance foyer, spiral stairway. Furnished with antiques. Porch and balcony. Small private parties accommodated.*

Coffee Tree Cabin
980 McCubbins Lane, Bardstown, KY 40004
(502) 348-1151
Innkeeper: J.L. and JoAnn Bland
Rooms: 3 w/pvt. bath, incl. 1 w/TV, plus 1 suite w/pvt. bath w/whirlpool, TV
Rates: $75/room, $85/suite, all incl. full brk., desserts, soups during winter. Seasonal variations. Discount avail. for extended stay.
Credit cards: Most major cards
Restrictions: No children, pets. Smoking restricted. 50% deposit req. 3-day cancellation notice req., less 50% deposit fee.
Notes: Hand hewn log house built in 1988. Located on 17.5 acres. Cathedral and natural plank ceiling, coach lighting. 22' balcony overlooking lodge room and breakfast room. Skylights and cobblestone fireplace. Furnished with some antiques. Porches with rockers and benches. Courtyard with fountain. Spring fed lake. Small private parties accommodated. *

Jailer's Inn
111 W. Stephen Foster Ave., Bardstown, KY 40004
(502) 348-5551, (800) 948-5551
Innkeeper: Fran and Challen McCoy
Rooms: 6 w/pvt. bath, incl. 3 w/TV, 1 w/Jacuzzi. Located in 2 bldgs.

Rates: $55-$85, incl. cont. brk., afternoon refreshment
Credit cards: Most major cards
Restrictions: No pets, smoking. Deposit req. 5-day cancellation notice req.
Notes: Colonial limestone jail with thirty inch-thick walls built in 1819. Expanded in 1874. Renovated in and has operated as inn since 1988. Furnished with antiques, Oriental rugs. Landscaped courtyard with pavilion, wishing well. Listed on the National Register of Historic Places. Limited handicapped access.*

Kenmore Farms B&B
1050 Bloomfield Rd. US 62E, Bardstown, KY 40004
(502) 348-8023, (800) 831-6159
Innkeeper: Dorothy and Bernie Keene
Rooms: 3 w/pvt. bath, plus 1 suite w/pvt bath, phone
Rates: $70/room, $125/suite, all incl. full brk., afternoon refreshment
Credit cards: None
Restrictions: No children under 12, pets, smoking. Deposit req. 72-hour cancellation notice
Notes: Two-story Victorian house with poplar floors, cherry stairway, built in the 1860s. Located in a farm setting. Sitting room, dining room. Furnishsed with antiques, Oriental rugs.*

BELLEVUE (1)

Weller Haus B & B
319 Poplar, Bellevue, KY 41073
(606) 431-6829
Innkeeper: Mary and Vernon Weller
Rooms: 1 w/pvt. bath, TV, plus 4 suites w/pvt. bath, incl. 3 w/TV. Located in 2 bldgs.
Rates: $68/room, $70-$85/suite, $120/Jacuzzi suite, all incl. cont. brk. Seasonal variations.
Credit cards: Most major cards
Restrictions: No pets. Smoking restricted. Deposit req.
Notes: Two Victorian Gothic houses with original millwork, built in 1880. Guests have access to 'ivy-covered' gathering kitchen, sky-lit common room with cathedral ceiling opening onto English garden. Furnished with antiques and 18th-century period pieces. Lawn and patio area. Small private parties accommodated. Listed with the National Trust in Washington, D.C.*

BRANDENBURG (9)

Doe Run Inn
500 Doe Run Hotel Rd. Rte. 2, Brandenburg, KY 40108
(502) 422-2982, (502) 422-4916
Innkeeper: Mr. & Mrs. Henry Hockman
Rooms: 11, incl. 8 w/pvt. bath, plus cabin
Rates: $33/room, $75/cabin
Credit cards: Most major cards
Restrictions: No pets. Deposit req. 7-day cancellation notice req.
Notes: Three-story structure built in 1821 from hand-hewn timber and native limestone as a mill. Converted to inn in 1927. Family owned for five generations. Original period decor. Smorgasbord Friday and Sunday. Gift shop with prize-winning quilts on premises.

COVINGTON (2)

The Carneal House Inn
405 E. Second, Covington, KY 41011
(606) 431-6130, (606) 581-6041

Innkeeper: Karen and Peter Rafuse
Rooms: 6 w/pvt. bath, incl. 3 w/fireplace
Rates: $70-$120, incl. full brk., afternoon refreshment. Seasonal variations. Discount avail. for mid-week stay.
Credit cards: Most major cards
Restrictions: No children under 14. Deposit req. 2-day cancellation notice req.
Notes: Two-story, Palladian Georgian sytle ante-bellum mansion built in 1815. Overlooks Licking River. Dining room, marble-floored gallery. Limestone terrace. Furnished in Victorian style with four poster beds. Surrounded by lawns and gardens. Horse-drawn carriage rides available. Small private parties accommodated. Fax machine, portable phone, and TV available. Spanish spoken.*

SANDFORD HOUSE

Sandford House
1026 Russell St., Covington, KY 41011
(606) 291-9133

Innkeeper: Dan and Linda Carter
Rooms: 1 w/pvt. bath, TV, plus 3 suites w/pvt. bath, phone, TV, incl. 1 w/whirlpool bath, original cooking fireplace. Plus Carriage House. Located in 2 bldgs.
Rates: $55/room, $85/suite, $85-$120/Carriage House, all incl. full brk., afternoon refreshment. Discount avail. for senior citizen, AAA, and extended stays.
Credit cards: Most major cards
Restrictions: Pets, smoking restricted. Deposit req. 24-hour cancellation notice.
Notes: Federal style house built in 1820. Victorianized after fire with Second Empire Mansard roof added. Has operated as Inn since 1990. Gazebo, garden. Listed on the National Register. Some suite guests have access to laundry facilities.*

DANVILLE (3)

Randolph House
463 W. Lexington, Danville, KY 40422
(606) 236-9594

Innkeeper: Georgie Heizer
Rooms: 3 w/pvt. bath, incl. 2 w/phone, TV
Rates: $55-$65, incl. full brk., reserved dinner. Discount avail for extended stay.
Credit cards: Most major cards
Restrictions: No pets. Smoking restricted. One night's deposit req. $10.00 cancellation fee.
Notes: Federal house with floor-length windows, thirteen foot ceilings, built in 1850s for Professor S.C. Randolph. Library, parlor. Furnished with European and Victorian antiques.*

Twin Hollies Retreat B & B
406 Maple Ave., Danville, KY 40422
(606) 236-8954

Innkeeper: Mary Joe and John W.D. Bowling
Rooms: 3 w/fireplace, incl. 1 w/pvt. bath
Rates: $75, incl. full brk. Discount avail. for corporate stay.
Credit cards: Most major cards
Restrictions: No pets. Smoking restricted. Deposit required. 7-night min. stay.
Notes: Two-story antebellum house built approx. 1833. Common room with fireplace. Jacuzzi overlooking gardens. Listed on the National Register of Historic Places.*

PINEAPPLE INN

GEORGETOWN (3)

Pineapple Inn
645 S. Broadway, Georgetown, KY 40324
(502) 868-5453

Innkeeper: Muriel and Les
Rooms: 4 w/pvt. bath, incl. 1 w/TV
Rates: $60, incl. full brk.
Credit cards: MC, V
Restrictions: No children under 12, pets. Smoking restricted. 50% deposit req. 48-hour cancellation notice req.

Notes: Two-story Victorian-style house with many gables, decorative vergeboards, applied pilasters, a bay window and bracketed eaves, built in 1876. Located on 3 acres. FUnique siding simulates cut stone. Kitchen, dining room, living room, foyer, TV room, sitting room. Front porch with swing and wicker furniture. Yard with tables and chairs.*

GHENT (1)

GHENT HOUSE B & B

Ghent House B & B
411 Main St., US 42, Box 478, Ghent, KY 41011
(502) 347-5807, (606) 291-0168
Innkeeper: Wayne and Diane Young
Rooms: 3 suites w/pvt. bath, incl. 2 w/phone, 1 w/fireplace, TV
Rates: $90-$110, incl. full brk., afternoon refreshment
Credit cards: Most major cards
Restrictions: No pets. Smoking restricted. $25.00 deposit req. 7-day cancellation notice req.
Notes: Two-storyFederal style antebellum house with crystal chandeliers, fireplaces, Jacuzzis and private porches, built in 1833. View of the Ohio River. Rose garden with gazebo, English walking garden.

GLASGOW (5)

Four Seasons Country Inn
4107 Scottsville Rd., Glasgow, KY 42141
(502) 678-1000
Innkeeper: Henry Carter
Rooms: 17 w/pvt. bath, phone, cable TV
Rates: $52-$62, incl. cont. brk. Discount avail. for extended stay.
Credit cards: Most major cards
Restrictions: No pets.
Notes: Victorian style inn built in 1989. Lobby with fireplace. Some rooms with deck. Furnished with antique reproductions. Swimming pool, veranda. Guests have access to health club. Handicapped access.*

LOUISVILLE (1)

Inn at the Park
1332 S. 4th St., Louisville, KY 40208
(502) 637-6930, (800) 700-7275
Innkeeper: Rob and Theresa Carskie
Rooms: 5 w/TV, incl. 3 w/pvt. bath, fireplace, 2 w/phone, plus 1 suite w/pvt. bath, fireplace, TV
Rates: $60-$79/room, $95/suite, all incl. full brk., evening refreshment
Credit cards: Most major cards
Restrictions: No pets. Smoking restricted. 48-hour cancellation notice req.
Notes: Three-story Victorian mansion of Richardsonian Romanesque architecture with 14-ft. ceilings, marble fireplaces and hardwood floors, built in 1886. Fully restored in 1985. Foyer with sweeping staircase, dining room. Five porches overlooking Central Park. Furnished with Victorian antiques and reproductions. Small private parties accommodated. Guests have access to fax and photocopy machine. Spanish spoken.*

INN AT THE PARK

Old Louisville Inn
1359 S. Third St., Louisville, KY 40208
(502) 635-1574, (502) 637-5892
Innkeeper: Marianne Lesker
Rooms: 8, incl. 5 w/pvt. bath, plus 3 suites w/pvt. bath
Rates: $95/room, $110-$195/suite, all incl. expanded cont. brk. Discount avail. for group stay. Seasonal variations. Special pkgs. avail.
Credit cards: MC, V
Restrictions: No pets. Smoking restricted. 50% deposit req. 48-hour cancellation notice req. 2-night min. stay on some holidays and special events.
Notes: Three-story house with leaded-glass, sculptured cornices, Corinthian columns built in 1901. Fully restored in the early 1970s. Has operated as inn since 1990. Lobby with twelve-foot ceiling. Parlor with fireplace. Game room with TV. Library, dining room. Furnished with antiques. Front porch, courtyard. Small private parties accommodated.*

Victorian Secret B & B
1132 S. First St., Louisville, KY 40203
(502) 581-1914
Innkeeper: Nan and Steve Roosa
Rooms: 3 w/TV, incl. 1 w/pvt. bath, phone, plus 1 suite w/pvt. bath, phone, TV
Rates: $48-$68/room, $78-$89/suite, all incl. cont. brk. Discount avail. for extended
   stay.
Credit cards: None
Restrictions: No pets. Smoking restricted. Deposit req. 3-day cancellation notice req.
Notes: Three-story brick Victorian Mansion with original woodwork, 11 fireplaces,
built approx. 1890. Renovated with central air conditioning, sundecks. Furnished
with antiques and period pieces. Guests have access to laundry facilities.*

MARION (4)

Lafayette Heights Clubhouse
173 Lafayette Heights, Marion, KY 42064
(502) 965-3889
Innkeeper: Harley and Joyce Haegelin
Rooms: 6, incl. 4 w/pvt. bath, 2 w/TV
Rates: $30-$45, incl. full brk. Discount avail. for extended stay.
Credit cards: MC, V
Restrictions: No pets, smoking.
Notes: Original clubhouse was built in the early 1920s. Most recent remodeling
added an 80 seat dining room, as well as more bedrooms and bathrooms. Dinner
available by request. Small private parties accommodated. Handicapped access.

MIDDLESBORO (8)

The RidgeRunner
208 Arthur Heights, Middlesboro, KY 40965
(606) 248-4299
Innkeeper: Susan Richards and associate, Irma Gall
Rooms: 4, incl. 2 w/pvt. bath. Suite avail.
Rates: $55-$65, incl. full brk., evening refreshment
Credit cards: MC, V
Restrictions: No children under 16, pets, smoking. One night's non-refundable
   deposit req. 7-day cancellation notice req.
Notes: Two-story Victorian mansion with original wood floors, woodwork, stained-
glass windows built in 1890. President Abraham Lincoln stayed here the night before delivering the Gettsburg Address. Fully restored in 1976. Dining room, library,
parlor. Jigsaw puzzles, antique game boards, knick-knacks. Furnished with heirloom
antiques. Front porch with rockers and swing, overlooking Cumberland Gap National Park Mountains. Lawn games, hammock. Small private parties accommodated. Special dietary needs met. Resident dog.

MOREHEAD (2)

Appalachian House
910 Willow Dr., Morehead, KY 40351
(606) 784-5421
Innkeeper: Allen and Betty Lake
Rooms: 2

Rates: $48/room, incl. full brk. Discount avail. for extended stay.
Credit cards: None
Restrictions: No children under 8, pets, smoking. $10.00 deposit req. 24-hour cancellation notice req., less $5.00 fee.
Notes: Furnished with antiques, handmade Appalachian toys, collectibles.

NICHOLASVILLE (3)

SANDUSKY HOUSE

Sandusky House
1626 Delaney Ferry Rd., Nicholasville, KY 40356
(606) 223-4730

Innkeeper: Jim and Linda Humphrey
Rooms: 3 w/pvt. bath, incl. 1 w/TV
Rates: $69, incl. full brk. Discount avail. for extended stay.
Credit cards: MC, V
Restrictions: No children under 12, pets. Smoking restricted. One night's deposit req. 3-day cancellation notice req. 2-night min. stay on holidays.
Notes: Two story Greek Revival house built in the 1850s. Located on 10 acres. Six porches, seven fireplaces, and brick columns.

PADUCAH (4)

The 1857s
127 Market House Square, Paducah, KY 42001
(502) 444-3960, (800) 264-5607

Innkeeper: Deborah Bohnert
Rooms: 1, plus 1 suite w/phone all w/pvt. bath, cable TV
Rates: $55/room, $65/suite, all incl. cont. brk., afternoon refreshment. Discount avail. for extended stay. Special pkgs. avail.
Credit cards: MC, V
Restrictions: No pets. Smoking restricted. 7-day cancellation notice req.
Notes: Three-story brick house built in 1857, located downtown. Inn on second and third floors, restaurant on first floor. Renovated in Victorian-era style. Parlor. Billiard table. Hot tub. Game room. Listed on the National Historic Register since 1977.*

RUSSELL SPRINGS (7)

White Pillars
100 Thrasher Ct., Russell Springs, KY 42642
(502) 866-7231, (502) 866-4132
Innkeeper: Margaret Thrasher
Rooms: 1 plus 3 suites, all w/pvt. bath, incl. 1 w/phone, fireplace, 2 w/TV
Rates: $65, incl. full brk., fruit basket. Discount avail. for extended stay.
Credit cards: MC, V
Restrictions: No smoking. Deposit req. 7-day cancellation notice req., less one
night's fee.
Notes: Two-story Country house built in 1876. Restored in 1992. Dining room. Sun-
room. Private second floor deck. Decorated in period furnishings.

SOMERSET (7)

Osborne's of Cabin Hollow
111 Fietz Orchard Rd., Somerset, KY 42501
(606) 382-5495
Innkeeper: Robert and Mary Osborne
Rooms: 1 w/pvt. bath, deck, plus 2 suites
Rates: $40-$50/room, $60-$70/suite, all incl. full brk., evening refreshment. Discount avail. for extended stay.
Credit cards: MC, V
Restrictions: No children under 12, pets, smoking. Deposit req. 10-day cancellation
notice req. Closed Dec. 1–April 31.
Notes: Log house built in 1990. Located on wooded hill. Decorated with country
furnishings. Porches with swings. Deck with rocker. Homemade jellies, preserves,
relishes, pickles, and specialty goods available.

Shadwick House
411 S. Main St., Somerset, KY 42501
(606) 678-4675
Innkeeper: Ann Epperson
Rooms: 4, no pvt. bath
Rates: $40, incl. full brk.
Credit cards: Most major cards
Restrictions: No pets, smoking. Deposit req. Min. 2-day cancellation notice req.
Notes: Two-story house built in 1920 as boarding house for railroad workers. Has
operated as Inn since 1990. Breakfast room. Furnished with antiques. Antique and
craft shop on premises.

SPRINGFIELD (6)

Maple Hill Manor
2941 Perryville Rd., Springfield, KY 40069
(606) 336-3075
Innkeeper: Bob and Kay Carroll
Rooms: 7 w/pvt. bath
Rates: $60-$80, incl. full brk., evening dessert. Seasonal variations. Special pkgs.
avail.
Credit cards: MC, V
Restrictions: No pets, smoking. Deposit req. 14-day cancellation notice req.

Notes: Two-story brick antebellum Italianate Revival house built in 1851. Foyer with free-standing cherry spiral staircase. Located on fourteen acres. Parlor with fireplace. Formal dining room. Library with board games. Patio with picnic tables, BBQ. Furnished with antiques, crystal chandeliers. Honeymoon hideaway with Jacuzzi. Giftshop on premises. Kentucky Landmark Home and listed on the National Register of Historic Places.*

VERSAILLES (3)

Bed & Breakfast at Sills Inn
270 Montgomery Ave., Versailles, KY 40383
(606) 873-4478, (606) 873-4726
Innkeeper: Tony Sills
Rooms: 6 plus 2 suites, all w/pvt. bath, cable TV. Located in 2 bldgs.
Rates: $59-$79/room, $89-$99/suite, all incl. full brk.
Credit cards: Most major cards
Restrictions: No pets. Smoking restricted. Full deposit req. for special events. 7-day cancellation notice req. 30-day cancellation notice req. for special events. 3-night min. stay for KY Derby, basket tournaments, and Rolex.
Notes: Three-story Victorian house built in 1911. Formal dining room. Common room with Victrola. Wrap-around porch with wicker rockers. Furnished with antiques, family heirlooms. Guests have access to kitchen. Airport pick-up available.*

Peacham
Rte. 1, Box 263, Versailles, KY 40383
(606) 873-3208
Innkeeper: Betsy Pratt
Rooms: 1 w/pvt. bath, plus 1 suite w/pvt. bath, phone
Rates: $60/room, $75/suite, all incl. full brk., afternoon refreshment
Credit cards: MC, V
Restrictions: No children under 12, pets, smoking. Deposit req. 48-hour cancellation notice, less $10.00 fee. 2-night min. stay during race meets in April and October.
Notes: 1½ story Federal style built in 1829. Made of Flemish bond brick with Palladiau windows. Front porch. 1½ acre pond. Fields, Thoroughbred mares.

Shepherd Place
31 Heritage Rd., Versailles, KY 40383
(606) 873-7843, (800) 278-0864
Innkeeper: Marlin and Sylvia Yawn
Rooms: 2 w/pvt. bath, phone, fireplace
Rates: $65, incl. full brk.
Credit cards: MC, V
Restrictions: No children under 12, pets, smoking
Notes: Built approx. 1815. Porch with swing. Yarn and/or hand-knitted sweaters available. Resident sheep.

Victorian Rose
160 S. Main, Versailles, KY 40383
(606) 873-5252, (606) 873-2525
Innkeeper: Tim and Judy Thompson
Rooms: 1 suite w/pvt. bath, phone, TV

Rates: $79/suite, $285/week, all incl. full brk.
Credit cards: Most major cards
Restrictions: No pets, smoking. Deposit req.
Notes: Located on the second floor of Victorian style building. Recently completed renovation includes bedroom with queen-size bed, full bath, complete kitchen, dining area, and living room with queen-size sleeper couch.

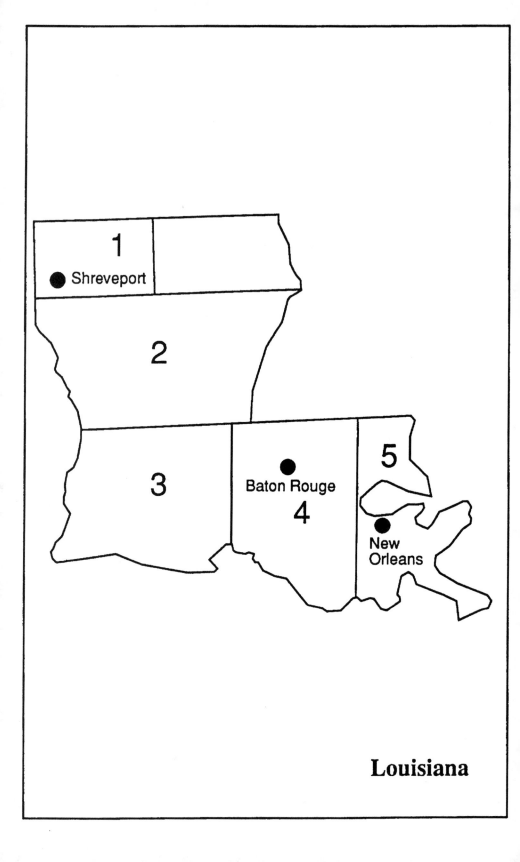

Louisiana

ABBEVILLE (3)

A la Bonne Veillee Guest House
Rte. 2, HWY 339, Box 2270, Abbeville, LA 70510
(318) 937-5495
Innkeeper: Ron Ray and Carolyn Doerle Ray
Rooms: 1 guesthouse w/2 bedrooms, incl. 1 bath, 2 fireplaces, phone, TV, kitchen
Rates: $100, incl. cont. brk. Discount avail. for extended stay.
Credit cards: Most major cards
Restrictions: No pets, smoking. One night's deposit req. Closed Thanksgiving Day,
Dec. 25, Jan. 1.
Notes: Two-story French-style cottage built about 1850. Fully restored. Surrounded
by thirty farmland acres. Front gallery. Modern kitchen, dining area. Furnished
with period antiques. Duck pond. Air-conditioned. Listed on the National Register
of Historic Places. French spoken.*

CARENCRO (3)

La Maison De Champagne
825 Kidder Rd., Carencro, LA 70520
(318) 896-6529
Innkeeper: Fred and Joeann McLemore
Rooms: 4 w/pvt. bath, incl. 3 w/phone, 1 w/TV. Located in 2 bldgs.
Rates: $90, incl. full brk.
Credit cards: MC, V
Restrictions: No children under 12, pets, smoking. Min. one night's deposit req.
Min 5-day cancellation notice req.
Notes: Country Victorian house built approx. 1900. Located on 9 wooded acres in
heart of Cajun Country. Decorated w/antiques. Seasonal pool. French spoken.*

KENNER (5)

Seven Oaks Plantation
2600 Gay Lynn Dr., Kenner, LA 70065
(504) 888-8649
Innkeeper: Kay and Henry Andressen
Rooms: 2 w/pvt bath.
Rates: $95-$115, incl. full brk., afternoon refreshment
Credit cards: Most major cards
Restrictions: No pets, smoking. One night's deposit req. 7-day cancellation notice
req., less $15.00 fee.
Notes: Two-story Plantation style house overlooking Lake Pontchartrain. Living
room with fireplace and piano. Furnished with Louisiana antiques. Landscaped gar-
dens with natural fish pond, pigeonnaire, herb garden. Collection of New Orleans
Madri Gras memorabilia.

LAFAYETTE (3)

T' Frere's House
1905 Verot School Rd., Lafayette, LA 70508
(318) 984-9347

Innkeeper: Pat and Maugie Pastor
Rooms: 3, incl. 1 suite all w/pvt. bath, TV, incl. 1 w/fireplace
Rates: $75-$85/room, $75-$85/suite, all incl. full brk., afternoon refreshment
Credit cards: Most major cards
Restrictions: No children under 14, pets. Smoking restricted. Credit card deposit
     req. 7-day cancellation notice req. 2-night min. stay during festivals.
Notes: Two-story French colonial building with steep piched roof built in 1880.
Front porch and balcony with hand-turned balustrade. Luminaires adorn tops of
doors of twelve foot ceilings. Three handcarved cypress fireplaces. Furnished with
antiques. Parlor, dining foom, front gallery, garden room, gazebo. Cajun breakfast
served. French spoken.

TANTE DA'S, A BED & BREAKFAST

Tante Da's, A Bed & Breakfast
2631 S.E. Evangeline Thwy., Lafayette, LA 70508-2168
(318) 264-1191, (800) 853-7378
Innkeeper: Tanya and Douglas Greenwald
Rooms: 4 w/pvt. bath
Rates: $75-$85, incl. full brk., evening refreshment. Discount avail. for extended
     stay.
Credit cards: Most major cards
Restrictions: Children welcome with prior notification. No pets. Smoking re-
     stricted. 72-hour cancellation notice req. 2-night min. stay on special event
     wknds.
Notes: Queen Anne revival cottage built in 1902. Fully restored in 1989. Has oper-
ated as inn since 1993. Parlor with TV. Front porch with swing. Rear patio. French
spoken.*

LAFITTE (3)

Victoria Inn
Hwy 45, Box 0545, Lafitte, LA 70067
(504) 689-4757, (504) 689-3399

VICTORIA INN

Innkeeper: Roy & Dale Ross
Rooms: 5 w/TV, incl. 3 w/pvt. bath, plus 2 suites w/pvt. bath, TV. Located in 2 bldgs.
Rates: $50-$75/room, $90-$120/suite, all incl. full brk., afternoon refreshment.
Credit cards: Most major cards
Restrictions: Smoking restricted. Call about pets. One night's deposit req. 10-day cancellation notice req.
Notes: West Indies-style cottage overlooking Bayou Barataria. Spanish, French, and Arabic spoken.

NATCHITOCHES (2)

Fleur-de-Lis
336 Second St., Natchitoches, LA 71457
(318) 352-6621, (800) 489-6621

Innkeeper: Tom and Harriette Palmer
Rooms: 5 w/pvt. bath
Rates: $60, incl. full brk., evening refreshment. Seasonal variations.
Credit cards: Most major cards
Restrictions: No children under 12, pets. Smoking restricted. One night's deposit req. Min. 3-day cancellation notice req.
Notes: Two-story Victorian house built in 1900. Has operated as inn since 1983. Living room with board games, TV, stereo. Wrap-around porch with rockers and swing. Furnished with antiques. Listed on National Register of Historic Places. Handicapped access.

NEW IBERIA (4)

Inn at LeRosier
314 E. Main St., New Iberia, LA 70560
(318) 367-5306

Innkeeper: Hallman and Mary Beth Woods
Rooms: 4 w/pvt. bath, phone, TV. Located in 2 bldgs.
Rates: $100, incl. full brk., stocked refrigerator
Credit cards: Most major cards

INN AT LE ROSIER

Restrictions: No children under 12, pets, smoking. One night's deposit req. 3-day cancellation notice req.

Notes: Two-story wood house built in 1870. Restored and opened as a restaurant and inn in 1990. Three parlors with fireplaces. Dining room. Separate cottage is of Acadian raised style. Furnished with antiques and reproductions. Restaurant on premises. Rose gardens. Deck, patio, veranda. Handicapped access.*

Pourtos House
4018 Old Jeanerette Rd., New Iberia, LA 70560
(318) 367-7045, (318) 364-8905

Innkeeper: Emma Fox

Rooms: 5, incl. 1 cabin, all w/pvt bath, phone. Located in 2 bldgs.

Rates: $65-$100, incl. full brk.

Credit cards: Most major cards

Restrictions: No children, pets, smoking restricted. 48-hr. cancellation req. 2-night min. stay.

Notes: Acadian Plantation style house located on three acres of tree-lined grounds. Strolling exotic birds. Furnished with antiques. Swimming pool, billiard table, and tennis court. Survival French spoken.*

NEW ORLEANS (5)

Beau Sejour
1930 Napoleon Ave., New Orleans, LA 70115
(504) 897-3746

Innkeeper: Gilles and Kim Gagnon

Rooms: 5 w/pvt. bath incl. 1 w/TV, plus 1 suite w/pvt. bath, TV.

Rates: $80/room, $100/suite, all incl. cont. brk.

Credit cards: Most major cards

Restrictions: Deposit req. 5-day cancellation notice req., less fee. 2-night min. stay.

Notes: Turn-of-the-century residence, recently renovated. Furnished with mix of European and American antiques. French spoken.

BEAU SEJOUR

La Maison
608 Kerlerec St., New Orleans, LA 70116
(504) 271-0228, (504) 271-0228, (800) 307-7179
Innkeeper: Alma and Don Hulin
Rooms: 2 w/pvt. bath, phone, TV; mini-suites avail.
Rates: $85-$165, incl. cont. brk., evening refreshment
Credit cards: None
Restrictions: No children, pets. Smoking restricted. Deposit req. Min. 14-day cancellation notice req.
Notes: Creole cottage built in 1805. Decorated in French Quarter style with wrought-iron furniture. Courtyard.*

La Maison Marigny
Bourbon at Esplanade, Box 52257, New Orleans, LA 70152-2257
(504) 488-4640, (800) 729-4640, (504) 488-4639
Innkeeper: Jeremy Bazata and Hazel Boyce
Rooms: 3 w/pvt. bath
Rates: $76-$136, incl. cont. brk. Seasonal variations.
Credit cards: Most major cards
Restrictions: No pets. Smoking restricted. Deposit req. 5-day cancellation notice req., 30-day cancellation notice req. for special events. 2-5 night min. stay.
Notes: Two-story inn, recently renovated. Sitting room, front gallery.*

Lafitte Guest House
1003 Bourbon St., New Orleans, LA 70116
(504) 581-2678, (800) 331-7971
Innkeeper: Dr. Robert Guyton and William B. Stuart
Rooms: 12 plus 2 suites, all w/pvt. bath, phone, TV
Rates: $95-$125/room, $165/suite, incl. expanded cont. brk, evening refreshment. Seasonal variations. Discount avail. for mid-week stay. Special pkgs. avail.
Credit cards: Most major cards
Restrictions: No pets. Smoking restricted. One night's deposit req. 7-day cancellation notice req. 2-night min. stay on wknds.
Notes: Three-story French manor house built in 1849. Located in the heart of the French Quarter. Double front and side balconies with wrought ironwork, courtyard.

Parlor. Elevator. Furnished with period antiques, reproductions, paintings. Some rooms with a balcony.*

Lamothe House
621 Esplanade Ave., New Orleans, LA 70116
(504) 947-1161, (504) 943-6536
Innkeeper: Carol Chauppette
Rooms: 11 plus 9 suites, all w/pvt. bath, phone, TV. Located in 3 bldgs.
Rates: $105/room, $165/suite, all incl. cont. brk. Discount avail. for extended, mid-week, and senior citizen stays. Seasonal variations.
Credit cards: Most major cards
Restrictions: No pets. Deposit req. 5-day cancellation notice req. 2-night min. stay on wknds. 5-night min. stay for special events.
Notes: French-style inn built in 1840. Restored in Victorian style. Dining room, parlor. Furnished with perioid antiques. Courtyard. Private parking available. Handicapped access.*

New Orleans Guest House
1118 Ursulines, New Orleans, LA 70116
(504) 566-1177, (800) 562-1177
Innkeeper: Ray and Alvin
Rooms: 14 w/pvt. bath, phone, TV. Located in 2 bldgs.
Rates: $69-$89, incl. cont. brk.
Credit cards: Most major cards
Restrictions: No pets. One night's deposit req. 3-day cancellation notice req. 3-night min. stay. Closed at Christmas.
Notes: Creole cottage built in 1848. Fully restored. Furnished with antiques and contemporary design. Air conditioning, fans. Courtyard. Free parking available.

Nine-O-Five Royal Hotel
905 Rue Royal, New Orleans, LA 70116
(504) 523-0219
Innkeeper: Mrs. J. Morell
Rooms: 10, no pvt. bath, plus 3 suites w/pvt. bath, kitchen, TV
Rates: From $65/room, from $110/suite. Seasonal variations.
Credit cards: Most major cards
Restrictions: No pets, smoking. Deposit req. 30-day cancellation notice req. 3-night min. stay.
Notes: Built in 1890. Located in heart of Old French Quarter.

St. Charles Guest House
1748 Prytania St., New Orleans, LA 70130
(504) 523-6556
Innkeeper: Dennis and Joanne Hilton
Rooms: 38, incl. 25 w/pvt. bath. Located in 4 bldgs.
Rates: $25-$85, incl. cont. brk. Seasonal variations.
Credit cards: Most major cards
Restrictions: One night's deposit req. 3-night min. on some holidays, special events.
Notes: European pension-style inn. Located in the lower Garden District on streetcar line. Has operated as inn since 1960. Under current ownership since 1980. Patio and pool area with banana trees. Frequented by European travelers, artists.*

Terrell House Mansion
1441 Magazine St., New Orleans, LA 70130
(504) 524-9859

Innkeeper: Harry Lucas

Rooms: 8 plus 1 suite, all w/pvt. bath, cable TV, phone. Located in 2 bldgs.

Rates: $70-$100/room, $130/suite, all incl. cont. brk., evening refreshment. Seasonal variations. Discount avail. for senior citizen and AAA stays.

Credit cards: Most major cards.

Restrictions: No pets, smoking. One night's deposit req. 7-day cancellation notice req. 5-night min. stay during special events.

Notes: Two-story Classical Revival style inn with gaslight fixtures, marble fireplaces, gold-leaf mirrors, built about 1858. Located in the Lower Garden District. Operated as inn since 1984. Double parlors, dining room, courtyard, kitchen. Furnished with period antiques, Oriental carpets. Many pieces of furniture built by Prudent Mallard in the 1850s. Small private parties accommodated.*

Whitney Inn
1509 St. Charles Ave., New Orleans, LA 70130
(502) 521-8000, (501) 525-5532

Innkeeper: Sally Cates, Mitchell Cumbow

Rooms: 10 w/pvt. bath, phone, fireplace, TV

Rates: $75-$125, incl. cont. brk. Seasonal variations.

Credit cards: Most major cards

Restrictions: No pets. Deposit required. 7-day cancellation notice req. 3-night min. stay during peak season.

Notes: Greek Revival townhouse built in the 1880s. Coffee room and garden deck. Handicapped access.

PRAIRIEVILLE (4)

Tree House in the Park
16520 Airport Rd., Prairieville, LA 70769-6600
(504) 622-2850, (800) 532-2246

Innkeeper: Julius and Fran Schmieder

Rooms: 2, plus 1 suite, all w/pvt. bath, phone, satellite TV, Jacuzzi on pvt. deck.

Rates: $110-$125/room, $150-$200/suite, all incl. full brk., first dinner. Discount avail. for senior citizens.

Credit cards: Most major cards

Restrictions: No children under 13, pets, smoking. Deposit req. 7-day cancellation notice req., less $50.00 fee.

Notes: Two-story Cajun cabin-in-the-swamp, built on 11' stilts. Located on three and one-half acres with three ponds in Port Vincent. Two rooms with private entrance. Heated swimming pool. Guests have access to TV, VCR, microwave, laundry facilities. Island with gazebo. Foot bridges. Hammock. Swings. Picnic areas. Boat slip, fishing dock, boats, paddles, cane poles and bait available. Double kayak float trips on Amite River organized.*

SAINT FRANCISVILLE (4)

Barrow House Inn
524 Royal St., Box 1461, Saint Francisville, LA 70775
(504) 635-4791, (504) 635-4769

BARROW HOUSE INN

Innkeeper: Shirley and Lyle Dittloff
Rooms: 5, plus 3 suites, all w/pvt. bath, TV. Located in 2 bldgs.
Rates: $85-$90/room, $100-$115/suite, all incl. cont. brk., evening refreshment
Credit cards: Most major cards
Restrictions: Well-mannered children welcome. No pets. $20.00 deposit req. 72-hr.
cancellation notice req. Closed Dec. 23–25.
Notes: Two guesthouses, built circa 1809 and the late 1700s. Enlarged just before
the Civil War with a Greek Revival facade. Fully restored in 1985. Formal dining
room, screened porch. Furnished with period antiques. Grounds include 200-year-
old oak tree. Cassette walking tour of historic district available. Listed on the National Register of Historic Places.*

Green Springs B & B
7463 Tunica Trace, Saint Francisville, LA 70775
(504) 635-4232, (504) 635-3355

Innkeeper: Madeline and Ivan Nevill
Rooms: 2, plus 1 suite, all w/pvt. bath, TV
Rates: $85/room, $120-$225/suite, all incl. full brk.
Credit cards: Most major cards
Restrictions: No pets. Smoking restricted. Deposit req.
Notes: Louisiana bluffland style house with ceiling fans and gallery swings. Located
near fields for walking trails and bird watching. Rooms decorated with contempo-
rary and antique furnishings and art.*

SHREVEPORT (1)

2439 Fairfield "A B & B"
2439 Fairfield Ave., Shreveport, LA 71104
(318) 424-2424, (318) 424-3658

Innkeeper: Jimmy and Vicki Harris
Rooms: 4 suites w/pvt. bath, phone, TV
Rates: $85-$150, incl. full brk., cont. brk. w/mid-week stay. Discount avail. for mid-
week stay.
Credit cards: Most major cards
Restrictions: No children, smoking. Deposit req. 7-day cancellation notice req.

Notes: Built circa 1905, this Bed and Breakfast features an 1893 concert grand piano, a 1900 pump organ, a victrola, a carved oak staircase, crystal chandeliers, period antiques. Each room includes whirlpool bath, private balcony with rocking chairs, cable television. Fax machine and copier available. Outside are rose and herb gardens, a Victorian swing, gazebo, and water fountain.*

SLIDELL (5)

SALMEN-FRITCHIE HOUSE B & B

Salmen-Fritchie House B & B
127 Cleveland Ave., Slidell, LA 70458
(504) 643-1405, (800) 235-4168, (504) 643-2251
Innkeeper: Sharon and Homer Fritchie
Rooms: 2, plus 3 suites, all w/pvt. bath, incl. 4 w/phone, TV, incl. 3 w/fireplace
Rates: $75-$95/room, $115/suite, all incl. full brk., afternoon refreshment. Discount avail for senior citizens.
Credit cards: Most major cards
Restrictions: No children under 10, pets, smoking. One-night's deposit req. 7-day cancellation notice req. less $35.00 fee. 3-night min. stay during Mardi Gras and Jazz Fest.
Notes: Two-story house built in 1895 on 4½ wooden acres. Located 25 minutes from New Orleans French Quarter and the Mississippi Gulf Coast. Furnished with period antiques.*

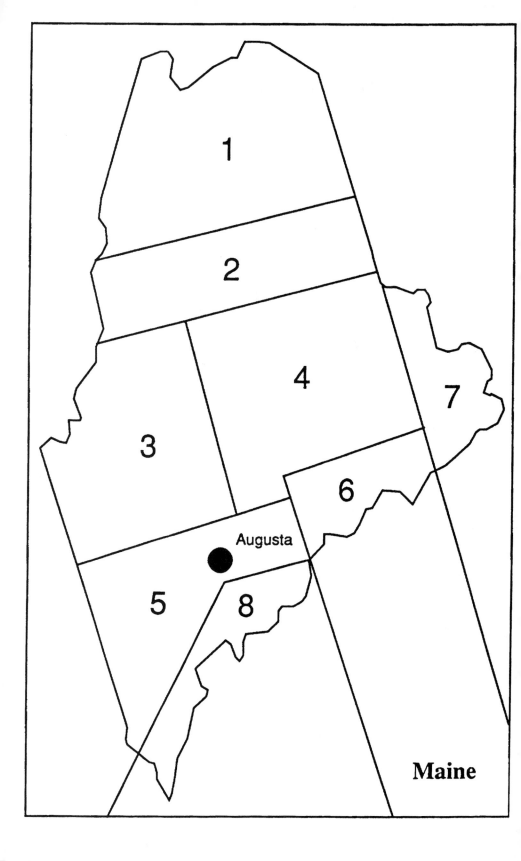

Maine

ATHENS (3)

Hilltop Lodging Bed & Breakfast
5088 Fox Hill Rd., Athens, ME 04912
(207) 654-3141
Innkeeper: Doris Elsa Brown
Rooms: 6, no pvt. bath, incl. 5 w/TV
Rates: $40, incl. cont. brk.
Credit cards: None
Restrictions: None
Notes: Farm house built in 1853. Fully remodeled. Located on 200 acres. Dining room. Ground include snowmobile trail. German spoken.

BANGOR (6)

Phenix Inn
20 Broad St., W. Mkt. Square, Bangor, ME 04401
(207) 947-3850, (207) 947-3550
Innkeeper: Kimberly Jurgiewich
Rooms: 35 plus 2 suites, all w/pvt. bath, phone, TV
Rates: $40-$60/room, $50-$75/suite, all incl. cont. brk. Seasonal variations, July 15–October 15.
Credit cards: Most major cards
Restrictions: None
Notes: Three-story inn built in 1873. Handicapped access. Listed on the National Register of Historic Places.*

BAR HARBOR (6)

Castlemaine Inn
39 Holland Ave., Bar Harbor, ME 04609
(207) 288-4563, (800) 338-4563, (207) 288-4525
Innkeeper: Terry O'Connell and Norah O'Brien
Rooms: 13 plus 2 suites, all w/pvt. bath, TV, incl. 6 w/fireplace
Rates: $78/room, $138/suite, all incl. cont. brk. Discount avail. for extended stay. Seasonal variations.
Credit cards: MC, V
Restrictions: No children under 13, pets. Smoking restricted. Min. 50% deposit req. Min. 15-day cancellation notice req.
Notes: Three-story, Queen Anne inn with twisting corridors and unexpected alcoves built in 1886. Innkeepers rebuilt inn from ground up, inside and outside. Landscaped grounds with flower garden, stone wall. Served as summer residence of the Austro-Hungarian ambassador, Baron Hengelmueler. Morning room with fireplace, veranda. Furnished with antiques and modern pieces. Some rooms have private entry to deck and balcony.

Graycote Inn
40 Holland Ave., Bar Harbor, ME 04609
(207) 288-3044

Innkeeper: Joe and Judy Losquadro
Rooms: 10 w/pvt. bath, incl. 3 w/fireplace, plus 2 suites w/pvt. bath, TV. Located in 2 bldgs.
Rates: $85-$135/room, $135-$175/suite, all incl. full brk., afternoon refreshment. Seasonal variations.
Credit cards: Most major cards
Restrictions: No children under 12, pets, smoking. 2-night's deposit req. 2-week cancellation notice req., less $25.00 fee. 2-night min. stay from June 16–Oct. 15. Closed Dec.–April 14.
Notes: Victorian cottage built in 1881. Located on one wooded acre with lawns, hammock. Foyer, parlor with fireplace, library, sunporch. Off-street parking available.

Hearthside Inn
7 High St., Bar Harbor, ME 04609
(207) 288-4533

Innkeeper: Susan and Barry Schwartz
Rooms: 9 w/pvt. bath, incl. 3 w/fireplace
Rates: $75-$115, incl. full brk., afternoon and evening refreshment. Seasonal variations.
Credit cards: MC, V
Restrictions: No children under 10, pets, smoking. 2-night deposit req. 7-day cancellation notice req. 2-night min. stay in summer.
Notes: Three-story arts and craft-style house built in 1907. Located on Mount Desert Island. Walled patio. Living room with library, fireplace. Dining room. Music room with studio grand piano, board games. Upstairs porch. Front porch with tables and chairs. Furnished in Victorian and country style with antiques, contemporary pieces.

Heathwood Inn
RR 1, Box 1938, Rte. 3, Bar Harbor, ME 04609
(207) 288-5591, (800) 582-3681

Innkeeper: Richard and Cindy Cassey
Rooms: 5 w/pvt. bath, incl. 1 w/fireplace. Suites avail. w/fireplace, balcony, sauna, Jacuzzi.
Rates: $87-$140, incl. cont. brk. Seasonal variations.
Credit cards: MC, V
Restrictions: No children, pets. Smoking restricted. Deposit req. 7-day cancellation notice req., less $10.00 fee.
Notes: Two-story Victorian farmhouse. Decorated with antique furnishings, old family photos.

Manor House Inn
106 West St., Bar Harbor, ME 04609
(207) 288-3759, (800) 437-0088

Innkeeper: Mac Noyes
Rooms: 9 w/pvt. bath, plus 5 suites, incl. 2 w/cable TV, 4 w/fireplace. Located in 3 bldgs.
Rates: $85-$135/room, $95-$155/suite, all incl. full brk. afternoon refreshment.
Credit cards: MC, V
Restrictions: No children under 8, pets, smoking. One night's deposit req. 14-day cancellation notice req., less $25.00 fee. 2-night min. stay.

Notes: Three-story Victorian mansion built in 1887. Located on one acre with gardens. Surrounded by Acadia National Park. Two sitting rooms with Victorian fireplaces, baby grand piano. Veranda. Furnished with period antiques. Guests have pool and tennis privileges at the Bar Harbor Club, across the street. Listed on the National Register of Historic Places.

The Maples Inn
16 Roberts Ave., Bar Harbor, ME 04609
(207) 288-3443
Innkeeper: Susan Sinclair
Rooms: 5 w/pvt. bath, plus 1 suite w/pvt. bath, fireplace, sofa bed
Rates: $90-$110/room, $135/suite, all incl. full brk., afternoon refreshment, picnic lunch. Seasonal variations.
Credit cards: Most major cards
Restrictions: No children under 8, pets, smoking. 2-night deposit req. 2-week cancellation notice req. 2-night min. stay on holiday wknds. Closed at Christmas.
Notes: 3-story Victorian cottage built in 1903 as inn. Parlor with fireplace, porch. Furnished with mixture of Colonial and Victorian antiques, paintings, accessories. Library. Spanish spoken.

Mira Monte Inn
69 Mount Desert St., Bar Harbor, ME 04609
(207) 288-4263, (800) 553-5109, 846-4784 in winter, (207) 288-3115
Innkeeper: Marian Burns
Rooms: 9 w/pvt. bath, phone, cable TV, fireplace, plus 3 suites w/pvt. bath, cable TV, phone, incl. 2 w/fireplace. Located in 2 bldgs.
Rates: $90-$145/room, $120-$180/suite, all incl. full brk., afternoon refreshment. Seasonal variations. Special pkgs. avail.
Credit cards: Most major cards
Restrictions: No children under 5, pets. Smoking restricted. 2-night's deposit req. 7-day cancellation fee req., less $10.00 fee. 2-night min. stay in summer. Closed Oct. 30–May 8.
Notes: Victorian house built in 1864. Located on 1.5 landscaped acres. Living room with piano, fireplace. Furnished in Victorian antiques. Library with fireplace. Wraparound porch, balconies, gardens, terrace. Handicapped access.*

The Tides
119 West St., Bar Harbor, ME 04609
(207) 288-4968
Innkeeper: Margaret Eden
Rooms: 3 suites w/pvt. bath, TV, incl. 2 w/fireplace
Rates: $195-$235, incl. full brk., afternoon refreshment. Seasonal variations.
Credit cards: MC, V
Restrictions: No children under 12, pets, smoking. Two night's deposit req. Cancellation notice req. 2-night min. stay for holiday wknds.
Notes: Three-story Greek Revival waterfront mansion built in 1887. Renovated in 1980. Located on one acre on shore of Frenchman's Bay. Upstairs sitting room with fireplace. Living room, dining room, each with fireplace and ocean view. Wraparound veranda with fireplace overlooking lawns. Two balconies. Furnished with period antiques. Decorated with Laura Ashley wallpapers and spreads.*

Twin Gables Inn
P.O. Box 282, Bar Harbor, ME 04609
(207) 288-3064
Innkeeper: Mindy Hill
Rooms: 6 w/pvt bath, incl. 2 w/TV
Rates: $69-99, incl. full brk. Seasonal variations.
Credit cards: MC, V
Restrictions: No pets, smoking. One night's deposit required. 7-day cancellation notice req.
Notes: Built in 1894. Completely restored and renovated. Living room with fireplace. Dining room. Country kitchen.

Wayside Inn
11 Atlantic Ave., Bar Harbor, ME 04609
(207) 288-5703, (800) 722-6671
Innkeeper: Steve and Sandi Straubel
Rooms: 5 plus 3 suites, incl. 6 w/pvt. bath, phone, 4 w/fireplace, TV
Rates: $70-$140, incl. full brk. Discount avail. for mid-week stay. Seasonal variations.
Credit cards: MC, V
Restrictions: No infants, pets, smoking. Deposit req.
Notes: *

BATH (8)

Fairhaven Inn
North Bath Rd., RR 2, Box 85, Bath, ME 04530
(207) 443-4391
Innkeeper: George and Sallie Pollard
Rooms: 8 w/pvt. bath
Rates: $60-$75, incl. full brk. Discount avail. for extended stay.
Credit cards: Most major cards
Restrictions: No smoking. Children, pets restricted. 7-day cancellation notice req. 2-night min. stay on wknds. in season and holidays.
Notes: Colonial inn built in 1790. Located on 23 hillside acres overlooking Kennebec River. Fully restored. Has operated as inn since 1979. Dining room with fireplace, parlor. Decorated with antique and country furnishings. Tavern with cable TV, wood stove on premises.*

BELFAST (6)

The Thomas Pitcher House
5 Franklin St., Belfast, ME 04915
(207) 338-6454
Innkeeper: Fran and Ron Kresge
Rooms: 4 w/pvt bath
Rates: $55-$80, incl. full brk., afternoon refreshment
Credit cards: None
Restrictions: No children under 12, pets, smoking. One night's deposit req. 72-hour cancellation notice req.
Notes: Victorian house built in 1873. Recently restored. Parlor with bay windows, marble fireplace. Library with cable TV, VCR, board games. Chippendale dining room. Furnished with antiques, reproduction and contemporary pieces. German, some French spoken.

BELGRADE LAKES (3)

Wings Hill
Rte. 27, Box 386, Belgrade Lakes, ME 04918
(207) 495-2400, (800) 509-4647
Innkeeper: Dick and Sharon Hofmann
Rooms: 8 w/pvt. bath, phone
Rates: $95, incl. full brk. Seasonal variations. Special pkgs. avail. Discount avail. for extended stay.
Credit cards: MC, V
Restrictions: No children under 10, pets. Smoking restricted. Min. 50% deposit req. 15-day cancellation notice req., less 15% fee. 2-night min. stay in summer. 3-night min. stay for holiday wknds.
Notes: Farmhouse built in 1800. Fully renovated. Dining room, country kitchen with woodburning stove. 100-ft. screened, wrap-around porch. Decorated with antiques and works of art*

BETHEL (5)

Abbott House
P.O. Box 933, Bethel, ME 04217
(207) 824-7600, (800) 240-2377
Innkeeper: Joe Cardello and Penny Bohac
Rooms: 4, no pvt. bath. 2 suites avail.
Rates: $40-$70/room, $90-$180/suite, all incl. full brk., afternoon refreshment. Seasonal variations. Discount avail. for mid-week or extended stays.
Credit cards: Most major cards
Restrictions: No children under 6, pets, smoking. 50% deposit req. 14-day cancellation notice. 2-night min. stay on winter wknds. 3-night min. stay for holidays.
Notes: Two-story Cape Cod-style house wide pine floors built approx. 1790. Massage therapist on staff. Outdoor hot tub, pool. All meals available. Spanish spoken.

BLUE HILL (6)

Blue Hill Farm Country Inn
Rte. 15, Box 437, Blue Hill, ME 04614
(207) 374-5126
Innkeeper: Jim and Marcia Schatz
Rooms: 14, incl. 7 w/pvt. bath, phone
Rates: $70-$85, incl. cont. brk. Seasonal variations.
Credit cards: MC, V
Restrictions: No children under 10, pets, smoking. Deposit req. 7-day cancellation notice req.
Notes: Farmhouse built at turn of the century. Located on forty-eight wooded acres overlooking field, trout pond, brooks. Living room with woodstove. Kitchen with Clarion stove. Library, parlor. Board games available. Limited handicapped access.*

Mountain Road House
RR 1, Box 2040, Mountain Rd., Blue Hill, ME 04614
(207) 374-2794
Innkeeper: Carol and John McCulloch
Rooms: 3 w/pvt. bath

MOUNTAIN ROAD HOUSE

Rates: $55-$75, incl. full brk., afternoon refreshment. Discount avail. for extended
  stay.
Credit cards: MC, V
Restrictions: No pets, smoking. One night's deposit req. 5-day cancellation notice
  req.
Notes: Two-story Victorian farmhouse with enclosed sun porch built in the 1890s.
Guests have access to parlor and den. Board games available. Resident dog and
cats.*

BOOTHBAY (8)

Kenniston Hill Inn
P.O. Box 125, Boothbay, ME 04537
(207) 633-2159, (207) 633-2159
Innkeeper: David and Susan Straight
Rooms: 10 w/pvt. bath, incl. 5 w/fireplace. Located in 2 bldgs.
Rates: $65-$110, incl. full brk. Seasonal variations.
Credit cards: MC, V
Restrictions: No children under 10, pets, smoking. Min. one night's deposit req. 14-
  day cancellation notice req., less $20.00 fee.
Notes: Two-story Georgian Colonial mansion built in 1786. Located on four
wooded acres with gardens bordered by public golf course. Living room with open-
hearth fireplace. Porch. Furnished with antiques. Decorated with handmade
quilts.*

BOOTHBAY HARBOR (8)

Admiral's Quarters Inn
105 Commercial St., Boothbay Harbor, ME 04538
(207) 633-2474
Innkeeper: Jean E. Duffy

Rooms: 2 plus 5 suites, all w/pvt. bath, cable TV
Rates: $65-$70/room, $75-$85/suite, all incl. cont. brk. Seasonal variations.
Credit cards: Most major cards
Restrictions: No children under 12, pets. One night's deposit req. 7-day cancellation notice req.
Notes: Sea captain's house built approx. 1825. Located on knoll overlooking harbor. Dining room. Deck, terrace. Furnished with antiques and white wicker. Handicapped access.

Anchor Watch B & B
3 Eames Rd., Boothbay Harbor, ME 04538-1003
(207) 633-7565
Innkeeper: Diane Campbell
Rooms: 4 w/pvt. bath
Rates: incl. full brk., afternoon refreshment. Seasonal variations.
Credit cards: MC, V
Restrictions: No children, pets, smoking. Min. one night's deposit req. 7-day cancellation notice req. 2-night min. stay on Col. Dy wknd. Closed Dec. 15–Feb. 15.
Notes: Two-story sea captain's shorefront house. Breakfast nook overlooking harbor, two lighthouses. Sitting room with TV, VCR, games. Porch. Rooms named after Monhegan ferries and many original Monhegan artists' works are displayed. Private pier. Innkeeper operates the ferry.*

Atlantic Ark Inn
64 Atlantic Ave., Boothbay Harbor, ME 04538
(207) 633-5690
Innkeeper: Donna Piggott
Rooms: 5, plus 1 suite, 1 cottage, all w/pvt. bath. Located in 2 bldgs.
Rates: $75-$149/room, $215/suite, all incl. full brk., afternoon and evening refreshment. Seasonal variations.
Credit cards: Most major cards
Restrictions: No children under 12, pets, smoking. 50% deposit req. 14-day cancellation notice req. Min. stay on some holiday wknds. Closed Nov. 1–May 29.
Notes: Traditional century-old Maine house built approx. 1894. Living room, dining room, sitting porch. Furnished with antiques and Oriental rugs. Some rooms with balcony, Jacuzzi, Greek tub, panoramic harbor view.

Harbour Towne Inn
71 Townsend Ave., Boothbay Harbor, ME 04538
(207) 633-4300, (800) 722-4240, (203)633-7584
Innkeeper: George Thomas
Rooms: 11 plus 1 suite all w/pvt. bath
Rates: $69-$120/room, $195-$225/suite, all incl. cont. brk. Seasonal variations. Discount avail for extended, mid-week stay.
Credit cards: Most major cards
Restrictions: No pets. Well-behaved children welcome. Smoking restricted. Deposit req. 7-day cancellation notice req., less fee.
Notes: Three-story Victorian town house, refurbished in traditional style. Rooms overlook waterfront or village, some with decks. Penthouse with private deck and panoramic view of harbor sleeps six. Sunroom. Gardens. Off-street parking available. Limited handicapped access.*

BRIDGTON (5)

THE NOBLE HOUSE

The Noble House
37 Highland Rd., Box 180, Bridgton, ME 04009
(207) 647-3733
Innkeeper: Dick and Jane Starets
Rooms: 4 plus 2 suites, all w/pvt. bath, some w/whirlpool baths. TV avail.
Rates: $74-$88/room, $94-$115/suite, all incl. full brk. Seasonal variations.
Credit cards: Most major cards
Restrictions: No pets. Smoking restricted. One night's deposit req. 10-day cancellation notice req., less $15.00 fee. 2-night min. stay on wknds. in season.
Notes: Turn-of-the-century Queen Anne. Located on three parklike hilly, wooded acres overlooking Highland Lake, Mount Washington and the Presidential Mountain Range. Victorian dining room with corner fireplace. Parlor with library, grand piano, pump organ, hearth. Lounge with TV, VCR, refrigerator. Decorated with period antiques. Porches with rockers. Private lake frontage with canoe, foot pedal boat, BBQ, hammock available.*

Tarry-A-While B & B Resort
Highland Ridge Rd., Bridgton, ME 04009
(207) 647-2522
Innkeeper: Hans and Barbara Jenni
Rooms: 36, all w/pvt. bath, plus 3 housekeeping units. Located in 6 bldgs.
Rates: $100-$120, $500-$950/cottages, all incl. brk. Discount avail. for children under 10.
Credit cards: None
Restrictions: No pets. Smoking restricted. $50.00 deposit req. 14-day cancellation notice req., less $15.00 fee. 2-night min. stay on wknds. Closed Labor Day–June 10.
Notes: Located on thirty-four acres with two sandy beaches on Highland Lake. Recreational hall with fireplace. Lobby. Tennis court, putting green. Swiss restaurant on premises. Row boats, sail boats, canoes, aqua bikes, pedal boats, lawn games available. German spoken. Handicapped access.

BROOKSVILLE (6)

Oakland House
Herricks, Brooksville, ME 04617-9702
(800) 359-7352
Innkeeper: James Littlefield
Rooms: 12, incl. 9 w/pvt. bath, 2 w/fireplace, plus 15 cottages w/pvt. bath, fireplace, incl. 3 w/phone, 2 w/TV. Located in 17 bldgs.
Rates: $80-$146/room, $100-$202/cottage, all incl. full brk. and lunch in summer. Seasonal variations. Discount avail. for extended stay.
Credit cards: None
Restrictions: No smoking in dining room. No pets other than dogs. Min. one night's deposit req. 30-day cancellation notice req. 4-night min. stay in August.
Notes: Has operated as inn under same family since 1889. Located on 100+ acres. Living room with fireplace, dining rooms, library. Recreation hall with TV, VCR. Private freshwater and saltwater beaches. Rowboats, lawn games, hot-air balloon rides available. Fishing trips arranged.*

BRUNSWICK (8)

Bethel Point B & B
RR5 Bethel Point Rd. 2387, Brunswick, ME 01044
(207) 725-1115
Innkeeper: Peter and Betsy Packard
Rooms: 3, incl. 1 w/pvt. bath, 1 w/fireplace
Rates: $60-$80, incl. full brk. Seasonal variations.
Credit cards: None
Restrictions: No pets, smoking. Min. one night's deposit req.
Notes: Colonial-style house built in 1834. Located on the ocean. Furnished with antiques. Resident pets.

Samuel Newman House
7 South St., Brunswick, ME 04011
(207) 729-6959
Innkeeper: Guenter Rose
Rooms: 6 plus 1 suite, no pvt. bath
Rates: $90-$150, incl. expanded cont. brk. Seasonal variations.
Credit cards: MC, V
Restrictions: No pets, smoking. One night's deposit req. 24-hour cancellation notice req.
Notes: Federal-style inn built in 1821. Some French, Indonesian spoken.

CAMDEN (8)

A Little Dream
66 High St., Camden, ME 04843
(207) 236-8742
Innkeeper: Joanna Ball and Bill Fontana
Rooms: 3 w/pvt. bath, phone, incl. 2 w/TV, plus 1 suite w/pvt. bath, phone, TV, fireplace. Located in 2 bldgs.
Rates: $85-$139/room, $139/suite, all incl. full brk, afternoon refreshment. Seasonal variations.
Credit cards: Most major cards

Restrictions: No pets, smoking. Deposit req., 14-day cancellation notice, less $15.00 fee, 2-night min. stay on holiday wknds.

Notes: Two-story turreted Victorian farmhouse with wrap-around porch. Renovated and in operation as an inn since 1988. Furnished with Victorian antiques. Listed on the National Register for Historic Places. Some rooms have private deck, view. Italian, German and some French spoken.

Camden Harbour Inn
83 Bayview St., Camden, ME 04843
(207) 236-4200

Innkeeper: Sal Vella, Patti Babij
Rooms: 22 w/pvt. bath, incl. 8 w/fireplace
Rates: $95-$195, incl. full brk. Seasonal variations. Special pkgs. avail.
Credit cards: Most major cards
Restrictions: No children under 12, pets. Deposit req. 7-day cancellation notice req.
Notes: Victorian inn built in 1874 on hill overlooking Penobscot Bay and Camden Harbour. Remodeled in 1984. Tavern with live music, TV, dining room, solarium, glass-enclosed porch, living room with TV. Furnished in Victorian style with some antiques. All meals available. Handicapped access.*

Hawthorn Inn
9 High St., Camden, ME 04843
(207) 236-8842

Innkeeper: Ken and Abigail Stern
Rooms: 10 w/pvt. bath, incl. 4 w/cable TV. Located in 2 bldgs.
Rates: $75-170, incl. full brk., afternoon refreshment. Discount avail. for extended stay. Seasonal variations.
Credit cards: MC, V
Restrictions: No children under 10, pets. Smoking restricted. 2-night's deposit req. 14-day cancellation notice req. 2-night min. stay from July 1–Aug. 31 and holiday wknds.
Notes: Victorian mansion with turret built in 1894. Carriage House. Dining room with fireplace. Two parlors with original stained-glass. Grand piano. Foyer with three-story curved staircase. Some private balconies and deck or patio. Deck overlooking Camden Harbor. Jacuzzi. Listed on the National Register of Historic Places. Resident cat.*

The Maine Stay Inn
22 High St., Camden, ME 04843
(207) 236-9636

Innkeeper: Peter and Donny Smith, Diana Robson
Rooms: 8 incl. 4 w/pvt. bath, 1 w/fireplace
Rates: $75-$115, incl. full brk. Seasonal variations.
Credit cards: Most major cards
Restrictions: No children under 8, pets, smoking. One night's deposit req. 3-day cancellation notice req.
Notes: Federal-style inn. Built in 1802. Operated as inn since 1988. Decorated with mementos. Private patio overlooking garden. Listed in National Register of Historic Places. *

Windward House
6 High St., Camden, ME 04843
(207) 236-9656

Innkeeper: Jon and Mary Davis
Rooms: 6 plus 1 suite, all w/pvt. bath
Rates: $65-$135/room $80-$135/suite, all incl. full brk., afternoon refreshment. Seasonal variations.
Credit cards: Most major cards
Restrictions: No children under 12, pets. Smoking restricted. Min. one night's deposit req. 21-day cancellation notice req., less $20.00 fee.
Notes: Three-story Greek Revival house built in 1854. Furnished with period antiques. Formal dining room with bay window. Living room with soapstone fireplace. Library with stereo, TV. Patio-deck overlooking orchard, gardens, and Mount Battie. Wicker room exhibits local art. Listed on National Register of Historic Places.

CAPE ELIZABETH (8)

Inn by the Sea
40 Bowery Beach Rd., Cape Elizabeth, ME 04107
(207) 799-3134, (800) 888-IBTS, (207) 799-4779
Innkeeper: Maureen McQuade
Rooms: 43 suites w/pvt. bath, phone, TV, VCR, incl. 6 w/fireplace. Located in 3 bldgs.
Rates: $100-$370. Seasonal variations.
Credit cards: Most major cards
Restrictions: No pets, smoking. One night's deposit req. 14-day cancellation notice req., less $50.00 fee. 2-night min. stay on wknds. 3-night min. stay on holidays.
Notes: Has operated as Inn since 1986. Private boardwalk overlooking Atlantic Ocean. Decorated with Chippendale furniture, wicker and light pine. All suites have kitchens, a living/dining area, patios or porches. Grounds with heated swimming pool, rose-trellised tea garden, gazebo, lawn games. Handicapped access.*

CAPE NEDDICK (8)

Cape Neddick House
1300 Rte. 1, Box 70, Cape Neddick, ME 03902
(207) 363-2500, (207) 363-4499
Innkeeper: John and Dianne Goodwin
Rooms: 4, plus 1 suite w/fireplace, all w/pvt. bath
Rates: $50-$75/room, $75-$95/suite, all incl. full brk.
Credit cards: None
Restrictions: No children under 7, pets. Smoking restricted. Min. 1-night deposit req. 14-day written cancellation notice req. 2-night min. stay on wknds.
Notes: Victorian farmhouse built in the 1800s. Fully restored. Located on 10 wooded acres. Living room, parlor with board games, deck, porch. Decorated with antiques, quilts.

CARIBOU (1)

The Old Iron Inn
155 High St., Caribou, ME 04736
(207) 492-4766, (207) 492-4766
Innkeeper: Kate and Kevin McCartney
Rooms: 4, incl. 1 w/pvt. bath
Rates: $35-$40, incl. full brk.

Credit cards: MC, V

Restrictions: No children under 5. Pets, smoking restricted. Deposit req. 24-hour cancellation notice req.

Notes: Built in 1914 with interior oak woodwork. Decorated with antiques and artwork. Guests have access to office with computer, laser printer, and FAX. Innkeepers collect antique irons.

CENTER LOVELL (5)

Center Lovell Inn
Rte. 5, Box 261, Center Lovell, ME 04016-0261
(207) 925-1575

Innkeeper: Richard and Janice Cox

Rooms: 8 w/pvt. bath, plus 2 suites w/pvt. bath, TV. Located in 2 bldgs.

Rates: $98-$185/room, $170-$335/suite, all incl. full brk., dinner. Seasonal variations.

Credit cards: Most major cards

Restrictions: No pets. Smoking restricted. Deposit req. Min 14-day cancellation notice req. 2-night min. stay on July wknds. Closed Nov. 1–Mar. 30.

Notes: Three-story main structure built in 1805. Enlarged and renovated in 1850. Remodeled in and has operated as inn since 1975. Norton House built in 1835. Parlor with TV, fireplace. Dining room with open-hearth iron fireplace built in early 1800s. Wrap-around porch overlooking the White Mountains.

CHERRYFIELD (6)

Ricker House
Park St., Box 256, Cherryfield, ME 04622
(207) 546-2780

Innkeeper: Bill and Jean Conway

Rooms: 3, no pvt. bath, incl. 1 w/fireplace

Rates: $40-$50, incl. full brk.

Credit cards: None

Restrictions: No children under 12, pets, smoking. 50% deposit req. 10-day cancellation notice req.

Notes: Two-story Federal-Colonial house built in 1803. Located along the Narraguagus River. Dining area. Double parlor overlooking river.

CLARK ISLAND (8)

Craignair Inn
533 Clark Island Rd., Clark Island, ME 04859
(207) 594-7644, (207) 596-7124

Innkeeper: Terry and Norman Smith

Rooms: 20 w/phone, incl. 8 w/pvt. bath, plus 2 suites w/pvt. bath, phone. Located in 2 bldgs.

Rates: $62-$92/room, $125/suite, all incl. full brk. Seasonal variations.

Credit cards: Most major cards

Restrictions: One night's deposit req. 48-hour cancellation notice req., less 10% fee. 2-night min. stay on holiday wknds.

Notes: Built in 1930. Converted in 1942 to an Inn. Located on four acres of shorefront. Parlor/library, dining room, old-fashioned kitchen with an antique cast-iron working stove. Furnished with antiques and wall hangings from both U.S. and other countries. Cots and cribs available. Restaurant on premises. Bridge connects property with island full of wildlife, swimming hole.*

COREA (6)

The Black Duck on Corea Harbor
Crowley Island Rd., Box 39, Corea, ME 04624
(207) 963-2689
Innkeeper: Barry Canner, Bob Travers
Rooms: 5 w/pvt. bath. Suites avail. Located in 2 bldgs.
Rates: $60-$80/room, $60-$125/suite, $80/cottage, all incl. full brk. Seasonal variations.
Credit cards: None
Restrictions: No children under 9, pets, smoking. Min. one night's deposit req. 2-week cancellation notice req., less $25.00 fee.
Notes: Built in late 1800s. Renovated, expanded and furnished with art and antiques. Located on 12 wooded acres with blueberry fields. Common rooms with fireplaces, wood stove, cable TV. Library, board games available. Resident pets. Limited French, Danish spoken.*

DAMARISCOTTA (8)

Brannon-Bunker Inn
H.C.R. 64, Box 045, Damariscotta, ME 04543
(207) 563-5941
Innkeeper: Joe and Jeanne Hovance
Rooms: 7 plus 2 suites, all w/pvt. bath. Located in 2 bldgs.
Rates: $55-$65/room, $75-$115/suite, all incl. cont. brk. Discount avail. for off-season stay.
Credit cards: MC, V
Restrictions: No pets, smoking. Min. 50% deposit req. 7-day cancellation notice req., less one night's stay. Closed Christmas week. No alcohol avail., but guests may bring their own.
Notes: Rural barn and carriage house built in the 1820s. Located on 28 acres overlooking Damariscotta River. Has operated as inn since the 1950s. Lobby. Common room with fireplace, TV, board games. Upstairs sitting area, breakfast nook. Furnished with American antiques from different periods and World War I memorabilia. Guests have access to kitchen. Limited handicapped access.*

DEER ISLE (6)

The Inn at Ferry Landing
108 Old Ferry Rd., RR1, Box 163, Deer Isle, ME 04627
(207) 348-7760
Innkeeper: John and Maureen Deis
Rooms: 5 plus 2 suites, all w/pvt. bath, incl. 1 w/woodstove
Rates: $70-$80/room, $85-$95/suite, all incl. full brk., afternoon refreshment. Seasonal variations.
Credit cards: MC, V
Restrictions: No children under 8, pets, smoking. One night's deposit req. 7-day cancellation notice req.
Notes: Two-story farmhouse built in the 1850s. Great room overlooking Eggemoggin Reach. Deck. Furnished with antiques, patchwork quilts. Guests have access to sand and gravel beach. Mooring and skiff available.*

EAST WATERFORD (5)

Waterford Inne
Chadbourne Rd., Box 49, East Waterford, ME 04088-0149
(207) 583-4037, (207) 583-4037

Innkeeper: Barbara and Rosalie Vanderzanden
Rooms: 9 plus 1 suite, incl. 6 w/pvt. bath, 1 w/fireplace
Rates: $74-$99/room, $99/suite, all incl. full brk.
Credit cards: AE
Restrictions: Smoking restricted. $50.00 deposit req. 14-day cancellation notice
  req., less $10.00 fee. 2-night min. stay on holiday wknds.
Notes: Two-story farmhouse located on 25 acres. Rolling terrain, farm pond, old
red barn. Dining room. Common room. Library. Decorated with antiques and art.
Board games available.

EASTPORT (7)

WESTON HOUSE

Weston House
26 Boynton St., Eastport, ME 04631
(207) 853-2907

Innkeeper: Jett Peterson
Rooms: 4, incl. 1 w/pvt. bath w/prior arrangement, 1 w/fireplace, 1 w/TV plus 1
  suite w/pvt. bath, fireplace, TV
Rates: $50-$75, incl. full brk., evening refreshment
Credit cards: None
Restrictions: No pets. Smoking restricted. Deposit req. 7-day cancellation notice
  req., less $10.00 fee.
Notes: Federal-style house built in 1810. Operated as inn since 1985. Located on
hill overlooking Passamaquoddy Bay. Dining room. Furnished with antiques, Oriental rugs, family treasures. Board games, all meals, picnic lunch, lawn games available. Listed on the National Register of Historic Places.

ELIOT (8)

Farmstead B & B
379 Goodwin Rd., Rte. 236, Eliot, ME 03903
(207) 439-5033, (207) 748-3145
Innkeeper: John and Meb Lippincott
Rooms: 7 plus 2 suites, all w/pvt. bath, phone
Rates: $54/room, $76/suite, all incl. full brk. Children under 6 free. Seasonal variations.
Credit cards: Most major cards.
Restrictions: Deposit req. 14-day cancellation notice req.
Notes: Built in 1704. Expanded to three-storys in 1894. Three-seater with Montgomery Ward catalog still stands. Handicapped access.*

ELLSWORTH (6)

Capt'n N Eve's Eden
RFD 2, Box 173A, Rte. 184, Ellsworth, ME 04605
(207) 667-3109
Innkeeper: Evelyn Farrell
Rooms: 3, incl. 1 w/pvt. bath
Rates: $35-$45, incl. full brk. Seasonal variations.
Credit cards: None
Restrictions: No pets. Smoking, children restricted. One night's deposit req. 7-day cancellation notice req.
Notes: Two-story house overlooking Frenchman's Bay. Sun room. Sitting room with color cable TV. Hot tub.

FARMINGTON (3)

Blackberry Farm B & B
Town Farm Rd., Box 7048, Farmington, ME 04938
(207) 778-2035
Innkeeper: Ruth and Glen Evans
Rooms: 3, incl. 1 w/pvt. bath
Rates: $40-$55, incl. full brk.
Credit cards: None
Restrictions: No infants. Smoking restricted. One night's deposit req. 2-week cancellation notice req., less 15% fee.
Notes: Two-story farmhouse with wood stoves built in 1878. Located on ten acres with vegetable and flower gardens, pond stocked with Rainbow trout. Parlor with fireplace. Furnished with antiques, family heirlooms. Deck overlooking swimming pool. Resident cats.*

FREEPORT (8)

Cottage Street Inn
13 Cottage St., Freeport, ME 04032
(207) 865-0932, (207) 865-0932,
Innkeeper: Tom and Anita Willet
Rooms: 3, plus 1 suite w/phone, all w/pvt bath, cable, HBO TV
Rates: $50-$95/room, $75-$150/suite incl. full brk.
Credit cards: Most major cards
Restrictions: No children under one. No pets, smoking.

Notes: Two-story inn decorated with Laura Ashley decor and linens. Located on dead end street in wooded area. Skylight in bedrooms. Off-street parking.*

Country At Heart B & B
37 Bow St., Freeport, ME 04032
(207) 865-0512
Innkeeper: Roger and Kim Dubay
Rooms: 3 w/pvt. bath
Rates: $65-$85, incl. full brk. Seasonal variations. Discount avail. for extended stay.
Credit cards: MC, V for deposit only
Restrictions: No pets, smoking. One night's deposit req. 7-day cancellation notice
   req., less $10.00 fee. Closed Thanksgiving and Christmas.
Notes: Two-story house built in 1870. Living room. Dining room with fireplace. Kitchen with wood stove. Furnished with antiques, reproductions and handmade crafts. Giftshop on premises. Innkeeper specializes in counted cross stitch and rug hooking. Resident dog.*

Isaac Randall House
5 Independence Dr., Freeport, ME 04032
(207) 865-9295
Innkeeper: Jim and Glynrose Friedlander
Rooms: 8 w/pvt. bath, incl. 2 w/fireplace
Rates: $85-$105, incl. full brk., afternoon refreshment. Seasonal variations. Discount
   avail. for senior citizen, extended stays.
Credit cards: MC, V
Restrictions: No children under 2, smoking. One night's deposit req. 7-day cancel-
   lation notice req., less $10.00 fee.
Notes: Federal-style farmhouse built in 1823. Operated as a stop on the Under-ground Railway. Located on six wooded acres with spring-fed pond. Common room with cable TV, board games, library. Country kitchen with beamed ceiling. Fur-nished with antiques, Oriental rugs, handsewn quilts, collectibles. Lawn games, BBQ available. Made-to-order quilts for sale. French, Spanish spoken. Handicapped access. Resident cats.*

FRYEBURG (5)

The Oxford House Inn
105 Main St., Fryeburg, ME 04037
(207) 935-3442
Innkeeper: John and Phyllis Morris
Rooms: 5 w/pvt. bath, TV
Rates: $75-$95, incl. full brk.
Credit cards: Most major cards
Restrictions: No smoking. Deposit req. 10-day cancellation notice req.
Notes: Two-story Edwardian mission-style house built in 1913. Lounge with cock-tails, TV, darts, reading. Dining room. Enclosed back porch. Furnished with an-tiques.*

ISLE AU HAUT (6)

The Keeper's House
Lighthouse Point, Box 26, Isle Au Haut, ME 04645
(207) 677-3678, (207) 367-2261

THE KEEPER'S HOUSE

Innkeeper: Jeff and Judi Burke
Rooms: 6, no pvt. bath, incl. 3 w/wood stove. Located in 3 bldgs.
Rates: $250, incl. 3 meals per day
Credit cards: None
Restrictions: No pets, smoking, telephone, electricity. $100 deposit req. 14-day cancellation notice req. 2-night min. stay in July and Aug. Closed Nov. 1–April 30.
Notes: Three-story stone house built for the keeper of a working lighthouse, lit for the first time on Christmas Eve, 1907. Located on island within Acadia National Park. Restored in 1986. Living room, dining room, kitchen. The Oil House Cottage includes outdoor shower and backhouse. Furnished with painted-wood antiques. Listed on the National Register of Historic Places. Guests park at Ken Gross' house across street from Square Deal Garage in Stonington and continue on mail boat except Sundays and U.S. Postal Holidays. Check in advance for boat schedule. Spanish spoken.

KENNEBUNK (8)

Arundel Meadows Inn
P.O. Box 1129, Kennebunk, ME 04043-1129
(207) 985-3770

Innkeeper: Mark Bachelder, Murray Yaeger
Rooms: 5 w/pvt. bath, incl. 2 w/fireplace, TV, plus 2 suites w/pvt. bath, incl. 1 w/fireplace, TV
Rates: $75-$95/room, $100-$110/suite, all incl. full brk., afternoon refreshment. Seasonal variations. Discount avail. for extended stay.
Credit cards: MC, V
Restrictions: No children under 12, pets, smoking. Deposit req. 14-day cancellation notice req. 2-night min. stay on holiday wknds.
Notes: Two-story farmhouse built in 1825. Located on 3.5 acres. Decorated with art and antiques collected both locally and around the world. Lawn chairs overlooking gardens. Innkeeper is a professional chef.*

Sundial Inn
48 Beach Ave, Box 1147, Kennebunk, ME 04043
(207) 967-3850, (207) 967-4719

Innkeeper: Larry Kenny
Rooms: 34 w/pvt. bath, phone, TV
Rates: $65-$151, incl. cont. brk. Discount avail. for extended stay.
Credit cards: Most major cards
Restrictions: No children under 13, pets, smoking. One night's deposit req. 10-day cancellation notice req., less $15.00 fee.
Notes: Three-story Victorian-style inn with elevator built as summer cottage. Renovated in 1987. Living room with ocean view. Decorated in Victorian country antiques. Handicapped access.

KENNEBUNK BEACH (8)

The Ocean View
72 Beach Ave., Kennebunk Beach, ME 04043
(207) 967-2750

Innkeeper: Bob and Carole Arena
Rooms: 4 plus 5 suites, all w/pvt. bath, incl. 4 w/cable TV. Located in 2 bldgs.
Rates: $75-$130/room, $85-$170/suite, all incl. cont. brk. Discount avail. for extended stay.
Credit cards: MC, V
Restrictions: No children under 13, pets. Smoking restricted. Min. 50% deposit req. 14-day cancellation notice req. less $15.00 fee.
Notes: Built in the late 1800s. Living room with fireplace. TV room, breakfast room, covered front porch. Some French spoken. All rooms overlook ocean.

KENNEBUNKPORT (8)

1802 House
15 Locke St., Box 646A, Kennebunkport, ME 04046-1646
(207) 967-5632, (800) 932-5632

Innkeeper: Ron and Carol Perry
Rooms: 6 w/pvt. bath, incl. 2 w/fireplace
Rates: $65-$125, incl. full brk. Discount avail. for senior citizens, airline employees. Seasonal variations.
Credit cards: Most major cards
Restrictions: No children under 12, pets, smoking. Min. one night's deposit req. 14-day cancellation notice req., less $15.00 fee.
Notes: Built as private house in 1802. Renovated in and has operated as inn since 1975. Located on 15th hole of golf course. Some rooms feature sitting areas with fireplaces, other have four poster queen-sized beds. Sitting room with potbellied stove, board games. Breakfast room with wicker furniture overlooking golf course. Two porches. Furnished in Colonial style.*

The Captain Lord Mansion
P.O. Box 800, Kennebunkport, ME 04046-0800
(207) 969-3141, (800) 522-3141, (207) 967-3172

Innkeeper: Rick Litchfield, Bev Davis
Rooms: 14 plus 2 suites, all w/pvt. bath, phone, incl. 11 w/fireplace, 3 w/whirlpool bath
Rates: $125-$199/room, $169-$189/suite, all incl. full brk., afternoon refreshment. Discount avail. for extended stay. Seasonal variations.
Credit cards: Most major cards

Restrictions: No children under 6, pets. Smoking restricted. Min. one night's deposit req. 15-day cancellation notice req., less $15.00 fee. 2-night min. stay on wknds.

Notes: Four-story mansion with octagonal cupola, spiral and elliptical staircases, working hand-pulled elevator and blown-glass windows built in 1812 overlooking the Kennebunk River. Renovated in and has operated as inn since 1978. Main hallway. Gathering room with fireplace, board games. Country kitchen. Decorated with period antiques and Oriental rugs. Giftshop on premises. Parking passes for beaches available. Small private parties accommodated. Audio/visual equipment available. Pumpkin-carving party with reception, scavenger hunt, and games during last weekend in October.*

Cove House
11 S. Main St., RR 3, Box 1615, Kennebunkport, ME 04046
(207) 967-3704

Innkeeper: Kathy, Bob and Barry Jones

Rooms: 3 w/pvt. bath, plus cottage

Rates: $70/room, $350-$500/cottage/week, all incl. full brk., afternoon refreshment. Seasonal variations.

Credit cards: Most major cards

Restrictions: No pets, smoking. One night's deposit req. 7-day cancellation notice req. 2-night min. stay from July 1–Aug. 31 and on holiday wknds.

Notes: Two-story colonial house built in 1700s. Located on 1.3 acres with gardens. Living room with library, fireplace. Cottage with screened front porch, living room, dining room. Resident pets.*

English Meadows Inn
141 Port Rd., Kennebunkport, ME 04043
(207) 967-5766

Innkeeper: Charles Doane

Rooms: 11 incl. 7 w/pvt. bath, plus 1 suite w/pvt. bath, TV, plus 1 cottage w/pvt. bath, TV. Located in 2 bldgs.

Rates: $78-$95/room, $120/suite, $120/cottage, all incl. full brk., afternoon refreshment. Seasonal variations. Discount avail. for extended stay.

Credit cards: MC, V

Restrictions: No children under 10, pets, smoking. Min. 50% deposit req. 10-day cancellation notice req. 2-night min. stay on wknds., June–October.

Notes: Three-story Victorian farmhouse built in 1860. Has operated as inn since 1910. Main house with sitting room. Attached carriage house with fireplaced livingroom. Cottage with screened porch. Furnished with antiques, brass and iron beds, hooked rugs, colorful quilts, works by local artists. Common rooms with TV, phone, board games. Grounds include gardens, fruit trees, pine grove.

The Inn on South Street
South St., Box 478A, Kennebunkport, ME 04046
(207) 967-5151

Innkeeper: Jacques and Eva Downs

Rooms: 3 w/pvt. bath, phone, incl. 1 w/fireplace, plus 1 suite w/pvt. bath, phone, fireplace, Jacuzzi

Rates: $90-$105/room, $160-$185/suite, all incl. full brk., afternoon refreshment. Seasonal variations. Discount avail. for extended stay.

Credit cards: MC, V

Restrictions: No children under 10, pets, smoking. Deposit req. 14-day cancellation notice req., less $15.00 fee. 2-night min. stay in-season and holidays.

Notes: Two-story Greek Revival/Federal-style house built about 1823. Living room with fireplace. Country kitchen overlooking river and ocean. Porch. Flower gardens with lawn furniture. Furnished with antiques. Listed on the National Register of Historic Places. German, Spanish spoken.*

The Kennebunkport Inn
One Dock Square, Box 111, Kennebunkport, ME 04046-0111
(207) 967-2621, (207) 967-3705

Innkeeper: Rick and Martha Griffin

Rooms: 34 w/pvt. bath, TV, incl. 14 w/phone, 1 w/fireplace. Located in 2 bldgs.

Rates: $63-$179, incl. cont. brk. Special pkgs. avail. Discount avail. for senior citizen, AAA and extended stays.

Credit cards: Most major cards

Restrictions: No pets. Smoking restricted. One night's deposit req. 7-day cancellation notice req., less $10.00 fee. 2-night min. stay on spring and fall wknds. 3-night min. stay on summer and holiday wknds.

Notes: Sea captain's mansion built in late 1800s. Two dining rooms, Victorian Pub, piano bar. Furnished with antiques, period pieces. Swimming pool overlooking Kennebunk River. Dinner available April–October. French spoken.*

KYLEMERE HOUSE 1818

Kylemere House 1818
South St., Box 1333, Kennebunkport, ME 04046-1333
(207) 967-2780

Innkeeper: Ruth and Helen Toohey

Rooms: 4 w/pvt. bath, incl. 1 w/fireplace

Rates: $80-$135, incl. full brk. Discount avail. for senior citizen and extended stays. Seasonal variations.

Credit cards: MC, V

Restrictions: No children under 12, pets, smoking. Min. one night's deposit req. 14-day cancellation notice req., less $15.00 fee. 2-night min. stay on wknds. 3-night min. stay on holiday wknds.
Notes: Two-story Federal-style inn built in 1818. Dining room. Parlor. Decorated with antiques and period furniture. Perennial garden, pond. French spoken.*

Lake Brook Guest House
57 Western Ave., Kennebunkport, ME 04043
(207) 967-4069
Innkeeper: Carolyn Anne McAdams
Rooms: 3 plus 1 suite, all w/pvt. bath
Rates: $75-$90/room, $95/suite, all incl. full brk. Seasonal variations. Discount avail. for extended stay.
Credit cards: None
Restrictions: No pets, smoking. Deposit req. 10-day cancellation notice req. less $15.00 fee. 2-night min. stay on wknds. 3-night min. stay on holiday wknds.
Notes: Two-story farmhouse built at the turn of the century. Located in Lower Harbor Village. Wrap-around porch with rockers overlooking gardens, marsh, tidal brook. Spanish spoken.*

Maine Stay Inn
34 Maine St., Box 500 A, Kennebunkport, ME 04046
(207) 967-2117, (800) 950-2117, (207) 967-8757
Innkeeper: Carol and Lindsay Copeland
Rooms: 13 w/pvt. bath, TV, incl. 3 w/fireplace, plus 4 suites w/pvt. bath, TV, incl. 2 w/fireplace. Located in 5 bldgs.
Rates: $75-$145/room, $100-$185/suite, all incl. full brk., afternoon refreshment. Discount avail. for extended stay.
Credit cards: Most major cards
Restrictions: No pets. Smoking restricted. 50% deposit req. 2-week cancellation notice req. 2-night min. stay on wknds.
Notes: Two-story Victorian Italianate-style house with cupola built in 1860. Queen Anne colonial revival touches added in 1900. Has operated as inn since 1941. Wrap-around porch with wicker furniture. Living room with flying staircase, crystal chandeliers, fireplace. Dining room. Furnished with Queen Anne revival antiques, reproductions. Lawn games available. Small private parties accommodated. Main house listed on the National Register of Historic Places.*

Old Fort Inn
Old Fort Ave., Box M, Kennebunkport, ME 04046
(207) 967-5353, (207) 967-4547
Innkeeper: Sheila and David Aldrich
Rooms: 16 w/pvt. bath, phone, cable TV, wet bar. Located in 2 bldgs.
Rates: $120-$230, incl. full brk. Seasonal variations.
Credit cards: Most major cards
Restrictions: No pets, smoking. Deposit req. 15-day cancellation notice 2-night min. stay on wknds. and high season. Closed Dec.-April.
Notes: Converted brick and stone carriage house built in 1880. Lodge in converted barn built about 1880 with brick fireplace. Located on Arundel Point. Dining room. Furnished with country antiques, hand-stenciled walls. Freshwater swimming pool, patio, tennis court, shuffleboard. Bicycles may be rented. Antique shop on premises. Laundry facilities available.*

Schooners Inn
Ocean Ave., Box 79, Kennebunkport, ME 04046
(207) 967-5333, (800) 525-5599, (207) 967-2040
Innkeeper: Diane Mailhot
Rooms: 10 plus 7 suites, all w/pvt. bath, phone, cable TV
Rates: $105-$130/room $150-235/suite, all incl. cont. brk. Seasonal variations.
Credit cards: Most major cards
Restrictions: No pets. Smoking restricted. 50% deposit req. 14-day cancellation notice req., less $15.00 fee. 2-night min. stay on wknds. and holidays.
Notes: Decorated in classic and contemporary styles with original paintings and prints of shipbuilding heritage. Furnished with Thomas Moser furniture. Cribs, free parking available. Handicapped access. French spoken.*

White Barn Inn
RR 3, Box 387, Beach St., Kennebunkport, ME 04046
(207) 967-2321, (207) 967-1100
Innkeeper: Laurie Cameron
Rooms: 24 plus 6 suites, all w/pvt. bath, incl. 11 w/phone, fireplace, TV. Located in 3 bldgs.
Rates: $100-$150/room, $190-$275/suite, $150-$185 gatehouse, all incl. cont. brk., afternoon refreshment. Seasonal variations.
Credit cards: Most major cards
Restrictions: No pets. Smoking restricted. Deposit req. 14-day cancellation notice req. 2-night min. stay on wknds. 3-night min. stay on holiday wknds.
Notes: Three-story coastline homestead built in the 1800s. Reception area, sitting rooms, colonial dining room, piano bar. Furnished with antiques. Restaurant on premises. Gatehouse suites have whirlpool tubs, robes. German and French spoken.*

KINGFIELD (3)

The Herbert
67 Main St., Kingfield, ME 04947
(207) 265-2000, (800) 843-4372, (207) 265-4594
Innkeeper: Brenda and Bud Faye
Rooms: 32, incl. 4 suites, all w/pvt. bath
Rates: $49-$80/room, $79-$150/suite, all incl. cont. brk. Seasonal variations.
Credit cards: Most major cards
Restrictions: Smoking restricted. 50% deposit req. 21-day cancellation notice req. during winter, less 20% fee. Min. stay during winter holidays.
Notes: Built in 1918. Restaurant with marble floors on premises. All rooms have whirlpool tubs or steambaths, some feature brass beds. French spoken. Handicapped access.*

KITTERY (8)

Enchanted Nights B & B
29 Wentworth St., Rte. 103, Kittery, ME 03904-1720
(207) 439-1489
Innkeeper: Nancy Bogenberger and Peto Lamandia
Rooms: 5, plus 2 suites, all w/pvt. bath, cable TV
Rates: $47-$92/room, $82-$120/suite, all incl. full brk.

Credit cards: Most major cards
Restrictions: No smoking. Min. one night's deposit req. Min. 8-day cancellation notice req., less $15.00 fee. 2-night min. stay on holidays.
Notes: Princess Anne Gothic Victorian house built in 1890. Decorated with ecclectic collection of French-Victorian furnishings. Bicycles, board games available. Handicapped access available.*

GUNDALOW INN

Gundalow Inn
6 Water St., Kittery, ME 03904
(207) 439-4040

Innkeeper: Cevia and George Rosol
Rooms: 6 w/pvt. bath
Rates: $80-$105, incl. full brk., afternoon refreshment. Seasonal variations.
Credit cards: Most major cards
Restrictions: No children under 16, pets, smoking. One night's deposit req. 10-day cancellation notice req.
Notes: Brick Italianate Victorian with ceiling fans built in 1889. Breakfast room with fireplace, parlor. Sitting room with books, board games, piano. Furnished with antiques, lace curtains, Oriental rugs. Porch with rocking chairs. Patio. Perennial and herb gardens. Slovak, French spoken. Handicapped access.

LINCOLNVILLE (8)

The Victorian B & B
The Other Rd., Box 258, Lincolnville, ME 04849
(207) 236-3785, (800) 382-9817

Innkeeper: Ray and Marie Donner
Rooms: 4 plus 2 suites, all w/pvt. bath, incl. 4 w/fireplace
Rates: $85-$100/room, $125-$175/suite, all incl. full brk., afternoon refreshment. Seasonal variations. Discount avail. for extended and group stays. Special pkgs. avail.
Credit cards: Most major cards

Restrictions: No children under 7, pets. Smoking restricted. Min. one night's deposit req. 14-day cancellation notice req.
Notes: Victorian Inn with fireplaces built in 1889. Wrap-around porch overlooking Penobscot Bay. Gazebo. Small private parties accommodated. Resident pets.*

MOUNT DESERT (6)

The Bed & Breakfast Year 'Round
P.O. Box 52, Mount Desert, ME 04660
(207) 244-3316

Innkeeper: Binnie and Stan MacDonald
Rooms: 3, incl. 1 w/pvt. bath
Rates: $65-$75, incl. full brk. Seasonal variations.
Credit cards: MC, V
Restrictions: No children under 5, pets, smoking. Min. one night's deposit req. 2-week cancellation notice req. 2-night min. stay.
Notes: Two-story house built in 1850. Furnished with antiques. Living room, music room, screened porch, garden courtyard, backyard with Adirondack chairs. Fireplace, books, games, puzzles. Listed on the National Register of Historic Places. Resident cat.

Long Pond Inn
Pond's End, Mount Desert, ME 04660
(207) 244-5854

Innkeeper: Bob and Pam Mensink
Rooms: 4, w/pvt. bath, incl. 1 w/Jacuzzi
Rates: $75-$95 incl. cont. brk. Discount avail. for extended stay.
Credit cards: MC, V
Restrictions: No children under 12 pets, smoking. Deposit req. 14-day cancellation notice req. 2-night min. stay.
Notes: Built with materials collected from dismantled estates, hotels. Greenhouse. Flower, herb, and vegetable gardens. Guests have access to canoes. Resident dogs. Dutch spoken.

NAPLES (5)

The Augustus Bove House
RR 1, Box 501, Naples, ME 04055
(207) 693-6365

Innkeeper: Dave and Arlene Stetson
Rooms: 10 plus 1 suite, all w/TV, incl. 7 w/pvt. bath, 4 w/fireplace
Rates: $55-$85, incl. full brk. Discount avail. for extended, mid-week, and senior citizen stays. Seasonal variations. Special pkgs. avail.
Credit cards: Most major cards
Restrictions: Pets welcome with prior arrangement. Smoking restricted. Deposit req. 28-day cancellation notice req., less $10.00 fee.
Notes: Three-story brick colonial hotel built in 1856. Restored in 1984. Located along Long Lake. Common room, veranda. Furnished with antiques. Handicapped access.*

Lamb's Mill Inn
Lambs Mill Rd., Box 676, Naples, ME 04055
(207) 693-6253

LAMB'S MILL INN

Innkeeper: Laurel Tinkham, Sandy Long
Rooms: 6 w/pvt. bath, TV
Rates: $75-$85, incl. full brk. Seasonal variations. Discount avail. for mid-week, extended stay.
Credit cards: V
Restrictions: No children under 10, pets, smoking. One night's deposit req. 14-day cancellation notice req., less $15.00 fee.
Notes: Country inn located on twenty wooded acres with two lakes. Boating, swimming available.*

NEWCASTLE (8)

Mill Pond Inn
R.F.D. 1, Box 245, Newcastle, ME 04553
(207) 563-8014
Innkeeper: Bobby and Sherry Whear
Rooms: 5 w/pvt. bath, incl. 1 w/phone, 3 w/fireplace
Rates: $40-$57, incl. full brk. Seasonal variations.
Credit cards: None
Restrictions: No children under 5, pets.
Notes: Located on shore of Damariscotta Lake. Sitting room with fireplace, dining room, deck overlooking Mill Pond. Boat, hammock available.

The Newcastle Inn
River Road, R.R. 2, Box 24, Newcastle, ME 04553
(207) 563-5685, (800) 832-8669
Innkeeper: Ted and Chris Sprague
Rooms: 15 w/pvt. bath, incl. 1 w/fireplace
Rates: $60-$190, incl. full brk., dinner. Special pkgs. avail.
Credit cards: MC, V
Restrictions: No children under 12, pets, smoking. One night's deposit req. 7-day cancellation notice req., less $20.00 fee.
Notes: Overlooking the Damariscotta River. Has operated as inn since about 1924. Formal living room with fireplace. Two dining rooms. Stencil room with hand stencilled floors. Screened porch overlooking gardens and river. Most rooms have view of river.*

NORTH HAVEN (6)

The Pulpit Harbor Inn
Crabtree Point Rd., North Haven, ME 04853-9706
(207) 867-2219
Innkeeper: Marnelle Bubar and Amanda Frankowski
Rooms: 6, incl. 3 w/pvt. bath
Rates: $70-$90, incl. full. brk.
Credit cards: Most major cards
Restrictions: Smoking restricted. Min. one night's deposit req. 10-day cancellation
   notice req., less $10.00 fee.
Notes: Two-story farmhouse built in the 19th-century. Recently renovated. Living
room with fireplace. Main dining room with wood stove. Greenhouse dining room,
library, screened porch, brick courtyard. Furnished with country prints, home-
made quilts. For ferry access from Rockland call (207) 596-2202. Restaurant on
premises. Bicycles available for rent. Some French spoken.

OGUNQUIT (8)

Beachmere Inn
12 Beachmere Place, Box 2340, Ogunquit, ME 03907
(207) 646-2021, (207) 646-2231
Innkeeper: Louesa Mace Gillespie
Rooms: 37 w/pvt. bath, phone, incl. 3 w/fireplace, plus 17 suites w/pvt. bath, incl.
   10 w/phone, 2 w/fireplace. Located in 5 bldgs.
Rates: $50-$160/room, $65-$200/suite, all incl. cont. brk. Special pkgs. avail.
Credit cards: Most major cards
Restrictions: No pets. 2-night's deposit req. 14-day cancellation notice req., less
   $15.00 fee. 3-night min. stay.
Notes: Victorian inn built at the turn of the century. Rooms overlook Little Beach
and sculptured gardens. Some guests have access to kitchennette. Limited handi-
capped access.*

Hartwell House
118 Shore Rd., Box 393, Ogunquit, ME 03907
(207) 646-7210, (207) 646-6032
Innkeeper: Jim and Trisha Hartwell, Alec and Renee Adams
Rooms: 11, plus 3 suites, 2 studios, all w/pvt. bath. Located in 2 bldgs.
Rates: $80-$135/room, $125-$175/suite, $100-$120/studio, all incl. full brk., after-
noon refreshment. Discount avail. for extended stay. Seasonal variations.
Credit cards: Most major cards
Restrictions: No children under 10, pets. Smoking restricted. One night's deposit
   req. 14-day cancellation notice req. 2-night min. stay from July 1-Aug. 31. 3-night
   min. stay for holidays.
Notes: Located on 1.5 acres of sculptured lawns and flower gardens. Dining room.
Common room with TV, fireplace, phones. Furnished with early American and English antiques. Front porch. French doors connecting to private balconies overlooking sculpted flower gardens. Decks, patios. Lawn games. available. Limousine service
available from airport. Small private parties accommodated. Handicapped access.*

Morning Dove
5 Bourne Ln., Box 1940, Ogunquit, ME 03907
(207) 646-3891

Innkeeper: Eeta Sachon
Rooms: 5, incl. 3 w/pvt. bath
Rates: $75-$100, incl. cont. brk, evening refreshment. Seasonal variations. Discount avail. for extended stay.
Credit cards: Most major cards
Restrictions: No children under 12, pets. Smoking restricted. 50% deposit req. 10-day cancellation notice req., less $10.00 fee. 2-night seasonal min. stay. 3-night min. stay on wknds. Closed Nov. 1–May 1.
Notes: Farmhouse built in the 1860s. Fully restored. Dining room, Victorian porch. Furnished with antiques, paintings by local artists. French spoken.

Puffin Inn
233 U.S. RT. 1, Box 2232, Ogunquit, ME 03907
(207) 646-5496

Innkeeper: Maurice and Lee . Williams
Rooms: 10 w/pvt. bath, refrigerator, incl. 2 w/TV. Located in 2 bldgs.
Rates: $80-$90, incl. cont. brk. Seasonal variations.
Credit cards: MC, V
Restrictions: No children under 12, pets. Smoking restricted. Min. one night's deposit req. 10-day cancellation notice req., less $10.00 fee. 2-night min. stay during July–Aug.
Notes: Three-story Victorian sea captain's house built about 1830. Living room, porch. Furnished with mixture of traditional and antique furniture. Flower gardens. Trolley stops at inn. Off-street parking available. French spoken. Limited handicapped access.

ORLAND (6)

The Sign of the Amiable Pig
Main St., Rte. 175, Box 232, Orland, ME 04472
(207) 469-2561

Innkeeper: Charlotte and Wes Pipher
Rooms: 3 w/fireplace, incl. 1 w/pvt. bath
Rates: $55, incl. full brk. Seasonal variations.
Credit cards: Most major cards
Restrictions: No pets, smoking. One night's deposit req. 7-day cancellation req.
Notes: Two-story house with pegged soft wood floors, square spiral front stair, six fireplaces, built in the 1800s. Located on four acres. Dining room, keeping room. Furnished with antiques, Oriental rugs.

PORTLAND (8)

Andrews Lodging
417 Auburn St., Portland, ME 04103
(207) 797-9157, (207) 797-9040

Innkeeper: Douglas and Elizabeth Andrews
Rooms: 5 w/phone, no pvt. bath plus 1 suite w/pvt. bath, phone, TV.
Rates: $58-$68/room, $85-$125/suite, incl. cont. brk. Discount for mid-week and extended stays. Seasonal variation.
Credit cards: Most major cards
Restrictions: No children under 6. Smoking restricted. Deposit req. 2-night wknd. min. from July–Oct.

ANDREWS LODGING

Notes: Two-story Colonial house built in 1744, fully renovated. Located on 1.75 acres. Sitting room with TV. Solarium overlookin gardens. Formal dining room. Decks, ice-skating rink. Furnished with antiques. Lawn games available. Guests have access to kitchen.*

Inn on Carleton
46 Carleton St., Portland, ME 04102
(207) 775-1910, (207) 761-2160
Innkeeper: Phil and Susan Cox
Rooms: 7, incl. 4 w/pvt. bath, phone
Rates: $49-$95, incl. full brk. Seasonal variations.
Credit cards: Most major cards
Restrictions: No pets, smoking. One night's deposit req. 7-day cancellation notice req., less $20.00 fee. 2-night min. stay on wknds. June 1–Oct. 31.
Notes: Three-story brick Victorian townhouse built in 1869. Front hall with curving stairway. Parlor with bay window, grandfather clock. Dining room. Furnished with period antiques. Bookbindery on premises. Resident cat.

West End Inn
146 Pine St., Portland, ME 04102
(207) 772-1377
Innkeeper: John Leonard
Rooms: 5 w/pvt. bath, phone, TV
Rates: $65-$129, incl. full brk., evening refreshment. Discount avail. for senior citizen, extended, and mid-week stays. Seasonal variations.
Credit cards: Most major cards
Restrictions: No children under 12, pets, smoking. Deposit req. 3-day cancellation notice req. 2-night min. stay during high season.
Notes: Spanish spoken.*

RANGELEY (3)

Northwoods B & B
Main St., Box 79, Rangeley, ME 04970
(207) 864-2440

Innkeeper: Robert and Carol Scofield
Rooms: 4, incl 3 w/pvt. bath
Rates: $60-$75, incl. full brk. Discount avail. for extended stay. Seasonal variations.
Credit cards: MC, V
Restrictions: No children under 8, pets, smoking. Deposit req. 14-day cancellation
  notice req.
Notes: Three-story house built in 1912. Living room with fireplace, cable TV, VCR.
Furnished with antiques. Front porch woverlooking lake. Private boat dock.*

RAYMOND (6)

Northern Pines
559 Rte. 85, Raymond, ME 04071
(207) 655-7624, (207) 655-3321

Innkeeper: Marlee Turner
Rooms: 50, incl. 20 w/pvt. bath, 2 w/fireplace. Located in 8 bldgs.
Rates: $35-$50, incl. full brk.
Credit cards: Most major cards
Restrictions: No smoking. Deposit req. Min. cancellation notice req., less 15% fee.
Notes: Lakeside lodge built in the 1920s. Located on 70 acres on Crescent Lake with
three artesian wells. Created as a camp for women at business or in college. Library,
fireplace. Conference Center and wedding facilities available. Health resort with ac-
tivities, meals and classes available. Hot Tub, sauna, boats, dock. Small private parties accommodated. Some French, Spanish, Russian spoken. Handicapped access.*

ROCKPORT (6)

ROCKPORT HARBOR HOUSE

Rockport Harbor House
11 Mechanic St., Rockport, ME 04856
(207) 236-2422

Innkeeper: Lynne Twentyman, Jessica Ward
Rooms: 2, w/pvt. bath, incl. 1 w/fireplace
Rates: $100-$165, incl. full brk.
Credit cards: None
Restrictions: 50% deposit req. 10-day cancellation notice req., less $20.00 fee. 2-night min. stay.
Notes: Some rooms with skylights and Jacuzzi. Deck overlooks mountains and sea. Private pier with 30' sloop, available for charter.

SACO (8)

Crown 'n' Anchor Inn
121 North St., Box 228, Saco, ME 04072
(207) 282-3829
Innkeeper: Martha Forester, John Barclay
Rooms: 6 w/pvt. bath, incl. 2 w/TV, plus 1 suite w/2 fireplaces, whirlpool
Rates: $60-$85/room, $85/suite, all incl. full brk. Discount avail. for extended stay.
Credit cards: MC, V
Restrictions: No children under 12, smoking. One-night's deposit req. 10-day cancellation notice req.
Notes: Two-story Adamesque-style, 19-room house built in 1827. Located on 2 wooded acres. Dining room. Listed on the National Register of Historic Places. Some French spoken.*

SEARSPORT (6)

Brass Lantern Inn
Rte. 1, Box 407, Searsport, ME 04974
(207) 548-0150, (800) 691-0150
Innkeeper: Pat Gatto, Dan and Lee Ann Lee
Rooms: 4 w/pvt. bath
Rates: $50-$75, incl. full brk. Seasonal variations.
Credit cards: MC, V
Restrictions: No pets. Smoking restricted. 50% deposit req. 14-day cancellation notice req.
Notes: Two-story Victorian inn built in 1850. Dining room, two parlors. Antique toy train shop on premises. 300 dolls on display.*

House of Three Chimneys
Black Rd., Box 397, Searsport, ME 04974
(207) 548-6117
Innkeeper: Patricia Collins-Stockton
Rooms: 4 w/pvt. bath, incl. 1 w/Jacuzzi
Rates: $40-$70/room, incl. full brk. Seasonal variations. Discount avail. for senior citizen and extended stays.
Credit cards: Most major cards
Restrictions: Children, pets, smoking restricted. $50 deposit req. 14-day cancellation notice req., less $10.00 fee.
Notes: Sea captain's Greek Revival-style house built around 1850. Front parlor, back parlor, library, study, "pub" with fireplace, TV, VCR, videotape collection. Board games available. French, German spoken.

SOUTH BROOKSVILLE (5)

Buck's Harbor Inn
P.O. Box 268, South Brooksville, ME 04617
(207) 326-8660
Innkeeper: Peter and Ann Ebeling
Rooms: 6, no pvt. bath. Suite avail.
Rates: $65/room, $75/suite, all incl. full brk. Discount avail. for extended stay.
Credit cards: MC, V
Restrictions: No pets, smoking. One night's deposit req. 14-day cancellation notice req. Closed Jan. 1–June 1.
Notes: Three-story country inn built in 1901. Completely renovated in 1982. Dining room, Library/sitting room. Dinners available on Saturday by reservation Oct 15–May 15.

SOUTH FREEPORT (8)

Harborside B & B
14 Main St., South Freeport, ME 04078-0036
(207) 865-3281
Innkeeper: James and Caroline Hendry
Rooms: 3 w/pvt. bath
Rates: $85, incl. full brk. Seasonal variations.
Credit cards: MC V
Restrictions: No children under 6, smoking. Deposit req. 7-day cancellation notice req. Closed Nov. 1–April 30
Notes: Resident dog. French, Italian spoken.

SOUTHWEST HARBOR (6)

The Harbour Cottage Inn
P.O. Box 258, Southwest Harbor, ME 04679-0258
(207) 244-5738
Innkeeper: Ann and Mike Pedreschi
Rooms: 7 plus 1 suite, all w/pvt. bath, phone
Rates: $55-$95/room, $85-$125/suite, all incl. brk., afternoon refreshment. Seasonal variations. Discount avail. for extended stay.
Credit cards: Most major cards
Restrictions: No children under 2, pets, smoking. One night's deposit req. 10-day cancellation notice req.
Notes: Three-story house with mansard roof built in 1870. Located on 1.2 acres with gardens. Sitting room with cable TV, VCR, antique piano, games. Reference books and novels. Dining room with door to deck overlooking lawn, harbor.*

The Island House
Clark Point Rd., Box 1006, Southwest Harbor, ME 04679-1006
(207) 244-5180
Innkeeper: Ann Bradford
Rooms: 4 plus 1 apt., incl. 1 w/pvt. bath, 2 w/cable TV, 2 w/fireplace
Rates: $45-$70/room, $95/carriage house, $120/apt, all incl. full brk. Seasonal variation. Discount avail. for extended stay.
Credit cards: MC, V

Restrictions: No children under 5, pets, smoking. Min. one night's deposit req. 14-day cancellation notice req., less min. $25.00 fee. 2-night min. stay, July/August. Closed Nov. 1–April 30.
Notes: Two-story main house with pumpkin board floors plus apartment over carriage house. Has operated as inn since 1832. Double living rooms with two fireplaces. Sitting room, dining area. Ralph Waldo Emerson, John Greenleaf Whittier slept here. Some French, Malay spoken.*

Island Watch B & B
Freeman Ridge Rd., Box 1359, Southwest Harbor, ME 04679-1359
(207) 244-7229
Innkeeper: Maxine M. Clark
Rooms: 4. plus 2 suites, all w/pvt. bath
Rates: $65-$75, incl. full brk. Discount avail. for extended stay. Seasonal variations.
Credit cards: None
Restrictions: No children under 12, pets, smoking. Deposit req. 7-day cancellation notice req. 2-night min. stay.
Notes: Twenty-five year old family-built inn. Common room with TV. Wrap-around decks overlooking ocean and mountains. Handicapped access.*

The Kingsleigh Inn
100 Main St., Box 1426, Southwest Harbor, ME 04679
(207) 244-5302
Innkeeper: Tom and Nancy Cervelli
Rooms: 7 w/pvt bath, plus 1 suite w/pvt. bath, TV, fireplace
Rates: $55-$95/room, $95-$155/suite, all incl. full brk., afternoon refreshment. Seasonal variations.
Credit cards: Most major cards
Restrictions: No children under 12, pets, smoking. One night's deposit req. 10-day cancellation notice req.
Notes: Three-story Colonial Revival Style inn built in 1904. Sitting room and living room with fireplace. Library and games. Furnished with period pieces. Wrap-around veranda with white wicker furniture. Guests have access to country kitchen.

The Lamb's Ear Inn
Clark Pt. Rd., Box 30, Southwest Harbor, ME 04679
(207) 244-9828
Innkeeper: Elizabeth and George Hoke
Rooms: 4 w/pvt. bath plus 2 suites w/pvt. bath, incl. 1 w/TV
Rates: $75-$95/room, $125/suite, all incl. full brk. Seasonal variations.
Credit cards: MC, V
Restrictions: No children under 8, pets, smoking. Min. one night's deposit req. 10-day cancellation notice req.
Notes: Two-story inn built in 1857. Common room with fireplace. Sun porch with wicker furniture, deck overlooking harbor.*

Lindenwood Inn
P.O. Box 1328, Southwest Harbor, ME 04679-1328
(207) 244-5335
Innkeeper: Jim King
Rooms: 16 w/TV, incl. 14 w/fireplace, 12 w/pvt. bath. Suites, housekeeping apartments and cottages avail. Located in 2 bldgs.

Rates: $55-$105/room, $85-$135/suite, $85-$155/housekeeping apartments and cottages, all incl. full brk. Seasonal variations.
Credit cards: Most major cards
Restrictions: No pets, smoking. One night's deposit req. 14-day cancellation notice req., less $10.00 fee. 3-night min. stay August and holiday wknds.
Notes: Two-story sea captain's house built in 1902 overlooking harbor. Sitting rooms open onto front porch. Living room with fireplace and TV. Guest rooms feature balconies. Dining room with fireplace.*

Moorings Inn
P.O. Box 744, Southwest Harbor, ME 04679
(207) 244-5523
Innkeeper: Leslie and Betty King
Rooms: 12 plus 7 suites, all w/pvt. bath, phone, incl. 1 w/fireplace, 1 apt. w/fireplace, 7 w/TV. Located in 6 bldgs.
Rates: $50-$75/room, $65-$75/suite, $75-$95/cottages & apt., all incl. cont. brk. Discount avail. for extended stay.
Credit cards: None
Restrictions: No pets. Smoking restricted. Min. one night's deposit req., Cancellation notice req., less $30.00 fee.
Notes: Two-story Main House built about 1784. Expanded in 1830. Lookout Cottage built in 1937. Pilot House converted from a barn in 1937. Has operated as inn since 1916. Decorated and furnished with antiques, ship models, decoys and nautical items. Sitting room with fireplace. Lounge with TV. Library, dining room, screened porches. Furnished with antiques. Restaurant on premises. Bicycles, canoes, gas grills available.

Penury Hall
Main St., Box 68, Southwest Harbor, ME 04679
(207) 244-7102
Innkeeper: Toby and Gretchen Strong
Rooms: 3, no pvt. bath
Rates: $60, incl. full brk. Seasonal variations.
Credit cards: None
Restrictions: No children under 12, pets, smoking. Deposit req. 14-day cancellation notice req. 2-week min. stay in July, Aug.
Notes: Built in 1830. Enlarged and remodeled. Has operated as inn since 1982. Living room with cable TV, fireplace. Dining room with fireplace. 17-foot canoe, 21-foot sloop, windsurfer, sauna available. Resident cats.

STRATTON (3)

Widow's Walk
171 Main St., Box 150, Stratton, ME 04982
(207) 246-6901
Innkeeper: Mary and Jerry Hopson
Rooms: 6, no pvt. bath
Rates: $46. Seasonal variation.
Credit cards: MC, V
Restrictions: No children under 6, pets, smoking. 50% deposit req. 21-day cancellation notice req., less $10.00 fee.

Notes: Two-story Steamboat Gothic design built in 1892. Two livings room. Ping pong/darts room with TV. Resident pets. Listed in National Register of Historic Places.

SUNSET (6)

Goose Cove Lodge
Goose Cove Road, Box 40, Sunset, ME 04683-0040
(207) 348-2508, (207) 348-2624
Innkeeper: Joanne and Dom Parisi
Rooms: 8 cottages plus 9 suites, all w/pvt. bath, most w/fireplace. Located in 10 bldgs.
Rates: $70-$88/suite, $80-$104/cottage, all incl. full brk. Seasonal variations. Special pkgs. avail.
Credit cards: MC, V
Restrictions: No pets. Smoking restricted. Deposit req. 14-day cancellation notice req., less $15.00 fee. 2-night min. stay from May 15-June 25 and from Sept. 3-Oct. 15. 7-night min. stay in July, Aug.
Notes: Lodge built in 1948. Located on 70 wooded acres on the ocean with 2500 feet of shoreline. Common room with library. Recreational hall with ping pong, pool table, games, video library. After dinner entertainment. Outdoor activities available. Small private parties accommodated. Handicapped access.*

TENANTS HARBOR (8)

East Wind Inn
Mechanic St., Box 149, Tenants Harbor, ME 04860-0149
(207) 372-6366, (207) 372-6320
Innkeeper: Tim Watts
Rooms: 17, incl. 9 w/pvt. bath, phone, plus 3 suites w/pvt. bath, phone, plus apt. Located in 2 bldgs.
Rates: $74-$96/room, $110/suite, $130/apt., all incl. cont. brk. Discount avail. for extended stay. Seasonal variations.
Credit cards: Most major cards
Restrictions: Pets welcome with prior notice. One night's deposit req. 14-day cancellation notice req., less $10.00 fee.
Notes: Built in 1890 as a sail loft. Restored in and has operated as inn since 1974. Small private parties accommodated.*

VINALHAVEN (6)

Fox Island Inn
Carver St., Box 451, Vinalhaven, ME 04863
(207) 863-2122
Innkeeper: Gail Reinertsen
Rooms: 6, no pvt. bath, plus 1 suite w/pvt. bath
Rates: $40-$60/room, $110/suite, all incl. cont brk.
Credit cards: None
Restrictions: No children under 10. No pet, smoking. One night's deposit req. 7-day cancellation notice req. Closed December-April.
Notes: Three-story inn. Reached by state-operated ferry departing from Rockland. Ferry reservations: (207) 596-2202. Bicycles available. Guests have access to kitchen. Off-season address: 1551 Live Oak Dr., P.O. Box 451, Tallahassee, FL 32301

WEST BOOTHBAY HARBOR (8)

The Lawnmeer Inn
P.O. Box 505, West Boothbay Harbor, ME 04575
(207) 633-2544, (800) 633-7645
Innkeeper: Jim and Lee Metgzer
Rooms: 30, incl. 22 w/TV, plus 2 suites w/TV, all w/pvt. bath. Located in 3 bldgs.
Rates: $60-$120/room, $80-$110/suite. Seasonal variations.
Credit cards: MC, V
Restrictions: Pets welcome with prior arrangement. Smoking restricted. One
  night's deposit req. 7-day cancellation notice req. 2-night min. stay on holiday
  and event wknds.
Notes: Three-story Victorian inn built in 1898. Located on island, surrounded by
woods on three sides and the ocean on the fourth. Common rooms. Porches with
Adirondack chairs overlooking flower and herb gardens. Cribs available. Restaurant
on primeses. Handicapped access. Resident cat.*

WINTER HARBOR (7)

Main Stay Inn
P.O. Box 459, Winter Harbor, ME 04693
(207) 963-2601, 963-5561
Innkeeper: Roger and Pearl Barto
Rooms: 3 rooms plus 1 efficiency unit, all w/pvt. bath, fireplace. Located in 3 bldgs.
Rates: $40-$50. Seasonal variations.
Credit cards: MC, V
Restrictions: One night's deposit required.
Notes: Seven-gabled Victorian house built in 1874. Remodeled in 1986. Living
room with TV. Two cottages, each with kitchen.

SQUIRE TARBOX INN

WISCASSET (8)

Squire Tarbox Inn
RR 2, Box 620, Wiscasset, ME 04578
(207) 882-7693
Innkeeper: Karen and Bill Mitman

Rooms: 11 w/pvt. bath, incl. 4 w/fireplace
Rates: $75-$210, incl. cont. brk., 5-course dinner. Special pkgs. avail.
Credit cards: Most major cards
Restrictions: No children under 14, pets. Smoking restricted. Min. one night's deposit req. 10-day cancellation notice req., less $5.00 fee. Closed Oct. 22–May 18. 12% gratuity added to all bills.
Notes: Colonial farmhouse with original floors, carvings, beams, moldings built 1763-1825. Fully restored. Located on twelve wooded acres. Dining room, deck. Lounge with fireplace. Barn houses pure-bred dairy goats. Cheese dairy on premises. Listed on the National Register of Historic Places. Bikes and rowboat on small cove avail.*

YORK (8)

Dockside Guest Quarters
P.O. Box 205, York, ME 03909
(207) 363-2868, (800) 270-1977

Innkeeper: David Lusty Family
Rooms: 15 w/pvt. bath, TV, plus 6 suites w/pvt. bath, TV, incl. 1 w/fireplace, 2 w/phone. Located in 5 bldgs.
Rates: $56-$96/room, $98-$142/suite. Seasonal variations. Discount avail. for extended stay. Special pkgs. avail.
Credit cards: Most major cards
Restrictions: No pets. Smoking restricted. Min. one night's deposit req. 2-week cancellation notice req., less $10.00 fee. 2-night min. stay in season. 3-night min. stay on holiday wknds.
Notes: Three-story main house with porches on two stories, plus four cottages, all overlooking harbor. Located on private peninsula. Furnished with antiques, ship models, marine paintings. Full restaurant on premises. Small private parties accommodated. Limited handicapped access.*

YORK BEACH (8)

Homestead Inn B & B
8 S. Main, Box 15, York Beach, ME 03910
(207) 363-8952

Innkeeper: Dan and Danielle Duffy
Rooms: 4, no pvt. bath
Rates: $49-$59, incl. cont. brk., afternoon refreshment. Seasonal variations. Discount avail. for senior citizen and extended stays.
Credit cards: None
Restrictions: No children under 15, pets, smoking. Min. one night's deposit req. 10-day written cancellation notice req.
Notes: Three-story guesthouse built in the early 1905. Converted in the 1960s. Located on Short Sands Beach. Living room with fireplace. Dining room with wood burning stove. Library, sun deck, front porch. French spoken.*

The Tide Watch Bed & Breakfast
46 Shore Rd., Box 192, York Beach, ME 03910
(207) 363-4713

Innkeeper: Alanna and Craig Schriefer
Rooms: 3, incl. 2 w/pvt. bath
Rates: $45-$65, incl. full. brk. Seasonal variations.

Credit cards: None

Restrictions: No pets, smoking. 50% deposit req. 14-day cancellation notice req.

Notes: Gambrel-style house built in 1960. Recently renovated. Parlor. Decorated in country decor. Private deck overlooking Cape Neddick River. Yard with private dock.

YORK HARBOR (8)

YORK HARBOR INN

York Harbor Inn
Rte. 1 A, Box 573, York Harbor, ME 03911
(800) 343-3869, (207) 363-3545, ext. 295

Innkeeper: Joseph and Garry Dominguez

Rooms: 31 w/phone, incl. 26 w/pvt. bath, 2 w/fireplace plus 1 suite w/pvt. bath, phone, spa. Located in 2 bldgs.

Rates: $79-$105, $119-$139/suite, all incl. cont. brk., soft drinks. Seasonal variations. Discount avail. for senior citizens.

Credit cards: Most major cards

Restrictions: No pets. Smoking restricted. 50% deposit req. 2-week cancellation notice req., less $10.00 fee.

Notes: Country inn in operation for over 100 years. Overlooks ocean. Common room with fieldstone fireplace. Cellar pub with entertainment, Dining Room. Cabin lounge with fireplace, light weekend entertainment, library. Reassembled former fisherman's cabin from the Isles of Shoals (circa 1637) sits in the center of the inn. Furnished with English antiques. Back yard with tables, chairs. Bicycles available. Small private parties accommodated. Handicapped access. Listed on the National Register of Historic Places. German and Spanish spoken.*

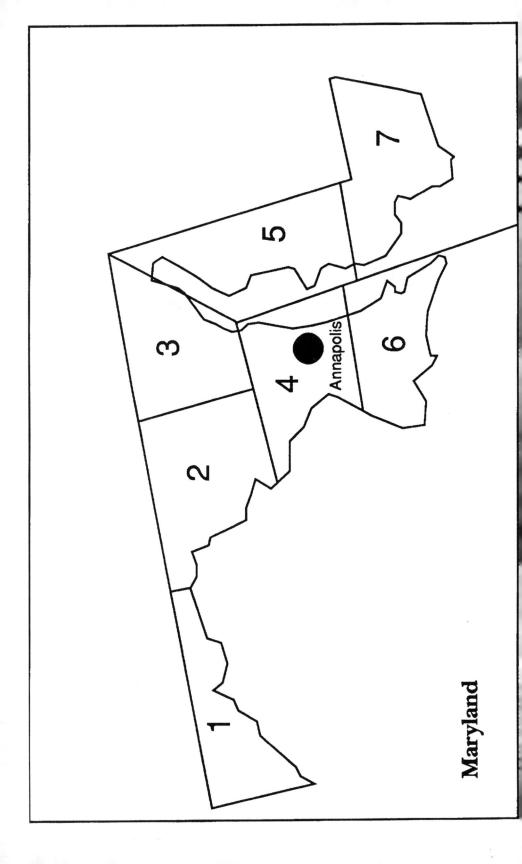

Maryland

Maryland

ANNAPOLIS (4)

The Ark and Dove
149 Prince George St., Annapolis, MD 21401
(410) 268-6277

Innkeeper: Susan Liedlich and Sandra Huffer
Rooms: 4 plus 1 suite, all w/pvt. bath, TV
Rates: $65-$75/room, $95/suite, all incl. full brk. Discount avail. for extended stay.
Credit cards: MC, V
Restrictions: No children under 10, pets, smoking. Deposit req. 10-day cancellation
  notice req. 2-night min. stay from Apr–Oct.
Notes: Early 1800s house with original pine floors. Furnished with Colonial and English antiques, Oriental and braided rugs.

Barn on Howards Cove
500 Wilson Rd., Annapolis, MD 21401
(410) 266-6840

Innkeeper: Libbie and Graham Gutsche
Rooms: 2 w/TV, no pvt. bath
Rates: $70, incl. full brk., afternoon refreshment. Discount avail. for extended stay.
Credit cards: None
Restrictions: No pets, smoking. One night's deposit req. 10-day cancellation notice
  req.
Notes: Two-story restored horsebarn built in 1850. Located on 6.2 wooded acres.
Furnished with antiques, arts and crafts. Common room, solarium, deck with view
of the water.*

BARN ON HOWARDS COVE

Chez Amis B & B
85 East St., Annapolis, MD 21401
(410) 263-6631, (800) 474-6631

Innkeeper: Don and Mickie Deline
Rooms: 4, incl. 2 w/pvt. bath, all w/TV
Rates: $75-$95, incl. full brk. Discount avail for mid-week stay. Seasonal variations.
Credit cards: None
Restrictions: No children under 10, pets, smoking. Min. one night's deposit req.
3-day cancellation notice req., less $15.00 fee.
Notes: Turn-of-the-century corner grocery store with original tin ceiling, Georgia pine floors, and oak display counter. Dining room on main floor. Furnished with antique quilts on the walls, country and European antiques. Garage parking available.*

College House Suites
One College Ave., Annapolis, MD 21401-1603
(410) 263-6124
Innkeeper: Don and Jo Anne Wolfrey
Rooms: 2 suites w/pvt. bath, phone, cable TV, incl. 1 w/fireplace
Rates: $160, incl. cont. brk., afternoon refreshment. Special pkgs. avail. Discount avail. for extended stay.
Credit cards: Most major cards
Restrictions: No children, pets, smoking. One night's deposit req. 21-day cancellation notice req., less $15.00 fee. 2-night min. stay.
Notes: Three-story Federal-style brick townhouse built in 1810. Formal dining room. Furnished with antiques, art deco and contemporary pieces. Decorated with fine art. Ivy-covered courtyard. Small private parties accommodated.*

DUKE & DUCHESS B & B

Duke & Duchess B & B
151 Duke of Gloucester St., Annapolis, MD 21401
(410) 268-6323, (410) 841-5456
Innkeeper: Doris Marsh
Rooms: 1 plus 1 suite, both w/pvt. bath, phone, A/C, TV, plus 1 suite.
Rates: $95/room, $150/suite, both incl. full brk.
Credit cards: Most major cards

Restrictions: Well-behaved children welcome. No pets, smoking. One night's deposit req. 7-day cancellation notice req. 2-night min. stay.
Notes: Three-story renovated house built in 1850. Furnished with antiques and artwork. Dining room, garden.

Gibson's Lodgings
110 Prince George St., Annapolis, MD 21401
(301) 268-5555
Innkeeper: Claude and Jeanne Schrift
Rooms: 19 plus 2 suites, incl. 7 w/pvt. bath, TV. Located in 2 bldgs.
Rates: $68-$98/room, $120/suite, all incl. cont. brk.
Credit cards: Most major cards
Restrictions: No pets, smoking. Deposit req. Min. 7-day cancellation notice req., less 40% fee.
Notes: Two-story Federal-style house built in 1768. Two-story Annex built in 1988. Two-story house renovated in 1988. Parlors, dining rooms, conference rooms. Furnished with antiques. Parking available. Handicapped access. Small private parties accommodated.*

Riverwatch
145 Edgewater Dr., Edgewater, Annapolis, MD 21037
(410) 974-8152
Innkeeper: Karen Dennis and Donald Silawsky
Rooms: 2 w/pvt bath
Rates: $65-$80, incl. cont. brk.
Credit cards: None
Restrictions: No pets. Smoking restricted. One night's deposit req. Refunded upon cancellation only if room re-rented. 4-night min. stay during Naval Academy Commissioning Week and October boat shows.
Notes: Located on the shore of the South River. Lounge, patio, dining room. Decorated in contempoary/Oriental style. Private dock. Swimming pool (seasonal). Hot tub. Resident cats.*

The William Page Inn
8 Martin St., Annapolis, MD 21401
(410) 626-1506, (410) 263-4841
Innkeeper: Robert Zuchelli, Greg Page
Rooms: 4, incl. 2 w/pvt. bath, plus 1 suite w/pvt. bath, TV
Rates: $125/room, $150/suite, all incl. full brk. Special pkgs. avail.
Credit cards: MC, V
Restrictions: No children under 12, smoking. 50% deposit req. 10-day cancellation notice req. 2-night min. stay on wknds. from Mar. 15–Nov. 30
Notes: Three-story inn built at the turn of the century. Common room, wraparound porch. Decorated in Victorian style. Furnished with antiques and period reproductions. Small private parties accommodated. Off-street parking available. Resident dog.*

BALTIMORE (3)

Betsy's Bed & Breakfast
1428 Park Ave., Baltimore, MD 21217-4230
(410) 383-1274, (410) 728-8957

Innkeeper: Betsy Grater
Rooms: 3 w/pvt. bath, incl. 1 w/phone
Rates: $75, incl. full brk. Discount avail. for mid-week, extended stays.
Credit cards: Most major cards
Restrictions: No pets, smoking. One night's deposit req. 10-day cancellation notice req., less $25.00 fee.
Notes: Bolton Hill town house built about 1870. Open-center staircase to fourth floor skylight and hallway floor laid in alternating strips of oak and walnut. Dining room with carved marble fireplace. Living room with high ceiling, French doors opening onto private garden. Furnished with country antiques, heirloom quilts, kitchen implements, and wall groupings including brass rubbings designed by the innkeeper. Patio, hot tub.*

Celie's Waterfront B & B
1714 Thames St., Baltimore, MD 21231
(301) 522-2323, (800) 432-0184, (410) 522-2324

Innkeeper: Celie Ives
Rooms: 5 w/pvt. bath, phone, TV, incl. 2 w/fireplace, plus 2 suites w/pvt. bath, phone, TV
Rates: $160, incl. cont. brk. Seasonal variations
Credit cards: Most major cards
Restrictions: No children under 10. pets, smoking. 50% deposit req. Min. 10-day cancellation notice req. 2-night min. stay in whirlpool rooms on wknds.
Notes: Federal-style inn. Roof deck with skyline, harbor views. Enclosed garden. Furnished with antiques and collectibles. Some rooms with private hot tub. Guests have access to FAX and modem. Small private parties accommodated. Off-street parking available. Handicapped access.*

Mr. Mole B & B
1601 Bolton St., Baltimore, MD 21217
(410) 728-1179, (410) 728-3379

Innkeeper: Collin Clarke, Paul Bragaw
Rooms: 5 suites w/pvt. bath, phone
Rates: $75-$145, incl. cont. brk.
Credit cards: Most major cards
Restrictions: No children under 10, pets, smoking. One-night's deposit req. Min. 14-day cancellation notice req. 2-night min. stay on wknds. Mar.–Nov.
Notes: Three-story house built in 1870. Living room, breakfast room, drawing room, with 14-foot ceiling, bay windows, and marble fireplaces. Decorated in English style, antiques, oriental pots. Grand piano. Garage parking available. French, German, Dutch spoken.*

Union Square House
23 S. Stricker St., Baltimore, MD 21233
(410) 233-9064, (410) 233-4046

Innkeeper: Patrice and Joe Debes
Rooms: 2 w/pvt bath, incl. 1 w/fireplace, TV, plus 1 suite w/pvt. bath, fireplace, TV
Rates: $80-$90/room, $115/suite, all incl. full brk, afternoon refreshment. Discount avail. for senior citizen and extended stays.
Credit cards: Most major cards
Restrictions: No pets. Smoking restricted. One night's deposit req. 14-day cancellation notice req.

Notes: Three-story Victorian Italianate style house with original plaster moldings and woodworkbuilt in 1874. Formal living room with fireplace, board games. Dining room. Furnished with period pieces. Garden with fountain and sundial. Small private parties accommodated. Partial handicapped access.*

BERLIN (7)

MERRY SHERWOOD PLANTATION

Merry Sherwood Plantation
8909 Worcester Hwy., Berlin, MD 21811
(410) 641-2112, (410) 641-3605
Innkeeper: Kirk and Ginny Burbage
Rooms: 7, incl. 5 w/pvt. bath, 3 w/fireplace plus 1 suite w/pvt. bath, fireplace.
Rates: $125/room, $150/suite, all incl. full brk., afternoon refreshment. Seasonal variations.
Credit cards: Most major cards
Restrictions: No children, pets, smoking. One night's deposit req. 7-day cancellation notice req. 2-night min. stay during high season.
Notes: 27-room Greek Revival, Classic Italianate, and Gothic mansion with 9 fireplaces built in 1859. Private baths, ballroom, parlors, a sun porch, and a library. Breakfast is served in formal dining room. Recently restored, furnished with authentic Victorian antiques. Wrought-iron main gates. Ballroom with marble fireplaces, peer mirrors, square grand piano, original Victorian furniture, and art pieces. Dining room features hand-carved sideboards, rosewood dining chairs, and chandelier. Located on 18 acres. Member of National Register of Historic Places.*

BETHESDA (5)

The Winslow Home
8217 Caraway St., Cabin John, Bethesda, MD 20818
(301) 229-4654
Innkeeper: Jane Winslow

Rooms: 2, no pvt. bath
Rates: $45, incl. full brk.
Credit cards: None
Restrictions: No pets, smoking, alcohol
Notes: Private home. Operating as inn since early 1980s. Kitchen, laundry facilities and piano. Garden. Patio.

BETTERTON (5)

Lantern Inn
P.O. Box 29, Betterton, MD 21610
(301) 348-5809
Innkeeper: Ken and Ann Washburn
Rooms: 13, incl. 2 w/pvt. bath
Rates: $68-$85, incl. cont. brk.
Credit cards: MC, V
Restrictions: No children under 12, pets, no smoking. Deposit req. 2-day cancellation notice req.
Notes: The three-story Victorian inn built in 1904. Recently restored and refurbished. Two living rooms with board games, TV. Dining room.

BUCKEYSTOWN (2)

The Catoctin Inn and Antiques
3613 Buckeystown Pike, Box 243, Buckeystown, MD 21717
(301) 874-5555, (800) 730-5550, (301) 831-8102
Innkeeper: Terry and Sarah Mac Gillivray
Rooms: 6 plus 1 suite, all w/pvt. bath, phone, incl. 1 w/Jacuzzi
Rates: $65-$85/room, $115-$125/suite, all incl.full brk., afternoon refreshment. Discount avail. for mid-week stay.
Credit cards: Most major cards
Restrictions: No pets, smoking. 2-day cancellation notice req.
Notes: Two-story house built in the 1780s. Parlor, library w/marble fireplaces, dining room, sun room. Located on 4 wooded acres w/gazebo. Furnished with antiques. 30 antique dealers located in 1890s Carriage House. Small private parties accommodated.*

CAMBRIDGE (5)

Glasgow Inn B & B
1500 Hambrooks Blvd., Cambridge, MD 21613
(410) 228-0575, (800) 373-7890, (410) 228-1000
Innkeeper: Louiselee Roche and Martha Ann Rayne
Rooms: 8, incl. 4 w/pvt. bath, fireplace
Rates: $75-$125, incl. full brk. Discount avail. for mid-week and extended stays.
Credit cards: MC, V
Restrictions: No pets, smoking. 2-night min. stay on wknds.
Notes: Colonial riverside plantation house built in 1760. Located on 7 acres. Listed on the National Register of Historic Places. Small private parties accommodated. Pick-up service from Marinas/Airport. Handicapped access.*

Sarke Plantation Inn
6033 Todd Point Rd., Box 139, Cambridge, MD 21613
(410) 228-7020

GLASGOW INN B & B

Innkeeper: Genevieve Finley
Rooms: 3 plus 1 suite, all w/pvt. bath, plus 1 w/TV, 1 w/fireplace
Rates: $50-$90/room, $110/suite, all incl. cont. brk. Discount avail. for extended
  stay.
Credit cards: Most major cards
Restrictions: No children under 10. Deposit req. 4-day cancellation notice req.
  Closed Dec. 31.
Notes: Two-story Plantation style house located on twenty seven acres. Living room
with fireplace, grand piano. Common room with pool table. Furnished with an-
tiques. Small private parties accommodated.*

CASCADE (2)

Bluebird on the Mountain
14700 Eyler Ave., Cascade, MD 21719
(800) 362-9526

Innkeeper: Eda Smith-Eley
Rooms: 2 plus 2 suites, all w/pvt. bath, fireplace, incl. 1 w/TV
Rates: $95-$105/room, $115/suite, all incl. cont. brk. Discount avail. for senior cit-
  izens.
Credit cards: MC, V
Restrictions: No children under 12. Smoking restricted. 50% deposit req. 7-day can-
  cellation notice req. 2-night min. stay on wknds.
Notes: Two-story manor house built in 1900. Dining room. Three porches with
rockers. Furnished with antiques, Oriental rugs, original artwork. Resident cats.*

CHESTERTOWN (5)

Brampton
25227 Chestertown Rd., Chestertown, MD 21620
(410) 778-1860

Innkeeper: Michael and Danielle Hanscom
Rooms: 6 w/pvt. bath, incl. 5 w/fireplace, plus 2 suites w/pvt. bath, incl. 1 w/fire-
place, TV. Located in 2 bldgs.
Rates: $90-$125/room, $110-$140/suite, all incl. full brk., afternoon refreshment
Credit cards: MC, V
Restrictions: No pets, smoking. Children restricted. One night's deposit req. 7-day
cancellation notice req. 2-night min. stay on wknds.
Notes: Three-story Greek Revival/Italian Renaissance house built in 1860. Located
on thirty-five acres. Dining room, parlor, mud room. Three-story walnut spiral staircase. Front porch with wicker furniture. Furnished with period antiques, reproductions. Listed on the National Register of Historic Places. Small private parties
accommodated. German, French spoken.

Hill's Inn B & B
114 Washington Ave., Chestertown, MD 21620
(301) 778-1926, (800) 345-4665

Innkeeper: Jill Brady
Rooms: 8 w/pvt. bath
Rates: $50-$110, incl. cont. brk. Discount avail. for extended, mid-week, and senior
citizen stays.
Credit cards: Most major cards
Restrictions: No pets. Deposit req. 2-day cancellation notice req.
Notes: 3-story Victorian house built in 1877. Fully restored. Dining room, double
parlors. German spoken.*

The River Inn at Rolph's Wharf
1008 Rolph's Wharf Rd., Chestertown, MD 21620
(410) 778-6347, (800) 894-6346

Innkeeper: Sandy Strouse
Rooms: 6 plus 1 suite, all w/pvt. bath
Rates: $85/room, $115/suite, cont. brk. Seasonal variations. Discount avail. for se-
nior citizens.
Credit cards: Most major cards
Restrictions: No children under 5, pets. Credit card deposit req., 5-day cancellation
notice req., less $25.00 fee. 2-night min. stay on holiday wknds.
Notes: 1830s Victorian house located on five acres of the Chester River. Restaurant
and bar on the premises. All rooms have air conditioning. Pool and bikes are avail-
able. Boaters welcome at full-service marina.*

CHEVY CHASE (4)

Chevy Chase Bed 'n Breakfast
6815 Connecticut Ave., Chevy Chase, MD 20815
(301) 656-5867, (301) 656-5867

Innkeeper: Sarah Gotbaum
Rooms: 2 w/pvt. bath, phone, TV
Rates: $65, incl. full brk. Discount avail. for extended stay.
Credit cards: None
Restrictions: No pets, smoking. Deposit req. 3-week cancellation notice req.
Notes: Two-story house with beamed ceilings built at the turn of the century. Fur-
nished with arts and crafts from around the world. Living room with fireplace.

CHEVY CHASE BED 'N BREAKFAST

Music room with piano. Innkeeper is a sociologist working on programs that promote and protect human rights in Africa. Many books available.*

EASTON (5)

The McDaniel House
14 N. Aurora St., Easton, MD 21601-3617
(410) 822-3704, (800) 787-4667
Innkeeper: Rosemary and S.D. Garrett
Rooms: 7, incl. 5 w/pvt. bath
Rates: $60-$80, incl. expanded cont. brk. Seasonal variations.
Credit cards: Most major cards
Restrictions: No pets. Smoking restricted. One-night's deposit req. 5-night cancellation notice req., less $25.00 fee. 2-night min. stay on wknds.
Notes: Three-story Victorian house with octagonal tower, pavilion, gable built in 1890. Wrap-around porch with wicker furniture. Dining room. Bike and boat rentals available. Small private parties accommodated. Off-street parking available.

ELLICOTT CITY (3)

White Duck B & B
3920 College Ave., Ellicott City, MD 21043-5502
(410) 992-8994
Innkeeper: Bruce and Marty Kennedy
Rooms: 2, w/pvt. bath, phone
Rates: $65, incl. cont. brk. Discount avail. for extended stay.
Credit cards: MC, V
Restrictions: No pets, smoking. 24-hour cancellation notice req., less one night's fee.
Notes: Three-story Queen Anne Victorian house with hardwood floors built in 1899. Located on two acres. Living room with fireplace. Dining room, shaded porch. Furnished with antiques, Oriental carpets. Custom desserts available. Innkeepers are

dietitian, nutritional counselor and are interested in woodworking, gardening, computers, wine tasting. German spoken.*

FREDERICK (2)

Middle Plantation Inn
9549 Liberty Rd., Frederick, MD 21701-3246
(301) 898-7128
Innkeeper: Shirley and Dwight Mullican
Rooms: 4 w/pvt. bath, TV, incl. cont. brk.
Rates: $95. Discount avail. for extended stay.
Credit cards: AE, MC
Restrictions: No children under 15, pets, smoking. One night's deposit req.
Notes: Rustic stone and log colonial house built in 1988 out of components of the old house dating to 1810. Located on 26 acres. Keeping Room with fireplace, stained-glass windows. Antiques. Garden with hen house.*

Spring Bank, A B & B Inn
7945 Worman's Mill Rd., Frederick, MD 21701
(301) 694-0440
Innkeeper: Ray and Bev Compton
Rooms: 5, incl. 1 w/pvt. bath
Rates: $75-$90, incl. cont. brk. Discount avail. for extended stay.
Credit cards: Most major cards
Restrictions: No children under 12, pets, smoking. 50% deposit req., refunded
   upon cancellation only if room is re-rented. 2-night min. stay on some Spring/
   Fall wknds.
Notes: Brick Romanesque house built in 1880. Located on two acres, surrounded by eight farmland acres. Furnished in Victorian style with antiques. Has operated as inn since 1980. Double parlor with TV. Sitting room with fireplace. Listed on the National Register of Historic Places.*

Turning Point Inn
3406 Urbana Pike, Frederick, MD 21701
(301) 874-2421, (301) 874-5773
Innkeeper: Charlie Seymour
Rooms: 5, incl. 3 w/pvt. bath, plus 2 cottages, incl. 1 w/pvt. bath, all w/TV
Rates: $75-$85/room, $100-$150/cottage, all incl. full brk., fresh fruit bowl in room
Credit cards: Most major cards
Restrictions: No pets. Smoking restricted. Deposit req. Cancellation notice flexible.
   Closed July 4, December 24, 25.
Notes: Edwardian-era estate house with Georgian Colonial features built in 1910. Located on five acres of lawn. Fully renovated and operated as inn since 1985. Living room, glass-enclosed porch. Furnished with antiques, reproductions. Restaurant on premises. French spoken. Handicapped access.

GAITHERSBURG (4)

Gaithersburg Hospitality B & B
18908 Chimney Place, Gaithersburg, MD 20879
(301) 977-7377
Innkeeper: Joe and Suzanne Danilowicz

Rooms: 4, incl. 2 w/pvt. bath
Rates: $42-$52, incl. full brk.
Credit cards: None
Restrictions: No children under 4, pets. Smoking restricted. Deposit req.
Notes: Contemporary Colonial-style house located in Montgomery Village. Has operated as Inn since 1987. Dining room, screened porch. Furnished with Oriental rugs.

BEAVER CREEK HOUSE B & B

HAGERSTOWN (2)

Beaver Creek House B & B
20432 Beaver Creek Rd., Hagerstown, MD 21740
(301) 797-4764

Innkeeper: Don and Shirley Day
Rooms: 5 w/TV, phone, incl. 3 w/pvt. bath
Rates: $55-$85, incl. full brk., afternoon refreshment. Discount avail. for mid-week stay.
Credit cards: Most major cards
Restrictions: No children under 10, pets, smoking. One night's deposit req. 72-hour cancellation notice req.
Notes: Two-story Victorian country house built at the turn of the century. Sitting room with TV, library. Parlor, dining room. Furnished with family antiques, memorabilia. Screened porch overlooking South Mountain. Patio overlooking country gardens, pond, fountain.*

HAVRE DE GRACE (3)

Spencer Silver Mansion
200 S. Union Ave., Havre de Grace, MD 21078
(800) 780-1485

Innkeeper: Jim and Carol Nemeth
Rooms: 4, incl. 1 w/pvt. bath, 2 w/phone
Rates: $60-$85, incl. full brk., fruit basket. Discount avail. for mid-week stay.

SPENCER SILVER MANSION

Credit cards: None
Restrictions: No pets. Smoking restricted. One night's deposit req. 7-day cancellation notice req. Closed Dec. 25.
Notes: Three-story Victorian house with parquet floors, oak woodwork, five fireplace mantles, oak parlor doors built in 1896 from locally quarried granite. Fully restored. Two parlors, one with fireplace, dining room, reading nook, wrap-around porch. TV, telephone available. Furnished in Victorian style with antiques. German spoken.*

HENDERSON (5)

The Chesapeake Gun Club
16090 Oakland Rd., Henderson, MD 21640
(800) 787-4667, (410) 482-7189

Innkeeper: Janet, Roz, Erlene, Teresa
Rooms: 7, plus 2 suites, all w/pvt. bath
Rates: $50-$110/room, $110-$150/suite, all incl. cont. brk.
Credit cards: Most major cards
Restrictions: No pets. Deposit req. 48-hour cancellation notice req.
Notes: Three-story shooting estate. Located on 700 wooded acres and open fields. Library, parlor, dining porch, dining room, steam room, sauna, gun room, wine cellar, rathskeller. Deer, goose, duck, wild turkey, quail, dove and other wild game hunting available. "Fairfield Shooting School," offering state-of-the-art Sporting Clays, on premises. Kennel with trainers available. Operated by "Chesapeake Inns" German spoken.*

KEEDYSVILLE (2)

Antietam Overlook Farm
P.O. Box 30, Keedysville, MD 21756
(800) 878-4241, (410) 313-1861

Innkeeper: Barbara and John Dreisch
Rooms: 5 suites w/pvt. bath, fireplace
Rates: $113-$148, incl. full brk.
Credit cards: Most major cards

Restrictions: No children, pets, smoking. 50% deposit req. 7-day cancellation notice req., less $20.00 fee. 2-night min. stay on wknds. and holidays.

Notes: 19th-century-style farmhouse located on 95 acres. Common room with fireplace. Country room with screened porch. Decorated with rustic wood finishes, French lace curtains, antiques, and flowered furnishings.*

NEW MARKET (2)

National Pike Inn
9 W. Main St., Box 299, New Market, MD 21774
(301) 865-5055

Innkeeper: Tom and Terry Rimel

Rooms: 4, incl. 3 w/pvt. bath plus 1 suite w/pvt. bath

Rates: $75-$125/room, $140-$160/suite, all incl. full brk. Discount for mid-week, military, and senior stays.

Credit cards: MC, V

Restrictions: No children under 10, pets, smoking. $30.00 deposit req. 7-day cancellation notice req., less $10.00 fee. 2-night min. stay during New Market Days, Christmas.

Notes: Federal-type house built from 1796 to 1804, named after the nation's first federally-funded highway. Widow's watch added in 1900. Completely restored. Colonial sitting room with TV, dining room, private courtyard. Furnished in Colonial decor with period reproductions. Grounds include Carriage House built in 1830, smoke house. Staff occasionally dresses in period costumes.

ROCK HALL (5)

INN AT OSPREY

Inn at Osprey
20786 Rock Hall Ave., Rock Hall, MD 21661
(410) 639-2194

Innkeeper: Dan and Dee Mullin and Susannah Ford

Rooms: 6, incl. 1 w/fireplace, TV, plus 1 suite w/TV, all w/pvt. bath

Rates: $110-$140/room, $150/suite. Seasonal variations. Discount avail. for group, mid-week stays.

Credit cards: MC, V

Restrictions: No children under 6, pets. Deposit req. 2-day cancellation notice req. 2-night min. stay on holiday wknds.

Notes: Built in 1993. Located on 30 acres of waterfront grounds. Clubhouse room with television. Sitting room. Gallery art. Marina with repair service available. Picnic area with grills. Teak deck with wrought iron furniture. Nature walk. Swimming pool and pool house. Bicycles. Small private parties accommodated.*

SAINT MICHAELS (5)

Inn at Perry Cabin
308 Watkins Lane, Box 247, Saint Michaels, MD 21663
(410) 745-5178, (800) 722-2949, (410) 745-3348

Innkeeper: Tom Ward

Rooms: 35, plus 6 suites, all w/pvt. bath, phone, TV

Rates: $175-$475/room, $525/suite, all incl. full brk., afternoon refreshment.

Credit cards: Most major cards

Restrictions: No children under 10, pets. Smoking restricted. One night's deposit req. 5-day cancellation notice req. Closed Christmas Day.

Notes: Three-story Colonial mansion built 1816. Has operated as inn since 1980. Now owned by the co-founder of the Laura Ashley Company, operating as the first of the Ashley Inns in America. Located on 25 acres. 3 dining rooms, gazebo bar overlooking Chesapeake Bay. Restaurant on premises with live music on weekends. Furnished with English and American antiques. Heated indoor swimming pool, health facility, exercise room, sauna & steam room. Full audio-visual and teleconferencing system available. Small private parties accommodated.*

PARSONAGE INN

Parsonage Inn
210 N. Talbot St., Saint Michaels, MD 21663
(800) 394-5519

Innkeeper: Peggy and Bill Parsons

Rooms: 7 w/pvt. bath, phone, incl. 3 w/fireplace, 1 w/cable TV, plus 1 suite w/pvt. bath, phone, TV

Rates: $100-$130, incl. full brk. Seasonal variations. Discount avail. for mid-week stay.

Credit cards: Most major cards

Restrictions: No children under 4, pets, smoking. One night's deposit req. 7-day cancellation notice req. 2-night min. stay on wknds.

Notes: Brick Victorian house with panelled chimneys built in 1883. Restored in 1983. Parlor with fireplace. Dining room, library, gingerbread porches. Decorated with Laura Ashley linens. Handicapped access. Bicycles, charcoal grill, audio/visual equipment available. Small private parties accommodated. Handicapped access.*

Wades Point Inn on the Bay
P.O. Box 7, Saint Michaels, MD 21663
(301) 745-2500

Innkeeper: Betsy and John Feiler

Rooms: 24, incl. 15 w/pvt. bath. Located in 3 bldgs.

Rates: $74-$165, incl. cont. brk. Seasonal variations. Discount avail. for extended and senior citizen stays.

Credit cards: MC, V

Restrictions: No pets, smoking. Full prepayment req. 72-hour cancellation notice req. 2-night min. stay on wknds. and holidays.

Notes: Georgian colonial main house built in 1819. Located on 120 acres. Common room with TV overlooking Chesapeake Bay. Screened porches, balconies. Dock for fishing/crabbing. Hiking/jogging trail. Small private parties accommodated.

SNOW HILL (7)

The River House Inn
201 E. Market St., Snow Hill, MD 21863
(410) 632-2722

Innkeeper: Larry and Susanne Knudson

Rooms: 7 w/pvt. bath, incl. 5 w/fireplace, plus 2 suites w/pvt bath, incl. 1 w/fireplace. Located in 3 bldgs.

Rates: $85-120, incl. full brk., evening refreshment. Seasonal variations. Discount avail. for military, AAA, and senior citizen stays.

Credit cards: MC, V

Restrictions: No pets. Smoking restricted. One night's deposit req. 7-day cancellation notice req. 2-night min. stay in July/August and on holiday wknds.

Notes: Main house: 1860 Gothic style. Little House: 1835 Tidewater Colonial. River Cottage: 1898 converted carriage house. Four common rooms, all with fireplaces. 2 acres of lawns on the Pocomok River. Lawn furniture and bicycles available.*

SOLOMONS (6)

Back Creek Inn
P.O. Box 520, Solomons, MD 20688
(301) 326-2022

Innkeeper: Lin Cochran, Carol Pennock

Rooms: 7, incl. 5 w/pvt. bath, 2 w/fireplace, 3 w/TV. Located in 2 bldgs.

Rates: $65-$125, incl. full brk., afternoon refreshment. Discount avail. for extended stay.

Credit cards: Most major cards

Restrictions: No children under 12, pets, smoking. One night's deposit req. 72-hour cancellation notice req., less $5.00 fee. 2-night min. stay on holiday wknds.
Notes: Three-story main house built in 1880. Located on .5 acre with two deep-water slips, accommodating boats with ten-ft. draft. Front screened porch, deck overlooking Back Creek, Chesapeake Bay. Common room with TV. Furnished with period antiques. Rose gardens, lily pond, white garden, herb garden. Jacuzzi. Innkeeper is avid gardener. Semi-handicapped access.

STEVENSON (3)

Gramercy B & B
1400 Greenspring Valley Rd., Box 119, Stevenson, MD 21153
(410) 486-2405
Innkeeper: Anne Pomykala, Cristin Pomykala
Rooms: 5 w/pvt. bath, TV, incl. 3 w/fireplace, 2 w/Jacuzzi, VCR. Suites avail.
Rates: $90-$150, incl. full brk., afternoon refreshment
Credit cards: Most major cards
Restrictions: No pets. Cancellation notice req. 2-night min. stay on holidays.
Notes: English Tudor mansion built in 1902. Located on 45 acres. Pool, tennis court, woodland trails, stream, flower and herb gardens. Organic farm. Fireplace, porch. Resident dog and cat. Small private parties accommodated.

TILGHMAN ISLAND (5)

Black Walnut Point B and B
Black Walnut Rd., Box 308, Tilghman Island, MD 21671
(410) 886-2452, (410) 886-2053
Innkeeper: Tom and Brenda Ward
Rooms: 6, plus 1 cottage, all w/pvt. bath, TV. Located in 3 bldgs.
Rates: $120/room, $140/cottage, incl. cont. brk. Discount avail. for mid-week, senior citizen stays.
Credit cards: MC, V
Restrictions: No children under 15, pets. Smoking restricted. One night's deposit req. 7-day cancellation notice req. 2-night min. stay on wknds. 3-night min. stay on holiday wknds.
Notes: Two-story house located on 57 acres. Common room with fireplace, piano, jukebox. Screened porch with rockers. Swimming pool, hammocks, lighted tennis court. Small private parties accommodated. Bicycle available.

Chesapeake Wood Duck Inn
Gibsontown Rd., Box 202, Tilghman Island, MD 21671
(410) 886-2070, (800) 956-2070, (410) 886-2263
Innkeeper: Dave and Stephanie Feith
Rooms: 6 suites w/pvt. bath
Rates: $115-$135, incl. full brk. afternoon refreshment. Discount avail. for extended and senior citizen stays. Special pkgs. avail. Seasonal variations.
Credit cards: MC, V
Restrictions: No children under 14. No pets. Smoking restricted. One night's deposit req. 7-day cancellation notice req. less $15.00 fee. Min. stay req.
Notes: 1890 Victorian house. Fully restored. Furnished with period furnishings, oriental rugs and original art. Bicycles available. Guests have access to swimming, tennis. French, Spanish spoken.*

VIENNA (7)

The Tavern House
111 Water St., Box 98, Vienna, MD 21869-0098
(301) 376-3347
Innkeeper: Harvey and Elise Altergott
Rooms: 4, incl. 2 w/fireplace
Rates: $60-$70, incl. full brk., afternoon and evening refreshment
Credit cards: MC, V
Restrictions: No children under 12, pets. Deposit req. 48-hour cancellation notice req.
Notes: Colonial tavern built in the early 1700s. Located on Nanticoke River and the Eastern Shore. Sitting room. Cellar with cooking fireplace. Furnished in Colonial style.*

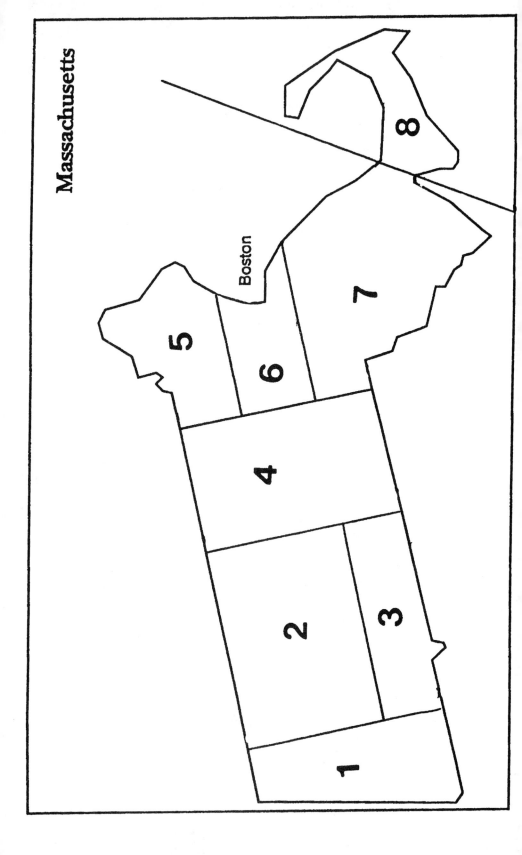

Massachusetts

Boston

Massachusetts

ALFORD (1)

Hidden Acres B & B
35 Tremont Dr., Alford, MA 01230
(413) 528-1028
Innkeeper: Lorraine and Daniel Miller
Rooms: 3, incl. 1 w/pvt. bath
Rates: $65-$95, incl. full brk. Discount avail. for extended and mid-week stays.
Credit cards: None
Restrictions: No children under 12, pets. Smoking restricted. One night's deposit req. 10-day cancellation notice req., less 10% fee. 2-night min. stay, July–August and on holidays wknds.
Notes: Built in 1987. Located on five acres surrounded by stone walls and tall trees. Living room with fireplace, TV, library. Sitting room with piano. Country kitchen. Decorated in country style.

AMHERST (2)

ALLEN HOUSE VICTORIAN INN

Allen House Victorian Inn
599 Main St., Amherst, MA 01002
(413) 253-5000
Innkeeper: Alan and Ann Zieminski
Rooms: 5 w/pvt. bath
Rates: $55-$95, incl. full brk., afternoon refreshment. Seasonal variations. Discount avail. for extended stay.
Credit cards: None
Restrictions: No children under 8, pets. Smoking restricted. Deposit req. 14-day cancellation notice req.

Notes: Three-story Queen Anne Stick Style house with peaked roofs, rectangular windows, cherry fireplace mantles built in 1886. Located on 3 acres. Living room with cable TV, breakfast room, ceiling fans. Guest rooms feature period-reproduction wallpapers, wicker 'steamship' chairs, pedestal sinks, screens, carved golden oak or brass beds, goose-down comforters, painted wooden floors and claw-foot tubs.

AUBURN (4)

Captain Samuel Eddy House
609 Oxford St., S., Auburn, MA 01501
(508) 832-7282

Innkeeper: Diedre and Mike Meddaugh
Rooms: 4 plus 1 suite, all w/pvt. bath
Rates: $65/room, $90/suite, all incl. full brk., afternoon refreshment. Discount avail. for extended stay.
Credit cards: V
Restrictions: No children under 5, pets, smoking. One night's deposit req. 7-day cancellation notice req., less $15.00 fee.
Notes: Center chimney colonial built in 1765. Recently restored. Has operated as Inn since 1986. Keeping room with fireplace. Two parlors with fireplaces, one with TV, board games. Solarium, and private gardensce. decorated with antiques. Perennial and herb gardens. Small private parties accommodated.

BARNSTABLE (8)

Ashley Manor
3660 Rt. 6A, Box 856, Barnstable, MA 02630
(508) 362-8044

Innkeeper: Fay and Donald Bain
Rooms: 2 w/pvt. bath, incl. 1 w/fireplace, plus 4 suites w/pvt. bath, fireplace. Located in 2 bldgs.
Rates: $115-$135/room, $160-$175/suite, all incl. full brk., evening refreshment. Seasonal variations.
Credit cards: Most major cards
Restrictions: No children under 14, pets. Smoking restricted. Min. 50% deposit req. 15-day cancellation notice req., less 5% fee. 2-night min. stay on some wknds. Longer min. stay on some holidays.
Notes: Built in 1699 with wide-board flooring, blown-glass windows, secret passageway. Expanded many times. Fully restored in 1970 by descendant of original owner. Located on two acres of manicured lawns with apple and cherry trees, boxwood hedges, gazebo, tennis court. Living room with beehive oven, formal dining room, and parlor with grand piano, each with fireplace. 40-foot brick terrace overlooking grounds. Furnished with antiques, Oriental rugs. French spoken.*

Crocker Tavern B & B
3095 Main St., Barnstable, MA 02630
(508) 362-5115

Innkeeper: Sue and Jeff Carlson
Rooms: 3 suites w/pvt. bath, incl. 2 w/fireplace
Rates: $85-$100, incl. cont. brk., afternoon refreshment. Seasonal variations.
Credit cards: None

Restrictions: No children under 11, pets, smoking. 50% deposit req. 14-day cancellation notice req., less $5.00 fee, 2-night min. stay on wknds. 3-night min. on holiday wknds.

Notes: Two-story colonial Inn built in 1754. Served as headquarters for the Whigs during the Revolution. Fully restored. Two common rooms with fireplaces, window seats, wide beam ceilings. Furnished with period antiques. Board games and reading material available. Handicapped access. Award winning restoration overseen by the Society for the Preservation of New England Antiquities.*

BARNSTABLE VILLAGE (8)

Beechwood Inn
2839 Main St., Barnstable Village, MA 02630
(508) 362-6618

Innkeeper: Ken and Debbie Traugot

Rooms: 5, incl. 2 w/fireplace, plus 1 suite, all w/pvt. bath

Rates: $110-$140/room, $135/suite, all incl. full brk., afternoon refreshment. Seasonal variations. Discount avail. for extended stay.

Credit cards: Most major cards

Restrictions: No children under 12, pets, smoking. Min. one night's deposit req. 15-day cancellation notice req., less 10% fee.

Notes: Two-story Queen Anne Victorian house built in 1853. Fully restored. Wraparound veranda. Panelled dining room with fireplace. Parlor. Furnished with period antiques. All bedrooms have either ocean or garden views. Lawn games available. Limited handicapped access.

BOSTON (6)

Beacon Hill Bed & Breakfast
27 Brimmer St., Boston, MA 02108
(617) 523-7376

Innkeeper: Susan Butterworth

Rooms: 3 w/pvt. bath, TV

Rates: $115-$140, incl. full brk. Discount avail. for extended stay. Seasonal variations.

Credit cards: None

Restrictions: No pets, smoking. Min. one night's deposit req. Min. 21-day cancellation notice req. less $10.00 fee. 2-night min. stay. 3-night min. stay on fall wknds. and holidays.

Notes: Six-story Victorian brick row house with high ceilings, oriel windows, original mouldings and elevator, built in 1869. Overlooking the Charles River. Innkeeper is caterer and has lived in this house since 1965. French spoken.*

Oasis Guest House
22 Edgerly Rd., Boston, MA 02115
(617) 267-2262, (617) 267-1920

Innkeeper: Joe Haley

Rooms: 16, w/pvt. bath, phone, TV

Rates: $60-$78, incl. cont. brk. Seasonal variations.

Credit cards: Most major cards

Restrictions: No children, pets. Smoking restricted. Deposit req. 14-day cancellation notice req.

Notes: Back Bay townhouses. Outside deck. Parking available.*

BREWSTER (8)

The Inn at the Egg
1944 Main St., Box 453, Brewster, MA 02631
(508) 896-3123, (508) 896-6821

Innkeeper: Diane McDonald and Joan Vergnani

Rooms: 3 plus 2 suites, all w/pvt. bath, TV

Rates: $65-$125, incl. full brk., afternoon refreshment. Seasonal variations. Discount avail. for extended stay.

Credit cards: MC, V

Restrictions: No pets, smoking. 50% deposit req. 14-day cancellation notice req., less $15.00 fee. 2-night min. stay, Jul.–Aug., holidays and special events.

Notes: Two-story Colonial house. Formerely the First Parish Church Parsonage. In 1865 home to author and preacher Horatio Alger, Jr. Gift gallery on premises. Furnished with antiques. Spanish spoken. Innkeepers publish cookbook.*

Old Sea Pines Inn
2553 Main St., Brewster, MA 02631
(508) 896-6114

Innkeeper: Michele and Stephen Rowan

Rooms: 19 plus 2 suites, incl. 16 w/pvt. bath, 8 w/cable TV, 3 w/fireplace. Located in 2 bldgs.

Rates: $43-$95/room, $95-$135/suite, incl. full brk., afternoon refreshment.

Credit cards: Most major cards

Restrictions: No children under 8, pets, smoking. Min. one night's deposit req. 14-day cancellation notice req. 2-night min. stay on wknds. from May 31–Nov. 1.

Notes: Three-story Sea Pines School of Charm and Personality for Young Women built in 1907. Renovated in and has operated as inn since 1977. Located on 3.25 acres. Dining room. Living room with fireplace. Two porches with rockers. Furnished with antiques from the 1920s and 1930s. Back yard with hammock. Restaurant on premises. Beach towels, off-street parking available. Complimentary bottle of champagne for honeymooners. Small private parties accommodated. German, Italian spoken.*

The Poore House
2311 Main St., Brewster, MA 02631
(508) 896-2094, (800) 233-6662

Innkeeper: Paul Anderson and Randy Guy

Rooms: 5 w/pvt. bath, incl. 4 w/phone, 2 w/fireplace

Rates: $45-$85, incl. cont. brk. Seasonal variations. Discount avail. for extended stay.

Credit cards: Most major cards

Restrictions: No children under 6, smoking. One night's deposit req. 10-day cancellation notice req., less $10.00 fee. 2-night min. stay on wknds., and holidays in season.

Notes: Two-story inn built in 1837 to house the poor. Recently renovated. Great room, patio. French spoken.*

BRIMFIELD (3)

Elias Carter House on the Common
No. Main St., Box 557, Brimfield, MA 01010-0557
(413) 245-3267, (413) 245-7619

Innkeeper: Carolyn Haley and family
Rooms: 2 w/pvt. bath, incl. 1 w/TV, plus 1 suite w/pvt. bath, pvt. entrance
Rates: $60-$115/room, $75-$135/suite, all incl. cont. brk. Seasonal variations. Discount avail. for extended and mid-week stays. Special rates during Brimfield Antique Shows.
Credit cards: None
Restrictions: No pets. Children, smoking restricted. Deposit req. 14-day cancellation notice during show weeks, less 50% fee.
Notes: Two-story Colonial house located on Town Common.*

BROOKLINE (6)

Beacon Inn
1087 & 1750 Beacon St., Brookline, MA 02146
(617) 566-0088, (617) 397-9267

Innkeeper: Dan McMann and Megan Rockett
Rooms: 24 w/TV, incl. 15 w/pvt. bath. Located in 2 bldgs.
Rates: $44-$86, incl. cont. brk.
Credit cards: Most major cards
Restrictions: No pets. Deposit req. Cancellation notice req.
Notes: Two turn-of-the-century townhouses have original woodwork and lobby fireplaces.*

Beech Tree Inn
83 Longwood Ave., Brookline, MA 02146
(800) 544-9660, (617) 277-0657

Innkeeper: Kathrine Anderson and Bette Allen
Rooms: 9, incl. 4 w/pvt. bath
Rates: $48-$72, incl. cont. brk. Seasonal variations.
Credit cards: None
Restrictions: Well behaved children and pets welcome. No smoking. 3-day cancellation notice req. 2-night min. stay on wknds.
Notes: Three-story turn of the century Victorian-style private house. Guests have access to fully equipped kitchen. Located near subway. German spoken.

CAMBRIDGE (6)

A B & B in Cambridge
1657 Cambridge, Cambridge, MA 01238-4316
(617) 876-8991, (800) 795-7122

Innkeeper: Doane Perry
Rooms: 3 w/pvt. bath, phone, TV
Rates: $65-$95, incl cont. brk., evening refreshment
Credit cards: Most major cards
Restrictions: No children under 6, pets, smoking
Notes: Three-story Colonial revival house built in 1897. Located in historical district. Decorated with antique oriental rugs, original paintings, antique mahogany desks, inlaid carved headboards, down comforters and pillows. Cane rockers. French, German spoken. *

A Cambridge House
2218 Massachusetts Ave., Cambridge, MA 02140
(617) 491-6300, (800) 232-9989, (617) 868-2848

Innkeeper: Ellen Riley, Tony Femmino
Rooms: 14 w/phone, cable TV, incl. 10 w/pvt. bath, 2 w/fireplace. Located in 2
  bldgs.
Rates: $89-$195, incl. full brk.
Credit cards: Most major cards
Restrictions: No children under 6, pets. Deposit req. 10-day cancellation notice req.
  2-night min. stay on wknds. from May 1–Dec. 1.
Notes: Two-story Federal-style house built in 1892. Fully renovated. Library, parlor,
each with fireplace. Exercise room. Furnished with antiques. Listed on the National
Register of Historic Places. Small private parties accommodated. Off-street parking
available.*

Mary Prentiss Inn
6 Prentiss St., Cambridge, MA 02140
(617) 661-2929, (617) 661-5989
Innkeeper: Charlotte and Briar Rose Forsythe
Rooms: 13 w/pvt. bath, phone, TV, plus 5/suites w/pvt. bath, phone, TV, fireplace
Rates: $79-$139/room, $125-$169/suite, all incl. cont. brk. Seasonal variations. Dis-
  count avail. for extended and group stays.
Credit cards: Most major cards
Restrictions: No pets, smoking. Min. one night's deposit req. 14-day cancellation
  notice req.
Notes: Neoclassic Greek Revival style hoom built in 1843. Parlor w/fireplace. Full
front porch, 1000-sq.-ft. deck. Furnished with unique antiques. Listed on National
Register of Historic Places. Small private parties accommodated. Handicapped access to common areas only.*

COPPER BEECH INN

CENTERVILLE (8)

Copper Beech Inn
497 Main St., Centerville, MA 02632-2913
(508) 771-5488

Innkeeper: Joyce Diehl
Rooms: 3 w/pvt. bath. Suite avail.
Rates: $90, incl. full brk. Seasonal variations.
Credit cards: Most major cards
Restrictions: No children under 12, pets. Smoking restricted. One-night's deposit req. 7-day cancellation notice req., less $20.00 fee. 2-night min. stay, May 15–October 31.
Notes: Two-story house built in 1830. Recently restored. Kitchen with wood stove from 1898. Parlor, common room. Furnished in traditional style. Sunning areas outside. Listed in the National Register of Historic Places.

CHATHAM (8)

Captain's House Inn of Chatham
369-377 Old Harbor Rd., Chatham, MA 02633
(508) 945-0127, (508) 945-0866

Innkeeper: Jan and Dave McMaster
Rooms: 11 w/pvt. bath, phone, incl. 4 w/fireplace plus 5 suites w/pvt. bath, incl. 1 w/fireplace. Located in 3 bldgs.
Rates: $125-$185/room, $160-$195/suite, all incl. brk.
Credit cards: Most major cards
Restrictions: No children under 12, pets, smoking. Min. one night's deposit req. 7-day cancellation notice req. 2-night min. stay on summer wknds.
Notes: Greek Revival-style house and Carriage House built in 1839. Cottage built in 1930. Located on two acres. Entrance hall. Living room with pine floors, fireplace. Breakfast room with floor-length windows overlooking gardens. Carriage House features living room, dining room, kitchen. Decorated with furnishings reminiscent of Williamsburg, including many antiques, period wallpaper. Bicycles available. Handicapped access.*

Carriage House Inn
407 Old Harbor Rd., Chatham, MA 02633
(508) 945-4688

Innkeeper: Pam and Tom Patton
Rooms: 3, no pvt. bath
Rates: $75-$130, incl. full brk., evening refreshment. Seasonal variations.
Credit cards: Most major cards
Restrictions: No children under 14, pets, smoking. 50% deposit req. 14-day cancellation notice req., less $20.00 fee. 2-night min. stay on wknds. in season. 3-night min. stay on holiday wknds.
Notes: Living room with fireplace and piano. Farmer's porch, deck. Furnished with antiques and family pieces. Bicycles, beach towels available. Resident golden retriever.*

Chatham Town House Inn
11 Library Ln., Chatham, MA 02633
(508) 945-2180, (508) 945-3990

Innkeeper: Russell and Svea Peterson
Rooms: 21 plus 2 suites, 2 cottages, all w/pvt. bath, phone, cable TV, incl. 2 w/fireplace. Located in 4 bldgs.
Rates: $165-$195/room, $195/suite, $270/cottage, all incl. cont. brk. Seasonal variations.

Credit cards: Most major cards

Restrictions: No pets, smoking. Min. one night's deposit req. 14-day cancellation notice req. (inn), 45-day cancellation notice req. (cottage), less 10% fee. 3-night min. stay, July–August and major holidays.

Notes: Two-story Victorian country mansion with high ceilings, old woodwork and hemlock floors, built in 1881. Located on 2 acres. Decorated with photos, paintings, prints. Heated swimming pool, spa. Restaurant with full liquor license on premises. Handicapped access. Swedish, Spanish spoken.*

Cranberry Inn at Chatham
359 Main St., Chatham, MA 02633
(508) 945-9232, (800) 332-4667, (508) 945-3769

Innkeeper: Jim and Debbie Bradley

Rooms: 16 plus 2 suites, all w/pvt. bath, phone, TV, incl. 8 w/fireplace

Rates: $85-$185, incl. cont. brk. Seasonal variations

Credit cards: Most major cards

Restrictions: No children under 8, pets. Smoking restricted. 50% deposit req. 14-day cancellation notice req., less $20.00 fee. 2-night min. stay during high season. 3-night min. stay on high season holidays. Closed Dec. 15–Mar. 15.

Notes: Colonial-style inn with wide plank floors, handmade drapes built in the 1830s. Fully renovated in 1988 and 1994. Has operated as inn since 1830. Main lobby with baby grand piano. Front porch, tap room, dining room, living room, landscaped rear patio. Decorated with traditional and country furnishings, American and English antiques, reproductions. Small private parties accommodated.*

Cyrus Kent House Inn
63 Cross St., Chatham, MA 02633
(800) 338-5368, (508) 945-9104

Innkeeper: Sharon Swan

Rooms: 6 plus 3 suites, all w/pvt. bath, phone, TV, incl. 3 w/fireplace. Located in 2 bldgs.

Rates: $75-$145/room, $85-$165/suite, all incl. cont. brk. Seasonal variations.

Credit cards: Most major cards

Restrictions: No children under 13, pets, smoking. One night's deposit req. 7-day cancellation notice req. 2-night min. stay on wknds. and holidays.

Notes: Two-story Sea captain's house with ceiling rosettes, plaster moldings, brass hardware and Carriage House built of Maine timber in 1877. Renovated in 1985. Has operated as inn since 1988. Landscaped grounds. Living room, dining room, each with marble fireplace. Front porch. Furnished with English and French antiques, reproductions.

Moses Nickerson House
364 Old Harbor Rd., Chatham, MA 02633
(508) 945-5859, (800) 628-6972

Innkeeper: Carl and Elsie Picola

Rooms: 7 w/pvt. bath, incl. 3 w/fireplace

Rates: $110-$159, incl. cont. brk., evening refreshment. Seasonal variations.

Credit cards: Most major cards

Restrictions: No children under under 14, pets, smoking. Deposit req. 2-week cancellation notice req., less $25.00 fee. 2-night min. stay on wknds. and June–October.

Notes: Two-story Federal-style whaling captain's house with wide pine floors and three staircases built in 1839. Refurnished in and has operated as inn since 1987. Sitting room with fireplace. English parlor, glass-enclosed breakfast room. Furnished with antiques, Oriental rugs. Flower gardens, fish pond, arbor.*

The Old Harbor Inn
22 Old Harbor Rd., Chatham, MA 02633
(508) 945-4434
Innkeeper: Sharon and Tom Ferguson
Rooms: 6 w/pvt. bath, incl. 1 w/phone, fireplace
Rates: $85-$170, incl. brk. Seasonal variations. Discount avail. for extended stay.
Credit cards: Most major cards
Restrictions: No children under 16, pets, smoking. Min. one night's deposit req. 2-week cancellation notice req., less $15.00 fee. 2-night min. stay, July 1–Sept. 6. 2-night min. stay on holiday wknds.
Notes: Two-story English country inn built in 1936. Gathering room with fireplace, baby grand piano. Sunroom, deck. Furnished with antiques, wicker, Oriental rugs. Decorated with Laura Ashley fabrics, Waverly wall coverings. King, queen, or twin-sized beds. Small private parties accommodated.*

CHESTERFIELD (2)

Seven Hearths B & B
412 Main Rd., Rte. 143, Chesterfield, MA 01012-0852
(413) 296-4312, (413) 296-4599
Innkeeper: Doc and Denise LeDuc
Rooms: 3 w/fireplace, incl. 1 w/pvt. bath
Rates: $55-$65, incl. full brk. Discount avail. for extended stay. Special pkgs. avail.
Credit cards: None
Restrictions: No children under 13, pets. Smoking restricted. One night's deposit req. 7-day cancellation notice req. 2-night min. stay during fall foliage season and graduation.
Notes: Two-story Dutch gambrel house built in 1891. Sitting area. Living room with TV, fireplace. Decorated with country decor, antique furnishings, art, and nature photography. Hot tub and sauna.

CHILMARK (8)

Breakfast at Tiasquam
RR 1, Box 296, Chilmark, MA 02535
(508) 645-3685
Innkeeper: Ron Crowe
Rooms: 6, incl. 2 w/pvt. bath, 1 w/fireplace, plus 2 suites w/pvt. bath, incl. 1 w/fireplace.
Rates: $70-$195, incl. full brk., beach pass. Seasonal variations.
Credit cards: Most major cards
Restrictions: No pets, smoking. Two-night's deposit req., refunded, less 10% fee, upon cancellation only if room re-rented.
Notes: Located on 4.5 acre hill. Decks, 20 skylights, hammocks. Handicapped access.*

BREAKFAST AT TIASQUAM

CONCORD (6)

The Colonial Inn
48 Monument Square, Concord, MA 01742
(508) 369-9200, (800) 873-3929, (508) 369-2170
Innkeeper: Jurgen Demisch
Rooms: 45 plus 2 suites, all w/pvt. bath, phone, TV
Rates: $85-$140/room, $130-$140/suite, incl. coffee. Seasonal variations. Discount
   avail. for senior citizens.
Credit cards: Most major cards
Restrictions: No pets, smoking. One night's cancellation notice req.
Notes: Three-story colonial Inn built in 1716. Has operated as inn since 1889. Merchants Row dining room, Thoreau Room, cafe, Heritage Room, two lounges include nightly entertainment. Gift Shop on premises. Small private parties accommodated. Spanish, German spoken. Handicapped access.*

Hawthorne Inn
462 Lexington Rd., Concord, MA 01742
(508) 369-5610
Innkeeper: Marilyn Mudry
Rooms: 7 w/pvt. bath
Rates: $85-$160, incl. cont. brk. Discount avail. for extended stay. Seasonal variations.
Credit cards: Most major cards
Restrictions: No pets, smoking. Min. one-night's deposit req. 14-day cancellation
   notice req., less 10% fee. 2-night min. stay on holiday and fall wknds.
Notes: Built in 1870 on land that once belonged to Ralph Waldo Emerson, the Alcotts, and Nathaniel Hawthorne. Common room with fireplace, library. Furnished with antiques, handmade quilts, Oriental rugs, artworks. Pond, vegetable gardens, fruit trees, grape vines, berry bushes, flower gardens.*

North Bridge Inn
21 Monument St., Concord, MA 01742
(508) 371-0014, (508) 371-6460

Innkeeper: Cheryl Roderick
Rooms: 6 suites w/pvt. bath, phone, TV
Rates: $125-$145, incl. full brk. Discount avail. for extended and mid-week stays.
Credit cards: Most major cards
Restrictions: No pets, smoking. Deposit req. 15-day cancellation notice req., less
   $10.00 fee.
Notes: Two-story European style hotel. Tea room. Furnished with contemporary and traditional reproductions. Small private parties accommodated.

CUMMINGTON (2)

Cumworth Farm
Rte. 112, 472 W. Cummington Rd., Cummington, MA 01026
(413) 634-5529
Innkeeper: Ed and Mary McColgan
Rooms: 6, no pvt. bath, incl. 1 w/fireplace, plus cottage
Rates: $60, incl. full brk., evening refreshment. Special pkgs. avail.
Credit cards: None
Restrictions: No pets. Smoking restricted.
Notes: Farmhouse built in 1780. Located on twenty five wooded acre working farm with pasture, blueberry and raspberry fields. (Guest can pick own berries July and August.) Operating maple sugarhouse in spring. Furnished with some antiques. Large Colonial living room. Parlor with fireplace, wood stove. Patio overlooking large yard. Hot tub available. Barn houses sheep where guests can witness birth of new lambs from late January to April.

WINDFIELDS FARM

Windfields Farm
154 Windsor Bush Rd., R.R. 1, Box 170, Cummington, MA 01026
(413) 684-3786
Innkeeper: Carolyn and Arnold Westwood
Rooms: 2, no pvt. bath.

Rates: $60, incl. full brk., afternoon refreshment
Credit cards: None
Restrictions: No children under 12, pets, smoking. One night's deposit req. 2-week cancellation notice req. Closed Mar.–Apr. 2-night min. stay on most wknds.
Notes: Two-story farmhouse built in 1830. Living room with piano, hi-fi, extensive library. Located on 100 acres of field and forest in the Berkshire hills. Hiking and skiing trails, brook, swimming pond, blueberry pastures, organic gardens, flower beds, solar greenhouse.

DENNIS (8)

Four Chimneys
946 Main St., Route 6A, Dennis, MA 02638
(508) 385-6317

Innkeeper: Russell and Kathy Tomasetti
Rooms: 8, incl. 6 w/pvt. bath, plus 1 suite w/TV
Rates: $55-$95/room, $95/suite, all incl. cont. brk. Seasonal variations. Discount avail. for extended stay.
Credit cards: Most major cards
Restrictions: No children under 6, pets. Smoking restricted. Min. 50% deposit req. 14-day cancellation notice req. less 10% fee. 2-night min. stay on wknds. 3-night min. stay on holiday wknds. Closed Oct. 17–April 28.
Notes: Victorian house with decorative woodwork, high ceilings, built in 1881. Newly restored. Located across from Scargo Lake. Living room with marble fireplace. Medallions with paddle fans. Dining room. Library with TV. Screened porch. Lawn with perennial gardens. Small private parties accommodated.*

Isaiah Hall B&B Inn

ISAIAH HALL B & B INN

152 Whig St., Dennis, MA 02638-1917
(508) 385-9928, (800) 736-0160, (508) 385-5879

Innkeeper: Marie Brophy
Rooms: 11, incl. 10 w/pvt. bath, 1 w/fireplace. Located in 2 bldgs.

Rates: $57-$102, incl. cont. brk. Seasonal variations. Discount avail. for extended stay.

Credit cards: Most major cards

Restrictions: No children under 7, pets. Smoking restricted. 50% deposit req. 10-day cancellation notice req. 2-night min. stay in season. 2-3 night min. stay on holidays.

Notes: Greek Revival farmhouse built in 1857. Parlor with stained-glass lamps, Victorian coal stove. Second sitting room with wood-paneled walls, games, TV. Dining room with cherry table. Front porch with rockers. Furnished with Oriental rugs, quilts, wicker, pine and oak antiques. Antique iron-and-brass beds. Lawn games available. Gardens. Guest telephone for incoming and outgoing calls. Small private parties accommodated. Handicapped access.*

Weatherly House
36 New Boston Rd., Dennis, MA 02638
(508) 385-7458

Innkeeper: Christopher and Krista Diego
Rooms: 2 w/pvt. bath, TV
Rates: $75-$95, incl. full brk. Seasonal variations.
Credit cards: Most major cards
Restrictions: No children, pets. Smoking restricted.
Notes: Two-story Greek Revival house built in 1835. Located on .75 acre. Sitting room, private terrace. Furnished with period antiques. Innkeepers are hotel school graduates, worked for Marriott and Hyatt in New York City and previously owned larger inn. Resident pets.

WEATHERLY HOUSE

Drawing by Merwin Freeman

DENNISPORT (8)

The Rose Petal B & B
152 Sea St., Box 974, Dennisport, MA 02639-0010
(508) 398-8470

THE ROSE PETAL B & B

Innkeeper: Gayle and Dan Kelly
Rooms: 3, incl. 2 w/pvt. bath
Rates: $59-$84, incl. full brk., afternoon refreshment. Seasonal variations.
Credit cards: Most major cards
Restrictions: No pets. Smoking restricted. Min. one night's deposit req. 14-day cancellation notice req.
Notes: Two-story house with picket fence. Built in 1872. Fully restored and redecorated in 1986. Has operated as inn since 1987. Parlor with TV, piano, games, reading material. Dining room. Guests have access to refrigerator. Furnished with antiques. Landscaped yard. Some French spoken.

EAST ORLEANS (8)

Nauset House Inn
143 Beach Rd., Box 774, East Orleans, MA 02643
(508) 255-2195
Innkeeper: Diane and Al Johnson, Cindy and John Vessella
Rooms: 14, incl. 8 w/pvt. bath. Located in 3 bldgs.
Rates: $65-$105, incl. cont. brk., evening refreshment. Discount avail. for extended stay.
Credit cards: AE, MC
Restrictions: No children under 12, pets, smoking. Min. one night's deposit req., 14-day cancellation notice req. 2-night min. stay on wknds.
Notes: Two-story farmhouse built in 1810. Located on three acres. 1904 Conservatory with wicker furniture. Living room, dining room, each with fireplace. Brick terrace. Furnished with antiques, country pieces. Decorated with local art.

The Parsonage Inn
202 Main Street, Box 1501, East Orleans, MA 02643
(508) 255-8217
Innkeeper: Chris and Lloyd Shand
Rooms: 6 w/pvt. bath, incl. 1 w/TV, plus 2 suites w/pvt. bath, TV
Rates: $75-$90/room, $100/suite, all incl. full brk., evening refreshment. Seasonal variations.
Credit cards: Most major cards

Restrictions: No children under 6, pets, smoking. Two night's deposit req. 14-day cancellation notice req. 2-night min. stay on summer and holiday wknds. Closed Thanksgiving and Christmas.

Notes: Two-story full-Cape style house and cottage built in 1770. Fireplace in parlor. Furnished in country style with antiques. Brick courtyard, gardens.*

Ship's Knees Inn
186 Beach Rd., Box 756, East Orleans, MA 02643
(508) 255-1312, (508) 240-1351

Innkeeper: Jean and Ken Pitchford

Rooms: 21, incl. 11 w/pvt. bath, 14 w/cable TV, plus 1 suite w/pvt. bath, fireplace, TV. 2 cottages w/fireplace, deck, living room, kitchen, bath, TV. Located in 4 bldgs.

Rates: $45-$100, incl. cont. brk. Special pkgs. avail.

Credit cards: MC, V

Restrictions: No children under 12, pets. Smoking restricted. Deposit req. 15-day cancellation notice req., less $10.00 fee. 2-night min. stay for room with pvt. bath.

Notes: Two-story sea captain's house built in 1820. Expanded in 1970. Cove House overlooking Orleans Cove. Lounge with TV, patio. Furnished in period nautical style with antiques, clipper ship models, braided rugs. Swimming pool, tennis court, lawn games.

SHIP'S KNEES INN

EASTHAM (8)

The Over Look Inn
3085 County Rd. 6, Box 771, Eastham, MA 02642
(508) 255-1886, (508) 240-0345

Innkeeper: The Aitchison Family

Rooms: 10 w/pvt. bath, incl. 1 w/fireplace

Rates: $75-$125, incl. full brk.

Credit cards: Most major cards

Restrictions: No children under 12, pets. Smoking restricted. Min. 50% deposit req. 10-day cancellation notice req., less 10% fee.

Notes: Three-story Victorian sea captain's house built in 1869. Fully restored. Located on 1.5 acres. Dining room, Victorian parlor, billiard room. Library with fireplace specializing in works by Winston Churchill overlooking front gardens. Furnished with Victorian antiques, period reproductions. French/Spanish spoken. Handicapped access.*

THE WHALEWALK INN

The Whalewalk Inn
220 Bridge Rd., Eastham, MA 02642
(508) 255-0617, (508) 240-0017

Innkeeper: Carolyn and Richard Smith
Rooms: 7 w/pvt. bath, plus 5 suites w/pvt. bath, incl. 3 w/fireplace. Located in 3 bldgs.
Rates: $90-$145/room, $150-$165/suite, all incl. full brk., afternoon refreshment. Seasonal variations. Discount avail. for extended stay.
Credit cards: MC, V
Restrictions: No children under 12, pets, smoking. Min. one night's deposit req. 2-week cancellation notice req. 2-night min. stay in season.
Notes: Georgian-style house built in 1833. Three buildings inlcude the inn, the barn, the guesthouse. Located on three acres of lawns, formal gardens, meadowlands. Dining room, garden patio. Two common rooms, each with fireplace. Bicycles available.*

EDGARTOWN (8)

The Arbor
222 Upper Main, Box 1228, Edgartown, MA 02539
(508) 627-8137

Innkeeper: Peggy Hall
Rooms: 10, incl. 8 w/pvt. bath
Rates: $65-$135, incl. cont. brk., afternoon refreshment. Seasonal variations. Discount avail. for extended stay.
Credit cards: MC, V
Restrictions: No children under 12, pets. Smoking restricted. Full prepayment req. 14-day cancellation notice req., less 10% fee. 3-night min. stay, July–August.

Notes: Victorian house built in the late 1800s. Living room, balcony, parlor, library, garden, fireplace, dining and breakfast room. Furnished with antiques, vintage furniture. Hammock. Woods Hole pick-up available.*

Captain Dexter House of Edgartown
35 Pease's Pt. Way, Box 2798, Edgartown, MA 02539
(508) 627-7289
Innkeeper: Michael Maultz
Rooms: 11 w/pvt. bath, incl. 4 w/fireplace
Rates: $65-$190, incl. cont. brk., evening refreshment. Seasonal variations. Discount avail. for mid-week and off-season stays.
Credit cards: Most major cards
Restrictions: No pets. Smoking restricted. Min. 50% deposit req. 14-day cancellation notice req.
Notes: Built in 1840 with exposed wooden beams, hardwood floors, original mouldings, New England-style dormers. Formal dining room, main parlor with fireplace. Decorated with period antiques. Swing-for-two. Landscaped garden. Guests have access to refrigerator. Small private parties accommodated.*

Colonial Inn of Martha's Vineyard
38 N. Water St., Box 68, Edgartown, MA 02539-0068
(800) 627-4701, (508) 627-5904
Innkeeper: Linda Malcouronne
Rooms: 39 plus 3 suites, all w/pvt. bath, phone, cable TV, A/C, heat, AM/FM clock radio
Rates: $60-$178/room, $85-$199/suite, all incl. cont. brk. Seasonal variations. Discount avail. for senior citizen, group, mid-week, and extended stays.
Credit cards: Most major cards
Restrictions: No pets. Deposit req. 14-day cancellation notice req. 2-night min. stay on wknds. 3-night min. stay on holiday wknds.
Notes: Built at the turn-of-the-century. Fully remodeled and refurbished. Porches overlooking harbor. Three verandas. Solarium overlooking garden courtyard. Handicapped access. Ten shops and boutiques, two restaurants on premises. Portuguese, French, Spanish spoken.*

The Daggett House
59 N. Water St., Edgartown, MA 02539
(508) 627-4600, (800) 946-3400, (508) 627-4611
Innkeeper: Celeste Emily Jones
Rooms: 21 plus 5 suites, all w/pvt. bath, phone, fireplace, incl. 8 w/TV. Located in 3 bldgs.
Rates: $140-$195/room, $230-$395/suite, brk. incl. Seasonal variations.
Credit cards: Most major cards
Restrictions: No pets, smoking. One night's deposit req. 2-week cancellation notice req., less $20.00 fee. 2-night min. stay on wknds. 3-night min. stay on holidays.
Notes: Colonial house with hidden stairway built in the 1600s. Breakfast room with fireplace. Main House with porch built as whaling captain's house in the early 1800s. Cottage built as schoolhouse in the 1800s. Sitting room with TV. Breakfast room with ancient panelled fireplace-beehive fireplace, bookcase opens to secret staircase. Dining room. Chimney room with fireplace overlooking harbor. Private pier, off-street parking available.

The Governor Bradford Inn of Edgartown
128 Main St., Edgartown, MA 02539-0239
(508) 627-9510
Innkeeper: Ray and Brenda Raffurty
Rooms: 16 w/pvt. bath, incl. 15 w/TV. Suite avail.
Rates: $95-$185/room, $210/suite, all incl. full brk., afternoon refreshment. Seasonal variations.
Credit cards: Most major cards
Restrictions: No children under 12, pets. Smoking restricted. 50% deposit req. 14-day cancellation notice req., less $15.00 fee. 2-night min.stay on summer, spring, and fall wknds.
Notes: Three-story Victorian whaling captain's house with gables built in 1865. Fully renovated in 1982. Breakfast room. Garden room with bar. Formal living room, parlor. Library with fireplace, terrace. Wicker room with bar. Furnished with antiques.*

Point Way Inn
104 Main St., Box 5255, Edgartown, MA 02539-5255
(508) 627-8633
Innkeeper: Linda and Ben Smith
Rooms: 14 w/pvt. bath, incl. 9 w/fireplace, 1 w/TV, plus 1 suite w/pvt. bath, fireplace
Rates: $65-$240, incl. cont. brk., afternoon refreshment. Seasonal variations. Discount avail. for senior citizen, AAA, government employees and extended stays. Special pkgs. avail.
Credit cards: Most major cards
Restrictions: No pets. 50% deposit req. 15-day cancellation notice req., less 10% fee. 2-night min. stay. 3-night min. stay on holidays.
Notes: Three-story sea captain's house built about 1832. Has operated as inn since 1980. Living room/library with fireplace, wet bar, puzzles, word and board games. Breakfast room with Franklin stove. Furnished with Colonial antiques, reflecting the innkeepers' sailing experiences. Front porch with swing. Enclosed garden and gazebo. Lawn games available. Small private parties accommodated. Guests have access to Inn's convertible. Handicapped access.*

ESSEX (5)

George Fuller House
148 Main St., Essex, MA 01929
(508) 768-7766
Innkeeper: Bob and Cindy Cameron
Rooms: 5 w/pvt. bath, phone, TV, incl 2 w/fireplace, plus 2 suites w/pvt. bath, phone, TV, incl. 1 w/fireplace
Rates: $75-$89/room, $115/suite, all incl. full brk., afternoon refreshment. Seasonal variations.
Credit cards: Most major cards.
Restrictions: No children under 6, pets, smoking. One night's deposit req. 14-day cancellation notice req. 2-night min. stay on holiday wknds.
Notes: Three-story Federalist house built in 1830, has original Indian shutters, panelling and wood carvings. Living and dining room each with fireplace. Three porches. Furnished in country style with period antiques. Innkeepers are sailor and registered nurse. FAX, off-street parking available. Resident cat.*

FAIRHAVEN (7)

Edgewater Bed & Breakfast
2 Oxford St., Fairhaven, MA 02719
(508) 997-5512

Innkeeper: Kathy Reed
Rooms: 3 plus 2 suites, all w/pvt. bath, TV, incl. 2 w/fireplace
Rates: $60-$70/room, $75-$80/suite, all incl. cont. brk. Discount avail. for extended
stay. Seasonal variations.
Credit cards: Most major cards
Restrictions: No children under 5, pets. Smoking restricted. Deposit req. 3-day
cancellation notice req. 2-night min. stay on holiday wknds.
Notes: Three-story house built in 1760s overlooking the New Bedford harbor. For-
mal dining room. Sunken in living room with fireplace. Decorated with period
furnishings. Off-street parking available.*

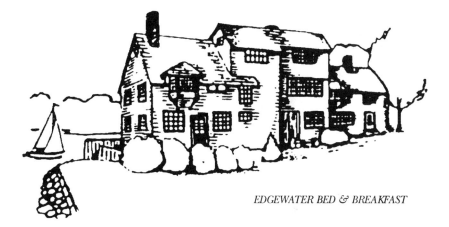

EDGEWATER BED & BREAKFAST

FALMOUTH (8)

Capt. Tom Lawrence House
75 Locust St., Falmouth, MA 02540
(508) 540-1445

Innkeeper: Barbara Sabo-Feller
Rooms: 6 w/pvt. bath
Rates: $75-$104, incl. full brk. Seasonal variations.
Credit cards: MC, V
Restrictions: No children under 12, pets, smoking. 50% deposit req. 2-week cancel-
lation notice req., less $20.00 fee. 2-night min. stay.
Notes: Two-story Victorian whaling captain's house built in 1861. Living room with
fireplace, Steinway piano. Furnished with antiques. German spoken.*

The Elms
495 W. Falmouth, Rte. 28A, Falmouth, MA 02574
(508) 540-7232

Innkeeper: Betty and Joe Mazzucchelli

Rooms: 9, incl. 7 w/pvt. bath
Rates: $65-$85, incl. cont brk., evening refreshment
Credit cards: None
Restrictions: No children. No smoking. One night's deposit req. 7-day cancellation notice req. 2-night min. stay on April 30–Oct. 12 wknds.
Notes: Victorian house built in 1739. Expanded in 1850. Fully refurbished and furnished with antiques. Parlor. Landscaped grounds with flower beds, English herb garden, silver garden, highbred hosta garden. Victorian gazebo. Handicapped access.

Gladstone Inn
219 Grand Ave. South, Falmouth, MA 02540
(508) 548-9851, (508) 548-9851

Innkeeper: James and Gayle Carroll
Rooms: 15, no pvt. bath, plus Carriage House suite, w/pvt. bath, kitchen, pvt. deck, TV. Located in 2 bldgs.
Rates: $60/room, $85/suite, all incl. full brk.
Credit cards: MC, V
Restrictions: No children under 14, pets. One night's deposit req. 5-day cancellation notice req. 2-night min. stay. Closed Oct. 15–May 15.
Notes: Three-story Victorian inn established in 1910 overlooking Martha's Vineyard. Decorated with antiques. Common room decorated in nautical motif with cable TV, refrigerator. Glassed-in porch. Bicycles and gas grill provided.

GRAFTON INN

Grafton Inn
261 Grand Ave. South, Falmouth, MA 02540
(508) 540-8688, (800) 642-4069, (508) 540-1861

Innkeeper: Liz and Rudy Cvitan
Rooms: 11 w/pvt. bath, phone, incl. 4 w/TV
Rates: $95-$135, incl. full brk., evening refreshment. Special pkgs. avail.
Credit cards: Most major cards

Restrictions: No children under 16, pets, smoking. 50% deposit req. 14-day written cancellation notice req., less $20.00 fee. 2-night min. stay on wknds. Closed Jan.1–Apr. 30.

Notes: 2-story Queen Anne-style Victorian inn with turret built about 1850 on oceanfront. Living room with cable TV, VCR. Enclosed porch overlooking Martha's Vineyard and Nantucket Sound. Furnished with period antiques. Artist's gallery on premises. Bicycles available.

The Inn at One Main St.
One Main St., Falmouth, MA 02540
(508) 540-7469

Innkeeper: Karen Hart and Mari Zylinski
Rooms: 6 w/pvt. bath
Rates: $65-$85, incl. full brk. Seasonal variations. Discount avail. for extended stay.
Credit cards: Most major cards
Restrictions: No children under 10, pets. Smoking restricted. One night's deposit req. 14-day cancellation notice req., less $20.00 fee. 2-night min. stay on holidays.
Notes: Victorian house with open front porch, 2-story turret, built in 1892. Located in historic area of Falmouth. Surrounded by white picket fence. Common room with phone and TV. Sitting room with fireplace.

MOSTLY HALL B & B INN

Mostly Hall B & B Inn
27 Main St., Falmouth, MA 02540
(508) 548-3786, (800) 682-0565,

Innkeeper: Caroline and Jim Lloyd
Rooms: 6 w/pvt. bath
Rates: $95-$110, incl. full brk., afternoon refreshment. Special pkgs. avail.
Credit cards: Most major cards
Restrictions: No children under 16, pets, smoking. 50% deposit req. 14-day cancellation notice req., less $20.00 fee. 2-night min. stay on wknds. & May–October. 3-night min. stay on holiday wknds.
Notes: Four-story Louisiana-style mansion with thirteen-ft. ceilings built in 1849. Located on 1.5 wooded acres on village green. Has operated as inn since 1980. Living

room with spinet piano, French coal stove. Common rooms with fireplace, TV. Dining room. Covered wrap-around veranda with chairs and tables. Enclosed widow's walk used as sitting room. Furnished in eclectic style with some antiques, Oriental rugs. Guest rooms feature queen-sized four poster canopy beds. Gazebo with swing. Lawn games, bicycles available. Some German spoken.

THE PALMER HOUSE INN

The Palmer House Inn
81 Palmer Ave., Falmouth, MA 02540
(508) 548-1230, (800) 472-2632, (508) 540-1878

Innkeeper: Ken and Joanne Baker
Rooms: 12 plus 1 suite, all w/pvt. bath, incl. 1 w/phone, 5 w/TV. Located in 3 bldgs.
Rates: $90-$130/room, $149/suite, all incl. full brk. Discount avail. for extended stay. Seasonal variations. Special pkgs. avail.
Credit cards: Most major cards
Restrictions: No children under 10, pets. Smoking restricted. Min. 2-night's deposit req. 14-day cancellation notice req. 2-night min. stay in season. 3-night min. stay on holidays.
Notes: Three-story Queen Anne Victorian inn with three-story turret, stained-glass windows, hardwood floors built in 1901. Wrap-around front porch with rocker. Dining room. Parlor with fireplace, board games, cable TV, upright piano. Furnished with period antiques. Bicycles available. Pet resident. Handicapped access.*

Village Green Inn
40 West Main St., Falmouth, MA 02540
(508) 548-5621

Innkeeper: Don and Linda Long
Rooms: 4 w/pvt. bath, incl. 2 w/fireplace, plus 1 suite w/pvt. bath, TV
Rates: $85-$100/room, $95-$120/suite, all incl. full brk., afternoon refreshment. Discount avail. for extended stay.
Credit cards: None
Restrictions: No children under 16, pets. Smoking restricted. One night's deposit req. 14-day cancellation notice req., less $20.00 fee. 2-night min. stay on holiday wknds. Closed Jan. and early Nov.
Notes: Two-story Federal-style Colonial house built in 1804. Fully remodeled in 1894 in Victorian-style. Located on Village Green. Formal parlor with mirrored

VILLAGE GREEN INN

fireplace, piano. Study. Two porches with white wicker furniture overlooking land-scaped lawns, gardens. Furnished with antiques, reproductions. Board games, beach passes, Bicycles available.

GAY HEAD (8)

Duck Inn
P.O. Box 160, Gay Head, MA 02535
(508) 645-9018
Innkeeper: Elise LeBovit
Rooms: 4 w/pvt. bath, phone, 1 w/TV, plus 1 suite w/pvt. bath, phone, TV, fireplace
Rates: $65-$150/room, $85-$175/suite, all incl. full brk., afternoon refreshment.
  Discount avail. for extended stay.
Credit cards: Most major cards
Restrictions: Smoking restricted. 50% deposit req. 14-day cancellation notice req.
Notes: Two-story stone foundation house built in 1794. Common area with fire-place, toys, cable TV, movies. Large deck with gas grill. Furnished in eclectic style. Beach lunches can be catered. Organic food served. Hot tub. Bike rentals. Masseuse, canoes, kayaks available. Resident cat and pig. French spoken.

GREAT BARRINGTON (1)

Baldwin Hill Farm B & B
RD 3, Box 125, Great Barrington, MA 01230
(413) 528-4092
Innkeeper: Richard and Priscilla Burdsall
Rooms: 4, no pvt. bath, incl. 2 suites w/pvt. bath
Rates: $75-$94, incl. full brk., afternoon refreshment. Seasonal variations. Discount
  avail. for extended stay.
Credit cards: Most major cards
Restrictions: No children under 12, pets, smoking restricted. One night's deposit
  req. 10-day cancellation notice req., less $10.00 fee. 2 or 3-night min. stay on
  wknds.
Notes: Victorian farm house, part of which was built in the 1700s. Opened as an inn in 1990. Located on hilltop. Two living rooms with TV, VCR, fieldstone fireplace, library, board games, piano. Lawns, vegetable gardens, and orchards which provide produce to guests in season. Some French spoken.*

Elling's Bed & Breakfast
R.D. 3, Box 6, Great Barrington, MA 01230
(413) 528-4103

Innkeeper: Jo and Ray Elling
Rooms: 6, incl. 4 w/pvt. bath
Rates: $55-$85, incl. cont. brk. Seasonal variations.
Credit cards: None
Restrictions: No children under 10, pets, smoking. One night's deposit req. 10-day cancellation notice req., less 10% fee. 2-night min. stay in summer and fall foliage season. 3-night min. stay on holiday wknds.
Notes: 2.5-story Georgian Cape house built about 1742. Located on six-acre wooded knoll. Has operated as inn since 1972. Parlor and dining room with fireplaces, porches, with rocking chairs overlooking mountains. Furnished with period antiques and Colonial reproductions. Lawns and gardens, games available.

Seekonk Pines Inn
142 Seekonk Cross Rd., Great Barrington, MA 01230
(413) 528-4192, (800) 292-4192

Innkeeper: Christian and Linda Best
Rooms: 6 w/pvt. bath
Rates: $70-$99, incl. full brk. Discount avail. for extended stay. Seasonal variations.
Credit cards: MC, V
Restrictions: Pets restricted. No smoking. Min. one night's deposit req. 14-day cancellation notice req., less $10.00 fee. 2-night min. stay, June, Sept., and Oct. wknds. 3-night min. stay, July–Aug. and most holiday wknds.
Notes: Post and beam farmhouse built in 1832. Common room with baby grand piano. Furnished with antique quilts. Decorated with innkeeper's watercolors. Swimming pool, bicycles available. German spoken.

Turning Point Inn
3 Lake Buel Rd., Great Barrington, MA 01230
(413) 528-4777

Innkeeper: Irving and Jamie Yost
Rooms: 7, incl. 4 w/pvt. bath, plus 1 suite w/pvt. bath, TV. Located in 2 bldgs.
Rates: $80-$100/room, $200/suite, all incl. full brk. Discount avail. for mid-week and extended stays.
Credit cards: Most major cards
Restrictions: No pets, smoking. Deposit req. 2-week cancellation notice req., less $10.00 fee. Min. stay varies.
Notes: Federal Colonial style house with wide floor boards, built about 1800. Located on eleven acres next to Butternut ski slope. Fully restored with antiques and reproductions. Two sitting rooms, each with fireplace, one with baby grand piano. Play room with cable TV, chess, games, fireplace. Guests have access to kitchen. Small private parties accommodated.

Windflower Inn
684S. Egremont Rd., Box 25, Great Barrington, MA 01230
(413) 528-2720, (413) 528-5147

Innkeeper: Barbara and Gerald Liebert, John and Claudia Ryan
Rooms: 13 w/pvt. bath, TV, incl. 6 w/fireplace
Rates: $160-$210, incl. cont. brk., dinner
Credit cards: Most major cards

Restrictions: No pets. Smoking restricted. $150.00 deposit req., 3-week cancellation notice req., less min. $5.00 fee. 2-night min. stay on wknds. 3-night min. stay on summer wknds.

Notes: Federal-style inn built in 1820. Located on 10 wooded acres. Living room with fireplace. Reading room with oak piano. Dining room with fireplace. Spacious porches. Swimming pool. Furnished with antiques. Limited handicapped access.

GREENFIELD (2)

Brandt House
29 Highland Ave., Greenfield, MA 01301
(413) 774-3329, (800) 235-3329, (413) 772-2908
Innkeeper: Phoebe Compton
Rooms: 7, incl. 2 w/fireplace, plus 3 suites, all w/pvt. bath, TV
Rates: $50-$135, incl. full brk. Seasonal variations. Discount avail. for mid-week and extended stays.
Credit cards: MC, V
Restrictions: Children, pets welcome with prior approval only. Smoking restricted. One night's deposit req. 50% cancellation fee req.
Notes: Two-story Colonial Revival house built in the 1890s. Fully renovated in 1987. Located on 3.5 wooded, hilltop acres. Living room. Dining room. Patio. Wrap-around porches. Library with billiard table. Board and yard games available. Clay tennis court. German spoken.*

HARWICH (8)

Harbor Breeze Bed and Breakfast
326 Lower Country Rd., Harwich, MA 02646
(508) 432-0337, (800) 272-4343
Innkeeper: Kathleen and David Van Gelder
Rooms: 8 w/pvt. bath, TV, plus 1 suite w/pvt bath, TV
Rates: $75-$85/room, $95-$120/suite, all incl. cont. brk. Seasonal variations. Discount avail. for extended stay.
Credit cards: Most major cards
Restrictions: No pets. 50% deposit req. 14-day cancellation notice req., less $10.00 fee. 2-night min. stay on wknds. and holidays.
Notes: Cape Cod house with rambling connection of cedar shake additions located across the street from the town harbor. Swimming pool, garden courtyard. Guests have access to nearby tennis court. Handicapped access.*

HARWICH PORT (8)

Country Inn
86 Sisson Rd., Route 39, Harwich Port, MA 02646
(508) 432-2769, (800) 231-1722
Innkeeper: Kathleen and David Van Gelder
Rooms: 6 w/pvt. bath, TV, incl. 2 w/fireplace, plus 1 suite w/pvt. bath, fireplace, TV
Rates: $75-$120/room, $95-$140/suite, all incl. cont. brk. Seasonal variations. Special pkgs. avail.
Credit cards: Most major cards
Restrictions: No children, pets. Smoking restricted. 50% deposit req. 14-day cancellation notice req., less $10.00 fee. 2-night min. stay on wknds. and holidays.

Notes: Two-story Cape Cod inn located on six acres. Parlor, TV room, dining room. Living room with fireplace. Swimming pool, three tennis courts, Private beach privileges available. Handicapped access.*

HYANNIS (8)

The Inn on Sea Street
358 Sea St., Hyannis, MA 02601
(508) 775-8030

Innkeeper: Lois Nelson, J. B. Whitehead
Rooms: 9, incl. 7 w/pvt. bath, 6 w/TV, plus cottage. Located in 2 bldgs.
Rates: $88-$98/room, $110/cottage, all incl. full, gourmet brk.
Credit cards: Most major cards
Restrictions: No children, pets. Smoking restricted. One night's deposit req., refunded, less 10% fee upon cancellation only if room is re-rented. Closed Nov. 1–Apr. l.
Notes: Two-story Victorian sea captain's house with decorative exterior Victorian woodwork, interior curved staircase, crystal chandelier, built in 1849. Living room with fireplace, TV, library, board games. Dining room. Furnished with period pieces, Oriental rugs, sterling silver, objets d'art. Listed on Hyannis' Register of historic houses.*

Mansfield House
70 Gosnold St., Hyannis, MA 02601
(508) 771-9455, (212) 262-6207

Innkeeper: Donald Patell
Rooms: 4 w/pvt. bath, TV
Rates: $65-$80, incl full brk. Seasonal variations. Discount avail. for extended stay.
Credit cards: None
Restrictions: Well-behaved children welcome. Pets welcome with prior approval. Smoking restricted. Min. one night's deposit req. 48-hour cancellation notice req.
Notes: Reception room with wicker furniture. Porch. Garden. Patio with garden, benches, chairs. Dining room. Babysitting arranged with prior notice. *

MANSFIELD HOUSE

The Salt Winds
319 Sea St., Hyannis, MA 02601-4508
(508) 775-2038
Innkeeper: Ginny and Craig Conroy
Rooms: 9 plus 3 suites, some w/pvt. bath, incl. 8 w/TV. Located in 3 bldgs.
Rates: $55-$80/room, $90-$145/suite, all incl. full brk.
Credit cards: Most major cards
Restrictions: No pets, smoking. Deposit req. 25% fee for cancellations.
Notes: 200 year old establishment. Outdoor heated pool. Gas grill and picnic tables available, board games, transportation to ferries available.

Sea Beach Inn
388 Sea St., Hyannis, MA 02601
(508) 775-4612
Innkeeper: Neil and Elizabeth Carr
Rooms: 9, incl. 7 w/pvt. bath, incl. 1 w/TV
Rates: $45-$75, incl. cont. brk. Seasonal variations. Discount avail. for senior citizen and extended stays.
Credit cards: Most major cards
Restrictions: No pets. Smoking restricted. One night's deposit req. 14-day cancellation notice req., less 15% fee. 2-night min. stay on holiday wknds. Closed Nov.–Mar.
Notes: Three-story sea captain's house built in 1860 with attached carriage barn. Has operated as inn, on and off, since the turn-of-the-century. Living room with cable TV. Breakfast room. Porch overlooking ocean. Patio overlooking gardens. Furnished in eclectic style. Small private parties accommodated. Resident dog.*

Sea Breeze Inn
397 Sea St., Hyannis, MA 02601
(508) 771-7213
Innkeeper: Patricia and Martin Battle
Rooms: 14 w/pvt. bath. Located in 2 bldgs.
Rates: $65-$95, incl. cont. brk.
Credit cards: Most major cards
Restrictions: Smoking restricted. Deposit req. 7-day cancellation notice req.
Notes: Two-story Victorian inn. Dining room, lobby. Furnished with antiques. Lawn with outdoor furniture.*

HYANNIS PORT (8)

The Simmons Homestead Inn
288 Scudder Ave., Hyannis Port, MA 02647-0578
(800) 637-1649, (508) 790-1342
Innkeeper: Bill Putman
Rooms: 10 w/pvt. bath, incl. 2 w/fireplace, 1 w/pvt. deck
Rates: $90-$130, incl. full brk., evening refreshment. Seasonal variations. Discount avail. for extended stay.
Credit cards: Most major cards
Notes: No pets. Smoking restricted. Min. 50% deposit req. 7-day cancellation notice req., less 15% fee. 2-night min. stay from June 1–Oct. 31. 3-night min. stay on holidays.

Notes: Two-story farmhouse built by sea captain in 1820. Restored in and has operated as inn since 1987. Formal dining room, common room, each with fireplace. Brick entry patio, covered wrap-around porch overlooking Simmons Pond. Decorated with fine furniture, brass, ceramic and papier-mache lifelike animals, needlepoint wall displays. Bicycles, beach chairs available.*

LANESBOROUGH (1)

Whippletree B and B
10 Bailey Rd., Rt. 7, Lanesborough, MA 01237
(413) 442-7468, (413) 443-9874
Innkeeper: Chuck and Kristin Lynch
Rooms: 4, incl. 1 w/pvt. bath, plus 1 suite w/pvt. bath, TV, kitchen, living room. Located in 2 bldgs.
Rates: $60-$75/room, $85/suite, all incl. cont. brk. Discount avail. for mid-week stay.
Credit cards: None
Restrictions: No pets, smoking. One night's deposit req. 10-day cancellation notice req., less $10.00 fee. 2-night min. stay on holiday wknds.
Notes: Two-story Federal Colonial farmhouse with random-width plank floors, built in 1753. Fully restored. Common rooms with games, books, wood-burning stove. Dining room, pool, porch. Decorated with hand-crafted items. Resident dog.*

LEE (1)

APPLEGATE

Applegate
279 W. Park St., Lee, MA 01238
(413) 243-4451
Innkeeper: Nancy Begbie-Cannata, Richard Cannata
Rooms: 6 w/pvt. bath, incl. 2 w/fireplace, plus carriage house for long-term stays. Located in 2 bldgs.
Rates: $80-$195, incl. expanded cont. brk., evening refreshment. Seasonal variations. Discount avail. for extended stay. Special pkgs. avail.
Credit cards: MC, V

Restrictions: No children under 12, pets. Smoking restricted. One night's deposit req. 14-day cancellation notice req., less min. one night's fee. 2-night min. stay on June, Sept. & Oct. wknds. 3-night min. stay on July, Aug. & holiday wknds.

Notes: Two-story Georgian colonial house with portico built in 1920s. Located on six acres of manicured lawns and flower gardens. Living room with fireplace, baby grand piano, library. Foyer, TV room with VCR, dining room with fireplace. Screened porch with wicker furniture. Furnished with antiques, reproductions and Oriental carpets. Lawn games, bicycles available. Carriage House apartment with 2 bedrooms, Jacuzzi, deck, grill TV, VCR.

The Morgan House Inn
33 Main St., Lee, MA 01238
(413) 243-0181

Innkeeper: Stuart and Lenora Bowen

Rooms: 12, incl. 1 w/pvt. bath, plus 1 suite w/pvt. bath, TV

Rates: $40-$90/room, $65-$135/suite, incl. full brk. Seasonal variations. Discount avail. for mid-week stay.

Credit cards: Most major cards

Restrictions: No pets. Min. one night's deposit req. 2-week cancellation notice req., less $10.00 fee. 2-night min. stay on wknds., July, August, and October.

Notes: Three-story house built in 1817 as a private residence. Converted to a stage-coach stop in 1855. Family room with library, TV, board games. Restaurant with fireplace, tavern with 100-year-old square grand piano on premises. Private second-floor dining room. Decorated with antique and reproduction furniture in Early American style.

LENOX (1)

AMADEUS HOUSE

Amadeus House
15 Cliffwood St., Lenox, MA 01240
(413) 637-4770, (800) 205-4770, (413) 637-4484

Innkeeper: John Felton and Martha Gottron

Rooms: 5 w/pvt. bath, incl. 1 w/fireplace, pvt. porch, plus 1 suite w/pvt. bath, phone, living room, full kitchen.

Rates: $55-$145/room, $90-$175/suite, all incl. full brk., afternoon refreshment. Seasonal variations. Discount avail. for extended and mid-week stays.

Credit cards: None

Restrictions: No children under 6, pets, smoking. Min. 50% deposit req. 14-day cancellation notice req., less $10.00 fee. 3-night min. stay on wknds. from July 1–Aug. 31. 2-night min. stay on holiday wknds. and October.

Notes: Two-story house built approx. 1824. Located on ½ acre. Dining room with three tables. Living room with fireplace. Library of several hundred compact discs, books, and magazines on music, history, art, literature, travel. Wrap-around porch with rockers and cafe chairs. Board games available. Off-street parking available. Handicapped access.

Apple Tree Inn
224 West St., Lenox, MA 01240
(413) 637-1477

Innkeeper: Aurora and Greg Smith

Rooms: 33 rooms, incl. 31 w/pvt. bath, 21 w/TV, 3 w/fireplace, plus 2 suites w/pvt. bath, TV, incl. 1 w/fireplace. Located in 2 bldgs.

Rates: $60-$80/room, $200-$240/suite, all incl. cont. brk. Seasonal variations. Discount avail. for extended stay.

Credit cards: Most major cards

Restrictions: No children under 10, pets. Smoking restricted. 50% deposit req. 2-week cancellation notice req., less 15% fee. 2-night min. stay in main house. 3-night min. stay on summer wknds.

Notes: Located on twenty landscaped hilltop acres with apple orchard, flower gardens. Parlor, dining room. Heated swimming pool, clay tennis court. Restaurant, tavern on premises.

Birchwood Inn
7 Hubbard St., Box 2020, Lenox, MA 01240
(413) 637-2600

Innkeeper: Dick, Dan and Joan Toner

Rooms: 10, incl. 8 w/pvt. bath, 3 w/fireplace, 1 w/TV, plus 2 carriage house efficiency suites w/pvt. bath, phone, TV. Located in 2 bldgs.

Rates: $50-$195/room, $90-$195/suite, all incl. full brk., afternoon refreshment. Seasonal variations. Discount avail. for extended and mid-week stays.

Credit cards: Most major cards

Restrictions: No children under 12, pets, smoking. Deposit req. 10-day cancellation notice req., less 10% fee. 2-night min. stay on holidays & Oct. wknds. 3-night min. stay on July and Aug. wknds.

Notes: Three-story Colonial house built in 1767. Located hilltop overlooking village. Eighteenth century library. Porch. Common rooms all have fireplaces. Decorated with antiques. Gardens. Yard games available. Listed on National Register of Historic Places.

Blantyre
16 Blantyre Rd., Box 995, Lenox, MA 01240-0995
(413) 637-3556, (413) 637-4282

Innkeeper: Roderick W. Anderson

Rooms: 17 w/pvt. bath, phone, TV, incl. 2 w/fireplace, plus 6 suites w/pvt. bath, phone, TV, incl. 3 w/fireplace. Located in 3 bldgs.

Rates: $220-$370/room, $250-$550/suite, all incl. cont. brk. Seasonal variations.

Credit cards: Most major cards
Restrictions: No children under 12, pets. Min. one night's deposit req. 2-week cancellation notice req., less $25.00 fee. 2-night min. stay on wknds. 3-night min. stay on holiday wknds. Evening dress req. in Main House after 6:00.
Notes: Three-story Tudor-style mansion with turrets, gargoyles, carved friezes, Carriage House, three cottages built in 1902. Fully restored. Located on eighty five acres. Great Hall with oak door, lofty beamed ceilings, heirloom furnishings, stockwide fireplace. Music room with fireplace, piano. Covered terrace with French doors. Dining room, moire room. Furnished with antiques. Some suites with 2 baths, sitting room, spiral staircases. Swimming pool, Jacuzzi, sauna, Har-Tru tennis courts, bent grass tournament croquet lawns on premises. All meals available. Small private parties accommodated. French, German spoken.*

BROOK FARM INN

Brook Farm Inn
15 Hawthorne St., Lenox, MA 01240
(413) 637-3013, (800) 285-POET
Innkeeper: Joe and Anne Miller
Rooms: 12 w/pvt. bath, incl. 6 w/fireplace
Rates: $65-$170, incl. full brk., afternoon refreshment. Seasonal variations. Special pkgs. avail. Discount avail. for extended stay.
Credit cards: Most major cards
Restrictions: No children under 15, pets, smoking. 50% deposit req. 2-week cancellation notice req., less 10% fee. 2-night min. stay on wknds. 3-night min. stay in summer.
Notes: Victorian Inn built in 1879. Operating under current management with renovations and redecorations since 1992. Foyer and living room, each with fireplace. Dining room. Library with fireplace, jig-saw puzzle, 500 volumes of poetry and 41 poets on tape. Poetry readings every Saturday night. Garden, heated swimming pool.

Cornell Inn
203 Main St., Lenox, MA 01240
(413) 637-0562
Innkeeper: Jack D'Elia

Rooms: 24 plus 6 suites, all w/pvt. bath, phone, incl. 19 w/fireplace, 26 w/TV. Located in 3 bldgs.
Rates: $69-$125/room, $99-$199/suite, all incl. cont. brk. Special pkgs. avail.
Credit cards: Most major cards
Restrictions: No pets. Deposit req. 14-day cancellation notice req., less $25.00 fee. 2-night min. stay on fall and winter wknds. 3-night min. stay in summer.
Notes: Three-story Victorian house with turret and carriage house built in 1888. Renovated in 1985. Dining room and Pub. Two common rooms with fireplace. Health spa, exercise room, and deck. Handicapped access.*

The Gables Inn
81 Walker St., Lenox, MA 01240
(413) 637-3416
Innkeeper: Mary and Frank Newton
Rooms: 15 w/pvt. bath, incl. 8 w/fireplace, 3 w/TV, plus 3 suites w/pvt. bath, fireplace, incl. 2 w/TV.
Rates: $75-$150/room, $150-$195/suite, all incl. full brk., evening refreshment
Credit cards: Most major cards
Restrictions: No children under 12, pets, cigar smoking. Deposit req. 2-week cancellation notice req., less 5% fee. 3-night min. stay July–August.
Notes: Fully recreated three-story Queen Anne Cottage built in 1885. Former home of Edith Wharton. Eight-sided library. Furnished with period pieces, fine art. Heated swimming pool with Jacuzzi, private tennis court, garden.

Garden Gables Inn
135 Main St., Box 52, Lenox, MA 01240
(413) 637-0193, (413) 637-4554
Innkeeper: Mario and Lynn Mekinda
Rooms: 18 w/pvt. bath, phone, incl. 8 w/fireplace, 4 w/TV. Some w/pvt. porches, whirlpool tubs. Suites avail. Located in 2 bldgs.
Rates: $65-$190/room, $115-$190/suite, all incl. full brk. Seasonal variations. Discount avail. for extended stay.
Credit cards: Most major cards
Restrictions: No children under 12, pets. Smoking restricted. Deposit req. 2-week cancellation notice req., less 10%. 3-night min. stay on wknds. from July–August, and holidays.
Notes: Two-story inn with gables built in 1780. Located on five wooded acres. Furnished with antiques, paintings. Living rooms, dining room featuere English antiques and 19th-century Dutch watercolors. Swimming pool. Handicapped access. French, German spoken.

Rookwood Inn
11 Stockbridge Rd., Box 1717, Lenox, MA 01240
(800) 223-9750
Innkeeper: Tom and Betsy Sherman, Maureen Hall
Rooms: 15 plus 5 suites, all w/pvt. bath, incl. 8 w/fireplace
Rates: $75-$225, incl. cont. brk. Discount avail. for mid-week stay. Seasonal variations.
Credit cards: DC
Restrictions: No pets, smoking. Deposit req. 14-day cancellation notice req. 3-night min. stay on summer wknds.

Notes: Two-story Victorian house with tower built in the 1830s. Veranda. Porch. Handicapped access.*

The Village Inn
16 Church St., Box 1810, Lenox, MA 01240
(413) 637-0020, (413) 637-9756
Innkeeper: Clifford Rudisill and Ray Wilson
Rooms: 32 w/pvt. bath, phone, incl. 6 w/fireplace, plus 1 suite w/pvt. bath, phone, TV
Rates: $50-$165/room, $210-$315/suite. Seasonal variations. Discount avail. for mid-week stay. Special pkgs. avail.
Credit cards: Most major cards
Restrictions: No children under 6, pets, smoking. Deposit req. 30-day cancellation notice req. 2-night min. stay on wknds. 3-night min. stay on holiday and summer wknds.
Notes: Two-story Federal/Colonial building built in 1771. Has operated as inn since 1775. Tavern, dining room, sitting room. Decorated with country antique furniture, oriental rugs, and small print wallpaper. Handicapped access.*

Walker House
74 Walker St., Lenox, MA 01240
(413) 637-1271, (413) 637-2387
Innkeeper: Peggy and Richard Houdek
Rooms: 8 w/pvt. bath, incl. 5 w/fireplace
Rates: $60-$170, incl. expanded cont. brk., afternoon refreshment. Discount avail. for mid-week and extended stays. Special pkgs. avail. Seasonal variations.
Credit cards: None
Restrictions: No children under 11, smoking. Pets welcome with prior approval. Min. one night's deposit req. 14-day cancellation notice req., less 15% fee. 2-night min. stay on wknds. 3-night min. stay on wknds. from July 1–Aug. 31 and holidays.
Notes: Two-story Federal Colonial inn built in 1804. Located on three wooded and landscaped acres. Guest rooms named and decorated for composers and furnished with antiques. Parlor with grand piano, fireplace, books, games. Dining room, indoor screened verandas. Library with big-screen TV, VCR, video collection. Bicycles available. Guests have acceess to nearby tennis courts. Handicapped access. French, Spanish spoken.

Whistler's Inn
5 Greenwood St., Lenox, MA 01240
(413) 637-0975, (413) 637-2190
Innkeeper: Richard and Joan Mears
Rooms: 12 w/pvt. bath, phone, incl. 3 w/fireplace, 2 w/TV. Located in 2 bldgs.
Rates: $70-$190, incl. full brk., afternoon refreshment. Seasonal variations.
Credit cards: Most major cards
Restrictions: No pets, smoking. 50% deposit req. 14-day cancellation notice req., less 10% fee. 3-night min. stay July–Aug. wknds.
Notes: French/English Tudor mansion built in 1820. Located on seven wooded acres with gardens. Library, music room, sun porch, terrace. Furnished with many antiques. Polish, French, Spanish spoken.*

LYNN (6)

Diamond District B & B
142 Ocean St., Lynn, MA 01902-2007
(617) 599-4470, (800) 666-3076, (617) 599-4470
Innkeeper: Sandra and Jerry Caron
Rooms: 4 suites w/pvt. bath
Rates: $58-$105, incl. full brk. Seasonal variations. Discount avail. for mid-week and
    extended stays.
Credit cards: Most major cards
Restrictions: Pets restricted. No smoking. One night's deposit req. 14-day cancellation
    notice req., less 20% fee. 2-night min. stay on holidays and Oct. wknds.
Notes: Three-story Georgian-style clapboard mansion with three-story grand stair-
case, built in 1911. Has operated as inn since 1989. Living room with fireplace over-
looking ocean. Dining room, porch, foyer. Common room with 1895 rosewood
Knabe concert grand piano. Veranda overlooking ocean and gardens. Furnished
with antiques, Oriental rugs. Beach umbrellas, towels, fax and business services
available.*

MARBLEHEAD (5)

Brimblecomb Hill
33 Mechanic St., Marblehead, MA 01945
(617) 631-3172, (617) 631-6366
Innkeeper: Gene Arnold
Rooms: 3, incl. 2 w/pvt. entrance, 1 w/pvt. bath
Rates: $55-$75, incl. cont. brk.
Credit cards: MC, V
Restrictions: No pets, smoking. Deposit req. 2-week cancellation notice req., less
    10% of deposit fee. 2-night min. stay on wknds.
Notes: Two-story Old Town House built in 1721. Features first floor guest rooms.
Sitting room with fireplace. Garden.

THE HARBOR LIGHT INN

The Harbor Light Inn
58 Washington St., Marblehead, MA 01945
(617) 631-2186, (617) 631-2216
Innkeeper: Peter and Suzanne Conway

Rooms: 19, incl. 11 w/fireplace, plus 1 suite, all w/pvt. bath, TV, phone. Located in 2 bldgs.

Rates: $85-$185/room, $150/suite, all incl. cont. brk.

Credit cards: None

Restrictions: No children under 6, pets. Smoking restricted. Min. one night's deposit req. 14-day cancellation notice req., less 10% fee. 2-night min. stay on wknds.

Notes: Three-story Federalist mansion built in the 18th century. Living room with fireplace. Rooftop walk overlooking Marblehead. Sundeck. Furnished with antiques, Oriental carpets, paintings, etchings, prints. Jacuzzi. Small private parties accommodated.

The Nesting Place
16 Village St., Marblehead, MA 01945
(617) 631-6655

Innkeeper: Louise Hirshberg

Rooms: 2

Rates: $125, incl. cont. brk. Seasonal variations. Discount avail. for mid-week and extended stays.

Credit cards: MC, V

Restrictions: No smoking. Min. one night's deposit req. 7-day cancellation notice req.

Notes: 19th-century house. Special therapy packages available.*

Spray Cliff "On the Ocean"
25 Spray Ave., Marblehead, MA 01945
(508) 744-8924, (800) 626-1530, (508) 744-8924

Innkeeper: Diane and Richard Pabich

Rooms: 7 w/pvt. bath, incl. 3 w/fireplace

Rates: $115-$200, incl. cont. brk., evening refreshment

Credit cards: Most major cards

Restrictions: No children under 12, pets. Smoking restricted. One-night's deposit req. 7-day cancellation notice req., less $15.00 fee. 2-night min. stay on wknds.

Notes: Tudor-style mansion built in 1910. Located atop seawall above rocky beach. Common room with fireplace overlooking ocean. Brick terrace in flower gardens. Furnished with some wicker furniture.*

Stillpoint
27 Gregory St., Marblehead, MA 01945
(617) 631-1667, (800) 882-3891

Innkeeper: Sarah Lincoln-Harrison

Rooms: 3, incl. 2 w/pvt. bath

Rates: $70-$95, incl. expanded cont. brk. Discount avail. for extended stay.

Credit cards: MC, V

Restrictions: No children under 10, pets, smoking. Min. one night's deposit req. 21-day cancellation notice req. 2-night min. stay on holiday wknds.

Notes: Three-story house built in 1930. Living room with fireplace, piano. Dining room. Deck overlooking gardens. Selection of local crafts for sale. Innkeeper takes an active role in the environment with an edible landscape. French spoken.*

MARTHA'S VINEYARD (8)

Menemsha Inn & Cottages
North Rd., Menemsha, Martha's Vineyard, MA 02552
(508) 645-2521

Innkeeper: Richard and Nancy Steves
Rooms: 9 inn rooms, plus 6 suites w/privacy deck; also 12 cottages w/fireplace, TV, all w/pvt. bath. Located in 14 bldgs.
Rates: $75-$120/room, $90-$160/suite, $975/wk/cottage, all incl. cont. brk. Seasonal variations.
Credit cards: None
Restrictions: No pets. 50% deposit req. 30-day cancellation notice req., less 10% fee. 2-night min. stay on off-season wknds. in cottages. Closed Dec.1–Apr. 29.
Notes: Cottage inn located on ten acres with stone walls in up-island Martha's Vineyard overlooking Vineyard Sound. Has operated as inn since 1989. Cottages with kitchen, screened-in porch. Living room, waterview porch in main inn. All weather tennis court. Meadows. Beach passes. Small private parties accommodated.

NANTUCKET (8)

Cobblestone Inn
5 Ash St., Nantucket, MA 02554
(508) 228-1987, (508) 228-6698

Innkeeper: Robin Hammer-Yankow
Rooms: 5 w/pvt. bath
Rates: $50-$140, incl. cont. brk. Seasonal variations.
Credit cards: MC, V
Restrictions: No children under 5, pets, smoking. Full prepayment req. for 1 to 3 nights, 50% deposit req. for 4 nights or more, 14-day cancellation notice, less 10% fee.
Notes: Three-story house built in 1725. Fully renovated. Has operated as inn since 1986. Living room with fireplace, cable TV, board games. Sun porch with wicker furniture and refrigerator. Brick patio overlooking garden. Furnished with period pieces.*

Eighteen Gardner Street Inn
18 Gardner St., Nantucket, MA 02554
(800) 435-1450

Innkeeper: Mary Schmidt
Rooms: 14, incl. 12 w/pvt. bath, 14 w/TV, 7 w/fireplace, plus 3 suites incl. 1 w/fireplace, all w/pvt. bath, TV, and Apt. no pvt. bath. Located in 2 bldgs.
Rates: $150-$160/room, $185/suite, $300/apt., all incl. cont. brk. Seasonal variations. Discount avail. for extended stay from Oct. 20–April 30.
Credit cards: Most major cards
Restrictions: No pets, smoking. Deposit req. 14-day cancellation notice req. 2-night min. stay in season.
Notes: 2.5-story Colonial whaling captain's house built in 1835. Furnished with antiques, reproductions, Oriental rugs. Living room. Dining room. Garden. Parlor with fireplace. Bicycles, off-street parking available.*

House of the Seven Gables
32 Cliff Rd., Nantucket, MA 02554
(508) 228-4706

HOUSE OF THE SEVEN GABLES

Innkeeper: Suzanne Walton
Rooms: 10, incl. 8 w/pvt. bath
Rates: $40-$150, incl. cont. brk. Seasonal variations.
Credit cards: Most major cards
Restrictions: No children under 8, pets. Min. 50% deposit req., refunded, less 20% fee, upon cancellation only if room is re-rented.
Notes: Victorian structure overlooking the mouth of the harbor built in the 1880s as annex for the Sea Cliff Inn. Parlor with TV, fireplace. Rear brick patio overlooking honeysuckle and wild roses. Furnished with period antiques.

Lynda Watts Bed & Breakfast
30 Vestal St., Box 478, Nantucket, MA 02554-0478
(508) 228-3828, (508) 228-4162
Innkeeper: David and Lynda Watts
Rooms: 2 w/TV, no pvt. bath
Rates: $70, incl. cont. brk. 50% deposit req.
Credit cards: MC, V
Restrictions: No pets. 50% deposit req. 10-day cancellation notice req. 2-night min. stay.
Notes: *

Martin House Inn
61 Center St., Box 743, Nantucket, MA 02554
(508) 228-0678
Innkeeper: Channing and Ceci Moore
Rooms: 13, incl. 9 w/pvt. bath, 2 w/fireplace
Rates: $55-$145, incl. expanded cont. brk., evening refreshment. Special pkgs. avail.
Credit cards: Most major cards
Restrictions: No children under 5, pets. Smoking restricted. Min. 50% deposit req. 10-day cancellation notice req., less $10.00 fee. 2-night min. stay on most wknds. 3-night min. stay, July, Aug.
Notes: 3-story Mariner's house built in 1803. Has operated as inn since 1920. Dining room, living room with fireplace, furnished with antiques. Veranda furnished with wicker furniture. Beach towel available.*

Parker Guest House
4 E. Chestnut St., Nantucket, MA 02554-3510
(508) 228-4625, (800) 248-4625, (508) 228-4638
Innkeeper: Paul and Beverly Sheets
Rooms: 6 w/pvt. bath, TV, refrigerator, coffee maker
Rates: $125, incl. cont. brk. Seasonal variations.
Credit cards: Most major cards
Restrictions: No children, pets, smoking. Min. 50% deposit req. 15-day cancellation
notice req., less 10% fee. 2-night min. stay on wknds. 3-night min. stay on holiday
wknds.
Notes: Three-story house built in 1930. Common room with books, magazines,
games, telephone. Patio with tables and chairs.*

Quaker House Inn & Restaurant
5 Chestnut St., Nantucket, MA 02554
(508) 228-0400, (508) 228-6205
Innkeeper: Bob and Caroline Taylor
Rooms: 8 w/pvt. bath
Rates: $100-$150, incl. full brk. Seasonal variations.
Credit cards: Most major cards
Restrictions: No children under school age, pets, smoking. One night's min. de-
posit req. 15-day cancellation notice req., less $10.00 fee. 2-night min. stay.
Notes: Two-story house. Furnished in period style with antiques.

Seven Sea Street Inn
7 Sea St., Nantucket, MA 02554
(508) 228-3577
Innkeeper: Matthew and Mary Parker
Rooms: 9 plus 1 apartment, all w/pvt. bath, cable TV, phone, refrigerator. Suites
avail.
Rates: $95-$165/room, $125-$210/suite, $165-$245/apt., all incl. cont. brk., Jacuzzi
whirlpool. Seasonal variations.
Credit cards: Most major cards
Restrictions: No children under 7, pets, smoking. Deposit req. 14-day cancellation
notice req. 2-night min. stay on wknds. 3-night min. stay on holiday wknds.
Notes: Red oak post and beam Inn with pine floors, built in 1993. Widow's walk
overlooking Nantucket Harbor. Common room with fireplace. Roof deck with harbor view. Furnished in Colonial style with canopy beds, early American reproductions, braided rugs. Jacuzzis. Small private parties accommodated. French spoken.*

Tuckernuck Inn
60 Union St., Nantucket, MA 02554
(800) 228-4886, (508) 228-4890
Innkeeper: Ken and Phyllis Parker
Rooms: 16 plus 2 suites, all w/pvt. bath, incl. 1 w/fireplace
Rates: $70-$145/room, $120-$210/suite, all incl. 50% discount on breakfast. Discount avail. for mid-week stay. Seasonal variations.
Credit cards: Most major cards
Restrictions: No children under 10, pets. Smoking restricted. 50% deposit req. 15-
day cancellation notice req., less 10% fee. 2-night min. stay on wknds. 3-night
min. stay on holiday wknds.

Notes: Three-story inn. Dining room with phone, TV. Library. Decorated in colonial style. Board games available. Guests have access to laundry facilities. Roof deck with view of Nantucket Harbor. Lawn games available. Small private parties accommodated. Japanese, German spoken.*

The Woodbox Inn
29 Fair St., Nantucket, MA 02554
(508) 228-0587
Innkeeper: Dexter Tutein
Rooms: 3 plus 6 suites, all w/pvt. bath, incl. 3 w/phone, 6 w/fireplace. Located in 2 bldgs.
Rates: $120/room, $150-$195/suite. Seasonal variations.
Credit cards: None
Restrictions: No pets. 50% deposit req., refunded upon cancellation only if re-rented. 3-night min. stay, July. 4-night min. stay, Aug. Closed on Mondays.
Notes: Built in 1709. Dinner available. Handicapped access. French, German spoken.

NEWBURYPORT (5)

Clark Currier Inn
45 Green St., Newburyport, MA 01950
(508) 465-8363
Innkeeper: Mary, Bob and Melissa Nolan
Rooms: 8 w/pvt. bath, incl. 5 w/phone
Rates: $65-$125, incl. cont. brk., afternoon refreshment. Seasonal variations.
Credit cards: Most major cards
Restrictions: No pets, smoking. One night's deposit req. 7-day cancellation notice req. 2-night min. stay during peak season. 3-night min. stay on holidays.
Notes: Three-story square, Federal-period house built in 1803. Features window seats, dentil mouldings, indian shutters, wide pumpkin pine flooring. Wide center hall, "good-morning staircase." Garden room. Parlor with original Samual McIntyre fireplace. Decorated with antiques. Restored garden, gazebo. Small private parties accommodated.

The Windsor House
38 Federal St., Newburyport, MA 01950
(508) 462-3778
Innkeeper: Judith and John Harris
Rooms: 6 w/phone, incl. 3 w/pvt. bath
Rates: $75-$115, incl. full brk., afternoon refreshment. Seasonal variations. Discount avail. for extended stay.
Credit cards: Most major cards
Restrictions: Pets welcome with prior arrangement. No smoking. One night's deposit req. 15-day cancellation notice req., less $5.00 fee. 2-night min. stay on wknds. from May–Nov. 3-night min. stay on holiday wknds.
Notes: 3½-story English country mansion built in 1786 as a wedding present in combination of Federal, Georgian, Colonial styles. Recently refurbished. Parlor. Sitting room with TV. Formal dining room with fireplace, beehive ovens. Decorated with period furniture. Brick courtyard. Cornish weekends and Celtic festivals organized.*

NORWELL (7)

1810 House B & B
147 Old Oaken Bucket Rd., Norwell, MA 02061
(617) 659-2532
Innkeeper: Susanne and Harold Tuttle
Rooms: 3, incl. 1 w/pvt. bath
Rates: $55, incl. full brk.
Credit cards: None
Restrictions: No children under 6, smoking. One-night's deposit req. 14-day cancellation notice req., less $10.00 fee.
Notes: Two-story house with beamed ceilings, 3 working fireplaces, wide pine floors, and hand stenciled walls. Family room with piano, TV/VCR. Furnished with antiques, oriental carpets, period pieces.*

OAK BLUFFS (8)

Tivoli Inn Bed & Breakfast
222 Circuit Ave., Box 1033, Oak Bluffs, MA 02557
(508) 693-7928
Innkeeper: Lisa and Lori Katsounakis
Rooms: 7, incl. 6 w/TV, 3 w/pvt. bath
Rates: $50-$135, incl. cont. brk., afternoon refreshment. Seasonal variations. Discount avail. for extended stay.
Credit cards: Most major cards
Restrictions: No pets. 50% deposit req. 14-day cancellation notice req., less 10% fee. 2-night min. stay on wknds.
Notes: Two-story inn with balcony and wrap-around latticed porch. Recently renovated. Living room with piano. Guests have access to phone.*

ORLEANS (8)

Academy Place Bed and Breakfast
8 Academy Pl., Box 1407, Orleans, MA 02653
(508) 255-3181
Innkeeper: Sandy and Charlres Terrell
Rooms: 5, incl 3 w/pvt bath. All
Rates: $55-$75, incl. cont. brk., afternoon refreshment. Discount avail. for extended stay. Seasonal variations.
Credit cards: None
Restrictions: No children under 6, pets, smoking. One night's deposit req. 48-hour cancellation notice req., less $20 fee. 2-night min. stay on wknds. July 1–Labor Day. Closed Columbus Day–Memorial Day.
Notes: Cape Code house built in 1752. Dining room. Guest lounge with TV, games, books. Beamed ceilings, leaded-glass windows. Farmer's porch. Furnished with antiques, Oriental rugs, handmade quilts.

The Farmhouse
163 Beach Rd., Orleans, MA 02653
(508) 255-6654
Innkeeper: Dot Standish
Rooms: 8 w/fireplace, incl. 5 w/pvt. bath, 2 w/TV. Located in 2 bldgs.
Rates: $52-$95, incl. cont. brk. Seasonal variations. Discount avail. for extended stay.

THE FARMHOUSE

Credit cards: MC, V
Restrictions: No children under 6, pets. Smoking restricted. Deposit req. 2-week cancellation notice req.
Notes: Farmhouse built in 1870. Fully restored. Furnished with antiques. Some rooms with ocean views. Deck.

Morgan's Way Bed and Breakfast
Nine Morgan's Way, Orleans, MA 02653
(508) 255-0831, (508) 255-0831
Innkeeper: Page McMahan and Will Joy
Rooms: 3, incl. 2 w/pvt. bath, plus cottage w/pvt. bath, phone, TV. Located in 2 bldgs.
Rates: $90/room, incl. full brk., $650/cottage/week, incl. cont. brk., champagne for special occasions. Seasonal variations.
Credit cards: Most major cards
Restrictions: No children under 12, pets, smoking. Full prepayment req. 14-day cancellation notice req. 2-night min. stay/rooms, 7-night min. stay/cottage.
Notes: Contemporary house with cathedral ceilings, oak beams, arched windows, oriental carpets, porcelains. Located on 5 wooded acres with gardens. Two living rooms with TV, VCR. Guests have access to heated swimming pool, deck, refrigerator. Handicapped access.*

MORGAN'S WAY BED AND BREAKFAST

PETERSHAM (4)

Winterwood at Petersham
19 N. Main St., Box 176, Petersham, MA 01366
(508) 724-8885
Innkeeper: Jean and Robert Day
Rooms: 6 w/pvt. bath, incl. 5 w/fireplace
Rates: $80, incl. cont. brk.
Credit cards: Most major cards
Restrictions: No pets. Smoking restricted. Deposit req. 2-week cancellation notice
   req.
Notes: Two-story Greek Revival inn built in 1842 as private summer home. Recently
restored. Located just off the common, across from a thirty-two-acre wildlife
meadow preserve. Living room with fireplace, porches. Small private parties ac-
commodated. Listed on the National Register of Historic Homes.*

PLYMOUTH (7)

Foxglove Cottage Bed & Breakfast
101 Sandwich Rd., Plymouth, MA 02360
(508) 747-6576, (508) 747-7622
Innkeeper: Mr. and Mrs. Charles K. Cowan
Rooms: 2 w/pvt. bath, fireplace
Rates: $75, incl. full brk., afternoon refreshment. Discount avail. for extended stay.
Credit cards: Most major cards
Restrictions: No children under 12, pets, smoking. One night's deposit req. 7-day
   cancellation req.
Notes: Restored Cape Cod house with wide pine board floors, built in 1820. Com-
mon room with video library, TV. Deck. Furnished in Victorian English and Amer-
ican antiques.*

PROVINCETOWN (8)

Captain Lysander Inn
96 Commercial St., Provincetown, MA 02657
(508) 487-2253, (508) 487-7579
Innkeeper: Mark Burdwell
Rooms: 13 w/pvt. bath, incl. 9 w/phone, 1 w/fireplace, plus cottage. Located in 2
   bldgs.
Rates: $75-$95/room, $125/suite, $150/cottage, all incl. cont. brk. Seasonal variations.
Credit cards: MC, V
Restrictions: No pets. Smoking restricted. 50% deposit req. 7-day cancellation notice req., refunded, less 15% fee, upon cancellation only if room re-rented. 4-
   night min. stay on holiday wknds.
Notes: Federal-style sea captain's house built in 1852. Bow deck overlooking
Provincetown Harbor. Sun porch, front parlor. Reading room with fireplace. Furnished with Queen Anne-style antiques, Oriental rugs. Off-street parking available.*

The Chicago House
6 Winslow St., Provincetown, MA 02657
(508) 487-0437, (800) 733-7869
Innkeeper: Randy Godfrey

Rooms: 10, plus 1 suite w/cable TV, 1 apt. w/cable TV, kitchen, 1 townhouse w/cable TV, kitchen, all w/pvt. bath. Located in 2 bldgs.
Rates: $49-$105/room, $130/suite, all incl. cont. brk. Seasonal variations.
Credit cards: Most major cards
Restrictions: Children welcome in season. Pets welcome with prior approval. 50% deposit req. 21-day cancellation notice req. 3-night min. stay on holiday wknds.
Notes: Main house dates back to 1830s, and annex building early 1780s. Common room. Living room with TV, VCR. Two decks. Garden. Limited free parking available. Limited handicapped access. Airport pickup available.

The Lamplighter Inn
26 Bradford St., Provincetown, MA 02657
(508) 487-2529, (508) 487-0079
Innkeeper: Michael Novik, Joe Czarnecki
Rooms: 7 w/TV, incl. 5 w/pvt. bath, plus 2 suites w/pvt. bath, TV, plus 1 cottage
Rates: $95/room, $125/suite, $140/cottage, all incl. cont. brk. Special pkgs. avail.
Credit cards: Most major cards
Restrictions: No children, pets, alchohol. Smoking restricted. 50% deposit req. 2-week cancellation notice req., less 20% fee. 3-night min. stay in cottage. 3-night min. stay on summer wknds. 5-night min. stay on 4th of July and Labor Day wknds.
Notes: Antique Federal Style two-story sea captain's house built in the early 1853. Located on hilltop overlooking Bay and Cape. Dining room, common room. Patio, third floor deck. Ice, telephone, bike rack and discount passes on whale watches available. Airport and boat pickup, parking available.*

Land's End Inn
22 Commercial St., Provincetown, MA 02657-1997
(508) 487-0706
Innkeeper: David Schoolman, Jordan Grossl
Rooms: 14 w/pvt. bath, plus 2 suites w/pvt. bath, cooking facilities
Rates: $98-$155/room, $130-$240/suite, all incl. cont. brk. Seasonal variations. Discount avail. for extended stay. Special pkgs. avail.
Credit cards: None
Restrictions: No children under 10, pets. Min. 50% deposit req. 10-day cancellation notice req., less 15% fee. 2-night min. stay on wknds. from September 12–June 27. 7-night min. stay from June 18–September 12.
Notes: Victorian shingle-style summer bungalow built in 1904. Located on a West End hill overlooking Provincetown and Cape Cod Bay. Living rooms, common areas, porch overlooking gardens. Common rooms with classical music, books, magazines. Furnished in eclectic Victorian style. Suites sleep 4, some rooms sleep 5. Resident pets.

Windamar House
568 Commercial St., Provincetown, MA 02657
(508) 487-0599, (508) 487-7505
Innkeeper: Bette Adams
Rooms: 6, incl. 2 w/pvt. bath, 2 w/TV, plus 2 apts. w/pvt. bath, TV
Rates: $60-$125/room, $110-$135/apts., all incl. cont. brk. Seasonal variations. Discount avail. for extended stay during mid & off-seasons.
Credit cards: None

Restrictions: No children, pets, smoking. 50% deposit req. 21-day cancellation notice req. less 25% fee. 4-night min. stay in apt.

Notes: Three-story, white clapboard sea captain's house built in 1840. Landscaped grounds with English flower gardens, grape arbor overlooking Cape Cod Bay. Common room with TV, VCR, film library. Furnished with antiques, original artwork. Guests have access to refrigerator, microwave.*

REHOBOTH (7)

Perryville Inn
157 Perryville Rd., Rehoboth, MA 02769
(508) 252-9239, (508) 252-5718

Innkeeper: Tom and Betsy Charnecki
Rooms: 4 plus 1 suite, incl. 3 w/pvt. bath
Rates: $50-$85/room, $85/suite, all incl. cont. brk.
Credit cards: Most major cards
Restrictions: No pets, smoking. Deposit req. 14-day cancellation notice req. 2-night min. stay on Summer and Fall wknds.
Notes: Three-story 19th-century Victorian farmhouse built in 1820s. Located on 4½ acres. Inn overlooks 18-hole golf course. Two sitting rooms. Furnished with antiques and handmade quilts. Mill pond. Bicycles available. Outdoor activities available. Listed on the National Register of Historic Places.*

ROCKPORT (5)

ADDISON CHOATE INN

Addison Choate Inn
49 Broadway, Rockport, MA 01966-1527
(508) 546-7543, (800) 245-7543

Innkeeper: Knox and Shirley Johnson
Rooms: 6 w/pvt. bath, plus 3 suites w/pvt. bath, TV. Located in 2 bldgs.
Rates: $65-$85/room, $85-$110/suite, all incl. expanded cont. brk. Seasonal variations. Discount avail. for extended stay.
Credit cards: Most major cards
Restrictions: No pets, smoking. One night's deposit req. 10-day cancellation notice req., less $15.00 fee. 2-night min. stay on summer wknds. Closed Jan.

Notes: Two-story Colonial farmhouse with pine plank flooring built in 1851. Carriage House. Located on landscaped grounds. Living room with library, stereo, TV. Dining room. Porch with flower boxes. Swimming pool, BBQ. Furnished with antiques, original artwork.*

The Inn on Cove Hill
37 Mount Pleasant St., Rockport, MA 01966
(508) 546-2701

Innkeeper: Marjorie and John Pratt
Rooms: 11 w/TV, incl. 9 w/pvt. bath
Rates: $49-$99, incl. cont. brk. Seasonal variations.
Credit cards: None
Restrictions: Children restricted. No pets, smoking. One night's deposit req. 10-day cancellation notice req. 2-night min. stay, July, August, September wknds.
Notes: Three-story Federal-style inn built in 1791 from proceeds of pirate's gold found at nearby Gully Point. Fully restored in 1985. Entrance hall with crafted spiral staircase. Living room, two outdoor porches with view of harbor and ocean, garden patio. Canopy beds. Furnished with antiques and period furniture. Off-street parking available.

Rocky Shores Inn & Cottages
65 Eden Rd., Rockport, MA 01966
(800) 348-4003

Innkeeper: Gunter and Renate Kostka
Rooms: 11, incl. 1 w/pvt. entrance, plus 11 cottages, all w/pvt. bath, TV. Located in 12 bldgs.
Rates: $103/room, incl. cont. brk., $106/cottage. Seasonal variations.
Credit cards: Most major cards
Restrictions: No pets. Smoking restricted. Min. one night's deposit req. 14-day written cancellation notice req., less $10.00 fee. 3-night min. stay for cottages.
Notes: Two-story house built on hilltop in 1905, cottages built in 1950s. Some overlook gardens. New England decor. Operated as inn since 1948. Most rooms and dining room overlook ocean. Living room, sun room, porch. German spoken.

Sally Webster Inn
34 Mt. Pleasant St., Rockport, MA 01966
(508) 546-9251

Innkeeper: Tiffany Traynor, David Muhlenberg
Rooms: 8 w/pvt. bath.
Rates: $55-$90, incl. full brk. Discount avail. for extended stay.
Credit cards: Most major cards
Restrictions: No children under 12, pets. Smoking restricted. One night's deposit req. 10-day cancellation notice req.
Notes: Two-story house built in 1832. Dining room. Common room with 1 of 6 fireplaces. Decorated with period antiques and reproductions. Brick terraces. Colonial flower and herb gardens.

Seacrest Manor
131 Marmion Way, Rockport, MA 01966
(508) 546-2211

Innkeeper: Leighton Saville, Dwight MacCormack, Jr.
Rooms: 8 w/cable TV, incl. 6 w/pvt. bath. Suites avail.

SEACREST MANOR

Rates: $88-$120, incl. full brk., afternoon refreshment. Seasonal variations.
Credit cards: None
Restrictions: No children under 16, pets, smoking. Min. one night's deposit req. 14-
day cancellation notice req., less $10 fee. 2-night min. stay on wknds. 3-night min.
stay on holiday wknds. Closed Dec.–Mar.
Notes: Built as 2-story private home. Located on 2 wooded acres with ocean and
garden view. Deck overlooks Mount Agamenticus. Dining room with fireplace overlooks gardens. Library with fireplace. Living room. Furnished with antiques. Bicycles available. Gardens. Off-street parking available. Limited French, Spanish
spoken.

SALEM (5)

Coach House Inn
284 Lafayette St., Salem, MA 01970
(508) 744-4092

Innkeeper: Patricia Kessler
Rooms: 6 w/TV, incl. 4 w/pvt. bath plus 5 suites, w/pvt. bath, TV
Rates: $72-$85/room, $79-$155/suite, all incl. cont. brk.
Credit cards: Most major cards
Restrictions: No pets, smoking. One night's deposit req. Min. 72-hour cancellation
notice req. 2-night min. stay on some wknds. and holidays.
Notes: Victorian sea captain's mansion built in 1879. Fully restored, redecorated
with antiques. Off-street parking available.*

The Inn at Seven Winter Street
7 Winter St., Salem, MA 01970
(508) 745-9520, (508) 745-5052

Innkeeper: Mr. D.L. and Jill E. Coté and Sally Flint
Rooms: 8 w/pvt. bath, phone, TV, incl. 4 w/fireplace, plus 2 suites w/pvt. bath,
phone, TV
Rates: $85-$115/room, $100-$135/suite, all incl. cont. brk., evening refreshment
Credit cards: Most major cards
Restrictions: No pets, smoking. One night's deposit req. 7-day cancellation req. 2-
night min. stay on July–Oct. wknds.
Notes: Three story French Second-Empire Victorian house. Built in 1870. Parlor
with fireplace. Furnished with period antiques. *

Salem Inn
7 Summer St., Salem, MA 01970
(508) 741-0680, (800) 446-2995, (508) 744-8924
Innkeeper: Richard and Diane Pabich
Rooms: 16 w/pvt. bath, phone, TV, incl. 10 w/fireplace, plus 5 suites w/pvt. bath, phone, cable TV, incl. 1 w/fireplace
Rates: $80-$125/room, $100-$150/suite, all incl. cont. brk., evening refreshment
Credit cards: Most major cards
Restrictions: Smoking restricted. One-night's deposit req. 7-day cancellation notice req., less $15.00 fee.
Notes: Two-story Federal-style townhouse built in 1834. Fully restored. Restaurant with two dining rooms on lower level. Enclosed brick courtyard with rose gardens. Furnished with period antiques.*

The Suzannah Flint House
98 Essex St., Salem, MA 01970
(508) 744-5281, (800) 752-5281
Innkeeper: Scott Eklind
Rooms: 4 w/pvt. bath, TV
Rates: $49-$109, incl. cont. brk. Discount avail. for extended stay, AARP members, and students.
Credit cards: Most major cards
Restrictions: No pets. Deposit req. 72-hour cancellation notice req.
Notes: Federalist house built in 1806. Located one block from waterfront. Antique fireplaces. Garden.

SANDWICH (8)

Bay Beach Bed & Breakfast
1-3 Bay Beach Ln., Box 151, Sandwich, MA 02563
(508) 888-8813
Innkeeper: Emily and Reale J. Lemieux
Rooms: Sandwich3 plus 2/suites all w/pvt. bath, TV, fireplace. Located in two bldgs.
Rates: $125-$175/room, $150-$195/suite, all incl. full brk. Seasonal variations.
Credit cards: MC, V
Restrictions: No children under 16, pets, smoking. One night's deposit req. 21-day cancellation notice req. 2-night min. stay on wknds. 3-night min. stay on holiday wknds.
Notes: Three-story Cape Cod-style house built in 1987. Living rooms with fireplace, piano. Sitting room with fireplace, board games, library. Dining area. Private decks overlooking ocean. Furnished with wicker. French spoken.*

Captain Ezra Nye House
152 Main St., Sandwich, MA 02563
(508) 888-6142, (800) 388-2278, (508) 833-2897
Innkeeper: Harry and Elaine Dickson
Rooms: 6, incl. 4 w/pvt. bath, 1 w/fireplace, plus 1 suite w/pvt. bath
Rates: $55-$90/room, $85-$90/suite, all incl. full brk. Seasonal variations.
Credit cards: Most major cards
Restrictions: No children under 6, pets, smoking. One night's deposit req. 48-hr. cancellation notice req. 2-night min. stay on holidays and wknds.

Notes: Two-story Federal sea captain's house built in 1829. Fully restored. Dining room, parlor with piano, den with fireplace, TV, games, library. Decorated with heirlooms, Oriental rugs, antiques. Spanish spoken.*

Dillingham House
71 Main St., Sandwich, MA 02563
(508) 833-0065

Innkeeper: Kathleen Kenney
Rooms: 4, incl. 2 w/pvt. bath, 1 w/fireplace
Rates: $65-$75, incl. cont. brk. Seasonal variations.
Credit cards: None
Restrictions: No children under 12. One night's deposit req. 7-day cancellation notice req.
Notes: Two-story Colonial house with wide pine floors built about 1650. Keeping room with baby grand piano, library. Sitting room with TV. Furnished with period antiques.

SUMMER HOUSE

Summer House
158 Old Main St., Sandwich, MA 02563
(508) 888-4991

Innkeeper: David and Kay Merrell
Rooms: 5, incl. 1 w/pvt. bath, 4 w/fireplace
Rates: $55-$75, incl. full brk., afternoon refreshment. Discount avail. for extended stay. Seasonal variations.
Credit cards: Most major cards
Restrictions: No children under 6, pets. Smoking restricted. Min 50% deposit req. 10-day cancellation notice req. 2-night min. stay on holiday, summer, and fall wknds.
Notes: Greek Revival house built in 1835. Fully restored. Formal breakfast room with library, parlor, each with marble fireplace, original woodwork. Furnished with antiques, hand-stitched quilts, heirloom linens. Sunporch with wicker furniture.*

Villaqe Inn at Sandwich
4 Jarvis St., Box 951, Sandwich, MA 02563
(508) 833-0363, (800) 922-9989

Innkeeper: Patricia and Winifried Platz
Rooms: 8 rooms, incl. 6 w/pvt. bath, 2 w/fireplace
Rates: $80-$95, incl. expanded cont. brk. Seasonal variations.
Credit cards: Most major cards
Restrictions: No children under 12, pets, smoking. 14-day cancellation notice req.
   2-night min. stay on wknds.
Notes: Federal-style house built approx. 1844. Fully restored. Property is surrounded by gardens and 250 rose bushes. Two common rooms and a wrap-around porch with rocking chairs. All furniture is custom-made by owner. German spoken.*

SCITUATE (6)

The Allen House
18 Allen Place, Scituate, MA 02066-1302
(617) 545-8221, (617) 545-4470
Innkeeper: Christine and Ian Gilmour
Rooms: 6, incl. 4 w/pvt. bath, 1 w/TV
Rates: $79-$119, incl. full brk. Discount avail. for mid-week stay. Seasonal variations.
Credit cards: Most major cards
Restrictions: No children under 12, pets. Smoking restricted. One night's deposit
   req. 10-day cancellation notice req., less $10.00 fee.
Notes: Three-story Victorian house built in 1905. Formal dining room and parlor with fireplace, TV. Library. Decorated with antiques. Some French, German, Spanish spoken. Off-street parking available. Handicapped access. Resident cats.*

SHEFFIELD (1)

Race Brook Lodge
864 S. Undermountain Rd., Sheffield, MA 01257
(413) 229-2916, (413) 229-6629
Innkeeper: Eve Van Syckle
Rooms: 20 in summer, 14 in winter, incl. 18 w/pvt. bath. Suites avail. Located in 3
   bldgs.
Rates: $65-$155, incl. cont. brk. Seasonal variations.
Credit cards: Most major cards
Restrictions: Smoking restricted. 14-day cancellation notice req. 2-night min. stay
   on 3-day wknds.
Notes: Two-story hand-hewn and timber peg barn built in the 1790s. Renovated in and has operated as inn since 1992. Central hall, books, games, maps, TV corner. Furnished in informal country style. Guests have access to kitchen. Jazz sessions hosted on Sundays. Small private parties accommodated. Handicapped access. Spanish spoken.

Ramblewood Inn
Rte. 41, Box 729, Sheffield, MA 01257
(413) 229-3363
Innkeeper: June and Martin Ederer
Rooms: 6 w/phone, incl. 5 w/pvt. bath, plus 1 suite w/pvt. bath, phone, TV
Rates: $85-$110/room, $180/suite, all incl. full brk. Seasonal variations. Discount
   avail. for extended stay.
Credit cards: MC, V

RAMBLEWOOD INN

Restrictions: No pets, smoking. 50% deposit req. 14-day cancellation notice req. 2-night min. stay on summer and holiday wknds.
Notes: Country-style lake-side house surrounded with pines, overlooking mountain Common room with fireplace, board games. Furnished with antiques. Garden. Small private parties accommodated.*

SOUTH CHATHAM (8)

Ye Olde Nantucket House
2647 Main St., Box 468, South Chatham, MA 02659
(508) 432-5641
Innkeeper: Steve and Ellen Londo
Rooms: 5 w/pvt. bath
Rates: $68-$85, incl. cont. brk. Seasonal variations.
Credit cards: Most major cards
Restrictions: No children under 8, pets. Smoking restricted. 50% deposit req. 7-day cancellation notice req., less $15.00 fee. 2-night min. stay on wknds. from Memorial Day–Sept. 15. 3-night min. stay on major holidays.
Notes: Two-story Greek Revival house built on Nantucket Island in 1830. Moved to its present location in 1867. Decorated with stenciled walls, pine floors. Furnished with antiques.*

THE LITTLE RED HOUSE

SOUTH DARTMOUTH (7)

The Little Red House
631 Elm St., South Dartmouth, MA 02748
(508) 996-4554

Innkeeper: Meryl Zwirblis
Rooms: 3, no pvt. bath
Rates: $55-$65, incl. full brk.
Credit cards: Most major cards
Restrictions: No children under 15, pets, smoking. 50% deposit req. 14-day cancellation notice req., less $10.00 fee. 2-night min. stay on wknds. from July 1–Aug. 31. Closed Christmas week and Thanksgiving.
Notes: Two-story Dutch Colonial house. Living room with fireplace. Dining room, gazebo. Furnished in country style with antiques.*

Salt Marsh Farm
322 Smith Neck Rd., South Dartmouth, MA 02748
(508) 992-0980

Innkeeper: Sally and Larry Brownell
Rooms: 2 w/pvt. bath
Rates: $65-$85, incl. full brk., afternoon refreshment. Seasonal variations. Discount avail. for extended stay.
Credit cards: MC, V
Restrictions: No children under 5, pets, smoking. Deposit req. 14-day cancellation notice req., less $10.00 fee. 2-night min. stay on holidays and summer wknds.
Notes: Two-story Federal farmhouse built in 1790. Located on ninety acre nature preserve. Has operated as inn since 1988. Living room/library with fireplace, board games, puzzles. Keeping room, dining room. Furnished with family antiques. Bicycles, including tandem available. Lawn for games and chairs or hammock for reading.

CAPTAIN NICKERSON INN

SOUTH DENNIS (8)

Captain Nickerson Inn
333 Main St., South Dennis, MA 02660
(508) 398-5966, (800) 282-1619

Innkeeper: David and Patricia York

Rooms: 5, incl. 3 w/pvt. bath,
Rates: $60-$85 incl. full brk., afternoon refreshment. Discount avail. for senior citizen, extended stays. Seasonal variations.
Credit cards: Most major cards
Restrictions: Smoking restricted. Deposit req. 14-day cancellation notice req. Min. 2-night min. stay for most holidays.
Notes: Two-story Victorian sea captain's house built in 1828 and changed to present Queen Anne style in 1879. Living room with fireplace, cable TV, VCR and stained-glass windows. Dining room with fireplace and stained-glass picture window. Front porch with wicker rockers and tables. Decorated with Oriental and hand woven rugs. Bicycles, board games, video movie available.*

MERRELL TAVERN INN

SOUTH LEE (1)

Merrell Tavern Inn
1565 Pleasant St., South Lee, MA 01260
(413) 243-1794

Innkeeper: Charles and Faith Reynolds
Rooms: 9 w/pvt. bath, phone, incl. 3 w/fireplace
Rates: $85-$145, incl. full brk, afternoon refreshment. Seasonal variations.
Credit cards: MC, V
Restrictions: No children, pets, smoking. Full prepayment req. 14-day cancellation notice req. 2-night min. stay on wknds. 3-night min. stay on summer wknds.
Notes: Built in 1794 as private residence with antique woodwork, fixtures, and original circular Colonial bar on Housatonic River and later used as stagecoach inn. Guest parlor, TV room. Central hallway with period grandfather clock. Common room with Colonial fireplace and beehive oven. Furnished with antiques, canopy beds. Gazebo, tea house, porches. Recipient of 1982 Preservation Award-Massachusetts Historical Commission. Listed on the National Register of Historic Places.

STERLING (4)

Sterling Orchards' B & B
60 Kendall Hill Rd., Sterling, MA 01564-0455
(508) 422-6595, 422-6170

STERLING ORCHARD'S B & B

Innkeeper: Robert and Shirley P. Smiley
Rooms: 2 suites w/pvt. bath, TV
Rates: $65-$80, incl. full brk., afternoon refreshment. Discount avail. for extended and senior citizen stays.
Credit cards: None
Restrictions: No pets, smoking. Deposit req. 2-night min. stay on Columbus wknd.
Notes: Two story colonial farmhouse with post and beam construction, 12-ft. center chimney, original wide pine floors, built in 1740. Breakfast solarium added in 1985. Lap pool in fenced yard. Yard and board games available.

STOCKBRIDGE (1)

Arbor Rose B & B
8 Yale Hill, Box 114, Stockbridge, MA 01262
(413) 298-4744
Innkeeper: Christina Alsop & family
Rooms: 4, incl. 2 w/pvt. bath
Rates: $60-$140, incl. full brk. Discount avail. for mid-week and extended stays.
Credit cards: Most major cards
Restrictions: No pets. One night's deposit req. 10-day cancellation notice req.
Notes: New England millhouse with pond. Parlor with fireplace and TV. Gardens. Mountain view. Decorated with antiques, and paintings.

Berkshire Thistle B & B
P.O. Box 1227 RT. 7, Stockbridge, MA 01262
(413) 298-3188
Innkeeper: Gene and Diane Elling
Rooms: 4 plus 1 suite, all w/pvt. bath, incl. 2 w/TV
Rates: $65-$120, incl. full brk. Seasonal variations. Discount avail. for extended stay.
Credit cards: Most major cards
Restrictions: No children under 12, pets, smoking. One night's deposit req. 10-day cancellation notice req. less 10% fee. 2-night min. stay on wknds., June 1–October 31.
Notes: A Colonial reproduction house on a hill on five acres. Common room has multi-use game table, TV, reading area. Wrap-around porch. Outside pool and lawn.

The Inn at Stockbridge
P.O. Box 618, Stockbridge, MA 01262
(413) 298-3337, (413) 298-3406

Innkeeper: Lee and Don Weitz
Rooms: 6 plus 2 suites, all w/pvt. bath, phone, incl. 1 w/TV
Rates: $80-$95/room, $160-$135/suite, all incl. full brk., evening refreshment. Discount avail. for extended and mid-week stays. Seasonal variations. Special pkgs. avail.
Credit cards: Most major cards
Restrictions: No children under 12, pets, smoking. One night's deposit req. 14-day cancellation notice req. 2-night min. stay on wknds. 3-night min. stay during Tanglewood season and holidays. Closed Mar. and Apr.
Notes: Pillared Georgian Colonial-style house built in 1906 as private residence. Located on twelve landscaped acres. Two living rooms, each with fireplace, one with baby grand piano and other musical instruments, the other with library. Dining room. Furnished with antiques and reproductions. Swimming pool, deck, lounge area. Small private parties accommodated.*

STURBRIDGE (4)

Colonel Ebenezer Crafts Inn
Rte. 131, Box 187, Sturbridge, MA 01566
(508) 347-3313, (800) 782-5425, (508) 347-5073

Innkeeper: Shirley Washburn
Rooms: 7 w/pvt. bath, incl. 1 w/TV, phone, plus 1 cottage suite w/pvt. bath
Rates: $69/room, $150/suite, all incl. cont. brk., afternoon refreshment. Seasonal variations.
Credit cards: Most major cards
Restrictions: No pets. Smoking restricted. One night's deposit req. 2-day cancellation notice req. 2-night min. stay on wknds. 3-night min. stay on holiday wknds.
Notes: Farmhouse built in 1786. Located on 51 acres with 3½ acres of manicured lawns. Formal sitting room with grand piano, phone. Library with fireplace. Sun room with TV. Terrace. Decorated in Colonial style with antiques. Swimming pool. Small private parties accommodated.

Sturbridge Country Inn
P.O. Box 60, Sturbridge, MA 01566
(508) 347-5503, (508) 347-4319

Innkeeper: Kevin MacConnell
Rooms: 8 plus 1 suite, all w/pvt. bath, whirlpool tub, fireplace, TV
Rates: $69-$129/room, $119-$149/suite, all incl. cont. brk., evening refreshment. Seasonal variations. Discount avail. for mid-week stay.
Credit cards: Most major cards
Restrictions: No children under 5. 7-day cancellation notice req.
Notes: Two-story inn built in the 1840s. Some rooms w/sunporch, vaulted ceiling. Suite w/skylights, sitting room, wet bar.*

TYRINGHAM (1)

The Golden Goose
123 Main Rd., Box 336, Tyringham, MA 01264-0336
(413) 243-3008

Innkeeper: Lilja and Joseph Rizzo
Rooms: 7, incl. 4 w/pvt. bath, plus 1 studio w/pvt. bath
Rates: $80-$110/room, $120-$125/apt., all incl. full brk., afternoon and evening refreshment. Seasonal variations. Discount avail. for extended stay.
Credit cards: Most major cards
Restrictions: No pets. Smoking restricted. Deposit req. 14-day min cancellation notice req. less 15% service fee. 2-night min. stay during some wknds. 3-night min. stay during holidays.
Notes: Two-story Colonial farmhouse. Has operated as inn since the early 1800s. Located on six landscaped acres. Two sitting rooms, each with fireplace, one with collection of classical and jazz records and tapes from 1940-70. Dining room with French doors leading to deck overlooking Appalachian Trail. Furnished with Victorian antiques. Lawn games, BBQ available.*

VINEYARD HAVEN (8)

Captain Dexter House
100 Main St., Box 2457, Vineyard Haven, MA 02568
(508) 693-6564
Innkeeper: Alisa Lengel
Rooms: 7, incl. 2 w/fireplace, plus 1 suite, all w/pvt. bath
Rates: $65-$160/room, $105-$160/suite, incl. cont. brk., evening refreshment. Seasonal variations. Discount avail. for mid-week and offseason stays.
Credit cards: Most major cards
Restrictions: No pets. Smoking restricted. Min. 50% deposit req. 14-day written cancellation notice req.
Notes: Early Victorian-style sea captain's house built in 1843. Living room/library with Rumford fireplace, formal dining room. Parlor with fireplace. Wrap-around porch. Restored and refurbished with 18th-century antiques, original woodwork and wide floorboards, period reproduction wallpaper, Oriental rugs. Some bedrooms have canopied four-poster beds. Flower gardens. Guests have access to refrigerator, locked garage. Car reservations should be made for ferry by calling (617) 540-2022 in Woods Hole. Passenger ferry service also available from New Bedford, Hyannis, and Falmouth.*

Nancy's Auberge
102 Main St., Box 4433, Vineyard Haven, MA 02568
(508) 693-4433
Innkeeper: Nancy Hurd
Rooms: 3, incl. 1 w/pvt. bath
Rates: $78-$98, incl. cont. brk. Seasonal variations.
Credit cards: Most major cards
Restrictions: No pets, smoking. Deposit req. 15-day cancellation notice req., less 10% fee. 2-night min. stay on summer wknds. 3-night min. stay on holiday wknds.
Notes: Off-street parking available. Handicapped access.*

Thorncroft Inn
278 Main St., Box 1022, Vineyard Haven, MA 02568-1022
(508) 693-3333, (800) 332-1236
Innkeeper: Karl and Lynn Buder
Rooms: 12 plus 1 suite, all w/pvt. bath, phone, TV, incl. 8 rooms plus 1 suite w/fireplace. Located in 2 bldgs.

Rates: $149-$349/room, $299/suite, all incl. full brk., afternoon refreshment. Seasonal variations.

Credit cards: Most major cards

Restrictions: No children, pets, smoking. Min. one night's deposit req. 14-day cancellation notice req. 3-night min. stay on major holidays, seasonal wknds. Couples only.

Notes: Main House built in 1918. Located on 3.5 wooded and landscaped acres. Two-story Carriage House reconstructed in 1985. Three-story Greenwood House built in 1906. Craftsman bungalow built in 1920. Located one mile from ferry dock on Martha's Vineyard. Formal dining room, Victorian reading room, wicker sun room with TV, outdoor shower. Furnished with antiques. Guests have access to refrigerator, in-room computer hook-up. Small private parties accommodated. Five-course dinners, off-street parking available. Contact Steamship Authority for reservations on ferry departing from Woods Hole on Cape Cod (508) 540-2022. French and Russian spoken.*

Twin Oaks Inn
8 Edgartown Rd., Box 1767, Vineyard Haven, MA 02568
(508) 693-8633, (508) 693-7332

Innkeeper: Doris L. Stewart

Rooms: 2, incl. 1 w/pvt. bath, plus 2 suites, incl. 1 w/pvt. bath, plus 1 apartment w/pvt. entrance, fireplace, sunroom, kitchen, bath

Rates: $80-$135/room, $145/suite, all incl. cont. brk., afternoon refreshment. Seasonal variations. Discount avail. for extended stay.

Credit cards: MC, V

Restrictions: No pets, smoking. Deposit req.

Notes: Two-story Dutch Colonial-style inn was built in 1906. Wrap-around enclosed front porch. Living room, dining room. Backyard.*

WAKEFIELD (5)

Heywood Wakefield Bed and Breakfast
87 Elm St., Wakefield, MA 01880
(617) 245-2627, (617) 246-4916

Innkeeper: Charles and Shirley Townshend

Rooms: 2, no pvt. bath

Rates: $55-$65, incl. cont. brk. Discount avail. for extended stay. Seasonal variations.

Credit cards: None

Restrictions: No children under 12, pets, smoking. Deposit req. 3-day cancellation notice req.

Notes: Living room with TV.

WARE (2)

The 1880 Inn Bed & Breakfast
14 Pleasant St., Ware, MA 01082
(413) 967-7847

Innkeeper: Margaret and Stan Skutnik

Rooms: 5, incl. 2 w/pvt. bath

Rates: $45-$65, incl. full brk. Discount avail. for senior citizens.

Credit cards: None

Restrictions: No pets, smoking. Deposit req. Min. 14-day cancellation notice req.

Notes: Colonial building with hardwood floors built in 1876. Common room with board games. Furnished with antiques.

Wildwood Inn
121 Church St., Ware, MA 01082
(413) 967-7798
Innkeeper: Fraidell Fenster, Richard Watson
Rooms: 7, no pvt. bath
Rates: $38-$85, incl. full brk. Seasonal variation. Discount avail. for extended stay.
Credit cards: Most major cards
Restrictions: No children under 6, pets. Smoking restricted. Min. one night's deposit req. 14-day cancellation notice req.
Notes: Three-story Victorian house built in the 1880s. Located on two landscaped acres with brook-fed swimming hole bordering 100-acre park. Wrap-around porch with wicker rockers, swing. Parlor with Victorian fireplace, 18th-century spinning wheel, board games. Dining room. Furnished in American Primitive style with heirloom quilts, collection of early cradles. Stone BBQ, hammock, lawn games, canoe available.*

WELLFLEET (8)

Inn at Duck Creeke
Main St. P.O. Box 364, Wellfleet, MA 02667
(508) 349-9333
Innkeeper: Robert Morrill, Judith Pihl
Rooms: 25, incl. 17 w/pvt. bath. Located in 3 bldgs.
Rates: $65-$90, incl. cont. brk. Seasonal variations. Special pkgs. avail.
Credit cards: Most major cards
Restrictions: No pets. Min. $100 deposit req. 3-day cancellation notice req., less $10.00 fee. 2-night min. stay on wknds. 3-night min. stay on holiday wknds.
Notes: 3-story Federal-style sea captain's house built in 1800s. Located on 5 acres overlooking Duck Pond. Screened porches. Common room. Decorated with antiques. Restaurant on premises. Some French and Spanish spoken. Handicapped access.

WEST BARNSTABLE (8)

Honeysuckle Hill
591 Main St., West Barnstable, MA 02668
(508) 362-8418, (800) 441-8418, (508) 362-4914
Innkeeper: Barbara Rosenthal
Rooms: 3 w/pvt. bath, incl. 1 w/fireplace
Rates: $95-$110, incl. full brk., afternoon refreshment. Seasonal variations. Discount avail. for extended stay.
Credit cards: Most major cards
Restrictions: No children under 5. Smoking restricted. Min. one night's desposit req. 14-day cancellation notice req. 2-night min. stay on wknds. in season.
Notes: Two-story Victorian farmhouse built about 1810. Renovated in and has operated as inn since 1984. Dining room with in-window, fly-in bird feeder. Garden great room with wood stove, TV. Front porch. Furnished with antiques. Side yard with hammock. Gardens with lily pond, waterfall. Some French, Italian spoken. Resident dogs.*

WEST BOYLSTON (4)

The Rose Cottage
24 Worcester St., Rts. 12 and 140, West Boylston, MA 01583
(508) 835-4034

Innkeeper: Michael and Loretta Kittredge
Rooms: 4 plus 1 suite, incl. 3 w/fireplace. Executive apartment avail. Located in 2
  bldgs.
Rates: $70/room, suite, $325 per week/apt., all incl. full brk., afternoon refreshment
Credit cards: None
Restrictions: No pets, smoking. One night's deposit req. 7-day cancellation notice
  req. 2-night min. stay on holidays, college parent wknds. Discount avail. for extended stay.
Notes: Gothic Revival house with gingerbread dormer, gabled roof built in 1850 as
a private summer house. Located on two landscaped acres with swing set, porch and
benches, wicker set, umbrella table and chairs, overlooking the Wachusett Reservoir. Victorian common room with wide pine board floor, fireplace, TV, books.
Cordless phone for guest use. Dining room with hardwood floor. Conference room.
Music room available. Furnished with 19th-century antiques. Barn with antique
shop on premises. Special meals available. Small private parties accommodated.*

WEST FALMOUTH (8)

Sjoholm Bed and Breakfast Inn
17 Chase Rd., Box 430, West Falmouth, MA 02574
(508) 540-5706, (800) 498-5706

Innkeeper: Barbara Eck
Rooms: 15, incl. 7 w/pvt. bath. Located in 2 bldgs.
Rates: $55-$90, incl. full brk. Seasonal variations. Discount avail. for senior citizen
  and extended stays.
Credit cards: None
Restrictions: No children under 5, pets, smoking. 50% deposit req. 14-day cancel-
  lation notice req., less $20.00 fee. 2-night min. stay on summer wknds.
Notes: Two-story Cape Cod-style farmhouse and Carriage House built about 1830.
Fully restored. Located on 2.5 acres. Living room with TV. Dining room with wood-
burning stove. Screened porch. Furnished with antiques, collectibles. Lawn chairs,
picnic table, outdoor shower, bike rack. Resident dogs. Sjoholm (pronounced Sha
holm) is Swedish for *safe place surrounded by water.* Handicapped access.*

WEST HARWICH (8)

Cape Cod Claddagh Country Inn
77 Main St., Box 667, West Harwich, MA 02671
(508) 432-9628, (800) 356-9628

Innkeeper: Jack and Eileen Connell
Rooms: 8 suites w/pvt. bath, cable TV
Rates: $75-$120, incl. full brk., boxed lunch, evening refreshment. Discount avail.
  for extended stay.
Credit cards: Most major cards
Restrictions: No pets. Smoking restricted. Min. one night's deposit req. 14-day can-
  cellation notice req., less 10% fee. 2-night min. stay.

Notes: Two-story Victorian house built about 1900 as parsonage. Operated as inn since 1940. Decorated with antiques, Oriental rugs. Two living rooms, one with fireplace. Formal dining room. Jacuzzi on wrap-around porch overlooking swimming pool and gardens. Irish hospitality in a Victorian ambiance.*

WEST TISBURY (8)

The Bayberry Inn
Old Courthouse Rd., Box 654, West Tisbury, MA 02575
(508) 693-1984
Innkeeper: Rosalie H. Powell
Rooms: 5, no pvt. bath
Rates: $110-$150, incl. full brk. Seasonal variations.
Credit cards: Most major cards
Restrictions: No children under 12, pets, smoking. Deposit req. 14-day cancellation notice req., less $20.00 fee. 2-night min. stay on wknds. 3-night min. stay on 3-day wknds.
Notes: New England Cape Cod style house w/brick chimneys and silver gray weathered shingles. Located on acres of land surrounded with lakes. Common room with fireplace. Terrace. Guests have access to refrigerator. Furnished in country atmosphere with antiques.*

WILLIAMSTOWN (1)

Steep Acres Farm
520 White Oaks Rd., Williamstown, MA 01267
(413) 458-3774
Innkeeper: Marvin and Mary Gangemi
Rooms: 4, no pvt. bath
Rates: $70, incl. full brk.
Credit cards: None
Restrictions: No children under 7, pets, smoking
Notes: Country house built approx. 1894. Located on 50-acre knoll with view of Berkshire Hills and Green Mountains. Furnished with antiques. Swimming pond. Trout fishing.

WOODS HOLE (8)

The Marlborough
320 Woods Hole Rd., Woods Hole, MA 02543
(508) 548-6218, (508) 457-7519
Innkeeper: Diana Smith
Rooms: 5 w/pvt. bath
Rates: $85-$105, incl. full brk., afternoon refreshment. Seasonal variations. Discount for extended and off-season mid-week stays. Special pkgs. avail.
Credit cards: MC, V
Restrictions: Children under 2 restricted. No pets, smoking. Full prepayment req. 14-day cancellation notice req., less 10% fee. 2-night min. stay on summer wknds. 3-night min. stay on holiday wknds.
Notes: Turn of the century reproduction of Cape Cod cottage. Located on .5 wooded acre. Parlor with fireplace, TV. Furnished with antiques, wicker, brass collectibles, handmade quilts. Swimming pool, hammock. Lawn games available. Antique shop on premises. Some French spoken.*

THE MARLBOROUGH

WORTHINGTON (2)

The Hill Gallery
137 E. Windsor Rd., Worthington, MA 01098
(413) 238-5914

Innkeeper: Walter and Ellen Korzec
Rooms: 2 w/pvt. bath, plus cottage w/pvt. bath, phone, TV
Rates: $60/room, call for cottage rates, all incl. full brk.
Credit cards: None
Restrictions: No children under 10, pets, smoking. 50% deposit req. 2-night min.
  stay on holiday wknds.
Notes: Two-story country inn. Art gallery, sundeck, patios.

YARMOUTH PORT (8)

Olde Captain's Inn
101 Main St., Yarmouth Port, MA 02675
(508) 362-4496

Innkeeper: Sven Tilly, Betsy O'Connor
Rooms: 3 w/pvt. bath, phone, TV, plus 2 suites w/pvt. bath, TV
Rates: $35-$80/room, $100/suite incl. expanded cont. brk. Discount for extended
  stay.
Credit cards: None
Restrictions: No pets, smoking. Min. 50% deposit req., refunded upon cancellation
  only if room is re-rented.
Notes: Captain's house built approx. 1830. Fully restored. Located on landscaped
grounds. Dining room, private patios. Lawn furniture, BBQ. Guests have access to
golf-driving net.

One Centre Street Inn
Rt 6A & Old Kings Hwy., Yarmouth Port, MA 02675
(508) 362-8910

Innkeeper: Karen Iannello
Rooms: 4, no pvt. bath, plus 1/suite w/pvt. bath, fireplace
Rates: $75-$95/room, $110/suite, all incl. full brk. Seasonal variations.

Credit cards: MC, V
Restrictions: No children under 12, pets, smoking. Deposit req. 14-day cancellation
   notice req.
Notes: Two-story Colonial house. Newly redecorated in Julin Anne furnishing.
Front hall, parlor. Dining room with brick hearth. Library/sitting room with fire-
place. Furnished with antiques.*

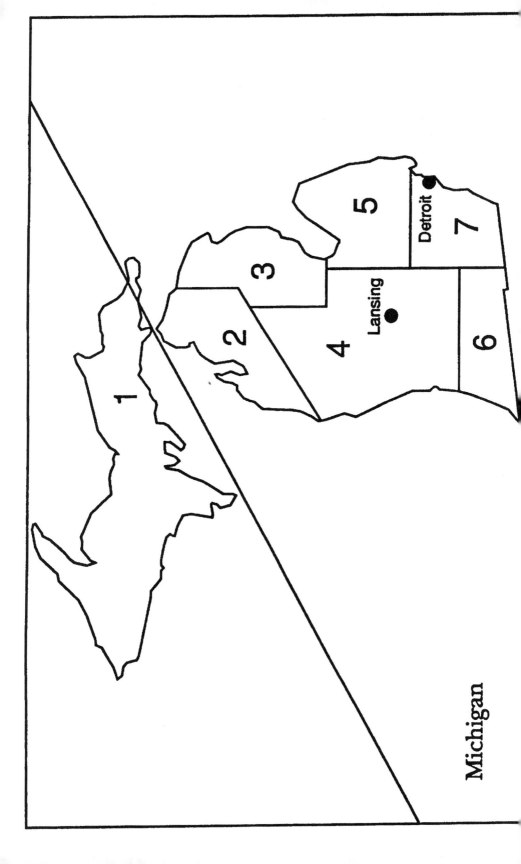

Michigan

Michigan

ANN ARBOR (7)

Urban Retreat
2759 Canterbury Rd., Ann Arbor, MI 48104
(313) 971-8110
Innkeeper: Gloria Krys, Andre Rosalik
Rooms: 2 w/phone, incl. 1 w/pvt. bath
Rates: $40-$60, incl. full brk. Discount avail. for mid-week and extended stays.
Credit cards: Most major cards
Restrictions: No children under 10, pets. Smoking restricted. Min. one night's deposit req. 5-day cancellation notice req., less $10.00 fee.
Notes: Ranch-style house built in the 1950s. Located adjacent to County Farm Park. Has operated as inn since 1986. Living room with fireplace, cable TV. Porch. Furnished with antiques, birdseye maple furniture. Cottage garden with patio. Resident cat. Designated a Backyard Wildlife Habitat by the National Wildlife Federation. Innkeepers work in the mental health field and strive to provide a quiet, relaxed atmosphere. *

Wood's Inn
2887 Newport Rd., Ann Arbor, MI 48103
(313) 665-8394
Innkeeper: Barbara Inwood
Rooms: 4, incl. 2 w/pvt. bath, 1 w/TV
Rates: $50-$60, incl. full brk.
Credit cards: None
Restrictions: No pets, smoking. $20.00 deposit req.
Notes: Two-story stone and wood early-American house built in 1859. Has operated as inn since 1984. Located on three wooded acres with gardens. Listed as one of the oldest structures in Washtenaw County. Dining room, parlor, kitchen. Screened porch with wicker furniture. Furnished with early-American and period pieces. Innkeeper collects colored art glass, Staffordshire figurines, and breeds Dalmatians.

AU GRES (3)

Point Au Gres Hotel
3279 S. Pointe Lane, Au Gres, MI 48703
(517) 876-7217
Innkeeper: Bob and Biba Jennings
Rooms: 5 w/cable TV, no pvt. bath
Rates: $49, incl. cont. brk. Seasonal variations. Discount avail. for mid-week stay.
Credit cards: MC, V
Restrictions: Deposit req. 2-day cancellation notice req.
Notes: Three-story white masonary building was built in 1938, overlooking Lake Huron. Dining room. Patio, deck overlooking Saginaw Bay. Pub with fieldstone bar and fireplace on premises. All meals, bicycles, row boat, sail boat, canoe available. French, Spanish spoken.*

POINT AU GRES HOTEL

AU TRAIN (1)

Pinewood Lodge
M28 West, Box 176, Au Train, MI 49806
(906) 892-8300
Innkeeper: Jerry and Jenny Krieg
Rooms: 7 w/TV, incl. 3 w/pvt. bath, plus 1 suite w/pvt. bath, TV
Rates: $55-$110, incl. full brk.
Credit cards: Most major cards
Restrictions: No pets, smoking. One night's deposit req. 48-hour cancellation notice req.
Notes: Log house built in 1991. Loft, great room, media room, front porch. Deck overlooking Lake Superior. Handicapped access.

PINEWOOD LODGE

BATTLE CREEK (6)

Greencrest Manor
6174 Halbert, Battle Creek, MI 49017
(616) 962-8633
Innkeeper: Kathy and Tom VanDaff
Rooms: 7, incl. 5 w/pvt. bath, 7 w/phone, 1 w/fireplace, 2 w/double whirlpools
Rates: $75-$170, incl. cont. brk.
Credit cards: Most major cards
No smoking. Min. one night's deposit req. 7-day cancellation notice req.
Notes: 56-year-old French Normandy mansion constructed of sandstone, slate and copper. Completely restored and decorated in the European style. Antique furnishings. Three levels of formal gardens and fountains on 15 acres. Small groups accommodated.

BAY CITY (5)

Clements Inn
1712 Center Ave., Bay City, MI 48708
(517) 892-1541, (517) 895-8535
Innkeeper: Brian and Karen Hepp
Rooms: 5, incl. 2 w/fireplace, plus 1 suite w/complete kitchen, whirlpool, all w/pvt. bath, phone, TV
Rates: $70-$125/room, $125/suite, all incl. cont brk. Discount avail. for mid-week stay, whole house.
Credit cards: Most major cards
Restrictions: No pets. Smoking restricted. Min. one night's deposit req. 7-day cancellation notice req.
Notes: Three-story Queen Anne-style Victorian house with oak ceilings, winding oak staircase, six fireplaces, built in 1886. Third-floor ballroom. Amber-paned glass windows and eight-foot window seat. Dining room, living room, library. Board games, fax service available. Screened porch with wicker furniture. Exercise room, pool table. Small private parties accommodated. Resident dog.*

BLACK RIVER (3)

Silver Creek
4361 S. US-23, Black River, MI 48721
(517) 471-2198
Innkeeper: Larry and Gladys Farlow
Rooms: 4 w/pvt. bath
Rates: $55, incl. full brk. Discount avail. for extended stay.
Credit cards: None
Restrictions: No children under 5, pets, smoking. One night's deposit req. 24-hour cancellation notice req., less $10.00 fee. 3-night min. stay on holidays.
Notes: Two-story house built in 1955. Located on 60 acres. Craft and antique room. Great room with cathedral ceilings. Picnic tables, grills available.*

BLANEY PARK (1)

Blaney Cottages
R.R. 1, Box 55, Blaney Park, MI 49836
(906) 283-3163

Innkeeper: Paul Oestrike
Rooms: 4 plus 7 suites, all w/pvt. bath. Located in 7 bldgs.
Rates: $35-$40/room, $55-$90/suite, all incl. cont. brk. Special pkgs. avail.
Credit cards: MC, V
Restrictions: No large animals. Smoking restricted. 50% deposit req. 7-day cancellation notice req.
Notes: Fully renovated and operated as inn since 1990. Furnished with Lazy Boy furniture. Landscaped. Kids playground on premises. Guests have access to picnic tables, gas grills, RV sites.*

BROOKLYN (6)

DEWEY LAKE MANOR B & B

Dewey Lake Manor B & B
11811 Laird Rd., Brooklyn, MI 49230
(517) 467-7122

Innkeeper: Joe, Barb, Barry and Tandy Phillips
Rooms: 4 w/pvt. bath, TV, incl. 1 w/phone
Rates: $55-$65, incl. cont. brk., afternoon refreshment. Special pkgs. avail.
Credit cards: MC, V
Restrictions: No pets, smoking. 50% deposit req. 5-day cancellation notice req. 3-night min. stay on race wknds.
Notes: Two-story Italianate house built in 1860s. Located on 18 acres on the shore of Dewey Lake. Parlor with baby grand piano. Sitting room with bay window. Dining room, porch. Furnished with antiques. Lawn games available. Small parties accommodated.*

CADILLAC (4)

Hermann's European Inn
214 N. Mitchell St., Cadillac, MI 49601
(616) 775-9563, (616) 775-2090

Innkeeper: Hermann and Martha Suhs
Rooms: 7, incl. 3 suites, all w/pvt. bath
Rates: $70-$85, incl. cont. brk. Discount for mid-week stay.
Credit cards: MC, V
Restrictions: No pets. Smoking restricted. 48-hour cancellation notice req.
Notes: Located atop European Cafe and Chef's Deli. German spoken.

CHASSELL (1)

Palosaari's Rolling Acres B & B
Rte. 1, Box 354, Chassell, MI 49916
(906) 523-4947

Innkeeper: Evey and Cliff Palosaari
Rooms: 3, no pvt. bath
Rates: $40, incl. full brk. Discount avail. for extended stay.
Credit cards: None
Restrictions: No pets. Smoking restricted. Deposit may be req.
Notes: Country-style house built in the 1940s. Located on a working dairy farm.
Finnish spoken.

COLDWATER (6)

Batavia Inn
1824 W. Chicago Rd., US 12, Coldwater, MI 49036
(517) 278-5146

Innkeeper: Fred Marquardt
Rooms: 4 plus 1 suite, all w/pvt. bath
Rates: $59/room, $99/suite, all incl. full brk. Special pkgs. avail.
Credit cards: None
Restrictions: Children welcome with prearrangement. No pets. Smoking restricted.
    Deposit req. 7-day cancellation notice req., less $10.00 per room fee.
Notes: Two-story Italianate farm house with ten and twelve foot ceilings built in
1872. Located on fifteen acres of wild-life habitat. Natural walnut and butternut
woodwork cut and milled from property. Library with bay windows overlooking gar-
den. Swimming pool. Lawn games available. Small private parties accommodated.
German spoken.

Chicago Pike Inn
215 E. Chicago St., Coldwater, MI 49036
(517) 279-8744

Innkeeper: Becky Schultz
Rooms: 4 plus 4 suites, all w/pvt. bath, phone, cable TV, incl 1 w/fireplace. Located
    in 2 bldgs.
Rates: $80-$105/room, $140-$165/suite, all incl. full brk., afternoon refreshment.
    Special pkgs. avail.
Credit cards: Most major cards
Restrictions: No children under 12, pets. Smoking restricted. One night's deposit
    req. 7-day cancellation notice req., less $10.00 fee. 2-night min. stay on some
    wknds. Closed Thanksgiving, Christmas.
Notes: Two-story Colonial Revival house with cherry staircase, parquet floors built
in 1903. Fully restored. Library with fireplace. Reception room with cherry panel-
ing, ten-ft. ceilings. Dining room with built-in mirrored buffet. Conference room.
Furnished with period antiques. Dinner, bicycles available. Small private parties accommodated.

EMPIRE (2)

Clipper House Inn
10085 Front St., Box 207, Empire, MI 49630
(616) 326-5518, (616) 326-5526

Innkeeper: Jeri Kallush
Rooms: 4, plus 1 suite, no pvt. bath
Rates: $55/room, $65/suite, all incl. full brk. Special pkgs. avail. Seasonal variations.
Credit cards: Most major cards
Restrictions: No children, pets, smoking. %50 deposit req. 3-day cancellation notice req.
Notes: Two-story western-style brick Inn with stenciled walls and hardwood floors built in 1897. Originally a dry goods store. Living room with cable TV, VCR. Furnished with antiques and country decor. Guests have access to kitchen.

HIDDEN POND B & B

FENNVILLE (4)

Hidden Pond B & B
5975 128th Ave., Box 461, Fennville, MI 49408
(616) 561-2491
Innkeeper: Larry and Priscilla Fuerst
Rooms: 2 w/pvt. bath
Rates: $64-$110, incl. full brk., afternoon refreshment. Discount avail. for extended and mid-week stays. Seasonal variations.
Credit cards: None
Restrictions: No children under 15, pets. Smoking restricted. 50% deposit req. 10-day cancellation notice req. less $15.00 fee. 2-night min. stay on holiday wknds.
Notes: Located on 28 wooded acres. Has operated as inn since 1983. Living room with fireplace. Dining room. Library. Kitchen and breakfast porch. Outdoor deck. Patio. Birdwatching. Ravine with pond. Resident outdoor cat.*

The Kingsley House B & B
626 W. Main St., Fennville, MI 49408
(616) 561-6425
Innkeeper: David and Shirley Witt
Rooms: 5 w/pvt. bath, incl. 3 w/TV, plus 3 suites w/pvt. bath, fireplace, TV. Located in 2 bldgs.

THE KINGSLEY HOUSE B & B

Rates: $75-$85/room, $125/suite, all incl. full brk., afternoon refreshment. Discount avail. for senior citizen and mid-week stays.
Credit cards: Most major cards
Restrictions: No children, pets, smoking. Deposit req. 10-day cancellation notice req. 2-night min. stay on wknds.
Notes: Queen Anne Victorian house with three-story turret built in 1886. Fully restored and redecorated. Oak open stairway. Formal dining room. Wrap-around porch with wicker chairs. Furnished with period antiques, family heirlooms. Bicycles available. Handicapped access. Dutch, Friesian spoken.*

FLINT (5)

Avon House B & B
518 Avon St., Flint, MI 48503
(810) 232-6861
Innkeeper: Arletta Minore
Rooms: 3, incl. 1 w/pvt. bath
Rates: $35-$40, incl. full brk. Discount avail. for extended stay.
Credit cards: None
Restrictions: No pets. Smoking restricted. 50% deposit req. 7-day cancellation notice req.
Notes: Victorian house built in the 1880s. Decorated with woodwork in Victorian tradition. Parlor with window benches, antique Steinway grand piano. Formal dining room.*

FRUITPORT-GRAND HAVEN (4)

Village Park B & B
60 W. Park St., Fruitport-Grand Haven, MI 49415-9668
(616) 865-6289
Innkeeper: John and Virginia Hewett
Rooms: 6 w/pvt. bath, incl. 2 w/TV, 1 w/fireplace
Rates: $60-$80, incl. full brk. Special pkgs. avail.
Credit cards: Most major cards
Restrictions: No pets, smoking. $50.00 deposit req. 7-day cancellation req., less $10.00 fee.
Notes: Three story house built in 1873. Living room with fireplace. Deck, roof-top balcony, hot tub. Special Wellness Weekend packages available.*

VILLAGE PARK B & B

GLEN ARBOR (2)

The Sylvan Inn
6680 Western Ave., Box 648, Glen Arbor, MI 49636
(616) 334-4333

Innkeeper: Bill and Jenny Olson

Rooms: 13, incl. 6 w/pvt. bath, TV, plus 1 suite w/pvt. bath, TV, all w/phone

Rates: $60-$120/room, $90-$95/suite, all incl. cont. brk. Discount avail. for extended stay.

Credit cards: None

Restrictions: Children welcome w/prior arrangment. No pets. Smoking restricted. One night's deposit req. 7-day cancellation notice req., less $10.00 fee. Min. stay on holiday wknds. Closed March, April, Nov.

Notes: Two-story house built in 1885, expanded in 1983. Refurbished and operated as inn since 1987. Parlor, porches, whirlpool, sauna. Handicapped access.*

THE SYLVAN INN

GRAND HAVEN (4)

Harbor House Inn
114 S. Harbor Dr., Grand Haven, MI 49417
(800) 841-0610, (616) 846-0530

Innkeeper: Emily Ehlert and Tiia Arrak
Rooms: 16, incl. 10 w/fireplace, plus 1 suite w/fireplace, TV, all w/pvt. bath. Some w/whirlpool bath. Located in 2 bldgs.
Rates: $85-$135/room, $175/suite, all incl. cont brk., afternoon refreshment. Seasonal variations.
Credit cards: MC, V
Restrictions: No pets. Smoking restricted. Min. one night's deposit req. 5-day cancellation notice req. 2-night min. stay on summer wknds.
Notes: Victorian-era house with pine floors built in 1987. Screened porch with white wicker furniture. Catering, easels, overhead projectors, TV/VCR available. Small private parties accommodated. Handicapped access.

GRAND RAPIDS (4)

Fountain Hill Bed & Breakfast
222 Fountain N.E., Grand Rapids, MI 49503
(616) 458-6621
Innkeeper: Chuck Carter, Sally Hale
Rooms: 4 w/pvt. bath, phone, cable TV, VCR. Located in 2 bldgs.
Rates: $60-$125, incl. full brk., evening refreshment. Discount avail. for extended stay.
Credit cards: Most major cards
Restrictions: No pets, smoking. Deposit req. 7-day cancellation notice req.
Notes: Two-story Italianate house built in 1874. Restored in 1986. Has operated as inn since 1987. Front parlor with staircase. Living room with fireplace. Dining room, conference room, three porches. Small private parties accommodated. Off-street parking available.

HOLLAND (4)

Dutch Colonial Inn
560 Central Ave., Holland, MI 49423
(616) 396-3664, (616) 396-0461
Innkeeper: Bob and Pat Elenbaas, Diana Klungel
Rooms: 3, plus 2 suites, all w/pvt. bath, phone
Rates: $70-$90/room, $100-$125/suite, all incl. full brk. Discount avail. for extended stay.
Credit cards: Most major cards
Restrictions: No pets. Smoking restricted. 4-day cancellation notice req., less $20.00 fee. 3-night min. stay on holiday wknds. in whirlpool room.
Notes: Dutch Colonial house built in 1930. Sitting room with cable TV, VCR. Sunporch, formal dining room. Furnished with heirloom antiques in period style. Whirlpool tubs available.

JONES (6)

The Sanctuary at Wildwood
58318 M-40 N, Jones, MI 49061
(616) 244-5910, (616) 244-5910
Innkeeper: Dick and Dolly Buerkle, Judy Krupka
Rooms: 11 suites, all w/pvt bath, Jacuzzi, service bar, fireplace, TV, pvt. deck. Located in 4 bldgs.
Rates: $169-$170, incl. cont brk. Discount avail. for extended stay.

Credit cards: Most major cards

Restrictions: No children under 12. No pets. Smoking restricted. Min. one night's deposit req. 7-day cancellation notice req., less $10.00 fee. 2-night min. stay.

Notes: Contemporary building. Located on 94+ wooded acres in State Game area. Common room with fireplace, satellite TV. Library. Great room. Formal dining room. Buffet breakfast. Deck overlooking pond with island. Canoe provided. Swimming pool. Walking trails. Cross country ski trails. Small private parties accommodated. Handicapped access.*

JONESVILLE (6)

Munro House
202 Maumee St., Jonesville, MI 49250
(517) 849-9292

Innkeeper: Joyce A. Yarde

Rooms: 5 w/pvt. bath, phone, TV, incl. 3 w/fireplace

Rates: $50-$68, incl. full brk., evening dessert, coffee. Discount avail. for extended stay.

Credit cards: MC, V

Restrictions: No children under 6, pets. Smoking restricted. $25.00 deposit req. 24-hour cancellation notice req.

Notes: Two-story Greek Revival house with 10 fireplaces built in 1834. Operated as a station on the underground railroad. Four common areas for reading or watching TV. Library with books, VCR. Gathering room with games. Colonial breakfast room with brick open hearth fireplace. Gardens. Small private parties accommodated.

CENTENNIAL

LEXINGTON (5)

Centennial
5774 Main St., Box 54, Lexington, MI 48450
(810) 359-8762

Innkeeper: Daniel and Dilla Miller

Rooms: 4 w/pvt. bath

Rates: $55-$75, incl. full brk., afternoon refreshment. Seasonal variations. Discount avail. for senior citizen and mid-week stays.

Credit cards: MC, V

Restrictions: No children under 10, pets, smoking. 50% deposit req. 48-hour cancellation notice req. 3-night min. stay on holiday wknds.

Notes: Two-story electic-style house built in 1879. Front parlor, center parlor, dining room, side porch with wicker. Furnished with antiques and reproduction furniture. Lawns and gardens. Listed on the Michigan State Historical Register. Resident pet.

McGEE HOMESTEAD

LOWELL (6)

McGee Homestead
2534 Alden Nash Northeast, Lowell, MI 49331
(616) 897-8142

Innkeeper: Bill and Ardie Barber

Rooms: 4 w/pvt. bath, TV

Rates: $38-$55, incl. full brk., afternoon refreshment. Discount avail. for extended stay.

Credit cards: MC, V

Restrictions: No smoking.

Notes: Two-story brick farmhouse built in the 1880s. Located on five acres. Separate common area with fireplace, library. Furnished with antiques. Barn with petting animals. Breakfast is made with "own" fresh eggs. Board games, reading material, TV, VCR, movies, lawn games, hammock available.

LUDINGTON (4)

The Inn at Ludington
701 E. Ludington Ave., Ludington, MI 49431
(616) 845-7055

Innkeeper: Diane Shields

Rooms: 5 plus 1 suite, all w/pvt. bath, incl. 2 w/fireplace

Rates: $55-$75/room, $75-$85/suite, all incl. full brk. Discount avail. for off-season and mid-week stays. Seasonal variations.

THE INN AT LUDINGTON

Credit cards: Most major cards
Restrictions: No pets. Smoking restricted. One night's deposit req. 7-day cancellation notice req. Min. 2-night min. stay on wknds. in July and Aug.
Notes: Queen Anne Victorian house built in 1889. Three-story turret, parlor, library, dining room. Furnished with antiques, reproductions, family heirlooms. Resident mini-dachshund. Innkeepers collect Teddy bears.*

MACKINAC ISLAND (1)

Cloghaun
P.O. Box 203, Mackinac Island, MI 49757
(906) 847-3885, (313) 331-7110

Innkeeper: James and Dorothy Bond
Rooms: 10, incl. 9 w/pvt bath
Rates: $60-$105, include cont. brk. Seasonal variations.
Credit cards: None
Restrictions: No pets, smoking. One night's deposit req. 2-night min. stay on holiday wknds. and Mackinac boat races. 10-day cancellation notice req., less $15.00 fee.
Notes: Victorian house built in 1884. Family owned and operated since 1884. Library with TV/VCR. Family antiques on display. No cars or motor vehicles allowed on island.

Haan's 1830 Inn
P.O. Box 123, Mackinac Island, MI 49757
(906) 847-6244, (708) 234-2662 (off-season)

Innkeeper: Joy, Vernon, Nicholas and Nancy Haan
Rooms: 6, incl. 5 w/pvt. bath plus 1 suite
Rates: $75-105/room, $115/suite, all incl. expanded cont. brk. Seasonal variations. Discount avail. for mid-week stay during spring and fall.
Credit cards: None
Restrictions: No pets. Smoking restricted. One night's deposit req. 14-day cancellation notice req., less $10.00 fee. No cars allowed on Mackinac Island.

Notes: Two-story Greek Revival house built in 1830 on foundations of a trader cabin. Expanded in 1847. Fully restored in 1976. Has operated as inn since 1984. Dining room with fireplace. Parlor, two open porches, screened porch. Furnished with period antiques. Off-season address: 3418 Oakwood Dr. Island Lake, IL 60042 (708) 526-2662.

MENDON (6)

Mendon Country Inn
440 W. Main, Mendon, MI 49072
(616) 496-8132, (616) 496-8403
Innkeeper: Richard and Dolly Buerkle
Rooms: 9 plus 9 suites, incl. 17 w/pvt bath, 13 w/fireplace. Located in 3 bldgs.
Rates: $65-$85/room, $125-$150/suite, all incl. cont. brk. Discount avail. for mid-week stay.
Credit cards: Most major cards
Restrictions: No children under 12, pets. Smoking restricted. One-night's deposit req. 7-day cancellation notice req., less $10.00 fee. 2-night min. stay on wknds. 3-night min. stay on special holidays.
Notes: Two-story country inn built in 1843. Rebuilt in 1873. Roof top garden. Winding walnut spiral staircase. Common area with TV, fireplace. Meeting area and game room. Decorated with antiques. Suites with Jacuzzi. Full cedar sauna. Covered deck. Bar-b-que and picnic area. Bicycles and canoeing available. Little Spanish spoken. Handicapped access. Small private parties accommodated.*

NEW BUFFALO (6)

Sans Souci Euro Inn B & B
19265 S. Lakeside Rd., New Buffalo, MI 49117
(616) 756-3141, (616) 756-5511
Innkeeper: Angelika Siewert
Rooms: 6 plus 2 suites, all w/pvt. bath, incl. 7 w/fireplace, 6 w/kitchen, 3 w/phone, 2 w/TV. Located in 2 bldgs.
Rates: $160-$166/room, $175/suite, all incl. full brk. except guest homes, which incl. full kitchen. Discount avail. for mid-week and extended stays. Special pkgs. avail.
Credit cards: Most major cards
Restrictions: No pets. Smoking restricted. 50% deposit req. 2-week cancellation notice req., less 50% fee which is applied to future visit. 2-night min. stay on wknds. 7-night min. stay in guest homes during summer.
Notes: European-style country estate with two guesthouses and two cottages, located on fifty acres with private lake. Has operated as inn since 1988. Living rooms with fireplace, cable TV. Furnished with old-world collectables. Guests have access to fully equipped kitchen. Lawn games available. Handicapped access. German, Spanish spoken.

NILES (6)

Yesterday's Inn
518 N. 4th, Niles, MI 49120
(616) 683-6079
Innkeeper: Elizabeth and Bob Baker
Rooms: 4 w/pvt. bath, incl. 1 w/phone

Rates: $60-$75, incl. full brk., afternoon refreshment, dessert on wknds. Discount avail. for extended and mid-week stays.
Credit cards: Most major cards
Restrictions: No pets, smoking. Min. 50% deposit req. 8-day cancellation notice req., less $10.00 fee. 2-night min. stay on holiday and football wknds.
Notes: Two-story Italinate house with high ceilings, original woodwork, original wooden staircase, built in 1875. Parlor with antique oriental chests. Breakfast room. Spa with hot tub. Small private parties accommodated. Resident cat.*

OWOSSO (4)

R & R Ranch
308 E. Hibbard Rd., Owosso, MI 48867
(517) 723-3232, (517) 723-2553
Innkeeper: Carl and Jeanne Rossman
Rooms: 3, incl. 1 w/pvt. bath, 2 w/phone, 1 w/fireplace, plus 1 suite w/phone, TV
Rates: $45-$60, incl. cont. brk., afternoon refreshment. Seasonal variations. Special pkgs. avail.
Credit cards: None
Restrictions: No smoking. 50% deposit req. 10-day cancellation notice req.
Notes: Farmhouse built in the early 1900s. Fully remodeled. Located on 150 acres overlooking Maple River Valley. Parlor with fireplace. Game room. Gardens. Outdoor deck. Large concrete circular drive and white board fences lead to stables of horses and cattle.

PENTWATER (4)

Historic Nickerson Inn
262 Lowell, Box 986, Pentwater, MI 49449
(616) 869-8241, (616) 869-6151
Innkeeper: Harry and Gretchen Shiparski
Rooms: 10 plus 2 suites w/Jacuzzi, balcony, all w/pvt. bath
Rates: $75-$95/room, $150-$175/suite, all incl. full brk., afternoon refreshment.
Credit cards: MC, V
Restrictions: Well behaved children over 12 welcome. No pets, smoking. 50% deposit req. 7-day cancellation notice req. less $15.00 fee. 2-night min. stay for insseason wknds.
Notes: Two-story inn built in 1913. Has operated as Inn since 1914. Verandah. Lobby with fireplace. Handicapped access to dining. Restaurant on premises. Spanish spoken.*

PETOSKEY (2)

Stafford's Bay View Inn
613 Woodland Ave., Petoskey, MI 49770
(616) 347-2771, (616) 347-0636
Innkeeper: Reginald Smith
Rooms: 25 w/pvt. bath, plus 8 suites w/pvt. bath, incl. 7 w/fireplace
Rates: $88-$138/room, $145-$160/suite, all incl. full brk. Seasonal variations. Special pkgs. available.
Credit cards: Most major cards
Restrictions: No pets. Deposit req. 10-day cancellation notice req.

Notes: Three-story inn with elevator established in 1886 overlooking Little Travers Bay. Has operated as Inn since 1961. Victorian parlor, garden dining room, sun room, front porch. Furnished with period antiques. Lawn games and bikes available for guests. Sunday brunch is available and small private parties accommodated. Listed on the Michigan State Register of Historic Places. Handicapped access available. *

RAPID RIVER (1)

The Buck Stop Plus
P.O. Box 156, Rapid River, MI 49878
(906) 446-3360
Innkeeper: Charlie Muntwyler
Rooms: 3, no pvt. bath
Rates: $69, incl. full brk. Seasonal variations. Discount avail. for senior citizen and extended stays. Special pkgs. avail.
Credit cards: Most major cards
Restrictions: Smoking restricted. Deposit req. 10-day cancellation notice req., less one night's fee.
Notes: Ranch-style solar electric house. Located on several hundred wooded acres with stocked forty-two acre private lake. Common room with fireplace, player piano. Living room, dining area. Deck, whirlpool. Boats, lawn games, winter dog sledding available. Fishing, hunting trips organized. Resident animals.*

ROCHESTER HILLS (7)

Paint Creek B & B
971 Dutton Rd., Rochester Hills, MI 48306
(810) 651-6785
Innkeeper: Loren and Rea Siffring
Rooms: 3 w/phone, no pvt. bath
Rates: $35-$45, incl. full brk. Discount avail. for senior citizen and extended stays.
Credit cards: None
Restrictions: No smoking. Deposit req. 2-day cancellation req.
Notes: Ranch style house located on three and a half wooded acres. Mostly glass family room overlooks pond and trout stream below. Feeding platform for wildlife on balcony. Tours of school with Leader Dogs for the Blind arranged in advance. *

SAGINAW (4)

Brockway House B & B
1631 Brockway, Saginaw, MI 48602
(517) 792-0746
Innkeeper: Richard Zuehlke Ina Carpentar (Zoe)
Rooms: 3, incl. 2 w/TV, plus 1 suite w/Jacuzzi, all w/pvt. bath, phone
Rates: $85-$95/room, $175/suite, all incl. full brk. Discount avail. for mid-week and extended stays.
Credit cards: MC, V
Restrictions: No pets, smoking. 50% deposit req. 10-day cancellation notice req.
Notes: Traditional "Southern plantation" house built in 1864. Decorated in Victorian decor. Furnished with primitive antiques, reproductions. Listed on the National Register of Historic Sites.

SAUGATUCK (4)

Kemah Guest House
633 Pleasant St., Saugatuck, MI 49453
(616) 857-2919
Innkeeper: Cindi and Terry Tatsch
Rooms: 6, no pvt. bath
Rates: $85-$140, incl. cont. brk., afternoon refreshment. Seasonal variations.
Credit cards: Most major cards
Restrictions: No children under 16, pets, smoking. One night's deposit req. 7-day
cancellation notice req., less one night's fee. 2-night min. stay on wknds., holidays, and special events.
Notes: Turn-of-the-century mansion with hand-carved woodwork, beamed ceilings,
stained-glass. Located on two wooded acres with cave, Indian grave. Rathskeller,
games room with billiard table, TV. Study with stone and tile fireplace. Parlor with
board games. Solarium. Formal dining room with bay window. Furnished in eclectic style with antiques. Sun porch. Small private parties accommodated. Registered
historic site.*

Maplewood Hotel
428 Butler St., Box 1059, Saugatuck, MI 49453
(616) 857-1771, (616) 857-1773
Innkeeper: Sam Burnell and Catherine Simon
Rooms: 10, incl. 4 w/fireplace, plus 5 suites, incl. 3 w/fireplace, all w/pvt. bath,
phone, cable TV, incl. some w/double Jacuzzi tubs
Rates: $65-$155/room, $155/suite, all incl. full brk. Seasonal variations. Discount
avail. for extended stay.
Credit cards: Most major cards
Restrictions: No pets, smoking. One night's deposit req. 7-day cancellation notice
req. 2-night min. stay on wknds. 3-night min. stay on holidays.
Notes: Greek Revival-style hotel built about 1861. Recently remodeled and refurbished. Furnished with antiques and period furniture made in Grand Rapids. Library. Dining room. Lounge. Sun room. Screened porch. Wood deck with
full-length lap pool. Dining room serves lunch, high tea. Limited handicapped access.*

The Park House
888 Holland St., Saugatuck, MI 49453
(616) 857-4535 (800) 321-4535, (616) 857-1065
Innkeeper: Joe and Lynda Petty
Rooms: 5, incl. 1 w/phone, cable TV, 3 w/fireplace, plus 6 suites all w/pvt. bath,
phone, cable TV, 5 w/fireplace, 1 w/Jacuzzi, pvt. balcony. Located in 4 bldgs. Cottages avail.
Rates: $85-$115/room, $120/suite, $130-$225 Cottages, all incl. cont. brk.
Credit cards: Most major cards
Restrictions: No pets. Smoking restricted. One night's deposit req., 7-day cancellation notice req. 2-night min. stay on wknds. 3-night min. stay on wknds. in July &
Aug.
Notes: Two-story clap-board house with wide-plank pine floors built in 1857. Parlor
with French doors overlooking garden. Common room with refrigerator, cable TV,
fireplace. Sitting room, patio with picnic table. Furnished in country decor. Decorated with antiques. Wrap-around porch. Jacuzzi. Listed on the National Register of

Historic Places. Murder Mystery weekends and Gourmet Holidays available. Special dietary needs accommodated with advanced notice. Limited handicapped access.*

The Red Dog Bed & Breakfast
132 Mason St., Box 956, Saugatuck. MI (616) 857-8851

Innkeeper: Dan Indurante
Rooms: 7, incl. 4 w/pvt. bath, 6 w/fireplace, plus 1 suite w/pvt bath, fireplace, TV
Rates: $55-$70/room, $85/suite, all incl. cont. brk. Seasonal variations.
Credit cards: Most major cards
Restrictions: No pets. Smoking limited. One night's deposit req. 7-day cancellation notice req.
Notes: Two-story house built in 1879. Living room with fireplace. Dining room. Second-floor porch.*

Sherwood Forest B & B
938 Center St., Box 315, Saugatuck, MI 49453
(800) 838-1246, (616) 857-1246

Innkeeper: Susan and Keith Charak
Rooms: 5 w/pvt. bath, incl. 2 w/fireplace, 1 w/Jacuzzi, plus 1 cottage
Rates: $60-$130, incl. cont. brk. Seasonal variations.
Credit cards: MC, V
Restrictions: No children under 12, pets. Smoking restricted. Deposit req. 10-day cancellation notice, less $10.00 fee. 2-night min. stay, May 1–October 31. 3-night min. stay on holidays.
Notes: Two-story Victorian house built in the 1890s. Surrounded by woods. Wraparound porch, outside heated pool and deck. Cottage sleeps seven.

Twin Gables Country Inn
900 Lake St., Box 881, Saugatuck, MI 49453
(616) 857-4346

Innkeeper: Michael and Denise Simcik
Rooms: 14, plus 3 cottages, incl. 1 w/fireplace, all w/pvt. bath
Rates: $68-$98, incl. cont. brk. Seasonal variations.
Credit cards: Most major cards
Restrictions: No children under 3, pets. Smoking restricted. 50% deposit req. 10-day cancellation notice req., less $10.00 fee. 2-night min. stay on wknds. 3-night min. stay on holiday wknds.
Notes: Built in 1865. Recently restored with hard rock maple floors, embossed tin ceiling. Operated as inn since 1983. Overlooks Kalamazoo Lake. Furnished with antiques, wicker, country crafts. Breakfast room. Common room with fireplace, cable TV. Front veranda overlooking Kalamazoo Lake. Side garden park with pond. Indoor hot tub. Swimming pool. Off-street parking, bicycles, cross-country ski equipment available. Small private parties accommodated. Limited handicapped access. Maltese, French, Italian spoken.*

Twin Oaks Inn
227 Griffith St., Box 867, Saugatuck, MI 49453
(616) 857-1600

Innkeeper: Jerry and Nancy Horney
Rooms: 4, plus 3 suites and 1 cottage, all w/pvt. bath, TV. Located in 2 bldgs.
Rates: $64-$74/room, $74-84/suite, $84-$94/cottage, all incl. full brk., afternoon refreshment. Discount avail. for extended stay.

Credit cards: Most major cards
Restrictions: No pets. Smoking restricted. Deposit req. 7-day cancellation notice
  req. 2-night min. stay on wknds. 3-night min. stay on holidays.
Notes: Built in 1860. Fully renovated. Common room with firplace. 2 porches. Outdoor hot tub. Horseshoes, bicycles, private parking available.*

SOUTH HAVEN (6)

Yelton Manor Bed & Breakfast
140 N. Shore Dr., South Haven, MI 49090
(616) 637-5220, (616) 637-4957

Innkeeper: Elaine Herbert and Robert Kripaitis
Rooms: 12 w/pvt. bath, TV, incl. 4 w/fireplace, plus 5 suites w/pvt. bath, TV, incl. 3
  w/fireplace. Located in 2 bldgs.
Rates: $90-$175, incl. brk., evening refreshment. Seasonal variations.
Credit cards: Most major cards
Restrictions: No children, pets, smoking. 50% deposit req. 10-day cancellation no-
  tice req., less $10.00 fee. Min. 2-night stay during high season and wknds.
Notes: Three-story Victorian mansion built in 1890. Fully renovated in 1989. Two
parlors with fireplaces, two porches, den with a bar, lounge with library, Widow's
Watch overlooking lake. Two-story Victorian Guest House built in 1993 with parlor,
nooks, porch with wicker furniture. Jacuzzi bath in some rooms. Decks with garden
swing and wicker porch. Furnished with antiques. Perennial and rose gardens.
Handicapped access available.

SEASCAPE BED AND BREAKFAST

SPRING LAKE (4)

Seascape Bed and Breakfast
20009 Breton, Spring Lake, MI 49456
(616) 842-8409

Innkeeper: Susan Meyer
Rooms: 2, plus 1 suite, all w/pvt. bath

Rates: $60-$95/room, $85-$145/suite, all incl. full brk. Discount avail. for extended and mid-week stays. Seasonal variations.

Credit cards: MC, V

Restrictions: No children under 10, pets, smoking. One night's deposit req. Min. 7-day cancellation notice req. 2-night min. stay on summer wknds. Closed Dec. 22-25.

Notes: 2-story ranch-style house with exposed wooden beams. Gathering room with fieldstone fireplace. Wrap-around deck overlooking Grand Haven Harbor. Located 140 feet from Lake Michigan, with private beach. Furnished with antiques.

THE VICTORIANA 1898

TRAVERSE CITY (2)

The Victoriana 1898
622 Washington St., Traverse City, MI 49684
(616) 929-1009

Innkeeper: Flo and Bob Schermerhorn
Rooms: 3 plus 1 suite, all w/pvt. bath, incl. 1 w/fireplace
Rates: $65/room, $75/suite, all incl. full brk.
Credit cards: MC, V
Restrictions: No pets, smoking. 50% deposit req. 7-day cancellation notice req.
Notes: Two-story Victorian house with tile fireplace, oak staircase built in 1898. Library with TV. Parlor, dining room. Furnished with antiques, Victorian pieces. Board games available. Gazebo.*

UNION PIER (6)

Gordon Beach Inn
16220 Lakeshore Rd., Union Pier, MI 49129
(616) 469-0800, (616) 469-1914

Innkeeper: Sharon Hawkes
Rooms: 20, incl. some w/Jacuzzi, wet bar, refrigerator, all w/pvt. bath, phone, cable TV
Rates: $75-$125, incl. full brk. Discount avail. for senior citizens.
Credit cards: MC, V
Restrictions: No pets. Smoking restricted. 7-day cancellation notice req. 2-night min. stay on holidays. Closed mid-week Nov.1–May 1.

Notes: Two-story lodge built in 1920s as resort hotel. Fully restored in 1985. Located in wooded community. Decorated with antiques, rocking chairs, and hand stenciling throughout. Lobby with fireplace, library, board games. Dining hall, bar, 2 front porches with wicker furniture, patio with iron tables and chairs. Restaurant and not-for-profit art gallery on premisis. Small private parties accommodated. Handicapped access.*

INN AT UNION PIER

Inn at Union Pier
9708 Berrien, Box 222, Union Pier, MI 49129
(616) 469-4700, (616) 469-4720

Innkeeper: Mark and Joyce Erickson Pitts

Rooms: 14, incl. 13 w/phone, 10 w/fireplace, plus 2 suites w/phone and fireplace, incl. 1 w/TV, all w/pvt. bath. Located in 3 bldgs.

Rates: $105-$130/room, $150-160/suite. Discount avail. for mid-week and extended stays. Seasonal variations.

Credit cards: Most major cards

Restrictions: No children under 12, pets. Smoking restricted. 50% deposit req. 14-day cancellation notice req., less $10.00 fee. 2-night min. stay on wknds. 3-night min. stay for holidays.

Notes: Built in 1920s as summer resort. Renovated in 1980s. Decorated in Scandanavian country and lakeside cottage styles. Antique Swedish fireplaces. Porches or Balconies overlook landscaped grounds. Hot tub and sauna. Yard games. Bikes. Michigan wines and popcorn in Great Room every evening. Beach towels provided. Small private parties accommodated. Limited handicapped access.

Minnesota

ANNANDALE (4)

Thayer Inn
Hwy 55, Box 246, Annandale, MN 55302
(612) 274-8222, (800) 944-6595

Innkeeper: Warren and Sharon Gammell
Rooms: 11, plus 2 suites, all w/pvt. bath, TV
Rates: $70-$125/room, $125/suite, all incl. full brk., evening refreshment. Discount avail. for mid-week stay.
Credit cards: Most major cards
Restrictions: Children welcome with prior approval. Deposit req. 2-day cancellation notice req.
Notes: Three-story Victorian style hotel built in 1895. Lounge. Furnished with authentic period antiques and handmade quilts. Hot tub and sauna. Psychic readings available. Small private parties accommodated. Listed on the National Register of Historic Places.*

BROOKLYN CENTER (6)

The Inn on the Farm
6150 Summit Dr. N, Brooklyn Center, MN 55430
(612) 569-6330, (612) 569-6320

Innkeeper: Stephen M. Barrett
Rooms: 9, plus 1 suite, all w/pvt. bath, phone, TV. Located in 4 bldgs.
Rates: $90-$110/room, $120-$130/suite, all incl. full brk., evening refreshment.
Credit cards: Most major cards
Restrictions: No children under 12, pets, smoking. Deposit req. 72-hour cancellation notice.
Notes: Handicapped access.

CANNON FALLS (7)

Quill & Quilt B & B
615 W. Hoffman St., Cannon Falls, MN 55009
(507) 263-5507

Innkeeper: Dennis and Marcia Flom
Rooms: 3, plus 1 suite w/double whirlpool, all w/pvt. bath
Rates: $55-$75/room, $100-$120/suite, all incl. full brk., evening dessert. Discount avail. for mid-week and extended stays.
Credit cards: MC, V
Restrictions: No children under 13, pets, smoking. One night's deposit req. 3-day cancellation notice req.
Notes: 3-story Colonial Revival house, built in 1897. Has operated as inn since 1987. Library, dining room. Parlor with oak and marble fireplace. Decorated with antiques and handmade quilts. Board games available. Porch with swing. Decks. Certified massage therapist arranged by appointment. Handicapped access.*

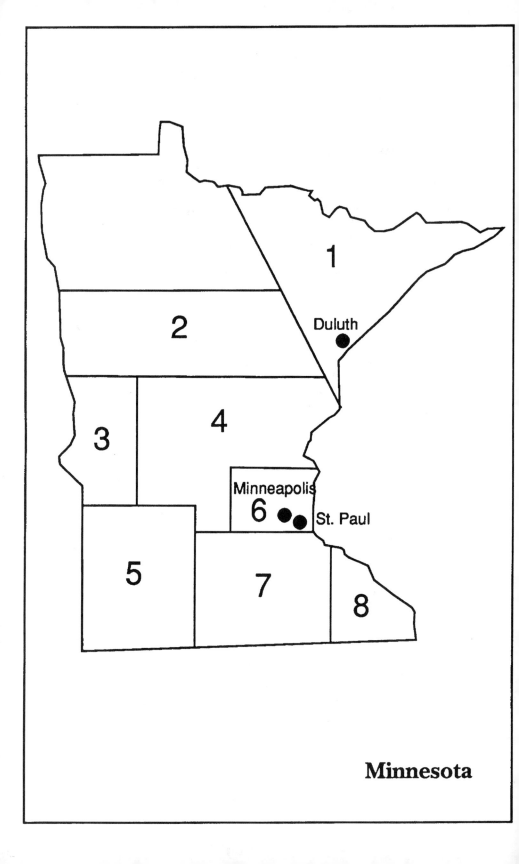

Minnesota

QUILL & QUILT B & B

CROOKSTON (2)

Elm Street Inn
422 Elm St., Crookston, MN 56716
(218) 281-2343, (800) 568-3476, (218) 281-1756
Innkeeper: John and Shirley Winters
Rooms: 4, incl. 2 w/pvt. bath
Rates: $45-$65, incl. full brk., afternoon refreshment
Credit cards: Most major cards
Restrictions: No pets, smoking. $25.00 deposit req. 2-day cancellation notice req.
Notes: Spanish and French spoken.*

FERGUS FALLS (3)

BAKKETOPP HUS

Bakketopp Hus
R.R.2, Box 187A, Fergus Falls, MN 56537
(218) 739-2915
Innkeeper: Judy and Dennis Nims

Rooms: 3 suites w/pvt. bath, phone, TV, incl. 1 w/fireplace, spa, pool table
Rates: $60-$95, incl. full brk., evening refreshment. Seasonal variations. Discount avail. for mid-week stay.
Credit cards: Most major cards
Restrictions: Children welcome with prior notification. No pets, smoking. Deposit req. Cancellation notice req., less $15.00 fee.
Notes: Two-story contemporary house located on several wooded acres. Living room with vaulted ceiling, loft area, fireplace. Furnished with family antiques. Upper deck overlooking Long Lake. Sunken flower gardens with fountains.*

GRAND MARAIS (1)

Dream Catcher Bed & Breakfast
H.C. 86, Box 122, Grand Marais, MN 55604-9501
(800) 682-3119, (218) 387-2876
Innkeeper: Jack and Sue McDonnell
Rooms: 3 w/pvt. bath, phone
Rates: $85-$95, incl. full brk. Seasonal variations. Discount avail. for mid-week stay, Jan. 1–June 15.
Credit cards: Most major cards
Restrictions: No children under 12, pets, smoking. One night's deposit req. 21-day cancellation notice req., less $25.00 fee. 2-night min. stay on wknds.
Notes: B&B built in 1992. Located on a hill in a 26-acre forest with view of Lake Superior. Each bedroom has view of forest and lake. 3-season porch. Living room with fireplace. Sauna.

Pincushion Mountain B & B
220 Gunflint Trail, Grand Marais, MN 55604-9701
(218) 387-1276, (800) 542-1226
Innkeeper: Scott Beattie
Rooms: 4 w/pvt. bath
Rates: $70-$95, incl. full brk. Seasonal variations.
Credit cards: Most major cards
Restrictions: No children under 12, pets, smoking. One night's deposit req. Min. 14-day cancellation notice req., less $10.00 fee. 2-night min. stay on holiday and winter wknds.
Notes: Two-story inn built in 1986. Located on 44 forested acres at 1,000-ft. elevation. Living room/dining area with wood stove overlooking Devil Track River valley and Lake Superior. Lodge-to-lodge hiking programs organized. Ski rentals, instruction available.*

GRAND RAPIDS (1)

Judge Thwing House
1604 County Rd. A, Grand Rapids, MN 55744
(218) 326-5618, (218) 326-9698
Innkeeper: Lilah Crowe
Rooms: 4, incl. 2 w/pvt. bath, plus 1 suite w/pvt. bath
Rates: $50-$85/room, $75-90/suite, all incl. full brk.
Credit cards: Most major cards
Restrictions: No smoking. $20.00 deposit req.
Notes: Two-story Colonial house with oak columns and woodwork, built in 1910 surrounded by fields and forest. Living room with VCR. Decorated with antiques.*

LAKE CITY (8)

RED GABLES INN

Red Gables Inn
403 N. High St., Lake City, MN 55041
(612) 345-2605

Innkeeper: Doug and Mary De Roos
Rooms: 5 w/pvt. bath
Rates: $75-$95, incl. full brk., evening refreshment. Discount avail. for cash, extended, and mid-week stays. Seasonal variations.
Credit cards: MC, V
Restrictions: No children under 13, pets. Smoking restricted. One night's deposit req. 7-day cancellation notice req., less $15.00 fee.
Notes: Two-story Italianate and Greek Revival inn built in 1865. Fully restored. Dining room with fireplace. Parlor with piano. Social hour. Screened porch. Furnished with antiques. Bicycles available. Mystery evening available. Small private parties accommodated.*

LANESBORO (8)

Mrs. B's Historic Lanesboro Inn
101 Parkway, Box 411, Lanesboro, MN 55949
(507) 467-2154, (800) 657-4710

Innkeeper: Bill Sermens and Mimi Abell
Rooms: 10 w/pvt. bath, incl. 2 w/fireplace
Rates: $58-$95, incl. full brk. Discount avail. for mid-week stay. Special pkgs. avail.
Credit cards: None
Restrictions: Children restricted. No pets, smoking. Deposit req. 7-day cancellation notice req., less $10.00 fee.
Notes: Two-story limestone building built in 1872. Has operated as inn since 1984. Parlor with baby grand pian0o, fireplace, library. Dining room, lobby, bar. Balcony with rockers overlooking the Root River. Decks, porches overlooking garden. Furnished with antiques. Dinner available. All meals made from organically grown foods. Small private parties accommodated. Handicapped access.

Scanlan House Bed and Breakfast
708 Parkway Ave. S., Lanesboro, MN 55949
(507) 467-2158, (800) 944-2158

Innkeeper: Gene, Kirsten, and Mary Mensing
Rooms: 2 plus 3 suites, incl. 1 w/fireplace, all w/pvt. bath, cable TV, 1 w/balcony
Rates: $55-$85/room, $85-$135/suite, all incl. full brk., evening refreshment. Discount avail. for wknd., extended and mid-week stays.
Credit cards: Most major cards
Restrictions: No children under 6, pets, smoking. Full prepayment req. 7-day cancellation notice req.
Notes: Gingerbread-style, two-story onion-dome tower house built in 1889. Located on the Root River. Furnished with period antiques, original woodwork, and stained-glass throughout. Balcony, patio, garden, carriage port. Listed on the National Register of Historic Places.*

LUTSEN (1)

Lindgren's Bed & Breakfast
P.O. Box 56, County Road 35, Lutsen, MN 55612-0056
(218) 663-7450
Innkeeper: Shirley Lindgren
Rooms: 4 w/pvt bath, TV, incl. 1 w/fireplace
Rates: $80-$110, incl. full brk. Special pkgs. avail.
Credit cards: MC, V
Restrictions: No children under 12, pets, smoking. One night's deposit req. Refunded upon cancellation only if room is re-rented, less $15.00 fee. 2-night min. stay on wknds. 3-night min. stay on holiday wknds.
Notes: Two-story log inn built in the 1920s. Knotty cedar living room with eighteen-ft. ceiling, stone fireplace, baby grand piano overlooking Lake Superior. Furnished with period pieces, 31 full mounts and assorted other taxidermy. Finnish sauna. Whirlpool. Lawn games available. Innkeeper enjoys hunting, fishing, golf, but mostly people.*

MINNEAPOLIS (6)

LeBlanc House
302 University Ave., N.E., Minneapolis, MN 55413
(612) 379-2570
Innkeeper: Barbara Fahasky, Bob Shulstad
Rooms: 3 w/phone, incl. 1 w/pvt. bath, 1 w/TV
Rates: $75-$95, incl. full brk. Discount avail. for extended stay.
Credit cards: Most major cards
Restrictions: No children under 12. Smoking restricted. 2-day cancellation notice req.
Notes: Three-story Queen Anne house. Furnished with antiques.*

Nan's Bed and Breakfast
2304 Fremont Ave. S., Minneapolis, MN 55405-2645
(612) 377-5118, (800) 214-5118
Innkeeper: Nan and Jim Zosel
Rooms: 3, no pvt. bath
Rates: $40-$50, incl. full brk. Discount avail. for extended stay.
Credit cards: Most major cards
Restrictions: One night's deposit req. 48-hour cancellation notice req.
Notes: Victorian house built in 1895. Furnished with antiques. Sitting room with wood stove. Three-season porch.*

MORRIS (3)

The American House
410 E. 3rd St., Morris, MN 56267
(612) 589-4054

Innkeeper: Karen and Kyle Berget
Rooms: 3, no pvt. bath
Rates: $30-$50, incl. full brk. Discount avail. for mid-week stay.
Credit cards: None
Restrictions: No pets. Smoking restricted. 50% deposit req. 24-hour cancellation
notice req.
Notes: Victorian house with stained-glass windows, beaded woodwork built in 1900.
Dining room with original stencil design, parquet hardwood floor. Toy room with
cable TV, antique toy collection. Furnished with family heirlooms and antiques.
Veranda. Small private parties accommodated.

ONAMIA (4)

Cour Du Lac Bed & Breakfast
RR 1, Box 269A, Onamia, MN 56359
(612) 532-4627

Innkeeper: Frank and Susan Courteau
Rooms: 3 w/pvt. bath, incl. 1 w/fireplace, window seat
Rates: $75-$95, incl. full brk. Seasonal variations.
Credit cards: MC, V
Restrictions: No children, pets. Smoking restricted. One night's deposit req. 14-day
cancellation notice req., less $5.00 fee.
Notes: Two-story house with spindle staircase. Sitting room with light oak wood-
work, overlooking lake. Dining room with view of lake. Furnished with antiques and
old family pictures. Board games available. Resident dog and cat.

PARK RAPIDS (2)

Dickson Viking Huss B & B
202 E. Fourth, Park Rapids, MN 56470
(218) 732-8089

Innkeeper: Helen Dickson
Rooms: 3 w/phone, TV, incl. 1 w/pvt. bath, fireplace
Rates: $25-$45, incl. full brk. Discount avail. for extended stay.
Credit cards: MC, V
Restrictions: No pets. Smoking restricted. Deposit req.
Notes: Contemporary cedar-sided house. Living room with fireplace, TV, games.

PELICAN RAPIDS (3)

Prairie View Estate
Rt. 2, Box 443, Pelican Rapids, MN 56572
(218) 863-4321

Innkeeper: Phyllis Haugrud, Janet Malakowsky and Carol Moses
Rooms: 3, incl. 1 w/pvt. bath
Rates: $35-$50, incl., brk. Discount avail. for extended stay.
Credit cards: Most major cards
Restrictions: No pets, smoking. Deposit req., 7-day cancellation notice req.

Notes: Scandinavian-American family house built in 1927. Country dining room, porch. Living room with TV. Furnished with family heirlooms. All meals available.

PRINCETON (4)

Oakhurst Inn Bed & Breakfast
212 Eighth Ave. S., Princeton, MN 55371
(612) 389-3553
Innkeeper: Suzie and Dave Spain
Rooms: 3 w/pvt. bath
Rates: $60-$75, incl. full brk., afternoon refreshment. Discount avail. for mid-week stay.
Credit cards: MC, V
Restrictions: No children under 12, pets. Smoking restricted. 50% deposit req. 2-week cancellation notice req., less $10.00 fee.
Notes: Two-story Victorian Cottage style house built in 1906. Front parlor with Richardson Romanesque-style working fireplace. Library with TV, VCR. Formal dining room. Wrap-around porch. Furnished with a combination of antique and reproduction items. Bicycles, books, board games, lawn games available. Horse-drawn carriage rides at additional charge. Small private parties accommodated.

OAKHURST INN BED & BREAKFAST

SAINT PAUL (6)

Chatsworth B & B
984 Ashland Ave., Saint Paul, MN 55104
(612) 227-4288
Innkeeper: Donna and Earl Gustafson
Rooms: 5, incl. 3 w/pvt. bath
Rates: $60-$115, incl. expanded cont. brk. Special pkgs. avail.
Credit cards: None
Restrictions: No pets, smoking. One night's deposit req. 5-day cancellation notice req.
Notes: Victorian house built in 1902. Fully remodeled in 1984. Located on wooded corner lot two blocks from the governor's mansion. Panelled dining room. Living

room with fireplace. Roof deck. Furnished in international style. Innkeeper is involved in yoga, nutrition, holistic health, therapeutic massage.*

Garden Gate B & B
925 Goodrich Ave., Saint Paul, MN 55105
(612) 227-8430, (800) 967-2703
Innkeeper: Mary and Miles Conway
Rooms: 4, incl. 1 suite. No pvt. bath.
Rates: $60/room, $85/suite, incl. full brk. Discount avail. for extended stay.
Credit cards: None
Restrictions: No pets, smoking. Deposit req.
Notes: Three-story Victorian built in 1906. Porch.

Prior's On Desoto
1522 DeSoto St., Saint Paul, MN 55101-3253
(612) 774-2695
Innkeeper: Mrs. Mary E. Prior
Rooms: 3, incl. 2 w/pvt. bath, TV
Rates: $57-$79, incl. full brk., afternoon refreshment. Seasonal variations. Discount avail. for extended stay.
Credit cards: None
Restrictions: No children, pets, smoking. One night's deposit req.
Notes: Custom-designed house built in 1991. Living room with fireplace and cathedral ceiling. Dining room, sundeck. Owners have travelled to 50 states and 23 countries. Limited French, German, Spanish, Japanese spoken.*

PRIOR'S ON DESOTO

SAINT PETER (7)

Engesser House
1202 South Minnesota Ave., Saint Peter, MN 56082
(800) 688-2646, (507) 931-9622
Innkeeper: Charles and Julie Storm
Rooms: 4 w/pvt. bath, cable TV, VCR

ENGESSER HOUSE

Rates: $45-$75, incl. full brk., evening refreshment. Discount avail. for extended stay.
Credit cards: MC, V
Restrictions: No children under 12, pets, smoking. 50% deposit req., 3-day cancellation notice req. 2-night min. stay during graduation wknd.
Notes: Two-story, Eastlake-style, Kasota stone and brick house built in 1880. Corner bay-tower with mansard roof, weather vane. Queen Anne features include large horizontal oval window. Parlor with black walnut, floor to ceiling fireplace. Gothic arch stained-glass window. Furnished in eclectic syle with antiques and owners' own art collection. Library with TV, VCR, movies. Guests have access to fax, photocopier, and MacIntosh Classic computer.*

SHERBURN (7)

Four Columns Inn
Rte. 2, Box 75, Sherburn, MN 56171
(507) 764-8861, (800) 944-2523
Innkeeper: Norman and Pennie Kittleson
Rooms: 4, incl. 3 w/pvt. bath, 2 w/phone, 2 w/TV. Bridal Suite avail. w/pull-down entrance to roof, deck and widow's walk.
Rates: $50-$70, incl. full brk.
Credit cards: None
Restrictions: No children under 12, pets, smoking.
Notes: Three-story Greek Revival inn with circular stairway built in 1884 as stagecoach stop. Fully remodeled with etched and stained-glass, brick from old school, cedar from old railroad trestle, redwood from watertower. Living room with library, grand piano. Music room with 1950s jukebox, player piano, musical instruments. Sun room with sauna. Den with fireplace. Great room with brick fireplace. Formal dining room, solarium, Victorian gazebo. Decorated with antiques. Small private parties accommodated.*

SPRING VALLEY (8)

Chase's B & B
508 N. Huron Ave., Spring Valley, MN 55975
(507) 346-2850

FOUR COLUMNS INN

Innkeeper: Bob and Jeannine Chase
Rooms: 5 w/pvt. bath
Rates: $75, incl. full brk., afternoon refreshment
Credit cards: Most major cards
Restrictions: No pets, smoking. Deposit req. 7-day cancellation notice req. 2-night min. stay on Sept., Oct. wknds. Closed Nov. 1–Feb. 28.
Notes: Two-story brick French Second Empire-style house with mansard roof and tower built in 1879. Parlors, library, porches. Dining room, second-floor sitting room. Furnished with antiques. Gardens. Picnic table, BBQ, vegetable garden, board games available. Listed on the National Register of Historic Places.

STILLWATER (6)

The Elephant Walk
801 W. Pine St., Stillwater, MN 55082
(612) 430-0359
Innkeeper: Rita Graybill
Rooms: 4 w/pvt. bath, phone, incl. 3/fireplace. Suite avail.
Rates: $115-$129/room, $119/suite, all incl. full brk. Seasonal variations. Discount avail. for mid-week stay.
Credit cards: MC, V
Restrictions: No children under 12, pets, smoking. Deposit req. 7-day cancellation notice req.
Notes: Two-story house built in 1883. Has operated as inn since 1992. Each room represents a different country and is furnished with collectibles and antiques collected worldwide. Two parlors, one with fireplace. Formal dining room. Whirlpools. Wrap-around front porch with swing, peacock chairs. Gardens.

James A. Mulvey Residence Inn
622 W. Churchill, Stillwater, MN 55082
(612) 430-3453
Innkeeper: Truett and Jill Lawson

Rooms: 4 w/pvt. bath, incl. 2 w/fireplace, plus 1 suite w/pvt. bath, fireplace. Located in 2 bldgs.

Rates: $95-$125/room, $139/suite, all incl. full brk., afternoon refreshment. Seasonal variations. Discount avail. for senior citizen, mid-week, and extended stays.

Credit cards: Most major cards

Restrictions: No children, pets, smoking. Deposit req. 7-day cancellation notice req.

Notes: Italianate Victorian house and stone carriage house located on one acre. Fully restored. Double parlor, formal dining room, Victorian screened porch. Furnished with collection of art pottery and antiques. Pool and Jacuzzi. Mountain bikes available. Handicapped access.*

Rivertown Inn
306 W. Olive St., Stillwater, MN 55082
(612) 430-2955, (612) 430-9292

Innkeeper: Chuck and Judy Dougherty

Rooms: 13 w/pvt. bath, incl. 5 w/whirlpool, 3 w/fireplace, plus 7 suites w/pvt. bath, incl. 4 w/phone, TV. Located in 2 bldgs.

Rates: $49-$129/room, $129-$159/suite, all incl. full brk., evening refreshment. Discount avail. for extended and holiday wknd. stays.

Credit cards: Most major cards

Restrictions: No children under 12, pets. Smoking restricted.

Notes: Three-story Italianate-style mansion built in 1882. Decorated with turn-of-the-century Victorian antiques. Small private parties accommodated.*

WALKER (2)

PEACE CLIFF

Peace Cliff
HCR 73, Box 998D, Walker, MN 56484
(218) 547-2832

Innkeeper: Dave and Kathy Laursen

Rooms: 5, incl. 1 w/pvt. bath, fireplace

Rates: $58-$95, incl. full brk. Discount avail. for extended and off-season group stays. Special pkgs. avail.

Credit cards: Most major cards

Restrictions: No children under 8, pets, smoking. Deposit req. 2-week cancellation notice, less 10% fee. 2-night min. stay in July, August, and for holidays.

Notes: Two-story inn located on 85-foot bluff overlooking Walker Bay. Tower library, trophy room with fireplace, TV room with cable, living room. Furnished with antiques, old books.

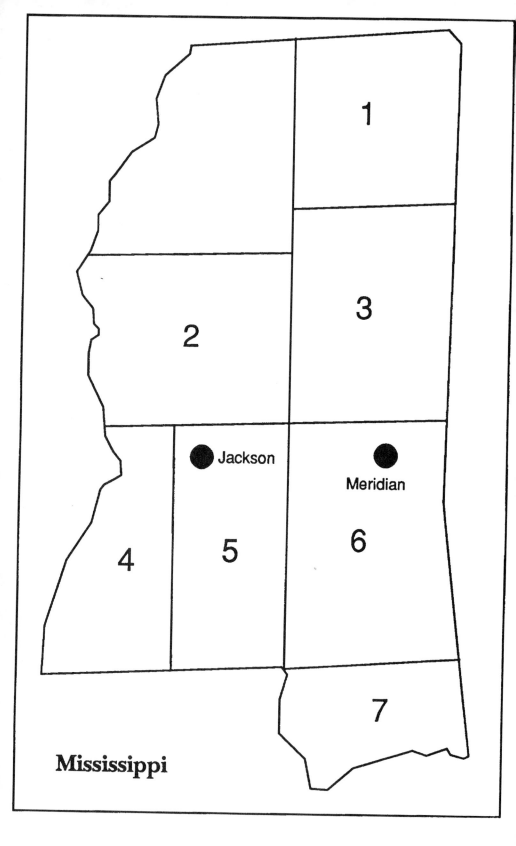

Mississippi

COLUMBUS (3)

Columbus Historic Foundation
P.O. Box 46, Columbus, MS 39703
(601) 329-3533
Innkeeper: various
Rooms: 16 w/pvt. bath, phone, TV, incl. 3 w/fireplace. Suites avail. Located in 5 bldgs.
Rates: $85/room, $115-$160/suite, all incl. full brk., afternoon refreshment. Discount avail. for extended stay. Special pkgs. avail.
Credit cards: MC, V
Restrictions: Children, pets, smoking restricted. One night's deposit req. 7-day cancellation notice req.
Notes: Columbus Historic Foundation operates five Antebellum inns in Columbus, built from 1828-1857, including small city cottage, palatial mansion, working plantation home. Common rooms, usually with fireplace. Each house furnished with authentic period furnishings. Some with extensive grounds, some with private gardens. All on the National Register of Historic Places. Small private parties accommodated. Board games, dinner available.*

CORINTH (1)

General's Quarters
924 Fillmore St., Box 1505, Corinth, MS 38834
(601) 286-3325
Innkeeper: John and Rosemary Aldridge
Rooms: 3 plus 1 suite, all w/pvt. bath, phone, TV
Rates: $75, incl. full brk. Discount avail. for mid-week stay.
Credit cards: Most major cards
Restrictions: One night's deposit req. 48-hour cancellation notice req., less one nights' fee.
Notes: Two-story built in 1870s. Located in historic district. Furnished with period antiques.

HATTIESBURG (6)

Tally House
402 Rebecca Ave., Hattiesburg, MS 39401
(601) 582-3467
Innkeeper: C.E. and Sydney Bailey
Rooms: 4 w/pvt. bath, fireplace
Rates: $65, incl. brk. Discount avail. for senior citizen and extended stays.
Credit cards: MC, V
Restrictions: No children under 12, pets. Smoking restricted.
Notes: Two-and-a-half-story house with 11 fireplaces built in 1907. Fully restored. 2-story wrap-around porch. Wicker-furnished sitting rooms. Listed on the National Register of Historic Places. Collection of antiques and artifacts.*

KOSCIUSKO (2)

The Redbudd Inn
121 N. Wells St., Kosciusko, MS 39090
(601) 289-5086, (800) 379-5086
Innkeeper: Maggie Garret Rose Mary Burge
Rooms: 4 plus 1 suite, all w/pvt. bath, phone, TV
Rates: $75-$100/room, $125/suite, all incl. full brk. afternoon refreshment. Special
　pkgs. avail.
Credit cards: MC, V
Restrictions: Deposit req. 48-hour cancellation notice req.
Notes: Two-story Queen Anne house. Has operated as inn since 1890s. Wide center
hall, square staircase. Windows with original interior blinds. Gallery. Balconies with
turned posts, balustrades, spindles, and carved brackets. Three-story octagonal corner tower. Restaurant and antique shop on premises. French spoken. Handicapped
access.*

LONG BEACH (7)

Red Creek Colonial Inn
7416 Red Creek Rd., Long Beach, MS 39560
(601) 452-3080, (800) 729-9670
Innkeeper: David and Christina Smith
Rooms: 4, incl. 3 w/pvt. bath, 1 w/fireplace, plus 1 suite w/pvt. bath, fireplace
Rates: $49-$69/room, $89/suite, all incl. cont. brk. Discount avail. for extended
　stay. Special pkgs. avail.
Credit cards: None
Restrictions: No pets, smoking. One night's deposit req. 14-day cancellation notice
　req., less credit for future stay within year. 2-night min. stay req. on wknds. from
　June–Aug.
Notes: Three-story raised French cottage built in 1899. Has operated as Inn since
1989. Located on eleven wooded acres. Sixty-four-ft. front porch with swings. Fur-
nished with antiques.*

NATCHEZ (4)

Dunleith
84 Homochitto St., Natchez, MS 39120
(601) 446-8500
Innkeeper: Nancy Gibbs
Rooms: 11 w/pvt. bath, phone, TV, fireplace
Rates: $85, incl. full brk., afternoon refreshment
Credit cards: Most major cards
Restrictions: No children, pets. Smoking restricted. Min. one night's deposit req.
　3-day cancellation notice req.
Notes: Three-story Greek Revival house built in 1856. Located on 40-acre land-
scaped park. Breakfast room is restored poultry house. Gallery with wicker chairs.
Dining room decorated with French Zuber wallpaper before World War I from
woodblocks carved in 1855. Staircase. Listed on Nattional Register of Historic
Places. A National Historic Landmark. Used in films *Huckleberry Finn*, and *Showboat*.

The Governor Holmes House
207 S. Wall St., Natchez, MS 39120
(601) 442-2366

THE GOVERNOR HOLMES HOUSE

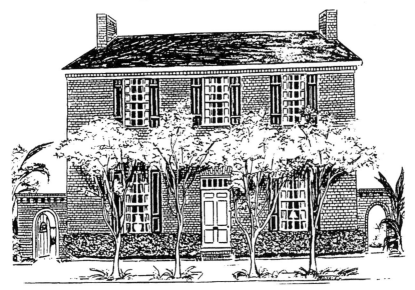

Innkeeper: Robert Pully
Rooms: 4 w/pvt. bath, fireplace, TV
Rates: $85, incl. full brk. Special pkgs. avail.
Credit cards: MC, V
Restrictions: No children under 12. Smoking restricted. Deposit req. 7-day cancellation notice.
Notes: Two-story house built in 1794. Dining room, breakfst room. Decorated with period furnishings, porcelain, oriental carpets and period paintings. Listed on National Register of Historic Places. *

The Guest House Historic Hotel
201 N. Pearl St., Natchez, MS 39120
(601) 442-1054, (800) 442-1054, (601) 442-1374
Innkeeper: Brenda Moon
Rooms: 18 w/pvt. bath, phone, TV, stocked minibar, coffee maker
Rates: $94, incl. cont. brk., evening refreshment. Seasonal variations. Discount avail. for senior citizen and mid-week stays.
Credit cards: Most major cards
Restrictions: No pets. Credit card deposit req., 48-hour cancellation notice req.
Notes: Two-story southern-style house built in 1840. Furnished with antiques and reproductions. Small private parties accommodated. Handicapped access.*

Harper House
201 Arlington Ave., Natchez, MS 39120
(601) 445-5557, (800) 571-8848
Innkeeper: John and Kay Warren

Rooms: 1 w/pvt. bath, TV, plus 1 suite, w/pvt. bath, TV
Rates: $70, incl. full brk.
Credit cards: Most major cards
Restrictions: No children under 12, pets, smoking. Deposit req. 7-day cancellation req.
Notes: Two-story Victorian house built in 1892. Custom stenciled rooms. Gazebo, wicker-filled porches. Furnished in antiques. Walk to historic district.*

Oakland Plantation
1124 Lower Woodville Rd., Natchez, MS 39120
(601) 442-1630 day, (601) 445-5101 night
Innkeeper: Andy and Jean Peabody
Rooms: 3, incl. 1 w/pvt. bath, plus 1 suite w/pvt. bath, TV
Rates: $65-$75, incl. full brk. Discount avail. for extended stay.
Credit cards: Most major cards
Restrictions: No pets. Smoking restricted. Deposit req. 2-day cancellation notice req.
Notes: Guests have access to tennis courts, pond fishing, canoeing, trail hiking. Handicapped access.*

PORT GIBSON (4)

Oak Square
1207 Church St., Port Gibson, MS 39150
(601) 437-4350, (800) 729-0240, (601) 437-5768
Innkeeper: Mr. and Mrs. William Lum
Rooms: 12 w/pvt. bath, phone, cable TV. Located in 3 bldgs.
Rates: $75-$95, incl. full brk. Discount avail. for families.
Credit cards: Most major cards
Restrictions: No pets. Smoking restricted. 3-day cancellation notice req.
Notes: 2-story Greek Revival, antebellum house built in 1850. Canopied beds. Parlors, formal dining room, courtyard, fountain, gazebo, massive oak trees. Furnished with heirloom antiques. Collection of rare Civil War memorabilia. Carriage house suite available. Listed on the National Register of Historic Places, and Mississippi's First National Historic District.

OAK SQUARE

TUPELO (1)

The Mockingbird Inn
305 N. Gloster, Tupelo, MS 38801
(601) 841-0286, (601) 840-4158

Innkeeper: Jim and Sandy Gilmer
Rooms: 6 plus 1 suite, all w/pvt. bath, phone, cable TV
Rates: $65-$95, incl. full brk., afternoon refreshment
Credit cards: Most major cards
Restrictions: No children under 13. Smoking restricted. One night's deposit req. 3-day cancellation notice req.
Notes: Two-story brick house built in 1925 in combination of Colonial, Prairie and Arts and Crafts styles. Fully renovated in 1993. Dining room, living room. Glass-enclosed porch. Each bedroom decorated to represent a city or country. Furnished with antiques, tapestry, and artwork. Guests have access to full kitchen, double Jacuzzi, and fax machine. Small private parties accommodated. Handicapped access. Some Spanish spoken.*

ANNABELLE

VICKSBURG (4)

Annabelle
501 Speed St., Vicksburg, MS 39180
(601) 638-2000, (800) 791-2000

Innkeeper: Carolyn and George Mayer
Rooms: 5 w/pvt. bath, cable TV, incl. 3 w/phone, plus 2 suites w/pvt bath, cable TV, incl. 1 w/phone. Located in 2 bldgs.
Rates: $80-$90/room, $125-$155/suite, all incl. full brk. Discount avail. for extended stay.
Credit cards: Most major cards
Restrictions: No children under 6. Smoking restricted. Desposit req. 2-day cancellation notice req.
Notes: Two-story Victorian-Italianate home built circa 1868. Dining room with 12' ceilings. New Orleans Vieux Carre patio. Period antiques. Pecan and magnolia trees. German, Portugese spoken. Resident cat.*

Flowerree Cottage
2309 Pearl St., Vicksburg, MS 39180
(601) 638-2704, (800) 262-6315, (601) 636-0052
Innkeeper: Gayle Tuminello
Rooms: 7 plus 2 suites, cottage, all w/pvt. bath, phone, cable TV. Located in 4 bldgs.
Rates: $85-$160/room, $110-130/suite, $220/cottage, all incl. full brk., evening re-
    freshment. Discount avail. for extended stay.
Credit cards: Most major cards
Restrictions: No children under 6, pets. Min. one night's deposit req. 3-day cancel-
    lation notice req. Closed Christmas Day.
Notes: Italianate mansion built about 1870. Fully restored in 1961. Double parlor.
Furnished with period antiques. Listed on the National Register of Historical
Places.*

WEST (2)

Alexander House B & B
210 Green St., Box 187, West, MS 39192
(601) 350-8034, (601) 967-2266, (601) 967-2417
Innkeeper: Ruth Ray, Woody Dinstel
Rooms: 3 w/pvt. bath, plus 2 suites, no pvt. bath
Rates: $65/room, $110/suite, all incl. full brk.
Credit cards: Most major cards
Restrictions: No children, pets, smoking.
Notes: Two-story house built about 1880. Has operated as inn since 1994. Parlor,
dining room. Furnished in Victorian style. Mountain bicycles available. Dinner
available by appointment. Resident outside cats.

Missouri

AUGUSTA (5)

Lindenhof Bed & Breakfast
Walnut & Jackson, Box 52, Augusta, MO 63332
(314) 228-4617
Innkeeper: Mary L Peters
Rooms: 4, incl. 3 w/pvt. bath
Rates: $55-$65, incl. full brk. Discount avail. for mid-week stay.
Credit cards: Most major cards
Restrictions: No pets, smoking. $35.00 deposit req. 7-day cancellation notice req.
Notes: Two story Country-Victorian farmhouse. Has operated as inn since 1987. Parlour, dining room. Furnished in antiques. Yard enclosed by wrought-iron fence.*

LINDENHOF BED & BREAKFAST

BRANSON (6)

The Brass Swan
202 River Bend Rd., Branson, MO 65616
(800) 280-6873
Innkeeper: Dick and Gigi House
Rooms: 4 w/pvt. bath, TV
Rates: $70-$80, incl. full brk.
Credit cards: Most major cards
Restrictions: No children, pets. Smoking restricted. One-night's deposit req. 14-day cancellation notice req.
Notes: Contemporary house overlooking Lake Taneycomo. Common room with fireplace. Game room with treadmill, pin-ball machine. Guests have access to wet bar, refrigerator, microwave. Hot tub available. Small private parties accommodated.*

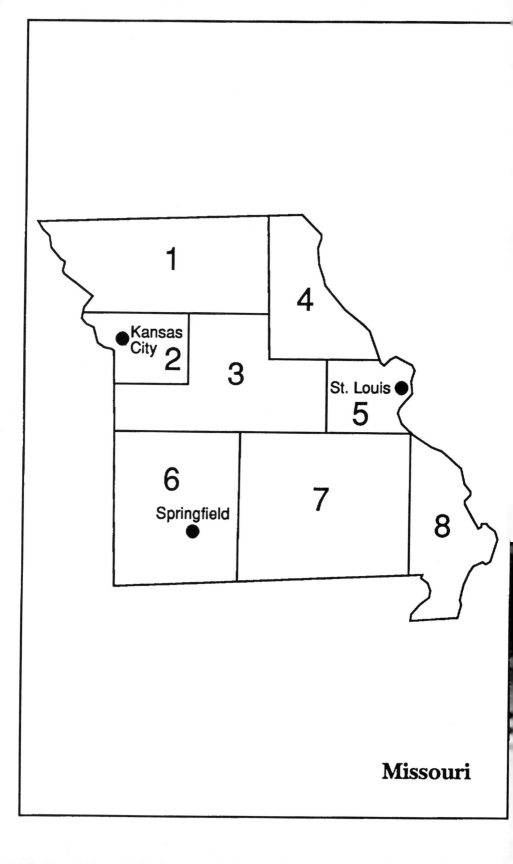

Missouri

Country Gardens
1824 Lakeshore Dr., H.C.R. 4, Box 2202, Branson, MO 65616
(417) 334-8564

Innkeeper: Bob and Pat Cameron
Rooms: 2 plus 1 suite, all w/pvt. bath, cable TV
Rates: $70/room, $95/suite, all incl. full brk. Discount avail. for extended stay.
Credit cards: Most major cards
Restrictions: No children under 12, pets, smoking. Deposit req. 21-day cancellation
notice req., less $15.00 fee.
Notes: Woodframe and rock house. Common room overlooking garden. Furnished
with antiques. Private dock on Lake Taneycomo. Swimming pool, deck spa. Boats
available.*

CARTHAGE (6)

Grand Avenue Inn
1615 Grand Ave., Carthage, MO 64836
(417) 358-7265

Innkeeper: Betty Nisich and Paula Hunt
Rooms: 3 w/pvt. bath, incl. 1 w/fireplace, plus 2 suites w/pvt. bath, incl. 1 w/TV
Rates: $75/room, $30/suite, all incl. full brk., afternoon refreshment. Seasonal vari-
ations. Discount avail. for mid-week stay.
Credit cards: MC, V
Restrictions: No children under 10, pets, smoking. 50% deposit req. 7-day cancel-
lation notice req., less $20.00 fee.
Notes: Two-story Victorian house with stained-glass windows built in the 1900s.
Library with TV. Dining room with oak dining table. Foyer, veranda. Furnished with
antiques. Lap pool. Small private parties accommodated. Listed on the National
Register of Historic Places. French spoken.*

HANNIBAL (4)

Garth Woodside Mansion
RR 1, off Route 61, Hannibal, MO 63401
(314) 221-2789

Innkeeper: Diane and Irv Feinberg
Rooms: 8 w/pvt. bath
Rates: $65-$105, incl. full brk., night shirt
Credit cards: MC, V
Restrictions: No children under 12, pets. Smoking restricted. Deposit req. Min.
7-day cancellation notice req., less $10.00 fee. 2-night min. stay on some wknds.
Notes: Three-story Victorian Second Empire mansion with three-story vaulted
staircase built in 1871. Located on thirty-nine acres with pond. Dining room, two
parlors, library. Furnished with antiques and original pieces. Veranda, two-person
Jacuzzi. Mark Twain spent several nights here when it was owned by his boyhood
friends John and Helen Garth. Listed on the National Register of Historic Places.

HERMANN (5)

Die Gillig Heimat
HCR 62 Box 30, Hermann, MO 65041
(314) 943-6942

Innkeeper: Ann and Armin Gillig

Rooms: 1 w/pvt. bath, plus 1 suite w/pvt. bath, phone, TV, sitting room
Rates: $55/room, $65/suite, all incl. full brk., afternoon refreshment
Credit cards: None
Restrictions: No pets, smoking. 50% deposit req. 10-day cancellation notice req. 3-week cancellation notice for festivals. 2-night min. stay during festivals.
Notes: Two-story house built in 1842. Expanded in 1878. Located on 250-acre working farm homesteaded by Innkeeper's German ancestors in the 1840s. Resident farm animals. German spoken.

JACKSON (8)

Trisha's Bed and Breakfast
203 Bellevue, Jackson, MO 63755
(314) 243-7427, (800) 651-0408
Innkeeper: Trisha and Gus Wischmann
Rooms: 4, incl. 3 w/pvt. bath, 1 w/TV
Rates: $65-$75, incl. full brk., afternoon refreshment. Discount avail. for mid-week stay. Special pkgs. avail.
Credit cards: Most major cards
Restrictions: No children under 5, pets. Smoking restricted. $25 per room non-refundable deposit req. Closed 3rd week in June.
Notes: Two-story Victorian house built in 1905. Expanded in 1935. Has operated as inn since 1988. Dining room, sitting room, family room, library, foyer. Furnished with antiques, collectables. Dinner available, special diets accommodated. Small private parties accommodated. Innkeeper is a relative of Abraham Lincoln and is collecting family pictures.*

TRISHA'S BED AND BREAKFAST

JAMESPORT (2)

Richardson House
P.O. Box 227, Jamesport, MO 64648
(816) 842-4211
Innkeeper: Rebecca Richardson

Rooms: 4 w/phone, TV

Rates: $75, incl. full brk. Seasonal variations. Discount avail. for mid-week stay. Children under 6 free.

Credit cards: MC, V

Restrictions: Pets, smoking restricted. One night's deposit req. 14-day cancellations req. less $10.00 fee.

Notes: Restored turn-of-the-century Victorian farmhouse in Amish country. Located on 7-acre Christmas tree farm. Family-owned since 1927. Furnished with antiques. Guests have access to kitchen. Cable TV, radio, books, board games available. Picnic baskets and all meals available. Small private parties accommodated.*

JOPLIN (6)

Visages
327 N. Jackson, Joplin, MO 64801
(417) 624-1397

Innkeeper: Bill and Marge Meeker

Rooms: 2, incl. 1 w/phone, TV, plus 1 suite w/pvt. bath, phone, TV, sunroom

Rates: $40-$50/room, $60/suite, all incl. full brk.

Credit cards: AE, DC

Restrictions: No infants. Pets welome with prior arrangement. Smoking restricted. Deposit req. 24-hour cancellation notice req.

Notes: Two-story Dutch Colonial inn built in 1898. Fully renovated in 1977. Decorated in eclectic turn-of-the-century Victorian and country decor, paintings and craftsmanship of innkeepers. Balcony overlooking gardens with stone walls. Cribs.*

KANSAS CITY (2)

Doanleigh Wallagh Inn
217 E. 37th St., Kansas City, MO 64111-1473
(816) 753-2667, (816) 753-2408

Innkeeper: Ed and Carolyn Litchfield

Rooms: 5 w/pvt. bath, phone, cable TV, incl. 1 w/fireplace

Rates: $80-$110, incl. full brk, cookies in room, afternoon refreshment. Discount avail. for extended stay.

Credit cards: Most major cards

Restrictions: No pets. Smoking restricted. One night's deposit req. Min. 7-day cancellation notice req., less $20.00 fee. 2-night min. stay on some holidays.

Notes: Two-story Georgian-style house built in 1907. Two living rooms, one with fireplace, grand piano, pump organ. Two dining rooms, porch. Furnished with American and English antiques. Off-street parking available. Small private parties accommodated. Some French, Romanian spoken.*

KIRKWOOD (5)

Eastlake Inn
703 N. Kirkwood, Kirkwood, MO 63122
(314) 965-0066

Innkeeper: Lori and Dan Ashdown

Rooms: 3 w/pvt. bath

Rates: $55-$70, incl. full brk.

Credit cards: Most major cards

Restrictions: No children under 10, pets, smoking. One night's deposit req. 2-week cancellation notice req.

Notes: Two-story Eastlake-style inn. Main dining room. Parlor with board games. A 1,100-piece hand-poured crystal chandelier over dining table. Furnished with period antiques. Gardens and brick patio.*

EASTLAKE INN

LIBERTY (2)

Lindgrens' Landing B & B
222 W. Franklin St., Liberty, MO 64068-1642
(816) 781-8742

Innkeeper: James and Esther Lindgren

Rooms: 2 plus 1 suite, incl. 1 w/pvt. bath, 3 w/phone jacks

Rates: $35-$50/room, $65-$80/suite, all incl. full brk.

Credit cards: None

Restrictions: Pets welcome with prior arrangement. Smoking restricted. Deposit may be required.

Notes: Brick Prairie Four Square-style house built in 1912. Living room with fireplace. Dining room. Board games, bicycles available. French spoken.*

MEXICO (4)

Hylas House Inn
811 S. Jefferson, Mexico, MO 65265
(314) 581-2011

Innkeeper: Tom and Linda Hylas

Rooms: 3, incl. 1 w/pvt. bath, 2 w/TV, phone, plus 1 suite w/living room, TV, VCR, phone, balcony, pvt. bath. Robes provided.

Rates: $65-$85/room, $95/suite, all incl.full brk., afternoon refreshment. Discount avail. for mid-week stay.

Credit cards: MC, V

Restrictions: No children under 12, pets. Smoking restricted. Full deposit req.

Notes: Two-story Italianate house with Delarobia archways, leaded-glass windows, cherry wood.

HYLAS HOUSE INN

PARKVILLE (2)

Down to Earth Lifestyles
Rte. 22, Parkville, MO 64152
(816) 891-1018

Innkeeper: Bill and Lola Coons
Rooms: 4 w/pvt. bath, phone
Rates: $75, incl. full brk., afternoon refreshment. Discount avail. for families.
Credit cards: None
Restrictions: No pets. Smoking restricted.
Notes: Mid-western style, earth-integrated house located on an 86-acre wooded, working farm. Roll-away bed and crib available. Lounge with TV. Great room with fireplace, piano, board games. Patio. Heated indoor swimming pool. Two stocked ponds.*

PLATTE CITY (2)

Basswood Country Inn
15880 Interurban Rd., Platte City, MO 64079-9185
(816) 858-5556, (816) 858-5556

Innkeeper: Don and Betty Soper
Rooms: 8 suites plus 1 cottage, all w/pvt. bath, phone, TV, mini-kitchen, incl. 2
   w/fireplace. Located in 3 bldgs.
Rates: $63-$125, all incl. cont. brk.
Credit cards: Most major cards
Restrictions: No pets. One night's deposit req. 72-hour cancellation notice req.
Notes: Country contemporary cottage built in 1987. Lakeside cottage built in 1935. Located on Seventy-four wooded acres. Once operated as private sportsman's club. Outdoor heated swimming pool. Four fishing lakes. Volleyball, shuffle board. Sign language spoken.*

SAINT LOUIS (5)

Lehmann House
10 Benton Pl., Saint Louis, MO 63104
(314) 231-6724

Innkeeper: Michael and Marie Davies
Rooms: 4 incl. 2 w/fireplace, 1 w/pvt. bath
Rates: $45-$70, incl. full brk., afternoon refreshment. Discount avail. for extended stay.
Credit cards: Most major cards
Restrictions: No pets, smoking. Min. 50% deposit req. 2-week cancellation notice req., less $15.00 fee.
Notes: Victorian Romanesque Revival house built in 1893. Restoration in progress. Located on a 3/4 acre. Entry foyer with fireplace. Parlor with TV, music. Dining room, library. Board games available. Furnished with antiques appropriate to the late-19th and early-20th centuries. Swimming during the summer. Tennis courts. Listed on the National Register of Historic Places. Italian, German spoken.*

LEHMANN HOUSE

The Winter House
3522 Arsenal St., Saint Louis, MO 63118
(314) 664-4399

Innkeeper: Kendall and Sarah Winter
Rooms: 2 plus 1 suite, all w/pvt. bath, incl. 1 w/cable TV
Rates: $70/room, $85/suite, all incl. expanded cont. brk., wknd. refreshment. Discount avail. for extended stay.
Credit cards: Most major cards
Restrictions: No children under 12, pets. Smoking restricted. Min. 50% deposit req. 7-day cancellation notice req. Closed Dec. 25–29.
Notes: Two and one-half story Victorian inn with turret built in 1897. Expanded in 1921. Has operated as Inn since 1989. Downstairs ceilings are pressed tin, doors feature original brass knobs. Parlor with cast iron log fireplace. Dining room with turret. Balconies, porches. Furnished in period decor with antiques, family heirlooms. Live piano music with breakfast on restored 1918 Bush and Gerts piano by advance reservation. Amtrak pick-up available for additional fee.*

SPRINGFIELD (6)

Walnut Street B and B
900 E. Walnut St., Springfield, MO 65806
(417) 864-6346, (417) 864-6184
Innkeeper: Karol Brown

THE WINTER HOUSE

Rooms: 10 plus 4 suites, all w/pvt. bath, phone, most w/fireplace, TV. Located in 3 bldgs.
Rates: $80-$95/room, $135-$150/suite, all incl. full brk. Discount avail. for midweek stay. Special pkgs. avail.
Credit cards: Most major cards
Restrictions: No children under 3, pets, smoking. One-night's deposit req. 14-day cancellation notice req., less $15.00 fee.
Notes: Victorian inn with hardwood floors built in 1894. Dining room. Sitting room with fireplace, board games, library, TV. Gathering room with fireplace, game table. Furnished with antiques. Porch with swing and rockers. Small private parties accommodated. Handicapped access in 1 bldg. Listed on the National Register of Historic Places. Featured as the city's designer showcase house.*

WARRENSBURG (2)

Cedarcroft Farm B & B
431 SE "Y" Hwy., Warrensburg, MO 64093
(816) 747-5728
Innkeeper: Sandra and Bill Wayne
Rooms: 2, no pvt. bath
Rates: $48-$53, incl. full brk., evening refreshment
Credit cards: Most major cards
Restrictions: No pets. Children, smoking restricted. Min. one night's deposit req. Min. 5-day cancellation notice req., less $15.00 fee.
Notes: Farmhouse built in 1867. Fully renovated. Located on 80 wooded acres. Has operated as inn since 1988. Victorian parlor, gathering room, dining area, front porch, kitchen. Furnished with antiques and primitive pieces. All meals available with prior notification. Innkeeper is retired Air Force officer, Civil War re-enactor.*

WASHINGTON (5)

Washington House B and B Inn
3 Lafayette St., Washington, MO 63090
(314) 239-2417
Innkeeper: Chuck and Kathy Davis
Rooms: 3 w/pvt. bath

Rates: $55-$75, incl. full brk., evening refreshment
Credit cards: Most major cards
Restrictions: No pets, smoking. 50% deposit req. 2-week cancellation notice req., less $10.00 fee.
Notes: Built as an inn in 1837 overlooking Missouri River. Recently restored. Parlor, terrace. Furnished with period antiques, reproductions. Complimentary bottle of wine and cheese on arrival.

WEST PLAINS (7)

Blue Spruce Inn
429 Aid Ave., West Plains, MO 65775
(417) 256-3209
Innkeeper: Rich and Terree Funesti
Rooms: 3, w/pvt. bath
Rates: $50, incl. full brk. Discount avail. for extended stay. Special pkgs. avail.
Credit cards: MC, V
Restrictions: No pets, smoking. Deposit req., 24-hour cancellation notice req., less $15.00 fee.
Notes: Two-story colonial house built in 1887. Family Room with stereo, VCR, and TV. Parlor and country dining room. Breakfast served in the gazebo. Furnished with antiques, handmade quilts, linens, and handwoven rugs. Dinners available by prior arrangement. Picnic baskets available. Small private parties accommodated.*

Montana

ANACONDA (3)

The Summit B & B
P.O. Box 217, Anaconda, MT 59711
(406) 563-6578
Innkeeper: Kerry and Colleen Hatcher
Rooms: 4, incl. 2 w/pvt. bath, 1 w/fireplace
Rates: $65-$95, incl. full brk. Discount avail. for senior citizen and extended stays.
Credit cards: MC, V
Restrictions: No children under 2, pets. Smoking restricted. Deposit req.
Notes: Two-story Cedar-sided house. Located on top of 7000-foot mountain overlooking lake and ski hill. Living room. Study with fireplace. Deck overlooking lake. Decorated with local antiques. Hot tub. Small private parties accommodated.*

BIGFORK (1)

O'Duach'ain Country Inn
675 Ferndale, Bigfork, MT 59911
(406) 837-6851, (406) 837-4390
Innkeeper: Tom and Margot Doohan
Rooms: 3 w/TV, phone, incl. 2 w/pvt. bath, plus 2 suites w/pvt. bath
Rates: $75/room, $95/suite, all incl. full brk. Special pkgs. avail.
Credit cards: Most major cards
Restrictions: Pets welcome with prior approval. Smoking restricted. 50% deposit req. 14-day cancellation notice req., less min. $25.00 fee.
Notes: Three-story log home well-hidden on five wooded acres. Decorated with eclectic furniture, artifacts and artistry. Game area, balconies, outdoor hot tub. Spanish spoken. Resident dog, peacock, horses, and miniature donkey.*

BOZEMAN (4)

Lindley House
202 Lindley Pl., Bozeman, MT 59715
(406) 587-8403, (800) 787-8404, (406) 582-8112
Innkeeper: Mary Jo Schneider, Stephanie Volz
Rooms: 2, plus 2 suites, all w/pvt. bath, phone, TV, incl. 1 w/fireplace
Rates: $110-$135/room, $175-$275/suite, all incl. full brk., evening refreshment. Seasonal variations.
Credit cards: MC, V
Restrictions: No children under 10, pets. Smoking restricted. 50% deposit req. 7-day cancellation notice req. 2-night min. stay.
Notes: Two-story Victorian manor house with stained-glass windows, built in 1889. Enclosed English garden. Hot tub, sauna. Mountain bikes available. Listed on the National Register of Historic Places.*

The Voss Inn
319 S. Willson, Bozeman, MT 59715
(406) 587-0982
Innkeeper: Bruce and Frankee Muller

Rooms: 6 w/pvt. bath, phone
Rates: $60-$80, incl. full brk., evening refreshment
Credit cards: Most major cards
Restrictions: No children under 5, pets, smoking. First and last nights' deposit req.
  7-day cancellation notice req., less $10.00 fee.
Notes: Two-story, Victorian mansion built in 1883. Victorian parlor with cable TV.
Furnished with some antiques. Guided day trips offered to Yellowstone. Dutch, Italian, Spanish spoken.*

BUTTE (3)

Copper King Mansion
219 W. Granite, Butte, MT 59701
(406) 782-7580
Innkeeper: Maria Sigl
Rooms: 2, plus 2 suites, incl. 2 w/pvt. bath, 1 w/phone, TV
Rates: $55/room, $75-$95/suite, all incl. full brk.
Credit cards: Most major cards
Restrictions: 2-day cancellation notice, less 25% fee.
Notes: Three-story Victorian inn built in 1884. Stained glass-windows, frescoed ceilings, hand-carved woodwork. Decorated with antique furnishings.*

COLUMBIA FALLS (1)

Bad Rock Country B & B
480 Bad Rock Dr., Columbia Falls, MT 59912
(406) 892-2829, (406) 892-2930
Innkeeper: Jon and Sue Alper
Rooms: 7 w/pvt. bath, phone, incl. 4 w/fireplace. Located in 3 bldgs.
Rates: $80-$125, incl. full brk, afternoon refreshment. Seasonal variations.
Credit cards: Most major cards
Restrictions: No children under 10, smoking. Pets restricted. Deposit req. Cancellation notice req., less $20.00 fee.
Notes: Main house and guest cabins located on 30-acre working farm. Each cabin has two guest rooms, with private entrances, fireplaces, private patio. Main house with three living rooms, book collection, dining room, and a family room with satellite TV. Hot tub. Innkeepers collect bunny rabbit creations.*

DARBY (3)

Triple Creek
5551 W. Fork Stage Rte., Darby, MT 59829
(406) 821-4664, (406) 821-4666
Innkeeper: Wayne and Judy Kilpatrick
Rooms: 17 cabins w/TV, phone, pvt. bath, fireplace, coffee maker, stocked refrigerator, incl. 6 w/outdoor hot tubs, 4 w/indoor whirlpool tubs.
Rates: $150-$175, incl. cont. brk., evening refreshment. Seasonal variations.
Credit cards: Most major cards
Restrictions: No children under 16. 50% deposit req. 7-day cancellation notice req.,
  less 50% fee. Closed Sunday–Thursday.
Notes: Lounge, sitting room. Grounds with creek, pond. Restaurant on premises.*

EMIGRANT (4)

PARADISE GATEWAY B & B

Paradise Gateway B & B
P.O. Box 84, Emigrant, MT 59027
(406) 333-4063

Innkeeper: Pete and Carol Reed
Rooms: 3 w/pvt. bath
Rates: $85-$95, incl. full brk., afternoon refreshment. Seasonal variations.
Credit cards: MC, V
Restrictions: No children, pets. Smoking restricted. One night's deposit req. 14-day
    cancellation notice req., less $15.00 fee. 2-night min. stay, July 1–Aug. 31.
Notes: Country house located on twenty-plus acres between two Rocky Mountain
ranges on banks of Yellowstone River. Parlor with fireplace, satellite TV, VCR. Dec-
orated with art and antiques. Fly-fish from doorway. Will assist with kennel arrangements.*

EUREKA (1)

Scenic Adventures B & B
US 93 N, Box 301, Eureka, MT 59917
(406) 889-3556

Innkeeper: Randy and Barbara Schermerhorn
Rooms: 8, no pvt. bath. Located in 2 bldgs.
Rates: $60, incl. full brk. Seasonal variations. Discount avail. for senior citizens. Spe-
    cial pkgs. avail.
Credit cards: MC, V
Restrictions: No pets. Smoking restricted. $35.00 deposit req. 14-day cancellation
    notice req.
Notes: Two-story inn. Guided day trips, mountain biking available.

GARDINER (4)

Yellowstone Inn B & B
US 89 & Main, Box 515, Gardiner, MT 59030
(406) 848-7000, (406) 848-7000

Innkeeper: Brad and Carmen Harbach

Rooms: 8, incl. 3 w/pvt bath, plus 1 suite w/pvt. bath, TV, plus stone cottage. Located in 3 bldgs.

Rates: $64-$74/room, $84/suite, $94/cottage, all incl. full brk. Seasonal variations.

Credit cards: MC, V

Restrictions: No pets, smoking. One night's deposit req. 2-day cancellation notice req.

Notes: Two turn-of-the-century stone houses located in Gardiner, the north entrance to Yellowstone National Park. Parlors with fireplaces. Tours, fishing, pack trips whitewater rafting arrangements through Inn. Hot tub. *

THE HOSTETLER HOUSE B & B

GLENDIVE (6)

The Hostetler House B & B
113 N. Douglas, Glendive, MT 59330
(406) 365-4505, (406) 365-8456

Innkeeper: Craig and Dea Hostetler

Rooms: 2, no pvt. bath

Rates: $45, incl. full brk. Discount avail. for mid-week, senior citizen, and extended stays.

Credit cards: None

Restrictions: No children, pets, smoking. One night's deposit req. 7-day cancellation notice req.

Notes: Two-story house with three-tiered brick planter built in 1912. Gazebo, sitting room, dining room, enclosed sun porch, deck, hot tub, cable TV, VCR, board games. Decorated with handmade quilts, family heirlooms, and collectibles. German spoken.*

HARDIN (5)

Kendrick House Inn
206 N. Custer Ave., Hardin, MT 59034
(406) 665-3035, (406) 665-3035
Innkeeper: Steve and Marcie Smith
Rooms: 7, no pvt. bath.
Rates: $55, incl. full brk.
Credit cards: MC, V
Restrictions: Well-behaved, older children welcome. Small pets welcome with prior approval. Smoking restricted. One night's deposit req. 14-day cancellation notice req.
Notes: Boarding house built in 1914. First rooming house to advertise modern facilities. Served as emergency hospital from 1943 to 1945. Located on border of Crow/Cheyenne Indian reservations. Restored in 1988. Decorated with period antiques, turn-of-the-century collectables, and memorabilia. Library with collection of Civil War and pre-WWI novels, TV/VCR. Sun porch. Two verandas—one with porch swing, one with wicker furniture. Listed on the National Register of Historic Buildings.*

HELENA (1)

The Sanders
328 N. Ewing, Helena, MT 59601
(406) 442-3309
Innkeeper: Bobbi Uecker, Rock Ringling
Rooms: 7 w/pvt. bath, phone, TV
Rates: $60-$98, incl. full brk.
Credit cards: Most major cards
Restrictions: No pets, smoking. One night's deposit req. 7-day cancellation notice req., less $10.00 fee.
Notes: Queen Anne-style house built in 1875. Fully restored in 1987. Dining room, sitting room, parlor, front porch. Furnished with antiques. Listed on the National Historic Register. Small private parties accommodated. Guests have access to fax machine. Off-street parking available.*

HELMVILLE (1)

McCormick's Sunset Guest Ranch
50 Cutoff Rd., Helmville, MT 59843
(406) 793-5574
Innkeeper: Mike and Janice McCormick
Rooms: 2, no pvt. bath
Rates: $69, incl. full brk. Seasonal variations.
Credit cards: None
Restrictions: No pets. 50% deposit req. 4-day cancellation notice req.
Notes: Located on 1,100-acre working cattle ranch bordering the Blackfoot River, homesteaded by the McCormicks in the 1870s. Horseback riding available.

KALISPELL (1)

Bonnie's B & B
265 Lake Blaine Rd., Kalispell, MT 59901
(406) 755-3776, (800) 755-3778

Innkeeper: Leonard and Bonnie Boles
Rooms: 2, no pvt. bath, incl. 1 w/phone plus 1 suite w/pvt. bath, phone, Jaccuzi.
Rates: $60-$80/room, $95/suite, all incl cont brk. Discount avail. for senior citizens.
Credit cards: None
Restrictions: No children under 12. No pets, smoking. One night's deposit req. 14-
day cancellation notice req.
Notes: English Tudor house with berry garden. Common room with rock fireplace.

Creston Inn
70 Creston Rd., Kalispell, MT 59901
(406) 755-7517, (800) 257-7517
Innkeeper: Tomas and Marlene Brunaugh
Rooms: 4 w/pvt. bath
Rates: $75-$85, incl. full brk. Seasonal variations.
Credit cards: MC, V
Restrictions: No children under 7, pets. Smoking restricted. One night's deposit
req. 14-day cancellation notice req., less $15.00 fee.
Notes: Two-story farmhouse build in 1920s. Located on wooded area with view of
mountains and valley. Living room with wood stove. Furnished in country decor, an-
tiques, and handcrafted items. Porch. Flower beds.*

CRESTON INN

Demersville School B & B
855 Demersville Rd., Kalispell, MT 59901
(406) 756-7587
Innkeeper: Sandi and Pat LaSalle
Rooms: 4 w/pvt. bath
Rates: $68, incl. full brk. Seasonal variations. Special hunting pkgs. avail.
Credit cards: MC, V
Restrictions: No children under 12. Pets, smoking restricted. Min. one night's de-
posit req., 14-day cancellation notice req., less $15.00 fee.
Notes: Schoolhouse built in 1908. Expanded in 1967. Dining room, decks over-
looking valley. Some Japanese and Spanish spoken.*

DEMERSVILLE SCHOOL B & B

River Rock B & B
179 Shrade Rd., Kalispell, MT 59901
(406) 756-6901
Innkeeper: Betty Lou Armstrong
Rooms: 3 w/phone, TV, incl. 2 w/pvt. bath
Rates: $75-$120, incl. cont. brk. Discount avail. for senior citizen and extended
stays. Seasonal variations.
Credit cards: MC, V
Restrictions: No children under 12, pets. Smoking restricted. One night's deposit
req. 14-day cancellation notice req., less $15.00 fee.
Notes: Decorated with unique designs.*

LAKESIDE (1)

Angel Point Guest Suites
829 Angel Point Rd., Box 768, Lakeside, MT 59922
(406) 844-2204
Innkeeper: Linda and Wayne Muhlestein
Rooms: 3 suites w/pvt. bath
Rates: $110-$120, incl. full brk.
Credit cards: MC, V
Restrictions: No children under 12, pets, smoking. 2-nights deposit req. Min. 14-day
cancellation notice req., less $15.00 fee. 2-night min. stay.
Notes: Two-story wood house located on Angel Point peninsula on Flathead Lake.
Suites display original artwork. Balcony with log railings, large windows with
panoramic views, sitting area with couches, recliner, TV, and piano. Private beach,
dock, lake platforms, gazebo, firepit, and bench swings.*

Fat Bear B & B
P.O. Box 694, Lakeside, MT 59922
(406) 857-2555
Innkeeper: Mary Corrao and Doug Bell
Rooms: 2, no pvt. bath
Rates: $60-$65, incl. full brk, afternoon refreshment. Seasonal variations. Discount
avail. for extended stay.
Credit cards: None
Restrictions: No children under 9. Smoking restricted. One night's deposit req. 14-
day cancellation notice req.
Notes: Rustic house located in forest overlooking Flathead Lake. Decks. Volleyball,
horseshoes, hammocks, campfire available.

LIBBY (1)

Kootenai Country Inn
264 Mack Rd., Libby, MT 59923
(406) 293-7878
Innkeeper: Mel and Amy Siefke
Rooms: 2, plus 1 suite w/phone, TV. No pvt. bath.
Rates: $60, incl. full brk. Discount avail. for senior citizens.
Credit cards: MC, V
Restrictions: Pets welcome with prearrangement. No smoking. One night's deposit req. 7-day cancellation notice req.
Notes: Two-story house located above Kootenai River on 40-acre ponderosa forest. Guests have access to kitchen, laundry room.*

POLSON (1)

Hidden Pines
792 Lost Quartz Rd., Polson, MT 59860-9428
(406) 849-5612, (800) 505-5612
Innkeeper: Earl and Emy Atchley
Rooms: 4, incl. 2 w/pvt. bath, phone, TV
Rates: $45-$60, incl. full brk., lunch
Credit cards: None
Restrictions: No children under 10, pets, Smoking restricted.
Notes: Built in 1977. Has operated as inn since 1989. Located in wooded area. Circular driveway with pines. Living room with fireplace, TV, VCR, board games, reading material. Porch, hot tub, picnic table, lawn chairs. Guests have access to lake. Swimming.*

RED LODGE (4)

Willows Inn
224 S. Platt Ave., Red Lodge, MT 59068
(406) 446-3913
Innkeeper: Kerry, Carolyn, and Elven Boggio
Rooms: 5 plus 2 cottages, incl. 3 w/pvt. bath. Located in 3 bldgs.
Rates: $50-$65/room, $60-$100/cottage, all incl. cont. brk., afternoon refreshment. Discount avail. for senior citizens and extended stays.
Credit cards: Most major cards
Restrictions: No children under 10, pets smoking. Min. one night's deposit req. Min. 24-hour cancellation notice req., less $10.00 fee. 2-night min. stay in cottage.
Notes: Three-story house built in 1903 overlooking Bear Tooth Mountain. Renovated in and has operated as inn since 1989. Living room with library, TV, VCR, video library, board games. Parlor. Dining room with wood stove. Furnished with antiques, wicker. Front porch with Amish swing. Patio overlooking gardens, mountains. Guests have access to kitchen. Finnish, Spanish spoken.*

RONAN (1)

The Timbers B & B
1184 Timberlane Rd., Ronan, MT 59864
(406) 676-4373, (800) 775-4373
Innkeeper: Doris and Leonard McCravey

THE TIMBERS B & B

Rooms: 1 suite w/pvt. bath, phone, TV, pvt. entrance
Rates: $95-$115, incl. full brk., afternoon refreshment. Seasonal variations.
Credit cards: MC, V
Restrictions: No children under 12, pets. Smoking restricted. One night's deposit
    req. Min. 7-day cancellation notice req., less $20.00 fee.
Notes: Built in 1990 with cathedral ceilings and hand-hewn beams. Located on 21
acres. Common room with fireplace, library, TV, overlooking the Rocky Mountain
Mission Range. Wrap-around deck. BBQ and picnic area available. Innkeeper was
on the Professional Rodeo Circuit for 27 years riding bucking horses. Resident dog
and cat.*

THREE FORKS (4)

Sacajawea Inn
5 North Main, Box 648, Three Forks, MT 59752
(406) 285-6515, (800) 821-7326, (406) 285-4210

Innkeeper: Smith and Jane Roedel
Rooms: 33 w/pvt. bath, phone, TV
Rates: $49-$99. Seasonal variations. Discount avail. to senior citizen and AAA stays.
    Children under 12 free.
Credit cards: Most major cards

SACAJAWEA INN

Restrictions: Pets, smoking restricted. Min. one night's deposit req. 2-day cancellation notice req.

Notes: Three-story inn with columned front porch, rocking chairs.

VALIER (2)

Pine Terrace B & B
Rte. 3, Box 909, Valier, MT 59486
(406) 279-3401, (800) 446-6924
Innkeeper: Dick and Carole DeBoo
Rooms: 2, no pvt. bath
Rates: $38, incl. cont. brk.
Credit cards: MC, V
Restrictions: No children under 5, pets, smoking. Closed Dec.–June.
Notes: Private home decorated with antique furnishings, including black wedding dress from 1886. Vegetable and fruit gardens. Resident peacocks, quineas, turkeys, pheasants' and bantam chicks.

WEST YELLOWSTONE (4)

Sportsman's High Bed & Breakfast
750 Deer St., HC 66, Box 16, West Yellowstone, MT 59758
(406) 646-7865, (800) 272-4227, (406) 646-9434
Innkeeper: Diana and Gary Baxter
Rooms: 5, no pvt. bath
Rates: $55-$85, incl. full brk. Seasonal variations.
Credit cards: Most major cards
Restrictions: No children under 10, pets, smoking. Min. one night's deposit req. 2-week cancellation notice req., less $15.00 fee. 2-night min. stay.
Notes: Two-story farmhouse with wainscotting, tongue, and groove ceilings, pine floors built in 1984. Located on one acre. Reading room, games room with pool table, board games. Keeping room with wood stove. Living room with TV, VCR, tape library. Furnished with antiques. Wrap-around porch overlooking grounds with pond. Hot tub.*

WHITEFISH (1)

Castle Bed & Breakfast
900 S. Baker, Whitefish, MT 59937
(406) 862-1257
Innkeeper: Jim and Pat Egan
Rooms: 3, incl. 1 w/pvt. bath
Rates: $60-$95, incl. full brk. Seasonal variations. Special pkgs. avail.
Credit cards: MC, V
Restrictions: No children under 10, pets, smoking. 50% deposit req. 7-day cancellation notice req.

WOLF CREEK (2)

Bungalow B & B
P.O. Box 202, Wolf Creek, MT 59648
(406) 235-4276
Innkeeper: Pat Anderson
Rooms: 4, incl. 1 w/pvt. bath, 2 w/fireplace

Rates: $65-$75, incl. full brk.

Credit cards: None

Restrictions: No pets, smoking. One night's deposit req. 72-hour cancellation notice req., less 20% fee.

Notes: Historic cedar lodge built circa 1911. Living room with *u*-shaped balcony. Dining room. Enclosed sun porch.*

Nebraska

BARTLEY (3)

Pheasant Hill Farm
HCR 68, Box 12, Bartley, NE 69020
(308) 692-3278
Innkeeper: Dona Nelms
Rooms: 2, no pvt. bath, plus 2 suites w/pvt. bath, incl. 1 w/TV
Rates: $40-$55. Discount avail. for extended stay.
Credit cards: None
Restrictions: No pets. Smoking restricted. Deposit req. 14-day cancellation notice req.
Notes: Stucco structure with oak floors and woodwork, built in 1937. Family room with TV, VCR, CD. Sunroom with views. Collectibles on display.

CRETE (4)

The Parson's House
638 Forest Ave., Crete, NE 68333
(402) 826-2634
Innkeeper: Harold and Sandy Richardson
Rooms: 2, no pvt. bath
Rates: $35, incl. full brk.
Credit cards: None
Restrictions: No children under 10, pets, smoking. 50% deposit req.
Notes: Two-story four-square house built in 1910. Located on three city lots with gardens. Living room with fireplace. Formal dining room. Den with TV, VCR. Front porch with swing. Patio. Furnished with antiques. Whirlpool tub, lawn games available.*

GRAND ISLAND (4)

Kirschke House
1124 W. 3rd St., Grand Island, NE 68801
(308) 381-6851
Innkeeper: Lois Hank
Rooms: 4, no pvt. bath
Rates: $45-$55, incl. full brk.
Credit cards: Most major cards
Restrictions: No pets, smoking. Min. 50% deposit req., 48-hour cancellation notice req.
Notes: Two-story brick house with turret, windowed cupola, and stained-glass windows built in 1902. Fully renovated in and has operated as inn since 1989. Entry with open oak stairway. Parlor with fireplace, TV, VCR. Brick wash house with wooden hot tub. Furnished with period antiques. All meals, lawn games, children's toy trunk available. Porch and garden patio areas.*

HASTINGS (4)

Grandma's Victorian Inn
1826 W. 3rd St., Hastings, NE 68901
(402) 462-2013

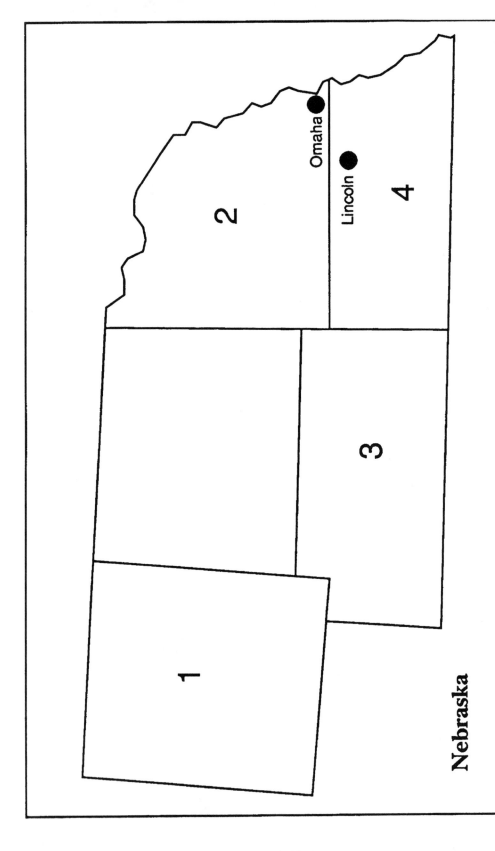

Nebraska

GRANDMA'S VICTORIAN INN

Innkeeper: Marilyn DiMartino
Rooms: 5 w/pvt. bath
Rates: $50-$55, incl full brk. Discount avail. for extended stay.
Credit cards: MC, V
Restrictions: No children under 12. Smoking restricted. $15.00 deposit req. 5-day
cancellation notice req.
Notes: Three-story Victorian house with open staircase built approx. 1886. Antique
furniture exhibited. Balcony. Porch with swings. Handicapped access.

HOLDREGE (3)

Crow's Nest Inn
503 Grant, Holdrege, NE 68949
(308) 995-5440

Innkeeper: James and Shirley Michael
Rooms: 2, no pvt. bath
Rates: $45, incl full brk. Discount avail. for payment by cash or check.
Credit cards: MC, V
Restrictions: No pets, smoking. $15.00 per room deposit req. 48-hour cancellation
notice req.
Notes: Two-story house with walk-in closets, glass door knobs, some original light
fixtures, built in 1926. Fireplace. Sunporch with TV, VCR. Resident dog.

LINCOLN (4)

Sweet Dream
2721 P St., Lincoln, NE 68503
(402) 435-6949, 438-1416

Innkeeper: Dimitrij and Magdalena Krynsky
Rooms: 1, plus 1 suite w/Jacuzzi, all w/pvt. bath, TV
Rates: $65/room, $95/suite, all incl. cont. brk., afternoon refreshment. Discount
avail. for mid-week stay.
Credit cards: None
Restrictions: No children under 10. No pets, smoking. 100% deposit req. 7-day can-
cellation notice req., less $10.00 fee.

Notes: Remodeled two-story house built in 19th-century. Declared a local historic landmark in 1993. Dining room. Free tickets to swimming pool in summer. Handicapped access. Czech, Polish spoken.

OAKLAND (2)

Benson Bed & Breakfast
402 N. Oakland Ave., Oakland, NE 68045-1135
(402) 685-6051
Innkeeper: Stan and Norma Anderson
Rooms: 3, incl. 1 w/washer/dryer, 1 w/Jacuzzi. No pvt. bath.
Rates: $38-$55, incl. full brk., afternoon refreshment. Discount avail. for senior citizens.
Credit cards: None
Restrictions: Well-behaved children over 12 welcome. No pets, smoking. $10 min. deposit req. 7-day cancellation notice req. less 20% fee.
Notes: Inn located on second floor of restored two-story building built in 1905. Decorated in traditional style with some antiques. Family room has cable TV, and soft-drink collectables. Dining room. Beauty shop and Giftshop on first floor. *

OMAHA (2)

The Offutt House B & B
140 N. 39th St., Omaha, NE 68131
(402) 553-0951
Innkeeper: Jeannie Swoboda
Rooms: 7 w/pvt. bath, incl. 6 w/phone, 2 w/TV, 2 w/fireplace, plus 2 suites w/TV, incl. 1 w/pvt bath, 1 w/phone
Rates: $45-$85/room, $85/suite, all incl. brk. Discount avail. for extended stay.
Credit cards: Most major cards
Restrictions: Smoking restricted. 50% deposit req. 5-day cancellation notice req.
Notes: Three-story *Chateauesque* mansion with 5 fireplaces, built in 1894. Brick garage added in 1916. Library with books, board games, grand piano. Dining room. Furnished with antiques. Small private parties accommodated.*

WATERLOO (2)

Journey's End
102 Lincoln Ave., Box 190, Waterloo, NE 68069-0190
(402) 779-2704
Innkeeper: Bill and Linda Clark
Rooms: 3, incl. 1 w/pvt bath
Rates: $40-$75, incl. full brk. Seasonal variations. Discounts avail.
Credit cards: None
Restrictions: No children under 12, pets, smoking. 25% deposit req. 7-day cancellation notice req.
Notes: Three-story neo-classic house with hardwood floors, hand carved paneling, stained and leaded-glass, tiled fireplaces, and pocket doors, built in 1905. Fully restored. Decorated with antiques, including clock collection dating back to 1735. Small private parties accommodated. Gift certificates available. Listed on National Register of Historic Places. Spanish spoken.

WILBER (4)

Hotel Wilber
203 S. Wilson, Box 641, Wilber, NE 68465
(402) 821-2020

Innkeeper: Frances Erb
Rooms: 10 w/TV, no pvt. bath
Rates: $45-$69, incl. full brk. Seasonal variations.
Credit cards: MC, V
Restrictions: No pets. Smoking restricted. 50% deposit req. 14-day cancellation notice req.
Notes: Two-story brick hotel with rich, red oak in lobby and on staircase extending to second floor. Located in Czech Capital of USA. Recently renovated. Decorated in blend of country and Victorian styles. Guide dogs and hunting dogs accepted during pheasant season. Kennels available. Listed on National Register of Historic Places. Handicapped access in dining room only.

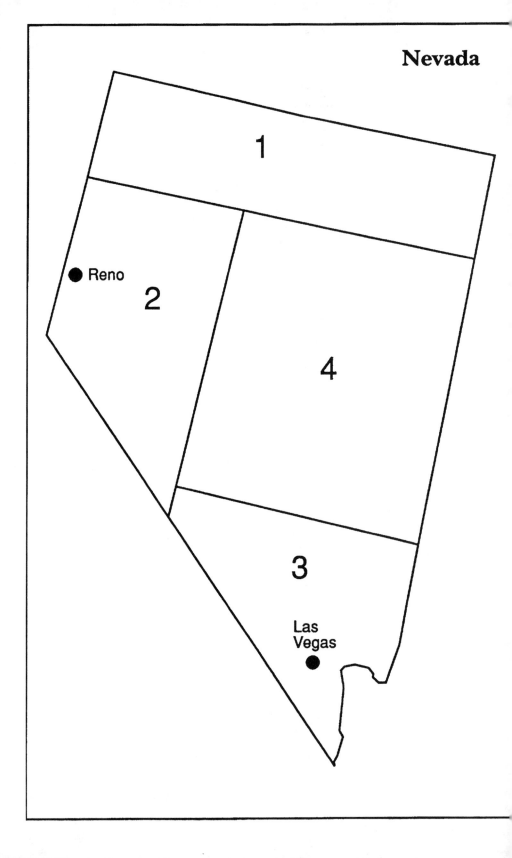

Nevada

1

● Reno

2

4

3

Las
Vegas
●

Nevada

EAST ELY (4)

Steptoe Valley Inn
220 E. 11th St., Box 151110, East Ely, NV 89315-1110
(702) 289-8687, (702) 435-1196 (Oct.–May)
Innkeeper: Jane and Norman Lindley
Rooms: 5 w/pvt. bath
Rates: $58-$85, incl. full brk., afternoon refreshment. Seasonal variations.
Credit cards: Most major cards
Restrictions: No pets, smoking. One night's deposit req. Full prepayment for July 4th and Labor day wknds. 48-hour cancellation notice req. 7-day cancellation notice req. for July 4th or Labor day wknds. Closed Oct. 1–May 31.
Notes: Two-story inn built in 1907 as grocery store. Fully reconstructed in and has operated as inn since 1990. Victorian dining room, library. Second-floor back porch. Furnished in country style. Rose garden and gazebo. Innkeepers operate back-country tours to the Great Basin National Park. Jeep rental available. Spanish spoken.*

STEPTOE VALLEY INN

INCLINE VILLAGE (2)

Haus Bavaira
593 N. Dyer Circ., Box 3308, Incline Village, NV 89450
(702) 831-6122
Innkeeper: Bick Hewitt
Rooms: 5 w/pvt. bath
Rates: $75-$110, incl. full brk. Discount avail. for extended, mid-week, and senior citizen stays.
Credit cards: Most major cards

Restrictions: No children under 10, pets. Smoking restricted. Deposit req. 10-day cancellation notice req.

Notes: European-style guesthouse built in 1980. Each room with balcony overlooking mountains. Living room with wood panelling and collection of German bric-a-brac. Located on Lake Tahoe. Reservations required.*

UNIONVILLE (1)

Old Pioneer Garden Country Inn
HC-64, Box 79, Unionville, NV 89418
(702) 538-7585

Innkeeper: Lew and Mitzi Jones
Rooms: 9, incl. 3 w/pvt. bath, 2 w/fireplace. Located in 3 bldgs.
Rates: $65, incl. full brk.
Credit cards: None
Restrictions: No smoking. $20.00 deposit req. Cancellation notice req.
Notes: Built about 1860. Located on trout creek on west side of Buena Vista Valley. Living room and library with fireplace. All meals available. Two barns, one with antique and junk shop and two corrals for guests with horses. Resident farm animals. Handicapped access. German spoken.*

New Hampshire

ALBANY (4)

Darby Field Inn
Bald Hill, Albany, NH 03818
(603) 447-2181, (603) 447-5726
Innkeeper: Marc and Maria Donaldson
Rooms: 15 w/pvt. bath, plus 1 suite w/pvt. bath
Rates: $120–$160/room, $130–$140/suite all incl. full brk., dinner. Discount avail. for extended and mid-week stays
Credit cards: Most Major Cards
Restrictions: No children under 2, pets. Smoking restricted. 50% deposit req. 2-week cancellation notice req. 2-night min. on most wknds., fall foliage season. 3-night min., Columbus Day, New Year's.
Notes: Wooden farmhouse with stonework around three sides built in 1826. Addition built in the 1940s. Dining room overlooking mountains. Living room with fieldstone fireplace. Common room with library, TV, VCR. Outdoor pool, croquet, and vollyball. Private cross-country ski trails. patio. Tavern with woodburning stove, live music. Furnished with antiques, reproductions. Swimming pool. Spanish spoken.*

ANDOVER (4)

ANDOVER ARMS GUEST HOUSE

Andover Arms Guest House
P.O. Box 256, Andover, NH 03216
(603) 735-5953
Innkeeper: Rick and Michelle Kettwig, Cynthia Zautner
Rooms: 4 plus 1 suite, all w/pvt. bath, TV
Rates: $50/room, $75-90/suite, all incl. cont. brk.
Credit cards: None
Restrictions: 50% deposit req. 7-day cancellation notice
Notes: Two-story Victorian-style farmhouse built in 1860s. Kitchen, common room with TV, two living rooms with fireplace. Parlor games available. Summer porches overlooking mountains. Furnished with antiques. Small private parties accommodated.

The English House
P.O. Box 162, Andover, NH 03216
(603) 735-5987

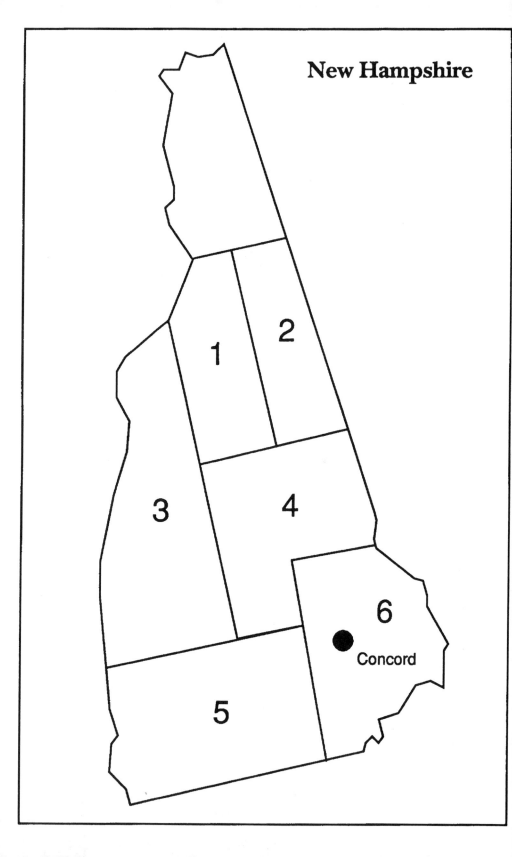

Innkeeper: Ken and Gillian Smith
Rooms: 7 w/pvt. bath
Rates: $55-$75, incl. full brk., afternoon and evening refreshment
Credit cards: MC, V
Restrictions: No children under 8, pets. Smoking restricted. Min. 50% deposit req.
2-week cancellation notice req., less $5.00 fee. 2-night min. stay on holiday and
special wknds.
Notes: Three-story Edwardian shingled house with fieldstone base built in 1906. Located on two wooded acres. Has operated as inn since 1985. Sitting room with cable
TV, phone. Furnished with period antiques. French, German spoken.*

ANTRIM (5)

Steele Homestead Inn
R.R. 1, Box 78, Antrim, NH 03440
(603) 588-2215

Innkeeper: Barbara and Carl Beehner
Rooms: 3 w/pvt. bath, incl. 2 w/fireplace
Rates: $68, incl. full brk. Discount avail. for senior citizen and extended stays.
Credit cards: None
Restrictions: No pets, smoking. Deposit req. 7-day cancellation notice req.
Notes: Built in 1810. Fully restored. Has operated as inn since 1983. Located on 4
acres with flower gardens, fruit orchard. Dining room, parlor, each with fireplace.
Furnished with Early American antiques, artwork.*

ASHLAND (4)

Glynn House Victorian Inn
43 Highland St., Box 719, Ashland, NH 03217
(603) 968-3775

Innkeeper: Karol and Betsy Patter
Rooms: 4 w/pvt. bath, incl. 1 w/fireplace, 1 w/cable TV, plus 2 suites w/pvt. bath,
incl. 1 w/fireplace, 1 w/TV
Rates: $85-$95/room, $125-$150/suite, all incl. full brk. Seasonal variations.
Credit cards: MC, V
Restrictions: No children under 6, pets. Smoking restricted. Deposit req. 2-week
cancellation notice req.
Notes: Three-story Victorian house with turret and gables built in 1895. Foyer, parlor, living room, conference room, verandas, Jacuzzi. Furnished with period antiques. Polish, Russian spoken.*

BETHLEHEM (1)

The Mulburn Inn
Main St., Rt. 302, Bethlehem, NH 03574-3389
(603) 869-3389

Innkeeper: Gary, Twila, Tim and Lisa Skeels
Rooms: 7 w/pvt. bath
Rates: $55-$70, incl. full brk., evening refreshment. Discount avail. for mid-week
stay. Seasonal variations.
Credit cards: Most major cards
Restrictions: No pets, smoking. 50% deposit req.

Notes: Two-story summer cottage with oak staircase, stained-glass windows, built on the Woolworth estate in 1913. Located on three acres. Furnished with period antiques. Common room with marble fireplace. Dining room, library.*

BRADFORD (3)

BRADFORD INN

Bradford Inn
RFD 1, Box 40, Main St., Bradford, NH 03221
(603) 938-5309
Innkeeper: Connie and Tom Mazol
Rooms: 6 plus 6 suites, all w/pvt. bath
Rates: $69/room, $79-$99/suite, all incl. full brk. Discount avail. for extended stay. Special pkgs. avail.
Credit cards: Most major cards
Restrictions: Pets restricted. One night's deposit req. 14-day cancellation notice req., less $10.00 fee. Min. stay req. for special event or holiday wknds.
Notes: Built as a Federal Revival country hotel in 1898. Two parlors with cable TV. Dining room with fireplace. Furnished with period antiques. Restaurant and full service bar on premises. Limited handicapped access.*

Candlelite Inn
RFD 1, Box 408, Old Center Rd., Bradford, NH 03221
(603) 938-5571
Innkeeper: Les and Marilyn Gordon
Rooms: 6, incl. 1 suite, all w/pvt. bath
Rates: $65-$70/room, $75/suite, all incl. full brk. Discount avail. for extended stay.
Credit cards: Most major cards
Restrictions: No pets, smoking. One night's deposit req. 14-day cancellation notice req., less $10.00 fee.
Notes: Victorian house built in 1897. Located on 3 acres. Parlor with fireplace, bay windows. Dining room, sunroom overlooking pond and brook. Gazebo porch. 3-story tressle-barn.

Rosewood Country Inn
Pleasant View Rd., Bradford, NH 03221
(603) 938-5253

Innkeeper: Dick and Leslie Marquis
Rooms: 7 w/pvt. bath, plus 1 suite
Rates: $85/room, $99-$110/suite, all incl. full brk. Seasonal variations. Special pkgs. avail.
Credit cards: Most major cards
Restrictions: No children under 10, pets, smoking. One night's deposit req., 7-day cancellation notice req., less $15.00 fee.
Notes: Two-story Country Victorian inn built in 1896. Located on twelve hilltop acres with stone walls. Living room with four fireplaces. Den, kitchen, dining room. Tavern room with TV. Parlor. Furnished with antiques. "Candlelight & Crystal" breakfast, lawn and board games available. French spoken.

CAMPTON (1)

Mountain-Fare Inn
Mad River Rd., Box 553, Campton, NH 03223
(603) 726-4283

Innkeeper: Susan and Nick Preston
Rooms: 7 plus 3 suites, incl. 8 w/pvt. bath, 1 w/fireplace
Rates: $56-$80, incl. full brk., afternoon refreshment plus Sat. dinner during ski season.
Credit cards: Most major cards
Restrictions: No pets, smoking. One night's deposit req. 10-day cancellation notice req., less $10.00 fee. 2-night min. stay during fall foliage, holiday, and ski seasons. Closed Dec. 24, 25.
Notes: Multi-gabled, white clapboard farmhouse built in the late 1840s. Located on six acres. Entry room with woodburning stove. Living room with fireplace. Game room with billiards, sauna. Dining room, porch. Vegetable, flower gardens. Small private parties accommodated. Innkeepers are professional ski coaches at Waterville Valley Ski Area. Guided hiking available for small groups.*

CAMPTON VILLAGE (1)

Campton Inn
R. R. 2, Box 282, Campton Village, NH 03223
(603) 726-4449

Innkeeper: Robbin and Peter Adams
Rooms: 6, incl. 1 w/pvt. bath, 2 w/TV
Rates: $35-$65, incl. full brk. Seasonal variations.
Credit cards: None
Restrictions: Pets restricted. No smoking. Deposit req. 2-week cancellation notice req. less $10 fee. 2-night min. stay during peak season wknds.
Notes: Two-story New England farmhouse with original pine floors, built in 1836. Has operated as inn since 1984. Screened porch. Common room with piano, wood stove, board games, books. Furnished in country style with antiques.

CENTER HARBOR (4)

Kona Mansion Inn
P.O. Box 458, Center Harbor, NH 03226-0458
(603) 253-4900, (603) 253-7350

Innkeeper: The Crowley Family
Rooms: 9, incl. 4 cottages, 2 chalets, all w/pvt. bath, TV, incl. 1 w/fireplace

Rates: $60-$140/room, $495 wk/cottage, $695 wk/chalet
Credit cards: MC, V
Restrictions: Pets restricted. One night's deposit req., refunded upon cancellation only if room re-rented.
Notes: Three-story mansion built in 1900 of local fieldstone with mock Tudor styling. Located on 130 acres along Lake Winnipesaukee overlooking the Belknap and White Mountains. Lounge, restaurant on premises. Tennis courts, nine hole, par three golf course on premises. Small private parties accommodated.

Red Hill Inn
RFD 1, Box 99M, Center Harbor, NH 03226
(603) 279-7001, (603) 279-7003
Innkeeper: Don Leavitt, Rick Miller
Rooms: 16 w/pvt. bath, phone, incl. 12 w/fireplace, plus 5 suites w/pvt. bath, phone, incl. 1 w/fireplace. Located in 5 bldgs.
Rates: $85-$145/room, $85-$125/suite, all incl. full brk. Discount avail. for mid-week stay.
Credit cards: Most major cards
Restrictions: No pets. Min. $50.00 deposit req. 14-day cancellation notice req., less 10% fee. 2-night min. stay on wknds.
Notes: Main inn built in 1900. Located on sixty acres overlooking Squam Lake and the White Mountains. Four dining rooms. Common rooms with fireplace. Country gourmet restaurant, lounge with weekend entertainment on premises. Cross-country ski trails and rentals available. Limited handicapped access.*

CHARLESTOWN (5)

Maple Hedge
Main St. Rte. 12, Charlestown, NH 03603
(603) 826-5237
Innkeeper: Dick and Joan DeBrine
Rooms: 4, plus 1 suite, all w/pvt. bath
Rates: $80-$89/room, $90-$110/suite, all incl. full brk., afternoon refreshment. Discount avail. for extended stay.
Credit cards: MC, V
Restrictions: No children under 12, pets. Smoking restricted. 2-night min. stay during foilage.
Notes: Early eighteenth-century Federal-style house located in meadow with ancient cedars and maples. Double parlored sitting room, formal dining room. Decorated with antiques. Board and yard games available.*

CONWAY (2)

Mountain Valley Manner
148 Washington St., Box 1649, Conway, NH 03818
(603) 447-3988
Innkeeper: Bob and Lynn Lein
Rooms: 3, incl. 1 w/pvt. bath
Rates: $45-$75, incl. full brk., afternoon refreshment. Discount avail. for extended stay.
Credit cards: Most major cards
Restrictions: No pets, smoking. One night's deposit req. 10-day cancellation notice req. 2-night min. stay on wknds.

Notes: 3-story restored country Victorian house. Furnished with mixture of country furnishings and period antiques. Victorian gardens, patio and pool. Guests have access to local health club.*

Darby Field Inn
Bald Hill, Conway, NH 03818
(603) 447-2181, (6003) 447-5726
Innkeeper: Marc and Maria Donaldson
Rooms: 15 w/pvt. bath, plus 1 suite w/pvt. bath
Rates: $120-$160/room, $130-$140/suite, all incl. full brk., dinner. Discount avail. for extended and mid-week stays.
Credit cards: Most major cards
Restrictions: No children under 2, pets. Smoking restricted. 50% deposit req. 2-week cancellation notice req. 2-night min. stay on most wknds., fall foliage season. 3-night min. stay for Columbus Day, New Year's.
Notes: Wooden farmhouse with stonework around three sides built in 1826. Addition built in the 1940s. Dining room overlooking mountains. Living room with fieldstone fireplace. Common room with library, TV, VCR. Outdoor pool, croquet, and volleyball. Private cross-country ski trails. patio. Tavern with woodburning stove, live music. Furnished with antiques, reproductions. Swimming pool. Spanish spoken.*

CORNISH (3)

Chase House
Rte. 12A, RR 2, Box 909, Cornish, NH 03745
(603) 675-5391, (603) 675-5010
Innkeeper: Bill and Barbara Lewis
Rooms: 6 w/pvt. bath, incl. 1 w/phone, 1 w/TV, plus 1 suite w/pvt. bath, phone, TV.
Rates: $85-$95/room, $95-$105/suite, all incl. full brk., evening refreshment.
Credit cards: MC, V
Restrictions: No children under 12, pets, smoking. One night's deposit req. 14-day cancellation notice req. 2-night min. stay on wknds. and from Sept. 10–Oct. 20.
Notes: Two-story Colonial-style house built in 1766 relocated and combined in 1845 with Federal-style house built in 1775. Fully restored in 1986. Expanded in 1992. Located on 160 wooded acres along banks of Connecticut River. Gathering room with fieldstone, raised-hearth fireplace. Dining room, terrace, parlor, sitting room. National Historic Landmark. Small private parties accommodated. Limited handicapped access.

EATON CENTER (2)

The Inn at Crystal Lake
Rte. 153, Box 12, Eaton Center, NH 03832
(603) 447-2120, (800) 343-7336
Innkeeper: Richard and Janice Octeau
Rooms: 11 w/pvt. bath, incl. loft in attached barn
Rates: $42-$70, incl. full brk., dinner. Special pkgs. avail. Seasonal variations.
Credit cards: Most major cards
Restrictions: No pets. Smoking restricted. Min. one night's deposit req. 2-week cancellation notice req., less $10.00 fee. 2-night min. stay on holidays and 3-day Columbus Day wknd. 15% gratuity added to all charges.
Notes: Greek Revival split-level house built with Victorian influence in 1884 overlooking Crystal Lake. Fully renovated since 1986. Furnished with Victorian antiques.

Parlor, three-level dining room and lounge, each with fireplace or woodburning stove. Lounge with 60-inch TV. Porch with wicker furniture. International gourmet dinners available. Small private parties accommodated. Innkeeper is an expert on the geology of New Hampshire. Resident cat.*

THE INN AT CRYSTAL LAKE

FRANCONIA (1)

Blanche's B and B
351 Easton Valley Rd., Franconia, NH 03580
(603) 823-7061

Innkeeper: John Vail, Brenda Shannon
Rooms: 5, incl. 2 w/pvt. bath
Rates: $35-$85, incl. full brk. Discount avail. for extended stay.
Credit cards: Most major cards
Restrictions: No pets, smoking. Min. one night's non-refundable deposit req. 15-day cancellation notice req., less $15.00 fee. 2-night min. stay on holidays and fall foliage wknds.
Notes: Gothic Revival farmhouse built in 1887. Located at base of Kinsman Ridge, on the Appalachian Trail. Sitting room with Glenwood stove, books, board games. Furnished with antiques, family heirlooms. Decorated with stenciled walls, ceilings.

BLANCHE'S B AND B

Foxglove, A Country Inn
P.O. Box 771, Franconia, NH 03580
(603) 823-8840, (603) 823-5755
Innkeeper: Janet Boyd and family
Rooms: 5, plus 1 suite, all w/pvt. bath
Rates: $85-$125/room, $170/suite, all incl. full brk., evening refreshment. Seasonal variations.
Credit cards: MC, V
Restrictions: No young children, pets, smoking. Deposit req. 14-day cancellation notice req.
Notes: Two-story, gabled inn built in 1898. Recently renovated. Located at 1500 ft. elevation overlooking the White and Green Mountains. Rooms decorated in country French style. Furnished with antiques.*

Franconia Inn
1300 Easton Valley Rd., Rte. 116, Franconia, NH 03580
(603) 823-5542, (800) 473-5299, (603) 823-8078
Innkeeper: The Morris Family
Rooms: 31 w/pvt. bath, plus 3 suites w/pvt. bath, incl. 2 w/fireplace
Rates: $58-$93/room, $98-$123/suite
Credit cards: Most major cards
Restrictions: No pets, smoking. Deposit req. 5-day cancellation notice req.
Notes: Colonial house built in 1868. Located on 107 acres overlooking Franconia Mountains. Has operated as inn since 1886. Rebuilt after fire in 1934. Recently remodeled. Living room, library, dining room, Rathskeller Lounge, and two spacious verandas with mountain views. Library with four fireplaces, board games. Stable with horses, clay tennis courts, fishing, various lawn games available. Skiing, sledding, and ice-skating availble during winter. German spoken. Handicapped access.*

The Horse & Hound Inn
205 Wells Rd., Franconia, NH 03580
(603) 823-5501
Innkeeper: Bill Steele and Jim Cantlon
Rooms: 8 w/pvt. bath, phone, plus 2 suites w/pvt. bath, incl. 1 w/phone
Rates: $60-$80/room, $120/suite, all incl. full brk. Discount avail. for mid-week, off-season, and group stays.
Credit cards: Most major cards
Restrictions: Pets welcome with prior arrangement. One night's deposit req. 48-hour cancellation notice req. Closed April.
Notes: Center Cape Farmhouse built in early 1800s. Has operated as inn since 1946. Located on 8.5 acres at base of Cannon Mountain, adjacent to White Mountain National Forest. Lobby with fireplace, lounge, library. Two dining rooms, each with fireplace. Furnished with some antiques. Covered patio overlooking flower garden. Restaurant with extensive wine list on premises.*

GILMANTON (4)

The Temperance Tavern
Old Province Rd., Box 369, Gilmanton, NH 03237
(603) 267-7349, (603) 267-7503
Innkeeper: Steve and Kristie Owens
Rooms: 3 w/pvt. bath, plus 2 suites w/pvt. bath, fireplace
Rates: $65-$125/room, $150-$250/suite, all incl. full brk. Seasonal variations. Discount avail. for senior citizen and extended stays.

Credit cards: MC, V

Restrictions: No children under 4, smoking. 50% deposit req., 10-day cancellation notice req., less $10.00 fee. 2-night min. stay on Race wknds., Foliage season and major holidays.

Notes: Two-story Colonial tavern with indian shutters, wainscotting, wide plank floor boards of 'the Kings's Lumber," and original 18th century stenciling by Moses Eaton, built in 1793. Commons Room, Tap Room, six working, open-hearth fireplaces. Small private parties accommodated. Gourmet lunches and dinners by The Tavern's French-trained chef available. French spoken.*

THE BERNERHOF

GLEN (2)

The Bernerhof
Rte. 302, Box 240, Glen, NH 03838-0240
(603) 383-4414, (800) 548-8007, (603) 383-0809

Innkeeper: Sharon Wroblewski

Rooms: 7 w/pvt. bath , phone, TV, incl. 4 w/spa, plus 2 suites w/pvt. bath, phone, TV, spa

Rates: $69-$89/room, $119-$139/suite, all incl. full brk. Seasonal variations. Discount avail. for mid-week stay.

Credit cards: Most major cards

Restrictions: Smoking restricted. Min. 50% deposit req. 2-week cancellation notice req., less $10.00 fee. 2-night min. stay for some wknds.

Notes: Three-story building built as an inn in the 1890s. Located in the foothills of White Mountains. Second floor sitting room with TV. Taproom with fireplace. Dining room. Furnished with antiques. Finnish sauna, swimming pool, children's playground, gourmet restaurant on premises. Site of A Taste of the Mountains Cooking School, a classical French cooking school.

GREENFIELD (5)

Greenfield B & B Inn
Forest Rd., Box 400, Greenfield, NH 03047
(603) 547-6327, (800) 678-4144, (603) 547-2418

Innkeeper: Barbara and Vic Mangini

Rooms: 12, incl. 9 w/pvt. bath, phone, TV, plus 3 suites w/pvt. bath, phone, TV. Located in 2 bldgs.
Rates: $49-$69/room, $99/suite, all incl. full brk. Discount avail. for senior citizen and extended stays. Special pkgs. avail.
Credit cards: MC, V
Restrictions: No pets. Smoking restricted. Deposit req. 7-day cancellation notice req.
Notes: Two-story inn. Common room with wicker rockers. Sundeck overlooking mountains. Glass-walled deckhouse. Small private parties accommodated. Limited handicapped access.*

THE INN AT ELMWOOD CORNERS

HAMPTON (6)

The Inn at Elmwood Corners
252 Winnacunnet Rd., Hampton, NH 03842-2627
(603) 929-0443, (800) 253-5691

Innkeeper: John and Mary Hornberger
Rooms: 5, no pvt. bath, plus 2 suites w/pvt. bath
Rates: $50-$65/room, $75-$85/suite, all incl. full brk., evening refreshment. Seasonal variations.
Credit cards: MC, V
Restrictions: No pets. Smoking restricted. One night's deposit req. 3-day cancellation notice req. 2-night min. stay on holiday wknds. 2-night min. stay, July and Aug. wknds., for suites.
Notes: Three-story Colonial house with hardwood floors built in 1870. Fully renovated in 1988. Sitting room with TV, board games, library. Breakfast room. Furnished in country style with collections of thimbles, baskets, quilts, braided rugs, dolls. Wrap-around porch with wicker furniture. Some French spoken.

HAMPTON BEACH (6)

The Oceanside
365 Ocean Blvd., Hampton Beach, NH 03842
(603) 926-3642, (603) 926-3549

Innkeeper: Skip and Debbie Windemiller
Rooms: 10 w/pvt. bath
Rates: $95-$110, incl. cont. brk. in off season, but not in July & Aug., Discount avail. for extended stay. Seasonal variations.
Credit cards: Most major cards
Restrictions: No children under 10, pets, smoking. One night's deposit req. 4-week cancellation notice req., less $15.00 fee.
Notes: Built in the early 1900s. Living room, dining room, each with fireplace. Two decks, enclosed sidewalk terrace. Furnished with period antiques. Self-service bar, cafe on premises.*

HARTS LOCATION (2)

The Notchland Inn
Route 302, Harts Location, NH 03812-9999
(603) 374-6131, (603) 374-6168
Innkeeper: Lee Schoof and Ed Butler
Rooms: 7 plus 4 suites, all w/pvt. bath, fireplace. Located in 2 bldgs.
Rates: $73-$100/room, $85-$105/suite, all incl. full brk., dinner, afternoon refreshment. Discount avail. for mid-week and extended stays. Special pkgs. avail.
Credit cards: Most major cards
Restrictions: No children under 12, pets, smoking. 50% deposit req. 14-day cancellation notice req., less $10.00 per night fee. 2-night min. stay on most wknds.
Notes: English-style manor house with hardwood interior, embossed metal ceilings built of native granite and timbers in 1862. Located on 400 acres in White Mountain National Forest on knoll overlooking the Saco River valley. Has operated as inn since 1920. Dining room with fireplace. Parlor with fireplace. Music room with piano, stereo, board games. Porch with rockers. Refuge for rare and endangered animals on premises. Resident llamas, sheep, angora goats, miniature horse, pygmy goats.*

HAVERHILL (3)

Haverhill Inn
Dartmouth College Hwy., Haverhill, NH 03765
(603) 989-5961
Innkeeper: Stephen Campbell and Anne Baird
Rooms: 4 w/pvt. bath, fireplace
Rates: $85, incl. full brk.
Credit cards: None
Restrictions: No children under 8, pets. Smoking restricted. Min. one night's deposit req. 14-day cancellation notice req. 2-night min. stay during fall foliage. Closed Mar., April, Nov.
Notes: Two-story Federal and Classical Revival-style house built in 1810. Located on five acres of meadow overlooking Connecticut River Valley in Haverhill Corner National Historic District. Furnished with antiques. Parlor with fireplace, library with fireplace, TV.

HENNIKER (5)

Colby Hill Inn
The Oaks, Box 778, Henniker, NH 03242
(603) 428-3281, (800) 531-0330, (603) 428-9218

Innkeeper: John, Eleanor and Laurel Day
Rooms: 16 w/pvt. bath, phone, incl. 2 w/fireplace. Located in 2 bldgs.
Rates: $85-$155, incl. full brk. Discount avail. for mid-week stay.
Credit cards: Most major cards
Restrictions: No children under 7. Pets, smoking restricted. Deposit req. 2-night min. stay on some wknds.
Notes: Two-story Colonial country inn with wide-board floors, wainscots, Indian shutters built in 1790. Barn built in 1893. Restored in 1959. Has operated as inn since 1964. Located on five acres. Library, lounge, dining room, each with fireplace. Board games available. Furnished with antiques, oil paintings, watercolors. Garden, swimming pool. Small private parties accommodated. Dinner available except on Monday and Tuesday. Resident dogs.*

Meeting House Inn
35 Flanders Rd., Henniker, NH 03242
(603) 428-3228
Innkeeper: Bill and June Davis, Cheryl and Peter Bakke
Rooms: 4 plus 2 suites, all w/pvt. bath
Rates: $65-$85/room, $93/suite, all incl. full brk.
Credit cards: Most major cards
Restrictions: No children under 12, pets, smoking. 3-day cancellation notice req. 2-night min. stay on wknds. in October and February.
Notes: Country-style inn built in 1794. Solar dining area. Decorated with family antiques. Hot tub. Sauna. Small private parties accommodated.

HILLSBOROUGH (5)

Inn at Maplewood Farm
447 Center Road, Box 1478, Hillsborough, NH 03244
(603) 464-4242, (603) 464-4242
Innkeeper: Laura and Jayme Simoes
Rooms: 3 w/pvt. bath, incl. 1 w/fireplace, plus 2 suites w/pvt. bath
Rates: $50-$65/room, $110/suite, all incl. full brk., afternoon refreshment. Seasonal variations. Discount avail. for extended stay.
Credit cards: Most major cards
Restrictions: No infants, pets, smoking. Deposit req., 14-day cancellation notice req., less $30.00 per room/per night fee. 2-night min. stay on holiday and special occasion wknds.
Notes: Two-story New England Colonial farm built in 1794. Restored by current owners. Furnished with mixture of antiques and new furniture. Dining room with guest refrigerator, fireplace. Parlor with fireplace, TV, guest phone. Board and lawn games available. Spanish, Portuguese spoken.*

HOLDERNESS (4)

The Inn on Golden Pond
Rt. 3, Box 680, Holderness, NH 03245
(603) 968-7269
Innkeeper: Bill and Bonnie Webb
Rooms: 9 w/pvt. bath, plus 2 suites w/pvt. bath, incl. 1 w/TV
Rates: $85-$95/room, $120-$135/suite, all incl. full brk.
Credit cards: Most major cards

Restrictions: No children under 12, pets, smoking. One night's deposit req. 14-day cancellation notice req., less $5.00 fee. 2-night min. stay on some wknds.

Notes: Two-story traditional Colonial house built in 1879. Located on fifty wooded acres across street from Squam Lake, setting for the movie On Golden Pond. All rooms decorated country style. Two sitting rooms, one with TV, and one with fireplace. 60-foot screened front porch. Ping pong and darts in outbuilding. Lawn games available.*

INTERVALE (2)

Wildflowers Inn
Rte. 16, Box 802, Intervale, NH 03845
(603) 356-2224

Innkeeper: Eileen Davis, Dean Franke
Rooms: 6, incl. 2 w/pvt. bath
Rates: $50-$92, incl. cont. brk. Seasonal variations.
Credit cards: MC, V
Restrictions: No pets. One night's deposit req. 14-day cancellation notice req., less $15.00 fee. Closed Nov. 1–April 30.
Notes: Two-story house with high ceilings built in 1878. Restored with natural woodwork. Dining room with fireplace. Parlor with library. Furnished with Victorian antiques. Some French spoken.

JACKSON (2)

Dana Place Inn
Rte. 16, Pinkham Notch, Box L, Jackson, NH 03846
(603) 383-6822, (800) 537-9276, (603) 383-6822

Innkeeper: The Levine Family
Rooms: 35, incl. 32 w/pvt. bath, 22 w/phone, 7 w/TV. Located in 3 bldgs.
Rates: $120-$185, incl. full brk., dinner, afternoon refreshment, box lunches. Special pkgs. avail. Seasonal variations.
Credit cards: Most major cards
Restrictions: One night's deposit req. 15-day cancellation notice req. 2-3 night min. stay on holidays. 2-night min. stay on wknds. during season.
Notes: Three-story colonial farmhouse. Located on 300 acres. Has operated as inn since the 1890s. Common room with fireplace, library. Four dining rooms, pub. Indoor swimming pool, Jacuzzi. Natural river swimming hole. Two tennis courts. French, Spanish spoken.*

Paisley and Parsley
Rte. 16B, Box 572, Jackson, NH 03846
(603) 383-0859

Innkeeper: Beatrice and Charles G. Stone
Rooms: 2 plus 1 suite, all w/pvt. bath, phone, TV
Rates: $75-$95/room, $65/suite, all incl. full brk., afternoon refreshment. Seasonal variations. Discount avail. for extended stay.
Credit cards: MC, V
Restrictions: No children under 6, pets, smoking. One night's deposit req. 14-day cancellation notice req., less $10.00 fee. 2-night min. stay on wknds., foliage season, holidays.

Notes: Two-story house built in 1989 facing Mt. Washington. Herb and perennial gardens. Two common rooms, one with fireplace, board games, books. Furnished with antiques. Brick terrace. Snow shoes, bicycles available. Handicapped access.*

Village House
Rte. 16A, Box 359, Jackson, NH 03846
(603) 383-6666, (800) 972-8343, (603) 383-6464
Innkeeper: Robin Crocker
Rooms: 13 w/phone, plus 2 suites, all w/pvt. bath, incl. 5 w/TV. Located in 2 bldgs.
Rates: $55-$150, incl. brk., afternoon refreshment. Seasonal variations. Discount avail. for extended stay. Special pkgs. avail.
Credit cards: Most major cards
Restrictions: No pets. Smoking restricted. Min. 50% deposit req. 14-day cancellation notice req. 2-night min. stay on winter wknds.
Notes: Early American-style Colonial house built in 1860. Operating as Inn over 100 years. Located on 6.5 wooded acres adjoining Wildcat and Ellis rivers. Furnished with period pieces. Living room with fireplace, cable TV. Sun room. Wrap-around porch with wicker furniture. Greenhouse with games. Bar. Swimming pool. Outdoor Jacuzzi. Clay tennis court. Gazebo. Ski trails. Cross-country skiing.

JAFFREY (5)

Benjamin Prescott Inn
Rt. 124 East, Jaffrey, NH 03452
(603) 532-6637, (603) 532-6637
Innkeeper: Barry and Jan Miller
Rooms: 7 w/pvt. bath, incl. 5 w/phone, plus 3 suites w/pvt. bath, phone, TV
$60-$80/room, $85-130/suite, all incl. full brk. Discount avail. for extended stay.
Credit cards: MC, V
Restrictions: No children under 10, pets. Smoking restricted. Min. 50% deposit req. 10-day cancellation notice req., less $15.00 fee. 2-night min. stay on some wknds.
Notes: Three-story Greek Revival house built in 1853 on 700-acre, working dairy farm. Living room with fireplace. Summer porch. Furnished in country style with antiques. Safe deposit box available. Small private parties accommodated. Resident cats.*

Lilac Hill Acres B & B
5 Ingalls Rd., Jaffrey, NH 03452
(603) 532-7278
Innkeeper: Frank and Ellen McNeill
Rooms: 5, no pvt. bath, incl. 2 w/phone
Rates: $60-$70, incl. full brk.
Credit cards: None
Restrictions: No children under 14, pets, smoking. Deposit req. 10-day cancellation notice req., less $10.00 fee. 2-night min. stay on Oct. wknds.
Notes: Two-story private house built in the early 1800s. Located high on 50-acre hill overlooking mountains and 115-acre pond stocked with trout. Sitting room with fireplace.

Woodbound Inn
62 Woodbound Rd., Jaffrey, NH 03452
(603) 532-8341, (603) 532-8341

LILAC HILL ACRES B & B

Innkeeper: Rick, Ken, Barbara, and Janet Kohlmorgen
Rooms: 33 plus 1 cabin, all w/pvt. bath, incl. 14 w/phone, 8 w/fireplace, 4 w/TV. Located in 2 bldgs.
Rates: $49-$92/room, $80-$150/cabin, all incl. cont. brk. Discount avail. for extended and senior citizen stays. Special pkgs. avail. Seasonal variations.
Credit cards: Most major cards
Restrictions: Pets, smoking restricted. Deposit req. 14-day cancellation notice req., less $10.00 fee.
Notes: Built in 1894. Located on 162 acres with nine hole, par 3 golf course and clay tennis court. Small private parties accommodated. Handicapped access.*

JEFFERSON (1)

The Jefferson Inn
Rte. 2, Jefferson, NH 03583
(603) 586-7998, (800) 729-7908
Innkeeper: Bertie Koelwijn, Greg Brown
Rooms: 11 w/pvt. bath, incl. 4 w/phone, 3 w/TV, plus 2 suites w/pvt. bath, TV, incl. 1 w/phone
Rates: $53-$78/room, $75-$110/suite, all incl. full brk., afternoon refreshment. Seasonal variations. Discount avail. for senior citizen, extended stays.
Credit cards: Most major cards
Restrictions: Well-behaved children welcome. No pets, smoking. 7-day cancellation notice req.
Notes: Victorian house built in 1896. Special wing designed for families provides isolation and family-friendly furnishings. Wrap-around porch with rockers overlooking the White Mountains. Swimming pond. Dutch, German spoken.*

LINCOLN (1)

Red Sleigh Inn B and B
Pollard Rd., Box 562, Lincoln, NH 03251-0562
(603) 745-8517
Innkeeper: Bill and Loretta Deppe
Rooms: 6, incl. 3 w/pvt. bath

Rates: $55-$75, incl. full brk.
Credit cards: MC, V
Restrictions: No children under 12, pets, smoking. Min. one night's deposit req. 10-day cancellation notice req., less $10.00 fee. 2-night min. stay on holiday wknds.
Notes: Three-story house. Common room with fireplace, board games. Furnished with antiques.

LITTLETON (1)

Beal House Inn
247 W. Main St., Littleton, NH 03561
(603) 444-2661

Innkeeper: Catherine and Jean-Marie Fisher-Motheu
Rooms: 13, incl. 9 w/pvt. bath
Rates: $55-$80, incl. cont. brk., afternoon refreshment. Seasonal variations. Discount avail. for extended stay.
Credit cards: MC, V
Restrictions: No pets, smoking. 50% deposit req. 14-day cancellation notice req.
Notes: Federal Renaissance farmhouse built in 1833. Victorian parlor with fireplace, books, player piano. Game room with TV, billiards, board games, collection of battery-operated toys of the 1950s and 1960s. Several porches, one glassed, with wicker rockers. Dining room with fireplace. Redwood deck overlooking White Mountain. Furnished with formal and country antiques, hooked and braided rugs. Antique shop on premises. French spoken.*

MARLBOROUGH (5)

Peep-Willow Farm
51 Bixby St., Marlborough, NH 03455
(603) 876-3807

Innkeeper: Noel Aderer
Rooms: 3, no pvt. bath
Rates: $45, incl. full brk. Special pkgs. avail.
Credit cards: None
Restrictions: No smoking. Pets welcome with prior notification. Deposit req. 7-day cancellation notice req.
Notes: Colonial gambrel house. Located on twenty-acre working Thoroughbred horse farm with *eventing* training. Innkeeper's team won gold medal at Montreal Olympics. French spoken. Handicapped access.*

MOULTONBORO (4)

Overlook Farm B & B
RD 1, Box 404, Moultonboro, NH 03254
(603) 284-6485

Innkeeper: Phyllis Olafsen
Rooms: 4, incl. 1 w/pvt. bath
Rates: $65-$80, incl. full brk. Discount avail. for extended stay.
Credit cards: None
Restrictions: No children under 8, smoking. One night's deposit req. 10-day cancellation notice req. 2-night min. stay from July 1–Aug. 31. and 1st wk. in Oct. Closed mid-Oct.–April.

Notes: Two-story, colonial farmhouse built circa 1800. Dining room. Screened porch. Furnished with antiques, pottery and quilts made by owner. Canoe provided. Hiking guide available.

NEW LONDON (3)

Pleasant Lake Inn
125 Pleasant St., Box 1030, New London, NH 03257-1030
(603) 526-6271, (800) 626-4907
Innkeeper: Grant and Margaret Rich
Rooms: 10 plus 1 suite, all w/pvt. bath
Rates: $75-$90/room, $95/suite, all incl. full brk., afternoon refreshment. Special pkgs. avail. Seasonal variations. Discount avail. for extended stay.
Credit cards: MC, V
Restrictions: No children under 6, pets. Smoking restricted. Min. one night's deposit req. 2-week cancellation notice req., less $15.00 fee. 2-night min. stay on peak wknds. 3-night min. stay on holiday wknds.
Notes: Cape farmhouse built in 1790. Fully renovated in 1985. Has operated as inn since 1878. Located on five wooded acres. Dining room with fireplace. Enclosed patio overlooking Pleasant Lake. Furnished with antiques. Private beach. Dinner, canoe, row boat available. Small private parties accommodated.*

NEWPORT (3)

The Inn at Coit Mountain
523 North Main St., HCR 63, Box 3, Newport, NH 03773
(603) 863-3583, (800) 367-2364, (603) 863-7816
Innkeeper: Dick and Judi Tatem
Rooms: 5, incl. 3 w/pvt. bath plus 2 suites w/pvt. bath, fireplace
Rates: $85-$140/room, $175/suite, all incl. full brk. Discount avail. for group and extended stays. Special pkgs. avail.
Credit cards: Most major cards
Restrictions: Well-behaved children welcome. No pets. Smoking restricted. One night's deposit req. 10-day cancellation notice req., less $10.00 fee. 2-night min. stay on holiday wknds.
Notes: Two-story Georgian mansion built in 1790. Located on 14 acres at foot of Coit Mountain. Oak-paneled library with granite fireplace, library, board games. Dining room with fireplace. All meals available with prior arrangement. Small private parties accommodated. Custom picture frame shop on premises. Limited handicapped access.*

NORTH CONWAY (2)

1785 Inn
P.O. Box 1785, North Conway, NH 03860
(603) 356-9025, (800) 421-1785, (603) 356-6081
Innkeeper: Charlie and Becky Mallar
Rooms: 16, incl. 11 w/pvt. bath, plus 1 suite w/pvt. bath, TV
Rates: $49/room, $99/suite, all incl. full brk. Discount avail. for extended stay. Seasonal variations.
Credit cards: Most major cards
Restrictions: No pets. Smoking restricted. One-night's deposit req. 7-day cancellation notice req., less $15.00 fee.

1785 INN

Notes: Two-story main house built in 1785. Located on 6 acres. Recently renovated. Living room, dining room, and pub, all with fireplace. Furnished in country antiques. Outdoor swimming pool. Lawn games available. Skiing and sledding in winter. Various languages spoken.*

The Buttonwood Inn
Mt. Surprise Rd., Box 1817GA, North Conway, NH 03860
(603) 356-2625, (800) 258-2625, (603) 356-3140
Innkeeper: Claudia and Peter Needham
Rooms: 9, incl. 3 w/pvt. bath
Rates: $40-$100, incl. full brk. Discount avail. for winter mid-week stay.
Credit cards: Most major cards
Restrictions: No pets. Smoking restricted. Min. 50% deposit req. 2-week cancellation notice req., less $10.00 fee. 2-night min. stay on wknds. from Jan. 1–Feb. 28 and fall foliage. 3-night min. stay on holiday wknds.
Notes: New England-style Cape Cod house built in the 1820s. Located on five wooded acres on the side of Mount Surprise in Mount Washington Valley. Living room with wood stove, TV. Sitting room with TV. Apres ski room with fireplace, dry bar, board games. Dining room. Furnished with antiques. Outdoor swimming pool. Lawn games available. Small private parties accommodated.*

Cabernet Inn
Rte. 16, North Conway, NH 03845
(603) 356-4704, (800) 866-4704
Innkeeper: Vickie and Bruce Pantti
Rooms: 9 w/pvt. bath
Rates: $89-$169, incl. full brk. Seasonal variations. Discount avail. for extended and mid-week stays.
Credit cards: Most major cards
Restrictions: No children under 8, pets, smoking. Min. 50% deposit req. 14-day cancellation notice req., less $25.00 fee. Min. stay during holidays and fall.
Notes: Two-story Victorian cottage built in 1842. Refurbished and enhanced in 1992 into non-smoking Vintage B&B. Two living rooms with woodburning fireplaces. Shaded outdoor patios. Limited handicapped access.*

The Center Chimney - 1787
River Rd., Box 1220, North Conway, NH 03860-1220
(603) 356-6788
Innkeeper: Farley Ames Whitley
Rooms: 4, incl. 1 w/TV
Rates: $49-$55, incl. cont. brk. Discount avail. for mid-week stay.
Credit cards: None
Restrictions: No pets. Deposit req. 10-day cancellation notice req. 2-night min. stay on holidays wknds.
Notes: Two-story house built in 1787. Living room with fireplace, cable TV, board games. Furnished with antiques.

Cranmore Mountain Lodge
Kearsarge Rd., Box 1194, North Conway, NH 03860-1194
(603) 356-2044, (800) 356-3596
Innkeeper: Dennis and Judy Helfand
Rooms: 16, plus 1 suite, 40-bed bunkhouse, incl. 5 w/pvt. bath, cable TV, 2 w/fireplace. Located in 2 bldgs.
Rates: $69-$104, $130-$190/suite, $220/townhouse, all incl. full brk. Discount avail. for group stay. Seasonal variations.
Credit cards: Most major cards
Restrictions: No pets. 50% deposit req. 14-day cancellation req., less $10.00 fee.
Notes: Farmhouse once owned by Babe Ruth's daughter. Located on eight acres with stream, trout pond. Sitting room with fireplace, TV. Game room, dining room. Decorated with antiques, Babe Ruth memorabilia. Ski rental and waxing shop on premises. Tennis court, basketball court, forty-foot swimming pool, volleyball court, Jacuzzi, BBQ. Townhouse sleeps 6-8.*

The Forest, A Country Inn
P.O. Box 1736, North Conway, NH 03845-0037
(603) 356-9772, (800) 448-3534, (603) 356-5652
Innkeeper: Ken and Rae Wyman
Rooms: 8, incl. 2 w/fireplace, plus 6 suites, incl. 3 w/pvt. bath. Located in 2 bldgs.
Rates: $60-$110/room, $85-$135/suite, all incl. full brk. Seasonal variations. Special pkgs. avail. Discount avail. for extended mid-week stay.
Credit cards: Most major cards
Restrictions: No children under 3, pets, smoking. Min. 50% deposit req. 14-day cancellation notice req., less min. $10.00 fee. 2-night min. stay on summer and winter wknds. and fall foliage season. Closed April.
Notes: Three-story Victorian inn built as general store in 1890. Stone cottage built at the turn-of-the-century. Expanded and has operated as inn since 1890. Renovated in 1984. Located on twenty-five wooded acres in the White Mountains. Living room with piano, fireplace. Dining room. Common room with cable TV. Glassed porch with wood stove. Screened veranda. Solar-heated swimming pool, cross-country ski trails. Furnished with antiques.*

Nereledge Inn
River Road, Box 547, North Conway, NH 03860
(603) 356-2831
Innkeeper: Valerie and Dave Halpin
Rooms: 9, incl. 3 w/pvt. bath
Rates: $59-$89, incl. full brk. Seasonal variations.

Credit cards: Most major cards
Restrictions: No pets, smoking. 2 night's deposit req. 2-week cancellation notice req. 2-night min. stay on most wknds., holidays, fall foliage season.
Notes: Built in 1787. Has operated as inn since 1922. Dining room with wood stove overlooking Saco River Valley, Cathedral Ledge, Moat Mountains. Two sitting rooms, one with wood stove, library, TV. Porch with rockers. English-style pub with board games open on Friday and Saturday evenings.

NERELEDGE INN

Stonehurst Manor
Rte. 16, Box 1937, North Conway, NH 03860-3217
(800) 525-9100, (603) 356-3271

Innkeeper: Peter Rattay
Rooms: 17, incl. 15 w/pvt. bath, plus 7 suites w/pvt. bath, fireplace, cable TV. Located in 2 bldgs.
Rates: $96-$116/room, $156/suite, all incl. cont. brk.
Credit cards: Most major cards
Restrictions: No pets. One night's deposit req. 14-day cancellation notice req., less $25.00 fee.
Notes: Three-story English country manor house with many gables, hand-carved oak woodwork, rebuilt after fire in 1875. Has operated as inn since 1940s. Located on thirty-three wooded acres. Four dining rooms. Living room with fireplace. Library, conference room. Furnished with antiques, wicker. Decorated with Victorian stained-glass and leaded windows. Tile and stone terrace overlooking swimming pool, tennis court. Lawn games, all meals available. Small private parties accommodated. Resident cat. German spoken.

Sunny Side Inn
PO Box 557, North Conway, NH 03860
(800) 600-6239

Innkeeper: Peter and Diane Watson
Rooms: 9 w/pvt. bath, phone, fireplace
Rates: $49-$99, incl. full brk. Seasonal variations.

STONEHURST MANOR

Credit cards: Most major cards
Restrictions: No pets, smoking. 50% deposit req. 14-day cancellation notice req., less $10.00 fee.
Notes: Farmhouse built in 1850. Has operated as inn since 1936. Sitting room with fireplace. Porches with flower boxes. German spoken.*

PORTSMOUTH (6)

Bow Street Inn
121 Bow St., Portsmouth, NH 03801
(603) 431-7760, (603) 433-1680

Innkeeper: Liz Hurley
Rooms: 9 plus 1 suite, all w/pvt. bath, phone, TV
Rates: $89-$105/room, $119-$139/suite, all incl. cont. brk. Discount avail. for mid-week and extended stays. Seasonal variations.
Credit cards: MC, V
Restrictions: No children under 5, pets, smoking. Min. one night's deposit req. 7-day cancellation notice req.
Notes: Located on second floor of 19th-century brick brewery located on Piscataqua River. Shares building with performing arts theater. Sitting room overlooking the Piscataqua River. FAX available. Spanish spoken.*

Governor's House
32 Miller Ave., Portsmouth, NH 03801
(603) 431-6546, (603) 427-0803

Innkeeper: John and Nancy Grossman
Rooms: 4, incl. 1 w/jaccuzi, all w/pvt bath, phone
Rates: $70-$140 incl. full brk., afternoon refreshment. Seasonal variations. Discount avail. for mid-week stay.
Credit cards: MC, V
Restrictions: No children under 14. No pets, smoking. One night's deposit req. 10-day cancellations notice req.
Notes: Turn-of-the-century Georgian colonial house built in 1917. located in historic district. Sitting room. Baby grand piano. Library. Tennis court. Boarding arrangements available. Off-street parking available.*

RYE (6)

The Cable House
20 Old Beach Road, Rye, NH 03870
(603) 964-5000
Innkeeper: Katherine Kazakis
Rooms: 6, no pvt. bath
Rates: $40, incl. cont. brk. Discount avail for extended stay.
Credit cards: None
Restrictions: No children. 50% deposit req. Closed Sept. 30–May 30.
Notes: Built in 1874 to house the first trans-Atlantic cable. Common room with TV. Breakfast room. Listed on the National Register of Historic Places.

SANBORNTON (4)

Ferry Point House on Lake Winnisquam
100 Lower Bay Rd., Sanbornton, NH 03269
(603) 524-0087, (508) 692-6022 (off-season)
Innkeeper: Joe and Diane Damato
Rooms: 7 w/pvt. bath
Rates: $70-$85, incl. full gourmet brk., afternoon refreshment. Discount avail. for extended stays.
Credit cards: None
Restrictions: No children under 12, pets, smoking. Min. one night's deposit req. 2-week cancellation notice req. 2-night min. stay on wknds. Closed Nov. 1–Memorial Day.
Notes: Located in Laconia. Country Victorian house built in the early 1800s. Dining room. Living room with fireplace, TV. Furnished with antiques. Sixty-ft. veranda overlooking Lake Winnisquam. Gazebo. Guests have access to private beach, row boat and paddle boat. French spoken.

SNOWVILLE (1)

Snowvillage Inn
Stuart Rd., Snowville, NH 03849
(603) 447-2818

SNOWVILLAGE INN

Innkeeper: Trudy and Frank Cutrone
Rooms: 18 w/pvt. bath, incl. 4 w/fireplace. Located in 3 bldgs.
Rates: $76-$156, incl. full brk. Discount avail. for mid-week and extended stays. Seasonal variations.
Credit cards: Most major cards
Restrictions: No children under 7, pets. Smoking restricted. 50% deposit req. 14-day cancellation notice req., less $10.00 fee. 2-night min. stay on wknds. and during fall foliage season.
Notes: Two-story inn built in 1900s. Located at 1,100-foot elevation on Foss Mountain. Common rooms with fireplace, grand piano, TV, VCR, board games, library. Dining room. Decorated in country style with antiques, crafts. Clay tennis courts, award-winning flower gardens, sauna, screened porch. Lawn games available. Steven Raichlen Cooking School on premises. Small private parties accommodated. German spoken.*

SUGAR HILL (1)

Sunset Hill House
Sunset Hill Rd., Sugar Hill, NH 03585
(603) 823-5522, (800) 786-4455, (603) 823-5738
Innkeeper: The Coyle family
Rooms: 30 w/pvt. bath. Located in 2 bldgs.
Rates: $35-$55, incl. full brk. Special pkgs. avail. Discount avail. for extended stay.
Credit cards: Most major cards
Restrictions: No pets, smoking. One night's deposit req. 2-week cancellation notice req. 2-night min. stay on holiday wknds. and during fall foliage season.
Notes: Colonial house built in 1882. Fully restored. Located at 1,700 ft. elevation overlooking Presidential and Green Mountains. Three parlors, each with fireplace. Function room, deck, patio. Furnished in New England style. Swimming pool, 9-hole golf course, hammock. Restaurant, tavern on premises. Cross-country skiing clubhouse offering instruction and rental. Small private parties accommodated. Gourmet cooking school, artist workshop, fly fishing instruction and other special events planned. Handicapped access.

THORNTON (1)

Amber Lights Inn B & B
Route 3, Thornton, NH 03223
(603) 726-4077
Innkeeper: Paul Sears and Carola Warnsman
Rooms: 3, incl. 1 w/pvt. bath, plus 2 suites w/pvt. bath, incl. 1 w/TV
Rates: $60-$75/room, $95-$140/suite, all incl. full brk., evening refreshment. Special pkgs. avail.
Credit cards: Most major cards
Restrictions: No children under 7, pets, smoking. One night's deposit req. 14-day cancellation notice req., less $10.00 fee. 2-night min. stay on foliage and ski wknds.
Notes: Colonial house built in 1815. Located on 5 acres with brook. Library, garden room. Lawn games available.*

WAKEFIELD (4)

The Wakefield Inn
Mountain Laurel Rd., RR 1, Box 2185, Wakefield, NH 03872
(603) 522-8272, (800) 245-0841

Innkeeper: Lou and Harry Sisson
Rooms: 7 w/pvt. bath
Rates: $65, incl. full brk. Discount avail. for extended stay. Special pkgs. avail.
Credit cards: MC, V
Restrictions: No children under 10, pets. Smoking restricted. 50% deposit req. 7-day cancellation notice req. 2-night min. stay on holiday wknds.
Notes: Three-story inn with spiral staircase, built in 1803. Renovated in 1890. Sitting room. Dining room with fireplace. Porch.

AMBER LIGHTS INN B & B

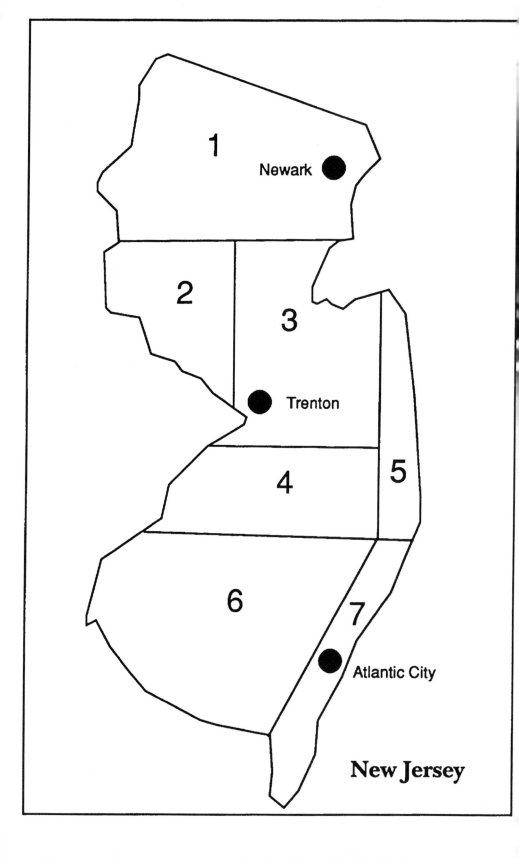

New Jersey

New Jersey

ANDOVER (1)

Crossed Keys
289 Pequest Rd., Andover, NJ 07821
(201) 786-5260, (201) 786-6320
Innkeeper: Pat Toye, Peter Belder
Rooms: 4, incl. 2 w/pvt. bath, fireplace, phone, TV, plus 1 suite w/pvt. bath, TV. Located in 2 bldgs.
Rates: $95-$110/room, $125/suite, $135/cottage, all incl. full brk.
Credit cards: Most major cards
Restrictions: No children under 12, pets, smoking. Min. 50% deposit req. 15-day cancellation notice req., less 10% fee. 2-night min. stay on wknds.
Notes: Built in 1790, restored in 1986. Has operated as inn since 1993. Dining room, living room. Library with pool table, fireplace. Separate stone cottage is part of the old barn. Furnished in 18th-century style. Lawn games avail. Small private parties accommodated.

AVON BY THE SEA (5)

The Avon Manor
109 Sylvania Ave., Avon By The Sea, NJ 07717
(908) 774-0110
Innkeeper: Jim and Kathleen Curley
Rooms: 8, incl. 6 w/pvt. bath
Rates: $80-$110, incl. full brk. Seasonal variations. Discount avail. for cash, midweek and extended stays.
Credit cards: Most major cards
Restrictions: No pets. Smoking restricted. 50% deposit req. 15-day cancellation notice req., les $15.00 fee. 2-night min. stay on wknds. 3-night min. stay on holiday wknds.
Notes: Two-story Colonial Revival house built in 1907. Operated as inn since 1948. Decorated with antiques, period pieces and wicker furniture. Parlor with fireplace. Library. Dining room with original chestnut wood. Wrap-around porch. Small private parties accommodated. *

BASKING RIDGE (3)

Olde Mill Inn
225 Rt. 202, Basking Ridge, NJ 07920
(908) 221-1100, (908) 221-1560
Innkeeper: Bocina Group
Rooms: 96 w/pvt. bath, incl. 1 w/fireplace, plus 6 suites w/pvt. bath, phone, TV
Rates: $125/room, $150/suite, all incl. cont. brk. Discount avail. for mid-week stay.
Credit cards: Most major cards
Restrictions: No pets. Smoking restricted. 24-hour cancellation notice req.
Notes: Handicapped access. Spanish spoken.*

BAY HEAD (5)

Bay Head Harbor Inn
676 Main Ave., Bay Head, NJ 08742-5346
(908) 899-0767

Innkeeper: Dan and Janice Eskesen
Rooms: 10, no pvt. bath, incl. 4 w/porches
Rates: $65-$95, incl. cont. brk., afternoon and evening refreshment. Discount avail.
   for group stay. Seasonal variations.
Credit cards: MC, V
Restrictions: No children under 5, pets, smoking. One night's deposit req. 14-day
   cancellation notice req., less $30.00 fee. 2-night min. stay on summer wknds. 3-
   night min. stay for holidays.
Notes: Three-story inn with hardwood floors, built in 1890s. Has operated as Inn
since 1990. Common room and porches. Furnished in country style with folk art
and antiques. Beach badges available during summer.

CONOVER'S BAY HEAD INN

Conover's Bay Head Inn
646 Main Ave., Bay Head, NJ 08742
(908) 892-4664

Innkeeper: Carl, Beverly and Timothy Conover
Rooms: 11 plus 1 suite, all w/pvt. bath, plus carriage house
Rates: $110-$175/room, $185/suite, $195/cariage house, all incl. full brk., afternoon refreshment. Seasonal variations. Discount avail. for mid-week, extended
   stays.
Credit cards: Most major cards
Restrictions: No children under 10, pets. Smoking restricted. Min. 50% deposit req.
   2-week cancellation notice req., less $5.00 per night fee. 2-night min. stay on
   wknds. 3-night min. stay on holidays.
Notes: Three-story house built in 1912 as private summer cottage. Reconstructed as
inn in 1916. Views of ocean, bay, marina and yacht club. Sitting room with cutstone
fireplace. Porches with rockers overlooking garden. Furnished with antiques, family pictures, original art. Dining room. Beach passes, off-street parking available.

BEACH HAVEN (7)

Bayberry Barque B & B Inn
117 Centre St., Beach Haven, NJ 08008
(609) 492-5216
Innkeeper: Tom and Barbara DeSanto
Rooms: 8 w/pvt. bath
Rates: $65-$80, incl cont. brk. Seasonal variations. Discount avail. for mid-week stay.
Credit cards: Most major cards
Restrictions: No children under 10, pets, smoking. 50% deposit req. 10-day cancellation notice req., less $5.00 fee. 2-night min. stay. 3-night min. stay on holiday wknds.
Notes: Victorian house with Oriel stained-glass window, built in the 19th-century. Located on Long Beach Island, one block from the ocean. Decorated with antiques. Listed in National and New Jersey Registers of Historic Places.

BELMAR (5)

Down the Shore B & B
201 7th Ave., Belmar, NJ 07719-2204
Innkeeper: Annette and Al Bergins
Rooms: 3, incl. 1 w/pvt. bath
Rates: $70-$80, incl. full brk., afternoon refreshment. Seasonal variations. Discount avail. for mid-week and extended stays.
Credit cards: None
Restrictions: No pets. Smoking restricted. One night's deposit req. 7-day cancellation notice req., less $15.00 fee. 2-night min. stay on wknds. and holidays.
Notes: Built in 1994 as a B&B. Located one block from the boardwalk. Parlor with TV, board games. Shaded proch. Off-street parking available.*

CAPE MAY (7)

The Abbey
34 Gurney St. at Columbia Ave., Cape May, NJ 08204
(609) 884-4506
Innkeeper: Jay and Marianne Schatz
Rooms: 12 plus 2 suites, all w/pvt. bath, refrigerator. Located in 2 bldgs.
Rates: $95-$150/room, $150-$190/suite, all incl. full brk., afternoon refreshment. Seasonal variations. Discount avail. for mid-week stay.
Credit cards: Most major cards
Restrictions: No children under 12, pets. Smoking restricted. Full prepayment req. Refunded less $20.00 fee only if room is re-rented. 2, 3, or 4-night min. stay on wknds.
Notes: Gothic Revival villa with 60-ft. tower built in 1869. Summer cottage built in 1873. Two parlors, two dining rooms, shaded verandas. Furnished with Victorian antiques, twelve-foot mirrors, marble-top dressers, stenciled and ruby glass arched windows. Board and table games, some on-site parking, beach chairs, beach passes, house phone available. Small private parties accommodated. Resident cats.*

The Albert Stevens Inn
127 Myrtle Ave., Cape May, NJ 08204
(609) 884-4717
Innkeeper: Curt and Diane Diviney-Rangen

Rooms: 7, plus 2 suites, incl. 1 w.TV, all w/pvt. bath,
Rates: $80-$105/room, $155/suite, all incl. full brk., afternoon, evening refreshments. Seasonal Variations. Discount avail.
Credit cards: Most major cards
Restrictions: No children under 15. No pets, smoking. Deposit secured w/cr. card. 14-day cancellation notice req., less $25.00 fee. 3-night min. on holidays.
Notes: Three-story Queen Anne Victorian, house built in 1898. Fully restored and operated as inn since 1980. Decorated in period antiques. Floating staircase suspended from the third floor. Two formal dining rooms and parlors. Two verandas. Hot tub. Groomed yards and gardens. Cat's Garden and Tea Tour available. Beach tags. Dinner available from February to April with a two-night stay. Resident cats.*

Angel of the Sea
5 Trenton Ave., Cape May, NJ 08204
(609) 884-3369, (800) 848-3369, (609) 884-3331

Innkeeper: John and Barbara Gurton
Rooms: 27 w/pvt. bath, TV. Located in 2 bldgs.
Rates: $95-$250, incl. full brk., evening refreshment. Seasonal variations.
Credit cards: None
Restrictions: No children under 8, pets, smoking. 15-day cancellation notice req. 2-night min. stay on wknds. 3-night min. stay on July–August wknds.
Notes: Three-story Victorian mansion with turret and tower built in 1850. Moved in 1881 and 1962. Fully restored. Common room with fireplace. Furnished with Victorian antiques.*

Barnard-Good House
238 Perry St., Cape May, NJ 08204
(609) 884-5381

Innkeeper: Tom and Nan Hawkins
Rooms: 3 plus 2 suites, all w/pvt. bath
Rates: $88-$118/room, $120/suite, all incl. full brk. Discount avail for extended stay.
Credit cards: MC, V
Restrictions: No children under 14, pets, smoking. 50% deposit req. 14-day cancellation notice req., less fee. 3-night min. room stay on wknds. 4-night min. suite stay on wknds. from June 15–Sept. 15. Closed Nov.
Notes: Victorian house with mansard roof built in 1858. Fully restored. Has operated as inn since 1979. Parlor, formal dining room, wrap-around veranda. Sitting room with antique pump organ. Furnished with Victorian antiques. Original concrete planting bed. Bicycles, beach tags, outdoor showers, dressing room, private off-street parking available.

Captain Mey's Inn
202 Ocean St., Cape May, NJ 08204
(609) 884-7793

Innkeeper: George and Kathleen Blinn
Rooms: 8, incl. 6 w/pvt. bath, plus 1 suite w/pvt. bath.
Rates: $98-$159/room, incl. full brk., afternoon refreshment. Seasonal variations.
Credit cards: MC, V
Restrictions: No children under 8, pets, smoking. 50% deposit req. 10-day cancellation notice req. 2-night min. summer stay. 3-night min. stay on wknds. from May–mid-Oct. 4-night min. stay on holiday wknds.

Notes: Two-story Colonial Revival-style Victorian house built in 1890. Fully restored. Dining room with fireplace bordered with Dutch ceramic tile. Vestibule with leaded-glass windows. Wrap-around veranda with wicker furniture Hanging ferns and Victorian wind curtains. Courtyard. Furnished with period antiques, Dutch accents. Decorated with Persian rugs on table tops, Delft Blue china. Beach towels, passes and sand chairs available. Center of tulip festival in the spring with 600 tulips blooming on property.*

CAPTAIN MEY'S INN

The Chalfonte
301 Howard St., Cape May, NJ 08204
(609) 884-8409

Innkeeper: Anne LeDuc and Judy Barhella
Rooms: 72, incl. 14 w/pvt. bath. Located in 3 bldgs.
Rates: $72-$154/room, $165/cottage, all incl. full brk., dinner. Discount avail. for group and mid-week stays. Special pkgs. avail. Seasonal variations.
Credit cards: MC, V
Restrictions: No pets. Smoking restricted. 50% deposit req. 14-day cancellation notice req., less $15.00 fee. 2-night min. stay on wknds. 3-night min. stay on holidays. Closed October–May. Jacket req. at dinner.
Notes: Three-story Italianate hotel with rickrack gingerbread built in 1876. Expanded in 1888 and 1895. Three cottages built in 1860, 1910, 1870. Up- and downstairs porches with rockers. Bar. Live professional theatre, classical concert series, folk nights, vintage films organized. Murder mystery, wine tasting, writing and painting workshops offered in summer. Small private parties accommodated. German, French spoken.*

The Duke of Windsor Inn
817 Washington St., Cape May, NJ 08204
(609) 884-1355, (800) 826-8973

Innkeeper: Bruce and Fran Prichard
Rooms: 10, incl. 8 w/pvt. bath
Rates: $70-$165, incl. full brk., afternoon refreshment
Credit cards: MC, V

Restrictions: No children under 12, pets, smoking. 50% deposit req. Deposit refunded, less $20.00 fee, upon cancellation only if room re-rented. 3-night min.
stay on holidays and from July–Sept. 15.

Notes: Three-story Queen Anne-style Victorian house with 45-foot turret built in
1896. Fully restored. Foyer with three-story carved oak open staircase, fireplace. Sitting room, library, front porch. Formal parlor with corner fireplace. Grand dining
room with five chandeliers. Furnished in Victorian decor with period antiques,
marble-topped tables, Tiffany stained-glass. Beach tags, hot and cold outdoor showers, off-street parking available. Inn known for its relaxed, friendly, informal atmosphere. On Grand Tour of Christmas Inns of Cape May.

Fairthorne B & B
111 Ocean St., Cape May, NJ 08204
(609) 884-8791, (800) 438-8742

Innkeeper: Ed and Diane Hutchinson

Rooms: 5 w/pvt. bath, incl. 3 w/TV, 1 w/fireplace, plus 1 suite w/pvt. bath, TV

Rates: $105-$140/room, $155-$195/suite, all incl. full brk., afternoon refreshment.
Seasonal variations. Discount avail. for extended, mid-week and group stays. Special pkgs. avail.

Credit cards: MC, V

Restrictions: No children under 14, pets, smoking. Min. one night's deposit req. 14-
day cancellation notice req., less $25.00 fee. 2-night min. stay on wknds. 3-night
min. stay on wknds, July and Aug.

Notes: Two-story Colonial Revival-style inn built in 1892. Wrap-around veranda with
wicker furniture. Furnished with period antiques. Sand chairs, outside hot beach
shower, beach tags available. Resident cats.*

Gingerbread House
28 Gurney St., Cape May, NJ 08204
(609) 884-0211

Innkeeper: Fred and Joan Echevarria

Rooms: 5, incl. 2 w/pvt. bath, plus 1 suite w/pvt. bath

Rates: $95-$145/room, $150-$155/suite, all incl. full brk., afternoon refreshment.
Seasonal variations. Discount avail. for extended stay.

Credit cards: MC, V

Restrictions: No children under 7, pets. Smoking restricted. Deposit req. 2-night
min. stay in spring and fall. 3-4 night min. stay in summer and holidays.

Notes: Victorian cottage with Gingerbread woodwork, double entrance doors of
teakwood with beveled glass, built in 1869 as summer retreat. Fully restored. Has
operated as inn since 1979. Parlor with fireplace. Dining room. Front porch with
wicker furniture. Decorated with period antiques. Gardens. Summer beach passes
available. Listed on the National Register of Historic Places.

The Humphrey Hughes House
29 Ocean St., Cape May, NJ 08204
(609) 884-4428, (800) 582-3634

Innkeeper: Lorraine and Terry Schmidt

Rooms: 7 w/pvt. bath, phone, incl. 1 w/fireplace, plus 3 suites w/pvt. bath, phone,
incl. 1 w/fireplace

Rates: $85-$160/room, $125-$205/suite, all incl. full brk., afternoon refreshment.
Discount avail. for mid-week and extended stays.

Credit cards: MC, V

Restrictions: No children under 16, pets, smoking. 50% deposit req. 14-day cancellation notice req., less $20.00 fee. 3-night min. stay in season.

Notes: Three-story house built in 1903. Has operated as inn since 1980. Common room with fireplace. Wrap-around veranda with wicker furniture. Glass-enclosed sun porch overlooking garden. Furnished in late Victorian style with antiques. Outdoor shower available. Handicapped access.

Inn on the Ocean
25 Ocean St., Cape May, NJ 08204
(800) 304-4477

Innkeeper: Jack and Katha Davis

Rooms: 5 suites, all w/pvt. bath

Rates: $95-$250, incl. full brk., afternoon refreshment

Credit cards: Most major cards

Restrictions: No children under 14, pets. Smoking restricted. Deposit req. Cancellation notice req., less fee.

Notes: Second Empire-style inn with French windows. Recently restored. Located in Historic District. Parlor and dining room, each with fireplace. On site parking available. Small private parties accommodated.*

The King's Cottage
9 Perry St., Cape May, NJ 08204
(609) 884-0415

Innkeeper: Tony and Pat Marino

Rooms: 8, plus 1 suite, all w/pvt. bath

Rates: $95-$195, incl full brk., afternoon refreshment. Discount avail. for extended stay.

Credit cards: None

Restrictions: No children under 12, pets. Smoking restricted. Deposit req. Cancellation notice req., less 20% fee. 2-night min. stay on wknds.

Notes: Three-story 'Stick style' inn with 2 enclosed and open wrap around verandas with ceramic tiles in railings from Philadelphia Centennial of 1876. Common room overlooking ocean. Decorated with antique wicker. Declared a national historic building in 1977.

Mainstay Inn
635 Columbia Ave., Cape May, NJ 08204
(609) 884-8690

Innkeeper: Tom and Sue Carroll

Rooms: 9 plus 3 suites, all w/pvt. bath. Located in 2 bldgs.

Rates: $135-$190/room, $140/suite, all incl. brk., afternoon refreshment

Credit cards: None

Restrictions: No children under 12, pets. Smoking restricted. Min. one night's deposit req. Cancellation notice req., less $10.00 fee. 3-night min. stay on most wknds. Closed mid-Dec.–mid-Mar.

Notes: Italianate villa inn with fourteen-foot ceilings and Cottage built in 1872 as exclusive gentlemen's gambling club. Fully restored with many original furnishings including lavish chandeliers, huge mirrors, lofty beds. Furnished with Victorian antiques. Three parlors. Victorian dining room. Two wrap-around verandas. Color TV/V. Private off street parking available. Small private parties accommodated. Handicapped access.

Mason Cottage
625 Columbia Ave., Cape May, NJ 08204
(609) 884-3358, (800) 716-2766
Innkeeper: Dave and Joan Mason
Rooms: 5, plus 4 suites, all w/pvt. bath
Rates: $85-$135/room, $135-$255/suite, all incl. full brk., afternoon refreshment.
  Discount avail. for senior citizen, extended and mid-week stays. Seasonal variations.
Credit cards: MC, V
Restrictions: No children under 12, pets. Smoking restricted. Min. one night's deposit req. 2-night min. stay on wknds. 3-night min. stay in summer & holidays.
  Closed Jan.
Notes: French Second Empire style inn with mansard roof, built in 1871. Parlor. Veranda. Furnished with restored, original period antiques. Beach passes available.*

MASON COTTAGE

Mission Inn
1117 New Jersey Ave., Cape May, NJ 08204
(609) 884-8380, (800) 800-8380
Innkeeper: Judith DeOrio and Diane Fischer
Rooms: 5, plus 1 suite, all w/pvt. bath
Rates: $85-$165/room, $115-$175/suite, all incl. full brk., afternoon refreshment.
  Discount avail. for mid-week stay.
Credit cards: Most major cards
Restrictions: No children, pets. Smoking restricted. Deposit req. Min. 15-day cancellation notice req., less $25.00 fee.
Notes: California Mission-style inn with latticed pergola. Veranda.

Mooring Guest House
801 Stockton Ave., Cape May, NJ 08204
(609) 884-5425
Innkeeper: Leslie Valenza
Rooms: 11, plus 1 suite w/TV, all w/pvt. bath

Rates: $80-$150/room, $550/week/suite, all incl. full brk., afternoon refreshment. Seasonal variations. Discount avail. for mid-week and extended stays.

Credit cards: MC, V

Restrictions: No children under 5, pets. Smoking restricted. 50% deposit req. 14-day cancellation notice req., less $20.00 fee. 2-night min. stay on wknds. 3-night min. stay on summer wknds. and holidays.

Notes: Three-story, second Empire style inn, built in 1882 as guesthouse. Victorian mansard structure. Furnished with 19th-century antiques, carved oak, wicker, lace and contemporary reproduction pieces. Dining room. Gardens around veranda. French doors onto second floor veranda. Off-street parking. Beach tags and towels. Some French spoken.*

Perry Street Inn
29 Perry St., Cape May, NJ 08204
(609) 884-4590

Innkeeper: John and Cynthia Curtis

Rooms: 10, incl. 7 w/pvt. bath, plus 10 motel efficiency units w/pvt. bath, phone

Rates: $45-$115/room, $55-$135/suite, all incl. full brk. Discount avail. for mid-week, extended and senior citizen stays. Seasonal variations.

Credit cards: Most major cards

Restrictions: No children under 12, pets. 50% deposit req. 14-day cancellation notice req. 3-night min. stay on holidays and Victorian Week wknd.

Notes: Two-story house, and adjacent motel, built about 1903. Completely refurbished in 1984. Front porch overlooking ocean. Lobby with early Edison phonograph that plays cylinders. Dining room. Furnished with Victorian pieces. On-site parking available. Small private parties accommodated. "Murder Mystery" Weekends organized.*

POOR RICHARD'S INN

Poor Richard's Inn
17 Jackson St., Cape May, NJ 08204
(609) 884-3536

Innkeeper: Richard Samuelson

Rooms: 7 plus 3 suites, incl. 3 w/pvt. bath, all w/cable TV

Rates: $64-$128/room, $600 per week/suite, all incl. cont. brk. Discount avail. for off-season stay.

Credit cards: MC, V

Restrictions: No pets, smoking. Deposit req., returned upon cancellation only if room re-rented. 2-3 night min. stay. Closed Jan. 1–Feb. 13.

Notes: Three-story Empire-style inn built in 1882. Renovated with new slate roof in and has operated as inn since 1977. Furnished in eclectic Victorian style with antiques. Porches with arched gingerbread. Listed on the National Register of Historic Places. Innkeepers strike a blend between today's informality and yesterday's charm without affectation or being overbearing. Beach tags available.

The Primrose
1102 Lafayette St., Cape May, NJ 08204
(800) 606-8288

Innkeeper: Buddy and Jan Wood, Sheryl Henry

Rooms: 4, w/pvt. bath

Rates: $80-$135, incl. full brk. Discount avail. for mid-week stay.

Credit cards: MC, V

Restrictions: No children. Deposit req. 7-day cancellation notice req. 2-night min. stay on winter wknds. 3-night min. stay on summer wknds.

Notes: Country Victorian. Porches. Courtyard. Gardens. Off-street parking. Bikes provided. Beach passes. Handicapped access.*

The Puffin
32 Jackson St., Cape May, NJ 08204
(609) 884-2664

Innkeeper: Toni and Bob Green

Rooms: 5 w/pvt. bath, TV.

Rates: $85-$150. Discount avail. for mid-week stay. Seasonal variations. Special pkgs. avail.

Credit cards: None

Restrictions: No pets, smoking. 50% deposit req., refunded, less $20.00 fee, upon cancellation only if room re-rented. 7-night min. stay from mid June–mid September.

Notes: Three-story Dutch Colonial Revival-style cottage built in 1906. Porch with wicker furniture. Decorated with Victorian and seashore motifs, antiques, family heirlooms. French spoken.

The Queen Victoria
102 Ocean St., Cape May, NJ 08204
(609) 884-8702

Innkeeper: Dane and Joan Wells

Rooms: 16, incl. 1 w/fireplace, plus 7 suites, incl. 1 w/fireplace, 1 w/phone, all w/pvt. bath. Located in 3 bldgs.

Rates: $75-$198/room, $145-$240/suite, all incl. full brk., afternoon refreshment. Discount avail. for mid-week and extended stays.

Credit cards: MC, V

Restrictions: No pets, smoking. Min. 50% deposit req. 21-day cancellation notice req., less $15.00 fee. 2-night min. stay on wknds. in Nov. and March. 3-night min. stay on wknds. in Apr. and Oct. and holidays.

Notes: Three-story stick-style mansion built in 1879. Library, dining room. Two parlors, one with fireplace, player piano, the other with board games, TV. Porches with rocking chairs overlooking Victorian gardens. Decorated with authentic Victorian furnishings in walnut, wicker, oak, pine. Bicycles, beach tags available. Special workshops and programs organized with special emphasis on Christmas. Small private parties accommodated. Handicapped access. French spoken. Resident cats.

Sea Holly Inn
815 Stockton Ave., Cape May, NJ 08204
(609) 884-6294
Innkeeper: Christy and Christopher Igoe
Rooms: 6 plus 2 suites, all w/pvt. bath
Rates: $95-$140/room, $140-$180/suite, all incl. full brk., evening refreshment. Seasonal variations. Discount avail. for extended stay. Special pkgs. avail.
Credit cards: Most major cards
Restrictions: No children, pets, smoking. Min. one night's deposit req., refunded upon cancellation, less 15% fee, only if room re-rented. 2-night min. stay off season. 3-night min. stay, mid-June–Oct. Closed Jan.
Notes: Three-story Gothic cottage with Italianate detailing built in 1875 as summer home. Parlor/dining area. Furnished with Renaissance Revival and Eastlake antiques. All front rooms overlook ocean. Beach tags, sand chairs, hot and cold outdoor showers, bicycles available. Small private parties accommodated.

The Stetson Inn
725 Kearney Ave., Cape May, NJ 08204
(609) 884-1724
Innkeeper: Carol & Lou Elwell
Rooms: 7 w/pvt. bath, phone
Rates: $75-$115, incl. full brk. Discount avail. for mid-week stay. Seasonal variations.
Credit cards: MC, V
Restrictions: No children under 12, pets. Smoking restricted. One-night's deposit req. 14-day cancellation notice req., less $20.00 fee. 2-night min. stay on wknds. 3-night min. stay on July-Aug. and holiday wknds.
Notes: Two-story seaside cottage built in 1915. Sun/shade porches. Parlor with fireplace and piano. Decorated with Laura Ashley wallpaper in country English and Victorian decor.*

SUMMER COTTAGE

Summer Cottage
613 Columbia Ave., Cape May, NJ 08204
(609) 884-4948

Innkeeper: Skip and Linda Loughlin
Rooms: 8, incl. 6 w/pvt. bath, 1 w/TV
Rates: $85-$160, incl full brk., afternoon refreshment
Credit cards: MC, V
Restrictions: No pets. Smoking restricted. 50% deposit req. Cancellation notice
   req., less $20.00 fee.
Notes: Italianate-style cottage with cupola, built around 1867. Veranda with wicker,
rockers, porch swing. Parlor with fireplace. Decorated with period Victorian fur-
nishings. Board games, beach tags, parking stickers available.*

The Victorian Rose
715 Columbia Ave., Cape May, NJ 08204
(609) 884-2497

Innkeeper: Robert and Linda Mullock
Rooms: 7 w/pvt bath, phone, plus 2 suites w/pvt. bath, TV, phone, plus cottage
   w/cable TV
Rates: $85-$135/room, $135/suite, $125/cottage, all incl. full brk., evening re-
   freshment. Discount avail. for extended stay.
Credit cards: None
Restrictions: Children over 12 welcome in cottages. No pets. One night's deposit
   req. Deposit refundable upon cancellation only if room re-rented. 3-night min.
   stay on wknds. from Jun.–Sept. Closed Jan. 1–Mar. 31.
Notes: Has operated as inn since 1880. Fully restored. Located in center of Cape
May Historic District. Parlor with fireplace. Dining room. Wide veranda with rockers. Furnished with rose theme throughout. Garden with 100 rose bushes. Beach
tags available.

White Dove Cottage
619 Hughes St., Cape May, NJ 08204
(609) 884-0613, (800) 321-3683

Innkeeper: Frank and Sue Smith
Rooms: 5 w/pvt. bath, plus suite w/pvt. bath, TV, fireplace
Rates: $75-$125/room, $120-$175/suite, all incl. full brk., afternoon refreshment.
   Discount avail. for senior citizen, extended and mid-week stays. Special pkgs.
   avail.
Credit cards: None
Restrictions: No children under 10, pets, smoking. 50% deposit req. 21-day cancellation notice req., less $20.00 fee. 2-night min. stay on wknds. and in season. 3-
   night min. stay, July 1–Aug. 31.
Notes: Three-story Second Empire-style house with mansard roof built in 1866. Has
operated as inn since 1950. Recently renovated. Living room with player piano. Dining room. Veranda with rockers. Furnished in country style with period country English antiques, family heirlooms, handmade quilts. Off-street parking, beach towels,
chairs available.*

Wilbraham Mansion
133 Myrtle Ave., Cape May, NJ 08204
(609) 884-2046

Innkeeper: Patty Carnes
Rooms: 7, plus 3 suites all w/pvt. bath
Rates: $95-$135/room, $150-$175/suite, all incl. full brk., evening refreshment. Dis-
   count avail. for off-season and extended stays. Seasonal variations.

Credit cards: AE, MC

Restrictions: No children under 16, pets. Smoking restricted. One night's deposit req. 10% cancellation fee. 2-night min. stay on wknds. 3-night min. stay on holiday and special event wknds.

Notes: Two-story Queen Anne Victorian mansion with 12-ft. ceilings built in 1840. Enlarged in 1895. Has operated as inn since 1988. Formal dining room, parlors with fireplace. Terrace, glassed sun porch. Furnished with original pieces, antiques. Indoor heated swimming pool. Tulip gardens. Lawn games, off-street parking available. Small private parties accommodated. Resident cat.

Windward House
24 Jackson St., Cape May, NJ 08204
(609) 884-3368

Innkeeper: Owen and Sandy Miller

Rooms: 6 w/pvt. bath, incl. 1 w/cable TV, plus 2 suites w/pvt. bath, cable TV

Rates: $85-$145/room, $90-$125/suite, all incl. full brk., evening refreshment. Discount avail. for mid-week stay. Seasonal variations.

Credit cards: MC, V

Restrictions: No children under 12, pets. Smoking restricted. Min. one night's deposit req. 14-day cancellation notice req., less $20.00 fee. Occasional 2 or 3-night min. stay.

Notes: Two-story, shingled, Edwardian-style seaside house built in 1905. Located in the historic district. Wrap-around porch with wicker furniture. Second floor porch private to two guest rooms. Third floor sun deck. Parlor with fireplace. Common room. Stained, leaded, and beveled glass. Furnished with Victorian antiques and collectables. Off-street parking, bicycles, free beach passes available. Female ghost in residence.

THE WOODEN RABBIT

The Wooden Rabbit
609 Hughes St., Cape May, NJ 08204
(609) 884-7293

Innkeeper: Greg and Debby Burow

Rooms: 2 plus 1 suite, all w/pvt. bath, phone, TV

Rates: $145/room, $165/suite, all incl. cont. brk. Seasonal variations.

Credit cards: Most major cards

Restrictions: No pets, smoking. Min. one night's, non-refundable deposit req. 2-night min. stay. 4-night min. stay in Summer.
Notes: Three-story house. Dining room with fireplace. Living room. Sun porch with wicker rockers. Furnished in country style.

Woodleigh House
808 Washington St., Cape May, NJ 08204
(609) 884-7123, (800) 399-7123

Innkeeper: Buddy and Jan Wood, Virginia Walsh
Rooms: 4, plus 1 suite, all w/pvt. bath
Rates: $80-$135/room, $110-$150/suite, all incl. cont. brk. Discount avail. for mid-week stay.
Credit cards: MC, V
Restrictions: No pets, smoking. 50% deposit req. 7-day cancellation notice req. 2-night min. stay on wknds. 3-night min. stay on summer wknds.
Notes: Two-story Victorian sea captain's house built in 1850s. Parlor with cable TV. Dining room. Porches with rockers and wicker overlooking brick courtyard and garden. Furnished with Victorian antiques. Innkeepers collect glass and Royal Copenhagen. Off-street parking, beach bicycles available.*

FLEMINGTON (2)

The Cabbage Rose Inn
162 Main St., Flemington, NJ 08822
(908) 788-0247

Innkeeper: Al Scott and Pam Venosa
Rooms: 5 w/pvt. bath, incl. 1 w/fireplace
Rates: $80-$110, incl. expanded cont. brk., afternoon refreshment. Discount avail. for mid-week and extended stays.
Credit cards: Most major cards
Restrictions: No children under 8, pets, smoking. 50% deposit req. 10-day cancellation notice req. 2-night min. wknd. stay, May–Nov.
Notes: Turret-crowned Victorian mansion with open-air gazebo built in 1890. Located on .5 acre. Entry hall with grand staircase. Parlor with cable TV. Dining room with baby grand piano. Sunporch. Front porch with wicker furniture. Furnished in light Victorian style. Flagstone patio, gardens. Lawn games, picnic baskets available.*

Jerica Hill Bed & Breakfast Inn
96 Broad St., Flemington, NJ 08822
(908) 782-8234

Innkeeper: Judith Studer
Rooms: 5 w/pvt. bath
Rates: $70-$105, incl. cont. brk. afternoon and evening refreshment. Discount avail. for senior citizen and mid-week stays.
Credit cards: Most major cards
Restrictions: No children under 12, pets. Smoking restricted. 50% deposit req. 10-day cancellation notice req. 2-night min. stay on most wknds.
Notes: Two-story, Queen Anne, Victorian country house Oak and wideboard pine floors, built in 1901. Has operated as inn since 1984. Center entrance hall with grand staircase. Dining room, living room with fireplace, library, cable TV. Screened porch with wicker furniture. Furnished with antiques. Off-street parking

available. Hot air balloon rides, country picnics and winery tours arranged. Resident pets.*

FRENCHTOWN (2)

Hunterdon House
12 Bridge St., Frenchtown, NJ 08825
(908) 996-3632, (800) 382-0375, (800) 473-2167
Innkeeper: Gene Refalvy
Rooms: 6 w/pvt. bath, incl. 1 w/fireplace, plus 1 suite w/pvt. bath
Rates: $110-$145/room, $145/suite, all incl. full brk., afternoon refreshment. Discount avail. for mid-week, extended, and senior citizen stays.
Credit cards: Most major cards
Restrictions: No children, pets, smoking. One night's deposit req. 10-day cancellation notice req. 2-night min. stay on wknds. 3-night min. stay on holidays.
Notes: Itanianate mansion with belvedere, built in 1864. Located one half block from Delawar River. Parlor. Dining room. Sitting porch. Furnished with period pieces, family memorabilia, and antiques. Concierge service available.*

GLENWOOD (1)

Apple Valley Inn
Box 302, Rt. 517 at Rt. 565, Glenwood, NJ 07418
(201) 764-3735
Innkeeper: Mitzi and John Durham
Rooms: 6, incl. 1 w/pvt. bath
Rates: $60-$75, incl. full brk., evening refreshment. Discount avail. for extended and mid-week stays.
Credit cards: None
Restrictions: No children under 12, pets. Smoking restricted. Deposit req. 3-day cancellation notice req. 2-night min. stay for major holidays.
Notes: Three-story colonial mansion built in 1831. Located on 3-acres with brook, apple orchard, grist mill. Sun room, kitchen, dining room. Glass-front woodstove. Parlor with fireplace. Common area. Furnished in period antiques. Swimming pool. Antique shop on premises. Resident pets.

LAMBERTVILLE (2)

Chimney Hill Farm
207 Goat Hill Rd., Lambertville, NJ 08530
(609) 397-1516
Innkeeper: Terry Ann and Richard Anderson
Rooms: 8 w/pvt. bath, incl. 2 w/fireplace
Rates: $80-$150, incl. full brk. Seasonal variations. Discount avail. for senior citizen stay.
Credit cards: Most major cards
Restrictions: No pets, smoking. One night's deposit req. 10-day cancellation notice req., less $10.00 fee. 2-night min. stay on wknds. 3-night min. stay on holidays.
Notes: Two-story stone and frame Colonial inn with three stairwells, wide plank pine floors, built in 1820. Expanded in 1927. Has operated as inn since 1988. Located on ten wooded acres with formal and raspberry gardens. Formal living room. Dining room with fireplace. Library, sun room. Furnished with antiques.*

CHIMNEY HILL FARM

NEWTON (1)

The Wooden Duck
140 Goodale Rd., Newton, NJ 07860
(201) 300-0395, (201) 300-0141
Innkeeper: Bob and Barbara Hadden
Rooms: 3 plus 1 suite, all w/pvt. bath, phone, TV. Located in 2 bldgs.
Rates: $85-$100/room, $150/suite, all incl. full brk., afternoon refreshment. Discount avail. for mid-week stay.
Credit cards: Most major cards
Restrictions: No children under 12, pets, smoking. One night's deposit req. 14-day cancellation notice req.
Notes: Two-story inn custom built in 1980. Located on 17 acres. Has operated as inn since 1995. Common room with fireplace, board games, library. Game room with fireplace, video library. Furnished with antiques and reproductions. Guests have access to kitchen. Innkeeper collects hand-carved ducks and pewter ice cream molds. Patio, swimming pool.

OCEAN CITY (7)

The Adelmann's
1228 Ocean Ave., Ocean City, NJ 08226
(609) 399-2786
Innkeeper: Anne Adelmann
Rooms: 7 w/TV, refrigerator, incl. 3 w/pvt. bath, plus 1 suite w/pvt. bath, TV, refrigerator. Some rooms w/pvt. access to front porch, flower deck
Rates: $50-$75/room, $80/suite, all incl. cont. brk. Discount avail. for group and extended stays. Special pkgs. avail.
Credit cards: None
Restrictions: No pets. Smoking restricted. One night's deposit req.
Notes: Three-story house. Has operated as inn by the same family since 1977. Sitting room with TV, refrigerator. Parlor. Front porch overlooking ocean. Patio with gas grill, picnic table. Outdoor showers, dressing rooms, beach towels available.

Guests have access to storage for beach and fishing gear, bicycles, etc. Small private parties accommodated. Some German spoken.

BarnaGate Bed & Breakfast
637 Wesley Ave., Ocean City, NJ 08226
(609) 391-9366

Innkeeper: Frank and Lois Barna
Rooms: 5, incl. 1 w/pvt. bath
Rates: $65-$75, incl. cont. brk. Discount avail. for mid-week stay.
Credit cards: MC, V
Restrictions: No children under 10. 50% deposit req. 3-day cancellation notice req. 2-night min. stay on holidays.
Notes: Country Victorian house built about 1895. Front porch. Common room with TV. Decorated in country style. Furnished with antiques.

Beachfront B&B
5447 Central Ave., Ocean City, NJ 08226
(609) 399-0477, (609) 399-6964

Innkeeper: Des and Dolly Nunan
Rooms: 3 suites w/pvt. bath, cable TV
Rates: $110-$150, incl. cont. brk. Discount avail. for extended and senior citizen stays. Seasonal variations.
Credit cards: None
Restrictions: No pets, smoking. Min. 50% deposit req. Min. 3-day cancellation notice req. 2-night min. stay on wknds. 3-night min. stay in summer.
Notes: Two-story inn built in 1912. Fully renovated and expanded in 1985. Furnished in contemporary style. Beachfront deck off living/dining room overlooking ocean. All meals available. Handicapped access. Italian, Spanish, some French spoken. *

The Charleston
928 Ocean Ave., Ocean City, NJ 08226
(609) 399-6049

Innkeeper: Ed and Jane Spangler
Rooms: 6 w/pvt. bath, incl 4 w/TV
Rates: $50-$70. Discount avail. for extended stay. Seasonal variations.
Credit cards: None
Restrictions: No pets, smoking. 2-night min. stay on wknds.
Notes: Two-story cottage built in 1920. Has operated as inn since 1950. Common room with TV, board games. Enclosed outdoor shower. Off-street parking available.*

Scarborough Inn
720 Ocean Ave., Ocean City, NJ 08226
(609) 399-1558, (800) 399-1558, (609) 399-4472

Innkeeper: Gus and Carol Bruno
Rooms: 25 plus 4 suites, all w/pvt. bath
Rates: $65-$100/room, $70-$90/suite, all incl. cont. brk. Seasonal variations. Discount avail. for mid-week and extended stays.
Credit cards: Most major cards
Restrictions: No pets. One night's deposit req. 7-day cancellation notice req. 2-night min. stay on wknds. 3-night min. stay on holidays.

Notes: Four-story Queen Anne-style Victorian house built in 1898. Parlor with ceiling fans, upright piano. Library, wraparound porch. Lobby with TV, VCR, videos. Board games available. Italian spoken. Complimentary beach tags provided to guests staying three or more consecutive nights.*

Serendipity Bed & Breakfast
712 9th St., Ocean City, NJ 08226-3554
(609) 399-1554
Innkeeper: Clara and Bill Plowfield
Rooms: 6, incl. 2 w/pvt. bath
Rates: $48-$80, incl. cont. brk. Seasonal variations. Special pkgs. avail.
Credit cards: Most major cards
Restrictions: No children under 10, pets, smoking. 50% deposit req. Deposit refunded, less $10.00 fee, upon cancellation only if room re-rented. 2-night min. stay on wknds. in rooms w/pvt. bath. 3-night min. stay in all rooms on summer holiday wknds.
Notes: Three-story house built in 1912. Fully renovated. Located ½ block from beach. Living room with fireplace, TV, VCR, stereo, library. Dining room, sitting room, porch. Board games available. Gourmet, natural foods vegetarian dinners available Oct.–May.*

OCEAN GROVE (5)

Cordova
26 Webb Ave., Ocean Grove, NJ 07756
(908) 774-3084 in summer, (212) 751-9577 in winter
Innkeeper: Doris Chernik
Rooms: 14 w/pvt. bath, incl. 2 w/phone, plus 2 suites w/pvt. bath, kitchen, plus 2 cottages w/pvt. bath, kitchen, TV, incl. 1 w/balcony. Located in 2 bldgs.
Rates: $29-$62/room, $54/suite, $95-$115/cottage, all incl. cont. brk. Discount avail. for senior citizen, mid-week and extended stays. Special pkgs. avail.
Credit cards: None
Restrictions: No pets. Smoking restricted. Min. 50% deposit req. 4-week cancellation notice req. 2-night min. stay on wknds. and holidays. Closed September–May.
Notes: Four-story Victorian inn built in 1886. Living room with library, music, TV. Furnished with antiques. Three porches, communal kitchen, BBQ, picnic tables. Saturday night wine/cheese parties. Listed on the National Register of Historical Places. Small private parties accommodated.*

SPRING LAKE (5)

Ashling Cottage
106 Sussex Ave., Spring Lake, NJ 07762
(908) 449-3553
Innkeeper: Jack and Goodi Stewart
Rooms: 10, incl. 8 w/pvt. bath
Rates: $97-$150, incl. full brk. Discount avail. for extended stay. Seasonal variations.
Credit cards: None
Restrictions: No children under 12, pets, smoking. One night's deposit req. 10-day cancellation notice req., less 15% fee. 2-night min. stay on wknds. 3-night min. stay on holiday wknds. Closed Jan.–March.

Notes: Two-story Victorian "carpenter Gothic" building with mansard roof built in 1877 as private residence. Decorated with antiques, reproductions. Living room with TV, VCR. Parlor with board games. Solarium, library, three porches, patio with BBQ. Small private parties accommodated. German spoken.*

The Hollycroft Inn
P.O. Box 448, Spring Lake, NJ 07762
(908) 681-2254

Innkeeper: Mark and Linda Fessler
Rooms: 7 w/pvt. bath, incl. 1 w/porch, 1 w/balcony, 2/w/fireplace
Rates: $95-$135, incl. full brk. Discount avail. for extended stay.
Credit cards: AE
Restrictions: No children, pets. Smoking restricted. One night's deposit req. 7-day cancellation notice req., less $10.00 fee.
Notes: Mountain lodge-style inn built of whole log beams and columns in 1908. Located in sheltered area. Common room with stone fireplace. Dining room. Latticed morning room. Flagstone patio. Resident cats.

Normandy Inn
21 Tuttle Ave., Spring Lake, NJ 07762
(908) 449-7172, (908) 449-1070

Innkeeper: Michael and Susan Ingino
Rooms: 15, plus 2 suites, all w/pvt. bath, phones, incl. 1 w/fireplace, 2 w/TV. Located in 2 bldgs.
Rates: $102-$152/room, $235/suite, all incl. full brk., evening refreshment. Discount avail. for mid-week and extended stays. Seasonal variations.
Credit cards: Most major cards
Restrictions: No pets. Smoking restricted. Min. one night's deposit req. 10-day cancellation notice req., less $10.00 fee. 2-night min. stay on wknds. from Mar.–Nov. 3-night min. stay on holidays. 4-night min. stay on July and Aug. wknds.
Notes: Victorian Italianate villa built in 1888. Enlarged in the early 1900s with Queen Anne accents. Fully restored. Has operated as inn since 1910. Two living rooms, dining room. Enclosed and wrap-around porches with wicker furniture. Decorated with Victorian antiques. Train and bus station pickup available. Bicycles available.*

The Sandpiper Restaurant & Hotel
7 Atlantic Ave., Spring Lake, NJ 07762
(908) 449-6060, (908) 449-8409

Innkeeper: Rosemary Richards
Rooms: 10 w/pvt. bath, incl. 3 w/fireplace, plus 5 suites w/pvt. bath
Rates: $60-$70, incl. cont. brk. Discount avail. for mid-week stay.
Credit cards: Most major cards
Restrictions: No pets. 50% deposit req. 14-day cancellation notice req.
Notes: Built in 1888 by Spanish Ambassador to United States. Exceptionally large rooms with 10-foot ceilings, most with ocean view. Indoor pool. Operated in casual style.

Sea Crest By The Sea
19 Tuttle Ave., Spring Lake, NJ 07762
(908) 449-9031, (800) 803-9031, (908) 974-0403

Innkeeper: John and Carol Kirby

Rooms: 10 plus 1 suite, all w/pvt. bath, incl. 7 w/fireplace, 1 w/TV
Rates: $92-$159/room, $189-$239/suite, all incl. full brk. Seasonal variations
Credit cards: MC, V
Restrictions: No children, pets. Smoking restricted. 50% deposit req., refunded, less $20.00 fee, upon cancellation only if room re-rented. 2-night min. stay on wknds. from Sept.–June. 2-night min. mid-week stay from July–August, 3-night min. wknd. stay from July–August.
Notes: Three-story Victorian mansion. Dining room, library. Living room with antique player piano overlooking ocean. Furnished with French and English antiques and family heirlooms. Veranda. Croquet court, bicycles, beach towels, beach passes available.

STANHOPE (1)

Whistling Swan Inn
110 Main St., Stanhope, NJ 07874
(201) 347-6369, (201) 347-3391

Innkeeper: Joe and Paula Williams-Mulay
Rooms: 9 plus 1 suite, all w/pvt. bath, phone
Rates: $85-$95/room, $110/suite, all incl. full brk., afternoon refreshment. Seasonal variations. Discount avail. for mid-week and extended stays.
Credit cards: Most major cards
Restrictions: No children under 12, pets, smoking. One night's deposit req. 3-day cancellation notice req. 2-night min. on holiday wknds.
Notes: Three-story Queen Anne Victorian house with pocket doors built in 1905. Fully renovated and extended in 1990. Has operated as inn since 1986. Located on one acre. Parlor with victrola, upright player piano and concealed cable TV. Dining room with fireplace. Furnished with antiques. Wrap-around veranda, stone pillar porch. Hammock, picnic table, business services available. Small private parties accommodated.*

STOCKTON (2)

Stockton Inn
One Main St., Box C, Stockton, NJ 08559
(609) 397-1250

Innkeeper: Andy McDermott and Bruce Monti
Rooms: 3 w/pvt. bath, TV, incl. 1 w/fireplace, plus 8 suites w/pvt. bath, TV, incl. 7 w/fireplace. Many w/balcony, veranda. Located in 4 bldgs.
Rates: $60-$105/room, $90-$145/suite, all incl. cont. brk. Special pkgs. avail.
Credit cards: Most major cards
Restrictions: No children under 12, pets. Full prepayment req. 7-day cancellation notice req., less 10% fee. 2-night min. stay on wknds. 3-night min. stay for holidays.
Notes: Three-story inn built in 1710. Has operated as inn since 1796. Main Inn, Wagon, Carriage and Federal Houses. Restaurant with 5 fireplaces, murals, full bar and wine service, live entertainment, dancing on premises. Seasonal garden dining amid waterfalls and pond.

Woolverton Inn
R.D. 3, Box 233, Stockton, NJ 08559
(609) 397-0802

Innkeeper: Elizabeth and Michael Palmer

Rooms: 8 w/pvt. bath, plus 3 suites w/pvt. bath, incl. 2 w/fireplace. Located in 2 bldgs.

Rates: $95-$115/room, $135-$150/suite, all incl. full brk. Discount avail. for midweek and group stays.

Credit cards: Most major cards

Restrictions: No children under 12, pets, smoking. One-night's deposit req. 14-day cancellation notice req. 2-night min. stay on wknds. 3-night min. stay on holidays wknds.

Notes: Three-story stone structure with wood plank flooring and a mansard slate roof, built in 1792. Remodeled in 1800s. Porch with garden. Has operated as inn since 1980. Dining room, patio, living room. Furnished with period pieces. Lawn games available. Small private parties accommodated.

WOOLVERTON INN

WHITEHOUSE STATION (1)

Holly Thorne House
141 Readington Rd., Whitehouse Station, NJ 08889
(908) 534-1616, (908) 534-9017

Innkeeper: Anne and Joe Fosbre
Rooms: 4 rooms w/pvt. bath
Rates: $80-$90, incl. full brk.
Credit cards: Most major cards
Restrictions: No children under 14, pets. 7-day cancellation notice req., less 10% fee.

Notes: English Manor Inn converted from cow barn. Gathering room wit fireplace, TV, VCR, FAX, refridgerator. Billiard room with fireplace, gym, whirpool tub. Swimming pool, cabana. Handicapped access.*

WOODBINE (7)

Henry Ludlam Inn
1336 Rte. 47, Woodbine, NJ 08270
(609) 861-5847

Innkeeper: Ann & Marty Thurlow
Rooms: 5 w/pvt. bath, incl. 3 w/fireplace

Rates: $85-$110, incl. full brk. Discount avail. for extended stay.
Credit cards: Most major cards
Restrictions: No children under 12. Min. one night's deposit req. 7-day cancellation notice req. 2-night min. stay on wknds. from May–October. 3-night min. stay on holiday wknds.
Notes: Three-story Federal Colonial style built in 1740. Located on 3 acres. Land leads down to fifty-six acre Ludlam's Pond. Parlor with wood-burning stove. Common room with TV/VCR, rolltop desk, fireplace. Decorated with antiques, braided rugs, handmade quilts. Porch overlooking the lake. Outdoor activities available. Gazebo.*

New Mexico

Casita Chamisa
850 Chamisal Rd. N.W., Albuquerque, NM 87107
(505) 897-4644
Innkeeper: Arnold and Kit Sargeant
Rooms: 1, plus 1 guesthouse, w/pvt. bath, fireplace, TV. Located in 2 bldgs.
Rates: $85, incl. cont. brk. Discount avail. for extended stay.
Credit cards: Most major cards
Restrictions: Pets welcome with prior arrangement. Smoking restricted. 50% deposit req. 10-day cancellation notice req. Closed Nov.
Notes: Adobe casita built about 1850. Guest house with Southwestern decor, kitchenette. Located on .5 wooded acre with vegetable garden. Deck, enclosed patio. Heated indoor swimming pool, hot tub. Therapeutic massage available. Archeological project sponsored by the Maxwell Museum of Anthropology on premises. Innkeeper is archeologist. Some Spanish, French spoken.*

Catherine Kelly's B & B
311 Smokey Bear Blvd, Box 444, Albuquerque, NM 88316
(505) 354-2335
Innkeeper: Amanda Tudor
Rooms: 4 plus 2 suites, incl. 2 w/pvt. bath
Rates: $50-$125, incl. cont. brk. Discount avail. for mid-week and senior citizen stays.
Credit cards: MC, V
Restrictions: No smoking. One night's deposit req. 10-day cancellation notice req., less 15% fee.
Notes: Ranch house located in the Village of Capitan. Handicapped access.

Las Palomas Valley B & B
2303 Candelaria Rd., NW, Albuquerque, NM 87107
(505) 345-7228, (505) 345-7328
Innkeeper: Andrew and Lori Caldwell
Rooms: 3, plus 5 suites, all w/pvt bath, TV. Located in 2 bldgs.
Rates: $65-$80/room, $85-$125/suite, all incl. full brk., evening refreshment. Discount avail. for group, extended and senior citizen stays.
Credit cards: Most major cards
Restrictions: No pets, smoking. Min. one night's deposit req. 2-day cancellation notice req.
Notes: Adobe estate built in 1939. Located on 3 acres. Dining room, sun porch, kitchen. Hot tub, tennis court, Barbeque, courtyard, rose garden, orchard. Furnished with antiques. Private courtyards available. Lawn games, FAX and wordprocessing facilities available. Handicapped access. Spanish spoken.*

Old Town B & B
707 17th St. NW, Albuquerque, NM 87104
(505) 764-9144
Innkeeper: Nancy Hoffman

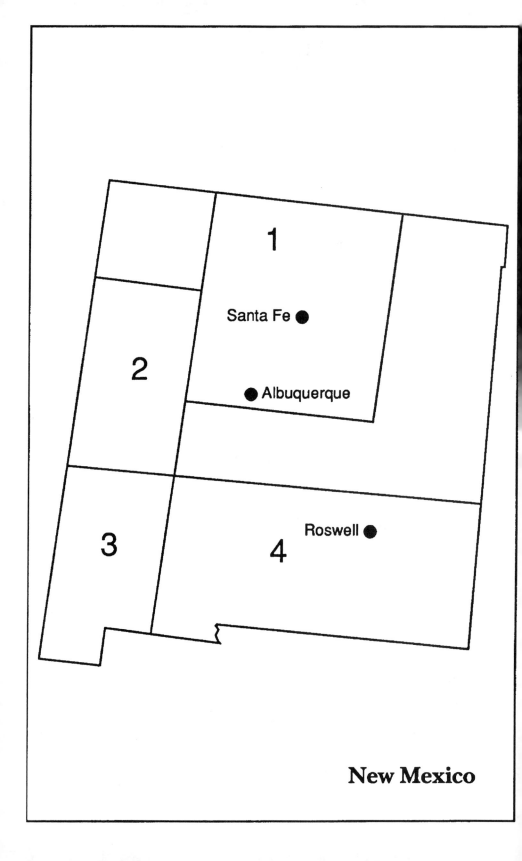

1

Santa Fe ●

2

● Albuquerque

3

4

Roswell ●

New Mexico

Rooms: 1 w/pvt. bath, phone, TV, pvt. entrance, plus 1 suite w/pvt. bath, phone, fireplace, TV, pvt. entrance, Jacuzzi bath
Rates: $60/room, $75/suite, all incl. cont. brk., afternoon refreshment. Discount avail. for extended stay.
Credit cards: None
Restrictions: No pets, smoking. 50% deposit req. 2-night min. stay during Balloon Fiesta.
Notes: Two-story adobe house built in 1840. Garden, patio, dining room.*

W. J. Marsh House/Snyder Cottage
301 Edith S.E., Albuquerque, NM 87102
(505) 247-1001
Innkeeper: Janice Lee Sperling, M.D.
Rooms: 8, incl. 2 suites, plus 1 cottage w/TV. All w/pvt. bath
Rates: $59-$109, incl. full brk. Discount avail. for singles and extended stays.
Credit cards: None
Restrictions: No pets, smoking. Children restricted. Deposit req. 14-day cancellation notice req., less $25.00 per night fee. Min. stay during October Balloon Fiesta.
Notes: Two-story Queen Anne Victorian inn with original California redwood floors, doors and trim, hand-tiled fireplace, gas lighting fixtures, stained-glass, built in 1895. 2 parlors, dining room, porch. Two resident ghosts. Cottage built in 1890 with clawfoot rub, fully-equipped kitchen sleeps six. Listed on National Register of Historic Places. French, Spanish spoken.*

BERNALILLO (1)

La Hacienda Grande
21 Baros Lane, Bernalillo, NM 87004
(505) 867-1887, (800) 353-1887, (505) 867-4621
Innkeeper: Daniel Buop, Shoshana Zimmerman
Rooms: 6 suites w/pvt. bath, phone, incl. 4 w/kiva fireplace, 4 w/TV
Rates: $89-$110, incl. full brk., afternoon refreshment. Discount avail. for extended stay. Special pkgs. avail. Seasonal variations.
Credit cards: Most major cards
Restrictions: No children under 12, pets. Smoking restricted. Deposit req. 10-day cancellation notice req., less 10% fee.
Notes: Spanish hacienda with 2' thick adobe walls, wood ceilings, tile, stone or brick floors, built in 1745 around a central courtyard with covered portico. Located on 3.5 acres. Fully restored. Living room with kiva fireplace. Dining room, porch. Furnished with handmade items and original artwork. Dinner, massage therapy, board games available. Small private parties accommodated.*

CHAMA (1)

Jones House
311 Terrace Ave., Box 887, Chama, NM 87520
(505) 756-2908
Innkeeper: Phil and Sara Cole
Rooms: 5 incl. 3 w/pvt. bath, 2 w/TV. Located in 2 bldgs.
Rates: $87, incl. full brk.
Credit cards: Most major cards

Restrictions: No children under 7, pets, smoking. Deposit req. 7-day cancellation notice req. 2-night min. stay.
Notes: The Innkeepers are 'Rail Fans' and enjoy sharing their knowledge of the train. Handicapped access.

CHIMAYO (1)

Casa Escondida
P.O. Box 142, Chimayo, NM 87522
(505) 351-4805, (800) 643-7201
Innkeeper: Irenka Taurek
Rooms: 5, incl. 1 w/fireplace, plus 1 suite w/fireplace, all w/pvt. bath. Located in 2 bldgs.
Rates: $75-$110/room, $130/suite, all incl. full brk., afternoon, and evening refreshments.
Credit cards: MC, V
Restrictions: No children under 1. Smoking restricted.
Notes: Spanish adobe Hacienda located on six acres, surrounded by mountains. Furnished with American Arts & Crafts antiques, down comforters. Some rooms with Kiva fireplaces. Secured grounds, outdoor hot tub, gardens, roof deck, patios. German, Russian, Polish spoken.*

La Posada de Chimayo
P.O. Box 463, Chimayo, NM 87522
(505) 351-4605, (505) 351-4605
Innkeeper: Sue Farrington
Restrictions: 2 plus 2 suites, all w/pvt. bath, fireplace. Located in 2 bldgs.
Rates: $90-$100/room, $80/suite, all incl. full brk. Discount avail. for extended winter stay.
Credit cards: MC, V
Restrictions: No children under 12. Pets welcome with prior arrangement. Smoking restricted. Deposit req. 10-day cancellation notice req. 2-night min. stay on wknds. Min. stay on holidays and certain festival periods.
Notes: Adobe guesthouse with viga ceilings, brick floors built in 1981 in rural setting. Sitting rooms, patio, pool, sun and shade decks. Furnished with Mexican rugs and furniture, handmade quilts. Spanish spoken. Resident dog.

CLOUDCROFT (4)

The Lodge at Cloudcroft
One Corona Place, Box 497, Cloudcroft, NM 88317
(505) 682-2566, (800) 395-6343, (505) 682-2715
Innkeeper: Mark Streander, Lisa Thomassie
Rooms: 50, incl. 40 w/phone, plus 8 suites, incl. 7 w/phone, all w/pvt. bath, cable TV. Located in 2 bldgs.
Rates: $49-$99/room, $109-$179/suite. Discount avail. for group stays.
Credit cards: Most major cards
Restrictions: No pets, smoking. Deposit req. 14-day cancellation notice req. less $10.00 fee. 2-night min. stay on holidays.
Notes: Two-story Lodge built in 1899. Located at 9,000-ft. elevation. Furnished with antiques. Heated swimming pool, sauna, spa. Two restaurants, two lounges, gift-

shop, jewelry shop, 9-hole golf course on premises. Handicapped access. Spanish, German spoken.*

CORRALES (1)

Sandhill Crane B & B
389 Camino Hermosa, Corrales, NM 87048
(505) 898-2445, (505) 898-2445
Innkeeper: Carol Hogan, Philip Thorpe
Rooms: 2 plus 1 suite, all w/pvt. bath, phone
Rates: $75-$95/room, $135-$175/suite, all incl. cont. brk. Discount avail. for extended, mid-week, and senior citizen stays.
Credit cards: MC, V
Restrictions: No pets. Smoking restricted. Min. one-night's deposit req. 14-day cancellation notice req.
Notes: Adobe hacienda surrounded by adobe walls draped with wisteria, honeysuckle and trumpet vines. Veranda overlooking mountains. Decorated with American Indian wall pieces and rugs. Furnished with paintings, weavings, and native craft work. Outdoor patio. Outdoor activities available. Handicapped access.*

SANDHILL CRANE B & B

DIXON (1)

La Casita
P.O. Box 103, Dixon, NM 87527
(505) 579-4297
Innkeeper: Sara Pene, Celeste Miller
Rooms: 1 cottage w/pvt. bath
Rates: $60-$100, incl. cont. brk.
Credit cards: None
Restrictions: No smoking. Pets restricted. 50% deposit req.
Notes: Traditional New Mexico adobe cottage with vigas, latillas and Mexican tile floors. Living room, patio. Guests have access to fully-equiped kitchen. Spanish spoken.

EL PRADO (1)

Salsa Del Salto
P.O. Box 1468, El Prado, NM 87529
(505) 776-2422
Innkeeper: Mary Hackett
Rooms: 8 w/pvt. bath, incl. 1 w/fireplace, 2 w/TV. Located in 2 bldgs.
Rates: $85-$160, incl. full brk. Special pkgs. avail.
Credit cards: MC, V
Restrictions: No children under 6, pets. Smoking restricted. 50% deposit req. 14-day cancellation notice req. Min. stay varies.
Notes: Two-story house. Common area with fireplace. Swimming pool, tennis court, hot tub. French, German, Spanish spoken.*

THE GALISTEO INN

GALISTEO (1)

The Galisteo Inn
Box 4, H.C. 75, Galisteo, NM 87540
(505) 466-4000, (505) 466-4008
Innkeeper: Joanna Kaufman and Wayne Aarniotoski
Rooms: 12, incl. 8 w/pvt. bath, 4 w/fireplace, 3 w/TV. Located in 3 bldgs.
Rates: $95-$170, incl. cont. brk. Discount avail. for extended stay. Seasonal variations.
Credit cards: Most major cards
Restrictions: No children under 12, pets. Smoking Restricted. Full prepayment req. 14-day cancellation notice req., less $10.00 fee. 2-night min. stay from May 1–Labor Day.
Notes: Adobe hacienda built about 1740. Located on eight acres with duck pond, giant cottonwoods. Library, dining room, entrance hall, each with fireplace. Living room, conference room. Furnished in New Mexico-style with plank and Mexican tile floors. Swimming pool, sauna, hot tub, exercise room, courtyard. Mountain bicycles, horseback riding, massage, board and lawn games available. Open to public for dinner. Small private parties accommodated. Limited handicapped access. Spanish spoken.*

LINCOLN (4)

Casa de Patron
P.O. Box 27, Lincoln, NM 88338
(505) 653-4676, (505) 653-4671
Innkeeper: Cleis and Jeremy Jordan
Rooms: 3 w/pvt. bath, plus 2-story casita w/pvt. bath, kitchenette, vigas, plus casita w/pvt. bath, refrigerator. Located in 3 bldgs.
Rates: $73/room, $93/casita, all incl. brk., dinner by reservation. Discount avail. for extended stay.
Credit cards: MC, V
Restrictions: No pets, smoking. Deposit req. 7-day cancellation notice req. 2-night min. stay for first full wknd. in Aug. Closed Feb.
Notes: Adobe house built in 1860s. Dining room with organ. Living room, courtyard patio, garden. Furnished with antiques, collectibles. Listed on the National Register of Historic Places. Small private parties accommodated. Innkeeper is professional organist.*

LOS ALAMOS (1)

Canyon Inn
80 Canyon Rd., Los Alamos, NM 87544
(505) 662-9595, (800) 662-2565
Innkeeper: Rick Kraemer
Rooms: 4, incl. 2 w/pvt bath, 1 w/fireplace, all w/phone
Rates: $55-$60, incl. cont brk. Seasonal variations. Discount avail. for extended stay. Special pkgs. avail.
Credit cards: MC, V
Restrictions: No smoking. One night's deposit req. 5-day cancellation notice req.
Notes: Laundry and kitchen facilities, pet boarding available.

Orange Street Inn
3496 Orange St., Los Alamos, NM 87544
(505) 662-2651, (505) 662-2651
Innkeeper: Susanne McGraham-Paisley and Michael Paisley
Rooms: 7, incl. 3 w/pvt. bath, plus 1 suite w/pvt. bath, phone, TV
Rates: $55-$67/room, $65-$75/suite, all incl. full brk., evening refreshment. Special pkgs. avail.
Credit cards: Most major cards
Restrictions: No children under 6, pets, smoking. Deposit req. 72-hour cancellation notice req., less $15.00 fee.
Notes: Two-story inn on back of Mountain Canyon in the 1940s. Located at 7,300-foot elevation. Sitting room with library, TV, board games. Dining room. Furnished in southwestern style with antiques. Guests have access to refrigerator. Small private parties accommodated. Computer services available. Handicapped access.*

NOGAL (4)

Monjeau Shadows Inn
HC 67, Box 87, Nogal, NM 88341
(505) 336-4191
Innkeeper: J.R. and Kay Newton
Rooms: 3, plus 2 suites, all w/pvt. bath, TV

Rates: $65-$75/room, $100-$150/suite, all incl. full brk. Discount avail. for extended stay.

Credit cards: MC, V

Restrictions: No children under 12, pets, smoking. One night's deposit req. 5-day cancellation notice req.

Notes: Four-level Victorian farmhouse built in 1980s. Located on 8.5 landscaped acres. Living room with stained-glass cathedral ceiling. Entertainment room with billard table, board games and TV. Basketball court. Picnic areas.

THE RED VIOLET INN

RATON (1)

The Red Violet Inn
344 N. Second St., Raton, NM 87740
(505) 445-9778

Innkeeper: John and Ruth Hanrahan

Rooms: 4, incl. 2 w/pvt. bath

Rates: $45-$65, incl. full brk., evening refreshment. Discount avail. for off-season, group, extended, and senior citizen stays.

Credit cards: MC, V

Restrictions: No children under 8, pets, smoking. 50% deposit req., 7-day cancellation notice, less $15.00 fee

Notes: Red brick Victorian house built in 1902. Parlor, dining room, porches. Furnished with antiques. Landscaped gardens. All meals, picnic lunches available with advance notice. Small private parties accommodated. BBQ grill, train, and bus pickup available. Innkeepers collect pitchers, bowls, chamber pots, and plates. Some Spanish spoken.*

SANTA FE (1)

A Starry Night
324 McKenzie, Santa Fe, NM 87501-1883
(505) 820-7117, (800) 830-0081

Innkeeper: Lee Purcell

Rooms: 1 w/pvt. bath, phone, TV, pvt. entrance, plus 1 suite w/pvt. bath, phone, TV, pvt. entrance, gas fireplace, mini-refrigerator

Rates: $96-$115/room, $115-$125/suite, all incl. cont. brk. Seasonal variations.
Credit cards: MC, V
Restrictions: No children, pets. Smoking restricted. 50% deposit req. 2-week cancellation notice req., less $15.00 fee. 2-night min. stay on wknds.
Notes: Historic adobe house with a garden of flowers and herbs.*

Adobe Abode
202 Chapelle, Santa Fe, NM 87501
(505) 983-3133, (505) 983-3133
Innkeeper: Pat Harbour
Rooms: 3 w/pvt. bath, phone, TV, plus 2 suites w/pvt. bath, phone, fireplace, pvt. patios, vigas, TV. Located in 3 bldgs.
Rates: $90-$115/room, $135-$140/suite, all incl. full brk., evening refreshment.
Credit cards: Most major cards
Restrictions: No children under 10, pets. Smoking restricted. One night's deposit req. 10-day cancellation notice req., less 10% fee. 2-night min. stay on wknds.
Notes: Adobe house built in 1910. Living room with fireplace, art collections, travel info. Decorated with New Mexican furniture, Indian art, rugs, and artifacts. Guesthouse has private entrance, brick patio, private bath. Fax available. Handicapped access.*

Alexander's Inn
529 E. Palace Ave., Santa Fe, NM 87501
(505) 986-1431
Innkeeper: Carolyn Lee
Rooms: 4 plus 3 suites, incl. 5 w/pvt. bath, 3 w/fireplace, 2 w/TV. Located in 2 bldgs.
Rates: $70-$90/room, $115-$150/suite, all incl. cont. brk., afternoon refreshment. Discount avail. for extended stay. Seasonal variations.
Credit cards: MC, V
Restrictions: No children under 6, smoking. Dogs allowed. Deposit req. 7-day cancellation notice req. 2-night min. stay on wknds. 3-night min. stay on holidays.
Notes: Two-story, brick Craftsman-style house built with hardwood floors, winding staircase, and stained-glass in 1903. Fully restored in and has operated as Inn since 1986. Front and rear porches overlooking gardens. Common room with kiva fireplace. Furnished with antiques. Spa facilities and bicycles available. French spoken.

Arius Compound
1018½ Canyon Rd., P.O. Box 1111, Santa Fe, NM 87504-1111
(800) 735-8453, (505) 982-2621, (505) 989-8280
Innkeeper: Len and Roberta Goodman
Rooms: 3 casitas w/pvt. bath, phone, cable TV, fireplace. Located in 2 bldgs.
Rates: $90-$150. Seasonal variations.
Credit cards: Most major cards
Restrictions: No smoking. 50% deposit req. Cancellation notice req.
Notes: Built in old Mexican style with tile and flagstone floors, ceiling vigas, central courtyard. Located on .5 acre. Living rooms, kitchens. Private patios with high adobe walls. Resident dog.

Canyon Road Casitas
652 Canyon Rd., Santa Fe, NM 84501
(505) 988-5888

Rooms: 1 plus 1 suite, all w/pvt. bath. Located in 2 bldgs.
Rates: $95/room, $125-$169/suite, all incl. cont. brk.
Credit cards: Most major cards
Restrictions: None
Notes: *

Casa de la Cuma B & B
105 Paseo de la Cuma, Santa Fe, NM 87501
(505) 983-1717
Innkeeper: Art and Donna Bailey
Rooms: 3, incl. 1 w/pvt. bath, plus 4 suites, all w/phone, TV. Located in 2 bldgs.
Rates: $65-$125/room, $90-$135/suite. all incl. cont. brk., afternoon refreshment.
  Discount avail. for extended stay. Seasonal variations.
Credit cards: MC, V
Restrictions: No pets, smoking. 50% deposit req. 7-day cancellation notice req., less
  15% fee. 2-night min. stay on wknds.
Notes: Located in the center of Sante Fe overlooking Sangre De Cristo mountain.
Sun room/breakfast area. Living room with fireplace. Decorated with Southwest-
ern handcrafted or period pieces, Navajo textiles, and original artwork. Patio with
50-year-old Blue Spruce pine. Small private parties accommodated. Spanish spoken.*

Don Gaspar Compound
623 Don Gaspar, Santa Fe, NM 87501
(505) 986-8664, (505) 986-0696
Innkeeper: Shirley and David Alford
Rooms: 6 w/pvt. bath, phone, TV, incl. 5 suites w/fireplace. Located in 2 bldgs.
Rates: $85-$95/room, $110-$195/suite, all incl. full brk. Discount avail. for extended stay.
Credit cards: None
Restrictions: Children welcome at Innkeeper's discretion. No pets, smoking. 50%
  deposit req. 2-week cancellation notice req., less $30.00 fee. 2-night min. stay in
  high season.
Notes: Mission and Adobe southwestern style Inn built in 1912. Garden courtyard
with fountain.

Dunshee's
986 Acequia Madre, Santa Fe, NM 87501
(505) 982-0988
Innkeeper: Susan Dunshee
Rooms: 2 suites w/pvt. bath, phone, fireplace, TV. Located in 2 bldgs.
Rates: $110-$120, incl. full brk. Discount avail. for extended stay.
Credit cards: MC, V
Restrictions: Pets restricted. No smoking. Two night's deposit req. 10-day cancella-
  tion notice req. 2-night min. stay on wknds.
Notes: Located in Santa Fe's historic zone. Living room with kiva fireplace. Patio.
Decorated with Mexican tile, viga ceilings, antiques, folk art. Small private parties
accommodated.

Four Kachinas Inn
512 Webber St., Santa Fe, NM 87501-4454
(800) 397-2564

Innkeeper: John Daw, Andrew Beckerman
Rooms: 4 w/pvt. bath, phone, TV, incl. 3 w/pvt. entrance, garden patio
Rates: $88-$113, incl. cont. brk., afternoon refreshment. Seasonal variations.
Credit cards: MC, V
Restrictions: No children under 10, pets, smoking. 50% deposit req. 14-day cancellation notice req., less 15% fee. 2-night min. stay on wknds.
Notes: Two-story Victorian pitched-roof style house built in 1991. Library of art and travel books. Guest lounge with woodburning stove. Furnished with handmade furniture, Navajo rugs, Kachina dolls. Off-street parking available. Handicapped access. Spanish, French spoken.*

Grant Corner Inn
122 Grant Ave., Santa Fe, NM 87501
(505) 983-6678

Innkeeper: Louise Stewart
Rooms: 11 w/cable TV, phone, incl 9 w/pvt. bath, 1 w/fireplace, plus 1 suite w/pvt. bath, phone, TV. Located in 2 bldgs.
Rates: $70-$140/room, $115-$150/suite, all incl. full brk., evening refreshment. Seasonal variations.
Credit cards: MC, V
Restrictions: No children under 8, pets, smoking. 50% deposit req. 10-day cancellation notice req. Min. stay for some holidays.
Notes: Three-story Colonial manor house built in 1905. Fully renovated in and has operated as inn since 1982. Dining room with fireplace. Wrap-around porch, gazebo. Decorated with international antiques. Small private parties accommodated. Handicapped access. Spanish spoken.*

Hacienda Vargas
P.O. Box 307, Algodones, Santa Fe, NM 87001
(505) 867-9115, (505) 867-9115

Innkeeper: Pablo and Julia De Vargas
Rooms: 4 plus 2 suites, all w/pvt. bath, incl. 4 w/fireplace
Rates: $69-$89/room, $89-$109/suite, all incl. full brk. Seasonal variations. Discount avail. for extended and senior citizen stays.
Credit cards: MC, V
Restrictions: No children under 12, pets, smoking. 50% deposit req. 10-day cancellation notice req. 2-3 night min. stay during Balloon Fiesta.
Notes: Adobe structure built circa 1792, fully renovated. Living room with Kiva fireplace, library, courtyard. Furnished with antiques. Barbeque area in the gardens. Hot tub overlooking New Mexico Mesas and Sandia Mountain. Adobe Chapel on premises. Handicapped access. German and Spanish spoken.*

Inn of the Animal Tracks
707 Paseo de Peralta, Santa Fe, NM 87501
(505) 988-1546

Innkeeper: Myrna Wheeler
Rooms: 5 w/pvt. bath, phone, TV, incl. 1 w/fireplace
Rates: $90-$130, incl. full brk. Seasonal variations.
Credit cards: Most major cards
Restrictions: No children under 16, pets, smoking. Deposit req. 8-day cancellation notice req., less $15.00 fee. 2-night min. stay on wknds.

Notes: Southwestern adobe-style house with hardwood floors built about 1890. Living room with kiva fireplace. Dining room. Shaded garden patio. Spanish spoken. Handicapped access.*

Preston House
106 Faithway St., Santa Fe, NM 87501
(505) 982-3465

Innkeeper: Signe Bergman
Rooms: 13 w/phone, TV, incl. 11 w/pvt. bath, 3 w/fireplace, plus 2 cottages w/pvt. bath, phone, TV, fireplace. Located in 4 bldgs.
Rates: $70-$140/room, $120-$145/cottage, all incl. cont. brk., afternoon refreshment. Seasonal variations.
Credit cards: Most major cards
Restrictions: No children under 10, smoking. 50% deposit req. 10-day cancellation notice req., less $15.00 fee.
Notes: Three-story Queen Anne-style house built in 1886 and Southwest-style adobe house. Once operated as a bordello. Porch, patio, garden. Dining room, parlor each with original Edwardian fireplaces. Library. Common area with two conference tables, fireplace. A/V, office equipment. Guests have access to full kitchen. Bedroom architectures are in Victorian and Southwest adobe styles. Furnished with antiques. Handicapped access. Small private parties accommodated. Resident cat.

Pueblo Bonito B & B Inn
138 W. Manhattan Ave., Santa Fe, NM 87501
(505) 984-8001

Innkeeper: Herb and Amy Behm
Rooms: 12, plus 6 suites, all w/pvt. bath, TV, phone. Located in 2 bldgs.
Rates: $65-$95/room, $105-$130/suite, all incl. cont. brk., afternoon refreshment.
Credit cards: MC, V
Restrictions: No pets. 50% deposit req. 10-day cancellation notice req., less $15.00 fee.
Notes: Two-story adobe compound with 12-inch thick walls built around turn of the century. Newly renovated. Dining room. Private courtyards. Furnished with Navajo rugs, baskets, sand paints, Pueblo and Mexican pottery, antiques, Spanish santos and works of local artisans. Shady gardens.*

Territorial Inn
215 Washington Ave., Santa Fe, NM 87501
(505) 989-7737, (505) 986-1411

Innkeeper: Lela McFerrin
Rooms: 11, incl. 8 w/pvt.bath, 2 w/phone, 2 w/fireplace, all w/cable TV
Rates: $80-$150, incl.cont. brk., evening refreshment
Credit cards: MC, V
Restrictions: No children under 10, pets, smoking. One night's deposit req. 2-week cancellation notice req. 2-night min. stay on wknds.
Notes: Two-story stone and adobe house built about 1890. Living room with fireplace. Rose garden. Gazebo with hot tub. Off-street parking, laundry service available. Handicapped access.*

SOCORRO (4)

Eaton House B & B Inn
403 Eaton Ave. Box 536, Socorro, NM 87801
(505) 835-1067
Innkeeper: Tom Harper and Anna Appleby
Rooms: 5 w/pvt. bath, incl. 2/fireplace. Located in 3 bldgs.
Rates: $75-$120, incl. full brk. Seasonal variations.
Credit cards: None
Restrictions: No children under 14 pets, smoking. Deposit req. 14-day cancellation notice req., 21-day cancellation notice req. for Festivals and holidays.
Notes: Territorial adobe inn with 10-foot high and two-foot thick walls built in 1881. Decorated with antique furniture and pieces crafted by local artisians. Handicapped access. Spanish, Chinese spoken.

TAOS (1)

American Artists Gallery House
Frontier Rd., Box 584, Taos, NM 87571
(505) 758-4446, (505) 758-0497
Innkeeper: Judie and Elliot Framan
Rooms: 4 plus 3 suites, all w/pvt. bath, fireplace. Located in 4 bldgs.
Rates: $70-$105, all incl. full brk. Seasonal variations. Special pkgs. avail.
Credit cards: MC, V
Restrictions: No children under 5, pets. Smoking restricted. 50% deposit req. 14-day cancellation notice req., less 15% fee.
Notes: Living room with fireplace. Dining room. Decorated with art collections, handpainted tiles, pottery, and native American-style rugs, to sculptures, oils and photographs. Landscaped garden. Hot tub. Fax available. Handicapped access.*

Brooks Street Inn
P.O. Box 4954, Taos, NM 87571
(505) 758-1489
Innkeeper: Carol Frank and Larry Moll
Rooms: 7, incl. 6 w/pvt bath, 3 w/fireplace
Rates: $75-$100, incl. full brk, evening refreshment. Seasonal variations. Discount avail. for frequent guests.
Credit cards: Most major cards
Restrictions: No pets, smoking. Children restricted. 50% deposit req. 10-day cancellation notice req., less $10.00 fee. 2-night min. stay on ski wknds.
Notes: Southwest adobe house built in 1956. Common room with stone fireplace. Beamed ceilings, wood floors. Southwest artwork/furniture. Espresso bar. Patio, walled garden. Named one of North America's Ten Best Inns for 1988 by *Country Inns* magazine.*

Casa de Milagros B & B
P.O. Box 2983, Taos, NM 87571
(800) 243-9334, (505) 758-8001
Innkeeper: Helen Victor and Janie Mansfield
Rooms: 5, incl. 4 w/fireplace, plus 1 suite, all w/pvt. bath, w/cable TV. Located in 2 bldgs.
Rates: $70-$120/room, $125-$185/suite, all incl. full brk. Seasonal variations.

Credit cards: MC, V

Restrictions: No smoking. Well behaved children and pets welcome. 50% deposit req. 10-day cancellation notice req., less 15% fee. 2-night min. stay.

Notes: Eclectically decorated. Dining room. Outdoor hot tub. FAX, off-street parking available. Handicapped access. Spanish spoken. *

Casa Zia
513 Zia, Box 5107, Taos, NM 87571
(505) 751-0697

Innkeeper: Ken Wright

Rooms: 5 suites

Rates: $50-$85, incl. cont. brk.

Credit cards: MC, V

Restrictions: No pets, smoking. 50% deposit req. 14-day cancellation notice req., less 15% fee.

Notes: Two-story house with gabled roof. Lounge with stone fireplace, TV, VCR. Geranium dining room. Decorated with southwestern furniture.*

El Rincon B & B
114 Kit Carson, Taos, NM 87571
(505) 758-4874

Innkeeper: Nina Meyers, Paul Castillo

Rooms: 10 plus 4 suites, all w/pvt. bath, TV, VCR. Located in 2 bldgs.

Rates: $49-$109, incl cont. brk.

Credit cards: Most major cards

Restrictions: Deposit required. 7-day cancellation notice req., less $7.00 fee.

Notes: Adobe inn built approx. 1894. Recently expanded with second story. Breakfast room with fireplace. Patio. Limited handicapped access. Spanish spoken.

La Posada de Taos
309 Juanita Lane, Box 1118, Taos, NM 87571
(505) 758-8164

Innkeeper: Bill Swan and Nancy Brooks-Swan

Rooms: 4 w/pvt. bath, incl. 2 w/fireplace, plus 2 suites w/pvt. bath, plus cottage w/kiva fireplace, pvt. bath, pvt. courtyard. Located in 2 bldgs.

Rates: $75-$115, incl. full brk. Discount avail. for extended stay.

Credit cards: None

Restrictions: Smoking restricted. 50% deposit req. 10-day cancellation notice req., less $10.00 fee. 2-night min. stay from January–October. 3-night min. stay for holidays.

Notes: Adobe house with oak floors built about 1910 plus Honeymoon House. Enclosed front porch. Living room with cable TV, fireplace, phone. Dining room with fireplace, library. Courtyard, Japanese garden with trickle fountain. Furnished in mixture of southwestern and international styles with some antiques. Music Month each spring and fall. Innkeeper has degree in architecture. Handicapped access. Spanish spoken.*

Little Tree B & B
P.O. Box 1100-225, Taos, NM 87571
(505) 776-8467, (505) 776-8467

Innkeeper: Kay and Charles Giddens

Rooms: 4 w/pvt. bath, incl. 3 w/TV, VCR, 2/fireplace. Located in 2 bldgs.

Rates: $65-$80, incl. cont. brk., evening refreshment. Seasonal variations. Discount avail. for senior citizen stay.

Credit cards: MC, V

Restrictions: No smoking. 50% deposit req., 10-day cancellation notice req., less $10.00 fee. 2-night min. stay on wknds.

Notes: Authentic all Adobe, Pueblo style house with log beams and small sticks for the ceiling, built in 1991. Has operated as inn since Christmas Day. Old Mexican tile in common areas. Furnished with antique and eclectic furniture. Quilts in every room handmade by owner. Breakfast served in dining room during winter, outside under the covered portal overlooking adobe walled courtyard in the summer. Two resident cats.*

LITTLE TREE B & B

Orinda
461 Valverde St., Box 4551, Taos, NM 87571
(505) 758-8581

Innkeeper: George and Cary Pratt

Rooms: 1, plus 2 suites, all w/pvt. bath, fireplace

Rates: $65-$85, incl full, meatless brk., afternoon refreshment. Seasonal variations.

Credit cards: MC, V

Restrictions: No children under 6, pets, smoking. 50% deposit req. 14-day cancellation notice req.

Notes: Updated, enlarged and remodelled adobe structure located in a meadow minutes from Plaza. Resident dog and cat.

Touchstone
0110 Mabel Dodge Ln, Box 2896, Taos, NM 87571-2896
(505) 758-0192, (505) 758-3498

Innkeeper: Bren Price

Rooms: 1, plus 3 suites, all w/pvt. bath, phone, cable TV, VCR, cassette player. Most w/fireplace.

Rates: $75-$150, incl. full brk. Special pkgs. avail. Discount avail. for off-season and extended stays.

Credit cards: None

Restrictions: No children under 12, pets. Smoking restricted. 50% deposit req. Min. 14-day cancellation notice req., less 15% fee.

Notes: Adobe house. Located on two wooded acres at 7000 ft. elevation. Common room with fireplace, TV, VCR, cassettes. Furnished with native American and fine art, antiques, Oriental rugs. Dining portal overlooking Taos Mountain. Outdoor hot tub.

TRUCHAS (1)

Rancho Arriba
P.O. Box 338, Truchas, NM 87578
(505) 689-2374

Innkeeper: Curtiss Frank
Rooms: 4, no pvt. bath. Located in 2 bldgs.
Rates: $55, incl. full brk.
Credit cards: Most major cards
Restrictions: No pets. Smoking restricted. One night's deposit req. 7-day cancellation notice req.
Notes: European-style traditional adobe haciendah with Viga and latilla ceilings. Located on working farm on historic Spanish land grant at gateway to Pecos Wilderness area. Built around central courtyard. Furnished with handmade colonial-style furniture. View of Sangre de Cristo Mountain.

New York

ALBANY (8)

Mansion Hill Inn & Restaurant
115 Philip St. at Park Ave., Albany, NY 12202
(518) 465-2038
Innkeeper: Stephen and Mary Ellen Stofelano, Jr.
Rooms: 7 plus 1 suite, all w/pvt. bath, phone, cable TV. Suites w/kitchen avail. Located in 4 bldgs.
Rates: $95-$125/room, $155/suite, all incl. full brk. Seasonal variations. Special pkgs. avail.
Credit cards: Most major cards
Restrictions: No pets. Smoking restricted. One night's deposit req. 5-day cancellation notice req.
Notes: Three-story brick and wood Victorian building built in 1861. Urban inn in heart of residential neighborhood within walking distance of downtown, overlooking the Helderberg Mountains, Hudson River, and Berkshire Mountains. Fully rehabilitated in 1984. Restaurant with fireplace on premises. Furnished with some antiques. Meeting rooms and business services available. Winner of Historic Albany Foundation's 1986 Preservation Merit Award. Handicapped access. Spanish spoken.

AMENIA (12)

Troutbeck
Leedsville Rd., Box 26, Amenia, NY 12501
(914) 373-9681, (914) 373-7080
Innkeeper: Jim Flaherty
Rooms: 28 plus 8 suites, incl. 31 w/pvt. bath, 34 w/phone, 8 w/fireplace. Located in 3 bldgs.
Rates: $350-$475, incl. 3 meals per day, evening refreshment. Discount avail. for extended stay. Special pkgs. avail.
Credit cards: Most major cards
Restrictions: No children under 12, pets. Smoking restricted. $200 deposit req., refunded upon cancellation only if room is re-rented. Closed mid-week to overnight guests. Conference Center open mid-week.
Notes: English Tudor house with slate roof and leaded windows built in 1918. Located on 442 wooded acres. Living room with TV, VCR. Sitting room, dining room, lounge, library with 13,000 books. Conference room with fireplaces. Heated swimming pool, summer swimming pool with deck, two tennis courts. Walled gardens. Furnished in English and American styles with antiques. Small private parties accommodated. Spanish, Italian, French, Portuguese spoken.*

AUBURN (6)

The Irish Rose B & B
102 South St., Auburn, NY 13021
(315) 255-0196, (315) 255-0899
Innkeeper: Patricia Fitzpatricks, Kevin McElligatt
Rooms: 4 plus 1 suite, incl. 3 w/pvt. bath, 1 w/fireplace

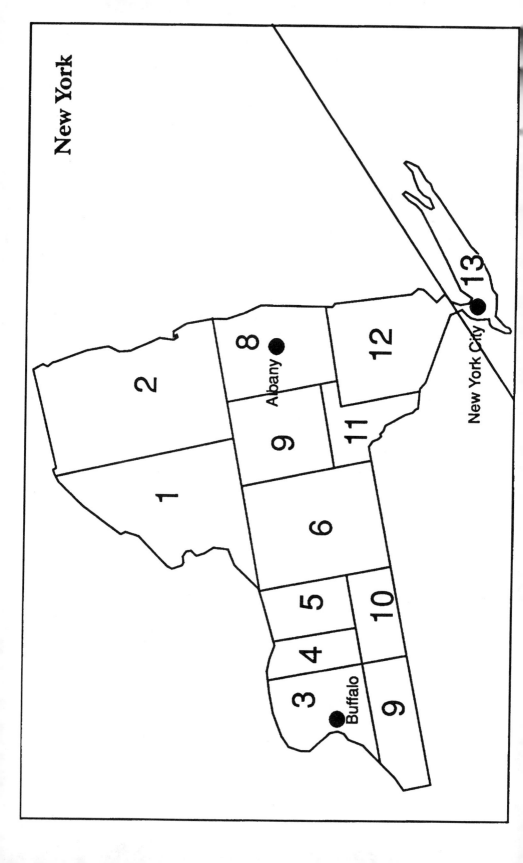

Rates: $85/room, $95-$125/suite, all incl. full brk. Discount avail. for AAA stay. Seasonal variations.

Credit cards: Most major cards

Restrictions: Pets, smoking restricted. $50.00 deposit req. 15-day cancellation notice req., less $20.00 fee. 2-night min. stay on wknds.

Notes: Three-story Queen Anne Victorian house with hand-carved cherry woodwork, built in 1807. Porch with swing. Parlor with TV, video movies. Board and lawn games available. Outdoor pool. Small private parties accommodated.*

BALDWINSVILLE (1)

Pandora's Getaway
83 Oswego St., Baldwinsville, NY 13027
(315) 635-9571

Innkeeper: Sandra Wheeler

Rooms: 3, incl. 1 w/pvt. bath, TV, plus 1 suite w/pvt. bath, phone, fireplace, TV

Rates: $50-$65/room, $80/suite, all incl. full brk. Special pkgs. avail.

Credit cards: MC, V

Restrictions: Well-behaved children welcome. No pets. Smoking restricted. Deposit req. 14-day cancellation notice req., less 10% fee.

Notes: Two-story Greek Revival house built in 1845. Located on hill. Living room with fireplace. Formal dining room. Front porch with rocking chairs. Furnished with antiques. Listed on the National Register of Historic Places. Resident cats.*

BINGHAMTON (6)

Pickle Hill B & B
795 Chenango St., Binghamton, NY 13901
(607) 723-0259

Innkeeper: Leslie and Tom Rossi

Rooms: 3, no pvt. bath

Rates: $40-$50, incl. cont. brk., ice cream and cider in season. Discount avail. for extended stay.

Credit cards: Most major cards

Restrictions: No pets, smoking. 24-cancellation notice req.

Notes: Two-story Victorian house with natural woodwork and stained-glass windows, built in 1890s. Lounge with books, music, board games. Living room with piano. Family room. Ice cream parlor breakfast nook on premises. Deck and rocking chairs on front porch. Bocci, basketball, badminton, picnic lunch available.

BOLTON LANDING (2)

Hilltop Cottage B & B
6883 Lakeshore Dr., Box 186, Bolton Landing, NY 12814
(518) 644-2492

Innkeeper: Anita and Charlie Richards

Rooms: 3 plus cabin, all w/pvt. bath, incl. 2 w/phone

Rates: $50-$65, incl. full brk.

Credit cards: MC, V

Restrictions: No pets. Smoking restricted. One night's deposit req. 7-day cancellation notice req. 2-night min. stay in cabin. Closed Easter, Thanksgiving, Christmas and New Years.

Notes: Two-story farmhouse built in 1926 as caretaker's cottage for the Stengel-DeCoppet estate. Fully renovated in and has operated as inn since 1986. Located on two acres. Furnished in traditional style with family pieces and antiques. Common room with piano, wood stove. Screened porch. Lawn furniture. German spoken. Resident cats, dog.*

BRONXVILLE (12)

The Villa
90 Rockledge Rd., Bronxville, NY 10708
(914) 337-7050, 337-5591, (914) 337-5661
Innkeeper: Helen Zuckermann
Rooms: 2, no pvt. bath, plus 1 suite w/pvt. bath, fireplace
Rates: $65-$85/room, $95/suite, all incl. cont. brk. Discount avail. for extended stay.
Credit cards: None
Restrictions: No pets. Deposit req.
Notes: Country-style residence centered on a balconied three-story 'Great Hall'. Formerly owned by Columbia University and served as weekend retreat for Dwight Eisenhower when he was president of the university. Located on quiet tree-shaded road. Comforatably furnished. Fireplaces throughout. Two large terraces, gardens. Outdoor hot tub. Guests have access to business center FAX. French, Italian, Spanish, German, and some Arabic spoken.

BROOKLYN (13)

Bed & Breakfast On The Park
113 Prospect Park W., Brooklyn, NY 11215
(718) 499-6115, (718) 499-1385
Innkeeper: Liana Paolella
Rooms: 4 plus 2 suites, incl. 4 w/pvt. bath, 3 w/phone, all w/TV
Rates: $100-$160/room, $150-$175/suite, all incl. full brk., afternoon refreshment. Seasonal variations. Discount avail. for group stay.
Credit cards: MC, V
Restrictions: No pets, smoking. 50% deposit req. 10-day cancellation notice req., less $25.00 fee. 2-night min. stay on wknds.
Notes: Four-story Park Slope brick limestone Victorian brownstone with intricately carved wood and stained-glass built in 1892. Fully restored and refurbished. Views of Statue of Liberty and New York City skyline and overlooking park. Has operated as inn since 1987. Parlor with TV, dining room. Furnished with family art collection, Victorian antiques, Oriental rugs. Garden. Guests have access to kitchen. Limited handicapped access. Valet parking available. French spoken.*

BURDETT (5)

The Red House Country Inn
4586 Picnic Area Rd., Burdett, NY 14818
(607) 546-8566
Innkeeper: Sandy Schmanke, Joan Martin
Rooms: 5, no pvt. bath, incl. 1 w/fireplace
Rates: $60-$85, incl. full brk.
Credit cards: Most major cards

Restrictions: No children under 12, pet, smoking. One night's deposit req. 2-week cancellation notice req. 2-night min. stay on wknds.

Notes: Farmhouse built about 1840. Located on five acres of groomed lawns, gardens in 13,000-acre Finger Lakes National Forest. Only residence within the National Forest. Fully restored. Public room, large veranda with wicker chairs. Decorated with antiques and Amish quilts. Swimming pool. Guests have access to kitchen. Dinner available with prior notification. Country store on premises. Resident goats and champion Samoyeds.*

CANADENSIS (5)

Brookview Manor
RR 1, Box 365, Canadensis, NY 18325
(717) 595-2451

Innkeeper: Lee and Nancie Cabana

Rooms: 3 w/pvt. bath, incl. 1 w/fireplace, plus 3 suites w/pvt. bath. Located in 2 bldgs.

Rates: $70-$145/room, $105-$145/suite, all incl. full brk., afternoon refreshment.

Credit cards: Most major cards

Restrictions: No children under 12. Smoking restricted. One night's deposit req. Min. 14-day cancellation notice req. 2-night min. stay on holidays.

Notes: Two-story house. Located on four acres. Dining room, sun porch. Wrap-around porch with glider. Furnished with antiques. Lawn games available. Small private parties accommodated.

CANANDAIGUA (5)

The Acorn
4508 Rte. 64 S., Box 334, Canandaigua, NY 14424
(716) 229-2834

Innkeeper: Joan & Louis Clark

Rooms: 4 w/pvt. bath, incl. 2 w/TV

Rates: $75-$140, incl. full brk., afternoon refreshment. Discount avail. for extended, mid-week, and senior citizen stays. Special pkgs. avail.

Credit cards: Most major cards

Restrictions: No children under 14, smoking. Pets restricted. 2-night min. stay on holidays and during Fall foliage season.

Notes: Two-story federal Stagecoach Inn built in 1795. Renovated in 1989. Common room with colonial fireplace, books. Furnished with antiques. Guest rooms have sitting area, beds warmed in cold weather. Private gardens.*

CANDOR (6)

Edge of Thyme Bed & Breakfast Inn
6 Main St., Candor, NY 13743
(607) 659-5155

Innkeeper: Frank and Eva Mae Musgrave

Rooms: 5, incl. 2 w/pvt. bath

Rates: $60-$70, incl. full brk. Discount avail. for extended stay.

Credit cards: MC, V

Restrictions: Well-behaved children welcome. No pets, smoking. Deposit req. 7-day cancellation notice req. Non-refundable deposit req. for certain wknds. 2-night min. stay on special event wknds.

Notes: Two-story Georgian house with parquet floors built in 1908. Library with fireplace, board games. Parlor with fireplace, TV. Porch with leaded-glass windows. Open porch. Furnished in turn-of-the-century style. Grounds with pergola built in 1860, gardens. Lawn games available.*

CAZENOVIA (6)

Brae Loch Inn
5 Albany St., Cazenovia, NY 13035
(315) 655-3431, (315) 655-4844
Innkeeper: James and Valerie Barr
Rooms: 14, incl. 12 w/pvt. bath, plus 1 suite, all w/phone, TV.
Rates: $75-$125, incl. cont. brk.
Credit cards: Most major cards
Restrictions: No pets. Full prepayment req. 10-day cancellation notice req.
Notes: Victorian inn built in 1805. Family owned and has operated as inn in Scottish tradition since 1946. Lounges, dining rooms, many with fireplaces. Meeting rooms, banquet facilities. Furnished with antiques, Stickley furniture, tartan plaids, original stained-glass. Scottish Giftshop, dinner theatre on premises. Small private parties accommodated.*

CHAPPAQUA (12)

Crabtree's Kittle House
11 Kittle Rd., Chappaqua, NY 10514
(914) 666-8044, (914) 666-2684
Innkeeper: John and Dick Crabtree
Rooms: 12 w/pvt. bath, phone, cable TV
Rates: $79-$89, incl. cont. brk.
Credit cards: Most major cards
Restrictions: No pets. Credit card deposit req. 24-hour cancellation notice req.
Notes: Originally built in 1790 as carriage house, nusery and fruit farm. Has operated as a roadhouse, school for girls, guesthouse for the Mount Kisco Little Theater. Each guest room uniquely different. Award-winning restaurant on premises. Mahogony bar originally purchased by Fanny Brice. Small private parties accommodated. Handicapped access. Spanish spoken.

CRABTREE'S KITTLE HOUSE

CHESTERTOWN (2)

Balsam House
Atateka Dr., Chestertown, NY 12817
(518) 494-2828, (800) 441-6856, (518) 494-4431
Innkeeper: Josef and Maggie Roettig
Rooms: 19, plus 2 suites, all w/pvt. bath, incl. 2 w/TV, fireplace
Rates: $75-$115/room, $135- $185/suite, all incl. full brk. Discount avail. for mid-
   week, AAA stays.
Credit cards: Most major cards
Restrictions: No pets. Smoking restricted. Deposit req. Cancellation notice req. 2-
   night min. stay on holidays and during local festivals.
Notes: Sprawling white building which has been an Adirondack landmark since
1845. Located on private lake teeming with bass and pike. Totally restored and refurbished to 'mountain elegance'. Parlor, living room, lounge, Victorian dining
room with copper fireplace serving French country cuisine. Decorated with a blend
of historic and modern, formal and informal. Bold Victorian decor with Oriental
rugs, marble fireplaces, ferns, antiques. *

The Chester Inn
Main St., Box 163, Chestertown, NY 12817
(518) 494-4148
Innkeeper: Bruce and Suzanne Robbins
Rooms: 2 plus 2 suites, all w/pvt. bath
Rates: $85-$100, incl. full brk., discount at local ice-cream parlor and restaurant.
   Seasonal variations.
Credit cards: MC, V
Restrictions: No children under 12, pets. Smoking restricted. One night's deposit
   req. 14-day cancellation notice req. 2 to 3-night min. stay on prime and holiday
   wknds.
Notes: Adirondack hotel with mahogony doors and hand rails, built in the 1880s.
Located on 13 acres of meadowlands. Grand hall with hand-grained woodwork.
Furnished with antiques. Front porch. Gardens. Listed on National Register of His-
toric Places.

Friends Lake Inn
Friends Lake Rd., Chestertown, NY 12817
(518) 494-4751, (518) 494-4616
Innkeeper: Sharon Taylor
Rooms: 6 plus 8 suites, all w/pvt. bath, incl. 1 w/fireplace
Rates: $155/room, $185-$225/suite, all incl. full brk., dinner. Special pkgs. avail.
   Discount avail. for group stay.
Credit cards: Most major cards
Restrictions: No pets, smoking. 50% deposit req. 14-day cancellation notice req.,
   less 10% fee. 2-night min. stay on wknds.
Notes: Country inn with original chestnut woodwork built in the 1860s. Fully re-
stored. Living room with TV, VCR. Dining room with fireplace. Study with board
games. Deck overlooking sandy beach on Friends Lake. Herb garden. Award-
winning restaurant, bar on premises. Canoes, windsurfers, mountain bicycles available. Small private parties accommodated. Swedish spoken.*

CLARENCE (3)

Asa Ransom House
10529 Main St., Clarence, NY 14031
(716) 759-2315, (716) 759-2791

Innkeeper: Judy and Robert Lenz
Rooms: 6, plus 3 suites, all w/pvt. bath, phone, TV, incl. 7 w/fireplace.
Rates: $85-$120/room, $145/suite, all incl. full brk. Special pkgs. avail.
Credit cards: DS, MC, V
Restrictions: No children under 5, pets, smoking. $75.00 per night deposit req. 7-day cancellation notice req.
Notes: Original building built in 1853 as tavern. Located on two acres. Library with fireplace, parlor games, books. Formal and country dining rooms, each with fireplace. Furnished with antiques and period reproductions. Giftshop, taproom on premises. Porch, pond, herb and flower gardens. Dinner available. Handicapped access.*

COLD SPRING (12)

One Market Street
1 Market St., Cold Spring, NY 10516
(914) 265-3912

Innkeeper: Philip and Esther Baumgarten
Rooms: 1 suite w/pvt. bath, kitchen
Rates: $75, incl. cont. brk.
Credit cards: V
Restrictions: No pets. Min. $30.00 deposit req. 7-day cancellation notice req.
Notes: Two-story Federal-style building built about 1820 located one block from the Hudson River in historic district. Garden. Country store on street level.

COOPERSTOWN (7)

Angelholm Bed & Breakfast
14 Elm St., Box 705, Cooperstown, NY 13326
(607) 547-2483, (607) 547-2309

Innkeeper: Fred and Jan Reynolds
Rooms: 5 w/pvt. bath
Rates: $85-$95, incl. full brk., afternoon refreshment. Seasonal variations.
Credit cards: MC, V
Restrictions: No children under 12, pets, smoking. One night's deposit req. 72-hr. cancellation notice req., less $15.00 fee. 2-night min. stay on wknds. from July–Aug. 3-night min. stay on holiday wknds.
Notes: Two-story Federal-period house built in 1805. Formal dining room. Living room with fireplace. Library with TV. Verandas overlooking English-style garden. Off-street parking available.*

Brown-Williams House
RR 1, Box 337, Rte. 28, Cooperstown, NY 13326
(607) 547-5569

Innkeeper: Deborah Bathen
Rooms: 5, incl. 4 w/pvt. bath
Rates: $60-$95, incl. cont. brk. Seasonal variations. Discount avail. for senior citizen and mid-week stays.

Credit cards: DS, MC, V
Restrictions: No pets. Smoking restricted. One night's deposit req. 72-hour cancellation notice req.
Notes: Two-story Federal-style inn built approx. 1825. Located on 5 acres. Common room with wide-screen TV, fireplace, board games. Furnished with Shaker and Federal style pieces. Porches.

Inn at Cooperstown
16 Chestnut St., Cooperstown, NY 13326
(607) 547-5756
Innkeeper: Michael Jerome
Rooms: 17 w/pvt. bath
Rates: $88-$95, incl. cont. brk. Seasonal variations.
Credit cards: Most major cards
Restrictions: No pets. Smoking restricted. One night's deposit req. 5-day cancellation notice req.
Notes: Second Empire-style inn with mansard roof, hardwood floors, wide baseboards and high ceilings, built in 1874 as annex to Fenimore Hotel. Designed by the architect who designed New York's Dakota and Plaza Hotel. Totally restored in and has operated as inn since 1985. Sitting room with fireplace, board games, TV, library. Furnished with antiques. Rocking chairs on the veranda. Handicapped access. Recipient of the 1986 New York State Certificate of Achievement in Historic Preservation.*

CORNING (10)

1865 White Birch B & B
69 E. First St., Corning, NY 14830
(607) 962-6355
Innkeeper: Kathy and Joe Donahue
Rooms: 4, incl. 2 w/pvt. bath
Rates: $55-72, incl. full brk.
Credit cards: Most major cards
Restrictions: No pets, smoking. Deposit req. 2-day cancellation notice req.
Notes: Two-story Victorian house with hardwood floors built in 1865. Fully refurbished. Has operated an an inn since 1984. Entry hall with winding staircase. Common room with fireplace, library, board games, TV. Dining room. Furnished in pine, oak, wicker, and brass. Backyard with picnic table, grill. Flower gardens.

Delevan House
188 Delevan Ave., Corning, NY 14830
(607) 962-2347
Innkeeper: Mary DePumpo
Rooms: 2 w/pvt. bath, TV, incl. 1 w/phone, plus 1 suite w/pvt. bath, phone, TV
Rates: $75/room, $85/suite, all incl. full brk., afternoon refreshment
Credit cards: MC
Restrictions: No children under 12. Deposit req. 3-day cancellation notice req.
Notes: Two-story southern Colonial house built in 1933 on hilltop. Dining room. Furnished with antiques. Screened porch overlooking town. Private yard. Airport pick-up available.

CROTON-ON-HUDSON (12)

Alexander Hamilton House
49 Van Wyck St., Croton-on-Hudson, NY 10520
(914) 271-6737, (914) 271-3927
Innkeeper: Barbara Notarius
Rooms: 2, incl. 1 w/fireplace, plus 5 suites, incl. 4 w/fireplace, all w/pvt. bath, phone, cable TV. Apt. avail.
Rates: $95-$105/room, $130-$250/suite, all incl. full brk. Discount avail. for extended stay.
Credit cards: Most major cards
Restrictions: No pets. Smoking restricted. Full pre-payment req. 7-day cancellation notice req., less one night's fee. 2-night min. stay on wknds.
Notes: Two-story Victorian house built in 1889. Located on cliff overlooking Hudson River. Decorated with period antiques and collections. Mini-orchard and in-ground swimming pool. Off-street parking available. French spoken.*

CROWN POINT (2)

Crown Point B & B
Main St., Box 490, Crown Point, NY 12928
(518) 597-3651
Innkeeper: Hugh and Sandy Johnson
Rooms: 5 plus 1 suite, all w/pvt. bath
Rates: $45-$65/room, $95/suite, all incl. expanded cont. brk. Discount avail. for senior citizen stay.
Credit cards: MC, V
Restrictions: No smoking. $25.00 per day deposit req. 7-day cancellation notice req., less fee. 2-night min. stay on holiday wknds.
Notes: Two-story manor house with six different kinds of paneled woodwork, pocket doors, built in 1887. Three parlors, each with fireplace. Dining room with fireplace. Three porches. Furnished with antiques. Handicapped access. Spanish spoken.

DOLGEVILLE (2)

Adrianna Bed & Breakfast
44 Stewart St., Dolgeville, NY 13329
(315) 429-3249, (800) 335-4233
Innkeeper: Adrianna Naizby
Rooms: 3, incl. 1 w/pvt. bath
Rates: $50-$65, incl. full brk., afternoon refreshment
Credit cards: Most major cards
Restrictions: No children under 5, pets. Smoking restricted. 50% deposit req. 7-day cancellation notice req.
Notes: Modern raised ranch house located in foothills of the Adirondacks. Living room with fireplace, TV, VCR. Swimming pool.*

DOWNSVILLE (11)

Adam's Antique Farm House B & B
Upper Main St., Box 18, Downsville, NY 13755
(607) 363-2757

Innkeeper: Harry and Nancy Adams
Rooms: 3, incl. 1 w/pvt. bath
Rates: $50, incl. full brk., afternoon and evening refreshment. Seasonal variations. Discount avail. for extended stay.
Credit cards: None
Restrictions: No pets, smoking. Deposit req.
Notes: Farm house built in 1892. Recently renovated. Located on two acres. Front porch with wicker furniture. Dining room with TV and games. Back deck overlooking brook. Antique store.

DRYDEN (6)

Serendipity B & B
15 North St., Box 287, Dryden, NY 13053-0287
(607) 844-9589, (607) 844-8311

Innkeeper: Kaaren Hoback
Rooms: 3 w/TV, no pvt. bath, plus 1 suite w/pvt. bath, phone
Rates: $59-$75/room, $75-$105/suite, all incl. full brk., afternoon refreshment. Discount avail. for mid-week stay.
Credit cards: Most major cards
Restrictions: No pets, smoking. Deposit req. 14-day cancellation notice req. Min. stay on certain wknds.
Notes: *

EAST HAMPTON (13)

Mill House Inn
33 N. Main St., East Hampton, NY 11937
(516) 324-9766

Innkeeper: Daniel and Katherine Hartnett
Rooms: 8 w/pvt. bath, incl. 3 w/fireplace. Phone avail.
Rates: $100-$190. Seasonal variations. Discount avail. for extended stay.
Credit cards: Most major cards
Restrictions: No pets, smoking. One night's deposit req. Deposit refunded, less $20.00 fee, upon cancellation only if room re-rented. 2-night min. stay on wknds. in-season. 3-night min. stay on summer holiday wknds.
Notes: Dutch Colonial inn built in 1790. Located near village and beach. Each room individually decorated. Common room with fireplace. Outdoor patio, hammock. Families welcome. Spanish spoken.*

The Pink House
26 James Lane, East Hampton, NY 11937
(516) 324-3400, (516) 324-5254

Innkeeper: Ron Steinhilber
Rooms: 5 w/pvt. bath, incl. 1 w/TV
Rates: $135-$245, incl. full brk. Seasonal variations.
Credit cards: Most major cards
Restrictions: No smoking. 50% deposit req. 3-night min. stay on summer wknds. 4-night min. stay on major holidays.
Notes: Two-story sea captain's House built in the mid-1800s. Fully renovated in 1990. Living room, screened porch. Dining room with fireplace. Swimming pool. Listed on the National Register of Historic Places.

ELBRIDGE (6)

Fox Ridge Farm B & B
4786 Foster Rd., Elbridge, NY 13060
(315) 673-4881, (315) 673-3691
Innkeeper: Marge and Bob Sykes
Rooms: 3, incl. 1 w/pvt. bath
Rates: $40-$65, incl. full brk. Discount avail. for extended stay.
Credit cards: None
Restrictions: No children under 6, pets, smoking. One night's deposit req. 7-day cancellation notice req.
Notes: Farmhouse. Family room with wood panelling, hardwood floors, grand piano, wood-burning stove, TV, VCR, stereo, library. Country kitchen with stone fireplace. Porch. Furnished with handmade quilts. Flower garden.

ESSEX (2)

The Stonehouse
Church & Elm St., Box 43, Essex, NY 12936
(518) 963-7713
Innkeeper: Sylvia Hobbs
Rooms: 1, plus 2 suites, all w/pvt. bath
Rates: $65/room, $85-$95/suite, all incl. cont. brk., evening refreshment. Discount avail. for extended, mid-week, senior citizen stays.
Credit cards: None
Restrictions: No pets. Smoking restricted. One night's deposit req. 10-day cancellation notice req. 2-night min. stay on holiday wknds. Closed Nov.–May.
Notes: Three-story Georgian house built in 1826. Fully restored. Located within walking distance to Charlotte-Essex ferry. Common room with fireplace. Dining room, garden terrace. Furnished with antiques. Small private parties accommodated. German, French spoken.*

BEARD MORGAN HOUSE

FAYETTEVILLE (1)

Beard Morgan House
126 E. Genesee St., Fayetteville, NY 13066
(315) 637-4234, (800) 775-4234, (315) 637-0010
Innkeeper: Bruce and Mary Coleman
Rooms: 5, incl. 2 w/pvt. bath, 1 w/TV
Rates: $55-$95, incl. full brk.
Credit cards: Most major cards
Restrictions: No pets, smoking. 50% deposit req. 7-day cancellation notice req.
Notes: Two-story Italianate-style house built in 3 sections, starting in 1830. Two living rooms, TV room. Wood-burning stove. Furnished with antiques. Screened-in porch under 150 year-old tulip tree. Limited handicapped access.

FULTON (1)

Battle Island Inn
R.D. 1, Box 176, Rt. 48 N, Fulton, NY 13069
(315) 593-3699
Innkeeper: Richard and Joyce Rici
Rooms: 5 w/pvt. bath, phone, TV
Rates: $55-$85, incl. full brk.
Credit cards: Most major cards
Restrictions: No children, pets, smoking. 50% deposit req.
Notes: Two-story house built in 1840. Fully restored. Located on four acres across street from golf course. Dining room, den. Sitting room with marble fireplace. Music room with piano, fireplace. Furnished with antiques, Oriental rugs. Three porches, patio overlooking the Oswego River, flower and herb gardens, orchard. Small private parties accommodated.

GARRISON (12)

The Bird & Bottle Inn
Rte. 9, Old Albany Post Rd., Garrison, NY 10524
(914) 424-3000, (914) 424-3283
Innkeeper: Ira Boyar
Rooms: 2 plus 1 suite, 1 cottage, all w/pvt. bath, fireplace. Located in 2 bldgs.
Rates: $195/room, $215/suite, cottage, all incl. brk., dinner. Mid-week pkgs. avail.
Credit cards: Most major cards
Restrictions: No children under 12, pets. Smoking restricted. $100.00 deposit req., refunded upon cancellation only if room is re-rented.
Notes: Opened as stagecoach stop in 1761. Fully restored in 1940. Enlarged and renovated in 1980. Each room individually decorated in colonial design with antiques. Three dining rooms, drinking room, each with fireplace. Award-winning Continental/American restaurant on premises. Brook with bridge, gazebo. Small private parties accommodated. Handicapped access.*

GENEVA (5)

Inn at Belhurst Castle
Rt. 145, Box 609, Geneva, NY 14456
(315) 781-0201, (315) 781-0201
Innkeeper: Duane R. Reeder

Rooms: 11 w/pvt. bath, phone, TV, incl. 3 w/fireplace, plus 2 suites w/pvt. bath, phone, TV, incl. 1 w/fireplace. Located in 2 bldgs.
Rates: $85-$130/room, $140-$225/suite, all incl. cont. brk., evening refreshment. Seasonal variations.
Credit cards: MC, V
Restrictions: No pets. One night's deposit req. 4-day cancellation notice req.
Notes: Romanesque, red medina stone 'castle' with two turrets, built in 1885. Located on 23-acre bluff overlooking Seneca Lake. Dining in the library, parlor, center room, consevatory, or on the veranda. Furnished with antiques and Oriental rugs. Lawn and tree-shaded vistas. All meals avail. Restaurant on premises. Small private parties accommodated.

GREENPORT (13)

The Bartlett House Inn
503 Front St., Greenport, NY 11944
(516) 477-0371
Innkeeper: John and Linda Sabatino
Rooms: 9 w/pvt. bath, incl. 1 w/fireplace, plus 1 suite w/pvt. bath
Rates: $62-$95/room, $75-$95/suite, incl. cont. brk. Seasonal variations.
Credit cards: Most major cards
Restrictions: No children under 11, pets. Smoking restricted. One night's deposit req. 3-day cancellation notice req. 7-day cancellation notice req. on holidays. 2-night min. stay on May–Oct wknds.
Notes: Three-story Victorian manor house with Corinthian columns, stained-glass windows, built in 1908. Living room with parquet floor, fireplace, board games, books. Guest phone avail. Furnished with period antiques, Oriental rugs. Front porch with wicker furniture. Limited handicapped access.

HAMLIN (3)

Sandy Creek Manor House
1960 Redman Rd., Hamlin, NY 14464-9635
(716) 964-7528
Innkeeper: Shirley Hollink, James Krempasky
Rooms: 3, incl. 1 w/pvt. bath
Rates: $45-$65, incl. full brk., evening refreshment. Discount avail. for frequent customers and extended stays.
Credit cards: Most major cards
Restrictions: No children under 12, smoking. Min. $20.00 deposit req. 7-day cancellation notice req., less $10.00 fee.
Notes: Two-story Tudor inn with natural woodwork and stained-glass windows built in 1910. Located on six wooded acres with perennial gardens and picnic tables. Common room with antique player piano. Decorated with Amish quilts. Large porch. Lawn and board games available. Resident cat.*

HAMMONDSPORT (10)

Blushing Rose B & B
11 William St., Hammondsport, NY 14840
(607) 569-3402
Innkeeper: Ellen and Becky Laufersweiler
Rooms: 4 w/pvt. bath

Rates: $75-$85, incl. full brk. Discount avail. for AAA stay. Seasonal variations.
Credit cards: None
Restrictions: No children, pets, smoking. One night's deposit req. 7-day cancellation notice req. 2-night min. stay on wknds. from June–Oct.
Notes: Italiante Victorian inn built in 1843. Located 3 doors from lakefront. Sitting room. Front porch with wicker furniture. Decorated with period antiques in warm Victorian style.*

HOUSE ON THE WATER

HAMPTON BAYS (13)

House on the Water
33 Rampasture Rd., Box 106, Hampton Bays, NY 11946-0012
(516) 728-3560
Innkeeper: Mrs. Ute
Rooms: 3 w/pvt. bath, incl. 2 w/phone, 1 w/cable TV
Rates: $75-$95, incl. full brk. Seasonal variations. Discount avail. for extended stay.
Credit cards: None
Restrictions: No children under 12, pets. Smoking restricted. One night's deposit req. 10-day cancellation notice req. 2-night min. stay on wknds. in season. 3-night min. stay for holidays.
Notes: One-story house located on 2 acres of waterfront garden on Shinnecock Bay. Terrace overlooking water. Guests have access to kitchen, laundry facilities. Bicycles, boat, beach lounges, beach umbrella available. Spanish, German, French spoken.*

HEMPSTEAD (13)

Country Life B & B
237 Cathedral Ave., Hempstead, NY 11550-1126
(516) 292-9219
Innkeeper: Wendy and Richard Duvall
Rooms: 3 w/TV, incl. 2 w/pvt. bath, plus 1 suite w/pvt. bath, fireplace, TV
Rates: $60-$95/room, $130/suite, all incl. full brk.
Credit cards: None
Restrictions: No pets, smoking. One night's deposit req. 10-day cancellation notice req. 2-night min. stay on wknds.

Notes: Two-story Dutch Colonial house built approx. 1924. Patio. Guests have access to antique 1929 Fords. Airport pick-up, free parking available. Handicapped access. French, Spanish spoken.*

HIGH FALLS (12)

Captain Schoonmaker's B & B
RD 2, Box 37, High Falls, NY 12440
(914) 687-7946
Innkeeper: Sam and Julia Krieg
Rooms: 12 plus 2 suites, incl. 2 w/pvt. bath, 3 w/fireplace. Located in 4 bldgs.
Rates: $80/room, $90/suite, all incl. full brk., afternoon refreshment
Credit cards: None
Restrictions: No children under 4, pets. Smoking restricted. One night's deposit req. 5-day cancellation notice req., less $10.00 fee. 2-night min. stay on wknds. from Sept. 1–Nov. 28.
Notes: Dutch stone main house built in 1760. Barn overlooking brook. Canal lock-tender's Towpath House. Victorian farmhouse built in 1875. Located on eight acres along Delaware-Hudson Canal. Living room with 225-year-old fireplace, den, each with TV. Decorated with authentic period furnishings. Porches overlooking trout stream with waterfall. Solarium with fireplace.

Locktender's Cottage
Route 213, Box 96, High Falls, NY 12440
(914) 687-7700, (914) 687-7073
Innkeeper: John Novi
Rooms: 2 plus 1 suite, all w/pvt. bath, phone, TV, fireplace
Rates: $65-$85/room, $$79-$99/suite, all incl. $10.00 voucher toward brunch or dinner.
Credit cards: Most major cards
Restrictions: No pets. Deposit req. 48-hour cancellation notice req. 2-night min. stay in peak season.
Notes: Colonial buiding dating back to days of Delaware and Hudson Canal which ran along side cottage. Restaurant on premises serves Sunday brunch and dinner Thu.–Sun.

HOBART (11)

Breezy Acres Farm B & B
Rural Delivery 1, Box 191, Hobart, NY 13788
(607) 538-9338
Innkeeper: Joyce and David Barber
Rooms: 2, plus 1 suite, all w/pvt. bath
Rates: $50-$60, incl. full brk. Discount avail. for extended stay.
Credit cards: Most major cards
Restrictions: No children under 6 without prior approval, pets, smoking. One night's deposit req. 2-week cancellation notice req.
Notes: 150-year-old rambling farmhouse on 300 wooded acres in the Catskills. Living room with fireplace, TV room. Pillared porches with wicker rockers. Sun deck with spa. Furnished with antiques, hand-crafted items and contemporary pieces. Swimming pond. Maple syrup, cream, sugar made and vegetables grown and sold on premises. In-home store features local handicrafted items.

HONEOYE (5)

The Greenwoods B & B
8136 Quayle Rd., Honeoye, NY 14471
(716) 229-2111

Innkeeper: Sue and Dave Green

Rooms: 4 w/pvt. bath, TV, plus 1 suite w/pvt. bath, fireplace, TV

Rates: $70-$90/room, $120/suite, all incl. full brk., afternoon refreshment. Special pkgs. avail.

Credit cards: Most major cards

Restrictions: No children under 12, pets. Smoking restricted. One night's deposit req. 7-day cancellation notice req.

Notes: Two-story log house built in 1990. Located on 5 acres. Common room with fireplace, board games. Library loft with telescope overlooking valley, stocked pond. Furnished in European-country decor.*

ITHACA (6)

The Federal House
P.O. Box 4914, Ithaca, NY 14852-4914
(607) 533-7362, (800) 533-7362, (607) 533-7899

Innkeeper: Diane Carroll

Rooms: 2 w/pvt. bath, incl. 1 w/fireplace, TV, plus 1 suite w/pvt. bath, fireplace

Rates: $65-$115/room, $89-$130/suite, all incl. full brk. Discount avail. for mid-week stay. Seasonal variations. Special pkgs. avail.

Credit cards: Most major cards

Restrictions: No children under 14, pets, smoking. One night's deposit req. 10-day cancellation notice req., less $10.00 fee. 2-night min. stay on wknds. from July–Aug. and Oct.

Notes: Two story house built in 1815. Parlor with hand-carved mantels. Sitting room with TV, refrigerator. Foyer with phone. Porch. Furnished with antiques. Located on one acre of landscaped grounds with garden and gazebo. Bicycles, airport pick-up available.*

La Tourelle Country Inn
1150 Danby Rd., Ithaca, NY 14850
(607) 273-2734, (607) 273-4821

Innkeeper: Leslie Leonard

Rooms: 35 w/pvt. bath, phone, TV, incl. 1 w/fireplace

Rates: $75-$125, incl. cont. brk.

Credit cards: Most major cards

Restrictions: Smoking restricted. Deposit req. 24-hour cancellation notice req.

Notes: European-style inn located on 70 acres in hills surrounding Ithaca. Lobby with fireplace. Ballroom. Furnished in old world and contemporary styles. Small private parties accommodated. Outdoor patio.*

Log Country Inn
P.O. Box 581, Ithaca, NY 14851
(607) 589-4771, (800) 274-4771, (607) 589-6151

Innkeeper: Wanda Grunberg

Rooms: 2 plus 1 suite, incl. 2 w/pvt. bath

Rates: $45-$65/room, $100/suite, all incl. full brk., afternoon refreshment. Discount avail. for mid-week stay.

Credit cards: MC, V

Restrictions: No smoking. Deposit required under certain circumstances. Min. stay req. for graduation and special event wknds.

Notes: Rustic log lodge built of Vermont logs inspired by American pioneer cabins of 18th and 19th centuries. Located on edge of 7,000-acre state forest. Living room with cathedral ceiling, exposed log beams. Gardens. Dinner available. Polish, Russian spoken.

Rose Inn
Rte. 34 N., Box 6576, Ithaca, NY 14851
(607) 533-7905, (607) 533-7908

Innkeeper: Sherry and Charles Rosemann

Rooms: 10 w/pvt. bath, phone, incl. 1 w/fireplace, plus 5 suites w/pvt. bath, phone, incl. 2 w/fireplace, TV

Rates: $1000-$160/room, $185-$250/suite, all incl. full brk.

Credit cards: MC, V

Restrictions: No children under 10, pets, smoking. Full prepayment req. for stays up to 3 days.

Notes: Two-story Italianate mansion with museum-quality circular Honduran mahagony staircase, oak inlaid parquet floors, built in the 1851. Located on twenty landscaped acres with fishing pond, flower gardens, century-old maple trees, apple orchard. Country kitchen, dining rooms, formal parlor, conference center. Furnished with 19th-century American and European antiques and collectibles. Dinner available Tuesday through Saturday. Small private parties accommodated. Spanish, German spoken.*

THE BOOK AND BLANKET B & B

JAY (2)

The Book and Blanket B & B
Rte. 9 N, Box 164, Jay, NY 12941
(518) 946-8323, (518) 946-8323

Innkeeper: Kathy and Fred and Daisy the bassset hound

Rooms: 3, incl. 1 w/pvt. whirlpool bath

Rates: $45-$65, incl. full brk., afternoon refreshment. Discount avail. for extended stay.

Credit cards: None

Restrictions: Pets, smoking restricted. One night's deposit req. 15-day cancellation notice req.

Notes: Two-story Greek Revival house built in the 1850s. Living room with board games, puzzles, TV, VCR, clasic movies on tape. Books in every room, which can be borrowed "indefinitely" by guests. Common area with fireplace. Furnished with antiques. Large porch with swing. Resident basset hound.

KEENE (2)

The Bark Eater Inn
Alstead Hill Rd., Keene, NY 12942
(518) 576-2221, (518) 576-2071

Innkeeper: Joe-Pete Wilson

Rooms: 11, incl. 4 w/pvt. bath, plus cottage w/fireplace. Located in 3 bldgs.

Rates: $90-$110/room, $180/cottage, all incl. full brk. Special pkgs. avail. Seasonal variations.

Credit cards: Most major cards

Restrictions: No pets. Smoking restricted. 50% deposit req. 7-day cancellation notice req., less 10% fee. 2-night min. stay on wknds. 3-night min. stay on holiday wknds.

Notes: Colonial-style farmhouse built in the early 1800s as stagecoach stop. Carriage House, Cottage. Dining room, living room, each with stone fireplace, wide-board floors. Meeting and conference rooms with PC, FAX, and phone hookups. Furnished with antiques. Riding stable with English and Western riding on premises. Ski center with rentals. All meals available. Innkeeper is former Olympic and World competitor in Nordic skiing, biathlon, bobsledding. Small private parties accommodated.*

KEENE VALLEY (2)

High Peaks Inn
Rte. 73, Box 73, Keene Valley, NY 12943
(518) 576-2003

Innkeeper: Jerry and Linda Limpert

Rooms: 7, incl. 2 w/pvt. bath, plus 1 suite w/pvt. bath

Rates: $65-$80/room, $80/suite, all incl. full brk., afternoon refreshment. Seasonal variations. Discount avail. for extended, mid-week stay.

Credit cards: MC, V

Restrictions: No pets, smoking. 50% deposit req. 21-day cancellation notice req. less 10% fee. 2-night min. stay on wknds. 3-night min. stay on holidays.

Notes: Adirondack lodge built in 1910. Dining room, library. Living room with granite fireplace and piano. Parlor with books, board games, TV, pool table. Wraparound porch. Patio with Bar-b-que grill. Dinners available. Resident pets.

LAKE GEORGE (2)

Corner Birches B & B
86 Montcalm St., Lake George, NY 12845
(518) 668-2837

Innkeeper: Ray and Janice Dunklee
Rooms: 4, no pvt. bath
Rates: $35-$45, incl. cont. brk.
Credit cards: None
Restrictions: No children, smoking. Well-behaved pets welcome. One night's deposit req. 48-hr. cancellation notice req.
Notes: Private home located 3 blocks from Lake George and village center. Has operated as inn since 1957. Living room with cable TV. Formal dining room, front porch with rocking chairs. Off-street parking available.

CORNER BIRCHES B & B

LAKE LUZERNE (2)

Lamplight Inn Bed and Breakfast
2129 Lake Ave., Box 70, Lake Luzerne, NY 12846
(518) 696-5294, (800) 262-4668

Innkeeper: Gene and Linda Merlino
Rooms: 10 w/pvt. bath, incl. 5 w/fireplace
Rates: $85-$140, incl. full brk. Discount avail. for extended stay. Special pkgs. avail. Seasonal variations.
Credit cards: Most major cards
Restrictions: No children under 12, pets. Smoking restricted. 50% deposit req. 14-day cancellation notice req. 2-night min. stay on wknds. 3-night min. stay on holiday wknds.
Notes: Victorian Gothic mini-mansion with oak woodwork, twelve-ft. beamed ceilings, carved chestnut keyhole staircase, chestnut wainscoting built in 1890 as summer home. Located on 2.5-acre knoll with garden. Has operated as inn since 1984. Living room, dining room with fireplaces. Wrap-around sun porch with wicker furniture, swing, board games. Furnished with antique oak, canopy, or brass and iron beds. Resident dog.*

LAKE PLACID (2)

Highland House Inn
3 Highland Pl., Lake Placid, NY 12946
(518) 523-2377, (518) 523-1863

Innkeeper: Teddy and Cathy Blazer
Rooms: 8 w/pvt. bath, TV, plus 1 cottage w/pvt. bath, fireplace, TV, VCR, stereo. Located in 2 bldgs.
Rates: $65-$75/room, $85-$105/cottage, all incl. full brk. Seasonal variations. Special pkgs. avail.
Credit cards: Most major cards
Restrictions: No pets, smoking. One night's deposit req. 3-week cancellation notice req. 2-night min. stay on wknds. 3-night min. stay on holidays
Notes: Adirondack style inn built in 1910 overlooking Mirror Lake. Living room with cable TV. Dining room with wood stove. Deck, glass-enclosed garden room. Hot tub. Cottage with kitchen, fireplace, balcony deck. Furnished with antiques.*

Interlaken Inn
15 Interlaken Ave., Lake Placid, NY 12946
(518) 523-3180, (800) 428-4369

Innkeeper: Roy and Carol Johnson
Rooms: 11 plus 1 suite, all w/pvt. bath, incl. 1 w/TV
Rates: $50-$110/room, $$110/suite, all incl. full brk., afternoon refreshment. Special pkgs. avail. Discount avail. for extended stay.
Credit cards: Most major cards
Restrictions: No children under 5, pets. Smoking restricted. One night's deposit req. 2-week cancellation notice req., less $10.00 fee. 2-night min. stay on fall and winter wknds. 3-night min. stay on holiday wknds. Dinner not served Tues. or Wed.
Notes: Victorian mansion with Swiss character built in 1906. Located on Signal Hill overlooking Lake Placid and Mirror Lake. Has operated as inn since 1947. Living room with fireplace, bar. Victorian dining room with tin ceiling, fireplace. Game room, sun porch, terrace. Furnished with period antiques. Gourmet restaurant on premises.*

Spruce Lodge
31 Sentinel Rd., Lake Placid, NY 12946
(800) 258-9350

Innkeeper: Carol Hoffman
Rooms: 7, incl. 2 w/pvt. bath, plus 1 cottage. Located in 2 bldgs.
Rates: $45-$60/room, $99/cottage, all incl. cont. brk.
Credit cards: MC, V
Restrictions: No pets, smoking. 7-day cancellation notice req. 2-night min. stay in cottage.
Notes: New England-style farmhouse. Has operated as a family-run inn since 1951. Living room, front porch. Furnished in Colonial style. Lawns with picnic area.

Stagecoach Inn
3700 Old Military Rd., Lake Placid, NY 12946
(518) 523-9474

Innkeeper: Peter Moreau
Rooms: 9, incl. 2 suites, incl. 7 w/pvt. bath, 1 w/fireplace
Rates: $70-$85/room, $110-$125/suite, all incl. full brk. Discount for extended stay, Apr.–June.
Credit cards: MC, V

Restrictions: No pets. Smoking restricted. One night's deposit req. 2-week cancellation notice req.

Notes: Only landmark in Lake Placid that remains of the romantic stagecoach era. Has operated as inn since before 1833, by current innkeepers since 1977. Completely restored in 1872 and 1979. Dining room with fireplace. Two story common room with balcony and fireplace. Front porch with rocking chairs. Furnished with country decor, including brass beds, iron beds, handmade quilts, wicker and antiques. Served as headquarters for CBS Sports during 1980 Winter Olympics.*

LEWISTON (3)

The Cameo Inn
4710 Lower River Rd., Lewiston, NY 14092
(716) 754-2075

Innkeeper: Gregory and Carolyn Fisher

Rooms: 5 plus 5 suites, incl. 6 w/pvt. bath, 3 w/phone, 2 w/cable TV, 1 w/fireplace. Located in 2 bldgs.

Rates: $65-$95/room, $95-$125/suite, all incl. full brk. Discount for extended, midweek and off-season stays.

Credit cards: None

Restrictions: No pets, smoking. Min. one night's deposit req. 72-hour cancellation notice req., less 10% fee.

Notes: Three-story Queen Anne Victorian and country-style houses. Located on three acres overlooking the Lower Niagara River. Dining room, meeting rooms. Small private parties accommodated.*

LIMA (4)

Fonda House B & B
1612 Rochester St., Box 551, Lima, NY 14485
(716) 582-1040

Innkeeper: Millie Fonda

Rooms: 3, incl. 1 w/pvt. bath

Rates: $50-$80, incl. full brk. Discount avail. for extended stay.

Credit cards: None

Restrictions: Children welcome with prior notification.

Notes: Italianate house built in 1853. Located on 2 wooded acres. Furnished in a Victorian manor.*

LOCKPORT (3)

Hambleton House B & B
130 Pine Ave., Lockport, NY 14094
(716) 439-9507, 634-3650

Innkeeper: Ted Hambleton

Rooms: 3 w/pvt. bath

Rates: $55-$75, incl. expanded cont. brk. Seasonal variations.

Credit cards: None

Restrictions: No children under 12. Smoking restricted. Deposit req. 72-hour cancellation notice req.

Notes: Two-story house with grand staircase built approx. 1850. Located within walking distance to Erie Barge Canal Locks. Parlor with TV. Dining room, wraparound porch.*

LOWVILLE (1)

Parkside Manor B & B
7701 N. State St., Lowville, NY 13367
(315) 376-4453

Innkeeper: Tim and Donna Moore
Rooms: 2, incl. 1 w/pvt. bath, TV, plus 1 suite w/pvt. bath, TV
Rates: $35-$45/room, $80/suite, all incl. full brk.
Credit cards: None
Restrictions: No pets, smoking.
Notes: Italianate Victorian house with grand staircase, solid oak paneling, three fireplaces, built in 1865 by the president of the Utica and Black River Railroad. Renovated in 1923. Recently restored. Located on the Village Green. Library, living room, dining room, three-season porch. Small private parties accommodated.

LYONS (5)

Roselawne B & B
101 Broad St., Lyons, NY 14489-1039
(315) 946-4218

Innkeeper: Marge and Bob MacDuffie
Rooms: 3, no pvt. bath, incl. 2 w/skylight
Rates: $50-$60, incl. full brk. on wknds., cont. brk. on wkdays. Discount avail. for extended stay.
Credit cards: None
Restrictions: No children under 10, pets. Smoking restricted. One night's deposit req. 7-day cancellation notice req.
Notes: Two-story Greek Revival house built in the mid-1840s. Remodeled in the 1880s with Victorian touches. Music room with organ, fireplace. Upstairs sitting room. Porch overlooking garden. Resident cats.

MOUNT TREMPER (12)

Mt. Tremper Inn
P.O. Box 51, Mount Tremper, NY 12457
(914) 688-5329

Innkeeper: Lou Caselli, Peter LaScala
Rooms: 11 plus 1 suite, incl. 2 w/pvt. bath
Rates: $60-$80/room, $95/suite, all incl. full brk.
Credit cards: MC, V
Restrictions: No children under 16, pets, smoking. 14-day cancellation notice req. 2-night min. stay.
Notes: Victorian mansion built in 1850 as guesthouse. Fully restored in 1985. Living room with blue-stone fireplace. Game room, library, dining room. Furnished in period style with red velvet walls, French lace curtains, hanging lamps. Covered outdoor veranda overlooking rose garden. Full wrap-around porch. Lawn games, parking available.

MUMFORD (4)

Genesee Country Inn
948 George St., Mumford, NY 14511
(716) 538-2500, (716) 538-4565

Innkeeper: Glenda Barcklow, Kim Rasmussen
Rooms: 8 w/pvt. bath, TV, phone, incl. 3 w/fireplace
Rates: $85-$125, incl. full brk., afternoon refreshment. Special pkgs. avail.
Credit cards: Most major cards
Restrictions: No pets, smoking. One-night's deposit req. 7-day cancellation notice
   req. 2-night min. stay on wknds. from May–Oct.
Notes: Stone mill house built in 1833. Totally refurbished. Located on six wooded
acres with three creeks, 16-foot natural waterfall, ponds and gardens. Furnished
with antiques and reproductions, some canopy beds. Small private parties accommodated. Trout fishing at inn.*

NEW PALTZ (12)

Nanna's Bed and Breakfast
54 Old Ford Road, New Paltz, NY 12561
(914) 255-5678
Innkeeper: Kathleen Maloney
Rooms: 2, no pvt. bath
Rates: $50, incl. full brk.
Credit cards: None
Restrictions: No pets, smoking. $20.00 deposit req. 7-day cancellation notice req.
Notes: Built in 1932. Located on 20 acres of extensive lawn, picnic areas and hiking
trails. Living room. Furnished with antiques.

NEW ROCHELLE (12)

Rose Hill Guest House
44 Rose Hill Ave., New Rochelle, NY 10804
(914) 632-6464
Innkeeper: Marilou Mayetta
Rooms: 3 w/phone, TV, incl. 1 w/pvt. bath, 2 w/fireplace
Rates: $65-$85, incl. cont. brk.
Credit cards: DC
Restrictions: Pets, smoking restricted. One night's deposit req. 3-day cancellation
   notice req., less $5.00 fee.
Notes: Two-story French Normandy house. Formal dining room. Living room with
fireplace. Flowered patio. Parking available.*

NEW YORK (13)

The Gracie Inn
502 E. 81st. St., New York, NY 10028
(212) 628-1700, (212) 628-6420
Innkeeper: Sandra Arcara, Daniel Chappuis
Rooms: 12 suites w/pvt. bath, kitchen, phone, TV, incl. penthouse duplex suite
   w/pvt. sundeck
Rates: $79-$279/1 bedroom suite, $199-$349/2 bedroom suite, all incl. cont. brk.
   Discount avail. for extended stay.
Credit cards: Most major cards
Restrictions: Deposit req. for weekly or monthly rates. 7-day cancellation notice req.
Notes: Five-floor European style apartment hotel located in the heart of the Upper
East Side just around the corner from Mayor's mansion. Elevator service. Furnished
with antiques, duvets, feather pillows, fresh flowers. Daily maid service. Business ser-

vices available. Nearby 24-hour parking. French, German, Spanish, Russian, Slovak spoken.*

Inn New York City
266 W. 71st St., New York, NY 10023
(212) 580-1900, (212) 580-4437

Innkeeper: Elyn and Ruth Mensch
Rooms: 4 suites w/pvt. bath, phone w/answering machine, cable TV, incl. 2 w/fireplace
Rates: $175-$250, incl. full brk., evening refreshment
Credit cards: Most major cards
Restrictions: No pets, smoking. Min. one night's deposit req. 14-day cancellation notice req. less $50.00 fee. 2-night min. stay. $25.00 surcharge for arrivals after 10:00 p.m.
Notes: Three-story brownstone with leaded-glass skylights built in the late 19th-century. Fully restored and soundproofed. Furnished in Victorian style. Library with board games. Living room with TV, VCR, stereo tape deck. Guests have access to kitchen.*

POUGHKEEPSIE (12)

Inn at the Falls
50 Red Oaks Mill Rd., Poughkeepsie, NY 12603
(914) 462-5770, (914) 462-5943

Innkeeper: Arnold and Barbara Sheer
Rooms: 24 plus 12 suites, all w/pvt. bath, phone, cable TV
Rates: $110-$127/room, $140-$150/suite, all incl. cont. brk., evening refreshment
Credit cards: Most major cards
Restrictions: No pets. Smoking restricted. 24-hour cancellation notice req.
Notes: Handicapped access.*

QUEENSBURY (2)

Crislip's Bed & Breakfast
693 Ridge Rd., Queensbury, NY 12804
(518) 793-6869

Innkeeper: Ned and Joyce Crislip
Rooms: 3 w/pvt. bath
Rates: $55-$75, incl. full brk. Seasonal variations.
Credit cards: MC, V
Restrictions: No smoking. Pets restricted. 50% deposit req. 2-day cancellation notice req.
Notes: Two-story restored Federal-style house built in 1820. Located on two wooded acres. Dining room, sun room overlooking lawn. Porch, terrace overlooking mountains, shade trees, old stone walls. Small private parties accommodated. Resident cats, dog. Some German spoken.

Sanford's Ridge
749 Ridge Rd., Queensbury, NY 12804
(518) 793-4923

Innkeeper: Carolyn and Robert Rudolph
Rooms: 2 w/pvt. bath, plus 1 suite w/pvt. bath

Rates: $60-$85/room, $75-$95/suite, all incl. full brk. Seasonal variations. Discount avail. for extended stay.

Credit cards: MC, V

Restrictions: No children under 12, pets, smoking. Deposit req. 14-day cancellation notice req., less $10.00 fee. 2-night min. stay on holiday and special wknds.

Notes: Two-story federal-style house with high ceilings, period fireplaces, pine floors, built in 1792. Fully restored. Mountain views. Common room with TV, phone. Furnished with antiques. Billiards. Swimming pool.*

RHINEBECK (12)

Village Victorian Inn
31 Center St., Rhinebeck, NY 12572
(914) 876-8345, (914) 266-4051

Innkeeper: Judy Kohler

Rooms: 5 w/pvt. bath, incl. 1 w/fireplace

Rates: $175-$250, incl. full brk.

Credit cards: AE

Restrictions: No children under 16, pets, smoking. Min. one night's deposit req. 21 day cancellation notice req. 2-night min. stay on wknds. 3-night min. stay on holiday wknds.

Notes: Two-story Victorian house built in 1860. Breakfast room with fireplace. Parlor with TV, board games. Oak dining room with fireplace. Porch with wicker furniture. Furnished with antiques. Off-street parking available.*

ROCK CITY FALLS (8)

Mansion Inn
Route 29, Box 77, Rock City Falls, NY 12863
(518) 885-1607, (518) 885-1607

Innkeeper: Tom Clark, Alan Churchill

Rooms: 4 plus 1 suite, all w/pvt. bath

Rates: $95/room, $110/suite, all incl. full brk. Seasonal variations.

Credit cards: None

Restrictions: No children under 12, pets. Smoking restricted. One night's deposit req. 14-day cancellation notice req. 2-night min. stay, May–October wknds.

Notes: Mansion built in 1866. Locted on 4 acres of landscaped grounds. Side porch with wicker seats. Dining room and sitting room with marble fireplace. Furnished with period armoires, antiques, brass and copper chandeliers. Library, pool. Resident pet.

ROCK STREAM (5)

Reading House B & B
4610 Rte. 14, Rock Stream, NY 14878
(607) 535-9785

Innkeeper: Rita and Bill Newell

Rooms: 4 w/pvt. bath

Rates: $55-$65, incl. full brk., afternoon refreshment. Seasonal variations. Special pkgs. avail.

Credit cards: Most major cards

Restrictions: No children under 9, pets. Smoking restricted. One night's deposit req. 10-day cancellation notice req. 2-night min. stay on holiday and race wknds.

Notes: Two-story Federal style farmhouse built in 1820. Located on three acres with two ponds and gardens, overlooking lake. Expanded with Greek Revival and Victorian details. Two parlors, dining room, bookery. Furnished with antiques and reproductions.

ROUND LAKE (2)

Olde Stone House Inn
P. O. Box 451, Round Lake, NY 12151
(518) 899-5048
Innkeeper: Mary and Walter Zielnicki
Rooms: 4, incl. 2 w/pvt. bath
Rates: $70-$100, incl. full brk., afternoon refreshment. Seasonal variations.
Credit cards: MC, V
Restrictions: No children under 12, pets. Smoking restricted. One night's deposit req. 14-day cancellation notice req. 2-night min. stay, July–Aug.
Notes: Two-story Colonial-style, cobblestone house with hardwood floors, ceiling fans, leaded-glass windows, built approx. 1820. Dining room with fireplace. Deck. Lawn games, BBQ available.*

SARATOGA SPRINGS (8)

Chestnut Tree Inn
9 Whitney Pl., Saratoga Springs, NY 12866
(518) 587-8681
Innkeeper: Cathleen and Bruce DeLuke
Rooms: 8 plus 1 mini-suite, 1 bungalow, incl. 5 w/pvt. bath. Located in 2 bldgs.
Rates: $65-$85/room, $95/suite, all incl. cont. brk. Seasonal variations.
Credit cards: MC, V
Restrictions: No pets, smoking. One night's deposit req. 10% fee for cancellation. 3-night min. stay during racing season and other special event wknds. Closed Nov. 1–March 31.
Notes: Second period Empire house with French mansard roof built in the 1860s. Living room with TV. Breakfast room. Furnished with antiques. Wrap-around front porch with antique wicker furniture. Garden with iron tables and chairs. Innkeepers are antique dealers.*

The Eddy House
Nelson Ave. Ext., Rd. 4, Saratoga Springs, NY 12866
(518) 587-2340
Innkeeper: Barbara Bertino
Rooms: 5, incl. 4 w/TV, no pvt. bath
Rates: $40-$160, incl. full brk., afternoon refreshment. Seasonal variations.
Credit cards: None
Restrictions: No children, pets. Smoking restricted. Min. one night's deposit req. 14-day cancellation notice req. 2-night min. stay.
Notes: Federal Colonial house built in 1947. Located on 1.5 acres across from harness racing track. Two living rooms, formal dining room, library, screened porch, country kitchen. Putting green, lawn games available.

Inn on Bacon Hill
200 Wall St., Box 1462, Saratoga Springs, NY 12866
(518) 695-3693

Innkeeper: Andrea Collins-Breslin
Rooms: 3 plus 1 suite, incl. 2 w/pvt. bath, phone
Rates: $65-$75/room, $85/suite, all incl. full brk. Seasonal variations.
Credit cards: MC, V
Restrictions: No children under 12, pets, smoking. One night's deposit req. 7-day cancellation notice req. 2-night min. stay on racing wknds.
Notes: Victorian mansion built in 1862. Lcoated in quiet, pastoral setting ten minutes east of Saratoga Springs. Fully restored. Guest parlor with marble fireplace, high ceilings, antique chandeliers, original plaster and wood mouldings. Victorian parlor suite with baby grand piano. Library with board games. Country dining room. Porch and flower gardens. Innkeeping course offered.*

INN ON BEACON HILL

The Six Sisters B & B
149 Union Ave., Saratoga Springs, NY 12866
(518) 583-1173, (518) 587-2470

Innkeeper: Kate Benton and Steve Ramirez
Rooms: 2 w/pvt. bath, plus 2 suites w/pvt. bath, 1 w/TV
Rates: $60-$80/room, $80-$100/suite, all incl. full brk. Discount avail. for extended, mid-week, senior citizen, and military stays.
Credit cards: Most major cards
Restrictions: No children under 10, pets, smoking. One night's deposit req. 14-day cancellation notice req. Occasional min. stay req.
Notes: Two-story Victorian inn with oak floors and Italian verd marble, built in 1880. Front entrance with Tiger Oak and multi-colored stained-glass. Master suite has private balcony. Furnished with antiques, Oriental carpets. Veranda with rocking chairs.*

Union Gables B & B
55 Union Ave., Saratoga Springs, NY 12866
(518) 584-1558, (518) 583-0649

Innkeeper: Jody and Tom Roohan
Rooms: 9, plus 10 suites, all w/pvt. bath, phone, TV
Rates: $80-$200, incl. cont. brk. Seasonal variations.

Credit cards: Most major cards

Restrictions: Smoking restricted. Credit card deposit req. 14-day cancellation notice req. in August only.

Notes: Queen Anne Victorian inn built approx. 1901. Newly restored. Large "Saratoga" porch. Outdoor hot tub, exercise equipment and bicycles. Listed on National Register of Historic Places. Family owned and operated. Limited French spoken.*

Westchester House
102 Lincoln Avenue, Box 944, Saratoga Springs, NY 12866
(518) 587-7613

Innkeeper: Bob and Stephanie Melvin

Rooms: 7 w/pvt. bath, phone

Rates: $75-$125, incl. cont. brk., afternoon refreshment. Seasonal variations. Discount avail. for extended, mid-week and senior citzen stays. Special pkgs. avail.

Credit cards: Most major cards

Restrictions: No children under 12, pets. Smoking restricted. Deposit req. 14-day cancellation notice req., less fee. 2-night min. stay on most wknds.

Notes: Two-story Queen Anne Victorian house with cupola, balcony, two elaborate fireplaces, large arched windows built in 1885. Fully restored in 1987. Has operated as inn since 1890. Double parlors with baby grand piano, library. Dining room. Furnished with antiques, Oriental carpets. Wrap-around porch overlooking gardens with sitting areas. Innkeepers collect art books. Small private parties accommodated.*

WESTCHESTER HOUSE

SAUGERTIES (12)

Bed by the Stream
7531 George Sickle Rd., Saugerties, NY 12477
(914) 246-2979, (914) 246-2680

Innkeeper: Odette Reinhardt

Rooms: 3 w/pvt. bath, fireplace, cable TV

Rates: $75, incl. full brk.

Credit cards: None

Restrictions: No pets, smoking. Deposit req. 7-day cancellation notice req.

Notes: Located on 5 acres. Enclosed porch overlooking stream. Swimming pool.

SHELTER ISLAND (13)

Bayberry B & B
36 S Menantic Rd., Box 538, Shelter Island, NY 11964-0538
(516) 749-3375
Innkeeper: Richard and Suzanne Boland
Rooms: 2 w/pvt. bath
Rates: $75-$125, incl. full brk. Seasonal variations. Special pkgs. avail.
Credit cards: Most major cards
Restrictions: No children under 12, pets, smoking. One night's deposit req. 10-day cancellation notice req. 2-night min. stay on wknds. 3-night min. stay on holiday wknds.
Notes: Living room with fireplace and piano. Furnished with antiques. Hammocks, swimming pool.

SHELTER ISLAND HEIGHTS (13)

The Chequit Inn
23 Grand Ave., Box 292, Shelter Island Hts., NY 11965-0292
(516) 749-0018, (516) 749-0183
Innkeeper: James and Linda Eklund
Rooms: 17, plus 3 suites, all w/pvt. bath. Located in 3 bldgs.
Rates: $80-$125/room, $95-$195/suite, all incl. cont. brk. Discount avail. for mid-week and extended stays. Special pkgs. avail.
Credit cards: Most major cards
Restrictions: No pets. Smoking restricted. Min. 50% deposit req. 10-day cancellation notice req. 2-night min. stay on wknds. 3-night min. stay on holiday wknds. Closed Oct. 31–May 1.
Notes: Victorian clapboard inn built in 1871. Has operated as inn since 1871. Fully restored in 1990. Lobby with fireplace. Dining room, terrace. Covered veranda overlooking Dering Harbor and Shelter Island Yacht Club. Furnished in eclectic country style with antiques. Two restaurants, piano bar on premises. Spanish, French spoken.*

Ram's Head Inn
108 Ram Island Dr., Shelter Island Hts., NY 11965-0638
(516) 749-0811, (516) 749-0059
Innkeeper: James and Linda Eklund
Rooms: 13, incl. 5 w/pvt. bath, 9 w/phone, plus 4 suites w/pvt. bath, phone.
Rates: $90-$115/room, $140-$195/suite, all incl. cont. brk. Seasonal variations. Discount avail. for mid-week stay.
Credit cards: Most major cards
Restrictions: No pets. Smoking restricted. Min. 50% deposit req. 10-day cancellation notice req. 2-night min. stay on wknds. 3-night min. stay on holiday wknds.
Notes: Two-story center hall Colonial house with 800 ft. of beachfront built in 1929. Patio overlooking Coecles Harbor. Sauna, private beach. O'Day sloops, sunfish, peddle boat, kayak available. Small private parties accommodated.

SKANEATELES (6)

Cozy Cottage
4987 Kingston Rd., Elbridge, Skaneateles, NY 13060
(315) 689-2082

Innkeeper: Elaine Samuels
Rooms: 2, no pvt. bath
Rates: $40-$50, incl. cont. brk. Discount for extended stay.
Credit cards: None
Restrictions: No children under 14, smoking. Cats welcome. Deposit req. Min. stay
during summer Skaneateles Music Festival.
Notes: Ranch house. Located on five country acres. Living room with TV, fireplace.
Elaine also operates a B & B Reservation Service.

SOUTHAMPTON (13)

Old Post House Inn
136 Main St., Southampton, NY 11968
(516) 283-1717
Innkeeper: Cecile and Ed Courville
Rooms: 7 w/pvt. bath
Rates: $80-$170, incl. cont. brk. Seasonal variations.
Credit cards: Most major cards
Restrictions: No children under 12, pets. 50% deposit req. 7-day cancellation notice
req., less 20% fee. 2-night min. stay on wknds. 3-night min. stay on holiday wknds.
Notes: Built in 1694 with chestnut plank floors. Restored to its original syle and located in heart of Southampton Village. Common room with hand-hewn beams and
fireplace. Wicker filled porch. Furnished in country decor with period antiques,
quilts, old bedsteads. Adjacent restaurant serves lunch and dinner. Archeological
dig completed in basement of inn. Listed on National Register of Historic Places.

SPENCER (6)

A Slice of Home
178 N. Main St., Spencer, NY 14883
(607) 589-6073
Innkeeper: Bea Brownell
Rooms: 3 plus 1 suite, incl. 1 w/phone
Rates: $35-$85, incl. full brk. Discount avail. for senior citizens.
Credit cards: None
Restrictions: No pets, smoking. Deposit req. 2-week cancellation notice req.
Notes: Italianate farmhouse built in 1844. Located on 12 acres between Watkins
Glen and Ithaca. Outside grill, picnic tables. Day or overnight bicycle tours
planned. Some German spoken.*

STANFORDVILLE (12)

The Lakehouse
Shelley Hill Rd., Stanfordville, NY 12581
(914) 266-8093, (914) 266-4051
Innkeeper: Judy Kohler
Rooms: 13 w/pvt. bath, TV, incl. 7 w/fireplace, 6 w/phone. Located in 4 bldgs.
Rates: $175-$395, incl. full brk., afternoon appetizers and pastries
Credit cards: AE
Restrictions: No infants, pets, smoking. Full prepayment req. 21-day cancellation
notice req. 2-night min. stay on wknds. 3-night min. stay on holidays.

Notes: Cedar-sided house. Located on twenty-two acres overlooking private seven-acre lake. Has operated as inn since 1990. Dining room with floor-to-ceiling fireplace. Living room with oak floor. Private redwood decks, dock.*

THE LAKEHOUSE

SYRACUSE (1)

Bed and Breakfast Wellington
707 Danforth St., Syracuse, NY 13208-1611
(315) 471-2433, (800) 724-5006, (315) 474-2557

Innkeeper: Wendy Wilber and Ray Borg
Rooms: 4 w/pvt. bath, TV, plus 1 suite w/pvt. bath, TV, fireplace
Rates: $65-$105, incl. full brk., afternoon refreshment. Discount avail. for extended, military and mid-week stays.
Credit cards: Most major cards
Restrictions: No children under 12, pets, smoking. Deposit req. 72-hour cancellation notice req. 2-night min. stay on some wknds.
Notes: Two-story brick and stucco Tudor-style house with canvas floors, arched foyer, built in 1914. Fully renovated. Has operated as inn since 1988. Dining room with fireplace. Living room, four porches. Furnished with antiques. Guests have access to exercise equipment. All meals available. Small private parties accommodated. Innkeeper collects porcelain bedpans, early farm tools and old books.

TANNERSVILLE (12)

The Eggery Inn
County Rd. 16, Box 4, Tannersville, NY 12485
(518) 589-5363

Innkeeper: Abe and Julie Abramczyk
Rooms: 13 w/pvt. bath, TV, plus 2 suites w/pvt. bath, TV. Located in 2 bldgs.
Rates: $90-$110, incl. full brk. Seasonal variations.
Credit cards: Most major cards
Restrictions: No children under 4. Smoking restricted. 50% deposit req. 14-day cancellation notice req. in high season. 2-night min. stay on high season wknds. 3-night min. stay on holiday wknds.

Notes: Three-story farmhouse built in 1900. Renovated in 1979. Has operated as inn since 1935. Located at 2,200-foot elevation in Catskill Park and Game Preserve. Sitting room with oak balustrade, Franklin stove, brick hearth, antique player piano. Dining room with handcrafted oak full-service bar. Furnished with period antiques. Wrap-around porch. Dinner available for small groups with prior arrangement. Handicapped access.*

TUPPER LAKE (2)

Green Gables B & B
24 Wawbeek Ave., Tupper Lake, NY 12986
(518) 359-7815
Innkeeper: Gail and Bob Caye
Rooms: 4 w/pvt. bath, phone, incl. 1 w/TV
Rates: $45-$55, incl. full brk.
Credit cards: MC, V
Restrictions: No pets, smoking. 33% deposit req. 5-day cancellation notice req. Closed Thanksgiving and Dec. 24, 25.
Notes: Three-story Victorian house built about 1903. Two living rooms with TV, fireplace. Front porch with rockers.

VERNON (6)

Lavender Inn
5950 State Route 5, Box 325, Vernon, NY 13476
(315) 829-2440
Innkeeper: Rose Degni, Lyn Doring
Rooms: 3 w/pvt. bath
Rates: $70, incl. brk. Seasonal variations.
Credit cards: AE, DC
Restrictions: No pets. Smoking restricted. One night's deposit req. 24-hour cancellation notice req. 30-day cancellation notice req. for priority wknds. 2-night min. stay on some wknds.
Notes: Two-story Federal-style house built in 1799. Dining room with brick fireplace with bread oven, slate hearth. Common room. Decorated with woodcrafts, quilts, weavings crafted by the innkeepers. Small private parties accommodated. Craft study weekends organized.*

VICTOR (5)

The Golden Rule B & B
6934 Rice Rd., Victor, NY 14564
(716) 924-0610
Innkeeper: Kalen and Dick de Mauriac
Rooms: 2 w/phone, TV, no pvt. bath
Rates: $55-$75, incl. full brk., afternoon refreshment. Discount avail. for extended, mid-week and senior citizen stays. Seasonal variations.
Credit cards: None
Restrictions: No children under 12, pets, smoking. One night's deposit req. 2-week cancellation notice req.
Notes: Original structure built as one room schoolhouse in 1865 (bell still rings) situated in Bristol Hills area. Major renovations and additions. Guest rooms with antiques, ceiling fans. Common room with fireplace. Swimming pool surrounded by

gardens, screened porch, deck, hammock, picnic table, gazebo. Lawn games available.

WAINSCOTT (13)

McErlean House
P.O. Box 1238, Wainscott, NY 11975
(516) 329-2212
Innkeeper: Artie and Leed McGurk
Rooms: 3, no pvt. bath
Rates: $75-$140, incl. full brk. Seasonal variations.
Credit cards: MC, V
Restrictions: Children welcome with prior notification only. Deposit req. 7-day cancellation notice req. 2-night min. stay.

WARRENSBURG (2)

Country Road Lodge
Hickory Hill Rd., HCR 1 #227, Warrensburg, NY 12885-9732
(518) 623-2207
Innkeeper: Sandi and Steve Parisi
Rooms: 4, incl. 3 w/pvt. bath
Rates: $52-$58, incl. full brk. Special pkgs. avail.
Credit cards: None
Restrictions: No children, pets. Smoking restricted. Min. $25.00 deposit req. 14-day
   cancellation notice req., less $5.00 fee. 2-night min. stay on holiday wknds.
Notes: Two-story cottage style house built in 1929. Located on 35 wooded acres
overlooking Adirondack Mountains. Sitting room with piano, board games, library.
Small private parties accommodated.*

Donegal Manor B & B
117 Main St., Warrensburg, NY 12885
(518) 623-3549
Innkeeper: Dorothy Wright
Rooms: 5, incl. 3 w/pvt. bath, 2 w/TV, 1 w/fireplace. Suite, efficiency apt. avail.
Rates: $55-$95/room, $70-$80/suite, all incl. full brk., afternoon refreshment. Sea-
   sonal variations. Discount avail. for extended stay. Special pkgs. avail.
Credit cards: MC, V
Restrictions: No children under 6, pets. Smoking restricted. Deposit req. 10-day
   cancellation notice req., less $3.00 fee. 2-night min. stay on summer wknds. and
   on holidays.
Notes: Italianate/Victorian house built about 1820. Horse barn built in 1860 which
now serves as antique shop. Parlor with Italian marble fireplace. Dining room.
Porch. Decorated with antiques, Oriental carpets, family heirlooms. James Fenni-
more Cooper stayed here.*

The Merrill Magee House
2 Hudson St., Warrensburg, NY 12885
(518) 623-2449
Innkeeper: Ken and Florence Carrington
Rooms: 10 plus 1 suite, all w/pvt. bath, fireplace, incl. 1 w/TV. Located in 2 bldgs.
Rates: $95-$105/room, $150/suite, all incl. full brk. Special pkgs. avail.
Credit cards: Most major cards

Restrictions: Children welcome in suite only. No pets. Smoking restricted. Min. one night's deposit req. 7-day cancellation notice req. 2-night min. stay for summer and holiday wknds.
Notes: Greek Revival house built in 1839. Screened porches with wicker chairs. Tavern, dining room, each with fireplace. Swimming pool, gazebo in secluded garden. Furnished with antiques, lace, chintz, original wallpapers. Restaurant on premises. Listed on the National Register of Historic Places. Handicapped access.*

White House Lodge
53 Main St., Warrensburg, NY 12885
(518) 623-3640
Innkeeper: James and Ruth Gibson
Rooms: 3, no pvt. bath
Rates: $85, incl. cont. brk., afternoon refreshment
Credit cards: MC, V
Restrictions: No children under 8, pets. Smoking restricted. Deposit req. 10-day cancellation notice req.
Notes: Victorian carriage house built in 1847. Lounge with TV. Wrap-around porch with wicker rockers and chairs. Furnished with Victorian antiques.

WATERVILLE (1)

Bed and Breakfast of Waterville
211 White Street, Waterville, NY 13480
(315) 841-8295
Innkeeper: Carol and Stanley Sambora
Rooms: 3, incl. 1 w/pvt. bath
Rates: $35-$65, incl. full brk.
Credit cards: Most major cards
Restrictions: No pets, smoking. 50% deposit req. 14-day cancellation notice req.
Notes: Two-story Victorian house. Located in Historic Triangle District. Sally's quilts are displayed throughout the house.*

WATKINS GLEN (10)

Clarke House Bed & Breakfast
102 Durland Place, Watkins Glen, NY 14891
(607) 535-7965
Innkeeper: Jack and Carolyn Clarke
Rooms: 4, incl. 2 w/pvt. bath
Rates: $50-$65, incl. full brk., afternoon refreshment
Credit cards: MC, V
Restrictions: No children, pets, smoking. Deposit req. 24-hour cancellation notice req.
Notes: English Tudor house built approx. 1920. Formal dining room, living room with fireplace. Furnished with antiques.*

WESTFIELD (9)

William Seward Inn
S. Portage Rd., Rte 394, Westfield, NY 14787
(716) 326-4151, (710) 326-4163
Innkeeper: Jim and Debbie Dahlberg

Rooms: 14 w/pvt. bath, incl. 1 w/fireplace. Located in 2 bldgs.
Rates: $85-$145, incl. full brk.
Credit cards: None
Restrictions: No children under 10, pets, smoking. One night's deposit req. 3-day
    cancellation notice req., less $25.00 fee. 2-night min. stay on most wknds.
Notes: 2-story Greek Revival house built in 1821. Located on knoll overlooking
Lake Erie. 3 2-story Greek pillars and second story porch. Former residence of
William Seward, secretary of state to Abraham Lincoln. Library with fireplace over-
looking garden. Parlor. Furnished with period antiques. Four rooms with double
Jacuzzi. Antique shop on premises. Dinner available Thursday through Sunday.
Small private parties accommodated. Handicapped access.*

1880 HOUSE BED & BREAKFAST

WESTHAMPTON BEACH (13)

1880 House Bed & Breakfast
2 Seafield Lane, Box 648, Westhampton Beach, NY 11978
(516) 288-1559, (800) 346-3290

Innkeeper: Elsie Collins
Rooms: 3 suites w/pvt. bath, cable TV. Located in 2 bldgs.
Rates: $100-$200, incl. full brk., afternoon refreshment. Seasonal variations.
Credit cards: Most major cards
Restrictions: No pets, smoking. One night's deposit req., credit for future stay upon
    cancellation. 2-night min. stay, June–Aug.
Notes: Two-story house built in 1880. Located within walking distance of the beach.
Parlor with fireplace. Victorian lounge with caned rocker, piano. Furnished in
eclectic style with antiques, Shaker benches. Swimming pool, tennis court.

WESTPORT (2)

Inn on the Library Lawn
1 Washington St., Westport, NY 12993
(518) 962-8666

Innkeeper: Ron & Elizabeth Van Nostrand

Rooms: 10 w/pvt. bath, incl. 9 w/TV
Rates: $65-$95, incl. full brk., afternoon refreshment. Discount avail. for senior citizen and extended stays
Credit cards: Most major cards
Restrictions: No pets, smoking. Deposit req. 2-week cancellation notice req.
Notes: Restored Victorian built in the 1875 overlooking Lake Champlain. Entry with columned portico. Guest rooms furnished with period antiques, some with lake view. Fireplaced lounge, library and common area with library and games. Dining room. Antiques and Artists Galleries on premises. Lunch available. Off-season dinner available.*

INN ON THE LIBRARY LAWN

WILLET (6)

Woven Waters
HC 73, Box 193 E, Willet, NY 13863-9707
(607) 656-8672
Innkeeper: Erika and John Kuryla
Rooms: 4, no pvt. bath
Rates: $50-$58, incl. full brk. Discount avail. for extended stay.
Credit cards: Most major cards
Restrictions: No children under 10, pets. Smoking restricted. 50% deposit req., Deposit refunded, less $10.00 fee, upon cancellation only if room re-rented.
Notes: Two-story barn. Dining room, glass-enclosed porch, open porch. Furnished with antiques. German spoken.

WILMINGTON (2)

The Inn at Whiteface Mountain
HCR-33, Rte. 86, Wilmington, NY 12997-9707
(518) 946-2232
Innkeeper: The Tsouros Family
Rooms: 14 w/pvt. bath, cable TV
Rates: $45-$95, incl. full brk., dinner. Seasonal variations. Special pkgs. avail.
Credit cards: Most major cards
Restrictions: Deposit req. 24-hour cancellation notice req.

Notes: Colonial Old World-style Inn with European Atmosphere, built in 1926 as farmhouse. Recently expanded. Decorated in European decor. Lounge with full bar and fireplace. Serving homecooked meals in dining room. Handicapped access. German spoken.*

North Carolina

The Doctor's Inn
716 S. Park St., Asheboro, NC 27203
(910) 625-4916
Innkeeper: Marion and Beth Griffin
Rooms: 1, no pvt. bath, plus 1 suite w/pvt. bath, all w/phone, TV
Rates: $50-$75, incl. full brk. afternoon refreshement
Credit cards: None
Restrictions: No children under 5, pets.
Notes: Two-story Dutch Colonial house. Decorated with antiques. Summer and winter porches.

ASHEVILLE (1)

Abbington Green B & B
46 Cumberland Cir., Asheville, NC 28801
(704) 251-2454, (704) 251-2872
Innkeeper: Valerie Larrea
Rooms: 5 plus 1 suite, all w/pvt. bath
Rates: $90-$110/room, $120/suite, all incl. full brk. Discount avail. for extended stay.
Credit cards: Most major cards
Restrictions: No children under 10, pets, smoking. One night's deposit req., 3-day cancellation notice req., less $15.00 fee in Oct. and Dec., 2-night min. stay on most wknds.
Notes: Three-story Colonial Revival-style house built about 1908. Fully restored in 1993 with an English flavor. Furnished in an eclectic style. Front porch (40 feet), rear porch, deck, second floor veranda have rocking chairs, porch swings and glidres. Third floor balcony balustrade is Chinese Chippendale design. Parlor games, audio and VCR tapes, reading material and piano available. Guests may use bicycles.

ABBINGTON GREEN B & B

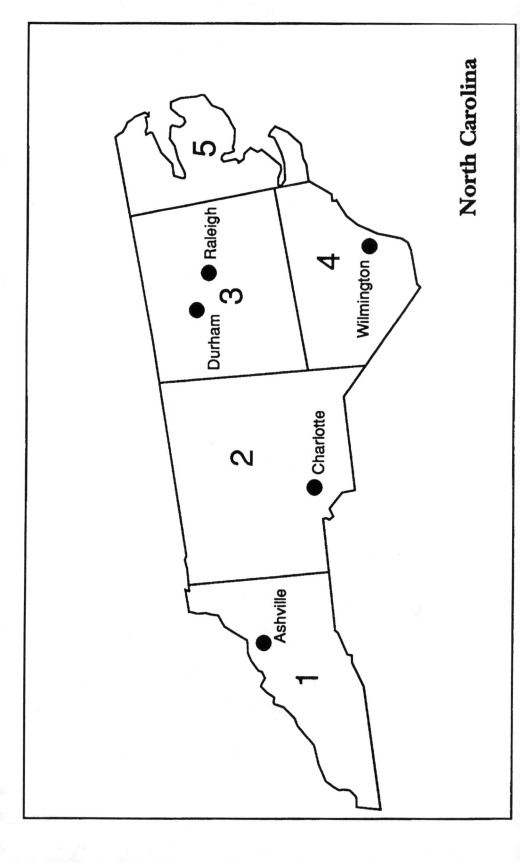

North Carolina

Albemarle Inn
86 Edgemont Rd., Asheville, NC 28801
(704) 255-0027

Innkeeper: Kathy and Dick Hemes
Rooms: 10 plus 1 suite, all w/pvt. bath, phone, TV, clawfoot tubs
Rates: $75-$130/room, $130/suite, all incl. full brk., evening refreshment. Discount avail. for mid-week stay.
Credit cards: Most major cards
Restrictions: No children under 13, pets. Smoking restricted. Deposit req. 7-day cancellation notice req. 2-night min. stay on wknds. from April–New Year's Day.
Notes: Greek Revival mansion with high ceilings, oak paneling, carved oak stairway with circular landing and balcony built in 1909. Dining room, sunporch, two living rooms. Bela Bartok wrote his third concert while living here. Listed in the National Register of Historic Places.*

Applewood Manor
62 Cumberland Circle, Asheville, NC 28801-1718
(704) 254-2244

Innkeeper: Maryanne Young, Susan Poole
Rooms: 3 plus 1 suite, 1 cottage, all w/pvt. bath, incl. 4 w/TV. Located in 2 bldgs.
Rates: $85-$95/room, $105/suite, $115/cottage, all incl. full brk., afternoon refreshment.
Credit cards: MC, V
Restrictions: No children under 12, pets, smoking. No deposit req. 3-day cancellation notice req. 2-night min. stay on wknds. & Oct. 3-night min. stay on holiday wknds.
Notes: Colonial Revival manor located on two acres. Parlor, library. 6 porches/balconies. Croquet, badminton, bicycles available.

BEAUFORT HOUSE VICTORIAN B & B

Beaufort House Victorian B & B
61 N. Liberty St., Asheville, NC 28801-1829
(704) 254-8334, (704) 251-2082

Innkeeper: Robert and Jacqueline Glasgow
Rooms: 7 plus 1 suite, all w/pvt. bath, phone, TV, incl. 2 w/fireplace

Rates: $85-$150/room, $195/suite, all full brk., afternoon refreshment. Seasonal variations
Credit cards: MC, V
Restrictions: No smoking. 50% deposit req., Min. 48-hour cancellation notice req. 2-night min. stay on wknds. May–Dec.
Notes: 3-story Queen Anne style house built in 1894. Wood interior, porch, gardens. Listed on the National Register of Historic Places. Handicapped access.

Black Walnut Inn
288 Montford Ave., Asheville, NC 28801
(704) 254-3878

Innkeeper: Jeanette Syprzak
Rooms: 4, incl. 2 w/pvt. bath, 3 w/fireplace, plus 2 suites w/pvt. bath, incl. 1 w/fireplace
Rates: $80-$110/room, $90-$130/suite, all incl. full brk., afternoon refreshment. Discount avail. for mid-week stay. Seasonal variations.
Credit cards: Most major cards
Restrictions: No pets. Smoking restricted. Deposit req. 7-day cancellation notice req., less $10.00 fee.
Notes: Two-story shingle-style house built in 1899. Restored in 1992. Foyer with fireplace, dining room, living room, sitting room. Decorated with antiques and traditional furnishings. VCR/movies available. Awarded the 1994 Griffin Preservation Award. Private parking.

Blake House Inn and Restaurant
150 Royal Pines Dr., Asheville, NC 28704
(704) 684-1847

Innkeeper: Bob, Eloise, and Pati Roesler
Rooms: 5 w/pvt. bath, TV, incl. 2 w/fireplace
Rates: $70-$90, incl. full brk., evening refreshment. Seasonal variations. Discount avail. for extended stay.
Credit cards: Most major cards
Restrictions: No children under 12, pets, smoking. Deposit req., 3-day cancellation notice req., less 10% fee, 2-night min. stay on wknds. and holidays.
Notes: Two-story Gothic mansion built in 1847. Two dining rooms, one with fireplace. Wrap-around porch with wicker furniture. Decorated with antiques, family heirlooms. The house served as a field hospital for Confederate armies.

Cairn Brae
217 Patton Mtn. Rd., Asheville, NC 28804
(704) 252-9219

Innkeeper: Milli and Ed Adams
Rooms: 3 plus 1 suite, all w/pvt. bath
Rates: $85-$100/room, $130/suite, all incl. full brk., afternoon and evening refreshment. Discount available for senior citizens.
Credit cards: MC, V
Restrictions: No children under 10, pets, smoking. One night's deposit req. 3-day cancellation notice req. 2-night min. stay on wknds. and holidays.
Notes: The name of the Inn is Scottish for "Rocky Hillside." Located on four wooded acres. All rooms have large picture windows. Dining room, living room with fireplace, cable TV, game table. Terrace, hammock, walking trails through wooded acreage. Spanish spoken.*

Carolina Bed & Breakfast
177 Cumberland Ave., Asheville, NC 28801
(704) 254-3608
Innkeeper: Sam and Karen Fain
Rooms: 5 w/pvt. bath, incl. 4 w/fireplace
Rates: $75-$85 incl. full brk., afternoon refreshment
Credit cards: Most major cards
Restrictions: No children under 12, pets, smoking. One night's deposit req. 72-hour
 cancellation notice req. 2-night min. stay on wknds. in season.
Notes: Two-story Colonial Revival house built at the turn-of-the-century. Fully re-
stored. Located on one wooded acre with gardens. Sitting room, parlor, each with
fireplace. Furnished with antiques and collectables. Two porches, deck.*

Cedar Crest Victorian Inn
674 Biltmore Ave., Asheville, NC 28803
(704) 252-1389, (704) 252-1806
Innkeeper: Jack and Barbara McEwan
Rooms: 8 plus 3 suites, all w/pvt. bath, phone, incl. 5 w/fireplace, 2 w/TV. Located
 in 2 bldgs.
Rates: $110-$140/room, $115-$185/suite, all incl. full brk., evening refreshment.
 Seasonal variations. Special pkgs. avail.
Credit cards: Most major cards
Restrictions: No children under 10, pets, smoking. One night's deposit req. 7-day
 cancellation notice req., less $10.00 fee. 2-night min. stay on some wknds. and
 holidays.
Notes: Three-story Victorian style inn built in 1891. Located on 4 acres. Dining
room. Parlor with fireplace. Furnished with period antiques. Victorian garden. Ve-
randa. Lawn games available. Listed on the National Register of Historic Places.

Colby House
230 Pearson Dr., Asheville, NC 28801
(704) 253-5644, (800) 982-2118, (704) 259-9479
Innkeeper: Everett and Ann Colby
Rooms: 4, incl. 1 w/fireplace, all w/pvt. bath, phone
Rates: $80-$110, incl. full brk. evening refreshment.
Credit cards: Most major cards
Restrictions: No children, pets. Smoking restricted. 3-day cancellation notice req.
Notes: Located in Historic District. Flower gardens. Porch with rocking chairs.

Corner Oak Manor
53 St. Dunstans Rd., Asheville, NC 28803
(704) 253-3525
Innkeeper: Karen and Andy Spradley
Rooms: 3 rooms, 1 suite, all w/pvt. bath. Located in 2 bldgs.
Rates: $85-$90/room, $100/suite, all incl. full brk.
Credit cards: Most major cards
Restrictions: No smoking, pets. Children restricted. One night's deposit req. 72-
 hour cancellation notice required. 2-night min. stay on wknds., April–Dec.
Notes: Two-story English Tudor Revival built in 1924. Renovated. Living room with
fireplace, baby grand piano. Dining room. Patio. Furnished with antiques and local
crafts. Resident cat.*

Dogwood Cottage
40 Canterbury Rd., Asheville, NC 28801-1535
(704) 258-9725

Innkeeper: Joan and Don Tracy
Rooms: 4 w/pvt. bath, fireplace
Rates: $90-$95, incl. full brk. Special pkgs. avail.
Credit cards: Most major cards
Restrictions: Smoking restricted. Deposit req. 7-day cancellation notice req. 2-night min. stay.
Notes: Built in 1910. Old fashioned country porch. Living room with fireplace. English library/den with TV, games, books, fireplace. Dining room. Veranda decorated with white wicker and chintz prints. Furnished with period pieces, chintz fabrics, and whimsical accessories. French doors in dining room and living room. Poolside patio. Handicapped access.*

Flint Street Inns
100 & 116 Flint St., Asheville, NC 28801
(704) 253-6723

Innkeeper: Rick, Lynne and Marion Vogel
Rooms: 8 w/pvt. bath, incl. 3 w/fireplace. Located in 2 bldgs.
Rates: $85, incl. full brk., afternoon refreshment.
Credit cards: Most major cards
Restrictions: No children under 14, pets. Smoking restricted. One night's deposit req. 24-hr. cancellation notice req. 2-night min. stay on some wknds.
Notes: Built about 1915. Located on one wooded acre with flower gardens in Montford Historic District. Front parlor, living room. Dining room with fireplace. Deck, front porch with sofa, chairs. Second house is three-story Tudor-style wood and stucco house built in the 1920s. Furnished in turn-of-the-century style.*

Inn on Montford
296 Montford Ave., Asheville, NC 28801-1660
(704) 254-9569, (704) 254-9518

Innkeeper: Ripley Hotch, Owen Sullivan
Rooms: 3 w/pvt. bath, fireplace, incl. 1 w/pvt. bath, fireplace, TV
Rates: $90-$130, incl. full brk., afternoon refreshment. Seasonal variations.
Credit cards: Most major cards
Restrictions: No children under 2, pets, smoking. One night's deposit req. 4-day cancellation notice req. Deposit refunded if room can be re-rented. 2-night min. stay on wknds. from Apr.–Dec.
Notes: Two-story inn built in 1900. Three common rooms with fireplaces. Garden room. English and American antiques and artwork. Resident pets.*

The Old Reynolds Mansion
100 Reynolds Heights, Asheville, NC 28804
(704) 254-0496

Innkeeper: Fred and Helen Faber
Rooms: 10, incl. 8 w/pvt. bath, 4 w/fireplace, plus 1 suite w/pvt. bath, fireplace, TV
Rates: $50-$90/room, $125/suite, incl. cont. brk., afternoon refreshment.
Credit cards: None
Restrictions: No children under 12, pets. One night's deposit req. 7-day cancellation notice req. 14-day cancellation req. 2-night min. stay on wknds., holidays.

Notes: Three-story brick antebellum mansion built in 1855. Located on four wooded acres overlooking mountains. Renovations begun in 1981. Has operated as inn since 1983. Front parlor with handcarved staircase, fireplace, board games, library. Dining room. Furnished with antiques. Wrap-around verandas on two levels. Swimming pool. Poolside suite w/kitchen, living room, and balcony. Listed on the National Register of Historic Places.

Reed House
119 Dodge St., Asheville, NC 28803
(704) 274-1604
Innkeeper: Marge Turcot
Rooms: 3, no pvt. bath, plus cottage w/pvt. bath, TV. Suite avail.
Rates: $50/room, $70/suite, $95/cottage, all incl. cont. brk.
Credit cards: MC, V
Restrictions: No pets. One night's deposit req. 72-hr cancel not. Closed Nov. 1–May 1.
Notes: Two-story Queen Anne Victorian house with tower built in 1892. Located on 1.5 acres on hill above Biltmore Village. Library with pool table. Upstairs sitting room with TV. Upstairs hall with board games. Formal parlor with piano. Dining room with TV. Wrap-around porch with swings, rockers. Upstairs porch. Furnished with Victorian antiques. Listed in the National Register of Historic Places.

Richmond Hill Inn
87 Richmond Hill Dr., Asheville, NC 28806
(704) 252-7313, (704) 252-8726
Innkeeper: Susan Michel
Rooms: 33 plus 3 suites, all w/pvt. bath, phone, TV, incl. 28 w/fireplace. Located in 3 bldgs.
Restrictions: $130-$235/room, $200-$325/suite, all incl. full brk.
Credit cards: Most major cards
Restrictions: No pets. Smoking restricted. 50% deposit req. 3-day cancellation notice req. 2-night min. stay on wknds.
Notes: Three-story Victorian mansion built in 1889. Formal dining room. Library with fireplace. Portrait of Gabriell Pearson hangs over mantel. Decorated with Victorian furniture, Oriental rugs. Glass-enclosed sun porch. Croquet court. Restaurant on premises. Small private parties accommodated. Handicapped access. Listed on the National Register of Historic Places.*

BALSAM (1)

Balsam Mountain Inn
P.O. Box 40, Balsam, NC 28707
(704) 456-9498, (705) 456-9298
Innkeeper: Bill Graham and Merrily Teasley
Rooms: 31, incl. 7 bedsitting rooms, plus 3 suites, all w/pvt. bath
Rates: $80-$85/room, $90-$100/bedsitting, $115-$130/suite, all incl. full brk. Discount avail for senior citizen and extended stays. Seasonal variations.
Credit cards: MC, V
Restrictions: No children under 12, pets. Smoking restricted.
Notes: Three-story inn built in 1908. Restored in 1991. Two one-hundred-foot porches with rockers and mountain view. Library with two-thousand volumes.

Furnished in period style. Listed in the National Register of Historic Places. Handicapped access. French spoken.*

Hickory Haven
P.O. Box 88, Balsam, NC 28707
(704) 452-1106, (800) 684-2836
Innkeeper: Connie Nicholson
Rooms: 3, plus 2 suites, all w/pvt. bath, phone, fireplace, TV
Rates: $95/room, $105/suite, all incl. full brk., afternoon refreshment. Seasonal variations. Discount avail. for extended stay.
Credit cards: MC, V
Restrictions: No children under 12, pets, smoking. One night's deposit req. 7-day cancellation notice req. 2-night min. stay on wknds.
Notes: Three-story inn. Located at 3800-ft. elevation. Great room with fireplace, main dining, sitting and guest kitchen area. Library. Giftshop on premises with works by local artists and crafters. Wrap-around veranda with rocking chairs. Decorated in country Victorian style. Furnished with antiques and collectibles. Small private parties accommodated.

BANNER ELK (1)

Archers Inn
Route 2, Box 56A, Banner Elk, NC 28604
(704) 898-9004
Innkeeper: Toni and Bill Coleman
Rooms: 14 w/pvt. bath, fireplace, incl. 10 w/TV. Located in 2 bldgs.
Rates: $65-$125, incl full brk. Discount avail. for mid-week stay. Seasonal variations.
Credit cards: MC, V
Restrictions: No pets, smoking. 50% deposit req. 2-week cancellation notice req. 2-night min. stay on wknds.
Notes: Lodge built in 1974. Post and beam Annex built in 1984. Located on three acres on Beech Mountain. Living room with fieldstone fireplace, cable TV. Dining room. Decks overlooking Elk River Valley. Roof garden. Restaurant on premises. Outdoor activities available. Small private parties accommodated. German and some Spanish spoken.*

BEAUFORT (5)

Delamar Inn
217 Turner St., Beaufort, NC 28516
(919) 728-4300
Innkeeper: Mabel and Tom Steepy
Rooms: 3 w/pvt. bath
Rates: $58-$88, incl. cont. brk. Discount avail. for extended stay. Seasonal variations.
Credit cards: MC, V
Restrictions: No children under 10, pets. Smoking restricted. 2-day cancellation notice req.
Notes: Two story Greek revival inn built in 1866. Completely restored. Upper and lower porches. Common room with books, TV. Living room with CD player, fireplace. Furnished with antiques. Bicycles and beach chairs available.

Langdon House B & B
135 Craven St., Beaufort, NC 28516
(919) 728-5499

Innkeeper: Jimm Prest
Rooms: 4 w/pvt. bath
Rates: $75-$120, incl. full brk, afternoon refreshment. Seasonal variations. Discount
avail. for extended stay.
Credit cards: None
Restrictions: No children under 12, pets. Smoking restricted. Full prepayment req.
14-day cancellation notice req, less $25.00 fee. 2-night min. stay on wknds.
Notes: Three-story house built in 1733 with additions made in 1790, 1870, 1920,
and 1950. Fully restored. Two-story double-deck porches. Original heart pine flooring. Parlor with 19th-century Estes pump organ, fireplace. Antique furnishings. Bicycles, beach towels, fishing rods, ice chests provided.

PECAN TREE INN

Pecan Tree Inn
116 Queen St., Beaufort, NC 28516
(919) 728-6733

Innkeeper: Susan and Joseph Johnson
Rooms: 6 w/pvt. bath, plus 1 suite w/pvt. bath, Jacuzzi
Rates: $65-$85/room, $95-$100/suite, all incl. cont. brk., afternoon refreshment.
Seasonal variations. Discount avail. for extended stay.
Credit cards: MC, V
Restrictions: No children under 12, pets. Smoking restricted. One night's deposit
req. 10-day cancellation notice req.
Notes: Two-story inn built in 1866. Victorian porches, turrets, gingerbread trim.
Dining room, front porch. Parlor, study. Library with reading material, board
games, refrigerator with complimentary beverages, candy. English flower and herb
garden. Bikes, beach chairs, towels, box lunches available.*

BLOWING ROCK (1)

Maple Lodge Bed & Breakfast
Sunset Dr., Box 1236, Blowing Rock, NC 28605
(704) 295-3331

Innkeeper: David and Marilyn Bateman

Rooms: 8 plus 2 suites and cottage, all w/pvt. bath
Rates: $75-$105/room, $120-$140/suite, all incl. full brk. Discount avail. for midweek and extended stays. Seasonal variations.
Credit cards: Most major cards
Restrictions: No children under 12, po pets, smoking. One night's deposit req. 72-hour cancellation notice req. 2-night min. stay on wknds. Closed Mar.
Notes: Old-fashioned house built in 1946, remodeled in 1979. Two parlors, one with stone fireplace, one with piano and old-time pump organ. Cable TV in Wicker Room. Sun porch and garden. Furnished with antiques, quilts, and down comforters.*

BOONE (1)

Grandma Jean's B & B
254 Meadowview Dr., Boone, NC 28607
(704) 262-3670

Innkeeper: Dr. Jean Probinsky
Rooms: 3 w/pvt. bath, plus 1 suite w/semi pvt. bath
Rates: $50/room, $60/suite, all incl. cont. brk. Seasonal variations.
Credit cards: Most major cards
Restrictions: No pets. Deposit req. 7-day cancellation notice req., less $15.00 fee. 2-night min. stay.
Notes: Spanish spoken.*

BREVARD (1)

The Inn at Brevard
410 E. Main St., Brevard, NC 28712
(704) 884-2105

Innkeeper: Bertrand and Eileen Bourget
Rooms: 14 plus 1 suite, incl. 13 w/pvt. bath, phone. Located in 2 bldgs.
Rates: $59-$79/room, $125/suite, all incl. full brk.
Credit cards: MC, V
Restrictions: No pets. Smoking restricted. One night's deposit req. 3-day cancellation notice req. 2-night min. stay on summer wknds. Closed Jan.–Feb.
Notes: European-style southern mansion, Greek revival architecture, built in 1885. Two parlors, foyer with fireplace. Porch, veranda. Furnished with period antiques. Dinners, brunch available. Small private parties accommodated. Listed on the National Register of Historic Places.

Womble Inn
301 W. Main St., Brevard, NC 28712
(704) 884-4770

Innkeeper: Steve and Beth Womble
Rooms: 5, plus 1 suite, all w/pvt. bath
Rates: $40-$58, incl. cont. brk. Discount avail. for extended stay.
Credit cards: MC, V
Restrictions: No pets, smoking. One night's deposit req. 48-hour cancellation notice req. 2-night min. stay on summer wknds.
Notes: Two-story New Orleans-style house. Dining room. Parlor with TV, fireplace, board games, music center. Furnished with 18th- and 19th-century antiques. Upstairs and downstairs porches. Christmas giftshop on premises. Small private parties accommodated.

BRYSON CITY (7)

Fryemont Inn
P.O. Box 459, Bryson City, NC 28713
(800) 845-4879

Innkeeper: Sue and George Brown, and George and Monica Brown
Rooms: 37 w/pvt. bath, plus 3 suites w/pvt. bath, TV, fireplace. Located in 2 bldgs.
Rates: $84-$114/room, $129-$165/suite, all incl. full brk, dinner. Seasonal variations.
Credit cards: Most major cards
Restrictions: No pets. Smoking restricted. Min. $100 deposit req. 2-week cancellation notice req. 2-night min. stay on wknds.
Notes: Two-story oak and chestnut main lodge built in 1923. Stone cottage renovated in 1989. Has operated as inn since 1923. Lobby with cable TV, board games, stone fireplace. Porch with rockers overlooking Great Smoky Mountains National Park. Conference room. 37 chestnut paneled rooms and 3 suites in the cottage adjacent to the inn. Olympic-sized swimming pool. Restaurant, full service bar on premises. Listed on the National Register of Historic Places. Small private parties accommodated.

Peggy's Mountain Laurel
3324 Hwy. 28 S., Bryson City, NC 28713
(704) 488-2055

Innkeeper: Peggy and Robert Eckley
Rooms: 6, no pvt. bath
Rates: $55, incl. full brk., afternoon refreshment
Credit cards: MC, V
Restrictions: No pets, smoking. Deposit req. Cancellation notice req., less $10.00 fee.
Notes: Two-story, 7,000 square-foot house. Located atop mountain overlooking Smokey Mountains. Great room with fireplace, sunroom.

RANDOLPH HOUSE INN

Randolph House Inn
223 Fryemont Rd., Box 816, Bryson City, NC 28713
(704) 488-3472

Innkeeper: Bill and Ruth Randolph Adams
Rooms: 5, incl. 3 w/pvt. bath, 1 w/fireplace, 1 w/TV, plus 2 suites
Rates: $100-$120, incl. full brk., dinner. Discount avail. for senior citizen, AAA stays. Seasonal variations.
Credit cards: Most major cards
Restrictions: No pets. Smoking restricted. Min one night's deposit req. 7-day cancellation notice req. 2-night min. stay in Oct. and holiday wknds. Closed Nov. 1–March 31.
Notes: Two-story mansion with twelve gables built in 1895. Has operated as inn since 1980. Located on mountain shelf overlooking Bryson City. Furnished with period antiques. Parlor with fireplace. Granite pillared front porch with rockers. Dinner available. Listed on the National Register of Historic Places. Limited handicapped access. *

BURNSVILLE (1)

A Little Bit of Heaven B & B
937 Bear Wallow Rd., Burnsville, NC 28714-6539
(704) 675-5379

Innkeeper: John and Shelley Johnson
Rooms: 4 w/pvt. bath
Rates: $55-$65, incl. full brk. Discount avail. for extended stay.
Credit cards: None
Restrictions: No pets, smoking. Deposit req., 7-day cancellation notice req. Min. stay req. for some holidays and craft festival.
Notes: Located at 3,000 foot elevation overlooking Celo Knob. Stone vestibule, gathering room, dining room. Picnic baskets available.

Estes Mountain Inn
Rte. 1, Box 1316-A, Burnsville, NC 28714
(704) 682-7263

Innkeeper: Bruce and Maryallen Estes
Rooms: 1 plus 1 suite, all w/pvt. bath, phone, TV
Rates: $55-$60, incl full brk., evening dessert. Discount avail. for senior citizen and extended stays. Children under 7 free.
Credit cards: None
Restrictions: No children under 3, pets. Smoking restricted. One night's deposit req. 10-day cancellation notice req.
Notes: Two-story white cedar log house built in side of mountain in 1988. Located in heavily wooded, high-altitude Blue Ridge Mountain with stream. Limited French and Spanish spoken.

Nu-Wray Inn
Town Square, Box 156, Burnsville, NC 28714
(704) 682-2329, (800) 368-9729

Innkeeper: Chris and Pam Strickland
Rooms: 26 w/pvt. bath, TV
Rates: $70-$110, incl. full brk., afternoon refreshment
Credit cards: Most major cards
Restrictions: No pets, smoking. Min. one night's deposit req. 48-hour cancellation notice req. 2-night min. stay in Oct. and holidays.

Notes: Three story Colonial Revival country inn buillt in 1833. Has been operated by same family for 4 generations. Family-style dinners available. Handicapped access.*

CANDLER (1)

Owl's Nest Inn at Engadine
2630 Smokey Park Hwy., Candler, NC 28715
(704) 665-8325, (800) 665-8868, (704) 667-2539
Innkeeper: Jim and Mary Melaugh
Rooms: 4 w/pvt. bath
Rates: $90-$120, incl. full brk., afternoon refreshment. Discount avail. for extended
    stay.
Credit cards: MC, V
Restrictions: No pets. Smoking restricted. One night's deposit req. 7-day cancellation notice req.
Notes: Two-story Queen Anne Victorian inn built with heart of pine panelling in 1885. Fully restored. Located on over 4 acres. Formal dining room with fireplace. Living room with gas fireplace, TV. Den with piano, board games, library. Wraparound porches, patio. Innkeeper collects owls from around the world. Listed on the National Register of Historic Places.

CAPE CARTERET (5)

Harborlight Guest House
332 Live Oak Dr., Cape Carteret, NC 28584
(919) 393-6868, (800) 624-2439
Innkeeper: Anita and Bobby Gill
Rooms: 2 w/pvt. bath, TV, plus 5 suites w/pvt. bath, fireplace, TV
Rates: $75-$90/room, $110-$155/suite, all incl. full brk. Seasonal variations. Discount avail. for extended stay.
Credit cards: Most major cards
Restrictions: No children under 16, pets, smoking. One night's deposit req. 48-hour cancellation notice req. 2-night min. stay on wknds.
Notes: Three-story inn with elevator. 530 ft. of shoreline available. Dining room, conference room, terrace, private balconies. Small private parties accommodated. Partial handicapped access.

CHARLOTTE (2)

The Inn Uptown
129 N. Poplar St., Charlotte, NC 28202
(704) 342-2800, (800) 959-1990, (704) 342-2222
Innkeeper: Elizabeth J. Rich
Rooms: 6 w/pvt. bath, phone, fireplace, TV
Rates: $89-$149, incl. full brk., evening refreshment. Discount avail. for mid-week, senior, and extended stays. Special pkgs. avail.
Credit cards: Most major cards
Restrictions: No children under 7, pets. Smoking restricted. 50% deposit req., 5-day cancellation notice req. Min. stay for special events.
Notes: Three-story Chateauesque style brick house built in 1890. Fully restored. Small private parties accommodated. Copier, fax machine modem, custom gift

baskets, whirlpool available with prior arrangement. Located within walking distance of the NFL stadium.*

The Morehead
1122 E. Morehead St., Charlotte, NC 28204
(704) 376-3357, (704) 335-1110
Innkeeper: Bill Armstrong, Mgr.
Rooms: 8, plus 4 suites, incl. 1 w/fireplace, all w/pvt. bath, phone, cable TV. Located in 2 bldgs.
Rates: $89/room, $95-$115/suite, $175/apt, all incl. cont. brk. Discount avail. for senior citizen, AAA and extended stays.
Credit cards: Most major cards
Restrictions: No pets. Smoking restriacted. Deposit req. 2-day cancellation notice req.
Notes: Main House and gardens built in 1917. Carriage House built in 1920. Columned veranda built in 1980. Furnished with antiques. Great room with TV. Dining room, library. Fax and copy service available. Off-street parking available. French/Spanish spoken. Guests have access to YMCA.Inn certified by the N.C. Division of Archives and History in 1992. Listed on National Registry of Historic Places.*

Still Waters
6221 Amos Smith Rd., Charlotte, NC 28214-8955
(704) 399-6299
Innkeeper: Janet and Rob Dyer
Rooms: 3, incl. 2 w/pvt. bath, plus 1 suite w/pvt bath TV
Rates: $65-$75/room, $75-$85/suite, all incl. full brk. Seasonal variations. Discount avail. for extended stay.
Credit cards: Most major cards
Restrictions: No pets. Smoking restricted. One night's deposit req. 72-hour cancellation notice req. 2-night min. stay on wknds.
Notes: Log lakefront resort house built 1929. Great room with stone fireplace. Glassed-in porch. Dock, gazebo, boat ramp, swim ladder. Short court tennis, volleyball, basketball.*

CLYDE (1)

Windsong, A Mountain Inn
120 Ferguson Ridge, Clyde, NC 28721
(704) 627-6111, (704) 627-8080
Innkeeper: Gale and Donna Livengood
Rooms: 5 w/pvt. bath, phone, incl. 4 w/fireplace, VCR, deck or patio, plus 1 guesthouse w/pvt. bath, phone, fireplace, VCR. Located in 2 bldgs.
Rates: $85-$95/room, $120-$140/guesthouse, all incl. full brk. Discount avail. for extended stay.
Credit cards: MC, V
Restrictions: No children under 8, pets, smoking. Deposit req. 72-hour cancellation notice. 2-night min. stay in guesthouse.
Notes: Contemporary log inn. High beamed ceilings and Mexican tile floors. Lounge with wet/bar, small refrigerator, billiard table, videocassette library. Separate 2-bedroom guesthouse. Hiking trail, llama farm. Swimming pool in summer. Tennis court.*

DILLSBORO (1)

Applegate Inn
163 Hemlock St., Box 567, Dillsboro, NC 28725
(704) 586-2397
Innkeeper: Emil and Judy Milkey
Rooms: 4 plus 2 suites all w/pvt. bath, incl. 2 suites w/TV. Located in 2 bldgs.
Rates: $65/room, $75/suite, all incl. full brk. Seasonal variations. Discount avail. for senior citizen and extended stays.
Credit cards: MC, V
Restrictions: No pets, smoking. Deposit req. 14-day cancellation notice req.
Notes: Country style Inn situated on Scott's Creek in Dillsboro. Living room with fireplace, TV, piano overlooking creek. Limited handicapped access.

DURHAM (3)

The Blooming Garden Inn
513 Holloway St., Durham, NC 27701
(919) 687-0801
Innkeeper: Frank and Dolly Pokrass
Rooms: 3 plus 2 suites w/Jacuzzi, all w/pvt. bath
Rates: $75-$95/room, $135-$150/suite, all incl. full brk. Discount avail. for extended stay.
Credit cards: Most major cards
Restrictions: 25% deposit req. Min. 14-day cancellation notice req. 2-night min. stay for special events.
Notes: Two-story, six star-burst-gabled Victorian house with twenty Tuscan columns on wrap-around porch. Built in 1890. Has operated as inn since 1990. Decorated with fabrics, art and artifacts from innkeepers' world travels and antiques. Garden with picket fence. German spoken.*

Old North Durham Inn
922 N. Mangum St., Durham, NC 27701
(919) 683-1885
Innkeeper: Debbie and Jim Vickery
Rooms: 3 rooms w/pvt. bath, incl. 2 w/fireplace, 1 w/TV, plus 1 suite w/pvt. bath, fireplace, TV
Rates: $70-$85/room, $120/suite, all incl. full brk., afternoon refreshment, tickets to Durham Bulls' baseball games. Discount avail. for extended stay.
Credit cards: MC, V
Restrictions: No pets, smoking. Deposit req. 48-hour cancellation notice req.
Notes: 3-story Colonial Revival house built in 1900. Fully restored. Guest rooms with coffered ceilings, ceiling fans, period wall-coverings and furnishings, oak and pine floors. Sitting area with reference library. Wrap-around porch with rockers. Parlor with piano, fireplace, TV, VCR, music center.*

EDENTON (5)

Captain's Quarters Inn
202 W. Queen St., Edenton, NC 27932
(919) 482-8945
Innkeeper: William and Phyllis Pepper
Rooms: 6, plus 2 suites, all w/pvt. bath, phone, TV

Rates: $75/room, $85/suite, all incl. full brk., afternoon and evening refreshment. Discount avail. for mid-week stay. Special pkgs. avail.

Credit cards: MC, V

Restrictions: No children under 8, pets. Smoking restricted. Min. $50.00 deposit req. Min. 3-day cancellation notice req. 2-night min. stay on holiday wknds.

Notes: Colonial Revival-style inn built in 1907. Fully renovated in 1993. Living room with TV, VCR, books. Center hall, reception room. Wrap-around porch with rockers, chairs, tables and swings overlooking gardens. Decorated with nautical paintings and prints. Board games, bicycles available. Mystery week-ends and sailing excursions on 34-ft. sloop organized. Kennel arrangements available. Handicapped access.

The Lords Proprietors' Inn
300 N. Broad St., Edenton, NC 27932
(919) 482-3641, (919) 482-2432

Innkeeper: Arch and Jane Edwards

Rooms: 20 w/pvt. bath, phone. Located in 3 bldgs.

Rates: $140-$180, incl. full brk.

Credit cards: None

Restrictions: Smoking, pets restricted. $50.00 deposit req. 2-day cancellation notice req. Closed Dec. 24, 25.

Notes: Three restored houses located on over an acre of grounds. Four parlors, each with fireplace. Dining room, brick patio, front porch with rockers. Small private parties accommodated. Handicapped access.*

ELIZABETH CITY (5)

Culpepper Inn
609 W. Main St., Elizabeth City, NC 27909
(919) 335-1993

Innkeeper: Judy Smith and Henry Brinkman

Rooms: 10 plus 1 suite, all w/pvt. bath, incl. 4 w/fireplace, 7 w/hookups for TVs to loan. Located in 2 bldgs.

Rates: $85-$95/room, $95-$105/suite, all incl. full brk. Discount avail. for military, AAA, and mid-week stays.

Credit cards: Most major cards

Restrictions: No children under 12, pets. Smoking restricted. Deposit req. 5-day cancellation notice req.

Notes: Three-story Colonial Revival-style house built in 1935. Some rooms with garden tubs for two. Roman swimming pool. Goldfish pond. Small private parties accommodated. Handicapped access. Some German spoken.

Elizabeth City B & B
108 E. Fearing St., Elizabeth City, NC 27909
(919) 338-2177

Innkeeper: Darla and Joseph Semonich

Rooms: 3 plus 1 suite, all w/pvt. bath, phone, TV. Located in 2 bldgs.

Rates: $55-$70/room, $75/suite, all incl. full brk., dinner by reservation.

Credit cards: None

Restrictions: No children under 6, pets, smoking. Deposit req. 2-day cancellation notice req.

Notes: Colonial Revival House with elaborate Victorian maple leaf moldings, solid brick porch, double doored entrance, pine floors built in 1898. Parlor with faux marble Slate Eastlake Mantel. Two-story Greek Revival Fraternal Lodge with red pine floors, vaulted ceilings and fan window built in 1847. Completely renovated. Small private parties accommodated. Private brick court yard, fish pond, gazebo in the back of the main house. Private outdoor dining and formal dining inside. Both houses listed on the National Register of Historic Places.

ELIZABETHTOWN (4)

Warwick House
P.O. Box 156, Elizabethtown, NC 28337
(910) 862-4970
Innkeeper: Don and SSharon Natale
Rooms: 3, no pvt. bath
Rates: $60, incl. brk., evening refreshment
Credit cards: Most major cards
Restrictions: No pets, alchohol. Smoking restricted.
Notes: Three-story southern Colonial-style house built in 1922. Renovated in 1990. Common room with cable TV, telephone. Library.

ELLERBE (2)

Ellerbe Springs Inn
Rte. 1, Box 179-C, Ellerbe, NC 28338
(919) 652-5600, (800) 248-6467
Innkeeper: Beth Cadieu-Diaz
Rooms: plus 1 suite, all w/pvt. bath, phone, TV, incl. 4 w/fireplace
Rates: $48-$74/room, $88-$94/suite, all incl. full brk. Discount avail. for mid-week stay.
Credit cards: Most major cards
Restrictions: No pets, smoking. 50% desposit req. 24-hour cancellation notice req.
Notes: Established in 1857. Renovated in 1988. Dining room. Antiques and reproductions. 50 acres with small lake and pavillion with picnic tables. National Register of Historic Placec. Murder Mystery Wknds. Lunch and dinner available. Small private parties accommodated.*

EMERALD ISLE (5)

Emerald Isle Inn
502 Ocean Ave., Emerald Isle, NC 28594
(919) 354-3222
Innkeeper: Ak and Marilyn Detwiller
Rooms: 2, no pvt. bath, incl. 1 w/TV, plus 3 suites w/pvt. bath, phone, TV
Rates: $50-$75/room, $75-$95/suite, all incl. full brk., afternoon refreshment. Seasonal variations.
Credit cards: None
Restrictions: No pets. Smoking restricted. Deposit req. 10-day cancellation notice req. 2-night min. stay on wknds. from May 26–Sep. 4.
Notes: Built approx. 1975. Dining room overlooking ocean. Library with board games overlooking Bay. Furnished in whimsical Victorian, French Provincial, and Tropical styles. Limited handicapped access.

FAISON (4)

Magnolia Hall
701 W. Main St., Box 728, Faison, NC 28341
(910) 267-9241, (910) 267-9242
Innkeeper: Verna Taylor
Rooms: 4 plus cottage, all w/pvt. bath, phone, TV. Located in 2 bldgs.
Rates: $45-$75/room, $90/cottage, all incl. full brk., evening refreshment. Special pkgs. avail.
Credit cards: None
Restrictions: No pets, smoking. One night's deposit req. Min. 24-hour cancellation notice req., less $20.00 fee.
Notes: 2-story plantation house built in 1853. Has operated as Inn since 1991. Reception area, formal parlor, library, dining room. Sun parlor, decks, covered portico, back foyer, second story porch. Furnished with period antiques original to the house. Small private parties accommodated. Owner is local Magistrate and can perform wedding ceremonies. Catering, group tours, handicapped access available.*

FLAT ROCK (1)

HIGHLAND LAKE INN

Highland Lake Inn
Highland Lake Dr., Box 1026, Flat Rock, NC 28731
(704) 693-6812, (704) 696-8951
Innkeeper: Kerry Lindsey
Rooms: 49, incl. 45 w/phone, 29 w/TV, 5 w/fireplace, plus 10 suites w/phone, TV, pvt. bath, incl. 6 w/fireplace. Located in 12 bldgs.
Rates: $59-$99/room, $128-$179/suite. Special pkgs. avail. Seasonal variations.
Credit cards: Most major cards
Restrictions: No pets, smoking. 50% deposit req. 2-night min. stay on wknds.
Notes: Two-story, Tudor-style lodge located on 180 acres of water, meadows, woods, trails; barn, organic garden, and greenhouse with vegetables, herbs, and berries. Swimming pool, tennis courts. Lake for fishing, canoeing. Canoes provided. Lawn games, sports equipment available. Restaurant on premises. Small private parties

accommodated. Resident goats, turkey, yak, colt, hens. Limited handicapped access.*

Woodfield Inn
Greenville Hwy., Box 98, Flat Rock, NC 28731
(704) 693-6016
Innkeeper: Jeane Smith
Rooms: 16, incl. 9 w/pvt. bath, 12 w/fireplace, 2 w/TV, plus 2 suites w/pvt. bath, fireplace, TV
Rates: $65-$90/room, $95-$110/suite, all incl. cont. brk. Seasonal variations.
Credit cards: MC, V
Restrictions: No pets. One night's deposit req. 3-day cancellation notice req.
Notes: Built in 1852 as the Farmer Hotel. Oldest operating inn in North Carolina. Recently restored. Guest parlors, verandas, three dining rooms. Furnished in Victorian style. Small private parties accommodated. Handicapped access.

FRANKLIN (1)

Buttonwood Inn
190 Georgia Rd., Franklin, NC 28734
(704) 369-8985
Innkeeper: Liz Oehser
Rooms: 4, incl. 2 w/pvt. bath
Rates: $55-$70, incl. full brk.
Credit cards: None
Restrictions: No pets. Smoking restricted. Deposit req. Min 3-day cancellation notice req. 2-night min. on holidays and Oct. wknds. Closed Dec. 1–March 31.
Notes: Tongue and groove house built in 1920s. Located on Franklin Public Golf Course (between 5th and 7th holes). Decorated in country decor with antiques, crafts, collectibles. Common room, deck overlooking mountains, golf course.*

Franklin Terrace
67 Harrison Ave., Franklin, NC 28734
(704) 524-7907, (800) 633-2431
Innkeeper: Ed and Helen Henson
Rooms: 9 w/pvt. bath, TV
Rates: $52-$65, incl. full brk.
Credit cards: Most major cards
Restrictions: No children under 3, pets. Smoking restricted. Depost req. 72-hour cancellation notice req. Closed Nov. 15–April 1.
Notes: Two-story inn with porches, originally built as a school in 1887. Furnished with period antiques. Antique/giftshop on premises. Listed in The National Register of Historic Places.*

Snow Hill
531 Snow Hill Rd., Franklin, NC 28734
(704) 369-2100
Innkeeper: Jilli Ryan and Carole Coffman
Rooms: 8, plus 1 suite, all w/pvt. bath
Rates: $70/room, $90/suite, all incl. full brk., evening refreshment. Seasonal variations.
Credit cards: MC, V

Restrictions: No pets, smoking. One night's deposit req.

Notes: Two-story school inn with stone bell tower built as a school in 1914. Converted in early 1940s into private home. Has operated as inn since 1994. Located on 13.5 acres. Decorated with antique school desks, and armoires. Front proch with Adirondack chairs overlooking mountains. Gazebo. Some French spoken. Handicapped access.

GERMANTON (2)

MeadowHaven B & B
N.C. Hwy. 8, Box 222, Germanton, NC 27019-0222
(910) 593-3996, (910) 593-3996
Innkeeper: Samuel and Darlene Fain
Rooms: 3 w/pvt. bath, phone, TV, VCR, plus 4 cabins w/pvt. bath, fireplace, TV, VCR
Rates: $60-$90/room, $125-$200/cabin, all incl. brk., afternoon refreshment. Special pkgs. avail.
Credit cards: Most major cards
Restrictions: No children under 13, pets, smoking. Deposit req. 14-day cancellation notice req., less $10.00 fee. 2-night min. stay on holiday wknds. for rooms. 2-night min. stay on wknds. and holidays for cabins.
Notes: Contemporary, chalet-style house located on 25 country acres. Vaulted greatroom with fireplace overlooking mountains. Game room. Heated indoor pool, hot tub, fishing lake, archery range. Some spanish spoken.*

GREENSBORO (2)

Greenwood B & B
205 N. Park Dr., Greensboro, NC 27401
(919) 274-6350, (800) 535-9363, (910) 274-9943
Innkeeper: Jo Ann Green
Rooms: 4, incl. 1 suite, all w/pvt. bath, phone
Rates: $75-$90/room, $100-$125/suite, all incl. expanded cont. brk., afternoon refreshment. Seasonal variations.
Credit cards: Most major cards
Restrictions: No children under 5, pets. Smoking restricted. One night's deposit req. 24-hour cancellation notice req.
Notes: Three-story, Stick-style house built in 1910. Renovated in 1986. Foyer, parlor, each with fireplace. Swimming pool.*

HENDERSONVILLE (1)

Claddagh Inn
755 N. Main St., Hendersonville, NC 28792
(704) 697-7778
Innkeeper: Dennis and Vickie Pacilio
Rooms: 13, incl. 11 w/fireplace, plus 1 suite w/fireplace, all w/pvt. bath, phone, cable TV
Rates: $69-$85/room, $89/suite, all incl. full brk., evening refreshment. Discount avail. for AAA and senior citizen stays.
Credit cards: Most major cards
Restrictions: No pets. Smoking restricted. One night's deposit req. 2-day cancellation notice req.

Notes: Colonial Revival inn. Fully restored. Has operated as inn since 1905. Parlor with cable TV. Library with over 500 volumes. Shaded veranda. Shuffleboard on premises. Listed on the National Register of Historic Places.*

Echo Mountain Inn
2849 Laurel Park Hwy., Hendersonville, NC 28739
(704) 693-9626, (704) 697-2047
Innkeeper: Frank and Karen Kovacik
Rooms: 29, incl. 25 w/phone, 28 w/cable TV, 7 w/fireplace, plus 4 suites w/TV, incl. 1 w/fireplace, all w/pvt. bath. Located in 3 bldgs.
Rates: $45-$175, incl. cont. brk. Seasonal variations. Discount avail. for auto club, senior citizen, and extended stays. Special pkgs. avail.
Credit cards: Most major cards
Restrictions: Well behaved children welcome. No pets, smoking. Min. one night's deposit req. Min. 7-day cancellation notice req. 2-3 night min. stay on holidays and at peak times.
Notes: Stone and frame inn built in 1896 on top of Echo Mountain. Glass enclosed dining room. Decorated with antiques and reproductions. Swimming pool. Small private parties accommodated. Fax, secretarial services and lawn games available. Limited handicapped access.*

Stillwell House B & B
1300 Pinecrest Dr., Hendersonville, NC 28739
(704) 693-6475
Innkeeper: Ronnie Gobel
Rooms: 2 w/pvt. bath, incl. 1 w/TV
Rates: $45-$65, incl. cont. brk. Discount avail. for extended stay. Seasonal variations.
Credit cards: MC, V
Restrictions: No children, pets, smoking. One-night's deposit req. 7-day cancellation notice req.
Notes: Two-story brick house built in mid 1920s. Restored in 1990. Gardens. Decorated with artwork. Resident pet.

THE WAVERLY INN

The Waverly Inn
783 N. Main St., Hendersonville, NC 28792
(704) 693-9193, (704) 692-1010

Innkeeper: John and Diane Sheiry, darla Olmstead
Rooms: 14, incl. 1 w/cable TV, plus 1 suite w/cable TV, all w/pvt. bath, phone
Rates: $89-$109/room, $165/suite, all incl. full brk., evening refreshment. Discount avail. for AAA. Seasonal variations.
Credit cards: Most major cards
Restrictions: No pets. Smoking restricted. Min. on night's deposit req. 2-day cancellation notice req. 2-night min. stay on holiday wknds.
Notes: Three-story Victorian-style boarding house with Eastlake staircase, woodwork built in 1898. Library with TV. Parlor. Dining room. Furnished with claw-footed tubs, four poster canopy beds, spindle beds and other antiques. Veranda with rockers. Off-street parking available. Murder mystery and Wine Lovers weekends available. Listed on the National Register of Historic Places. Small private parties accommodated. Limited handicapped access.*

HERTFORD (5)

GINGERBREAD INN

Gingerbread Inn
103 S. Church St., Hertford, NC 27944
(919) 426-5809

Innkeeper: Hans and Jenny Harnisch
Rooms: 3 w/pvt. bath, phone, fireplace, cable TV
Rates: $45, incl. full brk., gingerbread boy souvenir
Credit cards: MC, V
Restrictions: No children under 5, pets, smoking. Full prepayment req. 3-day cancellation notice req.
Notes: Two-story house built in the early 1900s. Restored by hand. Breakfast room. Wrap-around porch with rockers. Furnished with 17th-century antiques. Bakery on premises. German and Russian spoken. Included on Hertford's historical tour.

HICKORY (2)

Hickory B & B
464 7th St. S.W., Hickory, NC 28602
(704) 324-0548, (800) 654-2961, (704) 345-1112

Innkeeper: Suzanne and Robert Ellis
Rooms: 3 w/pvt. bath, plus 1 suite w/pvt. bath, fireplace
Rates: $60/room, $70/suite, all incl. full brk., afternoon refreshment.
Credit cards: None
Restrictions: No children under 9, pets, alcohol, smoking. One night's deposit req.
   14-day cancellation notice req.
Notes: Two-story Georgian-style house built in 1908. Located on 1.5 acres. Parlor, library with board games. Decorated in a country flavor with antiques. Swimming pool. Small private parties accommodated. Handicapped access.*

HIGHLANDS (1)

The Guest House
U.S. 64 E., Rte. 2, Box 649N, Highlands, NC 28741
(704) 526-4536
Innkeeper: Juanita Hernandez
Rooms: 4 w/pvt. bath
Rates: $68-$85, incl. full brk., afternoon refreshment. Seasonal variations. Discount
   avail. for extended stay.
Credit cards: MC, V
Restrictions: No pets, smoking. One night's deposit req., 7-day cancellation notice
   req., less 25% fee. 2-night min. stay on wknds. and holidays during high season.
Notes: Alpine-style mountain chalet. Has operated as Inn since 1990. Living room with native stone fireplace, dining area. Furnished in a contemporary style with antiques and fine art collected from around the world. Outdoor deck overlooking mountains. Spanish, German spoken.

KILL DEVIL HILLS (5)

Cherokee Inn
500 N. Virginia Dare Trail, Kill Devil Hills, NC 27948
(919) 441-6127, (800) 554-2764
Innkeeper: Bob and Kaye Combs
Rooms: 6 w/pvt. bath, cable TV
Rates: $60-$90, incl. cont. brk. Seasonal variations.
Credit cards: Most major cards
Restrictions: No children under 12, pets, smoking. Min. one night's deposit req.
   7-day cancellation notice req. 3-night min. stay on holidays. Closed Nov.–Mar.
Notes: Built in the 1940s as hunting lodge with tongue and groove cypress walls and ceilings. Ceiling fans. Wrap-around porch with swing and redwood picnic furniture. Common room for reading, board games.*

LAKE TOXAWAY (1)

Earthshine Mountain Lodge
Rte. 1, Box 216-C, Lake Toxaway, NC 28747
(704) 862-4207
Innkeeper: Marion Boatwright and Kim Maurer
Rooms: 9 w/pvt. bath and loft. Located in 2 bldgs.
Rates: $170, incl. 3 daily meals, afternoon refreshment, evening programs
Credit cards: MC, V

Restrictions: No pets. Smoking restricted. 50% deposit req. 21-day cancellation notice req., less $10.00 fee. 2-night min. stay.

Notes: One-and-a-half-story, hand built, cedar log lodge with rock fireplaces. Located on 100-year-old homesteaded 70 acres with riding and hiking trails bordering Pisgah National Forest. Has operated as inn since 1990. Rockers, hammocks. Guests are invited to help with chores. Small private parties accommodated. Weekend adventure treks, "Murder mystery" weekends. organized. Limited handicapped access.*

Greystone Inn
Greystone Lake, Box 6, Lake Toxaway, NC 28747
(704) 966-4700, (800) 824-5766, (704) 862-5689

Innkeeper: Tim and BooBoo Lovelace

Rooms: 33, incl. 2 suites, all w/pvt. bath, Jacuzzi, phone, TV, incl. 14 w/fireplace

Rates: $285-$370, incl. full brk., afternoon refreshment, 6-course dinner. Discount avail. for mid-week stay. Seasonal variations.

Credit cards: Most major cards

Restrictions: No pets. Smoking restricted. $200 min. deposit req. 14-day cancellation notice req., less $25.00 fee. 2-night min. stay on wknds.

Notes: Six-level Swiss mansion with balconies and gabled roof, built in 1915. Renovated in 1984. Dining room, freestanding library building. Furnished with antique and period reproductions. Swimming pool, stables. Lawn games, party boat, water ski and fishing boat, all meals available. Golf course, 640-acre lake. Listed on the National Register of Historic Places.*

MADISON (2)

The Boxley Bed and Breakfast
117 E. Hunter St., Madison, NC 27025
(910) 427-0453

Innkeeper: Monte and JoAnn McIntosh

Rooms: 4 w/pvt. bath, incl. 2 w/fireplace. Located in 3 bldgs.

Rates: $60, incl. full brk. Discount avail. for extended stay.

Credit cards: MC, V

Restrictions: No children under 6, pets. Smoking restricted. Deposit req. 2-day cancellation notice req.

Notes: Two-story Greek Federal-style plantation house. Located in historic district. Front walk and gardens lined with boxwoods. Family room with TV. Living room with baby grand. Porch.

MANTEO (5)

Tranquil House Inn
Queen Eliz. St., Box 2045, Manteo, NC 27954
(919) 473-1404, (800) 458-7069, (919) 473-1526

Innkeeper: Don and Lauri Just

Rooms: 23 plus 2 suites, all w/pvt. bath, phone, TV

Rates: $69-$149/room, $99-$149/suite, all incl. cont. brk., evening refreshment. Seasonal variations. Discount avail. for extended, senior citizen, mid-week, military stays.

Credit cards: Most major cards

Restrictions: No pets. Smoking restricted. One night's deposit req. Min. 48-hour cancellation notice req. 2-night min. stay, May–Sept.

Notes: Three-story 9th-century replica inn with cypress woodwork, bevelled glass, stained-glass built in 1988. Located on the waterfront. Library with fireplace. Deck with Adirondack funiture. Pantry. Terrace overlooks the bay. Decorated with designer wallpaper, Oriental and Berber carpets. Bicycles available. Handicapped access.*

MARSHALL (1)

Marshall House B & B
5 Hill St., Box 865, Marshall, NC 28753
(704) 649-9205, (800) 562-9258, (704) 649-2999
Innkeeper: Jim and Ruth Boylan
Restrictions: 9, incl. 2 w/pvt. bath, 1 w/fireplace
Rates: $41-$65, incl. cont. brk., afternoon refreshment. Seasonal variations.
Credit cards: Most major cards
Restrictions: Deposit req. 3-day cancellation notice req.
Notes: Built as private residence in 1903. Formal dining room, parlor, upstairs reading/TV room. Veranda with rockers. Furnished with period antiques. Listed on the National Register of Historic Places. Handicapped access. Innkeepers collect tea cups, tea pots. Resident pets.*

MOCKSVILLE (2)

Boxwood Lodge
132 Becktown Rd., Mocksville, NC 27028
(704) 284-2031
Innkeeper: Martha Hoffner
Rooms: 8
Rates: $45-$95
Credit cards: None
Restrictions: No children, pets. Smoking restricted.
Notes: Colonial Revival mansion built in 1933. Located on 51 wooded acres. Common room with fireplace, billiards. Small private parties accommodated.

MOORESVILLE (2)

24 Spring Run B & B
24 Spring Run, Lake Norman, Mooresville, NC 28115
(704) 664-6686
Innkeeper: Mary Farley
Rooms: 2 w/pvt. bath, cable TV
Rates: $85, incl. full brk.
Credit cards: MC, V
Restrictions: No children, pets, smoking. Deposit req. 7-day cancellation notice req., less $30.00 fee.
Notes: Two-story house. Dining room, deck overlooking Lake Norman. Gathering room with phone, fireplace, 1960s jukebox. Kitchen with beverage cart. Excercise room w/equipment, board games. Each guest will receive free, a $40.00 signed and numbered print by a famous artist. Pier permit for fishing, use of boat dock, deck, pier, paddle boat available. Lake swimming.*

MOUNT AIRY (2)

MAYBERRY B & B

Mayberry B & B
329 W. Pine St., Mount Airy, NC 27030
(919) 786-2045
Innkeeper: Jack and Hazel Fallis
Rooms: 2 no pvt. bath
Rates: $40, incl. full brk.
Credit cards: None
Restrictions: No pets. $10.00 deposit req. 48-hour cancellation notice.
Notes: Two-story house. Sitting room with TV, books, magazines.

The William E. Merritt House
618 N. Main St., Mount Airy, NC 27030
(800) 290-6290, (910) 786-2174
Innkeeper: Rich and Pat Mangels
Rooms: 4, incl. 2 w/pvt. bath
Rates: $40-$75, incl. full brk., evening refreshment. Discount avail. for mid-week
    stay.
Credit cards: Most major cards
Restrictions: No pets, smoking. Deposit req.
Notes: Two-story brick Victorian house with steep hipped roof and bracketed eaves,
tall panelled chimneys, granite string courses and window trip, built in 1901. Wrap-
around porch with Classical posts, spindled frieze, 2.5-story tower projecting bay.
Decorated with antiques.

MOUNTAIN HOME (1)

Mountain Home B & B
10 Courtland Blvd., Box 234, Mountain Home, NC 28758
(800) 397-0066
Innkeeper: Bob and Donna Marriott
Rooms: 7 w/cable TV, phone, incl. 5 w/pvt. bath w/phone, some w/pvt. decks, sky-
    lights.
Rates: $70-$95, incl. full brk., afternoon refreshment. Discount avail. for AE card.
    Seasonal variations. Special pkgs. avail.

Credit cards: Most major cards
Restrictions: No children under 10. Smoking restricted. Deposit req. 7-day cancellation notice req. 2-night min. stay.
Notes: Victorian style country house built in 1936 using original stone walls. Located in residental area on site of stagecoach stop and hotel. Remodeled in 1988. Furnished with antiques and oriental rugs. Living room and guest kitchen with fireplace. Guests have access to laundry facilities and health and racquet club. Gift items and certificates available. Small private parties accommodated.

MURPHY (1)

Huntington Hall
500 Valley River Ave., Murphy, NC 28906
(704) 837-9567, (800) 824-6189, (704) 837-2527

Innkeeper: Bob and Kate DeLong
Rooms: 5 w/pvt. bath, cable TV
Rates: $49-$65, incl. full brk., afternoon refreshment. Special pkgs. avail.
Credit cards: Most major cards
Restrictions: No pets, smoking. One night's deposit req. 48-hour cancellation notice req.
Notes: Two-story Victorian house with clapboard siding built approx. 1881. Living room with TV. Dining room, sun porch. Front porch with columns. Decorated with antiques and reproduction furniture. Murder-mystery weekends. organized. Some French, German spoken.*

NAGS HEAD (5)

First Colony Inn
6720 S. Virginia Dare Tr., Nags Head, NC 27959
(919) 441-2343, (800) 368-9390, (919) 441-9234

Innkeeper: Alan Lawrence
Rooms: 26, incl 4 suites, all w/pvt. bath, phone, cable TV. Most w/wet bar, microwave, or kitchenettes w/dishwasher. Some w/whirlpool tub.
Rates: $125-$225/room, $175-225/suite, all incl. cont. brk., afternoon refreshment. Seasonal variations. Special pkgs. avail.
Credit cards: Most major cards
Restrictions: No pets, smoking. 2-night deposit req., 30-day cancellation notice req. 2-night min. stay on wknds. 3-night min. stay on some holiday wknds.
Notes: Two-story beach hotel built in 1932. Moved to five acres with private sandy beach and renovated in 1988. Library with fireplace, pump organ, board games. Dining room. Two-story wrap-around verandas with rockers. Furnished with antiques, reproductions. Lawn games available. Swimming pool, sundeck. Listed on the National Register of Historic Places. Small private parties accommodated. Handicapped access.*

NEW BERN (4)

The Aerie
509 Pollock St., New Bern, NC 28560
(800) 849-5553

Innkeeper: Howard and Dee Smith
Rooms: 7 w/pvt. bath, phone, TV
Rates: $79-$89, incl. full brk., afternoon refreshment

Credit cards: Most major cards
Restrictions: No pets, smoking. Deposit req.
Notes: Two-story Victorian house with turret built in the early 1880s. Restored in and has operated as inn since the mid-1980s. Furnished with antiques and reproductions. Sitting room with player piano, board games. Patio shaded by 100-year-old Pecan tree. All meals available. Off-street parking available. Small private parties accommodated.

Harmony House
215 Pollock St., New Bern, NC 28560
(919) 636-3810
Innkeeper: A.E. and Diane Hansen
Rooms: 9 w/pvt. bath, cable TV
Rates: $55-$85, incl. full brk., afternoon refreshment
Credit cards: Most major cards
Restrictions: No pets, smoking. One night's deposit req. 48-hour cancellation notice req.
Notes: Two-story Greek Revival inn built in 1850. Enlarged about 1900. Front Parlor with 1875 pump organ. Dining room. Front porch with rockers, swings. Furnished with antiques, reproductions, memorabilia, made by local craftsmen. Landscaped grounds with lawn furniture.*

King's Arms Inn
212 Pollock St., New Bern, NC 28560
(919) 638-4409
Innkeeper: Richard and Patricia Gulley
Rooms: 10, inc. 8 w/pvt. bath, phone, cable TV
Rates: $76, incl. expanded cont. brk., afternoon refreshment. Discount avail. for senior citizen, AAA stays.
Credit cards: Most major cards
Restrictions: No pets, smoking. Deposit req. 48-hour cancellation notice req.
Notes: Two-story Colonial house built in 1847. Enlarged in 1895. Completely restored in 1980. Located in Historic District. Private parking available. French spoken.*

PINEBLUFF (4)

Pine Cone Manor
450 E. Philadelphia Ave., Box 1208, Pinebluff, NC 28373
(919) 281-5307
Innkeeper: Virginia Keith
Rooms: 4, incl. 3 w/pvt. bath, 2 w/phone, 2 w/TV, 1 w/fireplace. Located in 2 bldgs.
Rates: $45-$55, incl. cont. brk. Discount avail. for extended stay.
Credit cards: MC, V
Restrictions: No pets. One night's deposit req. 48-hour cancellation notice req.
Notes: Turn-of-the-century, two-story inn. Located in Pinehurst Resort area. Sleeping porches. Front porch with rockors, swing. Garden.

PISGAH FOREST (1)

Key Falls In
151 Everett Rd., Pisgah Forest, NC 28768
(704) 884-7559

Innkeeper: Clark and Patricia Grosvenor, Janet Fogleman
Rooms: 5, incl. 1 suite, all w/pvt. bath, incl. 1 w/TV
Rates: $55-$70/room, $85/suite, all incl. full brk, afternoon refreshment. Discount avail. for extended stay.
Credit cards: Most major cards
Restrictions: No children under 3, pets, smoking. Deposit req. 5-day cancellation notice req.
Notes: Victorian farm house built in the 1860s. Located on 35 acres with waterfall, stream, pond, picnic area. Victorian parlor. Living room with TV, board games, books. Furnished with antiques. Porch. Tennis, lawn games avail. Some Spanish spoken.*

The Pines Country Inn
719 Hart Rd., Pisgah Forest, NC 28768
(704) 877-3131

Innkeeper: Tom and Mary McEntire
Rooms: 21 plus 1 suite, all w/pvt. bath. Located in 6 bldgs.
Rates: $68/room, $85/suite, all incl. full brk. Discount avail. for extended stay.
Credit cards: None
Restrictions: No pets. Smoking restricted. 33% deposit req. 10-day cancellation notice req. Closed Nov. 1–April 30. No alcohol, but guests may bring their own drinks.
Notes: Two-story inn built in 1883. Located on twelve mountainside acres. Two cottages, two log cabins. Living room with open fireplace, dining room, second-story veranda. Handicapped access. Airport pickup, all meals available.

SALISBURY (2)

Rowan Oak House
208 S. Fulton St., Salisbury, NC 28144
(704) 633-2086

Innkeeper: Ruth Ann and Bill Coffey
Rooms: 2 w/pvt. bath, phone, plus 2 suites w/pvt. bath, phone, incl. 1 w/fireplace
Rates: $65-$95, incl. full brk., afternoon refreshment. Discount avail. for senior citizen and extended stays.
Credit cards: Most major cards
Restrictions: No children under 10, pets. Smoking restricted. 50% deposit req. 7-day cancellation notice req., less $10.00 fee. 2-4-night min. stay for special events.
Notes: Three-story Queen Anne house with octagonal cupola built in 1901. Seven tiled fireplaces, each with a uniquely carved mantle. Victorian parlor, library. Upstairs lounge with TV. Dining room with original 1901 wallpaper, leaded windows, shutters, and wainscoting. Columned, wrap-around porch with rockers. Furnished with antiques, reproductions. Perennial gardens. Spanish spoken.*

SALUDA (1)

Ivy Terrace
P.O. Box 639, Saluda, NC 28773
(800) 749-9542, (704) 749-2017

Innkeeper: Herbert and Diane McGuire
Rooms: 8 w/pvt. bath
Rates: $85-$125, incl full brk., local-interest gift
Credit cards: MC, V

Restrictions: No children, pets. Smoking restricted. One night's deposit req. 48-hour cancellation notice req.

Notes: Built in 1890s. Operated as inn since 1920s. Renovated in 1993. Located on wooded area. Parlor with stone fireplace. Dining room, porches, patios, terraces, gardens. Decorated with country antiques. Small private parties accommodated. Computers, Fax machine, slide projectors available. Dietary considerations with prior notice. Handicapped access.*

SHELBY (2)

Inn at Webbley
403 S Washington St., Box 1000, Shelby, NC 28150
(800) 852-2346, (704) 487-0619

Innkeeper: O. Max Gardner III and Victoria H. Gardner

Rooms: 5 w/pvt. bath, phone, cable TV, incl. 4 w/fireplace

Rates: $95-$150, incl. full brk.

Credit cards: Most major cards

Restrictions: No children under 16, pets, smoking. Deposit req. Cancellation notice req. 2-night min. stay for holiday wknds.

Notes: Two-story Antebellum Mansion built in 1852. Located on landscaped grounds with gardens. Twin parlors, formal dining room, library with grand piano, bar, courtyard, porches with rocking chairs. Furnished with French and English antiques, Oriental rugs. Listed on the National Register of Historic Places. Small private parties accommodated. Nearby kennels are available for pets with prior notice. Handicapped access.*

SILER CITY (2)

B & B at Laurel Ridge
Rte. 1, Box 116, Siler City, NC 27344
(919) 742-6049

Innkeeper: Lisa Reynolds, Dave Simmons

Rooms: 2 plus 1 suite, incl. 1 w/pvt. bath, 3 w/phone, 1 w/TV

Rates: $30-$55/room, $85-$110/suite, all incl. full brk. Discount avail. for extended stay.

Credit cards: MC, V

Restrictions: No pets, smoking. One night's deposit req. 3-day cancellation notice req., less $5.00 fee.

Notes: Country house built in 1984. Located on 26 acres. Common room with TV/VCR. Decorated with antiques and traditional furniture. Board and lawn games available. English country garden. All meals included for groups of ten or more. Some Spanish spoken.

SPARTA (2)

Turby-Villa
Star Rte. 1, Box 48, Sparta, NC 28675
(910) 372-8490

Innkeeper: Maybelline Turbiville

Rooms: 3 w/pvt. bath, incl. 2 w/phone

Rates: $50, incl. full brk.

Credit cards: None

Restrictions: No pets.

Notes: Contemporary two-story brick house. Located on twenty wooded acres. Enclosed porch with wicker furniture, overlooking the Blue Ridge Mountains.

STATESVILLE (2)

Aunt Mae's B & B
532 E. Broad St., Statesville, NC 28677
(704) 873-9525
Innkeeper: Sue and Richard Rowland
Rooms: 2 w/pvt. bath, phone, TV
Rates: $60, incl. full brk., afternoon refreshment. Discount avail. for senior citizen and extended stays. Special pkgs. avail.
Credit cards: MC, V
Restrictions: Pets, smoking restricted. Deposit req. 24-hour cancellation notice req.
Notes: Two-story, century-old Victorian house. Sitting room with board games and antique puzzles. Parlor with antique radio, antique record players and records. Library with century-old books, magazines, love letters. Porch.*

Cedar Hill Farm B & B
778 Elmwood Rd., Statesville, NC 28677
(704) 873-4332, (800) 487-8457 ext. 1254
Innkeeper: Brenda and Jim Vernon
Rooms: 1 w/pvt. bath, phone, TV, plus 1 cottage w/pvt. bath, phone, TV, fireplace, porch, refrigerator. Located in 2 bldgs.
Rates: $60/room, $75/cottage, all incl. full brk. Seasonal variations. Discount avail. for extended stay.
Credit cards: MC, V
Restrictions: Pets, smoking restricted. 50% deposit req. 3-day cancellation notice req.
Notes: Two-story house, log barn, and outbuildings built in 1840. Located on 32 wooded acres with wildflowers, stream, pastures with sheep. Porch with swing and rockers. Furnished with family antiques. Swimming pool, badminton, volleyball, hiking, fishing. Resident geese and rooster.*

SWAN QUARTER (5)

Cutrell Inn B & B
P.O. Box 125 Hwy. 45, Swan Quarter, NC 27885-0125
(919) 926-9711
Innkeeper: Delores C. Emory
Rooms: 3, no pvt. bath
Rates: $45-$55, incl. cont. brk.
Credit cards: Most major cards
Restrictions: No children under 12, pets, smoking. Deposit req. 72-hour cancellation notice req., less $10.00 fee.
Notes: 2-story house. Living room with TV, reading material. Screened front porch with swing, back deck. Guests have access to kitchen. Small private parties accommodated. Overnight storage for bicycles available.

TARBORO (3)

Little Warren Bed & Breakfast
304 E. Park Ave., Tarboro, NC 27886
(919) 823-1314

Innkeeper: Tom and Patsy Miller
Rooms: 3 w/pvt. bath, phone
Rates: $58-$65, incl. full brk.
Credit cards: Most major cards
Restrictions: No children under 6, pets. Deposit req. 48-hour cancellation notice req.
Notes: Two-story Edwardian house built in 1913. Lounge/living room with fireplace. Den. Two porches, one a wrap-around overlooking Town Common. Furnished with English and American antiques, collectibles, memorabilia. Spanish spoken.*

TRYON (1)

Mimosa Inn
1 Mimosa Inn Lane, Tryon, NC 28782
(704) 859-7688
Innkeeper: Jay and Sandi Franks
Rooms: 9 w/pvt. bath
Rates: $55-$85, incl. full brk.
Credit cards: Most major cards
Restrictions: No children under 10, pets, smoking. One night's deposit req. 48-hour cancellation notice req., less $5.00 fee.
Notes: Built in 1903 as casino with billiard tables and a bowling alley. Remodeled and expanded in 1916. Bowling alley was parqued together to form a narrow board, hardwood surface in the main parlor. Lobby and sitting area. Furnished with antiques and reproductions. Patio with outdoor fireplace. Lawn games available.

Pine Crest Inn
200 Pine Crest Lane, Box 1030, Tryon, NC 28782
(800) 633-3001, (704) 859-9135
Innkeeper: Jeremy and Jennifer Wainwright
Rooms: 24, incl. 16 w/fireplace, plus 6 suites, all w/pvt. bath, phone, TV. Located in 8 bldgs.
Rates: $125-$165, incl. cont. brk., evening refreshment.
Credit cards: Most major cards
Restrictions: No pets. Smoking restricted. 2-day cancellation notice req.
Notes: Built in 1926 with stone fireplaces, verandas. Located on 9 acres. F. Scott Fitzgerald and Ernest Hemingway slept here. Restaurant and bar on premises. Picnic lunches available. Listed on National Register of Historic Places. Small private parties accommodated. French spoken.*

Stone Hedge Inn
Howard Gap Rd., Box 366, Tryon, NC 28782
(704) 859-9114
Innkeeper: Ray and Anneliese Weingartner
Rooms: 5 plus 1 suite, all w/pvt. bath, phone, TV, incl. 2 w/fireplace. Located in 3 bldgs.
Rates: $65-$80/room, $85/suite, all incl. full brk. Discount avail. for extended and mid-week stays.
Credit cards: MC, V
Restrictions: No children under 12, pets. Deposit req. 2-day cancellation notice req.

Notes: Stone inn built in 1935. Located on forty landscaped acres at base of Tryon Mountain. Dining room. Furnished with antiques. Swimming pool. German spoken. Handicapped access.*

VALLE CRUCIS (1)

Inn at the Taylor House
P.O. Box 713, Hwy 194, Valle Crucis, NC 28691
(704) 963-5581, (704) 963-5818
Innkeeper: Chip and Roland Schwab
Rooms: 5 plus 2 suites, all w/pvt. bath, plus 3 cabins
Rates: $110/room, $145/suite, $95-$135/cabin, all incl. full brk., afternoon refreshment.
Credit cards: MC, V
Restrictions: Children restricted. No pets, smoking. One night's deposit req. 7-day cancellation notice req., less $10.00 fee. 2-night min. stay on wknds. Closed December–April.
Notes: Three-story frame house built in 1911. Wrap-around porch with swing and antique wicker furniture. Furnished with personal antiques, art, oriental rugs. Handicapped access.*

INN AT THE TAYLOR HOUSE

Mast Farm Inn
P.O. Box 704, Valle Crucis, NC 28691
(704) 963-5857, (704) 963-6404
Innkeeper: Sibyl and Francis Pressly
Rooms: 9, incl. 7 w/pvt. bath, 1 w/fireplace, plus 3 suites w/pvt. bath, fireplace. Located in 4 bldgs.
Rates: $90-$140/room, $140-$165/suite, all incl. cont. brk., dinner. Seasonal variations. Discount avail. for mid-week, extended stays.
Credit cards: MC, V

Restrictions: No children under 12, pets. Smoking restricted. One night's deposit req. 7-day cancellation notice req., less $5.00 fee. 2-night min. stay on wknds. Closed March 7–April 20, November 8–December 27.
Notes: Three-story farmhouse built in 1855. Main house, renovated blacksmith shop, woodwork shop and loom house. Located on eighteen-acre working farm. Has operated as inn since the early 1900s. 2 dining rooms, parlor. Wrap-around front porch with swing, rockers. Furnished with simple antiques. Handicapped access. Listed on the National Register of Historic Places. Portuguese spoken.*

MAST FARM INN

Drawing by Jerry Miller, courtesy N.C. Historical Prints.

WARSAW (4)

The Squire's Vintage Inn
Rte. 2, Box 130R, Hwy. 24, Warsaw, NC 28398
(910) 296-1727
Innkeeper: Iris Lennon
Rooms: 12 w/pvt. bath, phone, TV
Rates: $61, incl. cont. brk.
Credit cards: Most major cards
Restrictions: No pets. Credit card deposit req. 24-hour cancellation notice req.
Notes: Built in 1973. Meeting room. Landscaped sunken gardens with gazebo. Restaurant on premises. Small private parties accommodated. Guests have access to golf course. Handicapped access.

WAYNESVILLE (1)

Hallcrest Inn
299 Halltop Circle, Waynesville, NC 28786
(704) 456-6457, (800) 334-6457
Innkeeper: Martin and Tesa Burson, David and Catherin Mitchell
Rooms: 12 w/pvt. bath, incl. 4 w/fireplace. Located in 2 bldgs.
Rates: $55-$90, incl. full brk., dinner. Discount avail.for extended stay.
Credit cards: Most major cards
Restrictions: No pets. Smoking restricted. Deposit req. 7-day cancellation notice req. Closed mid-Dec.—May 31.

Notes: Farmhouse built in 1880. Living room. Sitting room with TV. Dining room with fireplace. Porches with rockers overlooking mountains. Furnished with antiques, family memorabilia. Small private parties accommodated. Handicapped access.*

Heath Lodge
900 Dolan Rd., Waynesville, NC 28786
(704) 456-3333, (800) HEATH-99
Innkeeper: Robert and Cindy Zinser
Rooms: 20 plus 2 suites, all w/pvt. bath, cable TV. Located in 7 bldgs.
Rates: $95-$115/room, $125/suite, all incl. full brk., dinner. Discount avail. for extended stay.
Credit cards: Most major cards
Restrictions: No pets, smoking. Deposit req. 14-day cancellation notice req. less $10.00 fee, closed Nov.–Apr.
Notes: Poplar and stone lodge with beamed ceilings, hardwood floors. Located on 6½ acres at 3,200-foot elevation in the heart of the Smoky Mountains. Has operated as inn since 1946. Living room with library, piano, board games. Dining room with oak floors, stone fireplace. Wide covered porches with rockers. Decorated with hooked rugs. Hot tub. Small private parties accommodated. Limited handicapped access. Spanish spoken.*

The Palmer House
108 Pigeon St., Waynesville, NC 28786-4334
(704) 456-7521
Innkeeper: Jeff Minick, Kris Gillet
Rooms: 7 w/pvt. bath
Rates: $50-$60, incl. full brk., evening refreshment, bookstore discount
Credit cards: Most major cards
Restrictions: No children under 2, pets, smoking. 50% deposit req. 14-day cancellation notice req., less $10.00 fee. 2-night min. stay on wknds. 3-night min. stay on holidays.
Notes: Three-story hotel built in the 1880s. Parlor with piano. Dining room. Front porch with rockers. Nurse doll collection on display. Bookstore on premises. Kennels available.

Swag Country Inn
Rte. 2, Box 280A, Waynesville, NC 28786
(704) 926-0430, (704) 926-2036
Innkeeper: Deener Matthews
Rooms: 13 w/pvt. bath, incl 6 w/fireplace, plus 2 suites w/pvt. bath, fireplace. Located in 4 bldgs.
Rates: $175-$284/room, $250-$325/suite, all incl. 3 meals daily, special events. Seasonal variations.
Credit cards: MC, V
Restrictions: No pets. One night's deposit req. 14-day cancellation notice req. Closed Nov. 1–May 31.
Notes: Built mostly of handhewn poplar logs in 1970. Located on 250 wooded acres with pond near Great Smoky Mountains National Park. 2 living rooms with fireplaces. Library with player piano, board games. 2 front porches with rocking chairs. Furnished in primitive style. Boat available. Handicapped access.

WEAVERVILLE (1)

Inn on Main Street
88 S. Main St., Box 1153, Weaverville, NC 28787
(704) 645-3442

Innkeeper: Joel and Melba Goldsby
Rooms: 5 w/pvt. bath
Rates: $55, incl. full brk., afternoon refreshment.
Credit cards: None
Restrictions: No children under 12, pets, smoking. One night's deposit req. 7-day
    cancellation notice req. 2-night min. stay on wknds.
Notes: Two-story inn built in 1900. Fully renovated. Porches. Parlor with TV. Phone
in halls. Game room with pool table, board games, dart board. Lawn games available.

WELDON (3)

WELDON PLACE INN

Weldon Place Inn
500 Washington Ave., Weldon, NC 27890
(919) 536-4582, (800) 831-4470

Innkeeper: Andy and Angel Whitby
Rooms: 4, incl. 3 w/pvt. bath
Rates: $60-$85, incl. full brk. Discount avail. for mid-week stay.
Credit cards: MC, V
Restrictions: No children under 7, pets. Smoking restricted. One night's deposit
    req. 3-day cancellation notice req.
Notes: Two-story Colonial Revival inn built in 1913. Entry room with antique baby
grand piano. Garden room with TV/VCR, books, board games. Furnished with
many original antiques in Victorian decor. Small private parties accommodated.*

WILMINGTON (4)

Anderson Guest House
520 Orange St., Wilmington, NC 28401
(919) 343-8128

Innkeeper: Landon and Connie Anderson
Rooms: 2 w/pvt. bath, fireplace
Rates: $75, incl. full brk., afternoon refreshment
Credit cards: None
Restrictions: No children under 3, smoking. Pets restricted. One night's deposit req. 24-hour cancellation notice req.
Notes: Italianate townhouse built in 1851. Restored in 1979. Two-story guesthouse built in 1981. Has operated as inn since 1981. Dining room with gas lights, cherry woodwork. Private backyard, porches. Furnished with some Victorian pieces, ceiling fans. German, French spoken.

Catherine's Inn on Orange
410 South Front St., Wilmington, NC 28401
(919) 251-0863, (800) 476-0723

Innkeeper: Walter and Catherine Ackiss
Rooms: 3, plus 1 suite w/phone, all w/pvt. bath
Rates: $55-$80/room, $120/suite, all incl full brk., afternoon and evening refreshment.
Credit cards: MC, V
Restrictions: No children under 12, pets. Smoking restricted. Deposit req. 3-day cancellation notice req.
Notes: Two-story inn built in 1883. Located on Cape Fear River and Historic Downtown. Library with cable television. Wrap-around porch.*

The Inn on Orange
410 Orange St., Wilmington, NC 28401
(910) 815-0035

Innkeeper: Paul Marston
Rooms: 2 w/pvt. bath, incl. 1 w/TV plus 2 suites w/pvt. bath, phone, TV
Rates: $65-$85/room, $75-95/suite, all incl. full brk., afternoon refreshment.
Credit cards: MC, V
Restrictions: No children under 16, pets. Smoking restricted. Deposit req. 3-day cancellation notice req. 2-night min. stay on holidays.
Notes: Two-story inn built in 1875. Located in Historical District. Library, parlor, dining room. Sitting room with TV. Furnished with antiques, reproductions. Garden, swimming pool.*

Market Street B & B
1704 Market St., Wilmington, NC 28403
(919) 763-5442, (800) 242-5442

Innkeeper: Bob and Jo Anne Jarrett
Rooms: 2 w/pvt. bath plus 2 suites, incl. 1 w/pvt. bath
Rates: $65-$75/room, $90/suite, all incl. full brk. Discount avail. for extended stay.
Credit cards: MC, V
Restrictions: No children under 12, pets, smoking.
Notes: Two-story Georgian-style brick house. Formal dining room. Furnished with antiques and reproductions. Side porch with rockers. Listed on National Register of Historic Places. Off-street parking available.

The Taylor House
14 N. Seventh St., Wilmington, NC 28401
(910) 763-7581, (800) 382-9982

Innkeeper: Glenda Moreadith
Rooms: 3 plus 1 suite, all w/pvt. bath, phone, incl. 1 w/fireplace
Rates: $95-$100/room, $90-$160/suite, all incl. full brk., afternoon and evening refreshment. Seasonal variations.
Credit cards: Most major cards
Restrictions: No children under 12, pets, smoking. One night's deposit req. 72-hour cancellation notice req. 2-night min. stay on most wknds. and holidays.
Notes: Two-story, neo-Classic-style house with original woodwork, stained-glass windows and open staircase, built in 1905. Fully restored. Living room. Music room with antique French grand piano. Dining room with beamed ceiling, fireplace. Furnished with antiques and contemporary pieces. Porch with swings and rocking chairs. Full service hair salon on premises.*

WINSTON-SALEM (2)

Lady Anne's Victorian B & B
612 Summit St., Winston-Salem, NC 27101
(910) 724-1074

Innkeeper: Shelley Kirley
Rooms: 2, plus 3 suites, all w/pvt. bath, phone, TV
Rates: $55-$85/room, $85-$135/suite, all incl. full brk., afternoon refreshment. Discount avail. for mid-week stay.
Credit cards: Most major cards
Restrictions: No children under 12, pets. Smoking restricted. Deposit req. 7-day cancellation notice req., less $10.00 fee.
Notes: Two-story Queen Anne house built in 1890. Formal dining room, Victorian porch. Furnished with period antiques. Listed on the National Register of Historic Places.

North Dakota

The Big Red House
729 Belmont Rd., Grand Forks, ND 58201
(701) 775-3332
Innkeeper: Rick and Becky Schoeneck
Rooms: 2, no pvt. bath
Rates: $50, incl. full brk.
Credit cards: MC, V
Restrictions: No pets, smoking. Deposit req. 7-day cancellation notice req., less 10% fee.
Notes: Three-story house with quartersawn oak woodwork and leaded-glass windows built in 1909. Located one block from the Red River. Living room, family room, sitting room with phone, TV, futon. Decorated with antiques, collectibles, and Oriental furnishings. Small private parties accommodated.

THE BIG RED HOUSE

JAMESTOWN (5)

Country Charm Bed & Breakfast
R.R. 3, Box 71, Jamestown, ND 58401
(701) 251-1372
Innkeeper: Tom and Ethel Oxtoby
Rooms: 4, no pvt. bath
Rates: $53, incl. full brk.
Credit cards: None
Restrictions: No smoking. Non-refundable one night's deposit req. Refunds upon cancellation in the form of a gift certificate.
Notes: Two-story farmhouse built in the 1897. Dining room, glassed-in sun porch, great room, back deck, side porch. Furnished with antiques, collectibles, handmade

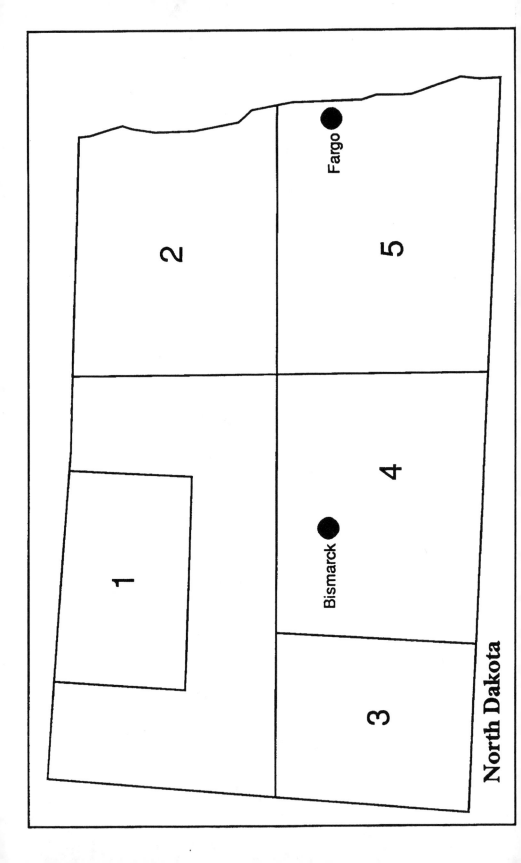

North Dakota

quilts. Small private parties accommodated. Innkeepers restore antique and classic cars, collect advertising signs, tins and postcards from early 1900s.

REGENT (3)

Prairie Vista
101 Rural Ave., Regent, ND 58650
(701) 563-4542, (701) 563-4642
Innkeeper: Marlys Prince
Rooms: 3, no pvt. bath
Rates: $50, incl. full brk.
Credit cards: None
Restrictions: No children under 10, smoking.
Notes: Brick house built in 1954. Located on seven acres surrounded by evergreens. Decorated in modern decor. Two-thousand-foot recreational area with swimming pool, exercise equipment, pool table.

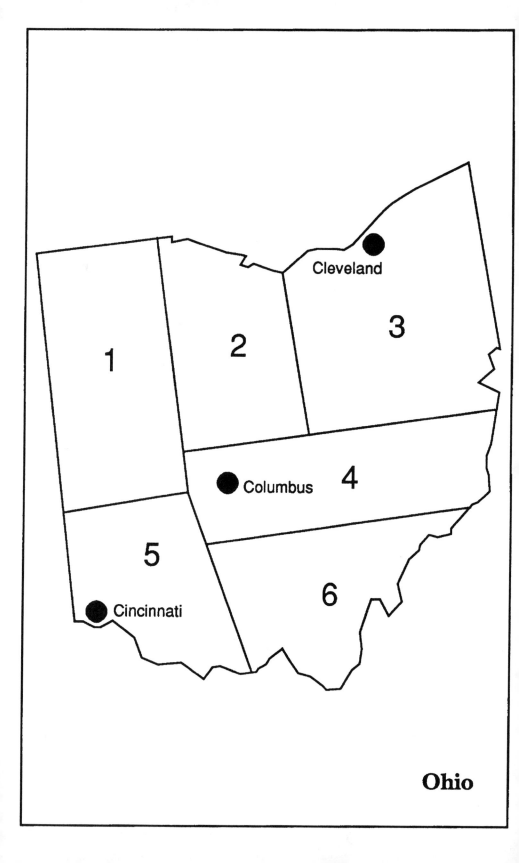

Ohio

ASHTABULA (3)

Michael Cahill B & B
1106 Walnut Blvd., Ashtabula, OH 44004
(216) 964-8449
Innkeeper: Paul and Pat Goode
Rooms: 4, incl. 2 w/pvt. bath
Rates: $45-$55, incl full brk. Discount avail. for extended stay.
Credit cards: None
Restrictions: Smoking restricted. Deposit req. 7-day cancellation notice req.
Notes: Two-story "stick style" architectural house built in 1887 with cherry wood-work, and original electric chandeliers. Located in Ashtaqbula Harbor Historic District. Furnished with antiques and period furnishings. Three sitting rooms. Small kitchenette upstairs. Wrap-around porch. Listed on National Register of Historic Places. Spanish, German, Italian spoken.*

CHARDON (3)

Bass Lake Inn
426 South St.(Rte.44), Chardon, OH 44024
(216) 285-3100, (216) 285-9393
Innkeeper: Bob Merkle
Rooms: 12 w/pvt bath, phone, fireplace, TV, refrigerator, Jacuzzi
Rates: $85-$95, incl full brk.
Credit cards: Most major cards
Restrictions: No pets. One night's deposit req. Min. 24-hour cancellation notice req.
Notes: Two-story house. Located in wooded area, surrounded by lake and 18-hole golf course. Small private parties accommodated. Handicapped access.

CINCINNATI (5)

Prospect Hill Bed & Breakfast Inn
408 Boal St., Cincinnati, OH 45210
(513) 421-4408
Innkeeper: Tony Jenkins, Gary Hackney
Rooms: 3 w/TV, incl. 1 w/pvt. bath, 2 w/fireplace
Rates: $79-$99, incl. cont. brk. Discount avail. for extended stay.
Credit cards: Most major cards
Restrictions: No children under 10, pets. Smoking restricted. Deposit req. 7-day cancellation notice req., less 10% fee.
Notes: Two-story Italianate townhouse built in 1867. Fully restored. Located on hillside overlooking Cincinnati. Formal dining room, side porch. Furnished with period antiques.*

Victoria Inn of Hyde Park
3567 Shaw Ave., Cincinnati, OH 45208
(513) 321-3567, (513) 321-3147
Innkeeper: Tom Possert & Debra Moore

Rooms: 2 plus 1 suite, all w/pvt. bath, phone, TV
Rates: $69-$79/room, $99/suite, all incl. full brk.
Credit cards: Most major cards
Restrictions: No children under 14, pets, smoking. 7-day cancellation req. 2-night min. stay on wknds.
Notes: Two-story Victorian style inn. Dining room. Decorated with antiques. In-ground pool. Guests have access to fax and copier. Small private parties accommodated. German spoken.

VICTORIA INN OF HYDE PARK

CLEVELAND (3)

Baricelli Inn
2203 Cornell Rd., Cleveland, OH 44106
(216) 791-6500, (216) 791-9131
Innkeeper: Kim Duda, Mike Moroni
Rooms: 3 plus 4 suites, all w/pvt. bath, phone, TV
Rates: $100/room, $130/suite, all incl. cont. brk. Discount avail. for extended stay.
Credit cards: Most major cards
Restrictions: No children under 5, pets. Deposit req. 7-day cancellation notice req., less 25% fee.
Notes: Turn-of-the-century brownstone built in 1896. Fully renovated in 1981. Located in Little Italy area. 5 dining rooms, incl. 3 with fireplace. Atrium, 2 glassed-in porches. Decorated with American and European antiques. Gourmet restaurant on premises. Guests have access to laundry, wine cellar. Off-street parking, passes to local fitness club available. Spanish spoken.

COLUMBUS (4)

Lansing Street B & B
180 Lansing St., Columbus, OH 43206
(614) 444-8488, (800) 383-7839
Innkeeper: Marcia A. Barck
Rooms: 2 suites w/pvt. bath, phone, TV
Rates: $65, incl. full brk., afternoon refreshment.
Credit cards: None

Restrictions: No smoking, 50% deposit req.
Notes: Two-story house with ten foot high ceilings and wood floors, located in the German Village. Greatroom with fireplace, courtyard with garden.

Penguin Crossing
295 E. N. Broadway, Columbus, OH 43214
(614) 261-7854, (800) 736-4846
Innkeeper: Ross and Tracey Irvin
Rooms: 3 w/phone, incl. 1 w/pvt. bath
Rates: $75-$125, incl. full brk. Discount avail. for extended and senior citizen stays.
Credit cards: Most major cards
Restrictions: Deposit req. 2-cancellation notice req. Total payment maybe req. for holidays and special events.
Notes: Two-story English Country inn built in 1923. Porch with swing and wicker furniture. Furnished with antiques, family heirlooms, and period pieces.

DANVILLE (2)

WHITE OAK INN

White Oak Inn
29683 Walhonding Rd., Danville, OH 43014
(614) 599-6107, (614) 599-9407
Innkeeper: Ian and Yvonne Martin
Rooms: 10 w/pvt. bath, phone, incl 3 w/fireplace, 1 w/TV. Located in 2 bldgs.
Rates: $75-$110, incl full brk., afternoon refreshment. Seasonal variations. Discount avail. for extended stay.
Credit cards: Most major cards
Restrictions: No children under 14, pets, smoking. Deposit req. 14-day cancellation notice. 2-night min. stay.
Notes: Two-story country house crafted by hand from red and white oak timber. Located on 14 wooded acres in the Walhonding Valley. Common room with antique square grand piano and fireplace. Furnished with antiques. Board and yard games, puzzles and bicycles available. Front porch with rockers and swings. Small private parties accommodated. Resident dog. French spoken.*

FORT RECOVERY (1)

Main Street Inn B & B
109 N. Main St., Fort Recovery, OH 45846
(419) 375-4955, (419) 375-4488
Innkeeper: Ginny Ruskin
Rooms: 3 plus 1 suite, all w/pvt. bath, incl. 1 w/fireplace, 2 w/TV
Rates: $48-$53/room, $58-$63/suite, all incl. full brk. Special pkgs. avail.
Credit cards: Most major cards
Restrictions: No pets, smoking.
Notes: Two-story Victorian styled house built in 1870. Grand foyer, high ceilings. Furnished with antiques.*

LANCASTER (6)

Butterfly Inn
6695 Lancaster-Circleville Rd., Lancaster, OH 43130
(614) 654-7654
Innkeeper: Ernie and Eloise Bolin
Rooms: 4, incl. 2 w/pvt. bath, all w/TV
Rates: $45. Discount avail. for extended stay.
Credit cards: None
Restrictions: No pets. Smoking restricted. $10.00 deposit req. 7-day cancellation notice req.
Notes: Ranch house located on 105 acres. Breakfast and dining and room. TV room, patio, gazebo, greenhouse, and butterfly flower bed.

LOUISVILLE (3)

The Mainstay
1320 Main St. E., Louisville, OH 44641
(216) 875-1021
Innkeeper: Joe and Mary Shurilla
Rooms: 2 plus 1 suite, all w/pvt. bath
Rates: $50/room, $60/suite, incl. full brk. afternoon refreshment. Discount avail. for extended stay.
Credit cards: MC, V
Restrictions: No pets, smoking. $20.00 deposit req. 7-day cancellation notice req.
Notes: Two-story Queen Anne Victorian house with carved oak, tin ceilings, built in 1886. Sitting room. Furnished with antiques. Guests have access to laundry. Off-street parking available. Resident dog.*

LUCASVILLE (6)

The Olde Lamplighter
9 West St., Box 820, Lucasville, OH 45648
(614) 259-3002
Innkeeper: Gaylord and Marilyn Liles
Rooms: 4, no pvt. bath
Rates: $48, incl. cont. brk. Discount avail. for extended stay.
Credit cards: MC, V
Restrictions: No children under 12, pets, smoking. One night's deposit req. 2-day cancellation notice req. 2-night min. stay on wknds.

Notes: Two-story brick house built in 1939. Living room with cable TV. Dining room. Furnished with family heirlooms, incl. Grandfather clock built in 1927. Rooftop sundeck. Piano and electric organ. Porch with wicker furniture.*

MARBLEHEAD (2)

Victorian Inn
5622 E. Harbor Rd., Marblehead, OH 43440
(419) 734-5611, (419) 734-6525
Innkeeper: Ron and Nancy Lehman
Rooms: 7, plus 1 suite, no pvt. bath
Rates: $65-$150/room, $85/suite, incl. expanded cont. brk.
Credit cards: Most major cards
Restrictions: No children under 12. Pets, smoking restricted. Three night's deposit req. 3-day cancellation notice req.
Notes: Victorian house built in the late 1800s. Restored and has operated as an inn since 1985. Formal living room with TV and fireplace, coffee room. Garden gazebo room. Brass beds in rooms. 10-person spa. Small private parties accommodated. Handicapped access.*

MARION (4)

The Olde Towne Manor
245 St. James St., Marion, OH 43302
(614) 382-2402
Innkeeper: Mary Louisa Rimbach
Rooms: 4 w/pvt. bath
Rates: $55-$65, incl. full brk.
Credit cards: MC, V
Restrictions: No children under 12, pets. Smoking restricted. Deposit req. 2-day cancellation notice req.
Notes: Two-story stone mansion built in 1920. Located on one acre in historic district. Fireside room. Library with 1,000 books. Pool table, sauna. Gazebo.

MOUNT VERNON (4)

Russell-Cooper House
115 E. Gambier St., Mount Vernon, OH 43050
(614) 397-8638
Innkeeper: Tim and Maureen Tyler
Rooms: 6 w/pvt. bath
Rates: $75, incl. full brk., afternoon and evening refreshment. Seasonal variations, Discount avail. for mid-week stay.
Credit cards: Most major cards
Restrictions: No children under 13, pets. Smoking restricted. Full prepayment req. 14-day cancellation notice req.
Notes: Two-story Victorian Gothic mansion built in 1829. Fully renovated and has operated as inn since 1987. Cherry-lined library with double-mantled fireplace. Dining hall with embossed tin ceiling, twin marble fireplaces. Sun room with wicker furniture, cable TV, refrigerator. Furnished with antiques, Civil War memorabilia. Listed on the National Register of Historic Places. Art gallery, studio on premises. Small private parties accommodated. Innkeepers are artist/crafters and preservation consultants.*

OLD WASHINGTON (4)

Zane Trace B & B
225 Old National Rd., Box 115, Old Washington, OH 43768
(614) 489-5970, (301) 757-4262 (off-season)
Innkeeper: Max and Ruth Wilson
Rooms: 3 plus 1 suite, incl. 1 w/fireplace, no pvt. bath
Rates: $40-$45/room, $68/suite, all incl. cont. brk.
Credit cards: None
Restrictions: Children under 12 welcome with prior notification. No pets. Restricted smoking. One night's deposit req. 7-day cancellation notice req., less $5.00 fee. Closed Nov. 1–May 1.
Notes: Italianate Victorian house built in 1859. Located on Old National Trail in Zane Grey territory. Parlor, card and reading room, screened porch, heated outdoor swimming pool, landscaped grounds.

ORRVILLE (3)

Grandma's House
5598 Chippewa Rd., Orrville, OH 44667-9750
(216) 682-5112
Innkeeper: Marilyn and David Farver
Rooms: 5, incl. 3 w/pvt. bath
Rates: $55-$90, incl. cont. brk. Discount avail. for extended, mid-week, and senior citizen stays.
Credit cards: V
Restrictions: No pets, smoking. Deposit req. 7-day cancellation notice req.
Notes: Solid brick farm house with original chestnut woodwork and wainscotting, built in the 1860s. Located in farm setting amongst corn, hay and wheat fields. Family owned for over 60 years. Parlor, dining room, kitchen. Board games, phone available. Lawns with picnic tables. Flower beds with benches. Front porch with hickory rockers. Resident dog, cats, and farm animals on premises. Limited handicapped access.

POLAND (3)

The Inn at the Green
500 S. Main St., Poland, OH 44514
(216) 757-4688
Innkeeper: Ginny and Steve Meloy
Rooms: 4 w/pvt. bath, TV, phone, incl. 3 w/fireplace
Rates: $50, incl. cont. brk., evening refreshment
Credit cards: Most major cards
Restrictions: No children under 5, pets. Deposit req. 7-day cancellation notice req.
Notes: Two-story Victorian townhouse with 12-ft. ceilings, original poplar floors built in 1876. Located on village green. Fully restored. Greeting room, parlor each with fireplace. Sitting room with TV, library. Meeting room. Enclosed porch with wicker furniture overlooking deck, patio, garden. Furnished with antiques, oriental rugs, and American art. Small private parties accommodated.*

RIPLEY (5)

The Baird House
201 N. 2nd St., Ripley, OH 45167
(513) 392-4918

Innkeeper: Glenn and Patricia Kittle
Rooms: 2 w/fireplace, incl. 1 w/pvt. bath, plus 1 suite w/pvt. bath, fireplace
Rates: $60-$75/room, $85/suite, all incl. full brk., afternoon refreshment
Credit cards: None
Restrictions: No children under 12, pets, smoking. 50% deposit req. 3-day cancellation notice req., less one night's fee. Closed one week in May, 2 weeks in Feb.
Notes: Two-story Italianate house built in 1825. Has operated as inn since 1989. Parlor, formal dining room, each with marble fireplace. Furnished with antiques, family keepsakes. Wrought-iron lace porch, balcony overlooking Ohio River. Library, books, and games available for guests enjoyment. Listed on the National Register of Historic Places.

Signal House
234 N. Front St., Ripley, OH 45167
(513) 392-1640
Innkeeper: Vic and Betsy Billingsley
Rooms: 2, no pvt. bath
Rates: $65-$754, incl. full brk., afternoon refreshment. Discount avail. for mid-week and extended stays.
Credit cards: None
Restrictions: No children, pets. Smoking restricted. Deposit req.
Notes: Two-story Greek Italianate style house with ornate plaster moldings, 12' ceilings, built on the Ohio River in the 1830s. Instrumental in Underground Railroad. Twin parlors with antique pump organ, piano. Board games, area history books available. Furnished with air of yesteryear. Three porches overlooking the river.*

SIGNAL HOUSE

SAINT MARYS (1)

Grand Lake St. Marys B & B
524 W. South St., Saint Marys, OH 45885-2239
(419) 394-1138, (800) 484-8409, ext. 1895
Innkeeper: Greg and Diane Hemsoth
Rooms: 4, incl. 1 w/pvt. bath, plus 1/suite w/pvt bath

Rates: $50, incl. cont. brk. Discount available for senior citizen, mid-week and extended stays.
Credit cards: MC, V
Restrictions: No children under nine, pets, smoking. Deposit req. 3-day cancellation notice req., less fee.
Notes: Three-story butter brick house with fireplaces, woodwork, staircases, built in late 1890s. Dining room backbar crafted from Black Forest lumber. Ballroom, front parlor. Small private parties accommodated.

SANDUSKY (2)

The Red Gables B & B
421 Wayne St., Sandusky, OH 44870
(419) 625-1189
Innkeeper: Jo Ellen Cuthbertson
Rooms: 4, incl. 2/pvt. bath
Rates: $50-$90, incl. cont. brk. Seasonal variations. Discount avail. for group stays.
Credit cards: None
Restrictions: No children Fri. & Sat. except by special arrangement. No pets, smoking. Deposit req. 14-day cancellation notice req. 2-night min stay on holiday wknds.
Notes: Two-story Tudor Revival house built around 1907. Located in Old Plat District. Great room with fireplace, bay window. Wicker-filled sitting area. Decorated in eclectic style with handmade slipcovers, curtains and comforters, and Oriental artifacts. Innkeeper is a semi-retired theatrical costume-maker.

Wagner's 1844 Inn
230 E. Washington St., Sandusky, OH 44870
(419) 626-1726
Innkeeper: Walt and Barb Wagner
Rooms: 3 w/phone, no pvt. bath
Rates: $50-$100, incl. cont. brk. Seasonal variations.
Credit cards: Most major cards
Restrictions: No children, pets, smoking. Full prepayment req., May–Oct. 7-day cancellation notice req. 2-night min. stay on holiday wknds.
Notes: Built in 1844. Located within walking distance of Sandusky's Historic District. Formal dining room, parlor with fireplace, billard room with TV. Screened veranda, enclosed courtyard. Furnished with antiques. Listed in National Register of Historic Places. Resident dog and cat.

SUGARCREEK (4)

Marbeyo B & B
2370 CR 144, Sugarcreek, OH 44681
(216) 852-4533
Innkeeper: Mark and Betty Yoder
Rooms: 3 w/pvt bath
Rates: $40-$55, incl cont. brk. Seasonal variations. Discount avail. for extended stay.
Credit cards: MC, V
Restrictions: No pets, smoking. $20.00 deposit req. 48-hour cancellation notice req.
Notes: Amish Mennonite family house located on 100 acre working dairy farm with petting animals. Dining room, porch. Homemade quilts for sale. German, Pennsylvania Dutch spoken. Resident farm animals.

TIPP CITY (1)

Willowtree Inn
1900 W. Rte. 571, Tipp City, OH 45371
(513) 667-2957
Innkeeper: Tom and Peggy Nordquist
Rooms: 3, plus 1 suite, all w/pvt. bath, TV
Rates: $48-$68/room, $120/suite, all incl. full brk. Discount avail. for extended, senior citizen, and mid-week stays.
Credit cards: MC, V
Restrictions: No children under 8, pets. Smoking restricted. Min. one night's deposit req. 7-day cancellation notice req.
Notes: Federal-style manor house built in 1830, located on 5 acres. Fully restored. Dining room with fireplace, living room with TV. Meeting rooms available. Original 1830 springhouse-smokehouse and pond on property. Furnished with antiques. Outdoor spa and deck overlooking pond. Small private parties accommodated. 18th- and 19th-century antique shop next door.*

TROY (1)

Allen Villa Bed & Breakfast
434 S. Market St., Troy, OH 45373
(513) 335-1181
Innkeeper: Robert and June Smith
Rooms: 5 plus 2 apts., all w/pvt. bath, phone, TV, VCR. Located in 2 bldgs.
Rates: $69-$74, incl. full brk., afternoon refreshment. Discount avail. for senior citizen stay.
Credit cards: Most major cards
Restrictions: No children under 12, pets. Smoking restricted. Deposit req. 24-hour cancellation notice req., less $10.00 fee.
Notes: Three-story Victorian mansion built in 1874. Formal dining room. Furnished with Victorian furniture, period antiques.

URBANA (4)

Northern Plantation B & B
3421 E. Rte. 296, Urbana, OH 43078
(513) 652-1782, (800) 652-1782
Innkeeper: Dave and Marsha Martin
Rooms: 4, incl. 1/pvt. bath
Rates: $65-$90, incl. full brk., evening refreshment
Credit cards: Most major cards
Restrictions: No children under 12. Smoking restricted. 50% deposit req. 48-hour cancellation notice req.
Notes: Two-story plantation house built in 1913. Located on 100 acres. Four generation family home since 1865. Parlor. Decorated with original furnishings. Fishing pond.

WEST LIBERTY (1)

Liberty House B & B
208 N. Detroit St., West Liberty, OH 43357-0673
(513) 465-1101, (800) 437-8109

Innkeeper: Russ and Sue Peterson
Rooms: 3 w/pvt. bath
Rates: $50-$65, incl. full brk. Discount avail. for extended stay.
Credit cards: Most major cards
Restrictions: Pets welcome with prior arrangement. Smoking restricted. Deposit req. 10-day cancellation notice req.
Notes: Two-story house with patterned oak floors and woodwork, built in early 1900s. Common room with phone and TV. Decorated with oriental rugs, antique furnishings, old and new quilts. Gardens. Wrap-around porch with swing.

WILLIAMSBURG (5)

Lewis McKever Farmhous
4475 McKeever Pike, Williamsburg, OH 45176
(513) 724-7044
Innkeeper: John and Carol Sandberg
Rooms: 3 w/pvt. bath
Rates: $65, incl. cont. brk., afternoon refreshment. Discount avail. for extended stay.
Credit cards: MC, V
Restrictions: No children under 12, pets, smoking. 24-hour cancellation notice req.
Notes: Two-story rural-Italianate brick farmhouse built in 1841. Located on ten acres. Parlor, dining room, second floor porch. Library with fireplace. Listed on the National Register of Historic Places.

MORGAN HOUSE

YELLOW SPRINGS (5)

Morgan House
120 W. Limestone St., Yellow Springs, OH 45387
(513) 767-7509
Innkeeper: M. Britton
Rooms: 4, no pvt. bath
Rates: $45-$55, incl. cont. brk. Discount avail. for extended and mid-week stays.
Credit cards: MC, V

Restrictions: No pets, smoking. Deposit req. 7-day cancellation notice req.
Notes: Three-story Tudor house built in 1921. Fully restored in 1986. Common room with TV. Screened porch overlooking gardens. Furnished with antiques, local artwork.

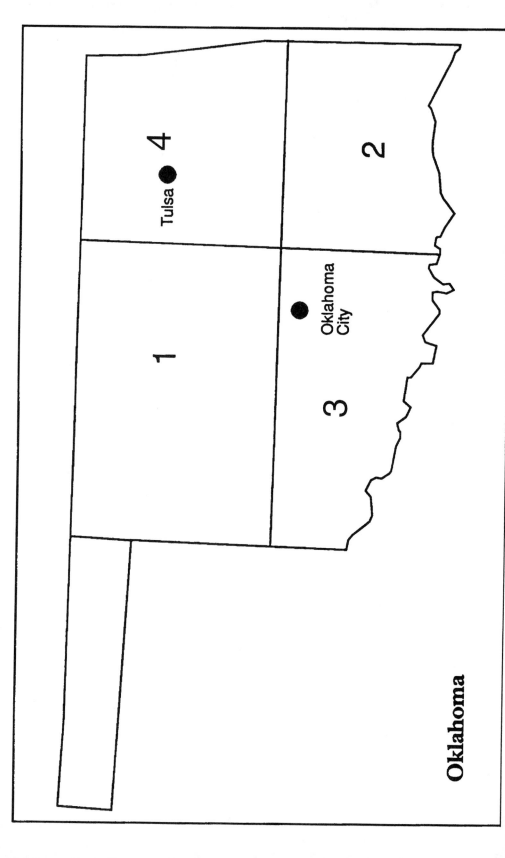

Oklahoma

Oklahoma

EDMOND (3)

The Arcadian Inn
328 E. 1st, Edmond, OK 73013
(405) 348-6347, (800) 299-6347
Innkeeper: Martha Hall
Rooms: 4 plus 1 suite, all w/pvt. bath, incl 2 w/phone
Rates: $65-$95/room, $120/suite, all incl. full brk. Discount avail. for mid-week stay.
Credit cards: Most major cards
Restrictions: No pets, smoking. Deposit req. 5-day cancellation notice req.
Notes: Three-story Victorian-style inn built in 1908. Wrap-around front porch with swing. Dining room. Parlor. Decorated with antiques. Garden spa.*

GROVE (4)

Oak Tree Bed & Breakfast
1007 S. Main, Grove, OK 74344
(918) 786-9119
Innkeeper: Mack and Mary Oyler
Rooms: 3, no pvt. bath
Rates: $45-$60, incl. full brk., evening refreshment
Credit cards: None
Restrictions: No children, pets, smoking. Deposit req. 2-day cancellation notice req., less $10.00 fee.
Notes: Located on Grand Lake o' the Cherokees. Living room with fireplace. Library with books, TV. Dining room. Furnished in traditional decor.

NORMAN (5)

Holmberg House B & B
766 DeBarr, Norman, OK 73069
(405) 321-6221, (800) 646-6221
Innkeeper: Richard Divelbiss, Jo Meacham
Rooms: 4 w/pvt. bath, TV
Rates: $55-$85, incl. full brk.
Credit cards: Most major cards
Restrictions: No children under 12, pets. Smoking restricted. One night's deposit req. 7-day cancellation notice req. 2-night min. stay on some wknds.
Notes: Two-story Craftsman-style house built in 1914 by the first dean of the University of Oklahoma's College of Fine Arts. Has operated as inn since 1994. Parlor with fireplace. Dining room. Front porch with rocking chairs. Furnished with antiques. Gardens. Small private parties accommodated. Listed on the National Register of Historic Places. Resident dog.

OKLAHOMA CITY (3)

Flora's B & B
2312 NW 46th, Oklahoma City, OK 73112
(405) 840-3157

Innkeeper: Newt and Joann Flora
Rooms: 2 suites w/pvt. bath, incl. 1 w/phone
Rates: $55, incl. full brk.
Credit cards: None
Restrictions: No children under 11, pets. Smoking restricted. Deposit req. 14-day cancellation notice req.
Notes: Common room with fireplace. Balcony, spa. Furnished with antiques and collectables. Covered guest parking available. Handicapped access.

WILBURTON (2)

The Dome House B & B
315 E. Main St., Wilburton, OK 74578
(918) 465-0092

Innkeeper: Raymen and Laverne McFerran
Rooms: 1 w/pvt. bath, phone, plus 3 suites w/pvt. bath, phone, TV, plus 1 cottage
Rates: $45/room, $55-$65/suite, $75/cottage, all incl. cont. brk., afternoon refreshment.
Credit cards: None
Restrictions: No children under 6, pets. Smoking restricted. Deposit req. 3-day cancellation notice req., less $5.00 fee.
Notes: Two-story house built in 1908. Named for its distinctive dome-topped, two-story turret. Parlor with fireplace, antique grand piano. Porches. Guest sitting area in turret. Cottage with private patio, barbeque.

Oregon

ASHLAND (5)

Ashland's Victory House
271 Beach St., Ashland, OR 97520
(503) 488-4428
Innkeeper: Dale Swire
Rooms: 5 w/pvt. bath, incl. 1 w/phone, 1 w/TV. Suite avail.
Rates: $75-$85/room, $175/suite, all incl. full brk. Seasonal variations. Discount avail. for extended stay. Special pkgs. avail.
Credit cards: None
Restrictions: No pets. Children over 12 restricted to suite. Smoking restricted. Min. one night's deposit req. 10-day cancellation notice req. 2-night min. stay on wknds. in high season.
Notes: Two-story, Tudor-style house with hardwood floors, built in 1940. Living room/dining room with fireplace. Den with jukebox, TV, VCR, classic film library. Furnished with 1940s memorabilia. Private backyard with redwood deck, hot tub, gardens. Limited handicapped access.*

ASHLAND'S VICTORY HOUSE

Chanticleer Inn
120 Gresham, Ashland, OR 97520
(503) 482-1919
Innkeeper: Pebby Kuan
Rooms: 6 w/pvt. bath, phone
Rates: $90-$155, incl. full brk., evening refreshment. Seasonal variations. Special pkgs. avail.
Credit cards: MC, V
Restrictions: No pets, smoking. One night's deposit req. 14-day cancellation notice req., less $25.00 per person fee. 2-night min. stay, March 15–Nov.31
Notes: Restored 1920s Craftsman-style house with country french decor. Small private parties accommodated.*

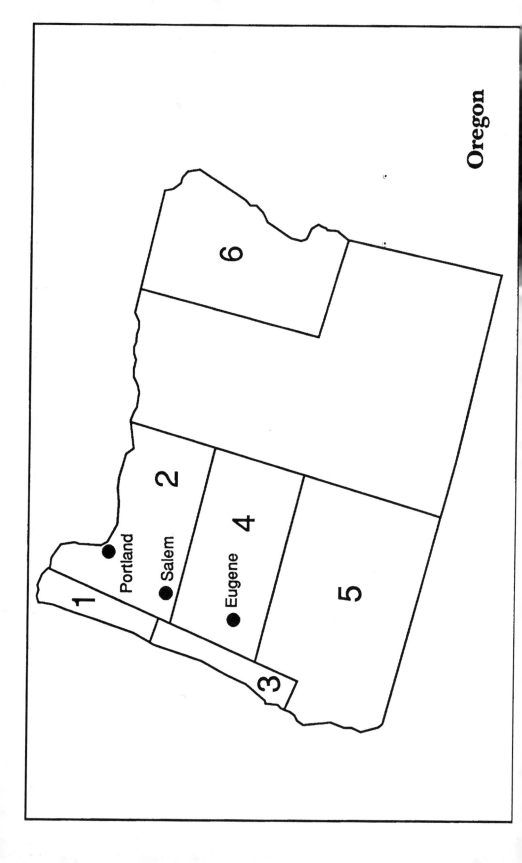

Country Willows
1313 Clay St., Ashland, OR 97520
(503) 488-1590, (800) WILLOWS, (503) 488-1611
Innkeeper: Dan Durant
Rooms: 5 plus 2 suites, all w/pvt. bath, incl. 1 suite w/fireplace. Located in 3 bldgs.
Rates: $90-$120/room, $120-$155/suite, all incl. full brk., afternoon refreshment.
Seasonal variations.
Credit cards: MC, V
Restrictions: No children under 12, pets, smoking. Deposit req. 14-cancellation notice req. 2-night min. stay on wknds. from June–Oct.
Notes: Two-story restored country farmhouse built in 1896. Located on 5 wooded, white-fenced acres with stream. Has operated as inn since 1985. Living room, dining room, den with fireplace, porches, patios, swimming pool. Resident geese, ducks and goats. Handicapped access.*

Cowslip's Belle
159 N. Main St., Ashland, OR 97520
(503) 488-2901, (800) 888-6819
Innkeeper: Jon and Carmen Reinhardt
Rooms: 3 plus 1 suite, all w/pvt. bath. Located in 2 bldgs.
Rates: $105-112/room, $120/suite, all incl. full brk., afternoon refreshment. Seasonal variations.
Credit cards: MC, V
Restrictions: No children under 10, pets, smoking. One night's deposit req. 30-day cancellation notice req. 2-night min. stay on wknds. June–Sept.
Notes: Two-story Craftsman bungalow and carriage house built in 1913. Dining room. Living room with piano. Decorated with vintage furnishings and Maxfield Parrish art. Garden patio.*

Iris Inn
59 Manzanita St., Ashland, OR 97520
(503) 488-2286
Innkeeper: Vicki Lamb
Rooms: 5 w/pvt. bath
Rates: $92, incl. full brk. Seasonal variations, November–February.
Credit cards: MC, V
Restrictions: No children under 7, pets. Smoking restricted. One night's deposit req. 10-day cancellation notice req., less $10.00 fee.
Notes: Two-story Victorian house built in 1905. Living room, dining room. Deck overlooking rose garden. Furnished with country antiques. Small private parties accommodated. Spanish, Greek spoken.

Mount Ashland Inn
550 Mt. Ashland, Box 944, Ashland, OR 97520
(503) 482-8707
Innkeeper: Jerry and Elaine Shanafelt
Rooms: 4 plus 1 suite, all w/pvt. bath, phone
Rates: $80-$130, incl. full brk., afternoon refreshment. Discount avail. for extended mid-week stay, Nov.–April.
Credit cards: MC, V

Restrictions: No children under 10, pets, smoking. One night's deposit req. 10-day cancellation notice req., less $10.00 fee. 2-night min. stay on wknds. and holidays, June 1–Sept. 30.

Notes: Two-story inn with decorative deck railing, log arches, log slab circular staircase designed and built in 1987 by innkeepers from cedar logs, most of which were cut and milled on the property. Located at 5,500 ft. elevation. Main room with stone fireplace, library. Deck overlooking Siskiyou Mountains. Decorated with antiques, hand-crafted furniture, homemade quilts, Oriental rugs, stained-glass. Dinner available Nov.–April.*

Oak Hill Country B & B
2190 Siskiyou Blvd., Ashland, OR 97520
(503) 482-1554, (800) 888-7434

Innkeeper: Tracy and Ron Bass
Rooms: 5 w/pvt. bath
Rates: $60-$90, incl. full brk. Seasonal variations. Special pkg. avail.
Credit cards: MC, V
Restrictions: No children uner 8, pets, smoking. One night's deposit req. 10-day cancellation notice req.
Notes: Two-story Craftsman-style farmhouse built in 1910. Living room with fireplace, dining room, veranda. Deck and garden. Bicycles available.

OAK HILL COUNTRY B & B

Pinehurst Inn at Jenny Creek
17250 Highway 66, Ashland, OR 97520
(503) 488-1002

Innkeeper: Mike and Mary Jo Moloney and Dan and Melissa Moloney
Rooms: 4 rooms, 2 suites, all w/pvt. bath
Rates: $75-$105/room, $110-$140/suite, all incl. brk., dinner. Discount avail. for mid-week stay.
Credit cards: Most major cards
Restrictions: No pets, smoking. Deposit req. 7-day cancellation notice req.
Notes: Roadhouse built in 1920. Fully restored. Located on 24 acres of the Cascade Mountains on Jenny Creek. Restaurant on premises.

Woods House
333 N. Main St., Ashland, OR 97520
(503) 488-1598, (800) 435-8260, (503) 482-7912

Innkeeper: Francoise and Lester Roddy
Rooms: 5 w/pvt. bath, plus carriage house suite. Located in 2 bldgs.
Rates: $65-$110, incl. full brk., afternoon and evening refreshment. Seasonal variations.
Credit cards: MC, V
Restrictions: No children under 5, pets, smoking. One night's deposit req. 14-day cancellation notice req. 2-night min. stay, June–Oct.
Notes: Two-story, Craftsman-style house built in 1908. Living room with fireplace, books, music. Dining room. Furnished with fresh flowers and lace. Grounds include majestic trees, grape arbors, rose gardens with tables and chairs. Front porch swing.*

WOODS HOUSE

ASTORIA (1)

Astoria Inn
3391 Irving Ave., Astoria, OR 97103-2632
(503) 325-8153

Innkeeper: Mickey Cox
Rooms: 3 w/pvt bath
Rates: $70-$85, incl. full brk. Seasonal variations.
Credit cards: MC, V
Restrictions: No children, pets. Smoking restricted. Deposit req. 2-day cancellation notice req.
Notes: Two-story Victorian house with veranda built in 1890s. Parlor with TV, VCR, video movies. Library with board games. Listed in the National Register of Historic Places. Small private parties accommodated. Resident dog.

Franklin St. Station B & B
1140 Franklin Ave., Astoria, OR 97103
(503) 325-4314, (800) 448-1098

Innkeeper: Renee Caldwell
Rooms: 4 plus 2 suites, incl. 1 suite w/fireplace, 2 w/TV, most w/pvt. bath
Rates: $63-$78/room, $85-$115/suite, all incl. full brk. Seasonal variations.
Credit cards: MC, V
Restrictions: No pets. Smoking restricted. One-night's deposit req. 3-day cancellation notice req. Min. stay req. for holiday and special event wknds.
Notes: Three-story inn built in 1900s. Decorated with ornate craftsmanship. New Captains Quarters.*

Grandview Bed & Breakfast
1574 Grand Ave., Astoria, OR 97103
(800) 488-3250

Innkeeper: Charleen Maxwell
Rooms: 3, no pvt. bath, plus 3 suites w/pvt. bath
Rates: $39-$92/room, $85-$110/suite, incl. cont. brk. Seasonal variations.
Credit cards: Most major cards
Restrictions: No children under 7, pets, smoking, alcohol. Unmarried couples will be uncomfortable. Deposit req. 2-day cancellation notice req.
Notes: Richardson shingle-style Victorian inn built in 1900. Open staircase, bay windows, bullet turret and inset balcony overlooking Columbia River. Located on the Historic Homes Walking Tour. Small private parties accommodated. Resident cats.

Inn-Chanted B & B
707 8th St., Astoria, OR 97103
(503) 325-5223

Innkeeper: Richard and Dixie Swart
Rooms: 2 w/pvt. bath, TV, incl. 1 w/fireplace, plus 1 suite w/pvt. bath, TV
Rates: $70-$80/room, $90/suite, all incl. full brk. afternoon refreshment. Seasonal variations. Discount avail. for extended stay.
Credit cards: Most major cards
Restrictions: No pets, smoking. Deposit req. 7-day cancellation notice req.
Notes: Some French spoken.*

BANDON (3)

Riverboat B & B
Rt. 2, Box 2485, Bandon, OR 97411
(503) 347-1922, (800) 348-1922

Innkeeper: Joe and Dixie Bolduc
Rooms: 8 staterooms w/pvt. bath
Rates: $125, incl. full brk.
Credit cards: Most major cards
Restrictions: No children, pets, smoking, high heels. One night's deposit req. 10-day cancellation notice req.
Notes: Authentic diesel-powered, three-story, sternwheel, 97-ft. riverboat built in 1993. Common room with woodburning stove, board games. Dining room. Open afterdeck. Breakfast served while underway, traveling up the Coquille River, under drawbridge. Remains moored in evening. Furnished with antiques.

Sea Star Guesthouse
375 Second St., Bandon, OR 97411
(503) 347-9632

Innkeeper: David and Monica Jennings
Rooms: 2 w/pvt. bath, TV, plus 2 suites w/pvt. bath, TV
Rates: $65-$75/room, $90-$100/suite, all incl. brk. allowance, evening refreshment. Seasonal variations. Discount avail. for extended stay.
Credit cards: Most major cards
Restrictions: No pets, smoking. One night's deposit req. 2-day cancellation notice req.
Notes: Two-story wood frame house with loft built 1987 overlooking harbor. Restaurant on premises.

BROOKINGS (5)

Holmes Sea Cove Bed & Breakfast
17350 Holmes Dr., Brookings, OR 97415
(503) 469-3025
Innkeeper: Jack and Lorene Holmes
Rooms: 3 suites w/pvt. bath, cable TV, refrigerator
Rates: $80-$95, incl. cont. brk. Discount avail. for extended stay.
Credit cards: MC, V
Restrictions: Children, smoking restricted. No pets. Min. one night's deposit req. 7-day cancellation notice req., less $10.00 fee. 2-night min. stay on major holidays.
Notes: Cedar house and guest cottage built in 1965. All rooms have ocean view and private entrance. Gazebo, private park with picnic tables. Furnished with antiques. Airport pick-up available.*

COTTAGE GROVE (4)

Lea House Inn Bed & Breakfast
433 Padific Hwy., (99S), Cottage Grove, OR 97424
(503) 942-5686
Innkeeper: Michelle & Keith Lawhorn
Rooms: 3, no pvt. bath, incl. 1 w/TV
Rates: $45-$55, incl. full brk., afternoon and evening refreshment. Seasonal variations. Special pkgs. avail.
Credit cards: Most major cards

Restrictions: Smoking restricted. One night's deposit req. 2-day cancellation notice req.
Notes: Two-story Victorian house built in 1890s. Upstairs parlor. May have breakfast in room. Furnished with antiques. Restaurant on premises. Picnic lunch and bicycles available.*

DAYVILLE (4)

Fish House Inn
P.O. Box 143, Dayville, OR 97825
(503) 987-2124
Innkeeper: Mike and Denise Smith
Rooms: 3, incl. 1 in the attic w/pvt. bath, plus cottage w/pvt. bath. Located in 2 bldgs.
Rates: $35-$50, incl. full brk.
Credit cards: None
Restrictions: No smoking. One-night deposit req.
Notes: Two-story house built in 1908. Originally home for first liquor store owner. Original tiny liquor store was turned into a dance studio for local children. Small cottage in back remodeled with two guest rooms. Decorated with finds from farm sales, things Piscean and baskets Denise wove from river willows. Guests have access to fruit trees, grapevines, and berry bushes. Horseshoe pits, and bar-b-que grills available.

ELMIRA (4)

McGillivray's Log Home B & B
88680 Evers Rd., Elmira, OR 97437
(503) 935-3564
Innkeeper: Evelyn McGillivray
Rooms: 2 w/pvt. bath, phone
Rates: $60-$70, incl. full brk.
Credit cards: MC, V
Restrictions: No pets, smoking. Deposit req. 3-day cancellation notice req.
Notes: Log house built in 1982. Has operated as inn since 1984. Located on five wooded acres. Kitchen with antique wood stove. Covered porches. Central heat and air conditioning. Handicapped access.

EUGENE (4)

The Campbell House
252 Pearl St., Eugene, OR 97401
(503) 343-1119, (503) 343-2258
Innkeeper: Myra Plant
Rooms: 14 w/pvt. bath, TV, VCR. Suites avail.
Rates: $75-$175, incl. brk. Discount avail. for mid-week stay. Seasonal variations.
Credit cards: Most major cards
Restrictions: No pets, smoking.
Notes: Two-story Queen Anne Victorian inn with gables built in 1892 with elements of the Shingle Style. Fully restored. Has operated as inn since 1993. Parlor, library, meeting room. Furnished with antiques. Guests have access to fax and photocopy machines. Small private parties accommodated. Handicapped access.

Duckworth Bed & Breakfast Inn
987 E. 19th Ave., Eugene, OR 97403
(503) 686-2451, (800) 713-2451
Innkeeper: Fred and Peggy Ward
Rooms: 3 w/TV, incl. 1 w/pvt. bath
Rates: $75-$85, incl. full brk. Discount avail. for extended, mid-week, and senior citizen stays. Seasonal variations.
Credit cards: None
Restrictions: No children under 12, pets, smoking. One night's deposit req. 7-day cancellation notice req., less one night's fee.
Notes: Two-story Crossman English Tudor cottage built in 1926. Parlor with fireplace, player piano, TV, VCR. Garden room with board games, library. Furnished with English and American antiques. Gardens with stone paths, tree swing, willow furniture. Bicycles available.

The Oval Door
988 Lawrence, Eugene, OR 97401-2827
(503) 683-3160, (502) 485-5339
Innkeeper: Judith McLane & Dianne Feist
Rooms: 4 w/pvt. bath
Rates: $65-$83, incl. full brk. Discount avail. for extended stay.
Credit cards: MC, V
Restrictions: No pets, smoking. One night's deposit req. 4-day cancellation notice req. 2-night min. stay during University functions, conventions.
Notes: Two-story inn built in 1990 with look of 1920s style. Living room with fireplace, library with TV, VCR, CDs. Dining room, tub room with whirlpool bath for two, music, candles. Furnished with antiques and traditional decor. Phone jacks in rooms. Wrap-around porch. Special dietary needs accommodated.*

Pookie's B & B on College Hill
2013 Charnelton St., Eugene, OR 97405
(503) 343-0383, (800) 558-0383, (503) 343-0383
Innkeeper: Pookie and Doug Walling
Rooms: 2 w/phone, incl. 1 w/pvt. bath
Rates: $65-$80, incl. full brk. Discount avail. for senior citizen, and group stays.
Credit cards: None
Restrictions: No children under 6, pets. Smoking restricted. One night's deposit req. 3-day cancellation notice req.
Notes: Two-story Craftsman style house with floor to ceiling wood moldings, built in 1918. Fully renovated. Formal dining room. Sitting area with TV, VCR, refrigerator. Furnished with period antiques of mahogany and oak. Special dietary needs accommodated.

GOVERNMENT CAMP (2)

Falcon's Crest
87287 Gov. Cp. Hwy., Box 185, Government Camp, OR 97028
(503) 272-3403, (800) 624-7384
Innkeeper: Robert and Melodie Johnson
Rooms: 3 w/pvt. bath, phone, plus 2 suites w/pvt. bath, phone
Rates: $85-$100/room, $110-$165/suite, all incl. full brk., afternoon refreshment. Discount avail. for extended stay. Special pkgs. avail.

Credit cards: Most major cards
Restrictions: No children under 6, pets, smoking. 50% of one night's deposit req. 48-hour cancellation notice req. 2-3 night min. stay in ski and holiday seasons.
Notes: Three-story chalet-style house. Renovated in 1983. Has operated as inn since 1987. Lobby with library. Dining room. Restaurant on premises. Great Room with wood stove, two decks overlooking Ski Bowl Mountain. Game table, board games. Selection of audio and visual tapes. Mystery Weekends organized. Small private parties accommodated.*

Mt. Hood Manor
P.O. Box 369, Government Camp, OR 97028
(503) 272-3440
Innkeeper: Mary Swanson
Rooms: 4 w/pvt. bath, phone, TV, VCR
Rates: $70-$140, incl. full brk. Discount avail. for extended stay.
Credit cards: None
Restrictions: No pets, smoking. Deposit req. 2-day cancellation notice req.
Notes: Tudor style inn built in 1993. Library of contemporary and classic films. Sitting room with fireplace. Outdoor hot tub.*

GRANTS PASS (5)

The Ahlf House Inn
762 N.W. 6th St., Grants Pass, OR 97526-1524
(503) 464-1374, (800) 863-1374
Innkeeper: Ken and Cathy Neuschafer
Rooms: 3 w/pvt. bath, TV, plus 1 suite w/pvt. bath, kitchen, Jacuzzi
Rates: $65-$75/room, $60/suite, all incl. full brk., evening refreshment. Seasonal variations. Discount avail. for extended, mid-week, and senior citizen stays.
Credit cards: Most major cards
Restrictions: No children under 10, pets, smoking. One night's deposit req. 3-day cancellation notice req.
Notes: Queen Anne Victorian house built in 1898. Recently remodeled.*

The Washington Inn
1002 N.W. Washington Blvd., Grants Pass, OR 97526
(503) 476-1131
Innkeeper: Bill Thompson
Rooms: 2 w/phone, incl. 1 w/pvt. bath plus 1 suite w/pvt. bath, balcony, phone
Rates: $55-$65. Seasonal variations.
Credit cards: None
Restrictions: No children under 15, pets. Smoking restricted. Min. one night's deposit req. 5-day cancellation notice req. Discount avail. for extended stay.
Notes: Victorian house once served as a maternity hospital and Episcopalian Parish. Treasures found during restoration on display. Porch swing. Listed on National Register of Historic Places.*

HARBOR (5)

Oceancrest House
15510 Pedrioli Dr., Harbor, OR 97415
(503) 469-9200, (503) 469-8864

Innkeeper: Georgine Paulin, Ronya Robinson
Rooms: 1 w/pvt. bath, TV
Rates: $70-$85, incl. cont. brk. Discount avail. for extended stay. Seasonal variations.
Credit cards: AE, MC
Restrictions: No children under 12, pets, smoking. Deposit req. 3-day cancellation
   notice req. 2-night min. stay on summer wknds. 3-night min. stay on holidays.
Notes: Private room with view of secluded beach. Luxurious furnishings. French
spoken.*

HOOD RIVER (2)

Brown's B & B
3000 Reed Rd., Hood River, OR 97031
(503) 386-1545
Innkeeper: Al and Marian Brown
Rooms: 2 w/pvt. bath
Rates: $60, incl. full brk. Seasonal variations.
Credit cards: MC, V
Restrictions: No children under 5, pets, smoking. Deposit req. 5-day cancellation
   notice req.
Notes: Two-story farmhouse built in the 1930s. Located on wooded rural hillside.
Remodeled in 1985. Organic orchard provides all fruit for guests.

State Street Inn B & B
1005 State St., Hood River, OR 97031
(503) 386-1899
Innkeeper: Mac and Amy Lee
Rooms: 4
Rates: $55-$75, incl. full brk.
Credit cards: MC, V
Restrictions: No pets. Smoking restricted. Min. one night's deposit req. 3-day can-
   cellation notice req.
Notes: Traditionally styled English house with gabled roof, pitched ceilings, oak
floors. Common room with leaded-glass windows overlooking the Columbia River.
Living room with sunroom. Dining room with plate glass window overlooking Mt.
Adams.*

JACKSONVILLE (5)

Reames House 1868
540 E. California St., Box 128, Jacksonville, OR 97530-0128
(503) 899-1868
Innkeeper: George and Charlotte Harrington-Winsley
Rooms: 4, incl. 2 w/pvt., bath
Rates: $80-$90, incl full brk. Seasonal variations
Credit cards: None
Restrictions: No children under 10, pets, smoking. Deposit req. 7-day cancellation
   notice req.
Notes: Victorian inn. Sitting room with white wicker, plants, twining pink rose sten-
ciling. Furnished with antiques. Perennial flower gardens, covered patio. Listed on
the National Register of Historic Places. Resident cat.*

REAMES HOUSE 1868

LA GRANDE (6)

Pitcher Inn
608 N Ave., La Grande, OR 97850
(503) 963-9152, (503) 963-2244
Innkeeper: Carl and Deanna Pitcher
Rooms: 3, no pvt. bath, incl 2 w/TV, plus 1 suite w/pvt bath, all w/phone
Rates: $55/room, $85/suite, all incl. full brk.
Credit cards: MC, V
Restrictions: No children under 12, smoking. Deposit req. 3-day cancellation notice req. Closed January 2–15.
Notes: Two-story Georgian house with oak floors, open staircase, built in 1925. Living room. Guest rooms decorated in different color themes, accented in roses, bows, and pitchers.

McMINNVILLE (2)

Baker Street B & B
129 S. Baker St., McMinnville, OR 97128
(503) 472-5575
Innkeeper: Cheryl and John Collins
Rooms: 2 w/pvt. bath, phone, incl. 1 w/TV, plus 1 suite w/pvt. bath, phone, TV
Rates: $65/room, $125/suite, all incl. full brk., evening refreshment. Discount avail. for mid-week stay.
Credit cards: MC, V
Restrictions: No pets. Smoking restricted. Deposit req. 14-day cancellation notice req., less $10.00 fee during peak periods.
Notes: Three-story Arts & Crafts style house built in 1914. Fully restored. Located in wine country. Parlor with fireplace. Dining room, porch. Furnished with Victorian antiques and oriental rugs. Some Spanish and German spoken.*

Steiger Haus
360 Wilson St., McMinnville, OR 97128
(503) 472-0821, 472-0238

Innkeeper: Doris & Lynn Steiger
Rooms: 3 w/pvt. bath, phone, plus 2 suites w/pvt. bath, phone, incl. 1 w/fireplace, 1 w/TV
Rates: $70-$75/room, $85-$100/suite, all incl. full brk., afternoon refreshment. Discount avail. for govt. employees and mid-week stay.
Credit cards: MC, V
Restrictions: No children under 10, pets, smoking. One night's deposit req. 7-day cancellation notice req., less $25.00 fee.
Notes: Three-story inn, operated with the theme "A Wool and Wine Country Inn." Dining room with fireplace. Sunroom weaving studio. Decks, terraces. German spoken.

MERLIN (5)

MORRISON'S ROUGE RIVER LODGE

Morrison's Rogue River Lodge
8500 Galice Rd., Merlin, OR 97526
(503) 476-3825, (800) 826-1963

Innkeeper: B.A., Elaine, and Michelle Hanten
Rooms: 13 w/pvt. bath, incl. 11 w/phone, TV, 9 w/fireplace. Located in 7 bldgs.
Rates: $160, incl. full brk., dinner. Seasonal variations.
Credit cards: MC, V
Restrictions: No pets. Min. 25% non-refundable, transferrable deposit req. Lunch served in fall only. Closed Nov. 15–May 1.
Notes: Two-story, country style river lodge built about 1945. Parlor with piano. Dining room. Deck overlooking Rogue River. Guests have access to hot tub, swimming pool, putting green, volleyball, tennis courts, and horseshoe pit. Fishing equipment furnished. White-water rafting organized. Private river beach on premises. All meals served family-style in ranch kitchen. Small private parties accommodated. Innkeepers make homemade jams, jellies, pickles, and spiced figs.*

Pine Meadow Inn
1000 Crow Rd., Merlin, OR 97532
(503) 471-6277, (800) 554-0806, (503) 471-6277

Innkeeper: Maloy and Nancy Murdock
Rooms: 3 w/pvt. bath, phone
Rates: $95-$110, incl. full brk. Discount avail. for extended stay.
Credit cards: None
Restrictions: No children under 8, pets, smoking. One night's deposit req. 7-day cancellation notice req., less fee.
Notes: Two-story country farmhouse located on nine wooded acres with meadow overlooking Mt. Walker, Mt. Sexton and Biuckhorn Mountain. Dining room with bay windows. Furnished with antiques. Wrap-around porch with wicker furniture. Deck with hot tub. English cutting and herb gardens.*

MYRTLE CREEK (5)

Havenshire B & B
901 N.W. Chadwick Lane, Myrtle Creek, OR 97457
(503) 863-5168

Innkeeper: Louis and Evelyn Sonka
Rooms: 3, no pvt. bath, plus 1 suite w/pvt. bath
$50-$60, incl. full brk.
Credit cards: None
Restrictions: No pets. Smoking restricted. One night's deposit req.
Notes: Two-story house located on 400-wooded-acre, working sheep ranch, along South Umpqua River. Decorated in country decor. Guesthouse with kitchen available. Guests invited to participate in shearing, lambing, and haying during season. Working dogs give herding demonstrations. Small private parties accommodated.

Sonka's Sheep Station Inn
901 N.W. Chadwick Lane, Myrtle Creek, OR 97457
(503) 863-5168

Innkeeper: Louis and Evelyn Sonka
Rooms: 3 w/pvt. bath, plus 1 suite. Located in 2 bldgs.
Rates: $50-$60, incl. full brk. Discount avail. for extended stay.
Credit cards: None
Restrictions: No pets, smoking. One night's deposit req. 48-hour cancellation notice req. Closed at Christmas.
Notes: Two-story working Dorset sheep ranch house and guesthouse built about 1940. Located on 400 acres along South Umpqua River. Kitchen, dining room. Furnished in country decor. All meals available. Guests may share ranch activities. Small private parties accommodated.*

NEWBERG (2)

Springbrook Hazelnut Farm
30295 N. Hwy. 99W, Newberg, OR 97132
(503) 538-4606, (800) 793-8528

Innkeeper: Ellen and Charles McClure
Rooms: 4 plus 1 suite, incl. 1 w/pvt. bath, 4 w/phone, TV. Located in 2 bldgs.
Rates: $90/room, $125/suite, all incl. full brk. Discount avail. for extended stay.
Credit cards: None
Restrictions: No pets, smoking. 50% deposit req. 7-day cancellation notice req., less $10.00 fee.
Notes: Two-story main house and carriage house. Located on 10 acres. Front porch with cover. Glassed-in sunporch with wicker furniture. Dining room. Sitting room.

Tennis court, pool, pond. Garden surrounded with orchards and vineyards. Spanish spoken. Listed on the National Register of Historic Places.*

SPRINGBROOK HAZELNUT FARM

NEWPORT (3)

Oar House Bed & Breakfast
520 S.W. Second St., Newport, OR 97365
(503) 265-9571
Innkeeper: Jan LeBrun
Rooms: 3 plus 1 suite, all w/pvt. bath
Rates: $80-$120/room, $100-$120/suite. Discount avail. for mid-week stay.
Credit cards: MC, V
Restrictions: No children, pets, smoking. Min. one night's deposit req. 3-day cancellation notice req., less $10.00 fee. 2-night min. stay on holiday wknds.
Notes: Built in 1900, renovated in 1993. Lighthouse tower with widow's walk reached from third floor by ship's ladder has 360 degree views of ocean. Located above five miles of beach. Two common rooms, one with fireplace and music system, and one with bar TV. Dining room. Living room. Guest refrigerator with soft drinks. Sheltered deck. Decorated with owner's art collection. Off-street parking. Some Spanish spoken.

Ocean House B & B
4920 N.W. Woody Way, Newport, OR 97365
(503) 265-6158, (800) 562-2632
Innkeeper: Bob and Bette Garrard
Rooms: 4 w/pvt. bath
Rates: $70-$115, incl. full brk., afternoon refreshment. Seasonal variations.
Credit cards: MC, V
Restrictions: No children under 14, pets, smoking. One night's deposit req. 3-day cancellation notice req.
Notes: Country-style house built in 1941 overlooking Agate Beach. Living room with fireplace, library, sun room, art gallery. Decks, porch overlooking floral garden. Private trail to beach and tide pools.

OREGON CITY (2)

Inn of the Oregon Trail
416 S. McLoughlin Blvd., Oregon City, OR 97045-3195
(503) 656-2089
Innkeeper: Mary and Tom Dehaven
Rooms: 2 w/pvt. bath, incl. 1 w/phone, plus 2 suites w/pvt. bath, fireplace, phone
Rates: $43-$58/room, $78/suite, all incl. full brk.
Credit cards: Most major cards
Restrictions: No pets, smoking. Children restricted.
Notes: Two-story Gothic Revival house with three cathedral-style windows built in 1867. Landscaped grounds with Japanese garden, loi-stocked pond. Restaurant on premises. Listed on the National Register of Historic Places. Limited hadicapped access. Japanese spoken.

Jagger House
512 Sixth St., Oregon City, OR 97045
(503) 657-7820

JAGGER HOUSE

Innkeeper: Claire Met
Rooms: 3, incl. 1 w/pvt. bath
Rates: $65-$75, incl. full brk. Discount avail. for extended stay.
Credit cards: MC, V
Restrictions: No children under 12, pets. Smoking restricted. One night's deposit req. 2-day cancellation notice req., less $10.00 fee.
Notes: Two-story vernacular-style house built about 1880. Restored in 1983. Decorated in oak and fir antiques, reproductions, wicker, quilts, lace, and chintz. Living room, dining room, library with board games. Wysteria-covered gazebo overlooking flower gardens with two benches. Handicapped access.*

PENDLETON (6)

Swift Station Inn B & B
602 S.E. Byers, Pendleton, OR 97801
(503) 276-3739

Innkeeper: Lorry and Ken Schippers
Rooms: 2 plus 1 suite, all w/phone, TV, incl. 1 w/pvt. bath
Rates: $60-$80/room, $75-$100/suite, all incl. full brk. Seasonal variations.
Credit cards: MC, V
Restrictions: No pets. Smoking restricted. One-night's deposit req. 2-day cancellation notice req.
Notes: Two-story Victorian house with gabled roofs, built in 1896. Wrap-around porch, parlor, living room.

PORTLAND (2)

General Hooker's B & B
125 S.W. Hooker, Portland, OR 97201
(503) 222-4435, (800) 745-4135, (503) 295-6727
Innkeeper: Lori Hall
Rooms: 4 w/phone, TV, VCR, incl. 2 w/pvt. bath
Rates: $65-$115, incl. expanded cont. brk., evening refreshment. Discount avail. for mid-week stay.
Credit cards: Most major cards
Restrictions: No children under 10, pets, smoking. Deposit req. 7-day cancellation notice req. 2-night min. stay, May–Oct.
Notes: Two-story Victorian house built in 1888. Roof deck overlooking downtown Portland. Library with book and film collection. Parlor/sitting room with fireplace. Furnished with antiques, modern art. Guests have access to refrigerator, fax machine, desk space. Resident cat.*

GENERAL HOOKER'S B & B

The John Palmer House
4314 N. Mississippi Ave., Portland, OR 97217
(503) 284-5893
Innkeeper: Mary, David, and Richard Sauter
Rooms: 5, no pvt. bath, plus 3 suites w/pvt. bath, phone, incl. 2 w/TV. Located in 2 bldgs.
Rates: $40-$75/room, $85-$125/suite, all incl. full brk. Discount avail. for extended and mid-week stays in 1 suite.
Credit cards: Most major cards

Restrictions: Children restricted. No pets, smoking. Deposit req. 7-day cancellation notice req. 2-night min. stay on wknds. and holidays.
Notes: Three-story Queen Anne Victorian house with stained-glass, built in 1890. Front parlor/music room with 1860 Gaveau piano. Formal dining room, veranda. Furnished with Victorian antiques. Walls covered with 1880 wallpapers by Christopher Dresser and William Morris. Gazebo with Jacuzzi. Dinner, concierge service, massage, horse-drawn carriage rides available. Listed on the National Register of Historic Places. Small private parties accommodated.*

Lion and the Rose
1810 NE 15th, Portland, OR 97212
(503) 287-9245, (503) 287-9247
Innkeeper: Kay Peffer
Rooms: 6 w/phone, incl. 4 w/pvt. bath
Rates: $70-$125, incl. full brk. Special pkgs. avail. Seasonal variations.
Credit cards: Most major cards
Restrictions: No children under 5, pets. Smoking restricted. Deposit req. 3-day cancellation notice req., less $10.00 fee.
Notes: Two-story Queen Anne house built in 1906. Dining room. Furnished with original antiques and reproductions. Gazebo.*

Pittock Acres Bed & Breakfast
103 N.W. Pittock Ave., Portland, OR 97210
(503) 226-1163
Innkeeper: Linda & Richard Matson
Rooms: 1, no pvt. bath, plus 2 suites w/pvt. bath, phone
Rates: $45/room, $70-$80/suite, all incl. full brk. Seasonal variations.
Credit cards: Most major cards
Restrictions: No children under 14, pets, smoking. One night's deposit req. 7-day cancellation notice req.
Notes: Two-story contemporary house built in 1974. Formal breakfast room. Sitting room with firieplace, TV. Victorian furnishings, wallpaper, wainscoting. One room with private deck. Special dietary needs accommodated. Resident dog and cat.*

Portland Guest House
1720 N.E. 15th Ave., Portland, OR 97212
(503) 282-1402
Innkeeper: Susan Gisvold
Rooms: 4, incl. 2 w/pvt. bath, phone, plus 3 suites w/pvt. bath, phone
Rates: $45-$75/room, $85/suite, all incl. full brk.
Credit cards: Most major cards
Restrictions: No pets, smoking. One-night's deposit req., 7-day cancellation notice req. 2-night min. stay on wknds.
Notes: Two-story Victorian house built in 1890. Fully restored. Furnished with antiques, vintage linens. Living room, dining room, upstairs deck.

ROSEBURG (5)

House of Hunter
813 S.E. Kane St., Roseburg, OR 97470
(503) 672-2335
Innkeeper: Jean and Walter Hunter

Rooms: 4, incl. 2 w/pvt. bath., plus 1 suite w/pvt. bath
Rates: $60-$75/room, $75-$105/suite, all incl. full brk. Discount avail. for senior citizen and mid-week stays. Seasonal variations.
Credit cards: MC, V
Restrictions: No children under 10, pets. Smoking restricted. Min. one-night's deposit req. 7-day cancellation notice req., less $10.00 fee.
Notes: Two-story, turn-of-the-century Italianate house fully restored in 1990. Located in "Tember Capital of the World." Library with fireplace and Grand room with TV. Patio. Furnishings include English wardrobe closet, and handmade quilts. Board games, putting green, off-street parking, airport pick-up available. Front garden.*

SALEM (2)

Marquee House
333 Wyatt Ct. N.E., Salem, OR 97301
(503) 391-0837
Innkeeper: Rickie Hart
Rooms: 5, incl. 3 w/pvt. bath, 1 w/fireplace
Rates: $48-$75, incl. full brk. Discount avail. for extended and senior citizen stays.
Credit cards: MC, V
Restrictions: No children under 14, pets. Smoking restricted. One night's deposit req. Min. 14-day cancellation notice req., less 10% fee. 2-night min. stay for major holidays.
Notes: Two-story Colonial Revival house built in the 1930s. Located on ½ acre. Dining room. Living room with fireplace. Decorated with antiques. Comedy movie theme throughout the house. Nightly film showing with popcorn. Off-street parking available. Small private parties accommodated.*

SANDLAKE (1)

Sandlake Country Inn
8505 Galloway Rd., Sandlake, OR 97112
(503) 965-6745
Innkeeper: Margo and Charles Underwood
Rooms: 2 plus 1 suite, cottage, all w/pvt. bath, incl. 3 w/phone, TV, 2 w/fireplace. Located in 2 bldgs.
Rates: $70-$100/room, $85/suite, $115/cottage, all incl. full brk.
Credit cards: Most major cards
Restrictions: No children under 14, pets. Smoking restricted. One night's deposit req. 7-day cancellation notice req. 2-night min. stay on wknds. and holidays.
Notes: Two-story shipwreck-timbered farmhouse and cottage built in 1894. Located on two acres. Parlor, sitting room, dining room. Furnished with antiques. Marble fireplaces. Porches, deck, garden spa. Hammock near creek. Bicycles available. Resident pet. Handicapped access.*

SISTERS (4)

Cascade Country Inn
15870 Barclay Dr., Box 834, Sisters, OR 97759
(503) 549-4666, (800) 316-0089
Innkeeper: Judy and Victoria Tolonen
Rooms: 6 w/pvt. bath

SANDLAKE COUNTRY INN

Rates: $100-$125, incl. full brk., evening refreshment. Seasonal variations. Discount avail. for group stay.

Credit cards: None

Restrictions: One night's deposit req. 3-day cancellation notice req. 2-night min. stay on wknds. from Memorial Day–Labor Day.

Notes: Built in 1994 at Sisters Eagle Air Airport. Furnished with antiques. Mountain bicycles available. Small private parties accommodated. Handicapped access.

SUBLIMITY (1)

Silver Mountain B & B
4672 Drift Creek Rd. S.E., Sublimity, OR 97385
(503) 769-7127, (503) 769-3549

Innkeeper: Jim and Shirley Heater

Rooms: 2 w/pvt. bath, incl full brk.

Rates: $55-$75

Credit cards: None

Restrictions: Well mannered children and pets are welcome. Smoking restricted. Min. one night's deposit req. 2-day cancellation notice req. Closed October–March.

Notes: Working farm in Cascade foothills. Settled in 1851. Modernized barn with adjacent pool, Jacuzzi, sauna, pool table, ping pong table, TV, VCR, fireplace, and kitchen. Guests invited to join in farm chores. Two ponds. Handicapped access.

TILLAMOOK (1)

Blue Haven Inn
3025 Gienger Rd., Tillamook, OR 97141
(503) 842-2265

Innkeeper: Ray and Joy Still

Rooms: 3, incl. 1 w/pvt. bath

Rates: $60-75, incl. full brk. Discount avail. for extended stay.

Credit cards: None

Restrictions: No children under 6, pets. Smoking restricted. One night's deposit req. 2-day cancellation notice req.

Notes: Two-story Craftsman-style house built in 1916. Restored in 1989. Located on two wooded acres. Formal dining room, living room. Library with board games and VCR. Country porch with swing. Furnished with antiques, collectibles. Picnic baskets, yard games available. Antique shop on premises. Handicapped access. *

WELCHES (2)

Old Welches Inn
26401 E. Welches Rd., Welches, OR 97067
(503) 622-3754

Innkeeper: Judith and Ted Mondun

Rooms: 3, no pvt. bath, plus cottage w/bath, kitchen, fireplace. Located in 2 bldgs.

Rates: $65-$75/room, $100-$175/cottage, all incl. full brk., afternoon refreshment, evening dessert. Seasonal variations.

Credit cards: Most major cards

Restrictions: No children under 12, smoking. Pets restricted. Deposit req. Min. 7-day cancellation notice req., less $15.00 fee. 2-night min. stay, July–Oct. 3-night min. stay for holidays.

Notes: Two-story, southern traditional-style inn with French windows, built in 1890. Operated as the first summer resort and hotel on Mt. Hood. Renovated and repaired. Dining room, living room with fireplace. Sun room with board games, puzzles. Fishing available on Salmon River behind inn. Lawn games in season. Patio, gazebo, overlooking river, mountains. Small private parties accommodated. Resident dog.*

OLD WELCHES INN

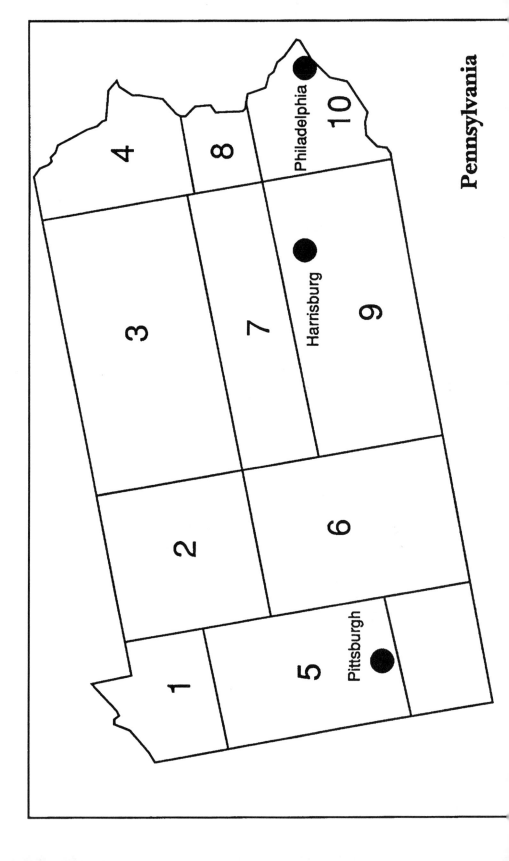

Pennsylvania

Pennsylvania

ADAMSTOWN (9)

The Adamstown Inn
62 W. Main St., Adamstown, PA 19501-0938
(712) 484-0800, (800) 594-4808
Innkeeper: Tom and Wanda Berman
Rooms: 4 w/pvt. bath, phone, incl. 2 w/TV
Rates: $65-$105, incl. cont. brk. Discount avail. for extended stay.
Credit cards: MC, V
Restrictions: No children under 12, pets. Smoking restricted. Deposit req. 14-day cancellation notice req., less $15.00 fee.
Notes: 2.5-story brick Victorian inn with leaded-glass doors, chestnut woodwork built in the early 1800s. Expanded in 1927. Renovated and operated as inn since 1989. Furnished with family heirlooms, handmade quilts, Oriental rugs. Innkeepers interested in skiing, volleyball, golf, chess, floral design, furniture refinishing, gardening, sewing, cooking. *

AIRVILLE (9)

Spring House
Muddy Creek Forks, Airville, PA 17302
(717) 927-6906
Innkeeper: Ray Hearne
Rooms: 4 plus 1 cottage, incl. 3 w/pvt. bath, wood burning stove. Located in 2 bldgs.
Rates: $50-$85, incl. full brk.
Credit cards: None
Restrictions: No pets, smoking. Full deposit req. 7-day cancellation notice req. 2-night min. stay on wknds.
Notes: Stone house built in 1798 by Pennsylvania legislator. Public room filled with paintings, art, pottery from around the world, Danish woodstove. Books, games, grand piano available. Furnished with country antiques, handwoven rugs, paintings, antique quilts. Spanish spoken.*

AKRON (9)

Boxwood Inn
12 Tobacco Rd., Box 203, Akron, PA 17501
(717) 859-3466, (800) 238-3466, (717) 859-4507
Innkeeper: June and Dick Klemm
Rooms: 4 w/pvt. bath, plus 1 suite w/pvt. bath, fireplace, TV. Located in 2 bldgs.
Rates: $75-$95/room, $125/suite, all incl. full brk., afternoon refreshment.
Credit cards: MC, V
Restrictions: No pets, smoking. One night's deposit req. 24-hour cancellation notice req.
Notes: Two-story stone farmhouse built in 1786. Renovated and decorated on 3.5 acres overlooking Amish farmlands. Garden room. Root cellar with arched ceiling. Furnished with American country antiques and Pennsylvania Dutch style. Vegetable gardens. Fruit trees. Lawns with boxwoods. German spoken.*

AVELLA (5)

Weatherbury Farm
RD 1, Box 250, Avella, PA 15312
(412) 587-3763, (412) 587-3763

Innkeeper: Dale, Marcy, Nigel Tudor
Rooms: 2 w/pvt. bath, phone, fireplace
Rates: $$50-$60, incl. full brk. Discount avail. for extended stay.
Credit cards: MC, V
Restrictions: No pets. Smoking restricted. One night's deposit req. 7-day cancellation notice req.
Notes: Farmhouse on working farm, built in 1864. Restored and redecorated. Living room, music room with piano. Dining room. Board games, puzzle table. Children's playroom. Furnished with old-fashioned country decor. Guest rooms have sitting areas. Gardens, lawn games, hammock. Porches, gazebo, swimmking pool. Children's playground. Resident farm animals. German spoken.*

AVONDALE (10)

BED & BREAKFAST AT WALNUT HILL

Bed & Breakfast at Walnut Hill
541 Chandler's Mill Rd., Avondale, PA 19311
(215) 444-3703

Innkeeper: Tom and Sandy Mills
Rooms: 3, no pvt. bath, incl. 1 w/TV
Rates: $80, incl. afternoon refreshment
Credit cards: None
Restrictions: No pets.
Notes: Two-story converted mill house overlooking meadow, built in 1840. Located in Kennett Square along Red Clay Creek. Parlor and porch w/swing. Hot tub, cable TV, VCR, oversized fireplace. Furnished with antiques. Some French, Spanish spoken.*

BANGOR (4)

Hurryback River House
RD2, Box 2177, Bangor, PA 18013
(610) 498-2131

Innkeeper: Arlene Prentiss
Rooms: 4, incl. 1 w/pvt. bath
Rates: $55, incl. cont. brk. Discount avail. for extended stay.
Credit cards: Most major cards
Restrictions: No pets, smoking.
Notes: Three-story house. Located on the Delaware River. Public room with large screen TV, antique pool table. Furnished with antiques.

BEACH LAKE (4)

Evergreen Lodge
P.O. Box 275, Beach Lake, PA 18405
(717) 729-8404
Innkeeper: Jerry and Emily Voshell
Rooms: 9 w/pvt. bath, incl. 8 w/TV. Located in 3 bldgs.
Rates: $35-$50, incl. cont. brk. Seasonal variations.
Credit cards: Most major cards
Restrictions: No pets. Deposit req. 24-hour cancellation notice req.
Notes: Two-story country lodge. Swimming pool, tennis/basketball court. Lawn games available. Handicapped access.*

EVERGREEN LODGE

BENTON (7)

Red Poppy B & B
RR 2, Box 82 (Rt 487), Benton, PA 17814
(717) 925-5823
Innkeeper: Carl and Madeleine Chiolan
Rooms: 4 w/TV, incl. 2 w/pvt. bath
Rates: $60-$80, incl. full brk., afternoon refreshment.
Credit cards: Most major cards
Restrictions: No smoking. Deposit req.

Notes: Two-story Victorian house. Living room with fireplace. Ceiling fans. Furnished with antiques. Screened porch with wicker furniture. Lawn swing. Giftshop on premises.

BIGLERVILLE (9)

Mulberry Farm
616 Flohrs Church Rd., Biglerville, PA 17307
(717) 334-5827
Innkeeper: Mimi Agard
Rooms: 3 w/pvt. bath, incl. 2 w/phone, 1 w/fireplace, plus 1 suite w/pvt. bath, fireplace
Rates: $100/room, $125/suite, all incl. full brk.
Credit cards: MC, V
Restrictions: No children under 12, pets. Smoking restricted. 50% deposit req. 7-day cancellation notice req., less $15.00 fee.
Notes: Two-story Georgian Colonial farm house with satin pine floors built in 1817. Located on 4.5 wooded acres with out-buildings, wisteria vines and grape arbor. Formal living room/library with two fireplaces, TV, VCR, CD. Dining room, terrace. Furnished with early pine and cherry antiques, Oriental rugs. Guests may take home cuttings from garden.*

BIRD-IN-HAND (9)

Village Inn of Bird-In-Hand
2695 Old Phil. Pike, Box 253, Bird-In-Hand, PA 17505
(717) 293-8369, (717) 768-1511
Innkeeper: Richmond and Janice Young
Rooms: 7 w/pvt. bath, phone, TV, plus 4 suites w/pvt. bath, phone, TV, incl. 2 w/fireplace
Rates: $59-$95/room, $79-$139/suite, all incl. cont. brk.
Credit cards: Most major cards
Restrictions: No pets. Smoking restricted. Deposit req. 48-hour cancellation notice req.
Notes: Three-story, five-bay country inn with turned Tuscan Order columns and fretwork railings, built in 1734. Sun porch. Listed in the Lancaster County Register of Historic Places.

BLOOMSBURG (7)

Irondale Inn B & B
100 Irondale Ave., Bloomsburg, PA 17815
(717) 784-1977
Innkeeper: Linda Wink
Rooms: 4, no pvt. bath, incl. 2 w/fireplace
Rates: $85, incl. full brk., evening refreshment. Seasonal variations. Discount avail. for mid-week and extended stays.
Credit cards: Most major cards
Restrictions: No children under 10, pets. Smoking restricted. Deposit req. 14-day cancellation notice req. 2-night min. stay on special wknds.
Notes: Two-story Colonial style house with seven working fireplaces, built in 1838. Located on 3 acres. Sun room with stained-glass and TV. Furnished with correct reproductions, fine antiques, Oriental rugs. Sun porch, lawns, gardens and gazebo. Hot tub and gold fish pond. Picnics arranged. Small private parties accommodated.

BOILING SPRINGS (9)

Highland House
108 Bucher Hill, Boiling Springs, PA 17007
(717) 258-3744
Innkeeper: Barry and Michaela Butcher
Rooms: 2 w/pvt. bath, incl. 1 w/fireplace, plus 1 suite w/pvt. bath
Rates: $75/room, $150/suite, all incl. full brk., evening refreshment
Credit cards: None
Restrictions: No children, pets. One night's deposit req.
Notes: Two and one half-story Federal brick house built around 1776. Yard is terraced to overlook Boiling Springs Lake. Used as an underground railroad stop. Three-story circular staircase. Use of swimming pool. Bicycle built for two, canoes available. Small private parties accommodated. Listed on National Register of Historic Places.*

BROGUE (9)

The Miller House
Rte. 1, Box 742, Brogue, PA 17309
(717) 927-9646, (717) 927-6528
Innkeeper: Sharon and Ed Marino
Rooms: 3, incl. 2 w/pvt. bath
Rates: $95, incl. full brk. Discount avail. for extended stay.
Credit cards: MC, V
Restrictions: Smoking restricted. Deposit req. 2-day cancellation notice req.
Notes: Guest house built in 1875. Located on 127 wooded acres. Renovated in 1993. Living room, dining room, sitting room. Outdoor activities available. Small private parties accommodated. Listed on the National Register of Historic places. Spanish spoken.

BUCKINGHAM (10)

Mill Creek Farm B & B
2348 Quarry Rd., Box 816, Buckingham, PA 18912
(215) 794-0776, (800) 562-1776, (215) 794-8113
Innkeeper: Paul Hoskinson
Rooms: 5, incl 3 w/pvt. bath, 1 w/fireplace, plus 1 suite w/pvt. bath
Rates: $90-$135/room, $135/suite. Discount avail. for senior citizens.
Credit cards: Most major cards
Restrictions: No children on wknds, pets, or smoking. Deposit req. 3-day cancellation notice req. 2-night min. stay.
Notes: Two-story 18th-century Field Manor house, located on 100+ acres with orchard, pond and paddocks, tennis court and pool. Decorated with country antiques. Fishing available. Small private parties accommodated. French spoken.*

CARLISLE (9)

Line Limousin Farmhouse
2070 Ritner Hwy., Carlisle, PA 17013-9303
(717) 243-1281
Innkeeper: Bob and Joan Line
Rooms: 4, incl. 2 w/pvt. bath, 1 w/phone, 3 w/TV

Rates: $65, incl. full brk. Discount avail. for extended stay.
Credit cards: None
Restrictions: Children restricted. No pets, smoking. One-night's deposit req. 7-day cancellation notice req., less $10.00 fee. 3-night min. stay during car shows.
Notes: Brick and stone farmhouse. Dining room with fireplace. Parlor with player piano. Furnished with antiques and modern pieces. Outdoor activities available. Resident animals.

LINE LIMOUSIN FARMHOUSE

CARROLL VALLEY (7)

The Old Barn
1 Main Trail, Carroll Valley, PA 17320
(717) 642-5711

Innkeeper: John and Janet Lee Malpeli
Rooms: 11 w/pvt. bath, phone, plus 3 suites w/kitchenette, pvt. bath
Rates: $80/room, $90/suite, all incl. cont. brk., full brk. on Sunday. Seasonal variations.
Credit cards: Most major cards
Restrictions: No children under 6, pets, smoking. Deposit req. 3-day cancellation notice req., less $10.00 fee. 2-night min. stay in season.
Notes: Barn built in 1843 and used as hospital in Civil War. Located on three acres. Fully restored in 1974. Living room, billiard room, library, social room with cable TV. Furnished with antiques and country period pieces. Swimming pool, ping pong, pool room. Limited handicapped access.*

CHALFONT (10)

Curley Mill Manor
776 N. Limekiln Pike, Chalfont, PA 18914
(215) 997-9015, (215) 997-9015

Innkeeper: Bob and Geogi Rauscher
Rooms: 4 w/pvt. bath, incl. 1 w/phone, 1 w/fireplace, 1 w/TV
Rates: $68-$105, incl. full brk., evening refreshment. Seasonal variations. Discount avail. for extended, senior citizen, and mid-week stays.

CURLEY MILL MANOR

Credit cards: Most major cards
Restrictions: No pets. Smoking restricted. Deposit req. 7-day cancellation notice req. 2-night min. stay on holidays and fall wknds.
Notes: Two-story Federal Stone manor with original millstone threshold, fireplace, built in 1825. Furnished with period antiques. Swimming pool, patio, lawn games.*

CHAMBERSBURG (9)

Falling Spring Inn
1838 Falling Spring Rd., Chambersburg, PA 17201
(717) 267-3654

Innkeeper: Adin and Janet Frey
Rooms: 5 w/pvt. bath, phone, 4 w/TV
Rates: $59.00, incl. full brk. Seasonal variations.
Credit cards: MC, V
Restrictions: No pets, smoking. One-night's deposit req. 3-day cancellation notice req., less $10.00 fee.
Notes: Three-story, mid-19th-century stone farmhouse. Dining room. Handicapped access.

The Ragged Edge Inn
1090 Ragged Edge Rd., Chambersburg, PA 17201
(717) 261-1195, (717) 263-7913

Innkeeper: Darlene Elders
Rooms: 7 w/pvt. bath, phone, TV, plus 3 suites w/pvt. bath, phone, TV, incl. 2 w/fireplace, plus apt. w/kitchen
Rates: $59/room, $110-$150/suite, $95/apt., all. incl. cont. brk. on weekdays, full brk. on wknds. Discount avail. for senior citizen and extended stays.
Credit cards: MC, V
Restrictions: No children, pets. Smoking restricted. One night's deposit req. 3-day cancellation notice req., less $10.00 fee.
Notes: Three-story Victorian mansion with hand-carved chestnut staircase, built in the early 1900s by the Moorhead C. Kennedy, President of Cumberland Valley Railroad. Fully restored and operated as Inn since 1993. Common rooms. Living room and dining room, each with mahogany walls, overlooking creek and forest. Deco-

rated with antiques including dolls and trains, and 'As If Everyday Was Christmas' sights. Whirlpool, sauna, video games, CD and cassett players available. Flower beds. Wrap-around porch has railroad arches. Fax, copy and computer service available. Small private parties accommodated.*

CLARION (2)

The Clarion House
77 S. 7th Ave., Clarion, PA 16214
(814) 226-4996
Innkeeper: Judy and Bill Miller
Rooms: 4, incl. 2 w/pvt. bath, phone
Rates: $60-$65, incl. expanded cont. brk.
Credit cards: Most major cards
Restrictions: No children, pets, smoking. One night's deposit req. 48-hour cancellation notice req.
Notes: Three-story house with stained-glass doors, wide center hall, built in 1894. Has operated as inn since 1992. Sitting room, formal living room, dining room. Hardwood stairway illuminated by octagonal stained-glass skylight. Landscaped grounds. Small private parties accommodated.

VICTORIAN LOFT B & B

CLEARFIELD (6)

Victorian Loft B & B
216 S. Front St., Clearfield, PA 16830
(814) 765-4805, (814) 765-1712, (800) 798-0456, (814) 765-9596
Innkeeper: Tim and Peggy Durant
Rooms: 2, no pvt. bath, plus cabin. Suite w/pvt. bath avail. Located in 2 bldgs.
Rates: $40-$65/room, $85-$100/suite, all incl. full brk., afternoon refreshment. Discount avail. for extended stay.
Credit cards: Most major cards
Restrictions: No smoking. Pets restricted. One night's deposit req. 2-day cancellation notice req.
Notes: Three-story, river-front Victorian house with cherry and oak woodwork, grand staircase, built in 1894. Double-decker Gingerbread sitting porches. Common room with entertainment center with movies, grand piano. Guests have access

to private kitchen. Sewing and weaving studios on premises with demonstrations. Furnished with antiques. Conversational Spanish spoken. Limited handicapped access.*

THE COLUMBIAN

COLUMBIA (9)

The Columbian
360 Chestnut St., Columbia, PA 17512
(717) 684-5869, (800) 422-5869

Innkeeper: Chris and Becky Will
Rooms: 5 w/pvt. bath, incl. 1 w/fireplace plus 1 suite w/pvt. balcony
Rates: $70-$80/room $85/suite, incl. full brk., afternoon refreshment. Discount avail. for extended and senior citizen stays. Seasonal variations.
Credit cards: MC, V
Restrictions: No pets. Smoking restricted. Deposit req. 2-day cancellation notice req. 2-night min. stay on holiday wknds.
Notes: Two-story Colonial Revival mansion with ornate stained-glass window, tiered oak staircase, built in 1897. Restored in 1988. Has operated as inn since 1989. Common room and dining room with fireplace. Wrap-around sun porches. Decorated with Victorian, English Country and antiques. Board games available.

COOKSBURG (2)

Clarion River Lodge
River Road, Box 150, Cooksburg, PA 16217
(800) 648-6743, (814) 744-8553

Innkeeper: Ellen O'Day
Rooms: 20 w/pvt. bath, phone, TV, refrigerator
Rates: $79-$129, incl. cont. brk. Seasonal variations. Discount avail. for AAA stay. Special pkgs. avail.
Credit cards: Most major cards
Restrictions: No children under 12, pets. $50.00 deposit req. 7-day cancellation notice req., less $10.00 fee. 2-night min. stay on wknds., holidays.
Notes: Two-story native cut stone lodge with wood paneling, oak beams, cathedral ceilings, built in 1987. Located along the Clarion River. Lobby with stone fireplace.

Dining room, library. Decorated with art reproductions, Danish furniture. Restaurant on premises. Small private parties accommodated.*

Gateway Lodge
Rte. 36, Box 125, Cooksburg, PA 16217-0125
(814) 744-8017, (814) 744-8017
Innkeeper: Joseph and Linda Burney
Rooms: 8, incl. 3 w/pvt. bath, plus 8 cottages w/pvt. bath, fireplace. Located in 9 bldgs.
Rates: $90-$170/room, $100-$130/cottages
Credit cards: Most major cards
Restrictions: No children under 8, pets. Smoking restricted. $100 deposit req. 3-day cancellation notice req. 2-night min. stay in cottages.
Notes: Two-story Colonial log cabin built in 1934. Located in Cook Forest State Park. Living room with stone fireplace. Pub room, game room, porch. Furnished in early American style with country antiques, quilts. Indoor heated swimming pool and sauna. All meals available. Handicapped access.

CRESCO (8)

La Anna Guest House
R.R. 2, Box 1051, Cresco, PA 18326
(717) 676-4225
Innkeeper: Kay Swingle and Julie Wilson
Rooms: 2, no pvt. bath
Rates: $25-$30, incl. cont. brk. Discount avail. for group stay.
Credit cards: Most major cards
Restrictions: No pets, smoking. $10.00 deposit req.
Notes: Three-story Victorian house with ten-foot ceilings, built in 1879. TV room. Furnished with Victorian and Empire antiques. Grounds include waterfalls, mountain views, pond.

DALLAS (4)

Ponda Rowland B & B
RR 1, Box 349, Dallas, PA 18612-9604
(800) 854-3286, (717) 639-5531
Innkeeper: Jeanette and Cliff Rowland
Rooms: 4 plus 1 suite, all w/pvt. bath, phone, incl. 4 w/fireplace, 2 w/TV
Rates: $55-$85/room, $75-$85/suite, all incl. full brk. Discount avail. for extended and mid-week stays. Special pkgs. avail.
Credit cards: Most major cards
Rooms: Pets welcome with prior notification. Smoking restricted. Min 50% deposit req. Gift certificates offered for cancellations. 2-night min. stay on some holidays.
Notes: Two-story timber frame and plank farmhouse built in 1850. Located on 130-acre farm with pond. Family room with fireplace. Living room, dining room, kitchen. Furnished with Colonial American antiques. Hay rides and pony rides available. Resident farm animals.*

DOVER (9)

Detters Acres B & B
6631 Old Carlisle Rd., Dover, PA 17315
(717) 292-3172

PONDA ROWLAND B & B

Innkeeper: Lorne and Ailean Detter
Rooms: 3 w/TV, incl. 1 w/pvt. bath. Located in 2 bldgs.
Rates: $60-$70, incl. full brk.
Credit cards: None
Restrictions: No pets, smoking. Min. one-night's deposit req. 4-day cancellation notice req.
Notes: Two-story farm house located on 76 acres. Recreation room with fireplace, piano, small game area. Gazebo. Picnic area. Horse and Amish buggy ride available.

DOYLESTOWN (10)

The Inn at Fordhook Farm
105 New Britain Rd., Doylestown, PA 18901
(215) 345-1766, (215) 345-1791
Innkeeper: Blanche Burpee Dohan, Elizabeth Romanella
Rooms: 7, incl. 3 w/pvt. bath, 2 w/fireplace, 2 w/balcony. Located in 2 bldgs.
Rates: $93-$135/room $175-$250/suite, all incl. full brk., afternoon refreshment.
Credit cards: Most major cards
Restrictions: No children under 12, pets, smoking. 50% deposit req. 7-day cancellation notice req. 2-night min. stay on wknds.
Notes: Colonial stone house with twelve-foot ceilings built in 1760. Carriage House with exposed beams, Gothic arches, chestnut paneling built in 1868. Formerly David Burpee's library. Located on sixty acres of woodlands, meadows, gardens with eight historical out-buildings. Library, study with TV. Main house furnished with family antiques, Oriental carpets. Decorated with grandfather clocks, fireplaces, gilded mirrors, family portraits. Lawn games available. Resident dog.*

Peace Valley B & B
75 Chapman Rd., Doylestown, PA 18901
(215) 230-7711
Innkeeper: Harry and Jane Beard

Rooms: 4, incl. 3 w/pvt. bath
Rates: $85-$120, incl. expanded cont. brk.
Credit cards: Most major cards
Restrictions: No pets, smoking. Children restricted. One night's deposit req. 2-day cancellation notice req. 2-night min. stay on wknds. from May–Oct.
Notes: Two-story stone farmhouse overlooking 1 acre pond, built in 1794. Located on 7.5 acres. Dining room, living room. Furnished with a mix of antiques and local reproductions. Board games, tennis court, off-street parking available. Limited handicapped access.*

PEACE VALLEY B & B

EAGLES MERE (3)

The Crestmont Inn
Crestmont Dr., Box 55, Eagles Mere, PA 17731-0055
(717) 525-3519

Innkeeper: John and Jane Wiley
Rooms: 14 w/pvt. bath, plus 3 suites w/pvt. bath, TV, plus 1 apt. w/pvt. bath, TV
Rates: $118-$148/room, $148-$178/suite, all incl. full brk., dinner, evening refreshment. Discount avail. for extended, mid-week, and senior citizen stays.
Credit cards: Most major cards
Restrictions: Pets and smoking restricted. One night's deposit req. 15-day cancellation notice req. 2-night min. stay June–Aug and Jan–Feb. wknds.
Notes: Located on 18,000 acres of forest. Dining room. Common room with fireplace, native cherry bar, and windows overlooking forest. Swimming pool, tennis courts, shuffleboard courts. Canoes, rowboats, sailboats, sunfish, paddleboats available. Small private parties accommodated. Limited handicapped access.*

Eagles Mere Inn
Mary & Sullivan Ave., Box 356, Eagles Mere, PA 17731-0356
(717) 525-3273, (800) 426-3273

Innkeeper: Susan and Peter Glaubitz
Rooms: 13 w/pvt. bath, plus 2 suites w/pvt. bath. Located in 2 bldgs.

Rates: $125-$175/room, $150-$195/suite, all incl. full brk., gourmet dinner. Discount avail. for mid-week stay.

Credit cards: MC, V

Restrictions: No pets. Smoking restricted. Deposit req. 14-day cancellation notice req. 2 or 3-night min. stay on some wknds.

Notes: Three-story inn built in 1878. Completely renovated. Has operated as inn since 1991. Protected by Nature Conservancy and State Forests. Living room with fireplace. Breakfast room and dining room. Pub, TV and game room. Walking path around lake. Guests have access to motor launch and Boat Club. Flowering trees.*

Shady Lane Lodge
Allegheny Ave., Eagles Mere, PA 17731
(717) 525-3394, (800) 524-1248, (717) 525-3344

Innkeeper: Pat and Dennis Dougherty

Rooms: 7 plus 1 suite, all w/pvt. bath

Rates: $75/room, $115/suite, all incl. full brk., evening refreshment. Seasonal variations. Discount avail. for mid-week stay.

Credit cards: None

Restrictions: No children under 12, pets. Smoking restricted. One night's deposit req. 10-day cancellation notice req. 2-night min. stay on wknds. 3-night min. stay on some holiday wknds.

Notes: Mountain resort with beamed ceiling, located in the Endless Mountains. Two sitting rooms, one with fireplace, library. Dining room overlooking the Endless Mountains. Hammock, board and lawn games available. Small private parties accommodated. Handicapped access.*

THE BECHTEL MANSION INN

EAST BERLIN (9)

The Bechtel Mansion Inn
400 W. King St., East Berlin, PA 17316
(717) 259-7760, (800) 331-1108

Innkeeper: Charles and Mariam Bechtel, Ruth Spangler

Rooms: 8 w/pvt. bath, incl. 2 suites w/phone, TV

Rates: $75-$115/room, $135/suite, all incl. full brk. Discount avail. for off-season and senior citizen stays.

Credit cards: Most major cards

Restrictions: No pets. Smoking restricted. 50% deposit req. 72-hr. cancellation notice req., less $10.00 fee. 2-night min. stay on holiday and October wknds.

Notes: Three-story Queen Anne-style mansion built in 1897 with turret, sliding oak shutters and etched glass. Three living rooms, each with TV. Air-conditioning. Dining room with window seat. Parlor and breakfast room with fireplace. Furnished with antiques and period furniture, lace curtains and handmade quilts. Victorian Carriage House has antique shop and sleeping facilities for bicyclists. Four porches. Garden. Small private parties accommodated. Listed on the National Register of Historic Places.*

ELIZABETHTOWN (9)

West Ridge Guest House
1285 West Ridge Rd., Elizabethtown, PA 17022
(717) 367-7783

Innkeeper: Alice P. Heisey

Rooms: 7 plus 2 suites, all w/pvt. bath, phone, TV, incl. 3 w/fireplace. Located in 2 bldgs.

Rates: $60-$85/room, $85-$110/suite, all incl. full brk. Discount avail. for mid-week and extended stays.

Credit cards: Most major cards

Restrictions: No pets, smoking. 25% deposit req. 7-day cancellation notice req. 2-night min. stay on holiday wknds.

Notes: Two-story, European ManorMain house built in 1894. Fully renovated. Guest house. Social room with TV. Guests have access to hot tub, exercise equipment. Handicapped access.*

CLEARVIEW FARM BED & BREAKFAST

EPHRATA (9)

Clearview Farm Bed & Breakfast
355 Clearview Rd., Ephrata, PA 17522
(717) 733-6333

Innkeeper: Glenn and Mildred Wissler

Rooms: 5, incl. 3 w/pvt. bath
Rates: $89, incl. full brk.
Credit cards: Most major cards
Restrictions: No children, pets, smoking. Deposit req. 10-day cancellation notice req. 2-night min. stay on wknds.
Notes: Three-story limestone farmhouse built in 1814. Fully restored. Located on 200 farmland acres. Has operated as inn since 1989. Formal dining room. Living room with fireplace. Screened porch overlooking pond with swans. Furnished with antiques.

Hackman's Country Inn
140 Hackman Rd., Ephrata, PA 17522
(717) 733-3498

Innkeeper: Kathryn Hackman
Rooms: 2, plus 2 suites, all w/pvt. bath
Rates: $45-$75, incl. full brk. Seasonal variations.
Credit cards: MC, V
Restrictions: No children under 10, pets. Smoking restricted. Deposit req. 7-day cancellation notice req.
Notes: Two-story farmhouse with bubble glass windows, built in 1857. Decorated with patchwork quilts.

The Inns at Doneckers
318-322 N. State St., Ephrata, PA 17522
(717) 738-9502

Innkeeper: Jan Grobengieser
Rooms: 27 w/phone, incl. 25 w/pvt. bath, 1 w/fireplace, 1 w/TV, plus 13 suites w/pvt. bath, phone, incl. 7 w/fireplace, 5 w/TV. Located in 4 bldgs.
Rates: $59-$125/room, $139-$175/suite, all incl. cont. brk., afternoon refreshment. Discount avail. for extended stay.
Credit cards: Most major cards
Restrictions: No pets. Smoking restricted. One night's deposit req. 2-day cancellation notice req. 2-night min. stay on holiday wknds.
Notes: Three connected turn-of-the-century houses with inlaid wood floors, stained-glass windows, balconies, porches. Guest House built in 1777. Parlor with TV, board games. Meeting room. Furnished with antiques. Decorated with hand-stenciled walls. Jacuzzi. Doneckers *Community* includes gourmet restaurant, department store, art gallery. Handicapped access. Small private parties accommodated.*

Smithton Inn
900 W. Main St., Ephrata, PA 17522
(717) 733-6094

Innkeeper: Dorothy Graybill
Rooms: 7 plus 1 suite, all w/pvt. bath, phone, fireplace
Rates: $65-$135/room, $140-$170/suite, all incl. full brk.
Credit cards: Most major cards
Restrictions: Children, pets welcome with prior arrangement. No smoking. Deposit req. 14-day cancellation notice req. 2-night min. on wknds. and holidays.
Notes: Three-story stone house built as inn in 1763. Garden house, parlor, library, dining room. Tavern room with fireplace. Furnished with antiques, handmade things, Amish quilts. Handicapped access.

SMITHTON INN

ERIE (1)

Spencer House
519 W. 6th St., Erie, PA 16507
(814) 454-5984

Innkeeper: Keith and Pat Hagenbuch
Rooms: 3 w/pvt. bath, phone, TV, plus 2 suites w/pvt. bath, phone, TV
Rates: $65-$85/room, $75-$120/suite, all incl. full brk., afternoon refreshment. Discount avail for mid-week stay.
Credit cards: Most major cards
Restrictions: No pets. Smoking restricted. Deposit req. Cancellation notice req., less $10.00 fee. 2-night min. stay on holiday and special event wknds.
Notes: Three-story Victorian mansion with original woodwook, 12' ceilings, interior folding shutters, built in 1876. Restored and has operated as an inn since 1992. Library. Parlor with fireplace, baby grand piano. Furnished with antiques. Front porch. Small private parties accommodated.*

Zion's Hill
9023 Miller Rd., Cranesville, Erie, PA 16410
(814) 774-2971

Innkeeper: John and Byrne
Rooms: 4 w/pvt bath
Rates: $60, incl cont. brk. Discount avail. for mid-week stay.
Credit cards: None
Restrictions: Smoking restricted. Deposit req. 7-day cancellation notice req.
Notes: Two-story house built in 1830. Furnished with antiques. Located on 100 acres. Once home of Dan Rice, model for American's "Uncle Sam".*

ERWINNA (10)

Evermay-on-the-Delaware
River Rd., Erwinna, PA 18920
(215) 294-9100, (610) 294-8249

Innkeeper: Ron Strouse, Fred Cresson
Rooms: 15 plus 1 suite, all w/pvt. bath, phone. Located in 3 bldgs.

Rates: $85$160/room, $200/suite, all incl. cont. brk., evening refreshment
Credit cards: MC, V
Restrictions: No children under 12, pets. Smoking restricted. One night's deposit req. 7-day cancellation notice req. 2-night min. stay on wknds. 3-night min. stay on holidays.
Notes: Three-story Victorian manor house built in the early 1700s. Located on twenty-five wooded acres overlooking Delaware River. Formal dining room. Parlor. Restaurant on premises. Dinner available on weekends and holidays. German spoken. Handicapped access. Listed on the National Register of Historic Places.*

ZION'S HILL

FELTON (9)

Feathering Farm
R.D. 2, Box 3420, Felton, PA 17322
(717) 927-6197

Innkeeper: Susan Green
Rooms: 2 plus 1 suite w/pvt. bath, phone, fireplace, TV
Rates: $95, incl. full brk., dinner. Discount avail. for extended stay.
Credit cards: None
Restrictions: No children under 10, smoking.
Notes: Two-story restored carriage house built in 1844 surrounded by stone walls built during the depression. Fully applianced kitchen. Dining and sitting room with fireplace. Library. Furnished with antiques and horse motifs. Screened porch. An in ground pool and bath house. Stabling arrangements can be made for guest's horses. Small private parties accommodated. Spanish spoken.

FOGELSVILLE (8)

The Glasbern
2141 Packhouse Rd., RD 1, Box 250, Fogelsville, PA 18051-9743
(215) 285-4723, (610) 285-2862

Innkeeper: Al and Beth Granger
Rooms: 10 w/pvt. bath, phone, TV, incl. 3 w/fireplace, plus 13 suites w/pvt. bath, phone, TV. Located in 4 bldgs.
Rates: $105-$170/room, $120-$235/suite, all incl. full brk., dinner

Credit cards: Most major cards
Restrictions: No pets. One night's deposit req. 7-day cancellation notice req., less
   10% fee. 2-night min. stay on wknds.
Notes: Two-story, 19th-century, post-and-beam German bank barn and farmhouse
with 26-foot cathedral ceiling, spiral staircase. Fully renovated. Has operated as inn
since 1985. Located in meadow on 100 acres of farmland. Living-dining room in
Great hall with stone walls and fireplace. Sunroom overlooking valley. Conference
room. Original rafters in the Gate House made from tree limbs. Carriage House
with fireplaces and whirlpool. Furnished in Victorian style. Patio overlooking
spring-fed pond. Vegetable and flower gardens, swimming pool. Small private parties accommodated. Lunch avail. for special groups only. Rental cars available. Resident dog.

QUO VADIS B AND B

FRANKLIN (5)

Quo Vadis B and B
1501 Liberty St., Franklin, PA 16323-1625
(814) 432-4208, (800) 360-6598

Innkeeper: Kristal and Stanton Bowner-Vath
Rooms: 6 w/pvt. bath
Rates: $60-$70, incl. full brk. Discount avail. for extended stay.
Credit cards: Most major cards
Restrictions: No pets. Children and smoking restricted. One night's deposit req.
Notes: Three-story brick Queen Anne house with parquet floors and terra cotta tile
built in 1867. Furnished with heirloom antiques. Handmade quilts and embroi-
dery.*

GAP (9)

Fassitt Mansion Bed & Breakfast
6051 Old Philadelphia Pike, Gap, PA 17527
(717) 442-3139, (800) 653-4139
Innkeeper: Tara and Ed Golish

Rooms: 4 w/pvt. bath, incl. 2 w/fireplace
Rates: $65-$85, incl. full brk. Seasonal variations.
Credit cards: MC, V
Restrictions: No pets. Smoking restricted. One night's deposit req. 7-day cancellation notice req., less $15.00 fee. 3-night min. stay on holiday wknds. 2-night min. stay on wknds. from July–Nov.
Notes: Two-story country mansion built in 1845. Front porch, living room, dining room. Furnished with antiques, handmade Amish quilts.*

BALADERRY INN

GETTYSBURG (9)

Baladerry Inn
40 Hospital Rd., Gettysburg, PA 17325
(717) 337-1342
Innkeeper: Tom and Caryl O'Gara
Rooms: 5 w/pvt. bath
Rates: $65-$95, incl. full brk.
Credit cards: Most major cards
Restrictions: No children under 8, pets. Smoking restricted. Deposit req. 5-day cancellation notice req. 2-night min. stay on holidays and for special events.
Notes: Two-story brick Federal-style house built in 1812. Fully restored. Located on edge of historic battlefield. Great room with brick fireplace. Dining terrace. Brick patio, gazebo, tennis court. Flower gardens, trees, lawns.*

The Brafferton Inn
44 York St., Gettysburg, PA 17325
(717) 337-3423
Innkeeper: Jane and Sam Back
Rooms: 8 w/pvt. bath, plus 2 suites w/pvt. bath, TV
Rates: $75-$95/room, $110-$120/suite, all incl. full brk.
Credit cards: Most major cards
Restrictions: No children under 8, pets. Smoking restricted. 50% deposit req. 7-day cancellation notice req.

Notes: Two-story stone house with 18th-century stencils, Williamsburg Collection trim, built about 1786 with pre-Civil War brick as the earliest deeded house in town. Clapboard addition. Living room with original fireplace, hardwood floors, chimney cupboard, player piano. Sitting room with library. Open glass-covered exterior atrium. Furnished with primitive antiques, oil paintings, prints. Flower garden. French spoken. Listed on the National Register of Historic Places. Handicapped access.*

Brierfield Bed & Breakfast
240 Baltimore St., Gettysburg, PA 17325
(717) 334-8725

Innkeeper: Nancy Rice
Rooms: 2 plus 3 suites, all w/pvt. bath, incl. 3 w/phone. Located in 2 bldgs.
Rates: $65-$75/room, $100-$110/suite, all incl. full brk.
Credit cards: None
Restrictions: No pets, smoking. Deposit req. 24-hour cancellation notice req.
Notes: Two-story house built approx. 1878. Located 2 blocks from Lincoln square. Front porch. Furnished with antiques in Victorian decor.*

Keystone Inn
231 Hanover St., Gettysburg, PA 17325
(717) 337-3888

Innkeeper: Doris Martin
Rooms: 4, incl. 2 w/pvt. bath, plus 1 suite w/pvt. bath, phone, TV
Rates: $59-$75/room, $100/suite, all incl. full brk., afternoon refreshment. Discount avail. for extended mid-week stay. Special pkgs. avail.
Credit cards: MC, V
Restrictions: No pets, smoking. One night's deposit req. 7-day cancellation notice req. 2-night min. stay in suite and on special and holiday wknds.
Notes: Three-story Late Victorian-style brick house with leaded-glass main entrance, three-story chestnut staircase, oak woodwork, built by local furniture maker in 1913. Living room with piano, fireplace, library. Dining room. Columned wraparound porch with wicker furniture overlooking flower gardens.Each guest room has reading nook with chairs, ottomans and writing desks. Special diets accommodated.

The Old Appleford Inn
218 Carlisle St., Gettysburg, PA 17325
(717) 337-1711, (717) 334-6228

Innkeeper: Frank and Maribeth Skradski
Rooms: 11 plus 1 suite, all w/pvt. bath. Located in 2 bldgs.
Rates: $93-$103/room, $118-138/suite, incl. full brk., afternoon refreshment. Seasonal variations. Discount avail. for extended stay.
Credit cards: Most major cards
Restrictions: No children under 14, pets, smoking. 50% deposit req. Min. 10-day cancellation notice req. 2-night min. stay on wknds. from May 1–Nov.
Notes: Italianate/Victorian brick mansion with original hardwood floors built in 1867. Has operated as inn since 1984. Living room with baby grand piano, fireplace. Library with fireplace. Dining room. Second floor sun room furnished with wicker. Balcony. Furnished with period country antiques, local artwork. Victorian garden. Antique shop on premises. Workshops, special events coordinated. Guests have ac-

cess to refrigerator and local YWCA. Small private parties accommodated. Resident dogs.*

THE OLD APPLEFORD INN

GREENSBURG (6)

Huntland Farm B & B
RD 9, Box 21, Greensburg, PA 15601
(412) 834-8483

Innkeeper: Robert and Elizabeth Weidlein
Rooms: 4, no pvt. bath
Rates: $55-$70, incl. full brk., afternoon and evening refreshment. Discount avail. for mid-week stay.
Credit cards: Most major cards
Restrictions: No children under 12, pets. Smoking restricted. Deposit req. 3-day cancellation notice req.
Notes: Three-story house built in 1848. Large living room. Porches and gardens. French spoken.*

HANOVER (9)

Beechmont Inn
315 Broadway, Hanover, PA 17331
(717) 632-3013, (800) 553-7009

Innkeeper: William and Susan Day
Rooms: 4 w/pvt. bath, phone, TV, plus 3 suites w/pvt. bath, phone, TV, fireplace
Rates: $80-$95/room, $115-$135/suite, all incl. full brk., afternoon refreshment. Special pkgs. avail.
Credit cards: Most major cards
Restrictions: No children under 12, pets. Smoking restricted. 50% deposit req. 2-day cancellation notice req. 2-night min. stay on wknds. in suites.
Notes: Two-story Federal-period inn built in 1834. Restored and redecorated in 1986. Located on three acres. Dining room, formal parlor, library. Furnished with

antiques. Landscaped flagstone courtyard with glider swing. Porch with wicker furniture.*

BEECHMONT INN

HARMONY (5)

Neff House
552 Main St., Harmony, PA 16037
(412) 452-7512
Innkeeper: Sally Jones
Rooms: 2 w/pvt. bath
Rates: $35-/$50, incl. full brk., afternoon refreshment. Special pkgs. avail.
Credit cards: Most major cards
Restrictions: No children under 12, pets, smoking. Deposit req. 14-day cancellation
    notice req.
Notes: Two-story house built in 1808. Guests have access to patio cooking and
kitchen. Garden. Airport pickup available. Studio giftshop on premises. Listed on
National Register of Historic Places.

HAWLEY (4)

Academy Street Bed & Breakfast
528 Academy St., Hawley, PA 18428
(717) 226-3430, (609) 395-8590, winter, (201) 335-5051
Innkeeper: Judith and Sheldon Lazan
Rooms: 7 w/cable TV, incl. 4 w/pvt. bath
Rates: $65-$75, incl. full gourmet brk., afternoon refreshment.
Credit cards: MC, V
Restrictions: No children under 13, pets. Closed Nov. 1–Apr. 30.
Notes: Two-story Italianate Victorian house with mahogany front door with original
glass paneling built in 1863. Located on hill near Lackawaxen River. Fully restored
in the 1970s. Living room with oak sideboard, polished marble mantle, yellow pine
floor. Original custom oak millwork. Innkeepers collect needlework antiques.*

HERSHEY (9)

Pinehurst Inn
50 Northeast Dr., Hershey, PA 17033
(717) 533-2603, (800) 743-9140, (217) 534-9140
Innkeeper: Roger and Phyllis Ingold
Rooms: 15, incl. 2 w/pvt. bath
Rates: $45-$69, incl. full brk. Seasonal variations.
Credit cards: MC, V
Restrictions: No pets, smoking. Deposit req. 2-day cancellation notice req. 2-night min. stay on holidays.
Notes: Built as brick student house for the Milton Hershey School in 1930. Located on two and a half acres. Common room with fireplace. Dining room. Sitting room with TV. Front porch with furniture and swing. Furnished in traditional style. Small private parties accommodated. Limited German spoken. Handicapped access. *

HOLICONG (10)

Ash Mill Farm
P.O. Box 202, Holicong, PA 18928
(215) 794-5373
Innkeeper: Jim and Patricia Auslander
Rooms: 3 plus 2 suites, incl. 1 w/TV, all w/pvt. bath
Rates: $90-$130/room, $115-$145/suite, all incl. full brk., evening refreshment. Discount avail. for mid-week, extended stay.
Credit cards: Most major cards
Restrictions: No children under 15, pets, smoking. One night's deposit req. 7-day cancellation notice req. 2-night min. stay on wknds. 3-night min. stay on holiday wknds.
Notes: Stucco-over-stone farmhouse built in 1790. Located on eleven acres. Dining room with fireplace. Living room, stone patio. Furnished with family antiques, collectibles. Decorated with Irish, Old and New World antiques, and patchwork quilts. Some French, Spanish spoken. Resident dogs, cats, lambs and sheep.*

HONEY BROOK (10)

Waynebrook Inn
Rtes. 10 & 322, Box 490, Honey Brook, PA 19344
(610) 273-2444, (800) 472-1057, (610) 273-2137
Innkeeper: Joseph Diequez III
Rooms: 17 plus 4/suites, all w/pvt. bath, phone, fireplace, TV and radio
Rates: $58-$88/room, $88-$120/suite, all incl. cont. brk.
Credit cards: Most major cards
Restrictions: No pets. Deposit req. 2-day cancellation notice req.
Notes: Four-story inn has been continuously occupied since it was built in 1738. Two banquet rooms with stage and dance floor. Furnished with handcrafted armoires, and Queen Anne writing desks. Small private parties accommodated. Handicapped access.*

JIM THORPE (8)

Harry Packer Mansion
Packer Hill, Box 458, Jim Thorpe, PA 18229
(717) 325-8566

Innkeeper: Rebert and Patricia Handwerk

Rooms: 10, incl. 6 w/pvt. bath, plus 3 suites w/pvt. bath. Located in 2 bldgs.

Rates: $75-$85/room, $95-$110/suite, all incl. full brk. Special pkgs. avail.

Credit cards: MC, V

Restrictions: No children, pets, stiletto heels. Smoking restricted. One night's non-refundable deposit req. 2-night min. stay on wknds.

Notes: Second Empire Victorian mansion with solid walnut woodwork, oak parquet floors, bronze and polished brass chandeliers built from local brick, stone in 1874. Expanded in 1881. Main entrance hall with hand-painted ceiling. Reception room with fireplace. Ladies formal parlor with Egyptian Revival mantle mirror. Gentleman's parlor with piano. Library, formal dining room. Front veranda with English Minton tile. Furnished with period antiques, Oriental rugs. Handicapped access. Small private parties accommodated. Murder Mystery Weekends organized.*

The Inn at Jim Thorpe
24 Broadway, Jim Thorpe, PA 18229
(717) 325-2599, (717) 325-9145

Innkeeper: David Drury

Rooms: 22 w/pvt. bath, phone, TV

Rates: $65-$100, incl. cont. brk. Discount avail. for mid-week and senior citizen stays.

Credit cards: Most major cards

Restrictions: No pets. Smoking restricted. Deposit req. 3-day cancellation notice req. 2-night min. stay on some wknds.

Notes: Handicapped access.*

KEMPTON (8)

Hawk Mountain Inn
RR1, Box 186, Kempton, PA 19529
(610) 756-4224

Innkeeper: Jim and Judy Gaffney

Rooms: 4 w/pvt. bath, phone, TV, incl. 2 w/fireplace, plus 2 suites w/pvt. bath, phone, TV

Rates: $65-$90/room, $90-$130/suite, all incl. full brk., afternoon refreshment. Discount avail. for extended and mid-week stays.

Credit cards: Most major cards

Restrictions: No children under 10, pets. Deposit req. 10-day cancellation notice req., less one night's fee. 2 night min. stay Sept–Oct. 3-night min. stay on holiday wknds.

Notes: Built in 1988 in rural setting. Common room with native stone fireplace, library, dining area. Furnished in eclectic style. Screened patio. Outdoor swimming pool. Pond and streams. All meals available on weekends.

KENNETT SQUARE (10)

Meadow Spring Farm
201 E. Street Rd. Rt. 926, Kennett Square, PA 19348
(610) 444-3903

Innkeeper: Anne Hicks, Debbie Hicks Aselrod

Rooms: 7, incl. 4 w/pvt. bath, 6 w/TV, 1 w/fireplace. Located in 2 bldgs.

Rates: $75-$85, incl. full brk.

Credit cards: None

Restrictions: No pets. $20.00 non-refundable deposit req. 2-night min. stay on wknds.

Notes: Two-story brick farmhouse built in 1836. Located on 125-acre working farm with pond. Dining room with fireplace. Games room with ping-pong, pool table, board games. Screened porch. Furnished with family antiques. Swimming pool, solarium with hot tub. Dinner available. Innkeeper collects dolls, cow figurines, and Santa Clauses. Handicapped access. Resident farm animals.*

KUTZTOWN (8)

Around the World B & B
30 S. Whiteoak St., Kutztown, PA 19530
(610) 683-8885, (610) 298-8414

Innkeeper: Jean F. Billig

Rooms: 2 w/pvt. bath, phone, plus 2 suites w/pvt. bath, phone, TV

Rates: $59-$70/room, $69-$129/suite, incl. full brk., afternoon refreshment. Seasonal variations. Discount avail. for senior citizen, AAA stays.

Credit cards: Most major cards

Restrictions: No children under 12, pets. Smoking restricted. One night's deposit req. 14-day cancellation notice req., less 15% fee. 2-night min. stay on summer and fall wknds.

Notes: Brick house with mahogony staircase built in the 1800s. Furnished in unique decor depicting different geographical areas including, American, Australian, Mexican, Canadian. Landscaped gardens with lily pond and gazebo. Off-street parking available. German spoken.*

LACKAWAXEN (4)

Roebling Inn on the Delaware
Scenic Dr., Lackawaxen, PA 18435
(717) 685-7900

Innkeeper: JoAnn and Donald Jahn

Rooms: 6 plus 1 cottage, all w/pvt. bath, fireplace, TV. Located in 2 bldgs.

Rates: $65-$95, incl. full brk. Discount avail. for extended and mid-week stays. Seasonal variations.

Credit cards: Most major cards

Restrictions: No pets. Smoking restricted. One-night's deposit req. 7-day cancellation notice req. 2-night min. stay on wknds. from May–Oct.

Notes: Two-story inn overlooking Pocono and Catskill Mountains, built in 1870s. Decorated with country antiques. Small private parties accommodated. Listed on the National Register of Historic Places.*

LAHASKA (9)

The Lahaska Hotel
Rte. 202, Box 500, Lahaska, PA 18931
(215) 794-0440

Innkeeper: Susan Kearney, Jim and Claire Eck

Rooms: 5, plus 1 suite, all w/pvt. bath

Rates: $65-$105/room, $110-$125/suite, all incl. cont. brk., afternoon and evening refreshment. Discount avail. for mid-week, extended and senior citizen stays. Seasonal variations.

Credit cards: None

Restrictions: No children under 12, pets. Smoking restricted. Full prepayment req. 2-day cancellation notice req. 2-night min. stay on wknds. 3-night min. stay on summer and holiday wknds.

Notes: Two-story Victorian house built in 1880. Converted to inn in 1971. Fully renovated and restored in 1986. Common room with TV, board games. Deck overlooking farmland. Small private parties accommodated. Restaurant on premises. Displayed artwork available for purchase. Week-end tours of vineyard and winery organized.

LAMPETER (9)

Walkabout Inn
837 Village Rd., Box 294, Lampeter, PA 17537
(717) 464-0707

Innkeeper: Richard and Magaret Mason

Rooms: 4 plus 1 suite, all w/pvt. bath, phone, TV

Rates: $79/room, $139/suite, all incl. full brk. Seasonal variations. Special pkgs. avail.

Credit cards: Most major cards

Restrictions: No children under 9, pets. Smoking restricted. Deposit req. 7-day cancellation notice req., less $35.00 fee.

Notes: Mennonite house built in 1925. Fully restored in country style. Dining room. Wrap-around porch with wicker furniture. Furnished with antiques, Oriental carpets, quilts, hand-painted wall stencilings. Landscaped grounds with English gardens. Dinner with Amish family arranged. Gift store on premises. Small private parties accommodated.*

LANCASTER (9)

The Dingeldein House
1105 E. King St., Lancaster, PA 17602
(717) 293-1723, (800) 779-7765

Innkeeper: Jack and Sue Flatley

Rooms: 4, incl. 2 w/pvt. bath

Rates: $60-$70, incl full brk.

Credit cards: Most major cards

Restrictions: No pets. Smoking restricted. One night's deposit req. 7-day cancellation notice req., less $15.00 fee. 2-night min. stay on wknds. from July–Oct.

Notes: Three-story Dutch Colonial house. Furnished in Queen Anne-style with antiques. Several common areas with fireplaces. Porch.

Gardens of Eden
1894 Eden Rd., Lancaster, PA 17601
(717) 393-5179

Innkeeper: Bill and Marilyn Ebel

Rooms: 4 w/pvt bath, incl. 1 w/phone, fireplace, TV, plus 1 suite w/phone, fireplace, TV, kitchen. Located in 2 bldgs.

Rates: $65-$85/room, $110/suite, all incl. full brk. Discount avail. for extended stay. Seasonal variations.

Credit cards: None

Restrictions: Children, smoking restricted. No pets. 2-night min. stay on wknds. from April–Nov.

Notes: Two-story Victorian house, built 1867. Located on 3.5 wooded acres overlooking Conestoga River. Furnished with antiques and family-made quilts, coverlets, and handwork. Screened porch and terraced grounds.*

Hollinger House Bed & Breakfast
2336 Hollinger Rd., Lancaster, PA 17602
(717) 464-3050
Innkeeper: Gina and Jeff Trost
Rooms: 5 w/pvt. bath, incl. 3 w/phone
Rates: $60-$90, incl. full brk., afternoon and evening refreshment. Seasonal variations. Discount avail. for extended and senior citizen stays.
Credit cards: Most major cards
Restrictions: No children under 12, pets, smoking. 50% deposit req. 7-day cancellation notice req., less $15.00 fee. 2-night min. stay on holiday wknds.
Notes: Three-story brick house built as leather tannery in 1870. Renovated in, and has operated as inn since 1984. Located on 5.5 wooded acres with stream. Living room with fireplace. Den with TV, VCR. Dining room. Board games available. Air conditioning. Giftshop on premises. Wrap-around veranda, double balconies. Picnic lunches available.

HOLLINGER HOUSE BED & BREAKFAST

The King's Cottage
1049 E. King St., Lancaster, PA 17602
(717) 397-1017, (717) 397-3447
Innkeeper: Karen and Jim Owens
Rooms: 8 w/pvt. bath
Rates: $80-$120, incl. full brk., afternoon refreshment. Discount avail. for extended stay. Seasonal variations.
Credit cards: Most major cards
Restrictions: No children under 12, pets. Smoking restricted. 50% deposit req. 7-day cancellation notice req., less $15.00 fee. 2-night min. stay on wknds. 3-night min. stay on holidays wknds.

Notes: 2-story Spanish-style mansion with hardwood floors built in 1913. Dining room. Living room with fireplace. Furnished in antiques and period reproductions. Small private parties accommodated. Listed on the National Register of Historic Places. Spanish spoken.*

Lincoln Haus Inn
1687 Lincoln Hwy. E., Lancaster, PA 17602
(717) 392-9412
Innkeeper: Mary Zook
Rooms: 5, plus 2 suites, all w/pvt. bath. Located in 2 bldgs.
Rates: $43-$60/room, $65-$75/suite, all incl. full brk. Discount avail. for extended stay. Seasonal variations.
Credit cards: None
Restrictions: No pets. Smoking restricted. Deposit req. 3-night min. stay for holiday wknds.
Notes: Built in 1915 with hip roofs and stained-glass entry. Living room with Amish gas lighting. Decorated with antique furniture and rugs. Limited handicapped access. German spoken.*

Witmer's Tavern–Historic 1725 Inn
2014 Old Philadelphia Pike, Lancaster, PA 17602
(717) 299-5305
Innkeeper: Brant Hartung
Rooms: 7 w/fireplace, incl. 2 w/pvt. bath
Rates: $60-$90, incl. expanded cont. brk.
Credit cards: None
Restrictions: Well-behaved children welcome. No pets. Non-refundable full prepayment req. 2-night min. stay on holiday and Oct. wknds. $15.00 fee for each night firewood used.
Notes: Four-story blue limestone inn built in 1725. Expanded in 1773. Restoration begun in 1975. Sitting room with library, fireplace, board games. Furnished with antiques. Antique and quilt shop on premises. Listed on the Local, State and National Registers of Historic Places. Resident chickens.*

LANDENBERG (10)

Cornerstone
Rd. 1, Box 155, Landenberg, PA 19350
(610) 274-2143, (610) 274-0734
Innkeeper: Linda Chamberlin, Marty Mulligan
Rooms: 7 w/pvt. bath, phone, TV, plus 5 suites w/pvt. bath, phone, TV, fireplace. Located in 7 bldgs.
Rates: $75-$150, incl. full brk.
Credit cards: Most major cards
Restrictions: No pets, smoking. Deposit req. 10-day cancellation notice req. 2-night min. stay.
Notes: Two-story 18th-century country inn built in 1700s. Den. Veranda with wicker chairs. Living room with two fireplaces. Furnished with 18th century pieces. Swimming pool with Jacuzzi. Bicycles available. Small private parties accommodated. German, French spoken.

LEBANON (9)

Zinns Mill Homestead
243 N. Zinns Mill Rd., Lebanon, PA 17402
(717) 272-1513
Innkeeper: Judy and Bob Heisey
Rooms: 4 w/TV, incl. 1 w/pvt. bath
Rates: $75-$95, incl. full brk. Discount avail. for extended stay.
Credit cards: MC, V
Restrictions: No children under 8, pets. Smoking restricted. One night's deposit
   req. 10-day cancellation notice req., less 10% fee.
Notes: Two-story limestone farmhouse built in early 1800s. Located on 13 acres
overlooking Snitz Creek. Family room with walk-in fireplace, TV, videos, classic
book collection. Living room with baby grand piano, game table. Limestone base-
ment with pool table, pin ball, darts. Furnished with antiques, ceiling fans.
Screened porch with wicker furniture, veranda. Hot tub room, swimming pool.
Gazebo next to pond. Limestone bridge. Lawn games available.

LIMA (10)

Hamanassett
P.O. Box 129, Lima, PA 19037-0129
(215) 459-3000, (610) 459-3000
Innkeeper: Mrs. Evelene H. Dohan
Rooms: 7, incl. 6 w/pvt. bath, TV, plus 1 suite w/pvt. bath, TV
Rates: $75-$100/room, $120/suite, all incl. full brk., afternoon refreshment. Dis-
count avail. for extended and group stays.
Credit cards: MC, V
Restrictions: No children under 14, pets. Smoking restricted. Deposit req. 5-day
   cancellation notice req., less $10.00 fee. 2-night min. stay, May–June, Nov., and
   on all holiday and graduation wknds.
Notes: Three-story manor house built in 1870. Located on 48 acres. Main living
room with Federal era fireplace. Library with over 2,000 volumnes. Green Room
with fireplace. Formal dining room with fireplace. Drawing room, Solarium. Furnished with antiques. Gardens, lawns, ancient trees. Murder Mystery weekends and
wine tasting parties organized. Small private parties accommodated. Limited handicapped access.*

LITITZ (9)

Swiss Woods B & B
500 Blantz Rd., Lititz, PA 17543
(717) 627-3358, (800) 594-8018, (717) 627-3483
Innkeeper: Werner and Debrah Mosimann
Rooms: 6 plus 1 suite, all w/pvt. bath
Rates: $80-$100/room, $110-$135/suite, all incl. full brk., afternoon refreshment.
   Seasonal variations. Discount avail. for extended stay.
Credit cards: Most major cards
Restrictions: No pets, smoking. One night's deposit req. 3-day cancellation notice
   req. 2-night min. stay on wknds. 3-night min. stay on holidays.
Notes: Built as an inn in 1985. Expanded in 1990. Located on 30 wooded acres over-
looking Speedwell Forge Lake. Common room with stone fireplace. Patio. Guests
have access to kitchen. Gardens, sandbox, children's playhouse. Picnic baskets, din-

ner with River Brethren family available with prior notification. Operated in Swiss-style. German, Swiss/German spoken.*

SWISS WOODS B & B

MACUNGIE (10)

Sycamore Inn
165 E. Main St., Macungie, PA 18062
(610) 966-5177
Innkeeper: Mark and Randeie Levisky
Rooms: 5, incl. 3 w/pvt. bath
Rates: $70-$80, incl. full brk.
Credit cards: MC, V
Restrictions: No children under 12, pets. Smoking restricted. Min. one night's deposit req. 7-day cancellation notice req., less 10% fee. Min. stay on special wknds.
Notes: Two-story farmhouse built in the early 1800s. Common room with walk-in fireplace, TV with movie library, games, reading material. Glass-enclosed porch. Furnished with antiques that are all for sale. Two resident dogs.

MALVERN (10)

The Great Valley House of Valley Forge
110 Swedesford Rd., RD 3, Malvern, PA 19355
(610) 644-6759, (610) 644-7019
Innkeeper: Pattye Benson
Rooms: 3, incl. 2 w/pvt. bath, all w/phone, cable TV
Rates: $70-$85, incl. full brk. Discount for extended stay.
Credit cards: Most major cards
Restrictions: No pets. Smoking restricted. One night's deposit req. Min. 7-day cancellation notice. 2-night min. stay on wknds. for rooms w/pvt. bath.

Notes: Built approx. 1690. Located on 4 acres with walking trails, swimming pool. Breakfast served in the 'Olde Kitchen' in front of a large walk-in fireplace. Furnised with antiques. French, Spanish spoken.*

MANCHESTER (9)

The Garden House B & B
350 Maple St., Manchester, PA 17345
(717) 266-6205
Innkeeper: Kim Gingerich, Treva Gingerich
Rooms: 1 plus 1 suite, no pvt. bath
Rates: $50/room, $55/suite, all incl. full brk.
Credit cards: None
Restrictions: No children under 12, pets, smoking. 50% deposit req. 7-day cancellation notice req., less $15.00 fee.
Notes: Two-story brick house built in 1910. Wrap-around porch. Dining room. 2 sitting rooms. Decorated with country flair. Board games, off-street parking available.

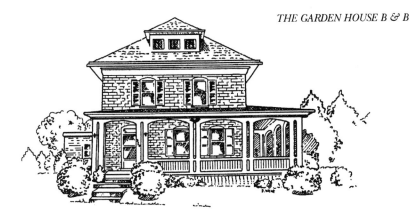

THE GARDEN HOUSE B & B

MANHEIM (9)

Herr Farmhouse Inn
2256 Huber Dr., Manheim, PA 17545
(717) 653-9852, (800) 584-0743
Innkeeper: Barry Herr
Rooms: 3, incl. 1 w/pvt. bath, 2 w/fireplace, plus 1 suite w/pvt. bath, TV
Rates: $70-$85/room, $95/suite, all incl. expanded cont. brk. Discount avail. for extended stay. Seasonal variations.
Credit cards: Most major cards
Restrictions: No children under 12, pets. Smoking restricted. Deposit req. 7-day cancellation notice req. 2-night min. stay on wknds. and holidays.
Notes: Two-story farmhouse with original pine floors built in 1738. Fully restored in 1988. Located on 11.5 farmland acres. Country kitchen with walk-in fireplace. Sun room. Furnished in Colonial style with antiques. Resident cat.*

MARIENVILLE (2)

Pioneer Lodge
P.O. Box 447, Marienville, PA 16239
(814) 927-6654
Innkeeper: Ronald and Mollie McDonald
Rooms: 4, no pvt. bath
Rates: $60, incl. full brk.
Credit cards: Most major cards
Restrictions: No children under 10, pets. Smoking restricted.
Notes: Lodge built in the 1800s. Located on 200 acres. Wrap-around porch. Living room with fireplace. Decorated with antiques, 100+ year old baby carriage, spinning wheel, cherry grandfather's clock owned by John Witherspoon, the only minister to sign the Declaration of Independence. Heated swimming pool. Outdoor activities.

MARIETTA (9)

The Noble House
113 W. Market St., Marietta, PA 17547-1411
(717) 426-4389
Innkeeper: Elissa and Paul Noble
Rooms: 2, incl. 1 w/pvt. bath, 1 w/fireplace, plus 1 suite w/pvt. bath, phone, TV
Rates: $55-$75/room, $75/suite, all incl. full brk., afternoon refreshment. Seasonal variations. Special pkgs. avail.
Credit cards: None
Restrictions: No pets, smoking. Deposit req.
Notes: Two-story Federal-style brick house built in the 1820s. Located in historic district. Dining room, living room with library, piano, fireplace, TV. Furnished with antiques and collectibles. Side porch, gardens. Catered dinners available.

The River Inn
258 West Front St., Marietta, PA 17547
(717) 426-2290
Innkeeper: Robert and Joyce Heiserman
Rooms: 3 w/pvt. bath, incl. 1 w/fireplace
Rates: $60-$70, incl. full brk., evening refreshment. Discount avail. for senior citizen and extended stays.
Credit cards: Most major cards
Restrictions: No children under 10, pets. Smoking restricted. 50% deposit req. 7-day cancellation notice req., less 25% fee.
Notes: Two-story house with 6 fireplaces, open stairway, hand-wrought tin lighting, built approx. 1794. Fully restored. Located in the historic district along the Susquehanna River. Sitting room with cable TV. Screened porch. Furnished with Colonial and country antiques and reproduction pieces. Herb and flower gardens. River fishing available.*

Vogt Farm Bed & Breakfast
1225 Colebrook Rd., Marietta, PA 17547
(717) 653-4810, (800) 854-0399
Innkeeper: Keith and Kathy Vogt
Rooms: 3 w/phone, no pvt. bath
Rates: $55, incl. full brk.

Credit cards: Most major cards
Restrictions: No pets. Smoking restricted. 50% deposit req. 48-hour cancellation notice req.
Notes: Two-story farmhouse built in 1868. Located on thirty-acre working farm. Family room with fireplace, TV. Living room with baby grand piano.

MERCERSBURG (9)

The Mercersburg Inn
405 S. Main St., Mercersburg, PA 17236
(717) 328-5231, (717) 328-3403
Innkeeper: Fran Wolfe
Rooms: 15 w/pvt. bath, phone, incl. 2 w/fireplace
Rates: $110-$180, incl. full brk. Seasonal variations.
Credit cards: Most major cards
Restrictions: No pets, smoking. One night's deposit req. 14-day cancellation notice req. 2-night min. stay for ski season and special events.
Notes: Three-story inn overlooking Mercersburg, Cumberland Valley, and Tuscarora Mountains. Conference rooms. Small private parties accommodated. Spanish spoken.*

MERTZTOWN (10)

Longswamp Bed and Breakfast
1605 State St., Mertztown, PA 19539
(610) 682-6197, (610) 682-4854
Innkeeper: Dean and Elsa Dimick
Rooms: 8, incl. 4 w/pvt. bath, 1 w/fireplace, plus 2 suites w/TV, incl. 1 w/fireplace. Located in 3 bldgs.
Rates: $60-$65/room, $65-$75/suite, all incl. full brk., evening refreshment.
Credit cards: Most major cards
Restrictions: No pets, smoking. Min. $25.00 deposit req. 48-hour cancellation notice req., less $5.00 fee.
Notes: Country farmhouse built in late 18th-century. Located on five wooded acres with fruit, herb and vegetable gardens. Living room with stone fireplace. TV room. Guest house and cottage, which has the original ceiling beams and a stone fireplace, a setting room and an adjoining bath, were formerly a way-station on the underground railroad. Innkeepers collect books and music. French spoken.*

MILFORD (4)

Black Walnut Country Inn
Rd 2, Box 9285, Fire Tower Rd., Milford, PA 18337
(800) 866-9870, (212) 721-5113
Innkeeper: Stewart and Effie Schneider
Rooms: 12, incl. 8 w/pvt. bath
Rates: $50-$100, incl. full brk. Discount avail. for mid-week stay. Seasonal variations.
Credit cards: Most major cards
Restrictions: No pets. Smoking restricted. 50% deposit req. 14-day cancellation notice req. 2-night min. stay on holiday wknds.
Notes: Tudor-style stone house built in 1940s. Located on 160 acres. Wrap-around porch. Historic marble fireplace. Parlor with TV/VCR, piano. Outdoor hot tub.

Petting zoo. Lawn games available. Greek spoken. Resident pet. Small private parties accommodated.

MONTOURSVILLE (3)

The Carriage House at Stonegate
RD 1, Box 11A, Montoursville, PA 17754
(717) 433-4340, (717) 433-4653
Innkeeper: Harold and Dena Mesaris
Rooms: 1 plus 1 suite w/phone, TV, no pvt. bath
Rates: $50/room, $70/suite, all incl. cont. brk.
Credit cards: None
Restrictions: $25.00 deposit req. 5-day cancellation notice req. 2-night min. stay on wknds.
Notes: Two-story Carriage House built in the early 1800s. Located on thirty acres along Mill Creek. Living/dining area with cable TV overlooking flower gardens, meadow. Furnished with antiques and period furniture. Guests have access to kitchen. Carriage House is rented to guests that are together as a group. Spanish spoken.*

MOUNT JOY (9)

Cedar Hill Farm
305 Longenecker Rd., Mount Joy, PA 17552
(717) 653-4655
Innkeeper: Russell and Gladys Swarr
Rooms: 5 w/pvt. bath
Rates: $55-$70, incl. cont. brk. Discount avail. for extended stay.
Credit cards: Most major cards
Restrictions: No pets, smoking. Deposit req. 48-hour min. stay on holiday wknds.
Notes: Two-story limestone farmhouse overlooking Little Chiques Creek built in 1817. Common room with game table. TV room with stereo, VCR, computer. Furnished with family heirlooms and antiques. Porch with wicker furniture. Small private parties accommodated.

Country Gardens Farm
686 Rock Point Rd., Mount Joy, PA 17552
(717) 426-3316
Innkeeper: Andy and Dotty Hess
Rooms: 3 w/pvt. bath
Rates: $60-$70, incl. full brk. Seasonal variations.
Credit cards: Most major cards
Restrictions: No pets, smoking.
Notes: Two-story brick farmhouse built in the 1860s. Family room with TV, books, fireplace, toys. Living room with piano and fireplace. Furnished with handmade crafts, original oil paintings, family heirlooms. Porches, lawns, swings. Flower gardens. Fruits and vegetables served are from garden on premises. Kittens and farm animals. Innkeepers spent most of their lives on this farm.

Green Acres Farm
1382 Pinkerton Rd., Mount Joy, PA 17552
(717) 653-4028, (717) 653-2840

Innkeeper: Wayne and Yvonne Miller
Rooms: 6 w/pvt. bath, incl. 1 suite w/pvt. bath
Rates: $55, incl. full brk.
Credit cards: None
Restrictions: No smoking. Deposit req. 14-day cancellation notice req. 2-night min. stay.
Notes: Three-story farmhouse built in 1840s. Has been in Miller family for over 30 years. Living room with fireplace. Two dining rooms, one with 150-year-old pewter cupboard. Kitchen with walk-in fireplace. Furnished with antiques. Pony cart rides available. Orchard with swing, trampoline. Balcony, porch. Resident kittens, farm animals.*

Hillside Farm Bed & Breakfast
607 Eby Chiques Rd., Mount Joy, PA 17552-8819
(717) 653-6697, (717) 653-6697

Innkeeper: Deb and Gary Lintner
Rooms: 5, incl. 3 w/pvt. bath
Rates: $50-$63, incl. full brk.
Credit cards: Most major cards
Restrictions: No children under 10, pets, smoking. Deposit req. 14-day cancellation notice req.
Notes: Two-story farmhouse built in 1866. Living room with TV, VCR, movies. Puzzles and board games available. Furnished in dairy antiques and milk bottles. Porch and second floor balcony. Tours to local dairy farms available.*

Olde Square Inn
127 E. Main St., Mount Joy, PA 17552
(717) 653-4525, (800) 742-3533, (717) 653-0749

Innkeeper: Dave and Fran Hand
Rooms: 4 w/pvt. bath, TV, incl. 2 w/phone
Rates: $75, incl. full brk. Discount avail. for extended stay.
Credit cards: MC, V
Restrictions: No children under 10, pets, smoking. One night's deposit req. 3-day cancellation notice req. 2-night min. stay on holiday wknds.
Notes: Recently restored Neo-Classic Inn. Located on "Olde Square." Computer and fax available.*

MUNCY (3)

Bodine House
307 S. Main St., Muncy, PA 17756
(717) 546-8949

Innkeeper: David and Marie Louise Smith
Rooms: 4 w/pvt. bath, TV, incl. 1 w/fireplace, 1 w/phone, plus 1 suite w/pvt. bath, phone, TV. Located in 2 bldgs.
Rates: $50-$70/room, $125/suite, all incl. full brk., evening refreshment. Discount avail. for mid-week stay.
Credit cards: Most major cards
Restrictions: No children under 6, pets, smoking. One night's deposit req. 3-day cancellation notice req. 2-night min. stay on selected wknds. Closed Christmas.

Notes: Federal town house built in 1805. Fully restored. Dining room, living room, sitting room, each with fireplace. Furnished with antiques. Suite is restored carriage house. Bicycles available. Listed on the National Register of Historic Places.*

NARVON (10)

Churchtown Inn
2100 Main St., Narvon, PA 17555
(717) 445-7794
Innkeeper: Hermine and Stuart Smith, Jim Kent
Rooms: 7 plus 1 suite, all w/pvt. bath, TV
Rates: $65-$95/room, $125/suite, all incl. full brk. Discount avail. for extended and mid-week stays. Special pkgs. avail.
Credit cards: MC, V
Restrictions: No children under 12, pets. Smoking restricted. Deposit req. 8-day cancellation notice req. less $15.00 fee. 2-night min. stay on wknds. 3-night min. stay on holiday wknds.
Notes: Two-story Federal Colonial fieldstone mansion built in 1735. Double Victorian parlor with baby grand piano. Glass-enclosed garden breakfast room. Furnished with antiques, collectibles, personal treasures. Dinner with Amish family available. Special events (i.e., mystery weekends, costume balls, musical evenings, etc.) organized. Small private parties accommodated. Some German spoken. Listed on the National Register of Historic Places.

NAZARETH (8)

CLASSIC VICTORIAN B & B

Classic Victorian B & B
35 N. New St., Nazareth, PA 18064
(610) 759-8276, (610) 434-1889
Innkeeper: Irene and Dan Sokolowski
Rooms: 3, incl. 1 w/pvt. bath, 2 w/TV
Rates: $65-$90, incl. full brk. Discount avail. for extended stay.
Credit cards: Most major cards

Restrictions: No children under 5, pets. Smoking restricted. 50% deposit req. 7-day cancellation notice req., less 10% fee. 2-night min. stay on holiday and college-event wknds.

Notes: Two-story Colonial Revival house built in 1908. Formal dining room. Parlor with carved Victorian mantle, TV. Furnished with antiques, traditional furnishings, oriental carpets. Veranda, balcony. Small private parties accommodated. Listed on the National Register of Historic Places. Resident pet.*

NEW BERLIN (7)

Inn at Olde New Berlin
321 Market St., New Berlin, PA 17855
(717) 966-0321, (717) 966-9557

Innkeeper: John and Nancy Showers
Rooms: 5 w/pvt. bath, phone, TV (upon request)
Rates: $70-$75, incl. full brk.
Credit cards: Most major cards
Restrictions: No pets. Smoking restricted. Deposit req. 7-day cancellation notice req. 2-night min. stay on college-event wknds. 2-night min. stay on August Heritage Day wknd.
Notes: Two-story Victorian inn built in 1906. Front porch, herb garden. Living room with piano. Dining room. Furnished with antiques, amish quilts, Oriental rugs. Restaurant on premises. Fax machine available. Small private parties accommodated.

NEW CUMBERLAND (9)

Farm Fortune
204 Limekiln Rd., New Cumberland, PA 17070
(717) 774-2683

Innkeeper: Chad and Phyllis Combs
Rooms: 3 plus 1 suite, incl. 2 w/pvt. bath, all w/phone
Rates: $60-$69, incl. full brk. Discount avail. for extended stay.
Credit cards: Most major cards
Restrictions: No children under 10, pets, smoking. One night's deposit req. 7-day cancellation notice req.
Notes: Two-story Limestone farmhouse with foyer staircase, three other sets of stairs, deep window sills, wide board floors, woodwork, built in 1700s. Located on 3 acres. Believed to be part of the underground railroad. Dining room. Family room with walk-in fireplace. Furnished with antiques. Board games available. Resident pet.*

NEW HOPE (10)

The Fox and Hound
246 W. Bridge St., New Hope, PA 18938
(215) 862-5082

Innkeeper: Dennis
Rooms: 5 w/pvt. bath
Rates: $55-$120, incl. cont. brk., full brk. on Sun.
Credit cards: Most major cards
Restrictions: No children, pets. Deposit req. 10-day cancellation notice req.
Notes: *

HollyHedge Estate B & B
6987 Upper York Rd., New Hope, PA 18938
(215) 862-3136, (215) 862-0960
Innkeeper: Joe and Amy Luccaro
Rooms: 13 plus 3 suites all w/pvt. bath, incl. 3 suites w/fireplaces. Located in 3 bldgs.
Rates: $95-$125/room, $150/suite, all incl. full brk. Seasonal variations.
Credit cards: Most major cards
Restrictions: No pets, smoking. Deposit req. 48-hour cancellation notice req., less $10.00 fee. 2-night min. stay.
Notes: Stone manor house and stone outbuildings located in English country gardens on twenty hillside acres. Dining room overlooking grounds, poolside terrace. Parlor with fireplace. Board games available. Guestrooms have access to private entrances and kitchen. Furnised with French, American and English antiques. Small private parties accommodated.*

Wedgwood Inn
111 W. Bridge St., New Hope, PA 18938-1401
(215) 862-2570
Innkeeper: Carl and Dinie Glassman
Rooms: 10 plus 2 suites, most w/pvt. bath, phone, incl. 6 w/fireplace, 6 w/TV. Located in 2 bldgs.
Rates: $65-$150/room, $120-$190/suite, all incl. full brk.
Credit cards: MC, V
Restrictions: No smoking. 50% deposit req. 10-day cancellation notice req., less $20.00 fee. 2-night min. stay on wknds. 3-night min. stay on holiday wknds.
Notes: 2.5-story Victorian inn with hardwood floors, gabled roof, bay windows built in 1870. Located on one wooded acre with flower gardens. Classic Revival stone manor house built in 1833. Has operated as inn since 1953. Parlor with fireplace, TV. Wrap-around veranda, Victorian gazebo, sun porch. Furnished with antiques. Guests have access to swimming pool at local club. Board and lawn games, horse-drawn carriage rides available. Revolutionary War reenactments hosted. Listed on the National Register of Historic Places. Handicapped access. French, Spanish, Dutch, Hebrew spoken. Resident pet.*

The Whitehall Inn
1370 Pineville Rd., New Hope, PA 18938
(215) 598-7945
Innkeeper: Mike and Suella Wass
Rooms: 5, incl. 3 w/pvt. bath, fireplace, plus 1 suite w/pvt. bath, fireplace
Rates: $130-$170/room, $180/suite, all incl. full brk., afternoon and evening refreshment.
Credit cards: Most major cards
Restrictions: No children under 12, pets, smoking. One night's deposit req. 21-day cancellation notice req., less $25.00 fee. 2-night min. stay on wknds. 3-night min. stay on holiday wknds.
Notes: 3-story stone manor house with high ceilings, 22' thick walls, built about 1794. Located on 12 acres. Has operated as inn since 1980. Parlor with library, fireplace, sun room. Furnished with family antiques. Tennis court, swimming pool, cabana. Horseback riding available. Occasional music concerts organized. Small private parties accommodated. Limited handicapped access.*

NEWFOUNDLAND (4)

White Cloud
RR 1, Box 215, Newfoundland, PA 18445
(717) 676-3162
Innkeeper: George Wilkinson
Rooms: 18, incl. 7 w/pvt. bath. Located in 3 bldgs.
Rates: $38-$53. Discount avail. for extended stay.
Credit cards: Most major cards
Restrictions: No smoking. $10.00 per person deposit req. 48-hour cancellation notice req., less fee.
Notes: Two-story farmhouse. Located on 50 wooded acres. Dining room, meeting room, library. Parlor with piano. Game room with table tennis and pool. Swimming pool, tennis court, shuffle board court. Chapel, restaurant on premises. Small private parties available.*

NEWTOWN (10)

The Brick Hotel
1 E. Washington St., Newtown, PA 18940
(215) 860-8313, (215) 860-8084
Rooms: 13 w/pvt. bath, phone, fireplace, TV. Suite avail.
Rates: $85-$120, incl. cont. brk. Special pkgs. avail.
Credit cards: Most major cards
Restrictions: No pets. Deposit req. 7-day cancellation notice req.
Notes: Two-story brick hotel built in 1764. Expanded in 1828. Fully renovated in 1985. Parlors, glass-enclosed veranda. Furnished in Victorian style. Restaurant, conference rooms on premises. Concierge available. Listed on the National Register of Historic Places.

NORTH WALES (10)

Joseph Ambler Inn
1005 Horsham Rd., North Wales, PA 19454
(215) 362-7500, (215) 361-5924
Innkeeper: Terry and Steve Kratz
Rooms: 28 w/pvt. bath, phone, TV, plus 1 suite w/pvt. bath, phone, TV. Located in 3 bldgs.
Rates: $95-$120/room, $140/suite, all incl. full brk.
Credit cards: Most major cards
Restrictions: No pets. Deposit req. 10-day cancellation notice req.
Notes: Three-story fieldstone Colonial farmhouse built in 1734. Renovated in and has operated as inn since 1983. Barn built in 1820. Renovated in 1987. Located on twelve acres. Three living rooms. Library with fireplace. Dining room. Lounge with bar. Furnished with antiques, Oriental rugs, and period reproductions. Restaurant on premises. Small private parties accommodated. Limited handicapped access.*

ORRTANNA (9)

Hickory Bridge Farm Inn
96 Hickory Bridge Rd., Orrtanna, PA 17353
(717) 642-5261
Innkeeper: Dr. and Nancy Jeane Hammett, Mary Lynn Martin

Rooms: 7, incl. 6 w/pvt. bath, 4 w/fireplace, 3 w/TV. Located in 5 bldgs.
Rates: $89, incl. full brk. Discount avail. for family stays.
Credit cards: MC, V
Restrictions: No pets, smoking. Min. $50.00 deposit req. 3-day cancellation notice req. 2-night min. stay on wknds. from March–Nov.
Notes: Three-story farmhouse built in late 1700s. Cottages overlook trout stream. Furnished with antiques. Back porch. All meals available. Handicapped access.

OTTSVILLE (10)

Auldridge Mead B & B
523 Geigle Hill Rd., Ottsville, PA 18942
(215) 847-5842, (215) 847-5842
Innkeeper: Karen Coigne, Craig Mattoli
Rooms: 4, incl. 2 w/pvt. bath, 1 w/fireplace, plus 1 suite w/pvt. bath, fireplace
Rates: $105-$145/room, $195/suite, all incl. full brk., afternoon refreshment. Discount avail. for extended stay.
Credit cards: AE
Restrictions: Children, smoking restricted. 50% deposit req. 7-day cancellation notice req. 2-night min. stay on wknds. from May–Dec.
Notes: Located on 15 acres. Common room with walk-in fireplace. Libraries of books, movies, music. Swimming pool, horse pasture. Guests have access to stone bank horse barn. Small private parties accommodated.

Frankenfield Farm B & B
93 Frankenfield Rd., Ottsville, PA 18942
(610) 847-2771
Innkeeper: Paul and Grace Ringheiser
Rooms: 4 w/pvt. bath, plus 2 suites w/pvt. bath, incl. 1 w/fireplace, TV. Located in 2 bldgs.
Rates: $100-$125/room, $150-$200/suite, all incl. full brk. Discount avail. for extended and mid-week stays.
Credit cards: Most major cards
Restrictions: No children under 12, pets, smoking. One night's deposit req. Ten day cancellation notice req., less $10.00 fee. 2-night min. stay on wknds. 3-night min. stay on holidays.
Notes: Two-story house built in 1879. Owned by current innkeepers since 1977. Stall space available in restored 8-horse, 2-pony barn.

PALMYRA (9)

The Hen-Apple B & B
409 S. Lingle Ave., Palmyra, PA 17078-9321
(717) 838-8282
Innkeeper: Flo and Harold Eckert
Rooms: 6 w/pvt. bath
Rates: $65, incl. full brk., afternoon refreshment. Special pkgs. avail. Seasonal variations.
Credit cards: MC, V
Restrictions: No children under 13, pets. Smoking restricted. 50% deposit req. Min. 14-day cancellation notice req., less $15.00 fee. 2-night min. stay on holidays.

Notes: Two-story Georgian-style farmhouse built in 1825. Located on 1 acre. Dining room. Parlour with TV. Wicker room with reading material, games. Furnished with antiques and reproductions. Screened porch. Resident cat.*

PARADISE (9)

Creekside Inn
44 Leacock Rd., Box 435, Paradise, PA 17562
(717) 687-0333, (717) 687-8200

Innkeeper: Cathy and Dennis Zimmerman
Rooms: 6, incl. 4 w/pvt. bath, 2 w/fireplace
Rates: $60-$110, incl. full brk., afternoon refreshment. Seasonal variations.
Credit cards: MC, V
Restrictions: No children under 12, pets, smoking. One night's deposit req. 5-day cancellation notice req., less $30.00 fee. 2-night min. stay on wknds. from Memorial Day–Labor Day.
Notes: Two-story Georgian limestone house built in 1781. Located on 1.75 acres on the Pequea Creek. Has operated as inn since 1990. Living room with fireplace. Two dining rooms. Porch with rockers. Furnished with antiques and collectibles. Limited handicapped access.

Maple Lane Guest House
505 Paradise Ln., Paradise, PA 17562
(717) 687-7479

Innkeeper: Edwin and Marion Rohrer
Rooms: 2 plus 2 suites, all w/pvt. bath
Rates: $45-$65/room, $70-$100/suite, all incl. cont. brk. Discount avail. for extended stays. Seasonal variations.
Credit cards: None
Restrictions: No pets, smoking. Deposit req. 7-day cancellation req. 2-night min. stay on wknds.
Notes: Modern colonial house with stenciled walls. Located on 250-acre working dairy farm with two acres of lawn and meadow. Parlor, front porch, lawn. Furnished with antiques, homemade quilts.

POINT PLEASANT (10)

Tattersall Inn
P.O. Box 569, Point Pleasant, PA 18950
(215) 297-8233

Innkeeper: Herb and Gerry Moss
Rooms: 4 plus 2 suites, all w/pvt. bath
Rates: $85-$94/room, $109/suite, all incl. cont. brk., afternoon refreshment. Discount for senior citizen and mid-week stays.
Credit cards: Most major cards
Restrictions: No pets. Smoking restricted. One night's deposit req. 10-day cancellation notice req. 2-night min. stay on wknds.
Notes: Two-story, 18th-century plastered fieldstone manor house built in 1740. Located on 1½ wooded acres with gardens. Common room with beamed ceiling, walk-in marble fireplace. Pillared porch, second floor veranda. Entrance hall, formal dining room with collection of antique phonographs, grand staircase. Furnished in Colonial style with antiques, needlework, paintings. Small private parties accommodated.*

QUAKERTOWN (10)

Country Inn
234 Old Bethleham Rd., Quakertown, PA 18951
(215) 536-3630, (215) 536-3881
Innkeeper: Carolyn Maxwell
Rooms: 6, incl. 5 w/pvt. bath
Rates: $85-$125, incl. cont. brk., afternoon and evening refreshment. Discount avail. for extended and mid-week stays.
Credit cards: Most major cards
Restrictions: No children under 14, pets. Smoking restricted. Non-refundable prepayment req. 7-day cancellation notice req.
Notes: Stone house built in 1749. Parlor. Decorated with eclectic art and accessories. Swimming pool. Lawn and board games available. Restaurant on premises. Small private parties accommodated. Limited handicapped access.

READING (10)

The House on the Canal
4020 River Rd., Reading, PA 19605-1065
(610) 921-3015
Innkeeper: Robert L. and Linda M. Yenser
Rooms: 1 w/pvt. bath, phone, TV, plus 1 suite w/pvt. bath, phone, TV
Rates: $75/room, $85/suite, all incl. full brk.
Credit cards: None
Restrictions: Smoking restricted. 20% deposit req. 14-day cancellation notice req.
Notes: Two-story farmhouse with hardwood floors, two-foot stone walls, built in the 1700s. Restored in 1985. Living room with fireplace. Dining room. Furnished with Victorian antiques. Suite has whirlpool tub. Porch and patio. Flower gardens.*

Hunter House
118 S. Fifth St., Reading, PA 19602
(610) 374-6608
Innkeeper: Norma and Ray Staron
Rooms: 2 plus 2 suites, all w/TV, incl. 2 w/pvt. bath
Rates: $60/room, $75/suite, all incl. full brk.
Credit cards: MC, V
Restrictions: No children under 6, pets. Smoking restricted. 25% deposit req. 2-day cancellation notice req.
Notes: Three-story townhouse built about 1840. Fully restored. Decorated with period furnishings. Italian spoken.*

RONKS (9)

Candlelight Inn
2574 Lincoln Hwy. E., Ronks, PA 17572
(717) 299-6005, (800) 772-2635, (717) 299-6397
Innkeeper: Heidi and Tim Soberick
Rooms: 5 plus 1 suite, incl. 4 w/pvt. bath
Rates: $65-$85, incl. full brk. Discount avail. for extended and mid-week stays.
Credit cards: MC, V
Restrictions: No pets, smoking. Deposit req. 2-night min. stay on wknds. from July 15–November 15.

Notes: Georgian-style rural house built in 1921. Parlor with fireplace. Furnished with Victorian antiques, fresh flowers, vintage furniture, handcrafted pillows. 2 porches overlook gardens and neighboring farms. French, Italian spoken.*

SCHAEFFERSTOWN (9)

The Franklin House
Main and Market Sts., Schaefferstown, PA 17088
(717) 949-3398
Innkeeper: Dottie Backenstose
Rooms: 5, no pvt. bath
Rates: $25-$35, incl cont. brk.
Credit cards: MC,V
Restrictions: No children under 10, pets. Smoking restricted.
Notes: Two-story inn built in 1746. Expanded to three stories in 1884. Germanic style wine cellars once used to protect townspeople from raids, restaurant, tavern on premises.

SCHELLSBURG (6)

BEDFORD'S COVERED BRIDGE INN

Bedford's Covered Bridge Inn
RD 1, Box 196, Schellsburg, PA 15559
(814) 733-4093
Innkeeper: Greg and Martha Lau
Rooms: 4, plus 2 suites, all w/pvt. bath
Rates: $65-$75/room, $85/suite, all incl. full brk.
Credit cards: Most major cards
Restrictions: No children under 12, pets, smoking. One night's deposit req. 7-day cancellation notice req. 2-night min. stay during fall foliage and holidays.
Notes: Three-story farm house built in 1866. Wrap-around porch. Common room with fireplace, library and refrigerator. Giftshop and warming hut on premises. Listed on the National Register of Historic Places.*

SHAWNEE-ON-DELAWARE (4)

Eagle Rock Lodge
River Rd., Box 265, Shawnee-on-Delaware, PA 18356
(717) 421-2139
Innkeeper: Jane and Jim Cox
Rooms: 6, no pvt. bath, plus 1 suite w/pvt. bath, plus house
Rates: $60-$75/room, $75-$100/suite, $175/house, all incl. full brk., afternoon refreshment. Discount avail. for extended stay.
Credit cards: AE
Restrictions: No pets. Smoking restricted. Deposit req. 5-day cancellation notice req. Min. stay req. on holiday wknds.
Notes: 18th-century inn located on ten acres. Lounge with cable TV, piano. Screened porch overlooking Delaware River. Furnished with wicker, antiques, country furnishings. Special diets accommodated. Board and lawn games available.*

SHIPPENSBURG (9)

Field and Pine B & B
2155 Ritner Hwy., Shippensburg, PA 17257
(717) 776-7179
Innkeeper: Allan and Mary Ellen Williams
Rooms: 4, no pvt. bath, incl. 2 w/TV, 1 w/fireplace
Rates: $65-$75, incl. full brk., afternoon refreshment. Discount avail. for senior citizens.
Credit cards: MC, V
Restrictions: No children under 12, pets. Smoking restricted. Deposit req. 10-day cancellation notice req., less $10.00 fee.
Notes: 18th-century, two-story limestone house with winding staircase, wide pine floors, stenciled walls. Originally served as inn and tavern for stagecoaches and weigh station. Located on wooded eighty-acre working farm with gardens. Formal dining room with fireplace. 8 restored fireplaces include walk-in cooking fireplace in kitchen. Furnished with antiques, quilts.

SMETHPORT (2)

The Christmas Inn
911 W. Main St., Smethport, PA 16749
(800) 653-6700
Innkeeper: Bob and Connie Lovell
Rooms: 6 plus 1 suite, all w/pvt. bath, phone
Rates: $65, incl. full brk., discount coupon for 'Christmas Store'
Credit cards: Most major cards
Restrictions: No children under 16, pets, smoking. Deposit req. 24-hour cancellation notice req. 2-night min. stay, Sept.–Oct.
Notes: Three-story Mansion built in 1900. Family owned until 1992. Fully renovated in 1994. Innkeepers are first owners not in the family of original owners. 'Christmas Store' on premises.

SMOKETOWN (9)

Homestead Lodging
184 E. Brook Rd., Rte. 896, Smoketown, PA 17576
(717) 393-6927

Innkeeper: Robert and Lori Kepiro
Rooms: 5 w/pvt. bath, TV, refrigerator
Rates: $35-$56, incl. cont. brk. Seasonal variations.
Credit cards: MC, V
Restrictions: No pets. Smoking restricted. Deposit req. 7-day cancellation notice
   req. 2-night min. stay on occasional holidays and special events.
Notes: Two-story brick house built in 1984. Porch. Guests have access to microwave
oven. Tennis court. Handicapped access. Giftshop on premises.

SOMERSET (6)

Bayberry Inn B & B
611 N. Center Ave. (Rt. 601), Somerset, PA 15501
(814) 445-8471
Innkeeper: Robert and Marilyn Lohr
Rooms: 11 w/pvt bath
Rates: $45-$55, incl cont brk.
Credit cards: Most major cards
Restrictions: No children under 12, po pets, smoking. Deposit req. 7-day cancella-
   tion notice req. 2-night min. stay on major holiday wknds.
Notes: Country inn located near Frank Lloyd Wright's Fallingwater.*

Glades Pike Inn
RD 6, Box 250, Somerset, PA 15501
(814) 443-4978, (412) 391-7607
Innkeeper: Janet L. Jones
Rooms: 5, incl. 3 w/pvt. bath, fireplace, TV
Rates: $60-$80, incl. full brk., wknd. afternoon refreshment. Seasonal variations.
Credit cards: Most major cards
Restrictions: One night's deposit req. 3-day cancellation notice req., less $5.00 fee.
   2-night min. stay, Dec. 15–Mar 1.
Notes: Two-story brick house with wood floors, high ceilings. Built as stagecoach
stop in 1842. Fully remodeled in and has operated as inn since 1987. Living room
with fireplace. Dining room. Guests have access to locked ski room.*

SPRING CREEK (1)

Spring Valley B & B
RD 1, Box 117, Spring Creek, PA 16436
(800) 382-1324, (814) 489-5657
Innkeeper: Deborah Regis
Rooms: 1 cottage, plus 2 suites, all w/pvt. bath, incl. 1 w/fireplace, 1 w/TV. Located
   in 2 bldgs.
Rates: $60-$125, incl. full brk. Discount avail. for extended, mid-week, and senior
   citizen stays. Seasonal variations.
Credit cards: MC, V
Restrictions: No children under 6, pets. Smoking restricted. 50% deposit req. 10-
   day cancellation notice req. 2-night min. stay on holiday wknds.
Notes: Located on 105-acre horseback and trail riding farm with indoor and out-
door riding areas. Porch, deck overlooking paddocks and horse riding areas. Boat
available for charter. Guests have access to charcoal grill. Clean horse box stalls and

pastures available. Trail rides organized. Some Portuguese spoken. Resident farm animals.*

STARLIGHT (4)

Inn at Starlight Lake
P.O. Box 27, Starlight, PA 18461
(717) 798-2519, (800) 248-2519, (717) 798-2672
Innkeeper: Jack and Judy McMahon
Rooms: 26, incl. 20 w/pvt. bath, 1 w/TV, plus 1 house w/pvt. bath, phone, fireplace. Located in 5 bldgs.
Rates: $65-$85/room, $170-$200/suite, all incl. full brk., dinner. Discount avail. for non-summer, mid-week, and extended stays. Seasonal Variations.
Credit cards: MC, V
Restrictions: No pets. Smoking restricted. Deposit req. 14-day cancellation notice req. 2-night min. stay. 3-night min. stay on holidays.
Notes: Three-story house. Located on private forty-five-acre Starlight Lake with access to fishing, swimming, biking, hiking and suffleboard. Has operated as inn since 1909. Lobby with fireplace, stove. Dining room overlooking lake. Three cottages, each with porch overlooking lake. Sun room, game room with TV, VCR, deck. Furnished with period pieces. Porch with rockers. Restaurant, bar, tennis court on premises. Children's play area, lawn games, boats, bicycles, off-street parking, all meals available. Resident dog.*

VALLEY FORGE (10)

Amsterdam B & B
P.O. Box 1139, Valley Forge, PA 19482
(610) 983-9620, (800) 952-1580
Innkeeper: Pamela and Ino Vandersteur
Rooms: 3 w/phone, TV, incl. 2 w/pvt. bath, plus apt. w/kitchen. Located in 2 bldgs.
Rates: $55-$75, incl. full brk., afternoon refreshment. Discount avail. for extended stay.
Credit cards: MC, V
Restrictions: No children under 8, pets. Smoking restricted. One night's deposit req. 7-day cancellation notice req. Min. stay req. in apartment.
Notes: Two-story house built as general store in the 1860s. Operated as part of the Underground Railroad. Has operated as inn since 1989. Dining room with wood burning stove. Living room. Furnished in Colonial Dutch decor. Front porch, indoor Jacuzzi. Lawn games, picnic table grill available. Guests have access to refrigerator, microwave. Dutch, French German, spoken.*

Valley Forge Mt. B & B
P.O. Box 562, Valley Forge, PA 19481-0562
(610) 783-7838, (800) 344-0123, (610) 783-7783
Innkeeper: Carolyn Williams
Rooms: 2 suites w/pvt. bath, phone, TV
Rates: $60, incl. full brk. Discount avail. for extended stay.
Credit cards: Most major cards
Restrictions: No pets. Smoking restricted. Deposit req. 3-day cancellation notice req., less $10.00 fee.

Notes: French Colonial house with 2 fireplaces, located on three wooded acres adjacent to Valley Forge National Historic Park. Guests have access to computer, printer, fax machine.*

WASHINGTON CROSSING (10)

Inn To The Woods
150 Glenwood Dr., Washington Crossing, PA 18977
(215) 493-1974, (800) 982-7619, (215) 493-3774
Innkeeper: Rosemary and Barry Rein
Rooms: 4 plus 2 suites, all w/pvt. bath, TV
Rates: $85-$110/room, $110-$140/suite, all incl. brk., afternoon and evening refreshment. Discount avail. for mid-week, extended, and senior citizen stays. Seasonal variations.
Credit cards: Most major cards
Restrictions: No children under 12, pets, smoking. 50% deposit req. 10-day cancellation notice req., less $10.00 fee.
Notes: Wood and stone Bavarian style inn built with beamed ceilings and parquet floors in 1978. Located on ten acres. Common room with fireplace, living garden, fishpond and antique nickelodeon. Furnished with American antiques. Small private parties accommodated. German spoken.*

WELLSBORO (3)

Kaltenbach's B & B
RD 6, Box 106 A, Stonyfork Rd., Wellsboro, PA 16901
(717) 724-4954, (800) 722-4954
Innkeeper: Lee Kaltenbach
Rooms: 8 w/TV, incl. 7 w/pvt. bath, 3 w/phone, 1 w/fireplace, plus 2 suites w/pvt. bath, phone, TV
Rates: $60-$70/room, $125/suite, all incl. full brk., afternoon refreshment. Seasonal variations. Discount avail. for mid-week, senior citizen stays. Special pkgs. avail.
Credit cards: MC, V
Restrictions: No pets, smoking. Deposit req. 7-day cancellation notice req., less $25.00 fee. 2-night min. stay for special events, holiday wknds. 4-night min. stay in hunting season.
Notes: Flagstone ranch house located on 72-acre working farm with cross country and hiking trails. Living room with fireplace. Decorated with homemade crafts. Picnic tables, outdoor girlls, playground, sites for motor homes, campers, tents available. Small private parties accommodated. Some Spanish spoken. Handicapped access. Resident farm animals and cat.

WEST CHESTER (10)

The Bed and Breakfast Bankhouse
875 Hillsdale Rd., West Chester, PA 19382
(215) 344-7388
Innkeeper: Diana and Michael Bove
Rooms: 1, no pvt. bath, plus 1 suite w/pvt. bath, phone
Rates: $65/room, $85/suite, all incl. full brk., afternoon refreshment. Discount avail. for extended and mid-week stays.
Credit cards: Most major cards

Restrictions: No children under 12, pets, smoking. Deposit req. 7-day cancellation notice req. 2-night min. stay on holiday wknds.
Notes: Two-story 18th-century house. Located across from pond and ten-acre horse farm. Sitting room/library, board games. porch. Furnished with antiques, folk art, stenciling.

THE BED AND BREAKFAST BANKHOUSE

Crooked Windsor
409 S. Church St., West Chester, PA 19382
(215) 692-4896
Innkeeper: Winifred Rupp
Rooms: 4, incl. 1 w/pvt bath
Rates: $65-$85, incl full brk., afternoon refreshment. Discount avail. for extended stay.
Credit cards: None
Restrictions: No pets, smoking. 20% deposit req.
Notes: Victorian house. Furnished with antiques. Pool and garden open in season. Spanish, German spoken.*

WILLOW STREET (9)

The Apple Bin Inn
2835 Willow St. Pike, Willow Street, PA 17584
(717) 464-5881, (800) 338-4296
Innkeeper: Barry and Debbie Hershey
Rooms: 4 w/TV, incl. 2 w/pvt. bath
Rates: $75-$85, incl. full brk., afternoon refreshment. Discount avail. for extended stay.
Credit cards: Most major cards
Restrictions: No children under 7, pets, smoking. Deposit req. 7-day cancellaton notice req. 3-night min. stay on holiday wknds.
Notes: Two-story Colonial house built in 1865. Served as general store. Dining room. Living room with books, handmade board games, maps, piano. Furnished with country and colonial reproductions. Porch, upstairs balcony, shaded patios. Picnic lunches, bicycle and equipment storage available. Limited handicapped access.

THE APPLE BIN INN

YORK (9)

Friendship House
728 E. Philadelphia St., York, PA 17403
(717) 843-8299

Innkeeper: Karen Maust and Becky Detwiler
Rooms: 3, incl. 2 w/pvt. bath, phone
Rates: $40-$60, incl. full brk. Discount avail. for extended and senior citizen stays.
Credit cards: None
Restrictions: No pets, smoking. Deposit req. 7-day cancellation notice req.
Notes: Three-story brick townhouse built in 1897. Located in historic district. Living room, kitchen. Furnished with some antiques and handmade pieces. Side yard, patio. Guests have access to locked garage.

FRIENDSHIP HOUSE

Smyser-Bair House
30 S. Beaver St., York, PA 17401
(717) 854-3411

Innkeeper: The King Family
Rooms: 4, no pvt. bath, plus 1 suite w/pvt. bath

SMYSER-BAIR HOUSE

Rates: $60/room, $80/suite, all incl. full brk., afternoon refreshment. Discount
   avail. for extended stay.
Credit cards: MC, V
Restrictions: No pets, smoking. One night's deposit req.
Notes: Four-story Italianate Victorian townhouse with four-floor winding walnut
staircase, parquet floors, stained-glass windows crystal chandlier, ceiling medallions,
built in 1880. Located in the historic district. Remodeled in 1897. Parlor with player
piano, floor-to-ceiling gold leaf pier mirrors. Dining room, office. Furnished with
antiques, reproductions, Oriental rugs. Fenced back yard. Listed on the National
Register of Historic Places.*

Rhode Island

The Barrington Inn
P.O. Box 397, Block Island, RI 02807
(401) 466-5510, (401) 466-5170

Innkeeper: Howard and Joan Ballard
Rooms: 6, incl. 1 w/TV, plus 2 apts. w/decks, all w/pvt. bath. Located in 2 bldgs.
Rates: $95-$145/room, $675-$700 per week/Apt., all incl. cont. brk. Discount avail.
for mid-week, off-season, and extended stays.
Credit cards: MC, V
Restrictions: No children under 12 in Inn. No pets. Deposit req. Smoking re-
stricted. Min. one night's deposit req. 15-day cancellation notice req., less $50.00
per wk. fee. 2-night min. stay on wknds. 3-night min. stay on holiday wknds.
Closed Nov. 25–Apr. 1.
Notes: Three-story Victorian farmhouse built in 1886. Housekeeping apartments in
converted barn. Renovated in 1981. Has operated as inn since 1976. Two common
rooms with games and books, one with TV and VCR. Located on knoll overlooking
New Harbor area. Dining room with wood stove. Furnished with early Block Island
furniture, wicker, family pieces. BBQ grill available. Rear deck overlooking fruit trees
on grounds. Outside shower available. Ferry pick-up, off-street parking available.*

THE BARRINGTON INN

The Bellevue House
High St., Box 1198, Block Island, RI 02807
(401) 466-2912

Innkeeper: Neva Flaherty
Rooms: 3 suites w/pvt. bath, TV, plus 2 apts., 2 cottages
Rates: $75-$90/room, $130-$180/suite, all incl. cont. brk. Discount avail. for mid-
week stay.
Credit cards: MC, V
Restrictions: No pets. Smoking restricted. 50% deposit req. 14-day cancellation no-
tice req., less $15.00 fee. 2-night min. stay. 3-night min. stay on wknds.
Notes: Two-story Colonial Revival-style house built about 1882. Located on 1.5 acres
with gardens. Front porch, sitting room. Furnished with Victorian pieces. Decorated

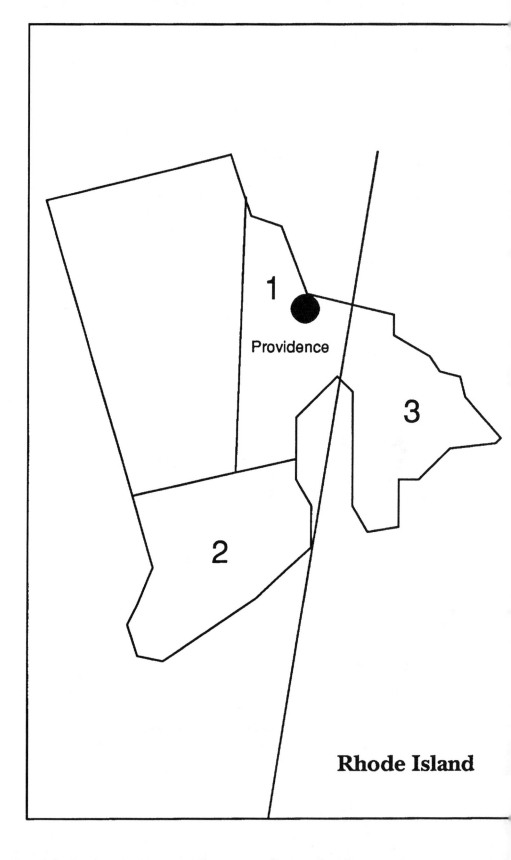

1

Providence

3

2

Rhode Island

with flowered wallpaper, white ruffled curtains. Lawn games available. Small private parties accommodated.*

Blue Dory Inn,
Dodge St., Box 488, Block Island, RI 02807
(401) 466-2254, (800) 992-7290, (401) 466-2909
Innkeeper: Ann Loedy
Rooms: 12 incl. 1 w/TV, plus 2 suites, incl. 1 w/TV, plus 2 cottages w/pvt. bath. Located in 4 bldgs.
Rates: $65-$175/room, $125-$245/suite, $140-$265/cottage, all incl. cont. brk., afternoon refreshment. Discount avail. for mid-week stay.
Credit cards: Most major cards
Restrictions: 50% deposit req.
Notes: Victorian Inn built about 1894. Located on the beach. Parlor with books, games TV, VCR. Decorated with floral wallpapers. Furnished with antiques. Deck and patio overlooking water. Beach towels and chairs available. Small private parties accommodated. Resident cat.*

The Continental
P.O. Box 575, Block Island, RI 02807
(401) 466-5136
Innkeeper: Lila Clerk
Rooms: 2, no pvt. bath
Rates: $65-$110, incl. full brk.
Credit cards: None
Restrictions: No children. 50% deposit req. 5-day cancellation notice req., less $25.00 fee. 2-night min. stay on wknds. in season.
Notes: Built in 1881. Restored in 1968. Common room with 8 ft. original fireplace and deck overlooking pond and wooded area. Furnished with country pine and French-Canadian antiques. Garden with 10-ft. hedge. Swimming available in pond fed by five springs. Board games available.

Hotel Manisses/1661 Inn
Spring St., Box 1, Block Island, RI 02807
(401) 466-2421, 466-2063, 466-2836,
Innkeeper: Joan and Justin Abrams, Steve and Rita Draper
Rooms: 36 plus 2 suites, incl. 34 w/pvt. bath, 29 w/phone, 3 w/fireplace, TV. Located in 3 bldgs.
Rates: $54-$325, incl. full brk. Discount avail. for mid-week stay. Special pkgs. avail.
Credit cards: Most major cards
Restrictions: No children under 13, pets. Smoking restricted. Min. 50% deposit req. 15-day cancellation notice req., less $25.00 fee. 3-night min. stay on high season wknds.
Notes: Victorian hotel built in 1874. Two-story inn built in 1900. Guest house. Fully renovated in 1972. Parlors, dining rooms, lobby, wine bar, library, deck. Decorated in Victorian style with antiques, period paintings. Flower gardens with fountain, garden terrace. Antique shop on premises. Small private parties accommodated. Ferry pickup available with prior arrangement. Island tours organized. Handicapped access. Variety of languages spoken.*

Rose Farm Inn
P.O. Box E, Block Island, RI 02807-0895
(401) 466-2034, (401) 466-2053

Innkeeper: Robert and Judith Rose
Rooms: 19, incl. 17 w/pvt. bath. Located in 2 bldgs.
Rates: $90-$175, incl. expanded cont. brk. Seasonal variations. Discount avail. for
extended stay.
Credit cards: Most major cards
Restrictions: No children under 12, pets. Smoking restricted. Min. 50% deposit req.
14-day cancellation notice req., less $20.00 fee. 3-night min. stay, June–Sept.
Notes: Farm house built in 1897 and has been in the rose family for 5 generations.
Reconstructed in and has operated as inn since 1980. Captain Rose House built in
1993. Stone porch, sun deck, Victorian parlors with wet bar. Furnished with antiques. German spoken. Handicapped access.

Sullivan House
P.O. Box 416, Block Island, RI 02807
(401) 466-5020

Innkeeper: The O'Brien Family
Rooms: 4, plus 1 suite, all w/pvt. bath
Rates: $140-$165/room, $195/suite, all incl. cont. brk. Seasonal variations. Dis-
count avail. for extended stay.
Credit cards: Most major cards
Restrictions: No children under 12, pets. Min. 50% deposit req. 14-day cancellation
notice req. 2-night min. stay on wknds.
Notes: Two-story inn built in 1904 with beachstone exterior. Located on hill. Wrap-
around varanda. Lawns. Stone fireplace. Private parties accommodated. Profes-
sional coordinators on staff.*

The White House
Spring St., Box 447, Block Island, RI 02807
(401) 466-2653

Innkeeper: Joseph and Violette Connolly
Rooms: 4 plus 1 suite, incl. 1 w/TV, 2 w/fireplace
Rates: $120, incl. full brk., evening refreshment. Discount avail. for extended stay.
Seasonal variations.
Credit cards: Most major cards

THE WHITE HOUSE

Restrictions: No children under 7, pets. One night's deposit req. 7-day cancellation notice req. less $20.00 fee. 3-night min. stay on holidays.
Notes: Built about 1790. Drawing room with TV. Decorated with French Provincial antiques, Oriental and French Royal family pictures and autographs. Innkeepers collect ceramics, Presidential autographs and documents. Airport or ferry pick-up available.

BRISTOL (3)

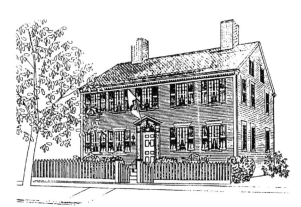

WILLIAMS GRANT B & B

Williams Grant B & B
154 High St., Bristol, RI 02809
(401) 253-4222, (800) 596-4222
Innkeeper: Mary and Mike Rose
Rooms: 5, incl. 3 w/pvt. bath
Rates: $65-$95, incl. full brk., evening refreshment. Special pkgs. avail. Seasonal variations.
Credit cards: Most major cards
Restrictions: No children under 12, pets. Smoking restricted. Deposit req. 10-day cancellation notice req., less $10.00 fee. 2-night min. stay on wknds. during high season.
Notes: Two-story Federal-style house built in 1800s. Restored in 1993. Located on 33 acres of Blithewolde gardens. Sitting room with piano. Resident pets.*

MIDDLETOWN (3)

Lindseys' Guest House
6 James St., Middletown, RI 02842
(401) 846-9386
Innkeeper: Anne Lindsey
Rooms: 3 w/TV, incl. 1 w/pvt., bath, phone
Rates: $55-$85, incl. cont. brk. Seasonal variations.
Credit cards: MC, V
Restrictions: No pets, smoking. One night's deposit req. 10-day cancellation notice req., less $10.00 fee. 2-night min. stay on holiday wknds.
Notes: Split-level house. Dining room, deck. Handicapped access. Off-street parking available.*

Sea Breeze
36 Kane Ave., Middletown, RI 02840
(401) 847-5626

Innkeeper: Sheila Harari
Rooms: 2 w/pvt. bath, TV
Rates: $95, incl. full brk. Discount avail. for mid-week stay. Seasonal variations.
Credit cards: None
Restrictions: No pets, smoking. One-night's deposit req. 24-hour cancellation notice req., less $15.00 fee.
Notes: Two-story modern style house built in 1978. Common breakfast room and deck overlooking lawn, trees, ocean. Decorated with modern furnishings.

NARRAGANSETT (2)

1900 HOUSE

1900 House
59 Kingtown Rd., Narragansett, RI 02882
(401) 789-7971

Innkeeper: Bill and Sandra Panzeri
Rooms: 2 w/pvt. bath
Rates: $45-$55, incl. full brk. Discount avail. for some extended stays. Seasonal variations.
Credit cards: None
Restrictions: No pets. Smoking restricted. One night's deposit req. 14-day cancellation notice req.
Notes: Three-story Victorian house built in 1900. Dining room with wood stove. Two reading rooms. Furnished with period pieces. Wrap-around screened porch with wicker furniture, rockers. Guests have access to refrigerator. Innkeepers interested in gardening, watercolor painting. Free beach parking available. Resident cats.

The Olds Clerk House B & B
49 Narragansett Ave., Narragansett, RI 02882
(401) 783-8008

Innkeeper: Patricia Watkins
Rooms: 2 w/pvt. bath, TV
Rates: $44-$95, incl. full brk., afternoon refreshment. Seasonal variations. Special pkgs. avail.
Credit cards: None
Restrictions: No children under 12, pets, smoking. Deposit req. 14-day cancellation notice req. 2-night min. stay on summer wknds.
Notes: Two-story Victorian house. Living room with TV, VCR, selection of movies, CD with music, board games, books. Sunroom. Guests have access to refrigerator. Furnished in eclectic style with antiques. Roses on front pathway. Resident dog and cats. French, German spoken.*

Richards Bed & Breakfast
144 Gibson Ave., Narragansett, RI 02882
(401) 789-7746
Innkeeper: Nancy and Steven Richards
Rooms: 4 w/fireplace, incl. 2 w/pvt. bath, plus 1 suite w/pvt. bath, fireplace
Rates: $60-$85/room, $100/suite, all incl. full brk.
Credit cards: None
Restrictions: No children under 12, pets, smoking. 50% deposit req. 14-day cancellation notice req., less $10.00 fee. 2-night min. stay on wknds. 3-night min. stay on holidays.
Notes: Cut granite house built in 1884. Library with fireplace. Formal dining room. Listed on the National Register of Historic Places.

NEWPORT (3)

Admiral Benbow Inn
93 Pelham St., Newport, RI 02840
(401) 848-8000, (800) 343-2863, (401) 848-8006
Innkeeper: Cathy Darigan
Rooms: 14 w/pvt. bath, phone, plus 1 suite w/pvt. bath, phone
Rates: $75/room, $95/suite, all incl. cont. brk. Seasonal variations. Discount avail. for mid-week and extended stays.
Credit cards: Most major cards
Restrictions: No children under 12, pets, smoking. 2-night min. stay. 3-night min. stay on holidays.
Notes: Two-story house built in 1855. Common room with cast-iron stove. Decorated with antiques. Listed on the National Register of Historic Places. 18th- and 19th-century barometers on display.

Brinley Victorian Inn
23 Brinley St., Newport, RI 02840
(401) 849-7645
Innkeeper: John and Jennifer Sweetman
Rooms: 15, incl. 11 w/pvt. bath, plus 2 suites w/pvt. bath. Located in 2 bldgs.
Rates: $59-$130/room, $75-$145/suite, all incl. cont. brk. Seasonal variations. Special pkgs. avail.
Credit cards: MC, V
Restrictions: No children under 8, pets. Deposit req. 7-day cancellation notice req., less $15.00 fee. 2 and 3-night min. stays on holidays and for special events.

Notes: Two-story Victorian house with polished wooden floors, curving staircases, built in 1850. Second house built in 1870. Buildings connected by breezeway and courtyard garden. Two parlors. Decorated with Victorian wallpaper, satin and lace window treatment, original faux finishes by Rita Rogers. Furnished with Victorian antiques. Porch with swing. Victorian courtyard. Concierge service available.*

The Burbank Rose
111 Memorial Blvd. West, Newport, RI 02840
(401) 849-9457
Innkeeper: John and Bonnie McNeely
Rooms: 3 w/pvt. bath
Rates: $39-$119, incl. full brk., afternoon refreshment. Discount avail. for extended, mid-week and senior citizen stays. Seasonal variations.
Credit cards: AE
Restrictions: No children under 8, pets, smoking. Deposit req. 48-hour cancellation notice req. 2-night min. stay on wknds, May–Sep.
Notes: Three-story house. Sitting room with cable TV.*

Covell Guest House
43 Farewell St., Newport, RI 02840
(401) 847-8872
Innkeeper: Jeanne Desrosiers
Rooms: 5 w/pvt. bath, incl. 1 w/fireplace
Rates: $100-$110, incl. cont. brk. Seasonal variations. Discount avail. for mid-week and extended stays.
Credit cards: MC, V
Restrictions: No children under 5, pets. One night's deposit req. 7-day cancellation notice req. 2-night min.stay. Closed part of Jan.
Notes: 2-story house built about 1810. Expanded and modernized in 1885 with mansard roof. Located in Historic Point section, 3 blocks from harbor. Two living rooms, incl. one with TV. Guests have access to kitchen. Furnished with antiques. Porch overlooking gardens. Off-street parking available.*

The Inn at Old Beach
19 Old Beach Rd., Newport, RI 02840
(401) 849-3479, (401) 847-1236
Innkeeper: Cyndi and Luke Murray
Rooms: 7 w/pvt. bath, incl. 3 w/fireplace, 2 w/TV. Located in 2 bldgs.
Rates: $130-$140, incl. cont. brk., afternoon refreshment. Discount avail. for extended, mid-week stays. Seasonal variations
Credit cards: Most major cards
Restrictions: No children under 12, pets, smoking. Min. one-night's deposit req. 14-day cancellation notice req., less 10% fee. 2-3 night min. stay for wknds. in-season.
Notes: Two-story Gothic Victorian house built in 1879. Victorian dining room, front parlor, living room. Guest pantry with refrigerator. Furnished in English country style. Gazebo, porches, brick patio. Garden with lily pond. Listed on the Rhode Island Historic Register.

Marian's Guest House
378 Spring St., Newport, RI 02840
(401) 848-0115

Innkeeper: Marian St. Pierre
Rooms: 6, incl. 2 w/pvt. bath, 1 w/fireplace, plus apt., all w/TV
Rates: $40-$120, incl. cont. brk. Seasonal variations. Discount avail. for extended, mid-week, senior citizen and group stays.
Credit cards: MC, V
Restrictions: Pets, smoking restricted. 50% deposit req. 3-day cancellation notice req.
Notes: Two-story Victorian inn built in 1861. Apartment has private entrance upon request. Small private parties accommodated. Off-street parking available.*

The Melville House
39 Clarke St., Newport, RI 02840
(401) 847-0640, (401) 847-0956
Innkeeper: Vince De Rico, David Horan
Rooms: 7, incl. 5 w/pvt. bath, 1 w/fireplace
Rates: $60-$110, incl. full brk., afternoon refreshment. Discount avail. for mid-week stay. Seasonal variations.
Credit cards: Most major cards
Restrictions: No children under 12, pets, smoking. Deposit req. 10-day cancellation req. 2-night min. stay on wknds. 3-night min. stay on holidays and special-event wknds.
Notes: Two-story house built about 1750. Breakfast room. Furnished in Colonial style. Off-street parking available. Listed on the National Register of Historic Places.*

The Merritt House Guests
57 2nd St., Newport, RI 02840
(401) 847-4289
Innkeeper: Angela and Joseph Vars
Rooms: 1 plus 1 suite, all w/pvt. bath, TV
Rates: $75-$85, all incl. full brk.
Credit cards: None
Restrictions: No children under 13, pets, smoking. One night's deposit req. 14-day cancellation notice req., less $15.00 fee. 2-night min. stay on wknds. 3-night min. stay on holiday wknds.
Notes: Dining room, living room, patio. Antique clocks in every room. Off-street parking available. Some French spoken.*

On The Point B & B
102 Third St., Newport, RI 02840
(401) 846-8377
Innkeeper: George Perry
Rooms: 2 w/pvt. bath, incl. 1 w/TV
Rates: $60-145, incl. cont. brk., afternoon refreshment. Seasonal variations.
Credit cards: Most major cards
Restrictions: No pets, smoking. One-night's deposit req. Min. 14-day cancellation notice req., less one-nights fee. 2-night min. stay on wknds. 3-night min. stay on holidays.
Notes: Victorian house built about 1894. Common room. Furnished with antique wicker. Innkeeper has extensive collection of old prints and photographs of Historic Newport.

The Pilgrim House Inn
123 Spring St., Newport, RI 02840
(401) 846-0040, (800) 525-8373

Innkeeper: Bruce and Pam Bayuk
Rooms: 10, incl. 8 w/pvt. bath
Rates: $45-$135, incl. cont. brk., evening refreshment. Seasonal variations.
Credit cards: MC, V
Restrictions: No children under 12, pets. Smoking restricted. Deposit req. 10-day cancellation notice req. 2-night min. stay on wknds. from June–Sept. 3-night min. stay on holidays. Closed Jan.
Notes: Three-story Victorian mansard house built in 1872. Located in the historic district of Newport, two doors from Trinity Church. Living room with Victorian fireplace, hand-turned mahogony mantle. Rooftop deck overlooking Newport Harbor. Furnished in Victorian style. Off-street parking available.*

Polly's Place
349 Valley Rd., Newport, RI 02842
(401) 847-2160

Innkeeper: Polly Canning
Rooms: 5w/pvt. bath, incl. 2 w/phone, plus 2 suites w/pvt. bath, phone, TV, plus apt. w/pvt. bath
Rates: $60-$85/room, $$80-$125/suite, all incl. full brk. Seasonal variations.
Credit cards: None
Restrictions: No children under 12, except babies in suite. No pets or smoking. Deposit req. 7-day cancellation notice req., less fee. 2-night min. stay on wknds. in season.
Notes: Private New England house with apartment. Kitchen, living room, patio. Grounds include weeping willow trees, brook.*

Spring Street Inn
353 Spring St., Newport, RI 02840
(401) 847-4767

Innkeeper: Parvin and Damian Latimore
Rooms: 7 w/pvt. bath, phone, plus 1 suite w/pvt. bath, phone

SPRING STREET INN

Rates: $65-$140/room, $100-$220/suite, all incl. full brk. Seasonal variations.
Credit cards: Most major cards
Restrictions: No children under 12, pets. Smoking restricted. Deposit req. 14-day cancellation notice req., less $10.00 fee. 2-night min. stay on high season wknds.
Notes: Empire Victorian house built in 1858. Sitting room with cable TV. All meals, off-street parking available. Small private parties accommodated. French, Spanish, Farsi spoken.*

Villa Liberte
22 Liberty St., Newport, RI 02840
(401) 846-7444, (800) 392-3717
Innkeeper: Leigh Anne Mosco
Rooms: 8 plus 4 suites, 3 apts., all w/pvt. bath, phone, TV. Located in 2 bldgs.
Rates: $69-$145/room, $99-$225/suite, all incl. cont. brk. Discount avail. for extended and mid-week stays.
Credit cards: None
Restrictions: No pets, smoking. 50% deposit req. 14-day cancellation notice, less $25.00 fee. 2-night min. stay on wknds.
Notes: Three-story inn and annex built in 1910. Renovated in and has operated as inn since 1986. Three lounges, lobby. Furnished in contemporary decor. Sundeck. Bar and Grill on premises. Off-street parking available.

PROVIDENCE (1)

The Cady House
127 Power St., Providence, RI 02906
(401) 273-5398, (401) 273-5398
Innkeeper: Anna and Bill Colaiace
Rooms: 2 w/pvt. bath, phone, incl. 1 w/TV, plus 1 suite w/pvt. bath, phone, fireplace, TV, plus 1 apt.
Rates: $65/room, from $75/suite, $150/wk./apt., all incl. brk.
Credit cards: None
Restrictions: No smoking. $25 deposit req.
Notes: Two-story Classical Revival house built in 1839. Located on Brown University campus. Screened veranda overlooking garden. Decorated with antiques, Oriental carpets, American and International folk art. Airport, bus and train station pick-up available. Hebrew and Spanish spoken. Resident dogs.*

The Old Court B & B
144 Benefit St., Providence, RI 02903
(401) 751-2002, (401) 272-6566
Innkeeper: Peter D. Kenney
Rooms: 10 w/pvt. bath, phone, incl. 2 w/cable TV, plus 1 suite w/pvt. bath, TV, phone. Located in 2 bldgs.
Rates: $95-$135/room, $150-$250/suite, all incl. full brk. Seasonal variations. Special pkgs. avail.
Credit cards: Most major cards
Restrictions: No children, pets. Smoking restricted. 50% deposit req. 7-day cancellation notice req. 2-night min. stay for holidays, special wknds., and Brown and R.I. School of Design graduations.
Notes: Italianate house with 12-ft. ceilings built in 1863. Furnished with period antiques, 19th-century memorabilia. Handicapped access. Spanish spoken.*

State House Inn
43 Jewett St., Providence, RI 02908
(401) 351-6111, (401) 351-4261
Innkeeper: Frank and Monica Hopton
Rooms: 10 w/pvt. bath, phone, TV, incl. 2 w/fireplace
Rates: $79-$99, incl. full brk., evening w/refreshment. Discount avail. for extended stay. Seasonal variations.
Credit cards: Most major cards
Restrictions: No pets. Smoking restricted. Deposit req. 48-hour cancellation notice req., less 10% fee.
Notes: Three-story house. Fully restored. Has operated as inn since 1990. Sitting room with fireplace. Dining room. Guests have access to complete working office with phone, fax, copier, PC. Off-street parking available. Small private parties accommodated. French spoken.*

WAKEFIELD (2)

The Larchwood Inn
521 Main St., Wakefield, RI 02879
(401) 783-5454, (401) 783-1800
Innkeeper: Francis and Diann Browning
Rooms: 20, incl. 13 w/pvt. bath, 9 w/phone. Located in 2 bldgs.
Rates: $30-$90
Credit cards: Most major cards
Restrictions: Deposit req. 7-day cancellation notice req.
Notes: Three-story manor house built about 1840. Four dining rooms, cocktail lounge with fireplace. Porch, patio overlooking gardens. Decorated in Scottish style and period pieces. Two-story Holly House with living room. All meals available. Live music on weekends. Small private parties accommodated. Spanish, French spoken.*

WARWICK (1)

Pawtuxet B and B
76 Bayside Ave., Warwick, RI 02886
(401) 941-4011
Innkeeper: Ron and Eileen Johnson
Rooms: 3, no pvt. bath
Rates: $55, incl. cont. brk.
Credit cards: None
Restrictions: No children under 7, pets. Smoking restricted. Deposit req. 7-day cancellation notice req.
Notes: Two-story, twelve-room Victorian house. Restored and renovated. Living room, wrap-around porch.*

WESTERLY (2)

The Villa
190 Shore Rd., Westerly, RI 02891
(401) 596-1054, (800) 722-9240, (401) 596-6268
Innkeeper: Jerry Maiorano
Rooms: 6 suites w/pvt. bath, TV, incl. 1 w/phone, 2 w/fireplace. Located in 2 bldgs.

Rates: $75-$175, incl. expanded cont. brk. Seasonal variations. Discount avail. for mid-week stay. Special pkgs. avail.

Credit cards: Most major cards

Restrictions: Smoking restricted. Min. 50% deposit req. 15-day cancellation notice req., less $10.00 fee. 2-night min. stay, Memorial Day–Labor Day and on holidays.

Notes: Dutch Colonial-style house with Mediterranean accents built in 1938. Located on 1.5 landscaped acre. Swimming pool, hot tub. Thursday buffet dinner available. Small private parties accommodated.*

Woody Hill Guest House
149 Woody Hill Rd., Westerly, RI 02891
(401) 322-0452

Innkeeper: Dr. Ellen Madison

Rooms: 3, plus 1 suite w/TV, all w/pvt. bath

Rates: $60-$105, incl. full brk. Seasonal variations. Discount avail. for extended stay.

Credit cards: None

Restrictions: No pets, smoking. One night's deposit req. 7-day cancellation notice req., less $10.00 fee. 2-night min. stay on summer wknds. preferred. Closed one week in Feb.

Notes: Two-story Colonial reproduction house with gambrel roof, wide-board floors. Located on hilltop. Library. Keeping room with beehive oven. Furnished with early American antiques, handmade quilts. Porch with rockers. Informal gardens. Swimming pool and pool house. Resident cats. Limited handicapped access.*

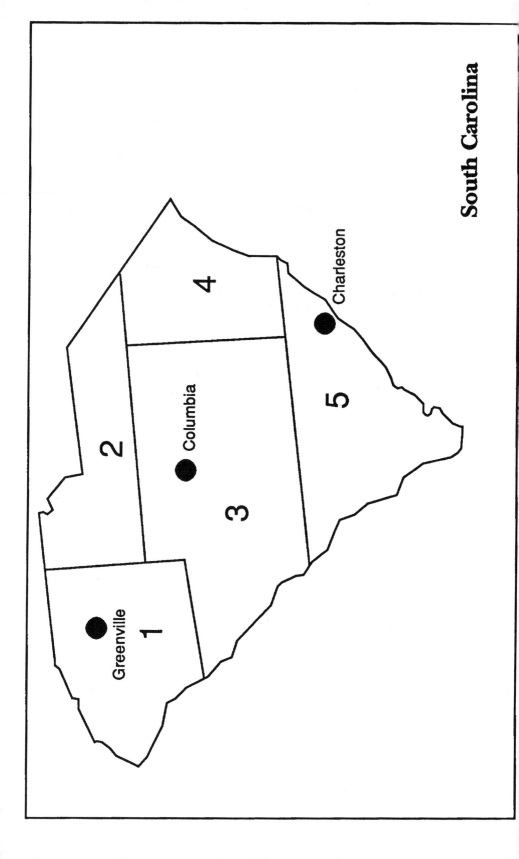

South Carolina

South Carolina

AIKEN (3)

New-Berry Inn
240 Newberry St., Aiken, SC 29801
(803) 649-2935
Innkeeper: Mary Ann and Hal Mackey
Rooms: 5 w/pvt. bath, phone, TV, incl. 2 w/fireplace, plus 1 suite w/pvt. bath, phone, fireplace, TV.
Rates: $55-65/room, $125-$150/suite, all incl. full brk. Seasonal variations. Discount avail. for mid-week stay.
Credit cards: Most major cards
Restrictions: No pets, smoking. Deposit preferred. 48-hour cancellation notice req.
Notes: Two-story Dutch Colonial house. Furnished with comfortable antiques. Handicapped access.*

ANDERSON (1)

River Inn
612 E. River St., Anderson, SC 29624
(803) 226-1431
Innkeeper: Wayne Hollingsworth, Pat Clark
Rooms: 3 w/pvt. bath, fireplace, TV
Rates: $65, incl. full brk. Discount avail. for mid-week, extended, and senior citizen stays. Seasonal variations.
Credit cards: Most major cards
Restrictions: No children under 12, pets. Smoking restricted. Deposit req. 14-day cancellation notice req.
Notes: Two-story, heart pine house with ten-foot, beamed ceilings, walnut stained woodwork, and crown moldings, built in 1914. Parlor with fireplace. Dining room with period pedestal table, sideboard, leaded-glass built-in china cabinets and firepalce. Side porch with swing and rockers. Hot tub in back yard.*

BEAUFORT (5)

TwoSuns Inn B & B
1705 Bay St., Beaufort, SC 29902
(803) 522-1122, (800) 532-4244, (803) 522-1122
Innkeeper: Carrol and Ron Kay
Rooms: 5 w/pvt. bath, phone
Rates: $99-$109, incl. full brk., afternoon refreshment. Seasonal variations. Discount avail. for extended, mid-week, and senior citizen stays.
Credit cards: Most major cards
Restrictions: No children under 12, pets. Smoking restricted. One night's deposit req. 48-hour cancellation notice req.
Notes: Three-story Neoclassic Revival house built in 1917. Fully restored and renovated in 1990. Living room with fireplace, library, board games, TV, VCR, movies. Parlor, dining room. Wrap-around veranda overlooking the bay. Widow's walk. Bicycles available. Small private parties accommodated. Murder mystery events available. Handicapped access. Innkeepers are a weaver and a commercial artist.*

TWOSUNS INN B & B

BENNETTSVILLE (2)

The Breeden Inn & Carriage House
404 E. Main St., Bennettsville, SC 29512
(803) 479-3665

Innkeeper: Wesley and Bonnie Park

Rooms: 6 w/pvt. bath, phone, cable TV, incl. 5 w/fireplace, plus cottage house w/kitchen. Located in 2 bldgs.

Rates: $55-$65, incl. full brk. Discount avail. for mid-week, senior citizen, and extended stays.

Credit cards: Most major cards

Restrictions: Supervised & well-behaved children welcome. No pets, smoking. One-night's deposit req. Min. 72-hour cancellation notice req. 2-night min. stay during special events.

Notes: Two-story southern Beaux Arts-style mansion with hardwood floors and Carriage House built in 1886. Refurnished in 1981. Has operated as inn since 1982. Located on 2 acres with six out buildings in Bennettsville's Historic District. Central

THE BREEDEN INN & CARRIAGE HOUSE

hall with stained, bevelled and leaded-glass. Two parlors, country kitchen, dining room. 29-columned wrap-around porch with wicker furniture, rockers, hammock, antique gliders. Furnished with antiques from 1700s to 1930s. Swimming pool, goldfish pond. Bicycles, lawn games available. Listed on the National Register of Historic Places.*

BLACKSBURG (2)

White House Inn
607 W. Pine St., Blacksburg, SC 29702
(803) 839-3000
Innkeeper: Jim White, Jo Ann Miller
Rooms: 4 plus 1 suite, incl. 3 w/pvt. bath, 5 w/phone, TV, 3 w/fireplace
Rates: $70-$75/room, $120/suite, all incl. full brk. Discount avail. for extended and mid-week stays.
Credit cards: MC, V
Restrictions: No children under 12, pets. Smoking restricted. 20% deposit req. 24-hour cancellation notice req.
Notes: Two-story Greek Revival mansion built in 1926. Fully restored with modern conviences. Common area. Furnished with antiques, Oriental rugs, oil paintings, and owner's collection of china. Screened back porch, brick patio overlooking grounds.*

CHARLESTON (5)

27 State Street B & B
27 State St., Charleston, SC 29401
(803) 722-4243
Innkeeper: Paul and Joye Craven
Rooms: 2 suites w/pvt. bath, phone, TV
Rates: $85-$150, incl. cont. brk. Discount avail. for extended stay. Seasonal variations.
Credit cards: None
Restrictions: No pets, smoking. Deposit req. 14-day cancellation notice req. 2-night min. stay on busy wknds.
Notes: Three-story house built in the 1800s. Veranda. Decorated with antiques and reproductions. Bicycles, parking, short-term leases available.*

27 STATE STREET B & B

Anchorage Inn
26 Vendue Range, Charleston, SC 29401
(803) 723-8300, (803) 723-9543
Innkeeper: Elizabeth Tucker, Lise Loux
Rooms: 17 plus 2 suites, all w/pvt. bath, phone, TV
Rates: $105-$184/room, $155-$229/suite, all incl. cont. brk. Special pkgs. avail. Seasonal variations.
Credit cards: Most major cards
Restrictions: No children under 12, pets. Smoking restricted. Deposit req. 48-hour cancellation notice req. 2-night min.stay on wknds. during high season.
Notes: Two-story English Coaching inn. Dining room, library. Furnished in 17th-century decor. Whirlpool tubs. Valet parking available.*

Ann Harper's B & B
56 Smith St., Charleston, SC 29401
(803) 723-3947
Innkeeper: Ann D. Harper
Rooms: 2, no pvt. bath, incl. 1 w/TV. Suite available.
Rates: $65-$75/room, $75-$90/suite, all incl. full brk. Seasonal variations.
Credit cards: None
Restrictions: No children under 10, pets. Smoking restricted. One night's deposit req. 14-day cancellation req. less $15.00 fee. 2-night min. stay on wknds.
Notes: Private house built in 1870. Located in historic district. Common room, second floor balcony, porch. Furnished with antiques, wicker and reproductions. Small wall garden in back. Off-street parking available.

Ashley Inn B & B
201 Ashley Ave., Charleston, SC 29403
(803) 723-1848, (803) 723-9080
Innkeeper: Bud and Sally Allen
Rooms: 6 plus 1 suite, all w/pvt. bath, phone, TV, incl. 2 w/fireplace
Rates: $69-$115/room, $110-$135/suite, all incl. full brk. Seasonal variations.
Credit cards: Most major cards
Restrictions: No children under 12, pets. Smoking restricted. Deposit req. 7-day cancellation notice req.
Notes: Two-story inn built in 1832. Furnished with antiques. Bicycle available.

Battery Carriage House Inn
20 S. Battery, Charleston, SC 29401
(800) 775-5575, (803) 727-3130
Innkeeper: Katharine Hastie
Rooms: 11 w/pvt. bath, cable TV, phone
Rates: $99-$199, incl. cont. brk., evening refreshment. Seasonal variations.
Credit cards: Most major cards
Restrictions: Children under 11 discouraged. No pets, smoking. Deposit req. 30-day cancellation notice req. 2-night min. stay on wknds.
Notes: Two-story antebellum mansion built in 1843. Renovated in 1870. Fully restored. Located on the waterfront. Wet bar, private courtyard. Decorated with period furnishings. Bicycles, whirlpool tubs available.*

Belvedere B & B
40 Rutledge Ave., Charleston, SC 29401
(803) 722-0973

Innkeeper: David Spell
Rooms: 3 w/pvt. bath, TV
Rates: $110, incl. cont. brk., evening refreshment. Deposit req. 14-day cancellation notice req. less $15.00 fee.
Credit cards: None
Restrictions: No children under 8, pets. Smoking restricted. Deposit req. 14-day cancellation notice req., less $15.00 fee. 2-night min. stay.
Notes: Colonial Revival mansion overlooking Colonial Lake built in 1900. Family room with cable TV. Furnished with Belvedere Plantation house interior.

Cannonboro Inn
184 Ashley Ave., Charleston, SC 29403
(803) 723-8572, (803) 723-9080
Innkeeper: Bud and Sally Allen
Rooms: 6 w/pvt. bath, TV, incl. 5 w/fireplace
Rates: $69-$115, incl. full brk. Seasonal variations.
Credit cards: Most major cards
Restrictions: No children under 12, pets. Smoking restricted. Deposit req. 7-day cancellation notice req.
Notes: Two-story antebellum house built about 1890. Formal dining room. Covered piazza overlooking low country garden. Furnished in period decor. Off-street parking available.*

Country Victorian B & B
105 Tradd St., Charleston, SC 29401-2422
(803) 577-0682
Innkeeper: Diane Deardurff Weed
Rooms: 2 w/pvt. bath, phone, fireplace, TV. Suite avail.
Rates: $75-$135, incl. expanded cont. brk., afternoon refreshment. Discount avail. for extended stay. Seasonal variations.
Credit cards: None
Restrictions: No children under 8, pets, smoking. Deposit req. 14-day cancellation notice req., less $15.00 fee. 2-night min. stay, March–July, October.
Notes: Two-story Country Victorian house with attached Carriage House built in 1820. Furnished with antiques, collectibles. Off-street parking, bicycles available.

John Rutledge House Inn
116 Broad St., Charleston, SC 29401
(803) 723-7999, (803) 723-2615
Innkeeper: Linda Bishop
Rooms: 16 plus 3 suites, all w/pvt. bath, phone, TV, incl. 11 w/fireplace. Located in 3 bldgs.
Rates: $130-$225/room, $235-$285/suite, all incl. cont. brk. Special pkg. avail. Seasonal variations.
Credit cards: Most major cards
Restrictions: No pets. Smoking restricted. Deposit req. 24-hour cancellation notice req. Min. stay req. during special events.
Notes: Two-story antebellum mansion with carved Italian marble fireplaces, original plaster moldings, inlaid floors, ironwork built in 1763 as the home of John Rutledge, a signer of the Constitution. Main House and two Carriage Houses. Redecorated and third floor added in 1853. Completely restored in 1988. Has operated as inn since 1989. Ballroom, balcony. Library with fireplace. Furnished with

antiques, historically accurate reproductions. Limited handicapped access. Listed of the National Register of Historic Places.*

King George Inn
32 George St., Charleston, SC 29401
(803) 723-9339
Innkeeper: Jean, Lynn, BJ, and Mike
Rooms: 7 w/pvt. bath, TV.
Rates: $65-$110, incl. cont. brk. Discount avail. for student's and extended stay. Seasonal variations.
Credit cards: MC, V
Restrictions: Pets welcome with prior notifications. Smoking restricted. 2-night's deposit req. 5-day cancellation notice req. 2-night min. stay.
Notes: Four-story federal-style house with 3 levels of Charleston porches built in 1794. Dining room. Furnished with antiques. Off-street parking. Handicapped access.

The Kitchen House
126 Tradd St., Charleston, SC 29401
(803) 577-6362
Innkeeper: Lois Evans
Rooms: 3 w/pvt bath, phone, TV, plus 2 suites w/pvt bath, phone, TV, fireplace
Rates: $100-$175/room, $175-$250/suite, all incl. full brk., evening refreshment. Discount avail. for extended stay. Seasonal variations.
Credit cards: MC, V
Restrictions: No pets. Smoking restricted. Min. one night's deposit req. 14-day cancellation notice req., less $15.00 fee. 2-night min. stay on wknds.
Notes: Three-story 18th-century pre-Revolutionary, midieval house. Fully restored. Located in Charleston's Historic District. Once the residence of the surgeon-general of Continental army and home of 2 confederate generals. Living room with fireplace. Dining room, pantry, patio, Colonial herb gardens.*

Maison Du Pré
317 E. Bay St., Charleston, SC 29401
(803) 723-8691, (800) 844-INNS, (803) 723-3722
Innkeeper: Robert, Lucille and Mark Mulholland
Rooms: 15, incl. 3 suites, all w/pvt. bath, phone, TV. Located in 5 bldgs.
Rates: $98-$145/room, $145-$200/suite, all incl. cont. brk., afternoon refreshment. Discount avail. for senior citizen, groups, and mid-week stays. Seasonal variations.
Credit cards: Most major cards
Restrictions: No pets, smoking
Notes: Two restored carriage houses and three "single houses" built in 1804. Located in the downtown Ansonborough Historic District. Furnished with period antiques and Oriental rugs. Features original paintings by owner. Three fountains and brick patios with flowering trees and shrubs, and a wishing well. Received Carolopolis Award from Preservation Society of Charleston. Small private parties accommodated. Some French spoken. Horse-drawn carriage tours, bus, and shuttle services arranged.*

Planters Inn
112 N. Market St., Charleston, SC 29401
(803) 722-2345, (800) 845-7082, (803) 577-2125

Innkeeper: Bill McDonald
Rooms: 36, plus 5 suites, all w/pvt. bath, phone, TV
Rates: $115-$149/room, $169-$229/suite, all incl. cont. brk., evening refreshment. Seasonal variations.
Credit cards: Most major cards
Restrictions: No pets. Smoking restricted. Credit card deposit req. 48-hour cancellation notice req. 2-night min. stay on some wknds.
Notes: Four-story Inn built in the 1840s. Restored in 1983 in historic detail w/high ceilings. Completely refurbished in 1994. Has operated as inn since 1981. Lobby. Furnished from the Historic Charleston Collection. Handicapped access. Restaurant on premises. Entrance-way opens onto the Historic Marketplace.*

Rutledge Victorian Inn
114 Rutledge Ave., Charleston, SC 29401
(803) 722-7551

Innkeeper: BJ, Jean, Lynn and Mike
Rooms: 10 w/TV, incl. 7 w/pvt. bath
Rates: $50-$110, incl. cont. brk. Discount avail. for student and extended stays.
Credit cards: Most major cards
Restrictions: No smoking. Small pets welcome with prior notification. 2-night's deposit req. 5-day cancellation notice req., less deposit fee. 2-night min. stay on wknds.
Notes: Victorian/Italianate house with columns, gingerbread details, 12-ft. ceilings and hardwood floors built about 1888. Furnished with antiques. Porch with rockers. Off-street parking available.

COLUMBIA (3)

Richland Street B & B
1425 Richland St., Columbia, SC 29202
(800) 779-7011

Innkeeper: Naomi Perryman
Rooms: 6 w/pvt. bath, TV, incl. 4 w/phone, plus 1 suite w/whirlpool bath, TV
Rates: $79-$99/room, $120/suite, all incl. cont. brk, afternoon refreshment. Discount avail. for senior citizens.
Credit cards: Most major cards

RICHLAND STREET B & B

Restrictions: No children under 12, pets. Smoking restricted. Min. one night's deposit req. 7-day cancellation notice req., less $10.00 fee.
Credit cards: Two-story Victorian house built in 1993. High ceilinged lobby. Second-story porch accessible from two of the front rooms.

GEORGETOWN (4)

1790 House Bed and Breakfast
630 Highmarket St., Georgetown, SC 29440
(803) 546-4821

Innkeeper: Patricia and John Wiley
Rooms: 5 w/pvt. bath, incl. 1 w/TV, 1 w/fireplace, plus 1 suite w/pvt. bath, phone, plus 1 cottage w/pvt. bath, Jacuzzi. Located in 2 bldgs.
Rates: $70-$80/room, $95/suite, $115/cottage, all incl. full brk., afternoon refreshment. Seasonal variations. Discount avail. for extended, mid-week, and senior citizen stays.
Credit cards: Most major cards
Restrictions: No pets, smoking. 50% deposit req. 72-hour cancellation notice req.
Notes: Two-story West Indies colonial plantation-style house built in 1790. Fully restored. Located in Georgetown Historic District. Wrap-around veranda. Drawing room with fireplace. Dining room, game room. Bicycles, table tennis, board games, hammock available. Gardens. Phones and TVs available upon request. Small private parties accommodated.

The Shaw House
613 Cypress Ct., Georgetown, SC 29440
(803) 546-9663

Innkeeper: Mary and Joe Shaw
Rooms: 3 w/pvt. bath, phone, incl. 1 w/TV
Rates: $50-$60, incl. full brk., afternoon refreshment. Special pkgs. avail.
Credit cards: None
Restrictions: No pets, smoking. Deposit req.
Notes: Two-story Colonial-style house. Has operated as inn since 1983. Den overlooking marsh. Columned front porch with large rocking chairs. Furnished with antiques.*

Shipwright's B & B
609 Cypress Ct., Georgetown, SC 29440
(803) 527-4475

Innkeeper: Leatrice Wright
Rooms: 1 plus 1 suite, all w/pvt. bath
Rates: $55/room, $60/suite, all incl. full brk. Discount avail. for extended stay.
Credit cards: None
Restrictions: 50% deposit req. 14-day cancellation notice req.
Notes: Brick ranch house located in Willow Bank Plantation. Great room. Decorated with family heirlooms and antiques. Front porch with rockers. Listed on the National Register of Historic Places. Marinas and anchorages pick-up available.

HILTON HEAD ISLAND (5)

Home Away Bed and Breakfast
3 Pender Ln., Hilton Head Island, SC 29928
(803) 671-5578

Innkeeper: Beverly Jones
Rooms: 1 w/pvt. bath, TV
Rates: $75, incl. cont. brk.
Credit cards: None.
Restrictions: Deposit req.

SUGARFOOT CASTLE

HONEA PATH (1)

Sugarfoot Castle
211 S. Main St., Honea Path, SC 29654-1522
(803) 369-6565
Innkeeper: Gale and Cecil Evans
Rooms: 3 w/phone, TV, no pvt. bath
Rates: $49, incl. cont. brk. Discount avail. for extended stay.
Credit cards: MC, V
Restrictions: No children under 10. Deposit req. 7-day cancellation notice req., less
    $2.00 fee.
Notes: Three-story brick Victorian house built in 1880. Fully restored. Living room.
Library with fireplace, VCR, desk and gametable. Screened back porch. Furnished
with family heirlooms.

LEESVILLE (3)

The Able House Inn
244 W. Church St., Leesville, SC 29070
(803) 532-2763
Innkeeper: Jack and Annabelle Wright
Rooms: 4 plus 1 suite, all w/pvt. bath, phone, incl. 1 w/TV
Rates: $50-$55/room, $60/suite, all incl. cont. brk., evening refreshment. Discount
    avail. for extended and senior citizen stays.
Credit cards: MC, V
Restrictions: No children under 12, pets. Smoking restricted. Deposit req. 2-day
    cancellation notice req.

Notes: Two-story house built in 1940. Located on one acre of private fenced yard. Living room with fireplace. Sunroom with TV. Dining room. Furnished with antiques. Flagstone patio with umbrella table overlooking swimming pool.

McCLELLANVILLE (5)

LAUREL HILL PLANTATION

Laurel Hill Plantation
8913 N. Hwy. 17, Box 190, McClellanville, SC 29458
(803) 887-3708
Innkeeper: Jackie and Lee Morrison
Rooms: 4 w/pvt. bath
Rates: $65-$85, incl. full brk.
Credit cards: Most major cards
Restrictions: No children under 6, pets. Smoking restricted. Deposit req. 3-day cancellation notice req., less $10.00 fee.
Notes: Two-story inn built in 1850s. Dining room. Wrap-around porches overlooking creek, marshes. Furnished with country and primitive antiques.*

MYRTLE BEACH (4)

Brustman House
400 25th Ave. S., Myrtle Beach, SC 29577
(803) 448-7699, (800) 448-7699, (803) 626-1500
Innkeeper: Dr. Wendell C. Brustman
Rooms: 3 w/pvt. bath, phone, plus 1 suite w/pvt. bath, phone, TV, kitchen
Rates: $55-$65/room, $80-$120/suite, incl. full brk., evening refreshment. Seasonal variations. Discount avail. for extended stay.
Credit cards: To hold reservation only
Restrictions: No children under 10, pets, smoking. One night's deposit req. 14-day cancellation notice req., less fee.
Notes: Two-story Georgian-style house located on one-acre. Furnished with Scandinavian classic furniture and down or Laura Ashley comforters. Rose garden. Bicycles, lawn games.*

Serendipity Inn
407 71st Ave. N., Myrtle Beach, SC 29572
(803) 449-5268
Innkeeper: Terry and Sheila Johnson
Rooms: 12, plus 2 suites, all w/pvt. bath, cable TV, refrigerator
Rates: $45-$92/room, $73-$110/suite, all incl. cont. brk. Seasonal variations.
Credit cards: Most major cards
Restrictions: No pets. Smoking restricted. Deposit req. 14-day cancellation notice req. 2-night min. stay on summer wknds.
Notes: Two-story Spanish mission-style complex built in 1984. Garden room. Guest rooms decorated individually in different periods. Heated swimming pool, spa, outdoor gas grill, brick patio with fountain. Lawn games available. Handicapped access. Spanish spoken.*

ROCK HILL (2)

East Main Guest House
600 E. Main St., Rock Hill, SC 29730
(803) 366-1161
Innkeeper: Melba and Jerry Peterson
Rooms: 2 w/pvt. bath, phone, TV, incl. 1 w/fireplace, plus 1 suite w/pvt. whirlpool bath, phone, fireplace, TV
Rates: $59-$69/room, $79/suite, all incl. cont. brk., afternoon refreshment. Special pkgs. avail.
Credit cards: Most major cards
Restrictions: No children under 12, pets, smoking. Deposit req.
Notes: Craftsman-style Bungalow completely renovated and decorated. Dining room. Sitting/game room. Arbor-pergola on patio.

SUMTER (3)

Sumter Bed and Breakfast
6 Park Ave., Sumter, SC 29150
(803) 773-2903, (803) 775-6943
Innkeeper: Jess and Suzanne Begley
Rooms: 5 w/pvt. bath, phone, TV, fireplace
Rates: $50-$65, incl. full brk. Discount avail. for extended stay.
Credit cards: MC, V
Restrictions: No children under 12, pets. Smoking restricted. One night's deposit req. 48-hour cancellation notice req.
Notes: Two-story house built about 1896. Foyer, dining room. Parlor with Victorian soap stone mantle, hand-carved mirror. Sitting room with TV. Furnished with antiques. Front porch with rocker overlooking Memorial Park. Innkeepers are enthusiastic about archeology, stone and wood sculpting, cooking, painting, handcrafts.*

SUNSET (1)

Laurel Springs Country Inn
1137 Moorefield Memorial Hwy., Sunset, SC 29685
(803) 878-2252
Innkeeper: Valdas Kotovas and Leslie Becker
Rooms: 2, no pvt. bath, plus 1 cabin. Located in 2 bldgs.
Rates: $60/room, $70/cabin, all incl. full brk. Seasonal variations.

Credit cards: None

Restrictions: No pets, smoking. One night's deposit req. 7-day cancellation notice req., less 50% fee.

Notes: One-story house on pond. Common room with fireplace. Fishing in pond, nature trails for hiking, late night bonfires. Italian and Lithuanian spoken.

South Dakota

CANOVA (4)

Skoglund Farm
Rte. 1, Box 45, Canova, SD 57321
(605) 247-3445
Innkeeper: Alden and Delores Skogland
Rooms: 4, no pvt. bath
Rates: $15-30, incl. full brk., dinner
Credit cards: Most major cards
Restrictions: Smoking restricted.
Notes: Farmhouse built in 1917. Common room with piano, TV. Resident farm animals.*

CORSICA (4)

Country Corner B & B
RR 2, Box 46, Corsica, SD 57328
(605) 946-5852
Innkeeper: Gene and Birdie Schoon
Rooms: 3, no pvt. bath. Suite avail.
Rates: $35/room, $50/suite, all incl. full brk. Seasonal variations. Special pkgs. avail.
Credit cards: None
Restrictions: Pets, smoking restricted. Deposit req. 7-day cancellation notice req.
Notes: Built in 1908. Restored in Victorian style in 1990. Dutch entry, formal dining room, living room. Southwestern basement with family room, snack bar. Game room, pool room. Furnished with antiques. Rose garden, patio. Yard with farm animals to pet. Horse drawn buggy and sleigh rides available. Limo service to and from casino available. Guests have access to laundry facilities. Dutch spoken.

CUSTER MANSION BED & BREAKFAST

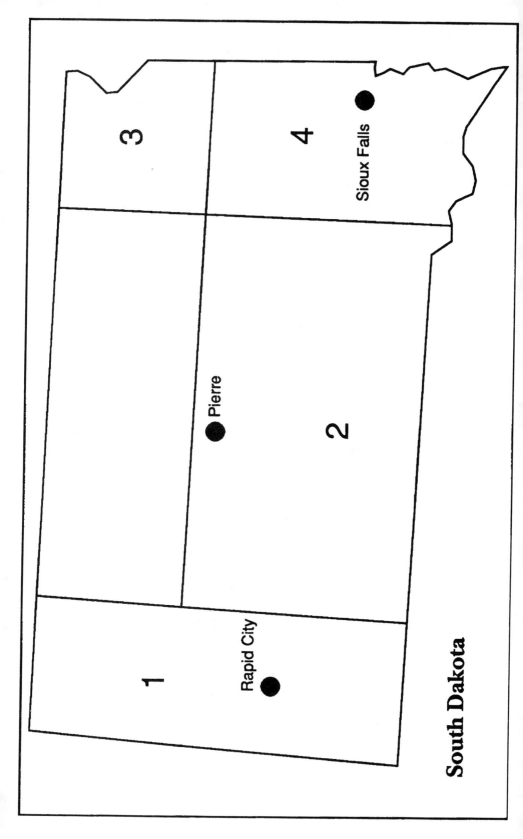

South Dakota

CUSTER (1)

Custer Mansion Bed & Breakfast
35 Centennial Dr., Custer, SD 57730
(605) 673-3333
Innkeeper: Mill and Carole Seaman
Rooms: 6, incl. 2 w/pvt. bath
Rates: $48-$73, incl. full brk. Seasonal variations. Discount avail. for extended, senior citizen stays.
Credit cards: None
Restrictions: No pets, smoking. 50% deposit req. 10-day cancellation notice req., less 5% fee
Notes: Two-story Victorian Gothic mansion built in 1891. Located on one acre with picket fence. Front parlor with lounge, TV. Dining room, library, Butler's pantry. Patio. Decorated in country style. Giftshop on premises. Listed on National Register of Historic Places. Spanish spoken.*

FREEMAN (4)

Farmers Inn B & B
RR 2, Box 39W, Freeman, SD 57029
(605) 925-7580
Innkeeper: Russell and MarJean Waltner
Rooms: 2 w/pvt. bath, phone, incl. 1 w/TV, plus 1 suite w/pvt. bath, phone, TV
Rates: $32-$40/room, $65/suite, all incl. full brk., afternoon refreshment. Discount avail. for extended stay.
Credit cards: Most major cards
Restrictions: No children under 10, pets, smoking.
Notes: Two-story, Victorian-style farmhouse built in 1914. Music room with piano, pump organ. Parlor with library. Sitting room and dining room. Furnished with antiques. Fitness center, sauna. All meals available. German spoken.

HERMOSA (1)

Bunkhouse B & B
14630 Lower Spring Creek Rd., Hermosa, SD 57744
(605) 342-5462
Innkeeper: Carol Hendrickson
Rooms: 1 w/pvt. bath, plus 2 suites, incl. 1 w/pvt. bath, 1 w/pvt. entrance, patio.
Rates: $65-$75/room, $110/suite, all incl. full brk.
Credit cards: MC, V
Restrictions: No pets or stallions. Restricted smoking. Deposit req. 14-day cancellation notice req.
Notes: Working ranch, settled in 1917, where the claim shack still stands. Family room on lower level with library, wood stove. Front porch with glider swing, benches, picnic tables. Furnished with western antiques. Play area for children. Giftshop on premises with handmade items crafted by Native American on nearby Sioux Reservation. Spring creek. Facilities for guest's horses. Resident farm animals. Handicapped access.*

HILL CITY (1)

High Country Ranch
12172 Deerfield Rd., Hill City, SD 57745
(605) 574-9003
Innkeeper: Larry and Bonnie McCaskell
Rooms: 4 cabins w/pvt. bath, phone, incl. 1 w/TV. Located in 4 bldgs.
Rates: $75, incl. full brk.
Credit cards: None
Restrictions: No smoking. Deposit req. 30-day cancellation notice req., less $20.00 fee.
Notes: Covered wagon dining room. Outdoor activities available. ½-hour trail ride included with stay. Horseback riding available. Handicapped access.*

HOT SPRINGS (1)

Villa Theresa Guest House
801 Almond St., Hot Springs, SD 57747
(605) 745-4633, (800) 523-4633
Innkeeper: Bob and Jan Scanlon
Rooms: 6 w/pvt. bath, incl. 1 w/Jacuzzi plus 1 suite w/pvt. bath, Jacuzzi, TV.
Rates: $65-$85/room, $95-$140 suite, all incl. full brk. Discount avail. for senior citizens, Sept.–May. Seasonal variations.
Credit cards: Most major cards
Restrictions: No pets, smoking. Deposit req. 7-day cancellation notice req.
Notes: Built in 1891. Located on bluff overlooking Hot Springs. Formal dining room, poker room with white wicker furniture, two-story octagonal living room with fireplace, eighteen ft. stenciled ceiling. Decorated in Victorian decor. Two porches. All guest rooms are theme decorated and include Old West, Oriental, Victorian, Mountain Cabin, Sioux, and Tropical Island furnishings. Listed on National Register of Historic Places. German, French, Russian spoken. *

RAPID CITY (1)

Anemarie's Country Bunny B & B
10430 Big Piney Rd., Rapid City, SD 57702
(605) 343-9234
Innkeeper: Randy and Cathy Blaseg
Rooms: 4 suites, w/pvt bath, TV, incl. 3 w/phone
Rates: $70-$90, incl full brk., afternoon refreshment. Seasonal variations.
Credit cards: None
Restrictions: No pets. Smoking restricted. 50% deposit req. 14-day cancellation notice req., less $10.00 fee.
Notes: Three-story redwood house. Furnished with European style. Guests have access to whirlpools, hot tubs, TV, VCR.*

WEBSTER (4)

Lakeside Farm B & B
RR 2, Box 52, Webster, SD 57274-9633
(605) 486-4430
Innkeeper: Joy and Glenn Hagen
Rooms: 3, no pvt. bath

Rates: $40, incl. full brk.
Credit cards: None
Restrictions: No pets, smoking, alcohol. Deposit req. 7-day cancellation notice req.
Notes: Two-story farmhouse.

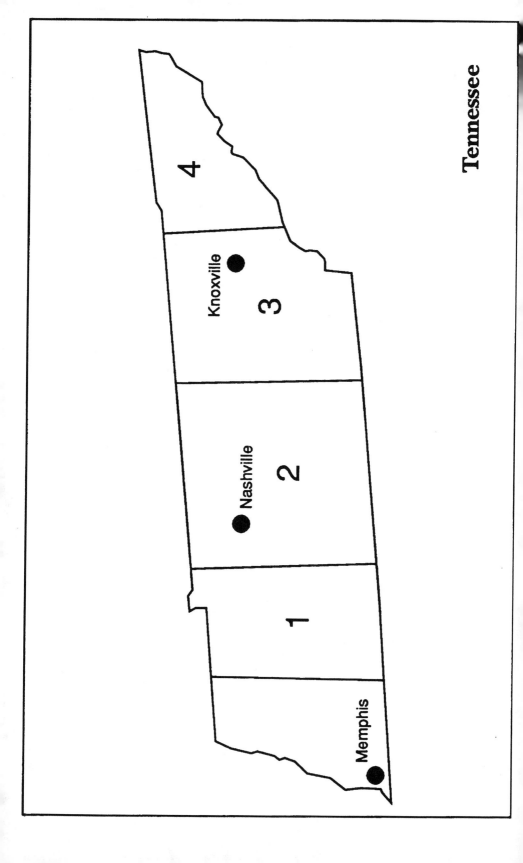

Tennessee

ARRINGTON (2)

Xanadu Farm
8155 Horton Hwy., Box 152, Arrington, TN 37014
(615) 395-4771
Innkeeper: Susan Freeman, Lisa Smith
Rooms: 1 cottage w/pvt. bath, phone, TV, kitchen
Rates: $75, incl. cont. brk. Discount avail. for extended stay.
Credit cards: None
Restrictions: No pets, smoking. 50% deposit req. 3-day cancellation notice req.
Notes: Country cottage located on 130-acre working horse farm. Main room with TV, phone, washer & dryer. Picnic shelter overlooking 1.5-acre pond stocked for fishing. 28-stall barn on property—bring your own horse. Resident Zebra.

CHATTANOOGA (3)

Adams Hilborne
801 Vine St., Chattanooga, TN 37403
(423) 265-5000, (423) 265-5555
Innkeeper: Wendy and David Adams
Rooms: 6 plus 6 suites, all w/pvt. bath, phone, TV, incl. 4 w/fireplace
Rates: $100-$295, incl. cont. brk. Discount avail. for corporate stay.
Credit cards: Most major cards
Restrictions: Children welcome by special arrangement. No pets. Smoking restricted.
   First and last night's deposit req. 14-day cancellation notice req., less $15.00 fee.
Notes: Three-story stone Romanesque mansion with 16-ft. ceilings, wide oak entry staircase, built in 1889. Fully renovated in 1995. Ladies drawing room , music room, banquet hall, Ambassador hall, all with fireplace. Ballroom, reception room, front and rear verandas. Decorated with antiques, original paintings. Small private parties accommodated. Dinner available for 2-200 by prior arrangement. Giftshop on premises. 1995 Chattanooga Decorator showhouse. Listed on the National Register of Historic Places. Off-street parking available. Handicapped access.*

DANDRIDGE (4)

Mill Dale Farm
140 Mill Dale Rd. Route 5, Dandridge, TN 37725
(615) 397-3470, (800) 767-3471
Innkeeper: Lucy Franklin
Rooms: 3 w/pvt. bath, phone
Rates: $65, incl full brk.
Credit cards: None
Restrictions: No pets. Smoking restricted. Deposit req. 7-day cancellation notice
   req., less $10.00 fee.
Notes: 19th-century farm house with circular stairway. Decorated with period furniture. Common room and kitchen with fireplaces. Handicapped access.

Mountain Harbor Inn
1199 Hwy. 139, Dandridge, TN 37725
(615) 397-3345, (615) 397-0264

Innkeeper: Rich and Pat Steinaway, Jim and Shirley McEwan
Rooms: 4 plus 8 suites, all w/pvt. bath, phone, TV
Rates: $60-$80/room, $75-$115/suite, all incl. full brk.
Credit cards: Most major cards
Restrictions: Deposit req. 50% cancellation fee. Closed Nov. 15–May 1.
Notes: Three-story inn with pillared porches. Decorated in antiques and quilts, and locally crafted rocking chairs. Located on lake. Boat launch and dock for fishing. Handicapped access.

FAYETTEVILLE (2)

Old Cowan Plantation
126 Old Boonshill Rd., Fayetteville, TN 37334
(615) 433-0225

Innkeeper: Paul and Betty Johnson
Rooms: 2 w/pvt. bath, TV, plus 1 suite w/pvt. bath, TV
Rates: $42/room, $45/suite, all incl. cont. brk.
Credit cards: Most major cards
Restrictions: No pets, smoking. Deposit req. 7-day cancellation notice req.
Notes: Colonial-style house built in 1886. Dining room. Porch with rocking chairs. Giftshop on premises. Handicapped access.

GATLINBURG (4)

7th HEAVEN LOG HOME INN

7th Heaven Log Home Inn
3944 Castle Rd., Gatlinburg, TN 37738
(615) 430-5000, (800) 248-2923, (615) 430-5000

Innkeeper: Ginger and Paul Wolcott
Rooms: 4 w/pvt. bath
Rates: $77-$117, incl. full brk. Seasonal variations. Discount avail. for group stay.
    Special pkgs. avail.
Credit cards: MC, V

Restrictions: No pets. Children and smoking restricted. 50% deposit req. 30-day cancellation notice req., less $15.00 fee. 2-night min. stay.

Notes: Two-story log house built in 1991. Located on 7th green of Bent Creek Golf Resort. Dining room, Guest kitchen. Recreation room with stone fireplace, TV/VCR. table, pool tables, games. Deck, log gazebo with Jacuzzi. Duck filled pond, golf course. Guests have access to pool, tennis. Resident dog.*

Butcher House
1520 Garrett Lane, Gatlinburg, TN 37738
(615) 436-9457
Innkeeper: Hugh and Gloria Butcher
Rooms: 4 w/pvt. bath, TV, plus 1 suite w/pvt. bath, TV
Rates: $79/room, $89/suite, incl. full brk., evening refreshment. Seasonal variations. Discount avail. for mid-week stay.
Credit cards: Most major cards
Restrictions: No children under 12, pets, smoking. Deposit req. 15-day cancellation notice req. 2-night min. stay on wknds.
Notes: Two-story house with balconies. Located at main entrance to Smokey Mountain National Park. Guests have access to kitchen. Furnished with Victorian, French, Queen Anne, and American Country antiques. Italian spoken.

Eight Gables Inn
219 N. Mountain Trail, Gatlinburg, TN 37738
(615) 430-3344
Innkeeper: Helen Smith
Rooms: 9, plus 1 suite.
Rates: $89-$98/room, $110/suite, all incl. full brk. Discount avail. for extended stay.
Credit cards: MC, V
Restrictions: Children under 12 welcome with prior arrangement. No pets. Smoking restricted. Deposit req. 10-day cancellation notice req.
Notes: One-story house. Located at the foot of Great Smokey Mountains National Park. Dining room, common room. Covered porch with rockers. Small private party accommodated. *

EIGHT GABLES INN

Hippensteal Mountain View Inn
P.O. Box 707, Gatlinburg, TN 37738
(615) 436-5761, (800) 527-8110, (615) 436-2354
Innkeeper: Vern and Lisa Hippensteal
Rooms: 8 w/pvt. bath, phone, fireplace, TV
Rates: $115, incl. full brk, afternoon refreshment
Credit cards: Most major cards
Restrictions: No pets, smoking. Deposit req. 10-day cancellation notice req. 2-night min. stay on wknds.
Notes: Three-story inn. Lobby with fireplace. Dining room, meeting room, library. Three-story wraparound porches with rocking chairs overlooking the Great Smokey Mountains. Furnished in eclectic style. Innkeeper is a watercolorist.

GOODLETTSVILLE (2)

Drake Farm on Lumsley Creek
P.O. Box 875, Goodlettsville, TN 37070-0875
(615) 859-2425, (615) 859-3671
Innkeeper: Rose Mary Drake
Rooms: 2 w/fireplace, incl. 1 w/phone, no pvt. bath
Rates: $55, incl. full brk.
Credit cards: Most major cards
Restrictions: Children and pets welcome with prior arrangements. No smoking. 50% deposit req. 7-day cancellation notice req.
Notes: Two-story antebellum farmhouse built in the 1850s. Located on 116 acres. Common room with TV. Library. Furnished with antiques. Porch, patio, swing, hammocks. Board games available. Outdoor activities available. Small private parties accommodated. German spoken. Handicapped access limited.*

Woodshire B & B
600 Woodshire Dr., Goodlettsville, TN 37072
(615) 859-7369
Innkeeper: John and Beverly Grayson
Rooms: 2 plus 1 cabin, all w/pvt. bath, pvt. entrance, cable TV
Rates: $50/room, $60-$75/cabin, all incl. cont brk. Discount avail. for extended stay.
Credit cards: None
Restrictions: Well behaved children welcome. No pets, smoking, alcohol. Min. one night's deposit req. 5-day cancellation notice req.
Notes: Two-story salt-box house built in New England style. Decorated with antiques and family craftwork. 150-year-old log cabin has front porch. Board games available. Deck. Benches in yard. Flower garden area.*

GREENEVILLE (4)

Big Spring Inn
315 N. Main St., Greeneville, TN 37743
(615) 638-2917
Innkeeper: Marshall and Nancy Ricker
Rooms: 4 plus 2 suites, all w/pvt. bath, phone. Located in 2 bldgs.
Rates: $76/room, $110/suite, all incl. full brk., afternoon refreshment. Discount avail. for mid-week stay.

Credit cards: Most major cards
Restrictions: No children under 4, pets, smoking. 50% deposit req. 3-day cancellation notice req.
Notes: Three-story Greek revival house located on 2 acres. Surrounded by 100-year-old trees and gardens. Front porch, dining room, library. Parlor with TV, piano, music collection. Board games, dinner available.*

BIG SPRING INN

Hilltop House
6 Sanford Circle, Greeneville, TN 37743
(615) 639-8202

Innkeeper: Denise M. Ashworth
Rooms: 3 w/pvt. bath, phone, incl. 2 w/TV
Rates: $60-$70, incl. full brk., afternoon refreshment. Seasonal variations. Discount avail. for extended stay. Special pkgs. avail.
Credit cards: Most major cards
Rates: No children under 3, pets, smoking. One night's deposit req. 7-day cancellation notice req.
Notes: Two-story house built in the 1920s. Located on three acres overlooking the Nolichucky River Valley. Common room with TV, VCR, books, board games, puzzles. Furnished with antiques and reproductions. Front porch with rocking chairs and swing. English gardens. Airport pick-up with prior notice. Lunch, dinner available.*

HENDERSONVILLE (2)

Monthaven
1154 W. Main St., Hendersonville, TN 37075
(615) 824-6319, (615) 822-7332

Innkeeper: Hugh Waddell and Alan Waddell
Rooms: 2 w/pvt. bath, phone, incl. 1 w/TV, plus 1 suite w/pvt. bath plus 1 log cabin w/prt. bath,fireplace. Located in 2 bldgs.
Rates: $75/room, suite, $85/cabin, all incl. cont. brk.
Credit cards: Most major cards

Restrictions: Smoking restricted. Deposit req. Min. 2-night stay for cabin

Notes: Two-story Greek Revival house built in mid-1880s on former Indian camp-ground soite. Furnished with white oadk and cedar and decorated inside and out with Victorian elements. Library features French provincial parlor and hallway has chandelier. Located on seventy-five wooded acres. Family owned since 1930. Handicapped access. Used as a military hospital for Union and Confederate soldiers in Civil War. Listed on the National Register of Historic Places. Resident cats and dog.*

LIMESTONE (4)

Snapp Inn B & B
1990 Davy Crockett Rd., Limestone, TN 37681
(615) 257-2482, (800) 524-0595

Innkeeper: Dan and Ruth Dorgan

Rooms: 3 w/pvt.bath, incl. 1 w/fireplace, 1 w/TV

Rates: $40-$50, incl. full brk. Discount avail. for extended stay.

Credit cards: Most major cards

Restrictions: No more than one child per room. No smoking. Deposit req. 7-day cancellation notice req.

Notes: Federal brick house built about 1815. Common room with pool table. Full back porch and front balcony. Furnished with antiques.*

SNAPP INN B & B

LOUDON (3)

The Mason Place B & B
600 Commerce St., Loudon, TN 37774
(615) 458-3921

Innkeeper: Bob and Donna Siewert

Rooms: 5 w/pvt. bath, fireplace

Rates: $96, incl. full brk., afternoon refreshment. Discount avail. for extended and mid-week stays.

Credit cards: MC, V

Restrictions: No children under 16, pets. Smoking restricted. Min. stay on some wknds.

Notes: Two-story Greek Revival plantation house built in 1865. Located on three acres. Grand entrance hall, 10 working fireplaces. Furnished with antiques. Grecian swimming pool, gazebo, wisteria-covered arbor. Porches with rockers and swings. Lawn games, gardens. Listed on National Registry of Historic Places. Limited handicapped access.*

McMINNVILLE (2)

FALCON MANOR B & B

Falcon Manor B & B
2645 Faulkner Springs Rd., McMinnville, TN 37110
(615) 668-4444

Innkeeper: George and Charlien McGlothin

Rooms: 5, incl. 1 w/pvt. bath

Rates: $75, incl. full brk. Discount avail. for extended stay.

Credit cards: MC, V

Restrictions: No children under 12, pets, smoking. Deposit req. 7-day cancellation notice req., less 5% fee for credit cards.

Notes: Two-story Queen-Anne Victorian mansion located on 3 acres shaded by century-old trees. Sitting room with library. 12-foot ceiling, sweeping staircase, exquisite woodwork, Victorian colors, antiques. Small private parties accommodated. Handicapped access to 2 rooms. Listed on the National Register of Historic Places.*

MONTEAGLE (2)

Adams Edgeworth Inn
Monteagle Assembly, Monteagle, TN 37356
(615) 924-4000, (619) 924-3236

Innkeeper: Wendy and David Adams

Rooms: 11 plus 1 suite, all w/pvt. bath, incl. 3 w/fireplace, 4 w/TV

Rates: $65-$100/room, $135-$150/suite, all incl. full brk. Discount avail. for extended, mid-week, and senior citizen stays.

Credit cards: Most major cards

Restrictions: Children welcome with prior arrangement. No pets, smoking. Deposit req. 14-day cancellation notice req., less $15.00 fee. 2-night min. stay on wknds. 3-night min. stay on some holidays.

Notes: Two-story Queen Anne Carpenter Victorian inn built in 1896. Dining room. Library. Common room with fireplace. Furnished in English Manor style with floral chintzes, antiques, and collection of original paintings. Veranda with rockers. Sauna, electric touring cart. Bicycles, board games available.*

NASHVILLE (2)

Monthaven Bed & Breakfast
1154 W. Main St., Hendersonville/Nashville, TN 37075
(615) 824-6319, (615) 822-7332

Innkeeper: Hugh and Alan Waddell

Rooms: 2 w/pvt. bath, phone, fireplace, incl. 1 w/TV plus 1 suite w/pvt. bath, phone, fireplace, TV, plus 1 log cabin w/pvt. bath, kitchen.

Rates: $75/room, suite, $85/log cabin. Discount avail. for extended stay.

Credit cards: Most major cards

Restrictions: Smoking restricted. Deposit req.

Notes: Two-story Greek Revival mansion with high ceilings, built as plantation house around 1840 on site of former Indian campground. Cabin reconstructed in 1938 with white oak and cedar, has living room with fireplace, and ping-pong table. Located on 75 wooded acres. Used as a military hospital for both Union and Confederate soldiers. Parlor, library. Decorated with antiques and four-poster beds in Victorian style. Museum-style glass case holds local memorabilia including old pharmaceuticals and Civil war bullets. Resident cats and dog. Handicapped access.*

PIKEVILLE (3)

Fall Creek Falls B & B
Rte. 3, Box 298B, Pikeville, TN 37367
(423) 881-5494, (423) 881-5040

Innkeeper: Rita and Doug Pruett

Rooms: 7 w/pvt. bath, phone, plus 1 suite w/pvt. bath, phone, fireplace

Rates: $65-$115/room, $115-$127/suite, all incl. full brk., afternoon refreshment. Seasonal variations. Discount avail. to nurses.

Credit cards: Most major cards

Restrictions: No children under 12, pets, smoking. Deposit req. 7-day cancellation notice req. 2-night min. stay req. on major holidays and Oct. wknds.

Notes: 1.5-story stenciled brick house built in 1982. Located on forty mountain acres with pond stocked with bass. Common rooms with TV. Furnished with antiques and crafts from local shops. Lunch, picnic area with charcoal grills and massage therapist available.*

RED BOILING SPRINGS (2)

Armour Hotel
321 E. Main St., Red Boiling Springs, TN 37150
(615) 699-2180, (615) 699-3639

Innkeeper: Brendy and Bobby Thomas

Rooms: 24 w/pvt. bath, plus 2 suites w/pvt. bath, incl. 1 w/TV
Rates: $70/room, $100/suite, all incl. full brk. and dinner.
Credit cards: None
Restrictions: Well-mannered children welcome. No pets.
Notes: Two-story native brick house built in 1924. Fully restored. Lobby, front porch with rocking chairs. All meals available by reservation only. Small private parties accommodated. Handicapped access.*

ROGERSVILLE (4)

Hale Springs Inn
110 W. Main St., Town Square, Rogersville, TN 37857
(615) 272-5171
Innkeeper: Capt. and Mrs. Carl Netherland-Brown, Ed Pace, Sue Livesay, Belle Elkins
Rooms: 5 plus 4 suites, all w/pvt. bath, cable TV, incl. 8 w/fireplace
Rates: $45-$60/room, $85/suite, all incl. cont. brk.
Credit cards: Most major cards
Restrictions: No pets. 25% deposit req.
Notes: Three-story Federal brick inn built in 1824. Fully restored. Colonial dining room with fireplace. Furnished with antiques, Oriental carpets, canopied beds. Formal gardens with gazebo. Dinner available. Andrew Jackson, Andrew Johnson, James K. Polk slept here. Spanish spoken.*

RUGBY (3)

Newbury House
Hwy. 52, Box 8, Rugby, TN 37733
(615) 628-2441
Innkeeper: Historic Rugby
Rooms: 5 incl. 3 w/pvt. bath, phone, plus cottage. Located in 2 bldgs.
Rates: $50-$70, incl. full brk., afternoon refreshment
Credit cards: MC, V
Restrictions: No children under 12, pets. Smoking restricted. One night's deposit req. 7-day cancellation notice req., less $10.00 fee.
Notes: Two-story house with mansard roof built as a boarding house in 1880. Cottage with kitchen built in 1879. Fully restored in 1985. Parlor, veranda. Furnished with Victorian-period antiques. Listed on the National Register of Historic Places. Guided tours organized. Limited handicapped access.

SAVANNAH (1)

Ross House B & B
504 Main St., Box 398, Savannah, TN 38372
(901) 925-3974, (901) 925-4472
Innkeeper: John Ross
Rooms: 2 suites w/pvt. bath, phone, TV
Rates: $75-$125, incl. cont. brk.
Credit cards: MC, V
Restrictions: No children under 10, pets, smoking. Deposit req. 10-day cancellation notice req., less $10.00 fee.
Notes: Two-story Neoclassical house with two-story portico with Ionic columns and pilasters, original metal shingle roof, built in 1908. Renovated in 1990. Entry hall

with three-section staircase. Music parlor with Victrola and original record collection. Library, dining room, family room, children's room. Furnished with antiques. Wrap-around porch. Yard contains collection of millstones. Flower garden shaded by grove of Bur Oaks. French, Spanish spoken.

SEVIERVILLE (4)

Blue Mountain Mist Country Inn
1811 Pullen Rd., Sevierville, TN 37862
(615) 428-2335
Innkeeper: Sarah and Norman Ball
Rooms: 11 w/pvt. bath, plus 1 suite w/pvt. bath, plus 5 cottages w/bath, phone, fireplace, TV, VCR, kitchenette. Located in 6 bldgs.
Rates: $79-$115/room, suite, $125/cottage, all incl. full brk., evening refreshment. Seasonal variations. Discount avail. for senior citizens.
Credit cards: MC, V
Restrictions: No pets, smoking. One night's deposit req. 10-day cancellation notice req. 2-night min. stay in Oct. and on holiday wknds.
Notes: Two-story Victorian-style farmhouse built in 1987. Located on hilltop overlooking farmland, Smoky Mountains. Two sitting rooms with fireplaces. Common room with TV. Dining room. Furnished with country antiques, crafts. Wrap-around porch with rockers. Lawns, flowers, trees, lily pond. Cottages have yard, grill, picnic table. Jacuzzi in some rooms. Small private parties accommodated. Handicapped access.*

CALICO INN

Calico Inn
757 Ranch Way, Sevierville, TN 37862
(615) 428-3833
Innkeeper: Jim and Lill Katzbeck
Rooms: 2 w/pvt. bath
Rates: $80-$85, incl. full brk. evening refreshment.
Credit cards: None
Restrictions: No children under 5. Smoking restricted. Deposit req. Min. 2-night stay on holiday wknds.

Notes: Log house located on 25 wooded, mountain acres in Great Smoky Mountain Park. Has operated as inn since 1990. Decorated with antiques. Front porch with rockers and swings overlooking Smoky Mountains. Back deck.

Huckleberry Inn Bed & Breakfast
1754 Sandstone Way, Sevierville, TN 37862
(615) 428-2475
Innkeeper: Rich and Barb Thomas
Rooms: 4 w/pvt. bath, whirlpool, incl. 2 w/fireplace
Rates: $69-$79, incl. full brk.
Credit cards: Most major cards
Restrictions: No pets. Children, smoking restricted. Deposit req. 7-day cancellation
   notice req.
Notes: Inn built from hand hewn oak and pine logs in 1992. Living room with fireplace. Country kitchen with fireplace. High-deck porch. Furnished with antiques. Decoarate with country curtains. Handicapped access.*

Von-Bryan Inn
2402 Hatcher Mtn Rd., Sevierville, TN 37862
(615) 453-9832
Innkeeper: D.J., JoAnn, David, and Patrick Vaughn
Rooms: 3 w/pvt. bath, plus 3 suites w/pvt. bath. Chalet available.
Rates: $80-$95/room, $120-$125/suite, $160/chalet, all incl. full brk., afternoon
   and evening refreshment. Discount avail. for mid-week stay.
Credit cards: Most major cards
Restrictions: No children under 10 in main house, no pets. Smoking restricted. Deposit req. 10-day cancellation notice req. 2-night min. stay in chalet and on holiday wknds.
Notes: Log house built in 1986. Located on mountaintop overlooking Great Smoky Mountains. Living room with stacked-stone fireplace. Sitting room with books and magazines. Dining room. Furnished with traditional and antique pieces, handmade quilts. Garden room with hot tub. Porch, deck. Patio with chairs, rockers, hammock. Swimming pool. Small private parties accommodated.*

RICHMONT INN

TOWNSEND (3)

Richmont Inn
220 Winterberry Lane, Townsend, TN 37882
(615) 448-6751
Innkeeper: Jim and Susan Hind
Rooms: 10 w/pvt. bath, incl. 8 w/fireplace
Rates: $85-$135, incl. full brk. evening refreshment
Credit cards: None
Restrictions: No children under 12, pets, smoking. Deposit req. 14-day cancellation notice req. 2-night min. stay on selected holiday wknds.
Notes: Two-story Appalachian cantilever barn-style inn located on 11 acres overlooking Lauren Valley. Has operated as Inn since 1991. Living room with wooden floors, floor to ceiling bookshelves. Panoramic dining area with stone floor. Furnished with 18th-centruy American-English antiques, American-French paintings, prints. Picnic lunches available. Handicapped access.*

Texas

ALTO (4)

Lincrest Lodge
P.O. Box 799, Hwy 21 E., Alto, TX 75925
(409) 858-2223, (409) 858-2232
Innkeeper: Chet & Charlene Woj
Rooms: 6 w/phone, TV, incl. 1 w/pvt. bath
Rates: $75, incl. full brk., evening refreshment. Special pkgs. avail.
Credit cards: Most major cards
Restrictions: No children under 10, pets, smoking. Deposit req. 7-day cancellation notice req.
Notes: Three-story Dutch Colonial-style inn located on 16-acre hilltop. Marble entrance hall, meeting rooms, porch cafe, dining room, living room. Club room with TV, VCR. Small private parties accommodated. Handicapped access.

AMARILLO (1)

Parkview House
1311 S. Jefferson, Amarillo, TX 79101
(806) 373-9464
Innkeeper: Nabil and Carol Dia
Rooms: 4 plus 1 suite, most w/pvt. bath, phone
Rates: $55-$65/room, $75/suite, all incl. cont. brk. Discount avail. for extended stay.
Credit cards: MC, V
Restrictions: No pets, smoking. Children welcome by prior arrangement only. One night's deposit req. 3-day cancellation notice req.
Notes: Two-story Victorian house built in 1908. Dining room, family room, common room with fireplace. Furnished with antiques in period decor. Tree-shaded L-shaped front porch, patio, hot tub. Board games available. Arabic spoken.*

ATHENS (4)

Dunsavage Farms
FM 804, Athens, TX 75751
(903) 675-2281, (800) 225-6982
Innkeeper: Lyn Dunsavage
Rooms: 2 w/pvt. bath, plus 2 suites w/pvt. bath, TV. Located in 2 bldgs.
Rates: $80, incl. full brk. Discount avail. for mid-week stay.
Credit cards: Most major cards
Restrictions: Smoking restricted. Credit card deposit req. 2-day cancellation notice req.
Notes: Two-story country farm house with two fireplaces, surrounded by grassy fields with seven-mile vistas. Libary. Furnished with art and antiques. Handicapped access. Spanish spoken.*

AUSTIN (5)

Austin's Wildflower Inn
1200 W. 22½ St., Austin, TX 78705
(512) 477-9639

Innkeeper: Kay Jackson
Rooms: 4, incl. 2 w/pvt. bath, phone
Rates: $59-$75, incl. full brk.
Credit cards: Most major cards
Restrictions: No children, pets, smoking. Deposit req. 2-day cancellation notice req.
Notes: Restored house. Dining room. Furnished with antiques. Decorated with lace or embroidered curtains. Back garden.

Fairview
1304 Newning Ave., Austin, TX 78704
(512) 444-4746, (800) 310-4746
Innkeeper: Duke and Nancy Waggoner
Rooms: 3 plus 3 suites, all w/pvt. bath, phone, TV. Located in 2 bldgs.
Rates: $89-$99/room, $109-$129/suite, all incl. full brk. Discount avail. for extended stay.
Credit cards: Most major cards
Restrictions: Children and smoking restricted. No pets. One night's deposit req. 3-day cancellation notice req., less $10.00 fee.
Notes: Two-story Texas Colonial Revival-style house. Great room. Parlor opening to Rose Garden. Conference room. Furnished with antiques. Small private parties accommodated.*

Governors' Inn
611 W. 22nd St., Austin, TX 78705
(512) 477-0711, (512) 477-0711
Innkeeper: Gwen and David Fullbrook
Rooms: 7 plus 1 suite, all w/pvt. bath, phone
Rates: $45-$89/room, $89-$99/suite, all incl. full brk. Discount avail. for extended and mid-week stays.
Credit cards: Most major cards
Restrictions: No children under 10, pets. Smoking restricted. Deposit req. 2-day cancellation notice req.
Notes: Two-story Neo-classical Victorian inn built in 1897. Three reception/dining rooms. Parlor. Decorated with antiques. Small private parties accommodated.*

GOVERNORS' INN

McCallum House
613 W. 32nd, Austin, TX 78705
(512) 451-6744, (512) 451-6744

Innkeeper: Roger and Nancy Danley

Rooms: 3 w/pvt. bath, phone, TV, kitchen, plus 2 suites w/pvt. bath, phone, TV, kitchen. Located in 2 bldgs.

Rates: $75/room, $95/suite, all incl. full brk. Discount avail. for extended stay. Special pkgs. avail.

Credit cards: Most major cards to hold reservation only

Restrictions: No children under 10, pets. Smoking restricted. Deposit req. 2-day cancellation notice req. 2-night min. stay on wknds.

Notes: Two-story Princess Anne Victorian house built in 1907. Garden apartment built in the 1920s. Fully renovated. Has operated as inn since 1983. Dining room, foyer. Furnished with period antiques, family pieces. Four rooms have private verandas. Screened porch under pecan tree. Victorian dollhouse. Designated an Austin landmark.*

McCALLUM HOUSE

Peaceful Hill B & B
6401 River Place Blvd., off Ranch Rd. 2222, Austin, TX 78730-1102
(512) 338-1817

Innkeeper: Peninnah Thurmond

Rooms: 2 w/pvt. bath, incl. 1 w/phone

Rates: $60, incl. full brk. Discount avail. for extended stay.

Credit cards: Most major cards

Restrictions: No pets. Smoking restricted. One night's deposit req. 2-day cancellation notice req. 2-night min. stay.

Notes: Country stone house built 1974. Located in rolling hills. Living room with grand stone fireplace. Country dining room. Furnished with country furniture. Porch with rocking chairs, swing. Hammock for two. Portable TV available.

Woodburn House Bed & Breakfast
4401 Avenue D, Austin, TX 78751-3714
(512) 458-4335

Innkeeper: Herb and Sandra Dickson

Rooms: 4 w/pvt. bath, phone
Rates: $72-$82, incl. full brk. Seasonal variations. Discount avail. for mid-week, extended stays.
Credit cards: None
Restrictions: No children under 7, pets. Smoking restricted. Min. one night's deposit req. 3-day cancellation notice req.
Notes: Common room with TV. Porches. Spanish spoken. Resident dog.

BRENHAM (6)

Mariposa Ranch B & B
Route 4, Box 172, Brenham, TX 77833
(409) 836-4545, (409) 836-4712, (409) 836-4545
Innkeeper: Johnna and Charles Chamberlain
Rooms: 8 w/TV, incl. 6 w/pvt. bath, 4 w/fireplace, plus 2 suites w/pvt. bath, fireplace, TV. Log cabin avail. Located in 6 bldgs.
Rates: $65-$85/room, $150/suite, $95/cabin, all incl. full brk., afternoon refreshment. Discount avail. for extended and mid-week stays.
Credit cards: MC, V
Restrictions: No pets, smoking. Deposit req. 7-day cancellation notice req., less $10.00 fee.
Notes: Two-story Texas Plantation house built in 1894. Located on working ranch overlooking Yegua Valley and Lake Somerville. Fully renovated. Parlor in main house. Other buildings include two cottages, Texas farmhouse built in 1850s, Texas Ranger log cabin built in 1830. Each building has covered porch. Furnished with period antiques. Seven veranda and patio areas. Resident horses, potbellied pigs, farm animals. Spanish spoken.

COLUMBUS (6)

Magnolia Oaks B & B
634 Spring St., Columbus, TX 78934
(409) 732-2726
Innkeeper: Bob and Nancy Stiles
Rooms: 5 plus 1 apt., all w/pvt. bath, incl. 3 w/phone, TV, 2 w/fireplace. Located in 2 bldgs.
Rates: $80-$120/room, incl. full brk. Discount avail. for extended stay.
Credit cards: None
Restrictions: No children, pets. Smoking restricted. One night's deposit req. 7-day cancellation notice req.
Notes: Two-story Eastlake Victorian house built in 1890. Located on 3/4 acres. Gingerbread decorated porch. Furnished with antiques and Texana. Board and lawn games available. Herb garden, fountain, arbor. Small private parties accommodated. Resident cat.

Raumonda Bed & Breakfast
1100 Bowie St., Box 112, Columbus, TX 78934
(409) 732-2190, FAX (409) 732-5135
Innkeeper: R.F. Rau
Rooms: 3 w/pvt. bath. Cottage available.
Rates: $80, incl. cont. brk., afternoon refreshment.
Credit cards: None

Restrictions: No children under 12, pets. Smoking restricted. One night's deposit req. 7-day cancellaiton notice req. 2-night min. stay on holidays.

Notes: Two-story Victorian house with two stairways, elevator, three fireplaces with white marble mantels, original grained painted woodwork, built in 1887. Purchased by the Rau family and completely restored in 1969. Glassed gallery. Living room with TV. Swimming pool, gardens. Furnished with antiques. Inn has Texas State Historical Medallion and is listed on National Register of Historic Places. Small private parties accommodated.

DALLAS (3)

Hotel St. Germain
2516 Maple Ave., Dallas, TX 75201
(214) 871-2516

Innkeeper: Claire Heymann

Rooms: 7 suites w/pvt. bath, phone, fireplace, TV

Rates: $225-600, incl. cont. brk., evening refreshment

Credit cards: Most major cards

Restrictions: No children under 12, pets. Deposit req. 7-day cancellation req.

Notes: Three-story Victorian mansion with 14-ft. ceilings, built in 1906. Has operated as inn since 1991. Parlor, foyer, library, New Orleans-style walled courtyard. Furnished with antiques. Restaurant on premises with room service. Small private parties accommodated. Valet parking. French, Spanish spoken.*

EL PASO (2)

Sunset Heights B & B
717 W. Yandell Ave., El Paso, TX 79902
(915) 544-1743, (915) 544-5119

Innkeeper: R. B0arnett, R. Martinez

Rooms: 5 plus 2 suites, most w/pvt. bath, phone, all w/TV, incl. 1 suite w/fireplace. Located in 2 bldgs.

Rates: $70-$100/room, $100-$145/suite, all incl. full brk. Discount avail. for extended stay and cash payments. Seasonal variations.

Credit cards: Most major cards

Restrictions: No children under 8, pets, smoking. Deposit req. Min. 21-day cancellation notice req.

Notes: Three-story Victorian style house built in 1905. Common room, dining room. Conference room on third floor. Decorated with vintage and period furnishings. Swimming pool with Jacuzzi. Outdoor fireplace. Small private parties accommodated. Spanish spoken.*

ENNIS (3)

Raphael House
500 W. Ennis Ave., Ennis, TX 75119
(214) 875-1555, (214) 875-0308

Innkeeper: Brian Wolf and Danna Cody Wolf

Rooms: 6 w/pvt. bath, phone, incl. 2 w/TV

Rates: $60-$100, incl. full brk., weekend afternoon refreshment. Discount avail. for extended, mid-week stays.

Credit cards: Most major cards

Restrictions: No pets. Smoking restricted. Deposit req. 7-day cancellation notice req., less $10.00 fee. Min. stay on special event wknds. Closed Dec. 24.
Notes: Two-story Greek Revival mansion built in 1906. Fully restored in and has operated as inn since 1988. Entry hall, living room, breakfast room, formal dining room, den kitchen. Furnished with period antiques, 25% being original to the Raphael House. Gardens, three porches. Swedish massage in your room available. Guests have access to Colonial Tennis Club. Golf cart available. Listed on the National Register of Historic Places. Small private parties accommodated. Some Spanish spoken.*

FLOYDADA (1)

Historic Lamplighter Inn
102 S. 5th St., Floydada, TX 79235
(806) 983-3035
Innkeeper: Evelyn Branch and Roxanne Cummings
Rooms: 18, incl. 5 w/pvt. bath, plus 2 suites w/pvt. bath
Rates: $45, incl. full brk. Discount avail. for extended and group stays. Special pkgs. avail.
Credit cards: None
Restrictions: No children under 12, pets, smoking. One night's deposit req., less 10% cancellation fee.
Notes: Two-story hotel built in 1912, opened in 1913. Fully restored in 1991. Lobby with pressed tin 11-ft. ceilings, piano, old phone booth, TV. Furnished with 'theme' memorabilia. Small private parties accommodated.*

FORT DAVIS (2)

The Hotel Limpia
P.O. Box 822, Fort Davis, TX 79734
(800) 662-5517
Innkeeper: Lanna and Joe Duncan
Rooms: 20 w/pvt. bath, TV, plus 10 suites w/kitchen. Located in 3 bldgs.
Rates: $58-80/room, $65-$112/suite, all incl. membership to private club.
Credit cards: Most major cards
Restrictions: Smoking restricted. 48-hr. cancellation req.

THE HOTEL LIMPIA

Notes: Pink limestone structure built in 1912, surrounded by mountains. Parlor with fireplace, board games. Furnished in Victorian, Mission, and 1940s style. Garden and veranda. Bookstore, giftshop, restaurant on premises. Spanish spoken. Handicapped access.

FREDERICKSBURG (5)

Country Cottage Inn
249 E. Main St., Fredericksburg, TX 78624
(210) 997-8549
Innkeeper: Jeffery and Ann Webb
Rooms: 3 w/pvt. bath, phone, TV, plus 4 suites w/pvt. bath, phone, TV, incl. 3 w/fireplace. Located in 2 bldgs.
Rates: $75-$95/room, $95-$110/suite, all incl. full brk.
Credit cards: MC, V
Restrictions: No pets. Smoking restricted. Deposit req. 72-hour cancellation notice req.
Notes: Two-story limestone house with two-ft. thick walls and exposed rafters built in 1850, expanded in 1860. Common room with fireplace. Porches, patio. Furnished with Texas primitive and German country antiques. Decorated with Laura Ashley linens. Listed on the National Register of Historic Places.*

COUNTRY COTTAGE INN

Das College Haus Bed & Breakfast
106 W. College, Fredericksburg, TX 78624
(210) 997-9047, (800) 654-2802
Innkeeper: Myrna and Tim Saska
Rooms: 1 plus 2 suites, all w/pvt. bath, phone, TV, incl. 1 w/fireplace
Rates: $70/room, $85/suite, all incl. full brk. Discount avail. for extended and midweek stays.
Credit cards: MC, V
Restrictions: No children under 10, pets, smoking. Deposit req. 3-day cancellation notice req.

Notes: Two-story Greek Revival Victorian house. Restored red barn. Dining room. Furnished with period furniture and original art. Porch and balcony with wicker furniture. Handicapped access.*

Schmidt Barn
231 W. Main St., Fredericksburg, TX 78624
(210) 997-5612, (512) 997-5612, (210) 997-8282
Innkeeper: Charles and Loretta Schmidt
Rooms: 1 rock barn
Rates: $73, incl. cont. brk.
Credit cards: Most major cards
Restrictions: Small pets welcome. 5-day cancellation notice req.
Notes: German spoken.*

GALVESTON (6)

Coppersmith Inn
1914 Ave. M, Galveston, TX 77550
(409) 763-7004
Innkeeper: Lisa, Kathy and Lee Hering
Rooms: 3, no pvt. bath, incl. 1 w/fireplace, plus 1 suite w/pvt. bath. Located in 2 bldgs.
Rates: $85-$120/room, $115-$135/cottage suite, all incl. brk., evening refreshment. Seasonal variations. Discount avail. for mid-week and extended stays.
Credit cards: Most major cards
Restrictions: No children under 5, pets, smoking. One night's deposit req. 14-day cancellation notice req., less $10.00 fee. 2-night min. stay on some peak wknds.
Notes: Three-story Queen Anne Victorian inn with gingerbread-trimmed double galleries and turret corner with bay windows, designed by Galveston architect Alfred Muller in 1887. Fully restored with teak, mahogany, curly pine and cypress staircase and banister. Common room with 11-ft. tall built-in china cabinet. Living room, veranda, deck. Furnished with antiques. Wisteria-covered arbor, bird bath, herb garden. Guests have access to kitchen. German, French spoken.*

GLEN ROSE (3)

Bussey's Something Special B & B
202 Hereford, Box 1425, Glen Rose, TX 76043
(817) 897-4843
Innkeeper: Susan and Morris Bussey
Rooms: 1 suite w/pvt. bath, 1 cottage
Rates: $80, incl. cont. brk. Discount avail. for extended and mid-week stays.
Credit cards: Most major cards
Restrictions: No pets. Smoking restricted. Deposit req. 7-day cancellation notice req.
Notes: Two-story cottage built in 1986. Living room with TV. Decorated with original paintings and handcrafted furniture. Porch with swing. Board games available. Small private parties accommodated.

Inn on the River
209 SW Barnard St., Box 1417, Glen Rose, TX 76043
(817) 897-2101, (817) 897-7729

Innkeeper: Peggy and Steve Allman
Rooms: 19 w/pvt. bath, plus 3 suites w/pvt. bath
Rates: $88-$115/room, $125-$145/suite, all incl. full brk.
Credit cards: Most major cards
Restrictions: No children, pets, smoking. Deposit req. Closed Thanksgiving week, Dec. 15–Jan. Located in dry county.
Notes: Built as 2-story drugless sanitarium in 1919. Fully renovated in 1993. Lobby, dining room. Furnished with antiques. Patio, veranda overlooking garden. Oak pavilion with picnic tables overlooking Paluxy River. Dinner available on Friday and Saturday. Handicapped access. Spanish spoken.*

Ye Ole' Maple Inn
P.O. Box 1141, Glen Rose, TX 76043
(817) 897-3456

Innkeeper: David and Roberta Maple
Rooms: 2 w/pvt. bath
Rates: $65-$75, incl. full brk., evening refreshment. Discount avail. for mid-week stay. Seasonal variations.
Credit cards: None
Restrictions: No children, pets, smoking. Min. one night's deposit req. 2-night min. stay on holiday wknds.
Notes: House built about 1950. Front porch with rocking chair overlooking Puluxy River. Den/dining room with fireplace, library. Furnished with antiques and grandfather clock from Germany. Handicapped access.

GOLIAD (5)

The Madison
736 N. Jefferson St., Goliad, TX 77963
(512) 645-8693

Innkeeper: Wallace and Joyce Benson
Rooms: 4 w/pvt. bath
Rates: $50-$65, incl. full brk. Discount avail. for mid-week stay.
Credit cards: Most major cards
Restrictions: No pets. Children, smoking restricted. Min. one-night's deposit req. Min. 14-day cancellation notice req.
Notes: Two-story Victorian Craftsman-style house built in 1888. Renovated in 1920s. Modernized in 1990. Common room with piano, fireplace. Library. Small private parties accommodated. Some Spanish spoken.

GONZALES (5)

St. James Inn
723 St. James St., Gonzales, TX 78629
(210) 672-7066

Innkeeper: Ann Covert
Rooms: 2 plus 3 suites, all w/pvt. bath, phone, fireplace, TV
Rates: $65/room, $130-$195/suite, all incl. full brk. Special pkgs. avail.
Credit cards: Most major cards
Restrictions: No children under 12, pets. Smoking restricted. Min. $100.00 deposit req. 2-day cancellation notice req. Prefer 2-night min. stay.
Notes: Three-story Greek-Victorian style house built in 1914. Reception hall, living room, dining room, conservatory. Furnished with antiques.*

GRANBURY (3)

Pearl Street Inn Bed & Breakfast
319 W. Pearl St., Granbury, TX 76048
(817) 279-7465

Innkeeper: Danette Hebda
Rooms: 3 plus 2 suites, all w/pvt bath, 1 suite w/phone, TV
Rates: $79-$84/room, $98/suite, all incl. full brk. Discount avail. for extended and mid-week stays.
Credit cards: None
Restrictions: No pets. Children, smoking restricted. One night's deposit req. Min. stay for certain local events.
Notes: Two-story prairie-style house built in 1800s. Wrap-around porch and yard. Dining room. Living room with stereo, TV/VCR. Decorated with antiques and period furnishings. Board and lawn games available. Small private parties accommodated. Resident pet.*

HOUSTON (6)

Sara's Bed & Breakfast Inn
941 Heights Blvd., Houston, TX 77008
(713) 868-1130, (800) 593-1130, (713) 868-1160

Innkeeper: Donna and Tillman Arledge
Rooms: 10 plus 3 suites, all w/phone, TV, incl. 11 w/pvt. bath. Located in 2 bldgs.
Rates: $50-$75/room, $120/suite, all incl. cont. brk. Discount avail. for extended stay.
Credit cards: Most major cards
Restrictions: No pets, smoking. One night's deposit req. 48-hour cancellation notice req.
Notes: Three-story Victorian cottage built at turn of the century. Second story with turret, widow's walk added in 1980. Fully restored in 1983. Has operated as inn since 1986. Three-story open space with spiral staircase under cupola. Parlor, 1,000-square-foot deck with spa, front balcony. Furnished with antiques, collectibles. Small private parties accommodated.*

SARA'S BED & BREAKFAST INN

River Bend B & B
Rte. 1, Box 114, Hunt, TX 78024
(210) 238-4681, (800) 472-3933, (210) 238-4681
Innkeeper: Conrad and Terri Pyle, Becky Key
Rooms: 9, plus 6 suites, all w/pvt. bath. Located in 3 bldgs.
Rates: $95/room, $100-$145/suite, all incl. full brk. Discount avail. for senior citizen and extended stays.
Credit cards: Most major cards
Restrictions: Children restricted. No pets, smoking. Min. one night's deposit req. 14-day cancellation notice req. 2-night min. stay, Memorial Day–Labor Day.
Notes: Native stone main lodge with cedar accents built in the 1930s. Located on fifty-five wooded acres with ½ mile of riverfront on the Guadalupe River. Dining room, front porch, back patio. Lounge with fireplace.

JEFFERSON (4)

Pride House
409 Broadway, Jefferson, TX 75657
(800) 894-3526
Innkeeper: Carol and Christel
Rooms: 9 w/pvt. bath, incl. 2 w/fireplace, plus 1 cottage w/pvt. bath, fireplace. Located in 2 bldgs.
Rates: $65-$100/room, $100/suite, all incl. full brk., evening refreshment. Discount avail. for mid-week and extended stays. Seasonal variations.
Credit cards: Most major cards
Restrictions: No children under 12, pets. Smoking restricted. Deposit req. 3-day cancellation notice req. 2-night min. stay on occasional wknds.
Notes: Two-story gingerbread Victorian main house with six guest rooms built in 1888. Restored in 1980. *The Dependency* guesthouse with four rooms and country kitchen. Has operated as an inn since 1980. Front parlor. Front porch with swing, rockers. Phone and TV available upon request. Side lawn with swing in pecan tree. Decorated with antiques and period furnishings. German spoken. Limited handicapped access.*

LEDBETTER (5)

Ledbetter Bed & Breakfast
P.O. Box 212, Ledbetter, TX 78946-0212
(409) 249-3066, (409) 249-3330
Innkeeper: Jay and Chris Jervis
Rooms: 16, incl. 6 w/pvt. bath, plus 11 suites, incl. 8 w/pvt. bath. Located in 6 bldgs.
Rates: $55-$100/room $70-$145/suite, all incl. cont. brk., afternoon refreshment. Discount avail. for mid-week, extended stays.
Credit cards: MC, V
Restrictions: No pets. Smoking restricted. 50% deposit req. 8-day cancellation notice req.
Notes: Vintage hotel and other houses date from 1860-1970. Pool house with hot tub, full kitchen. Lounge with fireplace, phone. Gameroom with TV, VCR, board games, jukebox. Furnished with antiques and reproductions. All meals, carriage and hay rides, lawn games available. Art Gallery, General Store with working museum, buggy shop, tavern, frame and mounting shop on premises. Small private parties accommodated. Limited handicapped access. Some Spanish spoken. Resident farm animals.*

MABANK (3)

Heavenly Acres Bed & Breakfast
Rt. 3 Box 470, Mabank, TX 75147-9803
(800) 283-0341, (903) 887-6108
Innkeeper: Vickie and Marshall Ragle
Rooms: 4 houses w/pvt. bath, TV, VCR, microwave, incl. 1 w/phone
Rates: From $75, incl. cont. brk. Special pkgs. avail.
Credit cards: Most major cards
Restrictions: Prior approval req. for pets. Smoking restricted. Deposit req. 7-day
cancellation notice req.
Notes: Located 12 miles SW of Canton. Located on 94 acres with 6-acre fishing lake
and 15-acre lower fishing lake, both spring fed and stocked with Bass, Crappie,
Bluegill, and Channel Catfish. Has operated as inn since 1990. Porch with rockers.
Gazebo and picnic areas. Paddle boats and boats w/trolling motors available. Pet-
ting zoo on premises. All meals available. Small private parties accommodated.
Handicapped access. Carport for guest parking. Resident animals.*

MINEOLA (4)

Munzesheimer Manor
202 N. Newsom, Mineola, TX 75773
(903) 569-6634
Innkeeper: Bob and Sherry Murray
Rooms: 6, incl. 3 w/fireplace, plus 1 suite, all w/pvt. bath. Located in 3 bldgs.
Rates: $65-$85/room, $90/suite, all incl. full brk., evening refreshment
Credit cards: Most major cards
Restrictions: Children welcome with prior arrangement. No pets. Smoking re-
stricted. One night's deposit req. Min. 10-day cancellation notice req.
Notes: Two-story Victorian Princess Anne-style pine and cedar manor house and
cottage built in 1898. Fully restored in 1987. Two parlors. Formal dining room.
Wrap-around porches with wicker furniture. Furnished with English and American
antiques. Picnic lunches, dinners available. Handicapped access. Small private parties accommodated.*

NEW BRAUNFELS (5)

Antik Haus Bed & Breakfast
118 S. Union Ave., New Braunfels, TX 78130
(210) 625-6666
Innkeeper: Donna and Jim Irwin
Rooms: 4, incl. 1 w/pvt. bath, TV
Rates: $30-$75, incl. full brk. Seasonal variations. Discount avail. for mid-week stay.
Special pkgs. avail.
Credit cards: None
Restrictions: No children under 12, pets. Smoking restricted. One night's deposit
req. 7-day cancellation notice req., less $5.00 fee. 2-night min. stay on wknds.
Notes: Two-story Victorian house built in 1907. Dining rooms with natural wood-
work, 12-ft. ceilings, fireplaces. Furnished with antiques. Gazebo and strombrella.
River rafting trip with picnic basket available. Outdoor spa, bicycle built for two,
tubes for river available.

SAN ANTONIO (5)

Beckmann Inn and Carriage House
222 E. Guenther St., San Antonio, TX 78204
(210) 229-1449
Innkeeper: Don and Betty Jo Schwartz
Rooms: 3 plus 2 suites, all w/pvt. bath, TV, incl. 2 suites w/phone. Located in 2 bldgs.
Rates: $80-$100/room, $110-$130/suite, all incl. full brk.
Credit cards: Most major cards
Restrictions: No children under 12, pets, smoking. Deposit req., 7-day cancellation notice, less $10.00 fee. 2-night min. stay on wknds.
Notes: Two-story Victorian house built in 1886. Wrap-around porch with white wicker furniture. Formal dining room, living room with fourteen-foot ceilings, tall windows with beveled glass inserts. Decorated with Victorian furniture. Adjoining Carraige House (suite) has a brick patio area. Listed in the National Register of Historic Places.

Bonner Garden
145 E. Agarita, San Antonio, TX 78212
(210) 733-4222, (800) 396-4222
Innkeeper: Jan and Noel Stenoien
Rooms: 4 plus 1 suite, all w/pvt. bath, phone, fireplace, TV. Located in 2 bldgs.
Rates: $75-$95/room, $95/suite, all incl. full brk. Discount avail. for extended and mid-week stays.
Credit cards: Most major cards
Restrictions: No children under 12, pets. Smoking restricted. One-night's deposit req. 3-day cancellation notice req. 2-night min. stay on wknds.
Notes: Two-story Italian Villa built in 1910 surrounded by gardens, walkways, and pool. Rooftop garden overlooking city. Dining room. Texana and home video library. Exercise facilities. Furnished with antiques, art, and architecture. Small private parties accommodated. Handicapped access.

Chabot Reed House
403 Madison, San Antonio, TX 78204
(210) 223-8697, (210) 734-2342
Innkeeper: Peter and Sister Reed
Rooms: 3 plus 2 suites, all w/pvt. bath, phone, TV, incl. 1 w/fireplace. Located in 2 bldgs.
Rates: $125, incl. full brk. Discount avail. for extended, mid-week, senior citizen stays.
Credit cards: None
Restrictions: No pets. Smoking restricted. One night's deposit req. 14-day cancellation notice req. 2-night min. stay on wknds.
Notes: Two-story Victorian style house built in 1876. Restored in 1985. Garden. Living room. Decorated with antiques, bronzes, Oriental pieces. Handicapped access. Listed on the National Register of Historic Places. Spanish spoken.*

Norton-Brackenridge House
230 Madison, San Antonio, TX 78204
(210) 271-3442
Innkeeper: Frances Bochat, Carolyn Cole

Rooms: 3 w/pvt. bath, phone, incl. 1 w/TV, plus 2 suites w/pvt. bath, phone, TV
Rates: $85-$105/room, $95/suite, all incl. full brk.
Credit cards: Most major cards
Restrictions: No children under 8, pets. Smoking restricted. One-night's deposit req. 7-day cancellation notice req. 2-night min. stay on wknds.
Notes: *

Oge House Inn on the Riverwalk
209 Washington St., San Antonio, TX 78204
(210) 223-2353, (800) 242-2770, (210) 226-5812

Innkeeper: Patrick and Sharrie Magatagan
Rooms: 5 plus 5 suites, all w/pvt. bath, phone, TV, most w/fireplace
Rates: $125-$135/room, $165-$195/suite, all incl. full brk. Discount avail. for extended and mid-week stays.
Credit cards: Most major cards
Restrictions: No children under 16, pets. Smoking restricted. 7-day cancellation notice req. 2-night min. stay on wknds. 3-night min. stay on holidays.
Notes: Some Spanish spoken.*

Riverwalk Inn
329 Old Guilbeau Rd., San Antonio, TX 78204
(210) 212-8300, (800) 254-4440, (210) 229-9422

Innkeeper: Johnny Halpenny, Jan and Tracy Hammer
Rooms: 9 plus 2 suites, all w/pvt. bath, phone, TV, incl. 9 w/fireplace. Located in 2 bldgs.
Rates: $89-$135/room, $160/suite, all incl. cont. brk. Discount avail. for mid-week stay. Seasonal variations.
Credit cards: Most major cards
Restrictions: No pets. Smoking restricted. One-night's deposit req. 10-day cancellation notice req., less $15.00 fee. 2-night min. stay on wknds. holidays, and special events.
Notes: Two-story 19th-century log inn built in the 1840s. Parlor. Furnished with antiques. Porch. Storytelling available. Spanish spoken. Handicapped access.*

San Antonio Yellow Rose
229 Madison, San Antonio, TX 78204
(210) 229-9903

Innkeeper: Jennifer and Cliff Tice
Rooms: 5 plus 1 suite, all w/pvt. bath, TV
Rates: $55-$95/room, $110/suite, all incl. full brk. Discount avail. for extended, mid-week, senior citizen stays. Seasonal variations.
Credit cards: Most major cards
Restrictions: No children under 11, pets, smoking. Deposit req. 7-day cancellation notice req., less $15.00 fee. 2-night min. stay on wknds.
Notes: Front and back porch, parlor, dining room. Covered off-street parking available.*

Summit Haus & Summit Haus II
427 W. Summit, San Antonio, TX 78212
(210) 736-6272, (800) 972-7266

Innkeeper: Adelynne H. Whitaker

Rooms: 3 w/pvt. bath, phone, incl. 1 w/TV, plus 3 suites w/pvt. bath, phone, TV, plus 1 cottage. Located in two bldgs.
Rates: $75-$85/room, $85-$95/suite, all incl. full brk. Discount avail. for extended stay.
Credit cards: Most major cards
Restrictions: No children under 10, pets. Smoking restricted. Deposit req. 7-day cancellation notice req. less $10.00 fee. 2-night min. stay on wknds.
Notes: Two-story house built in 1920. Parlor with fireplace, outdoor deck. Furnished with Biedermeier antiques, crystal, porcelains, Persian and Oriental rugs. Cottage has fireplace, dining room, breakfast room, full kitchen, and laundry facilities. Cottage furnished with 18th- and 19th-century French and English antiques. German spoken. Small private parties accommodated.

The Victorian Lady Inn
421 Howard St., San Antonio, TX 78212
(210) 224-2524, (800) 879-7116, (210) 224-4858
Innkeeper: Joe and Kathleen Bowski
Rooms: 5 incl. 2 w/fireplace, plus 2 suites, incl. 1 w/fireplace, all w/pvt. bath, phone, TV
Rates: $65-$110/room $100-$130/suite, all incl. full brk., afternoon refreshment. Discount avail. for extended and mid-week stays. Seasonal variations.
Credit cards: Most major cards
Restrictions: No children under 12, pets. Smoking restricted. Deposit req. 10-day cancellation notice req., less $20.00 fee. 2-night min. stay on wknds. and holidays.
Notes: Two-story Colonial Revival house built in 1898. Some rooms have private verandas or balconies. Grand foyer with sitting area and house phone. Dining area with leaded-glass windows, carved fireplace. Decorated with period antiques. Parking available.*

THE VICTORIAN LADY INN

SAN MARCOS (5)

Crystal River Inn
326 W. Hopkins, San Marcos, TX 78666
(512) 396-3739

Innkeeper: Mike and Cathy Dillon
Rooms: 7, plus 4 suites, incl. 10 w/pvt. bath, 8 w/phone, 8 w/cable TV, 5 w/fire-place, 4 w/sunken garden tub. Located in 3 bldgs.
Rates: $65-$85/room, $90-$110/suite, incl. full brk., evening refreshment. Special pkgs. available. Discount avail. extended and mid-week stays.
Credit cards: Most major cards
Restrictions: No children under 8, pets. Smoking restricted. 50% deposit req. 2-day cancellation notice req., less $5.00 fee. 2-night min. stay on wknds.
Notes: Two-story Victorian mansion built in 1883. Furnished with antiques. Decorated with designer fabrics. Library. Dining room with wet bar. Up- and downstairs verandas with wicker furniture, rockers. Grounds include brick courtyard with fishpond, gardens, waterfall, topiaries, BBQ. River trips arranged. Murder mysteries and other special weekends organized.*

SEABROOK (6)

Pelican House B & B Inn
1302 1st St., Seabrook, TX 77586
(713) 474-5295, (713) 474-7840

Innkeeper: Suzanne Silvin
Rooms: 4 w/pvt. bath, incl. 1 w/TV
Rates: $55-$65, incl. full brk., afternoon refreshment. Special pkgs. avail.
Credit cards: Most major cards
Restrictions: No children under 10, pets. Smoking restricted.
Notes: Cottage with original wood floors and 12-ft. ceilings, built about 1904.*

SOUTH PADRE ISLAND (7)

Brown Pelican Inn
207 W. Aries, Box 2667, South Padre Island, TX 78597-2667
(210) 761-2722

Innkeeper: Vicky Conway
Rooms: 7 plus 1 suite, all w/pvt. bath
Rates: $70-$135/room, $105-$150/suite, all incl. expanded cont. brk. Discount avail. for extended stay. 0Seasonal variations.
Credit cards: MC, V
Restrictions: No children under 11, pets. Smoking restricted. One night's deposit req. 10-day cancellation notice req.
Notes: Parlor. Porches overlooking bay. Furnished with European and American antiques.

Moonraker Bed & Breakfast
107 E. Marisol, Box CL-1-9, South Padre Island, TX 78597
(210) 761-2206

Innkeeper: Robert and Marcia Burns
Rooms: 3 w/pvt. bath, TV
Rates: $105-$140, incl. full brk. Seasonal variations.
Credit cards: V
Restrictions: No children, pets, smoking. 2 night's deposit req. 3-day cancellation notice req. 2-night min. stay.
Notes: Three-story European-style beach house. Living and dining rooms with gondola ceiling, organ. Furnished with Old World Antiques. Outdoor decks in front and back of house.

SPRING (6)

McLachlan Farm Bed & Breakfast
24907 Hardy, Box 538, Spring, TX 77383
(713) 350-2400, (800) 382-3988

Innkeeper: Jim and Joycelyn Clairmonte
Rooms: 4, incl. 3 w/pvt. bath, phone
Rates: $65-$100, incl. full brk.
Credit cards: MC, V
Restrictions: No children under 12, pets, smoking. Deposit req.
Notes: Farm house with wrap-around porches. Kitchen/greatroom, library, balcony with swing. Decorated in English-Country, Victorian style. Innkeeper collects cups and saucers, teapots and old glassware. Lawn games available. Handicapped access.*

STEPHENVILLE (3)

The Oxford House
563 N. Graham St., Stephenville, TX 76401
(817) 965-6885, (817) 965-7555

Innkeeper: Bill and Paula Oxford
Rooms: 4 w/pvt. bath, phone, incl. 1 w/fireplace, 1 w/TV
Rates: $58-$75, incl. full brk., evening refreshment
Credit cards: AE, MC
Restrictions: No children under 6. Deposit req. 3-day cancellation notice req. 2-night min. stay.
Notes: Three-story Victorian house built in 1898. Has operated as a bank and boarding house. Family room with piano. Dining room and gift nook. Furnished with antiques. Tearoom serving lunch on premises. Porch. Backyard with gazebo. Small private parties accommodated. Limited handicapped access.*

SWEETWATER (8)

Mulberry Manor
1400 Sam Houston, Sweetwater, TX 79556
(915) 235-3811, (800) 235-3811

Innkeeper: Raymond and Beverly Stone
Rooms: 2 w/pvt. bath, phone, incl. 1 w/TV, plus 2 suites w/pvt. bath, phone, incl. 1 w/fireplace, TV
Rates: $60-$80/room, $100-$175/suite, all incl. full brk., evening refreshment. Discount avail. for extended, mid-week, senior citizen, and govt. stays.

MULBERRY MANOR

Credit cards: Most major cards
Notes: Built in 1911. Living room with solid marble mantle. Formal dining room. Has operated as inn since 1993. Bar area with 52" TV. Private dinners and chauffeured 1929 Model A available. Small private parties accommodated. Handicapped access.

TEXARKANA (4)

Mansion on Main B & B
802 Main St., Texarkana, TX 75501
(903) 792-1835
Innkeeper: Kay and Jack Roberts
Rooms: 4 w/pvt. bath, TV, incl. 1 w/fireplace, 1 w/phone, plus 2 suites w/pvt. bath, TV, incl. 1 w/fireplace, 1 w/phone
Rates: $55-$75/room, $99-$110/suite, all incl. full brk. Discount avail. for extended stay.
Credit cards: Most major cards
Restrictions: No pets, smoking. Children restricted. One night's deposit req. 72-hour cancellation notice req.
Notes: Two-story mansion with Ionic columns built in 1985. Dining room with fireplace. Sitting areas in hall, books, magazines. Furnished with antiques. Victorian-style nightgowns and sleep0shirts available. Veranda, balcony. Handicapped access.*

TYLER (4)

Rosevine Inn Bed & Breakfast
415 S. Vine, Tyler, TX 75702
(903) 592-2221
Innkeeper: Bert and Rebecca Powell
Rooms: 5 w/pvt. bath. Located in 2 bldgs.
Rates: $65-$85, incl. full brk.
Credit cards: Most major cards
Restrictions: No children under 2, pets, smoking. One night's deposit req. 5-day cancellation notice req., less 10% fee. Closed Dec. 24, 25, and Thanksgiving.
Notes: Two-story Federal-style inn built in 1986. Sitting room with TV, board games. Living room with TV, player piano. Dining room. Furnished with antiques and country crafts in the 1920s style. Courtyard with fountain, fireplace, hot tub. Resident pet cat.*

VOLENTE (5)

Pickel's Lake Travis B&B at Volente
8010 Lakeview St., Volente, TX 78641-9671
(512) 331-8733, (800) 233-7378
Innkeeper: LaNoro Pickel, Gerry Cowan
Rooms: 4 w/pvt. bath, incl. 1 w/phone, TV. Located in 2 bldgs.
Rates: $60-$95, incl full brk. Special pkgs. avail.
Credit cards: Most major cards
Restrictions: No children, pets, smoking. One-night's deposit req. 7-day cancellation notice req.

Notes: Austin Stone Country French house with wood floors, high ceilings. Decks, porches with willow swing overlooking lake. Furnished with antiques. Boat dock, outdoor activities available.*

WIMBERLEY (5)

Blair House
1 Spoke Hill, Rte. 1, Box 122, Wimberley, TX 78676
(512) 847-8828
Innkeeper: Jonnie Stansbury
Rooms: 6 w/pvt. bath, phone. Located in 3 bldgs.
Rates: $90-$125, incl. full brk., evening refreshment
Credit cards: MC, V
Restrictions: No children, pets, smoking. Deposit req. $25.00 cancellation fee. 2-night min. stay on wknds.
Notes: Located on 90 acres of Texas Hill Country. Living room, library, two dining rooms, porches with rocking chairs, verandas, decks with hammocks, swings. Five-to seven-course dinner made from local fresh organic products served on Saturday evening and open to the public with reservations. Movie and CD collection. CD players in rooms. Handicapped access available. Spanish spoken.*

Eagles Nest Bed & Breakfast
Rte. 2, Box 73-D, Wimberley, TX 78676
(512) 847-3921, (800) 725-3909, (512) 847-3909
Innkeeper: Frank and Jimi Irby
Rooms: 3 suites w/pvt. bath, kitchen, fireplace, TV, incl. 2 w/phone
Rates: $60, incl brk. Discount avail. for extended, mid-week, and senior citizen stays.
Credit cards: Most major cards
Restrictions: Smoking restricted. Deposit req. 72-hour cancellation notice req., less $50 fee.
Notes: Overlooking the hill country. Furnished with antiques.

Old Oaks Ranch B & B
P.O. Box 912, Wimberley, TX 78676
(512) 847-9374, (512) 847-9374
Innkeeper: Bill and Susan Holt
Rooms: 3 w/pvt bath, TV, incl. 2 w/fireplace, plus 1 suite w/phone. Located in 3 bldgs.
Rates: $65-$85, incl full brk. Full prepayment req. 7-day cancellation notice req., less $5.00 fee. Discount avail. for mid-week stay.
Credit cards: MC, V
Restrictions: No children under 12, pets. Smoking restricted.
Notes: *

Southwind B & B
Rte. 2, Box 15, Wimberley, TX 78676
(512) 847-5277
Innkeeper: Carrie Watson
Rooms: 2 w/pvt. bath, plus 1 suite w/pvt. bath, fireplace
Rates: $70/room, $80/suite, all incl. full brk. Discount avail. for senior citizens.
Credit cards: Most major cards

Restrictions: No children under 12, pets, smoking. One night's deposit req. 3-day cancellation notice req. 2-night min. stay on holidays and the first Saturday of each month, April–Dec.

Notes: Two-story house built as an inn in 1985. Located on twenty-five wooded hilltop acres. Parlor with fireplace, library, board games. Kitchen, dining area. Upstairs and downstairs porches with rockers. Furnished with antiques, reproductions.*

WINNSBORO (4)

Thee Hubbell House
307 W. Elm, Winnsboro, TX 75494
(903) 342-5629, (903) 342-6627
Innkeeper: Dan and Laurel Hubbell
Rooms: 9 plus 3 suites, all w/pvt. bath, incl. 1 suite w/fireplace, TV. Located in 3 bldgs.
Rates: $75-$125/room, $150-$175/suite, all incl. full brk. Discount avail. for senior citizens.
Credit cards: Most major cards
Restrictions: No pets, smoking. Min. $50.00 deposit req. 24-hour cancellation notice req., less $25.00 fee.
Notes: Two-story Georgian house built in 1888. Reconstructed in Colonial-style in 1906. Restored in 1988. Formal living room with piano, fireplace. Entry hall, formal dining room, verandas, upstairs gallery. Dinner available. Small private parties accommodated. Innkeeper is town's mayor. Handicapped access available.*

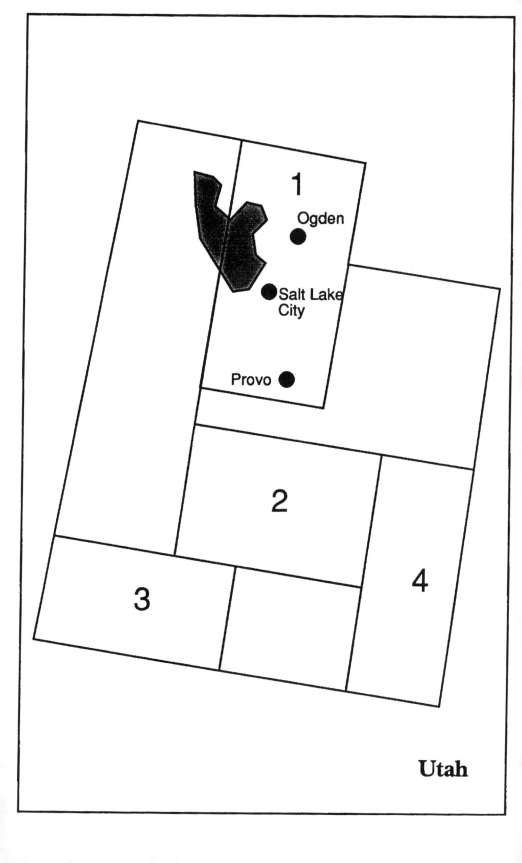

Utah

Utah

AMERICAN FORK (1)

American Fork B & B
1021 N. 150 W., American Fork, UT 84003
(801) 756-9459
Innkeeper: Fred and Marianne Roberts
Rooms: 1 plus 1 suite, all w/pvt. bath, TV
Rates: $40/room, $60/suite, all incl. full brk. Special pkgs. avail. Seasonal variations.
Credit cards: None
Restrictions: No children under 2. Pets, smoking restricted. Deposit req. Min. 14-day cancellation notice req. 2-night min. stay.
Notes: Two-story contemporary style house built in 1964. Located on 6 acres. Dining room. Family room with fireplace, big screen TV, piano, guitars, games. Outdoor activities available. Guests have access to nearby sports facility. Some French, Spanish spoken. Handicapped access.*

CEDAR CITY (3)

Paxman Summer House B & B
170 North 400 West, Cedar City, UT 84720
(801) 586-3755
Innkeeper: Karlene Paxman
Rooms: 4 w/pvt. bath, TV
Rates: $55-$75, incl. cont. brk. Seasonal variations.
Credit cards: Most major cards
Restrictions: No pets, Smoking restricted, $20.00 per night deposit req. 7-day cancellation notice req. 2-night min. stay on wknds. from July–Aug.
Notes: Victorian house built in 1900. Restored in 1963. Has operated as inn since 1985. Furnished in Queen Anne style. Dining room, private porch.*

DUCK CREEK VILLAGE (3)

Meadeau View Lodge
P.O. Box 1331, Duck Creek Village, UT 84762
(801) 682-2495, (801) 682-2075
Innkeeper: Craig and Kimberly Simmerman
Rooms: 6, plus 3 suites, all w/pvt. bath
Rates: $50/room, $60/suite, all incl. full brk., evening refreshment
Credit cards: MC, V
Restrictions: No large dogs, smoking. One-night's min. deposit req. 3-day cancellation notice req.
Notes: Mountain inn located within Dixie National Forest. Common area with circular fireplace. Decorated with country furnishings. Spanish spoken.*

EDEN (1)

The Snowberry Inn
1315 N. Hwy. 158, Eden, UT 84310
(801) 745-2634

Innkeeper: Roger and Kim Arave
Rooms: 5 w/phone
Rates: $75, incl. full brk. Discount avail. for extended stay.
Credit cards: MC, V
Restrictions: Smoking restricted. Deposit req. 7-day cancellation notice req., less $25.00 fee. 3-night min. stay on holiday wknds.
Notes: Log inn overlooking Pinewiew Reservoir and Ogden Valley. Common area, dining room, living room, TV/game room with pool table. Decorated with antiques and rustic furnishings. Dutch spoken. Handicapped access.*

LOGAN (1)

Alta Manor Suites
45 E 500 N, Logan, UT 84321
(801) 752-0808

Innkeeper: Julie Zufelt
Rooms: 8 suites w/pvt. bath, kitchen, gas fireplace, TV, VCR, whirlpool tub
Rates: $75-$95, incl. cont. brk. Discount avail. for extended stay.
Credit cards: MC, V
Restrictions: No pets, smoking. One night's deposit req. 2-day cancellation notice req.
Notes: Two-story English Tudor house built in 1992. Conference room equipped for P.C. and fax machines. Small private parties accommodated. Breakfast area located in separate building. Handicapped access.

ALTA MANOR SUITES

MOAB (4)

Castle Valley Inn
CVSR Box 2602, Moab, UT 84532
(801) 259-6012

Innkeeper: Eric Thomson and Lynn Forbes Thomson
Rooms: 8 w/pvt. bath, incl. 3 bungalows w/kitchenette, 3 w/VCR. Located in 3 bldgs.
Rates: $75-$140, incl. full brk., afternoon refreshment
Credit cards: Most major cards

Restrictions: No children under 10, pets. Smoking restricted. One night's deposit req. Min. 7-day cancellation notice req. 2-night min. stay on wknds.
Notes: Western-style country inn. Located on eleven acres of orchards, fields, lawns. Surrounded by redrock mesas. Common room with native rock fireplace, library of top-ranked films, TV, VCR. Rare art collection. Outdoor hot tub. Fixed price suppers available. Gourmet "Desert Survival Kit" lunches for take-out available. Lawn games available. Innkeepers are archeologist and furniture maker. Some French, German spoken.*

Sunflower Hill
185 N. 300 E, Moab, UT 84532
(801) 259-2974
Innkeeper: Richard and Marjorie Stucki
Rooms: 4 w/pvt. bath, TV, plus 2 suites w/pvt. bath, TV, incl. 1 w/phone. Located in 2 bldgs.
Rates: $78/room, $86/suite, all incl. full brk. Seasonal variations.
Credit cards: MC, V
Restrictions: No children under 8, pets, smoking. Min. one night's deposit req. 7-day cancellation notice req.
Notes: Two-story farmhouse built in 1890s. Located in canyonlands. Recently renovated with cottage added. Welcome room with books, maps, trail guides. Hot tub, patio, BBQ, picnic tables, flower gardens, wooded pathways. Bike storage available.*

MOUNT PLEASANT (2)

The Mansion House B & B Inn
298 S. State St., Mount Pleasant, UT 84647
(801) 462-3031
Innkeeper: Denis & Terri Andelin
Rooms: 4 w/pvt. bath, TV
Rates: $41-$62, incl. full brk.
Credit cards: MC, V
Restrictions: No children under 12, pets, smoking. Deposit req. 2-day cancellation notice req.
Notes: Two-story mansion with hand-painted ceiling, oak staircase, stained-glass windows, built in 1897. Swedish spoken.

NEPHI (2)

The Whitmore Mansion
110 S. Main St., Nephi, UT 84648
(801) 623-2047
Innkeeper: Bob and Dorothy Gliske
Rooms: 3 plus 2 suites, all w/pvt. bath
Rates: $60-$75/room, $75-$95/suite, all incl. full brk., evening refreshment
Credit cards: MC, V
Restrictions: No pets, smoking. Deposit req. 7-day cancellation notice req., less $10.00 fee.
Notes: Three-story Queen Anne Eastlake mansion with wood-carved stairway, sliding oak doors, original stained-glass windows and high ceilings built in 1898. Restored in 1979. Breakfast room. Furnished with antiques, hand-crocheted rag rugs. Small private parties accommodated. Dinner and phones available upon request. Listed on the National Register of Historic Places*

PARK CITY (1)

Blue Church Lodge and Townhouses
424 Park Ave, Box 1720, Park City, UT 84060
(801) 649-8009, (800) 626-5467, (801) 649-0686
Innkeeper: Nancy Schmidt
Rooms: 11 condos w/1-4 rooms, all w/pvt. bath, phone, fireplace, TV. Located in 2 bldgs.
Rates: $90-$475, incl. cont. brk. Seasonal variations.
Credit cards: Most major cards
Restrictions: No pets, smoking. Min $50.00 deposit req. Min 45-day cancellation notice req., less $50.00 fee.
Notes: Built as a church in 1897. Completely remodeled in 1983. Located in the heart of Park City's Historic District. Indoor and outdoor Jacuzzi, game room, laundry room. Furnished with antiques in country style. Listed on both the Utah and National Registers of Historic Sites.*

Imperial Hotel
221 Main St., Box 1628, Park City, UT 84060
(801) 649-1904, (800) 669-8824, (801) 645-7421
Innkeeper: Todd and Ann Hoover
Rooms: 10 w/pvt. bath, phone, TV
Rates: $75-$190, incl. full brk., afternoon refreshment. Seasonal variations. Discount avail. for group stay.
Credit cards: Most major cards
Restrictions: No pets, smoking. Deposit req. Cancellation policy variable. Occasional min. stay.
Notes: Three-story, Victorian-style, wood-frame building built in 1904. Entry hall and sitting room with stone floors and fireplace. Dining room. Furnished with period decor. Jacuzzi, ski lockers. Listed on National and State Registers of Historic Places. German spoken.*

OLD MINERS' LODGE B & B

Old Miners' Lodge B & B
615 Woodside, Box 2639, Park City, UT 84060-2639
(801) 645-8068, (800) 648-8068, TDD either line, (801) 645-7420

Innkeeper: Hugh Daniels, Susan Wynne, Liza Simpson
Rooms: 7 w/pvt. bath, plus 3 suites w/pvt. bath
Rates: $50-$150/room, $685-$190/suite, all incl. full brk., evening refreshment. Seasonal variations.
Credit cards: Most major cards
Restrictions: No pets, smoking. Deposit and cancellation policy variable. 2-night min. stay during Art Festival. 4-6 night min. stay on holidays. 4-night min. stay during Film Festival.
Notes: Two-story inn located in renovated 1893 building once used as housing for local miners. Living room with fireplace. Furnished with period antiques. Outdoor hot tub. Small private parties accommodated. Lunches and dinners available. Equipped for hearing and sight disabilities.*

Old Town Guest House
1011 Empire Ave., Box 162, Park City, UT 84060
(801) 649-2642
Innkeeper: Debi Lovci, John Hughes
Rooms: 3 plus 1 suite, all w/pvt. bath
Rates: $45-$175, incl. full brk. Seasonal variations.
Credit cards: None
Restrictions: No pets, smoking. 50% deposit req. 30-day cancellation notice req.
Notes: Two-story Victorian-style house. Family room with original fireplace. Decorated with country-style furnishings. Hot tub. Small private parties accommodated.*

Washington School Inn
543 Park Ave, Box 536, Park City, UT 84060
(801) 649-3800, (800) 824-1672
Innkeeper: Nancy Beaufort, Delphine Covington
Rooms: 12 w/pvt. bath, phone, incl 4 w/TV plus 3 suites w/pvt. bath, phone, incl. 2 w/fireplace
Rates: $85-$225/room, $130-$300/suite, all incl. full brk., afternoon refreshment. Seasonal variations.
Credit cards: Most major cards
Restrictions: No children under 12, pets. Smoking restricted. Min. one night's deposit req. Min. 60-day cancellation notice req., less $10.00 fee.
Notes: Four-level schoolhouse with bell tower built in 1889 of local limestone. Expanded in 1906. Fully restored and has operated as inn since 1985. Living room with twenty-foot ceiling, fireplace. Dining room. TV room with VCR. Game room. Lounge with Jacuzzi, sauna, shower rooms, ski lockers. Picnic lunch available. Small private parties accommodated. Guests have access to private athletics club. Listed on the National and Utah Registers of Historic Places. Handicapped access.*

SAINT GEORGE (3)

Green Gate Village
76 W. Tabernacle, Saint George, UT 84770
(801) 628-6999, (800) 350-6999, (801) 628-6989
Innkeeper: John and Barbara Greene
Rooms: 13 w/pvt. bath, phone, TV, plus 5 suites w/pvt. bath, phone, TV, fireplace, incl. 1 w/kitchen. Located in 8 bldgs.

Rates: $60/room, $75/suite, $110/house, all incl. full brk. Discount avail. for midweek stay.

Credit cards: Most major cards

Restrictions: Pets restricted. No smoking. Deposit req. 3-day cancellation notice req.

Notes: Greenhouse built in 1872. Orson Prat home listed on National Historic Register. Dining room. Swimming pool, tennis court, hot tub. Small private parties accommodated. Handicapped access.*

Seven Wives Inn
217 N. 100 West, Saint George, UT 84770
(801) 628-3737

Innkeeper: Donna and Jay Curtis, Alison and Jon Bowcutt

Rooms: 10 plus 2 suites, all w/pvt. bath, TV, incl. 3 w/fireplace. Located in 2 bldgs.

Rates: $50-$75/room, $100-$110/suite, all incl. full brk. Discount avail. for midweek stay.

Credit cards: Most major cards

Restrictions: Children welcome with prior arrangement. No pets, smoking. Deposit required. 3-day cancellation notice req., less $10.00 fee.

Notes: Two-story Colonial Main House with 12-ft. ceilings built in 1873. Parlor with fireplace, books, games. Furnished with antiques. Porch overlooking rose gardens. Swimming pool. Off-street parking available.*

SALT LAKE CITY (1)

Anton Boxrud B & B
57 S. 600 E., Salt Lake City, UT 84102
(800) 524-5511

Innkeeper: Mark Brown and Keith Lewis

Rooms: 6, incl. 2 w/pvt. bath, plus 1 suite w/pvt. bath

Rates: $35-$79/room, $89-$109/suite, all incl. full brk., evening refreshment. Discount avail. for birthday, anniversary and honeymoon.

Credit cards: Most major cards

Restrictions: No children, pets. Smoking restricted. One night's deposit req. 21-day cancellation notice req.

Notes: Victorian house with beveled and stained-glass windows, built in 1899. Restored according to original 1901 plans. Furnished in Victorian eclectic style. Dining room. Recognized by the Salt Lake Historic Society as one of Salt Lake's Grand Old Homes. 2 resident canine greeters.*

Brigham Street Inn
1135 E. South Temple, Salt Lake City, UT 84102-1605
(801) 364-4461, (801) 521-3201

Innkeeper: Nancy Pace

Rooms: 8 w/pvt. bath, phone, TV, incl. 5 w/fireplace, plus 1 suite w/pvt. bath, phone, TV, kitchen

Rates: $$75-$115/room, $150/suite, all incl. cont. brk.

Credit cards: Most major cards

Restrictions: No pets. Smoking restricted. One night's deposit req. 2-day cancellation notice req.

Notes: Victorian mansion built in 1898. Has operated as inn since 1982. Decorated by 12 interior designers. Formal dining room with chandelier. Parlor with bird's-eye maple fireplace. Living room with oak floors, Steinway grand piano, fireplace. Covered front porch. Received design awards from American Institute of Architects, American Society of Interior Designers, Utah Heritage Foundation, and Utah Historical Society. Listed on the National Register of Historic Places. Small private parties accommodated.*

Saltair B & B
164 S. 900 E., Salt Lake City, UT 84102
(801) 533-8184, (800) 733-8184, (801) 328-2060
Innkeeper: Nancy Saxton and Jan Bartlett
Rooms: 5, incl 2 pvt bath, plus 2 suites w/pvt. bath, phone, fireplace, TV. Located in 2 bldgs.
Rates: $38-99/room, $109-$139/suite, all incl full brk.
Credit cards: Most major cards
Restrictions: No pets, smoking. Full deposit req. 30-day cancellation notice req., Dec.–April, 10-day cancellation notice, May–Nov.
Notes: The oldest B & B in Salt Lake City. Listed on the National Historical Register. Common room with piano. Decorated in period decor.

Spruces B & B
6151 S. 900 East, Salt Lake City, UT 84121
(801) 268-8762
Innkeeper: Jane E. Johnson
Rooms: 2 plus 2 suites, all w/pvt. bath, phone, TV
Rates: $55-$75/room, $75-$135/suite, all incl. full brk. Discount avail. for extended and senior citizen stays.
Credit cards: Most major cards
Restrictions: No pets, smoking. One night's deposit req. 5-day cancellation notice req.
Notes: Gothic Victorian inn built in 1903. Renovated in 1985. Surrounded by small quarter horse breeding operation. Furnished with folk art and southwestern touches. French, German spoken. Handicapped access.*

WILDFLOWERS BED & BREAKFAST

Wildflowers Bed & Breakfast
936 E. 1700 South, Salt Lake City, UT 84105
(801) 466-0600, (801) 484-7832

Innkeeper: Cill Sparks and Jeri Parker
Rooms: 3 plus 1 suite all w/pvt. bath, TV, incl. 2 w/phone
Rates: $60-$70/room, $100-$150/suite, all incl. full brk. Discount avail. for extended, mid-week and senior citizen stays.
Credit cards: MC, V
Restrictions: No pets, smoking. 50% deposit req., 7-day cancellation notice req.
Notes: Three-story Victorian house built in 1891. Fully renovated in 1987. Located on .75 acre with fruit and nut trees, flower gardens. Parlor with fireplace. Covered deck. Listed on the National Register of Historic Places. Some French spoken.*

SANDY (1)

Alta Hills Farm
10852 S. 20th E., Sandy, UT 84092
(801) 571-1712

Innkeeper: Blaine and Diane Knight
Rooms: 5 w/TV, incl. 2 w/pvt. bath, 1 w/fireplace
Rates: $58-$78, incl. cont. brk.
Credit cards: V
Restrictions: No smoking. Deposit req.
Notes: Has operated as an English Huntseat Equestrian Center since 1974. Living room with fireplace. Furnished in English country style.

Mountain Hollow Inn
10209 S. Dimple Dell Rd., Sandy, UT 84092
(801) 942-3428

Innkeeper: Doug and Kathy Larson
Rooms: 9 rooms w/TV, plus 1 suite w/pvt. bath, fireplace, TV
Rates: $65/room, $150/suite, all incl. full brk. Discount avail. for senior citizens.
Credit cards: Most major cards
Restrictions: No children under 5, pets, smoking. 50% deposit req. Cancellation notice req., less $30.00 fee.
Notes: Built in 1981. Located on two wooded acres with stream, waterfall at the base of Little Cottonwood Canyon. Living room with two-story fireplace, cathedral ceiling, board games. Game room with pool table, ping-pong, TV, VCR, collection of over 100 video movies. Library. Furnished with western art, antiques. Decorated with antique quilts. Jacuzzi. Resident pets.*

TROPIC (3)

Bryce Point B & B
61 N. 400 W., Tropic, UT 84776
(801) 679-8629

Innkeeper: Lama and Ethel LeFevre
Rooms: 5 w/phone, TV, VCR
Rates: $55-$90, incl. full brk. Seasonal variations.
Credit cards: Most major cards
Restrictions: No children under 10, pets. Smoking restricted. One night's deposit req. 7-day cancellation notice req., less $5.00 fee.
Notes: Two-story inn built in 1930s and remodeled in 1987. Second-story, cedar, wrap-around decks overlooking valley. Living room.

Vermont

ALBURG (1)

Thomas Mott Homestead
Blue Rock Rd., R 2, Box 149B, Alburg, VT 05440
(802) 796-3736
Innkeeper: Dottie and Pat Schallert
Rooms: 4 w/pvt. bath, incl. 1 w/fireplace, plus 1 suite w/pvt. bath
Rates: $55-$70/room, $70/suite, all incl. full brk., afternoon refreshment
Credit cards: Most major cards
Restrictions: No children under 6, pets, smoking. One night's deposit req. 7-day
cancellation notice req., less $20.00 fee. Closed Jan.
Notes: Two-story farmhouse built in 1838. Fully restored. Lounge with library,
board games. Sitting area with TV overlooking Lake Champlain. Breakfast area. En-
closed porch and three outdoor porches. Lawn games, canoes. Dinner available
with prior notice. Gift room on premises.*

THOMAS MOTT HOMESTEAD

ANDOVER (5)

The Inn at Highview
RR 1, Box 201 A, Andover, VT 05143
(802) 875-2724, (802) 875-4021
Innkeeper: Gregory Bohan, Sal Massaro
Rooms: 6 plus 2 suites, all w/pvt. bath
Rates: $90-$105/room, $125/suite, all incl. full brk. Discount avail. for extended
and mid-week stays. Seasonal variations.
Credit cards: MC, V
Restrictions: No children under 12, smoking. One-night's deposit req. 10-day can-
cellation notice req., less 10% fee. 2-night min. stay on wknds. 3-night min. stay
on holiday wknds.

799

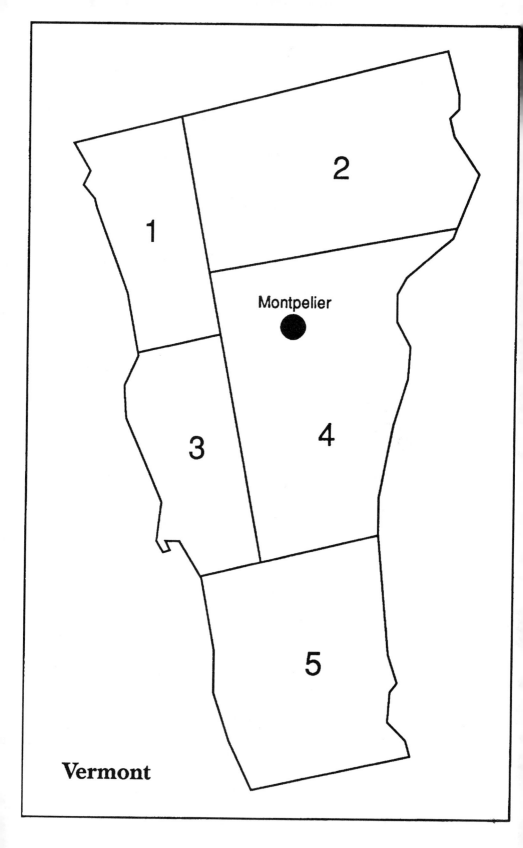

Montpelier

2

1

3

4

5

Vermont

Notes: Two-story 18th-century farmhouse. Located on 72 acres with hiking and cross-country ski trails. Dining room, library. Common area with fireplace. Garden pool, sauna. Italian, Spanish spoken.*

ARLINGTON (5)

Arlington Inn
Historic Rte. 7A, Box 369, Arlington, VT 05250
(800) 443-9442, (802) 375-6532
Innkeeper: Mark and Deborah Gagnon
Rooms: 7 w/pvt. bath, plus 6 suites w/pvt. bath, incl. 1 w/fireplace. Located in 2
    bldgs.
Rates: $65-$135/room, $115-$175/suite, all incl. full brk. Seasonal variations.
Credit cards: Most major cards
Restrictions: No pets, smoking. One night's deposit req. 2-week cancellation notice
    req. 2-night min. stay on peak season wknds.
Notes: Victorian Greek Revival mansion built in 1848. Parlor with fireplace. Dining
rooms, tavern. Game room with TV, VCR. Furnished with period antiques. Front
porch with rockers. Landscaped grounds with tennis court. Gourmet meals avail-
able. National Historic Trust Landmark. Small private parties accommodated.
French spoken.*

ARLINGTON INN

The Evergreen Inn
Sandgate Rd., Box 2480, Arlington, VT 05250
(802) 375-2272
Innkeeper: Mathilda and Kathleen Kenny
Rooms: 17, incl. 9 w/pvt. bath, plus 1 suite w/pvt. bath
Rates: $50-$60/room, $70/suite, incl. full brk., dinner. Discount avail. for extended
    stay.
Credit cards: None
Restrictions: No children under 3, smoking. $30.00 deposit req. 14-day cancellation
    notice req.

Notes: Two-story woodframe European-style country inn built in 1860. Expanded in and has operated as inn by the same family since 1935. Located on three acres in a mountain valley with stream. Living room with fireplace, TV, board games. Furnished with antiques. Dinner available. Buffet lunch offered during July and August. Handicapped access. German spoken. Resident pets.

Hill Farm Inn
R.R. 2, Box 2015, Arlington, VT 05250
(802) 375-2269, (800) 882-2545

Innkeeper: Regan and John Chichester

Rooms: 11 plus 2 suites plus 4 cabins, incl. 12 w/pvt. bath, 1 w/cable TV. Located in 2 bldgs.

Rates: $70-$100/room, $110-$120/suite, $80-$90/cabin, all incl. full brk., afternoon refreshment. Seasonal variations.

Credit cards: Most major cards

Restrictions: No smoking. Pets restricted. One night's deposit req. 14-day cancellation notice req., less $10.00 fee. 2-night min. stay on wknds. 3-night min. stay on holiday wknds. Dinner not avail. Wed.

Notes: Two-story main inn built in 1830. Located on fifty farmland acres along the Battenkill River. Has operated as inn since 1905. Guesthouse built in 1790. Dining room, living room with board games, each with fireplace. Furnished in country style with some antiques, handmade quilts, crocheted rugs. Porch with wicker rockers. Dinner, bus station pick-up available. Guests have access to Stratton Mountain's Sports Club. Resident dog. Limited handicapped access.*

Keelan House B&B
RD 1, Box 1272, Arlington, VT 05250
(802) 375-9029

Innkeeper: Verrall and Don Keelan

Rooms: 3 w/pvt. bath, plus 1 suite w/pvt. bath

Rates: $85/room, $85/suite, all incl. full brk. Seasonal variations.

Credit cards: None

Restrictions: No pets. Smoking restricted. One night's deposit req. 14-day cancellation notice req, less 10% fee. 2-night min. stay during fall foliage season. Closed Christas Day, New Year's Day.

Notes: Federal house with wide plank flooring, built in the 1820s. Restored in 1986. Located on 17 acres on Battenkill River. Dining room with fireplace. Living room with fireplace. Breakfast room, porch. Furnished with American antiques and crafts. Grounds include two ponds for swimming, fishing. Listed on National Register of Historic Places. Children's play equipment, canoeing, tubing, cross-country skiing, bicylces available.

BELLOWS FALLS (5)

River Mist Bed and Breakfast
7 Burt St., Bellows Falls, VT 05101
(802) 463-9023

Innkeeper: John and Linda Maresca

Rooms: 5, incl. 2 w/pvt. bath

Rates: $50-$75, incl. full brk. Seasonal variations. Discount avail. for extended and senior citizen stays.

Credit cards: Most major cards

Restrictions: No children under 5, pets, smoking. Deposit req. 48-hour cancellation notice req., less $10.00 fee. 2-night min. stay on foliage season and holiday wknds.
Notes: Two-story Queen Anne Victorian house built in 1903. Three common rooms, one with fireplace. Dining room, breakfast nook, wrap-around porch. Decorated in Country Victorian style.

RIVER MIST BED AND BREAKFAST

BENNINGTON (5)

Molly Stark Inn
1067 E. Main. St., Bennington, VT 05201-9631
(800) 356-3076
Innkeeper: Reed Fendler
Rooms: 5 w/pvt. bath, incl. 1 w/phone, 1 w/TV, plus 2 suites w/pvt. bath, incl. 1 w/phone, 1 w/TV, 1 w/fireplace. Located in 2 bldgs.
Rates: $65-$85/room, $125/suite, all incl. full brk. Seasonal variations. Discount avail. for senior citizen stay.
Credit cards: Most major cards
Restrictions: No children under 10, pets, smoking. Deposit req. 72-hour cancellation notice req. 2-night min. stay on wknds.
Notes: Two-story Queen Anne-style Victorian house with stenciled woodwork, wooden plank floors built in 1860. Has operated as inn since the 1940s. Fully renovated. Two common rooms, one with TV, fireplace. Furnished in country decor with antiques, clawfooted tubs, woodstove. Wrap-around front porch with rocking chairs.*

BETHEL (4)

Poplar Manor
Rte. 2, Box 136, Bethel, VT 05032
(802) 234-5426
Innkeeper: Carmen E. Jaynes
Rooms: 2, no pvt. bath, plus 1 suite, no pvt. bath
Rates: $38-$40, incl. expanded cont. brk.
Credit cards: None

Restrictions: Smoking restricted. $10.00 per night deposit req. 2-night min. stay during fall foliage season wknds.
Notes: Colonial house built in 1810 adjacent to White River. Dining room, living room with TV, phone. Furnished with antiques and collectibles. Spanish spoken.

BRANDON (3)

High Meadow
RD3, Box 3344, Brandon, VT 05733
(802) 247-3820
Innkeeper: Patrice Lopatin Reiner and Tom Reiner
Rooms: 3, no pvt. bath
Rates: $55-$65, incl. full brk. Seasonal variations.
Credit cards: None
Restrictions: No pets, smoking. Deposit req. 7-day cancellation notice req. Min. stay req. during holidays. Closed Feb.–April, and November.
Notes: Two-story country cottage built in the 1850s. Located in a mountain meadow in the National Forest area. Living room with fireplace. Dinner available. Resident goat, turkey, chickens, cat. 7 languages spoken.

Rosebelle's Victorian Inn
31 Franklin St., Rte. 7, Brandon, VT 05733
(802) 247-0098
Innkeeper: Ginette and Norm Milot
Rooms: 6, some w/pvt. bath
Rates: $65-$75, incl. full brk. Seasonal variations. Discount avail. for extended, mid-week, and senior citizen stays. Special pkgs. avail.
Credit cards: Most major cards
Restrictions: No children under 12, pets, smoking. One night's deposit req. 14-day cancellation notice req. 2-night min. stay on holiday wknds.
Notes: Three-story Victorian Inn built in 1839. Sitting room with fireplace. Living room with TV. Furnished with unique Victorian pieces. Porch with rockers. Small private parties accommodated. Listed on the National Register of Historic Places. French spoken.

BROOKFIELD (4)

Green Trails Country Inn by the Floating Bridge
P.O. Box 494, Brookfield, VT 05036
(802) 276-3412, (800) 243-3412
Innkeeper: Pat and Peter Simpson
Rooms: 15, incl. 9 w/pvt. bath. Located in 2 bldgs.
Rates: $68-$80, incl. full brk. Discount avail. for senior citizens.
Credit cards: None
Restrictions: No pets, smoking. Deposit req. 2-week cancellation notice req. 2-night min. stay during fall foliage and winter wknds.
Notes: Cape Cod structure built in 1790. Federal-style structure built in 1840. Both restored. Located at 1,200-ft. elevation near Sunset Lake and directly across from the only remaining wooden floating bridge in the U.S. Living room with library, TV, fireplace. Parlor with phone. Furnished with antiques, homemade quilts. Decorated with seasonal flowers, Norman Rockwell memorabilia, stencilling. Ski touring center on premises with complete rental equipment and instruction. Horse-drawn winter sleigh rides available. Swedish spoken.*

CHARLOTTE (1)

The Inn at Charlotte
RR 1, Box 1188, Charlotte, VT 05445
(802) 425-2934
Innkeeper: Letty Ellinger
Rooms: 6 w/pvt. bath, incl. 4 w/TV
Rates: $65-$85, incl. full brk., afternoon refreshment. Special pkgs. avail.
Credit cards: Most major cards
Restrictions: No children. Smoking restricted. One night's deposit req. 2-week cancellation notice req., less $15.00 fee. 2-night min. stay on wknds. from July–October.
Notes: Modern house furnished with country French furniture and 18th-century antiques. Common room with fireplace. Two dining rooms. Courtyard with flowers. Heated swimming pool and tennis court. Lunch, dinner, and picnic baskets available upon request. Mountain bikes available to rent. Spanish spoken.

CHELSEA (4)

Shire Inn
8 Main St., Box 37, Chelsea, VT 05038-0037
(802) 685-3031
Innkeeper: Jay and Karen Keller
Rooms: 6 w/pvt. bath, incl. 4 w/fireplace
Rates: $148-$178, incl. full brk., dinner. Seasonal variations. Special pkgs. avail.
Credit cards: Most major cards
Restrictions: No children under 6, pets, smoking. One night's deposit req. 14-day cancellation notice req. 2-night min. stay on wknds., holidays and fall foliage season.
Notes: Two-story red brick Federal house with original wide-board floors and spiral staircase, built in 1832. Recently redecorated. Located on twenty-four acres with trout stream and gardens. Parlor with fireplace. Library, porch. Furnished with period antiques. Dinners available.*

GREENLEAF INN

CHESTER (5)

Greenleaf Inn
P.O. Box 188, Chester, VT 05143
(802) 875-3171

Innkeeper: Dan and Elizabeth Duffield
Rooms: 5 w/pvt. bath
Rates: $65-$70, incl. full brk., afternoon refreshment. Discount avail. for group stay.
Credit cards: MC, V
Restrictions: No children under 6, pets. One night's deposit req. 15-day cancellation notice req.
Notes: Three-story Victorian country inn built in the 1850s. Located on one acre with brook. Dining room, front hall with art gallery. Fireplace. Furnished with antiques. Ski trails at back door.

HUGGING BEAR INN

Hugging Bear Inn
Main St., Chester, VT 05143
(802) 875-2412, (800) 325-0519

Innkeeper: Paul, Georgette and Diane Thomas
Rooms: 6 w/pvt. bath
Rates: $75-$90, incl. full brk. Seasonal variations.
Credit cards: Most major cards
Restrictions: No pets, smoking. 50% deposit req. Cancellation notice req., less fee. 2-night min. stay on holiday and high season wknds.
Notes: Three-story oak and black cherry Victorian house built in 1850. Colonial Revival carriage barn built in 1905. Located on .75 acre across from village green. Has operated as inn since 1983. Living room with tower section. Dining room, kitchen. Library/den with fireplace and audio-visual corner. Board games, toys available. Furnished in eclectic style with some antiques, teddy bears in every room. Porches on first and second floors. Large backyard and garden. Teddy Bear shop on premises. Resident cats. Bicycles available.

The Inn at Long Last
P.O. Box 589, Chester, VT 05143
(802) 875-2444

Innkeeper: Jack Coleman
Rooms: 24 plus 6 suites, all w/pvt. bath
Rates: $160, incl. full brk., dinner. Seasonal variations.
Credit cards: MC, V
Restrictions: No children under 2, pets, smoking. Deposit req. 7-day cancellation notice req. 2-night min. stay on fall foliage wknds. and Christmas. Closed during April and mid-November.
Notes: Two-story building built in the 18th century. Located on the village green. Library with fireplace. Victorian decor furnished with antiques. Gardens, tennis courts, fishing stream. Parlor and lawn games. Some French spoken.*

Inn Victoria
On the Green, Box 589, Chester, VT 05143
(800) 732-4288
Innkeeper: Tom and K.C. Lanagan
Rooms: 5 w/pvt. bath, incl. 1 w/phone, 1 w/fireplace, 1 w/TV, plus 2 suites w/pvt. bath, incl. 1 w/phone, 1 w/fireplace, 1 w/TV
Rates: $75-$110/room, $150/suite, all incl. full brk., afternoon refreshment. Seasonal variations. Discount avail. for mid-week stay.
Credit cards: Most major cards
Restrictions: No pets, smoking. Credit card deposit req. 14-day cancellation notice req. 2-night min. stay on fall foliage wknds.
Notes: Built in the 1850s. Parlor. Furnished with period antiques. Fireplace. Jacuzzi, bubble tubs, hot tub available. Tea pot shop on premises.*

The Madrigal Inn
61 Williams River Rd., Chester, VT 05143
(802) 463-2231, (800) 854-2208
Innkeeper: Ray and Nancy Dressler
Rooms: 10 w/pvt. bath, plus 1 suite w/pvt. bath
Rates: $85/room, $85/suite, all incl. full brk., evening refreshment. Discount avail. for senior citizen, military, clergy, and extended stays.
Credit cards: MC, V
Restrictions: No pets, smoking. One night's deposit req. 14-day cancellation notice req., less $5.00 fee. 3-night min. stay on holiday and fall foliage wknds.
Notes: Two-story inn built in 1992. Located on 60 acres. Dining room, loft library, meeting room, patio. Porcelain/cermaic and art studio with craft supplies and woodworking equipment on premises. Sunday afternoon classical music concerts. 1830s guesthouse is available for families/groups. Small private parties accommodated. Dinner available by reservation. Handicapped access.*

The Old Town Farm Inn
R.R.4, Box 383B (State Rt. 10), Chester, VT 05143
(802) 875-2346
Innkeeper: Fred and Jan Baldwin
Rooms: 11, incl. 3 w/pvt. bath
Rates: $58-$68, incl. full brk., afternoon refreshment. Discount avail. for mid-week, extended stay.
Credit cards: Most major cards
Restrictions: No children under 6, pets, smoking. One night's deposit req. Deposit refunded upon cancellation only if room re-rented, otherwise, less $10.00. fee. 2-3 night min. stay on holidays.

Notes: 2-story New England Colonial farm house built in 1861. Located on 11 wooded acres. Large barn, carriage house and milk house. Breakfast room overlooks brick patio and pond. Library, common room with stone fireplace, stone floor, BYOB bar, refrigerator, board games, dart board. Handmade spiral staircase. Furnished with period antiques, handmade quilts, and country curtains.

DANBY (5)

Quail's Nest B & B
Main St., Box 221, Danby, VT 05739
(802) 293-5099, (802) 293-6300
Innkeeper: Greg and Nancy Diaz
Rooms: 6, incl. 4 w/pvt. bath
Rates: $60-$70, incl. full brk., afternoon refreshment. Seasonal variations.
Credit cards: MC, V
Restrictions: No children under 8, pets, smoking. One night's deposit req. 5-day cancellation notice req. 14-day cancellation notice req. in season, less $10.00 fee
Notes: Two-story house built in 1835. Common room with fireplace, piano. Furnished with antiques, handmade quilts. Front porches with rockers. Hammock. German spoken.

Silas Griffith Inn
RR 1, Box 66F, Danby, VT 05739
(802) 293-5567
Innkeeper: Paul and Lois Dansereau
Rooms: 17, incl. 14 w/pvt. bath. Located in 2 bldgs.
Rates: $69-$86, incl. full brk, afternoon refreshment. Special pkgs. avail. Seasonal variations.
Credit cards: Most major cards
Restrictions: No pets, smoking. One-night's deposit req. 10-day cancellation notice req. 2-night min. stay on holiday wknds.
Notes: Three-story Victorian mansion with handcarved cherry woodwork, embossed tin ceilings, stained-glass windows, and Carriage House built in 1891. Fully restored in 1987. Sitting room with library, fireplace. Music room, game room, TV room. Swimming pool, flower gardens. Restaurant with fireplace on premises. Furnished with period antiques.*

DORSET (5)

Marble West Inn
Dorset West Rd., Dorset, VT 05251-0847
(802) 867-4155, (800) 453-7629
Innkeeper: Wayne and June Erla
Rooms: 7 w/pvt. bath, plus 1 suite w/pvt. bath
Rates: $75-$110/room, $125/suite, all incl. full brk., afternoon refreshment. Discount avail. for mid-week stay. Special pkgs. avail.
Credit cards: Most major cards
Restrictions: No children under 12, pets, smoking. One night's deposit req. 14-day cancellation notice req. 2-night min. stay on holiday and fall foliage wknds.
Notes: Greek Revival house with stenciled walls and staircase, built in the 1840s as a private home for owner of an early marble quarry. Has operated as inn since 1985. Located on 2 acres with two stocked trout ponds and mountain stream at the base of 3,300-ft. Mother Myrich Mountain. Seven marble columns supporting two front

marble porches overlooking meadow and Dorset mountains. Marble walkways and pieces placed throughout grounds. Common areas with dark wood floors. Piano room and library, both with marble fireplace. Furnished with antiques, Oriental rugs. Herb, vegetable, flower, and fern gardens. Listed in the National Register of Historic Places. Candlelight dinners available upon request.*

EAST BURKE (2)

Mountain View Creamery
Darling Hill Rd., Box 355, East Burke, VT 05832
(802) 626-9924
Innkeeper: Marilyn and John Pastore; Joy Chesley, Manager
Rooms: 8 w/pvt. bath, plus 2 suites w/pvt. bath
Rates: $90-120/room, $160/suite, all incl. full brk., afternoon refreshment. Seasonal variations. Discount avail. for extended stay. Special pkgs. avail.
Credit cards: MC, V
Restrictions: No pets, smoking. 2-night min. stay during fall foliage.
Notes: brick Georgian Colonial inn built in 1890. Located on 440-acre farm established in 1883. Fully restored. Parlor, dining room, function room. Furnished with country antiques. Table tennis, lawn bowling, croquet available. Small private parties accommodated. Russian spoken.

EAST MIDDLEBURY (3)

The Annex
Rte. 125, East Middlebury, VT 05740
(802) 388-3233
Innkeeper: Francis W. Hutchins
Rooms: 5, incl. 3 w/pvt. bath, plus 1 suite w/pvt. bath
Rates: $55-75/room, $85-$100/suite, all incl. cont. brk. Discount avail. for extended stay. Seasonal variations.
Credit cards: None
Restrictions: No pets, smoking. 50% deposit req. 10-day cancellation notice req., less $10.00 fee. 2-night min. stay on wknds.
Notes: Greek Revival house built in 1830. Recently restored. Living room with cable TV. Furnished with antiques. Grounds include perennial gardens, river.

ENOSBURG FALLS (1)

Berkson Farms
RR 1, Box 850, Enosburg Falls, VT 05450
(802) 933-2522, (802) 933-8331
Innkeeper: Susan and Terry Spoonire
Rooms: 4, incl. 1 w/pvt. bath
Rates: $55-$65, incl. 3 meals daily. Discount avail. for extended stay.
Credit cards: None
Restrictions: No smoking. Deposit req. 10-day cancellation notice req.
Notes: Two-story farmhouse built about 1890. Fully renovated. Located on 600-acre working dairy farm. Living room, library, dining room, family room, game room. Furnished with antiques. Guests are encouraged to help with farm chores. Children's play area. Picnic area. Bicycles, hay rides, trails, auctions, flea markets, fishing, hunting, swimming. Cross-country ski trails. Picnic lunches available. Resident farm animals.

BERKSON FARMS

ESSEX JUNCTION (1)

Mrs. B's B & B
23 East St., Essex Junction, VT 05452
(802) 878-5439
Innkeeper: Tom and Althea Banfield
Rooms: 2, no pvt. bath
Rates: $50, incl. full brk.
Credit cards: MC, V
Restrictions: No children under 12, pets, smoking. Deposit req. 24-hour cancellation notice req., less $10.00 fee
Notes: Two-story English house built in 1922. Decorated in Laura Ashley look.

FAIR HAVEN (3)

Maplewood Inn & Antiques
Route 22 A S., Fair Haven, VT 05743
(802) 265-8039, (800) 253-7729
Innkeeper: Cindy and Doug Baird
Rooms: 3 w/pvt. bath, phone, incl. 2 w/TV, plus 2 suites w/pvt. bath, phone, TV
Rates: $70-$85/room, $105/suite, all incl. expanded cont. brk., evening refreshment. Discount avail. for extended, group stays. Special pkgs. avail. Seasonal variations.
Credit cards: Most major cards
Restrictions: No children under 5, pets. Smoking restricted. Min. one night's deposit req. 14-day cancellation notice req., less $15.00 fee. 2-night min. stay, foliage wknds. 3-night min. stay, Christmas.
Notes: Two-story Greek Revival house with maple and wood plank floors, fancy moldings and wallpapers, built in 1843. Located on 3.5 acres. Once operated as dairy farm. Renovated in and has operated as inn since 1986. Keeping room with cable TV, fireplace. Breakfast room. Gathering room with library, board games. Front porch. Furnished with period pieces. Lawn games, canoe, and bicycles available. Innkeeper collects antique spinning wheels, yarn winders. Listed on the Vermont State Register of Historic Places. Antique shop on premises. Limited handicapped access.*

FAIRLEE (4)

Silver Maple Lodge
S. Main St., RR 1, Box 8, Fairlee, VT 05045
(802) 333-4326, (800) 666-1946

Innkeeper: Scott and Sharon Wright
Rooms: 16, incl. 14 w/pvt. bath, 8 w/TV, plus 8 cottages w/pvt. bath, incl. 2 w/kitchen, 3 w/fireplace. Located in 6 bldgs.
Rates: $48-68, incl. cont. brk. Discount avail. for extended stay. Special pkgs. avail.
Credit cards: Most major cards
Restrictions: Pets, smoking restricted. Min. one night's deposit req. 14-day cancellation notice req., less $2.00 fee. 2-night min. stay on holiday wknds. Special pkgs. avail.
Notes: Two-story Country farmhouse built in the 1700's, with Victorian addition added in 1855. Fully restored. Has operated as inn since 1926. Located opposite open farmland with views of White Mountains. Cottages with knotty pine walls, wide-board floors. Dining room, two sitting rooms. Wrap-around screened porch. Furnished in country style. Lawn games available. Picnic tables among apple trees. Hot air balloon inn-to-inn trips organized. Limited handicapped access.*

SILVER MAPLE LODGE

GAYSVILLE (3)

Cobble House Inn
P.O. Box 49, Gaysville, VT 05746
(802) 234-5458

Innkeeper: Beau, Phil, and Sam Benson
Rooms: 6 w/pvt. bath
Rates: $80-$100, incl. full brk., afternoon refreshment
Credit cards: Most major cards
Restrictions: No children under 8, pets, smoking. One night's deposit req. 14-day cancellation notice req. 2-night min stay on wknds. and fall foilage season. 3-night min. stay, Christmas.
Notes: Two-story Victorian mansion built in 1860s. Two parlors, two dining rooms. Porch overlooking mountains, White River. Italian, French dinners available. Handicapped access.

GRAFTON (5)

The Old Tavern at Grafton
Main St., Grafton, VT 05146
(802) 843-2231, (802) 843-2245

Innkeeper: Tom List

Rooms: 64 w/pvt. bath, plus 2 suites w/pvt bath. Located in 9 bldgs.

Rates: $110-$150/room, $200/suite, all incl. cont. brk, afternoon refreshment. Seasonal variations. Special pkgs. avail. Discount avail. for extended, senior citizen stays.

Credit cards: MC, V

Restrictions: No pets. Smoking restricted. One night's deposit req. 7-day cancellation notice req., less $10.00 fee. 2-night min. stay, fall foliage season. Jackets required at dinner. Closed Dec. 25, April.

Notes: Four-story federal-style main building built in 1801, plus cottages and guesthouses. Fully restored in 1965. Dining room, conference room, game room. Porch with rockers. Furnished with antiques. All meals, lawn games, bicycles, sleds, toboggans available. Tennis courts. Small private parties accommodated. Horse stable, natural swimming pond, cross-country ski center on premises. Theodore Roosevelt, Woodrow Wilson, Ulysses S. Grant, Daniel Webster, Rudyard Kipling, Nathaniel Hawthorne, Ralph Waldo Emerson and Henry David Thoreau slept here. Dutch, German, French, Spanish spoken.*

GREENSBORO (2)

Highland Lodge
RR1, Box 1290, Caspian Lake, Greensboro, VT 05841
(802) 533-2647

Innkeeper: David and Wilhelmina Smith

Restrictions: 11 w/pvt. bath, incl. 10 w/fireplace, plus 10 cottages w/pvt. bath, fireplace. Located in 11 bldgs.

Rates: $150-$210/room, $200/cottage, all incl. full brk., lunch & dinner. Seasonal variations.

Credit cards: MC, V

Restrictions: No pets. One night's deposit req. 7-day cancellation notice req. Closed mid-Oct.–mid-Dec., mid-March–May 31.

Notes: Two-story Victorian lodge built in the 1860s. Living room, dining rooms, play room. Porch overlooking Caspian Lake. Clay tennis court. Beach house with fireplace, grill on private beach. Lawn games, paddle boats, canoes, dock and swimming float, babysitter available. Restaurant on premises. Dutch spoken.*

JACKSONVILLE (5)

Engel House Bed and Breakfast
Rte. 112, Box 216, Jacksonville, VT 05342
(802) 368-2974

Innkeeper: Charles and Charlene Rinaldi

Rooms: 3, no pvt. bath

Rates: $45-$65, incl. full brk.

Credit cards: MC, V

Restrictions: No pets, smoking. Deposit req.

Notes: Two-story country village house built in 1840.*

JAMAICA (5)

Three Mountain Inn
P.O. Box 180, Jamaica, VT 05343
(802) 874-4140, (802) 874-4745

Innkeeper: Charles and Elaine Murray
Rooms: 14, incl. 13 w/pvt. bath, 2 w/fireplace, plus 1 suite w/pvt. bath, fireplace. Located in 2 bldgs.
Rates: $130-$180/room, $210/suite, all incl. full brk. Discount avail. for group stays.
Credit cards: Most major cards
Restrictions: No children under six, pets. Smoking restricted. Min. 50% deposit req. 14-day cancellation notice req., less $25.00 fee.
Notes: Two-story Colonial inn built in the 1790s. Fully restored with handhewn beams, wide-plank floors, rare "King's Wood" walls. Original beehive oven/fireplace. Landscaped pool. Separate meeting house. Has operated as inn since 1977. Small private parties accommodated.*

JAY PEAK (2)

Woodshed Lodge
Woodshed Rd., Jay Peak, VT 05859
(800) 9495-4445
Innkeeper: John and Christine Engler
Rooms: 7, incl. 3 w/pvt. bath
Rates: $25-$36, incl. full brk. Discount avail. for extended stay. Seasonal variations.
Credit cards: MC, V
Restrictions: No pets. Smoking restricted. One-night's deposit req. 21-day cancellation notice req.
Notes: Two-story restored farmhouse built in the 1900s. Located on 25 acres. Dining room with wood burning stove. Sitting room. Library/TV room with VCR. Board games available.

JERICHO (1)

Henry M. Field House
RR 2, Box 395, Jericho, VT 05465
(802) 899-3984
Innkeeper: MaryBeth and Terrence Horan
Rooms: 3 w/pvt. bath
Rates: $65-$95, incl. full brk.
Credit cards: MC, V
Restrictions: Children restricted. No pets, smoking. 50% deposit req. 14-day cancellation notice req., less $5.00 fee. 2-night min. stay on peak wknds. and holidays.
Notes: Victorian Italianate house with tall ceilings, ornamental plaster, etched glass, large paneled doors and moldings of butternut and mahogany, built in 1875. Located on 3.2 wooded acres with meadows bordering property. Three parlors with board games, TV, VCR. Library. Decorated with period furnishings. Three porches.

Homeplace Bed and Breakfast
RR 2, Box 367, Jericho, VT 05465
(802) 899-4694
Innkeeper: Hans and Mariot Huessy
Rooms: 3, no pvt. bath, incl. 2 w/phone, 1 w/TV
Rates: $55, incl. full brk. Discount avail. for extended stay.
Credit cards: None
Restrictions: No smoking. Pets restricted. $25.00 deposit req.

Notes: Two-story house built about 1970. Located on 100 wooded acres. Living room with board games, books, piano. Furnished with antiques and craftwork. Gardens and hiking trails. German spoken. Resident farm animals.*

KILLINGTON (3)

The Peak Chalet
South View Path, Box 511, Killington, VT 05751
(802) 422-4278
Innkeeper: Diane and Greg Becker
Rooms: 4 w/pvt. bath
Rates: $50-$110, incl. cont. brk. Discount avail. for senior citizens. Seasonal variations.
Credit cards: Most major cards
Restrictions: No children under 12, pets, smoking. 50% deposit req. Min. 30-day cancellation notice req., less $25.00 fee. 2-night min. stay on winter and fall wknds.
Notes: European Alpine-style inn. Has operated as inn since 1990. Living room with stone fireplace, cable TV, VCR, overlooking mountains. Decorated in country-inn style. Condominium available with full kitchen, bath, dining area, and living room with fireplace. German spoken.*

Snowed Inn
Miller Brook Rd., Box 2336, Killington, VT 05751
(802) 422-3407, (802) 422-3407
Innkeeper: Manfred and Jeanne Karlhuber
Rooms: 16 w/pvt. bath, TV, plus 2 suites w/pvt. bath, fireplace, incl. 2 w/TV, 1 w/phone. Located in 2 bldgs.
Rates: $40-$75/room, $70-$110/suite, all incl. cont. brk. Seasonal variations.
Credit cards: Most major cards
Restrictions: No pets. 50% deposit req. 14-day cancellation notice req., less 10% fee.
Notes: Woodland setting. Lounge with fieldstone fireplace and games. Furnished in country style. Outdoor hot tub. German spoken.*

SWISS INN

LONDONDERRY (5)

Swiss Inn
RR 1, Box 140, Rte. 11, Londonderry, VT 05148-9717
(802) 824-3442, (800) 847-9477, (802) 824-6313

Innkeeper: Joe and Pat Donahue
Rooms: 16 plus 2 suites, all w/pvt. bath, phone, cable TV
Rates: $59-$89/room, $99-$129/suite, all incl. full brk. Seasonal variations. Discount avail. for extended stay.
Credit cards: Most major cards
Restrictions: No pets. One night's deposit req. 7-day cancellation notice req. 2-night min. stay on wknds.
Notes: Two-story country inn located in the Green Mountains. Dining room serving Swiss Continental cuisine. Two sitting rooms with wood stoves. Lounge/bar with wood stove. Game room, library. Swimming pool, tennis court, trout pond.

The Village Inn at Landgrove
RR 1, Box 215 Landgrove, Londonderry, VT 05148
(802) 824-6673

Innkeeper: D. Jay and Kathy Snyder
Rooms: 16 w/pvt. bath
Rates: $75-$85, incl. full brk., afternoon refreshment, dinner
Credit cards: Most major cards
Restrictions: No pets. Smoking restricted. One night's deposit req. 10-day cancellation notice req. 2-night min. stay on wknds. Closed Apr.–Memorial Day, Nov. 1–Dec. 15.
Notes: Red brick clapboard building built as homestead in 1830. Has operated as inn since 1959, recently renovated and redecorated. Lobby with gift display. Game room, lounge. Furnished with antiques, hand painted furniture, stenciling. Swimming pool, tennis court, whirlpool, paddle court, stocked trout pond. Herb and flower gardens.*

LUDLOW (5)

The Andrie Rose Inn
13 Pleasant St., Ludlow, VT 05149
(802) 228-4846, (800) 223-4846, (802) 228-7910

Innkeeper: Jack and Ellen Fisher
Rooms: 10 w/pvt. bath, plus 11 suites w/pvt. bath, phone, fireplace, TV. Located in 3 bldgs.
Rates: $75-$150/room, incl. full brk., $185-$250/suite, incl. cont. brk. Discount avail. for senior citizen. Special ski pkgs. avail.
Credit cards: Most major cards
Restrictions: No pets, smoking. 50% deposit req. 14-day cancellation notice req., less $10.00 fee. 2-night min. stay in fall and winter.
Notes: Two-story Colonial inn with maple and fir hardwood floors built in 1829. Located at base of Okemo Mountain. Fully renovated in and has operated as inn since 1989. Furnished with period antiques, Laura Ashley linens. Wrap-around porch with rockers. Handicapped access.*

Black River Inn
100 Main St., Ludlow, VT 05149
(802) 228-5585

Innkeeper: Rick and Cheryl Del Mastro
Rooms: 10, incl. 8 w/pvt. bath
Rates: $60-$125, incl. full brk. Discount avail. for extended stay. Seasonal variations.
Credit cards: Most major cards

Restrictions: No children under 12, pets. 50% deposit req. 10-day cancellation notice req., less $10.00 fee. 3-night min. stay on fall and winter wknds.
Notes: Built in 1835 on the bank of the Black River. Living room with fireplace. Carriage House with TV. Furnished with antiques, including a walnut four-poster bed built in 1794 that Abraham Lincoln slept in. French country restaurant on premises.*

Combes Family Inn
RFD 1, Box 275, East Lake Rd., Ludlow, VT 05149
(802) 228-8799
Innkeeper: Ruth and Bill Combes
Rooms: 8 plus 3 suite, all w/pvt. bath. Located in 2 bldgs.
Rates: $90, incl. full brk. Special pkgs. avail. Seasonal variations.
Credit cards: Most major cards
Restrictions: One night's deposit req. 14-day cancellation notice req. 2-night min. stay on wknds.
Notes: Farmhouse built in 1880. Located on fifty wooded acres with vegetable garden, near Lake Rescue. Dining room with bay window overlooking Okemo Mountain. Lounge with fireplace. Furnished in casual, country style with turn-of-the-century oak pieces. Five motel units available. Resident farm animals. French spoken.*

Echo Lake Inn
P.O. Box 154, Ludlow, VT 05149-0154
(802) 228-8602, (800) 356-6844, (802) 228-3075
Innkeeper: John & Yvonne Pardieu, Chip Connelly
Rooms: 24, incl. 9 w/pvt. bath, plus 2 suites w/pvt. bath, incl. 1 w/TV
Rates: $60-$85/room, $70-$98/suite, all incl. full brk., dinner. Seasonal variations. Discount avail. for extended stay. Special pkgs. avail.
Credit cards: Most major cards
Restrictions: No children under 5, pets. Smoking restricted. 50% deposit req. 20-day cancellation notice req., less 10% fee. 2-night min. stay on holidays. Closed April.
Notes: Four-story gabled inn built in 1840. Living room with fireplace. Lounge, game room, tavern, porch. Furnished with early American antiques. Swimming pool, steam bath, lighted tennis court. All meals, lawn games available. Guests have access to dock and canoes. Innkeeper collects antique baskets.*

MANCHESTER (5)

Birch Hill Inn
West Rd., Box 346, Manchester, VT 05254-2761
(802) 362-2761
Innkeeper: Pat and Jim Lee
Rooms: 5 w/pvt. bath, incl. 1 w/fireplace, plus 1 cottage w/pvt. bath. Located in 2 bldgs.
Rates: $105-$130, incl. full brk., afternoon, evening refreshment
Credit cards: Most major cards
Restrictions: No children under 6, pets, smoking. $120 deposit req. 14-day cancellation notice req., less 10% fee. 2-night min. stay on wknds.
Notes: Two-story Colonial house and cottage built in 1790. Guest rooms overlooking mountains, farm, and pond. Living room with fireplace. Sun room, sitting

room, terrace. Furnished with antiques. Grounds include eight miles of cross-country skiing, swimming pool, private trout pond.

Manchester Highlands Inn
Highland Ave., Box 1754, Manchester, VT 05255-1754
(802) 362-4565, (800) 743-4565, (802) 362-4028

Innkeeper: Robert and Patricia Eichorn
Rooms: 15 w/pvt. bath. Located in 2 bldgs.
Rates: $85-$125/room, incl. full brk., afternoon refreshment. Seasonal variations. Discount avail. for mid-week stay.
Credit cards: Most major cards
Restrictions: No pets, smoking. Deposit req. 14-day cancellation notice req. less $10.00 fee. 2-night min. stay on wknds. and fall foliage season.
Notes: Three-story Queen Anne Victorian inn with turret and Carriage House built in 1898. Located on hilltop overlooking Manchester. Living room, wicker room, game room with billiards and table tennis. Front porch with hammock and rocking chairs. Outdoor swimming pool. French, German spoken. Resident cat.*

MANCHESTER HIGHLANDS INN

MANCHESTER CENTER (5)

The Inn at Ormsby Hill
Rte. 7A, RR2, Box 3264, Manchester Center, VT 05255
(802) 362-1163

Innkeeper: Nancy and Don Burd
Rooms: 4 w/pvt. bath, incl. 3 w/fireplace, plus 1 suite w/pvt. bath, fireplace
Rates: $95-$145/room, $145-$160/suite, all incl. expanded cont. brk., afternoon refreshment. Seasonal variations.
Credit cards: Most major cards
Restrictions: No children under 10, pets, smoking. One night's deposit req. 14-day cancellation notice req., less 10% fee. 2-night min. stay on most wknds.
Notes: Three-story manor house with hand-tooled staircases and woodwork, built in the late 1700s. Located on 2.5 acres overlooking the Green Mountains. Parlor,

dining room, conservatory, library, each with fireplace. Furnished with family antiques. Lawn games available. Innkeepers collect rare books.*

River Meadow Farm
P.O. Box 822, Manchester Center, VT 05255
(802) 362-1602, (802) 362-3700
Innkeeper: Patricia Dupree
Rooms: 5, no pvt. bath
Rates: $50, incl. full brk.
Credit cards: None
Restrictions: No pets, smoking. $25.00 deposit req. Prefer 2-night min. stay.
Notes: Farmhouse built circa 1800. Fully remodeled. Operated as Manchester "Poor Farm" from 1829 to 1945. Located on seventy acres. Kitchen with brick fireplace. Dining room. Den with TV. Living room with baby grand piano. Glassed and screen porch. Resident horses and cows.

Seth Warner Inn
Historic Rt. 7A, Box 281, Manchester Center, VT 05255
(802) 362-3830
Innkeeper: Stasia and Lee Tetreault
Rooms: 5 w/pvt. bath
Rates: $80-$95, incl. full brk., afternoon and evening refreshment
Credit cards: MC, V
Restrictions: No children under 12, pets, smoking. One night's deposit req. 14-day cancellation notice req., less 10% fee. 2-night min. stay on wknds. 3-night min. stay on holiday wknds.
Notes: Colonial inn with open beams, stenciling, built in 1800. Fully restored. Located between two mountain ranges. Parlor, library. Furnished with antiques. Pond, gardens. Polish spoken.*

MANCHESTER VILLAGE (5)

1811 House
Rt. 7A, Box 39, Manchester Village, VT 05254-0039
(802) 362-1811, (800) 432-1811, (802) 362-2443
Innkeeper: Bruce and Marnie Duff
Rooms: 13 w/pvt. bath, incl. 5 w/fireplace, plus 1 suite w/pvt. bath, fireplace. Located in 2 bldgs.
Rates: $110-$180/room, $180/suite, incl. full brk. Seasonal variations. Discount avail. for mid-week stay.
Credit cards: Most major cards
Restrictions: No children under 16, pets. Smoking restricted. Deposit req. 14-day cancellation notice req., less $20.00. 2-night min. stay during fall foliage season, holidays, and wknds. Closed 3 days at Christmas.
Notes: Two-story built in the 1770s and restored to the Federal period of the 1800s. Located on over seven acres of lawns with flower gardens. Has operated as inn since 1811. Sitting room, dining room, lounge, all with fireplaces. Decorated with English and American antiques, Oriental rugs.*

The Battenkill Inn
P.O. Box 948, Manchester Village, VT 05254
(800) 441-1628

THE BATTENKILL INN

Innkeeper: Ramsay and Mary Jo Gourd
Rooms: 10 w/pvt. bath, incl. 4 w/fireplace
Rates: $75-$130, incl. full brk., evening refreshment. Seasonal variations. Special
  pkgs. avail.
Credit cards: Most major cards
Restrictions: No pets, smoking. One night's deposit req. 14-day cancellation notice
  req., less $10.00 fee.
Notes: Two-story Victorian farmhouse with high ceilings, built in the 1840s. Lo-
cated on the Battenkill River at the base of Mount Equinox. Two dining rooms. Two
sitting rooms with fireplaces. Furnished with antiques. Pond with ducks, fishing.
Lawn games available. Handicapped access.

MENDON (3)

Red Clover Inn
RR 2, Box 7450, Woodward Rd., Mendon, VT 05701
(800) 752-0571, (802) 773-0594

Innkeeper: Sue and Harris Zuckerman
Rooms: 9 w/pvt. bath, incl. 2 w/TV, 2 w/whirlpool tubs, plus 3 suites w/pvt. bath,
  incl. 1 w/fireplace. Located in 2 bldgs.
Rates: $120-$225, incl. full brk., evening refreshment, dinner. Seasonal variations.
  Discount avail. for mid-week stay.

RED CLOVER INN

Credit cards: MC, V

Restrictions: No children under 8, smoking. Pets restricted. Deposit req. 14-day cancellation notice req., less $10.00 fee. 2-night min. stay on wknds. 3-night min. stay on holiday wknds.

Notes: Two-story farmhouse and carriage house built in 1840. Located on 13 acres of lawns and pasture. Decorated in country-style with antiques. 3 dining rooms, 2 with fireplaces. Common room with exposed wood beams, fireplace, TV, books, games. Pub, billiard room. Swimming pool. Pond, shade trees. Barn with horse, goat, cat. Resident dog.*

MIDDLEBURY (3)

BROOKSIDE MEADOWS

Brookside Meadows
R.D. 3, Box 2460, Middlebury, VT 05753
(802) 388-6429

Innkeeper: Linda and Robert Cole

Rooms: 3 w/pvt. bath, plus 1 suite w/pvt. bath, 2-bedrooms, living room, wood stove, dining area, kithcen, pvt. entrance, TV. Located in 2 bldgs.

Rates: $75-$85/room, $90-$100/suite, all incl. cont. brk.

Credit cards: MC, V

Restrictions: No children under 10, pets, smoking. Deposit req. 2-week cancellation notice req., less $15.00 fee.

Notes: Built in 1979. Located on 20 acres bordering the 'Muddy Branch' brook. Located 3 miles from Middlebury College. Patio with lawn chairs. Cross-country skiing, hiking on property. Resident goats, fowl, pigs, sheep, geese, dogs, and cats.*

MONTPELIER (4)

Betsy's Bed and Breakfast
74 E. State St., Montpelier, VT 05602
(802) 229-0466, (802) 229-0466

Innkeeper: Jon and Betsy Anderson

Rooms: 3 w/pvt. bath, phone, TV, plus 1 suite w/pvt. bath, phone, TV, kitchen. Located in 2 bldgs.
Rates: $45-$75/room, $85-$105/suite, all incl. full brk. Seasonal variations. Discount avail. for extended stay.
Credit cards: MC, V
Restrictions: No pets, smoking. One night's deposit req. 3-day cancellation notice req.
Notes: Three-story Queen Anne Victorian house with located in historic district. Dining room, formal parlor with fireplace. Exercise room. Furnished with antiques. Front porch with rockers. Adirondack chairs under apple tree. Outdoor hot tub. Perennial garden. FAX machine available.*

MORETOWN (4)

Camel's Hump View Inn
P.O. Box 720, Moretown, VT 05660
(802) 496-3614

Innkeeper: Wilma and Jerry Maynard
Rooms: 7 w/pvt. bath, plus 1 suite w/pvt. bath
Rates: $25-$35, incl. full brk. Special pkgs. avail.
Credit cards: Most major cards
Restrictions: No pets, smoking. 50% deposit req. 14-day cancellation notice req.
Notes: Farmhouse built in 1831. Renovated in 1958. Common room, game room. Furnished with antiques, braided rugs. Fruit, vegetable gardens. All meals available.

NORTH HERO (1)

Charlie's Northland Lodge
U.S. Rte. 2, Box 88, North Hero, VT 05474
(802) 372-8822

Innkeeper: Charles and Dorice Clark
Rooms: 3, no pvt. bath
Rates: $45-$50, incl. cont. brk.
Credit cards: Most major cards
Rooms: No children under 5, pets, smoking. Deposit req. 7-day cancellation notice req.
Notes: Guest parlor. Front porch overlooking Lake Champlain. Furnished with country antiques. Guests have access to kitchen. Sport and giftshop on premises with boat and motor rentals.

NORTHFIELD (4)

Long Way Inn
Rabbit Hollow Rd., Box 230, Northfield, VT 05663
(802) 485-3559, (802) 485-3474

Innkeeper: Allen and Ginnie Kelly
Rooms: 5 w/TV, incl. 3 w/pvt. bath
Rates: $1,000.00 for 3-night pkg. Additional nights are $300.00 each. Discount avail. for extended stay, returning guests.
Credit cards: Most major cards
Restrictions: Smoking restricted. One night's deposit req. 14-day cancellation notice req. 3-night min. stay.

Notes: Three-story inn. Kitchen. Living/meeting room with library. Greenhouses, spa, decks, porches, barbeque, and lawn.

The Northfield Inn
27 Highland Ave., Northfield, VT 05663
(802) 485-8558
Innkeeper: Aglaia and Alan Stalb
Rooms: 6 plus 2 suites, all w/pvt. bath, phone
Rates: $85/room, $130/suite, all incl. full brk. Discount avail. for extended stay.
Credit cards: MC, V
Restrictions: No children under 15, pets. Smoking restricted. One night's deposit req. 14-day cancellation notice req., less 20% fee.
Notes: Two-story house built at the turn of the century. Restored in Victorian style. Decorated in period furnishings. Formal dining room with fireplace. Library, parlor, game room. Porch with rockers. Outdoor activities available. Small private parties accommodated. Greek spoken.

NORTHFIELD FALLS (4)

Four Bridges Inn
School St., Box 117, Northfield Falls, VT 05664-0117
(802) 485-8995
Innkeeper: Sue and John Fisher
Rooms: 2, w/pvt. bath
Rates: $65, incl. full brk.
Credit cards: MC, V
Restrictions: Smoking restricted. One night's deposit req. 14-day cancellation notice req. 2-night min. stay at graduation time and for quilt festival.
Notes: Victorian house built in 1896. Restored in 1992. Dining room. Furnished with antiques. Gardens.*

ORLEANS (2)

Valley House Inn
4 Memorial Square, Orleans, VT 05860
(802) 754-6665, (800) 545-9711
Innkeeper: David and Louise Bolduc
Rooms: 20, w/TV
Rates: $35-$70. Discount avail. for extended stay.
Credit cards: Most major cards
Restrictions: Deposit req. 3-day cancellation notice req.
Notes: Two-story building built in the 1875. French spoken.*

ORWELL (3)

Historic Brookside Farms
Rte. 22A, Box 36, Orwell, VT 05760
(802) 948-2727, (802) 948-2015
Innkeeper: Joan and Murray Korda
Rooms: 5, incl. 2 w/pvt. bath, plus 1 suite w/pvt. bath. Located in 2 bldgs.
Rates: $85-$135/room, $150/suite, all incl. full brk. Discount avail. for senior citizens.
Credit cards: None

Restrictions: No pets. Smoking restricted. One night's deposit req. 14-day cancellation notice req., less $25.00 fee.
Notes: Two-story Greek Revival mansion built in 1789, enlarged in 1843. Farmhouse built in 1810, converted to guesthouse. Located on 300-acre working farm. Library with 10,000 volumes. Den with TV, board games. Dining room. Common room/family dining room. Listed on the National Register of Historic Places. All meals available. Innkeeper is a concert violinist. Maple syrup produced on premises. Antique shop. Some French, Spanish, German, Italian, Russian, Hungarian, Hebrew, Danish spoken. Resident farm animals.*

PERKINSVILLE (5)

THE INN AT WEATHERSFIELD

The Inn at Weathersfield
Rte. 106, Box 165, Perkinsville, VT 05151
(802) 263-9217, (800) 477-4828, (802) 263-9219
Innkeeper: Mary Louise and Ron Thorburn
Rooms: 9 plus 3 suites, all w/pvt. bath, incl. 9 w/fireplace
Rates: $180/room, $190-$210/suite, all incl. full brk., afternoon refreshment, dinner. Discount avail. for mid-week and extended stays.
Credit cards: Most major cards
Restrictions: No children under 8, pets. Smoking restricted. One night's deposit req. 14-day cancellation notice req., less $5.00 fee. 2-night min. stay on wknds. 3-night min. stay on holidays.
Notes: Original farmhouse built in the 1790s. Has operated as stagecoach stop, and in Underground Railroad during Civil War. Has operated as inn since 1961. 4,000-volume library. Dining room in carriage house with duo grand pianists. Parlor, keeping room, southern Colonial porch. Furnished with antiques, period reproductions. Horse-drawn sleigh and wagon rides, bicycles available. Special meals prepared in the 1795 open-hearth and beehive bake oven. Grounds include pond, recreation field, lawn games, sauna. Small private parties accommodated. German spoken.*

PERU (5)

THE WILEY INN

The Wiley Inn
1 Rte. 11, Box 37, Peru, VT 05152
(802) 824-6600

Innkeeper: Judy and Jerry Goodman
Rooms: 8 w/pvt. bath, incl. 1 w/fireplace, 1 w/TV, plus 8 suites w/pvt. bath, 1
 w/fireplace.
Rates: $75-$135/room, $150-$425 suite, all incl. full brk. Discount avail. for mid-
 week stay. Seasonal variations.
Credit cards: AE, V
Restrictions: No pets, smoking. 50% deposit req. 14-day cancellation notice req.,
 less 10% fee. 2-night min. stay on wknds. 3-night min. stay on holidays.
Notes: Main house built in 1835. Has served as stagecoach stop, farmhouse, and tea
 room. Renovated in 1989. Has operated as inn since 1943. Dining room with fireplace. Game room with TV and fireplace. Heated swimming Pool and ponds. Handicapped access.*

POULTNEY (3)

Lake St. Catherine Inn
Cones Point Rd., Box 129AM, Poultney, VT 05764
(802) 287-9347, (800) 626-5724

Innkeeper: Patricia and Raymond Endlich
Rooms: 35 w/pvt. bath. Located in 2 bldgs.
Rates: $148-$168/room, $825/wk for housekeeping cottage, all incl. full brk., din-
 ner. Special pkgs. avail. Seasonal variations.
Credit cards: None
Restrictions: No pets. Smoking restricted. $100 deposit req. 14-day cancellation no-
 tice req., less 15% fee. 2-night min. stay on holidays and peak periods. Closed
 mid-Oct–mid-May.
Notes: Built as inn on lake shore in 1932. Library, lounge. Lobby with wood stove,
 player piano, telephone, TV. Dining room. Furnished in country style. Sun deck
 overlooking lake, floating raft. Lawn games, docking space, boats, canoes, motors,
 bicycles available. Fishing licenses may be obtained at the inn. Bicycle tours organized. Handicapped access.*

PROCTORSVILLE (5)

The Depot Corner Inn and Restaurant
Rte. 131, Depot St., Box 78, Proctorsville, VT 05153
(802) 226-7970
Innkeeper: John and Deborah Davis
Rooms: 9 plus 2 suites, some w/pvt. bath
Rates: $75-$100, incl. full brk. Seasonal variations. Discount avail. for mid-week stay.
   Special pkgs. avail.
Credit cards: Most major cards
Restrictions: No children under 5, pets. Smoking restricted. Deposit req. 14-day
   cancellation notice req.
Notes: Built in the 1840s. Wrap-around porch. Library w/board games. Furnished
with period antiques. Cooking classes, boxed lunches, picnics available. Small private parties accommodated.*

Okemo Lantern Lodge
Main St., Box 247, Proctorsville, VT 05153
(802) 226-7770
Innkeeper: Dody Button
Rooms: 10 w/pvt. bath
Rates: $90, incl. full brk. Discount avail. for mid-week stay. Special pkgs. avail.
Credit cards: Most major cards
Restrictions: No pets, smoking. 50% deposit req. 15-day cancellation notice req.,
   less 10% fee. Closed April, Nov., Dec. 1–26.
Notes: Three-story Victorian house with natural butternut woodwork, winding
staircase and stained-glass windows built in the early 1800s. Living room with fireplace, bay window. Dining room, wrap-around porch. Furnished with antiques, wicker furniture. Heated outdoor swimming pool from May through September. Ride in rumble seat of 1935 Plymouth. French spoken.

QUECHEE (4)

Parker House
16 Main St., Quechee, VT 05059
(802) 295-6077
Innkeeper: Walt and Barbara Forrester
Rooms: 4 w/pvt. bath
Rates: $90-$125, incl. full brk.
Credit cards: MC, V
Restrictions: No children under 12, pets. Smoking restricted. Min. one night's deposit req. 10-day cancellation notice req. Closed April.
Notes: Two-story Victorian brick mansion built in 1857 by state senator. Fully restored in the 1970s and 1980s. 2 dining rooms, lounge, common room, balcony overlooking the Ottauquechee River. Guests have access to full club privileges at the Quechee Club, including golf courses, skiing, tennis, swimming and fitness center. Restaurant on premises. Gourmet dinners available. Innkeepers are graduates of the Culinary Institute of America. Small private parties accommodated. Registered as a National Historic Site.

Quechee Inn at Marshland Farm
Clubhouse Rd., Quechee, VT 05059
(802) 295-3133, (802) 295-6587

Innkeeper: Hal Lothrop
Rooms: 22 plus 2 suites w/pvt. bath, TV
Rates: $108-$188/room, $148-$208/suite, incl. full brk.
Credit cards: Most major cards
Restrictions: No children under 12, pets. Smoking restricted. Deposit req. 14-day
   cancellation notice req., less $10.00 fee. Min. 2-night stay on wknds.
Notes: Built in 1793. Restored in the mid-1970s. Lounge with fireplace, canopied
porch overlooking river, living room, library, dining room, 3 meeting rooms. Furnished with Queen Anne-style furniture. Cross-country skiing learning center and
fly-fishing school on premises. Bicycle and canoe rentals available. Guests have access to Quechee Club with swimming pools, tennis and squash courts, golf course.*

READING (5)

Bailey's Mills B&B
Bailey's Mills Rd., Reading, VT 05062
(802) 484-7809, (800) 639-3437
Innkeeper: Barbara Thaeder
Rooms: 2 w/pvt. bath, fireplace, plus 1 suite w/pvt. bath
Rates: $65-$75/room, $85-$95/suite, all incl. cont. brk. Seasonal variations.
Credit cards: MC, V
Restrictions: No smoking. 50% deposit req. 14-day cancellation notice req., less
   $10.00 fee. 2-night min. stay during fall foliage season.
Notes: Two-story house with 11 fireplaces with 2 original beehive ovens, built in the
early 1800s. Double deck front porch. Former general store, ballroom, dining room
with colonial style hearth, parlor, library, sunporch, pond.*

RIPTON (3)

The Chipman Inn
Rte. 125, Box 115, Ripton, VT 05766
(802) 388-2390
Innkeeper: Joyce Henderson, Bill Pierce
Rooms: 9 w/pvt. bath
Rates: $80-$100, incl. full brk. Seasonal variations.
Credit cards: Most major cards
Restrictions: No children, pets. Smoking restricted. Min. $40.00 deposit req. 2-night
   min. stay on wknds.
Notes: Built in 1828. Located on five mountain acres overlooking Middlebury. Sitting room/bar with Franklin fireplace. Dining room with fireplace, colonial stenciling. Reading room. Furnished with early American antiques. Dinners available.
French spoken.

ROCHESTER (3)

Liberty Hill Farm
RR 1, Box 158, Rochester, VT 05767
(802) 767-3926
Innkeeper: Bob and Beth Kennett
Rooms: 7, no pvt. bath
Rates: $100, incl. full brk., dinner
Credit cards: None

Restrictions: No pets, smoking. One night's deposit req. 14-day cancellation notice req.

Notes: Two-story farmhouse built in the 1820s. Located on 100-acre working dairy farm between White River and Green Mountain National Forest. Dining room. Living room with fireplace, butternut moldings. Kitchen. Swimming hole, hayloft. Herd of holsteins, farm animals. Guests are welcome to help with the farm chores.*

ROXBURY (4)

Inn at Johnnycake Flats
RFD 1, Carrie Howe Rd., Roxbury, VT 05669
(802) 485-8961
Innkeeper: Debra and Jim Rogler
Rooms: 3, incl. 1 w/pvt. bath. Suite avail.
Rates: $55-$65, incl. full brk., afternoon refreshment
Credit cards: Most major cards
Restrictions: Pets restricted. No smoking. 50% deposit req., refunded upon cancellation only if room re-rented.
Notes: Two-story stagecoach stop built in the 1880s. Fully restored. Has operated as inn since 1988. Furnished with family antiques. Gardens.

RUTLAND (3)

The Inn at Rutland
70 N. Main St., Rutland, VT 05701
(802) 773-0575, (802) 773-0699
Innkeeper: Bob and Tanya Liberman
Rooms: 7 w/pvt. bath, phone, TV, plus 3 suites w/pvt. bath, phone, TV
Rates: $65-$95/room, $110-$135/suite, all incl. expanded cont. brk. Discount avail. for group, corporate stays.
Credit cards: Most major cards
Restrictions: No children under 8, pets, smoking. 50% deposit req. 14-day cancellation notice req. 3-night min. stay on holiday wknds.
Notes: Two-story Victorian mansion built in 1890. Fully renovated. Two common rooms with fireplace, TV, video games. Leather wainscoting, leaded-glass window. Furnished with antiques.Porch. Carriage house available for storage. Small private parties accommodated. Russian spoken.*

SHELBURNE (1)

The Inn at Shelburne Farms
Shelburne Farms, Shelburne, VT 05482
(802) 985-8498, (802) 985-8123
Innkeeper: Kevin O'Donnell, Director
Rooms: 24 w/phone, incl. 17 w/pvt. bath
Rates: $85-$250
Credit cards: Most major cards
Restrictions: No pets. Smoking restricted. Deposit req. 15-day cancellation notice req., less $25.00 fee. 2-night min. stay on wknds. Closed mid-Oct.–mid-May.
Notes: English castle with turrets and gables built by heirs to the Vanderbilt fortune in 1899. Located on 1,000-acre farm on Lake Champlain. Landscaped gardens, lily pond with fountain. Renovated in and has operated as inn since 1986. Tea Room. Jacobean-designed Grand Foyer with marble fireplace. Dining room with marble

floors, carved ceilings, French doors overlooking Lake Champlain. Game room with pool table, board games. Library with fireplace. Furnished in period style with antiques. Listed on the National Register of Historic Places.

SPRINGFIELD (5)

HARTNESS HOUSE INN

Hartness House Inn
30 Orchard St., Springfield, VT 05156
(802) 885-2115, (802) 885-2207
Innkeeper: Eileen Gennette-Coughlin
Rooms: 40, incl. 2 suites, all w/pvt. bath, phone, cable TV. Located in 3 bldgs.
Rates: $69-$89/room, $111-$125/suite. Seasonal variations. Special pkgs. avail.
Credit cards: Most major cards
Restrictions: No pets. Smoking restricted. Min. one night's deposit req. 7-day cancellation notice req., less $10.00 fee.
Notes: Three-story mansion built in 1903. Reception room, lobby, living room, each with fireplace. Three dining rooms, music room, cocktail lounge. Deck overlooking swimming pool, gardens. Furnished with period antiques, Oriental rugs, fine artwork. Astronomy museum and 600-power telescope on premises. Listed on the National Register of Historic Places.

STOWE (1)

The Brass Lantern Inn
717 Maple St., Stowe, VT 05672
(802) 253-2229, (800) 729-2980, (802) 253-7425
Innkeeper: Andy Aldrich
Rooms: 9 w/pvt. bath, incl. 3 w/fireplace. TV avail.
Rates: $70-$150, incl. full brk., afternoon refreshment. Seasonal variations. Discount avail. for extended stay. Special pkgs. avail.
Credit cards: Most major cards
Restrictions: No pets, smoking. Deposit req. 15-day cancellation notice req., less $10.00 fee.
Notes: Two-story farmhouse with plank floors and carriage barn built in the early 1800s. Fully restored. Living room with fireplace. Dining room. Patio overlooking

mountains. Furnished with antiques, handmade quilts. Recipient of Northern Vermont Home Builders Association award.*

THE BRASS LANTERN INN

Fitch Hill Inn
RFD 1, Box 1879, Stowe, VT 05655
(802) 888-3834, (800) 639-2903
Innkeeper: Richard Pugliese
Rooms: 5 w/pvt. bath, incl. 1 w/TV, plus 1 suite w/pvt. bath, phone, TV
Rates: $50-$73/room, $105/suite, all incl. full brk., evening refreshment. Discount avail. for extended, senior citizen, AAA stays. Special pkgs. avail. Seasonal variations.
Credit cards: Most major cards
Restrictions: No children under 5, pets, smoking. One night's deposit req. 14-day cancellation notice req. 2-night min. stay on Christmas week and Presidents week.
Notes: Three-story Colonial farmhouse built in 1797. Located on four wooded acres. Country dining room. Family room with library, piano, cable TV. Furnished with antiques. Small private parties accommodated. All meals available. Spanish and French spoken.*

Guest House
4583 Mountain Rd., Box 1635, Stowe, VT 05672
(802) 253-4846, (800) 821-7891
Innkeeper: Christel and James Horman
Rooms: 8 w/pvt. bath
Rates: $60-$76, incl. full brk, afternoon refreshment in winter. Seasonal variations. Discount avail. for extended stay.
Credit cards: MC, V
Restrictions: No children under 10, pets, smoking. Min. one night's deposit req. 15-day cancellation notice req. 3-night min. stay on holiday wknds.. Closed April, Nov. 1–14.

Notes: Two-story Swiss-style chalet built in 1980. Located on five acres. Living room with cable TV, VCR, hearthstone fireplace, books. Outdoor swimming pool. BBQ available. German spoken.*

The Siebeness Inn
3681 Mountain Rd., Stowe, VT 05672
(802) 253-8942, (800) 426-9001, (802) 253-9232

Innkeeper: Sue and Nils Andersen
Rooms: 11 w/pvt. bath, incl. 2 w/TV, plus 1 cottage
Rates: $60-$95, incl. full brk., fall and winter dinner, $120-$200/cottage. Seasonal variations. Discount avail. for extended and mid-week stays. Special pkgs. avail.
Credit cards: Most major cards
Restrictions: No pets, smoking. One night's deposit req. 15-day cancellation notice req.
Notes: Two-story country inn built in 1952. Fully renovated in 1986. Lounge with fieldstone fireplace, library, *bring your own* bar. Dining room overlooking Mount Mansfield. TV room with VCR, board games. Game room with ping-pong. Rooms individually decorated with antiques, Laura Ashley country prints, handmade quilts, stenciling. Outdoor swimming pool, hot tub. Small private parties accommodated. Resident dog.*

THE SIEBENESS INN

Ski Inn
Rte. 108, Stowe, VT 05672
(802) 253-4050

Innkeeper: Harriet Heyer
Rooms: 10 w/TV, incl. 5 w/pvt. bath
Rates: $40-$60, incl. cont. brk. Special winter pkgs. avail.
Credit cards: Most major cards
Restrictions: Children, pets restricted. No smoking. Deposit may be req.
Notes: Two-story Colonial-style lodge built in 1940s. Located on twenty-eight acres of woodlands with brook. Dining room. Living room with fieldstone fireplace. Designed along New England architectural lines.*

Timberholm Inn
Cottage Club Rd., Box 810, Stowe, VT 05672
(802) 253-7603, (802) 253-8559
Innkeeper: Louise and Pete Hunter
Rooms: 10 plus 2 suites, all w/pvt. bath, suites w/TV
Rates: $50-$100/room, $90-$120/suite, incl. full brk., afternoon refreshment. Discount avail. for extended and mid-week stays. Seasonal variations.
Credit cards: MC, V
Restrictions: No pets. Smoking restricted. One night's deposit req. 15-day cancellation notice req. 5-night min. stay during Christmas week.
Notes: Two-story country inn built in 1949. Flower gardens. Great room with fieldstone fireplace. Game room. Furnished with antiques, artwork.*

TOWNSHEND (5)

Boardman House B & B
On the Green, Townshend, VT 05353
(802) 365-4086
Innkeeper: Sarah Messenger, Paul Weber
Rooms: 5 plus 1 suite, incl. all w/pvt. bath, suite w/TV
Rates: $65-$80/room, $90-$110/suite, all incl. full brk. Discount avail. for senior citizens. Seasonal variations.
Credit cards: None
Restrictions: Pets, smoking restricted.
Notes: Two-story house built in 1840 located on one acre. Living room, sitting room. Sauna, pool table, board and lawn games available.*

VERGENNES (1)

STRONG HOUSE INN

Strong House Inn
88 W. Main St., Vergennes, VT 05491
(802) 877-3337
Innkeeper: Mary and Hugh Bargiel

Rooms: 5, incl. 3 /pvt. bath, 1 w/phne, 2 w/fireplace, plus 2 suites w/pvt. bath, TV, incl. 1 w/phone, 1 w/fireplace

Rates: $65-$120/room, $110-$140/suite, all incl. full brk., evening refreshment. Seasonal variations.

Credit cards: Most major cards

Restrictions: No children under 10, pets, smoking. Deposit req. 14-day cancellation notice req.

Notes: Two-story Federal-style house with Greek Revival influences, free-standing main staircase with curly maple railings, formal fireplace, mouldings, built in 1834. Located on slight ridge with views of mountains. Has operated as inn since 1984. Parlor with fireplace. Furnished with antiques. All meals available. Listed on National Register of Historic Places.*

WAITSFIELD (1)

Lareau Farm Country Inn
P.O. Box 563, Waitsfield, VT 05673
(802) 496-4949, (800) 833-0766

Innkeeper: Dan and Sue Easley

Rooms: 12 plus 1 suite, most w/pvt. bath

Rates: $60-$100/room, $85-$125/suite, all incl. full brk. Discount avail. for midweek and extended stays. Seasonal variations.

Credit cards: MC, V

Restrictions: No pets. Smoking restricted. Deposit req. 21-day cancellation notice req.

Notes: Dairy farmhouse built about 1794. Dining room, 2 sitting rooms. Back porches. Furnished with antiques. Resident horses.*

Mad River Barn
Route 17, Box 88, Waitsfield, VT 05673
(802) 496-3310

Innkeeper: Betsy Pratt

Rooms: 15 w/pvt. bath, phone, incl. 8 w/cable TV. Located in 2 bldgs.

Rates: $50-$96, incl. full brk. Seasonal variations.

Credit cards: MC, V

Restrictions: No pets. Smoking restricted.

Notes: Located adjacent to 1,500 private acres. Has operated as inn since 1948. Game parlor, lounge with stone fireplace. Swimming pool uniquely located in quiet meadow. Full-service ski lodge in winter.*

Mad River Inn B & B
Tremblay Rd, Box 75, Waitsfield, VT 05673
(802) 496-7900, (800) 832-8278

Innkeeper: Luc and Rita Maranda

Rooms: 9 w/pvt. bath

Rates: $69-$125, incl. afternoon refreshment. Discount avail. for mid-week, airline, AAA, senior citizen stays. Seasonal variations.

Credit cards: Most major cards

Restrictions: No pets. Smoking restricted. 50% deposit req., 45-day cancellation notice req., less $25.00 fee. 4-night min. stay during Christmas.

Notes: Country Victorian built in the 1860s. Located along the Madison River. Porches, gardens, gazebo. Apres ski lounge with billiard table. Kids playroom, family room with toys, TV, VCR, music, games. Jacuzzi. French spoken.*

MAD RIVER INN B & B

Millbrook Inn
RFD Box 62, Waitsfield, VT 05673
(802) 496-2405

Innkeeper: Joan and Thom Gorman
Rooms: 7, incl. 4 w/pvt. bath
Rates: $80-$140, incl. full brk., dinner. Seasonal variations. Discount avail. for midweek stay.
Credit cards: Most major cards
Restrictions: No children under 5, smoking. Pets restricted. 50% deposit req. 3-week written cancellation notice req. 2-night min. stay on fall and winter wknds. 3-night min. stay on holiday wknds.
Notes: Two-story Cape Cod-style farmhouse built in 1850s. Warming room with antique Glenwood Parlor stove. Living room with fireplace, board games. Restaurant

MILLBROOK INN

on premises. 2 dining rooms, 1 with fireplace. Decorated with period furnishings. Yard with hammock, vegetable and herb gardens. Some French spoken.

Newtons' 1824 House Inn
Route 100, Box 159, Waitsfield, VT 05673
(802) 496-7555, (800) 426-3986, (802) 496-7558

Innkeeper: Nick and Joyce Newton
Rooms: 5 w/pvt. bath, phone, plus 1 suite w/pvt. bath, phone
Rates: $75-$125/room, $100-$115/suite, incl. full brk., afternoon refreshment. Seasonal variations. Discount avail. for mid-week stay.
Credit cards: Most major cards
Restrictions: No children under 8, pets, smoking. Deposit req. 14-day cancellation notice req. 2-night min. stay, wknds. 3-night min. stay, holidays.
Notes: Two-story, gabled, white-clapboard Victorian farmhouse built in 1824. Located on fifty-two acres along the Mad River. Renovated in and has operated as inn since 1989. Library with TV, VCR. Parlor with piano, fireplace. Drawing room, dining room each with fireplace. Furnished with English antiques, Oriental rugs, fine art. Swimming hole, cross-country ski trails. Horse pasturing available. Spanish spoken.*

NEWTONS' 1824 HOUSE INN

Valley Inn
Rt. 100, Box 8, Waitsfield, VT 05673
(802) 496-3450, (800) 638-8466

Innkeeper: Bill and Millie Stinson
Rooms: 20 w/pvt. bath
Rates: $69-$79, incl. full brk. Discount avail. for senior citizens. Seasonal variations.
Credit cards: Most major cards
Restrictions: No pets, smoking. 50% deposit req. 21-day cancellation notice req., less $25.00 fee. 3-night min. stay on holiday wknds.
Notes: Two-story Austrian-style inn built in 1949. Living room with fireplace. Lone Eagle Pub and game room. Cedar sauna. Decorated with hand stenciling, New England furnishings. Outdoor hot tub. Handicapped access.*

WALLINGFORD (5)

White Rocks Inn
RR1, Box 297, Wallingford, VT 05773
(802) 446-2077

VALLEY INN

Innkeeper: June and Alfred Matthews
Rooms: 5 w/pvt. bath, plus 1 cottage w/pvt. bath, whirlpool, kitchen
Rates: $75-$95, incl. full brk. Seasonal variations. Special pkgs. avail.
Credit cards: Most major cards
Restrictions: No children under 10, pets, smoking. 50% deposit req. 2-night min. stay on wknds., holidays and fall foliage season. Closed two weeks in April and all of Nov.
Notes: Two-story farmhouse and barn built in 1830. Located on river. Fully restored. Dining room with 18th-century English grandfather clock. Veranda overlooking Otter Creek. Furnished with antiques, Oriental rugs. Listed in National Register of Historic Places. Horses boarded. Spanish, French spoken.*

WARREN (4)

Beaver Pond Farm Inn
Golf Course Rd., Box 306, Warren, VT 05674
(802) 583-2861, (802) 583-2860

Innkeeper: Betty and Bob Hansen
Rooms: 6, incl. 4 w/pvt. bath
Rates: $72-$96, incl. full brk., afternoon refreshment. Discount avail. for mid-week stay. Special pkgs. avail.
Credit cards: Most major cards
Restrictions: No pets, smoking. 50% deposit req. 21-day cancellation notice req., less $25.00 fee. 2-night min. stay on wknds.
Notes: Two-story farmhouse built in 1860. Fully restored since 1977. Located adjacent to Robert Trent Jones golf course. Mountain views. Living room with fireplace. Deck. Furnished with antiques, handmade rugs. Dinner, available. French spoken. Listed on the Vermont Historic Buildings Register.*

The Sugartree
RR 1, Box 38, Sugarbush Access Rd., Warren, VT 05674
(800) 666-8907

Innkeeper: Frank and Kathy Partsch
Rooms: 7 w/pvt. bath, incl. 1 w/fireplace, plus 2 suites w/pvt. bath, incl. 1/fireplace
Rates: $80-$120/room, $90-$135/suite, all incl. full brk.
Credit cards: Most major cards

Restrictions: No children under 7, pets, smoking. Deposit req. 21-day cancellation notice req.

Notes: European-style salt box chalet. Has operated as inn since 1983. Living room with cable TV, fireplace. Furnished with handmade quilts, antiques, original art, custom stained-glass. Gardens, gazebo.*

West Hill House B and B
W. Hill Rd., RR 1, Box 292, Warren, VT 05674
(802) 496-7162
Innkeeper: Dotty Kyle and Eric Brattstrom
Rooms: 4 w/pvt. bath, incl. 1 w/TV
Rates: $85-$95 incl. full brk, afternoon refreshment. Discount avail. for mid-week, extended stays.
Credit cards: Most major cards
Restrictions: No children under 10, pets, smoking. 50% deposit req. 14-day cancellation notice req, less $20.00 fee. 2-night min. stay on wknds. 3-night min. stay on holiday wknds.
Notes: Two-story farmhouse built in 1860s. Located on 9 acres. Public room with books, VCR. Furnished with oriental rugs, art, antiques. Porch. Gardens, pond, apple orchards. Dinner available by reservation. Resident cat.*

WATERBURY (1)

INN AT BLUSH HILL

Inn at Blush Hill
P.O. Box 1266, R.R. 1, Waterbury, VT 05676
(802) 244-7529, (800) 736-7522, (802) 244-7314
Innkeeper: Pamela Gosselin
Rooms: 6, incl. 2 w/pvt. bath, 1 w/fireplace
Rates: $55-$90, incl. full brk., afternoon and evening refreshment. Seasonal variations. Discount avail. for extended stay. Special pkgs. avail.

Credit cards: Most major cards

Restrictions: No children under 7, pets, smoking. Deposit req. 14-day cancellation notice req. 2-night min. stay for some holidays, foliage wknds.

Notes: Cape Cod-style house built in 1790 as stagecoach stop. Located on 5.5 acres. Parlor with fireplace. Kitchen with double fireplace, bay window and view of Worcester Mountains. Library. Porch overlooking gardens, lawns. Furnished in eclectic style with Colonial antiques.*

The Old Stagecoach Inn
18 N. Main St., Waterbury, VT 05676
(802) 244-5056

Innkeeper: John Barwick

Rooms: 7, incl. 4 w/pvt. bath, plus 3 suites w/pvt. bath, incl. 1 w/fireplace

Rates: $40-$85/room, $60-$85/suite, all incl. full brk. Seasonal variations. Discount avail. for extended, mid-week, and senior citizen stays.

Credit cards: Most major cards

Restrictions: No pets. Smoking restricted. One night's deposit req. 14-day cancellation notice req., less $10.00 fee. 2-night min. stay during peak season wknds.

Notes: Three-story Victorian building with oak woodwork, stained-glass windows, fireplaces, tapestry, built in 1826 as a stagecoach stop. Fully restored. Located in valley surrounded by lakes, rivers, mountains. Dining room with fireplace. Library with tin ceiling. Furnished with period antiques. German spoken.

THE OLD STAGECOACH INN

Thatcher Brook Inn
Route 100 N., Box 490, Waterbury, VT 05676
(802) 244-5911, (802) 244-1294

Innkeeper: Peter and Kelly Vartey

Rooms: 23 plus 1 suite, all w/pvt. bath, phone, incl. 4 w/fireplace. Located in 2 bldgs.

Rates: $75-$145/room, $89/suite, all incl. full brk.

Credit cards: Most major cards

Restrictions: No pets, smoking. Deposit req. on holidays. 10-day cancellation notice req., less $10.00 per night fee. 2-night min. stay during peak season.

Notes: Victorian mansion with hand-carved stairway, pocket doors built in 1899. Restored in 1989. Study with library, TV, VCR, board games. Lobby with window seat. Gazebo-style front porch. Gourmet restaurant, tavern with fireplace on premises. Decorated with Laura Ashley fabrics. Dinner available. Small private parties accommodated. Handicapped access. Listed on the Vermont Register of Historic Buildings.*

WEST CHARLESTON (2)

Hunt's Hideaway
RR 1, Box 570, West Charleston, VT 05872
(802) 895-4432, (802) 334-8322
Innkeeper: Pat Hunt
Rooms: 3, no pvt. bath
Rates: $25-$35, incl. full brk. Discount avail. for extended stay.
Credit cards: None
Restrictions: None
Notes: Modern split-level house located on 100 wooded acres with brook, pond, fields. Has operated as inn since 1981. Swimming pool. Guests have access to kitchen.

WEST DOVER (5)

Snow Den Inn
Rte. 100N, Box 625, West Dover, VT 05356
(802) 464-9355, 464-5852
Innkeeper: Andy Trautwein
Rooms: 8 w/pvt. bath, TV, incl. 5 w/fireplace
Rates: $95-$275, incl. full brk., afternoon refreshment. Discount avail. for senior citizen stay. Special pkgs. available. Seasonal variations.
Credit cards: Most major cards
Restrictions: No children under 10, pets, smoking. Min. one night's deposit req. Min. 14-day cancellation notice req., less $15.00 fee. 2-night min. stay on wknds. 3-night min. stay on holidays.
Notes: Victorian farmhouse built in 1885. Has operated as inn since 1952. Living room with fireplace. Sitting room with TV. Dining room. Porch. Furnished with antiques. Listed on the National Register of Historic Places.*

WEST GLOVER (2)

Rodgers Farm Vacation
RFD 3, Box 57, West Glover, VT 05875
(802) 525-6677
Innkeeper: Jim and Nancy Rodgers
Rooms: 5, no pvt. bath
Rates: $35-$45, incl. brk. Discount avail. for extended stay.
Credit cards: MC, V
Restrictions: pets, smoking. 25% deposit req. 14-day cancellation notice req.
Notes: Farmhouse built in the 1840s. Located on 350 acres. Living room with TV. Kitchen/dining area. Enclosed porch. Swingset, ping-pong table available. Resident small farm animals to hold and pet. French spoken.

WESTON (5)

The Colonial House
287 Rt. 100, Weston, VT 05161
(800) 639-5033, (802) 824-3934

Innkeeper: John and Betty Nunnikhoven
Rooms: 15, incl. 9 w/pvt. bath, cable TV. Motel rooms avail.
Rates: $50-$84, incl. full brk., afternoon refreshment. Discount avail. for senior citizen, extended, and mid-week stays. Seasonal variations.
Credit cards: Most major cards
Restrictions: No pets, smoking. One night's deposit req. 14-day cancellation notice req. Dinner not avail. Wed. & Sun.
Notes: Farmhouse built about 1790. Has operated as inn since 1970. Living room with beamed ceilings, wide plank floors, woodburning stove. Dining room. Solarium, game room. Limited handicapped access.

The Wilder Homestead Inn
25 Lawrence Hill Rd., RR 1, Box 106D, Weston, VT 05161
(802) 824-8172

Innkeeper: Peggy and Roy Varner
Rooms: 7, incl. 5 w/pvt. bath
Rates: $70-$95, incl. full brk. Seasonal variations.
Credit cards: MC, V
Restrictions: No children under 6, pets, smoking. One night's deposit req. 14-day cancellation notice req., less $10.00 per day fee. 2-night min. stay, Aug.–Nov. and winter wknds.
Notes: Three-story brick Greek Revival house with original Moses Eaton stenciling, built in 1827. Restored with sitting porch. Five common rooms, three with fireplace, one with player piano. Furnished with early American antiques and reproductions. Decorated with handmade quilts. Listed on the National Register of Historic Places.

WILDER (4)

Stonecrest Farm
119 Christian St., Wilder, VT 05088-0504
(802) 296-2425, (603) 448-6077

Innkeeper: Gail Sanderson
Rooms: 5 w/pvt. bath
Rates: $100-$120, incl. full brk., afternoon refreshment. Seasonal variations. Discount avail. for extended stay.
Credit cards: MC, V
Restrictions: No children under 8, pets, smoking. One night's deposit req. 2-week cancellation notice req., less $10.00 fee. 2-night min. stay on special Dartmouth College wknds.
Notes: Two-story house with terraces, built in 1810. Located on two wooded acres with red barns, gardens. Living room with baby grand piano, fireplace, game table, books, curved oak stairway. Furnished with antiques. Inn hosts an 'Inn to Inn' canoeing trip. German spoken.*

WILMINGTON (5)

The Inn at Quail Run
HCR 63, Box 28, Smith Rd., Wilmington, VT 05363
(802) 464-3362, (800) 343-7227

Innkeeper: Thomas, Marie and Molly Martin
Rooms: 13 w/pvt. bath, incl. 3 w/fireplace, 2 w/TV, plus 2 suites w/pvt. bath. Located in 2 bldgs.
Rates: $85-$125, incl. full brk., afternoon refreshment. Discount avail. for extended stay. Seasonal variations.
Credit cards: Most major cards
Restrictions: No pets, smoking. One night's deposit req. 14-day cancellation notice req., less $25.00 fee.
Notes: Two-story inn located on twelve acres. Living room with fireplace. Game and TV rooms, sauna, exercise room. BYOB lounge and refrigerator available. Furnished with antiques. Solar heated pool, clay tennis court, Grounds include 40 kilometers of XC ski trails.*

Shearer Hill Farm B & B
P.O. Box 1453, Wilmington, VT 05363
(802) 464-3253, (800) 437-3104

Innkeeper: Bill and Patti Pusey
Rooms: 4 w/pvt. bath, incl. 1 w/TV. Located in 2 bldgs.
Rates: $80, incl. full brk., afternoon refreshment. Seasonal variations.
Credit cards: MC, V
Restrictions: No pets, smoking. One-night's deposit req. 10-day cancellation notice req., less $10.00 fee.
Notes: Farmhouse built about 1794. Fully restored. Living room with TV, VCR. Library.

Trail's End Country Inn
Smith Rd., Wilmington, VT 05363
(802) 464-2727, (800) 859-2585

Innkeeper: Bill and Mary Kilburn
Rooms: 13 w/pvt bath, incl. 4 w/fireplace, TV, plus 2 suites w/pvt. bath, fireplace, TV
Rates: $90-$150/room, $140-170/suite, all incl. full brk, afternoon refreshment. Discount avail. for mid-week stay. Special pkgs. avail.
Credit cards: MC, V
Restrictions: No pets. One night's deposit req. 14-day cancellation notice req., less 10% fee. 2-night min. stay on wknds. 3-night min. stay during holidays.
Notes: Former ski lodge, with major sprucing-up in 1988. Located on ten acres. Two-story great room with cathedral ceiling, fifteen-foot fieldstone fireplace, floor-to-ceiling solar windows. Balcony TV room. Recreation room. Dining room with antique kerosene lamps, serving Saturday night dinners. Furnished with family heirlooms. Grounds include outdoor swimming pool, clay tennis court, fully-stocked trout pond and English flower gardens.

The White House
Rte. 9, Box 757, Wilmington, VT 05363
(802) 464-2135, (800) 541-2135, (802) 464-5222

Innkeeper: Robert Grinold
Rooms: 16 w/pvt. bath, incl. 8 w/fireplace, plus, 1 suite w/pvt bath, fireplace
Rates: $190/room, $240/suite, all incl. full brk., dinner. Discount avail. for extended stays. Special pkgs. avail. Seasonal variations.
Credit cards: Most major cards

Restrictions: No children under 10, pets. 50% deposit req. 14-day cancellation notice req, less 5% fee. 2-night min. stay on wknds. Surcharge for use of credit cards. 15% gratuity added to final bill.

Notes: Three-story Victorian mansion with 2-story terraces, crafted French doors, built in 1915. Surrounded by formal flower gardens. Entrance hall with fireplace. Living room with fireplace, board games, 3 dining rooms serving Continental cuisine. Lounge overlooking Green Mountains. Furnished with period antiques. Heated indoor swimming pool with sauna, whirlpool, tanning room, outdoor swimming pool, spa facilities. Cross-country touring center on premises. Handicapped access. Some French spoken.*

WINDSOR (5)

Juniper Hill Inn
R.R. 1, Box 79, Windsor, VT 05089
(802) 674-5273, (800) 359-2541

Innkeeper: Robert and Suzanne Pearl
Rooms: 16 w/pvt. bath., incl. 9 w/fireplace
Rates: $85-$125, incl. full brk., afternoon refreshment. Discount avail. for mid-week stay. Special pkgs. avail.
Credit cards: Most major cards
Restrictions: No children under 12, pets, smoking. Deposit req. 14-day cancellation notice req. 2-night min. stay on holidays and during fall foliage season. Closed late-Oct.–Dec. 15, April.
Notes: Colonial Revival mansion built in 1902. Fully restored. Located on fourteen wooded acres with perennial gardens overlooking Mount Ascutney. Great hall with oak paneling, fireplace. Library, parlors. Furnished with antiques. Swimming pool. Formal gardens. Dinner, bicycle rental available. Listed on the National Historic Register of Historic Places. Small private parties accommodated.*

JUNIPER HILL INN

WOODSTOCK (4)

Applebutter Inn
Happy Valley Rd., Woodstock, VT 05091
(802) 457-4158

Innkeeper: Beverlee and Andrew Cook
Rooms: 5, incl. 1 w/pvt. bath, 4 w/fireplace, plus 1 suite w/pvt. bath
Rates: $80, incl. full brk. Seasonal variations.
Credit cards: MC, V
Restrictions: No infants, pets. Smoking restricted. Deposit req. 10-day cancellation
notice req.
Notes: Two-story restored Federal house built in 1840 as a dairy farm. Located on
4 acres in Taftsville. Furnished in 18th-century antiques, Oriental rugs, period sten-
ciling. Common room with fireplace, VCR, games. Parlor with books. Historic barn.
Handicapped access.

Canterbury House
43 Pleasant St., Woodstock, VT 05091
(802) 457-3077

Innkeeper: Fred and Celeste Holden
Rooms: 8 w/pvt. bath, incl. 2 w/cable TV, 1 w/fireplace
Rates: $85-$135, incl. full brk., afternoon refreshment. Discount avail. for extended
and senior citizen stays.
Credit cards: Most major cards
Restrictions: No children under 7, pets, smoking. Deposit req. 14-day cancellation
notice req.
Notes: Three-story Victorian townhouse built in 1880. Fully restored. Furnished
with Victorian antiques. Swimming hole. Bicycles available.*

The Charleston House
21 Pleasant St., Woodstock, VT 05091
(802) 457-3843

Innkeeper: Bill and Barbara Hough
Rooms: 7 w/pvt. bath, phone, fireplace, incl. 1 w/cable TV
Rates: $110-$145, incl. full brk.
Credit cards: Most major cards
Restrictions: No pets, smoking. Children restricted. Deposit req. 14-day cancella-
tion notice req. 2-night min. stay in season.
Notes: Greek Revival brick townhouse built in 1835. Restored. Furnished with pe-
riod antiques, Oriental rugs. Listed in the National Register of Historic Places.*

Kedron Valley Inn
Rte. 106, Woodstock, VT 05071
(802) 457-1473, (802) 457-4469

Innkeeper: Max and Merrily Comins
Rooms: 25 w/pvt. bath, TV, incl. 12 w/fireplace, plus 2 suites w/pvt. bath, fireplace,
TV. Located in 3 bldgs.
Rates: $114-$153/room, $189/suite, all incl. full brk. Seasonal variations. Discount
avail. for mid-week stay.
Credit cards: Most major cards
Restrictions: One night's deposit req. 14-day cancellation notice req. 2-night min.
stay, July–Feb. wknds. Closed April and for 10 days prior to Thanksgiving.
Notes: Three-story brick and clapboard Federal-style inn built in 1822. Located on
fifteen acres with 1.5 acre private swimming lake with white sand beach. Has operated as inn since 1840. Living room, dining room, reception room, each with fireplace. Meeting room, front porch, dining patio. Furnished with antiques,
collectables. Restaurant on premises. Flower gardens. Small private parties accom-

modated. Innkeepers collect heirloom quilts and antique clothing. Resident dog, cats. Handicapped access.*

KEDRON VALLEY INN

The Village Inn of Woodstock
41 Pleasant St., Woodstock, VT 05091
(802) 457-1255

Innkeeper: Kevin and Anita Clark
Rooms: 8, incl. 6 w/pvt. bath, 1 w/fireplace
Rates: $70-$150, incl. full brk., afternoon refreshment. Seasonal variations. Special
   pkgs. avail.
Credit cards: Most major cards
Restrictions: No pets, smoking. 50% deposit req. 2-week cancellation notice req. 2-
   night min. stay on wknds. and during foliage season.
Notes: Three-story Victorian mansion with tin ceilings, beveled glass windows, orig-
inal fireplaces, oak wainscoting, and carriage house built in 1899. Fully restored. Sit-
ting room with cable TV. Dining room, front porch. Furnished in country style.
Formal Victorian gardens. Gourmet dinner available. French and Spanish spoken.

The Winslow House
38 Rte. 4 West, Woodstock, VT 05091
(802) 457-1820

Innkeeper: Paul and Linda Noiseux
Rooms: 1 plus 3 suites, all w/pvt. bath
Rates: $68/room, $75-$95/suite, all incl. full brk.
Credit cards: Most major cards
Restrictions: No smoking. One night's deposit req. 15-day cancellation notice req.
   2-night min. stay during Sept. and Oct. 4-night min. stay from Christmas to New
   Year's week.
Notes: Two-story farmhouse with wide-board pine floors built in 1872. Has operated
as inn since 1987. Dining room. Sitting room with piano, wide board pine floors,
hand-stenciled walls, Oriental rugs. Furnished with period antiques, handmade
rugs.*

The Woodstocker
61 River St., Woodstock, VT 05091
(802) 457-3896, (800) 457-3896

THE WOODSTOCKER

Innkeeper: Jerry and JaNoel Lowe
Rooms: 7 w/pvt. bath, plus 2 suites w/pvt. bath, incl. 1 w/TV
Rates: $90-$100/room, $110-$125/suite, all incl. full brk., afternoon refreshment.
 Seasonal variations.
Credit cards: MC, V
Restrictions: No children under 12, pets, smoking. Min. one night's deposit req. 14-
 day cancellation notice req. 2-night min. stay on wknds. during high season.
Notes: Built in the 1800s. Located beside the Ottaqueechee River in a New England
setting. Recently redecorated. Living room framed by 170-year old timbers with
books, games, library of video tapes, TV, VCR, AM/FM cassettes, CD stereos. Furnished with antiques and reproductions. Limited handicapped access.*

Virginia

ALEXANDRIA (1)

Morrison House
116 S. Alfred St., Alexandria, VA 22314
(703) 838-8000, (800) 367-0800, (703) 684-6283
Innkeeper: Wanda McKeon
Rooms: 42, plus 3 suites, all w/pvt. bath, phone, cable TV
Rates: $185-$295/room, $250-$470/suite. Special pkgs. avail. Discount avail. for AAA, mid-week, and senior citizen stays.
Credit cards: Most major cards
Restrictions: No pets. Smoking restricted. Deposit req. 24-hour cancellation notice req.
Notes: Brick Federal-style house with black shutters, half-moon staircase, elliptical columned entrance. Formal parlor. Foyer with marble floor. Library with burnished mahogany paneling. Furnished with antique reproductions from the Federal era, Persian rugs. Piano cafe on premises. Small private parties accommodated. French, Spanish spoken.*

AMHERST (7)

Dulwich Manor
Rte. 5, Box 173 A, Amherst, VA 24521
(804) 946-7207
Innkeeper: Bob and Judy Reilly
Rooms: 6, incl. 4 w/pvt. bath, 2 w/fireplace, 1 w/whirlpool
Rates: $69-$89, incl. full brk., afternoon refreshment. Discount avail. for extended stay.
Credit cards: Most major cards
Restrictions: No pets. Smoking restricted. One night's deposit req. 14-day cancellation notice req. 2-night min. stay on May and Oct. wknds.
Notes: Two-and-a-half-story English-style brick manor house with Corinthian columns built in 1912. Living room, study with TV, each with fireplace. Formal dining room, veranda. Victorian gazebo, hot tub.*

CAPE CHARLES (10)

Nottingham Ridge
28184 Nottingham Ridge Lane, Cape Charles, VA 23310
(804) 331-1010
Innkeeper: Bonnie Nottingham
Rooms: 3 plus 1 suite, all w/pvt. bath, phone, TV
Rates: $65-$90/room, $115-$135/suite, all incl. full brk.
Credit cards: None
Restrictions: No children under 7, pets. Smoking restricted. Min. 50% deposit req. 7-day cancellation notice req. 2-night min. stay on wknds., April–Nov.
Notes: Two-story house located on 100 acres. Decorated with antiques, reproductions, collectibles. Screened porch overlooking bay.*

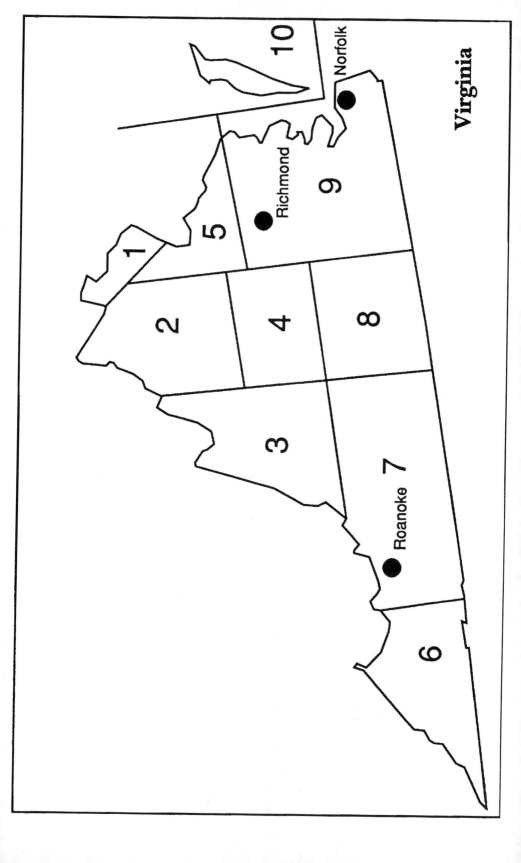

Virginia

Picketts Harbor
P.O. Box 97AA, Cape Charles, VA 23310
(804) 331-2212
Innkeeper: Sara and Cooke Goffigon
Rooms: 5 plus 1 suite, incl. 3 w/pvt. bath
Rates: $65-$125/room, $125/suite, all incl. full brk.
Credit cards: None
Restrictions: No children under 6. 50% deposit req. 2-night min. stay on holidays.
Notes: Two-story, 18th-century-style house with high ceilings, built in 1976. Located on 27 acres. Dining room. Living room with fireplace. Decorated with family furnishings and antiques.

CASTLETON (2)

Blue Knoll Farm
Rte. 1, Box 141, Castleton, VA 22716-9736
(703) 937-5234
Innkeeper: Mary and Gil Carlson
Rooms: w/pvt. bath, incl. 1 w/fireplace, 1 w/Jacuzzi tub
Rates: $95-$125, incl. full brk., afternoon refreshment
Credit cards: Most major cards
Restrictions: No children, pets. Smoking restricted. Deposit req. 48-hour cancellation notice req. 2-night min. stay on holiday and Oct. wknds.
Notes: Two-story, 19th-century farmhouse located on 5.5 acres. Parlor with antique wood-burning stove. Dining room. Furnished with antiques. Two porches, sundeck. Handicapped accessible.

CHARLES CITY (9)

Edgewood Plantation
4800 John Tyler Mem Hwy., Charles City, VA 23030
(804) 829-2962
Innkeeper: Dot and Julian Boulware
Rooms: 6 plus 2 suites, all w/pvt. bath, incl. 2 w/fireplace. Located in 2 bldgs.
Rates: $98-$148/room, $158-$168/suite, all incl. full brk. Seasonal variations.
Credit cards: MC, V
Restrictions: No children under 12, pets. Smoking restricted. 15-day cancellation notice req. 2-night min. stay on holiday and long wknds.
Notes: Three-story, Gothic-style plantation house built in 1849. Double parlor with two fireplaces. Formal dining room. Furnished with antiques. Gazebo, hot tub. Antique and giftshops on premises. Virginia Historic Landmark.

North Bend Plantation
12200 Weyanoke Rd., Charles City, VA 23030
(804) 829-5176
Innkeeper: George and Ridgely Copland
Rooms: 4 plus 1 suite, all w/pvt. bath, phone, incl. 4 w/TV
Rates: $95-$120/room, $145/suite, all incl. full brk. Discount avail. for extended and senior citizen stays.
Credit cards: None
Restrictions: No children under 6, pets. Smoking restricted. 50% deposit req. 2-week cancellation notice req. 2-night min. stay on holiday wknds.

Notes: Two-story Greek Revival-style house built in 1819 for the sister of President William Henry Harrison. Enlarged in 1853. Restored in and has operated as inn since 1984. Three porches. Living room with library. Den room with TV, board games. Billiard room. Furnished with antiques, family heirlooms, Civil War collectables. Swimming pool. Lawn games and bicycles available. Virginia Historic Landmark.*

CHARLOTTESVILLE (4)

200 SOUTH STREET INN

200 South Street Inn
200 South St., Charlottesville, VA 22902
(800) 964-7008, (804) 979-0200
Innkeeper: Brendan Clancy
Rooms: 17 w/pvt. bath, phone, incl. 6 w/fireplace, plus 3 suites w/pvt. bath, phone, fireplace. Located in 2 bldgs.
Rates: $95-$160/room, $175/suite, all incl. expanded cont. brk., evening refreshment. Discount avail. for senior citizen, AAA, Nat'l. Trust, military stays.
Credit cards: Most major cards
Restrictions: No pets. Deposit req. 7-day cancellation notice req. 2-night min. stay on spring and fall wknds.
Notes: Built in 1856. Renovated in 1986. Located in the Downtown Historic District of Charlottesville. Furnished with antiques. Whirlpool baths in some rooms.*

Clifton—The Country Inn
Rte. 13, Box 26, Charlottesville, VA 22901
(804) 971-1800, (804) 971-7098
Innkeeper: Craig and Donna Hartman
Rooms: 7 plus 7 suites, all w/pvt. bath, fireplace. Located in 4 bldgs.
Rates: $155-$188/room, $165-198/suite, iall ncl. brk., afternoon refreshment. Discount avail. for mid-week stay.
Credit cards: Most major cards
Restrictions: No pets, smoking. $100 deposit req. 15-day cancellation req., less 10% fee. 2-night min. stay on wknds.
Notes: Colonial mansion with six-columned Federal facade built in 1790 as part of the Thomas Jefferson estate. Located on forty wooded acres with pond. Double

entry foyer, living room with two fireplaces. Library with board games, dining room, each with fireplace. Slate veranda overlooking Blue Ridge Mountains and Rivanna River. Fully restored with English and American period furnishings. Croquet pitch, tennis court, full-sized pool and lake on property. Handicapped access.*

CHATHAM (7)

Eldon, The Inn at Chatham
Rte. 1, Box 254B, State Road 685, Chatham, VA 24531
(804) 432-0935

Innkeeper: Joy and Bob Lemm
Rooms: 3 w/pvt. bath, phone, plus 2 suites, incl. 1 w/pvt. bath, 1 w/phone
Rates: $55-$70/room, $90-$120/suite, all incl. full brk. Seasonal variations. Discount avail. for mid-week stay.
Credit cards: MC, V
Restrictions: No children under 12, pets. Smoking restricted. Deposit req. 2-night min. stay on some wknds.
Notes: Two-story Greek Rival plantaion manor house built in 1835. Fully restored. Located on 13 wooded acres. Furnished with antiques, Oriental rugs. Formal garden w/sculptures, orchard, fish pool. Original smoke house, ice house, stable, servants cottage. Gourmet restaurant on premises. Limited handicapped access.

House of Laird
335 S. Main St., Box 1131, Chatham, VA 24531-1131
(804) 462-2523

Innkeeper: Ed and Cecil Laird
Rooms: 3 plus 1 suite, all w/pvt. bath, phone, fireplace, TV
Rates: $60/room, $99/suite, all incl. full brk. Discount avail. for mid-week stay.
Credit cards: Most major cards
Restrictions: No children under 10, pets. Smoking restricted. 7-day cancellation notice req. 2-night min. stay on some wknds.
Notes: Two-story Greek Revival house built in 1880. Dining room. Decorated with antiques, quality reproductions, Oriental rugs. Handicapped access.*

CHINCOTEAGUE (10)

Island Manor House
4160 Main St., Chincoteague, VA 23336
(804) 336-6686

Innkeeper: Charles Kalmykow, Carol Rogers
Rooms: 8, incl. 4 w/pvt. bath. Located in 2 bldgs.
Rates: $70-$100, incl. full brk., afternoon refreshment. Discount avail. for extended stay.
Credit cards: Most major cards
Restrictions: No children under 12, pets. Smoking restricted. Full deposit req. 7-day cancellation notice req. 2-night min. stay on wkds. 3-night min. stay on holidays.
Notes: Two-story, two-building Victorian-style inn built in 1848. Common room with fireplace. Furnished in Federal style with collection of antiques, furniture, and art from the 1700s and 1800s. Board games available.*

Miss Molly's Inn
4141 Main St., Chincoteague, VA 23336
(804) 336-6686, (800) 221-5620

Innkeeper: David and Barbara Wiedenheft
Rooms: 7, incl. 5 w/pvt. bath
Rates: $69-$135, incl. full brk., afternoon refreshment. Discount avail. for extended, mid-week, senior citizen stays. Seasonal variations.
Credit cards: None
Restrictions: No children under 8, pets, smoking. Full prepayment req. 4-day cancellation notice req. 2 night min. stay on wknds.
Notes: Three-story Victorian house built in 1886. Fully restored. Wrap-around screened porch, five open porches. Furnished with lace curtains, stained-glass windows, period antiques. Small private parties accommodated. French, Dutch, German spoken.*

The Watson House
4240 Main St., Box 905, Chincoteague, VA 23336
(804) 336-1564

Innkeeper: Tom and Jacque Derrickson and David and JoAnne Snead
Rooms: 6 w/pvt. bath
Rates: $65-$105, incl. full brk., afternoon refreshment. Seasonal variations. Discount avail. for extended stay.
Credit cards: MC, V
Restrictions: No children under 10, pets, smoking. 50% deposit req. 7-day cancellation notice req. Min. stay req. on most wknds. and holidays.
Notes: Victorian house built in the late 1800s. Recently restored. Furnished with antiques. Guests have access to bicycles, beach chairs, beach towels.

THE WATSON HOUSE

CLUSTER SPRINGS (8)

Oak Grove Plantation
P.O. Box 45, Cluster Springs, VA 24535
(804) 575-7137

Innkeeper: Mary Pickett Craddock
Rooms: 2, no pvt. bath, incl. 1 w/fireplace

Rates: $45-$50, incl. full brk.
Credit cards: None
Restrictions: No pets. Smoking restricted. 50% deposit req. Deposit refunded upon cancellation only if room re-rented. Closed May & Sept. mid-weeks. Open full-time June–August.
Notes: Two-story house built in 1820. Located on 400 acres. Victorian dining room, parlor, sunporch. Furnished with period furniture and family pieces. Board and lawn games available. Spanish spoken. Resident pet.

COLUMBIA (4)

Upper Byrd Farm B & B
6452 River Rd. W., Columbia, VA 23038
(804) 842-2240
Innkeeper: Ivona Kaz-Jepsen, Maya Laurinaitis
Rooms: 3, incl. 2 w/pvt. bath
Rates: $60-$70, incl. full brk.
Credit cards: Most major cards
Restrictions: No children under 12. $20.00 deposit req.
Notes: Farmhouse located on 26 acres overlooking the James River. Furnished with antiques and original art.

DRAPER (7)

Claytor Lake Homestead Inn
Rte 651, Box 7, Draper, VA 24324
(703) 980-6777, (800) 676-5253
Innkeeper: Judy and Don Taylor
Rooms: 5 w/phone, TV, incl. 1 w/pvt. bath
Rates: $70-$140 incl. full brk. Seasonal variations.
Credit cards: Most major cards
Restrictions: No pets, smoking. Credit card deposit req. 7-day cancellation notice req. 2-night min. stay during first two weeks in May.
Notes: Two-story lakeside house. Brick and stone wrap-around porch with rocking chairs and lake view. Common room with fireplace. Dining room with bay window overlooking lake. Furnished with antiques. Private beach and boat dock. Rental boats available. Small private parties accommodated. Spanish spoken.*

DUBLIN (7)

Bell's B & B
13 Giles Ave., Box 405, Dublin, VA 24084
(703) 674-6331, (800) 437-0575
Innkeeper: Helga and David Bell
Rooms: 5, no pvt. bath, incl. 1 w/phone
Rates: $50-$65, incl. full brk. Discount avail. for senior citizen, mid-week, and extended stays.
Credit cards: V
Restrictions: Pets, smoking restricted. Deposit req. 7-day cancellation notice req.
Notes: German spoken.

FREDERICKSBURG (5)

La Vista Plantation
4420 Guinea Station Rd., Fredericksburg, VA 22408-8850
(703) 898-8444, (703) 898-1041
Innkeeper: Michele and Edward Schiesser
Rooms: 1 plus 1 suite, all w/pvt. bath, phone, TV, fireplace
Rates: $85, incl. full brk., afternoon refreshment. Discount avail. for extended stay.
Credit cards: Most major cards
Restrictions: No pets, smoking. Deposit req., refunded upon cancellation only if room re-rented.
Notes: Two-story Classical revival-style inn built in 1838. Located on ten landscaped acres with bass pond. Living room with fireplace. Sitting room, kitchen. 2-story front portico. Furnished with antiques and contemporary pieces. Row boat, bicycles available.*

FRONT ROYAL (2)

CHESTER HOUSE INN

Chester House Inn
43 Chester St., Front Royal, VA 22630
(703) 635-3937, (800) 621-0441
Innkeeper: Bill and Ann Wilson
Rooms: 5, incl. 4 w/pvt. bath, 1 w/fireplace, plus 1 suite w/pvt. bath, fireplace. Guesthouse w/kitchen avail.
Rates: $65-$105/room, $110/suite, incl. cont. brk., afternoon refreshment.
Credit cards: Most major cards
Restrictions: No children under 12, pets. Smoking restricted. One night's deposit req. Min. 72-hour cancellation notice req., less fee. 2-night min. stay on Oct., holiday and festival wknds.
Notes: Two-story Georgian mansion built in 1905. Located on two wooded acres. Living room, dining room. Parlor with TV. Card/game room. Portico and formal gardens with fountain and statuary.*

Constant Spring Inn
413 S. Royal Ave., Front Royal, VA 22630
(703) 635-7010 (800) 635-7011

Innkeeper: Joan and Bob Kaye
Rooms: 3 plus 5 suites, all w/pvt. bath, TV
Rates: $60/room, $70-$95/suite, all incl. full brk., afternoon refreshment. Special pkgs. avail.
Credit cards: MC, V
Restrictions: No pets, smoking. One night's deposit req. 72-hour cancellation notice req., less one night's fee unless room re-rented. 2-night min. stay for May and Oct.
Notes: Two-story, Colonial-style country inn. Game room, reading room, each with stone fireplaces. Board games available. Sun room and veranda with rocking chairs Front porch overlooking the Shenandoah River. Bicycles available. Small private parties accommodated.*

Killahevlin
1401 N. Royal Ave., Front Royal, VA 22630
(703) 636-7335, (800) 847-6132, (703) 636-8694

Innkeeper: Susan and John Lang
Rooms: 4 plus 2 suites, all w/pvt. bath, fireplace, incl. 3 w/whirlpool bath. Located in 2 bldgs.
Rates: $85-$105, incl. full brk., afternoon refreshment.
Credit cards: MC, V
Restrictions: No children under 12, pets, smoking. Deposit req. 72-hour cancellation notice req. 2-night min. stay in May and Oct.
Notes: Three-story Edwardian Mansion. Parlor with fireplace. French doors open to screened verandas. Decorated with Irish theme wallpaper. Two restored gazebos. Small private parties accommodated.*

GOSHEN (3)

Hummingbird Inn
Wood Lane, Box 147, Goshen, VA 24439-0147
(703) 997-9065, (800) 397-3214, (703) 997-9065

Innkeeper: Jeremy and Diana Robinson
Rooms: 3 w/pvt. bath, incl. 1 w/fireplace, plus 1 suite w/pvt. bath
Rates: $60-$75, incl. full brk. Seasonal variations. Discount avail. for senior citizen and extended stays. Special pkgs. avail.
Credit cards: MC, V
Restrictions: No children under 12, pets. Smoking restricted. One night's deposit req. 10-day cancellation notice req.
Notes: Two-story Victorian Carpenter Gothic villa with original pine floor built in 1780. Expanded in 1853. Located on one landscaped acre. Den with cable TV, stereo, fireplace. Solarium, parlor, two-story wraparound verandas. Furnished with antiques. Lawn games, dinner available with advance notice. Resident dog.*

LEESBURG (1)

Fleetwood Farm Bed & Breakfast
Rte. 1, Box 306-A, Leesburg, VA 22075
(703) 327-4325, (703) 777-8236

Innkeeper: Bill and Carol Chamberlin
Rooms: 2 w/pvt. bath, fireplace, incl. 1 w/Jacuzzi
Rates: $95-$120, incl. full brk., evening refreshment. Discount avail. for extended stay.

Credit cards: None

Restrictions: No children under 12, pets. Smoking restricted. One night's deposit req. 4-day cancellation notice req. Closed Dec. 23–27.

Notes: Two-story farmhouse built in 1745. Located on working natural-colored sheep farm. Has operated as inn since 1988. Living room with fireplace, stereo, TV, board games. Dining room. Furnished with antiques. Landscaped grounds with cookout area, hammock, vegetable, herb gardens, fruit trees. Lawn games, canoe, fishing equipment available. Picnics organized. Guests have access to refrigerator. Listed on the National Register of Historic Places. Resident outdoor sheep, llama, and cats.*

The Norris House Inn
108 Loudon St. S.W., Leesburg, VA 22075
(703) 777-1806, (800) 644-1806, (703) 771-8051

Innkeeper: Pam and Don McMurray

Rooms: 6 w/sitting area, no pvt. bath., incl. 3 w/fireplace

Rates: $70-$140, incl. full brk., evening refreshment. Seasonal variations.

Credit cards: Most major cards

tr No children, pets. Smoking restricted. Deposit req. 72-hour cancellation notice req. 2-night min. stay on wknds. in April, May, Sept. Oct. 3-night min. stay on holiday wknds.

Notes: Three-story brick Federal-style house built in 1806. Recently expanded. Has operated as inn since 1983. Library with cherry bookcases. Tea room and additional function rooms. Veranda and garden.*

THE NORRIS HOUSE INN

LEXINGTON (3)

Historic Country Inns of Lexington
11 N. Main St., Lexington, VA 24450
(703) 463-2044, (703) 463-7262

Innkeeper: Don Fredenburg, innkeeper; Peter Meredith family, owners

Rooms: 32 w/pvt. bath, TV, incl. 15 w/phone, 12 w/fireplace, plus 12 suites w/pvt. bath, TV, incl. 8 w/phone, 4 w/fireplace. Located in 5 bldgs.

Rates: $95-$115/room, $135-$155/suite, all incl. expanded cont. brk., evening refreshment. Seasonal variations. Discount avail. for mid-week, extended stays. Special pkgs. avail.

Credit cards: MC, V

Restrictions: Smoking restricted. Deposit req. 10-day cancellation notice req.

Notes: Three historic inns. Alexander-Withrow House built in 1789 with garden entrance. McCampbell Inn built in 1809 with porticos, balconies, rocking chairs. Maple Hall, built in 1850 on 56 acres with swimming pool, tennis court, fish pond, restaurant on premises, trails. All three inns furnished with variety of antiques, paintings.*

Lavender Hill Farm
Rte. 1, Box 515, Lexington, VA 24450
(703) 464-5877, (800) 446-4240

Innkeeper: Cindy and Colin Smith

Rooms: 2 w/pvt. bath, plus 1 suite w/pvt. bath

Rates: $60-$70/room, $100-$110/suite, all incl. full brk. Seasonal variations. Discount avail. for extended, senior citizen stays. Special pkgs. avail.

Credit cards: MC, V

Restrictions: No pets. Smoking restricted. Deposit req. 7-day cancellation notice req. 2-night min. stay on holidays and special events.

Notes: Two-story farmhouse built in 1790. Fully restored. Located on 20-acre working farm. Furnished in an English country decor. Vegetable garden. Front porch. Fishing, hiking. Horseback riding package avail. Dinner available. Resident farm animals.*

LAVENDER HILL FARM

LOCUST DALE (2)

Inn at Meander Plantation
HCR 5, Box 460A, Locust Dale, VA 22948
(703) 672-4912, (703) 672-4912

Innkeeper: Suzie Blanchard and Suzanne Thomas

Rooms: 3 w/pvt. bath, plus 1 cottage w/pvt. bath. Located in 2 bldgs.

Rates: $95-$155/room, $130-$175/cottage, all incl. full brk., afternoon refreshment. Discount avail. for extended, senior citizen stays.
Credit cards: MC, V
Restrictions: No children under 4. Smoking restricted. 50% deposit req. 14-day cancellation notice req.
Notes: Three-story brick Georgian mansion built in 1766 on 80 acres of pasture and woodlands. Parlor with baby grand piano, books. Formal dining room. Furnished with antiques and period reproductions. Columned from porch. Two-level wraparound porches in back overlooking Blue Ridge Mountains. Horseback riding, birdwatching, rafting on the Robinson River, trails. Hammock, lawn games, gardens. Picnic lunch and dinner available. Kennel boarding and stable boarding for horses available. Small private parties accommodated.*

LYNCHBURG (7)

Langhorne Manor B & B
313 Washington St., Lynchburg, VA 24504-4619
(804) 846-4667, (800) 851-1466
Innkeeper: Jaime and Jaynee Acevedo
Rooms: 3 w/pvt. bath, phone, incl. 1 w/fireplace, 1 w/TV, plus 1 suite w/pvt. bath, phone, fireplace, TV
Rates: $70-$95/room, $105/suite, all incl. full brk., afternoon refreshment. Discount avail. for extended, senior citizen and group stays.
Credit cards: Most major cards
Restrictions: No pets. Smoking restricted. Min. one night's deposit req. 15-day cancellation notice req. 2-night min. stay for some wknds.
Notes: Two-story neoclassical, antebellum mansion with Greek Revival flavor built about 1850. Located on landscaped lot with statued fountain, stone benches. Living room, formal parlor, music room, oak-panelled dining room. Furnished with antiques, family heirlooms. Second-floor art gallery. Spanish spoken.*

Lynchburg Mansion Inn
405 Madison St., Lynchburg, VA 24504
(804) 528-5400, (800) 352-1199
Innkeeper: Bob and Mauranna Sherman
Rooms: 3 w/pvt. bath, phone, TV, incl. 1 w/fireplace
Rates: $89-$99/room, $119/suite, all incl. full brk. Discount avail. for senior citizen, mid-week, and extended stays.
Credit cards: Most major cards
Restrictions: One night's deposit req. 10-day cancellation notice req. 2-night min. stay on Oct. and May wknds.
Notes: Two-story Spanish Georgian mansion built in 1914. Spanish tiled veranda with columns. 50-foot grand hall with high ceiling and cherry columns, wainscoting and moldings. Oak and cherry winding staircase. Dining room, library, solarium. Hot tub. Carriage house, gardens. Listed on the National Register of Historic Places. Small private parties accommodated.*

The Madison House B & B
413 Madison St., Lynchburg, VA 24504
(804) 528-1503, (800) 828-6422
Innkeeper: Irene and Dale Smith
Rooms: 3 w/pvt. bath, phone, incl. 1 suite w/pvt. bath, phone, TV

Rates: $70-$89/room, $109/suite, all incl. full brk., afternoon refreshment. Special pkgs. avail.

Credit cards: Most major cards

Restrictions: No pets, smoking. Deposit req. 10-day cancellation notice req., less $20.00 fee.

Notes: Two-story Italianate and Eastlake Victorian house with crystal chandeliers, stained-glass windows built in 1880. Has operated as inn since 1990. Seven fireplaces throughout. Double parlors, banquet room, wrought iron porch. Furnished with period antiques. Recipient of the Lynchburg Historical Foundation Merit Award for exterior renovation. Flower gardens. Picnic lunches available. Free Lynchburg Red Sox baseball tickets.*

MIDDLEBURG (1)

Welbourne
Middleburg, VA 22117
(703) 687-3201

Innkeeper: Nat and Sherry Morison

Rooms: 6 w/pvt. bath, fireplace, plus 2 suites w/pvt. bath. Located in 3 bldgs.

Rates: $86/room, $96/suite, all incl. full brk.

Credit cards: None

Restrictions: 50% deposit req. 7-day cancellation notice req.

Notes: 600-acre farm built in 1775. Expanded in 1870. Owned by same family for seven generations. Three common rooms. Dining room with fireplace, front porch. Furnished in classical eclectic style with antiques. Listed on the National Register of Historic Places. French spoken.

MILLBORO (3)

FORT LEWIS LODGE

Fort Lewis Lodge
HCR 3, Box 21A, Millboro, VA 24460
(703) 925-2314

Innkeeper: John and Caryl Cowden

Rooms: 13, incl. 9 w/pvt. bath, 2 w/fireplace, plus 4 suites w/pvt. bath. Log cabins available. Located in 3 bldgs.

Rates: $130-$140/room, $150/suite, $180/cabin, all incl. full brk., dinner

Credit cards: MC, V

Restrictions: No pets. Smoking restricted. One night's deposit req. 7-day cancellation notice req., less $10.00 fee. Closed Jan–Mar.

Notes: Two-story farm house, including other structures, on 3200 acres along the Cowpasture River. Originally a small stockade built in 1754. Has operated as inn by current innkeepers since 1986. Gathering room. Restaurant in 19th-century grist mill on property. Renovated silo with 3 guest rooms. 2 historic log cabins with stone fireplaces. Furnished with wildlife art and hand-crafted furniture. Decks, hot tub. Mountain bikes, picnic lunches available. Complete guide services available.*

River Ridge Guest Ranch
Rte. 1, Box 119-I, Millboro, VA 24460
(703) 996-4148

Innkeeper: Ann and Nancy Sams

Rooms: 2 plus 2 cabins plus family unit. Located in 4 bldgs.

Rates: $100/room, $120/cabin, $150/family unit, all incl. full brk. Discount avail. for extended stay.

Credit cards: MC, V

Restrictions: No pets. Smoking restricted. One night's deposit req. 2-day cancellation notice req. 2-night min. stay.

Notes: Two-story inn located on 400 acres. Common room with fireplace. TV room. Game room. Trail and hay wagon dinner rides available. German and French spoken. Opening scenes from the movie *Sommersby*, starring Richard Gere, were taken here.*

MOLLUSK (9)

The Guesthouses at Greenvale
Route 354, Box 70, Mollusk, VA 22517
(804) 462-5995

Innkeeper: Pam and Walt Smith

Rooms: 2 houses w/pvt. bath, kitchen, deck, phone, TV

Rates: $85-$115/house, incl. cont. brk. Seasonal variations. Discount avail. for midweek and extended stays.

Credit cards: MC, V

Restrictions: No children under 16, pets. Smoking restricted. One night's deposit req. 10-day cancellation notice req. 2-night min. stay on wknds. from Memorial Day–Labor Day.

Notes: Located on 13 acres on the Rappahannock River and Greenvale Creek. Furnished with antiques. Swimming pool, private beach, boat dock, bikes. Fishing, crabbing, lawn games available.

MONTEREY (3)

Highland Inn
Main St., Box 40, Monterey, VA 24465
(703) 468-2143

Innkeeper: Michael Strand and Cynthia Peel

Rooms: 13 plus 4 suites, all w/pvt. bath, TV

Rates: $49-$64/room, $69-$75/suite, all incl. cont. brk. Seasonal variations. Discount avail. for senior citizens and AAA stays.
Credit cards: MC, V
Restrictions: No pets. Smoking restricted. Deposit req. 24-hr. cancellation notice req. Min. stay on holiday and Oct. wknds.
Notes: Three-story Victorian house built in 1904. Located in the foothills of the Allegheny Mountains. Eastlake porches with gingerbread trim. Dining room. Parlor with antique piano. Giftshop, tavern on premises. Furnished with antiques, collectibles. Listed on the National Register of Historic Places. Virginia Historic Landmark.*

MOUNT JACKSON (2)

Widow Kip's Shenandoah Inn
Rte. 1, Box 117, Mount Jackson, VA 22842
(703) 477-2400
Innkeeper: Elizabeth A. Luse
Rooms: 5 plus 2 cottages, all w/pvt. bath, TV. Located in 3 bldgs.
Rates: $55-$70/room, $85/cottage, all incl. full brk.
Credit cards: MC, V
Restrictions: Children, pets restricted. No smoking. Deposit req. 5-day cancellation notice req.
Notes: Colonial house and two cottages built in 1830. Located on seven acres overlooking George Washington Mountains. Living room with fireplace. Library, dining room, side veranda, swimming pool. Furnished with antiques.*

WIDOW KIP'S SHENANDOAH INN

NATURAL BRIDGE (7)

Burger's Country Inn
Rte. 2, Box 564, Natural Bridge, VA 24578
(703) 291-2464
Innkeeper: Frances B. Burger
Rooms: 4, incl. 2 w/pvt. bath

Rates: $45-$50, incl. cont. brk.
Credit cards: None
Restrictions: Smoking restricted. Deposit preferred. 24-hour cancellation notice req.
Notes: Farmhouse built in 1900. Has operated as inn since the 1920s. Located on ten wooded acres in the Shenandoah Valley. Parlor with fireplace. Wrap-around porch with large columns. Furnished with antiques and collectibles. Lawn games available.*

BURGER'S COUNTRY INN

NELLYSFORD (4)

Trillium House
Wintergreen Dr., Box 280, Nellysford, VA 22958
(804) 325-9126, (804) 325-1099

Innkeeper: Ed and Betty Dinwiddie
Rooms: 10 plus 2 suites, all w/pvt. bath, phone
Rates: $90-$105/room, $120-$150/suite, all incl. full brk. Discount avail. for senior citizen and mid-week stays.
Credit cards: MC, V
Restrictions: No pets. No smoking in dining room. 50% deposit req. during ski season. 14-day cancellation notice. 2-3 night min. stay on wknds.
Notes: Country style inn built in 1983. Great room, dining room, library, garden room with cable TV, VCR, videotapes. Guests have access to TV. Handicapped access.*

NEW CHURCH (10)

The Garden and the Sea Inn
4188 Nelson Rd., New Church, VA 23415
(804) 824-0672, (800) 824-0672, (804) 824-5605

Innkeeper: Victoria Olian and Jack Betz
Rooms: 4 plus 1 suite, all w/pvt. bath, incl. 2 w/phone. Located in 2 bldgs.

Rates: $70-$140/room, $120-$140/suite, all incl. cont. brk., afternoon refreshment. Discount avail. for mid-week stay. Seasonal variations.

Credit cards: Most major cards

Restrictions: No pets. Smoking restricted. Deposit req. 7-day cancellation notice req. 2-night min. stay on wknds. 3-night min. stay on holidays and pony-penning wknds. Closed Nov. 1–March 31.

Notes: Victorian country house with gingerbread moldings, gabled roofs built in 1802. Enlarged in 1901. Located on the eastern shore near Chincoteage. Dining room, parlor. Library/music room. Furnished with antiques, Oriental rugs. Wraparound front porch. Restaurant, chamber music, art shows on premises. Some French spoken.*

THE GARDEN AND THE SEA INN

NEW MARKET (2)

Red Shutter Farm House
Rte. 1, Box 376, New Market, VA 22844
(703) 740-4281

Innkeeper: George W. and Juanita Miller

Rooms: 4, incl. 2 w/pvt. bath, 3 w/fireplce, plus 1 suite w/pvt. bath

Rates: $55-$70/room, $70/suite, all incl. full brk.

Credit cards: MC, V

Restrictions: No pets, smoking. One night's deposit req. 2-day cancellation notice req. 2-night min. stay on 3-day holiday wknds.

Notes: Two-story log farmhouse built in 1790. Enlarged in 1870, 1920, and 1930. Located on 20 acres. Has operated as inn since 1989. Living room, large center entrance hall, stairway. Library with TV. Conference room. Veranda with rocking chairs. Small private parties accommodated.

A Touch of Country
9329 Congress St., New Market, VA 22844
(703) 740-8030

Innkeeper: Dawn Kasow and Jean Schoellig

Rooms: 6 w/pvt. bath. Located in 2 bldgs.

Rates: $60-$70, incl. full brk.

Credit cards: MC, V

Restrictions: No children under 12, pets, smoking. 50% Deposit req. 7-day cancellation notice req. 2-night min. stay on holiday and Oct. wknds.

Notes: Two-story Shenandoah Valley house built in the 1870s. Fully restored. Dining room, family room, living room. Porch with swings. Furnished in country style with antiques, collectibles.

NORFOLK (9)

Page House Inn
323 Fairfax Ave., Norfolk, VA 23507
(804) 625-5033, (804) 623-9451

Innkeeper: Stephanie and Ezio DiBelardino

Rooms: 4 plus 2 suites, all w/pvt. bath, phone, TV, incl. 3 w/fireplace

Rates: $70-$120/room, $130-$145/suite, all incl. cont. brk., afternoon refreshment. Discount avail. for mid-week stay. Seasonal variations.

Credit cards: AE, MC

Restrictions: No children under 12, pets. Smoking restricted. One night's deposit req. 14-day cancellation notice req., less $25.00 fee. Min. stay req. for special event wknds. and some holidays.

Notes: Three-story Georgian Revival house built in the 1900s. Front porch. Formal dining room. Decorated in 19th- and early 20th-century antiques and art. Second-floor rooftop garden. Italian and some Spanish spoken. Resident dogs.*

NORTH GARDEN (4)

THE INN AT THE CROSSROADS

The Inn at the Crossroads
Rte. 2, Box 6, RR 692, North Garden, VA 22959
(804) 979-6452

Innkeeper: Lynn L. Neville, Christine N. Garrison

Rooms: 5, no pvt. bath

Rates: $65-$75, incl. full brk. Discount avail. for extended stay.

Credit cards: MC, V

Restrictions: No children under 8, pets, smoking. Deposit req. 3-day cancellation notice req. 2-night min. stay on special wknds.
Notes: Four-story brick Federal-style tavern built in 1820. Located on 4.5 acres overlooking the foothills of the Blue Ridge Mountains. Keeping room, common room, summer kitchen. Furnished with period antiques. Long front porch with rockers.*

ORANGE (2)

Hidden Inn
249 Caroline St., Orange, VA 22960
(703) 672-3625, (703) 672-5029

Innkeeper: Ray and Barbara Lonick
Rooms: 6 plus 4 suites, all w/pvt. bath, incl. 4 w/phone, 2 w/fireplace, 2 w/fireplace. Located in 4 bldgs.
Rates: $79-$129/room, $139-$159/suite, all incl. full brk., afternoon refreshment.
Credit cards: MC, V
Restrictions: No pets, smoking. Deposit req. 7-day cancellation notice req. 2-night min. stay on wknds.
Notes: Two-story Victorian house built at the turn-of-the-century. Located on seven wooded acres. Living room with fireplace, TV. Dining room. Furnished with antiques and handmade quilts. Wrap-around veranda overlooking tranquil garden and grounds. Gourmet dinners available. Spanish spoken.*

The Holladay House
155 W. Main St., Orange, VA 22960
(703) 672-4893, (703) 672-3028

Innkeeper: Pete and Phebe Holladay
Rooms: 5 plus 2 suites, all w/pvt. bath, incl. 1 w/phone, TV
Rates: $75/room, $185/suite, all incl. full brk. Discount avail. for mid-week stay.
Credit cards: MC, V
Restrictions: No pets. Smoking restricted. Deposit req. 7-day cancellation notice req. 2-night min. stay on holidays, in October, and on graduation wknds.
Notes: Two-story Federal style house built in 1830s. Dining room, parlor. Sun-porch with TV. Furnished with antiques, Victorian and Colonial-style pieces. Resident pet. Handicapped access.*

PETERSBURG (9)

Mayfield Inn
3348 W. Washington St., Petersburg, VA 23804
(804) 733-0866, (804) 861-6775

Innkeeper: Jamie and Dot Caudle and Cherry Turner
Rooms: 2 plus 2 suites, all w/pvt. bath
Rates: $60-$90/room, $70-$80/suite, all incl. full brk. Discount avail. for senior citizen and military stays.
Credit cards: MC, V
Restrictions: No pets. Smoking restricted. Deposit req. 3-day cancellation notice req.
Notes: Two-story manor brick house with clipped gable, wood shingle roof, five dormers, seven fireplaces, built in 1750. Fully restored in 1979. Located on 4 acres. Has operated as inn since 1986. Dining room. Decorated with oriental rugs, pine floors, antiques, period reproductions. Swimming pool, herb garden, gazebo.

Listed on the National Register of Historic Places. Small private parties accommodated.*

PULASKI (7)

The Count Pulaski B & B
821 N. Jefferson Ave., Pulaski, VA 24301
(703) 980-1163, (800) 980-1163
Innkeeper: Flo Stevenson
Rooms: 2 w/pvt. bath, phone, plus 1 suite w/pvt. bath, phone, fireplace.
Rates: $75/room, $95/suite, all incl. full brk., afternoon refreshment. Discount avail. for extended stay.
Credit cards: MC, V
Restrictions: No children, pets. Smoking restricted. Deposit req. Deposit refunded upon cancellation only if room re-rented.
Notes: Four-story brick Colonial Revival house built about 1914. Fully renovated in and has operated as inn since 1993. Dining room. Living room with fireplace and 1912 Steinway baby grand piano. Sunroom with fireplace. Porch overlooking gardens - one with lighted fountain, the other with a stream. Sunroom with cable TV. Furnished with family, European and Asian antiques. Listed on the National Register of Historic Places.*

RICHMOND (9)

Abbie Hill Bed & Breakfast
P.O. Box 4503, Richmond, VA 23220
(804) 355-5855, (804) 355-5855
Innkeeper: Barbara and Bill Fleming
Rooms: 2 plus 1 suite, all w/pvt. bath, fireplace, TV
Rates: $75-$95/room, $140-$150/suite, all incl. full brk., afternoon refreshment. Discount avail. for extended stay.
Credit cards: MC, V
Restrictions: No children under 12, pets, smoking. One night's deposit req. 7-day cancellation notice req., less $15.00 fee. 2-night min. stay on fall & spring wknds. Closed one week in fall, one week in spring.
Notes: Three-story brick Federal-style townhouse built in 1909. Parlor, dining room. Front porch with rockers. Furnished with period antiques. Listed in the National Register of Historic Places. Guests have access to laundry facilities, refrigerator. Off-street parking available.*

West-Bocock House
1107 Grove Ave., Richmond, VA 23220
(804) 358-6174
Innkeeper: Mr. and Mrs. James B. West, Jr.
Rooms: 2 w/pvt. bath, phone, TV, incl. 1 w/fireplace
Rates: $65-$75, incl. full brk., evening refreshment. Discount avail. for extended stay.
Credit cards: None
Restrictions: No pets. Smoking restricted.
Notes: Three-story brick house built in 1871. Dining room. Furnished with family antiques and eclectic art collection, french linens. Veranda, garden, courtyards. Small private parties accommodated.

The William Catlin House
2304 E. Broad St., Richmond, VA 23223
(804) 780-3746
Innkeeper: Robert and Josephine Martin
Rooms: 3 plus 2 suites, incl. 4 w/pvt. bath, 2 w/fireplace, 1 w/TV
Rates: $70-$90/room, $140/suite, all incl. full brk.
Credit cards: Most major cards
Restrictions: No children under 12, pets. Smoking restricted. 48-hour cancellation notice req.
Notes: Three-story brick Greek Revival house built in 1845. Located in the historic district. Furnished with antiques and period furniture.*

ROANOKE (7)

The Mary Bladon House
381 Washington Ave. S.W., Roanoke, VA 24016-4303
(703) 344-5361
Innkeeper: Bill and Sheri Bestpitch
Rooms: 2 w/pvt. bath, incl. 1 w/phone, plus 1 suite w/pvt. bath
Rates: $63-$80/room, $110-$130/suite, all incl. full brk., afternoon refreshment. Discount avail. for mid-week and extended stays.
Credit cards: MC, V
Restrictions: No pets, smoking. One night's deposit req. 72-hour cancellation notice req.
Notes: Two-story Victorian house built in 1890s. Verandas. Parlor with board games. Wrap-around front porch with swing. Furnished with Rococo Revival, Renaissance Revival and Eastlake-style pieces, crafts. Dinner available. Special diets accommodated. Airport pick-up available. Some German spoken.*

ROCKY MOUNT (7)

Claiborne House B & B
119 Claiborne Ave., Rocky Mount, VA 24151
(703) 483-4616, (703) 483-4616
Innkeeper: Margaret and Jim Young
Rooms: 3 w/pvt. bath, plus 2 suites w/pvt. bath, phone, TV
Rates: $65-$75/room, $85-$95/suite, all incl. full brk., afternoon refreshment.
Credit cards: MC, V
Restrictions: No pets, smoking. One night's deposit req. 7-day cancellation notice req.
Notes: Two-story turn-of-the-century Victorian house surrounded by English gardens. Furnished with Victorian Era antiques. 130-foot porch with wickered furniture.

SCOTTSVILLE (4)

High Meadows Inn
High Meadows Ln., Rte. 4, Box 6, Scottsville, VA 24590
(804) 286-2218
Innkeeper: Peter Sushka and Jae Abbitt
Rooms: 7 w/pvt. bath, incl. 5 w/fireplace, plus 5 suites w/pvt. bath, incl. 4 w/fireplace, 1 w/TV, plus 1 cottage. Located in 3 bldgs.

Rates: $95-$155/room, $125-$155/suite, all incl. full brk., dinner, evening refreshment. Seasonal variations. Discount avail. for AAA, senior citizen, extended, and mid-week stays.
Credit cards: MC, V
Restrictions: No smoking. Deposit req. 10-day cancellation notice req., less $15.00 fee. 2-night min. stay on fall and spring wknds. and holidays.
Notes: Three-story brick house built in 1832. Expanded in 1882. Restored in 1985. Has operated as inn since 1986. Located on 50 acres with two ponds, flower gardens, pino noir grape vines, gazebo. Grand hall, three common rooms, four porches. Furnished with period antiques, Oriental rugs. Listed on the National Register of Historic Places. Bicycles, lawn games, picnic lunches, dinner available. Small private parties accommodated. French and Italian spoken. Limited handicapped access.*

SMITH MOUNTAIN LAKE (7)

The Manor at Taylor's Store
Rte. 1, Box 533, Smith Mountain Lake, VA 24184
(800) 248-6267, (703) 721-5243
Innkeeper: Lee and Mary Lynn Tucker
Rooms: 6 plus 1 cottage, incl. 4 w/pvt. bath, 1 w/fireplace. Located in 2 bldgs.
Rates: $80-$125, incl. full brk. Discount avail. for mid-week stay.
Credit cards: MC, V
Restrictions: No pets. Children, smoking restricted. One night's deposit req. 7-day cancellation notice req. 2-night min. stay for wknds. from April 1–November 1.
Notes: Two-story Federal-style manor house built in 1799. Located on 120-acre estate with six spring-fed ponds in the foothills of the Blue Ridge Mountains. Formal parlor, sun room, billiard room, exercise room. Great room with big-screen TV, VCR, movie library. Furnished with antiques. Guests have access to kitchen. Hot tub. Some German spoken.*

SMITHFIELD (9)

Four Square
13357 Foursquare Rd., Smithfield, VA 23430
(804) 365-0749
Innkeeper: Roger and Amelia Healey
Rooms: 3 w/fireplace, TV, no pvt. bath
Rates: $75, incl. full brk.
Credit cards: MC, V
Restrictions: No children under 12, pets. Smoking restricted. 3-day cancellation notice req. 2-night min. stay on holidays.
Notes: Federal plantation house built in 1807. Located on 4 acres. Dining room. Parlor with fireplace. Furnished with family antiques and reproductions. Listed on the National Register of Historic Places. Spanish, Portuguese spoken.*

Isle of Wight Inn
1607 S. Church St., Smithfield, VA 23430
(804) 357-3176
Innkeeper: Bob and Sylvia Hart and Sam and Joan Earl
Rooms: 6 w/pvt. bath, phone, TV, plus 3 suites, w/pvt. bath, phone, TV, fireplace
Rates: $42-$59/room, $89-$99/suite, all incl. full brk. Discount avail. for senior citizens.

Credit cards: Most major cards
Restrictions: No pets. Smoking restricted. 50% deposit req. Min. 48-hour cancellation notice req.
Notes: Colonial inn. Jacuzzis. Antique shop on premises. Limited handicapped access.*

STAFFORD (5)

RENAISSANCE MANOR B & B

Renaissance Manor B & B
2247 Courthouse Rd., Stafford, VA 22554
(703) 720-3785, (703) 659-8999

Innkeeper: Tom and Joanne Houser, Joe and Dennen Bernard
Rooms: 3 w/pvt. bath, plus 1 suite w/pvt. bath, fireplace
Rates: $65/room, $95/suite, all incl. cont. brk., afternoon refreshment. Special pkgs. avail.
Credit cards: Most major cards
Restrictions: No pets, smoking. One night's deposit req. 7-day cancellation notice req.
Notes: Two-story manor with high ceilings, oak hardwood floors, fireplaces, and portico that resemble's George Washington's Mount Vernon. Dining room. Common room with library of classical literature and music. Furnished with period pieces and collectibles. Decorated with paintings by local artists. Formal garden. Small private parties accommodated. German spoken.*

STANLEY (2)

Jordan Hollow Farm Inn
Rte. 2, Box 375, Stanley, VA 22851
(703) 778-2285, (703) 778-1759

Innkeeper: Marley and Jetze Beers
Rooms: 21 w/pvt. bath, phone, incl. 5 w/cable TV, 4 w/fireplace. Located in 2 bldgs.
Rates: $140-$180, incl. full brk., dinner
Credit cards: Most major cards
Restrictions: No pets. Min. one night's deposit req. 2-day cancellation notice req.

Notes: Colonial farmhouse, log lodge, and frame lodge built about 1788. Located on forty-five-acre horse farm. Sitting room, four dining rooms, meeting room, game room. Private porches, veranda, sun decks, all overlooking Shenandoah National Park. Furnished with country antiques. Restaurant, cocktail lounge, riding stable on premises. Live weekend entertainment available. Dutch, German, French spoken. Resident farm animals. Handicapped access.*

JORDAN HOLLOW FARM INN

STAUNTON (3)

Ashton Country House
1205 Middlebrook Rd., Staunton, VA 24401-4546
(703) 885-7819, (800) 296-7819

Innkeeper: Sheila Kennedy and Stanley Polanski
Rooms: 3 plus 1 suite, all w/pvt. bath
Rates: $80/room, $95/suite , all incl. full brk., afternoon refreshment. Discount avail. for extended stay.
Credit cards: None
Restrictions: No children under 16, pets, smoking. 50% deposit req. 14-day cancellation notice req. 2-night min. stay on Memorial Day, 4th of July and Sept. and Oct. wknds.
Notes: Two-story Greek Revival brick house with three porches, original pine flooring, built in 1860. Forty-foot center hall and staircase. Empire style furnishings. Live piano music during breakfast. Bicycling maps available. Handicapped access. Resident cats, dogs, and goat.

Frederick House
28 North New St., Staunton, VA 24401
(703) 885-4220

Innkeeper: Joe and Evy Harman
Rooms: 8 plus 6 suites, all w/pvt. bath, phone, TV, incl. 3 suites w/fireplace. Located in 4 bldgs.
Rates: $55-$85/room, $85-$95/suite, all incl. full brk. Discount avail. for extended, mid-week, senior citizen stays. Seasonal variations.
Credit cards: Most major cards

Restrictions: No pets, smoking. 24-hour cancellation notice req.
Notes: Three townhouses built between 1810 and 1910. Fully restored. Furnished with antiques and period pieces. Guests have access to Staunton Athletic Club. Small private parties accommodated. Listed on the National Register of Historic Places.*

FREDERICK HOUSE

The Sampson Eagon Inn
238 E. Beverley St., Staunton, VA 24401
(800) 597-9722

Innkeeper: Frank and Laura Mattingly
Rooms: 3 plus 2 suites all w/pvt. bath, TV, VCR
Rates: $75-$85/room, $90-$95/suite, all incl. full brk.
Credit cards: None
Restrictions: No children under 12, pets, smoking. One night's deposit req. 10-day cancellation notice req., less deposit only if room re-rented. 2-night min. stay on wknds. in May & Oct.
Notes: Two-story Greek Revival mansion with Italianate Victorian elements built in 1795. Fully restored in 1992. Recipient of Historic Preservation Award for its restoration. Furnished with period antiques.*

Thornrose House at Gypsy Hill
531 Thornrose Ave., Staunton, VA 24401
(703) 885-7026

Innkeeper: Suzanne and Otis Huston
Rooms: 5 w/pvt. bath
Rates: $55-75, incl. full brk., afternoon refreshment
Credit cards: Most major cards
Restrictions: No children under 5, pets, smoking. One night's deposit req. 10-day cancellation notice req. 2-night min. stay on May and October wknds.
Notes: Georgian Revival house built at the turn of the century. Parlor with fireplace, grand piano, board games. Dining room with fireplace. Furnished with antiques. Shaded wrap-around veranda. Gardens and two sets of Pergolas.

STEELES TAVERN (3)

Steeles Tavern Manor
P.O. Box 38, Rt. 11, Steeles Tavern, VA 24476
(703) 377-644, (800), (703) 377-5937
Innkeeper: Eileen and Bill Hoernlein
Rooms: 3 w/pvt. bath, plus 2 suites w/pvt. bath, fireplace
Rates: $95-$140/room. $120/suite, all incl. full brk., afternoon refreshment. Seasonal variations. Discount avail. for mid-week stay.
Credit cards: MC,V
Restrictions: No children under 14, pets, smoking. Min. one night's deposit req. 14-day cancellation notice req., less $15.00 fee.
Notes: Two-story manor house built in 1916. Has operated as inn since 1995. Located on 55 acres with stocked fishing pond. Living room, two dining rooms, porch. Furnished with anitques. All meals available with prior notification.*

STRASBURG (2)

Hotel Strasburg
201 S. Holiday St., Strasburg, VA 22657
(800) 348-8327, (703) 465-4788
Innkeeper: Gary and Carol Rutherford
Rooms: 21 w/pvt. bath, phone, TV, plus 7 suites w/pvt. bath, phone, TV. Located in 3 bldgs.
Rates: $69/room, $79-$149/suite, all incl. wkday. cont. brk. Discount avail. for senior citizen, AAA stays.
Credit cards: Most major cards
Restrictions: Pets restricted. Credit card deposit req. 48-hour cancellation notice req.
Notes: Built as a hospital during the Civil War. Restored in Victorian style. Dining room. Furnished with period antiques, wall coverings, art collection.*

SWOOPE (3)

LAMBSGATE BED & BREAKFAST

Lambsgate Bed & Breakfast
Rte. 1, Box 63, Swoope, VA 24479
(703) 337-6929

Innkeeper: Elizabeth and Dan Fannon
Rooms: 3, no pvt. bath
Rates: $45, incl. full brk. Discount avail. for extended and family stays.
Credit cards: Most major cards
Restrictions: No pets, smoking. One night's deposit req. 14-day cancellation notice req. 2-night min. stay on July 4th.
Notes: Two-story brick vernacular farmhouse built in 1816. Located on seven-acre working sheep farm. Dining room, parlor with games, TV. Wrap-around veranda overlooking Allegheny Mountains. Furnished with antiques, collectibles.

UPPERVILLE (2)

1763 Inn
Rte. 1, Box 19D, Upperville, VA 22176
(703) 592-3848, (800) 669-1763, (703) 592-3114

Innkeeper: Uta Kirchner
Rooms: 16 w/pvt. bath, phone, TV, incl. 9 w/fireplace, plus 3 cabins
Rates: $95-$175, incl. full brk.
Credit cards: Most major cards
Restrictions: No pets. Credit card deposit req. 5-day cancellation notice req. 2-night min. stay on wknds.
Notes: Stone house restaurant built in 1763. Once owned by George Washington. Located on 50 wooded country acres. Bar/lounge with outside patio. Decorated with period furnishings and paintings. Swimming pool, pond, tennis court, barn. Small private parties accommodated. French, German spoken.

WASHINGTON (2)

CADEDONIA FARM - 1812

Caledonia Farm - 1812
Rte. 1, Box 2080, Flint Hill, Washington, VA 22627
(703) 675-3693, (800) 262-1812

Innkeeper: Phil Irwin
Rooms: 2 plus 1 suite, all w/fireplace, incl. 1 w/pvt. bath. Located in 2 bldgs.
Rates: $80/room, $140/suite, all incl. full brk., afternoon refreshment.
Credit cards: Most major cards

Restrictions: No children under 12, pets. Smoking restricted. One night's deposit req., refunded, less $20.00 fee, upon cancellation only if room re-rented. 2-night min. stay on holiday wknds. and Oct.

Notes: Two-story Federal-style stone house with two-ft.-thick walls, wide-pine floors, and summer kitchen built in 1812. Fully restored in 1965. Located on working cattle farm in Washington, VA. Winter kitchen with fireplace. Three porches. Candlelight dinner available with prior arrangement. Lawn games, bicycles, hayrides available. Listed as a Virginia Historic Landmark and on the National Register of Historic Places. Handicapped access. German, Danish spoken.*

Fairlea Farm B & B
Mount Salem Ave., Box 124, Washington, VA 22747-0124
(703) 675-3679, (703) 675-3679

Innkeeper: Walt and Susan Longyear
Rooms: 3 plus 1 suite, all w/pvt. bath, incl. 1 w/fireplace
Rates: $75-$105/room, $125/suite, all incl. full brk., afternoon refreshment. Special pkgs. avail.
Credit cards: None
Restrictions: Pets, smoking restricted. Deposit req. 7-day cancellation notice req., less $25.00 fee.
Notes: Two-story fieldstone manor house located on 40 acres. Common room with fireplace. Gazebo, terrace, pastures. French spoken. Resident sheep and cattle.*

Heritage House
Main St., Box 427, Washington, VA 22747
(703) 675-3207, (703) 675-1340

Innkeeper: Frank and Jean Scott
Rooms: 3 plus 1 suite, all w/pvt. bath
Rates: $95-$110/room, $125/suite, all incl. full brk., afternoon refreshment.
Credit cards: MC, V
Restrictions: No children, pets, smoking. One night's deposit req. Min. 7-day cancellation notice req., less $20.00 fee. 2 night min. stay during October wknds.
Notes: Two-story house built in 1837, said to have been General Jubal Early's headquarters. Living room with fireplace with original 1837 chimney. Furnished with antiques, Black Forest Cuckoo Clock, Spanish ship model.*

WHITE POST (2)

L'Auberge Provencale
P.O. Box 119, White Post, VA 22663
(800) 638-1702, (703) 837-2004

Innkeeper: Alain and Celeste Borel
Rooms: 8 w/pvt. bath, incl. 4 w/fireplace, plus 2 suites w/pvt. bath, incl. 1 w/TV, 1 w/fireplacle. Located in 3 bldgs.
Rates: $145-$155/room, $165-$185/suite, all incl. full brk., afternoon refreshment.
Credit cards: Most major cards
Restrictions: No children under 10, pets. Smoking restricted. One night's deposit req. 7-day cancellation notice req. Closed Jan. 1–Feb. 14.
Notes: Two-story stone house built in 1753. Front porch overlooking the Shenandoah Blue Ridge Mountains. Furnished with Victorian antiques. Operated in south-of-France style. Restaurant on premises. Small private parties accommodated. French, Spanish spoken.*

WILLIAMSBURG (9)

Applewood Colonial B & B
605 Richmond Rd., Williamsburg, VA 23185
(804) 229-0205, (800) 899-2753
Innkeeper: Fred Strout
Rooms: 3 w/pvt. bath, plus 1 suite w/pvt. bath, fireplace
Rates: $75-$90/room, $115/suite, all incl. expanded cont. brk., afternoon refreshment. Discount avail. for mid-week stay, Jan.–March.
Credit cards: MC, V
Restrictions: No pets, smoking. 50% deposit req. 14-day cancellation notice req. 2-night min. stay on wknds. and during special events.
Notes: Three-story Flemish-bond brick house built in the late 1920s. Parlor with dentil crown molding, fireplace, TV, board games. Dining room with crystal chandelier. Furnished in Colonial decor with antiques. Small private parties accommodated. Innkeepers collect apples.*

The Cedars
616 Jamestown Rd., Williamsburg, VA 23185
(804) 229-3591, (800) 296-3591
Innkeeper: Carol, Jim and Brona Malecha
Rooms: 7 w/pvt. bath, plus 2 suites w/pvt. bath, plus 1 cottage. Located in 2 bldgs.
Rates: $95-$135/room, $125-$155/suite, $150-$195/cottage, all incl. full brk. Discount avail. for extended stay.
Credit cards: MC, V
Restrictions: No pets, smoking. One night's deposit req. 14-day cancellation notice req., less $20.00 fee
Notes: Three-story brick Georgian/Colonial house built about 1925. Sitting room with fireplace. Porch with board games. Furnished with mixture of traditional and Colonial pieces, four poster and canopy beds.*

Governor's Trace
303 Capitol Landing Rd., Williamsburg, VA 23185-4314
(804) 229-7552, (800) 303-7552
Innkeeper: Sue and Dick Lake
Rooms: 3 w/pvt. bath, phone, incl. 1 w/fireplace
Rates: $95-$115, incl. cont. brk. Seasonal variations.
Credit cards: MC, V
Restrictions: No children, pets, smoking. Full prepayment req. 2-week cancellation notice req., less $5.00 fee. 2-night min. stay on holidays and wknds.
Notes: Georgian style brick house built in 1930. Located on a half-acre. Screened porch. Sitting room with fireplace. Furnished in eclectic style with antiques and collectibles. Historically Significant Designated Home.*

Homestay B & B
517 Richmond Rd., Williamsburg, VA 23185
(800) 836-7468
Innkeeper: Barbara and Jim Thomassen
Rooms: 3, no pvt. bath
Rates: $70-$80, incl. full brk. Seasonal variations.
Credit cards: MC, V

Restrictions: No children under 9, pets, smoking. Min. one night's deposit req. 14-day cancellation notice req., less deposit. 2-night min. stay on wknds., holidays, and for special events.

Notes: Two-story Colonial Revival house built in 1933. Living room with fireplace. Dining room. Furnished with turn of the century family antiques and country charm. Hosts have collection of handcrafted Noah's Arks and Pepsi collection of bottles from far-off places such as Russia, Spain, Morocco.*

Indian Springs B & B
330 Indian Springs Rd., Williamsburg, VA 23185
(804) 220-0726, (800) 262-9165

Innkeeper: Paul and Kelly Supplee

Rooms: 1 plus 2 suites, 1 cottage, all w/pvt. bath, TV, incl. 1 w/phone. Located in 2 bldgs.

Rates: $75/room, $90/suite, $105/cottage, all incl. full brk. Seasonal variations.

Credit cards: None

Restrictions: No pets, smoking. Deposit req. 14-day cancellation notice req., less $10.00 fee. 2-night min. stay on wknds.

Notes: Two-story wooded inn. Living room. Large deck with view. Veranda overlooking ravine.*

Liberty Rose Bed & Breakfast
1022 Jamestown Rd., Williamsburg, VA 23185
(804) 253-1260, (800) 545-1825

Innkeeper: Brad and Sandra Hirz

Rooms: 2 w/pvt. bath, TV, VCR, plus 2 suites, w/pvt. bath, TV, VCR, incl. 1 w/fireplace.

Rates: $105-175/suite, all incl. full brk.

Credit cards: MC, V

Restrictions: No children under 12, pets, smoking. Full prepayment req. 18-day cancellation notice req.

Notes: Two-story Country French colonial house with dormered slate roof built in the early 1920s. Located on wooded, hilltop. Has operated as inn since 1986. Entry porch. Parlor with fireplace, piano. Breakfast porch. Furnished with antiques. Gift-shop on premises.*

Newport House
710 S. Henry St., Williamsburg, VA 23185-4113
(804) 229-1775

Innkeeper: Cathy and John Millar

Rooms: 2 w/pvt. bath, phone, TV

Rates: $100-$115, incl. full brk. Discount avail. for extended stay.

Credit cards: None

Restrictions: No smoking, pets. 14-day cancellation notice req. 2-night min. stay on wknds.

Notes: Built in 1988 from a 1756 design by the architect of the Williamsburg Capitol. Living room, dining room, ball room. Colonial gardens with hammock. Furnished with English and American period antiques, reproductions, four-poster canopy beds. Colonial country dancing each Tuesday and Thursday evenings. Colonial clothing available. Resident rabbit. French spoken.*

Piney Grove at Southall's Plantation
P.O. Box 1359, Williamsburg, VA 23185-1359
(804) 829-2480
Innkeeper: Joseph, Joan, Brian, and Cindy Rae Gordineer
Rooms: 3, plus 1 suite, all w/pvt. bath, fireplace
Rates: $125-$140/room, $150/suite, all incl. full brk., evening refreshment.
Credit cards: Most major cards
Restrictions: No pets, smoking. Full prepayment req. 2-week cancellation notice
req., 2-night min. stay on holiday wknds.
Notes: Greek Revival plantation house built in 1857. Log house built about 1800.
Furnished with antiques. Swimming pool. German spoken. Resident farm animals.*

Primrose Cottage
706 Richmond Rd., Williamsburg, VA 23185
(804) 229-6421, (804) 259-0717
Innkeeper: Inge Curtis
Rooms: 2 w/pvt. bath, phone
Rates: $85-$95, incl. full brk.
Credit cards: Most major cards
Restrictions: No children, pets, smoking. One night's deposit req. 14-day cancellation notice req. 2-night min. stay on wknds.
Notes: European style Inn. Sitting room with TV. Bicycles available. German spoken.*

War Hill
4560 Long Hill Rd., Williamsburg, VA 23188
(800) 743-0248
Innkeeper: Shirley, Bill and Will Lee
Rooms: 7 w/pvt. bath, phone, plus cottage. Suite avail. Located in 2 bldgs.
Rates: $65-$85/room, $85-130/suite, $110-$155/cottage, all incl. full brk.
Credit cards: Most major cards
Restrictions: No pets, smoking. One night's deposit req. 10-day cancellation notice
req.
Notes: 18th-century style house built in 1986. Colonial cottage built in 1990. Located on 32 acres with orchards. Dining room. Parlor with fireplace. Furnished with antiques. Guests have access to whirlpool.

Williamsburg Manor B & B
600 Richmond Rd., Williamsburg, VA 23185
(804) 220-8011, (804) 220-0245
Innkeeper: Laura and Michael MacKnight
Rooms: 6 w/phone, TV, incl. 5 w/pvt. bath
Rates: $90, incl. full brk., dinner. Seasonal variations.
Credit cards: None
Restrictions: No children under 10, pets, smoking. One night's deposit req. 21-day
cancellation notice req. 2-night min. stay on wknds.
Notes: Two-story, Georgian brick Colonial house with arched doorways, grand staircase, built during the Reconstruction of Colonial Willimsburg. Recently restored. Games room, culinary library, dining room with fireplace. Furnished with antiques. Innkeeper Laura was previously the Director of Catering at Ford's Colony Country Club, and Michael, a graduate of Johnson and Wales Culinary Arts, served as Chef of Berkeley Plantation. Handicapped access.*

WILLIAMSBURG SAMPLER B & B

Williamsburg Sampler B & B
922 Jamestown Rd., Williamsburg, VA 23185
(800) 722-1169, (804) 220-0245

Innkeeper: Helen and Ike Sisane
Rooms: 4 w/pvt. bath, phone, TV
Rates: $85-$90, incl. full brk.
Credit cards: MC, V
Restrictions: No children under 10, pets, smoking. Deposit req. 14-day cancellation notice req. 2-night min. stay on wknds.
Notes: Three-story, Colonial-style house built in 1976. Foyer, living room. Dining room with Ethan Allen furniture, cut crystal glass, antiques, a tall-case clock, and organ. Sitting area with fireplace. Furnished in Colonial style with antiques. Garden. Colonial carriage house overlooking grounds.*

WOODSTOCK (2)

AZALEA HOUSE

Azalea House
551 S. Main St., Woodstock, VA 22664
(703) 459-3500

Innkeeper: Margaret and Price McDonald
Rooms: 2 w/pvt. bath, plus 1 suite w/pvt. bath
Rates: $50-$70/room, $$75-$80/suite, all incl. full brk.
Credit cards: Most major cards
Restrictions: No children under 5, pets, smoking. Deposit req. 3-day cancellation
   notice req. 2-night min. stay on Oct. wknds.
Notes: Two-story Victorian house built in 1890. Balcony overlooking mountains.
Furnished with antiques.

INN AT NARROW PASSAGE

Inn at Narrow Passage
US 11 S., Box 608, Woodstock, VA 22664
(703) 459-8000, (703) 459-8000

Innkeeper: Ellen and Ed Markel
Rooms: 12, incl. 10 w/pvt. bath, phone, 8 w/fireplace
Rates: %55-$95, incl. full brk.
Credit cards: MC, V
Restrictions: No pets, smoking. Deposit req. 3-day cancellation notice req. Min. stay
   req. on fall wknds., holidays.
Notes: Two-story log inn built in early 1740s on stagecoach route. Located on 5
acres overlooking the Shenandoah River. Headquarters for Stonewall Jackson in
1862. Fully restored. Living room with limestone fireplace. Paneled dining room.
Furnished with antiques and handcrafted Colonial reproductions. Back porches.
Small private parties accommodated.*

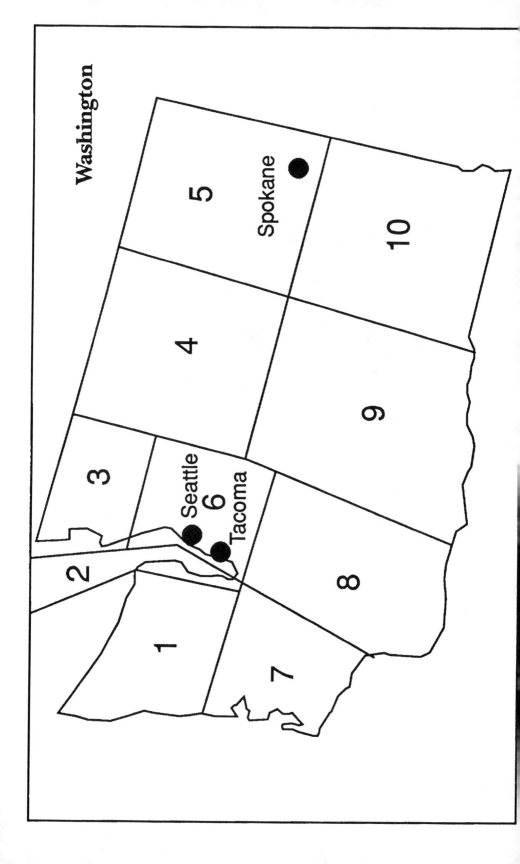

Washington

ANACORTES (2)

Albatross Bed & Breakfast
5708 Kingsway W., Anacortes, WA 98221
(360) 293-0677, (800) 484-9507, 5840
Innkeeper: Barbie and Ken
Rooms: 4 w/pvt. bath
Rates: $65-$85, incl. full brk., afternoon refreshment. Discount avail. for extended stay. Seasonal variations.
Credit cards: MC, V
Restrictions: No children under 6, pets. Smoking restricted. One night's deposit req. 72-hour cancellation notice req.
Notes: Two-story Cape Cod-style cedar house built in 1927. Located on one-acre. Guest rooms furnished with antiques and nautical decor. Living room with fireplace, TV, VCR, travel tapes. Dining room, deck overlooking Skyline Marina. Furnished in traditional style with a marine orientation. 46-foot sailboat for sightseeing. Bike rentals. Courtesy ferry pick-up available. Handicapped access.*

ALBATROSS BED & BREAKFAST

Channel House
2902 Oakes Ave., Anacortes, WA 98221
(206) 293-9382
Innkeeper: Dennis and Patricia McIntyre
Rooms: 6 w/pvt. bath, incl. 2 w/fireplace. Located in 2 bldgs.
Rates: $65-$95, incl. full brk., afternoon refreshment
Credit cards: Most major cards
Restrictions: No pets, smoking. One night's deposit req. 3-day cancellation notice req.

Notes: Victorian house overlooking Puget Sound built in 1902 by Italian count. Many of original windows intact, including mix of stained and leaded glass. Hardwood floors throughout. Library/music room, formal living room, dining room, all with fireplaces. Solarium, garden, hot tub. Furnished with period antiques. Guided kayak tours available. Small private parties accommodated.*

The Majestic Hotel
419 Commercial Ave., Anacortes, WA 98221
(360) 293-3355, (360) 293-5241
Innkeeper: Jeffrey and Virginia Wetmore
Rooms: 15 plus 8 suites, all w/pvt. bath, cable TV, phone
Rates: $89-$138/room, $177/suite, incl. cont. brk. Discount for corporate, senior, extended and AARP stays.
Credit cards: Most major cards
Restrictions: No pets. Smoking restricted. One night's deposit req. 7-day cancellation notice req.
Notes: Originally built in 1889 and restored as a small grand hotel. Located within walking distance of waterfront and downtown historic district. Guest rooms individually decorated with antiques. Some rooms have refrigerators, wet-bars, VCRs, large tubs, decks, or balconies. Courtyard Bistro and Rose and Crown Pub open daily for lunch and dinner. Function room for meetings and special events. Handicapped access.*

ANDERSON ISLAND (6)

The Inn at Burg's Landing
8808 Villa Beach Rd., Anderson Island, WA 98303
(206) 884-9185
Innkeeper: Ken and Annie Burg
Rooms: 1 plus 2 suites w/pvt. bath, TV
Rates: $65-$75/room, $90/suite, all incl. full brk.
Credit cards: Most major cards
Restrictions: No pets, smoking. $20.00 deposit req. 7-day cancellation notice req.
Notes: Contemporary log homestead with views of Mt. Ranier, Puget Sound, and Cascade Mountains. Living room overlooking Mount Ranier. Suite with skylight and private whirlpool bath. Hot tub. Resident dog.

ASHFORD (8)

Mountain Meadows Inn B & B
28912 SR 706E, Ashford, WA 98304
(206) 569-2788
Innkeeper: Chad Darrah
Rooms: 5 w/pvt. bath, located in 2 bldgs.
Rates: $75-$95/summer, $55-$75/winter, all incl. full brk., evening campfires, samores.
Credit cards: MC, V
Restrictions: No children under 10, pets, smoking. Deposit req. 10-day cancellation notice req.
Notes: Built in 1910 as mill superintendent's house. Extensive model railroad collection. Porch. Pond fishing, campfires, lawn games available.*

BAINBRIDGE ISLAND (2)

BOMBAY HOUSE B & B

Bombay House B & B
8490 Beck Rd., Bainbridge Island, WA 98110
(800) 598-3926, (206) 842-3926
Innkeeper: Bunny Cameron, Roger Kanchuk
Rooms: 4 plus 1 suite, incl. 3 w/pvt. bath, 1 w/fireplace, TV
Rates: $55-$85/room, $125/suite, all incl. full brk.
Credit cards: Most major cards
Restrictions: No children under 10, pets, smoking. 50% deposit req. 14-day cancellation notice req.
Notes: Captain's house built in 1907. Located on 5 hillside acres overlooking Puget Sound. 35-minute ferry ride from downtown Seattle. Surrounded by unstructured gardens, orchard. Furnished with country antiques. Parlor with woodburning stove. Country kitchen. Porches, deck, gazebo, widow's walk.*

BELLEVUE (6)

Bellevue Bed and Breakfast
830 100th Ave. S.E., Bellevue, WA 98004
(206) 453-1048
Innkeeper: Cy and Carol Garnett
Rooms: 2 plus 1 suite, incl. 2 w/pvt. bath, phone
Rates: $55/room, $100/suite, incl. full brk. Discount avail. for extended stay.
Credit cards: MC, V
Restrictions: No children under 8, pets, smoking. Credit card guarantee or one night's deposit req. 7-day cancellation notice req., less $5.00 fee.
Notes: Private home in Seattle suburb with hilltop, mountain and city views. Conference room. Private entrances. Guests have access to laundry facilities. Handicapped access. Small private parties accommodated. Lunch and dinner available. Some German spoken.*

BELLINGHAM (3)

BELLINGHAM'S DECANN HOUSE B & B

Bellingham's DeCann House B & B
2610 Eldridge Ave, Bellingham, WA 98225
(206) 734-9172
Innkeeper: Van and Barbara Hudson
Rooms: 2 w/pvt. bath, incl. 1 w/phone
Rates: $50-$70, incl. full brk. Discount avail. for extended stay.
Credit cards: None
Restrictions: No children under 12, pets, smoking. Deposit req. 14-day cancellation
notice req.
Notes: Restored Victorian house with stained glass and etchings created by
innkeeper. Located in historic neighborhood overlooking bay and islands. Guest
roooms decorated with family heirlooms. Parlor with pool table.*

North Garden Inn
1014 N. Garden, Bellingham, WA 98225
(206) 671-7828, (800) 922-6414
Innkeeper: Barbara and Frank DeFreytas
Rooms: 10 w/pvt. bath, 8 w/phone
Rates: $54-$59, incl. full brk. Discount avail. for seniors, extended stays
Credit cards: MC, V
Restrictions: No children under 10, pets, smoking. Deposit req. 24-hour cancella-
tion notice req.
Notes: Three-story Queen Anne Victorian house. Located on hill overlooking
Bellingham Bay. Two common rooms, each with Steinway grand piano. Some
rooms with handicapped access. Listed on the National Register of Historic Places.
Some French spoken.*

Schnauzer Crossing
4421 Lakeway Dr., Bellingham, WA 98226
(360) 733-0055, (360) 734-2808
Innkeeper: Vermont and Donna McAllister
Rooms: 2 plus 1 suite, 1 cottage, all w/pvt. bath, phone, incl. 2 w/cable TV, fireplace

Rates: $110/room, $160/suite, $180/cottage, all incl. full brk.
Credit cards: Most major cards
Restrictions: No smoking. One night's deposit req. 5-day cancellation notice req. 2-night min. stay on holidays and wknds.
Notes: Two-story house. Furnished with handmade furniture. Guest rooms with fresh flowers, goose down comforters, terry robes. Great room and deck overlooking Lake Whatcom. Library. Small private parties accommodated. Outdoor hot tub. Canoe, sailboat available. Handicapped access. Some French, Spanish spoken. Resident schnauzers.

CAMANO ISLAND (2)

Inn at Barnum Point
464 S. Barnum Rd., Camano Island, WA 98292-8510
(206) 387-2256, (206) 387-2256
Innkeeper: Carolin Barnum Dilorenzo
Rooms: 2 w/pvt. bath, phone, fireplace
Rates: $75, incl. full brk.
Credit cards: None
Restrictions: No pets, smoking. One night's deposit req. 5-day cancellation notice req., less $10.00 fee.
Notes: Cape Cod-style farmhouse. Located on the beach with orchard established in 1904, next to bird sanctuary. Dining room overlooking bluff.*

COSMOPOLIS (7)

Cooney Mansion
1705 Fifth St., Box 54, Cosmopolis, WA 98537
(206) 533-0602
Innkeeper: Judi and Jim Lohr
Rooms: 8, incl. 5 w/pvt. bath, 1 w/fireplace and TV
Rates: $50-$115, incl. full brk., afternoon and evening refreshment. Discount avail. for extended stay.
Credit cards: Most major cards
Restrictions: No pets, smoking. Children over 5 welcome on wkdays. or by special arrangement. Min. one night's deposit req. 7-day cancellation notice req., less $20.00 fee.
Notes: Built in 1908 as residence for lumber baron Neil Cooney. Beam and wood panelled first floor with living room, dining room, two parlors, sunroom. Library. Ballroom available for functions. Furnished with original turn-of-the-century American Arts and Crafts Period furniture and fixtures. Jacuzzi, sauna, exercise room. Rose garden, rhododendron grove, sprawling lawn. Listed as State and National Historic Register Landmark.

COUPEVILLE (2)

Colonel Crockett Farm B & B Inn
1012 S. Fort Casey Rd., Coupeville, WA 98239
(206) 678-3711
Innkeeper: Robert and Beulah Whitlow
Rooms: 5 w/pvt. bath
Rates: $65-$95, incl. full brk.
Credit cards: MC, V

Restrictions: No children under 14, pets, smoking. One night's deposit or credit card guarantee req. 7-day cancellation notice req.

Notes: Victorian farmhouse built in 1855. Located on ten wooded acres on the north shore of Crockett Lake overlooking Admiralty Bay. Oak-paneled library with slate fireplace. Solarium with Victorian-style wicker furniture. Breakfast room. Furnished with antiques. Listed on the National Register of Historic Places.*

COLONEL CROCKETT FARM B & B INN

DEER HARBOR (2)

Deep Meadow Farm B & B
P.O. Box 321, Deer Harbor, WA 98243
(206) 376-5866

Innkeeper: Gary and Anna Boyle
Rooms: 2, w/pvt bath
Rates: $95, incl. full brk., afternoon refreshment
Credit cards: None
Restrictions: No children under 12, pets, smoking. One night's deposit req. 14-day cancellation notice req., less $10.00 fee. 2-night min. stay from April–Oct.
Notes: Two-story homestead built approx. 1900. Located on 40 acres. Restored farmhouse built in 1938. Decorated with family heirlooms, antiques and memorabilia. Living room with fireplace, phone, TV. Veranda. Orchard with hot tub. Dairy barn. Vegetable garden. Hiking trails. Pond. Yard games. Resident cats and dog.

Palmer's Chart House
P.O. Box 51, Deer Harbor, WA 98243
(206) 376-4231

Innkeeper: Majean and Donald Palmer
Rooms: 2 w/pvt. bath, phone
Rates: $60, incl. full brk.
Credit cards: None
Restrictions: No children under 10, pets. Smoking restricted. Full prepayment req. 30-day cancellation notice req.
Notes: Located on one wooded acre on Orcas Island overlooking Deer Harbor. Has operated as inn since 1975. Living room with fireplace. Decks with lounge chairs.

Decorated with many Oriental furnishings. Flower garden. Accessible by Anacortes car ferry. Sailing excursions available on innkeeper's thirty-three-foot sloop. Spanish spoken.*

EASTSOUND (2)

Kangaroo House
North Beach Road, Box 334, Eastsound, WA 98245
(206) 376-2175
Innkeeper: Jan and Mike Russillo
Rooms: 4 plus 1 suite, incl. 2 w/pvt. bath
Rates: $70-$100/room, $110/suite, all incl. full brk.
Credit cards: MC, V
Restrictions: No pets, smoking. 50% deposit req. 7-day cancellation notice req.
Notes: 1907 Craftsman-style house. Located on Orcas Island. Sitting room with fieldstone fireplace. Study, breakfast room. Furnished in period style. Decks overlooking gardens. Spanish, Italian spoken.*

Outlook Inn on Orcas Island
Main St., Box 210, Eastsound, WA 98245-0210
(206) 376-2200, (206) 376-2256
Innkeeper: Jeanine
Rooms: 25, incl. 11 w/pvt. bath, phone, TV, plus 16 suites w/pvt. bath, phone, TV, fireplace. Located in 3 bldgs.
Rates: $29-$110/room, $210/suite, all incl. cont. brk.
Credit cards: Most major cards
Restrictions: No pets. Deposit req. 7-day cancellation notice req.
Notes: Thai spoken. Handicapped access.*

Turtleback Farm Inn
Rte. 1, Box 650, Eastsound, WA 98245
(206) 376-4914
Innkeeper: William and Susan Fletcher
Rooms: 7 w/pvt. bath
Rates: $70-$130, incl. full brk., evening refreshment
Credit cards: MC, V
Restrictions: No children under 8, pets, smoking. One night's deposit req. 10-day cancellation notice req., less $20.00 fee. 2-night min. stay on wknds. and in summer and holidays.
Notes: Two-story farmhouse located on Orcas Island on eighty-acres of forest and farmland. View of meadows, ponds. Renovated and expanded in 1985. Living room with Rumford fireplace, game table. Dining room with wet bar. Outside deck. Furnished with antiques and contemporary pieces. Small private parties accommodated. Handicapped access.*

EDMONDS (6)

Harrison House
210 Sunset Ave., Edmonds, WA 98020
(206) 776-4748
Innkeeper: Jody and Harve Harrison
Rooms: 2 w/pvt. bath, phone, TV, pvt. deck

Rates: $35-$65, incl. full brk.
Credit cards: None
Restrictions: No children, pets, smoking. Deposit req.
Notes: Waterfront house overlooking Puget Sound and Olympic Mountains built approx. 1990. Located near University of Washington.

FRIDAY HARBOR (2)

Friday's
35 First St., Friday Harbor, WA 98250
(206) 378-5848, (206) 378-3559
Innkeeper: Debbie and Steve Demarest
Rooms: 9, plus 1 suite, incl. 3 w/pvt. bath, 1 w/TV
Rates: $55-$125/room, $125-$155/suite, incl. cont. brk.
Credit cards: AE, MC, V
Restrictions: No pets, smoking. Deposit req. 7-day cancellation notice req.
Notes: Restored 1891 historic hotel and landmark one block from waterfront. Furnished with antiques, limited edition wildlife artwork, leaded glass, Victorian carpeting. Parlor. Some rooms with Jacuzzi tubs, private decks, water views.*

Mariella Inn & Cottages
630 Turn Point Rd., Friday Harbor, WA 98250
(360) 378-6868, (360) 378-6822
Innkeeper: Art and Alison Lohrey
Rooms: 10, incl. 3 w/pvt. bath, plus 1 suite w/pvt. bath, plus 7 cottages w/pvt. bath, fireplace. Located in 8 bldgs.
Rates: $100-$160/room, $160/suite, $175-$225/cottage, all incl. full brk. in season, cont. brk. off season. Seasonal variations.
Credit cards: MC, V
Restrictions: No children under 10 in main house. No pets, smoking. Min. one night's deposit req. 10-day cancellation notice req., less 10% fee. 2-night min. stay in main house in season. 3-night min. stay in cottages in season.
Notes: Victorian mansion built in 1902. Fully restored. Located on 7 landscaped, wooded acres 1/3 mile from ferry landing. Dining room overlooking water. Two parlors, each with fireplace. Private dock, hot tub. Lawn games available. Bicycles, kayaks, day sailors available to rent. Small private parties accommodated.*

States Inn
2039 W. Valley Rd., Friday Harbor, WA 98250
(206) 378-6240, (206) 378-6241
Innkeeper: Kip and Linda Taylor
Rooms: 6 plus 1 suite w/pvt. bath, fireplace
Rates: $80-$110/room, $175/suite, all incl. full brk. Discount avail. for AAA stay. Seasonal variations.
Credit cards: MC, V
Restrictions: No children under 10, pets, smoking. One night's deposit req., 7-day cancellation notice req., less $10.00 fee.
Notes: Country inn located on 44 acres on San Juan Island. Originally an old schoolhouse converted to a dance hall and then moved to current site as a ranch house. Now an active horse boarding ranch with trail rides available. Major renovation in 1991. Guest rooms decorated with theme of U.S. state it is named for. Liv-

ing room with stone fireplace, sunroom, reading room. Special handicapped access room. AAA 3-star rating.*

Wharfside B & B aboard 'Jacquelyn'
P.O. Box 1212, Friday Harbor, WA 98250
(360) 378-5661
Innkeeper: Clyde and Bette Rice
Rooms: 2, no pvt. bath
Rates: $70-$85, incl. full brk. Seasonal variations.
Credit cards: MC, V
Restrictions: One night's deposit req. 7-day cancellation notice req., less $10.00 fee. 2-night min. stay, July–Sept.
Notes: 60-ft. traditional sailing vessel. Main salon with fireplace. Furnished in Victorian style. Moored at the Friday Harbor Port Dock. Cruising charters available. Guests have access to ship's rowing gig.*

GREENBANK (2)

Guest House Cottages
3366 S. Hwy. 525, Greenbank, WA 98253
(206) 678-3115
Innkeeper: Mary Jane and Don Creger
Rooms: 5 cottages w/kitchen, plus 1 suite, 2 houses, all w/pvt. bath, TV, VCR, jacuzzi, fireplace. Located in 7 bldgs.
Rates: $285/Lodge, $155/farm house, $135-$185/cottage, all incl. expanded cont. brk. Discount avail. for extended stay. Seasonal variations.
Credit cards: Most major cards
Restrictions: No children, pets smoking. Min. one night's deposit req., 30-day cancellation notice req., less $10.00 fee. 2-night min. stay on wknds. 3-night min. stay during holidays.
Notes: Farmhouse with stained-glass windows built in the 1920s. Log house, two log cottages, two frame cottages. Located on twenty-five wooded acres with meadow overlooking water and mountains. Living room with fireplace. Country kitchen, dining room. Furnished with country antiques. Outdoor swimming pool, spa, exercise room, personal jacuzzis. Small private parties accommodated. Resident pet.*

KIRKLAND (6)

Shumway Mansion
11410 100 Ave., Juanita Bay, Kirkland, WA 98033
(206) 823-2303, (206) 822-0421
Innkeeper: Richard and Salli Harris, Julie Blakemore
Rooms: 6 plus 1 suite, all w/pvt. bath, phone, TV
Rates: $65-$85/room, $95/suite, all incl. full brk., evening refreshment
Credit cards: Most major cards
Restrictions: No children under 12, pets, smoking. Deposit or credit card guarantee req. 7-day cancellation notice req.
Notes: Built in 1910. Moved and renovated in 1985. Located on two-acres overlooking Juanita Bay. Ballroom, reception hall, two kitchens, porch, patio, gazebo. Furnished with antiques. Small private parties accommodated.*

LaCONNER (3)

HEATHER HOUSE

Heather House
505 Maple, Box 237, LaConner, WA 98257
(206) 466-4675
Innkeeper: Wayne and Bev Everton
Rooms: 3, incl. 1 w/pvt. bath, fireplace
Rates: $50-$70, incl. cont. brk., afternoon refreshment
Credit cards: MC, V
Restrictions: No children, pets, smoking. Credit card guarantee req. 24-hour cancellation notice req.
Notes: Cape Cod house with oak floors, wainscoting, built in 1979 as an exact replica of a turn-of-the-century home in Marblehead, Mass. with vista of farmland, the Cascades and Mt. Baker. Each guest room has terry robes, blow dryer. Walking distance to waterfront. Covered porch. Bicycles available.*

LANGLEY (2)

Country Cottage of Langley
215 6th St., Langley, WA 98260
(206) 221-8709
Innkeeper: Bob and Mary Decelles
Rooms: 5 plus 2 cottages all w/pvt. bath, incl. 3 w/fireplace. Located in 3 bldgs.
Rates: $90/room, $105/cottage, all incl. full brk. Seasonal variations. Discount avail. for extended stay
Credit cards: MC, V
Restrictions: No children, pets, smoking. One night's deposit req. 7-day cancellation notice req., less $10.00 fee. 2-night min. stay on wknds., June–Sept.
Notes: Restored farmhouse built in the 1920s plus two cottages. Located on two-acres with views of Puget Sound and Cascades. Living room with fireplace. Dining room, solar heated sun room. Gazebo, decks, hot tub. View of mountains and sea. Great to be in the country and in the city at the same time.*

COUNTRY COTTAGE OF LANGLEY

Eagle's Nest Inn
3236 E. Saratoga Rd., Langley, WA 98260
(360) 321-5331, (206) 221-5331
Innkeeper: Joanne and Jerry Lechner
Rooms: 3 plus 1 suite, all w/pvt. bath, TV/VCR
Rates: $95-$115/room, $95/suite, all incl. full brk., afternoon refreshment. Discount avail. Nov.–Mar.
Credit cards: Most major cards
Restrictions: No children under 12, pets, smoking. Credit card guarantee req. 7-day cancellation notice req., less $15.00 fee. 2-night min. stay on holiday wknds. for "view" rooms.
Notes: Two-story octagonal cedar house built in 1987. Located on 2.5 wooded-acres on hill overlooking Saratoga Passage, Mount Baker about 2½ miles from Langley. Most guest rooms with view, private balcony. Dining room. Lounge with TV, VCR, library, board games, window seat. Decks, spa.*

Log Castle
3273 E. Saratoga Rd., Langley, WA 98260
(360) 221-5483
Innkeeper: Jack and Norma Metcalf
Rooms: 3 plus suite, all w/pvt. bath, pvt. porch, incl. 2 w/TV
Rates: $80-$105/room, $105/suite, incl. full brk., afternoon refreshment
Credit cards: Most major cards
Restrictions: No children under 10, pets, smoking. Deposit req. 7-day cancellation notice req. Closed 3 days at Christmas.
Notes: Log lodge with three-story, eight-sided turret designed and built by innkeepers from trees on the property. Located on beach facing Mt. Baker and Cascade Mountains. Living/dining room with open-beam ceiling, stone fireplace, cable TV. Widow's walk. Canoe and rowboat available.*

LEAVENWORTH (4)

All Seasons River Inn
8751 Icicle Rd., Box 788, Leavenworth, WA 98826
(509) 548-1425, (800) 254-0555

Innkeeper: Kathy and Jeff Falconer
Rooms: 3 plus 2 suites, all w/pvt. bath, incl. 3 w/fireplace
Rates: $90-$105/room, $120-$125/suite, all incl. full brk. Seasonal variations.
Credit cards: MC, V
Restrictions: No children under 16, pets, smoking. Credit card guarantee or one night's deposit req. Min. 7-day cancellation notice req. 2-night min. stay on wknds. for suite and on other rooms for festivals and holiday wknds.
Notes: Cedar house built approx. 1990. Located on the banks of the Wenatchee River. All guest rooms have deck overlooking river. Common rooms for TV and video viewing, conversation or reading. Game room, library. Furnished with antiques, down comforters and handmade quilts, some with jacuzzi tubs. Terraced lawns and walkways to a sandy beach. Bicycles available.*

Mountain Home Lodge
P.O. Box 687, Leavenworth, WA 98826
(509) 548-7077

Innkeeper: Charlie Brooks and Chris Clark
Rooms: 9, plus 1 ste w/pvt. bath, in-room hot tub, fireplace
Rates: $78-$208/room, $118-$228/suite, all incl. three meals in winter
Credit cards: Most major cards
Restrictions: No children, pets, smoking. $50 deposit req. 3-week cancellation notice req. less $10.00 fee. 2-night min. stay from Thanksgiving–Mar. 30. accessible in winter only via lodge's Snowcat.
Notes: Mountain lodge located on 13-acres. Lounge with stone fireplace. Furnished with antiques and contemporary pieces. Outdoor hot tub, swimming pool. Lawn games available.*

Old Blewett Pass
3470 Highway 97, Leavenworth, WA 98826
(509) 548-4475

Innkeeper: Dave & Laura Wagner
Rooms: 4 w/pvt. bath
Rates: $75-$90, incl. full brk.
Credit cards: MC, V
Restrictions: No children, pets, smoking. 20% deposit req. 48-hour cancellation notice req. 2-night min. stay on local festival wknds., holidays.
Notes: Authentic frontier homestead built in 1908. Located in Cascade Mountain valley. Served as resting place for travelers in early 1900s. Main greeting room with fireplace. Swimming pool, volleyball, horseshoes, biking, cross-country skiing available.

Run of the River
P.O. Box 285, Leavenworth, WA 98826
(509) 548-7171, (800) 288-6491

Innkeeper: Monty and Karen Turner
Rooms: 5 plus 1 suite, all w/pvt. bath and TV, incl. 3 w/fireplace
Rates: $90/room, $140/suite, all incl. full brk. Discount avail. for senior citizens.
Credit cards: Most major cards
Restrictions: No children under 16, pets, smoking. One night's deposit req. 10-day cancellation notice req. 2-night min. stay on wknds. and holidays.
Notes: Natural log lodge with Cathedral pine ceilings, picture windows. Located adjacent to bird sanctuary. Furnished with hand-crafted log furniture, hand-stitched

quilts. Terrace with hot tub overlooking Icicle River. Lawn games available. Handicapped access.*

LOPEZ ISLAND (2)

Aleck Bay Inn
Rt. 1, Box 1920, Lopez Island, WA 98261
(206) 468-3535, (206) 468-3533
Innkeeper: David and May
Rooms: 4 suites w/pvt. bath, 2 w/fireplace, 1 w/TV
Rates: $110-$139, incl. full brk., afternoon refreshment
Credit cards: Most major cards
Restrictions: Children welcome by prior arrangement. No pets, smoking. One night's deposit or credit card guarantee req. 14-day cancellation notice req., less $10.00 fee.
Notes: Located on seven-acres with private beach on south end of Lopez Island. Music/play room overlooking bay with billiards, board games, piano, TV, piano, fireplace. Formal living room. Deck with adjoining hot tub. Bicycle rental available. Handicapped access. Chinese spoken.*

Inn at Swifts Bay
Rte. 2, Box 3402, Lopez Island, WA 98261
(206) 468-3636, (206) 468-3637
Innkeeper: Robert Herrmann, Christopher Brandmeir
Rooms: 2, plus 3 suites, incl. 3 w/pvt. bath
Rates: $75-$85/room, $110-$140/suite, all incl. full brk., afternoon refreshment
Credit cards: Most major cards
Restrictions: No children under 16, pets, smoking. One night's deposit req. 10-day cancellation notice req.
Notes: Northwest Tudor-style house located across the street from private beach and situated on three wooded acres. Living room with fireplace. Den with fireplace, TV, VCR, extensive book and video library. Outdoor hot tub. Pick-up at Lopez Ferry Landing, airstrip or Fisherman Bay Seaplane dock available. Portuguese, some German spoken.*

INN AT SWIFTS BAY

MacKaye Harbor Inn
Rte. 1, Box 1940,
Lopez Island, WA 98261
(206) 468-2253, (206) 468-9555
Innkeeper: Brooks and Sharon Broberg
Rooms: 4 plus 1 suites, incl. 1 w/pvt. bath, 1 w/fireplace, 1 w/pvt. deck
Rates: $69-$97/room, $97-$$115/suite, all incl. full brk., afternoon refreshment
Credit cards: MC, V
Restrictions: No children under 9, pets, smoking. Deposit req. 14-day cancellation
    notice req., less $10.00 fee. 2-night min. stay.
Notes: Victorian private house built in 1930 by a Norwegian sea captain. Restored.
Has operated as inn since 1985. Located on a low-bank sandy beach. Parlor with
harbor view, reading room, dining room. All meals available. Lawns and orchard on
property. Bicycles, windsurfers available for rent.*

MACKAYE HARBOR INN

LUMMI ISLAND (2)

Loganita By The Sea
2825 W. Shore Dr., Lummi Island, WA 98262
(206) 758-2651
Innkeeper: Ann and Glen Gossage
Rooms: 2 w/pvt. bath, plus 3 suites w/pvt. bath, fireplace, TV. Located in 2 bldgs.
Rates: $85-$135/room, $115-$175/suite, all incl. full brk., afternoon refreshment.
    Discount avail. for extended stay.
Credit cards: MC, V
Restrictions: Well-behaved children welcome. No pets, smoking. $200 damage de-
    posit req. 14-day cancellation notice req.
Notes: Two-story house built approx. 1894. Common rooms with floor-to-ceiling
stone fireplaces. Decks overlooking San Juan Islands. Hot tub.

The Willows Inn
2579 West Shore Dr., Lummi Island, WA 98262
(206) 758-2620
Innkeeper: Gary and Victoria Flynn
Rooms: 7, plus 2-bedroom guesthouse and cottage, all w/pvt. bath, incl. 2 w/fire-
    place, 3 w/TV

Rates: $95-$110/room, $135-$145/cottage, $210-$285/guest house, all incl. full brk., afternoon refreshment. Seasonal variations. Discount avail. for extended stay.
Credit cards: MC, V
Restrictions: No pets, smoking. One night's deposit req. 2-week cancellation notice req.
Notes: Island retreat established 70 years ago by current owner's grandparents. Restored with lattice work. Honeymoon cottage with private veranda. Sitting room with polished hardwood floors and grand oak fireplace. Game room with TV, darts, billiards, brewiana collection. Friday and Saturday night candlelight dinners available. Furnished with family antiques, personal mementos and fresh flowers. Long porch, sundeck, rhodedendron gardens, evergreens.

THE WILLOWS INN

MAPLE VALLEY (6)

Maple Valley Bed and Breakfast
20020 S.E. 228th, Maple Valley, WA 98038
(206) 432-1409
Innkeeper: Clarke and Jayne Hurlbut
Rooms: 2, no pvt. bath
Rates: $50-$65, incl. full brk. Discount avail. for extended stay.
Credit cards: None
Restrictions: No pets, smoking. Full prepayment req. 1-day cancellation notice req., less $10.00 fee.
Notes: Two-story house built by Clarke in 1970. Located on five acres with wildlife pond, peacocks. Cedar walls, detailed trim, unusual angles, ope-beamed ceilings, peeled-poled railings. Hand-hewn four poster bed in one guest room. Upstairs sitting room with books, wildlife guides, binoculars, games. Bed warmers on cool evenings. Deck overlooking orchard. Furnished with country collectables. BBQ, lawn games, board games available. Some Spanish spoken.*

MORTON (8)

St. Helens Manorhouse
7476 U.S. Hwy. 12, Morton, WA 98356
(206) 498-5243

Innkeeper: Susan and Kitty Baxter
Rooms: 4, incl. 2 w/pvt. bath
Rates: $59-$69, incl. full brk., afternoon refreshment. Discount for senior citizen and extended stays.
Credit cards: None
Restrictions: No children under 12, pets, smoking. Deposit req. 48-hour cancellation notice req., less $5.00 fee.
Notes: Old-growth, Douglas fir Queen Anne Classic house with etched beveled and leaded glass, built in 1910. Located on hill overlooking lake on 1,000-acre working produce farm. Parlor with board games, TV, VCR. Wrap-around porches, colonade. Furnished with antiques.

MOUNT VERNON (3)

White Swan Guest House
1388 Moore Rd., Mount Vernon, WA 98273
(206) 445-6805

Innkeeper: Peter Goldfarb
Rooms: 3 plus cottage, incl. 1 w/pvt. bath
Rates: $65-$75/room, $125/cottage, all incl. cont. brk., homemade chocolate chip cookies
Credit cards: MC, V
Restrictions: No smoking, pets. Children welcome in cottage. Credit card guarantee or deposit req. 5-day cancellation notice req. 2-night min. stay on Labor Day and July 4th wknds.
Notes: Farmhouse built in 1890s located 6 miles from fishing village of La Conner. Totally restored and redecorated in 1986. Parlor with wood stove. Dining room, library. Back porch with wicker furniture. Furnished with antiques. English cutting garden with picket fence, fruit trees.*

WHITE SWAN GUEST HOUSE

SPRING BAY INN

OLGA (1)

Spring Bay Inn
P.O. Box 97, Olga, WA 98279
(206) 376-5531, (206) 376-2193
Innkeeper: Carl Burger and Sandy Playa
Rooms: 4 w/pvt. bath, phone, fireplace, bay view, incl. 2 w/pvt. deck
Rates: $145-$165, incl. full brk., daily guided kayak tour. Discount avail. for extended stay. Group pkgs. avail.
Credit cards: MC, V
Restrictions: Non-refundable one night's deposit req. No smoking, pets.
Notes: Secluded retreat on Orcas Island located on 57 wooded acres adjacent to Obstruction Pass State Park. Inn operated by two retired park rangers. Frontage on private bay. Custom woodwork and masonry. All rooms individually decorated with high ceilings and custom windows, handmade quilts and afghans, nature illustrations. Baths with clawfooted tubs, tile. Living room with fireplace, bay front dining area. Bayside hot tub. Hiking trails, guided nature walks. German spoken.*

OLYMPIA (6)

Harbinger Inn
1136 E. Bay Dr., Olympia, WA 98506
(206) 754-0389
Innkeeper: Marisa and Terrell Williams
Rooms: 3 plus 1 suite, incl. 1 w/pvt. bath
Rates: $70/room, $90/suite, all incl. cont. brk., afternoon refreshment. Discount avail. for senior citizens.
Credit cards: Most major cards
Restrictions: No children under 10, pets, smoking. Deposit req. 72-hour cancellation req.
Notes: Restored house built in 1910 of finely detailed, grey, ashler block construction with white pillars and wide balconies. Turn-of-the-century furniture throughout inn. Library. Original wall stencils and oak pocket doors. Views of water and marina. Artesian waterfall on property.

Puget View Guest House
7924 61st NE, Olympia, WA 98516
(206) 459-1676
Innkeeper: Dick, Barb, and Britt Yunker
Rooms: 1 cottage w/pvt. bath
Rates: $79-$89, incl. cont. brk. Discount avail. for senior citizens.
Credit cards: MC, V
Restrictions: Pets accepted by prior arrangement. Deposit req. 5-day cancellation
    notice req.
Notes: Cottage overlooking the sea in a classic Northwest setting. Located on a cliff
on an acre of land next to forests of Tolmie State Park. Brown cedar shake cottage
sleeps four. Painted wood floors, braided rugs, white curtains. Porch, deck, BBQ,
small refrigerator.*

PACKWOOD (8)

Tatoosh Meadows
408 Craig Rd., Box 487, Packwood, WA 98361
(206) 494-2311, (800) 294-2311, (206) 494-2073
Innkeeper: Maree and Tom Lerchen
Rooms: 4 plus 5 suites, all w/pvt. bath, fireplace. 2 bedroom cabin w/pvt. bath. Lo-
    cated in five bldgs.
Rates: $100/room, $110-$135/suite, $200/cabin, all incl. cont. brk., evening re-
    freshment. Discount avail. for extended stay.
Credit cards: Most major cards
Restrictions: No smoking. One night's deposit req. No refund—reschedule of dates
    okay. 2-night min. stay. 3-night min. stay on holidays.
Notes: Accommodations in five cabins tucked among the foothills of the Cascades
on the banks of the Cowlitz River and surrounded by Gifford Pinchot National For-
est, Mount Ranier National Park and Goat Rocks Wilderness area. Units equipped
with kitchen facilities. Some with decks and hot tubs.*

PORT ANGELES (1)

The Tudor Inn
1108 S. Oak, Port Angeles, WA 98362
(206) 452-3138

THE TUDOR INN

Innkeeper: Jane and Jerry Glass
Rooms: 5, incl. 2 w/pvt. bath
Rates: $55-$90, incl. full brk., afternoon refreshment. Seasonal variations.
Credit cards: MC, V
Restrictions: No children under 12, pets. Smoking restricted. One night's deposit req. 5-day cancellation notice req., less $5.00 fee
Notes: Three-story frame Tudor house built in 1910. Fully restored and has operated as inn since 1983. Library with fireplace, living room, each with fireplace. Formal dining room, breakfast room. Furnished with antiques.*

PORT TOWNSEND (2)

The English Inn
718 F St., Port Townsend, WA 98368
(206) 385-5302, (206) 385-5302
Innkeeper: Juliette Swenson
Rooms: 5 w/pvt. bath
Rates: $65-$95, incl. full brk. Seasonal variations.
Credit cards: MC, V
Restrictions: No children under 12, pets, smoking. One night's deposit req. 72-hour cancellation notice req. 2-night min. stay on some wknds.
Notes: Two-story Italianate mansion with two-story bay windows, bracketed friezes, built in 1885. Located on hill overlooking the Olympic Mountains. Dining room. Lounge with TV, VCR. Furnished with English antiques. Garden with gazebo, hot tub. Bicycles available. French, German spoken.*

Heritage House
305 Pierce St., Port Townsend, WA 98368
(206) 385-6800
Innkeeper: Kathy, Gary and Shanon Hambley
Rooms: 5, plus 1 suite, incl. 4 w/pvt. bath, 1 w/fireplace
Rates: $60-$110, incl. full brk. Discount avail. for corporate stay.
Credit cards: Most major cards
Restrictions: No children under 12., pets, smoking. Deposit req. 10-day cancellation notice req.

HERITAGE HOUSE

Notes: Italianate inn built about 1878. Located on bluff overlooking Admiralty Bay and Olympic Mountains. Victorian parlor, dining room, breakfast nook. Each room distinctively furnished with Victorian antiques, period wallpapers. Listed on the National Register of Historic Places. Handicapped access.*

The James House
1238 Washington St., Port Townsend, WA 98368
(206) 385-1238, (800) 385-1238
Innkeeper: Carol McGough, Anne Tiernan
Rooms: 9 plus 2 suites, 1 cottage, incl. 4 w/pvt. bath, 2 w/fireplace
Rates: $65-$145/room, $100-$145/suite, incl. cont. brk.
Credit cards: Most major cards
Restrictions: Children under 12, pets, smoking. One night's deposit req. 5-day cancellation notice req.
Notes: Three-story Queen Anne mansion with oak, cherry and walnut parquet floors built in 1889. Located on bluff overlooking Puget Sound, Olympic and Cascade Mountain ranges. Renovated in 1960. Fully restored in and has operated as inn since 1973. Center hall with cherry staircase. Formal dining room, two parlors, all with fireplaces. Kitchen with wood stove. Furnished with Victorian furniture, period antiques. Garden. Listed on the National Register of Historic Places. Small private parties accommodated.

Lizzie's Victorian B & B
731 Pierce, Port Townsend, WA 98368
(206) 385-4168, (800) 700-4168
Innkeeper: Bill and Patti Wickline
Rooms: 8, incl. 5 w/pvt. bath, 1 w/fireplace
Rates: $58-$105, incl. full brk. Mid-week, winter discount avail.
Credit cards: MC, DC, V
Restrictions: No children under 10, pets, smoking. One night's deposit req. 4-day cancellation notice req. 2-night min. stay on holiday wknds.
Notes: Two-story Italianate Victorian house built in 1888. Two parlors, each with fireplace, one with grand piano. Library, kitchen. Furnished with antiques. Decorated with silk hangings from Broadway production of *Flower Drum Song*. Resident dog.*

POULSBO (2)

Edgewater Beach Bed and Breakfast
26818 Edgewater Blvd., Poulsbo, WA 98370
(800) 641-0955, (206) 779-6015
Innkeeper: Don Bell and Sandra
Rooms: 1, plus 2 suites, all w/pvt. bath, phone, microwave, stocked refregerator, incl. 1 w/TV
Rates: $75/room, $95-$125/suite, all incl. full brk., afternoon refreshment
Credit cards: Most major cards
Restrictions: No children under 8, pets, smoking. Deposit req. 2-day cancellation notice req.
Notes: Two-story cottage-style house overlooking the fjord of Hood Canal and Olympic Mountains. Each room has view. Glass-enclosed dining room, sun room with deck, Great Room surrounding a two-sided granite fireplace. Furnished in

eclectic and whimsical manner with antiques and treasures from throughout the United States. Ideal for birdwatching, especially of eagles. Handicapped access.*

Manor Farm Inn
26069 Big Valley Rd., Poulsbo, WA 98370
(206) 779-4628, (206) 779-4876
Innkeeper: Jill Hughes
Rooms: 7 w/pvt. bath, incl. 2 w/fireplace plus farm cottage and beach house
Rates: $95-$175, incl. full brk., afternoon refreshment. Seasonal variations.
Credit cards: MC, V
Restrictions: No children under 16, pets, smoking. Deposit req. 14-day cancellation notice req.
Notes: Farm built in 1890 located on 25 acres with fishing lake. All rooms have vaulted ceilings and are furnished with French pine antiques and eiderdown comforters. Drawing room with fireplace. Lawn games, mountain bikes available. Resident farm animals.

SEATTLE (6)

Bacon Mansion
959 Broadway E., Seattle, WA 98102
(206) 329-1864, (800) 240-1864, (206) 860-9025
Innkeeper: Daryl King, Timothy Stiles
Rooms: 5 w/phone, TV, incl. 3 w/pvt. bath, plus 3 suites w/pvt. bath, phone, TV, incl. 1 w/fireplace. Located in 2 bldgs.
Rates: $59-$89/room, $74-$125/suite, all incl. expanded cont. brk. Seasonal variations.
Credit cards: Most major cards
Restrictions: No pets. Smokiing restricted. Deposit req. 7-day cancellation notice req. 2-night min. stay on most wknds.
Notes: Four-story classical Edwardian-style tudor house built in 1909 on Capitol Hill. Fully renovated in and has operated as inn since 1985. Library. Features 3,000-crystal chandelier. Porches and patios. Small private parties accommodated.

BD Williams House Bed and Breakfast
1505 4th Ave. North, Seattle, WA 98109
(800) 880-0810, (206) 285-0810, (206) 285-8526
Innkeeper: Susan, Doug Williams and daughters
Rooms: 5, incl. 1 w/pvt. bath, 2 w/phone
Rates: $80-$90/shared bath, $85-$105/pvt. bath, all incl. full brk. Discount avail. for extended stay from Oct.–April.
Credit cards: AE, V
Restrictions: No pets, smoking resticted. Children welcome by prior arrangement. One night's deposit req. 7-day cancellation notice req.
Notes: Edwardian house with original woodwork, sculptured tin wall-coverings built at the turn-of-the-century. Located on Queen Anne Hill overlooking Cascade Mountains, Mount Ranier, downtown skyline, Puget Sound. Main living and dining areas. Formal entry Italian hand-tiled fireplace. Parlor with TV. Enclosed sun porch. Furnished with antiques.

Beechtree Manor
1405 Queen Anne Ave. N., Seattle, WA 98109
(206) 281-7037

Innkeeper: Virginia Lucero
Rooms: 6 plus 1 suite, incl. 4 w/pvt. bath, 1 w/TV
Rates: $49-$79/room, $95-$125, incl. full brk. Seasonal variations.
Credit cards: MC, V
Restrictions: No children under 5, smoking. One night's deposit req. 72-hour cancellation notice req. 2-night min. stay in July and Aug.
Notes: English country mansion built at turn of the century on Queen Anne Hill. Common room with fireplace, parlor, back porch with wicker rocking chairs, patio. Wood paneling. Furnished in English style with collections of original art, English wallpaper, Oriental rugs, antiques. Small private parties accommodated. Manager is a chef.*

Bellevue Place B & B
1111 Bellevue Place E., Seattle, WA 98102
(206) 325-9253, (800) 325-9253, (206) 455-0785

Innkeeper: Gunner Johnson, Joe Pruett
Rooms: 3, no pvt. bath.
Rates: $85, incl. full brk. Discount avail. for extended stay.
Credit cards: Most major cards
Restrictions: No children, pets, smoking. Deposit req. 14-day cancellation notice req., less $25.00 fee.
Notes: 1905 'Story Book' house with leaded glass. Located in Landmark Historic District of Capitol Hill. Guest rooms with pressed cotton bedding. Dining room with fireplace, grand piano. Solarium with formal patios. Furnished in Victorian style with Oriental rugs.*

CHAMBERED NAUTILUS INN

Chambered Nautilus Inn
5005 22nd Ave. N.E., Seattle, WA 98105
(206) 522-2536

Innkeeper: Bunny and Bill Hagemeyer
Rooms: 6, incl. 4 w/pvt. bath
Rates: $60-$98, incl. full brk., afternoon refreshment. Discount avail. for single, extended stay. Seasonal variations.
Credit cards: Most major cards
Restrictions: Guests restricted to one child under 12 with prior notice. No pets, smoking. Min. one night's deposit req. 7-day cancellation notice req. 2-night min. stay on wknds. 3-night min. stay on holiday wknds. No alcohol served, but guests may bring their own.
Notes: Three-story Georgian Colonial-style house built in 1915. Located in University District overlooking the Cascade Mountains. Dining room with fireplace. Living room with fireplace and grand piano. Fully-stocked bookcases in every room. Furnished with mixture of American and English antiques. Inn's name is taken from the seashell which, with its classic spiral shape, is a home of beauty, warmth and security for its sea animal. Small private parties accommodated. German spoken. Resident dog.*

College Inn Guest House
4000 University Way N.E., Seattle, WA 98105
(206) 633-4441
Innkeeper: Carol Wallace
Rooms: 25, no pvt. bath
Rates: $39-$69, incl. cont. brk. Discount avail. for extended stay.
Credit cards: MC, V
Restrictions: No pets, smoking. Credit card guarantee or one night's deposit req. 24-hour cancellation notice req.
Notes: Tudor style inn opened for Alaska-Yukon Exposition in 1909. Located in univerisy district. Electic furnishings including antiques. Fourth floor attic renovated to accommodate sitting, breakfast and TV area. Finnish, Spanish, some French spoken. Listed on the State Register of Historic Places.*

Prince of Wales
133 13th Ave. E., Seattle, WA 98102
(206) 325-9692, (800) 327-9692
Innkeeper: Carol Norton

PRINCE OF WALES

Rooms: 2 plus 2 suites, all w/pvt. bath, phone
Rates: $60-$95/room, $80-$95/suite, all incl. full brk. Discount avail. for extended stay.
Credit cards: Most major cards
Restrictions: No children under 3, pets, smoking. One night's deposit req. 7-day cancellation notice req. 2-night min. stay req., May 1–Oct. 1.
Notes: 3-story house built at the turn-of-the-century. Located on Capitol Hill overlooking the city and Puget Sound. Dining room. Some Spanish and Italian spoken. Resident cat and dog.

Queen Anne Hill Bed & Breakfast
1835 7th West, Seattle, WA 98119
(206) 284-9779

Innkeeper: Chuck and Mary McGrew
Rooms: 5, plus 2 suites, incl. 3 w/pvt. bath, 1 w/cable TV
Rates: $50-$65/room, $65-$79/suite, all incl. full brk. Discount avail. for extended stay.
Credit cards: MC, V
Restrictions: No pets, smoking. One night's deposit req. 72-hour cancellation notice req. 2-night min. stay on wknds.
Notes: Built at the turn-of-the-century. Located on Queen Anne Hill in residential area with view of the Olympic Mountains and Puget Sound. 10 minutes from downtown. Has operated as inn since 1982. Living room, TV room, kitchen. Furnished with antiques, unique collectibles and Oriental rugs*

Salisbury House
750 16th Ave. E., Seattle, WA 98112
(206) 328-8682, (206) 720-1019

Innkeeper: Cathryn and Mary Wiese
Rooms: 4 w/pvt. bath
Rates: $60-$97, incl. full brk.
Credit cards: Most major cards
Restrictions: No children under 12, pets, smoking. One night's deposit req. 7-day cancellation notice req. 2-night min. stay on wknds. 3-night min. stay on holidays.
Notes: Two-story house built about 1904 with maple floors, coffered ceilings, bay windows. Located on Capitol Hill. Has operated as inn since 1985. Library with fireplace and game table. Wrap-around porch. Second-floor sun porch/greenhouse. Landscaped gardens.

Shafer-Baillie Mansion
907 14th Ave. E., Seattle, WA 98112
(206) 329-4628, (206) 329-4654

Innkeeper: Erv Olssen
Rooms: 11 plus 2 suites, carriage house, all w/pvt. bath, phone, TV, refrigerator
Rates: $55-$85/room, $75-$115/suite, all incl. cont. brk. Discount avail. for extended stay.
Credit cards: AE, DS
Restrictions: No pets, smoking. One night's deposit req. 7-day cancellation notice req. 2-night min. stay on wknds. from May–Sept.
Notes: 15,000-square-foot mansion with original light fixtures, chandeliers and sconces, solid oak paneling, doors, bookcases and buit-in buffets, built in 1912. Located on on Capitol Hill. Oak-paneled dining room, winding staircase. Billiard

SALISBURY HOUSE

room with working fireplace and piano. Library with TV, VCR. Furnished with antiques. Small private parties accommodated. Landscaped lawn shaded by huge trees and shrubs.*

Villa Heidelberg
4845 45th Ave. S.W, Seattle, WA 98116
(206) 938-3658
Innkeeper: Barbara and John Thompson
Rooms: 4, incl. 1 w/pvt. bath, fireplace
Rates: $55-$85, incl. full brk.
Credit cards: Most major cards
Restrictions: No children, pets, smoking. One night's deposit req. 7-day cancellation notice req. 2-night min. stay.
Notes: 1909 Craftsman bungalow located in West Seattle 10 minutes from downtown. Views of Puget Sound. Wrap-around porch, gardens.

SEAVIEW (7)

Gumm's B & B Inn
3310 Hwy. 101 & 33rd, Box 447, Seaview, WA 98644
(206) 642-8887
Innkeeper: Esther and Mickey Slack
Rooms: 4 w/TV, incl. 2 w/pvt. bath
Rates: $65-$75, incl. full brk. Discount avail. for senior citizens.
Credit cards: MC, V

Restrictions: No infants, pets, smoking. One night's deposit req. 48-hour cancellation notice req.

Notes: Two-story house built in 1911. Living room with stone fireplace. Sun porch, hot tub. Dinner available.

The Shelburne Inn
P.O. Box 250, Seaview, WA 98644
(206) 642-2442, (206) 642-8904

Innkeeper: David Campiche, Laurie Anderson

Rooms: 13 plus 2 suites, all w/pvt. bath

Rates: $89-$125/room, $160/suite, all incl. full brk., afternoon refreshment. Discount for senors avail.

Credit cards: Most major cards

Restrictions: No pets, smoking. One night's deposit req. 5-day cancellation notice req. 2-night min. stay on wknds. Restaurant closed Wed. and for lunch on Mon. and Tues. in winter.

Notes: Victorian hotel built in 1896 and in continuous operation since. Enlarged in 1911. Rejuvenated in 1977. Renovated in 1983. Expanded in 1986. Dining room, lobby, sun deck. Furnished with 19th- and early 20th-century antiques. Restaurant, pub, gift shop on premises. Listed on the National Register of Historic Places. Small private parties accommodated. German spoken.*

SEQUIM (1)

Greywolf Inn
395 Keeler Rd., Sequim, WA 98382
(206) 683-5889

Innkeeper: Peggy and Bill Melang

Rooms: 4 plus 1 suite, all w/pvt. bath, incl. 1 w/TV

Rates: $62-$98/room, $140/suite, incl. full brk., afternoon refreshment. Seasonal variations. Discount avail. for senior citizen and extended stays.

Credit cards: Most major cards

GREYWOLF INN

Restrictions: No children under 12, pets, smoking. One night's deposit req. 72-hour cancellation notice req.

Notes: Country estate located on five wooded acres. Guestrooms decorated in themes ranging from Bavarian to Far Eastern. Audubon room for bird lovers. Gathering room with large fireplace, books, magazines, board games, music. Enclosed Japanese Shoji style spa.*

Margie's Inn on the Bay
120 Forrest Rd., Sequim, WA 98382
(206) 683-7011

Innkeeper: Margie L. and Donald A. Vorhies
Rooms: 4, plus 1 suite, all w/pvt. bath, TV, incl. 1 w/fireplace
Rates: $69/room, $125/suite, all incl. full brk. Seasonal variations.
Credit cards: MC, V
Restrictions: No children under 12, pets, smoking. Deposit req. 72-hour cancellation notice req.
Notes: Spacious, contemporary ranch-style hom on 180 feet of water frontage on Sequim Bay. Located on 2 acres in quiet area. Most guest room have water view. Large common room with woodburning stove, VCR, movies. Breakfast room, patio. Handicapped access. Resident Persian cats and parrot.*

SILVERDALE (2)

SeaBreeze Cottage
16609 Olympic View Rd., Silverdale, WA 98383
(206) 692-4648

Innkeeper: Dennis Fulton
Rooms: 2, incl. 1 w/pvt. bath, phone, TV, fireplace
Rates: $129-$149, incl. cont. brk., evening refreshment. Seasonal variations. Discount for extended and winter stays.
Credit cards: MC, V
Restrictions: No smoking. $100 deposit req. 10-day cancellation notice req., less $20 fee. 2-night min. stay on wknds.
Notes: Private 2-bedroom beach house with kitchen, fireplace, laundry facilities, private decks. Located on the beach of Hood Canal. Hot tub at water's edge. Offers total privacy.*

SPOKANE (5)

Marianna Stoltz House
427 E. Indiana Ave., Spokane, WA 99207
(509) 483-4316

Innkeeper: Jim and Phyllis Maguire
Rooms: 4 w/TV, incl. 3 w/phone, no pvt. bath. Suite avail.
Rates: $60-75/room, $69-$75/suite, all incl. full brk.
Credit cards: MC, V
Restrictions: No children under 12, pets, smoking. One night's deposit req. 7-day cancellation notice req.
Notes: Two-story foursquare house built in 1908. Has been in the same family since 1961. Has operated as inn since 1987. Dining room, parlor, sitting room, front and side verandas. Furnished in period style. Registered as a Spokane Historic Landmark. Train pick-up available.*

TACOMA (6)

Commencement Bay B & B
3312 N. Union Ave., Tacoma, WA 98407
(206) 752-8175, (206) 759-4025
Innkeeper: Bill and Sharon Kaufmann
Rooms: 3 w/pvt. bath, 2 w/cable TV
Rates: $75-$105, incl. full brk., evening refreshment. Seasonal variations. Discount avail. for extended stay.
Credit cards: Most major cards
Restrictions: No children under 12, pets. Smoking restricted. One night's deposit req. 7-day cancellation notice req.
Notes: Colonial house overlooking Tacoma, bay and mountains. Each guest room individually decorated. Common room with fireplace. Game room. Secluded hot tub and deck. Modem hookup available. Some Spanish spoken.*

VASHON ISLAND (2)

Old Tjomsland House
17011 Vashon Hwy. S.W., Box 913, Vashon Island, WA 98070
(206) 463-5275, (206) 463-3556 (booking agent), (206) 463-5275
Innkeeper: Jan and Bill Morosoff
Rooms: 1 suite w/pvt. bath, phone, TV, VCR, small appliances, plus cottage w/pvt. bath, phone, TV, VCR, small appliances. Located in 2 bldgs.
Rates: $100/suite, $85/cottage, all incl. full gourmet brk., afternoon refreshment. Discount avail. for mid-week stay and extended stays.
Credit cards: Most major cards
Restrictions: No pets, smoking, alcohol. One night's deposit req. 10-day cancellation notice. 2-night min. stay on wknds. and holidays.
Notes: Two-story Craftsman-style farmhouse built in 1890. Cottage built approx. 1940. Fully renovated. Located on two wooded acres with one-acre meadow across the street from bus stop. Upstairs suite has private entrance. Common room with piano, library. Family dining room with wood-burning stove. House furnished with family antiques. Cottage furnished in rattan and wicker. Children's play set. Bicycles available. French, German spoken. Resident dogs, cats, bird.*

Swallow's Nest Guest Cottages
6030 S.W. 248th St., Vashon Island, WA 98070
(206) 463-2646, (800) 269-6378
Innkeeper: Bob Keller and Robin Hughes
Rooms: 4 plus 1 studio, all w/pvt. bath and TV, incl. 2 w/woodstoves
Rates: $60-$85. Discount avail. for extended stays
Credit cards: Most major cards
Restrictions: No smoking. Pets restricted. Deposit req. 21-day cancellation notice req., less $20.00 fee.
Notes: Country cottages located one block from the beach, some with views and varying in size from studios to a 2-story Victorian which sleeps 8. Surrounded by several hundred acres of field and forest. Cottages furnished in comfortable style with plants, rockers, books. Guests have access to cooking facilities.*

WHITE SALMON (9)

Llama Ranch B & B
1980 Hwy. 141, White Salmon, WA 98672
(509) 395-2786, (800) 800-5262
Innkeeper: Jerry and Rebeka Stone
Rooms: 6, incl. 1 w/pvt. bath, plus 1 suite w/pvt. bath
Rates: $55-$65/room, $75/suite, all incl. full brk. Discount avail. for extended stay.
Credit cards: Most major cards
Restrictions: No smoking. 2-day cancellation notice req.
Notes: Farmhouse overlooking Mount Adams and Mount Hood. Located on ninety-seven-acre llama ranch. Lounge, kitchen. Guests have access to laundry facilities. Small private parties accommodated. All-day llama hikes organized.

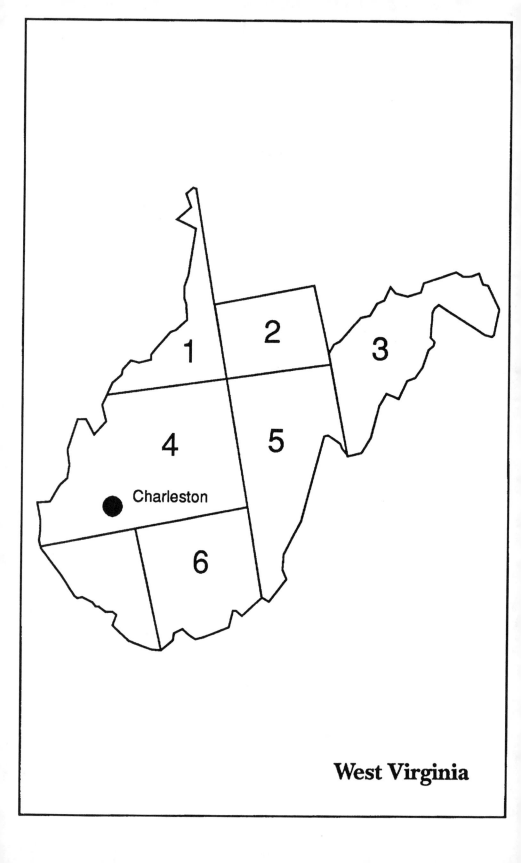

West Virginia

West Virginia

BEAVER (6)

House of Grandview
Rt. 9, Box 334, Beaver, WV 25813
(304) 763-4381
Innkeeper: Gordon and Imogene Dodd
Rooms: 2 plus cottage, all w/pvt. bath, phone, TV
Rates: $50-$65, incl. full brk. Discount avail. for extended stay.
Credit cards: MC, V
Restrictions: No pets. Smoking restricted. Deposit req. 48-hour cancellation notice
    req. 14-day cancalltion notice req. on holiday wknds.
Notes: Modern inn in country setting situated between Grandview National Park
and Little Beaver State Park. Each room is furnished with ceiling fans and individ-
ually decorated. Common room with fireplace, large screen TV, games. Reading
room. Screen porch, garden. One room with handicapped access.

BERKELEY SPRINGS (3)

Folkestone Bed & Breakfast
Rte. 2, Box 404, Berkeley Springs, WV 25411
(304) 258-3743
Innkeeper: Hettie Hawvermale
Rooms: 2, incl. 1 w/pvt. bath, plus apartment w/kitchen and deck
Rates: $60-$100, incl. full brk., evening refreshment
Credit cards: None
Restrictions: No children under 15, pets. $25.00 deposit req. Refunded upon can-
    cellation only if room rebooked. 2-night min. stay on holiday wknds.
Notes: Two-story English Tudor house built in 1929. Located on ten wooded acres.
Has operated as inn since 1939. Renovated in 1969. Sitting room, dining room,
screened porch. Furnished with antiques. Hot tub.

CHARLES TOWN (3)

Cottonwood Inn
RR 2, Box 61S, Charles Town, WV 25414
(304) 725-3371
Innkeeper: Eleanor and Colin Simpson
Rooms: 7 w/pvt. bath, TV, incl. 1 w/fireplace
Rates: $85-$105, incl. full brk.
Credit cards: Most major cards
Restrictions: No pets. Deposit req. 72-hour cancellation notice req.
Notes: Renovated Georigan farmhouse on 6 acres with trout stream running
through property. Quiet country setting near Harpers Ferry. Furnished with an-
tiques and period reproductions. Common rooms include living room and dining
room with fireplaces, library. Front porch with chairs and swing. Backyard pavillion for social events. Small private parties and business conferences accommodated.*

Gilbert House of Middleway
P.O. Box 1104, Charles Town, WV 25414
(304) 725-0637
Innkeeper: Bernie Heiler
Rooms: 2 plus 1 suite, all w/pvt. bath, incl. 2 w/fireplace
Rates: $100-$120/room, $140/suite, all incl. full brk., afternoon refreshment
Credit cards: Most major cards
Restrictions: No pets. Children, smoking restricted. Deposit req. 14-day cancellation notice req., less $25.00 fee.
Notes: Three-story L-shaped greystone inn of early Georgian style with 20-inch-thick walls. Built about 1760. Decorated in Old World atmosphere with historical antiques. Metal roof. Listed on the National Register of Historic Places. German, Spanish spoken.*

The Washington House Inn
216 S. George St., Charles Town, WV 25414
(304) 725-7923
Innkeeper: Mel and Nina Vogel
Rooms: 6 w/pvt. bath, incl. some w/fireplace, ceiling fan
Rates: $70-$95, incl. full brk., evening refreshment. Discount avail. for extended stay.
Credit cards: None
Restrictions: No children under 12, pets, smoking. One night's deposit req. 24-hour cancellation notice req.
Notes: Victorian built at turn-of-the-century. Antique furnishings, carved oak mantles. Dining room with fireplace. Wrap-around porch with swing and rocking chairs. Veranda.*

CHARLESTON (4)

Brass Pineapple Bed & Breakfast
1611 Virginia St. E., Charleston, WV 25311
(304) 344-0748, (304) 344-0748
Innkeeper: Sue Pepper
Rooms: 6 w/pvt. bath, phone, cable TV
Rates: $75-$95, incl. full brk., afternoon refreshment. Discount avail. for extended stay.
Credit cards: Most major cards
Restrictions: No children under 8, pets, smoking. Min. one night's deposit req. 7-day cancellation notice req. 2-night min. stay on holiday wknds.
Notes: Brick house built in 1910, combining an eclectic blend of Art Nouveau and Victorian styles. Contains ample stained glass, oak paneling, and Italian marble. Located in Charleston's historic East End ½ block from state Capitol. Guest rooms individually furnished with antiques, designer robes, soft linens. Dining room, veranda, rose garden.

Historic Charleston B & B
114 Elizabeth St., Charleston, WV 25311
(304) 345-8156, (800) CALL WVA
Innkeeper: Bob and Jean Lambert
Rooms: 3 w/pvt. bath
Rates: $60-$65, incl. full brk.
Credit cards: Most major cards

Restrictions: No pets, smoking. Deposit req. 48-hour cancellation notice req.
Notes: American Foursquare house with six fireplaces, built in 1905. Located one block from State Capitol. Guest rooms all have sitting area. Living room with TV, phone. Furnished with antiques and collectibles. Front porch with wicker chairs and great swing. Back deck.

ELKINS (4)

TUNNEL MOUNTAIN BED & BREAKFAST

Tunnel Mountain Bed & Breakfast
RT. 1, Box 59-1, Elkins, WV 26241
(304) 636-1684
Innkeeper: Ann and Paul Beardslee
Rooms: 3 w/pvt. bath
Rates: $50-$60, incl. full brk. Discount avail. for senior citizens.
Credit cards: None
Restrictions: No children under 13, pets. Smoking restricted. One night's deposit req. 7-day cancellation notice req., less $15.00 fee. 2-night min. stay on special wknds.
Notes: 3-story fieldstone house located on five wooded acres on Tunnel Mountain. Inn named for 1890 railroad tunnel that passes under hillside. Guest rooms furnished with antiques, hand-made comforters. Interior of inn finished in pine and rare wormy chestnut woodwork. Living room with fireplace, porch, patio.

GERRARDSTOWN (3)

Prospect Hill Farm Bed & Breakfast
P.O. Box 135, Gerrardstown, WV 25420
(304) 229-3346
Innkeeper: Hazel and Charles Hudock
Rooms: 2 plus cottage, all w/pvt. bath, incl. 3 w/fireplace, 2 w/phone, cottage w/kitchen
Rates: $85-$95/room, $95/cottage, all incl. full brk.
Credit cards: MC, V
Restrictions: No children in Guest House, pets. Smoking restricted. Deposit req. 7-day cancellation notice req. 2-night min. stay preferred.

Notes: Two-story Georgian antebellum mansion built in 1794 with four chimneys and former slave quarters, which house guests. Located on 225-acre working farm at foot of North Mountain. Grand staircase with 3-story mural. Furnished in country style with antiques. Fishing pond, extensive grounds.*

HARPERS FERRY (3)

FILMORE STREET B & B

Fillmore Street B & B
P.O. Box 34, Harpers Ferry, WV 25425
(304) 535-2619, (410) 321-5634
Innkeeper: James and Alden Addy
Rooms: 2 w/pvt. bath, TV
Rates: $70-$75, incl. full brk., evening refreshment
Credit cards: None
Restrictions: No children under 12, pets. $25.00 deposit req. 3-day cancellation notice req.
Notes: Victorian house on stone foundation of the Civil War era. Within walking distance of historic attractions. Dining room with fireplace. Parlors, library. Front porch with rockers. Furnished with Victorian antiques. Gardens.

Ranson-Armory House B & B
690 Washington St., Box 280, Harpers Ferry, WV 25425
(304) 535-2142
Innkeeper: John and Dorothy Hughes
Rooms: 2 w/pvt. bath
Rates: $60$75, incl. full brk. Discount available for extended and mid-week stays.
Credit cards: MC, V
Restrictions: No children under 10, pets, smoking. 2-night min. stay on holidays.
Notes: Farm house built in 1830.

HINTON (6)

Heritage House B & B
223 4th Ave., Hinton, WV 25951
(304) 466-6070

Innkeeper: Barbara Mc Lean
Rooms: 3 w/phone, TV, no pvt. bath
Rates: $30-$60, incl. full brk., evening refreshment. Seasonal variations.
Credit cards: None
Restrictions: No pets. Smoking restricted.
Notes: Two-story house built in 1896 as a commissary for the Chesapeake and Ohio Railroad. Converted to private residence in 1905. Fully renovated in and has operated as inn since 1993. Sitting room with cable TV. Furnished in period decor with antiques. Operated with a casual attitude. Garden with gazebo.

HUTTONSVILLE (5)

Mr. Richard's Olde Country Inn
RT. 1, 11-A-1, Rt. 219, Huttonsville, WV 26273
(304) 335-6659
Innkeeper: Richard S. Brown
Rooms: 11 plus 2 suites, incl. 8 w/pvt. bath, 3 w/fireplace
Rates: $55-$60, incl. full brk.
Credit cards: MC, V
Restrictions: Smoking restricted. Deposit req. 10-day cancellation notice req., less $10.00 fee. 2-night min. stay on holiday wknds.
Notes: Mansion built in 1853. Fully restored. Some guest rooms have private verandas. Restaurant and veranda open for light lunch and dinner.

LEWISBURG (6)

The General Lewis Inn
301 E. Washington St., Lewisburg, WV 24901
(304) 645-2600
Innkeeper: Mary Noel and Jim Morgan
Rooms: 25, incl. 2 suites, all w/pvt. bath, TV, phone
Rates: $55-$80/room, $80/suite
Credit cards: Most major cards
Restrictions: One night's deposit req. 7-day cancellation notice req.
Notes: Inn with sections dating back to 1834. Living room with fireplace. Dining room with hand-hewn beams. Furnished with historic antiques, products of the culture and craftsmanship of early settlers. Memorabilia collection of pioneer relics. Antique stagecoach. Listed on National Register of Historic Places.

MARTINSBURG (3)

Aspen Hall Inn
405 Boyd Ave., Martinsburg, WV 25401
(304) 263-4385
Innkeeper: Lou Anne and Gordon Claucherty
Rooms: 5 w/pvt. bath, incl. 1 w/fireplace
Rates: $95-$110, incl. full brk., afternoon refreshment
Credit cards: MC, V
Restrictions: No children under 12, pets, smoking. One night's deposit req. 5-day cancellation notice req. 2-night min. stay in Oct.
Notes: 200-year-old limestone mansion situated under canopy of giant locust trees on several acres. Parlor with grand piano, library. Formal dining room. Each guest

room furnished with antiques and has sitting area. Listed on National Register of Historic Places.*

ASPEN HALL INN

Boydville, the Inn at Martinsburg
601 S. Queen St., Martinsburg, WV 25401
(304) 263-1448

Innkeeper: LaRue Frye, Bob Boege, Carolyn Snyder, Pete Bailey
Rooms: 6, incl. 4 w/pvt. bath, incl. 1 w/fireplace, TV
Rates: $100-$125, incl. cont. brk., afternoon refreshment. Discount avail. for extended stay.
Credit cards: MC, V
Restrictions: No children under 12, pets, smoking. 50% deposit req. 7-day cancellation notice req. 2-night min. stay on Oct. wknds.
Notes: Two-story Federal mansion built in 1812. Located on fourteen wooded acres with original plantation out-buildings. Two-feet-thick stone walls. Music room with grand piano. Living room with stereo. Garden room with cable TV, library, board games. Front veranda with swings, rockers. Furnished with American and European antiques, Oriental rugs, oil paintings, murals, French chandeliers. Meeting/reception rooms available. Walled garden. Listed on the National Register of Historic Places.*

MOOREFIELD (3)

McMechen House B & B
109 N. Main St., Moorefield, WV 26836
(304) 538-7173, (800) 298-2466

Innkeeper: Linda, Bob and Larry Curtis
Rooms: 6, incl. 3 w/pvt. bath, plus 1 suite w/pvt. bath
Rates: $50-$75/room, $85/suite, all incl. full brk., afternoon refreshment. Discount avail. for mid-week and extended stays.
Credit cards: Most major cards

Restrictions: No pets. Smoking restricted. One night's deposit req. 2-day cancellation notice req., less 10% fee. 2-night min. stay for Heritage Wknd. Closed Dec. 15–Jan. 15.
Notes: Three-story brick Federal Greek Revival-style inn built in 1853. Served as Union and Confederate headquarters during the Civil War. Has operated as an inn since 1993. Center hall with spiral staircase. Parlor, dining room. Two-tiered porch with chairs. Furnished with period antiques. Weekend dinner available. Laundry facilities available. Small private parties accommodated. Handicapped access.

POINT PLEASANT (4)

Stone Manor
12 Main St., Point Pleasant, WV 25550
(304) 675-3442
Innkeeper: Janice and Tom Vance
Rooms: 3, no pvt. bath, all w/fireplace, incl. 1 w/phone
Rates: $50, incl. full brk.
Credit cards: None
Restrictions: No pets. Smoking restricted.
Notes: Restored house built in 1885 by Stone family who ran ferry boats from this site located on banks of Kanawha River. Victorian era furnishings throughout, handcrafted woodwork. Two sitting areas. Front porch facing river and park. Large yard with Victorian fish pond and fountain. Listed on National Register of Historic Places.

SHEPHERDSTOWN (3)

Thomas Shepherd Inn
300 W. German St., Box 1162, Shepherdstown, WV 25443
(304) 876-3715
Innkeeper: Margaret Perry
Rooms: 7 w/pvt. bath
Rates: $85-$125, incl. full brk., afternoon refreshment. Discount available for senior citizen, corporate stays.
Credit cards: Most major cards
Restrictions: No children under 7, pets, smoking. Credit card guarantee req. 7-day cancellation notice req. 2-night min. stay on wknds.
Notes: Two-story Federal-style house built in 1868 as the Lutheran Church's parsonage. Fully restored in and has operated as inn since 1984. Library with TV. Living room with fireplace. Two formal dining rooms. Upstairs back porch with rockers overlooking gardens. Furnished with period pieces. All meals available.

SUMMERSVILLE (6)

Historic Brock House
1400 W. Webster Rd., Summersville, WV 26651
(304) 872-4887
Innkeeper: Margie and Jim Martin
Restrictions: 6, incl. 3 w/pvt. bath
Rates: $69-$85, incl. full brk., afternoon refreshment. Discount avail. for senior citizens.
Credit cards: MC, V

Restrictions: No pets, smoking. One night's deposit req. 48-hour cancellation notice req.

Notes: Built in 1890 as hotel and farm house. Located on one wooded, landscaped acre. Living room with stone fireplace, game table, TV. Dining room. Wrap-around porch with wicker and rocking chairs, flower and fern baskets. Furnishings combine antiques with traditional furniture, brightly colored flowered fabric, Oriental rugs. Small private parties accommodated.*

VALLEY CHAPEL (2)

INGEBERG ACRES B & B

Ingeberg Acres B & B
Millstone Run Rd., Box 199, Valley Chapel, WV 26446
(304) 269-2834

Innkeeper: John and Inge Mann

Rooms: 3, no pvt. bath

Rates: $59, incl. full brk., afternoon refreshment. Discount avail. for senior citizens.

Credit cards: None

Restrictions: No pets, smoking. Deposit req. 24-hour cancellation notice req.

Notes: Dutch Colonial house built in 1980. Located on 450-acre working horse, cattle breeding farm. Recreation room. Living room with TV, library. Deck, patio. Swimming pool. Flower and vegetable gardens. Dinner available. Guests may participate in farm chores. Posted deer, grouse, squirrel, turkey, and rabbit hunting grounds. Stocked pond open to fishing. German spoken.

Wisconsin

ALBANY (9)

Albany Guest House
405 S. Mill St., Albany, WI 53502
(608) 862-3636
Innkeeper: Bob and Sally Braem
Rooms: 4 w/pvt. bath, incl. 1 w/fireplace
Rates: $55-$68, incl. full brk. Discount avail. for mid-week stay.
Credit cards: None
Restrictions: No children under 3, smoking, pets. Deposit req. 10-day cancellation notice req., less $10.00 fee
Notes: American Four Square house with original oak, maple, and pine floors, built circa 1908. Located on two acres of lawn and gardens plus eight more acres behind. Constructed of decorative concrete blocks formed on site. Furnished with antiques, Oriental or handwoven rugs and old interesting pieces. Front porch with swing, bench, table, and chairs. Yard for variety of sports.

ALBANY GUEST HOUSE

ALGOMA (7)

Amberwood Inn
N7136 Hwy. 42S, Lakeshore Dr., Algoma, WI 54201
(414) 487-3471
Innkeeper: Jan and George
Rooms: 1 plus 4 suites, incl. 4 w/pvt. bath, all w/TV
Rates: $65/room, $75-$85/suite, all incl. full brk.
Credit cards: MC, V
Restrictions: No pets. Smoking restricted. One night's deposit req. 10-day cancellation notice req. 2-night min. stay on wknds. Closed Nov. 1–Apr. 30.
Notes: Located on private wooded acreage on shores of Lake Michigan. Each suite uniquely furnished and has double French doors opening onto private deck overlooking the lake. Wet bars, refrigerators. Whirlpool, sauna, hot tub. Bikes available.

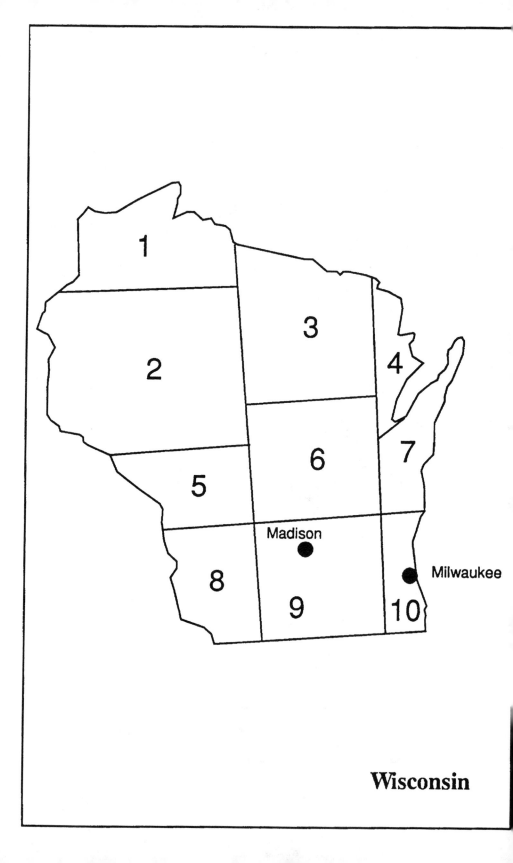

Wisconsin

ALMA (2)

Laue House Inn
1111 S. Main, Box 176, Alma, WI 54610
(608) 685-4923

Innkeeper: Jerry and Jan Schreiber
Rooms: 5 plus 1 suite, no pvt. bath, all w/cable TV
Rates: $25/room, $35/suite, all incl. cont. brk.
Credit cards: None
Restrictions: Inquire regarding children. No smoking. Deposit req. 2-day cancellation notice req.
Notes: Italianate house built in 1863 overlooking Mississippi River. Lounge with player piano. Porch overlooking Mississippi River. Guests have access to patio kitchen. Furnished with antiques. Canoe and bike rentals. Listed on National Register of Historic Places.

BARABOO (6)

PINEHAVEN B & B

Pinehaven B & B
E. 13083 Hwy. 33, Baraboo, WI 53913
(608) 356-3489

Innkeeper: Lyle and Marge Getschman
Rooms: 4 w/pvt. bath
Rates: $65-$76, incl. full brk.
Credit cards: MC, V
Restrictions: No children under 5, pets, smoking. One night's deposit req. 7-day cancellation notice req. 2-night min. stay on holiday wknds.
Notes: 20-year-old chalet style inn nestled in pine grove and situated in scenic valley. Guest rooms each distinctly different with antiques, quilts, wicker. Common room with fireplace, TV/VCR, game table and baby grand piano. Upper veranda, lower deck, screened in porch. Private lake.

The Victorian Rose
423 Third Ave., Baraboo, WI 53913
(608) 356-7828

Innkeeper: Bob & Carolyn Stearns
Rooms: 2, plus 1 suite, all w/pvt. bath
Rates: $65-$80/room, $80/suite, incl. full brk., social hour
Credit cards: None
Restrictions: No children, pets, smoking. One night's deposit req. 10-day cancellation notice req., less $25.00 fee.
Notes: Restored late-19th-century Queen Ann Victorian located within walking distance of historic downtown Baraboo. Surrounded by sugar maples and pine trees. Decorated with period antiques and heirloom collectibles. Hardwood floors, beveled mirror oak fireplace, sliding pocket doors, intricate woodwork. Parlor-library with TV, VCR plus sitting parlor. Wrap-around porch. Social hour with film classics.

BAYFIELD (1)

APPLE TREE INN

Apple Tree Inn
Rte. 1, Box 251, Bayfield, WI 54814
(715) 779-5572

Innkeeper: Joanna Barningham
Restrictions: 5 w/pvt. bath
Rates: $65-$80, incl. full brk.
Credit cards: MC, V
Restrictions: No pets, smoking. One night's deposit req. 7-day cancellation notice req.
Notes: Three-story frame house built in the early 1900s. Fully restored. Located on fifty-acre farm. Once the home of artist John Black, Sr. Front porch overlooking manicured lawns and gardens, Lake Superior and the Apostle Islands.

CEDARBURG (10)

Washington House Inn
W62 N573 Washington Ave., Cedarburg, WI 53012
(414) 375-3550, (800) 554-4717

Innkeeper: Wendy Porterfield
Rooms: 31 plus 3 suites, all w/pvt. bath, phone, cable TV, incl. 14 w/fireplace. Located in 2 bldgs.
Rates: $59-$159/room, $139-$159/suite, all incl. cont. brk., evening refreshment. Discount avail. for mid-week and senior citizen stays.
Credit cards: Most major cards
Restrictions: No pets. Smoking restricted. Deposit or credit card guarantee req. 24-hour cancellation notice req.
Notes: Cream city-brick inn with exposed brick walls, century-old ceiling timbers built in 1886. Restored in 1986. Located in heart of historic Cedarburg. Gathering room with tin ceiling, fireplace. Lobby, meeting rooms. Furnished in country Victorian style with antiques, Laura Ashley and Schumacher fabrics and wallpaper. Sauna. Listed on the National Register of Historic Places. Small private parties accommodated. Bicycles available for rent. Handicapped access.*

EAU CLAIRE (2)

Otter Creek Inn
2536 Hwy. 12, Eau Claire, WI 54701
(715) 832-2945
Innkeeper: Sheila and Randy Hansen
Rooms: 4 plus 1 suite, all w/pvt. whirlpool bath, phone, cable TV
Rates: $59-$109, incl. expanded cont. brk. Discount avail. for mid-week stay.
Credit cards: Most major cards
Restrictions: No children, pets, smoking. 50% deposit req. 7-day cancellation notice req.
Notes: English Tudor-style house built in 1950. Expanded in 1984 to bring it to current three-story, 6,000 square feet. Located on one wooded acre. Dining room, library area, reading lounge, two-story great room with woodburning firestove. Decorated in country Victorian theme, furnished with antiques and collectibles.

ELKHORN (9)

Ye Olde Manor House
Rte. 5, Box 390, Elkhorn, WI 53121
(414) 742-2450
Innkeeper: Babette and Marvin Henschel
Rooms: 3 plus 1 suite, incl. 2 w/pvt. bath
Rates: $50-$90, incl. full brk. Discounts avail.
Credit cards: Most major cards
Restrictions: Well-behaved children welcome. No pets, smoking. Deposit req. 48-hour cancellation notice req. 2-night min. stay on holiday wknds.
Notes: Country manor house built circa 1905, overlooking hillside and Lauderdale Lakes. Living room, dining room, enclosed front porch. Furnished with antiques.*

EPHRAIM (7)

Hillside Hotel of Ephraim
9980 Hwy. 42, Ephraim, WI 54211
(414) 854-2417, (800) 423-7023
Innkeeper: David and Karen McNeil
Rooms: 11 plus 1 suite, no pvt. bath. 2 cottages w/pvt. bath, fireplace, kitchen. Located in 3 bldgs.

Rates: $68-$89/room, $115-$158/suite, $140-$180/cottage, all incl. full brk., after-noon refreshment. Discount avail. for extended stay.
Credit cards: Most major cards
Restrictions: No pets, smoking. 50% deposit req. 21-day cancellation notice req., less $15.00 fee. 2-night min. stay on wknds. 3-night min. stay for holidays.
Notes: Two-story country Victorian hotel. Has operated as inn since 1890. Guest rooms with restored original country furnishings, hardwood floors, quilts. Dining room, music room, parlor. Veranda overlooking Green Bay. Side and back porches overlooking gardens. Private beach. All meals available. Listed on the National Register of Historic Places. Small private parties accommodated.

GILLS ROCK (7)

Harbor House Inn
12666 Hwy. 42, Gills Rock, WI 54210
(414) 854-5196
Innkeeper: David and Else Weborg
Rooms: 7 rooms plus 4 suites and 2 cottages, all w/pvt. bath, TV
Rates: $49-$75/room, $85/suite, $95/cottage, all incl. cont. brk.
Credit cards: Most major cards
Restrictions: No smoking. Credit card guarantee req. 14-day cancellation notice req. Min. stay required for some wknds.
Notes: Victorian house with new Scandanavian country wing overlooking a quaint fishing harbor, built in 1904. Decorated with period furnishings dating from early 1900s. Most rooms have refrigerator and microwave, some with private deck over-looking harbor. Sitting room with fireplace. Decks, gazebo. Private beach, bike rentals. Handicapped access. Danish spoken.

HAZEL GREEN (8)

Wisconsin House Stagecoach Inn
2105 E. Main St., Hazel Green, WI 53811
(608) 854-2233
Innkeeper: Ken and Pat Disch
Rooms: 6 plus 2 suites, incl. 6 w/pvt. bath
Rates: $55-$90/room, $100-$105/suite, all incl. full brk., afternoon refreshment. Discount avail. for extended and mid-week stays.
Credit cards: MC, V
Restrictions: No pets. Smoking restricted. Deposit req. 48-hour cancellation notice req.
Notes: Built in 1846 as stagecoach stop located 10 minutes from Galena, Ill. Has op-erated as inn since 1985. Parlor, pub, library, porches, gardens. Furnished with country antiques. Dinner available on weekends.*

HONEYCREEK (10)

Honeycreek Acres
N6360 Valley View Rd., Box 59, Honeycreek, WI 53138
(414) 763-7591, (800) 484-8081, (414) 763-7598
Innkeeper: Dr. Anne Hyman
Rooms: 3 plus 3 cabins w/fireplace, incl. 4 w/pvt. bath, 2 w/TV
Rates: $45-$65/room, $25 per person/cabin, incl. cont. brk. Discount avail. for ex-tended stay.

Credit cards: Most major cards

Restrictions: No pets, smoking. $25 per night deposit req. 48-hour cancellation notice req. Open May–Sept.

Notes: Contemporary glass and cedar chalet and cedar cabins on 55 acres in secluded valley. Remodeled barn for guests. Lounge with fieldstone fireplace. Dining area, patio. Music, singing, dancing. Located on private lake for boating, swimming, fishing. Lawn games. Hammock, hot tub.*

KANSASVILLE (10)

LINEN & LACE

Linen & Lace
26060 Washington Ave., Kansasville, WI 53139
(414) 534-4966

Innkeeper: Nancy & David Reckhouse

Rooms: 3, no pvt. bath

Rates: $60-$70, incl. full brk.

Credit cards: MC, V

Restrictions: No children, pets, smoking. Deposit req. 10-day cancellation notice req., less $10.00 fee.

Notes: Three-story house. Located on 4½ acres adjacent to a 200-acre game farm. Guest rooms feature period brass, iron or wood beds along with down comforters, ceiling fans, family heirlooms. Grand foyer with handcarved stair trims, pocket doors. Wrap-around porch.

KENOSHA (10)

The Manor House
6536 3rd Ave., Kenosha, WI 53143
(414) 658-0014

Innkeeper: Marc Giombetti

Rooms: 3 w/pvt. bath, cable TV, phone, incl. 1 w/fireplace, plus 1 suite w/pvt. bath, phone, cable TV, fireplace

Rates: $120/room, $140/suite, all incl. expanded cont. brk. Discount avail. for midweek stay. Special pkgs. avail.

Credit cards: Most major cards

Restrictions: No children under 12, pets. Smoking restricted. Deposit req. 21-day cancellation notice req., less 20% fee. 2-night min. stay on holidays.

Notes: Two-story brick Georgian mansion built about 1926 overlooking Lake Michigan. Fully refurnished in 1977. Living room with grand piano. Formal dining room, sun room, library. Furnished with 18th-century antiques, Oriental rugs. Landscaped wooded grounds with formal gardens, sunken lily pool, fountain, gazebo. Tennis court, bicycles, all meals available. Small private parties accommodated. Listed on the National Register of Historic Places.*

LA FARGE (5)

TRILLIUM

Trillium
Rte. 2, Box 121, La Farge, WI 54639
(608) 625-4492

Innkeeper: Rosanne Boyett
Rooms: 2 cottages w/pvt. bath, phone, fireplace, kitchen
Rates: $65-$70, incl. full brk. Discount for extended and winter stays.
Credit cards: None
Restrictions: No pets, smoking. 50% deposit req. 7-day cancellation notice req.
Notes: Located on eighty-five wooded-acre farm with brook in Amish community. Living room with stone fireplace. Kitchen/dining area with wood stove. Furnished with modern appliances. Hammock and porch overlooking organic garden, orchard.

LAKE GENEVA (9)

T. C. Smith Inn B & B
865 Main St., Lake Geneva, WI 53147
(414) 248-1097, (800) 423-0233

Innkeeper: Maureen Marks
Rooms: 6, plus 2 suites w/pvt. bath and TV, incl. 3 w/fireplace
Rates: $145-$175/room, $225/suite, all incl. full brk. Discount avail. for winter, midweek, and extended stays.
Credit cards: Most major cards
Restrictions: Deposit req. Cancellation notice req.

Notes: Two-story brick Victorian Greek Revival/Italianate mansion built in 1845. Foyer with parquet floor, brass and crystal chandelier. Sitting room with marble fireplace. Grand parlor with Tiffany chandelier, marble fireplace. Formal dining room with eleven-ft. ceilings. Billiard room. Second-floor sitting room. Furnished with period antiques, European paintings, Oriental carpets. Garden with waterfall. Listed on the National Register of Historic Places. Giftshop on premises. Bicycles available.*

MADISON (9)

Annie's Bed & Breakfast
2117 Sheridan Dr., Madison, WI 53704
(608) 244-2224, (608) 242-9611

Innkeeper: Anne and Larry Stuart
Rooms: 4 w/TV, incl. 2 w/pvt. bath. Suites avail.
Rates: $84-$94, incl. full brk. Special pkgs. avail.
Credit cards: Most major cards
Restrictions: No children under 12, pets. No smoking. One night's deposit req. 7-day written cancellation notice req.
Notes: Rustic cedar shake and stucco house. Located in quiet neighborhood. Has operated as inn since 1985. Furnished with antiques. VCR and refrigerator in rooms. Jacuzzi and gazebo. 3-star rating from AAA, 3-diamond rating from Mobil.

Canterbury Inn
315 W. Gorham at State, Madison, WI 53703
(800) 838-3850, (608) 258-8899, (608) 283-2541

Innkeeper: Harvey and Trudy Barash
Rooms: 5 w/pvt. bath, suite avail.
Rates: $100-$185/room, $220/suite, all incl cont. brk., evening refreshment, $10 gift certificate to bookstore. 15% rate increase on special-event wknds. Discount avail. for mid-week and frequent visitor stays.
Credit cards: MC, V
Restrictions: No pets, smoking. Deposit req. 14-day cancellation notice req. 2-night min. stay during special-event wknds.
Notes: Inn and bookstore located in historic building. Rooms decorated in gold, burgundy, forest green. Each room with Canterbury Tales theme including hand-painted murals. Amenities include high beamed ceilings, terrycloth robes. Parlor/conference room available for business meetings. VCRs, microwave ovens. Special events held in bookstore. Handicapped access.

Collins House Bed & Breakfast
704 E. Gorham St., Madison, WI 53703
(608) 255-4230

Innkeeper: Mike and Barb Pratzel
Restrictions: 5 suites w/pvt. bath, phone, incl. 1 w/balcony
Rates: $59-$125, incl. full brk., afternoon refreshment.
Credit cards: MC, V
Restrictions: No smoking. Pets considered. One night's deposit req. Min. 48-hrs. cancellation notice req. 2-night min. stay on football and special-event wknds.
Notes: Three-story Prairie school style inn with original leaded-glass windows built in 1911. Living room with fireplace. Sitting rooms overlooking Lake Mendota and the Capitol. Library with TV, VCR, cassettes. Meeting room. Furnished with

antiques, handmade quilts. Off-street parking available. Catering service available. Small private parties accommodated. Listed on the National Register of Historic Places.

The Plough Inn Bed & Breakfast
3402 Monroe St., Madison, WI 53711
(608) 238-2981
Innkeeper: John and Cathie Imes
Rooms: 4 plus 1 suite, all w/pvt. bath, phone, TV, incl. 1 w/fireplace, whirlpool, wet bar, refrigerator
Rates: $76-$96/room, $86-$96/suite, all incl. cont. brk. in mid-week, full brk. on wknds. Special pkgs. avail. Discount avail. for mid-week stay.
Credit cards: MC, V
Restrictions: No children under 10, pets, smoking. One night's deposit req. 7-day cancellation notice req. 2-night min. stay on special event wknds.
Notes: Two-story Greek Revival house built as a tavern in the mid-1800s. Fully renovated in 1986. Porch, terrace. Furnished in period style. A showcase for environmental products and processes for natural living.

MENOMONEE FALLS (10)

Dorshel's B & B
W140, N7616 Lilly Rd., Menomonee Falls, WI 53051
(414) 255-7866
Innkeeper: Dorothy and Sheldon Waggoner
Rooms: 3, incl. 2 w/pvt. bath. Phone avail.
Rates: $45-$60, incl. cont. brk. Discounted rates for extended stay negotiable
Credit cards: None
Restrictions: No children under 12, pets. Smoking restricted. One night's deposit req.
Notes: Country manor located on 1½ acres in residential area of village 20 minutes from Milwaukee. Furnished with antiques. 2 common areas with fireplaces. Formal dining room. Pool room. 2 screened porches, patio. Horseshoe pits, croquet, swings.

NEW GLARUS (9)

Jeanne-Marie's Bed & Breakfast
318 10th Ave., New Glarus, WI 53574
(608) 527-5059
Innkeeper: Jeanne Marie Meier
Rooms: 3, incl. 1 w/pvt. bath
Rates: $50-$70, incl. full brk.
Credit cards: MC, V
Restrictions: No pets, smoking. One night's nonrefundable deposit req. May be used for future visit if cancellation made 7 days ahead. 2-night min. stay on Festival wknds.
Notes: Red brick house built in 1915. Guest rooms with ceiling fans. Formal dining room. Old-fashioned screen porches. Furnished in nostalgic decor. Backyard gardens. Spanish spoken.

PORT WASHINGTON (10)

The Inn at Old Twelve Hundred
806 W. Grand Ave., Port Washington, WI 53074
(414) 268-1200

Innkeeper: Stephanie Bresett
Rooms: 2, no pvt. bath, plus 3 suites w/pvt. bath, TV, fireplace, incl. 2 w/whirlpool.
Rates: $75-$95/room, $125-$145/suite, all incl. expanded cont. brk. Discount avail.
for mid-week stay.
Credit cards: Most major cards
Restrictions: No children, pets, smoking. Credit card guarantee req. 72-hour cancellation notice req. 2-night min. stay on wknds. from mid-June–mid-Oct.
Notes: Queen Anne house. Fully restored. Grounds with gazebo. Lawn games, bicycles available.

RACINE (10)

LOCHNAIAR INN

Lochnaiar Inn
1121 Lake Ave., Racine, WI 53403
(414) 633-3300

Innkeeper: Dawn and Jennifer Weisbrod
Rooms: 6 plus 2 suites, all w/pvt. bath, phone, cable TV, incl. 2 w/fireplace
Rates: $75-$125/room, $175/suite, all incl. cont. mid-week brk., full brk. on wknds., evening refreshment. Discount avail. for extended, corporate and mid-week stays. Special pkgs. avail.
Credit cards: Most major cards
Restrictions: No pets. Smoking restricted. Credit card deposit req. 7-day cancellation notice req.
Notes: Three-story English tudor house with wood floors, copper-clad shingled roof, built in 1915. Recently restored. Located on bluff overlooking Lake Michigan. Each guest room displays it's own personality, uniquely decorated and furnished. Library, meeting room, parlor, veranda. Small private parties accommodated. Business services available. Spanish spoken. Handicapped access.

REEDSBURG (6)

Parkview Bed and Breakfast
211 N. Park St., Reedsburg, WI 53959
(608) 524-4333
Innkeeper: Tom and Donna Hofmann
Rooms: 4, incl. 2 w/pvt. bath, phone, TV
Rates: $55-$70, incl. full brk. Discount avail. for extended stay.
Credit cards: Most major cards
Restrictions: Children subject to prior arrangement. No pets, smoking. One night's deposit req. 48-hour cancellation notice req. 2-night min. stay on holiday wknds.
Notes: Queen Anne Victorian with woodwork, a suitor's window, open stairway, pocket door, leaded and etched windows, built in 1895. Located in historic district. Fully restored. Guest parlor with player piano, books, board games. Porch with rockers. Fish ponds, flower gardens and playhouse in park-like setting.

SPARTA (5)

Just-N-Trails B & B
Rte. 1, Box 274, Sparta, WI 54656
(608) 269-4522, (800) 488-4521
Innkeeper: Don and Donna Justin
Rooms: 9 plus 3 cottages, all w/pvt. bath, 1 w/phone. Located in 4 bldgs.
Rates: $70-$95/room, $125-$250/cottage, all incl. full brk.
Credit cards: Most major cards
Restrictions: No pets, smoking. Deposit req. 7-day cancellation notice req.
Notes: Two-story farmhouse with original maple floors and granary built in 1920. Log cottages. Modernized in 1940. Fully remodeled in 1970. Granary renovated in 1990. Has operated as inn since 1986. Located on third-generation 213-acre working dairy farm with landscaped lawn. Furnished with antiques. Guest rooms with Laura Ashley linens, log cagin pattern wall hangings, country accents. Dining room and garden room. Whirlpool. Porch with rocker. Decorated with Laura Ashley coverlets. Guests are welcome to help with the farm chores and visit with farm animals.*

SPOONER (2)

Aunt Martha's Guest House B&B
1602 Country Rd. A, HCR59, Spooner, WI 54801
(715) 635-6857
Innkeeper: Mary Askov and Robert Johnson
Rooms: 3, incl. 1 w/pvt. bath
Rates: $45-$55, incl. full brk.
Credit cards: None
Restrictions: No pets, smoking. Deposit req. 24-hour cancellation notice req.
Notes: Built in 1927 as a general store.

STEVENS POINT (6)

Dreams of Yesteryear B & B
1100 Brawley St., Stevens Point, WI 54481
(715) 341-4525, (715) 344-3407
Innkeeper: Bonnie and Bill Maher

Rooms: 3 plus 2 suites, all w/pvt. bath, incl. 1 w/phone, TV
Rates: $55-$80/room, $95-$105/suite, all incl. full brk., evening refreshment. Discount avail. for extended and corporate stays.
Credit cards: Most major cards
Restrictions: No children under 12, pets, smoking. One night's deposit req. 7-day cancellation notice req.
Notes: Turn-of-the-century Victorian Queen Anne style house built for local merchant. Recently restored. Golden oak woodwork, hardwood floors, leaded glass windows, footed tubs. Antique appointed rooms. Common room with original brass and iron fireplace. Porch overlooking gardens. Listed on National Register of Historic Places.

STONE LAKE (2)

NEW MOUNTAIN BED & BREAKFAST

New Mountain Bed & Breakfast
Route 1, Box 73C, Stone Lake, WI 54876
(715) 865-2486, (800) NEW-MT-BB

Innkeeper: Jim & Elaine Nyberg
Rooms: 4, incl. 1 w/pvt. bath, 2 w/TV
Rates: $50-$70, incl. full brk.
Credit cards: None
Restrictions: No pets. Smoking restricted. One night's deposit req. 7-day cancellation notice req., less $20.00 fee.
Notes: Hilltop extended cabin with skylights, French doors, overlooking Big Sissabagama Lake. Walls and ceilings of naturally aged knotty pine plus other woodwork throughout. Great room with wood stove, rockers, small library, puzzles. Loft overlooking great room. Dining area, screen porch. Boats, canoe paddle boat, dock, sauna for guest use. Handicapped access.*

STURGEON BAY (7)

White Lace Inn
16 N. 5th Ave., Sturgeon Bay, WI 54235
(414) 743-1105

Innkeeper: Dennis and Bonnie Statz
Rooms: 14 w/pvt. bath, incl. 9 w/fireplace, 5 w/TV, plus 1 suite w/pvt. bath, fireplace, TV. Located in 3 bldgs.
Rates: $45-$135/room, $130-$155/suite, all incl. cont. brk. Seasonal variations. Discount avail. for mid-week stay. Special pkgs. avail.
Credit cards: Most major cards
Restrictions: No children under 12, pets. Smoking restricted. One night's deposit req. 14-day cancellation notice req. 2-night min. stay on wknds. 3-night min. stay on holiday and some autumn wknds.
Notes: Three-story Victorian main house with turret built in 1903. Restored in and has operated as inn since 1982. Fully renovated in 1984. Located on one acre. Front parlor with fireplace. Sitting room with TV, board games. Dining room. Garden House built in 1880. Sitting room with fireplace, dining room. Washburn House opened in 1986. Furnished in country Victorian theme with antique 4-poster canopied beds, down comforters, period antiques. Handicapped access. Resident cat. Innkeepers say it is their guests that make the White Lace Inn special.

WHITE LACE INN

TWO RIVERS (7)

Red Forest Bed & Breakfast
1421 25th St., Two Rivers, WI 54241
(414) 793-1794
Innkeeper: Alan and Kay Rodewald
Rooms: 4, incl. 2 w/pvt. bath, phone
Rates: $60-$75, incl. full brk. Discount avail. for corporate stay.
Credit cards: Most major cards
Restrictions: No small children, pets. Smoking restricted. One night's deposit req. 7-day cancellation notice req.
Notes: Three-story shingle-style house with beveled and stained-glass windows, cross-beamed ceilings, ceiling fans, built in 1907. Fully renovated in and has operated as inn since 1990. Foyer with fireplace, window seats, oak stairway. Parlor, country dining room, front and back porches. Furnished with antiques.*

VIROQUA (5)

Viroqua Heritage Inn
220 E. Jefferson St., Viroqua, WI 54665
(608) 637-3306
Innkeeper: Nancy Rhodes-Seevers
Rooms: 4, incl. 2 w/pvt. bath
Rates: $50-$75, incl. full brk., afternoon refreshment
Credit cards: Most major cards
Restrictions: No pets, smoking
Notes: Victorian house with Queen Anne tower, hardwood floors, oak staircase, built about 1890. Recently restored. Porches with turned balusters, spindles, columns, leaded and beveled glass. Parlor/music room with antique baby grand piano, violin, Victrola. Living room with fireplace, turret alcove, board games. Formal dining room. Library, balcony overlooking garden, front porch. Furnished with antiques. Small private parties accommodated.*

WHITEWATER (9)

The Greene House Country Inn
Rte. 2, W5666, Whitewater, WI 53190-9412
(414) 495-8771, (800) 468-1959
Innkeeper: Lynn and Mayner Greene
Rooms: 3 w/TV, plus 1 suite, no pvt. bath
Rates: $49-$79/room, $79-$150/suite, all incl. full brk. Discount avail. for mid-week, group, and extended stays. Special pkgs. avail.
Credit cards: Most major cards
Restrictions: No children under 5, pets. Smoking restricted. One night's deposit req. 72-hour cancellation notice req., less $20.00 fee.
Notes: Farmhouse built in 1848. Parlor with fireplace, library, TV, VCR, movie library, board games. Decorated in turn-of-the-century style with antiques, quilts, musical instruments. Restaurant on premises. Grounds include mini-barnyard petting zoo, one-acre garden, lawn games, barn for group parties. Innkeeper collects guitars, banjos, mandolins, violins. Small private parties accommodated.*

Victoria-On-Main B & B
622 W. Main St. (Hwy 12), Whitewater, WI 53190
(414) 473-8400
Innkeeper: Nancy Wendt
Rooms: 3 w/sitting area, incl. 1 w/pvt. bath
Rates: $48-$75, incl. full brk., afternoon refreshment
Credit cards: MC, V
Restrictions: No children, pets, smoking. One night's deposit req. 48-hour cancellation notice req.
Notes: Queen Anne Victorian house built in 1895. Located adjacent to University of Wisconsin Whitewater campus in historic district. Reading room. Guest rooms feature different hardwoods of Wisconsin. Furnished with antiques, Laura Ashley prints, lace curtains, down comforters. Guests have access to kitchen, veranda.

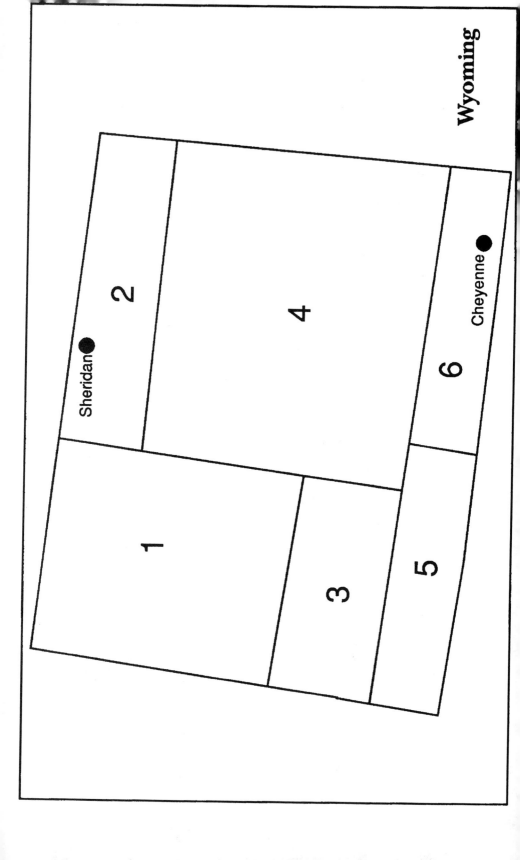

Wyoming

BIG HORN (2)

Spahn's Big Horn Mountain B & B
P.O. Box 579, Big Horn, WY 82833
(307) 674-8150
Innkeeper: Ron Spahn
Rooms: 3 w/pvt. bath, phone, plus 1 suite w/pvt. bath. Located in 3 bldgs.
Rates: $65-$95/room, $80-$100/suite, all incl. full brk. Special pkgs. avail.
Credit cards: MC, V
Restrictions: No pets, smoking. 50% deposit req. 21-day cancellation notice req.,
    less $10.00 fee.
Notes: Three-story main house built in 1976. 3-story log house with living room,
woodburning stove, outside deck. Cabin with sleeping loft, woodburning stove,
front porch. Solar-generated electricity. ½-mile border on Big Horn Mountain
forestland. Has operated as inn since 1985. Three-story high living room with fireplace. Dining room, deck. Operated with the adventurous spirit of a dude ranch.
Camping trips organized.*

SPAHN'S BIG HORN MOUNTAIN B & B

BUFFALO (2)

Cloud Peak Inn
590 N. Burritt, Buffalo, WY 82834
(307) 684-5794
Innkeeper: Rick and Kathy Brus
Rooms: 5, incl. 3 w/pvt. bath
Rates: $45-$55, incl. full brk., evening refreshment. Discount avail. for senior citi-
    zens, extended, and mid-week stays.
Credit cards: Most major cards
Restrictions: No pets. Smoking restricted. 50% deposit req. 7-day cancellation no-
    tice req.

Notes: Bungalow-style house with 10-foot wood beamed ceilings, built in 1912. Parlor, dining room with fireplace, sun room with Jacuzzi. Porch. Decorated with period antiques. Dinner available.*

TA Guest Ranch
P.O. Box 313, Buffalo, WY 82834
(307) 684-7002

Innkeeper: Earl and Barbara Madsen
Rooms: 5 w/pvt. bath. Located in 2 bldgs.
Rates: $80, incl. full brk. Seasonal variations. Special pkgs. avail.
Credit cards: MC, V
Restrictions: No pets, smoking. 50% deposit req. 7-day cancellation notice req., less $5.00 fee.
Notes: Living room.*

CASPER (4)

DURBIN STREET INN

Durbin Street Inn
843 S. Durbin, Casper, WY 82601
(307) 577-5774, (307) 266-5441

Innkeeper: Don and Sherry Frigon
Rooms: 5, no pvt. bath
Rates: $55-$70, incl. full brk., afternoon refreshment. Special pkgs. available.
Credit cards: Most major cards
Restrictions: No pets, smoking restricted. 50% deposit req. 72-hour cancellation notice req. or subject to $15.00 fee.
Notes: 1917 American Foursquare house situated in historical residential area within walking distance of Casper. Furnished with antiques. Large common area, small conference room. Other meals can be arranged.*

CODY (1)

Hunter Peak Ranch
Painter Rte., Box 1731, Cody, WY 82414
(307) 587-3711

Innkeeper: Louis and Shelley Carey
Rooms: 8 w/pvt. bath, equipped kitchen, incl. 2 w/fireplace. Located in 3 bldgs.
Rates: $57-$87, incl. full brk. Discount avail. for extended stay. Special pkgs. avail.
Credit cards: None
Restrictions: No pets, smoking. 30% deposit req. 60-day cancellation notice req. 3-night min. stay.
Notes: Ranch homesteaded in 1906 and operated by third generation hosts. Log buildings furnished with Indian rugs, paintings and tack in a Western style. Library, lodge room, dining room. Fishing, horsebackriding, volleyball, badminton, horseshoes, croquet, cross-country skiing, and snowmobiling available.

Lockhart Bed & Breakfast Inn
109 W. Yellowstone Ave., Cody, WY 82414
(800) 377-7255, (307) 587-6074, (307) 587-8644

Innkeeper: Cindy Baldwin
Rooms: 7 w/pvt. bath, phone, TV
Rates: $58-$82, incl. full brk. Discount avail. for extended stay.
Credit cards: Most major cards
Restrictions: No pets, smoking. One night's deposit req. 7-day cancellation notice req., less $20.00 fee
Notes: Built in 1890s. Fully restored and moved to original site overlooking Shoshone River. Former home of authoress Caroline Lockhart. Furnished with country antiques. Veranda. Lawn games available. Handicapped access.*

JACKSON (1)

The Alpine House
285 N. Glenwood, Box 20245, Jackson, WY 83001
(307) 739-1570, (800) 753-1421

Innkeeper: Hans and Nancy Johnstone
Rooms: 7 w/pvt. bath, pvt. balcony
Rates: $65-$110, incl. full brk., evening refreshment. Seasonal variations. Special pkgs. avail.
Credit cards: MC, V
Restrictions: No pets, smoking. 50% deposit req. Final pmt. due 30 days prior to arrival. 30-day cancellation notice req., less $20.00 fee.
Notes: Timber frame Scandinavian-style lodge. Dining area, living room with cathedral ceiling, library. Furnished with country antiques. Innkeepers are ex-Olympic skiers and currently mountain guides. Handicapped access.*

H. C. Richards B & B
160 W. Deloney, Box 2606, Jackson, WY 83001
(307) 733-6704, (307) 733-0930

Innkeeper: Jackie Williams
Rooms: 3 w/pvt. bath, phone, cable TV
Rates: $90, incl. full brk., afternoon and evening refreshment. Seasonal variations.
Credit cards: MC, V
Restrictions: No smoking. One night's deposit req. 7-day cancellation notice req.
Notes: 6,600-square-foot ranch-style house in building orginally homesteaded by innkeeper's grandfather in 1920s. Guest rooms with French phones, goosedown comforters, tapestry coverlets. Large dining room with massive chandelier, recreation

room with pool table, table tennis, games table. Decorated in French-English manner with antiques.*

Painted Porch B & B
P.O. Box 3965, Jackson, WY 83001
(307) 733-1981

Innkeeper: Martha and Matt MacEachern
Rooms: 1 plus 1 suite, all w/pvt. bath, Japanese soaking tub, TV, pvt. entrance
Rates: $115/room, $145/suite, all incl. full brk.
Credit cards: MC, V
Restrictions: No pets, smoking. 50% deposit req. 30-day cancellation notice req., less $20.00 fee. 2-night min. stay.
Notes: Farmhouse with hardwood floors, hand-painted tiles built in 1901. Moved in 1967 from Driggs, Idaho, over the Teton Pass to present location. Fully restored. Located on 3 wooded acres. Living room with moss rock fireplace. Furnished with antiques, family heirlooms. Spanish spoken.

Sassy Moose Inn
Teton Village Rd., H.C. 362, Jackson, WY 83001
(307) 733-1277, (800) 356-1277, (307) 739-0793

Innkeeper: Polly Englant
Rooms: 5 w/pvt. bath, TV, phone, incl. 2 w/fireplace. Suite avail.
Rates: $99-$129/room, $159/suite, all incl. full brk., afternoon and evening refreshment. Seasonal variations. Discount avail. for AAA, senior citizen, extended stays.
Credit cards: Most major cards
Restrictions: Some pets welcome by prior arrangement. No smoking. 50% deposit req. 30-day cancellation notice req. 2-night min. stay in July, August.
Notes: Log ranch house built in 1991 as an inn. Located on 3 acres. Porch and all guest rooms overlooking the Grand Teton Mtns. Dining room, lobby. Living room with wood-burning stove. Indoor/outdoor hot tub. Furnished in "Jackson Hole western" style. Guests have access to laundry facilities. Board and lawn games available.*

Twin Trees B & B
575 S. Willow, Box 7533, Jackson, WY 83001-7533
(307) 739-9737, (800) 728-7337

Innkeeper: Pat Martin
Rooms: 3 w/pvt. bath
Rates: $105, incl. full brk. Seasonal variations. Discount avail. for extended stay.
Credit cards: MC, V
Restrictions: No children under 15, pets, smoking. 50% deposit req. 10-day cancellation notice req., less $15.00 fee. 2-night min. stay.
Notes: Two-story country ranch-style house built as an inn in 1992. Living room, dining room. Furnished in eclectic style. Some Spanish spoken. Resident cats.*

The Wildflower Inn
Teton Village Rd., Box 3724, Jackson, WY 83001
(307) 733-4710, (307) 739-0914

Innkeeper: Ken and Sherrie Jern
Rooms: 5 w/pvt. bath, phone, cable TV, incl. 4 w/pvt. deck
Rates: $120-$130, incl. full brk.

Credit cards: MC, V
Restrictions: No pets, smoking. Full deposit req. 30-day cancellation notice req. for 50% refund if room re-rented.
Notes: Two-story log house designed and built by innkeepers. Located on three wooded acres. Has operated as inn since 1989. Guest rooms with down comforters. Dining room. Deck overlooking pond. Solarium with hot tub. Innkeeper is climbing guide, ski instructor.*

JACKSON HOLE (1)

Nowlin Creek Inn
660 E. Broadway, Box 2766, Jackson Hole, WY 83001
(307) 733-0882, (800) 542-2632, (307) 733-0106
Innkeeper: Mark and Susan Nowlin
Rooms: 4 plus 1 suite, all w/pvt. bath
Rates: $125/room, $155/suite, all incl. full brk., afternoon refreshment. Seasonal variations.
Credit cards: Most major cards
Restrictions: No children under 5, pets, smoking. Deposit req. 30-day cancellation notice req., less $20.00 fee. 2-night min. stay on wknds.
Notes: Located near heart of Jackson bordering the National Elk Refuge. Living room, dining room, library. Deck with hot tub. Both artists, innkeepers have decorated the inn with their own art, in addition to antique and historical prints and contemporary etchings. Western-style furnishings and Victorian antiques.*

LANDER (3)

Country Fare Bed and Breakfast
904 Main St., Lander, WY 82520
(307) 332-5906
Innkeeper: Tony and Mary Ann Hoyt
Rooms: 3 w/TV, VCR, no pvt. bath
Rates: $45-$60, incl. full brk., afternoon refreshment
Credit cards: MC, V
Restrictions: No children, pets, smoking. One night's deposit req. 7-day cancellation notice req., less $15.00 fee.
Notes: Victorian house located at the foot of Wind River Mountain Range. Fully restored. Great room w/TV, VCR library. Furnished with antiques, English duvets.

LARAMIE (6)

Annie Moore's Guest House
819 University, Laramie, WY 82070
(307) 721-4177, (800) 552-8992
Innkeeper: Ann Acuff and Joe Bundy
Rooms: 6, no pvt. bath
Rates: $40-$60, incl. cont. brk.
Credit cards: Most major cards
Restrictions: No children under 8, pets, smoking. Credit card guarantee or one night's deposit req. 7-day cancellation notice req.
Notes: Two-story Post-Victorian Queen Anne house built about 1910. Fully renovated. Has operated as inn since 1931. Colorfully decorated guest rooms. Located

directly across the street from University of Wyoming. Parlor, second-story sundeck. Furnished with antiques.

PINEDALE (3)

Window On The Winds
10151 Hwy. 191, Box 135, Pinedale, WY 82941
(307) 367-2600, (307) 367-2395
Innkeeper: Leanne McClain and Doug McKay
Rooms: 4, no pvt. bath
Rates: $50-$60, incl. full brk. Discount avail. for extended stay. **Seasonal variations.** Credit cards: Most major cards
Restrictions: No smoking. 50% deposit req. 7-day cancellation notice req.
Notes: Two-story log house built in 1968. Located at the base of the Wind River Mountains. Guest rooms with lodgepole pine queen beds, down comforters and pillows. Large common room with TV, fireplace, phone, games, books, overlooking Wind River Mountains. Sun room with hot tub. Decorated in western and plains Indian themes. Innkeepers are both archeologists.*

Contacts for Reservations

The following organizations may be contacted for reservations at bed and breakfast facilities in the areas listed:

ALASKA

Alaska Bed and Breakfast Association
369 S. Franklin, # 200, Juneau, AK 99801
Trish, Shari, Janice, Betty Lou, Karla
(907) 586-2959 (AK)
(907) 463-4453
Hours: 9:00—5:00, M—F
Rate range: $65—$150
Credit cards: Most major cards
Restrictions: 20% deposit req. 2-night min. stay in summer.
Notes: Accommodations regularly inspected. Reservations and deposit made through this service. Balance of payment made directly to host. A service of Alaska Rainforest Tours.

ARIZONA

Bed & Breakfast Inn Arizona
8900 E. Via Linda, Ste. 101, Scottsdale, AZ 85260
Scott Stuart
(602) 860-9338, (800) 266-7829
(602) 314-1193
Hours: 10:00—6:00
Rate range: $45—$300
Credit cards: Most major cards
Notes: Has operated as RSO since 1982, representing homestays, ranches, resorts, vacation apartments. Accommodations are inspected. All reservations made through this service. All payments made directly to host. Car rentals available.

Mi Casa Sue Casa B & B
P.O. Box 950, Tempe, AZ 85280-0950
Ruth Young
(602) 990-0682, (800) 456-0682
(602) 990-3390
Hours: 8:00—8:00
Rate range: $45—$175
Credit cards: None
Restrictions: Min. $20.00 deposit req. 7-day cancellation notice req., less $10.00 fee.
Notes: Accommodations in B&B Inns, ranches, homestays. All accommodations must meet B&B Reservation Services Worldwide and The National Network standards. Reservations and payments made through this service.

939

Old Pueblo Homestays RSO
5644 E. 6th St., Box 13603, Tucson, AZ 85732
Bill Janssen
(602) 790-0030, (800) 333-9776
(602) 790-2399
Hours: 8:30—6:30
Rate range: $45—$120
Credit cards: Please call for info.
Restrictions: Please call for info.
Notes: Accommodations available in homestays and B & B Inns. Reservations made through this service. Payments made through this service or directly with host. All accommodations are certified for comfort and cleanliness based on B & B Worldwide standards.

CALIFORNIA

Eye Openers Bed & Breakfast Reservations
P.O. Box 694, Altadena, CA 91003
Ruth Judkins, Betty Cox
(213) 684-4428, (818) 797-2055
(818) 798-3640
Hours: 9:00—5:00, M—TH
Rate range: $40—$200
Credit cards: MC, V
Restrictions: One-time $10.00 membership fee req. $25.00 deposit req. 7-day cancellation notice req., less $10.00 fee. Closed on major holidays.
Notes: Accommodations in country inns, B&B inns, homestays. Accommodations inspected annually. Reservations made through this service. Payments made through this service or directly to host.

Bed and Breakfast California
3924 E. 14th St., Long Beach, CA 90804
Robin Mahin
(310) 498-0552, (800) 383-3513
(310) 597-5220
Hours: 8:00—8:00
Rate range: $50—$175
Credit cards: All Major Cards
Restrictions: Please call for info. 2-night min.
Notes: Accommodations in B&B Inns, ranches, homestays, long-term hotels. Accommodations are inspected. Reservations made through this service. Payments made directly to host.

Dockside Boat & Bed
77 Jack London Square, Oakland, CA 94607
Rob and Mollie Harris
(510) 444-5858, (415) 392-5526
(510) 444-0420
Hours: 10:00—6:00, 7 days per week
Rate range: $95—$595

Credit cards: Most major cards
Restrictions: No children under 6, pets, smoking, high-heel shoes. 50% deposit req. 30-day cancellation notice req., less 25% fee.
Notes: Overnight dockside accommodations on sailing and motor yachts. Also available for private charter, catered dining. Reservations and payments made through this service.*

Point Reyes Lodging
P.O. Box 878, Point Reyes Station, CA 94956
Felicity Kirscal
(415) 663-1872, (800) 539-1872
(415) 663-8431
Hours: always
Rate range: $85—$225
Credit cards: Most major cards
Notes: Accommodations in small hotels, lodges, country inns, B&B inns, cottages. All accommodations have been inspected and certified by CABBI. Reservations and payments made directly to host. Small private parties accommodated. Swiss, Italian, Spanish spoken.

West Marin Network
P.O. Box 834, Point Reyes Station, CA 94956
Bobbi, Nina
(415) 663-9453, 663-9544
(415) 663-5458
Hours: 9:00—6:00, Mon.—Sat.
Rate range: $45—$175
Credit cards: None
Restrictions: Please call for info.
Notes: Accommodations available in B & B Inns, cottages, motels, hotels, lodges, homestays, guest houses. Reservations may be made through this service or directly with innkeeper. Payments made directly to host. Italian, German, Russian spoken.

B & B International
P.O. Box 282910, San Francisco, CA 94128
Sharon Klein
(415) 696-1690, (800) 872-4500
(415) 696-1699

B & B San Francisco
P.O. Box 420009, San Francisco, CA 94142
Susan and Richard Kreigich
(415) 479-1913, (800) 452-8249
(415) 921-2273
Hours: 9:30—5:00, M—F
Rate range: $65—$175
Credit cards: Most major cards
Restrictions: One night's deposit req.
Notes: Accommodations in B&B Inns, homestays and yachts. Accommdations are inspected annually. Reservations are made through this office. Payments made directly to host.

COLORADO

B & B Agency of Colorado at Vail
P.O. Box 491, Vail, CO 81658
Kathy Westerberg, Carol Walsh
(303) 949-1212, (800) 748-2666
(303) 949-1397
Hours: 9:00—6:00, M—F; 9:00—5:00, Sat.
Rate range: $45—$175
Credit cards: Most major cards
Restrictions: 50% deposit req. 60-day cancellation notice req. during ski season, less $25.00 per person fee. Closed April 15—May 15.
Notes: Accommodations in homestays, mountain lodges, inns and cabins. Has operated as Reservation Service since 1982. All properties personally inspected. Reservations and payments made through this service.

CONNECTICUT

Covered Bridge
P.O. Box 447, Norfolk, CT 06058
Hank and Diane Tremblay
(203) 542-5944
Hours: 10:00—8:00
Rate range: $85—$185
Credit cards: Most major cards
Restrictions: Full prepayment req. 10-day cancellation notice req., less $15.00 fee.
Notes: Accommodations in B&B Inns, homestays. All accommodations are inspected prior to joining this service. Reservations and payments made to this service. French spoken.

Nutmeg Bed & Breakfast Agency
P.O. Box 1117, West Hartford, CT 06127
Michelle Souza
(203) 236-6698, (800) 727-7592
Hours: 9:30—5:00, M—F
Rate range: $50—$150
Credit cards: Most major cards
Restrictions: Min. one night's deposit req. Min. $15.00 cancellation fee.
Notes: Accommodations in country inns, homestays, B&B inns. Accommodations inspected. Has operated as reservation service since 1981. Reservations made through this service. Payments made either to this service or directly to host.

DELAWARE

Bed & Breakfast of Delaware
3650 Silverside Rd., Box 177, Wilmington, DE 19810-2211
Millie Alford

(302) 479-9500
(302) 479-9500
Hours: 9:00—5:00, M—F
Rate range: $45—$125
Credit cards: Most major cards
Restrictions: Deposit req. 14-day cancellation notice req., less $25.00 fee.
Notes: Properties include country inns, southern plantation National Historical Register properties and home stays. All lodgings must pass a certified host inspection checklist published by Bed & Breakfast Worldwide. Reservations must be made through this office. Payments may be made either through this office or to host.

GEORGIA

R.S.V.P. GRITS
541 Londonberry Rd. N.W., Atlanta, GA 30327
Marty Barnes
(404) 843-3933, (800) 823-7787
(404) 252-8886
Hours: 9:00—6:00, M—F; 9:00—noon, Wknds.
Rate range: $65—$250
Credit cards: Most major cards
Restrictions: Closed Thanksgiving Day, Christmas Day, New Years Day.
Notes: Accommodations in country inns and B&B inns. Approx. 80% of properties are historic structures. All accommodations are properly licensed and inspected. Reservations made through this service. Payments made either through this service or directly to host.

Sonja's R.S.V.P. B & B Reservation Service
9489 Whitfield Ave., Box 49, Savannah, GA 31406
Sonja Lazzaro
(912) 232-7787, (800) 729-7787
Hours: 9:30—5:30, M—F
Rate range: $60—$225
Credit cards: Most major cards
Restrictions: One night's deposit req. 7-day cancellation notice req., less $15.00 per room fee. $5.00 additional charged for one night's stay.
Notes: Accommodations provided in country inns, homestays and B & B inns, all with private bath, breakfast, handicapped access, and antique furnishings, all located in or near historic districts. Properties inspected several time yearly. Reservations made through this service. Payments made directly to host. Also available — area maps, event lists, restaurant menus, tours organized.

HAWAII

Go Native - Hawaii
P.O. Box 11418, Hilo, HI 96721
Fred Diamond, Ken Wood
(808) 935-4178, (800) 662-8483

(808) 935-4178
Hours: 8:00—6:00
Rate range: $55—$150
Credit cards: None
Restrictions: 50% deposit req. 3-night min. stay.
Notes: Has operated as reservation service since 1982. Accommodations in country inns, B&B inns, homestays, cottages, guest houses, studios. All accommodations are inspected. Reservations and deposit made through this service. Balance of payment directly to host.

American International B & B
P.O. Box 240855, Honolulu, HI 96824
Michelle, Chris
(808) 941-0111, (800) 949-7878
Hours: 8:00—8:00
Rate range: from $35
Credit cards: None
Restrictions: Please call for info.
Notes: Accommodations in B & B inns, hotels, homestays. All properties required to be clean, friendly and licensed. Notes: Reservations and payments made to this service. German spoken.

Bed & Breakfast Honolulu (Statewide)
3242 Kaohinani Dr., Honolulu, HI 96817
Gene Bridges, Mary Lee
(808) 595-7533, (800) 288-4666
(808) 595-2030
Hours: 8:00—5:00, M—F; 8:00—noon, Sat.
Rate range: Please call for info. Discount for extended stay.
Credit cards: MC, V
Restrictions: Min. 50% deposit req. 2-week cancellation notice req., less $25.00 fee. $50.00 key deposit. $10.00 reservation fee. $10.00 fee to change a reservation already booked. Surcharge for less than 3-night stay.
Notes: 300 locations located on all Hawaiian islands. Has operated as reservation service since 1982. Car rentals, flower lei, fruit baskets, ferrys, cruises, tours, luaus organized.

All Islands Bed & Breakfast
823 Kainui Dr., Kailua, HI 96734-2025
Ann, Puahala, Carol, Aggie
(808) 263-2342, (800) 542-0344
(808) 263-0308
Hours: 8:00-5:00, Mon.—Fri.
Rate range: $45—$260
Credit cards: Most major cards
Restrictions: 20% deposit req.
Notes: Accommodations in homestays, studios, cottages. All accommodations regularly inspected. Reservations and deposit made through this service. Balance of payment made directly to host. Airport lei greetings, reservations for car rentals, air and boat trips available.*

ILLINOIS

Bed and Breakfast/Chicago, Inc.
P.O. Box 14088, Chicago, IL 60614
Mary Shaw, Lori Granoff
(312) 951-0085, (800) 484-4056
(312) 649-9243
Hours: 9:00—5:00, M—F
Rate range: $65—$185. Discount avail. for extended stay.
Credit cards: Most major cards
Restrictions: Deposit req. No pets. 2-night min. stay in homes. 3-night min. stay in unhosted apts.
Notes: Has operated as reservation service since 1980. Accommodations available in homestays, apartments, guest houses, inns. All properties personally inspected annually. All reservations made through this service. All payments made directly to host. Some Spanish, French spoken.

Heritage Bed & Breakfast Registry, The
75 E. Wacker Dr., Suite 3600, Chicago, IL 60601
Bill, Thor, Kyle
(312) 857-0800
(312) 857-0805
Hours: 9:00—5:00, M—F; 10:30—12:30, Sat.
Rate range: $65—$135
Credit cards: Most major cards
Restrictions: $15.00 non-refundable deposit req. 48-hour cancellation notice req.
Notes: Has operated as reservation service since 1984. Accommodations in homestays. All properties personally inspected. Reservations and payments made to this service. Spanish spoken.

LOUISIANA

New Orleans Bed and Breakfast and Accommodations
671 Rosa Ave., Metairie, LA 70005
Mary Di Benedetto, Myrle Dey, Adele Bornkessel, Barbara Mire
(504) 838-0071, 838-0072
(504) 838-0140
Hours: 8:00—5:00, M—F
Rate range: $50—$300
Credit cards: Most major cards
Restrictions: Please call for info.
Notes: Accommodations in plantation homes, country retreats, condos, apts., homestays. All accommodations are inspected. Reservations and payments made through this service. French, Spanish spoken.

MASSACHUSETTS

The Bed & Breakfast Folks
48 Springs Rd., Bedford, MA 01730
Phyllis Phillips
(617) 275-9025
Hours: 8:00 AM—10:00 PM, 7 days per week
Rate range: $40—$80
Credit cards: None
Restrictions: Please call for info.
Notes: Accommodations in private homes. All hosts are interviewed during a home visit prior to being listed. All reservations are made through this service. Fees may be paid to this office or to host directly.

A B&B Agency of Boston
47 Commercial Wharf, Boston, MA 02110
Ferne Mintz
(617) 720-3540, (800) 248-9262
(617) 523-5761
Hours: 9:00—9:00
Rate range: $55—$130
Credit cards: MC, V
Restrictions: Please call for info.
Notes: Accommodations in homestays, apts. and studios. Accommodations personally inspected. Reservation and deposit made to this service. Balance paid directly to host. Some Spanish and French spoken.

Bed & Breakfast Associates Bay Colony, Ltd.
P.O. Box 57166, Babson Park, Boston, MA 02157-0166
Barbara, Lynn, Lorraine, Cora, Marlilyn, Arline
(617) 449-5302, (800) 347-5088
(617) 449-5958
Hours: 9:00—5:00, M—F
Rate range: $55—$150. Discount for extended stay.
Credit cards: Most major cards
Restrictions: Min. One night's deposit req. 2-week cancellation notice req., less $25.00 fee. $10.00 surcharge for one night stay. Closed Christmas week.
Notes: Accommodations in inns, small hotels, unhosted apts. and homestays. Has operated as reservation service since 1981. All properties inspected annually. Reservations and deposits made through this service. Balance of payment either to this service or directly to host.

Greater Boston Hospitality
P.O. Box 1142, Brookline, MA 02146
Kelly Simpson
(617) 277-5430
(617) 277-5430
Hours: 8:30—5:30, M—Sat.
Rate range: $47—$125
Credit cards: Most major cards
Restrictions: Deposit req.

Notes: Accommodations in homestays, inns and unhosted condominiums. Accommodations are initially inspected by two staff members, with an annual follow-up visit. Reservations and most fees handled through this service. Relocation services offered.

Bed & Breakfast Cambridge & Greater Boston

P.O. Box 1344, Cambridge, MA 02238
Pamela Carruthers
(617) 576-1492, (800) 888-0178
(617) 576-1430
Hours: 10:00-6:00, M—F
Rate range: $55—$110
Credit cards: Most major cards
Restrictions: Deposit req. Closed Dec. 24—Jan. 2
Notes:Accommodations in B & B homestays, unhosted apts. and small inns. Notes: All accommodations are visited annually and evaluated on an on-going basis by guests. Reservations made and deposit paid through this service, balance paid directly to host.

B & B Marblehead & North Shore

P.O. Box 35, Newtonville, MA 02160
Suzanne Ross, Sheryl Felleman
(617) 964-1606, (800) 832-2632
(617) 332-8572
Hours: 8:30—6:00 & 7:00—9:00, M—F; 9:00—noon, Sat., 7:00—9:00, Sun.
Rate range: $45—$165. Discount avail. for extended and senior citizen stays.
Credit cards: Most major cards
Restrictions: Smoking restricted. $25.00 deposit req. 2-week cancellation notice req., less $15.00 fee. $15.00 non-refundable booking fee req. Closed wknds., Nov.—Apr., legal holidays and the third week in Nov.
Notes: Accommodations in B&B inns, cottages, apts., condos, homestays. All accommodations inspected annually and must be in conformity with local zoning regulations, carry liability insurance, pay annual host registration fee. Has operated as reservation service since 1984. Reservations and deposit paid to this agency. Balance of payment directly to host. Small private parties accommodated.*

Provincetown Reservation Service

293 Commercial St., Provincetown, MA 02657
Roz Hirsch, John Sorge, George Pohle, Carl Cefton
(508) 487-2400, (800) 648-0364
(508) 487-4887
Hours: 9:00—9:00 in season, 9:00—4:00 off season
Rate range: $50—$300
Credit cards: None
Restrictions: Please call for details.
Notes: This is a full-service travel agency, in business since 1987. Accommodations in guest houses, condos, homestays, motels. Accommodations are regularly inspected. Reservations made through this service. Payments made either through this service or directly to host.

Folkstone Bed & Breakfast Reservation Service

51 Sears Rd., Southborough, MA 01772
Abigail Miller

(508) 480-0380, (800) 726-2751
Hours: 9:30 AM—2:30 PM, 7:00 PM—9:00 PM, M—F
Rate range: $65—$150
Credit cards: MC, V
Restrictions: Deposit req. 14-day cancellation notice req., less $25.00 fee.
Notes: All properties have been visited and inspected for comfort, cleanliness and hospitality. All reservations and payments are made to this service. Spanish spoken.

Bed and Breakfast Cape Cod
P.O. Box 341, West Hyannisport, MA 02672-0841
Bernice, Joyce, Clark
(508) 775-2772
(508) 775-2884
Hours: 8:30—6:00
Rate range: $55—$200. Seasonal variations.
Credit cards: Most major cards
Restrictions: Children, smoking restricted. No pets. Min. one night's deposit req. 14-day cancellation notice req., less 5% fee. 2-night min. stay. 3-night min. stay for holidays.
Notes: Representing country inns, B & B inns and homestays. All reservations and payments made through this service. Each property is inspected at least once annually.

MARYLAND

Amanda's Bed and Breakfast Reservation Service
1428 Park Ave., Annapolis, MD 21217-4230
Betsy Grater
(410) 225-0001, (800) 899-7533
(410) 728-8957
Hours: 8:30—5:30, M—F; 8:30—12:00, Sat.
Rate range: $60 and up
Credit cards: Most major cards
Restrictions: Deposit req. 10-day cancellation notice req., less $25.00 fee. Closed Christmas and New Year's Day, Sundays
Notes: Has operated as service since 1985. Accommodations in pvt. homes, small inns, yachts. Accommodations meet local codes and zoning restrictions. Reservations made through this service. Payments made directly to host.

MISSOURI

Ozark Mountain Country B & B Service
P.O. Box 295, Branson, MO 65615
Kay Cameron
(417) 334-4720, (800) 695-1546
(417) 335-8134
Hours: 9:00—5:00 and 7:00—9:00, M—F, 1:00—5:00, S—S
Rate range: $30—$150

Credit cards: Most major cards
Restrictions: Please call for details.
Notes: Accommodations is country inns, homestays, B & B inns and cottages. All accommodations are visited and must be a place the agent would want to stay. All reservations made through this service. All payments made directly to host.

MISSISSIPPI

Columbus Historic Foundation
P.O. Box 46, Columbus, MS 39703
Pat Ross, Jane Lee
(601) 329-3533
(601) 329-9791
Hours: Always
Rate range: $85—$100
Credit cards: MC, V
Restrictions: Children restricted. One night's deposit req. 7-day cancellation notice req., less 25% fee. Closed during most holidays.
Notes: Accommodations provided in B & B Inns and antebellum homestays. Reservations may be made through this service or with the host. Payment is made directly to the host. Daily tours organized. Sponsor of the annual antiques show, Decorative Arts Forum, annual Spring Pilgrimage.

MONTANA

B & B Western Adventure
P.O. Box 4308, Bozeman, MT 59772
Paula Deigert
(406) 585-0557
(406) 585-2869
Hours: 9:00—1:00, Sept. 16—May 14, 9:00—5:00 balance of year
Rate range: $50—$150
Credit cards: MC, V
Restrictions: Closed afternoons, Sept. 16—May 14.
Notes: Accommodations in B&B Inns, homestays, ranches. All accommodations inspected. Reservations and first night's payment made through this office. Balance of payment made directly to host.

NEW HAMPSHIRE

Country Inns in the White Mountains
P.O. Box 2025, North Conway, NH 03860-2025
Agent
(603) 356-9460, (800) 562-1300
(603) 356-6081
Hours: 7:00—11:00

Rate range: Please call for details
Credit cards: Most major cards
Restrictions: Please call for details
Notes: Accommodations in country inns, B&B inns. All accommodations inspected regularly. Reservations made through this service or directly with host. Payments made directly to host.

NEW JERSEY

B & B Adventures
2310 Central Ave., Suite 132, North Wildwood, NJ 08260
Paul, Diane, Joan
(609) 522-4000, (800) 992-2632
(609) 522-6125
Hours: 9:00—5:00, M—F
Rate range: $50—$275
Credit cards: Most major cards
Restrictions: Please call for details.
Notes: Accommodations in country inns, B & B inns, cottages and homestays. All properties owned and operated by professional innkeepers, and inspected by this service. Reservations and paymnents made through this service.

Bed & Breakfast of Princeton
P.O. Box 571, Princeton, NJ 08542
John Hurley
(609) 924-3189
(609) 921-6271
Always
Rate range: Hours: $50—$60
Credit cards: None
Restrictions: One night's deposit req. 7-day cancellation notice req.
Notes: All accommodations inspected. Reservation and deposit made through this service. Balance of payment directly to host.

NEW YORK

American Country Collection of B & B
4 Greenwood Lane, Delmar, NY 12054
Arthur and Marie Copeland
(518) 439-7001
(518) 439-4301
Hours: 10:00—5:00, M—F
Rate range: $35—$250
Credit cards: Most major cards
Restrictions: Min. one night's deposit req. 14-day cancellation notice req., less $20.00 fee. $5.00—$10.00 administration fee charged on first booking in any six month period. Closed for one week at the end of March.

Notes: Accommodations in country inns, homestays, B&B inns, cottages. All accommodations are insured for B&B liability, and regularly inspected. Reservations and deposit made through this service. Balance of payment made directly to host.

Elaine's B & B Reservation Service
4978 Kingston Rd., Elbridge, NY 13060
Elaine Samuels
(315) 689-2082
Hours: 10:00—7:00, M—F
Rate range: $50—$150. Discount avail. for extended stay.
Credit cards: None
Restrictions: Deposit req. 2-week cancellation notice req., less $10.00 fee.
Notes: Accommodations in homestays and B&B Inns. All accommodations personally inspected. Reservations made through this service. Payments made directly to host. Small private parties accommodated.

Bed & Breakfast Network of New York
134 W. 32nd St., Suite 602, New York, NY 10001
Leslie Goldberg
(212) 645-8134, (800) 900-8134
Hours: 8:00—6:00, M—F
Rate range: $80—$300. Discount avail. for extended stay.
Credit cards: None
Restrictions: 25% deposit req.
Notes: Has been in business since 1986. Accommodations in host homes and furnished apts. All properties must meet specific standards. Reservations and deposit paid to this service. Balance of fee paid directly to host.

Urban Ventures, Inc.
38 W. 32 St., # 1412, New York, NY 10001
Mary, Myrna, Jim, Lynna, Judith
(212) 594-5650
(212) 947-9320
Hours: 8:00—5:00, M—F
Rate range: $55—$220
Credit cards: Most major cards
Restrictions: Closed on major holidays.
Notes: Accommodations in apts. All accommodations inspected. Has operated as reservation service since 1979. Reservations and payments made through this service. French, Spanish spoken.

OREGON

Northwest Bed & Breakfast, Travel Unlimited
610 S.W. Broadway, # 606, Portland, OR 97205
LaVonne Miller
(503) 243-7616
Hours: anytime
Rate range: $50—$175
Credit cards: Most major cards

Restrictions: Please call for info.
Notes: Accommodations in inns and homestays. Has operated as reservation service since 1979. All accommodations personally inspected. Reservations and payments made through this service. Itinerary-planning available.

PENNSYLVANIA

Hershey B & B Reservation Service
P.O. Box 208, Hershey, PA 17033-0208
Renee Deutel
(717) 533-2928
Hours: 9:30—6:30
Rate range: $50—$100
Credit cards: Most major cards
Restrictions: Children restricted. No smoking. Deposit req.
Notes: Accommodations in country inns, B&B inns, homestays. Accommodations personally inspected. Reservations and deposit made through this service. Balance of payment made directly to host.

Aunt Susie's Country Vacations
RD 1, Box 225, Hesston, PA 16647
Agent
(814) 658-3638
Hours: always
Rate range: $50—$75
Credit cards: None
Restrictions: Please call for details.
Notes: Accommodations in country inns, homestays. Reservations and payments made directly with host.

Guesthouses, Inc.
P.O. Box 2137, West Chester, PA 19380
Joan Mele
(610) 692-4575
Hours: 12:00—4:00, M—F
Rate range: $80—$200
Credit cards: Most major cards
Restrictions: First and last night's deposit req. 5-day cancellation notice req., less $5.00 fee.
Notes: Accomodations in country inns, B&B inns, homestays. Most properties are on the National or State Registers of Historic Places. Reservations and payments made through this office.

RHODE ISLAND

Anna's Victorian Connection
5 Fowler Ave., Newport, RI 02840
Susan, Heather

(401) 849-2489, (800) 884-4288
(401) 847-7309
Hours: 9:00—9:00, M—F; 9:00—7:00, Sat., Sun. Seasonal variations.
Rate range: $35—$300. Discount for extended stay.
Credit cards: Most major cards
Restrictions: 50% deposit req. 2-week cancellation notice req., less 10% fee.
Notes: Accommodations available in Country Inns, home stays, B & B Inns. Accommodations must pass inspection based on T.N.N. standards. Deposit payable to this service. Balance due directly to host. Reservations, gift certificates, guidebooks and concierge service available.

SOUTH CAROLINA

Southern Hospitality
110 Amelia Dr., Lexington, SC 29072
Mesa Faord
(803) 356-6238, (800) 374-7422
(803) 356-6238
Hours: 9:00-8:00, M—F, 1:00—4:00, Sat.
Rate range: $45—$150
Credit cards: MC, V
Restrictions: One night's deposit req. 7-day cancellation notice req. Closed New Year's Day and other major holidays.
Notes: Accommodations in country inns, homestays, B&B inns—all with less than 15 rooms. All accommodations licensed, insured and personally inspected. Reservations and deposit made through this service. Balance of payment made directly to host. Small private parties accommodated.

TENNESSEE

Natchez Trace B & B Reservation Service
P.O. Box 193, Hampshire, TN 38461
Kay and Bill Jones
(615) 285-2777, (800) 377-2770
Hours: 8:00—9:00
Rate range: $50—$115
Credit cards: MC, V
Restrictions: Please call for details
Notes: Accommodations in B&B Inns and homestays along the Natchez Trace National Parkway. Properties generally have been operating for at least one year and must pass inspection visit before being listed. Reservations and payments made through this service.

Bed & Breakfast About Tennessee
P.O. Box 110227, Nashville, TN 37222
Fredda Odom
(615) 331-5244, (800) 458-2421
(615) 833-7701

Hours: 9:00—5:00
Rate range: $55—$125
Credit cards: Most major cards
Restrictions: Full pre-payment req. 72-hour cancellation notice req., less 25% fee.
Notes: Accommodations in country inns, homestays, B&B inns, guesthouses. All properties visited by this service. Reservations and payments made through this service.

TEXAS

Sand Dollar Hospitality

3605 Mendenhall Dr., Corpus Christi, TX 78415
Pat and Paul Hirsbrunner, Mrs. Perry Tompkins
(512) 853-1222, 882-4123
Hours: 9:00—9:00
Rate range: $54—$150
Credit cards: MC, V
Restrictions: Closed Christmas day and one week in June
Notes: Accommodations in homestays, condos. Accommodations regularly inspected. Reservations and deposits made through this service. Balance of payment made directly to host.

Bed & Breakfast Texas Style, Inc.

4224 W. Red Bird Lane, Dallas, TX 75237
Ruth Wilson, Shelly Wilson, Joan Swanson, Amber Mathes
(214) 298-8586, 298-5433
Hours: 8:30—4:30, M—F
Rate range: $60—$150
Credit cards: Most major cards
Restrictions: One night's deposit req. 7-day cancellation notice req., less $10.00 fee. Closed on major holidays.
Notes: Accommodations in country inns, homestays, B&B inns, ranches, log cabins. Accommodations are regularly inspected. Reservations made through this service. Payments made either to this service or directly to host.

Bed and Breakfast Hosts of San Antonio

1777 NE Loop 410, # 600, San Antonio, TX 78217
Laverne Campbell, Brandy Williams
(210) 824-8036, 824-9931
(210) 824-9926
Hours: 9:00—5:00, M—F
Rate range: $43—$195
Credit cards: Most major cards
Restrictions: One night's deposit req. 7-day cancellation notice req., less $10.00 fee.
Notes: Has operated as a reservation service since 1982. Accommodations in B&B inns, guest houses. Accommodations are inspected and meet city regulations. Reservations made through this service. Payments made through this service or directly to host.

VIRGINIA

Princely B and B
819 Prince St., Alexandria, VA 22314
E.J. Mansmann
(703) 683-2159
Hours: 10:00—6:00, M—F
Rate range: $75—$105
Credit cards: None
Restrictions: Please call for info.
Notes: Representing homestays and guest houses built from 1750—1870. All accommodations inspected annually. Reservations and payments made through this service. French, Spanish spoken.

Guesthouses B & B, Inc.
P.O. Box 5737, Charlottesville, VA 22905
Mary Hill Caperton
(804) 979-7264
(804) 293-7791
Hours: 12:00—5:00, M—F
Rate range: $52—$200
Credit cards: Most major cards
Restrictions: Min. 25% deposit req.
Notes: Has operated as a reservation service since 1976. Accommodations in homestays, B & B inns, cottages. All properties inspected following T.N.N. guidelines. All reservations and deposits made through this service. Balance of fee paid directly to host.

The Travel Tree
P.O. Box 838, Williamsburg, VA 23187
Joann Proper
(804) 565-4747, (800) 989-1571
Hours: 6:00 PM—9:00 PM, M—TH
Rate range: $80—$150
Credit cards: Please call for info.
Restrictions: Deposit req. 15-day cancellation notice req., less $25.00 fee. Closed on national holidays.

WASHINGTON, D.C.

Bed 'n' Breakfast Accommodations, Ltd.
P.O. Box 12011, Washington, DC 20005
Wendy Serpan, Janet Armbruster
(202) 328-3510
(202) 332-3885
Hours: 10:00—5:00, M—F; 10:00—1:00, Sat.
Rate range: $45—$265
Credit cards: Most major cards

Restrictions: $50.00 deposit req. 3-day cancellation notice req., less $15.00 fee.
Notes: Eighty properties located in metropolitan Washington, D.C. Accommodations in apts., guest houses, small hotels, inns. Reservations and payments made through this service. Has operated as Reservation Service since 1978.